820.9 M927Li v. 7
Moulton, Charles Wells   9781344113373
The library of literary
criticism of English and

THE LIBRARY

OF

LITERARY CRITICISM

OF

ENGLISH AND AMERICAN AUTHORS

VOLUME VII
1875 - 1890

EDITED BY CHARLES WELLS MOULTON
ASSISTED BY A CORPS OF ABLE CONTRIBUTORS

GLOUCESTER, MASS.
PETER SMITH
1959

Copyright 1904
BY
THE MOULTON PUBLISHING COMPANY
Reprinted 1959
BY
PETER SMITH

To
William Dean Howells, A. M., L. H. D.

INTRODUCTION.

THE DRAMA

Good, my lord, will you see the players well bestowed? Do you hear, let them be well used; for they are the abstracts, and brief chronicles of the time. After your death you were better have a bad epitaph than their ill report while you lived.—SHAKESPEARE, WILLIAM, 1603, *Hamlet, Act II, Sc. 2.*

The words of a good writer, which describe it lively, will make a deeper impression of belief in us, than all the actor can insinuate into us, when he seems to fall dead before us; as a poet in the description of a beautiful garden, or a meadow, will please our imagination more than the place itself can please our sight. When we hear it related, our eyes (the strongest witnesses) are wanting, which might have undeceived us; and we all are willing to favour the slight when the poet does not too grossly impose on us. They, therefore, who imagine these relations would make no concernment in the audience, are deceived, by confounding them with the other, which are of things antecedent to the play: those are made often in cold blood, as I may say, to the audience; but these are warmed with our concernments, which were before awakened in the play. What the philosophers say of motion, that, when it is once begun, it continues of itself, and will do so to eternity, without some stop put to it, is clearly true on this occasion: the soul, being already moved with the characters and fortunes of those imaginary persons, continues going of its own accord; and we are no more weary to hear what becomes of them when they are not on the stage, than we are to listen to the news of an absent mistress.—DRYDEN, JOHN, 1668–93, *An Essay of Dramatic Poesy, Works,* ed. Scott and Saintsbury, vol. XV, p. 324.

O that, as oft I have at Athens seen
The stage arise, and the big clouds descend,
So now in very deed I might behold
The pond'rous earth, and all yon marble roof,
Meet like the hands of Jove.
—LEE, NATHANIEL, 1679, *Œdipus.*

In other things the knowing artist may
Judge better than the people; but a play
(Made for delight, and for no other use)
If you approve it not, has no excuse.
—WALLER, EDMUND, 1687(?), *The Maid's Tragedy, Prologue.*

To wake the soul by tender strokes of art,
To praise the genius, and to mend the heart;
To make mankind, in conscious virtue bold,
Live over each scene, and be what they behold:
For this the tragic Muse first trod the stage.
. . . .
Our scene precariously subsists too long
On French translation, and Italian song.
Dare to have sense yourselves; assert the stage,
Be justly warmed with your own native rage.
—POPE, ALEXANDER, 1713, *Addison's Cato, Prologue.*

I could wish there were a treaty made between the French and the English theatres, in which both parties should make considerable concessions. The English ought to give up their notorious violations of all the unities; and all their massacres, racks, dead bodies, and mangled carcasses, which they so frequently exhibit upon their stage. The French should engage to have more action and less declamation; and not to cram and crowd things together, to almost a degree of impossibility, from a too scrupulous adherence to the unities. The English should restrain the licentiousness of their poets, and the French enlarge the liberty of theirs: their poets are the greatest slaves in their country, and that is a bold word; ours are the most tumultuous subjects in England, and that is saying a good deal. Under such regulations one might hope to see a play in which one should not be lulled to sleep by the length of a monotonical declamation nor frightened and shocked by the barbarity of the action.—CHESTERFIELD, PHILIP STANHOPE LORD, 1752, *Letters to his Son.*

The invention of dramatic art, and that of a theatre, seem to lie very near one another. Man has a great disposition to mimicry; when he enters vividly into the situation, sentiments, and passions of others, he even involuntarily puts on a resemblance to them in his gestures. Children are perpetually going out of themselves; it is one of their chief amusements to represent those grown people whom they have had an opportunity of observing, or whatever comes in their way; and with the happy flexibility of their imagination, they can exhibit all the characteristics of assumed dignity in a father, a schoolmaster, or a king. The sole step which is requisite for the invention of a drama, namely, the separating and extracting the mimetic elements and fragments from social life, and representing them collected together into one mass, has not however been taken in many nations.—SCHLEGEL, AUGUSTUS WILLIAM, 1809, *Dramatic Art and Literature,* tr. Black, p. 14.

A drama (we adopt Dr. Johnson's definition, with some little extension) is a poem or fictitious composition in dialogue, in which the action is not related, but represented. A disposition to this fascinating amusement, considered in its rudest state, seems to be inherent in human nature. It is the earliest sport of children, to take upon themselves some fictitious character, and sustain it to the best of their skill, by such appropriate gestures and language, as their youthful fancies suggest, and such dress and decoration as circumstances place within their reach. The infancy of nations is as prone to this pastime as that of individuals. When the horde emerges out of a nearly brutal state, so far as to have holidays, public sports, and general rejoicings, the pageant of their imaginary deities, or of their fabulous ancestors, is usually introduced as the most pleasing and interesting part of the show. But however general the predisposition to the assumption of fictitious character may be, there is an immeasurable distance betwixt the rude games in which it first displays itself and that polished amusement which is numbered among the fine arts, which poetry, music, and painting have vied to adorn, to whose service genius has devoted her most sublime efforts, while philosophy has stooped from her loftier task, to regulate the progress of the action, and give probability to the representation and personification of the scene.—SCOTT, SIR WALTER, 1814-23, *The Drama.*

Everybody has his own theatre, in which he is manager, actor, prompter, playwright, sceneshifter, boxkeeper, doorkeeper, all in one, and audience into the bargain.—HARE, A. W. AND J. C., 1827-48, *Guesses at Truth.*

The excellence of these works is in a great measure the result of two peculiarities which the critics of the French school consider as defects,—from the mixture of tragedy and comedy, and from the length and extent of the action. The former is necessary to render the drama a just representation of a world in which the laughers and the weepers are perpetually jostling each other,—in which every event has its serious and ludicrous side. The latter enables us to form an intimate acquaintance with the characters with which we could not possibly become familiar during the few hours to which the unities restrict the poet. In this respect the works of Shakespeare, in particular, are miracles of art. In a piece which may be read aloud in three hours we see a character unfold all its recesses to us. We see it change with the change of circumstances. The petulant youth rises into the politic and warlike sovereign. The profuse and courteous philanthropist sours into a hater and scorner of his kind. The tyrant is altered, by the chastening of affliction, into a pensive moralist. The veteran general, distinguished by coolness, sagacity, and self-command, sinks under a conflict between love strong as death and jealousy cruel as the grave. The brave and loyal subject passes, step by step, to the extremities of human depravity. We trace his progress from the first dawnings of unlawful ambition to the cynical melancholy of his impenitent remorse. Yet in these pieces there are no unnatural transitions. Nothing is omitted; nothing is crowded. Great as are the changes, narrow as is the compass within which they are exhibited, they shock us as little as the gradual alterations of those familiar faces which we see every evening and every morning. The magical skill of the poet resembles that of the Dervise in the Spectator, who condensed all the events of seven years into the single moment during which the king held his head under the water.—MACAULAY, THOMAS BABINGTON, 1828, *John Dryden.*

It is a most difficult and laborious art; they know it that have tried. Men who decry it either console their own weakness with a contempt for the mechanical, as they call it, or blindly insist on its being superfluous. Let any man endeavour to construct a story of action which shall develop a passion—let him select characters to illustrate his passion, and let him put them into positive and appropriate action, such as does in truth develop the passion, and he will find the enormous difficulty of avoiding the temptation to let them *talk* this; to let them *reason on their feelings* rather than *feel;* to let them *determine* to act or *describe their actions* rather than positively *act;* and the difficulty of making them only do such things as are consistent with their characters and the problem of the piece; of preserving the spiritual force and integrity of his characters through all "circumstances," not allowing himself to be seduced by the temptation of letting circumstances in the play form and guide his characters, but to keep up their individualities through all these circumstances, whatever they may be, and to bring all deeds about naturally but not tediously; and of letting every act(*actus*) contain some deed, and every scene some positive advancement of the plot. These are the demands of this "mechanical part," and let those who think them easy, try!—LEWES, GEORGE HENRY, 1842, *Authors and Managers, Westminster Review, vol. 37, p. 81.*

That the technique of the drama is nothing absolute and unchangeable scarcely need be stated. Since Aristotle established a few of the highest laws of dramatic effect, the culture of the human race has grown more than two thousand years older. Not only have the artistic forms, the stage and method of representation undergone, a great change, but what is more important, the spiritual and moral nature of men, the relation of the individual to the race and to the highest forces of earthly life, the idea of freedom, the conception of the being of Divinity, have experienced great revolutions. A wide field of dramatic material has been lost; a new and greater range has been won. With the moral and political principles which control our life, our notion of the beautiful and the artistically effective has developed. Between the highest art effects of the Greek festivals, the *autos sacramentales*, and the drama of the time of Goethe and Iffland the difference is not less great than between the Hellenic choral theatre, the structure for the mystery play, and the complete inclosed room of the modern stage. It may be considered certain that some of the fundamental laws of dramatic production will remain in force for all time; in general, however, not only the vital requisites of the drama have been found in continuous development, but also the artistic means of producing its effects. Let no one think that the technique of poetry has been advanced through the creations of the greatest poets only; we may say without self-exaltation that we at present have clearer ideas upon the highest art effects in the drama and upon the use of technical equipment, than had Lessing, Schiller, and Goethe.—FREYTAG, GUSTAV, 1863-95,

Technique of the Drama, tr. MacEwan, Introduction, p. 1.

The drama is the necessary product of the age in which it lives, and of which it is the moral, social, and physical expression. It is divided into two classes. The first may be called the *contemporaneous* or *realistic* drama, which is a reflex of the features of the period, where the personages are life-size, the language partakes of their reality, and the incidents are natural. The object of this drama is to produce in the mind of the spectator sympathy with human suffering by effecting a perfect illusion that he is witnessing a destiny towards which the *dramatis personæ* are progressing. The other is the *transcendental* or *unreal drama*, where the personages are larger than life-size, their ideas and language more exalted than human conversation, and the incidents more important than we meet with in ordinary life. The object of this drama is to lift the spectator into a high atmosphere, and to expand his moral stature by association with *dramatis personæ* of gigantic proportions. In this region the drama cannot produce perfectly the theatrical illusion, because we cannot sympathize with beings more noble than ourselves. The contemporaneous drama possesses an archæological value. It is the only faithful record of its age. In it the features, expression, manners, thoughts, and passions of its period are reflected and retained.—BOUCICAULT, DION, 1877, *The Decline of the Drama, North American Review*, vol. 125, p. 236.

Why has no actor in your chief cities a stage of his own? Why do theatres belong to managers, business men who have acquired fortunes in this or that trade and now let them out, like bath-houses at great and stultifying rates to poor itinerant players? Have you no rich men—no men who will build and rent at a fair rental? No friends such as English art has in London? What a privilege to create great characters and play great plays for the suffering of paying three thousand dollars a week to a stranger? What is this trade in actors and plays, this speculating and gambling, this slave market, this crushing down of one that rises, this merchanting in actors and actresses, and the smiling octopus that sucks all things dry, this playing *down* to *people*, instead of playing *up* to *art*, and dragging the people after?—MANSFIELD, RICHARD, 1892, *A Plain Talk upon the Drama, North American Review*, vol. 155, p. 310.

The truth is that the immortal part of the stage is its noble part. Ignoble accidents and interludes come and go, but this lasts on forever. It lives like the human soul in the body of humanity, associated with much that is inferior, and hampered by many hindrances,—but it never sinks into nothingness, and never fails to find new and noble work in exactness of permanent and memorable excellence. Heaven forbid that I should seem to cover, even with a counterpane of courtesy, exhibitions of deliberate immorality. Happily this sort of thing is not common, and although it has hardly been practised by anyone who, without a strain of meaning, can be associated with the profession of acting; yet public censure not active enough to repress the evil, is ever ready to pass a sweeping condemnation on the stage which harbors it. Our cause is a good one. We go forth, armed with the luminous panoply which genius has forged for us, to do battle with dulness, with coarseness, with apathy, with every form of vice and evil. In every human heart there gleams a higher reflection of this shining armor. The stage has no lights or shadows that are not lights of life and shadows of the heart. To each human consciousness it appeals in alternating mirth and sadness, and will not be denied. Err it must, for it is human; but, being human, it must endure.—IRVING, HENRY, 1893, *The Drama*.

When the archbishop of York thus

effectually put an end to the Mysteries in 1579, the old dramas had produced all their fruit. They had kept alive the taste for spectacles; they left behind them troops of comedians throughout the provinces, numerous authors, and a public ready to listen. Already there was growing up in a little town upon the banks of the Avon a youth who should reach the highest summits of the art of the drama. At the time when those old representations were stopped, William Shakespeare was fifteen years old. —JUSSERAND, J. J., 1894, *The Drama of the Middle Ages, The Chautauquan, vol.* 14, *p.* 69.

It is generally held that the province of the drama is to amuse. I claim that it has a higher purpose—that its mission is to interest and to instruct. It should not *preach* objectively, but it should teach subjectively; and so I stand for truth in the drama, because it is elemental, it gets to the bottom of a question. It strikes at unequal standards and unjust systems. It is as unyielding as it is honest. It is as tender as it is inflexible. It has supreme faith in man. It believes that that which was good in the beginning cannot be bad at the end. It sets forth clearly that the concern of one is the concern of all. It stands for the higher development and thus the individual liberty of the human race.—HERNE, JAMES A., 1897, *Art for Truth's Sake in the Drama, The Arena, vol.* 17, *p.* 370.

I do not know that the fly in amber is of any particular use, but the Comic idea enclosed in a comedy makes it more generally perceptible and portable, and that is an advantage. There is a benefit to men in taking the lessons of Comedy in congregations, for it enlivens the wits; and to writers it is beneficial, for they must have a clear scheme, and even if they have no idea to present, they must prove that they have made the public sit to them before the sitting to see the picture. And writing for the stage would be a corrective of a too-incrusted scholarly style, into which some great ones fall at times. It keeps minor writers to a definite plan, and English. Many of them now swelling a plethoric market, in the composition of novels, in pun-manufactories and in journalism; attached to the machinery forcing perishable matter on a public that swallows voraciously and groans; might, with encouragement, be attending to the study of art in literature.—MEREDITH, GEORGE, 1897, *An Essay on Comedy and the Use of the Comic Spirit, p.* 98.

Nowadays, every second man is a would-be dramatist, every other woman a potential actress. The interest in the stage is not confined to that enthusiastic person, the constant playgoer—it extends to those platonic patrons of the drama who never enter the portals of a theatre; it embraces that sympathetic individual, the *laudator temporis acti*, who is ever prepared to bewail the death of the drama, and to weep the ready tear over its untenanted grave. . . . Whatever may be its ailments, the drama is not suffering from want of medical attendance, for disagreeing doctors are constantly warring over its prostrate but pulsating body.—TREE, HERBERT BEERBOHM, 1897, *Some Aspects of the Drama of To-Day, North American Review, vol.* 164, *pp.* 66, 67.

It is right and wholesome to have those light comedies and entertaining shows; and I shouldn't wish to see them diminished. But none of us is *always* in the comedy spirit; we have our graver moods; they come to us all; the lightest of us cannot escape them. These moods have their appetites,—healthy and legitimate appetites, —and there ought to be some way of satisfying them. It seems to me that New York ought to have one theatre devoted to tragedy. With her three millions of population, and seventy outside millions to draw upon, she can afford it, she can support it. America devotes more time, labor, money, and attention to distributing literary and musical culture among the general public than does any other nation, perhaps; yet here you find her neglecting what is possibly the most effective of all the breeders and nurses and disseminators of high literary taste and lofty emotion—the tragic stage. To leave that powerful agency out is to haul the culture-wagon with a crippled team. Nowadays, when a mood comes which only Shakespeare can set to music, what must we do? Read Shakespeare ourselves! Isn't it pitiful? It is playing an organ solo on a jew's-harp. We can't read. None but the Booths can do it.—CLEMENS, SAMUEL LANGHORNE (MARK TWAIN), 1898, *About Play-Acting, The Forum, vol.* 26, *p.* 150.

Solon, who was one of the traditional wise men of Greece—it is Plutarch who tells us the story—once went to see Thespis act. And after the play was done, he asked him if he were not ashamed of himself to tell so many lies before such a number of people. When Thespis replied that it was no harm to say or to do so in play, Solon vehemently struck his staff against the ground. "Ay," said he, "if we honour and commend such play as this, we shall find it some day in our business." Here is one of the earliest recorded instances of the judgment of the intellect on things of the imagination. Observe the two points which are found fault with in art. First, judged by a severe standard of experience, it is false; next, it has a deleterious influence on the practical conduct of life. Solon, no doubt, preserved his reputation for traditional wisdom by occasional lapses into folly, as is the habit of other wise men whose *obiter dicta* are apt to miss the highest aspect of things. But I begin with the story as indicative of a contrast you will find running through the history of Greek art, and also, to a large extent, of modern art—the wide divergence between the most cultured efforts of intelligent criticism, and the spontaneous outpouring of the artistic imagination. When it came to be the task of Plato and Aristotle to give a philosophical account of the work, which men like Pheidias and Praxiteles, Æschylus, Sophocles, and Euripides had done before them, they failed nearly as completely as Solon did, and for a similar reason. They applied the analytic processes of logic to a phenomenon, an artistic birth, an æsthetic illumination, which has little or nothing to do with mental processes at all. —COURTNEY, WILLIAM LEONARD, 1900, *The Idea of Tragedy in Ancient and Modern Drama, p.* 1.

There is not a more neglected branch of study than that concerned with the relation of amusement to ethical culture. The ideal of the stage, as an educational and religious force, which was so fully in accordance with the genius of classical Greece and was so naturally and completely worked out in practice by her people, was in less degree a recognized factor in the life of the Middle-Ages—until it was lost in the frozen fog that crept over the land with Puritanism, and doubly disappeared in the succeeding waves of materialism out of which we are just emerging.—POTTER, HELEN, 1900, *The Drama of the Twentieth Century, The Arena, vol.* 23, *p.* 157.

One art there is, and only one, which can avail itself at will of almost every device of all the other arts. One art there is which can reach out and borrow the aid of the poet, the painter, the sculptor, the musician, compelling them all to help it towards its own perfection. One art there is which, without danger of confusion, without departing from its own object, without loss of force, can, at one and the same time, tell a story, and give an impression of the visible world, and fill our eyes with the beauty of form, and charm our ears with rhythm and with harmony. This one art is the art of the drama, the art which most completely displays the life of man—"the youngest of the sister arts," the British poet called it, "where all their beauty blends."—MATTHEWS, BRANDER, 1903, *The Development of the Drama, p.* 3.

CONTENTS.

		PAGE.
AINSWORTH, WILLIAM HARRISON,	1805—1882	485
ALCOTT, AMOS BRONSON,	1799—1888	662
ALCOTT, LOUISA MAY,	1833—1888	665
ALLINGHAM, WILLIAM,	1824—1889	734
ARNOLD, MATTHEW,	1822—1888	627
BAGEHOT, WALTER,	1826—1877	96
BARNES, WILLIAM,	1810—1886	584
BEACONSFIELD, EARL OF,	1804—1881	276
BEECHER, HENRY WARD,	1813—1887	599
BOKER, GEORGE HENRY,	1823—1890	764
BORROW, GEORGE HENRY,	1803—1881	306
BOUCICAULT, DION,	1822—1890	762
BRIGHT, JOHN,	1811—1889	720
BROWN, JOHN,	1810—1882	477
BROWNING, ROBERT,	1812—1889	677
BROWNSON, ORESTES AUGUSTUS,	1803—1876	72
BUCKLAND, FRANCIS TREVELYAN,	1826—1880	210
BURTON, JOHN HILL,	1809—1881	315
BURTON, SIR RICHARD FRANCIS,	1821—1890	757
BUSHNELL, HORACE,	1802—1876	69
BRYANT, WILLIAM CULLEN,	1794—1878	109
CALVERLEY, CHARLES STUART	1831—1884	541
CARLYLE, THOMAS,	1795—1881	229
CHILD, LYDIA MARIA,	1802—1880	218
CHURCH, RICHARD WILLIAM,	1815—1889	728
CLARKE, JAMES FREEMAN,	1810—1888	672
COLENSO, JOHN WILLIAM,	1814—1883	522
COLLINS, MORTIMER,	1827—1876	81
COLLINS, WILLIAM WILKIE,	1824—1889	725
CRAIK, DINAH MARIA MULOCK,	1826—1887	623
CROSS, MARY ANN,	1819—1880	170
DANA, RICHARD HENRY,	1787—1879	152
DANA, RICHARD HENRY, JR.,	1815—1882	499
DARWIN, CHARLES ROBERT,	1809—1882	415

CONTENTS

		PAGE
DEWEY, ORVILLE,	1794—1882	495
DISRAELI, BENJAMIN,	1804—1881	276
DOYLE, SIR FRANCIS HASTINGS CHARLES,	1810—1888	649
DRAPER, JOHN WILLIAM,	1811—1882	502
ELIOT, GEORGE,	1819—1880	170
EMERSON, RALPH WALDO,	1803—1882	342
EVANS, MARIAN,	1819—1880	170
FAWCETT, HENRY,	1833—1884	548
FIELDS, JAMES THOMAS,	1816—1881	339
FINLAY, GEORGE,	1799—1875	48
FITZGERALD, EDWARD,	1809—1883	514
FORSTER, JOHN,	1812—1876	64
FULLERTON, GEORGIANA CHARLOTTE LADY,	1812—1885	566
GARRISON, WILLIAM LLOYD,	1805—1879	157
GILFILLAN, GEORGE,	1813—1878	150
GRAY, ASA,	1810—1888	669
GREEN, JOHN RICHARD,	1837—1883	504
GREG, WILLIAM RATHBONE,	1809—1881	320
HAVERGAL, FRANCES RIDLEY,	1836—1879	166
HAYNE, PAUL HAMILTON,	1831—1886	590
HELPS, SIR ARTHUR,	1813—1875	38
HOLLAND, JOSIAH GILBERT,	1819—1881	333
HOPKINS, MARK,	1802—1887	613
HORNE, RICHARD HENGIST,	1803—1884	544
HOUGHTON, LORD,	1809—1885	559
JACKSON, HELEN HUNT,	1831—1885	571
JEFFERIES, RICHARD,	1848—1887	618
JEVONS, WILLIAM STANLEY,	1835—1882	491
KINGSLEY, CHARLES,	1819—1875	17
KINGSLEY, HENRY,	1830—1876	79
LANE, EDWARD WILLIAM,	1801—1876	83
LANIER, SIDNEY,	1842—1881	325
LAZARUS, EMMA,	1849—1887	610
LAWRENCE, GEORGE ALFRED,	1827—1876	84
LEWES, GEORGE HENRY,	1817—1878	137
LEWES, MRS. GEORGE HENRY,	1819—1880	170
LIDDON, HENRY PARRY,	1829—1890	761
LONGFELLOW, HENRY WADSWORTH,	1807—1882	381
LYELL, SIR CHARLES,	1797—1875	33
MACKAY, CHARLES,	1814—1889	764
MAHON, LORD,	1805—1875	46

CONTENTS

			PAGE
MAINE, SIR HENRY JAMES SUMNER,	. .	1822—1888	651
MARSH, GEORGE PERKINS,	. . . .	1801—1882	492
MARSTON, PHILIP BOURKE,	. . . .	1852—1887	626
MARTINEAU, HARRIET,	. . . . .	1802—1876	54
MAXWELL, JAMES CLERK,	. . . .	1831—1879	168
MCCARTHY, DENNIS FLORENCE,	. . .	1820—1882	489
MILNES, RICHARD MONCKTON, .	. . .	1809—1885	559
MOTLEY, JOHN LOTHROP,	. . . . .	1814—1877	85
MOZLEY, JAMES BOWLING,	. . . .	1813—1878	147
NEAL, JOHN,	. . . .	1793—1876	76
NEWMAN, JOHN HENRY,	. . . . .	1801—1890	738
NORTON, CAROLINE ELIZABETH SHERIDAN,		1808—1877	101
OLIPHANT, LAURENCE, .	. . . . .	1829—1888	654
O'REILLY, JOHN BOYLE,	. . . . .	1844—1890	767
O'SHAUGHNESSY, ARTHUR WILLIAM EDGAR,		1844—1881	322
PALFREY, JOHN GORHAM,	. . . . .	1796—1881	337
PATTISON, MARK,	. . . .	1813—1884	538
PHILLIPS, WENDELL,	. . . . . .	1811—1884	552
PLANCHÉ, JAMES ROBINSON,	. . . .	1796—1880	216
PROCTOR, RICHARD ANTHONY, .	. . .	1837—1888	659
PUSEY, EDWARD BOUVERIE,	. . . .	1800—1882	466
READE. CHARLES, .	. . . . . .	1814—1884	526
RIPLEY, GEORGE, .	. . . . . .	1802—1880	223
ROE, EDWARD PAYSON,	. . . . .	1838—1888	674
ROSSETTI, GABRIEL CHARLES DANTE,	.	1828—1882	434
RUSSELL, JOHN LORD, .	. . . . .	1792—1878	143
RYAN, ABRAM JOSEPH, .	. . . . .	1839—1886	598
SAXE, JOHN GODFREY, .	. . . . .	1816—1887	616
SHAIRP, JOHN CAMPBELL, .	. . . .	1819—1885	568
SPEDDING, JAMES, .	. . . . . .	1808—1881	317
SPRAGUE, CHARLES,	. . . . . .	1791—1875	52
STANHOPE, PHILIP HERNY EARL,	. .	1805—1875	46
STANLEY, ARTHUR PENRHYN, .	. . .	1815—1881	296
STIRLING-MAXWELL, LADY,	. . . .	1808—1877	101
TAYLOR, BAYARD, .	. . . . . .	1825—1878	128
TAYLOR, SIR HENRY,	. . . . . .	1800—1886	579
TAYLOR, TOM, .	. . . .	1817—1880	213
THIRWALL, CONNOP,	. . . . . .	1797—1875	42
TITCOMB, TIMOTHY,	. . . . . .	1819—1881	333
THOMSON, JAMES, .	. . . . . .	1834—1882	473
TRENCH, RICHARD CHENEVIX, .	. . .	1807—1886	588

			PAGE.
TROLLOPE, ANTHONY,	1815—1882		456
TUPPER, MARTIN FARQUHAR,	1810—1889		731
TURNER, CHARLES TENNYSON,	1808—1879		161
VERY, JONES,	1813—1880		226
WARD, WILLIAM GEORGE,	1812—1882		481
WARREN, SAMUEL,	1807—1877		106
WELLS, CHARLES JEREMIAH,	1800—1879		164
WHIPPLE, EDWIN PERCY,	1819—1886		594
WHITE, RICHARD GRANT,	1822—1885		576
WILKINSON, SIR JOHN GARDNER,	1797—1875		50
WOOLSEY, THEODORE DWIGHT,	1805—1889		736

ENGRAVINGS.

	PAGE.
ARNOLD, MATTHEW, ...	627
From a Portrait by P. Sandys, 1881.	
BEECHER, HENRY WARD, ...	627
Engraving from a Photograph.	
BRIGHT, JOHN, ...	277
From Original Painting by Chappel.	
BROWNING, ROBERT, ...	677
Engraving from a Photograph.	
BRYANT, WILLIAM CULLEN, ...	109
Engraving by H. B. Hall & Sons.	
CARLYLE, THOMAS, ...	229
Engraving by Walker & Boutall, From a Painting by Sir J. E. Millais P. R. A.	
DISRAELI, BENJAMIN, ...	277
Engraving from a Photograph.	
ELIOT, GEORGE, ...	171
From a Drawing by Frederic Burton.	
EMERSON, RALPH WALDO, ...	343
Engraving by J. A. J. Wilcox.	
FITZGERALD, EDWARD, ...	229
Engraving from a Photograph.	
GARRISON, WILLIAM LLOYD, ...	553
From the Bust by Anne Whitney.	
GREEN, JOHN RICHARD, ...	739
Engraving by G. J. Stodart.	
HAYNE, PAUL HAMILTON, ...	591
Engraving by H. B. Hall & Sons, From a Photograph.	
HOLLAND, JOSIAH GILBERT, ...	591
Engraving by H. B. Hall & Sons.	
KINGSLEY, CHARLES, ...	17
From an Engraving by Sartain.	
LONGFELLOW, HENRY WADSWORTH, ...	343
From a Painting by C. P. A. Healey, 1862.	
LYELL, SIR CHARLES, ...	17
Engraving by C. H. Jeens, From a Photograph.	
MAINE, SIR HENRY JAMES SUMNER, ...	435
From a Portrait by Lowes Dickinson.	
MARSH, GEORGE PERKINS, ...	85
Engraving by H. B. Hall, Jr., From a Photograph.	
MARTINEAU, HARRIET, ...	55
Engraving from a Portrait, 1833.	
MILNES, RICHARD MONCKTON, ...	171
Engraving From the Original Painting by R. Lehmann.	
MOTLEY, JOHN LOTHROP, ...	85
Engraving by F. T. Stuart.	
NEWMAN, JOHN HENRY, ...	739
From a Drawing by G. Richmond, 1844.	
NORTON, CAROLINE ELIZABETH, ...	55
Engraving by W. O. Geller, From Original Painting by John Hayter.	
PHILLIPS, WENDELL, ...	553
Engraving by F. T. Stuart.	
PUSEY, EDWARD BOUVERIE, ...	297
Engraving by Walker & Boutall, From a Portrait by Miss Rosa Corder.	
ROSSETTI, DANTE GABRIEL, ...	435
From a Portrait by S. Hollyer.	
RUSSELL, JOHN LORD, ...	143
Engraving from a Painting by Francis Grant, R. A., 1853.	
STANLEY, ARTHUR PENRHYN, ...	297
Engraving by Francis Holt, A. R. A., Photograph by Samuel A. Walker.	
TAYLOR, BAYARD, ...	109
Engraving by F. T. Stuart, From a Photograph by Gutekunst.	
TAYLOR, SIR HENRY, ...	677
From a Photograph by Mr. Hawker.	
WARREN, SAMUEL, ...	143
Engraving by D. J. Pond, From a Photograph by Mayall.	

SIR CHARLES LYELL

Engraving by C. H. Jeens, from a Photograph.

CHARLES KINGSLEY

From an Engraving by Sartain.

The Library of Literary Criticism

of

English and American Authors

VOLUME VII

Charles Kingsley

1819–1875

Born, at Holne Vicarage, Devonshire, 12 June 1819. At school at Clifton, 1831–32; at Helston, Cornwall, 1832–36. Family removed to London, 1836. Student at King's Coll., London, 1836–38. Matric. Magdalene Coll., Camb., Oct. 1838; Scholar, 1839; B. A., 1842; M. A., 1860. Ordained Curate of Eversley, Hampshire, July 1842. Married Fanny Grenfell, 10 Jan. 1844; Rector of Eversley, same year. Clerk in Orders, St. Luke's, Chelsea, 1844–49. Canon of Middleham, 1845. Prof. of English Lit., Queen's Coll., London, 1848. Contrib. (under pseud. of "Parson Lot") to "Politics for the People," 1848; and to "The Christian Socialist," 1850–51. Contrib. to "Fraser's Mag.," 1848, etc. Ill-health, winter 1848–49. First visit to Continent, 1851. At Torquay, winter 1853–54. Chaplain in Ordinary to the Queen, 1859. Prof. of Modern History, Cambridge, 1860–69. Increasing ill-health from 1864. Pres. of Social Science Congress, 1869. Canon of Chester, 1869. Visit to West Indies, winter 1869–70. Resided at Chester, May 1870 to 1873. Pres. of Midland Institute, 1872. Canon of Westminster, 1873. Visit to America, 1874. Died, at Eversley, 23 Jan. 1875. Buried there. *Works:* "The Saint's Tragedy," 1848; "Twenty-five Village Sermons," 1849; "Alton Locke" (anon.), 1850; "Cheap Clothes and Nasty" (under pseu. "Parson Lot"), 1850; "The Application of Associative . . . Principles to Agriculture," 1851; "Yeast" (anon.), (from "Fraser's Mag."), 1851; "The Message of the Church to Labouring Men," 1851; "Phaethon," 1852; "Sermons on National Subjects" (2 ser.), 1852–54; "Hypatia" (from "Fraser's Mag."), 1853; "Alexandria and her Schools," 1854; "Who causes Pestilence?" 1854; "Sermons for the Times," 1855; "Westward Ho!" 1855; "Glaucus," 1855; "The Heroes," 1856 [1855]; "Two Years Ago," 1857; "Andromeda," 1858; "The Good News of God," 1859; "Miscellanies," 1859; "The Limits of Exact Sciences as applied to History," 1860; "Why should we pray for Fair Weather?" 1860; "Town and Country Sermons," 1861; "A Sermon on the death of . . . the Prince Consort," 1862 [1861]; "Speech of Lord Dundreary . . . on the great Hippocampus question" (anon.), 1862; "The Gospel of the Pentateuch," 1863; "The Water Babies," 1863; "What, then, does Dr. Newman mean?" 1864; "The Roman and the Teuton," 1864; "Hints to Stammerers" (anon.), 1864; "David," 1865; "Hereward the Wake," 1866; "The Temple of Wisdom," 1866; "Three Lectures on the Ancient Régime," 1867; "The Water of Life," 1867; "The Hermits," 1868; "Discipline," 1868; "God's Feast," 1869; "Madame How and Lady Why," 1870 [1869]; "At Last," 1871; "Poems," 1872 [1871]; "Town Geology," 1872; "Prose Idylls," 1873; "Plays and Puritans," 1873; "Health and Education," 1874; "Westminster Sermons," 1874; "Lectures delivered in America," 1875. *Posthumous:* "Letters to Young Men," 1877; "True Words for Brave Men," ed. by his wife, 1878; "All Saints' Day, and other Sermons," ed. by W. Harrison, 1878; "From Death to Life," ed. by his wife, 1887. He *edited:* Mansfield's "Paraguay," 1856; Tauler's

"History and Life," 1857; Brooke's "The Fool of Quality," 1859; Bunyan's "Pilgrim's Progress," 1860 [1859]; "South by West," 1874. *Collected Works:* in 28 vols., 1880–85. *Life:* "Letters and Memories," by his wife, 1877.—SHARP, R. FARQUHARSON, 1897, *A Dictionary of English Authors, p.* 157.

PERSONAL

Charles Kingsley spoke during two hours and twenty minutes, with such earnestness! such conviction! such passion! such beauty! There is nothing like real high eloquence. It is poetry living and breathing, and carrying you on like a torrent, in its magnificent course. Oh, how I longed for you! There was nothing to frighten any body. Of course the principles were large and general; but the whole address was most conciliatory. It was power in all its gentleness. He is a very great man.—MITFORD, MARY RUSSELL, 1844, *To Miss Barrett, Feb.* 28; *Life ed. L'Estrange, vol.* II, *p.* 272.

Few men have impressed me more agreeably than Mr. Kingsley. He is original and earnest, and full of a genial and almost tender kindliness which is delightful to me. Wild and theoretical in many ways he is of course, but I believe he could not be otherwise than good and noble, let him say or dream what he will.—BROWNING, ELIZABETH BARRETT, 1852, *To Mrs. Martin, Sept.* 2; *Letters, ed. Kenyon, vol.* II, *p.* 83.

He is tall, slender, with blue eyes, brown hair, and a hale, well-browned face, and somewhat loose-jointed withal. His wife is a real Spanish beauty. How we did talk and go on for three days! I guess he is tired. I'm sure we were. He is a nervous, excitable being, and talks with head, shoulders, arms, and hands, while his hesitance makes it the harder. Of his theology I will say more some other time. He, also, has been through the great distress, the "Conflict of Ages," but has come out at a different end from Edward, and stands with John Forster, though with more positiveness than he.—STOWE, HARRIET BEECHER, 1856, *To Mr. Stowe, Nov.* 7; *Life and Letters, ed. Fields, p.* 227.

Seems to have a stuttering way with him which one would think would interfere with that eloquence of preaching for which he is celebrated. He is tall, rather thin, with commonplace features, neither handsome nor the reverse, but seems a good fellow, and entirely unparsonical.—MOTLEY, JOHN LOTHROP, 1858, *Letter to his Wife, May* 28; *Correspondence, ed. Curtis, vol.* I, *p.* 232.

He has a little the look, when he first comes into a room, of a lion—*i. e.* of one who knows himself to be a lion. But I thought afterwards the impression might be due to the natural restlessness of his eye and manner—something of the same that Keble has. He is a most continuous talker, but fresh and interesting, and without affectation; and his hesitation of speech is not so much of a drawback as you might expect. He gave one the idea of a man who had a real wish to be manly and simple-minded, and made that his standard. He is made, of course, an immense deal of.—MOZLEY, JAMES BOWLING, 1862, *To Rev. R. W. Church, March* 31; *Letters, ed. his Sister, p.* 251.

A high noble forehead, large, earnest, deep-set eyes (which the lithograph had made hollow as if with thought and work) a firm, close-shut mouth, and large and powerful jaw; here was a poet as well as a parson, a fighter as well as a writer, a leader as well as a priest. Waving black hair, now thinned by time, adorned the head, and earnest, glowing, lustrous, and true-hearted eyes shone out from beneath the forehead, and seemed to speak openly to whomsoever listened, "Come, let us work together for the good of mankind. Love me, for I love you; or if I can't convince you, then——" Such was Charles Kingsley, as good and as free-natured a soul as one would care to see.—FRISWELL, JAMES HAIN, 1870, *Modern Men of Letters Honestly Criticised, p.* 315.

Rather tall, very angular, surprisingly awkward, with thin, staggering legs, a hatchet face adorned with scraggy gray whiskers, a faculty for falling into the most ungainly attitudes, and making the most hideous contortions of visage and frame; with a rough provincial accent and an uncouth way of speaking, which would be set down for absurd caricature on the boards of a comic theatre; such was the appearance which the author of "Glaucus" and "Hypatia" presented to his startled audience. Since Brougham's time nothing so ungainly, odd, and ludicrous had been displayed upon an English platform.—MCCARTHY, JUSTIN, 1872, *The Reverend Charles Kingsley, Modern Leaders,* p. 212.

He was what he was, not by virtue of his office, but by virtue of what God had made him in himself. He was, we might almost say, a layman in the guise or disguise—of a clergyman—fishing with the fishermen, hunting with the huntsmen, able to hold his own in tent and camp, with courtier or with soldier; an example that a genial companion may be a Christian gentleman—that a Christian clergyman need not be a member of a separate caste, and a stranger to the common interests of his countrymen. Yet human, genial layman as he was, he still was not the less —nay, he was ten times more—a pastor than he would have been had he shut himself out from the haunts and walks of men. He was sent by Providence, as it were, "far off to the Gentiles"—far off, not to other lands or other races of mankind, but far off from the usual sphere of minister or priest, "to fresh woods and pastures new," to find fresh worlds of thoughts and wild tracts of character, in which he found a response to himself, because he gave a response to them.—STANLEY, ARTHUR PENRHYN, 1875, *Funeral Sermon on Canon Kingsley in Westminster Abbey.*

I never thought to preach another sermon; but by the freshly covered grave of a friend all scruples and all hesitation vanish. It is a sad, sad task.... "Out of the abundance of the heart the mouth speaketh;" and if abounding sorrow and earnest love can give me words I will strive to address myself to the thoughts of your hearts.... But whatever his loss to the Church, much greater is his loss to us—whatever he was to others, much more was he to us; for he was the teacher and friend of every one of us. Of every one even of those who would none of his counsel, and despised his reproof; even to them he was the earnest affectionate friend.... We have known more of him than the most constant reader of his works, or the most ardent admirer of his talents. For until lately that the duties of well-deserved appointments took him away, he was always among us, and Sunday after Sunday we received his teaching.

You know how we hung on his lips.... Brethren, I have heard many preachers, but I never heard one whose hearty yet quiet manner appealed more earnestly to the mind and heart; or who had in so great a degree the power of explaining the truths of Scripture, and enforcing the practice of its precepts in such plain simple words. —COPE, SIR WILLIAM H., 1875, *Living unto God, Sermon Preached at Eversley, Jan. 31.*

Charles and Herbert Kingsley were brought to Helston Grammar School, in Cornwall, in the year 1832.... Charles was a tall, slight boy, of keen visage, and of great bodily activity, high-spirited, earnest, and energetic, giving full promise of the intellectual powers, and moral qualities, by which he was afterwards distinguished. Though not a close student, he was an eager reader and enquirer, sometimes in very out of the way quarters. I once found him busily engaged with an old copy of "Porphyry and Iamblichus," which he had ferreted out of my library. Truly a remarkable boy, original to the verge of eccentricity, and yet a thorough boy, fond of sport, and up to any enterprise—a genuine out-of-doors English boy. —COLERIDGE, DERWENT, 1875, *Letter to Mrs. Kingsley, Oct. 7; Charles Kingsley, his Letters and Memories of his Life,* ed. his Wife, vol. I, p. 23.

With regard to his moral qualities, he was a singularly affectionate man—very earnest, very kindly, feeling deeply for the labours and sufferings of others, and thoroughly devoted to the welfare of the poor. He was, indeed, the model of a parish priest; and, considering the temptations to higher flights which genius always offers, that he should have fulfilled these humbler duties so admirably is deserving of the highest praise.—HELPS, SIR ARTHUR, 1875, *Charles Kingsley, Macmillan's Magazine,* vol. 31, p. 376.

Kingsley's conversational powers [1849] were very remarkable. In the first place he had, as may be easily understood by the readers of his books, a rare command of racy and correct English, while he was so many sided that he could take keen interest in almost any subject which attracted those about him. He had read, and read much, not only in matters which every one ought to know, but had gone deeply into many out-of-the-way and unexpected studies. Old medicine, magic, the occult properties of plants, folklore, mesmerism, nooks and bye-ways of history, old legends; on all these he was at home. On the habits and dispositions of animals he would talk as though he were that king in the Arabian Nights who understood the language of beasts, or at least had lived among the gypsies who loved him so well. The stammer, which in those days was so much more marked than in later years, and which was a serious discomfort to himself, was no drawback to the charm of his conversation. . . . No man loved a good story better than he, but there was always in what he told or what he suffered himself to hear, a good and pure moral underlying what might be coarse in expression. While he would laugh with the keenest sense of amusement at what might be simply broad, he had the most utter scorn and loathing for all that could debase and degrade. And he was the most reverent of men, though he would say things which seemed daring because people were unaccustomed to hear sacred things named without a pious snuffle. This great reverence led him to be even unjust to some of the greatest humourists.—PAUL, C. KEGAN, 1876, *Letter to Mrs. Kingsley; Charles Kingsley, his Letters and Memories of his Life*, ed. his Wife, vol. I, pp. 225, 227.

All I saw of him left upon me the feeling that I was in contact with a powerfully earnest and reverent spirit. His heart seemed overcharged with interest in the welfare, physical, moral and spiritual, of his race. I was conscious in his presence of the bracing atmosphere of a noble nature. He seemed to me one of the manliest of men. I forbear to speak of the high estimate which, in common with all English-speaking people, I place upon his literary life-work. My copy of his "Hypatia" is worn by frequent perusal, and the echoes of his rare and beautiful lyrics never die out of my memory. But since I have seen *him*, the man seems greater than the author.—WHITTIER, JOHN GREENLEAF, 1876, *Letter to Mrs. Kingsley, Life and Letters*, ed. Pickard, vol. II, p. 627.

The green turf round the grave was soon worn by the tread of many footsteps; for months a day seldom passed without strangers being seen in the churchyard. On Bank holidays numbers would come to see his last resting-place—little children who had loved the "Waterbabies," and the "Heroes," would kneel down reverently and look at the beautiful wreaths of flowers, which kind hands had placed there, while the gipsies never passed the gate without turning in to stand over the grave in silence, sometimes scattering wild flowers there, believing, as they do, to use their own strange words, that "he went to heaven on the prayers of the gipsies."—KINGSLEY, MRS. CHARLES, 1876, ed. *Charles Kingsley, his Letters and Memories of his Life*, vol. II, p. 476.

That somewhat severe face belied one of the kindest hearts that ever beat; yet the handsome and chivalrous features not unworthily expressed one of the truest, bravest, and noblest of souls. Kingsley could not have done a mean or false thing: by his make it was as impossible as that water should run up hill.—BOYD, ANDREW H. K., 1877, *Charles Kingsley, Fraser's Magazine*, vol. 95, p. 255.

I have read every word of Canon Kingsley's "Life and Letters," and thought better of him for reading it. He was very decided in his opinions, but very modest in his notion of his own merits; and, though conservative in regard to the Anglican Church, tolerant and kind to those who did not agree with him. He was a friend to the humbler classes, and a most faithful and sympathetic pastor, wearing out his life for his flock; yet I cannot see that he contemplated doing them any good, save by personal effort and kind attentions. I do not find in any part of the memoir that he sought to improve the institutions under which the working class in England had been kept poor and degraded. But his personal attentions with respect to their comfort, their health, their spiritual condition, and their mental improvement, were constant, and these, along with his literary labors, undermined his health and broke it down once in two or three years. He was a worn-out man when he came to America. But read the book, if you can get it. If you skip anything, skip the letters in which he tries to be jocular and runs into slang—mere slang, which he seems to take for fun.—BRYANT, WILLIAM CULLEN, 1877, *To Miss J. Dewey, June 2*;

William Cullen Bryant, A Biography by Godwin, vol. II, *p.* 383.

He appears to us as a man of an extremely vigorous temperament and a decidedly simple intellect, with an appreciation of natural things and a power of expressing the pleasure of natural science that amount almost to genius, together with an adoration of all things English and Anglican which almost assimilates him to the typical John Bull of foreign caricature, and a hatred of "Popery" which strongly confirms this resemblance. His strongest quality was his great personal energy, which evidently had an influence of an agreeable and improving sort upon those with whom he came into contact.—JAMES, HENRY, 1877, *Charles Kingsley's Life and Letters, The Nation,* vol. 24, *p.* 60.

The life of this almost unique man will do much to give cheer and hope to the world's toilers of every grade; it will open the hearts of multitudes to the teachings of Christianity who would be repelled by the severities of other schools. We welcome it as a voice of gladness and melody.—PUTNAM, JAMES O., 1877-80, *Charles Kingsley; Addresses, Speeches and Miscellanies, p.* 220.

Charles Kingsley, who had shared his [Carlyle's] reaction in political affairs, kept away from him a good deal in later years because he felt himself to be one of the large number implicitly arraigned in the "Life of Sterling" as the disappointed young ladies who had taken the veil. But Carlyle always spoke affectionately of Kingsley. "I have a very vivid remembrance," he once said, "of Charles coming with his mother to see me. A lovely woman she was, with large, clear eyes, a somewhat pathetic expression of countenance, sincerely interested in all religious questions. The delicate boy she brought with her had much the same expression, and sat listening with intense and silent interest to all that was said. He was always of an eager, loving, poetic nature."—CONWAY, MONCURE DANIEL, 1881, *Thomas Carlyle, p.* 69.

Charles Kingsley has been one of the Forces of the present generation. He literally pitched heart-foremost, if not head-foremost, into all the social, scientific, and political problems, thoughtfully discussed by the more careful thinkers of the time, as a kind of "free lance," committed from the start to a championship of the emotional side of every question which his calmer contemporaries were inclined to consider from its reasonable side. If the difficulties which trouble all thinking-men in their endeavors to advance the human race could be overcome by gushes of philanthropic sentiment, Kingsley would have rapidly risen to be the first man of his time. . . . The real lesson taught by Charles Kingsley's life is this: that he was the most impulsive, the most inconsistent, the most passionate, and, at heart, the most conscientious, of human beings. . . . Kingsley never arrived at intellectual and moral manhood. He was a boy,—a grand, a glorious boy, when he first appeared as a dogmatic man, assuming to direct English thought; and a boy, a splendid boy, he remained to the last year of his life. All his vagaries of opinion and sentiment, all the strange inconsistencies of his career, all the sense and all the nonsense which alternately shocked or attracted his contemporaries, were properly to be referred to the plain fact that he never became a mature man. All the learning he acquired, all the experience of life he accumulated through long years, all his contacts and collisions with the minds of friends who represented the most advanced intellect of the age, never could cure him of the boyish defect of substituting impulse for intelligence, even in the consideration of those complicated problems in which intelligence should manifestly be the supreme guide and arbiter.—WHIPPLE, EDWIN PERCY, 1885, *Some Noted Princes, Authors, and Statesmen of Our Time,* ed. *Parton, pp.* 230, 231.

It is pleasing to recall the distinguished rector's attachment to dumb animals among the traits of his every-day life. Like Mrs. Somerville, he believed that some of the created beings inferior to man were destined to share the blessings of a future state of existence. His dog and his horse were his friends. As a perfect horseman, possessing the patience and much of the skill of a Rarey, he was a pattern to all who ride, reasoning with the animal he governed, and talking to it in gentle tones, mindful that the panic-fear both of horses and children is increased by harsh punishment.—EVERSHED, HENRY, 1886, *Canon Kingsley, National Review.*

No man was ever more sensitive to public opinion—felt its censure more keenly, or enjoyed its applause more frankly than he. He has often lamented his sensitiveness to me, and that he "was bred to think first, not whether a thing was right or wrong but, what Lady A or Mr. B would say about it." And yet with all this sensitiveness it would be hard to find any man of our time who was less warped by it—who wavered less in saying or doing the word or thing which he felt it was true and right to say or do, looking the storm, which he knew it would bring about his ears, straight in the face all the time. I am not aware that this has ever been fairly brought out, and it deserves a prominent place in studying and estimating his life's work. . . . I don't think anyone can appreciate Charles Kingsley rightly who is not aware of or does not take into account this almost painful sensitiveness.— HUGHES, THOMAS, 1892, *Charles Kingsley, Novelist, a Lecture by J. A. R. Marriott, Prefatory Note, p.* iv.

In all nature he saw something to admire, and his walks, to him, were as poems. On his lawn dwelt a family of toads, that lived on from year to year in the same hole in the green bank, which the scythe was never allowed to approach. He had two little friends in a pair of sand wasps, which lived in a crack of the window in his dressing-room; one of which he had rescued from drowning in a hand basin, taking it out tenderly and putting it in the sunshine to dry. The little fly-catcher which built its nest every year under his bedroom window was a constant joy to him. He had also a favourite slow-worm in the churchyard, which his parishioners were warned not to kill. Such tastes he encouraged in his children, and in the lads of the village, teaching them to love and handle gently, without disgust, all living things,—toads, beetles, frogs, etc., as being works and wonders from the hands of a living God; and though all this was true, and that he loved such humble creatures, yet to spiders he had the greatest aversion.—DAY, GEORGE, 1896, *Naturalists and their Investigations, p.* 148.

His keen interest in country sport, and in country pursuits generally, enabled him to sympathize with country gentlemen and sportsmen of all grades, and with agriculturists, farmers, and labourers alike; and his soldierly instincts, which he never lost, drew to him the soldier class, both officers and men, whom the neighbourhood of Eversley to Aldershot gave him rare opportunities of influencing. Hence, men were affected by him as they had not been affected by clergymen before; and he was regarded as the apostle of "muscular Christianity," a term which he thought most offensive, but which was understood at any rate by many, in a complimentary, not an offensive sense.—OVERTON, JOHN HENRY, 1897, *The Church in England, vol.* II, *p.* 391.

At Westminster he preached again many of the sermons which he had preached at Chester, and they produced a profound effect. It was curious to see him stand in the pulpit and gaze round him on the vast congregations with something of anxious curiosity. He felt the responsibility of those occasions, but he managed to create a sort of electric sympathy between his hearers and himself—a sympathy caused by the depth of his sincerity and earnestness.— FARRAR, FREDERIC WILLIAM, 1897, *Men I have Known, p.* 281.

Kingsley was a great martyr to stammering, it often was torture to him in a lively conversation to keep us all waiting till his thoughts could break through again. In church, however, whether he was reading or speaking extempore, there was no sign of stammering; apparently there was no effort to overcome it. But when he walked home from church he would say: "Oh, let me stammer now, you won't mind it."—MÜLLER, FRIEDRICH MAX, 1898, *Auld Lang Syne, p.* 109.

THE SAINT'S TRAGEDY
1848

We stayed at home reading the "Saint's Tragedy" by Charles Kingsley; the story of St. Elizabeth of Hungary, put into dramatic form with great power. I wish I had hit upon this theme for my Golden Legend, the mediæval part of my Trilogy. It is nobler and more characteristic than my obscure legend. Strange, that while I was writing a dramatic poem illustrating the Middle Ages, Kingsley should have been doing the same, and that we should have chosen precisely the same period, about 1230. His poem was published first, but I never saw it, or a review of it, till two days ago.—LONGFELLOW, HENRY WADSWORTH, 1852, *Journal, April* 2; *Life, ed. Longfellow, vol.* II, *p.* 219.

When Mr. Kingsley published his first poem, "The Saint's Tragedy," I was vain and conceited enough to write a preface to it. Soon enough the public had sense to perceive that, if recommendations were wanted, I should rather have begged one from him; soon enough I gave such offence to the public as would have rendered any recommendations of mine very damaging to the person who received them. That damage Mr. Kingsley has suffered, and has borne with kindness and generosity of which I may be excused for attempting to speak.—MAURICE, FREDERICK DENISON, 1859, *Mr. Kingsley and the "Saturday Review," Macmillan's Magazine, vol.* 1, *p.* 118.

It contained not only poetry of a very high order, but its character and its comedy are equally good.—FRISWELL, JAMES HAIN, 1870, *Modern Men of Letters Honestly Criticised, p.* 322.

The work by which his reputation in the world of letters was first established, and is likely to be longest maintained.—MARTIN, SIR THEODORE, 1879, *The Life of His Royal Highness the Prince Consort, vol.* IV, *p.* 283.

When the time has come for the literary history of England in the nineteenth century to be written by a competent hand, the "Saint's Tragedy" will have in it occupy an honoured place as a powerful dramatic expression of the social aspirations, from a religious point of view, in 1848, as conceived not too clearly, but entertained none the less fervently by one of the most generous spirits of that time.—KAUFMANN, MORITZ, 1892, *Charles Kingsley, Christian Socialist and Social Reformer, p.* 74.

ALTON LOCKE
1850

As for "Alton Locke," I totally forget all the miraculous part, and only read it as an intensely, frightfully practical book, and bought a more expensive pair of boots in consequence!—FOX, CAROLINE, 1853, *Letter to E. T. Carne, Jan.* 19; *Memories of Old Friends, ed. Pym. p.* 307.

Nowhere can you find any proof that the author is able to think about anything. An idea strikes him; he seizes it, and, to use Hawthorne's expression, "wields it like a flail." Then he throws it down and takes up something else, to employ it in the same wild and incoherent fashion. This is Kingsley all out, and always. He is not content with developing his one only gift of any literary value—the capacity to paint big, striking pictures with a strong glare or glow on them. He firmly believes himself a profound philosopher and social reformer, and he will insist on obtruding before the world on all occasions his absolute incapacity for any manner of reasoning on any subject whatsoever. Wild with intellectual egotism, and blind to all teaching from without, Kingsley rushes at great and difficult subjects head downwards like a bull.—McCARTHY, JUSTIN, 1872, *The Reverend Charles Kingsley, Modern Leaders, p.* 216.

"Alton Locke" may be fairly regarded as his best piece of work. . . . With all the genuine force of "Alton Locke"—and no living novelist has excelled the vividness of certain passages—there is an unsatisfactory side to the whole performance. It is marred by the feverishness which inspires most of his work. There is an attempt to crowd too much into the space, and the emphasis sometimes remains when the power is flagging. Greater reserve of power and more attention to unity of effect would have been required to make it a really great book.—STEPHEN, LESLIE, 1877-92, *Hours in a Library, vol.* III, *pp.* 47, 52.

As a novel it is almost a failure, but not so as a propagandist work of fiction. In its presentation of fact it is a complete success. In the description of fetid and filthy workshops and fever dens of the sweaters, in its exposure of the causes which turned honest and peaceable workmen into conspirators, the author of "Alton Locke" did the work of half a dozen labour commissions, and did it much more effectually by appealing in fervid tones of passionate sympathy to the well-to-do people of his day, calling upon them to rescue their fellow-men from destruction of soul and body, and stimulating private and public philanthropy to set about and face the social problem with honesty of purpose.—KAUFMANN, MORITZ, 1892, *Charles Kingsley, Christian Socialist and Social Reformer, p.* 130.

We can make sure of the fact that "Alton Locke" has been potent as a twofold protest: first against the cruel exploitation of labor, and second against the misdirected resentment of the sufferers. Its insurrection is on a far broader ground, and with a much wider intention than that of "Jane Eyre." It is human and that is personal; but because humanity is still so much weaker than personality, it has probably influenced vastly fewer readers. Then, it has failed of equal influence, undoubtedly, because it is not of equal art. It is a polemic, in which all the characters, of whatever party they apparently are, are always arguing for the author. . . . Neither Lillian Winnstay, the shallow-hearted, romantic beauty, who flatters the poor poet by her pleasure in his verse and his picturesque personality, nor Eleanor Staunton, who snubs him for his good, but is really his friend, and the faithful friend of all the poor, is more than an illustration.—HOWELLS, WILLIAM DEAN, 1901, *Heroines of Fiction*, vol. II, pp. 3, 4.

YEAST
1851

Canon Kingsley will be remembered longest by "Yeast" and "Alton Locke," the works of his "Sturm und Drang" period as "the Chartist Parson," before he had found a solution for everything. They are too bizarre to be permanently popular, but bizarre as they are, they are unmistakably powerful, and probably did much in their day to loosen the crust of callous prejudice into which the self-complacency of the comfortable classes always tends to harden. If everyone had worked as hard as Canon Kingsley to remedy the grievances which once excited him, it could not be said that he was premature in ceasing to be a revolutionist.—SIMCOX, GEORGE AUGUSTUS, 1875, *The Late Canon Kingsley, The Academy*, vol. 7, p. 115.

The verses given to Tregarva in "Yeast" sum up his diagnosis of the social disease with admirable vigour. Many scenes in that rather chaotic story are equally vivid in their presentation of the facts. The description of the village feast is a bit of startlingly impressive realism. The poor, sodden, hopeless, spiritless peasantry consoling themselves with strong drink and brutal songs, open to no impressions of beauty, with no sense of the romantic except in lawless passion, and too beaten down to have even a thought of rebellion except in the shape of agrarian outrage, are described with singular force.—STEPHEN, LESLIE, 1877-92, *Hours in a Library*, vol. III, p. 51.

"Yeast" is a book very difficult to classify. It is not exactly a novel, it is more than a "Dialogue," it is too romantic for a sermon, it is too imaginative for a pamphlet, it is too full of action for a political and social treatise. Incongruous as it is, it is interesting and effective, and contains some of Kingsley's best work. It has some of his most striking verses, some of his finest pictures of scenery, many of his most eloquent thoughts, all his solid ideas, the passion of his youth, and the first glow of his enthusiasm. It was written before he was thirty, before he thought himself to be a philosopher, before he professed to be entrusted with a direct message from God.— HARRISON, FREDERIC, 1895, *Studies in Early Victorian Literature*, p. 175.

HYPATIA
1853

"Hypatia" never came; but I cannot afford to be without it. Part of the conclusion seems to me particularly valuable. I mean the talk of the Christianized Jew to the classic boy. Hypatia's mistreatment by the Alexandrians I found almost too horrible. It is very powerful and tragic; but I objected to the word "naked." Pelagia's nakedness has nothing which revolts one . . . but I really was hurt at having Hypatia stript, tho' I see that it adds to the tragic, and the picture as well as the moral is a fine one.—TENNYSON, ALFRED LORD, 1853, *To Charles Kingsley; Alfred Lord Tennyson, A Memoir by his Son*, vol. I, p. 367.

You have performed a great and lasting work, but it is a bold undertaking. You fire over the heads of the public, οἷοι νυν ἄνθρωποι εἴσιν, as Nestor says, the pigmies of the circulating library. Besides, you have (pardon me) wronged your own child most cruelly. Are you aware that many people object to reading or allowing it to be read, because, the author says in the Preface, it is not written for those of pure mind? My daughters exclaimed when they read that in the Preface, after having read to their mamma the whole in numbers to general edification, as they do Bible and Shakspeare every day. I should wish you to have said, that in describing and picturing an age like that, there must be here and there nudities as in nature and as in the Bible. Nudities there are because there is truth. For God's sake, let that Preface not come before Germany without some modified expression. Impure must be the minds who can be offended or hurt by your picture! What offends and hurts is the modern

Lüsternheit, that veiling over indecency, exciting imagination to draw off the veil in order to see not God's naked nature, but corrupted man's indecency. Forgive that I take the child's part against the father! But, indeed, that expression is not the right, and unjust to yourself, and besides highly detrimental to the book.—BUNSEN, CHRISTIAN KARL JOSIAS BARON, 1853, *Letter to Kingsley, May; Charles Kingsley, his Letters and Memories of his Life*, ed. his Wife, vol. I, p. 367.

He leaves himself very much in the case of him who wrote a severe attack upon himself and neglected the intended vindication. We see the evil in full operation, there is a dramatic exhibition of that; but we discover only from a few didactic hints, that matters would have been mended by a different state of circumstances. With all its gorgeousness of coloring, and sustained intensity of interest, and general correctness of conclusion, "Hypatia" must be pronounced a failure.—BAYNE, PETER, 1858, *Essays in Biography and Criticism, Second Series*, p. 36.

It is difficult to believe that, either in "Hypatia" or in "Two Years Ago," he had laid his plot beforehand: in "Yeast" there does not pretend to be any plot at all. "Hypatia" especially might have been so grand, and is so disappointing. There is a consummate mastery of the costume and character of the epoch; there are magnificent materials of character and fancy brought together to the workshop; there are gorgeous descriptions of external beauty; there are individual scenes of thrilling interest; there are wonderful glimpses both of thought and passion. . . . The inconsiderate confusion in which the incidents of the story jostle and stumble over one another, and the indistinctness with which many of them are told, compel us to reserve our admiration for particular scenes and portions, and render it impossible to praise the work as a whole. . . . Still, with all its faults, it is unquestionably a work of genius; but of genius in a hurry,—of genius, as it were, shut up without fire or candle, like an inharmonious jury, and compelled to complete its task before it can regain its liberty.—GREG, WILLIAM RATHBONE, 1860-73, *Kingsley and Carlyle, Literary and Social Judgments*, p. 139.

It was his moral enthusiasm, which, in the pages of "Hypatia" has scathed with an everlasting brand the name of the Alexandrian Cyril and his followers, for their outrages on humanity and morality in the name of a hollow Christianity and a spurious orthodoxy. Read, if you would learn some of the most impressive lessons of Ecclesiastical history.—Read and inwardly digest those pages, perhaps the most powerful he ever wrote which close that wonderful story by discriminating the destinies which awaited each of its characters as they passed, one after another, "each to his own place." — STANLEY, ARTHUR PENRHYN, 1875, *Funeral Sermon on Canon Kingsley in Westminster Abbey*.

Among Kingsley's works, "Hypatia" is probably the one most widely known and appreciated, not only in England, but in Germany, France, and Italy also. Though a mere novel, it represents the struggle of the old Greek world with the new powers of Christendom with truly dramatic art.— MÜLLER, FRIEDRICH MAX, 1877-84, *Biographical Essays*, p. 366.

Apart from its other merits, many and conspicuous, "Hypatia" remains a monument of painstaking research. I should hesitate indeed to pledge myself to the accuracy of the minute details—though Kingsley took extraordinary pains to attain it— or even to the broad truth of the historical portraiture; it may be, as some one has said, that a sound historian would shudder at innumerable anachronisms and pick holes in every paragraph, but all I say is, produce me the "sound historian" who knew that period as Kingsley knew it, produce me the man as deeply read as Kingsley was in the Alexandrine mystics, and then we will argue about details. Meanwhile, in "Hypatia" we undoubtedly possess a wonderfully vivid—and in the main an accurate picture of one of the most important, pregnant, fateful epochs in the history of the world—a period which witnessed the death agonies of the Great Empire of the past, which saw the struggling to the birth of the new and vigorous nationalities of the future.—MARRIOTT, J. A. R., 1892, *Charles Kingsley Novelist, A Lecture*, p. 29.

The summer of 1863 added a third contest, which was provoked by the same theological bitterness. Stanley and Dr. Liddell had proposed that the University should confer the honorary degree of D. C. L. on the Rev. Charles Kingsley. The proposal was resisted by Dr. Pusey, partly on the ground of Kingsley's universalism, but more particularly on the ground that "Hypatia" was a work not fit to be read by our "wives and sisters." To Stanley the attack on "Hypatia" seemed the more unjustifiable and offensive because the book had been recommended to him by Mrs. Augustus Hare, and because he had himself urged his mother to read it. He carefully prepared a speech for the Council, in which he demanded "that the aspersions cast upon the moral character of the book, in the gross language which I have copied out from Pusey's lips, be withdrawn."—PROTHERO, ROWLAND E., 1893, *The Life and Correspondence of Arthur Penrhyn Stanley, vol.* II, *p.* 135.

An ambitious novel, at once historical and philosophical, impressive in parts, but on the whole heavy.—WALKER, HUGH, 1897, *The Age of Tennyson, p.* 270.

"Hypatia" still remains the sublimest subject that historical fiction has appropriated to its use—the death struggle between Greek and Christian civilization in the fifth century. . . . A second purpose is unmistakably conveyed in his sub-title to "Hypatia:" "New Foes with an Old Face." Kingsley was bitterly anti-Roman, and wished to arrest the movement toward Rome that Newman had given the Church of England. These ulterior aims lent to "Hypatia" a modern tone, making out of it a novel of aggressive purpose. But they stood in the way of real history. What purports to be historical facts in "Hypatia" Leslie Stephen has pronounced a bubble that bursts on the most delicate touch; the Church of Rome as therein represented is not the church of the fifth century, and the Goths are mythical.—CROSS, WILBUR L., 1899, *The Development of the English Novel, p.* 145.

It cannot be said by the unprejudiced reader that his Hypatia is an attractive personality. He has somehow failed to give her charm, though he has given her a beautiful body, perfectly moulded features, with blue eyes and yellow hair, and a glorious intellect. But the truth is his Hypatia remains as cold as the baths of Apollo, and it is not going too far to say that she is rather repellent. Of course she might answer that she did not mean to be otherwise, in her poet's hands, and that what he had shown her, that she was; rather arrogant in mind, holding matrimony in high scorn, and thinking but little better, if any, of maternity. The passion of the ardent young monk Philammon for this snow-cold divinity is not made altogether credible, and his sister, poor, pretty, Pelagia, who has lived the life of a wanton and is presently the paramour of the Gothic chief Amal, is more winning in some things that take the heart.—HOWELLS, WILLIAM DEAN, 1901, *Heroines of Fiction, vol.* II, *p.* 6.

WESTWARD HO!
1855

The construction of the romance we think, bears the marks of haste, and may perhaps be pronounced clumsy. . . . In beauties of detail no work of the author is more rich. Mr. Kingsley rarely constructs a character. But in the honest Jack Brimblecombe, that strange compound of imperfect literature and genuine feeling, of skin-deep valor and heart-sound faith, he has drawn a living man, less adequately developed indeed, but as fresh and original, as the inimitable Saunders Mackey of Alton Locke. . . . We hail it as a strong and a suggestive work.—HURLBUT, W. H., 1855, *Kingsley's Sir Amyas Leigh, Christian Examiner, vol.* 59, *pp.* 289, 290, 295.

"Westward Ho!" partakes much more of the character of biography and history than of the ordinary sentimental novel. Love plays a great part in the progress of the story, as it does in the lives of most men; but it is as motive influencing character and determining action that it is exhibited, not as itself the sole interest of life, the single feeling which redeems human existence from dulness and inward death. The love which acts on the career and character of Amyas Leigh does not spend itself in moonlight monologues or in passionate discourses with its object; nor does the story depend for its interest upon the easily roused sympathy of even the stupidest readers with the ups and downs, the fortunes and emotions, of a passion common in certain degrees and certain kinds to all the race. It is no such narrow view of life that is presented here, but rather that broad sympathy with human action and human feeling in its manifold completeness which gives to art a range as wide as life itself, and throws a consecrating beauty over existence from the cradle to the grave, wherever human affections act, wherever human energies find their object and their field, wherever the battle between right and wrong, between sense and spirit, is waged—wherever and by whatever means characters are trained, principles strengthened, and humanity developed.—BRIMLEY, GEORGE, 1855-58, "*Westward Ho!*" *Essays*, ed. Clark, p. 300.

Finished "Amyas Leigh." It is an ample and rather grand book, with magnificent passages of description; but too ponderous and melodramatic.—LONGFELLOW, HENRY WADSWORTH, 1856, *Journal, July 12; Life* ed. Longfellow, vol. II, p. 285.

A finer, nobler story for boys does not exist.—FRISWELL, JAMES HAIN, 1870, *Modern Men of Letters Honestly Criticised*, p. 330.

The most famous, and perhaps the best novel, of Charles Kingsley. Often one has read it since, and it is an example of those large, rich, well-fed romances, at which you can cut and come again, as it were, laying it down, and taking it up on occasion, with the certainty of being excited, amused—and preached at.—LANG, ANDREW, 1891, *Essays in Little*, p. 153.

When you read Charles Kingsley's story of "Westward Ho!" (which you surely should read, as well as such other matter as the same author has written relating to Raleigh) you will get a live glimpse of this noble knight of letters, and of those other brave and adventurous sailors of Devonshire, who in those times took the keels of Plymouth over great wastes of water. Kingsley writes of the heroes of his native Devon, in the true Elizabethan humor—putting fiery love and life into his writing; the roar of Atlantic gales breaks into his pages, and they show, up and down, splashes of storm-driven brine.—MITCHELL, DONALD G., 1890, *English Lands, Letters and Kings, Elizabeth to Anne*, p. 18.

His "Westward Ho!" may be regarded as an ideal example of the historical romance, so equably is a story of private life interwoven with public history.—MOULTON, RICHARD GREEN, 1895, *Kingsley's "Westward Ho!" The Chautauquan*, vol. 20, p. 548.

A historical romance, the scene of which is laid in the time of Elizabeth, is generally considered Kingsley's best work; and it is only a small minority, to which the writer happens to belong, who find it dreary. The power of some of the descriptions must be acknowledged; but whether "Westward Ho!" will live is a question on which there may be difference of opinion.—WALKER, HUGH, 1897, *The Age of Tennyson*, p. 270.

It is just the author's sympathy with the times, and with the men of the times, even down to their prejudices and fierce dislikes, that has given to "Westward Ho!" its unique success as a romance of that age of young and energetic enthusiasms. It is a manly book, and therefore pre-eminently a book for boys. From cover to cover there is nothing maudlin or weakly sentimental in it. Its verve and energy are infectious. All through the reader is conscious of that tingling of the blood that accompanies the excitement of a succession of high adventures.—GRAHAM, RICHARD D., 1897, *The Masters of Victorian Literature*, p. 91.

TWO YEARS AGO
1857

To us this appears the cleverest and the pleasantest of Mr. Kingsley's novels.—GREG, WILLIAM RATHBONE, 1860-73, *Kingsley and Carlyle, Literary and Social Judgments*, p. 141.

Is in many respects a painful performance. It contains, indeed, some admirable descriptions of scenery; but the sentiment is poor and fretful. Tom Thurnall, intended to be an embodiment of masculine vigour, has no real stuff in him. He is a bragging, excitable, and at bottom sentimental person. All his swagger fails to convince us that he is a true man. Put beside a really simple and masculine nature like Dandie Dinmont, or even beside Kingsley's own Amyas Leigh, one sees his hollowness. The whole story leads up to a distribution of poetical justice in Kingsley's worst manner. He has a lamentable weakness for taking upon himself the part of Providence.—STEPHEN, LESLIE, 1877-92, *Hours in a Library*, vol. III, p. 55.

The critical judgments on this novel are—as usual—singularly diverse. There are those who place it highest, while others place it lowest on the list of Kingsley's novels. For my part I should do neither. In construction it is perhaps the worst, but, on the other hand, in characterization and descriptive power it seems to me equal if not superior to the best. And after all it is in that gift of descriptive power, of dramatic delineation, of graphic word painting, that Kingsley surpassed all other novelists of his generation.—MARRIOTT, J. A. R., 1892, *Charles Kingsley Novelist, A Lecture*, p. 26.

ANDROMEDA
1858

His "Andromeda" is an admirable composition,—a poem laden with the Greek sensuousness, yet pure as crystal, and the best-sustained example of English hexameters produced up to the date of its composition. It is a matter of indifference whether the measure bearing that name is akin to the antique model, for it became, in the hands of Kingsley, Hawtrey, Longfellow, and Howells, an effective form of English verse. The author of "Andromeda" repeated the error of ignoring such quantities as do obtain in our prosody, and relying upon accent alone; but his fine ear and command of words kept him musical, interfluent, swift. — STEDMAN, EDMUND CLARENCE, 1875–87, *Victorian Poets*, p. 251.

In "Andromeda" Kingsley has shown a measure of power with which those who know him only through his lyrics would scarcely credit him. Many a canvas has gleamed with the statuesque figure of that old-world princess, but in none has it stood out more clearly than in the word-pictures of this fine poem. It is presented to us steeped in the clear golden air of the southern day; and the pure Pagan joy of existence, with its refusal to "look before and after," its absolute satisfaction with the present, and its shrinking even from the shadow of death, characterise most strikingly this late version of the oft-told tale.— GROSER, HORACE G., 1892, *The Poets and the Poetry of the Century, Kingsley to Thomson*, ed. Milnes, p. 4.

In "Andromeda" he has written the very best English hexameters ever produced, and perhaps the only ones in which that alien or rebel takes on at least the semblance of a loyal subject to the English tongue. The rise of the breeze after the passage of the Nereids, the expostulation of Andromeda with Perseus, and the approach of the monster, are simply admirable.— SAINTSBURY, GEORGE, 1896, *A History of Nineteenth Century Literature*, p. 325.

THE WATER BABIES
1863

His last great and spontaneous success.— SIMCOX, GEORGE AUGUSTUS, 1877, *Charles Kingsley, Fortnightly Review*, vol. 27, p. 23.

Perhaps there is no one book in which so many of the distinctive features of Charles Kingsley are combined as in the delightful "Water Babies," dedicated to his youngest son, Grenville Arthur, and to all other good little boys. In it we have his eager sympathy with suffering; his love for little children; his hatred of cruelty and injustice; his intolerance of ignorance which masquerades as knowledge; his delight in the wonderful things of Nature, which are the works of God. It is a dull soul who does not feel for poor little Tom, who spent his time between laughing and crying, and who thought it must be a very dirty lady who could need a bath-tub! Cousin Cramchild and Aunt Agitate seem, alas! like familiar friends. There is something as deep as there is delicious in the argument concerning the existence of water-babies.— ROGERS, ARTHUR, 1898, *Men and Movements in the English Church*, p. 329.

HEREWARD THE WAKE
1866

The story of "Hereward the Wake" has one peculiar charm which is not always to be found in stories. It is that charm which is found in matchless perfection in the Greatest of Story-books, and which gives to the life-histories recorded there such wonderful power and influence over our lives of nowadays, helping us, if we use the help rightly, to "make our lives sublime." It is the charm of perfect truth. The man Hereward is made to live and move before us as he lived and moved before his contemporaries, with all the strength and all the weakness of his character, a man of like passions with ourselves.— FIELD, MRS. E. M., 1893, *Great Characters of Fiction*, ed. Townsend, p. 145.

It has two great merits: it reproduces in a marvellous way the impression of the fen country; and, by vivid flashes, though not constantly, the reader seems to see before his eyes the very life of the old vikings.— WALKER, HUGH, 1897, *The Age of Tennyson*, p. 270.

POEMS

Kingsley's true poetic faculty is best expressed in various sounding lyrics for which he was popularly and justly esteemed. These are new, brimful of music, and national to the core. "The Sands o' Dee," "The Three Fishers," and "The Last Buccaneer" are very beautiful; not studies, but a true expression of the strong and tender English heart.— STEDMAN, EDMUND CLARENCE, 1875–87, *Victorian Poets*, p. 251.

His verse, however, has a great deal of merit, and may be read with some true pleasure. He had a capacity for poetry, as he had capacities for many things beside, and he cultivated it as he cultivated all the others. His sense of rhythm seems to have been imperfect. His ear was correct, and he often hit on a right and beautiful cadence; but his music grows monotonous, his rhythmical ideas are seldom well sustained or happily developed. His work abounds in charming phrases and in those verbal inspirations that catch the ear and linger long about the memory:—as witness the notes that are audible in the opening verses of "The Sands of Dee," the "pleasant Isle of Avès" of "The Last Buccaneer," and the whole first stanza of the song of the Old Schoolmistress in "The Water-Babies." But as it is with his music, so is it with his craftmanship as well. He would begin brilliantly and suggestively and end feebly and ill, so that of perfect work he has left little or none. It is also to be noted of him that his originality was decidedly eclectic—an originality informed with many memories and showing sign of many influences; and that his work, even when its purpose is most dramatic, is always very personal, and has always a strong dash in it of the sentimental manliness, the combination of muscularity and morality, peculiar to its author. For the rest, Kingsley had imagination, feeling, some insight, a great affection for man and nature, a true interest in things as they were and are and ought to be—above all, as they ought to be!—and a genuine vein of lyric song.—HENLEY, WILLIAM ERNEST, 1880, *The English Poets*, ed. Ward, vol. IV, p. 608.

Simple, brave, resolute, manly, a little given to "robustiousness," Kingsley transfigured all these qualities by possessing the soul and the heart of a poet. He was not a very great poet indeed, but a true poet—one of the very small band who are cut off, by a gulf that can never be passed, from mere writers of verse, however clever, educated, melodious, ingenious, amiable, and refined. He had the real spark of fire, the true note; though the spark might seldom break into flame, and the note was not always clear. Never let us confuse true poets with writers of verse, still less with writers of "poetic prose." Kingsley wrote a great deal of that—perhaps too much: his descriptions of scenes are not always as good as in Hereward's ride round the Fens, or when the tall, Spanish galleon staggers from the revenge of man to the vengeance of God, to her doom through the mist, to her rest in the sea. Perhaps only a poet could have written that prose; it is certain no writer of "poetic prose" could have written Kingsley's poems.—LANG, ANDREW, 1891, *Essays in Little*, p. 156.

Kingsley was, above all things, a worker, a worker with a keen moral consciousness, and a worker who sang at his work. His could never have been a life of mere æsthetic production. His best poems are those that he put forth, rhymeless and metreless, as stories; and these are instinct with the desire to promote nobility of conduct and character.—GROSER, HORACE G., 1892, *The Poets and the Poetry of the Century, Kingsley to Thomson*, ed. Miles, p. 2.

If Kingsley, with all his literary gifts, was never quite in the first rank in anything, he came nearest to being a poet of mark. Some of his ballads almost touch the high-water mark of true ballad poetry, with its abrupt fierce blows of tragedy and pathos, its simple touches of primitive rude speech, its reserve of force, its unspoken mysteries. At any rate, Kingsley's best ballads have no superior in the ballads of the Victorian era in lilt, in massiveness of stroke, in strange unexpected turns. "The Weird Lady" is an astonishing piece for a lad of twenty-one.—HARRISON, FREDERIC, 1895, *Studies in Early Victorian Literature*, p. 166.

Kingsley was one of those darlings—perhaps the rarest—of the Muses to whom they grant the gift not only of doing a little poetry exquisitely, but the further gift of abstaining from doing anything ill; and he seems to have recognised almost at once that "the other harmony," that of prose, was the one meant for him to do his day's work in.—SAINTSBURY, GEORGE, 1896, *A History of Nineteenth Century Literature*, p. 326.

GENERAL

The intensity of Mr. Kingsley's genius always secures to his productions a certain singleness of impression. The most heterogeneous materials, put into the crucible of his thoughts and brought to its white heat, flow down in the forms perfectly characteristic and distinct. The unity, however, is simply that of his own personality, meeting us again and again;—a phenomenon, let us say, ever delightful to us, and rich in whatever it is best to love and admire; but needing for its full power more elaboration of matter and harmony of plan than he exacts from himself.—MARTINEAU, JAMES, 1854, *Alexandria and her Schools, Essays Philosophical and Theological, vol.* II, *p.* 293.

In Mr. Kingsley's volumes the emotions play, we suspect, rather too important a part; yet their prevalence, attuned, as they always are, to nobleness and valor, spreads a general healthfulness around. To read his works, is like travelling in a pleasant hilly country, where the fresh hearty breeze brings you the strength of the mountains, and the clear atmosphere shows you every line, and curve, and streamer, of the clouds that race the wind. You may be compelled to remark that the cornfields are not so heavy as in the rich plain, that perhaps the poppy and the corn-flower, beautiful to the eye, but light on the granary-floor, are somewhat too abundant, and that there is an ample allowance of gay copse, and heath, and fern. But you feel that, at least, there is no miasma, that there is no haze, such as floats suspiciously over the rich, moist meadow, that you are in a land of freshness, freedom, health.—BAYNE, PETER, 1858, *Essays in Biography and Criticism, Second Series, p.* 11.

Whatever objections may be taken to his method, and whatever may be thought of his success, there can be no mistake as to his intention. His very rhetoric is surcharged, to the extent of a vehement mannerism, with the phrases of his Theology; and there is not one of his novels that has not the power of Christianity for its theme.—MASSON, DAVID, 1859, *British Novelists and Their Styles, p.* 280.

He reminds of nothing so much as of a war-horse panting for the battle; his usual style is marvellously like a neigh,—a "ha! ha! among the trumpets!" the dust of the combat is to him the breath of life; and when once, in the plenitude of grace and faith, fairly let loose upon his prey—human, moral, or material—all the Red Indian within him comes to the surface, and he wields his tomahawk with an unbaptized heartiness, slightly heathenish, no doubt, but withal unspeakably refreshing. It is amazing how hard one who is a gladiator by nature strikes when convinced that he is doing God service.—GREG, WILLIAM RATHBONE, 1860–73, *Kingsley and Carlyle, Literary and Social Judgments, p.* 117.

Men of far greater intellect have made their presence less strongly felt, and imprinted their image much less clearly on the minds of their contemporaries. He is an example of how much may be done by energetic temper, fearless faith in self, an absence of all sense of the ridiculous, a passionate sympathy, and a wealth of half-poetic descriptive power. If ever we have a woman's parliament in England, Charles Kingsley ought to be its chaplain; for I know of no clever man whose mind and temper more aptly illustrate the illogical impulsiveness, the rapid emotional changes, the generous, often wrong-headed vehemence, the copious flow of fervid words, the vivid freshness of description without analysis, and the various other peculiarities which, justly or unjustly, the world has generally agreed to regard as the special characteristics of woman. — MCCARTHY, JUSTIN, 1872, *The Reverend Charles Kingsley, Modern Leaders, p.* 221.

We cannot help regarding these letters and speeches of 1848–56 as a manly effort for order at a time when so many influences threatened instability and revolution in our country. There is much in them that may even now be found useful in reference to the question of bringing working-men into churches, and making them sober and loyal. Kingsley's words must have frequently acted as a corrective to the wild and feverish tirades of trades' leaders. In not a few respects, indeed, the direction which sanitary improvement, as well as wise philanthropical and political effort is taking now, may be regarded as a confirmation of much that Charles Kingsley said in these Reform Speeches and Letters. It is because we owe him such a deep debt of gratitude for pleasure, and for many wise and cheerful words, that we have taken it upon us to try to show that his "Chartism," which was the outcome of practical sympathy, rather than a reasoned political scheme, in any respect, was not of quite such a mad and dangerous sort as has often been asserted.—JAPP, ALEXANDER H., (H. A. PAGE), 1876, *Charles Kingsley's Chartism, Good Words, vol.* 17, *p.* 416.

With little subtlety of insight or feeling, with too much tendency to boisterous edification, he was still a most admirable descriptive writer. As a poet, it appears, he took himself too seriously; "Santa Maura" we see now was written with more emotion than it will be read with. The "Three Fishers" will probably live; it is too soon to guess whether the "Bad Squire" and the "Buccaneer" will follow the "Corn-Law Rhymes" to a premature grave. "Andromeda" has most of the merits of a Broad Church tract and an Alexandrian heroic idyll. His mantle as a novelist has fallen upon writers so unlike him as the author of "Guy Livingstone," "Ouida," and Miss Broughton.—SIMCOX, GEORGE AUGUSTUS, 1877, *Charles Kingsley, Fortnightly Review,* vol. 27, p. 31.

Kingsley's exuberant faith in his own message showed the high spirits of youth rather than a profound insight into the conditions of the great problems which he solved so fluently. At the time, however, this youthful zeal was contagious. If not an authority to obey, he was a fellow-worker in whom to trust heartily and rejoice unreservedly.—STEPHEN, LESLIE, 1877-92, *Hours in a Library,* vol. III, p. 32.

The Chartist movement in England called forth from him two novels, "Alton Locke" (1850) and "Yeast" (1851), which, amidst much that is crude and chaotic, are full of eloquent writing and breathe a spirit of earnest sympathy with the sufferings of the poor. . . . No more thoroughly healthy-souled man has adorned this generation, and few have been more potent for good.—NICOLL, HENRY J., 1882, *Landmarks of English Literature,* pp. 399, 400.

In both Lamennais and Kingsley we have the same admixture of humility and audacity, the charm of natural simplicity which attracts friends and attaches disciples, and the leonine defiance of falsities and wrongs which repels time-serving neutrals and opponents. In both, too, we observe the "passionate limitation of view" which looks on human affairs from the ideal standpoint of social reformers, rather than the realistic standpoint of social politicians or economic thinkers. This often impels them to dwell on social wrongs with the forcefulness of undisciplined exaggeration—a fault only partly corrected in Kingsley by his quasi-scientific habits of thought and social sympathies.—KAUFMANN, MORITZ, 1882-88, *Lamennais and Kingsley, Christian Socialism,* p. 80.

These lectures ["Roman and the Teuton"] throw no light upon any of the difficult and disputed points in the history of the Middle Ages. But this fact does not detract from their value. They were intended not as a history, but rather as a commentary on the significance and influence of historical events. They are to be judged, therefore, simply as the speculations of a remarkably ingenious and interesting mind; and, as such, they form, for the general reader, one of the most stimulating volumes ever written on this somewhat dreary period. Every lecture shows the fertility of imagination, the exuberance of fancy, and the ingenuity of expression that have made Kingsley's writings so delightful to a large number of readers. Few persons will read the books without being aroused and stimulated to new trains of thought.—ADAMS, CHARLES KENDALL, 1882, *A Manual of Historical Literature,* p. 154.

Kingsley was far less intense and theological. He had a broader nature, which took in more of the variety and beauty of life. He had, as Maurice acknowledged, a far higher capacity of natural enjoyment. But he, too, in everything—in his novel-writing, in his social efforts, in his history and science, as well as in his sermons—was a witness to the Divine. He did not glow, as Maurice did, with a Divine radiance in all he did; he had neither his "Master's subtlety nor his profundity; but he was more intelligible, healthy, and broad-minded, and he carried the spirit of Christianity as heartily, if not as profoundly, into all his work. Maurice was more of the Prophet both in his tenderness and occasional fierceness—Kingsley more of the Poet. Yet with all his more concrete poetic sympathies, the pupil was earnest as the theological master he delighted to honor.—TULLOCH, JOHN, 1885, *Movements of Religious Thought in Britain During the Nineteenth Century,* p. 182.

His novels have fine artistic qualities, but they are really parables rather than novels, pure and simple, and they can only be adequately valued by people who are in sympathy with the ethical thought and sentiment which they hold in solution.

Enthusiasm for Kingsley as a novelist is hardly ever found uncombined with enthusiasm for him as a theologian, a politician, and a social reformer; nor would Kingsley have valued even the most ardent appreciation of the body of his work unaccompanied by sympathy with its indwelling soul.—NOBLE, JAMES ASHCROFT, 1886. *Morality in English Fiction*, p. 44.

The minor prophets were many, but Charles Kingsley was the foremost among them.—BESANT, SIR WALTER, 1887, *Books which Have Influenced Me*, p. 23.

Of Kingsley more than of any other contemporary writer, it may be said that his works, in one way or another, are always the reflection of himself. He writes invariably from within, outwards. In what Goethe defines as true dramatic power—the power which is possessed by some men of putting themselves in the place of characters with whom they have nothing in common—"Wilhelm Meister" himself was not more deficient. Such of his creations, as are anything but painted, though often vividly painted, shadows, owe their life to the fact that they enshrine some portion of their creator's varied personality. . . . The "Wizard of the North" never makes himself visible amongst the scenes and persons he has conjured up; but the presence of Charles Kingsley, whether under the guise of philosopher, Viking, muscular Christian, gentleman adventurer, or at least as himself acting the part of chorus, can never for a moment be forgotten.—MALLOCK, MISS M. M., 1890, *Charles Kingsley, Dublin Review*, vol. 107, p. 13.

In the beginning of 1864 Kingsley had an unfortunate controversy with John Henry Newman. He had asserted in a review of Mr. Froude's "History" in "Macmillan's Magazine" for January 1860 that "Truth, for its own sake, had never been a virtue with the Roman catholic clergy," and attributed this opinon to Newman in particular. Upon Newman's protest, a correspondence followed, which was published by Newman (dated 31 Jan. 1864), with a brief, but cutting, comment. Kingsley replied in a pamphlet called "What, then, does Dr. Newman mean?" which produced Newman's famous "Apologia." Kingsley was clearly both rash in his first statement and unsatisfactory in the apology which he published in "Macmillan's Magazine" (this is given in the correspondence). That Newman triumphantly vindicated his personal character is also beyond doubt. The best that can be said for Kingsley is that he was aiming at a real blot on the philosophical system of his opponent; but, if so, it must also be allowed that he contrived to confuse the issue, and by obvious misunderstandings to give a complete victory to a powerful antagonist. With all his merits as an imaginative writer, Kingsley never showed any genuine dialectical ability.—STEPHEN, LESLIE, 1892, *Dictionary of National Biography*, vol. XXXI, p. 178.

To put it plainly, I cannot like Charles Kingsley. Those who have had opportunity to study the deportment of a certain class of Anglican divines at a foreign *table d'hôte* may perhaps understand the antipathy. There was almost always a certain sleek offensiveness about Charles Kingsley when he sat down to write. He had a knack of using the most insolent language, and attributing the vilest motives to all poor foreigners and Roman Catholics and other extra-parochial folk, and would exhibit a pained and completely ludicrous surprise on finding that he had hurt the feelings of these unhappy inferiors—a kind of indignant wonder that Providence should have given them any feelings to hurt. At length, encouraged by popular applause, this very second-rate man attacked a very first-rate man. He attacked with every advantage and with utter unscrupulousness; and the first-rate man handled him; handled him gently, scrupulously, decisively; returned him to his parish; and left him there, a trifle dazed, feeling his muscles. — QUILLER-COUCH, A. T., 1895, *Adventures in Criticism*, p. 139.

The merits of Kingsley as a writer, and especially as a writer of fiction, are so vivid, so various, and so unquestionable by any sound and dispassionate criticism, that while cynics may almost wonder at his immediate and lasting popularity with readers, serious judges may feel real surprise at his occasional disrepute with critics. The reasons of this latter, however, are not really very hard to find. He was himself a passionate partisan, and exceedingly heedless as to the when, where, and how of obtruding his partisanship. He had that unlucky foible of inaccuracy in fact which sometimes, though by no means always, attends the faculty of brilliant description and declamation, and which especially characterised his own set or coterie. Although possessed of the keenest sense both of beauty and of humour, he was a little uncritical in expressing himself in both these departments, and sometimes laid himself open in reality, while he did so much oftener in appearance, to the charge of lapses in taste. Although fond of arguing he was not the closest or most guarded of logicians. And lastly, the wonderful force and spontaneity of his eloquence, flowing (like the pool of Bourne, that he describes at the opening of his last novel) a river all at once from the spring, was a little apt to carry him away with it.—SAINTSBURY, GEORGE, 1896, *English Prose, ed. Craik, vol.* V, *p.* 647.

If his early socialistic novels begin to be obsolete, "Hypatia" and "Westward Ho!" have borne the strain of forty years, and are as fresh as ever. The vivid style of Kingsley was characteristic of his violent and ill-balanced, but exquisitely cheery nature.—GOSSE, EDMUND, 1897, *A Short History of Modern English Literature, p.* 372.

A popular writer, only superficially acquainted with history, but imbued with a magnificent enthusiasm and a manly and tender religious feeling.—HUTTON, WILLIAM HOLT, 1897, *Social England, ed. Traill, vol.* VI, *p.* 274.

The fact is that Kingsley was all his life, in everything he thought and in everything he did, a poet, a man of high ideals, and likewise of unswerving honesty.—MÜLLER, FRIEDRICH MAX, 1898, *Auld Lang Syne, p.* 109.

Kingsley, a man of aggressive energy, intense enthusiasms, varied interests, and lofty ideals, was one of the most stimulating and wholesome influences of his time.—PANCOAST, HENRY S., 1899, *Standard English Poems, Spenser to Tennyson, p.* 736, *note.*

There have been many writers, no doubt, of higher literary rank, but few who by their works have given their generation so much pleasure, and still fewer who have given it in such a thoroughly healthy and invigorating way. And certainly no intelligent reader ever rose from a perusal of Kingsley's books without feeling himself a little stronger, more natural, more sympathetic human being, or without an increased sense of that faith in God and nature which was always at the centre of Kingsley's thought. — STUBBS, CHARLES WILLIAM. 1899, *Charles Kingsley and the Christian Social Movement, p.* 182.

The passion of strenuous effort in these books has burned away the mist and fog of the earlier day. It is too much to say that "Alton Locke" brought on the political reforms of England—the demands of the Charter, the equal districts, the vote by ballot, the extended suffrage. It is too much to say that "Yeast" or "Alton Locke" freed the apprentice or emancipated the agricultural laborer. But it is not too much to say that they notably advanced the cause of freedom. When the influences are summed up which have made for social and political enlightenment in England, no small share will be found due to these purposeful novels of Charles Kingsley.—STODDARD, FRANCIS HOVEY, 1900, *The Evolution of the English Novel, p.* 173.

Sir Charles Lyell
1797–1875

Sir Charles Lyell, geologist, born at Kinnordy, Forfarshire, 14th November 1797, the eldest son of the mycologist and Dante student, Charles Lyell (1767–1849). Brought up in the New Forest, and educated at Ringwood, Salisbury, and Midhurst, in 1816 he entered Exeter College, Oxford, and took his B. A. in 1819. At Oxford in 1819 he attended the lectures of Buckland, and acquired a taste for the science he afterwards did so much to promote. He studied law, and was called to the bar; but devoting himself to geology, made European tours in 1824 and 1828–30, and published the results in the "Transactions of the Geological Society" and elsewhere. His "Principles of Geology (1830-33) may be ranked next after Darwin's "Origin of Species" among the books which have exercised the most powerful influence on scientific thought in the 19th century. It denied the necessity of stupendous convulsions, and taught that the greatest geological changes might have been produced by forces still at work. "The Elements of Geology" (1838) was a supplement. "The Geological Evidences of the Antiquity of Man" (1863) startled the public by its unbiased attitude towards Darwin. Lyell also published "Travels in North America" (1845) and "A Second Visit to the United States" (1849). In 1832-33 he was professor of Geology at King's College, London. Repeatedly president of the Historical Society, and in 1864 president of the British Association, he was knighted in 1848 and created a baronet in 1864. He died in London 22d February 1875, and was buried in Westminster Abbey. See "Life, Letters, and Journals" (1881), and Prof. Bonney's "Charles Lyell and Geology" (1895).—PATRICK AND GROOME, eds., 1897, *Chambers' Biographical Dictionary*, p. 609.

PERSONAL

CHARLES LYELL,
BARONET, F. R. S.,
AUTHOR OF
"THE PRINCIPLES OF GEOLOGY."
BORN AT KINNORDY, IN FORFARSHIRE,
NOVEMBER 14, 1797;
DIED IN LONDON,
FEBRUARY 22, 1875.
THROUGHOUT A LONG AND LABORIOUS LIFE
HE SOUGHT THE MEANS OF DECIPHERING
THE FRAGMENTARY RECORDS
OF THE EARTH'S HISTORY
IN THE PATIENT INVESTIGATION
OF THE PRESENT ORDER OF NATURE,
ENLARGING THE BOUNDARIES OF KNOWLEDGE
AND LEAVING ON SCIENTIFIC THOUGHT
AN ENDURING INFLUENCE.
"O LORD, HOW GREAT ARE THY WORKS,
AND THY THOUGHTS ARE VERY DEEP."
PSALM XCII. 5.
—INSCRIPTION ON GRAVE, 1875, *Westminster Abbey*.

He was in many ways a very interesting man. His scientific confrères were probably little aware of the vein of deeper sentiment in him which kept him in sympathy with moral and religious trusts too often disowned by them. Few men have found a more distinct work to do in science and in life; or have done it with more complete effect.—MARTINEAU, JAMES, 1875, *To A. J. Mott*, Feb. 25; *Life and Letters*, ed. Drummond, vol. II, p. 85.

Of him who is thus laid to rest, if of any one of our time, it may be said that he followed truth with a zeal as sanctified as ever fired the soul of a missionary, and with a humility as child-like as ever subdued the mind of a simple scholar. For discovering, confirming, rectifying his conclusions, there was no journey too distant to undertake. Never did he think of his own fame or name in comparison of the scientific results which he sought to establish. From early youth to extreme old age it was to him a solemn religious duty to be incessantly learning, constantly growing, fearlessly correcting his own mistakes, always ready to receive and reproduce from others that which he had not in himself. Science and religion for him not only were not divorced, but were one and indivisible.—STANLEY, ARTHUR PENRHYN, 1875, *Sermon in Westminster Abbey; Life, Letters and Journals of Sir Charles Lyell*, ed. Mrs. Lyell, vol. II p. 461.

I saw more of Lyell than any other man, both before and after my marriage. His mind was characterised, as it appeared to me, by clearness, caution, sound judgment, and a good deal of originality. When I made any remark to him on Geology, he never rested until he saw the whole case clearly, and often made me see it more clearly than I had done before. He would advance all possible objections to my suggestion, and even after these were exhausted would long remain dubious. A second characteristic was his hearty sympathy with the work of other scientific men. . . . His delight in science was ardent, and he felt the keenest interest in the future progress of mankind. He was very kind-hearted, and thoroughly liberal in his religious beliefs, or rather disbeliefs; but he was a strong theist. His candour was highly remarkable. He exhibited this by becoming a convert to the Descent theory, though he had gained much fame by opposing Lamarck's views, and this after he had grown old.—DARWIN, CHARLES, 1876, *Autobiography, The Life and Letters of Charles Darwin*, ed. his Son, vol. I, p. 59.

Above the medium height and having a well-shaped head and clear-cut intellectual features [with a forehead of surprising height and width], Lyell would have been a man of commanding presence if his extremely short sight had not obliged him to stoop and to peer into anything he wished to observe. In Lyell a keen insight into nature and human nature, a well-balanced judgment, and a strong sense of justice, were combined with a deep veneration for all that is noble and true. ... It was his warm sympathy and receptivity, combined with true philosophical candour, which kept him to the very last in touch with advancing knowledge. In his work Lyell was very methodical, beginning and ending at fixed hours. Accustomed to make use of the help of others on account of his weak sight, he was singularly unconscious of outward bodily movement, though highly sensitive to pain. When dictating, he was often restless, moving from his chair to his sofa, pacing the room, or sometimes flinging himself full length on two chairs, tracing a pattern with his finger on the floor, as some thoughtful or eloquent passage flowed from his lips. But though a rapid writer and dictator, he was sensitively conscientious in the correction of his manuscript, partly from a strong sense of the duty of accuracy, partly from a desire to save his publisher the expense of proof corrections. Hence passages once finished were rarely altered, even after many years, unless new facts arose.—FISHER, ARABELLA BUCKLEY, 1893, *Letter to Grenville A. J. Cole, Dictionary of National Biography, vol.* XXXIV, *p.* 323.

Sir Charles Lyell realized to my mind the man of science as he was of old; devout, and yet entirely free-thinking in the true sense; filled with admiring, almost adoring love for Nature, and also (all the more for that enthusiasm) simple and fresh-hearted as a child. ... Sir Charles's interest in his own particular science was eager as that of a boy.—COBBE, FRANCES POWER, 1894, *Life by Herself, vol.* II, *pp.* 404, 405.

PRINCIPLES OF GEOLOGY
1830–33

Mr. Lyell's system of geology is just half the truth, and no more. He affirms a great deal that is true; and he denies a great deal which is equally true; which is the general characteristic of all systems not embracing the whole truth.—COLERIDGE, SAMUEL TAYLOR, 1833, *Table Talk, June* 29; *Table Talk and Omniana, ed. Ashe, p.* 230.

I think his book by many degrees the best work, not only on his subject, but on any scientific subject with which I am acquainted. It reduces an intricate, obscure, and most enormously copious subject, to one which is almost mathematically arranged, clear and condensed. His generalisations are quite inimitable, except by the singular beauty and force of his detailed descriptions and his patient investigation of disputed points; to which I may add the calm, dispassionate, gentlemanlike style in which he handles, not one, but every controversial subject which the subject requires should be discussed. And yet he does this with so much liveliness both of manner and of diction, and with such genuine earnestness, that I, for one, cannot help being swept away with the gentle but irresistible current of his persuasive eloquence. For, indeed, his book contains the essence of eloquence; right reason, extensive and exact knowledge, cultivated taste, and a disinterested and philosophical desire to state the matter in such a way that truth may be the result. There is, moreover, an elegance of fancy throughout, and a touch of humour, or rather of wit, which are in happy companionship with the simplicity and general elegance of the composition. It is already, in my apprehension, the first book of the day, and every time I read it, I am filled the more and more with respect for the author's talents and his knowledge, and feel more and more grateful to him for the pleasure he has given me. I trust he will be able soon to print a cheaper edition, for the book would soon be very extensively circulated, if its form and price were such as to enable the great body of readers to get at it.—HALL, BASIL, 1833, *Letter to Leonard Horer, Sept.* 7; *Life, Letters and Journals of Sir Charles Lyell, ed. Mrs. Lyell, vol.* II, *Appendix A., p.* 465.

The appearance of this work will always form an epoch in the history of geology.... It is not less due to him than to our readers, that we should observe, in conclusion, how distinctly the general tendency of these volumes is to open up new, interesting, and expansive views of the mighty work of Creative Intelligence. ... No reader can peruse it without being deeply impressed by the fresh and striking proofs it affords, in every page, of the Almighty Power, Wisdom, and Goodness.—WHEWELL, WILLIAM, 1835, *Lyell's Principles of Geology, Quarterly Review, vol.* 53, *pp.* 407, 448.

I have recently read afresh the first

edition of the "Principles of Geology;" and when I consider that this remarkable book had been nearly thirty years in everybody's hands, and that it brings home to any reader of ordinary intelligence a great principle and a great fact—the principle, that the past must be explained by the present unless good cause be shown to the contrary; and the fact, that, so far as our knowledge of the past history of life on our globe goes, no such cause can be shown—I cannot but believe that Lyell, for others, as myself, was the chief agent for smoothing the road for Darwin. For consistent uniformitarianism postulates evolution as much in the organic as in the inorganic world. The origin of a new species by other than ordinary agencies would be vastly greater "catastrophe" than any of those which Lyell successfully eliminated from sober geological speculation. — HUXLEY, THOMAS HENRY, 1887, *On the Reception of the "Origin of Species," The Life and Letters of Charles Darwin*, ed. his Son, vol. I, p. 543.

The "Principles of Geology" is by no means light reading, but as a work of science it ranks deservedly high; in the days when it first appeared it was probably rendered more attractive by the delicately heretical flavour, which added a charm to all similar researches in those days, but has now become too much a matter of course to interest any one.—OLIPHANT, MARGARET O. W., 1892, *The Victorian Age of English Literature*, p. 365.

In 1871 he published a virtually new work, which has seen four editions, "The Student's Elements of Geology." For several years his was the only convenient modern text-book on the subject, and it may already be regarded as a classic. The life-work of the author is exemplified even here, by the treatment of the various systems in descending order, thus proceeding from the known towards the unknown, from existing phenomena to the endeavour to comprehend the past.—COLE, GRENVILLE A. J., 1893, *Dictionary of National Biography*, vol. XXXIV, p. 323.

It is the destiny of all books of science to be soon superseded and superannuated, while those of literature may live for all time. I suppose Sir Charles Lyell's "Principles of Geology" has undergone, or will undergo, this fate ere long; but the magnanimity and candor which made him, in issuing the tenth edition of that book, abjure all his previous arguments against evolution and candidly own himself Darwin's convert, was an evidence of genuine loyalty to truth which I trust can never be forgotten. He was, as Professor Huxley called him, the "greatest Geologist of his day"—the man "who found Geology an infant science feebly contending for a few scattered truths, and left it a giant, grasping all the ages of the past."—COBBE, FRANCES POWER, 1894, *Life, by Herself, vol.* II, p. 408.

The man who dealt the death-blow to the old uncritical view of geology was Sir Charles Lyell, whose "Principles of Geology" marks an epoch in the science. Lyell's central doctrine is that the past history of the earth must be inferred by ordinary processes of observation and reasoning from the present, and that it is possible to interpret "the testimony of the rocks" by means of principles which we still see at work. In other words he was a "uniformitarian." The victory of his view established "the reign of law" over the field of geology, and went far towards convincing men of its universality. Assuming no causes except such as he could point to in experience, Lyell showed how the geological formations of the earth arose. According to Darwin, the effect of Lyell's work could formerly be seen in the much more rapid progress of geology in England than in France; and the "Principles of Geology" was most helpful to Darwin himself.— WALKER, HUGH, 1897, *The Age of Tennyson*, p. 177.

Lyell's "Principles of Geology" will always rank as one of the classics of geology and must form an early part of the reading of every man who would wish to make himself an accomplished geologist.—GEIKIE, SIR ARCHIBALD, 1897, *The Founders of Geology*, p. 281.

ANTIQUITY OF MAN
1863

You asked me to tell you, when I had read it, what I thought of Sir Charles Lyell's book. I have only to-day finished the perusal of the copy he kindly sent me, that is, all but half of the matter on the glacial period, which I reserve till I can read it more attentively. Throughout it is a very interesting and to me a very satisfactory book. It is three books: 1. A capital résumé and examination of what we knew about the evidence of antiquity of man; no evidence we had not read of before, but very clearly presented, of course. 2. A treatise on the glacial period. Out of this I have much to learn, and must read it all again carefully; of a part I have not yet cut the leaves. 3. On transmutation matters. That part of the book I can judge somewhat of, and I declare it first-rate. It is just about what I expected, and is characteristic of the man. I think that you, and Hooker, are unreasonable in complaining of Lyell that he does not come out "flat-footed," as we say, as an advocate of natural-selection transmutation. For, 1st, it is evident that though inclined strongly towards it he is by no means satisfied that natural selection will do all the work you put upon it. 2nd, he very plainly implies nearly all you would have him say. And, 3d, he serves your cause (supposing it to be well-founded) quite as effectually, perhaps, by his guarded position, by his keeping the position of a judge rather than of an advocate, and by considering still the case as not yet ripe for a decision.—GRAY, ASA, 1863, *To Charles Darwin, April 20; Letters, ed. Gray, vol.* II, *p.* 503.

The book may seem, from the literary critic's point of view, rather composite in character, and this objection was made in a good-natured form by a writer in the "Saturday Review," who called it "a trilogy on the antiquity of man, ice, and Darwin." That, however is but a slight blemish, if blemish it be, and it was readily pardoned, because of the general interest of the book, the clearness of its style, and the lucidity of its reasoning.—BONNEY, THOMAS GEORGE, 1895, *Charles Lyell and Modern Geology, p.* 185.

GENERAL

Mr. Lyell's book, ["Travels in North America"] to borrow a term from his favourite science, may be likened to a *pudding-stone*, in which the geological plums are thickly set in a thin paste of travel. As the latter is seasoned with praise nearly to the American taste, the whole will be devoured by the omnivorous general reader, although much of it will be somewhat beyond his comprehension.—GRAY, ASA, 1845, *Lyell's Travels in North America, North American Review, vol.* 61, *p.* 498.

His scientific observations are full of information and entertainment, though we cannot always go along with him in his theories; but the materials which he has brought together to assist one in forming a correct view of the condition and prospects of various portions of our country, and of the character of the several classes of its inhabitants, are more complete and trustworthy than can be found in any single book of travels in America with which we are acquainted.—BOWEN, FRANCIS, 1849, *Lyell's Second Visit to America, North American Review, vol.* 69, *p.* 353.

Lyell . . . is an excellent and thoughtful writer, but not, I think, a great field observer . . . his mind is essentially deductive not inductive.—SEDGWICK, ADAM, 1865, *Life and Letters, vol.* II, *p.* 412.

I do not know whether I was quite so much interested by Lyell's work as by Lubbock's "Prehistoric Times;" but I do not think Lyell has left much room for doubt as to his opinions on any point on which he must be supposed to have made up his mind, nor did his book acquaint me with any as to the main question which I had not previously heard from himself in conversation.—THIRLWALL, CONNOP, 1865, *Letters to a Friend, Nov.* 24, *ed. Stanley, p.* 43.

Sir Charles Lyell has always maintained orthodoxy of opinion while boldly seeking the truths unfolded to his penetration by his favorite science. His writings have been rather noted for their pith than for their voluminousness; he has written *multum*, not *multa*, in accordance with the counsel of the old philosopher. His style is always positive, and his elucidations are clear and exhaustive. He was one of those who gave an impulse to the great intellectual movement which is bearing fruit in the animated scientific discussions of the present day, of which many of the writers have now got far beyond him.—TOWLE, GEORGE M., 1871, *Sir Charles Lyell, Appleton's Journal, vol.* 6, *p.* 214.

For somewhere about half a century he continued in the van of English geologists, and so identified himself with them and their pursuits as to be justly taken as the leader of geological speculation in this country. . . . Of his work among the Tertiary formations, with the nomenclature by which, through that work, they are now universally known, his observations on the rise of land in Sweden, his researches into the structure of volcanic cones, and other original contributions, over and above the solid additions to science supplied by the numerous editions of his popular works, it is not needful to make mention here. Enough is gained if at this time these few lines recall some of the services to which Sir Charles Lyell devoted a long, honourable, and illustrious life, which have graven his name in large letters on the front of the temple of science, and in memory of which that name will long be remembered with gratitude and enthusiasm as a watchword among the students of geology.—GEIKIE, SIR ARCHIBALD, 1875, *Scientific Worthies*, *Nature, vol.* 12, *pp.* 325, 327.

The science of Geology is enormously indebted to Lyell—more so, as I believe, than to any other man who ever lived.—DARWIN, CHARLES, 1876, *Autobiography, The Life and Letters of Charles Darwin*, ed. his Son, *vol.* I, ⨍ 60.

Many books have been written about Mont Blanc, its botany and its glaciers, but none have ever equalled, in truthfulness and freshness of description, the diary of Lyell. He seized upon all the remarkable points to be noticed, and shone both as a botanist and geologist. . . . Lyell's long-expected book on the "Principles of Geology" was published in 1830, and it made a very considerable sensation, and was warmly combated and abused. Now it is admitted as the most conclusive and useful of introductory books, fit for a youth, and eminently good in its tone.—DUNCAN, P. MARTIN, 1882, *Heroes of Science, pp.* 312, 326.

In reviewing the seventy-eight years of his labours, it is impossible to avoid seeing throughout how admirably his opportunities were adapted to the work he had to do. He was the right man, to start with; but the lines also fell to him in the right places. With equal abilities, equal ardour, and equal singleness of purpose, he could not have done so much without the happy conjunction of circumstances as well. On the other hand, the lesson of his valuable life throws only into stronger relief the utter waste of powers and opportunities on the part of most other Englishmen in like positions. Ninety-nine people out of a hundred, put in Lyell's place, would have been nothing better than masters of foxhounds or slaughterers of tame pheasants.—ALLEN, GRANT, 1882, *Sir Charles Lyell, Fortnightly Review, vol.* 37, *p.* 87.

It has been sometimes said that Lyell was not an original thinker. Possibly not; *vixere fortes ante Agamemnona* is true in science no less than in national history; there were mathematicians before Newton, philosophic naturalists before Darwin, geologists before Lyell. He did not claim to have discovered the principle of uniformity. He tells us himself what had been done by his predecessors in Italy and in Scotland: but he scattered the mists of error and illusion, he placed the idea upon a firm and logical basis; in a word, he found uniformitarianism an hypothesis, and he left it a theory. That surely is a more solid gift to science, a better claim to greatness, than any number of brilliant guesses and fancies, which, after coruscating for a brief season to the amazement of a gaping crowd, explode into darkness, and are no more seen.—BONNEY, THOMAS GEORGE, 1895, *Charles Lyell and Modern Geology, p.* 219.

The greatest geologist of his time.—WILLIAMS, HENRY SMITH, 1901, *The Story of Nineteenth-Century Science, p.* 99.

Sir Arthur Helps
1813–1875

Born, at Balham Hill, Streatham, 10 July 1813. At Eton, 1829–32. Matric. Trin. Coll., Camb., 1832; B. A., 1835; M. A., 1839. Priv. Sec. to Chancellor of Exchequer, 1836 [?]–39; to Sec. for Ireland, 1839. Commissioner of French, Danish and Spanish Claims. Married Bissel Fuller. Clerk of Privy Council, June 1860 to March 1875. Hon. D. C. L., Oxford, 8 June 1864. C. B., June 1871; K. C. B., July 1872. Died, in London, 7 March 1875. *Works:* "Thoughts in the Cloister and the Crowd" (anon:), 1835; "Essays written in the intervals of Business" (anon.), 1841; "Catherine Douglas" (anon.), 1843; "King Henry II." (anon.), 1843; "The Claims of Labour" (anon.), 1844; "Friends in Council," ser. i. (2 pts.), 1847–49; ser. ii., 1859; "A Letter from one of the Special

Constables in London" (anon.), 1848; "The Conquerors of the New World" (anon.), 1848; "Companions of my Solitude" (anon.), 1851; "A Letter on Uncle Tom's Cabin" (anon.) 1852; "The Spanish Conquest in America" (4 vols.), 1855–61; "Oulita the Serf" (anon.) 1858; "Organization in Daily Life" (anon.), 1862; "Life of Las Casas," 1868 [1867]; "Realmah" (anon.), 1868; "Life of Columbus" (with H. P. Thomas), 1869; "Life of Pizarro," 1869; "Casimir Maremma" (anon.), 1870; "Brevia" (anon.), 1871; "Conversations on War" (anon.), 1871; "Life of Hernando Cortes," 1871; "Life and Labours of Mr. Brassey," 1872 (3rd edn. same year); "Thoughts upon Government," 1872; "Some Talk about Animals" (anon.), 1873; "Ivan de Biron" (anon.), 1874; "Social Pressure" (anon.), 1875. He *edited:* the Prince Consort's "Speeches," 1862; the Queen's "Leaves from the Journal of our Life in the Highlands," 1868; the Queen's "Mountain, Loch and Glen," 1869; T. Brassey's "Work and Wages," 1872. — SHARP, R. FARQUHARSON, 1897, *A Dictionary of English Authors*, p. 130.

PERSONAL

I dined with Arthur Helps yesterday at Sir James Clark's—very snug—only he and myself. He is a sleek man, with close-snipped hair; has a quiet, humorous way of talking, like his books.—ELIOT, GEORGE, 1853, *To Mrs. Bray, Dec. 28; George Eliot's Life as related in her Letters and Journals*, ed. Cross, vol. I, p. 230.

A thin, scholarly, cold sort of a man.—HAWTHORNE, NATHANIEL, 1856, *English Note-Books*, vol. II, p. 24.

Next to humanity the object of Sir Arthur's greatest reverence was its most direct emanation—a book. His acquaintance with books was enormous. He read rapidly, for his power of attention was absolute; and he remembered what he read for that same reason. I am unable to say who were his favourite writers; for the writers he knew best he regarded as personal friends, and among personal friends there should be no favouritism. If I were called upon to say of what writer I have heard him speak the most often and with the greatest admiration, I think it would be one of the last my readers would be likely to name—Machiavelli. But then he had derived his opinion of him, not from the pages of Macaulay, but from the revelations of that great statesman concerning himself—to be found only in his writings and his life. Should a finished portrait of Sir Arthur Helps ever be achieved by a competent hand, it will present traits, moral and intellectual, too numerous and too beautiful to be truthfully attributable to more than a very few men of our own or any other time. One of these traits must not be omitted from the slightest sketch of him—the intensity and constancy of his personal attachments.—HULLAH, JOHN, 1875, *Sir Arthur Helps, Macmillan's Magazine*, vol. 31, p. 553.

He was an excellent host. . . . The admirable tact of the master of the house was always successful in putting people at ease with each other. He talked admirably, and had a marvellously retentive memory, but he never forgot the rule which he puts in the mouth of one of the "Friends in Council"—that "one ought always to be mindful of the first syllable of the word conversation, and talk *with* people, not to them." As head of an Office which had to enter into relation with nearly every department of Government, he gained universal esteem. He treated his subordinates almost as part of his own family, and was perpetually extending his hospitality to them. . . . He was, I think, over-sensitive to adverse criticism, of which he had perhaps not enough to allow him to grow callous to it; and the least misprints in his own books or articles annoyed him exceedingly.—PRESTON-THOMAS, H., 1890, *Arthur Helps, Blackwood's Magazine*, vol. 148, pp. 46, 47, 49.

GENERAL

"Casimir Maremma," by the same author, is an Oriental story. The form of the conversations is not attractive; while the tales, though daringly novel in conception, are not always skilfully worked out. The language throughout is pure and elegant, and the true worth of the matter lies in its earnest and enlightened speculation. . . . Helps's "History of Spanish Conquests in America" deals mainly with the slavery question and with the colonial policy of the Spaniards, and consequently does not trench on the ground so well occupied by Robertson and Prescott. The style of the work is chaste, the sentiment pure and elevated.—SPALDING, WILLIAM, 1852, *A History of English Literature*, pp. 417, 425.

I have been reading Helps' "Conquest" on your recommendation. It is a curiously told story—as if it was being *told* with all the narrator's little private ways of allusion or remark—but very interesting.— CHURCH, RICHARD WILLIAM, 1857, *To Sir Frederick Rogers*, Feb. 17; *Life and Letters of Dean Church*, ed. his Daughter, p. 178.

It ["Oulita"] is a noble and beautiful work. It is strongly marked with the same characteristics which distinguish its author's former writings. Its power and excellence are mainly in thoughtfulness, pathos, humour. There is a certain subtlety of thought,—a capacity gradually to surround the reader with an entire world and a complete life: we feel how heartily the writer has thrown himself into the state of things he describes, half believing the tale he tells, and using gently and tenderly the characters he draws. We have a most interesting story: we see before us beings of actual flesh and blood. . . . The language of the tragedy is such as might have been expected from its author. There is not a phrase, not a word from first to last, to which the most fastidious taste could take exception.—BOYD, ANDREW K. H., 1858, *Oulita the Serf*, *Fraser's Magazine*, vol. 57, p. 529.

Though he is capable of strong conclusiveness, he approaches conclusions by a zig-zag, and tries by a parting kick any god of his own setting up. He concludes, but his conclusions are half-regrets; and his despotism (for he can be despotic) is almost a genial rage; as of a man who should say, "Come, something must be possible; let us go and make that something real after all this vacillation." He says of the statesman—that is, Malverton says of him—that "he should doubt to the last, and then act like a man who has never doubted." To this Ellesmere replies, "Cleverly put, but untrue, after the fashion of you maxim-mongers. He should not act like a man who has never doubted, but like a man who was in the habit of doubting till he had received sufficient information." There is a good deal of Mr. Helps himself in that description; and it is not a bad sketch of the right temperament for a statesman.— HOLBEACH, HENRY, 1870, *The Author of "Friends in Council,"* *Contemporary Review*, vol. 14, p. 429.

No two men have done more, I believe, to save this generation from two or even three extremes of fanaticism, than Mr. Carlyle and Mr. Helps. . . . It is this vein of wise charity, running through all which Mr. Helps has ever written, which makes his books so wholesome to the student of his fellow-men; especially wholesome, I should think, to ministers of religion.—KINGSLEY, Charles, 1872, *Mr. Helps as an Essayist*, *Macmillan's Magazine*, vol. 25, p. 201, 203.

When Mr. Helps, twenty-five years ago, published "Friends in Council," he founded a school of essayists who undertook to apply what—to use one of their favorite expressions—is called "thought" to all the minor affairs of life. . . . Of Mr. Helps's school we confess we cannot with honesty say much good. Of Mr. Helps we gladly speak with considerable respect. He has, as an historian, produced works which place him high among historical writers of the second class. His earlier essays were graceful and intelligent, if not very profound or vigorous. There was a time when he wrote somewhat above the level of his readers, and strove rather to bring them up to him than to descend to their capacities. The candor, moreover, he claims he really possesses, and we suspect he might still as a critic produce works of considerable value. We greatly hope that he may cease to write vaguely on things in general, and produce once more works on history worthy of his considerable reputation. As an historian he has one great merit. He is one of the few men who still believe in moral force, since, in England at least, the limited number of persons who did not bow down and worship force when represented by Louis Napoleon, began to adore it when represented by Bismarck. From this passionate admiration for successful violence Mr. Helps is entirely free. — DICEY, A. V., 1872, *Mr. Arthur Helps*, *The Nation*, vol. 14, pp. 323, 324.

His most popular books are "Friends in Council" and "Companions of my Solitude." In these volumes are reported the conversations of a company of friends, who discuss questions of various kinds,— ethical, social, and literary. English literature contains nothing in the shape of colloquial essays that approaches these in merit. The individuality of the interlocutors is carefully preserved, and the reader acquires a personal interest in each hardly subordinate to the general effect of the wisdom which they interchange. The thought of these essays is effective not only by its intrinsic vigor and its wonderful affinity for the mind of average intelligence, but by the inimitable grace and almost insidious gentleness of its expression. No writer is more remote from dogmatism than Mr. Helps; but his opinions bear unmistakable marks of maturity and fixedness. His felicity of illustration is hardly surpassed, and the tender human sympathy which warms all his writings brings him very near to his readers. Mr. Helps is not a powerful original thinker; but he has the art of presenting the best thought in the most impressive and persuasive shape, in an almost unequaled degree, and of calling out or reanimating ideas which have been latent in the minds of his readers. There are no essays in the language, save perhaps those of Macaulay, that are at once so delightful and so instructive as Mr. Helps's.—CATHCART, GEORGE R., 1874, *ed., The Literary Reader*, p. 323.

I scarcely knew him except at Cambridge forty years ago: and could never relish his Writings, amiable and sensible as they are. I suppose they will help to swell that substratum of Intellectual *Peat* (Carlyle somewhere calls it) from [which] one or two living Trees stand out in a Century.— FITZGERALD, EDWARD, 1875, *Letter*, April 9; *Letters to Fanny Kemble, ed. Wright*, p. 65.

Sir Arthur Helps' books, if they possessed no other merit, would still be valuable to our hurry-skurry age by recalling to us the sense that there is—or used to be—such a thing as Leisure somewhere on the globe.— COBBE, FRANCES POWER, 1875, *Social Pressure*, *The Academy*, vol. 7, p. 5.

In the most characteristic series of his works, of which "Friends in Council" is the centre, he is persistently occupied with a rationale of things which most think it a gain not to think about; how to do things that most do well or ill, and are done with; how to mitigate the surprises and avoid the regrets which meet us by the way, for which most think callousness the only remedy and the best. Throughout, the vein of his speculation is coloured by a view that if we would take up the little difficulties of life and deal with them, the great ones would melt away. He did not treat the weariness of detail and the reluctance to spend thought in articulating statements that border upon truisms as facts to be reckoned with, but as mistakes to be corrected, as, indeed, the sensitive eagerness of his mind, however it was disciplined into patience, always led him to see much more clearly that in life which is modifiable, than that which is fixed. But within its range, his perception was singularly clear and accurate, and there can be little doubt that it was heightened by his keen disinterested sensibility to all concrete discomfort. Perhaps his great talent for the concrete did something to keep his mind in the byways of thought and affairs; the highways of both are paved with abstractions.—SIMCOX, GEORGE AUGUSTUS, 1875, *Sir Arthur Helps*, *The Academy*, vol. 7, p. 268.

Helps' literary career commenced at an early age with the publication in 1835 of "Thoughts in the Cloister and the Crowd." He afterwards attempted history, fiction, drama, but his social essays alone achieved any lasting popularity. . . . his views are for the most part commonplace and are often expressed at tedious length.—BOASE, GEORGE CLEMENT, 1891, *Dictionary of National Biography*, vol. XXV, p. 372.

His position in the world of letters was something of a paradox: he never rose to the highest sphere, yet was a universal favourite of the public, respected and merited every respect; and while treating the loftiest subjects in a manner considered by a mass of readers both original and striking, he never really in any of his works rose above the region of the respectable commonplace.—OLIPHANT, MARGARET O. W., 1892, *The Victorian Age of English Literature*, p. 154.

In different ways enough—for he was as quiet as the other was showy—Helps was the counterpart of Kinglake, as exhibiting a certain stage in the progress of English culture during the middle of the century—a stage in which the Briton was considerably more alive to foreign things than he had been, had enlarged his sphere in many ways, and was at least striving to be cosmopolitan, but had lost insular strength without acquiring Continental suppleness. —SAINTSBURY, GEORGE, 1896, *A History of Nineteenth Century Literature*, p. 384.

He was an overrated writer in his time. He is perhaps underrated now.—SHORTER, CLEMENT, 1897, *Victorian Literature*, p. 191.

Connop Thirlwall
1797–1875

Born, at Stepney, 11 Feb. 1797. Early education at Charterhouse School. Matric. Trin. Coll., Camb., 1814; Craven Scholar, 1815; Bell's Scholar, 1815; Chancellor's Medallist, 1818; B. A., 1818; Minor Fellow, Trin. Coll., 1818; M. A., 1821. Student of Lincoln's Inn, Feb. 1820. Called to Bar, 1825. Ordained Deacon, 1827; Priest, 1828. Rector of Kirby-under-Dale, Yorks, 1834–40. B. D. and D. D., 1840. Bishop of St. David's, July 1840 to May 1874. Died, at Bath, 27 July 1875. *Works:* [exclusive of separate sermons and episcopal charges, etc.]: "Primitiæ" (priv. ptd.), 1809; "History of Greece" (8 vols.), 1835–47; "The Advantages of Literary and Scientific Institutions," 1850; "Inaugural Address" [at the Edinburgh Philosophical Institution], 1861; "The Present State of Relations between Science and Literature," 1867. *Posthumous:* "Remains, literary and theological," ed. by J. J. S. Perowne (3 vols.), 1877–78; "Letters, literary and theological," ed. by J. J. S. Perowne and L. Stokes, 1881; "Letters to a Friend," ed. by Dean Stanley, 1881. He *translated:* Schleiermacher's "Critical Essay on the Gospel of St. Luke," 1825; Niebuhr's "History of Rome" (with J. C. Hare), 1828.—SHARP, R. FARQUHARSON, 1897, *A Dictionary of English Authors, p.* 279.

PERSONAL

My Bishop, I can discern, is a right solid honest-hearted man, full of knowledge and sense, excessively delicate withal, and, in spite of his positive temper, almost timid. No wonder he is a little embarrassed with me, till he feel gradually that I have not come here to eat him, or make scenes in his still house. But we are getting, or as good as got, out of that, and shall for a brief time do admirably well. Here is medicine for the soul, if the body fare worse for such sumptuosities, precisely the converse of Llandough. It is wholly an element of rigid, decently elegant *forms* that we live in. Very wholesome for the like of me to dip for a day or two into that, is it not? For the rest, I have got two other novels of Tieck, of which the admiring Bishop possesses a whole stock.—CARLYLE, THOMAS, 1843, *Letter to Jane Welsh Carlyle, A History of His Life in London,* ed. Froude, vol. I, p. 263.

CONNOP THIRLWALL
SCHOLAR, HISTORIAN, THEOLOGIAN,
FOR THIRTY-FOUR YEARS
BISHOP OF ST. DAVID'S.
BORN FEBRUARY 11, 1797.
DIED JULY 27, 1875.
COR SAPIENS ET INTELLIGENS
AD DISCERNENDUM JUDICIUM.
GWYN. EI. FYD.

—INSCRIPTION ON GRAVE, 1875, *Westminster Abbey, p.* 395.

The Bishop had but few intimate friends; and of those who were his contemporaries at Cambridge, most had passed away before him. To the world at large he was known as the scholar, the historian, the theologian, foremost in the first rank of these; but of the man they knew little or nothing. . . . The Bishop's life was not an eventful life. It was essentially the life of the student and the man of letters; it presented few of those incidents which make the ordinary biography. With the exception of the remarkable episode at Cambridge, there was little in it that attracted notice. Men far less distinguished made more noise in the world. He rarely spoke in the House of Lords; he never threw himself in the strife of parties. No man governed a diocese better, and the difficulties of his diocese were peculiar; but he did not belong to the modern type of bishop, whose efficiency is measured in common estimation by his power of speech and motion.—PEROWNE, J. J. STEWART, 1881, *Letters of Connop Thirlwall,* ed. Perowne and Stokes, *Preface*, pp. v, vi.

In April, 1875, the Bishop became almost totally blind, and lost the use of his right hand. His solitude was relieved as far as possible by those around him. He was kept acquainted with everything that happened, and his unabated interest in all religious and political matters was shown by the letters he dictated. His mind was kept in continual exercise; a letter from his nephew, written a short time before the Bishop's death, speaks of him as translating Sanscrit as it was read to him by one member of the family, Italian and Portuguese with another, and German and French with another. Even the little ones were employed in reading history and chemistry to him. His patience and gentleness touched the hearts of all about him. The loss of eyesight and the loss of power of using his pen must have tried him severely, yet no complaint ever escaped him.—STOKES, LOUIS, 1881, *Letters of Connop Thirlwall, ed. Perowne and Stokes, p. 394.*

The English Church will probably never again have a prelate of Thirlwall's power or character. — FROUDE, JAMES ANTHONY, 1884, *Thomas Carlyle, A History of his Life in London, vol. I, p. 159.*

It has often been observed that every great mind has its distinct phases, according as it is known to outsiders or to intimates. This was true of the late Bishop of St. David's whose claims to greatness are indisputable. You could not judge of him by his portraits and photographs, for which he sat only to please his friends, or by his effigy in Westminster Abbey. The broad forehead, the massive jaw, the intellectual but stern countenance revealed one phase, the smile which occasionally lit up his face revealed another. Under the grave face was an almost womanly tenderness, a sense of humour and an enjoyment of a merry thought, to be looked for in a Wilberforce but which was a revelation in a Thirlwall. But like the heat latent in an anvil, it needed the percussion of kindred influences to bring these warmer traits to the surface. Scholar, historian, theologian—so is he described on his monument; but he was much more than this. He might emphatically have said, *Humani nihil alienum.*— HUNTINGTON, GEORGE, 1886, *Lighter Phases of a Great Mind, Temple Bar, vol. 76, p. 188.*

The Bishop of St. David's, Thirlwall, was staying at the Rectory [1853] when I was at home. Excellent as he was, I was horribly afraid of him, for a more repellent, freezing manner than his I never saw. I hated the Rectory now more than ever, but was more than ever devoted to Lime.— HARE, AUGUSTUS J. C., 1896, *The Story of My Life, vol. I, p. 348.*

HISTORY OF GREECE
1835-47

I have lately read Thirlwall's fourth volume, which perhaps is the best. He has thrown much new light on the history of Athens at the close of the Peloponnesian war. After all, however, the history is so uncertain that one scarcely knows what to believe. He has succeeded in shaking Xenophon's credit to a greater degree than I should have thought possible.—LEWIS, SIR GEORGE CORNEWALL, 1837, *To E. W. Head, June 2; Letters to Various Friends, ed. Lewis, p. 80.*

You will be glad to hear, I think, that the volumes of Thirlwall's Greece seem to me to improve as the work advances. There never could be a doubt as to the learning and good sense of the book; but it seems to me to be growing in feeling and animation, and to be now a very delightful history, as well as a very valuable one.— ARNOLD, THOMAS, 1840, *Letter to Archdeacon Hare, Jan. 26; Life and Correspondence, ed. Stanley, vol. II, p. 174.*

If my early friend Dr. Thirlwall's "History of Greece" had appeared a few years sooner, I should probably never have conceived the design of the present work at all; I should certainly not have been prompted to the task by any deficiencies, such as those which I felt and regretted in Mitford. The comparison of the two authors affords indeed a striking proof of the progress of sound and enlarged views respecting the ancient world during the present generation. Having studied of course the same evidence as Dr. Thirlwall, I am better enabled than others to bear testimony to the learning, the sagacity, and the candour which pervades his excellent work.—GROTE, GEORGE, 1846, *A History of Greece, Preface.*

A work which, as a whole, is not perhaps to be compared favorably with that of Grote, but which still has some points of great advantage. It shows learning, sagacity, and candor; but it falls far short of Grote in that power of combination and generalization which has made the later work so justly famous. The English of Thirlwall is superior to that of Grote, although the style of neither of them is entitled to very high praise. Thirlwall's sympathies are aristocratic rather than democratic—the exact opposite of the sympathies of Grote. The books, therefore, may well be read at the same time, in order that conflicting views may be compared and weighed. Another difference between the two works is that while Grote is especially strong on the earlier history of Greece, Thirlwall is strong on the later history. Perhaps the best portion of Thirlwall's book is that which relates to the age beginning with the period at which Grote ends.—ADAMS, CHARLES KENDALL, 1882, *A Manual of Historical Literature*, p. 93.

Bishop Thirlwall certainly rivalled Gibbon and Macaulay in mental calibre, and the inferior reputation of his "History of Greece" is one proof among many of the supreme importance of striking diction. But still more powerful causes concurred. Writing for a cyclopædia, he inevitably worked with a feeling of constraint; and, though he cannot have underrated the difficulties, he seems to have imperfectly realised the grandeur of his undertaking. Hence he is always a little below his subject, and a little below himself; he delights and instructs, but he does not satisfy.—GARNETT, RICHARD, 1887, *The Reign of Queen Victoria*, ed. Ward, vol. II, p. 453.

It is a work full of interest and much more readable than the more elaborate history of Grote, though the latter has to a great extent supplanted it as a work of reference. Thirlwall's history will, however, always retain its value, and certainly deserves more attention than is generally paid to it.—OLIPHANT, MARGARET O. W., 1892, *The Victorian Age of English Literature*, p. 194.

He is seldom picturesque, and indeed he never tries to be so. But to a scholarship naturally far superior to Grote's, he united a much fairer and more judicial mind, and the faculty of writing—instead of loose stuff not exactly ungrammatical nor always uncomely, but entirely devoid of any grace of style—an excellent kind of classical English, but slightly changed from the best eighteenth century models. And he had what Grote lacked, the gift of seeing that the historian need not—nay, that he ought not to—parade every detail of the arguments by which he has reached his conclusions; but should state those conclusions themselves, reserving himself for occasional emergencies in which process as well as result may be properly exhibited. It is fair to say, in putting this curious pair forward as examples respectively of the popular and scholarly methods of historical writing, that Grote's learning and industry were very much more than popular, while Thirlwall's sense and style might with advantage have put on, now and then, a little more pomp and circumstance. But still the contrast holds; and until fresh discoveries like that of the "Athenian Polity" accumulate to an extent which calls for and obtains a new real historian of Greece, it is Thirlwall and not Grote who deserves the first rank as such in English.—SAINTSBURY, GEORGE, 1896, *A History of Nineteenth Century Literature*, p. 222.

As a historian, Thirlwall is undoubtedly a sounder scholar and a better writer than Grote; he has also a more judicial temper and a finer sense of proportion.—SANDYS, J. E., 1897, *Social England*, ed. Traill, vol. VI, p. 310.

GENERAL

Pray get Thirlwall's "Charge" and read it; it is well worth twice 2s. It is, I think, a specimen of clear, manly thought and expression, and of English equity, though perhaps with too little enthusiasm. There is, however, no want of practical faith, and there are indications of a more devout spirit than one has been wont to attribute to him.—MAURICE, FREDERICK DENISON, 1842, *Letter to Mr. Scratchey, Dec. 28; Life* ed. Maurice, vol. I, p. 336.

A fresh perusal of these remarkable "Charges" has only deepened my impression not merely of the extraordinary ability and learning which everywhere stamp them, but of their permanent value as a philosophical contribution to ecclesiastical literature. They were not merely counsels addressed by the Chief Pastor of a diocese to his clergy, or dissertations of more or less value on topics of transient interest: they were the review by a master mind of all the great questions which have agitated the Church of England during one of the most eventful periods of her history. . . . In the first place, their value consists to a great extent in the depth as well as the breadth of view which they everywhere exhibit. . . . In the next place, the combination of exact scholarship with a vast range of varied learning gave a singular weight to any opinion which fell from him on questions of criticism and interpretation. Here he had no rival on the Episcopal Bench, perhaps none among English scholars. There might be those who were not inferior to him in a critical knowledge of the Old Testament or of the New; none perhaps were equally sure of their ground in both. There were those who surpassed him in minute acquaintance with patristic and mediæval literature; there were none who possessed in the same degree the critical skill which could dissect a text, with the learning which could illustrate it. His range was wide, but he knew its limits. He was no pretender to knowledge; and hence on questions where an acquaintance with scientific investigations seemed necessary to speak with authority, he speaks with reserve and a caution which to many appeared disappointing. But this very reserve inspires confidence. We can trust a guide who resolutely keeps within the limits of his own knowledge.—PEROWNE, J. J. STEWART, 1876, ed. *Remains Literary and Theological of Connop Thirlwall, Preface, vol. I, pp. v, vii.*

Of that thirst for knowledge in all its parts of which the Bible speaks, of the mastery of all ancient and modern learning, few, if any, in his time have been more wonderful examples than he who from his eleventh till his threescore and eighteenth year was always gathering in fresh stores of understanding. Of him, as of Solomon, it might be said, "Thy soul covered the whole earth." There was hardly a civilized language which he had not explored both in its structure and literature. He was the chief of that illustrious group of English scholars who first revealed to this country the treasures of German research, and the insight which that research had opened into the mysterious origin of the races, institutions, and religions of mankind. . . . It may be disappointing to some that this prodigious acquisition of knowledge was not accompanied by a corresponding productiveness. With the exception of the few indications we have given, his learning perished with him.—STANLEY, ARTHUR PENRHYN, 1881, ed. *Letters to a Friend by Connop Thirlwall, Preface, pp, viii, x.*

We shall not attempt to trace the history of the Bishop through the thirty-four years of his episcopal life. The real record of that life consists in his charges, which, for the lucidity and completeness with which they handle every question that has come to the surface in the Church of England during the period over which they extend, and for the vast store of learning compressed into the positions which they establish, defy all comparison with anything which has been produced by any prelate of the present century.—BLAKESLEY, J. W., 1882, *Bishop Thirlwall's Letters, The Academy, vol. 21, p. 20.*

In the sphere, at any rate, of theology Thirlwall might have been expected to influence his age. In him profound learning and unrivalled dialectical skill and supreme soundness of judgment coexisted in a rare combination. The candid perusal of his letters makes it apparent that his mind was constantly occupied with the theological problems which have now exercised and tormented two generations of Englishmen. He was prepared to sum up the never-ending case of scepticism against revealed religion in favor of Christianity. His high character and his intellectual eminence were calculated to give to every expression of his convictions a weight, with the English public at least, as great as ought in reason to be attributed in matters of religious belief to the authority of any individual. But though Thirlwall was prepared to sum up the case, he never (if one may be allowed to follow out a metaphor irresistibly suggested by the idiosyncrasies of his genius) delivered judgment.—DICEY, A. V., 1882, *Bishop Thirlwall, The Nation, vol. 34, p. 149.*

Two of the undergraduates were discussing his "dryasdust" ways in the college library after a fashion a little irreverent, when a Fellow walked up to them. He was a somewhat pompous man, and his reproof was true to his character. "You are probably ignorant, young gentlemen, that the venerable person of whom you have been speaking with such levity is one of the profoundest scholars of our age—indeed, it may be doubted whether any man of our age has bathed more deeply in the sacred fountains of antiquity." "Or come up drier, sir," was the reply of the undergraduate.—DEVERE, AUBREY, 1897, *Recollections, p. 38.*

Connop Thirlwall was celebrated in his day as one of the best of English scholars; but no man was ever less of the mere grammarian. Trenchant intellect and sound judgment were his characteristics. He impressed all who encountered him with his capacity to be a leader of men; and his early enterprises seemed a guarantee that he would redeem his promise. As one of the translators of Niebuhr he moulded English historical thought; and his translations of Schleiermacher's essay on St. Luke made an equally deep impression on English theology.—WALKER, HUGH, 1897, *The Age of Tennyson, p. 123.*

Philip Henry Earl Stanhope
Lord Mahon
1805—1875

Born, at Walmer, 30 Jan. 1805. Matric., Ch. Ch., Oxford, 19 April 1823; B. A., 1827; Created D. C. L., 11 June 1834; M. A., 18 Dec. 1854; Hon. Student, Ch. Ch., 1858-75. M. P. for Wootton-Bassett, 1830-31; for Hertford, 1832-52. Under-Sec. of State for Foreign Affairs, 1834-35; Sec. to Board of Control, 1845-46. F. R. S., 1827. Married Emily Harriet Kerrison, 10 July 1834. F. S. A., 1841; Pres., 1846. Succeeded to Earldom, 1855. Founded Stanhope Modern History Prize at Oxford, 1855. Chairman of National Portrait Gallery, 1857. Lord Rector of Marischal Coll., Aberdeen, 1858. Hon. LL. D. Camb., 1864. Foreign Member of French Acad., 1872. Hon. Antiquary to Royal Academy. Governor of Wellington Coll. Trustee of British Museum. Died, at Bournemouth, 24 Dec. 1875. *Works:* "Life of Belisarius," 1829; "History of the War of the Succession in Spain" (2 pts.), 1832-33; "Lord John Russell and Mr. Macaulay on the French Revolution" (anon.), 1833; "Letters from Switzerland" (anon.; priv. ptd.), 1834; "History of England from the Peace of Utrecht to the Peace of Versailles" (7 vols.), 1836-54; "Speech . . . on the Law of Copyright," 1842; "Essai sur la Vie du Grand Condé" (priv. ptd.), 1842 (English version, 1845); "Historical Essays" (from "Quarterly Rev."), 1849; "The Forty-five," 1851; "Letter to Jared Sparks," 1852; "Secret Correspondence connected with Mr. Pitt's return to Office in 1804" (priv. ptd.), 1852; "Lord Chatham at Chevening" (priv. ptd), 1855; "Addresses delivered at Manchester, Leeds, and Birmingham," 1856; "Address delivered . . . as Lord Rector of Marischal Coll.," 1858; "Life of the Rt. Hon. William Pitt" (4 vols.), 1861-62; "Miscellanies, 1863; "History of England during the Reign of Queen Anne, until the Peace of Utrecht," 1870 (2nd edn. same year); "Miscellanies. second series," 1872. *Posthumous:* "The French Retreat from Moscow, etc." (from "Quarterly Rev."), 1876; "Notes of Conversations with the Duke of Wellington," 1888. He *edited:* Earl of Peterborough's "Letters to General Stanhope," 1834; Hon. A. Stanhope's "Spain under Charles the Second," 1840; "Extracts from Dispatches of the British Envoy at Florence" (priv. ptd. for Roxburghe Club), 1843; "Correspondence between . . . William Pitt and Charles Duke of Rutland," 1842; Earl of Chesterfield's "Letters," 1845; "Memoirs of Sir Robert Peel" (with E. Cardwell), 1856-57.—SHARP, R. FARQUHARSON, 1897, *A Dictionary of English Authors*, p. 265.

PERSONAL

He is a distinguished personage in the way of letters, science and art, and I found him particularly agreeable. He is a slender, thin man, with handsome features, curly hair, and spectacles. — MOTLEY, JOHN LOTHROP, 1858, *To his Wife, June 27; Correspondence*, ed. Curtis, vol. I, p. 284.

GENERAL

He has undoubtedly ["History of the War of Succession in Spain"] some of the most valuable qualities of an historian—great diligence in examining authorities, great judgment in weighing testimony, and great impartiality in estimating characters. . . . His narrative is very perspicuous, and is also entitled to the praise, seldom, we grieve to say, deserved by modern writers, of being very concise. It must be admitted however, that, with many of the best qualities of a literary veteran, he has some of the faults of a literary novice. He has no great command of words. His style is seldom easy, and is sometimes unpleasantly stiff.— MACAULAY, THOMAS BABINGTON, 1832, *Lord Mahon's War of the Succession, Critical and Miscellaneous Essays*.

Lord Mahon's "History" ["From the Peace of Utrecht to the Peace of Versailles"] contains a great quantity of valuable and *original* information, acquired from authentic sources never before opened to the public. It is written in a lively, entertaining style. . . . It is, in short, a substantial and permanent acquisition to one of the most important departments of English Literature. — WARREN, SAMUEL, 1845, *Popular and Practical Introduction to Law Studies, Second Ed.*, p. 1203.

A judicious and accurate writer, whose faithfulness and good sense may be depended on, though he has not the animation and spirit of style which a work of this kind requires.—PEABODY, W. B. O., 1846, *Mahon's Life of the Prince of Condé, North American Review. vol.* 63, p. 122.

Lord Mahon's excellent "History of the War of the Succession in Spain" leaves the same general impression on the mind of the reader as to the effect of that war on the Spanish character, that is left by the contemporary accounts of it. It is, no doubt, the true one.—TICKNOR, GEORGE, 1849, *History of Spanish Literature, Period* ii, *ch.* i, *note.*

An accurate, calmly-tempered, and attractive history, will be found in Lord Mahon's "History of England" during an important part of the last century.—REED, HENRY, 1850–55, *Lectures on English Literature*, p. 259.

We are not going to comment on these agreeable volumes at large. We have read them with great interest and enjoyment;—not with satisfaction; that is more than we can say. . . . Lord Mahon is not only an upright historian, but a writer, in the main, competent and accomplished for his work. If he makes no parade of philosophical disquisition, his exhibition of events and actors is such that the reader easily gets at the lessons, with the added pleasure of seeming to make them his own discovery. His style is perspicuous and flowing. Though not distinguished by vigor or grace, it gets over the ground evenly, and with speed enough, without Gibbon's stilts, or the grand and lofty tumbling of Carlyle. It has the great merit of a flexibility which makes it equal to dignified narrative, and which, at the same time, permits the introduction, without abruptness or jar, of personal anecdotes and illustrations of a lighter character.—PALFREY, JOHN GORHAM, 1852, *Lord Mahon's History of England, North American Review*, vol. 75, p. 125.

Lord Mahon has brought to the arduous task of continuing Hume's "History" through the eighteenth century, the taste of a scholar, the liberality of a gentleman, and the industry of an antiquarian.—ALISON, SIR ARCHIBALD, 1853, *History of Europe, 1815–1852, ch.* v.

There is no work that can be more safely put in the hands of the American historical student than Lord Mahon's, not only for its tolerant and philosophic views of English affairs, but as enabling a reasonable American to feel and understand how his own history appears to a generous and friendly foreign observer. Such a process is very salutary in this self-compiacent meridian.—REED, WILLIAM B., 1855, *ed., Lectures on English Literature, by Henry Reed*, p. 259, *note.*

Lord Stanhope's "Life of Mr. Pitt" has both the excellences and the defects which we should expect from him, and neither of them are what we expect in a great historical writer of the present age. . . . He is not anxious to be original. He travels if possible in the worn track of previous historians; he tells a plain tale in an easy plain way; he shrinks from wonderful novelties; with the cautious skepticism of true commonsense, he is always glad to find that the conclusions at which he arrives coincide with those of former inquirers. His style is characteristic of his matter: he narrates with a gentle sense and languid accuracy, very different from the stimulating rhetoric and exciting brilliancy of his more renowned contemporaries.—BAGEHOT, WALTER, 1861, *William Pitt, Works, ed. Morgan*, vol. III, p. 123.

Earl Stanhope has written from the best materials a most interesting biography of the younger Pitt, with whom he was connected by family ties, by sentiments of gratitude, and by the affinities of political principles; yet he has not hesitated to expose the very grave defects in his character and conduct, and has obtained approbation for candor.—BANCROFT, GEORGE, 1867, *Joseph Reed: A Historical Essay.*

Always writes with dignity and elegance, and inspires confidence in his candor if he does not transport the reader with enthusiasm for his brilliancy.—PORTER, NOAH, 1870, *Books and Reading*, p. 183.

Lord Mahon is a zealous investigator, and a clear and impartial writer. His "History of England" contains an able account,—the best, perhaps, yet written by one not a native,—of the American War of Independence. Unfortunately, however, it involved him in two disputes with American historians. He had charged Sparks with altering Washington's letters, and also with adding matter not contained in them. This charge was indignantly repelled and refuted, and was subsequently withdrawn by Lord Mahon himself. He had also characterized the execution of André as a "blot" upon Washington's career. This led to an exhaustive investigation of the entire subject by Major Charles Biddle of Philadelphia, who showed conclusively "that

Washington had no alternative; the prisoner was regularly tried before the proper tribunal, and received the fate which he had incurred."—HART, JOHN S., 1872, *A Manual of English Literature*, p. 571.

The very titles of most of Lord Stanhope's works are enough to show that the writer was totally devoid of enthusiasm. . . . What he brought to his work were the qualities of calm sense and clear judgment, together with a thorough love of truth for its own sake. No one will probably even rise from the perusal of his history, or of the life of Pitt, which is properly its continuation, with a sense that he has gained any clear insight into the inner life of the times of which they treat. But neither will anyone have cause to complain that his feet have been entangled in the meshes of paradox, or that he has been beguiled with party politics under the name of history. The external facts will have been set clearly before the reader, and it will be for him to interpret the riddle as best he can.—GARDINER, SAMUEL RAWSON, 1876, *Earl Stanhope*, The Academy, Vol. 9, p. 9.

The sympathies of Stanhope are with the Tories, and are therefore the very opposite of those of Macaulay. In point of style, too, the works are very dissimilar. Stanhope has shown great diligence in examining authorities, good judgment in weighing testimony, and great impartiality in estimating characters; but in the presentation of his results he is quite devoid of that literary skill which made his predecessor so famous. The style, though generally perspicuous, is formal and stiff, sometimes even incorrect.—ADAMS, CHARLES KENDALL, 1882, *A Manual of Historical Literature*, p. 465.

Was an active historical writer of great diligence and impartiality, and possessed of a fair though not very distinguished style.—SAINTSBURY, GEORGE, 1896, *A History of Nineteenth Century Literature*, p. 246.

He does not reach distinction either of thought or style.—WALKER, HUGH, 1897, *The Age of Tennyson*, p. 142.

George Finlay

1799–1875

An English historian of the first rank; born in Faversham, Kent, of Scotch blood, Dec. 21, 1799; died in Athens, Greece, Jan. 26, 1875. An ardent Philhellene, he joined Byron's company at Missolonghi in 1823 to assist in liberating Greece from the Turks; and ended by residing there permanently,—at first a cultivator, and then a student of and writer of Greek history. He was for many years the Athens correspondent of the London Times. His "Greece under the Romans, B. C. 146 to A. D. 717" (1844) raised him at once to a place among the few foremost historians: Edward A. Freeman declared it to be the most truly original historical work of modern times; and for sound broad humanity, acute judgment, and luminous common-sense on both the practical and the philosophic sides of history, it has few equals of any age. It is not in the form of detailed annals except in the last part, most of it being a set of essays on the political and social conditions of Greece as a subject province. Succeeding volumes carried the story more in detail down to modern times, ending with two volumes on the Greek Revolution. The whole, revised and some volumes wholly rewritten by the author, was published posthumously in 7 vols. (1877).—WARNER, CHARLES DUDLEY, ed. 1897, *Library of the World's Best Literature, Biographical Dictionary*, vol. XXIX, p. 189.

PERSONAL

Of Mr. Finlay it may be said that though he passed a lifetime in the Levant, he never became a Levantine. He was every inch an English gentleman from the beginning to the end, and his loss will be deeply felt by all of his countrymen who have had the advantage of enjoying at Athens his genial hospitality and instructive society.—NEWTON, SIR CHARLES T., 1875, *Recollections of Mr. Finlay*, The Academy, vol. 7, p. 167.

The world is said to know nothing of its greatest men, and certainly the *Times* seems to know very little of its greatest Correspondent. A man of whom Great Britain may well be proud has passed away in a distant land, and the greatest British newspaper, a paper which had been often honoured with his contributions, a paper commonly so ready with long biographies of every man of the smallest eminence, can give him only a few lines of small print without so much as the heading of his name. No one will grudge to the memory either of Mr. Kingsley or of Lord St. Leonards the full recognition which they have met with; but the most truly original historian of our time and language might surely claim a place alongside of the novelist and the lawyer.—FREEMAN, EDWARD AUGUSTUS, 1875, Mr. *Finlay, The Saturday Review, vol.* 39, *p.* 174.

His unfortunate investment had at least the good results of compelling his continual residence in the country, with which he became most thoroughly acquainted, and of stimulating his perception of the evils which, in the past as in the present, have deteriorated the Greek character and injured the credit and prosperity of the nation. The publication of his great series of histories commenced in 1844, and was completed in 1861, when he wrote the autobiographical fragment which is almost the sole authority for his life. His correspondence is lost or inaccessible, and, notwithstanding his courteous hospitality, acknowledged by many travellers, little more seems to be known of his life in Greece than his constant endeavours to benefit the country by good advice, sometimes expressed in language of excessive if excusable acerbity, but which, if little followed, was never resented by the objects of it. — GARNETT, RICHARD, 1889, *Dictionary of National Biography, vol.* XIX, *p.* 30.

GENERAL

It could hardly be said of his account of Greek politicians that he was "to their virtues very kind, and to their faults a little blind." He told the truth about Greece fearlessly, and with no tinge of partisanship, and it is to the credit of the nation that they appreciated his impartiality; and all through their many political vicissitudes respected the one foreigner who, living in their midst, had the courage to tell them of their faults.—NEWTON, SIR CHARLES T., 1875, *Recollections of Mr. Finlay, The Academy, vol.* 7, *p.* 167.

Different in every respect as were the two men in position and temper and line of study, far more widely-spread as the fame of the one is than the fame of the other, still he who wishes to master the history of the Greek nation as a whole can as little dispense with Mr. Finlay as he can with Mr. Grote. And it does kindle a certain feeling of indignation when we find the memory of such a man so unworthily dealt with in the quarter where he ought to have met with most honour. . . . He has left his mark on the historical learning of the age. It is easy to point out faults in his writings. It is plain that they would in some respects have gained if, instead of being written at Athens, they had been written in London, at Oxford, or at Göttingen. But we believe that by such an exchange they would have lost far more than they would have gained. Mr. Finlay was not, in his earlier life, a man of the closet. He went out to Greece to fight; he stayed there to till the ground. He was led to study and to write history in order to explain what he saw in the processes of fighting and tilling the ground. He saw that the phenomena of modern Greece could be understood only by going back to that stage in Grecian history when Greece, from one point of view, might be said to be conquered, while from another point of view she might be said to begin her own work of conquest. . . . This wide grasp of one side of his subject, of the side with which he was immediately concerned, would have been ill exchanged for any improvements in form and manner which his work would probably have gained had it been done in a Western capital or a Western university. As a contribution to the general history of the Greek nation, as a protest against those who would end Greek history with the fight of Chairôneia or with the burning of Corinth. Mr. Finlay's "History" marks an epoch. It is quite possible that some one else may tell the tale in some respects better, but it is Mr. Finlay who first showed that there was any tale to tell at all. And his works are hardly less valuable from the Roman than from the Greek side. No one after him, save the most ignorant and thoughtless, can babble any more about "Greeks of the Lower Empire." He sets before us the true nature and importance of that great and abiding power of the Eastern Rome on which the men of the eleventh century still looked with awe and wonder.—FREEMAN, EDWARD AUGUSTUS, 1875, *Mr. Finlay, The Saturday Review, vol.* 39, *pp.* 174, 175.

Finlay was almost the first to point out the permanence of the Greek local institutions, and his legal training and knowledge of political economy enabled him to seize the really important points in the history of the people of Eastern Europe, where others have merely given us personal anecdotes of the rulers. The political and social lessons to be learnt from the history of the Greeks during two thousand years of servitude are perhaps not less than those which we gain from Grote's sympathetic account of the rise and glory of ancient Hellas.—BOASE, CHARLES WILLIAM, 1878, *Finlay's History of Greece, The Academy, vol.* 13, *p.* 135.

It is no empty compliment to compare this work with that of the historian of the "Decline and Fall of the Roman Empire." While some of the qualifications of Gibbon are notably absent, others that Gibbon did not possess are conspicuously present. The author carried on his investigations in the very heart of the country whose turbulent vicissitudes he describes. Spending a large portion of his life in his library, immediately beneath the Acropolis, he had the good fortune not only to complete his great work, but also to subject it to such careful revision as the criticism of recent scholarship had made necessary. The most prominent characteristics of the work are learning, accuracy, and fidelity. In addition, it may be said that the author is severely critical. . . . As a help to those who would become acquainted with the history of the East, these learned and eloquent volumes have no equals. They are worthy to stand by the side of those of Grote.—ADAMS, CHARLES KENDALL, 1882, *A Manual of Historical Literature, pp.* 102, 103.

Finlay is a great historian of the type of Polybius, Procopius, and Machiavelli, a man of affairs, who has qualified himself for treating of public transactions by sharing in them, a soldier, a statesman, and an economist. He is not picturesque or eloquent, or a master of the delineation of character, but a singular charm attaches to his pages from the perpetual consciousness of contact with a vigorous intelligence. In the latter portion of his work he speaks with the authority of an acute, though not entirely dispassionate, eye-witness; in the earlier and more extensive portion it is his great glory to have shown how interesting the history of an age of slavery may be made and how much Gibbon had left undone. Gibbon, as his plan requires, exhibits the superficial aspects of the period in a grand panorama; Finlay plunges beneath the surface, and brings to light a wealth of social particulars of which the mere reader of Gibbon could have no notion. This being Finlay's special department, it is the more to his praise that he has not smothered his story beneath erudition. He may, indeed, even appear at a disadvantage beside the Germans as regards extent and profundity of research, but this inferiority is more than compensated by the advantages incidental to his prolonged residence in the country.— GARNETT, RICHARD, 1889, *Dictionary of National Biography, vol.* XIX, *p.* 31.

The history of Greece has been laid before the world as only a man possessing such an extensive and thorough knowledge of the country could do, by George Finlay. —OLIPHANT, MARGARET O. W., 1892, *The Victorian Age of English Literature, p.* 561.

Sir John Gardner Wilkinson
1797–1875

Orientalist, was born at Hardendale, Westmoreland, and educated at Harrow, and at Exeter College, Oxford. When quite a young man he visited Egypt for the sake of his health, and remained there for twelve years, during which time he devoted himself to the study of Egyptian antiquities. A paper of his on "A Part of the Eastern Desert of Upper Egypt" was read before the Geographical Society in 1830, and was a record of a journey of exploration made with Captain Burton. The paper had been written, however, as early as 1823. In 1827–8 Wilkinson published his "Materia Hieroglyphica," containing the Egyptian Pantheon and the succession of the Pharaohs; his "Extracts from the Hieroglyphical Subjects" in 1830; "Thebes and Ancient Egypt" in 1833; and "The Topography of Thebes, and General View of Egypt." in 1835. His *magnum opus*, "The Manners and Customs of the Ancient Egyptians" (1837–41; 3rd ed. by Dr. Birch, **1878**), is the standard authority on all matters relating to Egyptian art; and its value is enhanced by the beautiful illustrations with which it is enriched by its author. It is written to support no particular theory, but contents itself with picturesque description.

It was followed by the very popular "Modern Egypt and Thebes" (1844), and a condensed edition entitled "Handbook for Travelers in Egypt" (1847). Sir Gardner Wilkinson, who had been knighted in 1839, then published a work on "Dalmatia and Montenegro" (1848); and, returning to Egyptology, "A Popular Account of the Ancient Egyptians" (1854), "Egypt in the Time of the Pharaohs" (1857), and "The Architecture of Ancient Egypt" (1860); he also wrote "On Colour and the Necessity of a General Diffusion of Taste" (1858). He also contributed some most valuable notes and illustrations to the Egyptian chapters of Professor Rawlinson's translation of "Herodotus." Most of his Egyptian collections are in the British Museum, and Sir Gardner Wilkinson also presented Harrow School with a museum of Egyptian art.—SANDERS, LLOYD C., ed. 1887, *Celebrities of the Century*, p. 1052.

PERSONAL

I heard a lecture on digestion (part of a course on the physics of human nature), by Wilkinson at the Whittington Club. I was very much pleased with him: his voice clear, manner collected, like one who knew what he was about; his style rich, a good deal of originality in his metaphors and a little mysticism, tending to show that there is in the universe a digestive or assimilative process going on, which connects man with nature, and the present with the other life. —ROBINSON, HENRY CRABB, 1848, *Diary, Sept. 27; Diary, Reminiscences and Correspondence*, ed. Sadler, vol. II, p. 377.

Notwithstanding his numerous publications, filling no less than twenty-two volumes, four of which are of plates from the author's drawings,—in one case lithographed by himself,—besides contributing to the publications of Societies, a great mass of materials remains in Sir Gardner's hands. His note-books are full of drawings beautifully and clearly executed, as well as careful memoranda of every object he met interesting to a student of archælogy and art. His works exhibit but a selection, and it would be a boon to knowledge could he be prevailed upon to publish these note-books as they stand.—REEVE, LOVELL, 1863, *ed. Portraits of Men of Eminence*, p. 80.

Sir Gardner Wilkinson was one of the fortunate few of whom, despite a well-worn maxim, it could be asserted in his life-time that he was happy. He achieved success and he was rewarded with honours. He saw his principal work become a classic. And he enjoyed in equal proportion the gifts of culture, of fortune, and of taste. Not many scholars are also artists, and few artists are also distinguished for scholarship; but Sir Gardiner Wilkinson was both scholar and artist. He, moreover, added to this rare combination two tastes which are, perhaps above all others, delightful to their possessors—namely, the love of archæology and the love of travel. . . . Sir Gardner Wilkinson was not a witty man; but he had a playful humour, and a keen sense of the ludicrous. Even the staid pages of "Manners and Customs" sparkle occasionally with flashes of fun. His own manners were charming, and his good-nature was proverbial. His books, his notes, his sketches, were freely at the service of all who sought information at his hands; and with ladies he was a universal favourite. One who knew him writes of him to me as being "truly a courteous gentleman in all his ways and doings." He loved society, and society repaid him with interest. When in the intervals of foreign work and travel he resided in England, he lived in the gay world of forty years ago; kept his cab; and even while writing his "Manners and Customs" and drawing his own illustrations upon the wood, he used to be about every night at all the fashionable entertainments of the season.—EDWARDS, AMELIA B., 1879, *The Manners and Customs of the Ancient Egyptians, The Academy*, vol. 15, pp. 251, 252.

GENERAL

I need scarcely mention the admirable work of Sir Gardner Wilkinson, in which he has availed himself of the paintings, sculptures, and monuments of the ancient Egyptians to restore their manners and customs, and to place their public and private life before us, as fully as if they still occupied the banks of the Nile. I shall frequently have occasion to refer to it in the course of this and the following chapters.—LAYARD, AUSTEN HENRY, 1849, *Nineveh and its Remains*, vol. II, pt. ii, ch. i.

His volumes, on the whole, afford more materials for grave study and meditation than for the entertainment of the passing hour, so that the lovers of very light reading will be apt to pass them by altogether.

But he writes without prejudice or pretension, and throws considerable light upon what has recently become a political problem of no small moment,—the condition, tendencies, and prospects of the great Slavonic race in Europe.—BOWEN, FRANCIS, 1850, *Wilkinson's Dalmatia and Montenegro, North American Review, vol. 70, p. 391.*

If the work is in any respect open to criticism, it must be on the ground that the writer's learning is almost oppressive, and is not so thoroughly digested and assimilated with the personal narrative as to suit the appetite of the moderns for light reading. Our traveller is more frequently an instructive than an amusing companion; and many readers will therefore undertake no more than what we have proposed as the limits of our own endeavors; namely, to skim the cream of the book, and leave its weightier matters for subsequent study and reference.—BOWEN, FRANCIS, 1850, *Wilkinson's Dalmatia and Montenegro, North American Review, vol. 70, p. 371.*

The "larger work," too costly for general circulation, did more than all other English books towards erecting *Egyptology* into a distinct department of knowledge, and bringing into use its contributions to numerous branches of art and science. Yet more, it not only gave us archæological facts, but so combined and vitalized the results of the author's inquiries as to reproduce to the fancy the men and manners of ancient Egypt. The work now before us is a careful condensation of the former, with some important additions, which bring down the history of discovery to the year 1853. — PEABODY, ANDREW P., 1854, *A Popular Account of the Ancient Egyptians, North American Review, vol. 79, p. 527.*

The work of Sir Gardner Wilkinson upon Ancient Egypt, which speaks to the eye, is far more instructive than the efforts to address the mind through the restored language of the Egyptians. — LEWIS, SIR GEORGE CORNEWALL, 1862, *An Historical Survey of Astronomy of the Ancients.*

This work ["Ancient Egyptians"] may be said to have created a new era in the popular knowledge of Egypt, and given the impetus to such subsequent labors as those of Layard, Rawlinson, etc. . . . Wilkinson is a thorough scholar in whatever he undertakes, and all his works are full of valuable information, skilfully presented and suggesting reflection.—HART, JOHN S., 1872, *A Manual of English Literature, p. 563.*

Ever since the first appearance of this work, ["Ancient Egyptians"] in 1837, it has been recognized as having a classical value. The author was a patient and conscientious scholar and a good draughtsman; and for these reasons, notwithstanding the great advances of Oriental scholarship, the importance of his volume has not materially diminished. The modern editor, Dr. Birch, is a prominent Egyptologist, and he has greatly improved the work by correcting those portions which recent scholarship has shown to be defective. The author's chronology has generally been regarded as having very little value; indeed, in the opinion of most scholars, it is hopelessly wrong. But the work, in spite of some defects of this nature, is of so much importance that no student of ancient Egypt can afford to neglect it. As a representation of the manners and customs of the Egyptians, it has no superior.—ADAMS, CHARLES KENDALL, 1882, *A Manual of Historical Literature, p. 80.*

Charles Sprague
1791–1875

A cashier of the Globe Bank, Boston, 1825–65, well known in his life-time as a verse-writer, and still pleasantly remembered for the genuine sentiment in such poems as "The Family Meeting" and "The Winged Worshippers," though an "Ode to Shakespeare" was once much praised. His poems first appeared in 1841, the latest edition being that of 1876. —ADAMS, OSCAR FAY, 1897, *A Dictionary of American Authors, p. 355.*

PERSONAL

Few poets have been more respected for moral worth and nobility of character.— SARGENT, EPES, 1880–81, *Harper's Cyclopædia of British and American Poetry, p. 415.*

GENERAL

A young man of Boston, Massachusetts— a merchant's clerk, we believe, who obtained prize after prize, among the poets of his country, for his "Address" on the opening of sundry theatres. There is not much poetry in these papers, thus written; but—after all—they are about as good, and about as poetical, as the best of ours, by Johnson, Pope, Garrick, Byron, etc.—NEAL, JOHN, 1825, *American Writers*, *Blackwood's Magazine*, vol. 17. p. 202.

Mr. Sprague's language is simple and nervous, and his imagery brilliant and striking. There is a spirit of pervading good sense in this ["Curiosity"] poem, which shows that he gives poetry its right place in his mind. Above all there is a lofty tone of thought, which indicates superiority to the affectations of the day.—PEABODY, W. B. O., 1830, *Sprague's Poems*, *North American Review*, vol. 30, p. 323.

The ode recited in the Boston theatre, at a pageant in honour of Shakspeare, in 1823, is one of the most vigorous and beautiful lyrics in the English language. The first poet of the world, the greatness of his genius, the vast variety of his scenes and characters, formed a subject well fitted for the flowing and stately measure chosen by our author, and the universal acquaintance with the writings of the immortal dramatist enables every one to judge of the merits of his composition. Though to some extent but a reproduction of the creations of Shakspeare, it is such a reproduction as none but a man of genius could effect.—GRISWOLD, RUFUS WILMOT, 1842, *The Poets and Poetry of America*, p. 91.

Mr. Sprague is an accomplished belles-lettres scholar, so far as the usual ideas of scholarship extend. He is a very correct rhetorician of the old school. His versification has not been equalled by that of any American—has been surpassed by no one living or dead. In this regard there are to be found finer passages in his poems than any elsewhere. These are his chief merits. In the *essentials* of poetry he is excelled by twenty of our countrymen whom we could name. Except in a very few instances he gives no evidence of the loftier ideality.—POE, EDGAR ALLAN, 1842, *A Chapter on Autography*, Works ed. Stedman and Woodberry, vol. IX, p. 247.

The performance which has rendered Sprague best known to the country as a poet is his metrical essay on "Curiosity." . . . It is written in heroic measure, and recalls the couplets of Pope. The choice of a theme was singularly fortunate. He traces the passion which "tempted Eve to sin" through its loftiest and most vulgar manifestations; at one moment rivalling Crabbe in the lowliness of his details, and at another Campbell in the aspiration of his song. The serious and the comic alternate on every page. Good sense is the basis of the work; fancy, wit, and feeling warm and vivify it; and a nervous tone and finished versification, as well as excellent choice of words, impart a glow, polish, and grace that at once gratify the ear and captivate the mind.—TUCKERMAN, HENRY T., 1852, *A Sketch of American Literature*.

"The Shakespeare Ode" is a noble poem, and we think it his master-piece. The composition of the ode requires a rare union of great qualities: genius of a high order, boldness of metaphor, skill in versification, a delicate susceptibility to musical expression, all are requisite to success. Our author, by a single stroke of his pencil, sets before us the leading characters of the great dramatist, and they once more live again. If this be in any sense reproduction it seems more like a new creation. Not more vividly are the passions portrayed in "Alexander's Feast" or in Collins' famous Ode. Few poems have so felicitous a close.—RUGGLES, JOHN, 1875, *Charles Sprague*, *Unitarian Review*, vol. 4, p. 50.

His poem of "Curiosity," delivered in 1829 before the Phi Beta Society of Harvard College, is so excellent in description in the various pictures it gives of human life, in the pungency of its wit and satire, that it deserves a place among the best productions of the schools of Pope and Goldsmith. His odes are more open to criticism, though they contain many thoughtful, impassioned, and resounding lines. . . . Perhaps Sprague's most original poems are those in which he consecrated his domestic affections. Wordsworth himself would have hailed these with delight. Anybody who can read with unwet eyes "I See Still," "The Family Meeting," "The Brothers," and "Lines on the Death of M. S. C.," is a critic who has as little perception of the languages of natural emotion as of the reserves and refinements of poetic art.—WHIPPLE, EDWIN PERCY, 1876–86, *American Literature and Other Papers*, ed. Whittier, pp. 81, 82.

It would be, of course, absurd to claim

for Sprague a place by the side of the great singers of the world or of the English language. The moderation of his own claims was shown by his ceasing to write when he was only forty years old, and while he had yet more than forty years to live. Poetry was not the business, but the solace, of his life, and he was contented with a modest share of the rewards of genius. That he had the gift of poetic genius we think few readers of his poems will deny. His is not machine-made verse. His thoughts come flowing from his heart and mind, and they find fit words in which to clothe themselves. And this is what we understand to be meant by the "Vision and the Faculty Divine." Though Sprague may not deserve to rank with the great poets of the English language, we think that he merits a high place among the minor poets of our literature.—QUINCY, EDMUND, 1876 *Charles Sprague, The Nation, vol.* 23, *p.* 155.

Another example of the emptiness of contemporary fame. During the first half of the century he ranked second only to Bryant and Halleck, but to-day he is a little more than a vague memory.—PATTEE, FRED LEWIS, 1896, *A History of American Literature, p.* 169.

It is difficult to understand how such a production ["Curiosity"] could obtain such popularity. It is of exemplary form, finished versification, and approved rhetoric, but mechanical in design and treatment, and, on the whole, rather tedious. It was one of the successful poems of the day, was largely read and quoted in this country, and grossly plagiarized in England.—ONDERDONK, JAMES L., 1899–1901, *History of American Verse, p.* 127.

Harriet Martineau
1802–1876

Born, at Norwich, 12 June 1802. Early education at home. At a school at Norwich, 1813–15. At Bristol, 1818–19. Returned to Norwich, April 1819. Contrib. to "Monthly Repository," from 1821. Severe illness, 1827, followed by financial difficulties. Wrote three prize essays for Central Unitarian Association, 1830–31. Visit to her brother James at Dublin, 1831. Engaged on "Illustrations of Political Economy," Feb. 1832 to Feb. 1834. Settled in London. Visit to America, Aug. 1834 to Aug. 1836. Travelled on Continent, 1839. Refused Crown Pensions, 1834, 1841, and 1873. Testimonial raised to her by her friends, 1843. Lived at Tynemouth, 1839–45; at Ambleside, Westmoreland, 1845 till her death. Friendship with Wordsworth. Visit to Egypt and Palestine, Aug. 1846 to July 1847. Contrib. to "Daily News," 1852–66; to "Edinburgh Review," from 1859. Died, at Ambleside, 27 June 1876. *Works:* "Devotional Exercises" (anon.), 1823; "Addresses, with Prayers" (anon.), 1826; "Traditions of Palestine," 1830; "Five Years of Youth," 1831; "Essential Faith of the Universal Church," 1831; "The Faith as unfolded by many Prophets," 1832; "Providence as manifested through Israel," 1832; "Illustrations of Political Economy" (9 vols.), 1832–34; "Poor Laws and Paupers Illustrated," 1833–34; "Illustrations of Taxation," 1834; "Miscellanies" (2 vols., Boston), 1836; "Society in America," 1837; "Retrospect of Western Travel," 1838; "How to Observe," 1838; "Addresses," 1838; "Deerbrook," 1839; "The Martyr Age of the United States" (under initials: H. M.), 1840; "The Playfellow" (4 pts.: "The Settlers at Home;" "The Peasant and the Prince;" "Feats on the Fiord;" "The Crofton Boys"), 1841; "The Hour and the Man," 1841; "Life in the Sick Room" (anon.), 1844; "Letters on Mesmerism," 1845 (2nd edn. same year); "Forest and Game-Law Tales" (3 vols.), 1845–46; "Dawn Island," 1845; "The Billow and the Rock," 1846; contribution to "The Land we Live In" (with C. Knight and others), 1847, etc.; "Eastern Life," 1848; "History of England during the Thirty Years' Peace" (with C. Knight), 1849; "Household Education," 1849; "Introduction to the History of the Peace," 1851; "Letters on the Laws of Man's Nature" (with H. G. Atkinson), 1851; "Half a Century of the British Empire" (only 1 pt. pubd.), [1851]; "Sickness and Health of the people of Bleaburn" (anon.), 1853; "Letters from Ireland" (from "Daily News"), 1853; "Guide to Windermere" [1854]; "A Complete Guide to the English Lakes" [1855]; "The Factory Controversy," 1855; "History of the American Compromises" (from "Daily News") 1856; "Sketches from Life" [1856]; "Corporate Traditions and National Rights" [1857]; "British Rule in India," 1857; "Guide to Keswick" [1857]; "Suggestions towards the Future Government of India," 1858;

HARRIET MARTINEAU

Engraving from a Portrait, 1833.

CAROLINE ELIZABETH NORTON

Engraving by W. O. Geller. From Original Painting by John Hayter.

"England and her Soldiers," 1859; "Endowed Schools of Ireland" (from "Daily News"), 1859; "Health, Husbandry, and Handicraft," 1861; "Biographical Sketches" (from "Daily News"), 1869 [1868]. *Posthumous:* "Autobiography," ed. by M. W. Chapman, 1877 (3rd edn., same year); "The Hampdens," 1880 [1879]. She *translated:* Comte's "Positive Philosophy," 1853. *Life:* by Mrs. Fenwick Miller, 1884.—SHARP, R. FARQUHARSON, 1897, *A Dictionary of English Authors, p.* 188.

PERSONAL

I believe she will do much good; her motives and principles are pure and high, and success, as I predicted, has improved, not spoiled her. Indeed, she has very extraordinary talent and merit, and a noble independence of mind.—AIKIN, LUCY, 1832, *To Dr. Channing, Nov.* 19; *Correspondence of William Ellery Channing and Lucy Aikin,* ed. *LeBreton, p.* 156.

Her dress is simple, unexpensive, and appropriate. Her voice is too low-toned, but agreeable, the suitable organ of a refined spirit. Her manners, without any elegance, are pleasing, natural, and kind. She seldom speaks unless addressed, but in reply to a single touch she pours out a rich stream. She is never brilliant, never says a thing that is engraven on, or *cut in,* to your memory, but she talks on a greater variety of topics than any one I ever heard —agreeably, most agreeably, and with sense and information. She is *womanly,* strictly, with sympathies fresh from the heart, enthusiasms not always manifestly supported by reason, now and then bordering on the dogmatical, but too thorough a lover of human rights ever, I think, to overstep the boundary, and she is, I think, not conceited—no, not in the least, but quite aware of her own superiority, and perhaps a little too frank on this point. But this may be from a deficiency instead of excess of vanity.—SEDGWICK, CATHARINE M., 1835, *Journal, Aug.* 9; *Life and Letters,* ed. *Dewey, p.* 241.

Miss Martineau is a person of lively, agreeable conversation, kind and candid, but rather easily imposed upon, and somewhat spoiled, perhaps, by the praises she has received, and the importance allowed to her writings.—BRYANT, WILLIAM CULLEN, 1836, *Letter to his Wife, April 27; A Biography of William Cullen Bryant by Godwin, vol.* I, *p.* 314.

I was apprehensive, from her high literary reputation, that I should find her a little too blue to be agreeable. But it is not at all the case; she is pleasant and unaffected, has great vivacity, talks well upon all subjects, and is fond of laughing; with these qualifications she is, of course, an engaging companion. The only difficulty in conversing with her arises from her great deafness. — HONE, PHILIP, 1836, *Diary, April 5,* ed. *Tuckerman, vol.* I, *p.* 206.

Two or three days ago there came to call on us a Miss Martineau, whom you have perhaps often heard of in the "Examiner." A hideous portrait was given of her in the "Fraser" one month. She is a notable literary woman of her day, has been traveling in America these two years, and is now come home to write a book about it. She pleased us far beyond expectation. She is very intelligent-looking, really of pleasant countenance, was full of talk, though unhappily deaf almost as a post, so that you have to speak to her through an ear-trumpet. She must be some five-and-thirty. As she possesses very "favourable sentiments" towards this side of the street, I mean to cultivate the acquaintance a little.—CARLYLE, THOMAS, 1836, *Letter to His Mother, Nov.; Thomas Carlyle, A History of His Life in London,* ed. *Froude, vol.* I, *p.* 83.

She is a woman of one idea,—takes one view, that is, and knows nothing of qualification,—and hence is opinionated and confident to a degree that I think I never saw equalled.— DEWEY, ORVILLE, 1837, *To Rev. William Ware, July* 10; *Autobiography and Letters,* ed. *Dewey, p.* 163.

She is a heroine, or to speak more truly, her fine sense and her lofty principles, with the sincerest religion, give her a fortitude that is noble to the best height of heroism. — MACREADY, WILLIAM C., 1841, *Diary, March* 28; *Reminiscences,* ed. *Pollock, p.* 497.

She is a very admirable woman—and the most logical intellect of the age, for a woman. On this account it is that the men throw stones at her, and that many of her own sex throw dirt; but if I begin on this subject I shall end by gnashing my teeth. A righteous indignation fastens on me. I had a note from her the other day, written in a noble spirit, and saying, in reference to the insults lavished on her, that she was prepared from the first for *publicity,* and ventured it all for the sake of what she considered the truth—she was sustained, she said, by the recollection of Godiva.— BROWNING, ELIZABETH BARRETT, 1844, *To H. S. Boyd, Dec.* 24; *Letters, ed., Kenyon, vol.* I, *p.* 225.

Miss Martineau makes herself an object of envy by the success of her domestic arrangements. She has built a cottage near her house, placed in it a Norfolk dairy-maid, and has her poultry-yard, and her piggery, and her cow-shed; and Mrs. Wordsworth declares she is a model in her household economy, making her servants happy, and setting an example of activity to her neighbors.—ROBINSON, HENRY CRABB, 1849, *To Miss Fenwick, Jan.* 15; *Diary, Reminiscences and Correspondence, ed. Sadler, vol.* II, *p.* 386.

I trust to have derived benefit from my visit to Miss Martineau. A visit more interesting I certainly never paid. If self-sustaining strength can be acquired from example, I ought to have got good. But my nature is not hers; I could not make it so though I were to submit it seventy times seven to the furnace of affliction, and discipline it for an age under the hammer and anvil of toil and self-sacrifice. Perhaps if I was like her I should not admire her so much as I do. She is somewhat absolute, though quite unconsciously so; but she is likewise kind, with an affection at once abrupt and constant, whose sincerity you cannot doubt. It was delightful to sit near her in the evenings and hear her converse, myself mute. She speaks with what seems to me a wonderful fluency and eloquence. Her animal spirits are as unflagging as her intellectual powers. I was glad to find her health excellent. I believe neither solitude or loss of friends would break her down. I saw some faults in her, but somehow I like them for the sake of her good points. It gave me no pain to feel insignificant, mentally and corporeally, in comparison with her.—BRONTË, CHARLOTTE, 1850; *To W. S. Williams, Jan.* 1; *Charlotte Brontë and her Circle, ed. Shorter, p.* 5.

I think I neglected to record that I saw Miss Martineau a few weeks since. She is a large, robust, elderly woman, and plainly dressed; but withal she has so kind, cheerful, and intelligent a face that she is pleasanter to look at than most beauties. Her hair is of a decided gray, and she does not shrink from calling herself old. She is the most continual talker I ever heard; it is really like the babbling of a brook, and very lively and sensible too; and all the while she talks, she moves the bowl of her ear-trumpet from one auditor to another, so that it becomes quite an organ of intelligence and sympathy between her and yourself. The ear-trumpet seems a sensible part of her, like the antennæ of some insects. If you have any little remark to make, you drop it in; and she helps you to make remarks by this delicate little appeal of the trumpet, as she slightly directs it towards you; and if you have nothing to say, the appeal is not strong enough to embarrass you. All her talk was about herself and her affairs; but it did not seem like egotism, because it was so cheerful and free from morbidness. And this woman is an Atheist, and thinks that the principles of life will become extinct when her body is laid in the grave! I will not think so, were it only for her sake. What! only a few weeds to spring out of her mortality, instead of her intellect and sympathies flowering and fruiting forever.—HAWTHORNE, NATHANIEL, 1854, *English Note-Books, vol.* I, *p.* 110.

We Unitarians have reason to be proud that this remarkable woman was born and developed in our communion, and that Unitarian publishing-houses first printed and circulated her works, when other houses refused her books on political economy as dull and unmarketable. Thus the modest Unitarian publisher in Paternoster Row really brought her to the notice of the world. We, as Unitarian Christians, it may be said, have reason also to be sad, that the woman who began her successful literary career by writings that illustrated and defended our views of Christianity, should in later life have renounced her faith in historic Christianity, and the divine assurance of immortality contained in the Gospel of Jesus Christ.—LOWE, MARTHA PERRY, 1876, *Editor's Note-Book, Unitarian Review, vol.* 6, *p.* 336.

How well I remember the first sight of her, so long ago! We first saw her at church— Dr. Channing's. It was a presence one did not speedily tire of looking on—most attractive and impressive; yet the features were plain, and only saved from seeming heavily moulded by her thinness. She was rather taller and more strongly made than most American ladies. Her complexion was neither fair or sallow, nor yet of the pale, intellectual tone that is thought to belong to authorship. It was the hue of one severely tasked, but not with literary work. She had rich, brown, abundant hair, folded away in shining waves from the middle of a forehead totally unlike the flat one described by those who knew her as a child. It was now low over the eyes, like the Greek brows, and embossed rather than graven by the workings of thought. The eyes themselves were light and full, of a grayish greenish blue, varying in color with the time of day, or with the eye of the beholder—*les yeux pers* of the old French romance writers. They were steadily and quietly alert, as if constantly seeing something where another would have found nothing to notice. Her habitual expression was one of serene and self-sufficing dignity —the look of perfect and benevolent repose that comes to them whose long, unselfish struggle to wring its best from life has been crowned with complete victory. You might walk the livelong day, in any city streets, and not meet such a face of simple, cheerful strength, with so much light and sweetness in its play of feature.—CHAPMAN, MARIA WESTON, 1877, *Memorials of Harriet Martineau*, p. 29.

Looking back at this calm distance at the whole transaction, I think it open to reasonable doubt whether it was well for me to become the critic of the "Letters" at all, even in the impersonal form of an anonymous reviewer. And I might have anticipated the fruitlessness of my attempt to withdraw the master from the disciple and try conclusions with him alone. But in the substance of the critique I see nothing to correct or retract. And in its tone I do not notice an uncalled-for severity. If compared with Edward Forbes's review of the same book (fairly representing the purely scientific estimate of its character), it indubitably stands much further within the limits of patient and considerate controversy. . . . The estrangement produced by this cause and its antecedents was all on one side. My affection for my sister Harriet survived all reproaches and mistakes, and, if she had permitted, would at any moment have taken me to her side for unconditional return to the old relation. If time had lessened our sympathies of thought, it had enlarged those of character, and had developed in her a cheerful fortitude, an active benevolence, and unflinching fidelity to conviction, on which I looked with joyful honour, and in view of which all vexing memories were ready to die away.— MARTINEAU, JAMES, 1877, *To Rev. Charles Wicksteed, Aug. 5*; *Life and Letters*, ed. Drummond, vol. I, p. 225.

I do not want to overpraise a personage so antipathetic to me as H. M. My first impression of her is, in spite of her undeniable talent, energy, and merit—what an unpleasant life and unpleasant nature!—ARNOLD, MATTHEW, 1877, *To Rev. G. W. Boyle, March 11*; *Letters* ed. Russell, vol. II, p. 158.

She became at length almost another estate in the realm. Cabinet Ministers consulted her upon the gravest questions of policy. She interposed to settle disputes between leaders which were embarrassing the reform movements of the time. She brought about a reconciliation between Sir Robert Peel, when Prime Minister, and Cobden. She was full of diplomatic skill and social address. We cannot be surprised that without vanity, she felt herself a power, and became dogmatic and dictatorial. No man or woman ever lived who guarded more jealously a personal self-respect. The noble family of Lansdowne wished an introduction to her at a London party, at which her mother was present; but as they did not ask that her mother be presented to them, she rejected every overture for further acquaintance. She refused an introduction to the poet Tom Moore, because he published a poem of raillery in the *Times*. It wounded her and she never forgave it. Different administrations urged a government pension upon her, which she refused. This great, proud, toilsome, self-contained character, wrought her work until she attained the age of seventy-four years, and, measured either by the powers developed in her life, or by its results upon the thought and policy of her time, she appears a peerless woman. Indeed we almost forget she was a woman, and think of her as a human force thrown upon our century when great revolutions were demanding great leaders.—PUTNAM, JAMES O., 1877-80, *Harriet Martineau's*

Autobiography; Addresses, Speeches and Miscellanies, p. 226.

I confess I am very curious to see Mrs. Chapman's book. This stout-hearted woman (Martineau) lay down with a sort of grim satisfaction to die, at the age of fifty-one; and didn't she live quite twenty years afterwards? I will hazard the observation that her longevity may have been favoured by her supreme self-complacency. Also is she not a little cool (coarse? vulgar?) in the way she talks about "Old Wordsworth?" Mind, I can stand her contempt for parsons, and all that—it doesn't ruffle my feathers in the least. But I do feel that with Wordsworth we are upon sacred ground. I am all the more bothered because Miss Martineau was not a Philistine by any means, and she makes every now and then extraordinary good hits as to what constitutes true poetry.—BROWN, THOMAS EDWARD, 1878, *to Miss Cannan, May* 16; *Letters, ed. Irwin, vol.* I, *p.* 82.

I was pleased to find that, notwithstanding her heresies, the common people in Ambleside held her in gentle and kindly remembrance. She was a good neighbor, charitable to all, considerate toward the unlettered, never cynical or ill-tempered, always cheerful and happy as the roses and ivy of "The Knoll" she so much loved.— CONWAY, MONCURE DANIEL, 1881, *The English Lakes and Their Genii, Harper's Magazine, vol.* 62, *p.* 166.

Her form and features were repellent; she was the Lady Oracle in all things, and from her throne, her sofa, pronounced verdicts from which there was no appeal. Hers was a hard nature: it had neither geniality, indulgence, nor mercy. Always a physical sufferer, so deaf that a trumpet was constantly at her ear; plain of person—a drawback of which she could not have been unconscious; and awkward of form: she was entirely without the gifts that attract man to woman: even her friendships seem to have been cut out of stone; she may have excited admiration indeed, but from the affections that render woman only a little lower than the angels she was entirely estranged.—HALL, SAMUEL CARTER, 1883, *Retrospect of a Long Life, p.* 330.

Faults she had, of course—the necessary defects of her virtues. Let it be said that she held her own opinions too confidently— the uncertain cannot be teachers. Let it be said that her personal dislikes were many and strong—it is the necessary antithesis of powerful attachments. Let it be said that her powers of antagonism at times were not sufficiently restrained—how, without such oppugnancy, could she have stood forth for unpopular truths? Let all that detractors can say be said, and how much remains untouched? In the paths where Harriet Martineau trod at first almost alone, many women are now following. Serious studies, political activity, a share in social reforms, an independent, self-supporting career, and freedom of thought and expression, are by the conditions of our age, becoming open to the thousands of women who would never have dared to claim them in the circumstances in which she first did so. In a yet earlier age such a life, even to such powers as hers, would have been impossible. As it was, she was only a pioneer of the new order of things inevitable under the advance of civilization and knowledge. . . . She cared for nothing before the truth; her efforts to discover it were earnest and sincere, for she spared no pains in study and no labor in thought in the attempt to form her opinions correctly. Having found what she must believe to be a right cause to uphold, or a true word to speak, no selfish consideration intruded between her and her duty. She could risk fame, and position, and means of livelihood, when necessary, to unselfishly support and promulgate what she believed it to be important for mankind to do and believe. She longed for the well being of her kind; and so unaffectedly and honestly that men who came under her influence were stimulated and encouraged by her to share and avow similar high aims. Withal, those who lived with her loved her; she was a kind mistress, a good friend, and tender to little children; she was truly helpful to the poor at her gates, and her life was spotlessly pure.—MILLER, MRS. E. FENNICK, 1884, *Harriet Martineau (Famous Women Series), pp.* 301, 303.

Plain and, judging from her portraits, far from prepossessing in her young days, she had become with age a good-looking, comely, interesting old lady, very deaf, but cheerful and eager for news, which she did not always catch correctly. With all her manly self-dependence and strict intentional honesty, with all her credit for practical common sense, she was as much a poet at heart as her brother, the Rev. James. . . . A true and brave woman.—LINTON, WILLIAM JAMES, 1894. *Threescore and Ten Years*, p. 168.

My boyish recollection of Miss Martineau is very pleasant. She was always amiable. On one occasion, when she sat writing at a table in a parlor, I remember standing with my head just above it, and wondering at the ease and regularity with which she despatched, in her clear, round hand, letter after letter, never pausing for a word or an idea, or to read what she had written. Although there was no room for mystery, I felt something of the fascination which, we are told, riveted the observer who watched the unknown hand at the opposite window filling and throwing off with the tireless uniformity of a machine what proved to be the manuscript pages of "Waverley." As she tossed the last letter on the great pile before her, she said, "Now, my boy, isn't that a pretty good morning's work?" and while I hesitated for an answer that should do justice to her and credit to myself, she put on a hair glove of hers which was lying on the table, and gave my cheeks a playful rubbing, the tingle of which I seem to feel yet.—SEDGWICK, HENRY DWIGHT, 1895, *Reminiscences of Literary Berkshire, Century Magazine*, vol. 50, p. 556.

Within the household in Magdalen Street the severity of Puritan training still lingered, though perhaps it was less marked than in some other families; and Harriet Martineau, who was an abnormally sensitive child, delicate in health, and always longing for demonstrative tokens of affection, chafed against this strictness. It is easy to collect from the pages of her Autobiography passages which, taken by themselves, give a repellant picture of her mother; but this is unjust, both to the mother and to the daughter, and the Autobiography as a whole does not lay the latter open to the charge of disloyalty and ingratitude to which injudicious friends have exposed her. That there was a difference of temperament which, especially in Harriet's childhood, prevented a mutual understanding, does not lay either of them open to blame. According to the autobiography the gentle and unselfish father was likewise unable to read the heart of the young genius.—DRUMMOND, JAMES, 1902, ed. *Life and Letters of James Martineau.*

AUTOBIOGRAPHY

Her forthcoming "Autobiography" will be looked for with deep, if somewhat painful interest, for it is to contain "a full account of her faith and philosophy." In the sketch already referred to she tells us that the cast of her mind was "more decidedly of the religious order than any other, during the whole of her life," and that "her latest opinions were in her own view the most religious;" and at the same time "that she was not a believer in revelation at all" in her later years. Her firm grasp of her own meaning, and her singular power of expression will probably stand her in good stead in making her faith, whatever it may be, clear to those who have never yet been able to understand it. In any case it must command the most respectful attention, for even if not the motive power in, it was at least consistent with, a singularly noble and courageous life.—HUGHES, THOMAS, 1876, *Harriet Martineau, The Academy*, vol. 10, p. 35.

Deeply interesting as the work is, it is impossible to deny that it has given more pain than pleasure to large numbers of those friends who knew her best and valued her most truly. Her own autobiography does her so much less than justice, and the needless, tasteless, and ill-conditioned memorials of the lady to whom she injudiciously entrusted the duties of editor, have managed to convey such an unsound and disfiguring impression of her friend, that the testimony of one who enjoyed her intimacy for many years, and entertained a sincere regard for her throughout, seems wanting to rectify the picture.—GREG, WILLIAM RATHBONE, 1877, *Harriet Martineau, Miscellaneous Essays*, p. 176.

You must read Harriet Martineau's "Autobiography." The account of her childhood and early youth is most pathetic and interesting; but as in all books of the kind, the charm departs as the life advances, and the writer has to tell of her own triumphs. One regrets continually that she felt it necessary not only to tell of her intercourse with many more or less distinguished persons—which would have been quite pleasant to everybody—but also to pronounce upon their entire merits and demerits, especially when, if she had died as soon as she expected, these persons would nearly all have been living to read her gratuitous rudenesses. Still I hope the book will do more good than harm.—ELIOT, GEORGE, 1877, *To Mrs. Bray, March 20; George Eliot's Life as related in her Letters and Journals*, ed. Cross, vol. III, p. 219.

Miss Martineau knew herself unusually well, and she has determined that we should know all that she had to tell us. The knowledge will rather dim the brightness of the popular tradition which rests upon the first wonderful years in London and the first happy years at Ambleside; it will give some substance to the reserve of the minority which persisted in finding Miss Martineau disagreeable; it contains a most unsparing revelation of a most unattractive nature; but it contains also a picture of the diligent, unflinching heroism by which that nature was trained to a life of nobleness and at last of happiness. Nor is the picture less impressive for the austerity of the artist's method. She has resolved not only that we should know intimately, but that we should know her almost exclusively through her own deliberate judgment. She wrote her autobiography partly because she knew she could write it, but principally because she thought it a duty to withold her letters from publication. — SIMCOX, GEORGE AUGUSTUS, 1877, *Miss Martineau, Fortnightly Review*, vol. 27, p. 516.

It is written with ability, and there is much in it that is instructive and something that is interesting; but my interest is rather in the other subjects of which she writes than in the woman. She is undoubtedly honest and truthful; but I have seldom seen truth and honesty made to wear so repulsive an aspect; and this through what seems to me a pervading connection of it with presumption and pride. I get rather tired of her perpetual "principles," and in her devotion to truth I think she makes a mistake, not altogether uncommon, of what it is that she ought to be devoted to—mixing up one with another of the divers meanings of the word.—TAYLOR,. SIR HENRY, 1877, *To Mrs. C. Earle,. May 6; Correspondence*, ed. Dowden, p. 367.

I have even bought Miss Martineau; and am reading her as slowly as I can, to eke her out. For I can't help admiring, and being greatly interested in her, tho' I suppose she got conceited. Her Judgments on People seem to me mainly just.—FITZGERALD, ED-WARD, 1877, *To W. F. Pollock, May 24; More Letters*, p. 188.

I stop in the midst of reading Miss Martineau's memoir of her own life—an entertaining book for the most part, with one or two tedious places; but how immensely conceited the woman was! One would think, on reading what she says of herself, that the whole world stood still while it was waiting for her directions. She is very contemptuous in her judgments of almost every eminent person whom she had any acquaintance with, and expresses her contempt without the least reserve. I perceived that trait in her character when she was here. She seemed to fancy that she had crossed the Atlantic to enlighten us in regard to our duty and interest, and that all we had to do was to submit ourselves to her guidance.—BRYANT, WILLIAM CULLEN, 1877, *To Miss J. Dewey, June 2; William Cullen Bryant, A Biography by Godwin*, vol. II, p. 382.

GENERAL

Know that a great new light has arisen among English women. In the words of Lord Brougham, "There is a deaf girl at Norwich doing more good than any man in the country." You may have seen the name and some of the productions of Harriet Martineau in the "Monthly Repository," but what she is gaining glory by are "Illustrations of Political Economy," in a series of tales published periodically, of which nine or ten have appeared. It is impossible not to wonder at the skill with which, in the happiest of these pieces, for they are unequal, she has exemplified some of the deepest principles of her science, so as to make them plain to very ordinary capacities, and demonstrated their practical influence on the well-being, moral and physical, of the working classes first, and ultimately on the whole community. And with all this, she has given to her narratives a grace, an animation, and often a powerful pathos, rare even in the works of pure amusement.—AIKIN, LUCY, 1832, *To Dr. Channing, Oct. 15; Correspondence of William Ellery Channing and Lucy Aikin*, ed. LeBreton, p. 148.

I have not time to write to you about Miss Martineau's "Tales," of which of course you have heard, and we have read many. Some are, I think, excellent, and all are powerful where her imagination comes into play. Her reasoning is not and does not pretend to be original. It is taken verbatim from Malthus and McCulloch, a bad school, and her sectarianism not unfrequently peeps out; but I would recommend you strongly to read the "Manchester Strike," which might I think be useful to your poor people at Coventry hereafter, if the time should come when any such folly should be meditated.—HOOK, WALTER FARQUHAR, 1833, *To W. P. Wood, Dec. 7; Life and Letters, ed. Stephens, p.* 171.

I have no great faith in some of her doctrines, but I delight in her stories. The "Garveloch Tales" are particularly good. What a noble creature Ella is! To give us in a fishing-woman an example of magnanimity and the most touching affection, and still keep her in her sphere; to make all the manifestations of this glorious virtue appropriate to her condition and consistent with her nature,—this seems to me to indicate a very high order of mind, and to place Miss Martineau among the first moral teachers as well as first writers of her time. Perhaps I may be partial. I feel so grateful to her for doing such justice to the poor and to human nature, and I am strongly tempted to raise her to the highest rank.—CHANNING, WILLIAM ELLERY, 1833, *To Miss Aikin, May 30; Correspondence of William Ellery Channing and Lucy Aikin, ed. Le Breton, p.* 172.

Ah, welcome home, Martineau, turning statistics
To stories, and puzzling your philogamystics!
I own I can't see, any more than dame Nature,
Why love should await dear good Harriet's dictature!
But great is earth's want to some love-legislature.

—HUNT, LEIGH, 1837, *Blue-Stocking Revels.*

On one point, unfortunately, Miss Martineau could have been at no loss, from the moment of deciding to write a book of Travels in this country. America her theme, satire was to "be her song;" the bookseller and his patrons are to be satisfied with no less than a pungent piquancy of remark, and this they stand ready to compensate with no stinted bounty.—PALFREY, JOHN GORHAM, 1837, *Miss Martineau's Society in America, North American Review, vol.* 45, p. 418.

You say you are surprised I did not express more admiration of Harriet Martineau's book about America. But I *do* admire it—the spirit of it—extremely. I admire her extremely; but I think the moral, even more than the intellectual, woman. I do not mean that she may not be quite as wise as she is good; but she has devoted her mind to subjects which I have not, and probably could not, have given mine to, and writes upon matters of which I am too ignorant to estimate her merit in treating of them. Some of her political theories appear to me open to objection; for instance, female suffrage and community of property; but I have never thought enough upon these questions to judge her mode of advocating them. The details of her book are sometimes mistaken; but that was to be expected, especially as she was often subjected to the abominable impositions of persons who deceived her purposely in the information which she received from them with the perfect trust of a guileless nature. I do entire justice to her truth, her benevolence, and her fearlessness; and these are to me the chief merits of her book.—KEMBLE, FRANCES ANN, 1838, *Letter, Jan.* 8; *Records of Later Life, p.* 80.

Woman: "And we have now got another writer-lady down at Ambleside." Howitt: "A poet?" Woman: "Nay, nothing of the sort; another guess sort of person, I can tell you." Howitt: "Why, who is that?" Woman: "Who is that? why Miss Martineau they call her. They tell me she wrote up the Reform Bill for Lord Brougham: and that she's come from the Lambtons here; and that she's writing now about the taxes. Can she stop the steam, eh? can she, think you? Nay, nay I warrant, big and strong as she is. Ha! Ha! good lauk! as I met her the other day walking along the muddy road below here—'Is it a woman or a man, or what sort of an animal is it?' said I to myself. There she came, stride, stride—great heavy shoes, stout leather leggings on, and a knapsack on her back! Ha! Ha! that's a *political comicalist*, they say; what's that? Do they mean that they can stop steam? But I said to my husband: Goodness, but that *would* have been a wife for you! Why she'd ha' ploughed! and they say she mows her own grass, and digs her own cabbages and potatoes!"—HOWITT, WILLIAM, 1847, *Homes and Haunts of the Most Eminent British Poets, vol.* II, p. 140.

We have read Miss Martineau's book. It is, to my mind, the most awful book that was ever written by a woman. She and this wise Mr. Atkinson dethrone God, abuse Christ, and prefer Mahometanism to Christianity. It made me sick and ill to hear them talk of Jesus as a mere clever mesmerist. To me it is blasphemy. To show you how evil the book is, I must tell you that Alfred wanted the Inquisition for its authors, and I sympatised with him. It will make good people devilish in their indignation and anger, and it will set all the poor infidels crowing like cocks on a dunghill. And only think, in their large appendix, in which they support themselves by such authorities as Hobbes, Lord Bacon, Sir James Mackintosh, &c., I should see a long article with the innocent name of Mary Howitt to it! It is the account of the Preaching Epidemic in Sweden. Curious as it is, it proves nothing, and seems merely introduced to make me out an infidel. I think this has provoked your father more than anything else.—HOWITT, MARY, 1851, *Letter to her Daughter, Autobiography, ed. her Daughter, vol.* II, *p.* 69.

We cannot call to mind any woman of modern or of past times, who has produced a larger number and variety of solid, instructive, and interesting books. She has written well on political economy, on history, on foreign travel, on psychology, and on education; she has produced many clever tales and novels; her books for children and for men are alike good.—SMILES, SAMUEL, 1860, *Brief Biographies.*

The greatest among Englishwomen, except George Eliot, has just departed from among us. Her genius was not only various and remarkable in every line in which it was developed, but singularly masculine in its characteristics. She was a poet and a novelist; but she was much more distinguished in the more unusual developments of a female mind, namely, as political economist, theologian, and journalist. Of course she was precocious. Indeed, when one thinks of what she has done, and when she began to do it, it seems incredible that even three-quarters of a century should have sufficed for so much work. To the last generation she must have seemed one of the most familiar and well-established of English writers; to the present generation it is a marvel to see her death announced to-day, for to us she was a British classic, and hardly accounted among the moderns. . . . Upon the whole, I think, "Life in the Sick-Room" is the most delightful of her works, and will live almost as long as sickness is in the world. One proof of its intrinsic merit is that though published without the aid of her then famous name, it achieved a great success at once; nor is it too much to say it would have been the foundation-stone of her fame as a religious writer, had she confined her attention to similar topics.— PAYN, JAMES, 1876, *Harriet Martineau, Harper's Magazine, vol.* 53, *pp.* 715, 716.

Hard work and high courage were, to our thinking, her most noteworthy characteristics. Even those most familar with her life and work will have been startled at the list of her writings drawn up by herself, "to the best of her recollection," which appeared in the "Daily News" as an appendix to the autobiographical sketch left by her for publication with the editor of that journal, to which alone in her later years she had contributed no less than 1642 articles. From this list it appears that her first book, "My Servant Rachel," was published in 1827, her last, "Biographical Sketches," in 1869. In those fifty-two years more than 100 volumes (103 we believe to be the exact number) appeared from her pen, besides which she was a constant contributor to quarterlies, and monthly magazines, and newspapers, and carried on a correspondence which would of itself have been enough to use up the energy of most women. Apart from all the questions of its contents, the mere feat of getting such a mass of matter fairly printed and published could not easily be matched, and the more the matter is examined the more our wonder will grow. In all that long list there is not a volume, so far as we are aware, which bears marks of having been put together carelessly, or for mere book-making purposes, and her fugitive articles are as a rule upon burning topics, the questions by which men's minds were most exercised at the time. Indeed, though she lived by the pen, no writer ever wielded it with greater independence and single-mindedness. — HUGHES, THOMAS, 1876, *Harriet Martineau, The Academy, p.* 367.

I entirely agree with you in respect to Miss Martineau. The curious limited folly of her apparent common-sense struck me in St. Andrews, and I thought it would make a good article. The autobiography seems much worse than could have been expected. How such a common-place mind could have attained the literary position she did fills me with amazement. How did she manage it? I can only look and wonder.—OLIPHANT, MARGARET O. W., 1877, *To Mr. Blackwood, March 8; Letters, ed Coghill, p. 263.*

She is a most lucid writer, and often more than lucid. When we compare her intellectual force with that of her accomplished contemporary, Sara Coleridge, for example, we feel at once how much power there was in her. She nearly always grasps us; and if we are in haste to find her wrong we sometimes find we have to retrace our steps and pronounce her right after all.— RICHARDSON, HENRY S., 1877, *Harriet Martineau's Account of Herself, Contemporary Review, vol. 25, p. 1123.*

There were doubtless authors in England and America who had produced a higher quality of work, but not one perhaps who had accomplished so large an amount of solidly good and useful achievement. Miss Martineau certainly did much to refute the lingering tradition, if it still needs refuting, that the minds of women are wanting in clearness, method, and logic. Her arguments, if unsatisfactory, were always coherent, and those who tried to cope with her in controversy generally repented it. This conscious power did not diminish her positiveness, but rather increased it, and she was as often dogmatic in her assertions as if she had no arguments to back them. A very clever woman lately said to us, speaking of her young son, "I reasoned with him; I said to him, Charley, you are a great fool." Miss Martineau could supply the reasoning if needed, but she often came at once to the same decisive assertion.—HIGGINSON, THOMAS WENTWORTH, 1877, *Harriet Martineau's Autobiography, The Nation, vol. 24, p. 237.*

She had, early in life, cultivated a concise and ready style of composition, and was proud of her neat manuscripts. Statesmen, editors, publishers, and philanthropists felt that here was a writer—woman though she was—who could fill their coffers or sweep their stable clean. Hence her widespread-power. It needed all her honesty, her sense of the high purposes of literature and of her own vocation in it, and above all, her unfailing instinct for choosing the noble and liberal side in a controversy, to prevent her from becoming every man's drudge —a mere literary besom. But she was not this. One of the last acts she recorded of herself was her quarrel with "Household Words" because she thought the editor had behaved unfairly to the Roman Catholics. She was thoroughly honest, brave even to recklessness, a warm friend, and not a less spiteful foe. She was not half so admirable as a writer and thinker as she was in her more practical capacity of philanthropist. She began life a "radical reformer," and she died true to her colours.—MASSON, ROSALINE ORME, 1877, *Harriet Martineau's Autobiography, The Academy, vol. 11, p. 292.*

A work ["History of England"] containing much information of interest and value, and written with the author's well known spirit and vivacity. It is strongly tinged with personal feeling, and, for this reason, the work can hardly be said to have permanent value. Miss Martineau entered into the life and activity of political affairs with great zeal, and, as she grasped every subject with the energy of a strong mind, her opinions are always entertaining and are generally well worth listening to. Her description of the deplorable financial and social condition of England after the Napoleonic wars is perhaps the most successful part of the work. The volumes are pervaded with an ardent sympathy for the people in their struggles for greater liberties. —ADAMS, CHARLES KENDALL, 1882, *A Manual of Historical Literature, p. 470.*

In an epoch fertile of great genius among women, it may be said of Miss Martineau, that she was the peer of the noblest, and that her influence on the progress of the age was more than equal to that of all the others combined. She has the great honor of having always seen truth one generation ahead; and so consistent was she, so keen of insight, that there is no need of going back to explain by circumstances in order to justify the actions of her life. This can hardly be said of any great Englishman, even by his admirers..—PHILLIPS, WENDELL, 1883, *Remarks at the Unveiling of Miss Anne Whitney's statute of Miss Martineau in the Old South Meeting-House, Dec. 26; Speeches, Lectures and Letters, Second Series, ed. Pease, p. 473.*

Harriet Martineau is one of the most

distinguished literary women this century has produced. She is among the few women who have succeeded in the craft of journalism, and one of the still smaller number who succeeded for a time in moulding and shaping the current politics of her day.—FAWCETT, MILLICENT GARRETT, 1889, *Some Eminent Women of Our Times*, p. 57.

Some of her stories perhaps show an approach to genius; but neither her history nor her philosophical writings have the thoroughness of research or the originality of conception which would entitle them to such a name. As an interpreter of a rather rigid and prosaic school of thought, and a compiler of clear compendiums of knowledge, she certainly deserves a high place, and her independence and solidity of character give a value to her more personal utterances.—STEPHEN, LESLIE, 1893, *Dictionary of National Biography*, vol. XXXVI, p. 313.

Her gift to literature was for her own generation. She is the exponent of the infant century in many branches of thought: —its eager and sanguine philanthropy, its awakening interest in history and science, its rigid and prosaic philosophy. But her genuine humanity and real moral earnestness give a value to her more personal utterances, which do not lose their charm with the lapse of time.—JOHNSON, R. BRIMLEY, 1896, *English Prose, ed. Craik*, vol. V, p. 463.

Harriet Martineau was the object of rather absurd obloquy from Conservative critics as an advanced woman in her day, and of still more absurd eulogy by Liberal sympathisers both in that day and since.

Personally she seems to have been amiable and estimable enough. Intellectually she had no genius; but she had a good deal of the versatile talent and craftsmanship for which the literary conditions of this century have produced unusual stimulus and a fair reward.—SAINTSBURY, GEORGE, 1896, *A History of Nineteenth Century Literature*, p. 164.

She is however most memorable, not as an original thinker, but as a translator and expounder. She translated and condensed the philosophy of Comte, and did as much as anyone to make it known in England. She had the great merits of unshrinking courage, perfect sincerity and undoubting loyalty to truth.—WALKER, HUGH, 1897, *The Age of Tennyson*, p. 168.

Opinions may differ as to what constitutes Harriet Martineau's best work, but my view is that her translation and condensation of Auguste Comte's six volumes into two will live when all her other work is forgotten. Comte's own writings were filled with many repetitions and rhetorical flounderings. He was more of a philosopher than a writer. He had an idea too big for him to express, but he expressed at it right bravely. Miss Martineau, trained writer and thinker, did not translate verbally; she caught the idea, and translated the thought rather than the language. And so it has come about that her work has been translated literally back into French and is accepted as a text-book of Positivism, while the original books of the philosopher are merely collected by museums and bibliophiles as curiosities.—HUBBARD, ELBERT, 1897, *Little Journeys to the Homes of Famous Women*, p. 106.

John Forster
1812–1876

Born, at Newcastle, 2 April 1812. At school at Newcastle. Play, "Charles at Tunbridge," performed at Newcastle theatre, 2 May 1828. To Cambridge, Oct. 1828. Removed to University Coll., London, Nov. 1828. Student at Inner Temple, 10 Nov. 1828; called to Bar, 27 Jan. 1843. Contrib. to "Newcastle Magazine," 1829. Dramatic critic of "True Sun," 1832. Editor of "The Reflector" series of essays, 1832–33. Contrib. to "Courier" and "Athenæum." Literary and dramatic critic to "Examiner," 1833. Edited "Foreign Quarterly Review," 1842–43. Contrib. to "Shilling Magazine" and "Edinburgh Review," 1845, 1856. Editor of "Daily News," Feb. to Oct. 1846. Editor of "Examiner," 1847 to Dec. 1855. Contrib. to "Quarterly Review," Sept. 1854 to 1855. Secretary to Commissioners of Lunacy, Dec. 1855 to Feb. 1861. Married Mrs. Eliza Ann Colburn, 24 Sept. 1856. Commissioner of Lunacy, Feb. 1861 to 1872. Died, 2 Feb. 1876. Buried at Kensal Green. **Works:** "Rhyme and Reason" (anon.), 1832; "Lives of the

Statesmen of the Commonwealth" (5 vols., in "Lardner's Cyclopædia"), 1836-39; "The Life and Adventures of Oliver Goldsmith," 1848 (enlarged edn. called "Life and Times" of Goldsmith, 1854); "Historical and Biographical Essays," 1858; "The Arrest of the Five Members by Charles I.," 1860; "The Debates on the Grand Remonstrance," 1860; "Life of Landor" (2 vols.), 1869; "Life of Dickens" (3 vols.), 1872-74; "Life of Jonathan Swift," vol. i., 1876. He *edited:* Evelyn's "Diary," 1850-52.—SHARP, R. FARQUHARSON, 1897, *A Dictionary of English Authors, p.* 102.

PERSONAL

I have made the acquaintance of Mr. Forster, and like him exceedingly; he is very clever, and, what is better, very noble-minded. — BLESSINGTON, MARGUERITE COUNTESS, 1836, *Letter, Literary Life and Correspondence, ed. Madden, vol.* II, *p.* 143.

A very ugly and noseless likeness of a great tragedian whom he tried to imitate . . . even to his handwriting, . . . a sort of lick-dust to Mr. Fonnoir [Albany Fonblanque] and to Mr. Anybody and everybody else to whom he could gain access.— LYTTON, ROSINA BULWER LADY, 1839, *Chevley.*

There is alive at present in God's universe, and likely to live, a man, Forster by name, a barrister, without practice, residing at number fifty-eight Lincoln's-Inn Fields, not unknown to fame as "the second worst critic of the age," who has gained himself a tolerable footing in our house and hearts, by, I cannot precisely say, what merits: Latterly, Carlyle has not thought him "so very bad a critic;" for he finds him here and there taking up a notion of his own, "as if he understood it." For my part, I have always thought rather well of his judgment; for, from the first, he has displayed a most remarkable clear-sightedness, with respect to myself; thinking me little short of being as great a genius as my husband. And you, by you also his character as a critic has deserved to be redeemed from contempt; for he it was who wrote the article in the "Examiner" in praise of "The Election."—CARLYLE, JANE WELSH, 1842, *To John Sterling, Jan,* 19, *Letters and Memorials, ed. Froude, vol.* I, *p.* 100.

A disciple of Lavater or Gall and Spurzheim could not encounter Forster in any society, or position in it, without being struck with his appearance, his broad and ample forehead, his massive features, his clear, intelligent eye, his firm, fixed, and solemn look, and expressiveness of lips and other features. When we are ushered into the presence of Forster, we feel at home in his company, and well assured of our safety in it. We find ourselves in the company of a man of high integrity and moral character —of an enlarged mind and of a generous nature.—MADDEN, RICHARD ROBERT, 1855, *The Literary Life and Correspondence of the Countess of Blessington, vol.* II, *p.* 142.

So completely had he established his position in 1837 (he was then twenty-five) that he then became engaged to L. E. L., who was at the height of her fame and courted by hosts of admirers. . . . It has been often said, by many who knew the betrothed, that L. E. L. was piqued at the resignation with which Mr. Forster received his dismissal. That a feeling which was not love prompted her to accept the suit of Mr. Maclean was evident to all her friends. It is probable that the outhoress of "The Vow of the Peacock" expected her lover to treat her with extravagant chivalry; to refuse his *congé*, though given again and again; to listen to no reasoning away of his love, and to worship his mistress only the more passionately for the dark clouds that had settled over her head. Whereas she was met by a man of honour who, while maintaining the completest faith in her innocence and remaining ready to marry her, was sufficiently master of himself to defer to her arguments when she showed cause why their engagement should be at an end.—JERROLD, BLANCHARD, 1876, *John Forster, Gentleman's Magazine, N. S., vol.* 16, *pp.* 317, 319.

Forster may be truly said to have exhibited three, if not four, sorts of characters, or rather external styles. There was the inflated, loud, and rudely overbearing style; there was the attempt at this, now and then, among his equals in position, under cover of a half-jocose air, or holding himself in readiness to retreat upon, "Well, but to be serious;" thirdly, there was the style among his superiors in social position or public estimation, when he was all courtesy, though occasionally with a smiling dignity and pompous politeness; and, fourthly,—and a most striking impersonation this,—in addressing a lady on a first introduction, when his style was subdued to a most gentle, and even emotional tenderness of voice and manner, as though he were a physician standing before some goddess in a delicate state of health. He even carried this last style into public life; and I once heard him, when called upon, at a public dinner, to propose "The health of the ladies," assume a tone of voice so tremulous with affectionate solicitude and loving delicacy of allusion (to the heavenly presence of those in the gallery), that he very nearly carried it too far, so as to be obliged to stop with a broken voice, and shed tears. Everybody expected it. I was on the verge of some myself.—HORNE, RICHARD HENGIST, 1876, *John Forster, Temple Bar, vol.* 46. *p.* 510.

Those who knew Forster intimately were alone qualified to appreciate at their true worth his many noble and generous peculiarities. Regarded by strangers, his loud voice, his decisive manner, his features, which in any serious mood were rather stern and authoritative, would probably have appeared anything but prepossessing. Beneath his unflinching firmness and honesty of purpose were, however, the truest gentleness and sympathy. Outsiders might think him obstinate and overbearing, but in reality he was one of the tenderest and most generous of men. A staunch and faithful friend, he was always actively zealous as the peacemaker. While he had the heartiest enjoyment of society he had a curious impatience of little troubles, and yet the largest indulgence for the weakness of others.—KENT, CHARLES, 1889, *Dictionary of National Biography, vol.* XX. *p.* 18.

Forster's foibles were a source of occasional merriment to his friends. His resolute and rather despotic disposition procured for him, however, a good deal of outward respect, especially as he could be, in and out of the *Examiner*, very useful and helpful to all whom he liked. It was credibly reported of Dickens that Forster was the only man of whom he stood a little in awe. . . . He was an honourable as well as an able man, diligent and painstaking in business, and his friendship, when once won, was remarkably steadfast.—ESPINASSE, FRANCIS, 1893, *Literary Recollections and Sketches, p.* 116.

John Forster—Lady Bulwer's Butcher's Boy—was a self-made man, very agreeable to those who could keep him at a distance, but highly unpleasant when he chose.—HAZLITT, W. CAREW, 1897, *Four Generations of a Literary Family, vol.* II, *p.* 130.

GENERAL

Forster is a first-rate man, generous and high-minded; I know him by what he has written. His "Life of Goldsmith" is perfection of its kind — wise, charitable, thoughtful, written in vigorous and manly English. When my life is written after I am dead . . . may I get such a biographer, not to slur over my faults and weaknesses, but to meet them fairly, and present them in their just relation to the entire character.—MORLEY, HENRY, 1850, *Letter, May* 8; *Life of Henry Morley by Henry Shaen Solly, p.* 154.

The rarest and most advantageous of all combinations—the union of common sense and great intellectual endowments—constitutes the power and peculiarity of Mr. Forster's abilities alike in literature and journalism. One is reminded, by his lucid, plain, trenchant, and forcible style of writing, of Cobbett's best manner, with a large infusion into it of literary taste and scholarship.—MADDEN, RICHARD ROBERT, 1855, *The Literary Life and Correspondence of the Countess of Blessington, vol.* II, *p.* 142.

I have just finished the second volume of Forster's Dickens: and still have no reason not to rejoice in the Man Dickens. And surely Forster does his part well; but I can fancy that some other Correspondent but himself should be drawn in as Dickens' Life goes on, and thickens with Acquaintances.—FITZGERALD, EDWARD, 1873, *To W. F. Pollock, March* 30; *Letters, ed. Wright, vol.* I, *p.* 352.

Mr. Forster's "Life of Dickens," now completed in the third volume, is a thoroughly successful picture of the life of the great humourist, and an invariable aid to the attempt to estimate his genius. It was objected to Mr. Forster's earlier volumes, that he himself occupied too prominent a place in the narrative, and that he did not represent his friend in the most amiable and pleasing light. But it is not easy to see how the biographer could have obtruded himself less. An attachment so close, so long, and so unbroken, is perhaps unparalleled in the annals of literary friendships. There was no moment in the life of Dickens in which he did not appeal to Mr. Forster as to another self. Whether it was a question of putting off a dinner-party, or of going to America, of changing the name of a character, or of changing his domestic relations, or of giving public readings—these two last steps Mr. Dickens spoke of as the Plunge and the Dash—his constant cry to Mr. Forster was "advise, advise!" It was not possible to tell the story of the one life without admitting something of the other. Then as to the keenness, the hardness, the masterful side of Mr. Dickens' character, his restlessness, his uneasy endurance of society, his too lofty estimate of the importance of himself and his affairs, all these are easily accounted for by the story of a life which made such blemishes almost fatal. Thus Mr. Forster's book is an *apologia* for the life, and for the genius, with its defects.—LANG, ANDREW, 1874, *Forster's Life of Dickens, The Academy, vol.* 5, *p.* 190.

The merits and defects of his works sprang from the same source. He was an advocate, not a judge. He had sledgehammer blows to deal against the mere semblance of history which passed muster before him, and he was too impatient of the nonsense which was talked by writers like the elder Disraeli to enquire whether some residuum of sense might not be found beneath it all. He was deficient in that judicious scepticism with which an historian is bound to test his assertions which will not bear the test of serious investigation. Hence, too, his preference of biography to history. He had almost a feminine need for a personal attachment in his literary work; of some hero with whose cause he could thoroughly identify himself, and whose faults and mistakes could, if they were acknowledged at all, be covered with loving tenderness. He never attached himself to unworthy objects. Recent inquiry may throw doubt on some of his assertions and qualify some of his judgments. But the men whom he admired were deservedly the leaders of a great age, and the party whose greatness he appreciated was the party which justly merits the highest respect.— GARDINER, SAMUEL R., 1876, *John Forster, The Academy, vol.* 9, *p.* 122.

To offer a concise view of the writings of Mr. Forster, it may be said that they have seldom been awarded all the credit to which they are entitled for the varied labours of the research, the solidity of their substance, and the finish of their texture. They almost always, on great occasions, display force as well as choice diction, and a certain dramatic yet subdued eloquence that carries conviction by its dignity. At the same time, it would be difficult to detach half a dozen sentences, or even passing remarks, that can be ranked as original, or brilliant. We never see a quotation from them relating to philosophy, the fine arts, human passions, or social progress; though some good quotations might, here and there, be made with reference to certain historical characters. But the most important work he did in the literary field of his day, was by no means that of his substantive volumes: it was his anonymous and, comparatively, unknown writings and influences in the *Examiner*, and elsewhere after he had risen to sufficient importance. —HORNE, RICHARD HENGIST, 1876, *John Forster, Temple Bar, vol.* 46, *p.* 503.

The information supplied by Forster's work ["Life of Landor"] is full, precise, and trustworthy; great pains were taken to make the presentation of character complete; there is no approach to tampering with facts through an unwise zeal of friendship; the biographer, allowance being made for some necessary reserve, before all else endeavoured to be truthful, and because entirely just, he felt that in treating of such a man as Landor generosity is a part of justice. At the same time it must be confessed that the work to which we must turn for information about the events of Landor's life is far from being one of the rare and fortunate works of genius.—DOWDEN, EDWARD, 1877–78, *Studies in Literature, p.* 160.

Mr. Forster was appointed by Landor himself as his literary executor; he had command of all the necessary materials for his task, and his book ["Life of Landor"] is written with knowledge, industry, affection, and loyalty of purpose. But it is cumbrous in comment, inconclusive in criticism, and vague on vital points, especially on points of bibliography, which in the case of Landor are frequently both interesting and obscure. — COLVIN, SIDNEY, 1881, *Landor* (*English Men of Letters*), *p.* 5.

A work of the very first importance ["Life of Eliot"] to the student of this period. Sir John Eliot was the most eloquent leader of the first Parliament of Charles I.; but, until the appearance of his biography, there was no means of obtaining an account of the part he took. His speeches, of which MSS. generally remained, had not previously been published or even read. These volumes, therefore, contain a vast amount of valuable information not to be found elsewhere. This material comprises not only Eliot's speeches, but also a voluminous correspondence with all the prominent leaders of the popular movement. No one will ever understand thoroughly what the rising against the Stuarts meant until he is well acquainted with its beginning, and no one can get such an acquaintance better than by studying these volumes. Mr. Forster was long considered the best English biographer; and the "Life of Sir John Eliot" is his most valuable production.—ADAMS, CHARLES KENDALL, 1882, *A Manual of Historical Literature*, p. 457.

He always seemed to be the exemplar of the true literary man—no mere *writer*, like so many, able to write and write at any notice, and about everything or anything. He was a diligent student, and laboured hard to cultivate his talent. The most gratifying thing in his course was to note his work: conscientious throughout, in everything he did his best, looking on "giving *anything to the press*" as a sort of solemn, responsible thing, not to be lightly attempted. . . . A more entertaining book than the "Life of Dickens" was never written.—FITZGERALD, PERCY, 1882, *Recreations of a Literary Man*, vol. I, pp. 173, 174.

I think that that portion of the literary world which understands the fabrication of newspapers will admit that neither before his time, nor since, has there been a more capable editor of a weekly newspaper. As a literary man, he was not without his faults. That which the cabman is reported to have said of him before the magistrate is quite true. He was always "an arbitrary cove." As a critic, he belonged to the school of Bentley and Gifford—who would always bray in a literary mortar all critics who disagreed with them, as though such disagreement were a personal offence requiring personal castigation. But that very eagerness made him a good editor. Into whatever he did he put his very heart and soul. During his time the *Examiner* was almost all that a Liberal weekly paper should be.—TROLLOPE, ANTHONY, 1882–83, *An Autobiography*, p. 62.

Forster may be described as a useful, rather than an artistic biographer. In tone and manner of writing, as of speaking, he was loud and pompous, with a mighty opinion of himself, and a still greater one of his friends.—OLIPHANT, MARGARET O. W., 1892, *The Victorian Age of English Literature*, p. 567.

No one would wish to detract from the merits of Mr. Forster's book, ["Life of Swift"] but it is assuredly doing him no injustice to say that, had he paid more attention to the art of suppression and selection, it would have been better for his readers, and better for Swift's fame. But this is not the only blemish in his work. It is animated throughout by an unpleasant polemical spirit. He appears to have regarded the biographers who preceded him as jealous lovers regard rivals. He is continually going out of his way to exalt himself and to depreciate them. Here we have a digression on the incompetence of Deane Swift, there a sneer at Orrery. Now he pauses to carp at Delany; at another time he wearies us with an account of the deficiencies of Sheridan. He must himself have admitted that his own original contributions to Swift's biography were as a drop in the river, compared with those of Scott and Monck Mason, and yet Scott rarely appears in his pages, except in a disadvantageous light, and to Monck Mason's work, though he draws largely on it, he studiously refrains from acknowledging the slightest obligation. But, to do him justice, Mr. Forster's fragment is a solid and valuable addition to the literature of Swift. If he had added nothing of importance to what was known before, he has scrutinised with miscroscopic minuteness all that was known; he has thus accurately distinguished between what was fiction and what was fact.—COLLINS, JOHN CHURTON, 1893, *Jonathan Swift*, p. 9.

In contemporary biography his chief performances were lives of Landor and of Dickens, with both of whom he was extremely intimate. In private life Forster had the character of a bumptious busybody which character indeed the two books just mentioned, . . . abundantly establish. And towards the men of letters with whom he was intimate (Carlyle and Browning may be added to Landor and Dickens) he seems to have behaved like a Boswell-Podsnap, while in the latter half of the character he no doubt sat to Dickens himself. But he was an indefatigable literary inquirer, and seems, in a patronising kind of way, to have been liberal enough of the result of his inquiries. He had a real interest both in history and literature, and he wrote fairly enough.—SAINTSBURY, GEORGE, 1896, *A History of Nineteenth Century Literature*, p. 243.

Forster had little power of realising character, and the subjects of his biographies are never clearly outlined. His "Life of Dickens" has an importance beyond its intrinsic merits, because it is the most authoritative book on the great novelist.—WALKER, HUGH, 1897, *The Age of Tennyson*, p. 141.

Horace Bushnell
1802—1876

An American theologian. He was born in Litchfield, Conn., April 14, 1802; graduated at Yale in 1827, where he studied law and theology; in 1833 became pastor of the North Congregational Church in Hartford, resigned 1859, and died there February 17, 1876. He was a voluminous writer on theological subjects, some of his works being "Principles of National Greatness;" Christian Nurture" (1847); "God in Christ" (1849); "Christian Theology" (1851); "Sermons for the New Life" (1858); "Nature and the Supernatural" (1858); "Work and Play" (1864); "Christ and His Salvation" (1864); "Woman's Suffrage, the Reform Against Nature" (1869); "The Vicarious Sacrifice" (1865). He was also a writer for various periodicals and newspapers. He was a bold and original thinker, with peculiar eloquence of style. Though strongly evangelical in belief, he denied the Calvinistic theory of the atonement (known as the "satisfaction theory"), and gave less than the ordinary emphasis to the distinction between the persons in the Trinity. These, with other divergences, led to his being accused of heresy; but ultimately the fellowship of the Congregational churches was found broad enough to include him, and he kept his standing therein with growing influence until his death. . . . His select works appeared in a collected edition (8 vols., 1876-77). For his life, consult M. B. Cheney, "Life and Letters of Horace Bushnell" (New York, 1880); T. T. Munger (Boston, 1899).—GILMAN, PECK, AND COLBY, eds. 1900, *New International Encyclopædia*, vol. III, p. 655.

PERSONAL

Three years ago it was my privilege to spend the major part of a summer vacation with this rare man in the Green Mountains. Some impressions which I received of his mental structure, and of his theology, and of his religious character, deserve recording. . . . Few men have ever impressed me as being so electric with vitality at all points as he was. He was an enthusiast in his love of rural sights and sounds and sports. In little things as brimful as in great things, he seemed the *beau ideal* of a live man. The supremacy of mind over the body was something wonderful. . . . The *abandon* of his recreations in the bowling-alley, where he was a boy again, and his theological talks of a Sunday evening, told the same story. "Dying, and behold we live," recurred once and again in listening to the conversations in which he was sure to be the centre and the seer. I have never heard from any other man, in the same length of time, so much of original remark. One could not long discourse with him, even on the common things and in the undress of life, without discovering the secret of his solitude in the theological world. That solitude was not in him, as it is in some men, an affectation of independence. It was in the original make of the man. Nothing struck him as it did the average of men. He took in all things, and reflected back all things, at angles of his own. He never could have been a partisan. With many of the tastes of leadership, he could never have led a party or founded a school. Still less could he have been a follower of other leaders.—PHELPS, AUSTIN, 1876, *Horace Bushnell, Christian Union*.

During his years of failing health he always owned a horse, and many and great were the family excitements attending the sale of an old horse or the purchase of a new one. His occasional long absences from home in quest of health, during which he could not afford to keep a horse unused at home, made these changes somewhat frequent. His excessive honesty was certainly not good policy in dealing with horse-men. If his old horse had a fault or two, he did not content himself with mentioning it, but dwelt upon his failings and set them forth in all lights, till he had left the unfortunate animal not a leg to stand upon. He once sold a horse to a good friend, as honest as himself, who, after trying old Robin for a week or two, came to say that Dr. Bushnell had not asked enough for him, and generously handed over another hundred dollars. If, on the other hand, my father was about to buy a new horse, his easily roused enthusiasm would lead him to speak so heartily in praise of the animal, that the owner would at once see an added value in him, and fix his price accordingly. No experience of these facts availed to alter my father's course at the next opportunity; the temptation to say all he thought was too much for him; nor would he consent to limit his freedom of speech out of any paltry considerations of policy. It was the same with horses as with theology—he was a little more than honest.—CHENEY, MARY BUSHNELL, 1880, *Life and Letters of Horace Bushnell, p. 462.*

Playfulness I should call one of Dr. Bushnell's marked traits, seldom, if ever, exploding aloud. A native refinement kept him from public shouting or private noise. But some ghost of a smile seemed ever to haunt his face,—never hard or biting, but like the gracious beginning of a kiss. If the remark was incisive which he was about to make, the wreath of good-humor was always the more protective and soft.. The geniality began in his mind, and went through the expression of his features into his unconscious manner and slightest gesture. Indeed, it was his very atmosphere. The boy never quite left the man. Something even of the look of the babe was in the virile glance and tone.—BARTOL, CYRUS AUGUSTUS, 1880, *Letter to Mrs. Bushnell, Life and Letters of Horace Bushnell, ed. Cheney, p. 186.*

When, at the close of the war, Yale College, his alma mater, honored her many soldier sons by a commemorative celebration, Dr. Bushnell was invited to deliver the oration. It seemed to me that he was never grander than on that occasion. . . . The Doctor was himself the central figure of the hour, not merely because of his position, but by his character and mental and moral power. He stood there like an inspired prophet of old to give his message and to bear his witness. He had, in one sense, been in more battles than any veteran before him. His face and figure showed scars that came of conflicts with intellectual and spiritual giants. And in his countenance was the clear light of assured triumph of faith. All present looked up to him with admiration and reverence.—TRUMBULL, HENRY CLAY, 1899, *Sunday School Times, Aug. 12.*

GENERAL

Dr. Bushnell is a profound and therefore an independent thinker, and has consequently been arraigned by some of his clerical brethren as not soundly "orthodox,' because he does not choose to adopt all the old phraseology. Those who have attacked him, however, on this ground, have had abundant reason to repent of their rashness; for he has vindicated his faith in a manner that has completely silenced his opponents.—CLEVELAND, CHARLES D., 1859, *A Compendium of American Literature, p. 519.*

Neither his tastes nor his mental traits incline him to polemical theology; not that he is not a logical reasoner, but his nature is a sensitive one, and his discourses all show strong poetic feeling, and a tendency to illustrate spiritual truth by natural images and analogies, rather than to define it in exact formulas by sharp mathematical lines. It will be difficult to find in the sermons of any modern author so many passages of moral and intellectual beauty as Dr. Bushnell's discourses furnish. The current of his thought is strong, but not dogmatic; his piety is evidently the mainspring of his life, but it has no tinge of asceticism; his imagination is his strongest intellectual faculty, but it is made subservient to the noblest uses.—UNDERWOOD, FRANCIS H., 1872, *A Hand-Book of English Literature, American Authors, p. 212.*

He was a bold thinker because he sought for the truth. Near the end of his life, he said playfully, to one of his friends, as the two were fishing in the wilderness, "It is my joy to think that I have sought most earnestly and supremely to find and to live by the truth." He was broad-minded and many-sided, because he would look at the truth from every point of view. He was careless of traditions, because he sought solid standing place for his own feet. He was independent of others, because he must satisfy the consuming hunger of his own soul. When he found the truth, he applied it fearlessly to himself and to other men, to principles, institutions, and dogmas. He abhorred shams and conventional phrases in argument, because he believed so strongly in realities. What offended others as irreverent, often—not always— betokened his higher reverence for what he received as positive truth. He was also manly in the expression and defence of his faith. However he might appear to others, in the sanctuary of his inner self, there ever dwelt a prayerful, magnanimous, loving spirit toward God and man—PORTER, NOAH, 1876, *Memorial Sermon in Chapel of Yale College, March* 26, *p.* 8.

Those piercing glances of insight, and those singular felicities of expression, which so often startle Dr. Bushnell's readers, must surely have often been remarked in his letters and his conversation. And we may well ask, Is not his already large and constantly increasing audience to be satisfied with more knowledge, from these sources, of "the man and his communications?"—DREW, G. S., 1879, *Dr. Bushnell, Contemporary Review, vol.* 35, *p.* 831.

Horace Bushnell, a man congenitally compelled to see all things in the light of reason, espoused at the beginning and maintained to the end the cause of the Orthodox faith. It has had no other expounder of equal genius in our time. He was, however, no such severe dialectician as Calvin. While he would be logical, the forms of logic he despised. His method was that of suggestion. He was more a poet than an advocate. No man drew out his discriminations in sharper lines. But in his nature underneath every line of argument was mystical piety for a daily refuge, and no romance charmed him like a book of prayer. He had that charity for his opponents which sprang from an understanding of their positions as well as from the tenderness of his own heart. He knew why and how one could differ from him; and his imagination, alike fine and broad, showed him on what ground had stood any and every scheme of religion that had prevailed in the world.—BARTOL, CYRUS AUGUSTUS, 1880, *Principles and Portraits, p.* 366.

Great as was his enthusiasm in the pursuit of truth, it was chastened by docility and patience. His aim and prayer were to hold himself in integrity,—perfectly open to the teachings of truth,—never to decide any questions by his prepossessions and his will, nor on the authority of a great name. And it is especially worthy of note that he would not go an inch beyond what the truth, as clearly recognized, warranted. The gist of his alleged heresy in respect to the Trinity lay in his refusal to affirm three metaphysical personalities in the interior substance of the Godhead. He was open to suggestions from persons of the humblest grade. There was something wonderful, almost sublime, in his patience, by which he could bridle his fiery spirit and quietly wait until his knotty questions, of their own accord, opened to him their solutions. And when, under this process, the solutions came, cleaiing away obscurities, and giving his mind rest, is it at all surprising that he should accept them as gifts from God himself, or that he should affirm, what has been an offense to many, that in forming his views he seemed to have had only about the same agency that he had in preparing the blood he circulated, and the anatomic frame he occupied?—CHESEBOROUGH, A. S., 1886, *Relation of Bushnell's Opinions to his Character, Andover Review, vol.* 6, *p.* 117.

Bushnell the theologian was, like Robertson, Maurice, or Kingsley, in England, a genuine stimulating force upon many of the younger Congregationalists of New England; and Bushnell the essayist—now reminding one of Carlyle, now of Ruskin, but ever original—resembled Emerson, though, of course, in a small degree, in his broadcast spreading of seeds of thought.—RICHARDSON, CHARLES F., 1887, *American Literature*, 1607-1885, *vol.* I, *p.* 299.

Dr. Bushnell had a creative mind of a high order, striking out a path of his own, an innovator, indeed, turning the mind of the churches into new directions, in order that they might escape the wearisome confusion bred by the old controversies, and yet aware also that the full significance of the old doctrines had not been measured. If he did not always solve the issues which he raised, yet he never failed to shed light upon them, revealing by his personal disclosure of his own religious need the positive directions which theology must take.—ALLEN, ALEXANDER V. G., 1894, *Religious Progress,* p. 11.

Thirty years ago, Bushnell's great work, "The Vicarious Sacrifice," appeared and provoked a heated controversy. The author was excluded from many pulpits. But now his theory is more generally accepted than any other.— HARRIS, GEORGE, 1895, *Sermons.*

I have called him a man of rare gifts, not yet, as it seems to me, appreciated at their true worth by those who are our conventional measures of reputation. . . . His vocabulary, full and rich, gives him pigments of the rarest. Language indeed is a passion with him; and he sways its rhythmic treasures to his purpose.—MITCHELL, DONALD G., 1899, *American Lands and Letters, Leather-Stocking to Poe's "Raven,"* pp. 75, 88.

Valuable as the sermons of Bushnell are to all who read them, they are of special value to the teacher of homiletics. As he studies them, searching for the art that lends such power to the thought, he notes first their structural quality,—built, not thrown together, nor gathered up here and there. He traces the intertwined rhetoric and logic, each tempering the other,—the reasoning little except clear statement and the rhetoric as convincing as the logic. He follows the wide sweep of the thought which yet never wanders from the theme. He notes the Platonic use of the world as furnishing images of spiritual realities; and a kindred habit of condensing his meaning into apothegms that imbed themselves in the memory. He shows how the preacher begins by almost sharing a doubt with his hearer and leaves him wondering why he ever doubted; how theology is transformed into religion which becomes the judge of theology; and how while the whole sermon is instinct with thought and sentiment, it is practical down even to homeliest details;—this and more the teacher will point out to his students, but he has not compassed the preacher, nor can he measure these discourses by any analysis. They have that which defies analysis,—genius, the creative faculty, the gift of direct vision.—MUNGER, THEODORE T., 1899, *Horace Bushnell,* p. 284.

These political books and addresses of Dr. Bushnell reveal thoroughness of research and an intimate knowledge of contemporary conditions. They show him as the citizen, loving his city, and state, and country, the spokesman of the conscience of many, and the guide to their political thinking. They contain pointed sentences that stick, winged words that fly. While his civil interests were great, his ethical and religious interests were greater. He was a religious and moral teacher, but one who could not help applying his principle to life; so even his most abstruse theological reasonings become clear as appeals to a common humanity, which has its days to live in the streets and houses of an intricate civilization.—ADDISON, DANIEL DULANY, 1900, *The Clergy in American Life and Letters,* p. 289.

Except in some of his theological works, he seldom felt a need of reinforcing his opinions or illustrating them, much less of adorning them, by quotation. If he sometimes made his argument overstrenuous, it was through urgency of zeal rather than pride of power, and never in malice of temper. He cherished no animosities, and courted peace rather than strife, but not at the price of suppressing the message he was charged to deliver.—ALLEN, WALTER, 1900, *Horace Bushnell, Atlantic Monthly,* vol. 85, p. 424.

Orestes Augustus Brownson
1803–1876

An American theologian and author. He was born in Stockbridge, Vt., and was brought up as a Presbyterian, but became a Universalist preacher, and was a vigorous and indefatigable writer in support of whatever belief he for the time adopted. In 1828 he went into politics, and tried to establish a Workingmen's Party in New York, moved thereto by the ideas of Robert Owen. In 1832 he was enthusiastic over Dr. Channing, and became a Unitarian preacher. In 1836 he organized in Boston "The Society of Christian Progress" as a church, of which he was pastor. At this period, also, Brownson was one of the New England Transcendentalists, and published "New Views of Christianity," "Society and the Church," which was a moderate attack on Protestantism. In 1838 he started the *Boston Quarterly Review*, which had existence for about five years, and was then merged in the New York *Democratic Review*, and from 1844 was known as *Brownson's Quarterly Review*. This was written throughout almost entirely by Brownson himself. In 1840 he published "Charles Elwood: or, The Infidel Converted," a treatise, in the form of a story, in favor of the Roman Catholic Church, toward which the author was drifting, and which he joined in 1844. A deeply spiritual man, he gained a reputation as a philosopher and a powerful Catholic apologist, in spite of his frequent conflicts with the Church authorities. His most important writings, in addition to those mentioned above, are: "The Convert: or Leaves from My Experience" (1857); "The American Republic; Its Constitution, Tendencies, and Destiny" (1870). His "Works" have been republished by his son, H. F. Brownson, in 20 volumes (1882–87). The latter has also published a "Life," in 3 vols. (1898–1900).—GILMAN, PECK, AND COLBY, eds. 1902, *The New International Encyclopædia*, vol. III, p. 506.

PERSONAL

I am no saint, never was, and never shall be a saint; I am not, and never shall be, a great man; but I always had, and I trust I always shall have, the honor of being regarded by my friends and associates as impolitic, as rash, imprudent, and impracticable. I was and am, in my natural disposition, frank, truthful, straightforward, and earnest; and, therefore, have had, and, I doubt not, shall carry to the grave with me, the reputation of being reckless, ultra, a well-meaning man, perhaps an able man, but so fond of paradoxes and extremes, that he cannot be relied on, and is more likely to injure than serve the cause he espouses. So, wise and prudent men shake their heads when my name is mentioned, and disclaim all solidarity with me. — BROWNSON, ORESTES AUGUSTUS, 1857, *The Convert, Works*, ed. Brownson, vol. v, p. 45.

Dr. Brownson was then [1834] in the very prime of manhood. He was a handsome man, tall, stately, and of grave manners. His face was clean shaven. The first likeness of him that I remember appeared in the *Democratic Review*, published by O'Sullivan and Langtry. It made him look like Proudhon, the French socialist. This was all the more singular because at that time he was really the American Proudhon, though he never went so far as "La propriété, c'est le vol." As he appeared on the platform and received our greeting he was indeed a majestic man, displaying in his demeanor the power of a mind altogether above the ordinary. But he was essentially a philosopher, and that means that he never could be what is called popular. He was an interesting speaker, but he never sought popularity. He never seemed to care much about the reception his words received, but he exhibited anxiety to get his thoughts rightly expressed and to leave no doubt about what his convictions were. Yet among a limited class of minds he always awakened real enthusiasm—among minds, that is, of a philosophical tendency. He never used manuscript or notes; he was familiar with his topic, and his thoughts flowed out spontaneously in good, pure, strong, forcible English. He could control any reasonable mind, for he was a man of great thoughts and never without some grand truth to impart. But to stir the emotions was not in his power, though he sometimes attempted it; he never succeeded in being really pathetic.—HECKER, I. T., 1887, *Dr. Brownson and the Workingman's Party Fifty Years Ago, Catholic World*, vol. 45, p. 204.

He was so arbitrary and dogmatic [1844] that most people did not like him; but I appreciated his acquaintance, as he was a liberal thinker and had a world of information which he readily imparted to those of a teachable spirit.—STANTON, ELIZABETH CADY, 1898, *Eighty Years and More*, p. 133.

GENERAL

In logical accuracy, in comprehensiveness of thought, and in the evident frankness and desire for truth in which it is composed, ["Charles Elwood"] we know of few theological treatises which can be compared with it.—POE, EDGAR ALLAN, 1841, *A Chapter on Autography, Works*, ed. Stedman and Woodberry, vol. IX, p. 201.

With regard to Mr. Brownson's merits as a cultivator of that philosophy of society which he professes, a candid estimate would probably determine that his own contributions to it amount to nothing: we cannot discover any one element of opinion, any one definite view, any single principle of arrangement or detail, which a future historian will refer to his name as connected with its first appearance in the science. . . . The style of Mr. Brownson has some good qualities. It is commonplace, without purity, and destitute of any characteristic brilliancy or elegance; but it is natural, direct, and plain. It is that simple and unaffected manner which has the appearance of being formed, not upon any plan, but merely by practice and use. Occasionally his better taste is overcome by the faults of Carlyle, or some other favourite of the hour; but when he uses his own style, it would be difficult to name an author who renders abstruse subjects so familiar, or conducts the most arduous discussions with greater ease.—GRISWOLD, RUFUS WILMOT, 1847, *The Prose Writers of America*, pp. 423, 424.

Close behind him is Brownson, his mouth very full
With attempting to gulp a Gregorian bull;
Who contrives, spite of that, to pour out as he goes
A stream of transparent and forcible prose;
He shifts quite about, then proceeds to expound
That 'tis merely the earth, not himself, that turns round,
And wishes it clearly impressed on your mind
That the weathercock rules and not follows the wind;
Proving first, then as deftly confuting each side,
With no doctrine pleased that's not somewhere denied,
He lays the denier away on the shelf,
And then—down beside him lies gravely himself.
He's the Salt River boatman, who always stands willing
To convey friend or foe without charging a shilling,
And so fond of the trip that, when leisure's to spare,
He'll row himself up, if he can't get a fare.
The worst of it is, that his logic's so strong,
That of two sides he commonly chooses the wrong:
If there *is* only one, why, he'll split it in two,
And first pummel this half, then that, black and blue.
That white's white needs no proof, but it takes a deep fellow
To prove it's jet-black, and that jet-black is yellow.

—LOWELL, JAMES RUSSELL, 1848, *A Fable for Critics*.

Mr. Brownson is an active thinker, an energetic writer, and a man who has assumed an important position in American literature by years of steady labor. He has devoted himself during that time to the highest questions of philosophy, ethics, and theology, and has treated none of these subjects in a superficial or commonplace way. He has also belonged for a time, after a fashion of his own, to our communion. He has repeatedly created sensations by his ultraism on several subjects, and he finally astonished our community by going over from extreme Neology and Transcendentalism to Romanism of the most Ultramontane kind.— CLARKE, JAMES FREEMAN, 1850, *Brownson's Argument for the Roman Church, Christian Examiner*, vol. 48, p. 227.

The style of Mr. Brownson is a remarkably felicitous one for the discussion of abstract topics; full, fluent, easily intelligible, meeting the philosophic requirements of the subject, at the same time preserving a popular interest, it was well adapted to enlist the popular ear. As a vehicle for the speculations of the scholar it still preserves its attraction to those who delight in mental gladiatorial exercises, or are curious to note the reconciliation of the "chartered libertine" in doctrine to the authoritative voice of the Church.— DUYCKINCK, EVERT A., AND GEORGE L., 1865–75, *Cyclopædia of American Literature*, ed. Simons, vol. II, p. 145.

Dr. Brownson is an exceedingly able and acute reasoner, and a clear and forcible writer. As might be expected, his religious convictions permeate nearly every sentence. With most authors there are certain fields on which there is a truce to controversy: but Dr. Brownson, with more logic, perhaps, but with less amenity, treats every subject, from metaphysics to an album sonnet, in its relations to the church; and it is almost impossible to give the best specimens of his style without introducing topics that do not belong in a collection of literature. — UNDERWOOD, FRANCIS H., 1872, *A Hand-Book of English Literature, American Authors*, p. 236.

The power of Dr. Brownson as a writer lies principally in the exposition of the fundamental principles of faith or reason. When he developed these principles and their consequences, he appeared as if armed with the club and might of Hercules, with which he crushed the Hydra of error with its several heads of heresy, infidelity, and atheism. "His style was as clear and forcible as the train of thought and reasoning of which it was the expression." A certain childlike simplicity and candor, an apparent love of truth which sought for no disguise, and a boldness of spirit which took no account of earthly considerations, gave to his writings a singular charm and influence.—JENKENS, O. L., 1876, *The Student's Handbook of British and American Literature, p.* 473.

Mr. Brownson was a remarkable man, remarkable for intellectual force, and equally for intellectual wilfulness. His mind was restless, audacious, swift; his self assertion was immense; his thoughts came in floods; his literary style was admirable for freshness, terseness and vigor. Of rational stability of principle he had nothing, but was completely at the mercy of every novelty in speculation. That others thought as he did, was enough to make him think otherwise; that he thought as he had six months before was a signal that it was time for him to strike his tent and move on. An experimenter in systems, a taster of speculations, he passed rapidly from one phase to another, so that his friends ascribed his steadfastness to Romanism, to the fatigue of intellectual travelling. —FROTHINGHAM, OCTAVIUS BROOKS, 1876, *Transcendentalism in New England, p.* 128.

Those who may read the essays on political matters contained in these volumes, will not fail to note that the author's political opinions or views of government ran parallel with his religious or theological convictions. At first he was a radical, a believer in the majesty, the infallibility,—the divinity, I may say,—of the masses, placing the origin of all authority in the individual man, attempting to establish the association or community system of government; seeking the overthrow of all priesthood because it binds the conscience; of the banks, because they are in the interest of the business class or employers and opposed to the laboring class or employed; of the transmission of property by will or descent, because a man's right to his property ceased with his death, and he would have the State apportion it amongst the most needy. As he came to acknowledge the authority of God in matters of religion, he saw that power too was from him and thenceforth held that government was necessary for the preservation of order and the restraining of license, and although the political people are the means or channel through which the State derives its power, yet that power, whether monarchical, aristocratic, democratic, or mixed, is from God, and he that resists it resists God. Thus from a radical, a destroyer of all authority, he came to see in human Government a likeness and imitation of Divine Providence; not an evil to be hated and resisted, but a beneficent agent for the protection of right, the advancement of civilization, the aid of religion, science, art, and learning, and next to religion the greatest means by which man may attain his destiny, and as such to be loved, obeyed, and defended. The essays of Dr. Brownson on theology, politics, and morals, are all based on his philosophy, according to which nature and grace, reason and revelation, the order of reality and that of science are brought into the harmony which for three hundred years had been the aim of thinking men.—BROWNSON, HENRY F., 1882, *ed. The Works of Orestes A. Brownson, Introduction, p.* x.

This is not so much a history as a political study; but its author was so vigorous a thinker and writer that it is well worthy of the historical student's attention. Dr. Brownson was essentially a reviewer of books, and not a maker of them; but in the volume before us he has embodied the best part of his writings. . . . The reader will probably dissent from the writer quite as often as he agrees with him; but, in spite of this fact, he will find the vigor and originality of the work exceedingly suggestive.— ADAMS, CHARLES KENDALL, 1882, *A Manual of Historical Literature, p.* 567.

There are names connected with Catholic literature in America that we should ever hold in honor and benediction. Such is the name of Orestes A. Brownson. Do we realize all the greatness covered by that name? America has produced no more powerful intellect than Brownson's. There was no problem, social, political, religious, or philosophical, that he did not grapple with and find an answer for. . . . The very ring of his sentences was a trumpet-blast to us of the rising generation. He taught us how to take our stand upon his own high plane of thought, and thence survey the beautiful harmony of our creed with all that is good and noble in the natural world. He brought home, not to us alone, but to the cultured intellect throughout the Christian world—for he had admirers in all parts and among all creeds—the great truths of natural and revealed religion with a grasp, a force, and an energy of expression worthy of an Aquinas. We were led to hold up our heads and to be proud of the faith that could inspire such sublime thoughts and control such a noble nature. His great intellect was only equalled by his profound humility. — MULLANY, PATRICK FRANCIS (BROTHER AZARIAS), 1889, *Books and Reading*, pp. 59, 61.

One of the most powerful minds, the most intense personalities, in American literature is that of Orestes Brownson, whose distinguishing trait, at first glance, is the broad range of interests, of thought, and of knowledge over which his intellect plays with abiding and almost equal strength. Neither discursive, content with moving upon the surface, nor overborne by emotion, nor bound by prejudice nor pedantry, it seems to many of us to have surpassed in depth, comprehensiveness, and sincerity every other philosophic mind that this country has produced. In keeping with his intellect, Brownson's lucid, forceful style gives the impression of a prodigious and unchanging momentum. His collected works fill twenty ponderous volumes, some of which have claimed title to further remembrance by holding their vitality in tact after thirty or forty years.— LATHROP, GEORGE PARSONS, 1896, *Orestes Brownson, Atlantic Monthly*, vol. 77, p. 770.

Throughout, he was active in political discussion; oftenest radical, but at times severely conservative; writing sharply and strongly in journals of his own establishment; always trenchant in speech—always vagrant in thought: a strong, self-willed, and curious Vermonter!—MITCHELL, DONALD G., 1899, *American Lands and Letters, Leather-Stocking to Poe's "Raven,"* p. 176.

In the well-known work "Catholic Belief" a list is given of some of the more eminent converts to the Catholic Church in America. The lists include statesmen, judges, generals, authors of note, famous men of Science, and distinguished ecclesiastics; but one name towers like a mountain peak above the rest—the name of Orestes A. Brownson, who is stated, by the author of "Catholic Belief," to have been called by the famous English statesman, lawyer, and man of letters, Lord Brougham, the "master mind of America."—GILDEA, WILLIAM L., 1899, *An English View of Brownson's Conversion, Catholic World*, vol. 69, p. 24.

It is pathetic to have to recognize that Brownson is a really forgotten man, for at one time he stood between contending forces a seemingly powerful figure. But against the subtle individualism of the Protestant mind he contended with singularly little result. So doughty a champion probably inspired his new friends with a measure of dismay, while it may fairly be doubted if he ever succeeded in winning a notable convert to his own new way of thinking. In this respect the contrast between him and Father Hecker is striking. The unsympathetic mind commonly regards him as a sort of ecclesiastical recidivist, who, having tried one form of spiritual error, soon abandoned it, only to seek another, which in turn he would presently repudiate. His conceit, of which he always made frank acknowledgment, led him firmly to maintain that all this was consistent progress.—SWIFT, LINDSAY, 1900, *Brook Farm*, p. 246.

John Neal
1793–1876

A once famous littérateur of Portland, Maine, who early gained a hearing, and, as poet, novelist, dramatist, and magazinist, was constantly before the public for the rest of his long life, though little of his work can be said to survive, able as some of it is. The more important of his writings include, "Keep Cool," a novel; "The Battle of Niagara," a poem; "Goldau, and Other Poems;" "Rachel Dyer," a novel; "Downeasters," a novel; "True Womanhood;" "Bentham's Morals and Legislation;" "Great Mysteries and Little Plagues;" "Wandering Recollections of a Somewhat Busy Life" (1870).—ADAMS, OSCAR FAY, 1897, *A Dictionary of American Authors*, p. 268.

PERSONAL

A New Englander — a real brother Jonathan, or Yankee; one of those audacious, whimsical, obstinate, *self-educated* men, who are called by Dr. Ferguson the self-taught astronomer, while giving an account of himself—"The Scholars of God Almighty." Neal has written more volumes, if those that he does acknowledge be his; or, one-third part of those, which he does not acknowledge, though laid, with all due solemnity, at his door, by the beadles of literature—than, perhaps, any other four of his countrymen. Yet he is now only thirty-two years of age—with a constitution able to endure every kind of hardship—has only been writing, at intervals, for seven years—has only gone through his apprenticeship, as an author, and set up for himself, within a few months.—His life has been a course of continual adventure. It will be one of great profit, we hope, now that he is out of his time, to the people of this generation, at least. He is a Quaker; or *was*, till the society "read him out" for several transgressions—to wit—for knocking a man, who insulted him, head over heels; for paying a militia fine; for making a tragedy; and for desiring to be turned out whether or no.—NEAL, JOHN, 1825, *American Writers, Blackwood's Magazine*, vol. 17, p. 190.

There swaggers John Neal, who has wasted in Maine
The sinews and chords of his pugilist brain,
Who might have been poet, but that, in its stead, he
Preferred to believe that he was so already;
Too hasty to wait till Art's ripe fruit should drop,
He must pelt down an unripe and colicky crop;
Who took to the law, and had this sterling plea for it,
It required him to quarrel, and paid him a fee for it;
A man who's made less than he might have, because
He always has thought himself more than he was,—
Who, with very good natural gifts as a bard,
Broke the strings of his lyre out by striking too hard,
And cracked half the notes of a truly fine voice,
Because song drew less instant attention than noise.
—LOWELL, JAMES RUSSELL, 1848, *A Fable for Critics*.

In the evening had John Neal at tea, whom I found to be a character, one of the curiosities of literature, very entertaining, large, strong, with a spirited air, independent, quick in general, but with no malice, exceedingly egotistical, but not troublesome on that account.—DANA, RICHARD HENRY, 1854, *To his Wife, Sept.* 3; *Richard Henry Dana, A Biography*, ed. C. F. Adams, vol. I, p. 331.

Neal is a literary and social evergreen of the first quality: except a more silvery tinge to his hair and a somewhat thinner cheek, he is the same pleasant, genial, emphatic, and colloquial enthusiast as when he wrote "Seventy-Six" and the "American Eagle." It was a treat to hear him and Dr. J. W. Francis compare notes.—TUCKERMAN, HENRY THEODORE, 1858, *Letter, May* 21; *Allibone's Dictionary of English Literature*, vol. II, p. 1404.

GENERAL

Mr. Neal must be allowed to be among the most remarkable of our writers, whether of poetry or prose. He is gifted with an almost magical facility of literary composition. What to others is a work of careful study, and severe labor, is to him a pastime. His writings have in most cases been thrown off with a rapidity that almost surpasses belief. . . . Mr. Neal's poetry has not been so popular as that of many others who never possessed his power. The circumstance may be partly ascribed to the false taste in which his works are mostly composed, and partly to this, that it is addressed to the fancy, rather than the feeling; not that he wants poetical sensibility, or a delicate or refined conception of what is beautiful and tender and moving in the works of nature, or the emotions in the human bosom, for he has all these; and he has besides a passionate and overpowering sense of grandeur and sublimity. But his poetry is wanting in natural sentiment; it does not touch the heart—it does not awaken our sensibilities, or stir up from their recesses the "thoughts that lie too deep for words."—KETTELL, SAMUEL, 1829, *Specimens of American Poetry*, vol. III, pp. 86, 89.

John Neal's forces are multitudinous, and fire briskly at everything. They occupy all the provinces of letters, and are nearly useless from being spread over too much ground.—WHIPPLE, EDWIN PERCY, 1845, *Words, Essays and Reviews*, vol. I, p. 105.

Of Mr. Neal's poems, I may repeat what

I have remarked elsewhere. They have the unquestionable stamp of genius. He possesses imagination in a degree of sensibility and energy hardly surpassed in this age. The elements of poetry are poured forth in his verses with a prodigality and power altogether astonishing. But he is deficient in the constructive faculty. He has no just sense of proportion. No one with so rich and abundant materials had ever less skill in using them. Instead of bringing the fancy to adorn the structures of the imagination, he reverses the poetical law, giving to the imagination the secondary office, so that the points illustrated are quite forgotten in the accumulation and splendour of the imagery. . . . Of his novels it may be said that they contain many interesting and some striking and brilliant passages—filling enough, for books of their sort, but rarely any plot to serve for warp. They are original, written from the impulses of the author's heart, and pervaded by the peculiarities of his character; but most of them were produced rapidly and carelessly. . . . The best of them would be much improved by a judicious distribution of points, and the erasure of tasteless extravagancies. — GRISWOLD, RUFUS WILMOT, 1847, *The Prose Writers of America*, p. 315.

I hardly know how to account for the repeated failures of John Neal as regards the *construction* of his works. His art is great and of a high character—but it is massive and undetailed. He seems to be either deficient in a sense of completeness, or unstable in temperament; so that he becomes wearied with his work before getting it done. He always begins well—vigorously—startlingly—proceeds by fits—much at random—now prosing, now gossiping, now running away with his subject, now exciting vivid interest; but his conclusions are sure to be hurried and indistinct; so that the reader, perceiving a falling-off where he expects a climax, is pained, and, closing the book with dissatisfaction, is in no mood to give the author credit for the vivid sensations which have been aroused *during the progress* of perusal. Of all literary foibles the most fatal, perhaps, is that of defective climax. Nevertheless, I should be inclined to rank John Neal first, or at all events second, among our men of indisputable *genius.*—POE, EDGAR ALLAN, 1850 *Marginalia*, CXXXVIII.

There is a great deal of merit in the works we have mentioned; they are full of dramatic power and incident; but these verses are well nigh overbalanced by their extravagance, and the jerking, out-of-breath style in which they are often written. . . . The vigor of the man, however, pervades everything he has produced. He sees and thinks as well as writes, after his own fashion, and neither fears nor follows criticism. It is to be regretted that he has not more fully elaborated his prose productions, as that process would probably have given them a firmer hold on public favor than they appear to have secured. There is much strong vigorous sense, independence in speaking of men and things; good, close thought; analysis of character, and clear description, which the public should not lose, in these pages.—DUYCKINCK, EVERT A., AND GEORGE L., 1865–75, *Cyclopædia of American Literature,* ed. Simons, vol. I, p. 875.

Has chiefly distinguished himself as a most voluminous contributor to letters,—novels, plays, poems, history, and critical reviews without number bearing witness to his indefatigable industry, versatile talent, and ease and sprightliness of style.—ALIBONE, S. AUSTIN, 1870, *A Critical Dictionary of English Literature,* vol. II, p. 1404.

Neal wrote from the surface of his mind, which was frothy. His life was mixed, and his novels were equally so. The very plot is erratic, sometimes intensely, almost luridly, dramatic, sometimes weak, and attenuated beyond any reader's patience. As he had been shop-boy, dry goods merchant, lawyer, poet, and essayist, as well as novelist, he considered himself qualified to lecture on all subjects. . . . The style is slipshod, a perfect storm of words to the square inch of ideas, a huddle of incident and characters, with scarcely a clew to his purpose with them. Of the artistic element there is none whatever, no sense of proportion, no patient study of persons, no arrangement, no aim, and no fulfillment. There is only one character that clings to the mind, and that is John Neal—the universal Yankee, whittling his way through creation, with a half-genius for everything, a robust genius for nothing,—everything in the egg, and not a chick fully developed.—MORSE, JAMES HERBERT, 1883, *The Native Element in American Fiction, Century Magazine,* vol. 26, p. 290.

Henry Kingsley
1830-1876

Novelist, third son of the Rev. Charles Kingsley, and younger brother of Charles Kingsley and George Henry Kingsley, was born at Barnack, Northamptonshire, on 2 Jan. 1830. He was educated at King's College, London, and at Worcester College, Oxford, where he matriculated 6 March, 1850. He left college in 1853 to go to the Australian goldfields with some fellow-students. After five years' desultory and unremunerative employment he returned to England, and soon afterwards made himself known by the spirited and successful novel, "Geoffrey Hamlyn," in which his Australian experience was turned to account. It was followed in 1861 by "Ravenshoe," which also made its mark, and afterwards by many others. In 1864 he married his second cousin, Sarah Maria Kingsley, and settled at Wargrave, near Henley-on-Thames. He was afterwards for eighteen months editor of the "Edinburgh Daily Review," an organ of the free church. During his editorship the Franco-German war broke out, and Kingsley went out as correspondent for his paper. He was present at the battle of Sedan (1 Sept. 1870), and was the first Englishman to enter the town afterwards. After giving up the paper he settled for a time in London, and renewed his work as a novelist. He subsequently retired to the Attrees, Cuckfield, Sussex, where he died of a cancer in the tongue after some months' illness on 24 May 1876. Kingsley's works are: 1. "The Recollections of Geoffrey Hamlyn," 3 vols. 1859. 2. "Ravenshoe," 3 vols. 1862. 3. "Austin Elliott," 2 vols. 1863 (French translation by Daurand Forgues, 1866). 4. "The Hillyars and Burtons: a Story of two Families," 3 vols. 1865. 5. "Leighton Court: a Country House Story," 2 vols. 1866. 6. "Silcote of Silcotes," 3 vols. 1867. 7. "Mademoiselle Mathilde," 3 vols. 1868. 8. "Stretton," 3 vols. 1869. 9. "Old Margaret," 2 vols. 1871. 10. "The Lost Child" (illustrated by L. Frölich), 1871. 11. "The Boy in Grey," 1871. 12. "Hetty and other Stories," 1871. 13. "The Harveys," 2 vols. 1872. 14. "Hornby Mills, and other Stories," 1872. 15. "Valentin: a French Boy's Story of Sedan," 1872. 16. "Reginald Hetherege," 3 vols. 1874. 17. "Number Seventeen," 2 vols. 1875. . 18. "The Grange Garden: a Romance," 3 vols. 1876. 19. "Fireside Studies," 2 vols. 1876. He also edited the Globe edition of "Robinson Crusoe" in 1868, with a biographical introduction, and published in 1869 "Tales of Old Travels re-narrated."—STEPHEN, LESLIE, 1892, *Dictionary of National Biography*, vol. XXXI, p. 181.

PERSONAL

He found his proper place as an essayist and a novelist, and in all his works there is to me a strange and nameless charm—a quaint humor, a genuine sentiment, an atmosphere all his own, breezy, buoyant, boyish, seeming to show a personality behind all his creations, that of their creator, a fair, frank, fresh-hearted man. He had true artistic talent, too, inherited from his grandfather, and he may have been just in judging himself capable of gaining far greater reputation as a painter than as a novelist even. His skill in drawing was amazing, and the few water-colors and oils left to his family—and unknown outside of its members—are masterpieces.
—MARTIN, BENJAMIN ELLIS, 1886, *Old Chelsea, Century Magazine*, vol. 33, p. 234.

The story of Henry Kingsley's life may well be told in a few words, because that life was on the whole a failure. The world will not listen very tolerantly to a narrative of failure unaccompanied by the halo of remoteness. To write the life of Charles Kingsley would be a quite different task. Here was success, victorious success, sufficient indeed to gladden the heart even of Dr. Smiles—success in the way of Church preferment, success in the way of public veneration, success, above all, as a popular novelist, poet, and preacher. Canon Kingsley's life has been written in two substantial volumes containing abundant letters and no indiscretions. In this biography the name of Henry Kingsley is absolutely ignored. And yet it is not too much to say that, when time has softened his memory for us, as it has softened for us the memories of Marlowe and Burns and many another, the public interest in Henry Kingsley will be stronger than in his now more famous brother.—SHORTER, CLEMENT, 1895, ed. *The Recollections of Geoffrey Hamlyn, Memoir*, p. 137.

No one knows whether Henry Kingsley was precocious or dull at Oxford. Nobody seems to know anything about Henry

Kingsley, at Oxford or anywhere else. In "The Memoir of Charles Kingsley," by Mrs. Kingsley, she does not even mention the name of Henry Kingsley, her famous husband's equally famous brother. The Encyclopædias, the Dictionaries of Authors, ignore him, or dismiss him with a line or two; he is rarely if ever mentioned, in the Biographies, in the Auto-biographies, or in the Reminiscences of his contemporaries; and yet he wrote some of the most wholesome, most fascinating novels of his century. . . . That he loved Oxford, and went often back to Oxford, in spirit, if not in body, is shown throughout his work. He sent Ravenshoe to "St. Paul's" in Oxford, which was, perhaps, St. John's. He educated Lord Welter and Austin Elliot at Christ Church. John Thornton in "Austin Elliot," was a Servitor at Christ Church, who fell in love with the pretty daughter of a "well-to-do farmer living down the river not far from Oxford." Arthur Silcote was the youngest tutor at Balliol. And "Leighton Court" is described as being "very like Balliol, uncommonly like Oriel, and a perfect replica of University." Henry Kingsley, whatever was his life in Oxford, proved himself in after life to have been one of the best examples of the Oxford man. And if you care to see what sort of an imaginary Oxford man a real Oxford man can create, read the story of Charles Ravenshoe—who, like his creator, was brave, honest, simple, open-hearted, open-handed, and one of the noblest characters in modern fiction; and thereby you will see what Oxford has done, and can do, for the men she calls her sons.—HUTTON, LAURENCE, 1903, *Literary Landmarks of Oxford*, pp. 262, 263.

GENERAL

If nicknames were not rash as well as rude, we should be tempted to try our skill at one, and to call Mr. Henry Kingsley one of Heaven's Undergraduates. Almost all his characteristics as a novelist are those of the typical undergraduate, intensified and sublimated of course. His ideals of male and female character—particularly his usual hero, who is a tremendous fellow at everything, but gets into awful scrapes, and is invariably forgiven by an angelic father—are intensely undergraduate, and so is his style with its perpetual flow of rather forced humour, partaking freely of exaggeration and burlesque. Now, although an undergraduate is a noble and interesting product, he is or ought to be essentially transitional, and Mr. Henry Kingsley shows no signs of transition, except occasional retrogressions into the schoolboy stage. The man who could write "Geoffrey Hamlin," and "Ravenshoe," we hardly remember how many years ago, ought by this time to have turned out something of real permanent value, and we fear that "Reginald Hetherege" can hardly be said to possess much value of any kind, except such as most of the better class of ordinary novels may claim.—SAINTSBURY, GEORGE, 1874, *Reginald Hetherege, The Academy, vol. 6, p. 7*.

Many years ago Mr. Henry Kingsley . . . wrote "Geoffrey Hamlyn," a book which, without being exactly a well-constructed story, had several cleverly-devised situations and clearly-marked characters, besides containing descriptions of Australian life endued with much freshness and novelty; drawn from his own experience of five years' sojourn in the colony. He followed this up with a real good novel, "Ravenshoe;" and then came a second and third, "Austin Elliot" and the "Hillyars and Burtons," half of iron and half of miry clay, exhibiting in parts the former painstaking and literary merit, and elsewhere somewhat of the carelessness of a school-boy rhapsodist. After that time, with less regard for criticism and for his own reputation as an author than his friends could have wished, he poured out a long series of tales, only one of which, "Mademoiselle Mathilde," had as much pains bestowed on it as is essential to thoroughly good work. Sometimes, it is true, single passages and scenes of merit have redeemed a few of these later books, as "Silcote of Silcotes" and "Stretton," which in spite of much extravagance of plot, are undoubtedly amusing; but sheer dulness was occasionally reached, as in "Hetty," "Reginald Hetherege," and some others.—LITTLEDALE, RICHARD F., 1876, *New Novels, The Academy, vol. 9, p. 554*.

"Ravenshoe," his most successful work, published in 1861, has more of plot and more studied delineation of character than is found in the majority of his books; the well-known incident of the rough and rather brutal Welter's hesitation between right and wrong, when he is called upon to do his duty at the cost of a fortune to himself, shows a latent power which might have raised him to a very high place in literature.—OLIPHANT, MARGARET O. W., 1892, *The Victorian Age of English Literature*, p. 300.

I worshipped his books as a boy; to-day I find them full of faults—often preposterous, usually ill-constructed, at times unnatural beyond belief. John Gilpin never threw the wash about on both sides of the way more like unto a trundling mop or a wild goose at play than did Henry Kingsley the decent flow of fiction when the mood was on him. His notion of constructing a novel was to take equal parts of wooden melodrama and low comedy and stick them boldly together in a paste of impertinent drollery and serious but entirely irrelevant moralizing. And yet each time I read "Ravenshoe"—and I must be close upon "double figures"—I like it better.—QUILLER-COUCH, A. T., 1895, *Adventures in Criticism*, p. 138.

His novels are extremely loose in construction, and he is no rival to his brother in that exuberance of spirits which gives to the writings of the latter their most characteristic excellence.—WALKER, HUGH, 1897, *The Age of Tennyson*, p. 271.

A writer of distinctly lower literary merit [than Charles Kingsley] but of no little force and fascination as a storyteller, especially of Australian life.—TRAILL, HENRY DUFF, 1897, *Social England*, vol. VI, p. 284.

Mortimer Collins
1827-1876

Novelist, and writer of verse, was born at Plymouth and educated at a private school. Devoting himself to journalism and authorship, he became connected with various newspapers, especially the London *Globe*. He was well-known as a writer of "vers de société." Mr. Collins' separate publications in verse are "Summer Songs," 1860; "Idyls and Rhymes," 1865; "The Inn of Strange Meetings and other Poems," 1871. He was also the author of the following novels:—"Who is the Heir?" 1865; "Sweet Anne Page," 1868; "The Ivory Gate," 1869; "The Vivian Romance," 1870; "Marquis and Merchant," 1871; "Two Plunges for a Pearl," 1872; "Princess Clarice," 1872; "Miranda," 1873; "Squire Silchester's Whim," 1873; "Mr. Carrington" (written under the name of R. T. Cotton), 1873; "Transmigration," 1874: and "Frances," 1874. A volume of essays published anonymously in 1871 and entitled, "The Secret of Long Life," was also from the pen of Mr. Collins.—WARD, THOMAS HUMPHRY, ed., 1885, *Men of the Reign*, p. 207.

PERSONAL

"I wholly agree," he writes, "in the great saying, *Laborare est orare*: I add, *Laborare est vivere*." Again he writes: "I should grow very weary of life if I did not feel that I had God for friend." His marriage was an exceptionally happy one. He not only wrote poetry, but made life a poem. Says one of his friends: "He rejoiced in diffusing gladness; was intensely gentle and tender, and peculiarly sensitive to kindness." By intuition he seemed to have a thorough faith in God and a future life. His writings indicate a highly poetical temperament, and he preserved his intellectual vigor and kindly nature to the last.—SARGENT, EPES, 1880-81, *Harper's Cyclopædia of British and American Poetry*, p. 816.

He possessed one of those comprehensive intellects that can at once embrace the highest truths and yet be alive to all the commonplaces of human life. Variously read, he had a keen appreciation of the works of others and a humble reverence for everything great and good. He had neither conceit nor envy in his composition, nor was he ambitious for fame, except so far as it might help to brighten his material welfare. He was a frank, genial, openhearted man, and had a kindly, buoyant nature, as may be plainly seen from his writings. He was always happy, bore troubles patiently, and never grumbled at the hardness of his lot; was most helpful to others when they needed help, firm and affectionate in his friendships, a cheery companion and a delightful host, as those who visited him at Knowl Hill can testify. He was never ill-tempered or unsociable, was incapable of any kind of meanness or malice, and hated hypocrisy in every form; he was full of happy, wholesome life, believing that existence held more of joy than of misery.—HALL, CHARLES E., 1884, *Mortimer Collins, Gentleman's Magazine*, vol. 256, p. 281.

Collins was a man of great physical and mental vigour. He was over six feet high and powerfully built. He wrote several hours in the day, and again from ten to two at night. Besides contributing to newspapers, he wrote several novels and other works, and turned out an enormous quantity of playful verse for the amusement of his friends. He was a great athlete, a first-class pedestrian, a lover of dogs, and a keen observer of nature. He revered White of Selborne, and wrote many interesting letters upon the habits of birds in the *Times* and elsewhere. He was a mathematician and a good chess-player.—STEPHEN, LESLIE, ed. 1887, *Dictionary of National Biography, vol.* XI, *p.* 373.

GENERAL

"Frances" is not written in Mr. Mortimer Collins's most culinary vein. . . . We are sorry that the amiable author of this novel should be out of temper. He is particularly angry with his critics. We had believed that Mr. Collins was spoilt by his critics who call his style crisp, as he himself calls the bacon, and say that his sentiments are breezy and his heroines ideal. He is even angry with his quills, the quills which have carried him triumphantly through so many reams of rubbish, the quills with whose origin he might have been thought to have sympathy. Perhaps the cause of this displeasure is his desertion from the bill-of-fare style of literature. Rather than see him angry we would counsel him to abandon his new alliance and return to his cutlets.— MACLEANE, WALTER, 1874, *Frances, The Academy, vol.* 6, *pp.* 289, 290.

As a poet, without ever aiming very high, or, indeed, at doing more than producing facile *vers de société*, Mr. Collins succeeded more nearly than either Mr. Frederick Locker or Mr. Austin Dobson in reproducing the peculiar lyrical flow of the best and easiest French *chansons*, so that he suggests, at however great an interval, Béranger rather than Praed. The gift may not be accounted a very brilliant one, but it is so extremely rare (far rarer than more solid poetical qualities) that critics cannot afford to depreciate it, and many far more pretentious minor singers of the day could have been much more easily spared than Mr. Mortimer Collins.—LITTLEDALE, RICHARD F., 1876, *Mortimer Collins, The Academy, vol.* 10. *p.* 137.

He was a man of varied gifts; large and generous both in body and mind; very susceptible to all sights, sounds, and tastes, physical and mental; with a zest for enjoyment of all good things, from a poem or a picture to a cigar and a glass of claret, and a taste which was naturally healthy in almost all. . . . He was one of those men who suffered from over activity of mind, of whom it may be paradoxically said that their thoughts throng too quickly to let them think. Few can help regretting that he never permitted himself those reflective pauses in the midst of creation which are necessary for the production of sure work. Day after day he wrote, never caring to ascertain that his day's work was "good," content that it should be "good enough" for the immediate purpose. And it always was "good enough," always full of fresh impressions freshly expressed, studied with bright epigram, sparkling with pleasant verse, overflowing with animal and mental spirits—the clear current of an honest, manly, and scholarly mind. . . . With the exception of James Hannay, there has been no man of our time whose career has ended in so great a literary disappointment.— MONKHOUSE, COSMO, 1879, *Pen Sketches by a Vanished Hand, The Academy, vol.* 16, *p.* 419.

The novels are indeed, as it were, a reflex of the author's own mind—psychological studies rather than stories, pictures of himself and what he wished to be, full of bright refreshing bits that may be read again and again. They are readable if only for their terse, epigrammatic English, their original thought, and the purity of the moral tone which pervades them throughout. They depict all that is best and noblest in human nature, showing us the higher types of manhood in preference to the lower. The aim of the author seemed always to be directed against the follies of life; he stirs up all the manlier qualities of our nature, and those who read must needs feel refreshed in spirit.—HALL, CHARLES E., 1884, *Mortimer Collins, Gentleman's Magazine, vol.* 256, *p.* 277.

Whose light and musical verses have much charm, has also a right to be mentioned in a record of English contemporary poetry.—OLIPHANT, MARGARET O. W., 1892, *The Victorian Age of English Literature, p.* 455.

His novels are too romantic and wild to abide as works of Fiction; he avowedly drew his characters, and invented his incidents, as he desired them to be, not as he supposed they were in real life. But his books are always worth reading, on account of the pleasant writing therein, and the numerous lyrics which every now and then sparkle as gems in the mass. The best of them are, perhaps, "Sweet Anne Page," "Frances," and "Mr. Carington."—HAY, T. W. LITTLETON, 1892, *The Poets and the Poetry of the Century, Kingsley to Thomson, ed. Miles, p.* 286.

He was one of the last of the so-called Bohemian school in letters and journalism, something of a scholar, a fertile novelist, and a versatile journalist in most of the kinds which make up modern journalism.—SAINTSBURY, GEORGE, 1896, *A History of Nineteenth Century Literature, p.* 333.

Had a very happy knack for the lighter kinds of lyrical verse, half playful and half serious. Under pressure of circumstances he wrote too much, and the failure to "polish and refine" tells against a great deal of his work.—WALKER, HUGH, 1897, *The Age of Tennyson, p.* 257.

Whatever posthumous fame Mortimer Collins may gather will be won by his lyrics, and by passages in his longer poems. Here, even more clearly than in his prose, may be heard the jubilant ring of delight over the advent of the glorious climax of the year. Not the narrow purse nor the inevitable call to forced labor of the pen could mar the note of enjoyment or provoke a murmur of pessimism. . . . His work shows signs of the stress under which he worked from first to last, and literature is the poorer because leisure to perfect and polish was denied him. He had no weighty message to deliver, but he has left a legacy of consolation to the few who have learned his secret, a feat not always compassed by the greater prophets. Like his beloved birds, he sang because he must, a tendency which in itself would have been fatal to the proclamation of any serious evangel, for, let him start on any theme he might select, he would invariably drift back, after a little, to tell of some suggestive passage recently discovered in a book, or to chat about his dogs or his feathered friends, or some other delight of his little garden domain. . . . In all his work the influence of sound classical training is apparent. . . . Mortimer Collins was not a great writer in any sense, but he could treat with such subtle insight, such penetrating sympathy, those emotions and aspects of life which, for him, comprised the whole joy of living, that to all those who have fallen under his charm the sight or sound of his name will never fail to call up some pictures of the Thames in its summer glory, as he perceived or imagined it, of the chorus of the birds, of the quaint, loving humors of his dogs, of the jocund feast at the end of a hard day's toil, or of the perfect domestic happiness of his later years.—WATERS, W. G., 1899, *Among my Books, Literature, vol.* 5, *p.* 28, 29, 30.

Edward William Lane

1801–1876

An English Orientalist, one of the most accomplished men of his time; born at Hereford, Sept. 17, 1801; died at Worthing, Aug. 10, 1876. He published "Manners and Customs of the Modern Egyptians" (1836), and made one of the most famous translations of the "Arabian Nights" (1838–49). This work was the first translation of consequence into English which was made directly from the Arabic, all previous translations having been made through the French. It contained valuable illustrations and numerous scholarly and indispensable notes. The translations of Burton and Payne were subsequent to it. The world is indebted to him for many valuable works on Egypt, and especially for his "Arabic-English Lexicon" (1863–74), which cost him twenty years of unremitting labor. The succeeding parts came out from 1877 to 1889 under the editorship of S. Lane-Poole, the whole forming a dictionary indispensable to the student of Arabic.—WARNER, CHARLES DUDLEY, ed., 1897, *Library of the World's Best Literature, Biographical Dictionary, vol.* XXIX, *p.* 324.

PERSONAL

The world has lost an English scholar whom even Germany acknowledged to be the unapproachable master of his subject. . . . Mr. Lane's private life was that of a learned man. He allowed nothing but the claims of affection to interfere with his work, but his few spare moments endeared him to his family and his friends. His influence in his own circle being that of a noble example was potent, and his sympathies were never narrowed by his almost ascetic life. Public affairs shared with the history of discovery of every kind his warmest interest. A lofty faith and a blameless life added from time to time to the dignity of his form and the nobility of his countenance, in spite of the constant ill-health with which he battled while he did his work. A delicate constitution, enfeebled by severe study, at length gave way, and, notwithstanding the constant, and most tender affection of his family, and the unremitting care of his medical adviser, a short illness ended the career of this great scholar.—POOLE, REGINALD STUART, 1876, *The Academy, vol.* 10, *pp.* 188, 189.

Lane's third visit to Egypt was undertaken with the special object of preparing a lexicon of the Arabic language, of which his previous residence in Cairo had given him such a mastery that the very Ulema of the University of the Azhar were wont privately to seek his help in difficult questions of philology. He devoted the rest of his life to it, working from ten to twelve hours a day for nearly a third of a century.— POOLE, STANLEY LANE, 1887, *Celebrities of the Century, ed. Sanders, p.* 654.

GENERAL

The especial and exceptional manner of this work ["Manners and Customs of the Modern Egyptians"] is in its careful and minute account of the social conditions and habits of the people of Egypt. Mr. McCoan, in his recent work on Egypt, assures us that the descriptions are admirable portrayals of Egyptian life at the present day. —ADAMS, CHARLES KENDALL, 1882, *A Manual of Historical Literature, p.* 416.

This was the first accurate version of the celebrated Arabic stories, and still remains the best translation for all but professed students. It is not complete, and the coarseness of the original is necessarily excised in work which was intended for the general public; but the eastern tone, which was lost in the earlier versions, based upon Galland's French paraphrase, is faithfully reproduced, and the very stiffness of the style, not otherwise commendable, has been found to convey something of the impression of the Arabic. The work is enriched with copious notes, derived from the translator's personal knowledge of Mohammedan life and his wide acquaintance with Arabic literature, and forms a sort of encyclopædia of Muslim customs and beliefs. —POOLE, STANLEY LANE, 1892, *Dictionary of National Biography, vol.* XXXII, *p.* 73.

George Alfred Lawrence
1827–1876

George Alfred Lawrence, educated at Rugby, and at Balliol College, Oxford, where he graduated with honors 1850; called to the bar at the Inner Temple 1852; but devoted himself chiefly to literature. His novels were published anonymously. 1. Guy Livingstone; or, Thorough, Lon., 1857, p. 8vo; 4th ed., 1862. . . . 2. Barren Honour, 1862, 2 vols. p.8vo. 2d ed. same year. 3. Border and Bastile, 1863, 8vo. 4. (Ed.), A Bundle of Ballads, Lon., 1863, sq.16mo. 5. Maurice Dering; or, The Quadrilateral, Lon., 1864, p.8vo.; new ed. 1869. 6. Sans Merci; or, Kestrels and Falcons, Lon., 1866, 3 vols. p.8vo.; new ed. 1869, 1 vol. 12mo. 7. Brakespeare; or, The Fortunes of a Free-lance, Lon., 1868, 3 vols. p.8vo. 8. Sword and Gown, Lon., 1868, p.8vo.; new ed., 1870. 9. Breaking a Butterfly; or, Blanche Ellerslie's Ending, Lon., 1869, 3 vols. p.8vo. 10. Anteros, Lon., 1871, 3 vols. p.8vo. 11. Silverland, Lon., 1873, p.8vo. . . . 12. Hagarene, Lon., 1874, 3 vols. 8vo.—KIRK, JOHN FOSTER, 1891, *A Supplement to Allibone's Critical Dictionary of English Literature, vol.* II *p.* 979.

GENERAL

In 1857 he astonished novel-readers by his "Guy Livingstone, or, Thorough," with its deification of strength and very questionable morality. The hostile critics depicted the hero as a mixture of the prize-fighter and the libertine, while the admirers of the book praised the disregard of conventionalities and personal daring of both the hero and the author, and a report that in the work the author had described his own boyhood and college life lent an additional piquancy to the book. It had a large sale, and from this time forward Lawrence produced a work of fiction nearly every alternate year. One of the best of these was "Sword and Gown," 1868, which has a coherence and an air of probability

JOHN LOTHROP MOTLEY

Engraving by F. T. Stuart.

GEORGE PERKINS MARSH

Engraving by H. B. Hall, Jr.

hardly to be found elsewhere in his writings. . . . In his numerous books Lawrence's style is always vigorous, and he is never dull.—BOASE, GEORGE CLEMENT, 1892, *Dictionary of National Biography*, vol. XXXII, pp. 254, 255.

"Guy Livingstone," which was very popular, and much denounced as the Gospel of "muscular blackguardism"—a parody on the phrase "muscular Christianity," which had been applied to and not unwelcomed by Charles Kingsley. The book exhibited a very curious blend of divers of the motives and interests which have been specified as actuating the novel about this time. Lawrence, who was really a scholar, felt to the full the Præ-Raphaelite influence in art, though by no means in religion, and wrote in a style which is a sort of transition between the excessive floridness of the first Lord Lytton and the later Corinthianism of Mr. Symonds. But he retained also from his prototype, and new modelled, the tendency to take "society" and the manners, especially the amatory manners, of society very much as his province. . . . That Lawrence's total ideal, both in style and sentiment, was artificial, false, and flawed, may be admitted. But he has to a great extent been made to bear the blame of exaggerations of his own scheme by others; and he was really a novelist and a writer of great talent, which somehow came short, but not so very far short, of genius.—SAINTSBURY, GEORGE, 1896, *A History of Nineteenth Century Literature*.

John Lothrop Motley
1814–1877

Born, at Dorchester, Mass., 15 April 1814. To Harvard Univ., 1827; B. A., 1831. Studied at Berlin and Göttingen Universities, 1832–33. Married Mary Benjamin, 2 March 1837. Advocate, 1837. Sec. of American Legation, St. Petersburg, winter of 1841–42. Contrib. to "North American Rev." from 1845. Mem. of Massachusetts House of Representatives, 1849. In Europe, 1851–56. In Boston, 1856–57. Contrib. to first no. of "Atlantic Monthly," Nov. 1857. Returned to England, 1858. Hon. LL. D., Harvard, 1860; Hon. D. C. L., Oxford, 1860. To America, 1861. U. S. A. Ambassador at Vienna, 1861–67. Returned to Boston, June 1868. To England, 1868; resided there till his death. Ambassador to England, 1869–70. Foreign Assoc. of French Academy, 1876; Dr. Phil., Gröningen; Corresp. Mem. Institute of France; F. S. A., Hon. LL. D., Cambridge; Hon. LL. D., New York; Hon. LL. D., Leyden; Mem. of numerous American and foreign historical societies. Last visit to America, 1875. Died, near Dorchester, Devonshire, 29 May 1877. Buried at Kensal Green. *Works:* "Morton's Hope," 1839; "Merry Mount," 1849; "History of the Rise of the Dutch Republic," 1856; "History of the United Netherlands," vols. i., ii., 1860; vols. iii., iv., 1868; "Causes of the Civil War in America," 1861; "Historic Progress and American Democracy," 1869; "The Life and Death of John of Barneveld," 1874. *Posthumous:* "Correspondence," ed. by G. W. Curtis, 1889. *Life:* by O. W. Holmes, 1878.—SHARP, R. FARQUHARSON, 1897, *A Dictionary of English Authors*, p. 206.

PERSONAL

Allow me to thank you most warmly for your long and interesting letter, which, if it had been twice as long as it was, would only have pleased me more. There are few persons that I have only seen once with whom I so much desire to keep up a communication as with you; and the importance of what I learn from you respecting matters so full of momentous consequences to the world would make such communication most valuable to me, even if I did not wish for it on personal grounds.—MILL, JOHN STUART, 1862, *Letter to Motley*, Oct. 31; *Correspondence of John Lothrop Motley*, ed. Curtis, vol. II, p. 95.

Breakfasted with Layard, to meet Julian Fane, who told us an amusing story about Motley, who is now American Minister at Vienna, and a most furious Northerner; although before the War he said to Layard —"If our Sister of the South wants to leave us, let her part in peace." He had become, it appears, so excited that he had quite withdrawn from society, being unable to listen with toleration to any opinions hostile to his own. This had gone on for some time, when his friends arranged a little dinner, at which the greatest care was to be taken to keep the conversation quite away from all irritating subjects. Not a word was said about the

War, and everything was going on delightfully, when an unlucky Russian, leaning across the table, said—"Mr. Motley, I understand that you have given a great deal of attention to the history of the sixteenth century; I have done so too, and should like to know whether you agree with me in one opinion at which I have arrived. I think the Duke of Alva was one of the greatest and best statesmen who ever lived!" Motley completely lost his temper, and the well-laid plan was overthrown.—DUFF, SIR MOUNTSTUART E. GRANT, 1863, *Notes from a Diary, March 26, vol.* I, *p.* 227.

Jack My Dear,—Where the devil are you, and what do you do that you never write a line to me? I am working from morn to night like a nigger, and you have nothing to do at all—you might as well tip me a line as well as looking on your feet tilted against the wall of God knows what a dreary colour. I cannot entertain a regular correspondence; it happens to me that during five days I do not find a quarter of an hour for a walk; but you, lazy old chap, what keeps you from thinking of your old friends? When just going to bed in this moment my eye met with yours on your portrait, and I curtailed the sweet restorer, sleep, in order to remind you of Auld Lang Syne. Why do you never come to Berlin? It is not a quarter of an American's holiday journey from Vienna, and my wife and me should be so happy to see you once more in this sullen life.— BISMARCK, OTTO EDUARD LEOPOLD PRINCE VON, 1864, *Letter to Motley, May* 23; *The Correspondence of John Lothrop Motley, ed. Curtis, vol.* II, *p.* 159.

But there is a yet deeper key of harmony that has just been struck within the last week. The hand of death has removed from his dwelling-place amongst us one of the brightest lights of the Western Hemisphere—the high-spirited patriot, the faithful friend of England's best and purest spirits, the brilliant, the indefatigable historian who told, as none before him had told, the history of the rise and struggle of the Dutch Republic, almost a part of his own. We sometimes ask what room or place is left in the crowded temple of Europe's fame for one of the Western World to occupy. But a sufficient answer is given in the work which was reserved to be accomplished by him who has just departed. So long as the tale of greatness of the House of Orange, of the siege of Leyden, of the tragedy of Barneveld, interests mankind, so long will Holland be indissolubly connected with the name of Motley, in the union of the ancient culture of Europe, with the aspirations of America which was so remarkable in the ardent, laborious, soaring soul that has passed away.— STANLEY, ARTHUR PENRHYN, 1877, *Sermon in Westminster Abbey, June* 3.

JOHN LOTHROP MOTLEY,
BORN AT DORCHESTER, MASS.. APRIL 15, 1814.
DIED NEAR DORCHESTER, DORSET., MAY 29, 1877.
In God is light, and in him is no darkness at all.

MARY ELIZABETH, WIFE OF JOHN LOTHROP MOTLEY,
BORN APRIL 7, 1813.
DIED DECEMBER 31, 1874.
Truth shall make you free.
—INSCRIPTION ON GRAVE, 1877, *Kensal Green Cemetery.*

Having succeeded Mr. Motley at Vienna some two years after his departure, I had occasion to read most of his despatches, which exhibited a mastery of the subjects of which they treated, with much of the clear perception, the scholarly and philosophic tone and decided judgment, which, supplemented by his picturesque description, full of life and color, have given character to his histories. They are features which might well have served to extend the remark of Madame de Staël that a great historian is almost a statesman.— JAY, JOHN, 1877, *Paper Read at a Meeting of the New York Historical Society.*

I met Motley at Göttingen in 1832, I am not sure if at the beginning of Easter Term or Michaelmas Term. He kept company with German students, though more addicted to study than we members of the fighting clubs (corps). Although not having mastered yet the German language, he exercised a marked attraction by a conversation sparkling with wit, humor, and originality. In autumn of 1833, having both of us migrated from Göttingen to Berlin for the prosecution of our studies, we became fellow-lodgers in the house No. 161 Friedrich Strasse. There we lived in the closest intimacy, sharing meals and outdoor exercise. Motley by that time had arrived at talking German fluently; he occupied himself not only in translating

Goethe's poem "Faust," but tried his hand even in composing German verses. Enthusiastic admirer of Shakespeare, Byron, Goethe, he used to spice his conversation abundantly with quotations from these his favorite authors. A pertinacious arguer, so much so that sometimes he watched my awakening in order to continue a discussion on some topic of science, poetry, or practical life, cut short by the chime of the small hours, he never lost his mild and amiable temper. . . . The most striking feature of his handsome and delicate appearance was uncommonly large and beautiful eyes. He never entered a drawing-room without exciting the curiosity and sympathy of the ladies.—BISMARCK, OTTO EDUARD LEOPOLD PRINCE VON, 1878, *Reminiscences of Motley, per Lothair Bucher, Memoir of John Lothrop Motley by Holmes, Proceedings of the Massachusetts Historical Society, vol. 16, pp.* 410, 411.

He generally rose early, the hour varying somewhat at different parts of his life, according to his work and health. Sometimes, when much absorbed by literary labor, he would rise before seven, often lighting his own fire, and with a cup of tea or coffee writing until the family breakfast hour, after which his work was immediately resumed, and he usually sat over his writing table until late in the afternoon, when he would take a short walk. His dinner hour was late, and he rarely worked at night. During the early years of his literary studies he led a life of great retirement. Later, after the publication of the "Dutch Republic" and during the years of official place, he was much in society in England, Austria, and Holland. He enjoyed social life, and particularly dining out, keenly, but was very moderate and simple in all his personal habits, and for many years before his death had entirely given up smoking. His work, when not in his own library, was in the Archives of the Netherlands, Brussels, Paris, the English State Paper office, and the British Museum, where he made his own researches, patiently and laboriously consulting original manuscripts and reading masses of correspondence, from which he afterwards sometimes caused copies to be made, and where he worked for many consecutive hours a day. After his material had been thus painfully and toilfully amassed, the writing of his own story was always done at home, and his mind, having digested the necessary matter, always poured itself forth in writing so copiously that his revision was chiefly devoted to reducing the over-abundance. He never shrank from any of the drudgery of preparation, but I think his own part of the work was sheer pleasure to him.—HARCOURT, LADY, 1878, *Letter to Oliver Wendell Holmes, Proceedings of the Massachusetts Historical Society, vol.* 16, *p.* 472.

A very serious breach had taken place between the President and Mr. Sumner on the important San Domingo question. It was a quarrel, in short, neither more or less, at least so far as the President was concerned. The proposed San Domingo treaty had just been rejected by the Senate, on the thirtieth day of June, and immediately thereupon,—the very next day,—the letter requesting Mr. Motley's resignation was issued by the Executive. This fact was interpreted as implying something more than a mere coincidence. It was thought that Sumner's friend, who had been supported by him as a candidate for high office, who shared many of his political ideas and feelings, who was his intimate associate, his fellow-townsman, his companion in scholarship and cultivation, his sympathetic co-laborer in many ways, had been accounted and dealt with as the ally of an enemy, and that the shaft which struck to the heart of the sensitive Envoy had glanced from the *æs triplex* of the obdurate Senator. . . . The ostensible grounds on which Mr. Motley was recalled are plainly insufficient to account for the action of the Government. If it was in great measure a manifestation of personal feeling on the part of the high officials by whom and through whom the act was accomplished, it was a wrong which can never be repaired and never sufficiently regretted. — HOLMES, OLIVER WENDELL, 1878, *John Lothrop Motley, A Memoir, pp.* 160, 184.

When Motley had grown to man's estate Lady Byron declared that he more resembled her husband than any person she had ever met; but Wendell Phillips, his playmate and classmate, objects to this opinion on the ground that Motley was handsomer than Byron. . . . The beautiful boy was saved from being spoiled by a combination in his nature of an immense intellectual ambition with a corresponding self-distrust. To the end of his life he was consumed with a desire to perform great things, and to the end of his life he was painfully sensible that he had not come up to his lofty ideal.—WHIPPLE, EDWIN PERCY, 1886, *Recollections of Eminent Men, pp.* 158, 159.

MORTON'S HOPE
1839

There is a manliness and a concentration in the author's style, that at once evinces his power; and he possesses, in an eminent degree, that most rare and difficult art in story-telling, the knowing where to stop: he never launches out into digressions, nor wearies the reader with unnecessary remarks and explanations. His meaning is at once stamped clear and finished, and requires no after touching to render it more complete.—HOOK, THEODORE, 1839, *Morton of Morton's Hope, New Monthly Magazine, vol.* 57, *p.* 137.

It must be confessed that, as a story, "Morton's Hope" cannot endure a searching or even a moderately careful analysis. It is wanting in cohesion, in character, even in a proper regard to circumstances of time and place; it is a map of dissected incidents which has been flung out of its box and has arranged itself without the least regard to chronology or geography. It is not difficult to trace in it many of the influences which had helped in forming or deforming the mind of the young man of twenty-five not yet come into possession of his full inheritance of the slowly ripening qualities which were yet to assert their robust independence. How could he help admiring Byron and falling into more or less unconscious imitation of his moods, if not of his special affectations?—HOLMES, OLIVER WENDELL, 1878, *Memoir of John Lothrop Motley, Proceedings of the Massachusetts Historical Society, vol.* 16, *p.* 412.

The failure of this book was complete and almost ignominious, in spite of many admirable passages both of reflection and description, the merit of which was apparent amid all the anarchy of the narrative. It exhibited in an exaggerated form a mental defect which is more or less visible in his histories,—namely, a tendency to treat subordinate details with such fulness and richness as somewhat to interfere with a clear perception of the main design. In "Morton's Hope" this defect was so prominent as to enable scores of people, who were incompetent to write any half-dozen of its brilliant paragraphs, to sneer at the work as a whole. "Have you heard," said a wit of the family of Morton to his acquaintance, "that our friend Motley's failure is 'Morton's Hope?'" Motley himself came to hate his own book so much that it was dangerous to refer to it in his presence.—WHIPPLE, EDWIN PERCY, 1886, *Recollections of Eminent Men, p.* 163.

MERRY MOUNT
1849

The early history of Plymouth and Massachusetts, though it is a record of adventures, perils, and hardships, and many strongly marked characters appear in it, certainly presents few materials for romance. The whole foreground of the canvas is occupied by the grim figures of the Puritans, and in the distance appear only a few Indians flitting about like shadows in the interminable forests. It is a wild and stern scene, but its features are not pliable enough for the imagination to work upon. It does not offer those striking contrasts of situation and character, that variety of costume and scenery, or those rapid alterations of fortune, of light and gloom, in which the writer of fiction delights. The story is even a monotonous recital of exile, labor and suffering, bravely endured from the holiest of all motives. It claims attention and study from the moralist, the philosophical observer of human nature, and even from the statesman; but it hardly arrests the notice of those who crave only a pleasurable excitement of the fancy and the intellect.—BOWEN, FRANCIS, 1849, *Merry-Mount, North American Review, vol.* 68, *p.* 203.

Without rapidity of movement or stirring interest, its quiet style is certainly not dull. Its representations of the grim Puritans and the jovial and aggravating Anglicans of Wollaston Heights, are faithful portraitures; and we feel that we are instructed by an historian who is no special pleader on either side. The old hermit of Boston is a personage whom one remembers long after the book has been laid down. In scene, characterization, and accuracy of historical narration, "Merry Mount" was a fit precursor of the later and more important works of its author, devoted to other and higher subjects. The book has disappeared from notice, and it perhaps hardly deserves reprinting;

but it showed the trend of the author's mind, and proved that a future success was at least possible for him.—RICHARDSON, CHARLES F., 1887, *American Literature, 1607–1885, vol.* I, *p.* 503.

HISTORY OF THE DUTCH REPUBLIC
1856

A history . . . as complete as industry and genius can make it now lies before us, of the first twenty years of the Revolt of the United Provinces; of the period in which those provinces finally conquered their independence and established the Republic of Holland. It has been the result of many years of silent thoughtful, unobtrusive labor, and unless we are strangely mistaken, unless we are ourselves altogether unfit for this office of criticising which we have here undertaken, the book is one which will take its place among the finest histories in this or in any language. . . . All the essentials of a great writer Mr. Motley eminently possesses. His mind is broad, his industry unwearied. In power of dramatic description no modern historian, except perhaps Mr. Carlyle, surpasses him, and in analysis of character he is elaborate and distinct. His principles are those of honest love for all which is good and admirable in human character wherever he finds it, while he unaffectedly hates oppression, and despises selfishness with all his heart.—FROUDE, JAMES ANTHONY, 1856, *Westminster Review vol.* 65, *p.* 314.

For twenty years I have been in the habit of urging the students to study the history of the Netherlands, as next in importance among modern states to the history of our own country, to that of England; repeatedly I have advised them to take solitary "William of Orange" as a great theme for addresses or essays; and you may readily judge with what satisfaction I can now direct them to Motley's work. One or two things I could have wished differently; but the merits of the book are so great and of such general and public character that all of us owe thanks to the patient, diligent, skilful, right-minded, and truthful author. It is a wholesome and nutritious book. It is a good pabulum for commonwealth-men and commonwealth-lads. I know that it is but too often injurious to become acquainted with crime and vice, even when exhibited to be loathed; but it is a stern necessity for reflecting men of action to know how deep humanity can sink and what fearful capacity of relapse there is in every one of us in bewildering circumstances. Besides, the baseness of Philip and the crime of Alva are so stupendous that they lose the power of familiarizing the souls of men, when plainly represented, with baseness and crime; while side by side with these hideous pictures is exhibited the full-length image of a William,— the greatest of that worshipful band of exalted citizens to which Thrasybulus, Timoleon, Andrea Doria, and Washington belong. Congress and Parliament decree thanks for military exploits,—rarely for diplomatic achievements. If they ever voted their thanks for books,—and what deeds have influenced the course of human events more than some books?—Motley ought to have the thanks of our Congress; but I doubt not that he has already the thanks of every American who has read the work.—LIEBER, FRANCIS, 1857, *Letter to S. Austin Allibone, April* 14; *Allibone's Dictionary of English Literature, vol.* II, *p.* 1380.

Mr. Motley's "History of the Dutch Republic" is, in my judgment, a work of the highest merit. Unwearying research for years in the libraries of Europe, patience and judgment in arranging and digesting his materials, a fine historical tact, much skill in characterization, the perspective of narration, as it may be called, and a vigorous style, unite to make it a very capital work, and place the name of Motley by the side of those of our great American historical trio—Bancroft, Irving and Prescott. I name them alphabetically, for I know not how to arrange them on any other principle.—EVERETT, EDWARD, 1858, *Letter to S. Austin Allibone, June* 7; *Allibone's Dictionary of English Literature, vol.* II, *p.* 1380.

Alluding to a prediction which I had ventured in regard to Motley's "Rise of the Dutch Republic" a little while before its publication, you ask me if the results have corresponded with my expectations. I will answer you with much pleasure, though the opinion of any individual seems superfluous in respect to a work on the merits of which the public, both at home and abroad, have pronounced so unanimous a verdict. As Motley's path crosses my own historic field, I may be thought to possess some advantage over most critics in my familiarity with the ground. However this may be, I can honestly bear my testimony to the extent of his researches and to the accuracy with which he has given the results of them to the public. Far from making his book a mere register of events, he has penetrated deep below the surface and explored the causes of these events. He has carefully studied the physiognomy of the times and given finished portraits of the great men who conducted the march of the revolution. Every page is instinct with the love of freedom and with that personal knowledge of the working of free institutions which could alone enable him to do justice to his subject. We may congratulate ourselves that it was reserved for one of our countrymen to tell the story—better than it had yet been told—of this memorable revolution, which in so many of its features bears a striking resemblance to our own.—PRESCOTT, WILLIAM HICKLING, 1858, *Letter to S. Austin Allibone, June 28*; *Allibone's Dictionary of English Literature*, vol. II, p. 1380.

The labor of ten years was at last finished. Carrying his formidable manuscript with him,—and how formidable the manuscript which melts down in three solid octavo volumes, is, only writers and publishers know,—he knocked at the gate of that terrible fortress from which Lintot and Curll and Tonson looked down on the authors of an older generation. So large a work as the "History of the Rise of the Dutch Republic," offered for the press by an author as yet unknown to the British public, could hardly expect a warm welcome from the great dealers in literature as in merchandise. Mr. Murray civilly declined the manuscript which was offered to him, and it was published at its author's expense by Mr. John Chapman. The time came when the positions of the first-named celebrated publisher and the unknown writer were reversed. Mr. Murray wrote to Mr. Motley asking to be allowed to publish his second great work, the "History of the United Netherlands," expressing at the same time his regret at what he candidly called his mistake in the first instance, and thus they were at length brought into business connection as well as the most agreeable and friendly relations.—HOLMES, OLIVER WENDELL, 1878, *John Lothrop Motley, A Memoir*, p. 74.

The "Dutch Republic," precluded by the overture of a masterly and vivid historical survey, is a drama, which facts have made highly sensational, of the fiercest struggle against temporal and spiritual despotism that, within the same space of years, Europe has seen. It is divided, not inappropriately, though perhaps with some regard for effect, into a prologue and five acts, to each of which, in succession, the name of the Spanish governor for the time is attached. The portraits of the great emissaries—particularly those of Granvelle of Arras and Duchess Margaret of Alva, Don John of Lepanto, and Alexander of Parma—are drawn with bold strokes and in lasting colours. Behind the scenes, director of the assailing forces, is the evil genius, Philip himself, to whose ghastly figure, writing letters in the Escurial, our attention is called with a wearisome if not affected iteration of phrase; while the presence of the great champion, William the Silent, is felt at every crisis retrieving the retreat and urging on the victory. The most horrible chapter of modern times, that of the Inquisition, is set forth with a power that brands its records into the memory of the reader; amid a throng of scenes of pageantry and pathos, we may refer to those of Egmont's triumph at St. Quentin, of his execution, of the misery of Mook Heath, the siege of Leyden, and the hero's end.—NICHOL, JOHN, 1882-85, *American Literature*, p. 151.

This is a remarkable book. It is a vivid portrayal of one of the most dramatic portions of modern European history. Motley possessed nearly all the essentials of a great historical writer. His industry was unwearied, and his opportunities were all that could be desired. He penetrated deep below the surface of things, and explored their hidden causes. His pages are instinct with the love of freedom and hatred of tyranny. His style is clear, vivid, and eloquent. His analysis of character is remarkably distinct, and his power of dramatic narrative has not often been excelled. But the work, with all these excellent characteristics, has its drawbacks. The judicious reader constantly labors under the impression that there is another story to be told. The author's aversions are so strong and his predilections so extreme that they seem often to have taken absolute possession of his judgment.

At times he almost appears to be apprehensive that his words will not adequately express the energy of his thoughts, and consequently his language sometimes becomes so emphatic as to appear stilted and declamatory.—ADAMS, CHARLES KENDALL, 1882, *A Manual of Historical Literature*, p. 420.

It is the enthusiasm and warmth of feeling which have given the "Dutch Republic," to most minds, its chief charm; which have done more than anything else to make it, in the estimation of the world at large, one of the most interesting historical books ever written in any language. But it has also many elements of technical perfection. It is written with great care. Many of the sentences are exquisite in felicity and finish. The style is dignified, yet rich with the evidences of literary cultivation and fertile fancy. The larger matters of composition are managed with taste and power. Rarely has any historian in the whole history of literature so united laborious scholarship with dramatic intensity. — JAMESON, JOHN FRANKLIN, 1897, *Library of the World's Best Literature*, ed. Warner, vol. XVIII, p. 10376.

HISTORY OF THE UNITED NETHERLANDS
1860–68

It is gratifying to learn that before long such a history [on the Netherlands] may be expected,—if, indeed, it should not appear before the publication of this work,—from the pen of our accomplished countryman, Mr. J. Lothrop Motley, who, during the last few years, for the better prosecution of his labors, has established his residence in the neighborhood of the scenes of his narrative. No one acquainted with the fine powers of mind possessed by this scholar, and the earnestness with which he has devoted himself to his task, can doubt that he will do full justice to his important, but difficult subject.—PRESCOTT, WILLIAM HICKLING, 1855, *History of the Reign of Philip the Second*, Preface, p. XII.

His investigations into the manuscript records of the time have been so laborious, and he has brought to light so much curious and novel information, that it seems almost ungrateful to hint that we have somewhat too much of it. But the readers of this generation are an impatient race; and Mr. Motley does tell us of intrigues, and abortive negotiations, and diplomatic nothings with a painful minuteness. . . . The "History of the United Netherlands" is far less disfigured with uncouth expressions, meant to be effective, than was the "Rise of the Dutch Republic." Yet, even in the latter work, a very superficial search will detect many eccentricities of language. . . . In addition to the other excellencies which we have already mentioned, Mr. Motley possesses the rare merit of being able to sympathise with all the various characteristics of the era of which he writes. Nor is this a slight matter; for he has selected an era which presents, perhaps, more varied characteristics than any other in the history of the world.—LANCASTER, HENRY H., 1861–78, *Motley's "United Netherlands," Essays and Reviews*, ed. Jowett, pp. 172, 174, 175.

The history of Holland during the period treated by Mr. Motley is the history of European liberty. Every nation was in some way concerned in the great struggle between Spain and the Netherlands. The characters of Philip II., of his great minister, Cardinal Granvelle, of his sister, Margaret of Parma, and of his great general, the infamous Duke of Alva, as well as the principles and policies of the Spanish government, are painted in the strongest colors. English history also has a new illumination from this work, and the reader will probably get a more vivid and accurate conception of the vain and vacillating Queen Elizabeth, of the unprincipled Earl of Leicester, of Lord Burghley, Walsingham, Drake, and other prominent persons of the period than can be gained from any other source. Of famous Hollanders and Flemings the historian has made a national portrait gallery.—UNDERWOOD, FRANCIS, 1872, *A Hand-Book of English Literature, American Authors*, p. 396.

If the "History of the United Netherlands" is not so great a book as the "Rise of the Dutch Republic," the fault lies partly in the nature of the subject. The interest is more divided. The greater hero is at the head of the worst cause. Alexander of Parma is, as a man, a head and shoulders taller than Maurice of Nassau. But the fault was also in some degree Mr. Motley's. As long as he had to tell of the sieges of Antwerp and Ostend the reader felt no weariness, and the English reader of candid mind would feel special pleasure in being rescued from the delusion which had so long blinded his eyes to the share taken by the brave Dutch in causing the failure of the Armada, and in the victorious onslaught on Cadiz. But the fields of diplomacy were a sad temptation to Mr. Motley. An historian who neglects to study the countless despatches in which diplomacy has been wont to spin its airy web, will be certain to be ignorant of much that he ought to know. But the historian who will not resolutely content himself to omit entirely about three-quarters of what he has learned, and to boil down the remainder to a highly concentrated essence, will weary his readers. This is precisely what Mr. Motley too often did. His pages were crowded with move and countermove, with argument and rejoinder, till the thread of the negotiation could be seized with difficulty by the most attentive reader.— GARDINER, SAMUEL R., 1877, *The Late Mr. J. L. Motley, The Academy, vol.* 11, p. 509.

There were no names that sounded to our ears like those of Sir Philip Sidney and Leicester and Amy Robsart. But the main course of this narrative flowed on with the same breadth and depth of learning and the same brilliancy of expression. The monumental work continued as nobly as it had begun. The facts had been slowly, quietly gathered one by one, like pebbles from the empty channel of a brook. The style was fluent, impetuous, abundant, impatient, as it were at times, and leaping the sober boundaries prescribed to it, like the torrent which rushes through the same channel when the rains have filled it. Thus there was matter for criticism in his use of language. He was not always careful in the construction of his sentences. He introduced expressions now and then into his vocabulary which reminded one of his earlier literary efforts. He used stronger language at times than was necessary, coloring too highly, shading too deeply in his pictorial delineations. To come to the matter of his narrative, it must be granted that not every reader will care to follow him through all the details of diplomatic intrigues which he has with such industry and sagacity extricated from the old manuscripts in which they had long lain hidden. But we turn a few pages and we come to one of those descriptions which arrest us at once and show him in his power and brillancy as a literary artist. His characters move before us with the features of life; we can see Elizabeth, or Philip, or Maurice, not as a name connected with events, but as a breathing and acting human being, to be loved or hated, admired or despised as if he or she were our contemporary.—HOLMES, OLIVER WENDELL, 1878, *John Lothrop Motley, A Memoir,* p. 142.

With all the merits of the work, and these are many and conspicuous, it must be conceded that it is too controversial in its character to be accepted as the final judgment of mankind. Though these faults detract from the value of the history, they will not diminish in the least the interest of the reader in its pages.— ADAMS, CHARLES KENDALL, 1882, *A Manual of Historical Literature,* p. 421.

THE LIFE AND DEATH OF JOHN OF BARNEVELD
1874

Mr. Motley . . . would appear qualified beyond most men to write the life of the greatest of Dutch statesmen, and readers who take up his last work will naturally expect to find in it a thoroughly satisfactory life of "John of Barneveld." This expectation will be disappointed. The book has great merits. Mr. Motley's industry has collected together a large amount of information, all of which is new to his mass of readers, and a great deal of which he may be fairly said to have for the first time exhumed or discovered. There are, further, parts of the book . . . which are admirable specimens of animated narrative; but though the work is filled with materials from which it would be possible to construct a biography of Barneveld, it can hardly claim to be a life of the Advocate. Readers will put down the two volumes with a sense of having read a confused chronicle of perplexed events without being able to form to themselves a clear conception of the course of the narrative, of the character and policy of the man with whom it deals, or of the real causes of his tragic end. The work reads like chapters torn from their places in a larger consecutive history. The chapters are not without interest, but they fail to compose a biography.—DICEY, A. V., 1874, *The Nation, vol.* 18, *p.* 301.

It is with unfeigned regret that all who value Mr. Motley's work in his own sphere will see that he is despising the difficulties of a subject on which his knowledge is extremely limited. We feel very much towards his projected enterprise, as the engineer felt who reported on the terrible accident on the South-Western Railway last summer, in which a bullock got in the way of the train. Either the train, he said, if possible, should have been brought to a dead stop, or, if that was not possible, it should have pushed on at full speed. We had rather that Mr. Motley should bring his train to a full stop, and return to his old line. But if that is not to be hoped, we trust that he will push on at full speed. The real history of the Thirty Years' War is one which will probably take the lifetime of men to investigate thoroughly; and it would be a pity if Mr. Motley were to occupy much time in laboriously acquiring knowledge to which he has not as yet found the key. If Mr. Motley can be induced to continue to treat the subject as a mere episode deserving no serious study, he may possibly write a book as full of mistakes as those which we have signalised, and may then, after wasting three or four years of his valuable life, come back to that special work in which he stands alone, and in relation to which even those who venture to criticise him, are aware that they stand in the relation of scholars to a master.—GARDINER, SAMUEL R., 1874, *The Life and Death of John of Barneveld, The Academy*, vol. 5, p. 194.

With all Motley's efforts to be impartial, to which even his sternest critics bear witness, he could not help becoming a partisan to the cause which for him was that of religious liberty and progress, as against the accepted formula of an old ecclesiastical organization. For the quarrel which came near being a civil war, which convulsed the State, and cost Barneveld his head, was on certain points, and more especially on a single point, of religious doctrine.—HOLMES, OLIVER WENDELL, 1878, *Memoir of John Lothrop Motley, Proceedings of the Massachusetts Historical Society*, vol. 16, p. 458.

Valuable and interesting as the work is, it may be said that if he had shortened Barneveld's life by a half, he might have lengthened his own; for the materials were more intractable than any he had before encountered,—the handwriting especially of the great Advocate of Holland being so bad as almost to be undecipherable even by the aid of the microscope. On the last day of the year in which this noble work appeared, Mrs. Motley died. This blow, coming as it did in the midst of bodily illness and mental distress, broke his heart. —WHIPPLE, EDWIN PERCY, 1886, *Recollections of Eminent Men*, p. 189.

Thorough and conscientious, interesting and valuable as the book is, it is not to be denied that it takes sides with Oldenbarneveld, and that it is written with less freshness and brilliancy than the earlier volumes. JAMESON, JOHN FRANKLIN, 1897, *Library of the World's Best Literature*, ed. Warner, vol. XVIII, p. 10379.

GENERAL

What pictures yet slumber unborn in his loom,
Till their warriors shall breathe and their beauties shall bloom,
While the tapestry lengthens the life-glowing dyes
That caught from our sunsets the stain of their skies!
In the alcoves of death, in the charnels of time,
Where flit the gaunt spectres of passion and crime,
There are triumphs untold, there are martyrs unsung,
There are heroes yet silent to speak with his tongue!
Let us hear the proud story which time has bequeathed
From lips that are warm with the freedom they breathed!
Let him summon its tyrants, and tell us their doom,
Though he sweep the black past like Van Tromp with his broom!
—HOLMES, OLIVER WENDELL, 1857, *A Parting Health to J. L. Motley, Poetical Works, Cambridge Ed.*, p. 151.

His strong and ardent convictions on the subject of his work have also affected its style and literary character; his narrative sometimes lacks proportion and forbearance; he dwells to excess upon events and scenes of a nature to kindle in the mind of the reader the excitement he himself feels, and he studiously witholds from the opposite side the same amount of space and of colouring. His style is always copious, occasionally familiar, sometimes stilted and declamatory, as if he thought he could never say too much to convey the energy of his own impressions. The consequence is, that the perusal of his work is alternately attractive and fatiguing, persuasive and irritating. An accumulation of facts and details, all originating in the same feeling and directed to the same object, mingles our sympathy with some degree of distrust; and although the cause he defends is beyond all question gained, we are not impressed with the judgment of such an advocate. — GUIZOT, FRANÇOIS PIERRE GUILLAUME, 1857, *Philip II. and his Times, Edinburgh Review*, vol. 105, p. 45.

Whose name belongs to no single country, and to no single age. As a statesman and diplomatist and patriot, he belongs to America; as a scholar, to the world of letters; as a historian, all ages will claim him in the future.—FISH, HAMILTON, 1868, *Address Before the New York Historical Society*, Dec. 16.

He is especially remarkable for a certain breadth of mind which impels him to take comprehensive and exhaustive views of his subject. His style is a model of vigor and grace, and in dramatic quality it is equaled by that of no other historian of this century.—CATHCART, GEORGE R., 1874, ed. *The Literary Reader*, p. 307.

My first interview, more than twenty years ago, with Mr. Lothrop Motley, has left an indelible impression on my memory. It was the 8th of August, 1853. . . . My eagerness to make the acquaintance of such an associate in my sympathies and my labors may be well imagined. But how shall I picture my surprise, in presently discovering that this unknown and indefatigable fellow-worker has really read, I say read and reread our "Quartos," our "Folios," the enormous volumes of "Bor," of "Van Meteren," besides a multitude of books, of pamphlets, and even of unedited documents. Already he is familiar with the events, the changes of condition, the characteristic details of the life of his and my hero. Not only is he acquainted with my Archives, but it seems as if there was nothing in this voluminous collection of which he was ignorant. . . . The Archives are a specific collection, and my Manual of National History, written in Dutch, hardly gets beyond the limits of my own country. And here is a stranger, become a compatriot in virtue of the warmth of his sympathies, who has accomplished what was not in my power. By the detail and the charm of his narrative, by the matter and form of a work which the universality of the English language and numerous translations were to render cosmopolitan, Mr. Motley, like that other illustrious historian, Prescott, lost to science by too early death, has popularized in both hemispheres the sublime devotion of the Prince of Orange, the exceptional and providential destinies of my country, and the benedictions of the Eternal for all those who trust in Him and tremble only at His word.—VAN PRINSTERER, M. GROEN, 1875, *Maurice et Barnevelt, Étude Historique.*

His histories are, in some degree, epics. As he frequently crosses Prescott's path in his presentation of the ideas, passions, and persons of the sixteenth century, it is curious to note the serenity of Prescott's narrative as contrasted with the swift, chivalric impatience of a wrong which animates almost every page of Motley. Both imaginatively reproduce what they have investigated; both have the eye to see and the reason to discriminate; both substantially agree in their judgment as to events and characters; but Prescott quietly allows his readers, as a jury, to render their verdict on the statement of the facts, while Motley somewhat fiercely pushes forward to anticipate it. Prescott calmly represents; Motley intensely feels. Prescott is on a watch-tower surveying the battle; Motley plunges into the thickest of the fight. In temperament no two historians could be more apart; in judgment they are identical. As both historians are equally incapable of lying, Motley finds it necessary to overload his narrative with details which justify his vehemence, while Prescott can afford to omit them, on account of his reputation for a benign impartiality between the opposing parties. A Roman Catholic disputant would find it hard to fasten a quarrel on Prescott; but with Motley he could easily detect an occasion for a duel to the death. It is to be said that Motley's warmth of feeling never betrays him into intentional injustice to any human being; his histories rest on a basis of facts which no critic has shaken.—WHIPPLE, EDWIN PERCY, 1876-86, *American Literature and Other Papers*, ed. *Whittier*, p. 96.

Give evidence of the author's long and careful research, but are faulty in style and spirit. He neither weighs the meaning of his words, nor combines them skillfully. His misrepresentations of Catholics are so obvious that Protestant critics themselves have condemned his "over-zealous partisanship."—JENKINS, O. L., 1876, *The Student's Handbook of Literature*, p. 498.

I should have liked Stanley to have pointed out the thing which strikes me most in Motley, that alone of all men past and present he knit together·not only America and England, but that Older England which we left on Frisian shores, and which grew into the United Netherlands. A child of America, the historian of Holland, he made England his adopted country, and in England his body rests.—GREEN, JOHN RICHARD, 1877, *Letter, June 4; Letters, ed. Stephen, p. 468.*

Sleep, Motley, with the great of ancient days,
   Who wrote for all the years that yet shall be,
Sleep with Herodotus, whose name and praise
   Have reached the isles of earth's remotest sea.
Sleep, while, defiant of the slow delays
   Of Time, thy glorious writings speak for thee
And in the answering heart of millions raise
   The generous zeal for Right and Liberty.
And should the days o'ertake us, when, at last,
   The silence that—ere yet a human pen
Had traced the slenderest record of the past—
   Hushed the primæval languages of men
Upon our English tongue its spell shall cast,
   Thy memory shall perish only then.
—BRYANT, WILLIAM CULLEN, 1877, *In Memory of John Lothrop Motley.*

But there is a yet deeper key of harmony that has just been struck within the last week. The hand of death has removed from his dwelling place amongst us one of the brightest lights of the Western Hemisphere,—the high-spirited patriot, the faithful friend of England's best and purest spirits, the brilliant, the indefatigable historian who told as none before him has told the history of the rise and struggle of the Dutch Republic, almost a part of his own. We sometimes ask what room or place is left in the crowded temple of Europe's fame for one of the Western world to occupy. But a sufficient answer is given in the work which was reserved to be accomplished by him who has just departed. So long as the tale of the greatness of the house of Orange, of the siege of Leyden, of the tragedy of Barneveld, interests mankind, so long will Holland be indissolubly connected with the name of Motley in that union of the ancient culture of Europe with the aspirations of America which was so remarkable in the ardent, laborious, soaring soul that has passed away. He loved that land of his birth with a passionate zeal, he loved the land of his adoption with a surpassing love.—STANLEY, ARTHUR PENRHYN, 1877, *Sermon in Westminster Abbey, June 3.*

Since the death of Lord Macaulay no contribution, in our tongue, to historic literature, has been at once so original, solid, and popularly attractive as the nine volumes of Mr. Motley; nor has any event been more justly lamented than the premature close of the career of one, at once a student and an artist, whose often fiery zeal was always restrained by a resolute fairness, and who carried into the politics of his own day the quenchless love of liberty with which he animates the scenes and revivifies the actors of the past.— NICHOL, JOHN, 1882–85, *American Literature, p. 154.*

Of all the books I have read lately, "Motley's Letters" are the most delightful. He was a perfect letter-writer. His account of the great struggle of the Northern States has impressed me intensely.—EASTLAKE, ELIZABETH LADY, 1889, *To Sir Henry Layard, Dec. 1; Journals and Correspondence, vol. II, p. 298.*

Motley had the intense zeal of the born investigator, a rare and heroic quality of which the world takes little note in historians. He had likewise in full possession those qualities which engage the reader. No American has ever written a history more brilliant and dramatic. The subject was a noble one. It was full of picturesque incident, of opportunities for glowing description, of thrilling tales of heroism. But it was not simply these that so engaged Motley's interest that, as he afterwards said, he felt as if he *must* write upon it. It was a great national conflict for freedom, and as such was profoundly congenial to one who, above all things, loved liberty. The warm heart and enthusiastic, ardent temper of the historian laid him open to dangers of partiality which, it must be confessed, he was far from wholly escaping. The American public little appreciate the extent to which he was influenced by such feelings.—JAMESON, JOHN FRANKLIN, 1891, *The History of Historical Writing in America, p. 119.*

The greatest of the whole of American historians. . . . His "Rise of the Dutch Republic," 1856, and "History of the United Netherlands," published in installments from 1861 to 1868, equaled

Bancroft's work in scientific thoroughness and philosophic grasp, and Prescott's in the picturesque brilliancy of the narrative, while it excelled them both in its masterly analysis of great historic characters, reminding the reader, in this particular, of Macaulay's figure painting. — BEERS, HENRY A., 1895, *Initial Studies in American Letters*, p. 151.

Motley's high rank as an historian is secure. As searching as Bancroft, as graphic as Prescott, he outwent them both in comprehension of character, in dramatic quality, and impassioned force. He was too intense a lover of liberty and virtue to be quite impartial. William the Silent was his hero, and Philip II. his villain, but what prejudice he had was always of a noble sort.—BATES, KATHARINE LEE, 1897, *American Literature*, pp. 245, 246.

A born investigator, Motley toiled for years in the libraries and state archives of western Europe, his zest in the pursuit of truth transforming drudgery into delight. . . . Motley's style, which suggests that of Carlyle, is notably vigorous and brilliant, and certain passages are filled with sarcastic humor. Prescott excelled in the orderly movement of his narrative, but Motley possessed a dramatic instinct which enables him to seize upon some revealing situation and bring it vividly before us. This same dramatic power shows itself also in his delineation of character; certain figures stand out with life-like distinctness, and we can almost imagine ourselves alongside of those men and women of the past in whose company, Motley himself wrote, he was spending all his days.—PANCOAST, HENRY S., 1898, *An Introduction to American Literature*, p. 233.

Motley's historical work is obviously influenced by the vividly picturesque writings of Carlyle. It is clearly influenced, too, by intense sympathy with that liberal spirit which he believed to characterise the people of the Netherlands during their prolonged conflict with Spain. From these traits result several obvious faults. In trying to be vivid, he becomes artificial. In the matter of character, too, his Spaniards are apt to be intensely black, and his Netherlanders ripe for the heavenly rewards to which he sends them as serenely as romantic novelists provide for the earthly happiness of heroes and heroines. Yet, for all his sincerely partisan temper, Motley was so industrious in accumulating material, so untiring in his effort vividly to picture its external aspect, and so heartily in sympathy with his work, that he is almost always interesting. What most deeply stirred him was his belief in the abstract right of man to political liberty; and this he wished to celebrate with epic spirit. Belief and spirit alike were characteristically American; in the history of his own country there was abundant evidence of both.—WENDELL, BARRETT, 1900, *A Literary History of America*, p. 272.

Walter Bagehot
1826–1877

Born, at Langport, Somersetshire, 3 Feb. 1826. At school in Bristol. To Univ. College, London 1842; B. A. and Mathematical Scholarship, 1846; M. A. and gold medal for philosophy and political economy, 1848. In Paris, 1851. Contrib. letters to "The Inquirer," Dec. 1851. Called to Bar, 1852. Edited "National Review" (with R. H. Hutton), 1855–64. Married Miss Wilson, 1858. Editor of "The Economist," 1860–77. Died, at Langport, 24 March 1877. *Works:* "Estimates of some Englishmen and Scotchmen" (from "National Review"), 1858; "Parliamentary Reform" (from "Nat. Review"), 1859; "The History of the Unreformed Parliament" (from "Nat. Rev."), 1860; "Memoir of the Rt. Hon. J. Wilson" (from "Economist"), 1861; "Count your Enemies," 1862; "The English Constitution" (from Fortnightly Rev."), 1867 (new ed., enlarged, 1872); "A Practical Plan for Assimilating the English and American Money" (from "Economist"), 1869; "Physics and Politics," 1872; "Lombard Street," 1873 (2nd-4th edns., same year); "Some Articles on the Depreciation of Silver" (from "Economist"), 1877. *Posthumous:* "Literary Studies," ed. by R. H. Hutton (2 vols.), 1879 [1878]; "Economic Studies," ed. by Hutton, 1880; "Biographical Studies," ed. by Hutton 1881; "Essays on Parliamentary Reform," 1883; "The Postulates of English Political Economy," ed. by A. Marshall, 1885. *Collected Works:* ed. by F. Morgan, with *memoir* by R. H. Hutton (American ed., 5 vols.), 1889.—SHARP, R. FARQUHARSON, 1897, *A Dictionary of English Authors*, p. 14.

PERSONAL

Though himself extremely cool and sceptical about political improvement of every sort, he took abundant interest in more ardent friends. Perhaps it was that they amused him; in return his good-natured ironies put them wholesomely on their mettle. As has been well said of him, he had a unique power of animation without combat; it was all stimulous and yet no contest; his talk was full of youth, yet had all the wisdom of mature judgment (R. H. Hutton). Those who were least willing to assent to Bagehot's practical maxims in judging current affairs, yet were well aware how much they profited by his Socratic objections, and knew, too, what real acquaintance with men and business, what honest sympathy and friendliness, and what serious judgment and interest all lay under his playful and racy humour.—MORLEY, JOHN, 1882, *Valedictory, Studies in Literature*, p. 325.

Bagehot was one of the best conversers of his day. He was not only vivid, witty, and always apt to strike a light in conversation, but he helped in every real effort to get at the truth, with a unique and rare power, of lucid statement. One of his friends said of him: "I never knew a power of discussion, of co-operative investigation of truth," to approach to his. "It was all stimulus, and yet no contest."—HUTTON, RICHARD HOLT, 1885, *Dictionary of National Biography*, vol. II, p. 396.

The books which I have passed in rapid review form an immense output for a man who died at fifty-one, but I am not sure that the impression of power which was produced by his conversation was not even greater. Perhaps its most remarkable feature was its unexpectedness. However well you knew him you could not foresee how he would express himself on any subject, but when you knew it, you had in the immense majority of cases to admit that which he said was admirably said.—DUFF, SIR MOUNTSTUART GRANT, 1900, *The National Review*, vol. 34, p. 544.

GENERAL

It is inevitable, I suppose, that the world should judge of a man chiefly by what it has gained in him, and lost by his death, even though a very little reflection might sometimes show that the special qualities which made him so useful to the world implied others of a yet higher order, in which, to those who knew him well, these more conspicuous characteristics must have been well-nigh emerged. And while of course it has given me great pleasure, as it must have given pleasure to all Bagehot's friends, to hear the Chancellor of the Exchequer's evidently genuine tribute to his financial sagacity in the Budget speech, and Lord Granville's eloquent acknowledgments of the value of Bagehot's Political counsels as editor of the *Economist*, in the speech delivered at the London University on the 9th of May, I have sometimes felt somewhat unreasonably vexed that those who appreciated so well what I might almost call the smallest part of him, appeared to know so little of the essence of him,—of the high-spirited, buoyant, subtle, speculative nature in which the imaginative qualities were even more remarkable than the judgment, and were indeed at the root of all that was strongest in the judgment,—of the gay and dashing humour which was the life of every conversation in which he joined,—and of the visionary nature to which the commonest things often seem the most marvellous, and the marvellous things the most intrinsically probable. To those who hear of Bagehot only as an original political economist and a lucid political thinker, a curiously false image of him must be suggested. . . . This, at all events, I am quite sure of, that so far as his judgment was sounder than other men's—and on many subjects it was much sounder—it was not in spite of, but in consequence of, the excursive imagination and vivid humour which are so often accused of betraying otherwise sober minds into dangerous aberrations. In him both lucidity and caution were directly traceable to the force of his imagination.—HUTTON, RICHARD HOLT, 1877, *Walter Bagehot, The Fortnightly Review*, vol. 28, pp. 453, 454.

In some respects, the intellect of the gifted man whose name furnished the title of the present paper, was typical of the age. It was fearless and independent, accepting only that which came with well-established claims upon its credence; it was susceptible, yet capable of giving exact weight to the opinions and ideas which impinged upon its susceptibility; it was dissatisfied with the *status quo*, both in theology and politics; and, as in the case of all the best minds, it was not utterly devoid of some tinge of Utopianism. To a frank and liberal nature were united deep mental culture, considerable philosophical power, imaginative endowments of no mean order, and—what is more surprising than all, perhaps, after the qualities just enumerated—a large practical ability rarely witnessed in this order of brain. Few men of our own time have combined in so eminent a degree "the useful and the beautiful"—if we may use a common phrase in this connection. Yet his name and his writings are by no means so widely known as they deserve to be.—SMITH, GEORGE BARNETT, 1879, *Walter Bagehot, Fraser's Magazine, vol.* 99, *p.* 298.

So far from being dry or dull, his analytic force vivifies whatever it touches. His own enjoyment of his researches, finding vent in many quips and cranks and illustrative "excursuses" from his main theme, is contagious. The most careful student of Bishop Butler as an abstract writer would be astonished to find how many new lights are thrown on his celebrated "Analogy" by a reference to the circumstances in which it was composed; and the critic enters with equally fresh and keen-sighted delight into the underlying impulses of the songs of Béranger and Burns, the poems of Cowper and Wordsworth, the novels of Thackeray and Dickens, the historical writings of Gibbon and Macaulay, the political and literary essays of the first Edinburgh Reviewers. There is no affectation of universal knowledge; you feel unmistakably that Mr. Bagehot wrote about all these things because he was interested in them. You feel also that he had a deep undertsanding of everything that he handled.—MINTO, WILLIAM, 1879, *Literary Studies, The Academy, vol.* 15, *p.* 2.

I have recently read the "Literary Studies" of Mr. Walter Bagehot, published since his death. I was curious to see this book as a statement of his opinions upon the subjects which it discusses, but still more as an expression of the author. One is interested to observe the steps by which a man, attracted by many and diverse subjects, at last finds his way to the kind of work which he can do best. The essays are pleasant and amusing reading, but somewhat disappointing. The fault of them is that they are too theoretical and not sufficiently immediate. Instead of looking directly at the subject and describing it as he perceives it to be, he argues, infers, etc. But this was not Mr. Bagehot's way of writing upon other than literary subjects; the best things which occur in his far more valuable political works and his writings in the *Economist* are the results of a profound and subtle intuition. . . . It is as a journalist that Mr. Bagehot seems to me to have been particularly admirable and worthy of imitation. Among the admirable qualities of his writings in the *Economist*, that which ought especially to be imitated was his respect for business and public action. . . . His manner was that of a man who sits down among a number of friends, as honorable and intelligent as himself, to discuss things and not to make a vain and ineffectual display of words. His especial title to praise and imitation is that he looked upon journalism as action rather than literature, and upon himself as a partaker in the public business of the day rather than as a man of letters. . . . His style is an excellent model for writers who would do what he did. It was very conversational and cautious, and was therefore well suited to express the thoughts of one who was first of all an inquirer, who was rather a judge than an advocate, though he was capable of advocating effectively views which he had accepted with circumspection. . . . Mr. Bagehot's style moves with the caution of his thoughts. His mind scrutinizes the subject, and, from its careful way of proceeding, adopts a language which is cautious and has but little motion. There are other minds, however, to whom it is natural to express thoughts formed with the greatest deliberation with rapidity and rhythm. Both styles are true, although of the two the first is the less liable to exaggeration and affected imitation. — NADAL, EHRMAN SYME, 1879–82, *Journalism and Mr. Bagehot, Essays at Home and Elsewhere, pp.* 246, 248, 258, 259.

Every writer has the defect of his qualities, and I should say that Bagehot, while possessing the inventive and imaginative mind, which enabled him to discover and to describe so clearly, did not excel either in that laboured ratiocination or minute analysis which are essential to the highest success in some branches of economic study. He could both sustain a long argument and analyse minutely. Whatever he had to do he did thoroughly, and took what pains were necessary—in some cases he had conspicuously that transcendent capacity for taking trouble which Carlyle describes as the quality of genius. Still it did not "come naturally" to him to do either of these things, and he was not here conspicuously successful.—GIFFEN, ROBERT, 1880, *Bagehot as an Economist, The Fortnightly Review*, vol. 33, p. 555.

I find some good Stuff in Bagehot's Essays, in spite of his name, which is simply "Bagot," as men call it.—FITZGERALD, EDWARD, 1880, *Letter, Jan. 8; Letters to Fanny Kemble*, p. 165.

Bagehot has brought more knowledge of life and originality of mind to the elucidation of the theory and practice of English politics than any man since Burke. He is the only Englishman of first-rate talents who, during the last half-century, has applied the whole force of his mind to the analysis of the mass of laws, maxims, and habits which go to make up the English Constitution. In the course of a few years he will undoubtedly be recognized by all the world as the most eminent of constitutionalists. If this recognition has not yet been attained, the failure, such as it is, is due mainly to the versatility of Bagehot's interests, and to the consequent difficulty felt by ordinary students in believing that a writer who excelled in so many fields of speculation—in the sphere of criticism, of imaginative literature, and of political economy—could be pre-eminent in one field; and to the lucidity of Bagehot's explanations, which led even those who learnt most from his pages into the delusion that what their teacher explained so easily was in itself easy to explain and hardly needed explanation.—DICEY, A. V., 1881, *Bagehot's Biographical Studies, The Nation*, vol. 32, p. 426.

A series of essays on the various branches and functions of the English government. It is the most brilliant political work that has appeared in Europe in many years; the most brilliant that has appeared in England since the death of Burke. It should be thoughtfully studied by every student of political forms and methods. Bagehot's leading characteristic is not so much that he describes the English government as that he penetrates beyond its forms and examines the essence and significance of whatever part of it he has in hand. To a student, therefore, who already knows something of the organization of the government, Bagehot is likely to be the most suggestive and awakening of all writers. The work is so free from all controversial spirit that it is not easy to decide from it whether the author ranks himself as a Liberal or as a Conservative. While he admires the English government as a whole, he does not hesitate to criticise it sharply wherever he finds a weak point. Another feature of the volume is in the frequent comparisons into which the author enters of the results of English methods, and of the results of other methods elsewhere. These comparisons may not always be accepted as entirely just, but they are always suggestive and never commonplace. The author's style is exceedingly vivacious, and therefore the book is as interesting as it is valuable.—ADAMS, CHARLES KENDALL, 1882, *A Manual of Historical Literature*, p. 489.

No one who does not—as probably no one save a possible future editor ever will—compare this edition, word by word, with any former ones, can form any adequate conception of the shocking state of Bagehot's text as heretofore given to the world; there is nothing even remotely approaching it in the case of any other English writer of high rank since Shakespeare's time. This reflects no discredit on Mr. Hutton, who simply left it as he found it, and who shows in his memoir of Bagehot that he knew it was not in very good shape,—though apparently he did not realize how bad it was; but I think it does reflect a good deal on Bagehot, who could have saved the worst things by the most casual glance at his proofs, and who evidently never even looked at most of them at all. These slips cover almost the entire possible range of human blunders, and are sometimes of serious moment. Perhaps the most numerous sort resulted from misreading by the printers of Bagehot's not very legible handwriting, perpetuated by his failure to correct them. Through this, some of the review articles are perfect museums of grotesque errors. . . . Regarding the "English Constitution," appreciation of its immense merits must be taken for granted; praising it is as superfluous as praising Shakespeare. Every student knows that it has revolutionized the fashion of writing on its subject, that its classifications of governments are accepted commonplaces, that it is the leading authority in its own field and a valued store of general political thought.—MORGAN, FORREST, 1889, ed. *The Works of Walter Bagehot*, Editor's Preface, pp. ii, xii.

With his habitual sincerity.—GLADSTONE, WILLIAM EWART, 1895, *Bishop Butler and his Censors*, The Nineteenth Century, vol. 38, p. 718.

There is no acuter critic of men and books, and none with less literary bias.—MATTHEWS, BRANDER, 1897, *The Historical Novel*, The Forum, vol. 24, p. 91.

These are eminently businesslike sentences. They are not consciously concerned with style; they do not seem to stop for the turning of a phrase; their only purpose seems to be plain elucidation, such as will bring the matter within the comprehension of everybody. And yet there is a stirring quality in them which operates upon the mind like wit. They are tonic and full of stimulus. No man could have spoken them without a lively eye. I suppose their "secret of utility" to be a very interesting one indeed,—and nothing less than the secret of all Bagehot's power. Young writers should seek it out and ponder it studiously. It is this: he is never writing "in the air." He is always looking point-blank and with steady eyes upon a definite object; he takes pains to see it, alive and natural, as it really is; he uses a phrase, as the masters of painting use a color, not because it is beautiful,—he is not thinking of that,—but because it matches life, and is the veritable image of the thing of which he speaks. Moreover, he is not writing merely to succeed at that; he is writing, not to describe, but to make alive. And so the secret comes to light.—WILSON, WOODROW, 1898, *A Wit and a Seer*, Atlantic Monthly, vol. 82, p. 540.

Whatever the value of Bagehot's theories, his literary faculty was, of course, incomparably superior to Ricardo's. His books confirm what his friends tell us of his conversation. His mind was so alert, his interest in life so keen, and his powers of illustration so happy, that he could give freshness even to talk upon the British Constitution and liveliness to a discussion of the Bank reserve. He could not, that is, be dull or commonplace even on the driest or tritest of topics. . . . Bagehot's strong point, indeed, is insight into character: what one of his critics has called his "Shakespearean" power of perceiving the working of men's minds. . . . When a dull man of business talks of the currency question, says Bagehot, he puts "bills" and "bullion" into a sentence, and does not care what comes between them. He illustrates Hobbes' famous principle that words are the money of fools and the counters of the wise. The word currency loses all interest if we do not constantly look beyond the sign to the thing signified. Bagehot never forgets that condition of giving interest to his writing. Few readers will quite accept the opinion of his editor, that he has made "Lombard Street" as entertaining as a novel. But he has been wonderfully successful in tackling so arid a topic; and the statement gives the impression made by the book. It seems as though the ordinary treatises had left us in the full leaden cloud of a London fog, which, in Bagehot's treatment, disperses to let us see distinctly and vividly the human beings previously represented by vague, colourless phantoms.—STEPHEN, LESLIE, 1900, *Walter Bagehot*, National Review, vol. 35, pp. 936, 941, 949.

Mr. Bagehot's books are full of actuality. His pages are so animated that something seems to happen in almost every one of them. The hippopotamus sticks out his head, as does the ox with that wonderful wet nose on the foreground of Rubens' "Nativity" in the Antwerp gallery. . . . Mr. Bagehot is not only an original writer, but he presents you with his thoughts and fancies in an unworked state. He is not an artist; he does not stop to elaborate and dress up his material; but having said something which is worth saying and has not been said before, this strange writer is content to pass hurriedly on to say something else. There is more meat on Mr. Bagehot's bones for the critics than almost on anybody else's; hence his extreme utility to the nimble-minded and lighthearted gentry aforementioned. Bagehot crops up all over the country. His mind is lent out; his thoughts toss on all waters; his brew, mixed with a humbler element, may be tapped; elsewhere he has made a hundred small reputations. Nothing would have pleased him better; his fate would have jumped with his ironical humour. . . . A strain of very severe morality runs through all Mr. Bagehot's literary criticism. It is noticeable in his reviews of Thackeray and Dickens. I have no quarrel with it. I have heard Mr.

Bagehot called a paradoxical writer. This is absurd. A paradoxical talker he may have been. Conversation without paradox is apt to be as dull as still champagne, but in his considered writings, after he had outgrown his boyish ὕβρις, a love of the truth is conspicuous throughout. He is pre-eminently a sensible, truthful man. But, there is the rub; he hated dulness, apathy, pomposity, the time-worn phrase, the greasy platitude. His writings are an armoury of offensive weapons against pompous fools. The revenge taken by these paltry, meaningless persons is to hiss *paradox* whenever the name of their tormentor is mentioned.—BIRRELL, AUGUSTINE, 1901, *Walter Bagehot, Essays and Addresses, pp.* 133, 136, 150.

Caroline Elizabeth Sheridan Norton
Lady Stirling—Maxwell
1808–1877

Born [Caroline Elizabeth Sarah Sheridan], in London, 1808. Precocious literary ability. Married (i.) to Hon. George Chapple Norton, 30 June 1827; rupture with him, 1836. Edited "La Belle Assemblée," 1832–36; "The English Annual," 1834. Prolific writer of poems and novels; contributed frequently to periodicals. Husband died, 24 Feb. 1875. Married (ii.) to Sir William Stirling-Maxwell, 1 March 1877. Died, 15 June 1877. *Works:* "The Sorrows of Rosalie" (anon.), 1829; "The Undying One," 1830 (2nd edn. same year);" "Poems" (Boston), 1833; "The Wife and Woman's Reward" (anon.), 1835; "The Dream,' 1840; "Lines" [on the Queen], [1840]; "A Voice from the Factories" (anon.), 1836; "The Child of the Islands," 1845; "Aunt Carry's Ballads for Children," 1847; "Stuart of Dunleath," 1851; "English Laws for Women in the Nineteenth Century" (priv. ptd.), 1854; "A Letter to the Queen on Lord Chancellor Cranworth's Marriage and Divorce Bill," 1855; "The Centenary Festival" (from "Daily Scotsman"), [1859]; "The Lady of La Garaye," 1862 [1861]; "Lost and Saved," 1863; "Old Sir Douglas" (from "Macmillan's Mag."), 1868 [1867]. She *edited:* "A Residence at Sierra Leone," 1849; Miss Stapleton's "The Pastor of Silverdale," 1867; "The Rose of Jericho," 1870.—SHARP, R. FARQUHARSON, 1897, *A Dictionary of English Authors, p.* 214.

PERSONAL

Sheridan's daughter and poetess, sat nearer to us, looking like a queen, certainly one of the most beautiful women I ever looked upon.—WILLIS, NATHANIEL PARKER, 1835, *Pencillings by the Way, Letter* cxix.

I hope you will not take it ill if I implore you to try at least to be calm under these trials. You know that what is alleged (if it be alleged) is utterly false, and what is false can rarely be made to appear true. The steps which it will be prudent to take, it will be impossible to determine until we know more certainly the course that is intended to be pursued. You ought to know him better than I do, and must do so. But you seem to me to be hardly aware what a GNOME he is. In my opinion he has somehow or other made this whole matter subservient to his pecuniary interest. Since first I heard that I was to be proceeded against, I have suffered more intensely than I ever did in my life. I have had neither sleep nor appetite, and I attribute the whole of my illness to the uneasiness of my mind. Now, what is this uneasiness for? Not for my own character, because, as you justly say, the imputation upon me is as nothing. It is not for the political consequence to myself, although I deeply feel the consequences which my indiscretion may bring upon those who are attached to me, and follow my fortunes. The real and principal object of my anxiety and solicitude is you, and the situation in which you have been so unjustly placed by the circumstances which have taken place.—MELBOURNE, LORD, 1836, *Letter to Mrs. Norton, April; Lives of the Sheridans by Fitzgerald, vol.* II, *p.* 410.

I cannot contemplate without deep emotion the effect of your verdict upon the fate of this lady. In the pride of beauty, in the exuberance of youthful spirits, flattered by the admirers of her genius, she may have excited envy, and may not have borne her triumph with uniform moderation and meekness; but her principles have been unshaken, her heart has been pure. As a wife her conduct has been irreproachable; as a mother she has set a bright example to her sex.—CAMPBELL, LORD, 1836, *Address to the Jury, Lives of the Sheridans by Fitzgerald, vol.* II, *p.* 417.

One of the pleasantest dinners I ever enjoyed was with Mrs. Norton. She now lives with her uncle, Mr. Charles Sheridan, who is a bachelor. . . . The beauty of Mrs. Norton has never been exaggerated. It is brilliant and refined. Her countenance is lighted by eyes of the intensest brightness, and her features are of the greatest regularity. There is something tropical in her look; it is so intensely bright and burning, with large dark eyes, dark hair, and Italian complexion. And her conversation is so pleasant and powerful without being masculine, or rather it is masculine without being mannish; there is the grace and ease of the woman with a strength and skill of which any man might well be proud. Mrs. Norton is about twenty-eight years old, and is, I believe, a grossly slandered woman. She has been a woman of fashion, and has received many attentions which doubtless she would have declined had she been brought up under the advice of a mother; but which we may not wonder she did not decline, circumstanced as she was. It will be enough for you, and I doubt not you will be happy to hear it of so remarkable and beautiful a woman, that I believe her entirely innocent of the grave charges that have been brought against her. I count her one of the brightest intellects I have ever met.—SUMNER, CHARLES, 1839, *To George S. Hillard, Feb. 16; Memoir and Letters of Sumner, ed. Pierce, vol.* II, *pp.* 61, 62.

I dined this day with Rogers, the Dean of the poets. . . . It was not till dinner was half over that he was called out of the room, and returned with a lady under his arm. A lady, neither splendidly dressed nor strikingly beautiful, as it seemed to me, was placed at the table. A whisper ran along the company, which I could not make out. She instantly joined our conversation, with an ease and spirit that showed her quite used to society. She stepped a little too near my prejudices by a harsh sentence about Goethe, which I resented. And we had exchanged a few sentences when she named herself, and I then recognized the much-eulogized and calumniated Honorable Mrs. Norton, who, you may recollect, was purged by a jury finding for the defendant in a *crim. con.* action by her husband against Lord Melbourne. When I knew who she was, I felt that I ought to have distinguished her beauty and grace by my own discernment, and not waited for a formal announcement. You are aware that her position in society was, to a great degree, imperilled.—ROBINSON, HENRY CRABB, 1845, *To Thomas Robinson, Jan.* 31; *Diary, Reminiscences and Correspondence, ed. Sadler, vol.* II, *p.* 335.

At the Bunsens' yesterday. I saw Mrs. Norton and looked at her well. Her beauty is, perhaps, of too high an order to strike at first, especially as she is now above forty. It did not give me much artistic pleasure, but I could see that I should probably think her more and more beautiful. Also, I did not see her speak or smile, as she was listening to music.—EASTLAKE, ELIZABETH LADY, 1851, *Journal, Jan.* 29; *Journals and Correspondence, ed. Smith, vol.* I, *p.* 267.

She was at this time apparently about forty, still very handsome, and singularly attractive in her manners and conversation, her figure, though fine, was not tall or commanding; her countenance, of the Roman cast, was beautiful, and a profusion of black hair descending in curls on her shoulders set off the brilliant colour of her skin. Long acquainted with the men most celebrated for rank, talent, and fashion in her day, she had the ease of manner and varied conversation which, more than anything else, these advantages confer, but at the same time she had lost none of the native kindliness and sweetness of her disposition. She was uniformly courteous and affable to such a degree indeed, that no one could discover from her manner whose conversation, of those she met in society, she really preferred. There is no one perfect, however, in this world, and Mrs. Norton had one blemish in society, which increased rather than diminished with the lapse of time. She has associated so frequently with the first in talent and station, that her mind had become impregnated, as it were, with the atmosphere which they breathed. Hence her conversation consisted too much of anecdotes— many of them trivial enough—of eminent men.—ALISON, SIR ARCHIBALD, 1867?–83, *Some Account of My Life and Writings, vol.* II, *p.* 76.

When I first knew Caroline Sheridan, she had not long been married to the Hon. George Norton. She was splendidly handsome, of an un-English character of beauty, her rather large and heavy head and features recalling the grandest Grecian and Italian models, to the latter of whom her rich colouring and blue-black braids of hair give her an additional resemblance. Though neither as perfectly lovely as the Duchess of Somerset nor as perfectly charming as Lady Dufferin, she produced a far more striking impression than either of them, by the combination of the poetical genius with which she alone of the three was gifted, with the brilliant wit and power of repartee which they (especially Lady Dufferin) possessed in common with her, united to the exceptional beauty with which they were all three endowed. Mrs. Norton was extremely epigrammatic in her talk, and comically dramatic in her manner of relating things. I do not know whether she had any theatrical talent, though she sang pathetic and humorous songs admirably, and I remember shaking in my shoes when, soon after I came out, she told me she envied me, and would give anything to try the stage herself. I thought as I looked at her wonderfully, beautiful face, "Oh, if you did, what would become of me?"—KEMBLE, FRANCES ANN, 1879, *Records of a Girlhood*, p. 174.

It seems but yesterday—it is not so very long ago certainly—that I saw for the last time the Hon. Mrs. Norton. Her radiant beauty was then faded, but her stately form had been little impaired by years, and she had retained much of the grace that made her early womanhood so surpassingly attractive. She combined in a singular degree feminine delicacy with masculine vigor; though essentially womanly, she seemed to have the force of character of man. Remarkably handsome, she, perhaps, excited admiration rather than affection. I can easily imagine greater love to be given to a far plainer woman. She had, in more than full measure, the traditional beauty of her family, and no doubt inherited with it some of the waywardness that is associated with the name of Sheridan.—HALL, SAMUEL CARTER, 1883, *Retrospect of a Long Life*, p. 386.

One of the most charming persons whom I ever met in my life was the Hon. Mrs. Caroline Norton, and one of the most delightful dinners at which my wife and I were ever present was at her house. As I had been familiar with her poems from my boyhood, I was astonished to find her still so beautiful and young—if my memory does not deceive me, I thought her far younger looking than myself. Mrs. Norton had not only a graceful, fascinating expression of figure and motion, but narrated everything so well as to cast a peculiar life and interest into the most trifling anecdote. Mrs. Norton had marvellously beautiful and expressive eyes, such as one seldom meets thrice in a life. As a harp well played inspires tears or the impulse to dance, so her glances conveyed, almost in the same instant, deep emotion and exquisite merriment. — LELAND, CHARLES GODFREY, 1893, *Memoirs*, pp. 428, 429.

To account for the extraordinary fascination she exercised over old and young, even after she had attained the age when most women cease to exert an influence upon the mind masculine, we must remember that her magic was quite as much due to her mental as to her personal gifts. She had acquired the art, without using any so-called art, of looking half her age, and was sometimes mistaken for her son's wife.— GERARD, FRANCES A., 1897, *Some Fair Hibernians*, p. 240.

Was then [1843] very handsome. Her hair, which was decidedly black, was arranged in flat bandeaux, according to the fashion of the time. A diamond chain, formed of large links, encircled her fine head. Her eyes were dark and full of expression. Her dress was unusually *décolletée*, but most of the ladies present would in America have been considered extreme in this respect.—HOWE, JULIA WARD, 1899, *Reminiscences*, 1819–1899, p. 102.

GENERAL

Shepherd,—"Her poetry? That'll no be easy, sir; for there's a saftness and a sweetness, and a brichtness, and abune a' an indefinite, and indescribable, and undefinable, and unintelligible, general, vague, dim, fleetin' speerit o' feminine sympathy and attraction—na, na, na, these are no the richt words ava—a celestial atmosphere o' the balm o' a thousand flowers, especially lilies and roses, pinks, carnations, violets, honeysuckle, and sweetbriar—an intermingled mawgic o' the sweetest scents in natur—heaven and earth breathin' upon ane anither's faces and breasts— hangin' ower yon bit pathetic poem,

Rosalie, that inclines ane to remember the fair young lady that wrote it in his prayers!"—WILSON, JOHN, 1830, *Noctes Ambrosianæ, Blackwood's Magazine*, vol. 27, p. 686.

"Mrs. Norton." The God, stepping forward a pace,
Kiss'd her hand in return, with respect in his face,
But said, "Why indulge us with nothing but sighs?
You best prove your merits when cheerful and wise:
Be still so; be just to the depths of your eyes."
Then he turned to us all, and repeated in tones
Of approval so earnest as thrill'd to one's bones,
Some remarks of hers (bidding us learn them all too)
On the art of distinguishing false love from true.
After which, as he seated her near him, he cried,
"'Twas a large heart, and loving, that gave us this guide."
—HUNT, LEIGH, 1837, *Blue-stocking Revels*.

This lady is the Byron of our modern poetesses. She has very much of that intense personal passion by which Byron's poetry is distinguished from the larger grasp and deeper communion with man and nature of Wordsworth. She has also Byron's beautiful intervals of tenderness, his strong practical thought, and his forceful expression. It is not an artificial imitation, but a natural parallel: and we may add that it is this her latest production, which especially induces, and seems to us to justify, our criticism.—COLERIDGE, HENRY NELSON, 1840, *Modern English Poetesses, Quarterly Review*, vol. 66, p. 376.

The imagination of Mrs. Norton is chiefly occupied with domestic feelings and images, and breathes melodious plaints or indignations over the desecrations of her sex's loveliness; that of Miss Barrett often wanders amidst the supernatural darkness of Calvary, sometimes with anguish and tears of blood, sometimes like one who echoes the songs of triumphal quires. . . . Mrs. Norton is beautifully clear and intelligible in her narrative and course of thought and feeling; Miss Barrett has great inventiveness, but not an equal power in construction. The one is all womanhood; the other all wings. The one writes from the dictates of a human heart in all the eloquence of beauty and individuality; the other like an inspired **priestess**—not without a most truthful heart, but a heart that is devoted to religion, and whose individuality is cast upward in the divine afflatus, and dissolved and carried off in the recipient breath of angelic ministrants.—HORNE, RICHARD HENGIST, 1844, *A New Spirit of the Age*, p. 270.

Mrs. Norton has been styled the Byron of her sex. Though she resembles that great poet in the energy and mournfulness so often pervading her pages, it would be erroneous to confound her sorrowful craving for sympathy, womanly endurance, resignation, and religious trust, with the refined misanthropy of Childe Harold.—GRISWOLD, RUFUS WILMOT, 1844, *The Poets and Poetry of England in the Nineteenth Century*, p. 360.

This brilliant volume has not materially softened our suspicion that the present purveyors of our popular literature are on a false tack. We still doubt whether any great good will come of this eternal reproduction in imaginative works, of the "Condition of England Question." . . . She has been for years devoting her abilities to the cause which she now maintains;— none can have forgotten, in particular, her verses on the factory children, nor her letters on mendicancy in the public journals, though her claim to these last may have been unsuspected until her present avowal. Nor will Zoilus be able to point out any sentiment in these cantos at variance with the simplicity and generosity of their apparent scope and purpose. . . . It will be enjoyed now and remembered in honour hereafter, not because of its formal doctrine, but for the sake of its vivid and varied transcripts of human life and passion—pictures which would, we suspect, have been still more likely to further the artist's views, had her graceful drawing and rich colouring dispensed with the texts and commentaries now blazoned round them on too conspicuous frames. . . . We wish we had room for a score more of these masterly sketches—but we hope we have given enough, not to excite attention, for that such gifts employed with such energy must at once command, even were the name on the title-page a new one—but enough to show that we have not observed with indifference this manifestation of developed skill—this fairest wreath as yet won in the service of the graver Muses for the name of Sheridan.—LOCKHART, JOHN GIBSON, 1845, *The Child of the*

Islands, Quarterly Review, vol. 76, *pp.* 1, 2, 3, 11.

Her ear for the modulation of verse is exquisite; and many of her lyrics and songs carry in them the characteristic of the ancient Douglases, being alike "tender and true." It must be owned, however, that individuality is not the most prominent feature of Mrs. Norton's poetry.— MOIR, D. M., 1851-52, *Sketches of the Poetical Literature of the Past Half-Century.*

Melancholy is the prevailing tendency of her mind; and though we cannot but regret that one whose society never fails to confer pleasure should have so often been disappointed in its search herself, we can not but rejoice that circumstances should have thrown her genius in that which was perhaps its natural channel, and enriched our literature, both in poetry and prose, with so many gems of the pathetic, which are indelibly engraven on the memory of all who are acquainted with them.—ALISON, SIR ARCHIBALD, 1853, *History of Europe 1815-1852, ch.* V.

"The Child of the Islands" was written in the maturity of her youth and beauty. Under guise of a Birthday Ode to the Prince of Wales, it conveyed a tender appeal to the rich to consider the sufferings of the poor, and more especially of poor children. The subject was at that date a new and important one in politics. The Factory Bill had done something to better the condition of children, but they were still put to brutal uses in mines, and subject to solitary confinement in prisons; and Mrs. Norton's verses, and still more the prose "Notes" she appended to them, show her to have been in close and womanly sympathy with this kind of human misery. Here and there, too, in the same poem, is heard the true ring of poetic music; as when she recalls some happy hour,

"In meadow walks and lovely loitering lanes;"

or in this still prettier line, remembering a scene among Scottish hills loved in her girlhood—

"Still gleams my lone lake's unforgotten blue."

As famous as any of her more extensive works are some of her lyrics, set to music by popular composers. How often have tears started in response to her ballad—

"Love not! love not! the thing you love may die!"

And who does not know her rich half-Moorish melodies set by herself to her own words? How few men or women have succeeded in producing a really popular song—one so simple and attractive as to be heard all over the land, in the hush of lighted drawing-rooms and on hand-organs in dull London streets. This triumph has been hers, and it will be remembered now that she is gone.—MASSON, ROSALINE ORME, 1877, *Lady W. Stirling Maxwell, The Academy, vol..* 11, *p.* 555.

A sort of soda-water Byron.—GOSSE, EDMUND, 1881, *The Early Writings of Robert Browning, The Century, vol.* 23, *p.* 196.

What strikes us in her poetry is the earnestness of feeling, the masculine cast of thought, and the mode in which her own personality is made to furnish dramatic colour and action. It is thus evident that she wrote because she wished to express her own feelings, and leave a record of her many trials, and not from a *dilettante* longing to figure in print.—FITZGERALD, PERCY, 1886, *The Lives of the Sheridans, vol.* II, *p.* 373.

She is said to be the original of George Meredith's "Diana of the Crossways," that brilliant, complex character who stands out alive, humanly wrong and lovable among all the heroines of novels. Mrs. Norton was no mere fashionable writer of pretty trifles. Without her rank, her genius would have found her recognition, for she poured her warm, womanly heart-blood into her writings in defence of the poor and oppressed.—DORSEY, ANNA VERNON, 1891, *Society Women as Authors, The Cosmopolitan, vol.* 11, *p.* 590.

Mrs. Norton's work was not conceived in any dilettante spirit. It shows from first to last, that steady progress which only comes of conscientious application and continuous study. Her longer works lack the sustained interest which can alone make such poems permanently popular, but they contain stanzas which give felicitous expression to genuine feeling and ennobling thought. Lockhart, in the *Quarterly,* called her "the Byron of poetesses," but except for the connubial infelicity which withered both of their lives, and the occasional expression of the emotions stirred by their common experience, the analogy cannot be said to hold good. Each, like Wordsworth's nightingale, was "a creature of a fiery heart;" but Mrs. Norton was chastened and refined by the sufferings that irritated and degraded

Byron. Mrs. Norton's tender and womanly feeling was everywhere evident in her life and work. Her sympathy with the poor and the suffering was keen and constant.—MILES, ALFRED H., 1892, *The Poets and the Poetry of the Century, Joanna Baillie to Mathilde Blind*, p. 242.

A passage from "The Dream," quoted by Lockhart, rivals in passionate energy almost anything of Byron's; but there is no element of novelty in Mrs. Norton's verse, any more than there is any element of general human interest in the impassioned expression of her personal sorrows. Mrs. Norton had already (1856) proclaimed the sufferings of overworked operatives in "A Voice from the Factories," a poem accompanied by valuable notes. In "The Child of the Islands" (i. e. the Prince of Wales), 1845, a poem on the social condition of the English people, partly inspired by such works as Carlyle's "Chartism" and Disraeli's "Sybil," she ventured on a theme of general human interest, and proved that, while purely lyrical poetry came easily to her, compositions of greater weight and compass needed to be eked out with writing for writing's sake. Much of it is fine and even brilliant rhetoric, much too is mere padding, and its chief interest is as a symptom of that awakening feeling for the necessity of a closer union between the classes of society which was shortly to receive a still more energetic expression in Charles Kingsley's writings. . . . The emotion itself is usually sincere—always when her personal feelings are concerned—but the expression is conventional. She follows Byron as the dominant poet of her day, but one feels that her lyre could with equal ease have been tuned to any other note. Her standard of artistic execution was not exalted. Though almost all ·her lyrics have merit, few are sufficiently perfect to endure, and she will be best remembered as a poetess by the passages of impassioned rhetoric imbedded in her longer poems.—GARNETT, RICHARD, 1895, *Dictionary of National Biography*, vol. XLI, pp. 207, 208.

"The Outward Bound," "Bingen on the Rhine," and other things are at least passable, and one of the author's latest and most ambitious poems, "The Lady of La Garaye," has a sustained respectability.—SAINTSBURY, GEORGE, 1896, *A History of Nineteenth Century Literature*, p. 315.

Her poetic gift was not great, but her verse is spirited, and has frequently a ring of genuine pathos.—WALKER, HUGH, 1897, *The Age of Tennyson*, p. 260.

It was as a poetess that Mrs. Norton was chiefly known. Her verse was graceful and harmonious, but more emotional than intellectual. Wrath at injustice and cruelty stirred the depths of her soul; her heart was keenly alive to the social evils around her and she longed passionately for power to redress them. The effect of her own wrongs and sufferings was to quicken her ardour to help her fellow women smarting under English law as it at that time existed.—HECTOR, ANNIE ALEXANDER, (MRS. ALEXANDER), 1897, *Women Novelists of Queen Victoria's Reign*, p. 284.

Samuel Warren
1807–1877

Born, in Denbighshire, 1807. Studied medicine for a short time at Edinburgh University. Student of Inner Temple, 1828; Special Pleader, 1831–37; called to Bar, 1837. Contrib. to "Blackwood's Mag." from Aug. 1830. Q. C., 1851. Bencher of Inner Temple, 1851. Recorder of Hull, 1852–74. Hon. D. C. L., Oxford, 9 June 1853. M. P. for Midhurst, 1856–59. Master in Lunacy, 1859–77. Died, 29 July 1877. *Works:* "Passages from the Diary of a Late Physician" (3 vols.), 1832–38; "Popular and Practical Introduction to Law Studies," 1835; "The Opium Question," 1840 (4th edn. same year); "Ten Thousand a Year" (anon.), 1841; "Now and Then," 1847; "The Moral, Social and Professional Duties of Attorneys and Solicitors," 1848; "Correspondence . . . relative to the trial of Courvoisier," 1849; "Letter to the Queen on a late Court Martial," 1850; "The Lily and the Bee," 1851; "The Queen, or the Pope?" 1851; "Manual of the Parliamentary Election Law of the United Kingdom," 1852; "Intellectual and Moral Development of the Present Age," 1852; "The Law and Practice of Election Committees," 1853; "Charge to the Grand Jury," 1854, "Miscellanies" (from "Blackwood's Mag."; 2 vols.), 1854–55; "Works" (5 vols.), 1854–55; "Labour," 1856. He *edited:* "Select Extracts from Blackstone's

Commentaries" (with J. W. Smith), 1837; "Blackstone's Commentaries Systematically Abridged," 1855.—SHARP, R. FARQUHARSON, 1897, *A Dictionary of English Authors*, p. 293.

PERSONAL

Mr. Warren, of the "Ten Thousand a Year," was in court,—a pale, thin, intelligent face, evidently a nervous man, more unquiet than anybody else in court,—always restless in his seat, whispering to his neighbors, settling his wig, perhaps with an idea that people single him out.—HAWTHORNE, NATHANIEL, 1855, *English Note-Books*, vol. I, p. 152.

It was a curious coincidence that his first instructor in law should have been Samuel Warren, author subsequently of "Ten Thousand a Year." One might have presupposed that there would have been an almost perfect assimilation between the brain that conceived Tittlebat Titmouse and that which evolved Triplet. Yet, sad to relate, the two of a trade failed to agree, and after a year of Mr. Samuel Warren, Charles Reade shifted his seat to the chambers of Mr. Matthew Fortescue, a warm friend of his brother.—READE, CHARLES L., AND REV. COMPTON, 1887, *Memoir of Charles Reade*, p. 105.

It has been a temptation difficult to resist, to refrain from weaving into this history the most amusing record of the life of Warren, which is to be found in these pages. He was always the chief figure in those pleasant episodes of London life which diversified the story of the brothers, from the very first outset of Alexander and Robert; the most lively and diverting figure, often disapproved of, sometimes quite exasperating in his play with life and literature, never remembering that there were (usually) only thirty days in a month, and only so many pages in a magazine, almost always too late, too long, keeping the Editors on tenter-hooks of expectation, furious with them when they cut short his papers or excised some favourite passage, as we have seen the young men do with a courage almost super-editorial: though every controversy ended in tears and laughter of reconciliation, and the vain, overweening, open-hearted, and simple-minded man conquered all grievances with his exuberance of life and jest, the magnanimity with his vanity, and the real affection and friendship that lay under all. —OLIPHANT, MARGARET O. W., 1897, *William Blackwood and his Sons*, vol. II.

In his colossal literary vanity Warren resembled Boswell. The stories in which he appears as the butt of Sergeant Murphy and other experienced wags are numerous; but when his literary reputation was not involved he was one of the gentlest, best-hearted, and most reasonable of men. He was popular as a bencher of the Inner Temple.—SECCOMBE, THOMAS, 1899, *Dictionary of National Biography*, vol. LIX, p. 426.

DIARY OF A LATE PHYSICIAN
1832–38

The nature of these narratives may easily be guessed from their title, and Warren very skillfully maintained the disguise of a medical man, gained chiefly by his own early introduction into a humble branch of that profession. The tales themselves are of various lengths, and very unequal degrees of merit. They are all, with the exception of one or two (which are not important enough to change the general impression on the reader), of a very tragic and painful nature—dark and agonising pages from the vast book of human suffering. . . . The style, though occasionally rather too highly coloured, is very direct, powerful, and unaffected; and the too great prevalence of a tone of agony and extreme distress, which certainly injures the effect of the whole, by depriving the work of *relief*, which is, above all, indispensable in painful subjects, is perhaps rather attributable to the nature of the subjects than to any defect of the artist.—SHAW, THOMAS B., 1847, *Outlines of English Literature*, p. 390.

So intense was the air of reality about these sketches that one of Mr. Warren's critics found fault with them as a betrayal of professional confidence.—HART, JOHN S., 1872, *A Manual of English Literature*, p. 534.

His "Diary of a Late Physician" produced a great effect, partly, I think, under the mistaken impression that it had been bequeathed to the world by a real practising physician, and therefore dealt with interesting facts, and not only with amusing fancies. But partly also because, though somewhat rough, if not course in texture, it gave evidence of talent, and was reasonably held to be a work of promise.—DOYLE,

SIR FRANCIS HASTINGS, 1886, *Reminiscences and Opinions*, p. 234.

Printed in collective form (1832, and complete 1838), they went through numerous editions, were translated into several European languages, and extensively pirated in America, while they still sell largely in paper covers for sixpence. Their literary merit is slight, but their melodramatic power is considerable.—SECCOMBE, THOMAS, 1899, *Dictionary of National Biography*, vol. LIX, p. 424.

TEN THOUSAND A YEAR
1841

I finished yesterday the first volume of "Ten Thousand a Year," the commencement of which, as Aunt Margaret intends to testify in her next epistle, is very unpromising. As it proceeds however it becomes splendid; and, having completed the volume, I laid it down with the impression that it was equal to Dickens.—ROSSETTI, DANTE GABRIEL, 1843, *To his Mother, June 2; Family Letters*, ed. W. M. Rossetti, vol. II, p. 11.

This work portrays the unexpected elevation to immense wealth and importance of one of the most contemptible beings that the imagination can conceive, Mr. Tittlebat Titmouse, a vulgar, ignorant, coxcomb of the lowest order, a linen-draper's shopman in Oxford-street, and suddenly exalted, through the instrumentality of some rascally attorneys, who have discovered a defect in a pedigree, to the third heaven of English aristocracy. The book is crowded with "scenes of many-coloured life," and with an infinity of personages, all vigorously, and some admirably drawn. The gradual development of the plot is carried on, not only with considerable skill and probability, but with a great deal more attention to detail than is usual in modern fiction; and many of the scenes are highly dramatic and natural. . . . Mr. Warren is a barrister, and a distinguished writer on legal education; and we cannot, therefore, be surprised that he should exhibit great and accurate knowledge, not only of the profession itself, but of the habits of its members. The work is undeniably a production of great skill and genius, and setting aside a little political partiality (for all Mr. Warren's good people are Tories, and his bad ones as invariably Whigs), must be considered as giving a vivid, well-drawn, and impressive picture of modern English society.—SHAW, THOMAS B., 1847, *Outlines of English Literature*, pp. 390, 391.

Shows considerable power of comic, or rather grotesque, picturing, and might take a high rank in fiction but for the terribly virtuous and high-flown characters which were apparently the pride of the author's heart. Aubrey, his favourite hero, was chosen by Thackeray as an excellent example of several branches of snobbishness.—OLIPHANT, MARGARET O. W., 1892, *The Victorian Age of English Literature*, p. 290.

GENERAL

Samuel Warren, though able, yet vainest of men,
Could he guide with discretion his tongue and his pen,
His course would be clear for—"Ten Thousand a Year,"
But limited else to a brief—"Now and Then."
—ROSE, SIR GEORGE, 1847? *On Samuel Warren*.

He possesses, in a remarkable manner, the tenderness of heart and vividness of feeling, as well as powers of description, which are essential to the delineation of the pathetic, and which, when existing in the degree in which he enjoyed them, fill his pages with scenes which can never be forgotten. His "Diary of a Physician" and "Ten Thousand a Year" are a proof of this; they are, and chiefly for this reason, among the most popular works of imagination that this age has produced. Mr. Warren, like so many other romance writers of the age, has often filled his canvas with pictures of middle and humble life to an extent which those whose taste is fixed on the elevating and the lofty not altogether approve. But that is the fault of the age rather than the man. It is amply redeemed, even in the eyes of those who regard it as a blemish, by the gleams of a genius which shine through the dark clouds of melancholy with which his conceptions are so often invested; by the exquisite pathetic scenes with which they abound; and the pure and ennobling objects to which his compositions, even when painting ordinary life, are uniformly directed.—ALISON, SIR ARCHIBALD, 1853, *History of Europe, 1815-1852*, ch. V.

Few, if any, writers of fiction of the present century, hold a more powerful pen than Samuel Warren. In vivid painting

WILLIAM CULLEN BRYANT.

Engraving by H. B. Hall & Sons.

BAYARD TAYLOR.

Engraving by F. T. Stuart. From a
Photograph by Gutekunst.

of the passions, and in faithfully depicting scenes of modern life, his tales have enjoyed a very great and deserved popularity.—CLEVELAND, CHARLES D., 1853, *English Literature of the Nineteenth Century*, p. 697.

Turned from the study of Medicine to that of Law. . . . . At the beginning of the reign Samuel Warren published, in 1838-40, a series of tales or sketches of life called "The Diary of a Late Physician" which first appeared in "Blackwood's Magazine." In this there were touches of pathos; and there was comic power in his very successful novel "Ten Thousand a Year," which followed in 1841. "Now and Then," in 1848, sustained the author's credit; but in 1851 the opening of the great Exposition suggested a rhapsody of neither prose nor verse called "The Lily and the Bee" that showed how a clever novelist with a good sense of the ridiculous, and a clear headed lawyer to boot, may make himself ridiculous by failing to see the limits of his power. — MORLEY, HENRY, 1881, *Of English Literature in the Reign of Victoria, with a Glance at the Past*, p. 343.

If anything was ever written which could startle and horrify the imagination, and create in it an alarmed expectation of revelations to come, it was the paper called "The Man about Town," herein discussed, which for sheer horror exceeded anything that had been written, at least let us say since "Frankenstein." It is very possible it may have been a salutary revelation: there is no doubt it was a very dreadful one.—OLIPHANT, MARGARET O. W., 1897, *William Blackwood and His Sons*, vol. II, p. 34.

William Cullen Bryant
1794-1878

William Cullen Bryant born Nov. 3, 1794. First poems printed, March 18, 1807. "The Embargo" printed, 1808. "The Genius of Columbia," 1810. Enters Williams College, Oct., 1810. Leaves Williams College, May, 1811. "Thanatopsis" written, 1812. Begins the Study of Law, 1812. Admitted to the Bar, 1815. "Thanatopsis" printed, 1817. Marries Miss Fanny Fairchild, 1821. Delivers "The Ages" at Harvard, 1821. Removes to New-York City, 1825. Union of *The New-York Review* and *The New-York Literary Gazette*, March 17, 1826. Becomes Assistant Editor of "The Evening Post," 1826. Edits *The Talisman* with Verplanck and Sands, 1827-1830. Becomes chief Editor of *The Evening Post*, 1829. First European Tour, 1834-1836. "The Fountain, and others Poems," published, 1842. First Tour in the South, March-May, 1843. "The White-Footed Deer, and other Poems," published, 1844. Purchases the Estate at Roslyn, 1845. Second European Tour, April-Dec., 1845. Delivers the Oration on Thomas Cole, 1848. Second Tour in the South, and First Visit to Cuba, March-May, 1849. Third European Tour, June-Oct., 1849. "Letters of a Traveller" published, 1850. Presides at the Banquet to Kossuth, Dec. 9, 1851. Delivers the Oration on J. Fennimore Cooper, Feb. 25, 1852. Fourth European Tour, Visit to the Holy Land, and Second Visit to Cuba, 1852. A Complete Edition of Poems published, 1854. Fifth European Tour, and First Visit to Spain, 1857-1858. Baptized at Naples, April, 1858. Dangerous Illness of Mrs. Bryant at Naples, May, 1858. "Letters from Spain and other Countries," published, 1859. Address at the Schiller Festival, Nov. 11, 1859. Delivers the Oration on Washington Irving, 1860. Made Presidential Elector, 1860. "Thirty Poems" published, 1863. Seventieth Birthday Celebrated by the Century Club, Nov. 3, 1864. Death of Mrs. Bryant, June, 1866. Last European Tour, 1867. The Free-Trade Banquet to Bryant, Jan. 30, 1868. "Letters from the East" published, 1869. Delivers the Oration on Fitz-Greene Halleck, Feb. 3, 1869. Translation of "The Iliad" published, 1870. Delivers the Oration on Gulian C. Verplanck, May 17, 1870. Translation of "The Odyssey" published, 1871, Address on Italian Unity, Jan., 1871. Address on the Unveiling of the Morse Statue, June 10, 1871. Tour in Mexico, Winter of 1871-72. Address on the Unveiling of the Shakespeare Statue, May, 22, 1872. Address on Reform, Sept. 23, 1872. Address on the Scott Statue, Nov. 4, 1872. Visited by the Commemorative Committee, Nov. 3, 1874. "The Flood of Years" published, 1876. Presentation of the Commemorative Vase, June 20, 1876. Delivers the Oration on Mazzini, May 29, 1878. Death of Bryant, June 12, 1878. Burial, June 14, 1878.—HILL, DAVID J., 1879, *William Cullen Bryant*, p. 13.

PERSONAL

With one exception (and that's Irving) you are the man I most wanted to see in America. You have been here twice, and I have not seen you. The fault was not mine; for on the evening of my arrival committee-gentlemen were coming in and out until long after I had your card put into my hands. As I lost what I most eagerly longed for, I ask you for your sympathy, and not for your forgiveness. Now, I want to know when you will come and breakfast with me: and I don't call to leave a card at your door before asking you, because I love you too well to be ceremonious with you. I have a thumbed book at home, so well worn that it has nothing upon the back but one gilt "B," and the remotest possible traces of a "y." My credentials are in my earnest admiration of its beautiful contents.—DICKENS, CHARLES, 1842, *Letter to Bryant, Feb. 14; A Biography of William Cullen Bryant by Godwin, vol.* I, *p.* 395.

In height, he is, perhaps, five feet nine. His frame is rather robust. His features are large but thin. His countenance is sallow, nearly bloodless. His eyes are piercing gray, deep set, with large projecting eyebrows. His mouth is wide and massive, the expression of the smile hard, cold—even sardonic. The forehead is broad, with prominent organs of ideality; a good deal bald; the hair thin and grayish, as are also the whiskers, which he wears in a simple style. His bearing is quite distinguished, full of the aristocracy of intellect. . . . His dress is plain to the extreme of simplicity, although of late there is a certain degree of Anglicism about it. In character no man stands more loftily than Bryant. The peculiarly melancholy expression of his countenance has caused him to be accused of harshness, or coldness of heart. Never was there a greater mistake. His soul is charity itself, in all respects generous and noble. His manners are undoubtedly reserved.—POE, EDGAR ALLAN, 1846, *William Cullen Bryant, W rks, ed. Stedman and Woodberry, vol.* VI, *pp.*118, 119.

It is consistent when we find the poet's home a great, old-time mansion, so embosomed in trees and vines that we can hardly catch satisfactory glimpses of the bay on which it lies, through the leafy windows, of which an overhanging roof prolongs the shade. No greener, quieter, or more purely simple retreat can be found; none with which the owner and his tastes and occupations are more in keeping. It would be absurd to say that all appearance of show or style is carefully avoided for it requires very little observation to perceive that these are absent from the place simply because they never entered its master's mind. I suppose if anything could completely displease Mr. Bryant with this beloved home, it would be the addition of any outward costliness, or even elegance, calculated to attract the attention of the passing stranger. Friend Richard Kirk—a Quaker of the Quakers, if he may be judged by his works—little thought, when he built this great, ample, square dwelling-place, in the lap of the hills, in 1787, that he was fashioning the house of a poet—one worthy to be spared when temple and tower went to the ground, because it is the sanctuary of a priest of Nature.—KIRKLAND, CAROLINE M., 1853–96, *Homes of American Authors, ed. Hubbard, p.* 48.

Yesterday, while we were at dinner, Mr. ——— called. I never saw him but once before, and that was at the door of our little red cottage in Lenox, he sitting in a wagon with one or two of the Sedgwicks, merely exchanging a greeting with me from under the brim of his straw hat, and driving on. He presented himself now with a long white beard, such as a palmer might have worn as the growth of his long pilgrimages, a brow almost entirely bald, and what hair he has quite hoary; a forehead impending, yet not massive; dark, bushy eyebrows and keen eyes, without much softness in them; a dark and sallow complexion; a slender figure, bent a little with age, but at once alert and infirm. It surprised me to see him so venerable; for, as poets are Apollo's kinsmen, we are inclined to attribute to them his enviable quality of never growing old. There was a weary look in his face, as if he were tired of seeing things and doing things, though with certainly enough to see and do, if need were. My family gathered about him, and he conversed with great readiness and simplicity about his travels, and whatever other subject came up. . . . His maners and whole aspect are very particularly plain, though not affectedly so; but it seems as if in the decline of life, and the security of his position, he had put off whatever artificial polish he may have heretofore had, and resumed the simpler habits and deportment of his early New England breeding. Not but what you discover, nevertheless, that he is a man of refinement, who has seen the world, and is well aware of his own place in it. . . . He uttered neither passion nor poetry, but excellent good sense, and accurate information, on whatever subject transpired; a very pleasant man to associate with, but rather cold, I should imagine, if one should seek to touch his heart with one's own. He shook hands kindly all around, but not with any warmth of grip, although the ease of his deportment had put us all on sociable terms with him.—HAWTHORNE, NATHANIEL, 1858, *Passages from French and Italian Note Books, May 22,* pp. 210, 211, 212.

O poet whom our grandsires loved,
    And whom our sires revered and praised,
Not less do we,—last of the three
    Of generations thou hast graced. . . .
The Eastern pines thy love shall sing
    Across the land, to where, profound
By Western steeps, the wild wave sweeps,
    That, save its dashing, hears no sound.
The trees thy loving care didst tend
    Shall blossom still; and still shall run
The laughing rills among the hills
    And sunny vales of Cummington.
And Roslyn's fields be fair again
    With bloom, as in those marvelous hours
When thou, thy heart from cares apart,
    Walked lovingly among the flowers.
And Roslyn's woods be all atune
    With birds that warble forth thy name
In Springtime's green, or Summer's sheen,
    Or in the Autumn's tint of flame.
Sing forth his name, pour out his praise,
    O woods and streams, O birds and flowers!
Repeat, repeat his numbers sweet;
    His love and fame are yours and ours.
—BROWNE, FRANCIS F., 1874–95, *Bryant's Eightieth Birthday, Volunteer Grain.*

As a poet, as a journalist, as a patriot, as a pure and upright man, living to an almost patriarchal age, yet never losing his interest, or relaxing his efforts, in whatever might advance the honor or welfare of his fellow-men, he has won for himself an imperishable remembrance on the page of history.—WINTHROP, ROBERT C., 1878, *Addresses and Speeches, vol.* III, *p.* 510.

From his childhood and through all his eighty-four years his habits of life were temperate and careful. . . . He rose early, took active exercise, walked far and easily, spared work at night, yet had time for every duty of a fully occupied life, and at seventy-one sat down in the shadow of the great sorrow of his life to seek a wise distraction in translating the Iliad and the Odyssey. His sobriety was effortless; it was that of a sound man, not of an ascetic. He was not a vegetarian nor a total abstainer from wine; but of tobacco, he said, playfully, that he did not meddle with it except to quarrel with its use. No man ever bore the burden of years more lightly, and men of younger generations saw with admiration and amazement an agility that shamed their own. At four-score his eyes were undimmed, and his ears had a boy's acuteness. — CURTIS, GEORGE WILLIAM, 1878, *William Cullen Bryant, A Commemorative Address, p.* 61.

It is the glory of this man that his character outshone even his great talent and his large fame. Distinguished equally for his native gifts and his consummate culture, his poetic inspiration and his exquisite art, he is honored and loved today even more for his stainless purity of life, his unswerving rectitude of will, his devotion to the higher interests of his race, his unfeigned patriotism, and his broad humanity. It is remarkable that with none of the arts of popularity a man so little dependent on others' appreciation, so self-subsistent and so retiring, who never sought nor accepted office, who had little taste for coöperation, and no bustling zeal in ordinary philanthrophy, should have drawn to himself the confidence, the honor, and reverence of a great metropolis, and become, perhaps it is not too much to say, our first citizen.— BELLOWS, HENRY WHITNEY, 1878, *Funeral Sermon, June* 14; *William Cullen Bryant by John Bigelow, p.* 305.

And so the good, stainless, noble old citizen and poet lies in the closed coffin there—and this is his funeral. A solemn, impressive, simple scene, to spirit and senses. The remarkable gathering of gray heads, celebrities—the finely render'd anthem, and other music—the church, dim even now at approaching noon, in its light from the mellow-stain'd windows—the pronounc'd eulogy on the bard who loved Nature so fondly, and sung so well her shows and seasons.—WHITMAN, WALT, 1878, *Autobiographia, June* 14.

Mr. Bryant's face and figure was one well known to Americans. He was a handsome old man, having a slight, erect form, a fine head, and a white flowing beard. His eyes, when his mind was excited with a peculiar mirth which he had, glittered through their half-shut lids with a gem-like brilliancy. At the time when I knew him he was already past eighty. He wrote but little in his newspaper, and he never was a talkative man. But both in his conversation and in the little writing which he now and then did, it was common to meet with some stroke of his sense or exact imagination. . . . I have omitted one ingredient in the reputation of Mr. Bryant in America; there was in it something of Franklin. He was a man of rules, an early riser, and very nearly a vegetarian. Having been often asked as to the methods by which he had accomplished so much, he gave to the world the hygienic and literary regulations which he had observed throughout his long life. He had always much to say against affectation and against modern extravagance of living. He thus figured to the younger generation as the representative of old-fashioned New England sagacity and simplicity.—NADAL, EHRMAN SYME, 1878, *William Cullen Bryant, Macmillan's Magazine, vol.* 38, *pp.* 374, 375.

SACRED TO THE MEMORY OF
W. C. B.
IN ORDER OF TIME AND EXCELLENCE OF GENIUS
ONE OF THE FATHERS OF AMERICAN POETRY
A WRITER OF CONSUMATE ENGLISH PROSE;
BY HIS WISDOM AND INSIGHT A JOURNALIST OF MASTERLY POWER;
THOUGH HOLDING NO PUBLIC OFFICE OF HIS COUNTRY.
AS A MAN, AUSTERE, RELIGIOUS, SELF-CONTAINED; HIS LIFE WAS AN EXPRESSION OF HIS POETRY; HIS DEATH AN ILLUSTRATION OF THE SPIRIT OF
"THANATOPSIS."
B. NOV. 3, 1794.
D. JUNE 12, 1878.
—RIPLEY, GEORGE, 1878? ' *Epitaph on William Cullen Bryant, p.* 172.

Mr. Bryant was a poet who could take care of himself and get a living. He could not only do this, but he could do a wise and manly part in guiding the politics of the country. He could not only manage his own private and family affairs in a prosperous way, but he could discharge his duties as a citizen and a member of society. In his own personal character and history he associated probity with genius, purity with art, and the sweetest Christianity with the highest culture. He has proved to all the younger generation of poets that hysterics are not inspiration, that improvidence is not an unerring sign of genius, that Christian conviction and Christian character are not indications of weakness, but are rather a measure of strength, and that a man may be a poet and a poet a man.— HOLLAND, JOSIAH GILBERT, 1878, *Topics of the Times, Scribner's Monthly, vol.* 16.

This was not Thyrsis! no, the minstrel lone
And reverend, the woodland singer hoar,
Who was dear Nature's nursling, and the priest
Whom most she loved; nor had his office ceased
But for her mandate: "Seek again thine own;
The walks of men shall draw thy steps no more!"
Softly as from a feast
The guest departs that hears a low recall,
He went, and left behind his harp and coronal.
—STEDMAN, EDMUND CLARENCE, 1878, *The Death of Bryant.*

There was a mournful propriety in the circumstances of the death of Bryant. He was stricken just as he had discharged a characteristic duty with all the felicity for which he was noted, and he was probably never wholly conscious from that moment. Happily we may believe that he was sensible of no decay, and his intimate friends had noted little. He was hale, erect, and strong to the last. All his life a lover of nature and an advocate of liberty, he stood under the trees in the beautiful park on a bright June day, and paid an eloquent tribute to a devoted servant of liberty in another land. And while his words yet lingered in the ears of those who heard him, he passed from human sight. There is probably no eminent man in the country upon whose life and genius and career the verdict of his fellow-citizens would be more immediate and unanimous. His character and life had a simplicity and austerity of outline that had become universally familiar, like a neighbouring mountain or the sea. His convictions were very strong, and his temper uncompromising; he was independent beyond most Americans. He was an editor and a partisan; but he held politics and all other things subordinate to the truth and the common welfare, and his earnestness and sincerity and freedom from selfish ends took the sting of personality from his opposition, and constantly placated all who, like him, sought lofty and virtuous objects.—SWINTON, WILLIAM, 1880, *Studies in English Literature*, p. 408.

The serenity and dignity so manifest in Bryant's writings were notable also in his person. The poet was often depicted by pencil and pen. The phrenologists exhausted their skill upon his noble head, and the painters and engravers their art upon his face. The former believed him to approach the ideal of Spurzheim in his phrenological developments, and the latter deemed him to possess the fine artistic features of Titian and of the Greek poet whom he translated. It is a consolation to age, when protected by a wise and orderly regulated life, that its inherent dignity supplies the want, if not the place, of youth, and that the veneration and serenity which surround it more than compensate for the passions which turbulence renders dangerous. To such an honored age as this Bryant attained; calm, circumspect, and sedate, he passed the perilous portals of Parnassus with his crown of laurel untarnished and unwithered by the baser breath that sometimes lurks like a poison within its leaves. He more resembled Dante in the calm dignity of his nature, though happily not in the violent and oppressive affliction of his life, than any other poet in history.—WILSON, JAMES GRANT, 1886, *Bryant and his Friends*, p. 81.

Probably the title of the Great American could be as fittingly applied to Bryant as to any man our nation has produced. He has been happily called the Puritan Greek; and this epithet applies equally well to his life as to his writings. If he was a Stoic in his earlier years, he was as unmistakably a Christian in later life. During both periods he was pure as ice, lofty in thought, noble in deed,—an inspiration toward the True Life to all who watched his course. No errors of passion or of over-heated blood did he have to mourn over, even in youth; yet he was not cold or unimpassioned, as his deep devotion throughout life to the woman of his choice proved. He led emphatically the intellectual life, with as little admixture of the flesh as possible; yet the warm currents of feeling were never dried up in his nature, but bubbled up freshly to the end. He lived largely on the heights of life, yet he was not uncharitable to the weaknesses and follies he saw everywhere about him, but rather looked upon them with a half-pitying tenderness; and he dropped a tear occasionally where the integrity of his own nature counselled a stern reproof.—GRISWOLD, HATTIE TYNG, 1886, *Home Life of Great Authors*, p. 132.

Bryant's office desk was his newspaper Egeria. It was also a curiosity. Except for a space immediately in front of him about two feet long and eighteen inches deep, his desk was usually covered to the depth of from twelve to twenty inches with opened letters, manuscript, pamphlets, and books, the accumulation of years. During his absence in Europe in 1859-60, his associate thought to do Bryant a good turn by getting rid of this rubbish and clearing his table so that he should have room for at least one of his elbows on the table. When he returned and saw what had been done, it was manifest from his expression—he said nothing—that what had been so kindly intended was regarded as anything but a kindness. He had also one habit in common with Pope, of always writing his "copy" for the paper on the backs of these old letters and rejected MSS. One who was associated with him for many years in the management of the *Evening Post* affirms that he never knew Bryant to write an article for its columns on a fresh sheet of paper. He also used a quill pen, which he was in the habit of mending with a knife nearly as old as himself, and which might originally have cost him fifty cents. He has been heard to speak of this knife with affection, and to resent the suggestion that he should replace it with a better one. Every year had added a value to it which no new knife could possibly have in his eyes. The same attachment to old servants made him hold on to a blue cotton umbrella which had very little to commend it either in fair weather or foul but its age. The ladies of his household at last, and when he was about setting out for Mexico, conspired against the umbrella, hid it away, and in its place packed a nice new silk one. He discovered the fraud that had been practised upon him, turned his back upon the *parvenu*, and insisted upon the restoration of his old and injured friend to its accustomed post of honor by his side. To him age made everything sacred but abuses. He petted the old brutes of his barnyard and stables, and held to his old friends with hooks of steel, closing his eyes resolutely to everything about them which he could not admire.—BIGELOW, JOHN, 1890, *William Cullen Bryant (American Men of Letters)*, p. 109.

Mr. Bryant illustrated as truly as Burns himself the maxim that the poet is born and not made, yet no votary of the Muses ever reconciled more completely the exalted aspiration and inspiration of the poet with the commonplace desperations of active and useful life. As fond of rural beauty as Theocritus or Catullus, and as fascinated by country life as Horace or Virgil, he yet for half a century attended at his editorial desk with inexorable punctuality. His Pegasus was never chained to his cart-horse. When Pegasus took his flight to the skies, the cart-horse still turned his honest furrow in the ground.—SEDGWICK, HENRY DWIGHT, 1895, *Reminiscenses of Literary Berkshire, Century Magazine*, vol. 50, p. 564.

He was by no means the leonine Jupiter of Launt Thompson's colossal bust. His frame was small, his features were delicate, and at the last there was something a little over-powering in his full and flowing beard.—CHADWICK, JOHN W., 1895, *America's Seven Great Poets, The Arena*, vol. 15, p. 12.

The memory of that early married life never grew dim. Mr. Godwin says that fifty-five years after his marriage, and ten years after his wife's death, the poet visited once more the house where the marriage had taken place. He walked about for some time, saying nothing; but as he was about to turn away he exclaimed, "There is not a spire of grass her foot has not touched," and his eyes filled with tears. Beneath that calm and undemonstrative exterior lay hid the deepest and tenderest feeling.—LAWRENCE, ARTHUR, 1895, *Bryant and the Berkshire Hills, Century Magazine*, vol. 50, p. 375.

His firm old features, encircled by a cloud of snowy hair and beard, would have impressed anybody; but in the distinction of Bryant's appearance there was something more than accident of feature, and something far more significant in the history of literary America. One does not remember his mane as in the least assertive. Rather to those who, without knowing him, saw him at a distance, his aspect was gentle, kindly, calmly venerable. But it had not the simplicity of unconsciousness. Whatever he really felt, he looked like a man who felt himself considerable, and certainly the qualities for which he most valued himself were not those which as journalist and man of business had made him a man of fortune. The thing for which he most respected himself was his work as a poet; and beyond question it was his work as a poet which the public most willingly recognised. The distinction he may have felt,—the distinction which he certainly received from his contemporaries, and which came to be so embodied in his personal appearance,—was wholly due to his achievement as a man of letters.—WENDELL, BARRETT, 1900, *A Literary History of America*, p. 202

In my studio Bryant's head came out with wonderful picturesqueness. I had never before had such a model. It would have been a delight to make oil-color studies of it, strong in effects of light and shade; but this was not what Bryant had come for. I chose a view of the face which I thought was getting most directly at the man, though not his most characteristic appearance; but still, with the beautifully formed head and face, the long white hair mingling with the flowing white beard, there was no lack of the pictorial element. —EATON, WYATT, 1902, *Recollections of American Poets, Century Magazine*, vol. 64, p. 843.

EDITOR

I ought to answer your question about the New York "Evening Post." I am a small proprietor in the establishment, and am a gainer by the arrangement. It will afford me a comfortable livelihood after I have paid for the *eighth part*, which is the amount of my share. I do not like politics any better than you do; but they get only my mornings, and you know politics and a belly-full are better than poetry and starvation.—BRYANT, WILLIAM CULLEN, 1828, *To Richard H. Dana, Feb. 16; A Biography of William Cullen Bryant by Godwin*, vol. I, p. 235.

During Mr. Bryant's editorial career of more than fifty years, have been waged the most important political conflicts in the history of the Republic, and in these he has manfully participated. On questions of national policy concerning the old United States Bank, the war with Mexico, the admission of slavery into the territories and its abolition, the tariff, the Ashburton treaty, the war of the rebellion, amnesty, the Alabama claims, the San Domingo muddle, civil service, resumption of specie payments, and other subjects of vital importance, his utterances have been prompt, unequivocal, and just; and he has maintained his principles with an unshaken constancy. He has never waited to catch the breath of popular opinion before flinging abroad his standard. The question with him has always been, "What is right? What subserves human interests best? What is the province and duty of government?" And so he has been the uncompromising enemy of political rings, class legislation, and jobbery, and corruption of all sorts, and the friend and ally of humane and liberal institutions, righteous reform, and the administration of impartial justice. Indeed, there is no species of political iniquity that he has not vigorously assailed, and no doctrines of permanent advantage to the commonwealth that he has not judiciously advocated and set firmer in the minds and hearts of men. He is a statesman of the best type and, as has been said by a distinguished senator, "he is a teacher of statesmen." He has asked nothing of his country but the privilege to serve her interests. Not even his bitterest political opponents have ever accused him of a desire for public office. It is one of the marvels of his great career that, amid the engrossing labors and cares of editorial life, he has kept a sweet temper for scholastic pursuits.—POWERS, HORATIO N., 1878, *William Cullen Bryant, Scribner's Monthly*, vol. 16, p. 484.

Behind this editor's desk there sat a master of many languages, a traveler in foreign lands, a student of various sciences, a poet of unquestioned genius, a moralist of high principles, a critic of keen penetration. The man in whom all these were united made it a special object of endeavor always to write the best thoughts in the best manner.—HILL, DAVID J., 1879, *William Cullen Bryant, p. 171.*

But although as a journalist Bryant took high ground and defended it firmly, he was never carried away by the fury of partisan discussion. In his editorial writings, as in his poetry, the tone is full of dignity. Calm in his strength, he was both temperate in expressing his opinions and good-tempered. He fought fairly and he respected his adversary. He was never a snarling critic either of men or of measures. He elevated the level of the American newspaper, but it was by his practice, not by his preaching. He was choice in his own use of words, and there was in the office of the *Evening Post* a list of words and phrases not allowed in its pages. But he was not a stickler for trifles, and he had no fondness for petty pedantries.—MATTHEWS, BRANDER, 1896, *An Introduction to the Study of American Literature, p. 77.*

I obtained the position of fine-art editor of the "Evening Post," then edited by W. C. Bryant, a position which did not interfere with my work in the studio. . . . My relations with Bryant were intellectually profitable to me. He was a man who enjoyed the highest consideration amongst our contemporary journalists,—of inflexible integrity in politics as well as in business affairs. . . . Bryant was held to be a cold man, not only in his poetry, but in his personal relations; but I think that, so far as his personality was concerned, this was a mistake. He impressed me as a man of strong feelings, who had at some time been led by a too explosive expression of them to dread his own passions and who had, therefore, cultivated a repression which became the habit of his life. The character of his poetry, little sympathetic with human passion, and given to the worship of nature, confirmed the general impression of coldness which his manner suggested. I never saw him in anger, but I felt that the barrier which prevented it was too slight to make it safe for any one to venture to touch it. A supreme sense of justice went with a somewhat narrow personal horizon, a combination which, while it made him hold the balance of judgment level, so far as the large world of politics was concerned, made him often too bitter in his controversies touching political questions; but the American political daily paper has never had a nobler type than the "Evening Post" under Bryant. Demonstrative he never was, even with his intimates, but to the constancy and firmness of his friendship all who knew him well could testify, and, as long as he lived, our relations were unchanged, though my wandering ways

brought me seldom near him in later years.
—STILLMAN, WILLIAM JAMES, 1901, *The Autobiography of a Journalist*, vol. I, p. 217.

THE EMBARGO
1808

Among instances of literary precocity, there are few recorded more remarkable than that of Bryant. Tasso, when nine years old, wrote some lines to his mother, which have been praised; Cowley, at ten, finished his "Tragical History of Pyramus and Thisbe;" Pope, when twelve, the "Ode to Solitude;" and the "wondrous boy Chatterton," at the same age, some verses entitled "A Hymn for Christmas Day;" but none of these pieces evidence the possession of more genius than is displayed in Bryant's "Embargo" and "Spanish Revolution," written in his thirteenth year.— ANON, 1809, *The Embargo, Second Ed., Advertisement*.

It was just as good and just as bad as most American imitations of Pope; but the boy indicated a facility in using the accredited verse of the time which excited the wonder and admiration of his elders. Vigor, compactness, ringing emphasis in the constantly recurring rhymes, — all seemed to show that a new Pope had been born in Massachusetts.—WHIPPLE, EDWIN PERCY, 1876–86, *American Literature and Other Papers*, ed. *Whittier*, p. 36.

THANATOPSIS
1812–17

A noble example of true poetical enthusiasm. It alone would establish the author's claim to the honors of genius.—WILSON, JOHN, 1832, *American Poetry, Blackwood's Magazine*, vol. 31, p. 652.

"Thanatopsis" is the poem by which its author is best known, but is by no means his best poem. It owes the extent of its celebrity to its nearly absolute freedom from defect, in the ordinary understanding of the term. I mean to say that its negative merit recommends it to the public attention. It is a thoughtful, well-phrased, well-constructed, well-versified poem. The concluding thought is exceedingly noble, and has done wonders for the success of the whole composition.—POE, EDGAR ALLAN, 1846, *William Cullen Bryant, Works*, ed. *Stedman and Woodberry*, vol. VI, p. 113.

The poem which is, perhaps, the highest expression of his genius, and the best known of any American poem, is "Thanatopsis."

. . . There is not, probably, an educated man now living among our English race in whose mind this solemn and beautiful meditation is not associated with "the last bitter hour." Its pictured phrases occur at every coming up of the grisly thought that haunts us all. Its serene philosophy has touched thousands who could never reason calmly for themselves upon the inevitable order of nature. It leaves a clear impression upon the memory that defies the blur of misquotation, for its well chosen words are united by the cohesive power of genius, like the cemented blocks of Old World temples, into imperishable forms. — UNDERWOOD, FRANCIS H., 1872, *A Hand-Book of English Literature, American Authors*, p. 136.

The perfection of its rhythm, the majesty and dignity of the tone of matured reflection which breathes through it, the solemnity of its underlying sentiment, and the austere unity of the pervading thought, would deceive almost any critic into affirming it to be the product of an imaginative thinker to whom "years had brought the philosophic mind." . . . It is doubtful if Bryant's "Thanatopsis" has been excelled by the many deep and beautiful poems which he has written since. In his case, as in that of Wordsworth, we are puzzled by the old head suddenly erected on young shoulders. They leap over the age of passion by a single bound, and become poetic philosophers at an age when other poets are in the sensuous stage of imaginative development.—WHIPPLE, EDWIN PERCY, 1876–86, *American Literature and Other Papers*, ed. *Whittier*, pp. 36, 37.

It was the first adequate poetic voice of the solemn New England spirit; and in the grandeur of the hills, in the heroic Puritan tradition of sacrifice and endurance, in the daily life, saddened by imperious and awful theologic dogma, in the hard circumstances of the pioneer household, the contest with the wilderness, the grim legends of Indians and the war, have we not some outward clue to the strain of "Thanatopsis," the depthless and entrancing sadness, as of inexorable fate, that murmurs, like the autumn wind through the forest, in the melancholy cadences of this hymn to Death?—CURTIS, GEORGE WILLIAM, 1878, *William Cullen Bryant, A Commemorative Address*, p. 21.

"Thanatopsis" is a Saxon and New

England poem. Its view of death reflects the race characteristics of ten centuries. It shows "no trace of age, no fear to die." Its morality and its trust are ethnic rather than Christian. It nowhere expresses that belief in personal immortality which the author possessed and elsewhere stated. It is a piece of verse of which any language or age might be proud. Yet, as I have just said, this strong and serene utterance of philosophy and of poetry, expressed in the best blank verse of the period, came from a mere boy, who but a few years before had been writing political poems, dashed with fire and vitriol, on "The Embargo" and "The Spanish Revolution." In its earliest publication "Thanatopsis" was much less than perfect, and was manifestly inferior to the final version. But even then it was, as it is now, a microcosm of the author's mind and powers.—RICHARDSON, CHARLES F., 1888, *American Literature*, 1607–1885, vol. II, p. 37.

It appeared in the September number of the "North American Review" for 1817, and proved to be not only the finest poem which had yet been produced on this continent, but one of the most remarkable poems ever produced at such an early age, and a poem which would have added to the fame of almost any poet of any age, while it would have detracted from the fame of none. From the day this poem appeared, the name of its author, which till then had scarcely been heard farther from home than the range of the human voice, was classed among the most cherished literary assets of the nation. Like the mythic Hermes, who before the sun had reached its zenith on the day of his birth had stolen and slaughtered the cattle of Apollo, young William Cullen Bryant, with scarcely less startling precocity, before he was out of his teens had possessed himself of Apollo's lyre, and established himself as the undisputed laureate of America.— BIGELOW, JOHN, 1890, *William Cullen Bryant (American Men of Letters)*, p. 2.

Begotten in the woods not yet cleared from the neighborhood of his home, the edge of the primeval forests which for centuries had covered the shores of the New World—it revealed the secrets which lurked under their boughs, and was peopled with shadows and memories of vanished and forgotten races. By no poet before or since was the universality of Death so strongly stated, and so impressively expressed.— STODDARD, RICHARD HENRY, 1891, *A Box of Autographs, Scribner's Magazine*, vol. 9, p. 219.

THE AGES
1821

There is running through the whole of this little collection, a strain of pure and high sentiment, that expands and lifts up the soul and brings it nearer to the source of moral beauty. This is not indefinitely and obscurely shadowed but it animates bright images and clear thoughts. There is everywhere a simple and delicate portraiture of the subtle and ever vanishing beauties of nature, which she seems willing to conceal as her choicest things, and which none but minds the most susceptible can seize, and no other than a writer of great genius, can body forth in words. There is in this poetry something more than mere painting. It does not merely offer in rich colours what the eye may see or the heart feel, nor what may fill the imagination with a religious grandeur. It does not merely rise to sublime heights of thought, with the forms and allusions that obey none but master spirits. Besides these, there are wrought into the composition a luminous philosophy and deep reflection, that make the subjects as sensible to the understanding, as they are splendid to the imagination. There are no slender lines and unmeaning epithets, or words loosely used to fill out the measure. The whole is of rich materials, skilfully compacted. A throng of ideas crowds every part, and the reader's mind is continually and intensely occupied with "the thick-coming fancies."—PHILLIPS, WILLARD, 1821, *Bryant's Poems*, North American Review, vol. 13, p. 380.

It is the one improper theme of its author.—POE, EDGAR ALLAN, 1846, *William Cullen Bryant, Works*, ed. Stedman and Woodberry, vol. VI, p. 112.

The subject is admirably fitted for the display of power. What can be more susceptible of poetical thought and expression than a rapid review of the history of the world? The theme is a half-inspiration of itself. Mr. Bryant, however, looks with the eye of a philosopher on the varying phases of humanity, and although we read with an attentive pleasure, we do not feel that delight which we know the subject is so admirably calculated to afford. We miss those vigorous, golden passages, which compel us to pause, and read again out of the mere enthusiasm of admiration.—POWELL, THOMAS, 1850, *The Living Authors of America*, p. 190.

It is a simple, serious, and thoughtful survey of history, tracing a general law of progress; and the stately Spenserian measure is marked by the moderation, the sinewy simplicity, the maturity and freedom from mannerism, which are Bryant's signmanual.—CURTIS, GEORGE WILLIAM, 1878, *William Cullen Bryant, A Commemorative Address*, p. 28.

HOMER
1870–77

Mr. Bryant has long been known, by his original poems, as resembling the old epic poets, in his language, more than any other living writer of English. It may be said that contemporary poets have excelled his verse, one in splendor, another in suggestiveness, another in fulness of knowledge and in reach of thought, and more than one in nearness to the great mental conflicts of the age; but he has certainly not been surpassed, perhaps not approached by any writer since Wordsworth, in that majestic repose and that self-reliant simplicity which characterized the morning stars of song. He has adhered to the permanent element in our language; and the common perversions in the meaning of good old words, which make it so nearly impossible even for most men of culture to write a sentence that Chaucer could have understood, seem to be unknown to him. No qualification for a translator of Homer could be more essential than this; and the reader who has duly considered its importance will find that it has given Mr. Bryant's translation a vast superiority over all others. The simplicity of Professor Newman's ballad verse is gained only by the sacrifice of dignity; that of the writers of English hexameters is mere baldness; even that of Lord Derby is habitually weak, forced and halting; but that of Mr. Bryant is at once majestic and direct, at once noble, rapid, and vigorous; it is, in a large degree, the simplicity of Homer.—LEWIS, CHARLTON T., 1871, *Mr. Bryant's Translation of the Iliad, North American Review*, vol. 112, p. 360.

He worked only in the mornings, after his usual exercise, when both mind and body were fresh. With a copy of Homer open on his desk, and a lexicon near by, he wrote for three or four hours, and then laid his papers aside for the day. There were other translations on his bookshelves, Chapman, Pope, and Cowper, of course; Voss's German version, and one in Spanish and another in Italian; later on he procured Professor Blackie's; but these he consulted only at intervals, to settle some point of construction of which he had doubts. It confused and fettered him, he said, to know how others had done a passage before him. Besides, he intended his version for popular, not learned, use, and he could give it a more popular cast, he thought, with the original text alone for his guide. The fluency with which he commonly wrote is apparent from the manuscript, where page follows page without inconsiderable erasures. Yet, at times, there are pages almost illegible from the number of the interlineations and changes. In original composition his habit was to fix his verses in his head while he was walking the fields, and to commit them to paper afterward; and, as his verbal memory was a retentive one, it is probable he pursued the same method in translating the old Greek.—GODWIN, PARKE, 1883, *William Cullen Bryant, A Biography*, vol. II, p. 271.

The best characteristics of Bryant's "The Iliad" and "The Odyssey" are: (1), general, though not invariable, fidelity to the text, as compared with former versions by poets of equal rank; (2), simplicity of phrase and style; (3), approximate transfusion of the heroic spirit; (4), a purity of language that pleases a sensible reader. It is not likely that Bryant possessed a scholar's mastery of even the familiar Ionic Greek, but the text of Homer long has been substantially agreed upon by European editors, there are special lexicons devoted to it, and it is faithfully rendered in German and English translations: so that the poet could have little trouble in adjusting it to his metrical needs. His choice of words is meagre, and so—in a modern sense—was that of Homer; there is no lack of minstrels, nowadays, who ransack their vocabularies to fill our jaded ears with "words, words, words." As a presentment of standard English the value of these translations is beyond serious cavil. When they are compared with the most faithful and poetic blank-verse rendering which preceded them, the work of Cowper, they show an advance in both accuracy and poetic quality. Lord Derby's contemporaneous version is dull and inferior. Bryant naturally handled to best advantage his descriptive passages,—the verses in the Fifth Odyssey, which narrate the visit of Hermes to Calypso, furnishing a case in point. His rendering of these is more literal than the favorite transcript by Leigh Hunt, and excels all others in ease and choice of language.—STEDMAN, EDMUND CLARENCE, 1885, *Poets of America*, p. 84.

While giving his readers the genuine spirit of Homer, Bryant has also given them one of the finest specimens of pure Saxon English in our literature. It will reward the curiosity of the philologist to note the large proportion of words of one syllable, the scarcity of words of three or more syllables, and the yet more conspicuous absence of words of Greek or Latin derivation. The sale of the work was to Mr. Bryant at least one gratifying evidence of its merit. Up to May, 1888, 17,000 copies of the Iliad had been sold, yielding him in royalties $12,738. Of the Odyssey, 10,244 copies, yielding in royalties $4,713, making a total income from these translations up to the spring of 1888 of $17,451.—BIGELOW, JOHN, 1890, *William Cullen Bryant (American Men of Letters)*, p. 168.

GENERAL

Bryant, whose songs are thoughts that bless
The heart, its teachers, and its joy,
As mothers blend with their caress,
Lessons of truth and gentleness
And virtue for the listening boy.
Spring's lover, flowers for many a day
Have blossomed on his wandering way,
Beings of beauty and decay,
They slumber in their autumn tomb;
But those that graced his own Green River,
And wreathed the lattice of his home,
Charmed by his song from mortal doom,
Bloom on, and will bloom on for ever.
—HALLECK, FITZ-GREENE, 1828, *The Recorder*.

As a poet, he is entitled to rank with the most eminent among us for originality, and finished, chaste execution. He does not offend us by abruptness and inequality. He presents us with here and there a bold image, but the tenor of his poetry is even and sustained. He shows good judgment, and a careful study of the materials of his verse. He does not aim with an overdaring attempt at those lofty and bewildering flights which too often fill the poet's pages with cloudy and confused representations. His delineations are clear and distinct, and without any indications of an endeavor to be startling and brilliant by strange metaphors, or unlicensed boldness of phraseology. His writings are marked by correct sentiment and propriety of diction.—KETTELL, SAMUEL, 1829, *Specimens of American Poetry*, vol. III, p. 133.

His lines "To the Past," "Lament of Romero," "Summer Wind," and everything painting our scenery, I am sure can be eclipsed by nothing of our own day; the first, I have thought, by nothing in the language.—VERPLANCK, GULIAN CROMMELIN, 1831, *Letter to Washington Irving*, Dec. 31; *A Biography of William Cullen Bryant by Godwin*, vol. I, p. 266.

And last, not least, thou!—now nurtured in
  the land
Where thy bold-hearted fathers long ago
Rocked Freedom's cradle, till its infant hand
  Strangled the serpent fierceness of its foe,—
Thou, whose clear brow in early time was
  fanned
By the soft airs which from Castalia flow!
Where art thou now? feeding with hickory
  ladle
The curs of Faction with thy daily twaddle!
Men have looked up to thee, as one to be
  A portion of our glory; and the light
And fairy hands of woman beckoned thee
  On to thy laurel guerdon; and those bright
And gifted spirits, whom the broad blue sea
Hath shut from thy communion, bid thee,
  "*Write*,"
Like John of Patmos. Is all this forgotten,
  For Yankee brawls and Carolina cotton?
Are autumn's rainbow hues no longer seen?
  Flows the "Green River" through its vale
  no more?
Steals not thy "Rivulet" by its banks of green?
  Wheels upward from its dark and sedgy
  shore
Thy "Water Fowl" no longer?—that the mean
  And vulgar strife, the ranting and the *roar*
Extempore, like Bottom's should be thine,—
Thou feeblest truck-horse in the Hero's line!
—WHITTIER, JOHN GREENLEAF, 1832, *To a Poetical Trio in the City of Gotham, Haverhill "Iris" Sep. 29; Life and Letters*, ed. Pickard, vol. I, p. 107.

Bryant is, by very general consent, placed at the head of our poetic department. His writings are distinguished by those graces which belong to naturally fine perceptions and a chastised taste. A deep moral feeling, serious but not sad, tinctures most of his views of man and nature, and insensibly raises thought from the contemplation of these lower objects, to that of the Mind who formed them. Bryant has proved, beyond any other writer, the fruitlessness of our country in poetic topics and illustrations.—PRESCOTT, WILLIAM HICKLING, 1832, *English Literature of the Nineteenth Century, North American Review, vol. 35, p. 181.*

Others before him have sung the beauties of creation, and the greatness of God; but no one ever observed external things more closely, or transferred his impressions to paper in more vivid colors. A violet becomes, in his hands, a gem fit to be placed in an imperial diadem; a mountain leads his eyes to the canopy above it. . . . On the whole, we may pronounce the book before us, the best volume of American poetry that has yet appeared. The publication of such a volume is an important event in our literature.—SNELLING, W. J., 1832, *Bryant's Poems, North American Review, vol. 34, pp. 502, 512.*

The descriptive writings of Mr. Bryant are essentially American. They transport us into the depths of the primeval forest, to the shores of the lonely lake, the banks of the wild, nameless stream, or the brow of the rocky upland, rising like a promontory from amid a wild ocean of foliage, while they shed around us the glories of a climate fierce in its extremes, but splendid in all its vicissitudes. His close observation of the phenomena of nature and the graphic felicity of his details prevent his descriptions from ever becoming general and commonplace, while he has the gift of shedding over them a pensive grace that blends them all into harmony, and of clothing them with moral associations that make them speak to the heart. Neither, I am convinced, will it be the least of his merits, in your eyes, that his writings are imbued with the independent spirit and buoyant aspirations incident to a youthful, a free, and a rising country.—IRVING, WASHINGTON, 1832, *Poems of William Cullen Bryant, London Ed., Introduction.*

None of these poems are long; but condensation is not by any means their distinguishing merit, especially of the descriptive passages; we see much simplicity, but no sublimation; and to us the chief charm of Bryant's genius consists in a tender pensiveness, a moral melancholy, breathing over all his contemplations, dreams, and reveries, even such as in the main are glad, and giving assurance of a pure spirit, benevolent to all living creatures, and habitually pious in the felt omnipresence of the Creator. His poetry overflows with natural religion—with what Wordsworth calls the "religion of the woods." The reverential awe of the Invisible pervades the verses entitled "Thanatopsis" and "Forest Hymn," imparting to them a sweet solemnity which must affect all thinking hearts. There is little that is original either in the imagery of the "Forest Hymn," or in its language; but the sentiment is simple, natural, and sustained; and the close is beautiful. The one idea is that "the groves were God's first temples," and might have been solemnly illustrated; but there is not a single majestical line, and the imagination, hoping to be elevated by the hymn of the high-priest, at times feels languor in the elaborate worship.—WILSON, JOHN, 1832, *American Poetry, Blackwood's Magazine, vol. 31, p. 650.*

Mr. Bryant, during a long career of authorship, has written comparatively little; but that little is of untold price; ὀλίγον τε δίλον τε,—little, but precious and dear. What exquisite taste, what a delicate ear for the music of poetical language, what a fine and piercing sense of the beauties of nature, down to the minutest and most evanescent things! He walks forth in the fields and forests, and not a green or rosy tint, not a flower, or herb, or tree, not a tiny leaf or gossamer tissue, not a strange or familiar plant, escapes his vigilant glance. The naturalist is not keener in searching out the science of nature, than he in detecting all its poetical aspects, effects, analogies, and contrasts. To him, the landscape is a speaking and teaching page. He sees its pregnant meaning, and all its hidden relations to the life of man.—FELTON, CORNELIUS CONWAY, 1842, *Mr. Bryant's Poems, North American Review, vol. 55, p. 501.*

No poet has described with more fidelity the beauties of the creation, nor sung in nobler song the greatness of the Creator. He is the translator of the silent language of the universe to the world. His poetry is pervaded by a pure and genial philosophy, a solemn, religious tone, that influence the fancy, the understanding, and the heart. He is a national poet. His works are not only American in their subjects and their imagery, but in their spirit. They breathe a love of liberty, a hatred of wrong, and a sympathy with mankind. His genius is not versatile; he has related no history; he has not sung of the passion of love; he has not described artificial life. Still, the tenderness and feeling in the "Death of the Flowers," "Rizpah," "The Indian Girl's Lament," and other pieces, show that he might have excelled in delineations of the gentler passions, had he made them his study. The melodious flow of his verse, and the rigour and compactness of his language, prove him a perfect master of his art. But the loftiness of his imagination, the delicacy of his fancy, the dignity and truth of his thoughts, constitute a higher claim to our admiration than mastery of the intricacies of rhythm, and of the force and graces of expression.— GRISWOLD, RUFUS WILMOT, 1842, *The Poets and Poetry of America*, p. 126.

Wherever English poetry is read and loved, his poems are known by heart. Collections of poetry, elegant extracts, schoolbooks, "National Readers," and the like, draw largely upon his pieces. Among American poets his name stands, if not the very first, at least among the two or three foremost. Some of his pieces are perhaps greater favorites with the reading public, than any others written in the United States.—HILLARD, GEORGE STILLMAN, 1843, *Bryant's Poems, North American Review*, vol. 55, p. 500.

There is Bryant, as quiet, as cool, and as dignified,
As a smooth, silent iceberg, that never is ignified,
Save when by reflection 'tis kindled o' nights
With a semblance of flame by the chill Northern Lights.
He may rank (Griswold says so) first bard of your nation
(There's no doubt that he stands in supreme ice-olation),
Your topmost Parnassus he may set his heel on,
But no warm applauses come, peal following peal on,—
He's too smooth and too polished to hang any zeal on:
Unqualified merits, I'll grant, if you choose, he has 'em,
But he lacks the one merit of kindling enthusiasm;
If he stir you at all, it is just, on my soul,
Like being stirred up by the very North Pole.
—LOWELL, JAMES RUSSELL, 1848, *A Fable for Critics*.

A few other American poets may excel him in affluence of imagery and variety of tone and subject, but probably none is so essentially poetical in nature. He is so genuine that he testifies to nothing, in scenery or human life, of which he has not had a direct personal consciousness. He follows the primitive bias of his nature rather than the caprices of fancy. His sincerity is the sincerity of character, and not merely the sincerity of a swift imagination, that believes only while it is creating. He does not appear to have the capacity to assume the various points of view, to project himself into forms of being different from his own, to follow any inspiration other than that which springs up in his own individual heart. As a poet, his nature is not broad, sensitive, and genial, but intense, serious, and deep; and we should suppose that his sensibility, pure and earnest as it is, within the bounds of his own individual emotions, would cool from sympathy into antipathy, when exercised on objects beyond its self-limited range. The charge of coldness, which is sometimes brought against him, must have reference to the limitation, not the force of his sympathies.— WHIPPLE, EDWIN PERCY, 1849-71, *Bryant, Literature and Life*, p. 304.

The poem ["June"] has always affected me in a remarkable manner. The intense melancholy, which seems to well up, perforce, to the surface of all the poet's cheerful sayings about his grave, we find thrilling us to the soul, while there is the truest poetic elevation in the thrill. The impression left is one of a pleasurable sadness.— POE, EDGAR ALLAN, 1850, *The Poetical Principle, Works*, ed. Stedman and Woodberry, vol. VI, p. 16.

He is a sentimental and descriptive poet, neither rising into passion nor prompted to deep reflection; but his thoughts flow naturally and easily, his imagery is often fine, and his pathos as often quite touching. His blank verse is of rare excellence; and his diction, always refined, is sometimes very felicitous. He never fulfilled the promise of genius held out by his youthful "Thanatopsis;" but his most ambitious composition, "The Ages," is a beautiful representation of gentle fancy and kindly sympathy; and among his smaller pieces, if there be no decisive originality, there is an ideality of taste which has produced some lyrical gems—such as the "Hymn to the North Star," and the verses "To a Waterfowl." He produced, in his seventy-sixth year, a book of Eastern Travel, and a blank-verse translation of Homer's "Iliad," of considerable merit.—SPALDING, WILLIAM, 1852, *A History of English Literature*, p. 382.

Bryant has created nothing great; his voice is feeble, melodious, somewhat vague; but pure, solemn, and not imitative. More philosophic than picturesque, the expression of melancholy sensations, born of forest and lake, finds a sweet echo in his verse. The sublime is not his territory; his peculiar charm is chaste and pensive sadness, which associates itself with natural objects and the beings of the creation; he loves them, and the modest piety mingled with this affection, breathes a pathetic grace upon his verse. Christian and English poet, the gentle solemnity of his poetry emanates from his religious conviction. . . . Bryant by his contemplative gentleness and gravity reminds one of Klopstock; fantasy and free caprice are found in neither.—CHASLES, PHILARÈTE, 1852, *Anglo-American Literature and Manners*, pp. 186, 191.

The only fault we have to find with Mr. Bryant is that he has written so little, and has chosen to scatter his brilliance amidst a constellation of little poetic stars, rather than to concentrate the light of his genius in some immortal work, which should shine as a planet in the literary horizon to the latest generation.—ALLIBONE, S. AUSTIN, 1854–58, *A Critical Dictionary of English Literature*, vol. I, p. 271.

His present eminence among all parties, as the unquestioned first poet of the country, has been gained by him in connection with a career which has its daily trials and temptations,—a career which no one but an experienced editor of a newspaper would be likely fully to appreciate. Let me call the attention of the brother poets who are to celebrate his birthday to the undimmed lustre of the laurels worn so long. . . . For him to have thus set himself the task, and come from it as does Bryant,— the acknowledged most independently reliable editor, as well as the irreproachable first poet, is an example not given us by the ancients.—WILLIS, NATHANIEL PARKER, 1864, *Letter to the Century Club on Bryant's Seventieth Birthday, William Cullen Bryant by John Bigelow*, p. 229.

The voices of the hills did his obey;
The torrents flashed and tumbled in his song;
He brought our native fields from far away,
Or set us mid the innumerable throng
Of dateless woods, or where we heard the calm
Old homestead's evening psalm.
But now he sang of faith of things unseen,
Of freedom's birthright given to us in trust,
And words of doughty cheer he spoke between,
That made all earthly fortune seem as dust,
Matched with that duty, old as time and new,
Of being brave and true.
We listening, learned what makes the might of words—
Manhood to back them, constant as a star;
His voice rammed home our cannon, edged our swords,
And sent our borders shouting; shround and spar
Heard him and stiffened; the sails heard and wooed
The winds with loftier mood.
In our dark hour he manned our guns again;
Remanned ourselves from his own manhood's store;
Pride, honor, country, throbbed through all his strain;
And shall we praise? God's praise was his before;
And on our futile laurels he looks down,
Himself our bravest crown.
—LOWELL, JAMES RUSSELL, 1864, *On Board the Seventy-six, Nov. 3*.

I join with all my heart in your wish to honor this native, sincere, original, patriotic poet. I say original; I have heard him charged with being of a certain school. I heard it with surprise, and asked, What school? for he never reminded me of Goldsmith, or Wordsworth, or Byron, or Moore. I found him always original—a true painter of the face of this country, and of the sentiment of his own people. When I read the verses of popular American and English poets, I often think that they appear to have gone into the art galleries and to have seen pictures of mountains, but this man to have seen mountains. With his stout staff he has climbed Greylock and the White Hills, and sung what he saw. He renders Berkshire to me in verse, with the sober coloring, too, to which nature cleaves, only now and then permitting herself the scarlet and gold of the prism. It is his proper praise that he first, and he only, made known to mankind our northern landscape —its summer splendor, its autumn russet, its winter lights and glooms. And he is original because he is sincere.—EMERSON, RALPH WALDO, 1864, *Address Before the*

Century Club on Bryant's Seventieth Birthday.

It will perhaps take a little time, but should not take more than a little, for poetical students fresh from the poetry of to-day to adjust themselves properly to the study of such poems as these. Instead of a style "bourré par l'idée à en craquer," and subjects fetched from all heaven and earth, they will find a singularly simple and straightforward fashion of verse, dealing mainly with one theme and satisfied with that. With the mechanism of his art the poet apparently troubles himself very little, or conceals his efforts very cunningly. There is scarcely a new or unusual metrical effect throughout the book; the language is as little studied as the versification; and the subjects, however various, are generally treated in such a manner as to come very much under one head. But it would be a very great mistake to suppose that these poems, because they lack certain characteristics more or less effective, are either monotonous or trivial. . . . From his earliest poems, the "Waterfowl," the oddly named "Thanatopsis," and the rest, to those of only a year or two ago, he observes the worship of nature with no diminished zeal and no diminished power. Very rarely has any writer preserved such an even level of merit throughout his poems, the absence of any particularly absorbing theme being compensated by the steady attention which he pays to his one subject. —SAINTSBURY, GEORGE, 1874, *Bryant's Poems, The Academy, vol. 5, p. 84.*

William Cullen Bryant is able to hear the great harmony of nature in her gentlest and in her most powerful tones. But he paints by preference the quiet life of nature and of man, and the depth of his feeling enables him to find the most precious pearls of songs in the simplest scenes. Such are the "Indian's Complaint at the Graves of his Fathers" and the "Song of the Pitcairn Islander." His poetry much resembles that of Cowper and Gray, but there is such a specifically American tone in it that he has been rightly called the first original poet of his country.—SCHERR, J., 1874, *A History of English Literature, p. 301.*

The father of the present generation of American poets, and one of the most original of the brotherhood.—CHAMBERS, ROBERT, 1876, *Cyclopædia of English Literature, ed. Carruthers.*

Of course it would be absurd to rank Bryant with Wordsworth, but he was something more than a copy on a small scale of one side of a great poet. He sees that what is the whole of life to Wordsworth is only a part of his life and of the life of the world. And his preoccupation with death and with the transitoriness of life gives him an originality of his own. . . . His date and his nationality save him from being classed with English minor poets; they are always straining at the unattainable or else sinking back in conscious depression; whereas the sober dignity natural to Bryant was sustained by the consciousness that all his life he was one of the first poets of his age and country.— SIMCOX, GEORGE AUGUSTUS, 1878, *The Academy, vol.* 13, *p.* 556.

To Bryant, beyond all other modern poets, the earth was a theatre upon which the great drama of life was everlastingly played. . . . The qualities by which Mr. Bryant's poetry are chiefly distinguished are serenity and gravity of thought; an intense though repressed recognition of the morality of mankind; an ardent love for human freedom; an unrivalled skill in painting the scenery of his native land. He had no superior in his walk of poetic art—it might almost be said no equal, for his descriptions of nature are never inaccurate or redundant. "The Excursion" is a tiresome poem, which contains several exquisite episodes. Mr. Bryant knew how to write exquisite episodes, and to omit the platitudes through which we reach them in other poets.—STODDARD, RICHARD HENRY, 1878, *Poetical Works of William Cullen Bryant, Household Ed., p.* XXII.

His poetry kept its essential intelletual type, and did not glow with passion or burn with martial fire. He had neither epic fulness, nor dramatic compass and force. . . . He was in his way scholastic in poetry, a disciple of his own set school; and with his wonderful sense of beauty he never ventures to lose his calmness or in any way to be unwise. He never said a foolish thing, and rarely, if ever, did an unwise one. Even love, which makes so many men fools, made him thoughtful; and his one sacred love went forth in calm idyls and rose into godly hymns, and never burned with wasting fires. . . . His poetry was little personal, and shy of men and women, he was more at home, especially in earlier life, with Nature.—OSGOOD, SAMUEL, 1878, *Address at the Memorial Meeting of the Goethe Club, Oct.* 30.

That "rock-loving columbine" is better than Bryant's "columbines in purple dressed," as our flower is not purple, but yellow and scarlet. Yet Bryant set the example to the poets that have succeeded him of closely studying Nature as she appears under her own skies. I yield to none in my admiration of the sweetness and simplicity of his poems of nature, and in general of their correctness of observation. They are tender and heartfelt, and they touch chords that no other poet since Wordsworth has touched with so firm a hand. Yet he was not always an infallible observer; he sometimes tripped upon his facts, and at other times he deliberately moulded them, adding to, or cutting off, to suit the purposes of his verse.—BURROUGHS, JOHN, 1879-95, *Nature and the Poets, Pepacton, p.* 90.

His last word, as his first, was Liberty!
His last word, as his first, for Truth
Struck to the heart of age and youth:
He sought her everywhere,
In the loud city, forest, sea and air:
He bowed to wisdom other than his own,
To wisdom and to law,
Concealed or dimly shown
In all he knew not, all he knew and saw,
Trusting the Present, tolerant of the Past,
Firm-faithed in what shall come
When the vain noises of these days are dumb;
And his first word was noble as his last!
—TAYLOR, BAYARD, 1879, *Epicedium, William Cullen Bryant, Scribner's Monthly* vol. 17, *p.* 336.

"Bryant's sonnets are so few that I could repeat them all without wearying you; but as you are already familiar with them, I shall merely specialize several in the line wherein he excels all our modern poets, namely, the loving and reverent worship and interpretation of Nature in her serenest moods. I allude particularly to his sonnets on 'Midsummer,' 'October,' and 'November;' and, as I read them, give attention to the exceeding delicacy and minuteness of their detail coupled with their breadth and largeness, and also to the warmth and sober richness of their coloring. I have read them a hundred times, but never without discovering some new beauty to be enjoyed, or without marvelling at the power of dilatation and contraction of poetic vision, and the extraordinary poetic sensibility, which have made descriptions so glowing and so true possible to be transferred to words within a scope so limited. . . . Bryant and Whittier belong to different grades as artists, though both are pre-eminently gifted with quick poetic sensibility, and the faculty of picturesque poetic utterance. Bryant's imagination is the loftiest; his conceptions are grander, his thoughts more exalted, his style purer, his powers of generalization greater, his coloring firmer and truer than Whittier's."—DESHLER, CHARLES D., 1879, *Afternoons with the Poets, pp.* 290, 292.

Bryant pulsing the first interior verse-throbs of a mighty world—bard of the river and the wood, ever conveying a taste of open air, with scents as from hayfields, grapes, birch-borders—always lurkingly fond of threnodies—beginning and ending his long career with chants of death, with here and there through all, poems, or passages of poems, touching the highest universal truths, enthusiasms, duties—morals as grim and eternal, if not as stormy and fateful, as anything in Eschylus.—WHITMAN, WALT, 1881, *Autobiographia, April* 16.

His life, public and private, was in keeping with his speech and writings. We often say of a poet or artist that he should not be judged like other men by his outward irrelevant mark or habit; that to see his best, his truest self you must read his poems or study his paintings. In reading Bryant's prose and verse, and in observing the poet himself, our judgments were the same. He always held in view liberty, law, wisdom, piety, faith; his sentiment was unsentimental; he never whined nor found fault with condition or nature; he was robust, but not tyrannical; frugal, but not too severe; grave, yet full of shrewd and kindly humor. Absolute simplicity characterized him. Ethics were always in sight. He was, indeed, an "old man for counsel;" but he learned in youth from the lives and precepts of Washington, Hamilton, and their compeers, that he taught and practised to the last. His intellectual faculties, like his physical, were balanced to the discreetest level, and this without abasing his poetic fire. His genius was not shown by the advance of one faculty and the impediment of others; it was the spirit of an even combination, and a fine one. . . . The delights of nature, and meditations upon the universality of life and death, withdrew him from the study of the individual world. Thus he became a philosophic minstrel of the woods and waters, the foremost of American landscape poets. . . . No doubt Bryant's models confirmed his natural restrictions of speech. But even this narrow verbal range has made his poetry strong and pure; and now, when expression has been carried to its extreme, it is an occasional relief to recur to the clearness, to the exact appreciation of words, discoverable in every portion of his verse and prose. It is like a return from a florid renaissance to the antique; and indeed there was something Doric in Bryant's nature. His diction, like his thought, often refreshes us as the shadow of a great rock in a weary land. . . . Give his poems a study, and their simplicity is their charm.—STEDMAN, EDMUND CLARENCE, 1885, *Poets of America, pp.* 64, 67, 77.

The life of William Cullen Bryant is an integral part of American literature. His long, honorable career as a journalist and citizen have also identified him with the best interets of his native land. In the later years of his life he wrote quite a number of hymns. . . . His religious views also ripened and grew more spiritual as he neared the grave.—DUFFIELD, SAMUEL WILLOUGHBY, 1886, *English Hymns, p.* 43.

Bryant's genius is not seen to best advantage in his "Wild-Life" poems. It is in meditation verse, such as the "Thanatopsis" and "Lines to a Waterfowl," that the majesty and grave eloquence which characterise his genius become most readily apparent. —ROBERTS, CHARLES G. D., 1888, *ed. Poems of Wild Life, p.* 231, *note.*

His place was with Gray, not with Milton, Goethe, Browning, or Burns. Intense power was not his, nor broad creative range, nor soaring vision; his marks were thoughtfulness and serenity.— RICHARDSON, CHARLES F., 1888, *American Literature,* 1607–1885, *vol.* II, *p.* 40.

Bryant appears to me to be a poet of a less attractive but somewhat higher class than Longfellow. His versification is mannered, and his expressions are directly formed on European models, but his sense of style was so consistent that his careful work came to be recognisable. His poetry is a hybrid of two English stocks, closely related; he belongs partly to the Wordsworth of "Tintern Abbey," partly to the Coleridge of "Mont Blanc." The imaginative formula is Wordsworth's, the verse is the verse of Coleridge, and having in very early youth produced this dignified and novel flower, Bryant did not try to blossom into anything different, but went on cultivating the Coleridge-Wordsworth hybrid down to the days of Rossetti and of Villanelles. But Wordsworth and Coleridge had not stayed at the "Mont Blanc" and "Tintern Abbey" point. They went on advancing, developing, altering, and declining to the end of their days. The consequence is that the specimens of the Bryant variety do not strike us as remarkably like the general work of Wordsworth or of Coleridge. . . . He is exquisitely polished, full of noble suavity and music, but his irreparable fault is to be secondary, to remind us always of his masters first, and only on reflection of himself.—GOSSE, EDMUND, 1889, *Has America Produced a Poet? Questions at Issue, pp.* 83, 84.

Of Bryant's rank and merits as a poet there is, and for some time to come is likely to be, a great diversity of opinion. A partial explanation of this may be found in the fact that the most enduring qualities of his verse are readily appreciated by only a comparatively restricted class even of those who read poetry. He was essentially an ethical poet. His inspiration was always from above. In the flower, in the stream, in the tempest, in the rainbow, in the snow, in everything about him, nature was always telling him something new of the goodness of God and framing excuses for the frail and the erring. His verses are the record of these lessons as far as he apprehended and could express them. The number who comprehend the full force of them at a single reading, however, is comparatively small. Every one of his verses will bear the supreme test of a work of literary art, which discloses a wider horizon and new merits at each successive perusal. . . . As water in crystallizing excludes all foreign ingredients, and out of acids, alkalies, and other solutions yields a crystal of perfect purity and sweetness, so his thoughts in passing into verse seemed to separate themselves from everything that was transient or vulgar. His poems have come to us as completely freed from every trace of what is of the earth earthy as if, like St. Luke's pictures, they had received their finishing touch from the angels.—BIGELOW

JOHN, 1890, *William Cullen Bryant (American Men of Letters), pp* 140, 153.

My first romantic love of nature was awakened by the poems of William Cullen Bryant, then in the zenith of their popularity. There was something tangible in the pictures that he drew; his themes pointed out the charms of the woods and the mountains and the fields, which were all about me—before my eyes on every side. The distinguished poet was our neighbor, or, to be more exact, his birthplace was on a picturesque hillside in sight of my own birthplace, and he usually came to the old homestead every Summer. When a boy, he attended school with my father, and I had asked so many questions about how he looked in his youth and what he said and did, that I almost fancied I had actually seen him write "Thanatopsis."—LAMB, MARTHA J., 1891, *Formative Influences, The Forum, vol.* 11, *p.* 53.

His vocabulary was limited; his poetry was frigid. To be stirred by it is, in the words of Lowell, "like being stirred up by the very North Pole." It had little capacity for growth, and was at its best before the poet was out of his teens. But it had great virtues. Written in classic English, imbued with great dignity of thought and feeling, pervaded with what Wordsworth has called the "religion of the woods"—the devout and solemn reverence for the invisible powers of nature—its manly reserve and repose elevated not only his countrymen's ideals of literary excellence, but their ideals of life as well.— MABIE, HAMILTON W., 1892, *The Memorial Story of America, p.* 588.

Mr. Bryant was a wonderful worker; not only was his editorial industry remarkable, but his contributions to our American literature, both in prose and verse, afford abundant evidence of the fact. He was an accomplished student of the literature of many languages, and while his translations from other tongues are so felicitous that his fellow-master, Longfellow, praised some of his Spanish translations as rivalling the originals in beauty, yet his own verse is as free from the merely literary influence or reminiscence as the pure air of his native hills from the perfume of exotics. His last considerable poem, "The Flood of Years," but echoes in its meditative flow the solemn cadences of "Thanatopsis."—SAUNDERS, FREDERICK, 1894, *Character Studies, p.* 140.

Bryant is one of the few poets of genuine power whose poetic career shows no advance. The first arrow he drew from his quiver was the best, and with it he made his longest shot; many others he sent in the same direction, but they all fell behind the first. This accounts for the singleness and the depth of the impression he has left; he stands for two or three elementals, and thereby keeps his force unscattered. He was not, indeed, wholly insensible to the romanticist stirrings of his time, as such effusions as "The Damsel of Peru," "The Arctic Lover," and "The Hunter's Serenade," bear witness. He wrote several pieces about Indians—not the real red men, but those imaginary noble savages, possessors of all the primitive virtues, with whom our grandfathers peopled the American forests. He wrote strenuously in behalf of Greek emancipation and against slavery, but even here, though the subject lay very near his heart, he could not match the righteous vehemence of Whittier, or Lowell's alternate volleys of sarcasm and rebuke. Like Antæus, Bryant ceased to be powerful when he did not tread his native earth.— THAYER, WILLIAM R., 1894, *Bryant's Centennial, The Review of Reviews, vol.* 10, *p.* 406.

Bryant's genius was at its best in passages imaginatively descriptive of external loveliness, rather than in those expressive of moods and feelings when the spirit is aspiring or analytically reflective. His true strength lay in his powers of vivid delineation, in the art which could bring distinctly to mind, with a few graphic strokes, the rushing vehemence of the stream or the waterfall; the boundless stretch of the prairie magnificence; the terrors of the hurricane, no less than the gentle sweetness of the evening wind, as it "rocks the little wood-bird in his nest," or "curls the still waters bright with stars," or goes forth as "God's blessing breathed upon the fainting earth." His genius lingers lovingly over the splendours of mountain and valley scenery, as if at home with the sublimities of the "beetling verge" where storm and lightning "have tumbled down vast blocks, and at the base dashed them into fragments;" or where "upon the meadow's breast the shadow of the thicket lies." With these and similar scenes of natural charm Bryant's poetry abounds; but with regard to that mysterious land of spiritual longing and contemplation towards which the loftiest thoughts of man turn wistfully, his conceptions are limited and prescribed. Although his poetry is full of reference to the highest subjects which can engage the mind, these are all viewed from one standpoint. His spirit is enlisted on the affirmative side of the problem, and in every line that he has written we feel the influence of the faith of one who believes in Divine goodness ruling the universe.—BRADFIELD, THOMAS, 1895, *William Cullen Bryant, Westminster Review, vol.* 143, *p.* 90.

It is as a poet, and especially by a few distinctive compositions, that Bryant will be most widely and deeply held in remembrance. . . . Bryant's venerable aspect in old age—with erect form, white hair, and flowing snowy beard—gave him a resemblance to Homer; and there was something Homeric about his influence upon the literature of his country, in the dignity with which he invested the poetic art and the poet's relation to the people.— LATHROP, GEORGE PARSONS, 1897, *Library of the World's Best Literature, ed. Warner, vol.* v, *pp.* 2626, 2627.

Bryant's poems inevitably bring Wordsworth to our minds, yet it seems unfair to Bryant's talents to measure their increase by comparison with the fruits of Wordsworth's genius. Bryant's lot took him to the city, to newspapers and daily cares, while Wordsworth sauntered contemplative over Helvellyn and along the margin of Windermere. Great poetry has never been written by a man who was not able to give to it his concentrated thought and his whole heart. Chaucer, Shakespeare, Spenser, Pope, Wordsworth, Shelley, Byron, all the great poets of England have given undivided allegiance to poetry. Bryant could not do so, and his poems bear the marks of his involuntary disloyalty. A poet must be judged by his achievement alone. Bryant's verses, except at their best, show a lack of art. They are a little undisciplined; they betray truancy to the classics.—SEDGWICK, HENRY D., JR., 1897, *Bryant's Permanent Contribution to Literature, Atlantic Monthly, vol.* 79, *p.* 541.

Bryant's poetry is stately, lofty, clear. A man of practiced self-control, who from childhood to the day of his death rose early, ate sparingly, exercised regularly, his verse is equally subject to rule. No impetuous measures broke from his pen. Respect for law and order, personal reserve, and coldness of temperament are so far from being the traditional make-up of a poet that it is no wonder the critics are puzzled. —BATES, KATHARINE LEE, 1897, *American Literature, p.* 140.

By reason of his long-continued life, Bryant seems nearer to our own day than, as a poet, he really is. Historically he must be remembered as the first of American poets,—first in poetry as Irving was first in one form of prose, and Cooper in another. The body of his poetic work is small, and the greater portion of it is manifestly destined to be forgotten.— HOWE, M. A. DE-WOLFE, 1898, *American Bookmen, p.* 75.

Above and beyond all, he was nature's evangelist to man. He caught the spirit of the messages whispered by the trees, sung by the river and chanted by the sea. Trees and flowers, the forest and the prairies, the clouds, the sky and the stars, the sea, the tides, and the winds, the thunder-storm and the hurricane, spoke to him a "various language," which he interpreted to his fellow-men.—ONDERDONK, JAMES L., 1899–1901, *History of American Verse, p.* 177.

As one looks through his work, however, one is apt to wonder whether, even if his life had been destitute of personal bereavement, his verse might not still have hovered sentimentally about the dead. His most successful poem, "Thanatopsis," was apparently written before death had often come near him; and it is hardly excessive to say that if a single name were sought for his collected works, from beginning to end, a version of that barbarous Greek title might be found suitable, and the whole volume fairly entitled "Glimpses of the Grave." Of course he touched on other things; but he touched on mortality so constantly as to make one feel regretfully sure that whenever he felt stirred to poetry his fancy started for the Valley of the Shadow of Death.—WENDELL, BARRETT, 1900, *A Literary History of America, p* 200.

Bryant was not of a cold nature, but, on the contrary, a very passionate one, which he had learned to control perfectly, and I always had an impression from certain expressions in his poems that he had, in the past, suffered greatly from uncontrolled passion, and had found the necessity of great restraint. . . . I think that the apparent coldness in his verse was really due to his having learned to avoid passionate expression as treacherous, and liable to lead to repentance. His only safety was in the most supreme self-control. — STILLMAN, WILLIAM JAMES, 1901, *Letter to the Editor, Academy,* vol. 60, p. 130.

Bayard Taylor
1825–1878

Born at Kennett Square, Chester County, Pa., Jan. 11, 1825; died at Berlin, Dec. 19, 1878. An American poet, traveler, writer of travels, translator, and novelist. He was named after James A. Bayard, and in early life sometimes signed himself "J. Bayard Taylor." He was apprenticed to a printer in 1842. He traveled on foot in Great Britain, Germany, Switzerland, Italy, France, etc., 1844–46, writing letters to American papers; was connected with the New York "Tribune," and its correspondent in California 1849–50; and traveled in Egypt, Asia Minor, Syria and Europe 1851–52, and in Spain, India, China and Japan 1852–53, joining Perry's expedition in Japan. On his return, having traveled more than fifty thousand miles, he began his series of lectures. He traveled in Germany, Norway, and Lapland in 1855; traveled later in Greece, etc.; was secretary of legation and chargé d'affaires at St. Petersburg 1862-63; resided afterward on the Continent; visited Egypt and Iceland in 1874; and was appointed United States minister at Berlin 1878. His principal works are "Ximena, etc." (1844: poems), "Views Afoot" (1846), "Rhymes of Travel" (1849), "Eldorado, or Adventures in the Path of Empire" (1850), "Book of Romances, Lyrics, and Songs" (1851), "A Journey to Central Africa" (1854), "The Lands of the Saracen" (1854), "Poems and Ballads" (1854), "A Visit to India, China, and Japan" (1855), "Poems of the Orient" (1855), "Poems of Home and Travel" (1855), "Northern Travel" (1857), "Travels in Greece, etc." (1859), "At Home and Abroad" (1859-62), "The Poet's Journal" (1862), "Hannah Thurston" (1863: a novel), "John Godfrey's Fortunes" (1864), "The Story of Kennett" (1866), "Colorado" (1867), "Byways of Europe" (1869), "Joseph and his Friend" (1870), "The Masque of the Gods" (1872), "Beauty and the Beast" (1872), "Lars, etc." (1873), "School History of Germany to 1871" (1874), "Egypt and Iceland" (1874), "The Prophet" (1874: a tragedy of Mormonism), "Home Pastorals" (1875), "The Echo Club, and other Literary Diversions" (1876), "Boys of Other Countries" (1876), "The National Ode" (1876), "Prince Deucalion" (1878), "Studies in German Literature" (1879), "Critical Essays, etc." (1880), and "Dramatic Works" (1880: with notes by M. H. Taylor), He edited Tegner's "Frithjofs Saga" in 1867 (translated by Blackley), and translated Goethe's "Faust" in the original meters (1870–71).—SMITH, BENJAMIN E., *ed.* 1894–97, *Century Cyclopædia of Names,* p. 981.

PERSONAL

Here too, of answering love secure,
Have I not welcomed to my hearth
The gentle pilgrim troubadour,
Whose songs have girdled half the earth;
Whose pages, like the magic mat
Whereon the Eastern lover sat,
Have borne me over Rhine-land's purple vines,
And Nubia's tawny sands, and Phrygia's mountain pines!
—WHITTIER, JOHN GREENLEAF, 1856, *The Last Walk in Autumn,* st. XV.

Here under the flowers that grew in German soil, lies the mortal frame tenanted for fifty-three years by the richly-endowed genius whom men knew as Bayard Taylor. Thy name will be spoken by coming generations, who never looked into thy kindly, winning face, never grasped thy faithful hand, never heard a word from thy eloquent lips. Yet no: the breath of the mouth is exhaled and lost, but thy word, thy poet-word, is abiding. On behalf of those whom thou hast left behind, urged by my affection as thy oldest friend in the Old World, as thou didst often call me, and as a representative of German literature, I send after thee loving words of farewell. What thou hast become and shalt continue to be in the realms of mind, after ages will determine. Today our hearts are thrilled with grief and lamentation, and yet with exaltation too. . . . As from one power to another, so wast thou the accredited envoy from one realm of mind to another, and even in thy latest work thou dost show that thou livedst in that religion which embraces all confessions, and takes not the name of one to the exclusion of the rest. Nature gave thee a form full of grace and power, a spirit full of clearness and chaste cheerfulness, and the grace of melodious speech to set forth the movements and emotions springing from the eternal and never-fathomed source of being, as well as from the fleeting and never-exhausted joys of wedded and paternal love, of friendship, of the inspiration of nature, of patriotism, and of the ever-ascending revelations of human history.—AUERBACH, BERTHOLD, 1878, *Remarks at the American Embassy, Dec. 22; Life and Letters of Bayard Taylor, ed. Taylor and Scudder, vol.* II, *pp.* 766, 767.

> Dead he lay among his books!
> The peace of God was in his looks.
> As the statues in the gloom
> Watch o'er Maximilian's tomb,
> So those volumes from their shelves
> Watched him, silent as themselves.
> Ah! his hand will nevermore
> Turn their storied pages o'er;
> Nevermore his lips repeat
> Songs of theirs, however sweet.
> . . . .
> Thou hast sung, with organ tone,
> In Deukalion's life, thine own;
> On the ruins of the Past
> Blooms the perfect flower at last.
> Friend! but yesterday the bells
> Rang for thee their loud farewells;
> And to-day they toll for thee,
> Lying dead beyond the sea;
> Lying dead among thy books,
> The peace of God in all thy looks!

—LONGFELLOW, HENRY WADSWORTH, 1878, *Bayard Taylor, Ultima Thule.*

Bayard Taylor's death slices a huge cantle out of the world for me. I don't yet *know* it, at all; it only seems that he has gone to some other Germany, a little farther off. How strange it all is: he was such a fine fellow, one almost thinks he might have talked Death over and made him forego his stroke.—LANIER, SIDNEY, 1878, *To Gibson Peacock, Dec. 21; Letters, p.* 58.

No one could possibly look upon the manly young fellow at that time (1847), without loving him. He was tall and slight, with the bloom of youth mantling a face full of eager, joyous expectation. Health of that buoyant nature which betokens delight in existence was visible in every feature of the youthful traveler.

"The fresh air lodged within his cheek
As light within a cloud."

We all flocked about him like a swarm of brothers, heartily welcoming him to Boston. When we told him how charmed we all were with his travels, he blushed like a girl, and tears filled his sensitive eyes. "It is one of the most absorbingly interesting books I ever read!" cried one of our number, heightening the remark with an expletive savoring of strength more than of early piety. Taylor looked up, full of happiness at the opinion so earnestly expressed, and asked, with that simple naïveté which always belonged to his character, "Do you really think so? Well, I am so glad!"—FIELDS, JAMES T., 1878, *New York Tribune, Dec.* 24.

> In other years—lost youth's enchanted years,
> Seen now, and evermore, through blinding tears
> And empty longing for what may not be—
> The Desert gave him back to us; the Sea
> Yielded him up; the icy Norland strand
> Lured him not long, nor that soft German air
> He loved could keep him. Ever his own land
> Fettered his heart and brought him back again.
> What sounds are these of farewell and despair
> Borne on the winds across the wintry main!
> What unknown way is this that he is gone,
> Our Bayard, in such silence and alone?
> What new strange quest has tempted him once more
> To leave us? Vainly, standing by the shore,
> We strain our eyes. But patience! when the soft
> Spring gales are blowing over Cedarcroft,
> Whitening the hawthorne; when the violets bloom
> Along the Brandywine, and overhead
> The sky is blue as Italy's, he will come. . .
> In the wind's whisper, in the swaying pine,
> In song of bird and blossoming of vine,
> And all fair things he loved ere he was dead!

—ALDRICH, THOMAS BAILEY, 1878, *Bayard Taylor.*

He spoke of his appointment to Berlin, in the tone of a man who was modestly conscious of his worth; who knew that the distinction, brilliant as it was, had been fair earned, but who was none the less grateful for it. He knew that he was fit for the place, and that the honor bestowed on him was one to which he in turn was able to do honor. He had a just pride in hearing his name associated with the names of Irving, of Motley, of Marsh, of Lowell,—one and all men who had earned their fame in literature before they became diplomatists. He was far too frank and open-natured to care to hide his pleasure. With all his varied and ample experience, with all his knowledge of the world and mastery of social conventionalities, Mr. Taylor retained to the last a certain freshness and candor in expressing his inmost feelings, which belongs only to those souls that have no mean secrets to keep, no false pride or false modesty. He was pleased, and he was not ashamed of being pleased. It is only a man very sure of himself who can venture to take the world into his confidence as he did. Then, as often before, I thought it most honorable to him. It was consistent with great dignity of demeanor, and whoever fancied he could take advantage of it soon found out his mistake. He submitted readily and generously to all sorts of slight impositions. He gave five francs for some service which fifty centimes would have rewarded amply. He would never look too closely into matters where only his own interest was at stake, but where others were concerned, where it was his business to defend interests which had been confided to him, he could be hard, astute, immovable. That was one of his peculiar merits as a minister. In most points no two men could be more unlike than Mr. Taylor and Prince Bismarck, but they had this in common: that they told the truth fearlessly, and found it served their purpose where the most ingenious mystifications would have failed of their end.—SMALLEY, G. W., 1879, *New York Tribune.*

Ah then — farewell, young-hearted, genial friend!
Farewell, true poet, who didst grow and build
From thought to thought still upward and still new.
Farewell, unsullied toiler in a guild
Where others defile their hands, and where so few
With aims as pure strive faithful to the end.
—CRANCH, CHRISTOPHER P., 1879, *Scribner's Monthly, vol. 17, p. 731.*

To think of him is to recall a person larger in make and magnanimity than the common sort; a man of indescribable buoyancy, hopefulness, sweetness of temper, — reverent, loyal, shrinking from contention yet ready to do battle for a principle or in the just cause of a friend; a patriot and lover of his kind, stainless in morals, and of an honesty so pure and simple that he could not be surprised into an untruth or the commission of a mean and unworthy act. — STEDMAN, EDMUND CLARENCE, 1879, *Bayard Taylor, Scribner's Monthly, vol. 19, p. 89.*

People who knew Bayard Taylor but superficially were apt to accuse him of what they were pleased to call literary vanity. To me this charge seems to be based upon an imperfect comprehension of the rare simplicity and earnestness of the man. Of course he believed in himself and in his own poetic mission, and he was not disposed to admit into the circle of his more intimate friends any one who questioned the genuiness of his poetic talent. But who likes to have his merits questioned in his own presence? and who chooses his friends among his hostile critics? It is not to be denied that the conventional code of etiquette requires that a man should deprecate his own worth, and, especially in the case of an author, that he should put a very modest estimate upon his own productions. Bayard Taylor was too frank and honest to conform to this rule. If you told him that you thought his "Pæan to the Dawn" in the "Songs of the Orient" was a wonderful poem, his fine eyes would light up with pleasure, and he would describe too in vivid colors the situation which had suggested the song to him.—BOYESEN, HJALMAR H., 1879, *Reminiscences of Bayard Taylor, Lippincott's Magazine, vol. 24, p. 211.*

Never can I forget the conversation between Carlyle and Bayard Taylor, when the latter visited London on his way to take his place as minister at Berlin. Several years before, Bayard had called upon Carlyle, and audaciously announced that he meant to write the life of Goethe. The old man could not allow any such liberties taken with his literary hero without a challenge, and set a sort of trap for this ambitious American. "But," said he, "are there not already Lives of Goethe? There is Blank's Life of Goethe; what fault have you to find with that?" The tone was that Blank had exhausted the subject. Bayard immediately began showing the inadequacy and errors of Blank's book, and withal his own minute and critical knowledge of Goethe, when Carlyle broke out with a laugh, saying of the *Life* he had mentioned, "I couldn't read it through." From that moment he was cordial, and recognized the man before him.—CONWAY, MONCURE DANIEL, 1881, *Thomas Carlyle, p. 103.*

On the 17th a rapid change began, which was cruelly deceptive in its first form; for though his attendants knew the contrary, a sudden relief conveyed to Bayard Taylor the delusive hope that he had passed through a crisis and was now to get well. It was in reality a premonition of the immediate end. It was followed by extreme pain, which brought with it a bitter disappointment. On the 19th, after restlessness and wandering of mind, he was in his chair, where he now spent most of his time. His will flamed out in one final burst. "I want,"—he began, and found it impossible to make his want known or guessed until suddenly he broke forth, "I want, oh, you know what I mean, that *stuff of life!*" It was like Goethe's cry, the despair of one groping for that which had always been his in large measure. At two in the afternoon he fell asleep, and at four o'clock gently breathed his last.—TAYLOR, MARIE HANSEN, AND SCUDDER, HORACE E., 1884, *Life and Letters of Bayard Taylor, vol.* II, *p.* 765.

Passing from Taylor the author to Taylor the individual, we have in him a signal example of high, unspoiled manhood. His whole life was a practical epic, the keynote of which sounded the dignity of labor consecrated by ennobling ends. Self-trustful, with a healthy, well-poised mind, appreciating his own gifts, and knowing of what they were capable, he was still never arrogant or overbearing. As a companion, all who really knew, loved him. His heart dominated even his great intellect. —HAYNE, PAUL HAMILTON, 1884, *Bayard Taylor, The Andover Review, vol.* 2, *p.* 557.

Memory recalls to me that I was a schoolboy on College Hill, Poughkeepsie, when Taylor first lectured in that town, and when I first saw him at a supper party under my father's hospitable roof. He possessed what old Fuller quaintly called a "handsome man-case," and was, I think, the tallest of American poets, standing over six feet. Later in life he came to resemble a Teuton in look and bearing, and was greatly changed from my early recollections, when he possessed a slight figure and something of the Grecian type in head and face, as represented in an early portrait of him seated on the roof of a house in Damascus, painted by Thomas Hicks.—WILSON, JAMES GRANT, 1886, *Bryant and his Friends, p.* 356.

Bayard Taylor was at this period [about 1853] a bird of passage, on his way to other countries, and we did not see very much of him, though he spent an evening with us. But there are people whom you may like very much, and know to a considerable extent very quickly; and Bayard Taylor was I think one of these. He was quite a young man—not out of the "twenties" I am sure—and full of that hopeful enthusiasm and energy which are so becoming at that age. He had already travelled much and was planning further daring adventures. There was such an undercurrent of courage and chivalry about him that I have often thought how well suited to him was his Christian name. . . . In his youth Bayard Taylor was decidedly handsome, with a glow in his complexion which reminded one of his neighbors the Red Indians. He was tall and slim, with every limb expressive of agility.—CROSLAND, MRS. NEWTON (CAMILLA TOULMIN), 1893, *Landmarks of a Literary Life, pp.* 209, 210.

Taylor wrote with such rapidity that he could complete a duodecimo volume in a fortnight. His industry of hand was amazing. He seemed never to weary, and his handwriting was exceptionally neat and fine. A comparison of letters written in his seventeenth year and in his fiftieth shows almost no change of hand. His penmanship and his style were formed early and changed little. In the long manuscript of "Faust" there is scarcely a misformed or carelessly made letter. He was a genuine artist in black and white, and his highest happiness was to sit from morn till dewy eve, smoking a cigar that was not too good, and filling page after page with his neat chirography. A surprising instance is recorded of his facility and speed. In a night and a day he read Victor Hugo's voluminous "La Légende des Siècles," and wrote for the "Tribune" a review of it which fills eighteen pages of his "Essays and Literary Notes," and contains five considerable poems which are translations in the metre of the original.—SMYTH, ALBERT H., 1896, *Bayard Taylor (American Men of Letters), p.* 162.

POETRY

Ximena; | or | The Battle of the Sierra Morena | and | other Poems, | By James Bayard Taylor. | "I am a Youthful Traveler on the Way." | Henry Kirke White | Philadelphia:—Herman Hooker, 178 Chestnut Street | MDCCCXLIV. — TITLE PAGE TO FIRST EDITION, 1844.

My very soul revolts at such efforts (as the one I refer to) to depreciate such poems as Mr. Taylor's. Is there no honor—no chivalry left in the land? Are our most deserving writers to be forever sneered down, or hooted down, or damned down with faint praise, by a set of men who possess little other ability than that which assures temporary success to *them,* in common with Swaim's Panacea or Morrison's

Pills?— POE, EDGAR ALLAN, 1849, *Bayard Taylor, Works*, ed. Stedman and Woodberry, vol. VIII, p. 279.

He has written the tragedy of Mormonism, and taken Joe Smith and Brigham Young for his heroes. His experiment has not, to our taste, been remarkably successful, but it is creditable to his intellectual pluck. If he had succeeded, he would have achieved an extraordinary feat; but it must be confessed that, though we should certainly have boasted of his performance, we would not perhaps have admitted that he had attempted it at his peril. Of course Mr. Taylor has had in a measure to adapt his material to poetic conditions. He has changed the names of his personages, elaborated his plot, left certain details gracefully vague, and, for the most part, steered clear of local color. But his desire has evidently been to adhere to reality as much as was practically convenient and to enjoy whatever benefit there might be in leaving to his drama the savor of the soil. . . . It perturbs our faith a little to learn that the prophet is Mr. Joe Smith, and the *dénouement* is to be the founding of Salt Lake City by Mr. Brigham Young; we reflect that there is a magic in associations, and we are afraid that we scent vulgarity in these. But we are anxious to see what the author makes of them, and we grant that the presumption is in favor of his audacity. Mormonism we know to be a humbug and a rather nasty one. It needs at this time of day no "showing up," and Mr. Taylor has not wasted his time in making a poetical exposure. — JAMES, HENRY, 1875, *Taylor's Prophet, North American Review*, vol. 120, pp. 188, 189.

The richness of his vocabulary never impels him to sacrifice truth of representation to the transient effectiveness which is readily secured by indulgence in declamation. One sometimes wonders that the master of so many languages should be content to express himself with such rigid economy of word and phrase in the one he learned at his mother's knee. Among Taylor's minor poems it is difficult to select those which exhibit his genius at its topmost point. Perhaps "Camadeva" may be instanced as best showing his power of blending exquisite melody with serene, satisfying, uplifting thought. The song which begins with the invocation, "Daughter of Egypt, veil thine eyes!" is as good as could be selected from his many pieces to indicate the energy and healthiness of his lyric impulse. His longer poems would reward a careful criticism.—WHIPPLE, EDWIN PERCY, 1876-86, *American Literature and Other Papers*, ed. *Whittier*, p. 87.

Far be it from us to say he was not a poet. There are passages not a few in his books which would make it difficult to question his claim. Certainly he had a poetic mind. G. P. R. James described him as "the best landscape painter in words that he had ever known," and he was sometimes more than that. The poets of his own day—Longfellow, Whittier, and Bryant among them— regarded him as a poet, and his masterly translation of "Faust" is by itself almost enough to establish the position. Yet the world was so far right that he was something else in the first place, and a poet only in the second place.—LEWIN, WALTER, 1884, *Life and Letters of Bayard Taylor, The Academy*, vol. 26, p. 300.

His fanciful conceit that Shelley's spiritual influence had entered his own mind seems pardonable in one who, even before his acquaintance with the works of that poet, had voiced in his "Angel of the Soul" the same passionate appeal for the solution of life's mystery that Shelley had expressed in the introductory passage of his "Alastor " But while at even this early period his study of Shelley inspired him, and moved him to such songs as "The Ode to Shelley" and "Ariel in the Cloven Pine," it is but fair to point to another master-singer who might be said to have had, if not an equal, at the least a partial, influence on his lyrical expression. While in Germany he read, for the first time in the original, Schiller's poems. Appealing to his ear with their rhythmical beauty, they stirred his imagination, and through those early years of struggle for a "poetical individuality." as he himself termed it in letters of that time, there is in his verse the same exuberance of diction, the same fervor and passionate chase after the ideal, as is to be found in Schiller's "Poems of the First Period."— TAYLOR, MARIE, 1902, ed. *The Poetical Works of Bayard Taylor, Household Ed., Preface*, p. IV.

FAUST
1870–71

Your letter reached me on Tuesday last; the books on Friday. I go to bed usually as near ten as I can that I may rise at five;

your volumes kept me up till nearly two in the morning of Saturday; the like of which has not happened to me in five years. . . . The second part of "Faust" I studied seriously a year or two ago, using the commentary of Carrière. Your translation and notes would have saved me a world of trouble. You impart clearness to what is obscure, and give a thread of continuity to what might seem fantastic and unorganized. Here is seen the energy of Goethe's political feelings; his contempt for the follies and crimes of misgovernment of German princes was the sincere expression of the thoughts which he carried along with him all his life; only their vices were so deeply seated that he to the last appears to me to have despaired of German union.—BANCROFT, GEORGE, 1871, *To Bayard Taylor; Life and Letters of Bayard Taylor*, ed. Taylor and Scudder, vol. II, p. 562.

He was a poet. It may be said, indeed, that his poetic power lay at the foundation of all his linguistic attainments. He apprehended foreign speech and foreign life in all its forms through that poetic faculty which is of the nature of intuition. Not that labor was wanting, but labor served to bind and complete what had been caught at and appropriated by the appreciative and penetrative power of a poetic mind. Moreover, in the growth of his own nature, Bayard Taylor had come to think and create in sympathy with Goethe. No doubt the study which was given to "Faust" had much to do with the subsequent development of Bayard Taylor's genius, but it did not lay the foundation of that development; it came when from other causes his mind was ripe for Goethe's thought. When, therefore, he was absorbed in the work of translation, he was very far removed from a mechanical task, however delicate. On the contrary he was in a creative mood, constructing part by part a great poem which lay alongside of "Faust," singularly harmonious with the original, as all critics granted, because the harmony consisted in the very subtle likeness of the movement of his mind with that of Goethe's.—TAYLOR, MARIE HANSEN, AND SCUDDER, HORACE E., 1884, ed., *Life and Letters of Bayard Taylor*, vol. II, p. 556.

The scholarly character of this performance is now established. That to which more than one of his predecessors had given a lifetime, he apparently completed in three years. He had borne it in mind, however, for two decades, and it was his habit to think upon a task until able to execute it at a dash and with great perfection. The result was an advance upon any previous rendering of the entire work. . . . The characteristics of Taylor's "Faust" are sympathetic quality, rapid poetic handling, absolute fidelity to the text. Now and then his realistic version of the first part has an unusual or quaint effect, detracting from its imaginative design. — STEDMAN, EDMUND CLARENCE, 1885, *Poets of America*, pp. 422, 423.

VIEWS AFOOT
1844

The last chapter fills me with great wonder. How could you accomplish so much, with such slight help and appliances? It shows a strength of will—the central fire of all great deeds and words—that must lead you far in whatever you undertake.— LONGFELLOW, HENRY WADSWORTH, 1846, *Letter to Taylor*, Dec. 25

There is something which we like well in the title of this unpretending work; it is straightforward and expressive, suiting well with the character in which the writer presents himself to the world. . . . Most ancient men would say, that for a journeyman printer, without property, without friends, without encouragement, to undertake the tour of Europe, was the wildest of all human visions; and we doubt not that Mr. Taylor received rich presents of this kind of sympathy from those who knew his adventurous design. But those prudent and estimable persons were looking, all the while, to external advantages for the purpose, and making no account of inward resources; when experience shows that, whether to trudge through Europe, or to foot it through life,—for John Wesley says there is no carriage-road to heaven,— the strong mind and strong heart are more than a match for them all. . . . It is not necessary to give much account of a popular work like this, which is already in the hands of many, and which many more might read with profit and pleasure, not merely for the animated and intelligent account of most interesting countries which it contains, but for the example of energy in the pursuit of improvement here presented, without the self-complacency with which that bold trait of character is too often attended.—PEABODY, W. B. O., 1847, *Taylor's Views Afoot in Europe, North American Review*, vol. 64, *pp*. 483, 484, 499.

Then Bayard Taylor—protégé of Natty,
Dixon-like walked into the "literati!"
And first to proper use his genius put,
Like ballet-girls, by showing "Views Afoot!"
—DUGANNE, A. J. H., 1851, *Parnassus in Pillory*.

I say, then, most earnestly, to every youth anxious to go abroad, traverse Europe, and pay his way by writing for some journal, "Tarry at Jericho, till your beard be grown." I never knew but one of your class—Bayard Taylor—who achieved a real success in thus traveling; and he left home a good type-setter, with some knowledge of modern languages; so that he stopped and worked at his trade whenever his funds ran short; yet, even thus, he did not wholly pay his way during the two years he devoted to his delightful "Views Afoot." I know it, for I employed and paid him all that his letters were fairly worth, though not nearly so much as his letters *now* righteously command. He practiced a systematic and careful economy; yet he went away with money, and returned with the clothes on his back, and (I judge) very little more. My young friend, if you think yourself better qualified than he was go ahead, and "do" Europe! but don't ask me to further your scheme; for I hold that you may far better stay at home, apply yourself to some useful branch of productive industry, help pay our national debt, and accumulate a little independence whereon, by and by, to travel (if you chose) as a gentleman, and not with but a sheet of paper between you and starvation.—GREELEY, HORACE, 1868, *Recollections of a Busy Life*, p. 326.

The success of his book was undoubted, and was merited at the time, though it would attract but little attention now. If he had known more than he did, it would have been less interesting; he was lucky in not being too far ahead of his readers. He told them in a pleasant way of common things which were novelties to them. He was not accepted as a traveler among those who had traveled themselves. . . . He overlooked much that was important, and beheld too much that was merely trivial.—STODDARD, RICHARD HENRY, 1889, *Bayard Taylor, Lippincott's Magazine*, vol. 43, *p*. 572.

The poetic fervor of the book and its restrained vigor of style, the tenacity of purpose, the struggle, the courage, and the pluck that it revealed, fascinated the public, and sufficiently account for its great popularity.—SMYTH, ALBERT H., 1896, *Bayard Taylor (American Men of Letters)*, p. 50.

GENERAL

Putnam has sent us a few copies of your poems, and I cannot help writing a hasty line to say how grandly the ballads swell and tramp along, and how fine the other poems seem in this dress. Why, Bayard, man, you have done the thing in getting out this book. Your prefatory remarks I like hugely. George Lunt, to whom I handed the open book a few hours ago in the store, told me he had read and re-read your ballads over and over again, and knew not the hand that penned the lines. You have a capital reputation now in poetry, and must be careful of your muse. A good beginning is everything. I stand at a desk where I can gauge a man's depth in the public reading estimation, and I know no youngster who stands dearer than J. B. T., doffing the J.—FIELDS, JAMES T., 1848, *To Bayard Taylor, Dec.* 26; *Life and Letters of Bayard Taylor*, ed. Taylor and Scudder, vol. I, p. 139.

Were it only for his active life of enterprise and for the additions he has made to our knowledge, Mr. Taylor should be held in grateful esteem. His positive merits as a writer, however, deserve a warmer recognition. His descriptions are clearly and vividly portrayed, and his books are weighted with but little of the ordinary traveller's burden of unimportant personal details. They are interesting as mere narratives, and of permanent value for the facts they record. His Oriental poems have a natural warmth of color and vivacity of expression. He will be chiefly remembered, however, among poets, for his faithful and admirable translation of Faust, a work that testifies to his skill, poetic feeling, and mastery of expression.—UNDERWOOD, FRANCIS H., 1872, *A Hand-Book of English Literature, American Authors*, p. 518.

The author of this somewhat ante-dated volume is not unknown in Europe; in America not to know him is to proclaim oneself unknown. By turns, and sometimes all at once, he has figured as printer, journalist, dramatist, poet, special correspondent. That he has been a diplomatist we are almost certain; that he has figured as a tourist in every land under the sun, let the multitude of ephemeral travels which bear his name on the title-page testify. In a word, he is "one of the most remarkable men" of his country. But whether as a writer in the "Tribune," as translator of Goethe, as Bayard Taylor of Central Africa, Bayard Taylor of California, Bayard Taylor of Japan, or Bayard Taylor the Secretary of Legation, he has, while doing everything well, in none soared above respectable mediocrity.—BROWN, ROBERT, 1874, *Egypt and Iceland in 1874, Academy, vol.* 6, *p.* 649.

Taylor was too high a character, and he filled too large a place in our literature, to be subjected, in the helplessness of death, to the wrong of having his work tampered with, even by tender hands, devoted to fulfilling a purpose of his own. The master's hand is as stiff as the pencil which he held, his blood is as dry as the colors upon his palette: let the pupils stand before his unfinished work in the stillness of reverence; but let no one impose a tone or a tint upon the canvas, lest the world of today and the world of tomorrow should say that the picture is not his.—BOKER, GEORGE H., 1879, *Studies in German Literature, by Bayard Taylor, Introduction, p.* VIII.

He could roll off a poem on any subject to order. But it is mechanism. How, indeed, could he infuse life when he had no living faith or hope? Turning over these manifold poems, some of them of striking symmetry and finish, we confess to a feeling of sadness and disappointment. His poetry never took hold of the popular heart. His "Centennial Ode" was as great a failure as Sidney Lanier's. There is no thought, no soul, no *mens divinor* in it—a symphony of unmeaning sounds, but no inner music. He is best in his poetical descriptions of natural scenery. He had a good eye for this, and he manages to catch the expression. His translations are invariably good. Indeed, to speak phrenologically, he had imitation large but ideality small. So, too, the best reflections in his prose works are unconsciously copied from the vast stores of his reading, though he himself is perfectly honest. Still, he must pay the penalty of the versatile genius of the journalist in having most of his writings classed as ephemeral. — O'CONNOR, J. V., 1879, *Bayard Taylor, The Catholic World, vol.* 29, *p.* 115.

He brought us wonders of the new and old;
We shared all climes with him. The Arab's tent
To him its story-telling secret lent,
And, pleased, we listened to the tales he told.
His task, beguiled with songs that shall endure,
In manly, honest thoroughness he wrought;
From humble home-lays to the heights of thought
Slowly he climbed, but every step was sure.
—WHITTIER, JOHN GREENLEAF, 1881, *Bayard Taylor, The King's Missive and Other Poems.*

The value of "Hannah Thurston" as a bit of truthful local characterization has never been sufficiently acknowledged by the critics, while its defects as a work of art are plain. The life, at least, was distinctly American and local.—MORSE, JAMES HERBERT, 1883, *The Native Element in American Fiction, Century Magazine, vol.* 26, *p.* 363.

Some of his voluminous books of travel have become classics in their way. They are singularly free, upon the whole, not merely of poetical exaggeration, but even of a tendency in that direction,—being remarkable rather for clearness of statement and practical information. Not that the poet could aways hide himself behind the homespun mask of utilitarianism; for through it his brilliant mind flashed, as it were, arch humors and wonderful suggestions! Now and then, mere photographic details are followed by word-pictures so vivid, eloquent, and full of *vraisemblance* that they seem absolutely rhythmical. Each flowing period sets itself to music. Read, for example, his wonderful description of the "Taj Mahal!" Where, in recent English literature, has it been surpassed? . . . As a novelist Taylor hardly impresses us as being one "to the manner born." That indefinable ease, grace, and confidence, that steady-going power of the masters of prose fiction, he did not and he could not display. His novels were fairly successful for a time, and accomplished in some measure the purposes for which they were penned. They had not in them the stuff of perpetuity.—HAYNE, PAUL HAMILTON, 1884, *Bayard Taylor, Andover Review, vol.* 2, *pp.* 553, 554.

As a poet, the qualities of his mature style were now fairly displayed. From the beginning, rhythm, the *surreusis* of liquid measures, had much to do with his sense of the beautiful in verse, and reacted upon his imagination. He revelled in the effect of the broad English vowels, the "hollow ae's and oe's," and in the consonantal vigor of our language. He enjoyed reading aloud the poetry of Darley, of Byron and Shelley, and read his own with such melody and resonance that one who listened to its chanting sound was no more able than himself to tell whether it was of his poorest or his best. Its dominant quality, therefore, was often that of eloquence, as in the verse of Croly and Campbell. Poe quoted from one of his early pieces, to show that eloquence and imagination may go together. I have said that Bryant was "elemental" in his communion with sea and forest and the misty mountain winds. Taylor, as to the general range of his poetry, was ethnical and secular. — STEDMAN, EDMUND CLARENCE, 1885, *Poets of America*, p. 411.

Seldom does achievement lag so far behind the desire as in the case of the "Deukalion." Taylor sought to make it a poem fitly chronicling the entire upward and onward march of man, but overwork and failing powers are sadly manifest. Yet, after all, neither vain excuse nor word of deep disappointment need embitter our memories of one who produced (albeit in three years) a metrical version of Faust that for practical purposes is faultless, and who wrote (in four days) "The Masque of the Gods," our best addition to the loftiest or religious division of the drama, the highest form of literature. — RICHARDSON, CHARLES F., 1888, *American Literature*, 1607–1885, *vol.* II, *p.* 248.

Bayard Taylor, so beloved, so full of high hope, and so pathetically foredoomed to a fame that must grow scantier with advancing years.—SHARP, WILLIAM, 1889, *ed., American Sonnets, Introductory Note, p.* xxiii.

The predominant trait of Taylor's mind was a certain love of Nature in her larger forms: it was not so much the love of a naturalist as the love of a painter; his poetry was always picturesque. This quality, which is felt, rather than perceived, is conspicuous in the "Metempsychosis of the Pine,"—which he never surpassed. . . . His popularity as a traveller was greater than his popularity as a poet,— a circumstance which disappointed him and stimulated him into writing more poetry. Of the value of his contributions to the literature of travel, I am no judge. I read his books as they appeared, and was interested in them on his account, but they have left no definite impression on my mind. It was as a poet I most admired him, and it is as a poet, I think, that he will be chiefly remembered.—STODDARD, RICHARD HENRY, 1889, *Bayard Taylor, Lippincott's Magazine, vol.* 43, *pp.* 574, 578.

Taylor's novels had the qualities of his verse. They were profuse, eloquent, and faulty. "John Godfrey's Fortune," 1864, gave a picture of Bohemian life in New York. "Hannah Thurston," 1863, and "The Story of Kennett," 1866, introduced many incidents and persons from the old Quaker life of rural Pennsylvania, as Taylor remembered it in his boyhood. The former was like Hawthorne's "Blithedale Romance," a satire on fanatics and reformers, and its heroine is a nobly conceived character, though drawn with some exaggeration. "The Story of Kennett," which is largely autobiographic, has a greater freshness and reality than the others and is full of personal recollections. In these novels, as in his short stories, Taylor's pictorial skill is greater, on the whole, than his power of creating characters or inventing plots.—BEERS, HENRY A., 1895, *Initial Studies in American Letters, p.* 179.

His early life had been warped by sentimentality, and cribbed by repression. Two centuries of Quaker ancestry had condemned him to slow development. From the first there was a purely literary strain in his blood, but the nice sense of proportion and of harmony was slowly arrived at. He was, he said, ten years behind every other American author; but when those who had the start of him flowered and ceased he was stepping on with quick impatience to more novel experiments and to more conspicuous results. The really great things of which he was capable were still before him when he died, with more unfilled renown and unaccomplished growth within him than any other man in American letters. . . . Consider the work he did in the fifty-four years of his life; his far travels, his wide experience in all departments of journalism, his services as a diplomatist in Russia and in Germany, the variety of his literature,—essays, descriptive and critical, history and biography, novels and short stories, translations, odes, idyls, ballads, lyrics, pastorals, dramatic romances, and lyrical dramas,—and it is clear that his career comprehends the orbit of contemporary American life and letters. He was not our highest and most influential writer; he was rather a *meistersinger*,—a guild-singer,—a man of talent, and master of the mechanics of his craft. But on all sides he touched the life of his time. He was one of the most widely-known American authors. Art had graven him in romantic garb upon the public mind. Astonishing memory and prodigious industry in him had taken the place of genius, and they had won a signal triumph.—SMYTH, ALBERT H., 1896, *Bayard Taylor (American Men of Letters)*, pp. 179, 273.

Taylor's exuberant rhetoric is both his strength and his weakness. . . . In all his later writings he never surpassed the glowing passionate imagery of his "Poems of the Orient." He seemed to have caught the very spirit of the far East and interpreted it as none of our writers before or since. It was like an infusion of tropical blood into the somewhat stiff and formal body of our American verse. . . . The great gulf fixed between the so-called "Sacred Poems" of Willis and Taylor's "Poems of the Orient" represents only a dozen years in time, but an indefinite period in the development of the poetic spirit. By this publication Taylor at once placed himself at the head of our minor poets. In his higher strains he seemed to unite the lyrical music of Poe with the artistic finish of Longfellow.—ONDERDONK, JAMES L. 1899-1901. *History of American Verse.*

George Henry Lewes
1817–1878

Born, in London, 18 April 1817. At school in London, Jersey, Brittany, and Greenwich. For a time worked in a lawyer's office; afterwards studied medicine. After some years spent in France and Germany, became an actor. Acted in London at various times, 1841–50. Play, "The Noble Heart," produced in Manchester, 16 April 1849; at Olympic, London, Feb. 1850. Married Agnes Jervis, 18 Feb. 1841. Adopted literary career. Contributed to various periodicals. Wrote various plays and farces. Editor of "The Leader," 1850. Met Mary Ann Evans ("George Eliot"), 1851; lived with her, July 1854 till his death. To Germany with her, July 1854. Returned to England, March 1855. Editor of "Fortnightly Review," May 1865 to Dec. 1866. Died, in London, 30 Nov. 1878. *Works:* "Biographical History of Philosophy" (4 vols.), 1845–46; "The Spanish Drama," 1847; "Ranthorpe" (anon.) 1847; "Rose, Blanche and Violet," 1848; "Life of Maximilien Robespierre," 1849; "The Noble Heart," 1850; "A Chain of Events," (under pseud. "Slingsby Lawrence" with Charles J. Mathews, 1852); Comte's "Philosophy of the Sciences," 1853; "Life and Works of Goethe," 1855; "Seaside Studies" 1858; "Physiology of Common Life" (2 vols.), 1859–60; "Studies in Animal Life,"1862; "Aristotle, 1864; "Problems of Life and Mind" (5 vols.), 1874 [1873]–79; Selections from the "Modern British Dramatists" (2 vols.), 1867; text to "Female Characters of Goethe" [1874]; "On Actors and the Art of Acting," 1875. [Also several plays and farces, pubd. in Lacy's Acting Edition, written under pseud. of Slingsby Lawrence.] *Posthumous:* "The Study of Psychology," 1879. He *edited:* J. F. W. Johnston's "Chemistry of Common Life," 1859. —SHARP, R. FARQUHARSON, 1897, *A Dictionary of English Authors,* p. 168.

PERSONAL

I was introduced to Lewes the other day in Jeff's shop—a sort of miniature Mirabeau in appearance.—ELIOT, GEORGE, 1851, *To Mr. Bray, Sept.; George Eliot's Life as related in her Letters and Journals,* ed. Cross, vol. I, p. 189.

No one could say that he was handsome. The long bushy hair, and the thin cheeks, and the heavy moustache, joined as they were, alas! almost always to a look of sickness, were not attributes of beauty. But there was a brilliance in his eye, which was not to be tamed by any sickness, by any suffering, which overcame all other feelings on looking at him. I have a portrait of him, a finished photograph, which he gave me some years since, in which it would seem as though his face had blazed up suddenly, as it often would do, in strong indignation against the vapid vauntings of some literary pseudo-celebrity. But the smile would come again, and before the anger of his sarcasm had had half a minute's play, the natural drollery of the man, the full overflowing love of true humour, would overcome himself, and make us love the poor satirised sinner for the sake of the wit his sin had created.—TROLLOPE, ANTHONY, 1879, *George Henry Lewes, Fortnightly Review, vol.* 31, *p.* 23.

A sort of untamed lion he was in my day, sturdy, well set up, with a mop of curly, brown-coloured hair, worn long. He had a lion-like trick of shaking his mane—head, I mean—when the hair would fall round his face, over his collar and shoulders. Then he would throw his head well back with a vigorous jerk, and show a row of strong white teeth in a well-formed mouth, a broad forehead, and well-developed intellectual organs. I can see him now, standing just so at the piano, rolling out some jolly song, with powerful voice and good enunciation.—GRUNDY, FRANCIS H., 1879, *Pictures of the Past, p.* 170.

About Lewes's ugliness there could be no two opinions. There was not a good feature in his face, yet his face as a whole, was one which you would look twice at and which had at any rate the merit of not being commonplace.—SMALLEY, GEORGE W., 1880-91, *George Eliot, Dec.* 25; *London Letters and Some Others, vol.* I, *p.* 246.

Few men of his time excelled him as a converser. He had a large fund of anecdote at his command, and could tell a story so as to render it interesting to every hearer. . . . The richly stored mind and the seductive tongue of Lewes made him acceptable to any woman who could be impressed through the intellect rather than the eye; his face was his greatest defect, though it is an exaggeration to style him, as has been done, the ugliest man of his day. —RAE, W. FRASER, 1881, *George Eliot's Life and Writings, International Review, vol.* 10, *p.* 453.

The most alert, the most universal mind of his generation, equally remarkable as a critic, as a physiologist and as a philosopher, a brilliant talker, whose dazzling wit played over an abyss of deep reflection.—DARMESTETER, JAMES, 1883-96, *English Studies, tr. Mrs. Darmesteter, p.* 112.

Among others I fell in with that notorious group of Free Lovers, whose ultimate transaction was the most notable example of matrimony void of contract in our day. But though those who floated on the crest of the wave, [Lewes and George Eliot]— and whose informal union came to be regarded as a moral merit, even by the straitlaced, had the more genius and the better luck, he who made personal shipwreck,— [Thornton Hunt]—and from whose permitted trespass the whole thing started, had the nobler nature, the most fruitful heart, the more constant mind, and was in every way the braver and the truer man. He whom society set itself to honour, partly because of the transcendent genius of his companion, partly because of his own brilliancy and facility, was less solid than specious. The other, whom all men, not knowing him, reviled, was a moral hero. The former betrayed his own principles when he made capital out of his "desecrated hearth," and bewildered society by setting forth ingenious stories of impossible ceremonies which had made his informal union in a certain sense sacramental, so that he might fill his rooms with "names," and make his Sundays days of illustrious reception. — LINTON, ELIZABETH LYNN, 1885, *An Autobiography of Christopher Kirkland, vol.* I, *p.* 273.

Mr. Lewes was quite as good in a company of three as in a company of thirty. In fact, he was better, for his *verve* was not in the least dependent on the number of his audience, and the flow was less interrupted. Conversation was no effort to him; nor was it to her so long as the members engaged were not too many, and the topics were interesting enough to sustain discussion.—CROSS, J. W., 1885, *ed. George Eliot's Life as related in her Letters and Journals, vol.* III, *p.* 243.

Lewes had plenty of egotism, not to give it a more unamiable name, but it never mastered his intellectual sincerity. George Eliot describes him as one of the few human beings she has known who will, in the heat of an argument, see, and straightway confess, that he is in the wrong, instead of trying to shift his ground or use any other device of vanity.—MORLEY, JOHN, 1885, *The Life of George Eliot, Macmillan's Magazine, vol.* 51, *p.* 245.

Conceive a little, narrow-shouldered man of between forty and fifty, with long straight hair, a magnificent forehead, dark yet brilliant eyes, and a manner full of alertness and intellectual grace. This was George Lewes, whom Douglas Jerrold had once stigmatised as "the ugliest man in London," averring at the same time that he had caused the chimpanzee in the Zoological Gardens to die "out of jealousy, because there existed close by a creature more hideous than itself!" But George Lewes, though not an Adonis, was certainly not ugly. The great defects of his face were the coarse, almost sensual mouth with its protruding teeth partly covered by a bristly moustache, and the small retreating chin; but when the face lighted up, and the eyes sparkled, and the mouth began its eloquent discourse, every imperfection was forgotten.—BUCHANAN, ROBERT, 1886, *A Talk with George Eliot, A Look Round Literature*, p. 219.

If any man could ever be said to have lived in another person, Lewes in those days, and to the end of his life, lived in and for George Eliot. The talk of worshipping the ground she trod on, and the like, are pretty lovers' phrases, sometimes signifying much, and sometimes very little. But it is true accurately and literally of Lewes. That care for her, at once comprehensive and minute, unsleeping watchfulness, lest she should dash her foot against a stone, was *never* absent from his mind. She had become his real self, his genuine *ego* to all intents and purposes. And his talk and thoughts were egoistic accordingly. Of his own person, his ailments, his works, his ideas, his impressions, you might hear not a word from him in the intercourse of many days. But there was in his inmost heart a *naif* and never-doubting faith that talk on all these subjects as regarded *her* must be profoundly interesting to those he talked with.—TROLLOPE, THOMAS ADOLPHUS, 1888, *What I Remember*, p. 452.

After George Eliot saw Lewes for the first time, she described him as "a sort of miniature Mirabeau in appearance." As in Mirabeau's case, the ugliness and the remains of the ravages of the smallpox were undoubtedly there, but Lewes had a fine eye and an expressive countenance, which when lighted up by a smile was far from disagreeable. However it was Lewes's plainness of visage that led the Carlyles, as will be seen further on, to speak of him, though only for a time, as "The Ape."— ESPINASSE, FRANCIS, 1893, *Literary Recollections and Sketches*, p. 278.

Lewes's health had been often feeble during his later years. He had, however, a remarkable buoyancy of spirit, and was, till the last, most brilliant and agreeable in conversation. Whatever his faults, he was a man of singular generosity, genial and unpretentious, quick to recognise merit, and ready to help young authors. Though an incisive critic he was never bitter, and was fair and open-minded in controversy. His extraordinary versatility is shown by his writings, and was, perhaps, some hindrance to his eminence in special departments. He was short and slight, with a fine brow and very bright eyes, but the other features were such that Douglas Jerrold is said to have called him too unequivocally the "ugliest man in London;" yet in animated talk his personal defects would vanish.—STEPHEN, LESLIE, 1893, *Dictionary of National Biography*, vol. XXXIII, p. 167.

Mr. Lewes was very clever, acute and vivacious, with an essentially all-round intelligence; a ready man, able to turn the talent that was in him to full and immediate account. — LOCKER-LAMPSON, FREDERICK, 1895, *My Confidences*, p. 312.

The last time that my father saw George Henry Lewes, husband of George Eliot (Miss Mary Evans), he was standing, like Collier, at Charing Cross, and presented a singular appearance, being dressed from top to toe in white, and the only thing about him that was not white was his red hair and beard.—HAZLITT, W. CAREW, 1897, *Four Generations of a Literary Family*, vol. II, p. 17.

HISTORY OF PHILOSOPHY
1845-46

A distinctive characteristic of Mr. Lewes's work is, that it is written to prove that philosophy, properly so called, is impossible. It is a curious thing to find a history of metaphysics laboriously produced by an author who avows his belief in the utter futility of metaphysics, and who denies even the superior grandeur of the speculations through which that misty science leads. Most men, whether speaking or writing, are wont to begin a discussion of any subject by maintaining its vast importance and utility: Mr. Lewes writes his book to show that his subject is of no importance or utility at all. Any interest which philosophy may still retain, he holds to be purely historical.—BOYD, ANDREW K. H., 1857, *Recent Metaphysical Works, Fraser's Magazine*, vol. 56, p. 659.

Mr. G. H. Lewes' "History of Philosophy" is in some respects more erudite and acute than the work of Mr. Maurice, but it is written too decidedly in the *negative* spirit of the *positive* school to inspire entire confidence, especially as it is a cardinal doctrine of this school that philosophical speculation is vain and profitless.—PORTER, NOAH, 1870, *Books and Reading,* p. 311.

Mr. Lewes lacks the vocation of the scholar, which indeed is generally wanting in original minds. His history resembles rather that of Hegel, than that of Ritter. His review of the labours of philosophers is rather occupied with that which they have thought, than with their comparative importance. He judges rather than expounds: his history is fastidious and critical. It is the work of a clear, precise, and elegant mind, always that of a writer, often witty, measured, possessing no taste for declamation, avoiding exclusive solutions; and making its interest profitable to the reader whom he forces to think. There are many ideas in this book. — RIBOT, THÉODULE, 1874, *English Psychology,* p. 258.

It was a more characteristically audacious thing to attempt to cram the history of philosophy into a couple of medium-sized volumes, polishing off each philosopher in a few pages, draining him, plucking out the heart of his mystery and system, and stowing him away in the glass jar designed to exhibit him to an edified class of students. But it must be admitted that the "History of Philosophy" is a genuine and a valuable study, although the author, not then in the calmer maturity of his powers, crumples up the whole science of metaphysics, sweeps away transcendental philosophy, and demolishes *a priori* reasoning in a manner which strongly reminds one of Arthur Pendennis upsetting, in a dashing criticism, and on the faith of an hour's reading in an encyclopaedia, some great scientific theory of which he had never heard before, and the development of which had been the life's labor of a sage. —McCARTHY, JUSTIN, 1880, *A History of Our Own Times from the Accession of Queen Victoria to the Berlin Congress,* vol. iv, ch. lxvii.

One of the chief notes of this book—in its earliest and latest form alike, its characteristic note—was its antipathy to philosophical theology, and to all the fundamental conceptions on which it rests. Mr. Lewes's idea of the history of philosophy was very like the popular notion of the play of Hamlet with the part of Hamlet missed out. He did not believe in any higher or spiritual thought. All metaphysic was to him an absurdity. It was merely "the art of amusing one's self with method"—"*l'art de s'égarer avec méthode.*" No definition can be wittier or truer, he thought.—TULLOCH, JOHN, 1885, *Movements of Religious Thought During the Nineteenth Century,* p. 157.

This is undoubtedly a work of great importance and of considerable merit. The narrative is usually careful and sufficiently attractive, and the judgments for the most part well weighed and impartial. Some of the earlier articles on the Greek writers, the chapter devoted to the Sophists in particular, show a liveliness of style which brings us quite into the sphere of light reading; but there is plenty of good heavy solidity to counterbalance this. Yet the information and even the instruction is, as a rule, pleasantly conveyed. — OLIPHANT, MARGARET O. W., 1892, *The Victorian Age of English Literature,* p. 416.

Though occasionally superficial, and too much tinged with a sort of second-hand Positivism, had, as the qualities of these defects, an excellent though sometimes a rather treacherous clearness, and a unity of vision which is perhaps more valuable for fairly intelligent readers than desultory profundity. But it can hardly take rank as a book of philosophical scholarship, though it is almost a brilliant specimen of popular philosophical literature.—SAINTSBURY, GEORGE, 1896, *A History of Nineteenth Century Literature,* p. 355.

A work lacking in weight and authority in the philosophical part, but undoubtedly interesting in its sketches of famous philosophers, ancient and modern, from Thales and Pythagoras to Hegel and Comte.—GRAHAM, RICHARD D., 1897, *The Masters of Victorian Literature,* p. 233.

LIFE OF GOETHE
1855

Read in Lewes's "Life of Goethe,"—a very clever and judicious book. The best we have had as yet, giving the great German as he really was.—LONGFELLOW, HENRY WADSWORTH, 1855, *Journal, Dec.* 16; *Life by Longfellow,* vol. II, p. 299.

It is by this biography, perhaps, that he is best known to general readers. As a critical biography of one of the great heroes of literature it is almost perfect. It is short, easily understood by common readers, singularly graphic, exhaustive, and altogether devoted to the subject. It is one of these books of which one is tempted to say, that he who had it before him to read, is to be envied.—TROLLOPE, ANTHONY, 1879, *George Henry Lewes, Fortnightly Review, vol.* 31, *p.* 20.

Perhaps no other man then living could have shown himself competent to deal with Goethe's many-sidedness—to discuss "Faust" and "Tasso," "Hermann und Dorothea" at one moment, the poet's biological and botanical discoveries the next, and to estimate at their true worth the speculations on colours, which Goethe held to be more calculated than his poems to secure him immortality. The book remains the standard life of the great Weimar sage in this country, and is popular in Germany, in spite of a vast Goethe literature which has been published since its appearance.— SHORTER, CLEMENT K., 1897, *Victorian Literature, Sixty Years of Books and Bookmen, p.* 149.

PROBLEMS OF LIFE AND MIND
1874–79

Although Mr. Lewes has retained the name of Metaphysics, and offers his solution of what are universally called the problems of Metaphysics, he shows himself from title-page to colophon an unflinching adherent of the positive methods, and never travels a hair's-breadth from his canons which bind truth to experience. In his claim to have swept metaphysics into the fold of science, he is never found to be using metempirical expedients. Whether or not he has domesticated the untamed metaphysical Pegasus, and harnessed him to the car of terrestrial science, we leave to the future to decide; but we can say at once that he himself has never mounted the wild charger into the realms of cloudland, and if he has really got Pegasus as completely in hand as he thinks, he himself is certainly safe on mother earth.—HARRISON, FREDERIC, 1874, *Mr. Lewes's Problems of Life and Mind, The Fortnightly Review, vol.* 22, *p.* 92.

In the last chapter Mr. Lewes considers the place of sentiment in philosophy. What he has to show is that Sentiment, or Emotion, is one important source of knowledge. But what he says is more likely to impress his readers with its power of obscuring vision and obstructing research.—SPALDING, DOUGLAS A., 1874, *Lewes's Problems of Life and Mind, Nature, vol.* 10, *p.* 2.

In the first volume Mr. Lewes was chiefly occupied with forging new weapons for the armoury of empirical thought: in this he shows us how they can be used. Chief among these is the theory of abstraction: a theory more or less perceived and acted upon by all empirical philosophers, but now wrought into a finished instrument of various application and exceeding power. But any theory of abstraction, it may be said, must be still only an affair of logic: and how shall a purely logical doctrine throw light upon problems such as those of Matter, Cause, and Things in Themselves? The answer is short: By dispelling logical illusions. And in fact Mr. Lewes lets in light upon a whole series of metempirical phantoms in a manner of which we can here only give the slightest hints. One feels at the end that one has travelled a good way along the road which Mr. Lewes truly says that the scientific study of metaphysic has to pursue, namely the substitution of intelligible for unintelligible questions.—POLLOCK, FREDERICK, 1875, *Problems of Life and Mind, The Academy, vol.* 7, *p.* 533.

These five volumes ["Problems of Life and Mind"] conserve the well-matured thought of one who has hardly an equal in recent philosophical literature in breadth and accuracy of knowledge, and to whose restless and versatile mind originality of conception was a necessity. Combining this volume of special knowledge, biological, psychological, historical, and literary, with a high degree of generalising power, he has struck out conceptions which, while closely related to the scientific ideas of the hour, are also far in advance of them. Thus he is commonly looked on as heterodox in biology, though some of his ideas, as, for example, that of the fundamental identity of all nervous structures, are slowly being taken up by specialists. Whether such a range of exact special information as Mr. Lewes possessed is compatible with the highest quality of philosophical synthesis may perhaps be doubted. . . . Throughout, the writer never fails to be luminous and stimulating in thought and picturesque and forcible in language. No student of psychology who wants to be abreast with recent researches will be able to dispense with a repeated reference to this concluding volume of the series. Though deprived of artistic completeness, it is a worthy conclusion to a literary activity of a remarkable range and of a uniformly sustained earnestness.—SULLY, JAMES, 1880, *Problems of Life and Mind*, The Academy, vol. 17, pp. 308, 310.

GENERAL

Execrable, ["Rose Blanche"] that is; I could not have suspected even the ape of writing anything so silly. Lady H. read it all the way down, and decided it was "too vulgar to go on with." I myself should have also laid it aside in the first half volume if I had not felt a pitying interest in the man, that makes me read on in hope of coming to something a little better. Your marginal notes are the only real amusement I have got out of it hitherto.—CARLYLE, JANE WELSH, 1848, *To Thomas Carlyle*, Apr. 13; *Letters and Memorials*, ed. Froude, vol. I, p. 318.

I have a very high opinion of his literary judgment.—ARNOLD, MATTHEW, 1858, *To his Mother*, Jan 3; *Letters* ed. Russell, vol. I, p. 67.

What man of our day has done so many things and done them so well? He is the biographer of Goethe and of Robespierre; he has compiled the "History of Philosophy," in which he has something really his own to say of every great philosopher, from Thales to Schelling; he has translated Spinoza; he has published various scientific works; he has written at least two novels; he has made one of the most successful dramatic adaptions known to our stage; he is an accomplished theatrical critic; he was at one time so successful as an amateur actor that he seriously contemplated taking to the stage as a profession, in the full conviction, which he did not hesitate frankly to avow, that he was destined to be the successor to Macready. . . . There was a good deal of inflation, and audacity, and nonsense in it; ["Ranthorpe"] but at the same time it showed more brains and artistic impulse and constructive power than nine out of every ten novels published in England to-day.—MCCARTHY, JUSTIN, 1872, *Modern Leaders, George Eliot and George Lewes*, pp. 141, 142.

Almost any one of the essays ["On Actors and the Art of Acting"] would have sufficed to prove that Mr. Lewes was a competent theatrical critic, and as far as Mr. Lewes is personally concerned, the whole volume proves little more.—WEDMORE, FREDERICK, 1875, *On Actors and the Art of Acting*, The Academy, vol. 8, p. 76.

He is, I think, the acutest critic I know—and the severest. His severity, however, is a fault. His intention to be honest, even when honesty may give pain, has caused him to give pain when honesty has not required it. He is essentially a doubter, and has encouraged himself to doubt till the faculty of trusting has almost left him. I am not speaking of the personal trust which one man feels in another, but of that confidence in literary excellence which is, I think, necessary for the full enjoyment of literature.—TROLLOPE, ANTHONY, 1882-83, *An Autobiography*, p. 112.

Of these critical writings the most valuable are those on the drama, which were afterwards republished under the title "Actors and Acting." With this may be taken the volume on "The Spanish Drama." The combination of wide scholarship, philosophic culture, and practical acquaintance with the theatre gives these essays a high place among the best efforts in English dramatic criticism.—SULLY, JAMES, 1882, *The Enclyclopædia Britannica*, vol. XIV.

Mr. Lewes was not only an accomplished and practised literary critic, but he was also gifted with the inborn insight accompanying a fine artistic temperament, which gave unusual weight to his judgment.—CROSS, J. W., 1884, *George Eliot's Life as related in her Letters and Journals*, p. 277.

He originated no special line of thought. He was the bold usher of the modern scientific spirit, and his influence chiefly consisted in the unalloyed enthusiasm with which he pushed its premisses to their legitimate conclusion. . . . He had admirable gifts as a writer, whatever we may think of his powers as a thinker. His exposition was marked by a rare lucidity, and had the charm of interest, even when least satisfactory. Much of a Frenchman in many of his ways, he had the French gift of facile and happy expression.—TULLOCH, JOHN, 1885, *Movements of Religious Thought in Britain During the Nineteenth Century*, p. 157.

Of course, writing thus much and on such a great variety of themes, Lewes was not always effective. All along, indeed, he contributed more to "the literature of knowledge" than to "the literature of power." But whatever he wrote displayed a certain originality of view. Whether he was dealing with literature, philosophy, or science,

SAMUEL WARREN

Engraving by D. J. Pond. From a Photograph by Mayall.

LORD JOHN RUSSELL

Engraving from a Painting by Francis Grant, R.A., 1853.

he was never an echo of his predecessors or contemporaries. Lewes was no worshipper of great names, and had in a singular degree the courage of his opinions.—ESPINASSE, FRANCIS, 1893, *Literary Recollections and Sketches, p. 276.*

He was, despite his freakishness, probably the most highly-trained thinker who ever applied himself to the study of theatrical art in England. It was a happy chance which superadded to his other gifts that innate passion for the stage which is the condition precedent of helpful dramatic criticism.—ARCHER, WILLIAM, 1896, *George Henry Lewes and the Stage, The Fortnightly Review, vol. 65, p. 230.*

John Lord Russell
1792–1878

First Earl Russell: known as Lord John Russell till 1861. Born at London, Aug. 18, 1792: died May 28, 1878. An English statesman, orator, and author: third son of the sixth Duke of Bedford. He studied at Edinburgh; entered Parliament in 1813; began his advocacy of Parliamentary reform in 1819; advocated Catholic emancipation in 1826, and the repeal of the Test Acts in 1828; became paymaster of the forces in 1830; introduced the Reform Bill in 1831, and was one of its leading champions until its passage in 1832; became leader of the Whig party in 1834: was home secretary 1835–39, secretary for war and the colonies 1839–41, and prime minister and first lord of the treasury 1846–52; published the "Durham Letter" in 1850; was foreign secretary and later president of the council 1852–55; represented England at the Vienna Conference in 1855; was colonial secretary in 1855, foreign secretary in the Palmerston-Russell administration 1859–65; and prime minister and first lord of the treasury 1865–66; and was created Earl Russell in 1861. He edited the memorials and correspondence of Charles James Fox (1853–57); and of Moore (1852–56); and wrote "Life and Times of Fox" (1859–66), "Recollections and Suggestions" (1875), etc.—SMITH, BENJAMIN, E., ed. 1894–97, *The Century Cyclopedia of Names, p. 847.*

PERSONAL

Lord John Russell was born with a feeble intellect and a strong ambition. He was busied with the battle of valets. A feeble Cataline, he had a propensity to degrade everything to his own mean level, and to measure everything by his own malignant standard.—DISRAELI, BENJAMIN (EARL OF BEACONSFIELD), 1836, *Runnymede Letters.*

Bennoch pointed out Lord John Russell, a small, very short, elderly gentleman, in a brown coat, and so large a hat—not large of brim, but large like a peck-measure—that I saw really no face beneath it.—HAWTHORNE, NATHANIEL, 1856, *English Note-Books, vol. II, p. 19.*

Who does not know the personal characteristics of Lord Russell? Who has not seen the square and stunted figure, the large head, the big mouth, the pugnacious nose? No one who enters the House of Lords can mistake his identity. He sits below the gangway on the Liberal side of the House, his head and features almost hidden by a huge broad-brimmed hat. It appears to be a veritable Cave of Adullam which he has formed for himself in this part of the House. Here he is joined at times by Lord Clanricarde, Lord Westbury, or other discontented Liberals, and with them he holds frequent conversations in a voice which almost drowns that of the man who is supposed to have possession of the House for the time being. When he rises to speak, he places his hat upon the seat behind him, clasps his hands behind his back, turns away from the reporters, and says what he has to say in a grumbling monotone. His speech has become so indistinct now, that but little of what he says reaches the peers on the other side of the House, and men like Lord Grey, who do not care much for appearances, but who still regard Lord Russell's utterances as important, will seat themselves close to him whilst he is speaking, and, with hand to ear, endeavor to catch all that he says. It does not appear, however, that it is from inability to speak clearly and distinctly that he makes his speeches in this unsatisfactory manner. It would rather seem that it is from sheer contempt for the people he is addressing; since, when he chooses, he can speak out in such a manner as to make himself heard all over the House. When he does this, he allows those present to witness once again the old-fashioned peculiarities of pronunciation. — REID, THOMAS WEMYSS 1872, *Cabinet Portraits, p. 124.*

His manner was singularly cold and repelling. People said that his aristocratic *hauteur* was indomitable. The joyous *bonhomie* with which Palmerston could make himself at home amid a group of rural voters was utterly foreign to Russell's frigid manner. Lord John was said to be miserably parsimonious. He seemed only a formal, bloodless, and fishy sort of little man. He is a very little man, and he has or had a way of folding his arms and expanding his chest and deepening his voice, and, in fact, trying to swell himself into physical dignity, which oddly but inevitably reminded one of a frog trying to rival the ox. . . . Russell's voice is at once weak and husky; he is hardly taller than Louis Blanc, and he has not the bright eyes and the wonderfully mobile and expressive features of the French orator. But he studied the ways of the House of Commons, resolved to become a good debater there, and he succeeded. He always watched with keen eyes for any flaw in the reasoning or inconsistency in the statement of an adversary, and he made cruel work with anything of the kind. He was fluent and ready—a kind of slow fluency, a sort of forced readiness; but however achieved, the result was there in a capacity to reply on the spur of the moment, and to speak for as long a time as was necessary. His language was clear, precise, and expressive; there was a cold emphasis about it which impressed it on the listener's attention like the steady dropping of chilly water. Russell had a broad and general knowledge of history, and was sure to remember something which his antagonist had forgotten or did not know, and which came in with unexpected and damaging effect as an argument or illustration. He brought everything to the test of a cold, sharp intelligence, and had no pity for the enthusiasm or the crotchets of anybody.—McCarthy, Justin, 1873, *Earl Russell, The Galaxy*, vol. 15, p. 11.

The practical statesman and party leader were equally blended in Earl Russell. He led his party on several occasions triumphantly through times of crisis; and if occasionally he brought disaster upon it, he was exceedingly clever in retrieving its fortunes. . . . He imbibed much of the spirit and many of the aspirations of his ancestor, Lord William Russell, and in the history of this country his name will occupy an honoured and a distinguished place.—Smith, George Barnett, 1888, *The Prime Ministers of Queen Victoria*, pp. 173, 174.

Lord John owed but a small debt to Nature: undersized, undignified, ungraceful; a bad speaker, with no pretense to eloquence either in thought, word, or action, he yet held a foremost place in the arena, for more than half a century. He said of himself, "My capacity I always felt was very inferior to that of the men who have attained, in past time, the foremost places in our Parliament, and in the councils of our Sovereign."—Hall, Samuel Carter, 1883, *Retrospect of a Long Life*, p. 132.

All these gifts—wit, humour, playfulness, high spirits—were the graceful accessories of a nature essentially warm, tender, and true. To his wife and children, and to those who knew him well, nothing has been more amazing than the prevalence in the public mind of the notion, memorably expressed by Lord Lytton in the "New Timon," that his temperament was cold and repellant. That such a notion should ever become current is an illustration of the unfortunate magic of manner. It is touching to know that, within three months of his death, he said to his wife, "I have sometimes seemed cold to my friends, but it was not in my heart." They who knew that heart need no such assurance.—Russell, George W. E., 1889, *Lord Russell, The Contemporary Review*, vol. 56, p. 820.

In his advocacy of great legislative measures of reform, as in his desire to find practical remedies for existing grievances, Lord John showed not merely a mind singularly free from prevailing prejudice, but also a firm belief in the ultimate triumph of certain political principles. There was nothing spasmodic about the Liberalism of Lord John Russell. It was not his business, it was not his aspiration, to be always on the crest of the wave of popular feeling. He is the type of a brave, a steadfast, and a patriotic reformer, in fine weather and in foul alike adhering to the principles he professed; and for the simple reason that he believed in them. There was in him nothing of the opportunist or of the agitator. Foresight, steadfastness, courage, and patriotism are the qualities for which, amongst British statesmen, Lord John Russell will always be remembered.—Elliot, Arthur D., 1890, *Lord John Russell, Macmillan's Magazine*, vol. 61, p. 145.

His physical defects prevented him from

becoming an orator. His voice was poor, and he had an awkward manner. Men used to say that "when he placed his left elbow on the palm of his right hand, the house awaited a sentiment in favour of religious liberty." His weak physique and delicate health explain also why Lord John Russell was such a bad party leader. His manner to his supporters was cold and repellent; he lacked personal magnetism, and ill-health prevented him from properly discharging those social functions which, under the English system, are so important to the union of a party. His coldness was of manner only. "The popular idea of Johnny," wrote Motley, "is of a cold, cynical, reserved personage. But, in his own home, I never saw a more agreeable manner." But nevertheless it did as much harm among his supporters as if it had been real. To the same source may be traced that *unevenness*, which is so often a characteristic of small and weakly men. Lord John's personality lacked the massiveness of Peel or Palmerston. When he was great, men thought him merely clever; when he was moderate, he somehow failed to inspire all the confidence he deserved. At times he was too reticent; at times he spoke out too plainly, and was too unrestrained. His eternal resignations, always withdrawn under pressure, produced among his colleagues the impression that he was sometimes weak, and thus, though the acknowledged leader of his party, he was not always at the head of the government. To the ordinary reader of his life, this does not seem altogether natural to his character, which was as strong and manly as it was simple and straightforward. Perhaps it was not the consequence of character, but of physique.—TANNER, J. R., 1891, *Walpole's Life of Lord John Russell, English Historical Review, vol. 6, p. 185.*

GENERAL

Lord John Russell has sent us down what he calls a "tragedy" the other day—and upon a subject no less dangerous than the fate of Don Carlos. Schiller and Alfieri yet live. The Newspapers say Lord Byron is greatly obliged to his brother lord, the latter having even surpassed "Werner" in tameness and insipidity; so that Byron is no longer Author of the dullest tragedy ever printed by a lord. This is very foul to Byron; for though I fear he will never write a good play, it is impossible he can ever write anything so truly innocent as this "Don Carlos." I would have sent it to you; but it seemed superfluous. There is great regularity in the speeches, the lines have all ten syllables exactly—and precisely the same smooth ding-dong rhythm from the first page to the last; there are also little bits of metaphors scattered up and down at convenient intervals, and very fair whig sentiments here and there; but the whole is cold, flat, stale, and unprofitable, to a degree that "neither gods nor men nor columns can endure." You and I could write a better thing in two weeks, and then burn it. Yet he dedicates to Lord Holland, and seems to say like Correggio in the Vatican, *ed io anche son pittore*. Let us be of courage! we shall not be hindmost any way. —CARLYLE, THOMAS, 1822, *To Miss Welsh, Dec. 25; Early Letters, ed. Norton, p. 254.*

They [Speeches] afford a fair example of his Parliamentary oratory, and are in every way worthy of his great reputation. Indeed, he may well be content to rest his fame on them, for he could not appear to greater advantage; and the student of political history will find them full of suggestive materials. . . . They are replete both with study and with thought. Reflection, earnestness, nobility, and breadth of sentiment, coupled with a refined and cultivated power of expression, are the characteristics of his style; and lurking beneath, and only rarely rising to the surface, is the latent fire—the true inspiring genius of the orator. . . . Indeed, alongside any of his contemporaries, his published speeches need not fear comparison. Brougham soared a flight beyond him, though impulsive and erratic; but though Lord Russell had not the lively and sonorous cadence of Canning, nor the powerful ponderous precision of Peel, he has more depth than the first, and more versatility of thought than the last. The metal rings true throughout, nor do the solid and valuable materials of which they are composed lose anything in the setting. Above all, he had the true gift of eloquence—earnestness. He knew what he wanted, and he felt it, a spell which no arts of rhetoric can buy.—MONCRIEFF, J., 1870, *Earl Russell's Speeches, Edinburgh Review, vol. 131, p. 580.*

The attempt of Earl Russell to become a poet, by his tragedy of "Don Carlos, or Persecution," was for the time rather successful; at least the poem went through several editions in the course of a year, but it seems ever after to have been remembered only to the noble author's ridicule. I have not read it myself, and I do not know anybody who has. This tragedy was written at the time when Lord John Russell was in intimate relationship with the poets, scholars, and wits who frequented Holland House, and was doubtless fired with an ambition to do something which should entitle him to be regarded as one of their number. I fancy those poets, scholars, and wits must have knowingly or unintentionally, and out of mere good nature, flattered our young lord a good deal, and made him think much more of himself than the public outside were likely to think of him.—McCARTHY, JUSTIN, 1873, *Earl Russell, The Galaxy, vol.* 15, *p.* 8.

He was a writer from his earlier youth, and though he cannot be said to have any stable place in English literature, it is something to have tried his abilities as a dramatist, essayist, and historian. . . . The good temper and general moderation of these pages do not extend to the record of the party divisions that broke up the Government to which Lord Russell succeeded on the Death of Lord Palmerston. — MILNES, RICHARD MONCKTON (LORD HOUGHTON), 1875, *Recollections and Suggestions, The Academy, vol.* 7, *pp.* 105, 106.

On public grounds Lord John stands before posterity in a double capacity. He was not merely a distinguished statesman; he was a voluminous author. If, indeed, he had deserted, as he once thought of abandoning, politics for literature, it is not likely that he would have acquired fame. His best works would, no doubt, have brought credit to any writer. But their warmest admirers will hardly number them among the classics. Those of Lord John Russell's books which still survive are read because they were written by Lord John Russell; and the light which the author sheds is lustre borrowed from the eminence of the statesman. It is as a man of action, and not as a man of letters, that Lord John will descend to posterity; and it is by his achievements in Parliament, and not by the productions of his pen, that he must ultimately be judged.—WALPOLE, SPENCER, 1889, *The Life of Lord John Russell, vol.* II, *p.* 455.

From youth to age Lord John not merely possessed the pen of a ready writer, but employed it freely in history, biography, criticism, *belles-lettres*, and verse. His first book was published when George III. was King, and his last appeared when almost forty years of Queen Victoria's reign had elapsed. The Liverpool Administration was in power when his biography of his famous ancestor, William, Lord Russell, appeared, and that of Mr. Disraeli when the veteran statesman took the world into his confidence with "Recollections and Suggestions." . . . Literature often claimed his pen, for, besides many contributions in prose and verse to periodicals, to say nothing of writings which still remain in manuscript and prefaces to the books of other people, he published about twenty works, great and small. Yet, his strength lay elsewhere. His literary pursuits, with scarcely an exception, represent his hours of relaxation and the manner in which he sought relief from the cares of State. . . . The "Essay on English Government" is, in fact, not the confessions of an inquiring spirit entangled in the maze of political speculation, but the conclusions of a young statesman who has made up his mind, with the help of Somers and Fox. . . . Though it must be admitted that he performed some parts of it in rather a perfunctory manner, the eight volumes which appeared between 1853 and 1856 of the "Memoirs, Journal, and Correspondence of Thomas Moore" represent a severe tax upon friendship, as well as no ordinary labour on the part of a man who was always more or less immersed in public affairs.—REID, STUART J., 1895, *Lord John Russell, pp.* 273, 275, 278.

The excellence of Russell's literary achievement was not proportioned to its quantity. His historical work, entitled "Memoirs of the Affairs of Europe" (1824), is but a fragment, and is more than a creditable compilation. Mr. Gladstone has, however, affirmed that "Burke never wrote anything better" than some passages, especially that running "When I am asked if such or such a nation is fit to be free, I ask in return, is any man fit to be a despot?" Russell's "Essay on the English Constitution" (1821) is the best work from his pen, while that containing the "Letters of the Fourth Duke of Bedford" (3 vols., 1842-3-6), with an historical introduction, is the most successful and interesting. . . . His literary skill is most marked in his epistolary writing, and his speeches and writings abound in happy and telling phrases.—RAE, FRASER, 1897, *Dictionary of National Biography, vol.* IX, *p.* 462.

James Bowling Mozley
1813–1878

Born, at Gainsborough, Lincolnshire, 15 Sept. 1813. Family removed to Derby, 1815. At Grantham Grammar School, 1822–28. Matric. Oriel Coll., Oxford, 1 July 1830; B. A., 1834; English Essay Prize, 1835; M. A., 1838: Fellow of Magdalen Coll., 1840–56; B. D., 1846; D. D., 1871. Intimacy with Pusey at Oxford. Contrib. to "British Critic," and "Guardian." Part editor of "Christian Remembrancer," 1845–55. Rector of Old Shoreham, Sussex, 1856–78. Married Amelia Ogle, July 1856. Bampton Lecturer, Oxford, 1865; Select Preacher, 1869. Canon of Worcester, 1869–71. Regius Prof. of Divinity, Oxford, and Canon of Ch. Ch., 1871–78. Died, at Shoreham, 4 Jan. 1878. *Works:* "The Influence of Ancient Oracles," 1836; "Observations on the Propositions to be submitted to Convocation" (anon.), 1845; "A Treatise on the Augustinian Doctrine of Predestination," 1855; "The Primitive Doctrine of Baptismal Regeneration," 1856; "A Review of the Baptismal Controversy," 1862; "Subscription to the Articles," 1863; "Eight Lectures on Miracles," 1865; "Observations on the Colonial Church Question," 1867; "The Roman Council," 1870 [1869]; "The Principle of Causation," 1872; "Sermons preached before the University of Oxford," 1876; "Ruling Ideas in Early Ages," 1877; *Posthumous:* "Essays Historical and Theological," ed. by his sister, 1878; "The Theory of Development" (from "Christian Remembrancer"), 1878; "Sermons, Parochial and Occasional," 1879; "Lectures, and other Theological Papers," 1883; "Letters," ed. by his sister, with *life* 1885 [1884].—SHARP, R. FARQUHARSON, 1897, *A Dictionary of English Authors*, p. 207.

PERSONAL

Among Dr. Mozley's youthful characteristics were simplicity of habits, warm but undemonstrative affections, sincerity of thought, an almost stern purity of mind, carelessness of worldly advancement or distinction, and a deliberate desire to attach himself to a worthy object of life. . . . He was fond of his friends and of society, conscious of his own powers, without valuing himself on them, and ready and liberal in his appreciation of others. But partly from the modesty of a man who had before him a high standard of excellence, partly because he could not easily do himself justice in spoken words, partly because it was a kind of serious amusement to him to observe and ponder, he did not talk much in company. If he spoke, he seemed to speak because there was something which ought to be said, and nobody else to say it; expressing himself in short and even abrupt sentences and well-chosen words, which showed even a critical or eager interest in what was going on; but, when this was done falling back into his normal state of amused or inquiring attention, like a man who has discharged a duty and is glad to have done with it. He was not an artist or a writer of poems, but he had a keen and somewhat analytical appreciation of what was beautiful to the eye or ear, whether severe or florid, and his writings show that his sense of things was as vigorous in point of humour and poetry as in point of philosophy. Pomp he respectfully appreciated, as on proper occasions a fitting instrument for the adornment of truth, and he was fully aware that a battle of principle may occasionally have to be fought on a point of detail. But he was quite superior to the triviality which agitates itself about prettinesses, the pomposity which feels itself exalted by being part of a ceremonial, or the captiousness which finds occasion for petty quarrel. Of cant or pretentiousness he was intolerant, of unction implacable perhaps to a fault, so that those who did not know him might imagine him dry. He had not the special excellences or the defects of a great preacher, and, with all his power of thought and imagery, could scarcely, I think, have become one, even had his delivery been better than it was. He was wholly genuine.—BLACHFORD, LORD, 1879, *Mozley's Essays, Historical and Theological, The Nineteenth Century*, vol. 5, p. 1013.

From infancy his mind busied itself with grave thoughts, which took such hold of him that he was from the first ready to be their champion. It is told of him that in the nursery he did battle for free will against his nurse, who, led away by a popular curate, had adopted fatalistic opinions. The controversial spirit, by which is meant not partisanship, but the willingness to combat for what he believed to be great truths, went with him through life. The thoughts and interests with which he began it, he held to its close, whatever variation in form and colour they might be forced to assume. The strong grip of great truths—intense tenacity of thought and of affection—that was James Mozley's main characteristic from first to last.—SHAIRP, JOHN CAMPBELL, 1880, *The Late Canon Mozley, Fraser's Magazine, vol.* 101. *p.* 174.

He was always critical of his own work as though he had an ideal he had never reached. He had to be persuaded into the due amount of satisfaction. His real lasting pleasure in his friends' praise was because it came from them.—MOZLEY, ANNE, 1884, *Letters of the Rev. J. B. Mozley, p.* 350.

So much of Dr. Mozley's power depended upon his self-restraint, that he himself is almost impenetrable. If his intimate letters had been entirely held back we would have hardly known him at all. As it is, perhaps the first impression is that he is very hard to know. He tells us much less both of himself and of others than the author of "Reminiscences of Oriel." From one point of view this reserve is attractive. Few thoughtful persons of the present century have solved Carlyle's problem of consuming their own smoke so completely.—SIMCOX, GEORGE AUGUSTUS, 1884, *Letters of the Rev. J. B. Mozley, The Academy, vol.* 26. *p.* 370.

GENERAL

They [Bampton Lectures] are an example, and a very fine one, of a mode of theological writing which is characteristic of the Church of England, and almost peculiar to it. The distinguishing features of it are a combination of intense seriousness with a self-restrained, severe calmness, and of very vigorous and wide-ranging reasoning on the realities of the case with the least amount of care about artificial symmetry or scholastic completeness. Admirers of the Roman style call it cold, indefinite, wanting in dogmatic coherence, comprehensiveness, and grandeur. Admirers of the German style find little to praise in a cautious bit-by-bit method, content with the tests which have most affinity with common sense, incredulous of exhaustive theories, leaving a large margin for the unaccountable or the unexplained. But it has its merits, one of them being that, dealing very solidly and very acutely with large and real matters of experience, the interest of such writings endures as the starting-point and foundation for future work. . . . It is marked throughout with the most serious and earnest conviction, but it is without a single word, from first to last, of asperity or insinuation against opponents; and this, not from any deficiency of feeling as to the importance of the issue, but from a deliberate and resolutely maintained self-control, and from an overruling ever-present sense of the duty, on themes like these, of a more than judicial calmness. — CHURCH, RICHARD WILLIAM, 1866-97, *Mozley's Bampton Lectures, Occasional Papers, pp.* 85, 132.

We have here a mind instinct with the best temper of Butler's school, living and active in mature vigor in presence of the questions of our own day: and the influence of such a mind is likely to perpetuate that temper, as the writings of the master seem now to fail to do, because those who are excited about questions of the day, and feel rightly that they have an importance not of the day only, are yet unable to recognise the same questions as they appeared to a different generation. It is seldom that an author with so vigorous a personality as Dr. Mozley's can be so adequately characterized by referring him to a particular school. He is too thoughtful a writer to allow us to suppose that he has learnt nothing except what he learnt from Butler: still more unjust would it be to describe him as merely an old-fashioned Churchman. But that intellectual self-restraint which is one of the best and most constant features of the school has been exercised by him in the repression of those opinions which are individual with him, and not direct outgrowths of the Anglican spirit or the Butlerian method.—SIMCOX, WILLIAM HENRY, 1876, *University and Other Sermons, The Academy, vol.* 10, *p.* 127.

It is not often that a collection of miscellaneous writings bears throughout so genuine and strong an impress of the writer's personality. Dr. Mozley led a retired life, and only in the latter portion of it came to be widely known; but he seems to have made a deep impression upon those who were brought into personal contact with him, and this impression will be shared by all who become acquainted with him through these pages. Even without the help of the affectionate and appreciative sketch which opens the volumes it would be impossible not to arrive at the conclusion that the author was a very able, a very sincere, and a very honest man; a man equally strong in his convictions, tenacious in his grasp, and independent in arriving at his conclusions. . . . His strongest intellectual bent was in the line of metaphysical enquiry; when dealing with philosophical principles his grasp was always vigorous. Combined with his marked analytic faculty was a cognate disposition to study the workings of human character, a disposition in his case so strong that the habit of searching beneath the external act for the hidden motive amounted almost to an instinct. We are told that he habitually speculated on the character of all with whom he came in contact, a fact which accounts for the distinctive merits and distinctive defects of the volumes before us.— DIMAN, J. L., 1879, *Mozley's Essays, The Nation*, vol. 28, p. 169.

Since the day, now nearly five and thirty years ago, when the Rev. J. H. Newman left the Church of England, there has not arisen within it any so solid and powerful theological teacher as James B. Mozley, the late Professor of Divinity in the University of Oxford. A teacher I call him, though it was by the pen, rather than by the living voice, that he taught his fellow-men. Looking back over the long interval that has elapsed since that great crisis, among the many able preachers and teachers in the Church of England, no one appears with a mind so massive and so profound as his. His voice, indeed, was seldom heard from the pulpit, or in any public place; he took little or no outward part in the movements of ecclesiastical affairs; yet from the retirement of his study he furnished his Church and his country with a body of thought larger and more substantive, he produced more work that will be a permanent possession, than any other contemporary teacher of the Church to which he belonged. — SHAIRP, JOHN CAMPBELL, 1880, *The Late Canon Mozley, Fraser's Magazine*, vol. 101, p. 174.

One cannot read Mozley's writings without feeling some surprise that a man of such gifts did not exercise a greater influence during his lifetime. From 1871 until his death, he was Regius Professor of Divinity in Oxford, and his biographer tells that he possessed every qualification for the post except the faculty of popular teaching. But why should a man who was almost equally gifted with ratiocinative and imaginative powers have been destitute of the faculty of popular teaching? We can only account for it on the supposition that he did not possess the power of awakening enthusiasm. He possessed himself, as his writings show, the power of being stirred to enthusiasm by high thoughts, but he may have wanted the power of taking his hearers into his sympathy. A certain intellectual hauteur seemed to have kept him apart from the mass of men, and prevented him either from leading a party, or gathering disciples around him. A reserved, distant tone is perceptible in all his writings. This is visible in his language, whether he is speaking of God, or his fellow-men. He wrote an essay on Luther, in which he shows an almost personal aversion to the reformer, and a strange want of appreciation of his greatness. But it was just what he most disliked in Luther that he himself most wanted. Had his religion and his humanity been of a somewhat less reserved and distant character, had he possessed a greater stock of homely sympathies, he would have assuredly gained a wider personal recognition while he was still living to enjoy it. The two large volumes of Essays, which were published after his death, raised his reputation as a writer and as a thinker, but in some respects they disappointed those who had been accustomed to regard him as a rare example of an impartial religious thinker. They contain passages of great beauty, and they show how versatile he was; but, in some of his historical estimates, he manifests a narrow-minded prejudice, an unfair animus, such as we expect in writers of the level of Dean Hook.—GIBB, JOHN, 1881, *Theologians of the Day—Canon Mozley, The Catholic Presbyterian*, vol. 5, p. 88.

Mozley treated hackneyed themes with the vigour and freshness which can only be attained by a genuine thinker; he is never a mere retailer of the commonplaces of others. . . . We can hardly turn over a page of what Mozley has written without meeting with some striking thought, and we are everywhere conscious of the perfect good faith and sincerity which animated him. But we cannot fail also to be reminded not unfrequently of the fact that he generally presented himself as an advocate, though a perfectly sincere advocate, and not as a judge or a philosopher. Hence he not uncommonly states questionable propositions as if they admitted of no question; and, in pushing on a vigorous front attack, he is not always aware that he has uncovered his flank.—CHEETHAM S., 1883, *Lectures and other Theological Papers, The Academy*, vol. 23, p. 127.

As exhibited in his works the theology of Canon Mozley is fragmentary. It is not seen as a system well proportioned, each part fitly adjusted to every other. This characteristic is due, however, simply to the fact that his published writings relate in the main to a few particular doctrines. His views in reference to doctrines not thus considered can be gathered only crumb by crumb, by inference and suggestion.— THWING, CHARLES F., 1884, *Theology of Canon Mozley, Bibliotheca Sacra*, vol. 41, p. 287.

I am surprised that you do not appreciate J. Mozley, a different animal *generically*, I should say, from Tom, though like them both. And surely, as to style, Jem had both imagination and acuteness, two strong gifts, though he had but little humour, and was apt to analyze too much. —LAKE, WILLIAM CHARLES, 1885, *Letter to Dean Merivale, Jan.* 17; *Memorials, ed. his Widow*, p. 269.

A very acute and striking theological writer as well as critic.—OLIPHANT, MARGARET O. W., 1892, *The Victorian Age of English Literature*, p. 325.

Although his manner of delivery was somewhat lifeless and uninteresting owing to weakness of voice, the matter of his professorial lectures were excellent, and one of his best works consisted of a course delivered to graduates, mostly themselves engaged in tuition, and entitled "Ruling Ideas in early Ages, and their relation to the Old Testament Faith."—GREENHILL, W. A. 1894, *Dictionary of National Biography*, vol. XXXIX, p. 250.

George Gilfillan
1813–1878

Critic and essayist, was born in the pleasant village of Comrie, Perthshire, where his father, who wrote under the *nom de plume* of "Leumas," his own Christian name spelt backwards, was a minister of the Secession Church. Gilfillan himself was ordained as minister of a United Presbyterian congregation in Dundee in 1836, where he remained till his death. In 1846 he collected some sketches originally written for his friend Thomas Aird's paper, the *Dumfries Herald*, into a volume called "A Gallery of Literary Portraits." In 1843 he published a sermon on "Hades, or the Unseen," which gave great offence to many of his clerical brethren, as seeming to admit a kind of purgatory in the future world; and in 1869 a book on "Christian Heroism," in which he affirmed that the standards of the Church were "Seen now to contain many blunders." Both these works somewhat estranged Mr. Gilfillan from his brethren, and it was some time before he could satisfy them of his orthodoxy. In 1854 he brought out "The Grand Discovery, or the Fatherhood of God," followed the next year by "The Influence of Burns on Scottish Poetry and Song." Mr. Gilfillan was the author of numerous other works, and at his death he was engaged on the "History of British Poetry." In 1881 appeared some of his "Sketches, Literary and Theological," under the editorship of Mr. Frank Henderson, M. P.—SANDERS, LLOYD C., ed. 1887, *Celebrities of the Century*, p. 481.

PERSONAL

His funeral, 17 Aug., at Balgay cemetery, was attended by a procession two miles long. Gilfillan's many friends acknowledged that success never spoilt him, and all recognised his generosity and sincerity. Though living so busy a life, he found time in vacations for much foreign travel.—EBSWORTH, J. W., 1890, *Dictionary of National Biography*, vol. XXI, p. 351.

GENERAL

A poor, meritorious Scotchman, a burgher minister in Dundee, of the name of Gilfillan, has published a book—I believe at his own expense too, poor fellow—under the title "Gallery of Literary Portraits," or some such things; and is about sending, as in duty bound, a copy to the quarterly. I know not whether this poor book will in the least lie in your way; but to prevent you throwing it aside without so much as looking at it, I write now to bear witness that the man is really a person of superior parts; and that his book, of which I have read some of the sections, first published in a country newspaper that comes to me, is worthy of being looked at a little by you,— that you may decide then, with cause shown, whether there *is* anything to be done with it. I am afraid not very much! A strange, oriental, scriptural style; full of fervour, and crude gloomy fire—a kind of *opium* style. However, you must look a little, and say.—CARLYLE, THOMAS, 1845, *Letter to Lockhart, Nov. 20; The Life and Letters of John Gibson Lockhart,* ed. Lang, vol. II, p. 240.

With all due charity, and largest allowances for his peculiar temperament, we must aver that Mr. Gilfillan is the most flagrant example of the "episodical" that we ever happened upon. No leap is too magnificent for him. Had he power equal to his wish, he would swim the Hellespont, and, without taking breath, hurry up the loftiest of the Olympus, and then at a bound, clear half the countries of the Orient, and alight on the snows that gird the mountains of the moon: and this, for pastime merely, while making a promenade from the Tuileries to the Place de Vendome. When we took up his book, and traced him through the sketch of Jeffrey, we rather liked him; but after bearing with his "sophomorics" to the sketch of Coleridge, we lost all patience, and wrote him down an ass. Yes, poor Dogberry had not half done justice to himself had he been George Gilfillan. Not that this same writer has not a considerable share of a certain sort of genius, . . . yet so vain is he and "protrusive," that it requires a large degree of Christian charity to segregate his faults from his excellences, and give the latter their full weight in the balance of our judgment.—BACON, R. H., 1847, *Gilfillan's Literary Portraits, American Review,* vol. 5, p. 387.

I hear that you have had the misfortune to be publicly praised by that coxcomb of coxcombs, Gilfillan.—PATMORE, COVENTRY, 1850, *Letter to William Allingham.*

He is beyond all doubt, one of those "second-sighted" men, "who see a sight we cannot see, and hear a voice we cannot hear." . . . We have read the book, which is introduced to us by a title so repulsive to our taste, with mingled emotions. There are some passages in it, and many single expressions, which convey vivid ideas, and present pleasing images. We concede to him fancy, imagination, and a very considerable acquaintance with sources of poetical imagery. But these are not the only qualifications that are needed, to write instructively on Hebrew Poetry. . . . We go to that garden for nutritious vegetables and salutary fruits. But we are presented by Mr. Gilfillan with pretty nosegays and splendid boquets. We go looking for healthful nourishment, and we are told to lie down among the pinks and tulips and jessamines and roses, and that we shall, by so doing, be better satisfied than by any common-place affair of eating. . . . We say in all simplicity and earnestness, that we are sorry so noble a theme and so good a design should be so painfully marred by glaring conceits and accumulated prettinesses.—STUART, MOSES, 1851, *Gilfillan's Bards of the Bible, North American Review,* vol. 73, pp. 240, 241, 258.

Mr. Nichol of Edinburgh was by no means fortunate in his choice of an editor for a series of the English poets, when he selected this gentleman to preface every volume with "a critical dissertation." He is well known as a productive and very lively author, a sort of literary conjuror in the sober walks of criticism, who never appears without a blaze of fireworks about his head. He carries what is called fine writing to an excess which quite outdistances the usual range of sophomoric effort in that direction. Like Sir Hudibras,

"For rhetoric, he could not ope
His mouth, but out there flew a trope."

He is a standing example of the evil of possessing too much fancy, too much sublimity, too much excitability, and too ready a command of the English and Scottish vocabularies. His metaphors are entirely out of proportion with the necessities and fitnesses of his subjects. There are quite too many of them to be genuine. We see the prettiness, and admire the sparkle, but think the display too extensive to be real.—DUYCKINCK, E. A., 1854, *Edward Young, North American Review,* vol. 79, p. 270.

He possesses one of the most dangerous of arts for any one who would achieve solid and lasting reputation,—that of great verbal facility, approaching to conversational familiarity. He is sometimes happy in his metaphors and apt in his allusions, but is more likely to be extravagant in the one and grotesque in the other; reminding us forcibly of the bombast and egotism so generally observable in the prevailing style of second-rate American writers. Mr. Gilfillan is by no means devoid of talent; and it is well worth his while by a course of wholesome discipline of his natural abilities, to correct the errors of a critical pen which sometimes displays more passion than judgment and more vigour of language than depth of thought. . . . Whatever other charges Mr. Gilfillan's critics may bring against him, he certainly cannot be accused of indolence, as, in addition to his professional duties, he contributes to no less than five or six periodicals. It is no slight commendation—but one to which he may justly lay claim—that a high moral purpose, a kindly spirit, and a hearty appreciation of the good, the right, and the true, are prominent characteristics of his writings.—ALLIBONE, S. AUSTIN, 1854–58, *A Critical Dictionary of English Literature* vol. I, p. 670.

He has been a very voluminous writer, but has been more ambitious of quantity in his productions than of quality. A dangerous facility of expression, unrestrained by a severe taste, has led him too often into what certainly approaches bombast.— HART, JOHN S., 1872, *A Manual of English Literature*, p. 602.

The industry of Mr. Gilfillan is a remarkable and honourable feature in his character; and his writings, though too often disfigured by rash judgments and a gaudy rhetorical style, have an honest warmth and glow of expression which attests the writer's sincerity, while they occasionally present striking and happy illustrations. From his very unequal pages, many felicitous images and metaphors might be selected.—CHAMBERS, ROBERT, 1876, *Cyclopædia of English Literature*, ed. Carruthers, p. 215.

Gilfillan's glowing papers, always eloquent while not undiscriminating, excited considerable attention in their contrast to the general tameness (occasionally flavoured by cynicism) of English criticism.—ESPINASSE, FRANCIS, 1893, *Literary Recollections and Sketches*, p. 373.

Last of all, "The National Burns," edited by the Rev. George Gilfillan is mainly notable for the Gilfillanism of its gifted Editor.— HENLEY, WILLIAM ERNEST, AND HENDERSON, THOMAS F., 1896, ed. *The Poetry of Robert Burns*, vol. II, p. 290, note.

Richard Henry Dana
1787–1879

Richard Henry Dana, the Elder. An American poet and essayist; born at Cambridge, Mass., Nov. 15, 1787; died Feb. 2, 1879. His lectures on Shakespeare's characters, delivered in the principal cities of the Atlantic coast (1839–40) awakened a deep public interest. His principal poems are: "The Change of Home" (1824); "The Dying Raven" (1825); "The Buccaneers" (1827), specially noteworthy for its magnificent descriptions of the vicissitudes of ocean scenery. To a periodical publication, *The Idle Man* (N. Y., 1821–22), of which he was editor, he contributed critical papers and several short stories; among them "Paul Fenton," and "Edward and Mary."—WARNER, CHARLES DUDLEY, ed. 1897, *Library of the World's Best Literature, Biographical Dictionary*, vol. XXIX., p. 130.

PERSONAL

The most charming way to see Dana was on his own coast, on the rocks, under a gray sky, as the small black figure moved slowly up and down the beach, with the face to the sea. . . . He sat beneath his portrait, the work of William M. Hunt, and as I cast my eyes at the portrait the thought came that this was an octogenarian, but as he drew me into conversation upon current literatures I could not but feel that I was talking with a man of my own age. To one who was specially intimate with him he recently said "I never remember I am old. I feel young." In fact, he never grew old. His beard grew to be silver gray, but he never used glasses, and even the print of the London *Guardian* was not too close for him to read by gaslight only a few days before his death. And so I found him the youngest old man I have ever met. His conversation was as fresh as salt-sea spray; it was racy; it sparkled. I never met a man who put more meaning into words. . . . His religious life, if less prominent than his literary life, was what was chief and best in him. He took the conservative side in the famous controversy in which his cousin, Dr. Channing, led the liberal side. His opinions were broad and strong; they were his own. He was not satisfied with the Calvinism of his day, and finally found his home in the Episcopal church, in which communion he henceforth lived and in which he died. He was one of the original founders of the Church of the Advent, and as long as it kept to its old position was warmly attached to it, and worshipped there to the last.—WARD, JULIUS H., 1879, *Richard Henry Dana, Atlantic Monthly, vol.* 43. *pp.* 522, 523, 524.

He was under the usual height, broad-shouldered but slight, still holding himself tolerably erect, with sight and hearing unimpaired, his eloquent and expressive eyes undimmed, and his pale countenance and fine regular features presenting a mingled air of sadness and unmistakable refinement, combined with the sweet, high-born courtesy of the old school of gentlemen. His silvery hair, reaching to his shoulders, and his full, flowing beard and long mustache of the same color, assisted in making him in his *tout ensemble* one of the finest living pictures that I have ever seen of noble and venerable age. I stood in the presence of Richard Henry Dana, the patriarch of American poets. Although over ninety years of age, he was still in the possession of a fair measure of health and strength, and in the enjoyment of a serene and sunny old age.— WILSON, RICHARD GRANT, 1879, *Richard Henry Dana, Scribner's Monthly, vol.* 18, *p.* 106.

In the old churchyard of his native town,
  And in the ancestral tomb beside the wall,
  We laid him in the sleep that comes to all,
And left him to his rest and high renown.
The snow was falling, as if Heaven dropped down
  White flowers of Paradise to strew his pall;—
  The dead around him seemed to wake, and call
His name, as worthy of so white a crown.
—LONGFELLOW, HENRY WADSWORTH, 1880, *The Burial of the Poet, Ultima Thule, p.* 53.

THE BUCCANEER
1827

"The Buccaneer," is a story of supernatural agency, founded, as the author says in his Preface, on a tradition relating to an island off the New England coast. It is a narrative of a murder committed by a piratical, hardhearted man, of whom the whole island stood in awe, and who at last comes to a strange and horrible end. . . . The incidents are strongly conceived, and brought before the reader, with great distinctness of painting. It seems to us, however, that the rough brutality of the Buccaneer's character is sometimes brought out so broadly, as to have rather an unpleasing effect. Yet nothing, it seems to us, can be better in its way, than the passage in which his remorse is described, after it had finally mastered and subdued his spirit.—BRYANT, WILLIAM CULLEN, 1828, *Dana's Poems, North American Review, vol.* 26, *pp.* 243, 244.

There is a boldness in the outline of this poem, and a strength of conception in the incidents, which bespeak genius of no common stamp. The elements of the work are of a description to put to a rigorous test the powers of the writer. The feelings engendered in the darkest recesses of the human heart, and the workings of the stronger and sterner passions of our nature, demand great boldness in the mind that would explore their mysteries, and superior skill in the hand that would subdue them to the purposes of poetry. The spirits of the air come not at the bidding of common mortals; it is only the potent wand of the true enchanter which can summon them from their abodes and command them to do his pleasures. Mr. Dana has approached this subject evidently with a correct appreciation of the daring nature of his attempt, and the execution of his task indicates a careful study of his materials. His subject is one, which in its main features, has been turned to frequent use in poetry, yet he has treated it in a manner peculiarly his own. . . . The most striking effects of the poem relate more to the manner, than the matter. There is an abruptness in the progress of the narrative, which sometimes appears like a want of connection in the incidents, as if the minor developments, here and there, yet remained to be supplied. The style is remarkable for its plainness and severity; it has no labored elevation or brilliancy, but is at the same time neat and expressive. The language is on the whole in good keeping with the subject. Its simplicity is well adapted to the representation of vehement passions, and is suited to the service and naked grandeur of those feelings which it is the object of the narrative to depict. Notwithstanding the deficiency of ornament in the style, the descriptions are in a high degree striking and picturesque. — KETTELL, SAMUEL, 1829, *Specimens of American Poetry, pp.* 2, 3.

The characters in this poem are not elaborately drawn and filled out. A few bold touches, and a sketch of living power starts into being before the reader's eye. A word, an expression, a line, open deep glances into the inmost hiding-places of the soul, like a flash of lightning suddenly let in upon the recesses of some gloomy cavern. On these daring pencillings, if we may be allowed a term from a kindred art, the shading of supernatural incidents is made to fall with startling effect, and here and there a trait of softest light, mingles sweetly with the general sternness of the piece. The style is terse and strong. Few words, chosen with consummate art, and constructed with singular power, each being necessary to give the full meaning, and not always doing that, form its leading characteristic.—FELTON, CORNELIUS CONWAY, 1834, *Dana's Poems and Prose Writings, Christian Examiner*, vol. 15, p. 397.

The poetical literature of our country can scarcely be said to have a longer date than that of a single generation. As a matter of fact, the very fathers of it are still living. It really commenced with Bryant's "Thanatopsis" and Dana's "Buccaneer." The grave, philosophic tone, chaste simplicity of language, freedom of versification, and freshness and truth of illustration, which marked the former poem, and the terse realism of the "Buccaneer," with its stern pictures of life and nature drawn with few strokes sharp and vigorous as those of Retzsch's outlines, left the weak imitators of an artificial school without an audience. —WHITTIER, JOHN GREENLEAF, 1875, *ed. Songs of Three Centuries, Preface*, p. iv.

"The Buccaneer" is remarkable for its representation, equally clear, of external objects and internal moods of thought and passion. In one sense it is the most "objective" of poems; in another, the most "subjective." The truth would seem to be that Dana's over-powering conception of the terrible reality of sin—a conception almost as strong as that which was fixed in the imagination of Jonathan Edwards—interferes with the artistic disposition of his imagined scenes and characters, and touches even some of his most enchanting pictures with a certain baleful light.—WHIPPLE, EDWIN PERCY, 1876-86, *American Literature and Other Papers, ed. Whittier*, p. 40.

"Dana's imagination has none of the frisky lightness and celerity of an Ariel, but, combining something of the wild grandeur of a Salvator with the imposing darkness of a Rembrandt, is intent upon transferring to his sombre canvas the effect of crime to beget more appalling crime, to dry up the founts of human feeling in the soul, to blast the springing shoots of tenderness and manliness and honor in the heart, to render the man more cruel as he becomes more callous, to banish him from the circle of human sympathies and affections, and to separate him from the companionship of his kind by the solitariness of his unparalleled atrocities, till he becomes unendurable even to himself; and at last, stung by the ghost of unbidden memories, preyed upon by remorse, and maddened by spectral fears and terrors, he plunges beneath the angry waves of black despair."—DESHLER, CHARLES D.. 1879, *Afternoons with the Poets*, p. 277.

"The Buccaneer," on which Dana's reputation rests, is a very striking and graceful poem, dealing with a ghastly story of crime on the high seas which is a little out of keeping with a style as cold and severe as that of Akenside. It is written, moreover, in an unattractive stanza, of which this is an example:—

"A sweet, low voice, on starry nights,
 Chants to his ear a plaining song;
Its tones come winding up the heights,
 Telling of woe and wrong;
And he must listen, till the stars grow dim,
The song that gentle voice doth sing to him."

But the poem is well composed, and must be judged, not by the standard of to-day, but by that of the "Corsairs" and "Jacquelines" in competition with which it was written. In Dana's other poems he shows himself a tamer and less stately Bryant, always graceful, and sometimes very felicitous, preferring, however, the heroic measure to Bryant's eighteenth-century blank verse.— GOSSE, EDMUND, 1879, *Mr. Richard Henry Dana, Senior, The Academy*, vol. 15, p. 144.

In depicting the strongest human feelings and emotions, such as avarice and cruelty, bravado and cowardice, defiance and remorse, the poem possesses a certain power that both fascinates and repels the reader. There are passages of remarkable beauty that are almost sublime, yet one finishes its perusal with the feeling that the poet's execution falls short of the high design. There is a lack of melody in spite of its elaborate finish, as well as a lack of those essentials that appeal to the sympathies of the reader, and leave indelible impressions upon his memory. It is neither a great nor beautiful poem. . . . The great Scotch critic was perhaps correct in declaring, "We pronounce it by far the most powerful and original of American poetic compositions." —ONDERDONK, JAMES L., 1899-1901, *History of American Verse*, p. 124.

GENERAL

Notwithstanding the cold reception it ["The Idle Man"] met with from the public, we look upon as holding a place among the first productions of American literature. It will be referred to hereafter, we doubt not, as standing apart from the crowd of contemporary writings, and distinguished by a character of thought and expression peculiarly its own. . . . He seems to have fixed his attention only upon what he thought the permanent qualities of literature, and his work is one which will be read with the same pleasure a century hence, as at the present time. . . . The style of "The Idle Man" is genuine mother English, formed from a study of the elder authors of the language, with now and then a colloquial expression of the humblest kind, elevated into unexpected dignity, or an obsolete word or phrase revived, as if on purpose to excite the distaste of the admirers of a stately or a modernized diction. It is free from all commonplace ornaments, from all that multitude of stock metaphors and illustrations which have answered the uses of authors from time immemorial.—BRYANT, WILLIAM CULLEN, 1828, *Dana's Poems, North American Review*, vol. 26, p. 239.

In attempting to compress his language he is sometimes slightly obscure, and his verse is occasionally harsh, but never feeble, never without meaning. . . . All the writings of Dana belong to the permanent literature of the country. His prose and poetry will find every year more and more readers. —GRISWOLD, RUFUS WILMOT, 1842, *The Poets and Poetry of America*, p. 65.

Mr. Dana is, perhaps, our most original poet. No American productions, with which we are acquainted, are characterized by such intense subjectiveness, or bear so deep an impress of individuality, as those of the author of the "Buccaneer." We feel in reading them, that the inward life of the man has found utterance in the rugged music of the poet. He seems never to have written from hearsay, or taken any of his opinions at second-hand. Perhaps this is to be attributed, in a great degree, to his habits of retirement. . . . In description, he excels, perhaps, all his American contemporaries.—WHIPPLE, EDWIN PERCY, 1844, *Poets and Poetry of America, Essays and Reviews* vol. I, pp. 44, 46.

I fear, owing a very large portion of his reputation to his *quondam* editorial connection with the "North American Review."— POE, EDGAR ALLAN, 1846, *The Literati, Works*, ed. Stedman and Woodberry, vol. VIII.

Mr. Dana is a writer of great purity and power, of much acuteness and elegance in other walks than in those of philosophic sentiment, or of sentimental description; but in those he is a master, and ranks first among his contemporaries and countrymen. He has vast power in depicting the struggles of the darker passions, jealousy, hatred, suspicion and remorse. "Paul Felton" has touches of Byronic force, and discloses a similar vein to that so fully opened, and with such popular effect, in the works of Godwin and Charles Brockden Brown. In "Paul Felton," Mr. Dana has exhibited power in depicting passion, as well as sentiment; and the same criticism applies to his "Thornton," though in a much inferior degree. Yet he is most at home in pictures of domestic life; in describing the charm of home-scenes, in realizing the ideals of conjugal felicity. Strange that the author who, as a man, is so enthusiastic on such a theme, should, as a poet (for he is one, as much in "Tom Thornton" and "Paul Felton," as in the "Buccaneer"), delight in pictures also of gloom, of crime, of remorse. . . . A writer, equally excellent in prose and poetry, seems to be regarded as a sort of intellectual bigamist. The narrowness of vulgar judgments will no more allow a twofold excellence than the law will allow of more than one wedded wife. It is hence, perhaps, the poetry of Dana has been underrated. His prose fiction is so powerful and fine, his criticism so acute and searching, his moral writing so deep and subtle, that with most critics his poetry must suffer in proportion. Mr. Griswold has pointed out its principal defect, occasional harshness, (almost inseparable from vigorous earnestness), while he has dwelt justly upon its depth and richness of thought Mr. Dana is essentially a philosophic poet, with perhaps more of thought than imagination; a reflective rather than a creative genius, we mean in degree and relatively. Most of his poetry is grave, and much of it religious. There is a spirituality about it, highly characteristic of the writer and the man. Domestic life, and childhood, and feminine purity, are his favorite and frequent themes. —JONES, W. A., 1847, *The Writings and Literary Character of R. H. Dana, American Review*, vol. 5, pp. 270, 271.

Here comes Dana, abstractedly loitering along,
Involved in a paulo-post future of song,
Who'll be going to write what'll never be written
Till the Muse, ere he thinks of it, gives him the mitten,—
Who is so well aware of how things should be done,
That his own works displease him before they're begun,—
Who so well all that makes up good poetry knows,
That the best of his poems is written in prose;
All saddled and bridled stood Pegasus waiting,
He was booted and spurred, but he loitered debating;
In a very grave question his soul was immersed,—
Which foot in the stirrup he ought to put first,
And, while this point and that he judicially dwelt on,
He, somehow or other, had written Paul Felton;
Whose beauties or faults, whichsoever you see there,
You'll allow only genius could hit upon either.
That he once was the Idle Man none will deplore,
But I fear he will never be anything more;
The ocean of song heaves and glitters before him,
The depth and the vastness and longing sweep o'er him,
He knows every breaker and shoal on the chart,
He has the Coast Pilot and so on by heart,
Yet he spends his whole life, like the man in the fable,
In learning to swim on his library table.
—LOWELL, JAMES RUSSELL, 1848, *A Fable for Critics.*

There are a simplicity and individuality about Dana's writings, which give him the decided impress of being a man of more originality than he really possesses. There is less reliance upon foreign sources for his subjects; he likewise treats them in a manner of his own, which compels the reader to respect him for his intention, if he cannot applaud him for the successful result of his experiment.—POWELL, THOMAS, 1850, *The Living Authors of America,* p. 248.

The contents of the "Idle Man" have been long known to the lovers of Mr. Dana's writings. It is now nearly thirty years since that little publication was suspended, and nearly twenty, since its stories were collected, together with the poetry, and published in a single duodecimo volume. The most powerful of the fiction is "Paul Felton," —a terrible delineation of the course of a highly sensitive and educated mind, the victim of morbid feelings, perverting the good and innocent into causes of suspicion and jealousy, and dragged, as by the power of fiends, along its wretched path of misery to murder, exhaustion, and death. To depict such scenes demands very high powers, —a profound insight into the heart, and a certain experience of the sorrows of a morbidly sensitive mind.—BROWN, S. G., 1851, *Dana's Poems and Prose Writings, North American Review,* vol. 72, p. 131.

Dana was really the first poet who possessed power enough to delineate the natural peculiarities of his country and to discover the romantic treasures lying hid in its history.—SCHERR, J., 1874, *A History of English Literature,* tr. *M. V.,* p. 300.

The life of Richard Henry Dana has special interest for all Americans, from the circumstance that it includes the entire literary history of the nation, not excepting Barlow's "Vision of Columbus," which appeared about the time of his birth. He has seen the whole achievement, of which he is an honored part. His own contribution to it is none the less important, because so unobtrusively made. He has never been one of those who attach themselves to the structure as a flying buttress, or seek to shoot aloft at an ornate and conspicuous pinnacle; but when we examine the foundations, we shall find his chisel-mark on many of the most enduring blocks.—TAYLOR, BAYARD, 1877, *Richard Henry Dana, Essays and Notes,* p. 278.

The general impression which the poetry of Richard Henry Dana leaves upon the mind is that he is not so much a poet as a man of vigorous intellect who had determined to be a poet, and that he reached this determination too late in life. He moves like one who is shackled by his measures, whether they are simple, as in "The Buccaneer," or of a higher order, as in "The Husband and Wife's Grave" and "The Dying Raven." The literary career of Richard Henry Dana may be said to have practically ended with the publication of the little volume containing "The Buccaneer" (1827), though he afterward added to it as many more poems as were contained therein (nine in all), and brought out a collected edition of his works in two volumes.—STODDARD, RICHARD HENRY, 1879, *Richard Henry Dana, Harper's Magazine, vol.* 58, *p.* 775.

Brown's influence is apparent in two

novels of Richard Henry Dana, "Tom Thornton" and "Paul Felton," in which a more graceful, if still somewhat abrupt, style is employed, with almost equal vigour, if inferior originality, to illustrate similar monstrosities of character, on the basis of incidents almost equally unnatural, and directed to a moral purpose with such intensity that they are said to have rather frightened than amused their readers.—NICHOL, JOHN, 1882–85, *American Literature*, p. 162.

The reader will not go to Dana for any original work in prose. He was a reader and lover of books, and brought good ones to America; wrote about them in the "Review;" and, with the Channings—who were his cousins—with the Everetts, and Sparkses and Walkers, made a good centre about which a new literary culture formed itself; but after the literature began to grow, he was easily distanced by the young men who reverenced and outgrew him. Except for that rare and brilliant genius, William Ellery Channing, brought up in part like himself in Newport, he was the oldest of the group that welcomed Wordsworth and the "Lake" people, and blessed them because they loved Nature—the only poetical thing, except his fireside and his liberty, which the New Englander then found to love.—

MORSE, JAMES HERBERT, 1887, *Richard Henry Dana, Sr., The Critic*, vol. 11, p. 239.

His poems, published in 1827, under the title of "The Buccaneer, and Other Poems," were too psychological to be popular: but they picture with striking vividness both the outward and the inward world, and show a truly Calvinistic conception of the reality of sin. Their power is greater than their art: and their beauty is overshadowed by their gloom. Dana was one of those men who gave glimpses of powers apparently equal to any achievement, but who never —for whatever reason—achieve quite what is expected of them.—HAWTHORNE, JULIAN, AND LEMMON, LEONARD, 1891, *American Literature*, p. 116.

Wrote better prose than verse. "The Buccaneer" is based on a finely poetical sea-superstition, but is awkwardly told; all his poems seem manufactured, and most are dull. His reviews of Brown, Irving, and others, in *The North American*, are sensible, and the style is clear and strong. The tales, "Tom Thornton" and "Paul Felton" (in his periodical, *The Idle Man*,) have considerable power, although the didactism of the first is too obvious and the second is a rather violent imitation of Brown.—BRONSON, WALTER C., 1900, *A Short History of American Literature*, p. 170.

William Lloyd Garrison
1805–1879

Journalist and abolitionist, was born at Newburyport, Mass., December 10, 1805. He was apprenticed to the printer of the "Newburyport Herald," and at seventeen began to write for it. In 1824 he became editor of the "Herald," and in 1829 joint editor of the "Genius of Universal Emancipation," published in Baltimore. The vigorous expression of his anti-slavery views led to his imprisonment for libel; but friends paid his fine. He delivered emancipation lectures in New York and other places, and returning to Boston, in 1831 started the "Liberator," a paper which he carried on until slavery was abolished in the United States. For the first few years he was constantly threatened with assassination and prosecution, and was even subjected to personal violence, but he persevered. In 1833, 1846, and 1848 he visited Great Britain, and on his first return organised the Anti-slavery Society, of which he was president. In 1865, after the total abolition of slavery, Garrison's friends presented him with 30,000 dollars. He died at New York, 24th May 1879. He published "Sonnets and Other Poems" (1847). See Lives by his children (4 vols. 1885–89; new ed. 1893), Johnson (1881,) Grimke (1891), and Goldwin Smith (1892). —PATRICK AND GROOME, eds., 1897, *Chambers's Biographical Dictionary*, p. 397.

PERSONAL

Champion of those who groan beneath
  Oppression's iron hand:
In view of penury, hate, and death,
  I see thee fearless stand.
Still bearing up thy lofty brow,
  In the steadfast strength of truth,
In manhood sealing well the vow
  And promise of thy youth.
—WHITTIER, JOHN GREENLEAF, 1833, *To W. L. G.*

The haters of Garrison have lived to rejoice in that grand world-movement which, every age or two, casts out so masterly an agent for good. I cannot speak of that gentleman without respect. — EMERSON, RALPH WALDO, 1844, *Journal*; *A Memoir of Ralph Waldo Emerson*, ed. Cabot, vol. II, p. 430.

In a small chamber, friendless and unseen,
  Toiled o'er his types one poor, unlearned young man;
The place was dark, unfurnitured, and mean;—
  Yet there the freedom of a race began...
O small beginnings, ye are great and strong,
  Based on a faithful heart and weariless brain!
Ye build the future fair, ye conquer wrong,
  Ye earn the crown, and wear it not in vain.
—LOWELL, JAMES RUSSELL, 1848, *To W. L. Garrison*.

He never trifled, made no account of sharp points or minute particulars, was seldom humorous, not often sarcastic, and cared little for studied phrases. Although, to the surprise of most men, probably, there are more epigrammatic and pithy sayings in his speeches—"hits," as Brougham somewhat irreverently calls such bursts—*mots* which will pass into literature—than can be culled from the orations of Webster. His tone was that of a grave and serious indictment; his whole soul freighted his words. Entirely forgetting himself, an intense earnestness melted everyone into the hot current of his argument or appeal, and the influence, strong at the moment, haunted the hearer afterward, and was doubled the next day. He was master of a style of singular elevation and dignity. Windham said the younger Pitt "Could speak a king's speech off-hand." So far as dignity of tone was concerned, Garrison could have done it. No American of our day could state a case, or indite a public document, with more wary circumspection, impressive seriousness, or grave dignity than he could. The "Declaration of Sentiments" by the convention which formed the American Antislavery Society, and that Society's statement of its reasons for repudiating the United States Constitution, have a breadth, dignity, and impressive tone such as are found in few, if any, of our state papers since the Revolution, when Dickinson, Jay, Hamilton, and Adams won such emphatic praise from Lord Chatham. — PHILLIPS, WENDELL, 1879, *North American Review*, vol. 129, p. 150.

He stands out in the same distinct relief among his contemporaries as against his predecessors; for while others of his own party equaled or surpassed him in genius, wit, eloquence, personal attractiveness, social position, ingenuity of attack, brilliancy of defense; yet by his clearness and integrity of nature he surpassed them all, and was the natural leader of all. However keen others might be in moral discernment, he was keener; however ably others might deal with a sophist, his exposition was sure to be the most cogent and convincing. To preserve this mastery among his associates he used no manœuvres, exerted no devices, asked no favors. He never attitudinized, and he never evaded; but his power in his own circle was as irresistible as the law of gravitation. He was never hurried or disconcerted or even vexed; indeed, he did not expend himself on special contests or fret about particular measures. Where others fought to win he simply bore his testimony, which in the end proved the path to winning. I well remember how, at the height of some fugitive-slave case, when it seemed to his associates as if the very gate of freedom turned on keeping that particular slave from bondage, he would be found at his compositor's desk—for he always set up his own editorials—as equable as ever, and almost provokingly undisturbed by the excitement of that fleeting hour.— HIGGINSON, THOMAS WENTWORTH, 1885, *William Lloyd Garrison, Century Magazine*, vol 30, p. 588.

I never saw my father draw even a diagram, and he had not the least training in drawing; yet his penmanship was handsome, and wonderfully persistent in its uniformity. It was always, however, very labored and inflexible, and latterly he wrote much in pencil, having begun with quills, then taken to steel nibs, and sometimes used a gold pen.... His ambidextrousness abided with him to the end: he shaved himself with great facility, using either hand; at table he held his knife in his left. He was what would be called a handy man about the house, though not fertile in contrivances. He hung the window-shades and the pictures — the latter with a good eye to symmetry, squareness, and general effect. He *helped* in everything.... He had neither a Scientific nor, strictly speaking, a poetic love of nature. He had no botanical knowledge whatever, and small cognizance of the varieties of trees or flowers. A solitary walk in the country could hardly have been congenial to him, at least as an habitual diversion. . . . My father's love of pets never forsook him—or, rather, of cats: towards dogs he had an aversion. . . . The love of a pretty face was inextinguishable in my father. It pleased him, as it does many a man, more than any other beautiful thing in nature. His æsthetic sense in general was uncultivated, but it would have repaid cultivating. He had a great fondness for pictures, with but little artistic discrimination, his modest purchases being often dictated by pure sentiment. His visit to the Louvre gave him pleasure, in spite of much that seemed to him rubbish, while the scenes of gory battle canvases at Versailles offended his moral sensibilities. He took real delight and lingered long in the art section of the Paris Exposition of 1867, of which he especially enjoyed the statuary where the intent was chaste. It fell to his lot to befriend artists among other struggling and impecunious fellow-beings, and his charity to them was undoubtedly reïnforced by his love of art. To music he was attuned from infancy, and he never ceased to sing.—GARRISON, WENDELL PHILLIPS, 1889, *William Lloyd Garrison, The Story of his Life Told by his Children*, pp. 309, 311, 312.

I was a frequent visitor at the home of William Lloyd Garrison [1844]. Though he had a prolonged battle to fight in the rough outside world, his home was always a haven of rest. Mrs. Garrison was a sweet-tempered, conscientious woman, who tried, under all circumstances, to do what was right. She had sound judgment and rare common sense, was tall and fine-looking, with luxuriant brown hair, large tender blue eyes, delicate features, and affable manners. They had an exceptionally fine family of five sons and one daughter. Fanny, now the wife of Henry Villard, the financier, was the favorite and pet. All the children, in their maturer years, have fulfilled the promises of their childhood. Though always in straitened circumstances, the Garrisons were very hospitable. It was next to impossible for Mr. Garrison to meet a friend without inviting him to his house, especially at the close of a convention.—STANTON, ELIZABETH CADY, 1897, *Eighty Years and More*, p. 128.

It happened that I met him at one of Parker's Sunday evenings at home. I soon felt that this was not the man for whom I had cherished so great a distaste. Gentle and unassuming in manner, with a pleasant voice, a benevolent countenance, and a sort of glory of sincerity in his ways and words, I could only wonder at the falsehoods that I had heard and believed concerning him.— HOWE, JULIA WARD, 1899, *Reminiscences, 1819–1899*, p. 153.

There never was a more benevolent face than William Lloyd Garrison's. He had a kindly eye, a winning smile, a gentleness of way, a crisp, straightforward way of talking, and a merciless movement in straight lines of thought. — POND, MAJOR JAMES BURTON, 1900, *Eccentricities of Genius*, p. 13.

GENERAL

Next, your turning Author. You have no doubt read and heard the fate of such characters, that they generally starve to death in some garret or place that no one inhabits; so you may see what fortune and luck belong to you if you are of that class of people. Secondly, you think your time was wisely spent while you was writing political pieces. I cannot join with you there, for had you been searching the scriptures for truth, and praying for direction of the holy spirit to lead your mind into the path of holiness, your time would have been far more wisely spent, and your advance to the heavenly world more rapid. But instead of that you have taken the Hydra by the head, and now beware of his mouth; but as it is done, I suppose you think you had better go and seek the applause of mortals. But, my dear L., lose not the favour of God; have an eye single to his glory, and you will not lose your reward. — GARRISON, FANNY LLOYD, 1823, *Letter to William Lloyd Garrison, June 3*.

Garrison is so used to standing alone that, like Daniel Boone, he moves away as the world creeps up to him, and goes farther *into the wilderness*. He considers every step a step forward, though it be over the edge of a precipice. But, with all his faults (and they are the faults of his position), he is a great and extraordinary man. His work may be over, but it has been a great work. Posterity will forget his hard words and remember his hard work. I look upon him already as an historical personage, as one who is in his niche. You say it is a merit of Theodore Parker's letter that there is no "Garrisonism" in it. Why, it is full of Garrisonism from one end to the other. But for Garrison's seventeen years' toil, the book had never been written. I love you (and love includes respect); I respect Garrison (respect does not include love). There never has been a leader of Reform who was not also a blackguard. Remember that Garrison was so long in a position where he alone was right and all the world wrong, that such a position has created in him a habit of mind which may remain, though circumstances have wholly changed.—LOWELL, JAMES RUSSELL, 1848, *To C. F. Briggs, March 26; Letters, ed. Norton, vol.* I, *p.* 125.

Garrison will be recognised hereafter, not only as at present,—as the Moses of the enslaved race, leading them out of their captivity,—but as more truly the founder of the Republic than Washington himself.—MARTINEAU, HARRIET, 1855–77, *Autobiography, ed. Chapman, vol.* I, *p.* 373.

We ought to rejoice that he whose life has just closed has left to us an example grand like the hill-tops against a clear evening sky. It stands out to be a guide and direction to all of us who come after him. I can think of no funeral in the history of the world where those left behind had so much reason to rejoice. When we look back over his life of more than three-score years and ten, and see it filled with beneficient work, a work that leaves its mark on this age and on the ages to come,—it seems to me, instead of sorrowing we can rejoice that this example is left us. With the full possession of his powers, this friend has completed his work.—STONE, LUCY, 1879, *Tributes to William Lloyd Garrison at the Funeral Services, May 28, p.* 17.

If America had produced no other men of action besides Washington and Garrison, she would have gained the right to place these men amongst the very greatest of the race. Garrison is one of those men who have shown forth the living power of that religion which holds the Bible as the charter of human liberty and the source of our divinest hopes. He gained his influence over men through the appeal which he made to their consciences as believers in that Book. He was a *moral* reformer to the end, and during many years of the struggle left such of his friends as were inclined, to wage the battle in the political arena. As for him, his arguments, his inspiration, and his encouragement were drawn from sources to which the politician might, or might not choose to repair. That single-hearted, intrepid, clear-eyed printer's boy, fastening his heart upon high enterprises, looks, to our mind, far greater than a Hannibal or a Wellington; and only those who have been the greatest benefactors of the poor, the weary, and the sad, have a right to be mentioned beside him when the story of his brave life is recalled for the instruction and encouragement of mankind. — DORLING, WILLIAM, 1880, *William Lloyd Garrison, The Modern Review, vol.* 1, *p.* 374.

"An Appeal to South Carolina," tells the real story of the time to an intelligent reader and is historically significant. Mr. Garrison, as author of the pamphlet, comes before us as a narrator of plain facts, revealing virtually the growth of this South-Carolinian element, and prophetic of startling issues: hence it seemed to me that we should accept the two sets of facts with their particular meanings, discriminating between good and evil, and avoid confounding things that differ. In view of this state of things, it must be evident, even to the youngest reader, that when Mr. Garrison, through "The Liberator," denouncing slaveholding as a sin against God and humanity, called upon the nation for repentance of that sin, and immediate abjuration of it, there was a power of truth and right in his appeal that touched millions.—HAGUE, WILLIAM, 1887, *Life Notes, p.* 152.

He wrote poetry throughout his marvelous career, and some of his sonnets are hardly excelled in depth of feeling and poetic beauty.—PERLEY, SIDNEY, 1889, *The Poets of Essex County Massachusetts, p.* 58.

"I began the publication of the 'Liberator' without a subscriber, and I end it—it gives me unalloyed satisfaction to say—without a farthing as the pecuniary result of the patronage extended to it during thirty-five years of unremitted labors." These were Garrison's words when he brought his editorship to a close. The contrast is curious between the barrenness of the Abolitionist journalism and the immensely profitable circulation of the Abolitionist novel.—SMITH, GOLDWIN, 1892, *The Moral Crusader, William Lloyd Garrison, p.* 193.

The writings of Garrison, although very voluminous, would not in themselves give their author literary distinction. They were simply a means to an end, a by-product from a career devoted fixedly to the accomplishment of a great purpose. His ringing orations and scathing paragraphs are now as dead as the issue that called them forth. Yet Garrison will ever hold a high place in the history of American thought and literature. While it is yet too early to estimate the true extent of his influence on the spirit of his times, it can with safety be said that this influence was widespread and vital.—PATTEE, FRED LEWIS, 1896, *A History of American Literature*, p. 326.

Charles Tennyson Turner
1808–1879

Born, at Somersby, Lincs., 1808. Educated at Louth Grammar School till 1820; at home, 1820–28. Matric., Trin Coll., Camb., 1828; Bell Scholarship, 1828; B. A., 1832. Ordained Deacon, 1835. Curate of Tealby, 1835. Vicar of Grasby, Lincs., 1835–79. Married Louisa Sellwood, 1837. Took additional surname of Turner, on succeeding to estate of his great-uncle, 1838. Contrib. poems to "Macmillan's Mag.," 1860. Died, at Cheltenham, 25 April 1879. *Works:* "Poems by Two Brothers" (with Alfred and Frederick Tennyson), 1829; "Songs and Fugitive Pieces," 1830; "Sonnets," 1864; "Sonnets, Lyrics, and Translations," 1873. *Posthumous:* "Collected Sonnets, old and new," 1880.—SHARP, R. FARQUHARSON, 1897, *A Dictionary of English Authors*, p. 278.

PERSONAL

Midnight—in no midsummer tune
　The breakers lash the shores:
The cuckoo of a joyless June
　Is calling out of doors:
And thou hast vanish'd from thine own
　To that which looks like rest,
True brother, only to be known
　By those who love thee best.
Midnight—and joyless June gone by,
　And from the deluged park
The cuckoo of a worse July
　Is calling thro' the dark;
But thou art silent underground,
　And o'er thee streams the rain,
True poet, surely to be found
　When Truth is found again.
—TENNYSON, ALFRED, 1879, *Midnight, June 30.*

His ideal was high, his opinion of himself low; he was not stimulated to self-assertion by any disputes or jealousies—if he ever thought ill of anybody but himself (which I doubt), he never acted upon the thought:—in such cases a sensitive mind will turn to self-criticism and fall into delusions; and as a foreign enemy is the best cure for internal dissension, it may well be that when he called in his genius to defend his creed, his old quarrel with it for want of originality was forgotten, and he consented to employ it again in its proper work. . . . He was a scholar, a reader, and, though not a great traveler, he had seen strange lands. His memory was well stored with classical imagery. The great events and great biographies of the past, the struggles of the nations and the victories of humanity in the present, and the hidden future of his country and his race, filled him with emotion, and inspired strains which will probably take place hereafter, many of them, among the memorable utterances of our time. He was always original; his thoughts and language, both, were always his own, whether they had been used by others or not; and his range was wide.—SPEDDING, JAMES, 1879, *Charles Tennyson Turner, Nineteenth Century*, vol. 6. pp. 467, 470.

With wreaths of love we crown thy natal day,
Though thou hast vanished from thy fellowmen,
The sweet voice silenced, and the ready pen,
With all it might have painted, put away.
Never again to us will light-winged lay
New beauties waft, caught by the subtle ken,
Nor to our longing ears ever again
New music from thy cunning harp will stray.
But still thy gentle presence seems to brood
O'er the dim distance of the azure wold,
O'er summer cornfield, and o'er lonely wood:
Still in thy books communion I can hold
With all that is most lovely, true, and good,
And feel thy spirit stir me as of old.
—WILTON, RICHARD, 1879, *In Memory of Charles Tennyson Turner, July 4.*

A mere obituary sketch scarcely admits of detail, otherwise many anecdotes might be told of his delight in his garden, of his fondness for his dogs, of his training his horses to obey his voice rather than rein or whip, and of his playful gentleness with children. No one, however, who reads his poems, can well fail to perceive the "alma beata e bella" breathing through them; and those who best knew him feel that in these he almost lives again as he was in his daily life. Yet, when I talked with him a year ago, nothing of what he had written seemed to me to represent in full measure that simplicity of the man—at once childlike and heroic.—TENNYSON, HALLAM, 1880, ed. *Collected Sonnets Old and New*, p. x.

In reading the sonnets we can see him moving about in his parish, succouring the poor, consoling the sick, cheering the aged folk, and speaking kindly to the children; thinking, as he goes, of the news that had that day reached him from the great world, and with an eye ever open to new beauties and new phases of nature. One who knew Charles Tennyson well, could not help regarding Dr. Johnson's Latin epigram on Parnell as especially applicable to him, and thus turned it into English verse, and wrote it in the fly-leaf of his sonnet-book:—

"Poet and Priest alike, in neither least,
In both complete, though far too meek to know it;
For not the Poet's sweetness lacks the Priest
And not the Priestly holiness the Poet."

The slightest incident, the most ordinary event of his daily life, is enough to stir his retiring muse; the first budding green of the spring, the later yellowing leaves of autumn still clinging to the trees, the harvest-field, the first note of cuckoo or nightingale, the coming of the swallows, the first ice in winter, the beautiful play of light through the lattice, the setting free of a prisoned bird, the impression made on his children by some new book,—these are his themes; and he treats them with such simplicity, grace, and occasional sustained beauty of phrase, never affected or overdone.—JAPP, ALEXANDER H., 1892, *The Poets and the Poetry of the Century, Frederick Tennyson to A. H. Clough*, ed. Miles, p. 47.

GENERAL

In the present age it is next to impossible to predict from specimens, however favourable, that a young man will turn out a great poet, or rather a poet at all. Poetic taste, dexterity in composition, and ingenious imitation, often produce poems that are very promising in appearance. But genius, or the power of doing something new, is another thing. Mr. Tennyson's sonnets, such as I have seen, have many of the characteristic excellencies of those of Wordsworth and Southey.—COLERIDGE, SAMUEL TAYLOR, 1830, *Table Talk*, ed. Ashe, Apr. 18, p. 61.

I read last month C. Tennyson Turner's "Sonnets," than which there are none in the language more beautiful in their sincerity and truth.—TAYLOR, SIR HENRY, 1869, *To Mrs. Edward Villiers*, Jan. 24; *Correspondence*, ed. Dowden, p. 287.

The dominant charm of all these Sonnets is the pervading presence of the writer's personality, never obtruded, but always impalpably diffused. The light of a devout, gentle, and kindly spirit, a delicate and graceful fancy, a keen, if not very broad, intelligence, irradiates their thoughts, while to the language in which they are condensed, Art lends a power that

"Consolidates the flame,
And keeps its colours, hardening to a gem."

—HEWLETT, HENRY G., 1873, *English Sonneteers: Mr. Charles Turner, Contemporary Review*, vol. 22, p. 637.

I dare to say that Charles's share in the volume of 1830, and his onward all-too-widely sundered and timidly-put-forth triplet of volumes, will satisfy whosoever cares to take pains to master them, that if he had elected to be Poet rather than Cleric, he might have run neck-to-neck in the glorious race and crown-winning of our Laureate. Nay, more. There are elements of poetic inspiration and *motif* in Charles, that the world had been the richer for had they been shared by Alfred; for where the younger brother is hazy and indefinite, and growingly inarticulate on the deepest facts and problems, the elder is open-eyed and clear-spoken, and that not professionally or because he is a parson, but from the inevitableness of his whole-brained, whole-hearted, though unclamorous godliness.— GROSART, ALEXANDER B., 1875, *The Rev. Charles (Tennyson) Turner, Leisure Hour*, vol. 24, pp. 711, 716.

Although strikingly original, both in subject and treatment, Mr. Turner's muse cannot fail to suggest the piety, purity, and simplicity of Cowper; the deep, calm, reflective vein, with spirit analogies and teachings from nature, which is characteristic of Wordsworth; and also the condensation, felicitous epithet, and the exquisitely polished, careful art-finish of his brother—the poet laureate.—SYMINGTON, A. J., 1875, *Charles (Tennyson) Turner, International Review*, vol. 2, p. 602.

Like Violets, I say: to be overlooked by the "madding Crowd," but I believe to smell sweet and blossom when all the gaudy Growths now in fashion are faded and gone. He ought to be known in America—everywhere.—FITZGERALD, EDWARD, 1878, *To C. E. Norton*, Dec. 15; *Letters*, ed. Wright, vol. I, p. 433.

Charles Turner has a clear and loving eye

for outward Nature and her ways, but his bias was not towards the inner essence of her delicate idealism, nor was he enraptured into grave and mystic adoration in her venerable presence. He delighted in sunshine and shadow, he reflected on the singular powers of flying rain and tossing breeze, he was much with the sights and sounds of moorland and lea; but all these and their like were for him subordinate and instrumental, not so much guiding to ideal retreats and spiritual forces hidden away within and behind themselves, as co-operating with the individual soul towards the highest culture and the energies of pure Being. Nor is his attitude simply that of a moral disciplinarian or an ingenious artist of didactic allegories. To leave such an impression as that would be to entirely misrepresent the poet. His strength lies in that pure, healthy sentiment which depends on close and energetic association, and is illustrated rather in meditative gravity than in conclusive and axiomatic dogma. Undoubtedly there is a moral bias in these sonnets, but it never degenerates into monotonous advocacy or morbid appeal. Nature's impressions on the poet's mind are sharp and decisive, and they are invariably depicted so as to arrest and hold the reader; they are, moreover, inspiring and suggestive, and the feelings and reflections that arise out of them are natural and of pure and sterling quality.—BAYNE, THOMAS, 1881, *Charles Tennyson Turner, Fraser's Magazine*, vol. 104, p. 795.

The graceful and finished compositions. . . . Reminding one of no other person in his own family or out of it.—DOYLE, SIR FRANCIS HASTINGS, 1886, *Reminiscences and Opinions*, p. 76.

Charming, even permanently beautiful as many of his sonnet-stanzas are, their form cannot be admired: if we have been correct in considering the so-called pure types to be the true expression of certain metrical laws, then certainly these compositions of his are not sonnets, but only (to repeat Mr. Ashcroft Noble's appropriate term for similar productions) sonnet-stanzas. The rhythm is much broken up, and the charm of assured expectancy is destroyed.—SHARP, WILLIAM, 1886, *ed. Sonnets of this Century, Introduction*, p. lv.

He is delightfully single-minded, disinclined to any resource that may seem merely artistic or self-conscious. His mind is like a crystal to take the shape and colour of what is presented to it, and seen in that crystal all is transformed, beautified. He did not need to travel far—"to trundle back his soul a thousand years"—to find subjects for poetic treatment; the events, the sights, the scenes of every day, in his quiet rural parish, were enough. The book thus becomes a faithful mirror of a good man's life, whose wealth of good will and charity are not exhausted in it. In few cases have poems been more directly written from the heart and personal feeling.—JAPP, ALEXANDER H., 1892, *The Poets and the Poetry of the Century, Frederick Tennyson to A. H. Clough*, ed. Miles, p. 53.

Apart from the main stream of poetry, there were separate streams which represented distinct passages in the general movement. The "Sonnets" of Charles Tennyson Turner, which began in 1830, stand by their grace and tenderness at the head of a large production of poetry which describes with him the shy, sequestered, observant life of the English scholar and lover of nature, of country piety and country people.—BROOKE, STOPFORD A., 1896, *English Literature*, p. 246.

This poet's sympathy was so gracious, so all-pervading, that it has dyed with its own colours not only the landscape with all its smaller features,—birds and flowers, but also the very tools of the labourer, the steam-thresher, the distant railway—the poet's imagination not only personifying, but ensouling them with human life, under pressure of a strange personal energy. Henry Vaughan, two centuries before, has shown the same power, which is quite distinct from the gift of vivid description.— PALGRAVE, FRANCIS TURNER, 1896, *Landscape in Poetry*, p. 273.

Both as to fame, and probably as to his own productiveness, Charles Tennyson Turner was crushed, as it were, under his greater brother. He wrote little more, though he carefully revised and in some respects decidedly improved his sonnets. It is by virtue of them that he takes his place among English poets. They are graceful and sweet, but the substance is not always worthy of the form. They reveal everywhere the interests and the pursuits of the Vicar of Grasby, and they are honourable to his peaceful piety. It is evident that both Charles and Frederick Tennyson, and especially the latter, might have been disposed to adapt to themselves the humorous complaint of the second Duke of Wellington, and exclaim, "What can a man do with such a brother?"—WALKER, HUGH, 1897, *The Age of Tennyson*, p. 53.

Like the only other master of the sonnet with whom he can be compared, Wordsworth, he wrote, or rather printed, too many for his fame. Some are on topics such as the questions at issue between orthodoxy and scepticism, which are wholly unfitted for declamatory treatment in the sonnet form, while others are of inadequate interest or workmanship. But when all deductions are made there remains a considerable body of sonnets of rare distinction for delicate and spiritual beauty, combined with real imagination.—AINGER, ALFRED, 1899, *Dictionary of Nationa' Biography*, vol. LVII.

Charles Jeremiah Wells
1800–1879

In his youth became acquainted with the Keats brothers, and with R. H. Horne. In 1822 he published, anonymously, "Stories after Nature," and in 1824, "Joseph and His Brethren, a Scriptural Drama: in Two Acts," using the pseudonym "H. L. Howard." This was revived in 1876, with an introduction by Mr. Swinburne. Practised law early in life, and at one time held a professorship at Quimper. His closing years were passed at Marseilles.—STEDMAN, EDMUND CLARENCE, ed., 1895, *A Victorian Anthology*, p. 709.

PERSONAL

Anybody could see that Wells was fond of field sports and all out-of-door exercises. He was a fair horseman, a pretty good shot; and he liked to talk about fishing, though I seldom heard of his taking anything, at any rate before he left England. He understood floriculture, and would have been a really good gardener but for his impatient habit of now and then pulling up plants to see how the roots were getting on, carefully putting them back again. He would do this early in the morning, before anybody else was up, Mrs. Wells told me.—HORNE, RICHARD HENGIST, 1879, *Charles Wells, The Academy*, vol. 15, p. 349.

It was somewhere between 1845 and 1847. . . . A healthy, ruddy-faced, weather-hardened, fleshless man, bright and cheery, foxy-looking (if it may be said without prejudice), the very type of a wiry sporting squire, who looked as if he lived always out-of-doors, and had too keen a relish for fresh air and following the hounds to have ever dreamed upon the side of Parnassus. His talk even was not of poetry, but, as chiefly recurs to me, of Brittany and (he had become a Catholic) of the good Breton *curé:* a character which I suppose neither Scott nor myself had much cared to discuss, but in which he greatly interested us.—LINTON, WILLIAM JAMES, 1879, *Charles Wells, The Academy*, vol. 15, p. 325.

GENERAL

"Joseph" is, perhaps, the solitary instance, within our period, of poetry of the very first class falling quite unrecognised and continuing so for a long space of years. Its time, however, will most assuredly still come. It is impossible here to make any but a passing allusion to it, as affording, in its command of various character, including even the strongest and most earthly passion, but all working within a circle of spiritual influence,—a perfect parallel with the productions of Blake's genius, though rather, perhaps, with its more complete development in painting, than its always somewhat fragmentary written expression. —ROSSETTI, DANTE GABRIEL, 1863, *The Life of William Blake by Alexander Gilchrist, Supplementary Chapter*, vol. I, p. 381.

In whatever degree the undeniable presence of minor faults and mere stains of carelessness may excuse the neglect of Mr. Wells's prose stories, no such plea of passing defect can extenuate the scandal of the fact that to this day his great dramatic poem remains known perhaps on the whole to about half a dozen students of English art. . . Only once before had such a character been given with supreme success, and only by him who has given all things rightly, in whom there was no shadow of imperfection or shadow of failure. In the Cleopatra of Shakespeare and in the heroine of the present play there is the same imperious conscience of power by right of supreme beauty and supreme strength of will; the same subtle sweetness of speech; the same delicately rendered effect of perfection in word and gesture, never violated or made harsh even by extreme passion; the same evidence of luxurious and patient pleasure found in all things sensually pleasant; the same capacity of bitter shame and wrath, dormant until the insult of resistance or rebellion has been offered; the same contemptuous incapacity to understand a narrower passion or a more external morality than their own; the same rapid and supple power of practical action. All women in literature after these two seem coarse or trivial when they touch on anything sensual; but in their passion there is nothing common or unclean; nothing paltry, no taint of vulgar sin or more vulgar repentance, can touch these two. And this the later poet, at least, has made out of the slightest and thinnest material possible; his original being not only insufficient—the very bare bones of conjecture, the suggestion of a skeleton character—but actually, as far as it was anything at all, so associated with ideas simply ludicrous and base that the very name of "Potiphar's wife" has the sound of a coarse by-word.—SWINBURNE, ALGERNON CHARLES, 1875, *An Unknown Poet, Fortnightly Review*, vol. 23, p. 219, 222.

After making all allowance for the exceeding fertility of literature, which in this century has resembled a tropical forest where bird of rarest plumage or plant of strangest hue may lurk unnoticed mid the prodigality of fair things around it, the neglect of the poem is still inexplicable. If it be great work in the true sense of that term, as I for one think it is, then it is as great as dramatic work—not, indeed, as a drama to be acted, for no one who has read it will conceive that it could be brought successfully upon the stage, but as a poem distinguished by dramatic situations, by dramatic imagery, by the dramatic marking and sustaining of character.—SYMONDS, JOHN ADDINGTON, 1876, *Joseph and his Brethren, The Academy*, vol. 9, p. 375.

The adventures of his one known book form an extraordinary page of literary history. "Joseph and his Brethren" came into the world unnoticed, as veritable a stillbirth of genius as ever occurred. Hazlitt, it is true, said the book was "more than original, aboriginal, and a mere experiment in comparison with the vast things" Wells could do; but Hazlitt forebore to review it, and even constantly dissuaded the young poet from writing. About 1838 another neglected writer, Thomas Wade, author of "Mundi et Cordis Carmina," spoke out in loud commendation of the pseudonymous and forgotten drama. In 1844 Mr. R. H. Horne, writing his charming "New Spirit of the Age," made space for a clear and generous statement that "Joseph and his Brethren" was "full of the elements of true poetry—rich in passion, in imagination, and in thoughts resulting from reason, experience, and understanding"—but in vain. At last it happened to fall into the hands of Mr. D. G. Rossetti, and in 1863, while writing of Blake, he paid a princely tribute to Wells. The tide now turned at last; "Joseph and his Brethren" became a kind of Shibboleth —a rite of initiation into the true poetic culture—but still the world at large knew nothing of it. Finally, however, Mr. Swinburne, who is never tired of indulging in the "noble pleasure of praising," and whose eye is ever open to excellence of any kind, made it a duty to resuscitate the forgotten poet, and the results were his eloquent article in the *Fortnightly Review*, and the reprint of the drama issued by Messrs. Chatto and Windus in 1876.—GOSSE, EDMUND, 1879, *Charles J. Wells, The Academy*, vol. 15, p. 189.

But anything more unchastened than "Joseph and his Brethren" it has been the lot of but few poets to bring to the birth. Although for outpourings of pure poetry, the results of first-hand observation of life and nature, the work challenges the highest comparison, there was no serious attempt to endow its teeming beauties with a compact and fitting form, very little care concerning such details as spelling and punctuation— which seem to have been left to some one, as Wells says, "more ignorant than himself" —and not too much attention to grammar or metrical exactness. Indeed it is said that Wells positively would not see the work through the press, and, once having written it and found a publisher, seemed to regard the whole thing very much as a joke. . . . Wells's discrimination of character throughout the work, whether in its first, its second, or its final state, is of the very essence of the dramatic faculty. The earthly scenes between Joseph and his brothers, however little adapted for representation, are masterly both in the individual handling of the several characters, and in the vivid perception of surroundings. The character of Pharaxanor, the wife of Potiphar, is a still higher flight of creation: she is of the great unflinching women of all literature: she lives in that strenuous sense in which Medea, Clytemnestra, Cleopatra, Brynhild, Gudrun, and Hallgerda Long-coat live. The unpublished version depicts her in her fall and degradation, as well as in her power, and leaves her the same complete and consistent character, once known, never to be forgotten. There are few pages of "Joseph and his Brethren" that are not instinct with high criticism of life and vitalized by poetic utterances, in which true thought is recorded with rare felicity of expression.—FORMAN, H. BUXTON, 1894, *The Poets and the Poetry of the Century, John Keats to Edward Lord Lytton*, ed. *Miles, pp.* 363, 368.

Wells's "Stories after Nature," published anonymously in 1822 (London, 12mo) are the nearest approach to the Italian novelette that our literature can show. Simple in plot, yet generally founded on some striking idea, impressive in their conciseness, and highly imaginative, they are advantageously distinguished from their models by a larger infusion of the poetical element, but fall short of them in artistic structure and narrative power, and the style is occasionally florid. They would have been highly appreciated in the Elizabethan age, but the great subsequent enrichment and expansion of the novel left little room for them in Wells's day. . . .

"Stories from Nature" being but a slight though a charming book, Wells's reputation must rest chiefly upon his dramatic poem. It is truly poetical in diction, and often masterly in the delineation of character; but its especial merit is the fidelity with which the writer reproduces the grand Elizabethan manner with no approach to servility of imitation. He is as much a born Elizabethan as Keats is a born Greek; his style is that of his predecessors, and yet it seems his own. It must have been impossible for him to draw Potiphar's spouse without having Shakespeare's Cleopatra continually in his mind, and yet his Paraxanor is an original creation. The entire drama conveys the impression of an emanation from an opulent nature to which production was easy, and which under the stimulus of popular applause, might have gone on producing for an indefinite period. The defect which barred the way to fame for him was rather moral than literary; he had no very exalted standard of art and little disinterested passion for it, and when its reward seemed unjustly withheld, it cost him little to relinquish it.—GARNETT, RICHARD, 1899, *Dictionary of National Biography*, vol. LX, pp. 225, 226.

Frances Ridley Havergal
1836–1879

An English religious writer and poet; born at Astley, Worcestershire, Dec. 14, 1836; died at Swansea, Wales, June 3, 1879. She began to write hymns and letters in verse at the age of seven, but did not publish anything until 1860. She was a frequent contributor to Good Words. Among over 30 publications, which once enjoyed considerable popularity, may be noticed: "The Four Happy Days" (1873); "Under the Surface" (1874), poems; "Royal Graces and Loyal Gifts" (6 vols. 1879); "Under His Shadow" (1879); and a number of posthumous works by various editors.—WARNER, CHARLES DUDLEY, ed., 1897, *Library of the World's Best Literature, Biographical Dictionary*, vol. XXIX, p. 253.

PERSONAL

She received her education at English and German boarding-schools, and enjoyed exceptional advantages of culture and travel. In the midst of it all her Christianity became her predominant characteristic, and her piety was as attractive as it was profound. She mastered languages with great ease. French, German, Italian, Latin, Greek, and Hebrew were among her acquirements. She even learned enough Welsh from her donkey-girl to take part in the Welsh church services. The scholarly instinct was strong within her, and her Bible—noted and underlined—was one of the best of proofs that she applied herself earnestly to the noblest themes. She was also finely musical—a performer, vocalist and composer, whom Heller was glad to approve—and the "Songs of Grace and Glory" furnish good proof of this.—DUFFIELD, SAMUEL WILLOUGHBY, 1886, *English Hymns*, p. 189.

The last nine years of her life were very sad. She lost her father and beloved stepmother, and became an invalid herself, suffering fearfully from a painful and mortal disease. When very near her end her physician said, "Good-bye, I shall not see you again." She asked, "Do you really think I am going?" When he said, "Yes, probably to-day," she smiled and exclaimed,

"Beautiful; too good to be true. It is splendid to be so near the gates of heaven." She was thrown into fearful convulsions; when they ceased, she nestled down in the pillows, folded her hands on her breast and said, "There now, it is all over—blessed rest!"—RUTHERFORD, M., 1890, *English Authors*.

GENERAL

In her little book of poems, entitled 'Under the Surface," we have groups of doctrinal verse, which ring out in all their clearness, and tell of "true metal;" while, in her little books of prose, we search in vain to find even one doubtful or meretricious sentence. Solid simple truth, offered to us in the attractive language of a child bringing us a message from her father; this is the general style of her writing, and as such we prize it. . . . Oh! that the inspired mantle of spiritual, prayerful, praiseful song might descend on some heart amongst us, for the continuation of the great work begun, by God's almighty power, through the gifted pen and hallowed life of Frances Ridley Havergal!—HOPE, E. R., 1879, *Frances Ridley Havergal, Catholic Presbyterian, vol. 2, pp. 275, 277*.

Whilst it is true that Miss Havergal learned in suffering what she taught in song, it is also true that she had made her poetic purpose a subject of much reflection. It was owing to the fact that she very early apprehended that her poetical efforts must be strictly commensurate with her poetical strength, and that she correctly gauged her poetical capabilities, that we have received at her hands those hymns which for the rich quality of their music have not been surpassed; and which for chastity of thought, reverence of spirit, and piety of feeling, have not been excelled by any religious writer since the days of Keble. Her "song chalice" might be frail, but not less sure was she that it was a work divine. . . . The "Ministry of Song," however, showed that Miss Havergal was not merely a writer of devotional lyrics, but a close observer of human life and character. If the book made it apparent that a new lyrist had arisen, it made it also distinctly apparent that one was moving in society who, having meditated a great deal on various problems of human life, was industriously taking notes of all she heard and saw therein. Her secular pieces bring us into direct contact with those subtle and hidden forces which go to the moulding and upbuilding of character; they also give language to those great unseen griefs and those terrible unuttered agonies that lie immediately below the surface of apparently tranquil lives. To this class of her writing belongs her fine poem "Wounded." Although it is only the record of a drawing-room experience, yet it is impossible not to be struck by its inimitable literary precision, its animated force, and its truthful picturing of a too common incident.—ANTON, P., 1880, *Frances Ridley Havergal, Fraser's Magazine, vol. 102, p. 482, 484*.

Reverting again to the devotional lyrics of the present day, those of Frances Ridley Havergal take high rank, alike for their poetic beauty, their freshness and religious fervor. Her productions, which have been worthily collected into a volume, remind us sometimes of the muse of Keble and anon of Faber and of Adelaide Procter.—SAUNDERS, FREDERICK, 1885, *Evenings with the Sacred Poets, p. 492*.

In poetry she was intensely religious, intensely subjective, and intensely sensitive to all beautiful or inspiring things. Many of her verses (like the "Moonlight Sonata," of which, by the way, she was an almost unrivalled interpreter) are really autobiographic. — DUFFIELD, SAMUEL WILLOUGHBY, 1886, *English Hymns, p. 189*.

Her religious poetry became exceedingly popular in evangelical circles, and her hymns are to be found in all collections. In her poetical work there is a lack of concentration, and a tendency to meaningless repetition of phrase, but some of her hymns are excellent, and will permanently preserve her name. Her autobiography was published in "Memorials of Frances Ridley Havergal, by her Sister, M. V. G. Havergal," 2nd edition, 1880. The influence of this book has been as remarkable as that of Miss Havergal's poems. It presents a striking picture of an unusually eager, if somewhat narrow, spiritual life.—BAYNE, RONALD, 1891, *Dictionary of National Biography vol. XXV, p. 180*.

Among the writers of religious verse and song no one has won a more enduring place in the homes and hearts of English speaking people than Frances Ridley Havergal. . . . She learned through suffering to dedicate her gifts and her life to the service of Christianity and many a soul has found the long needed help and comfort through her words.—RENFREW, CARRIE, 1895, *Frances Ridley Havergal, The Magazine of Poetry*, vol. 7, p. 339.

Miss Havergal's verse owes its popularity more to its religious teaching than to its poetic merit—teaching which has been aptly described as "mildly Calvinistic without the severe dogmatic tenet of reprobation." Without making any pretensions to the *rôle* of a poet, she gave lyrical expression to her own spiritual experiences and aspirations, and in doing so voiced the feelings and desires of others less able to express themselves. In this, though it cannot be said that she showed any marked originality of thought or felicity of expression, she at least fulfilled one of the offices of poetry. Many of her hymns have become widely popular, and have been included in various hymn-books in England and America. Her "Consecration Hymn," beginning

Take my life, and let it be
Consecrated, Lord, to Thee,

has been, as we imagine she would have desired it to be, one of the most popular. Whatever qualities her verse may lack, there can be no doubt as to its sincerity; and this is a quality not always found in religious verse. The entire consecration she sought to make included her powers of versification; and had they been much greater than they were, they would doubtless have been devoted as unreservedly to Christian service.—MILES, ALFRED H., 1897, *The Poets and the Poetry of the Century, Sacred, Moral, and Religious Verse*, p. 635.

James Clerk Maxwell
1831–1879

Physicist, born at Edinburgh, June 13, 1831, was educated there at the Academy and the University, and ere he was fifteen wrote papers of scientific value. At Cambridge he was (1845) second wrangler and bracketed with the senior wrangler for the Smith's prize. In 1856 he became a professor in Marischal College, Aberdeen, in 1860 in King's College, London, and in 1871 professor of Experimental Physics at Cambridge. He died November 5, 1879. In the great work of his life "Electricity and Magnetism" (2 vols. 1873), he constructed a theory of electricity in which "action at a distance" should have no place. He was the first to make colour-sensation the subject of actual measurement. He obtained the Adams prize for his splendid discussion of the dynamical conditions of stability of the ring-system of Saturn. But he was best known to the public by his investigations on the kinetic theory of gases. His Bradford "Discourse on Molecules" is a classic. Besides many papers, he published a text-book of the "Theory of Heat" and a little treatise on "Matter and Motion." In 1879 he edited Cavendish's "Electrical Researches." See his "Scientific Papers" edited by Niven (8 vols. 1890); his Life by Lewis Campbell and Garnett (1882); and Glazebrook's "Clerk-Maxwell and Modern Physics" (1896).— PATRICK AND GROOME, eds., 1897, *Chambers's Biographical Dictionary*, p. 645.

PERSONAL

As a professor he was wonderfully admired by those who were truly his disciples. He had not the power of making himself clearly understood by those who listened but casually to his pithy sentences, and consequently he was not a so-called popular lecturer; nor was he a most successful teacher of careless students. But when he had those about him who could enter into his mind, and, receiving the golden truths from his lips, could alloy them in such a way as to make them acceptable to the ordinary student, no better teacher could be desired, even for the most elementary instruction. His wonderful imagination was of great value, not only in supplying illustrations for didactic purposes, but in suggesting analogies and opening up new fields for research.—GARNETT, WILLIAM, 1879, *James Clerk Maxwell, Nature*, vol. 21, p. 45.

One great charm of Maxwell's society was his readiness to converse on almost any topic with those whom he was accustomed to meet, although he always showed a certain degree of shyness when introduced to strangers. He would never tire of talking with boyish glee about the d—l on two sticks and similar topics, and no one ever conversed with him for five minutes without having some perfectly new ideas set before him; sometimes so startling as to utterly confound the listener, but always such as to well repay a thoughtful examination. Men have often asked, after listening to a conversation on some scientific question, whether Maxwell were in earnest or joking.

The charm of his conversation rendered it very difficult to carry on any independent work when he was present, but his suggestions for future work far more than compensated for the time thus spent. . . . The leading note of Maxwell's character is a grand simplicity. But in attempting to analyse it we find a complex of qualities which exist separately in smaller men. Extraordinary gentleness is combined with keen penetration, wonderful activity with a no less wonderful repose, personal humility and modesty with intellectual scorn. His deep reserve in common intercourse was commensurate with the fulness of his occasional outpourings to those he loved. . . . Great as was the range and depth of Maxwell's powers, that which is still more remarkable is the unity of his nature and of his life. This unity came, not from circumstances, for there were breaks in his outward career, but from the native strength of the spirit that was in him. In the eyes of those who knew him best, the whole man gained in beauty year by year. As son, friend, lover, husband; in science, in society, in religion; whether buried in retirement or immersed in business—he is absolutely single-hearted. This is true of his mental as well as his emotional being, for indeed they were inseparably blended. And the fixity of his devotion both to persons and ideas was compatible with all but universal sympathies and the most fearless openness of thought.—CAMPBELL, LEWIS, AND GARNETT, WILLIAM, 1882, *The Life of James Clerk Maxwell*, pp. 370, 425, 432.

As a man Maxwell was loved and honoured by all who knew him; to his pupils he was the kindest and most sympathetic teacher, to his friends he was the most charming of companions; brimful of fun, the life and soul of a Red Lion dinner at the British Association meetings, yet in due season grave and thoughtful, with a keen interest in problems that lay outside the domain of his work, and throughout his life a stern foe to all that was superficial or untrue. On religious questions his beliefs were strong and deeply rooted; the words which close his lecture on molecules, expressing his faith in "Him, who in the beginning created not only the heaven and the earth, but the materials of which heaven and earth consists," have often been quoted. There is a bust by Boehm in the Cavendish Laboratory, and also a portrait painted by his cousin, Miss Wedderburn. The bust was executed after his death from Jeens's engraving, which forms the frontispiece to his works; and a portrait by Mr. Lowes Dickenson, based on the same engraving, was presented to Trinity College by the subscribers to the memorial fund.—GLAZEBROOK, R. T., 1894, *Dictionary of National Biography*, vol. XXXVII, p. 121.

GENERAL

Maxwell's reputation in the scientific world rests chiefly upon his contributions to electrical science and his speculation in "Molecular Physics." . . . If we inquire what were the qualities of the man which enabled him to accomplish so much, we think the most important moment will be found in an almost unique union of certain mental and physical powers.—FERRIS, W. M., 1883, *James Clerk Maxwell, The Nation*, vol. 37, p. 102.

Maxwell's work, as a whole, is characterised by two qualities which, taken together, convey to the mind an extraordinary impression of his genius: the first, a direct gift of insight which enabled him to picture to himself with vividness the most complicated phenomena; the second, a corresponding command of precise and luminous expression. To attribute to him these two qualities may seem at first sight paradoxical, for it is admitted that he never was a good lecturer, and that even in private oral exposition he was often hesitating, and sometimes confused. But the hesitation and apparent confusion arose from no want of inner clearness, but from an exuberance of imagination which made him interrupt himself, and hurried him on from one illustration to another in a way which often taxed the attention of his hearers. Something of this turbid overflow of thought or fancy shows itself in his letters, nor can it be contended that, when he leaves the solid ground of physical reasoning for the more airy regions of mental and religious philosophy, his vision has the same distinctness, or his expressions the same convincing clearness. But on his own ground he fully justified the remark about him attributed to Mr. Hopkins, the great Cambridge tutor of the last generation: "It is impossible that that man should think incorrectly on physical subjects." — SMITH, HENRY J. S., 1883, *A Life of Professor Clerk Maxwell, The Academy*, vol. 23, p. 19.

Of the "Electricity and Magnetism" it

is difficult to predict the future, but there is no doubt that since its publication it has given direction and colour to the study of Electrical Science. It was the master's last word upon a subject to which he had devoted several years of his life, and most of what he wrote found its proper place in the treatise. Several of the chapters, notably those on electromagnetism, are practically reproductions of his memoirs in a modified or improved form. The treatise is also remarkable for the handling of the mathematical details no less than for the exposition of physical principles, and is enriched incidentally by chapters of much originality on mathematical subjects touched on in the course of the work.—NIVEN, W. D., 1890, ed., *The Scientific Papers of James Clerk Maxwell, vol.* I, *p.* 29.

"One who has enriched the inheritance left by Newton and has consolidated the work of Faraday—one who impelled the mind of Cambridge to a fresh course of real investigation—has clearly earned his place in human memory." It was thus that Professor Lewis Campbell and Mr. Garnett began in 1882 their life of James Clerk Maxwell. The years which have passed, since that date, have all tended to strengthen the belief in the greatness of Maxwell's work and in the fertility of his genius, which has inspired the labours of those who, not in Cambridge only, but throughout the world, have aided in developing the seeds sown by him. . . . Since Maxwell's death volumes have been written on electrical questions, which have all been inspired by his work. The standpoint from which electrical theory is regarded has been entirely changed. The greatest masters of mathematical physics have found, in the development of Maxwell's views, a task that called for all their powers, and the harvest of new truths which has been garnered has proved most rich.—GLAZEBROOK, R. T., 1896, *James Clerk Maxwell and Modern Physics, pp,* 9, 216.

Maxwell called himself the interpreter of Faraday's views; but he was more than this; he built up a mathematical theory of magnetism and electricity which will be a lasting monument to his genius. He also propounded his electro-magnetic theory of light, in which he supposes that electrical energy is propagated by vibrations of the same æther which is supposed to transmit energy in the form of light. His theory supposes, in fact, that electricity and light are simply different aspects of the same phenomenon—a vibrating æther. In recent years Hertz, a pupil of Helmholtz, has, in a series of brilliant experiments, gone far towards verifying the results of Maxwell's theory of light. Electric waves have been obtained, and have been shown to be capable of reflection and refraction in exactly the same way as waves of light. Maxwell died in 1879, and the scientific world lost its most brilliant genius.—RHODES, W. G., 1897, *Social England, ed. Traill, vol.* VI, *p.* 352.

The natural philosophy of electricity, which may be said to have begun with Örsted and Ampère, is due in no small measure to the experimental researches and truly philosophical ideas of Faraday. The first consistent statement of it was given by Thomson, who expressed in mathematical language Faraday's ideas of lines of force, and deduced by a dynamical process the consequences of Faraday's experimental discoveries. Thomson's theory was at bottom one of action in a medium, and from it he obtained by deduction and experimental verification important discoveries of his own. Upon this quantitative philosophical discussion Maxwell to a great extent based his form of the theory, the essence of which is its dynamical character, and its explicit transference of the phenomena from the conductors and magnets and circuits to the electromagnetic field. The theory of light, though far from being the end, is the crown of the whole work.—GRAY, A., 1898, *Clerk Maxwell's Influence on Modern Physics, Nature, vol.* 58, *P.* 219.

George Eliot
Mary Ann Cross
1819–1880

1819.—Mary Ann Evans, "George Eliot," born November 22 at South Farm, Arbury, in Warwickshire. 1820–1841.—Lived at Griff House, Nuneaton, in the midst of farmhouses, and scenery described in "Adam Bede" and "The Mill on the Floss." 1824–1827.—Attended Miss Lathom's boarding school. 1827–1831.—Attended Miss Wallington's school

GEORGE ELIOT

From a Drawing by Frederic Burton.

RICHARD MONCKTON MILNES

Engraving from the Original Painting by R. Lehman.

and read Bunyan, Defoe, Johnson, Scott, Lamb, etc. 1831-1834.—At the Misses Franklin's school at Coventry, under strong Calvinistic influences. 1836.—Death of her brother; domestic cares; learns Italian and German; studies music, science, metaphysics, mathematics, and the great English poets. 1841.— March, removed to Coventry with her father; friendship with the Brays, resulting in a change in her religious views to Unitarianism; domestic disturbances. 1846.—Translated Strauss's "Leben Jesu." 1849.—May 31, death of her father, Robert Evans. 1849-1850.—Visited France and Italy; resided eight months in Geneva. 1851-1857.—Wrote for the *Westminster Review*, of which she became assistant editor; met Lewes, Chapman, Spencer, and the Martineaus. 1853.—Removed to Hyde Park, London. 1854.—Translated Feuerbach's "Essence of Christianity." 1854-1858.—Union with George Henry Lewes, journalist and philosopher; spent eight months in Weimar and Berlin; wrote for the *Leader* and *Westminster*. 1856-1858.—Publication of "Scenes of Clerical Life;" end of her incognito. 1859.—Publication of "Adam Bede," her first long novel. 1860.—Publication of "The Mill on the Floss;" visited Italy. 1861.—Publication of "Silas Marner;" visited Florence in May. 1863.—Publication of her great Italian novel "Romola," begun in the *Cornhill Magazine* for July, 1862. 1866.— Publication of "Felix Holt," a socialistic novel. 1867.—Visited Spain. 1868.—Publication of "The Spanish Gypsy," a dramatic poem, and other poems, "Agatha," "How Liza Loved the King," "Brother and Sister," etc. 1870.—Journey to Berlin and Vienna. 1871-1872.—Publication of "Middlemarch." 1872-1873.—Visited Hamburg and Cambridge. 1874.—Publication of "Legend of Jubal," and other poems. 1876.—Publication of "Daniel Deronda," a Jewish novel. 1877.—Removed to "The Heights," her country home in Surrey. 1878.—Met Turgenev and the Crown Prince and Princess of Germany; death of Lewes, November 28. 1879.—Publication of "Theophrastus Such." 1880.—May 6, marriage with John Walter Cross; death December 22.—WAUCHOPE, GEORGE ARMSTRONG, 1899, *ed. George Eliot's Silas Marner, p.* 15.

PERSONAL

Miss Evans (who wrote "Adam Bede") was the daughter of a steward, and gained her exact knowledge of English rural life by the connection with which this origin brought her with the farmers. She was entirely self-educated, and has made herself an admirable scholar in classical as well as in modern languages. Those who knew her had always recognized her wonderful endowments, and only watched to see in what way they would develop themselves. She is a person of the simplest manners and character, amiable and unpretending, and Mrs. B— spoke of her with great affection and respect.—HAWTHORNE, NATHANIEL, 1860, *French and Italian Note-Books, p.* 555.

It was at Villino Trollope, [the Florentine residence of Mr. T. Adolphus Trollope] that we first saw. . . George Eliot. She is a woman of forty, perhaps, of large frame and fair Saxon coloring. In heaviness of jaw and height of cheek-bone she greatly resembles a German; nor are her features unlike those of Wordsworth, judging from his pictures. The expression of her face is gentle and amiable, while her manner is particularly timid and retiring. In conversation, Mrs. Lewes is most entertaining, and her interest in young writers is a trait which immediately takes captive all persons of this class. We shall not forget with what kindness and earnestness she addressed a young girl who had just began to handle a pen, how frankly she related her own literary experience, and how gently she *suggested* advice. True genius is always allied to humility, and in seeing Mrs. Lewes do the work of a good Samaritan so unobtrusively, we learned to respect the woman as much as we had ever admired the writer. "For years," said she to us, "I wrote reviews because I knew too little of humanity."— FIELD, KATE, 1864, *English Authors in Florence, Atlantic Monthly, vol.* 14, *p.* 665.

July 14*th*.—A. travelled down from London with G. H. Lewes, who took him to his home at Witley and introduced him to Mrs. Lewes (George Eliot). A. thought her "like the picture of Savonarola." . . . *July* 22*nd* —. . . A. and Hallam called on Mr. and Mrs. Lewes. She is delightful in a *tête-à-tête*, and speaks in a soft soprano voice, which almost sounds like a fine falsetto with her strong masculine face.—TENNYSON, HALLAM, 1871, *Journal; Alfred Lord Tennyson, A Memoir by his Son, vol.* II, *p.* 107.

She is an accomplished linguist, a brilliant talker, a musician of extraordinary skill. She has a musical sense so delicate and exquisite that there are tender, simple, true ballad melodies which fill her with a pathetic pain almost too keen to bear; and yet she has the firm, strong command of tone and touch, without which a really scientific musician cannot be made. I do not think this exceeding sensibility of nature is often to be found in combination with a genuine mastery of the practical science of music. But Mrs. Lewes has mastered many sciences as well as literatures. Probably no other novel writer, since novel writing became a business, ever possessed one tithe of her scientific knowledge. . . . Mrs. Lewes is all genius and culture. Had she never written a page of fiction, nay, had she never written a line of poetry or prose, she must have been regarded with wonder and admiration by all who knew her as a woman of vast and varied knowledge; a woman who could think deeply and talk brilliantly, who could play high and severe classical music like a professional performer, and could bring forth the most delicate and tender aroma of nature and poetry lying deep in the heart of some simple, old-fashioned Scotch or English ballad. Nature, indeed, seemed to have given to this extraordinary woman all the gifts a woman could ask or have—save one. It will not, I hope, be considered a piece of gossiping personality if I allude to a fact which must, some day or other, be part of literary history. Mrs. Lewes is not beautiful. In her appearance there is nothing whatever to attract admiration.—MCCARTHY, JUSTIN, 1872, *"George Eliot" and George Lewes, Modern Leaders*, p. 137.

No one who had ever seen her could mistake the large head (her brain must be heavier than most men's) covered with a mass of rich auburn hair. At first I thought her tall; for one could not think that such a head could rest on an ordinary woman's shoulders. But, as she rose up, her figure appeared but of medium height. She received me very kindly. In seeing, for the first time, one to whom we owed so many happy hours, it was impossible to feel towards her as a stranger. All distance was removed by her courtesy. Her manners are very sweet, because very simple, and free from affectation. To me her welcome was the more grateful as that of one woman to another. . . . Looking into that clear calm eye, one sees a transparent nature, a soul of goodness and truth, an impression which is deepened as you listen to her soft and gentle tones. A low voice is said to be an excellent thing in woman. It is a special charm of the most finely-cultured English ladies. But never did a sweeter voice fascinate a listener—so soft and low, that one must almost bend to hear. . . . I should do her great injustice, if I gave the impression that there was in her conversation any attempt at display. There is no wish to "shine." She is above that affectation of brilliancy which is often mere flippancy. Nor does she seek to attract homage and admiration. On the contrary, she is very averse to speak of herself, or even to hear the heart-felt praise of others. She does not engross the conversation, but is more eager to listen than to talk. She has that delicate tact—which is one of the fine arts among women—to make others talk, suggesting topics the most rich and fruitful, and by a word drawing the conversation into a channel where it may flow with a broad, free current.—FIELD, MRS. HENRY M., 1875, *Home Sketches in France and Other Papers*, pp. 284, 285.

George Eliot is too great for the judgment of any less a critic than posterity. It will read her books in a broader light than we, in the light, also, of personal history of her life and of the literary material which has gone to the making of her books. In the absence of anything authentic about Shakespeare, the legendary deer-stealing became an event in English history. There is no writer who has had a more remarkable personal history than Mrs. Lewes, though she is known to the biographical dictionaries only by the dates of publication of her books, or a history that has had more marked influence on the direction of literary activity.—BOWKER, RICHARD ROGERS, 1877, *Daniel Deronda, International Review* vol. 4, p. 76.

Her face, instead of beauty, possessed a sweet benignity, and at times flashed into absolute brilliancy. She was older than I had imagined, for her hair, once fair, was gray, and unmistakable lines of care and thought were on the low, broad brow. . . . Dressed in black velvet, with point lace on her hair, and repeated at throat and wrists, she made me think at once of Romola and Dorothea Brooke. . . . She talked as she wrote; in descriptive passages, with the same sort of humor, and the same manner of linking events by analogy and inference. The walls were covered with pictures. I remember Guido's Aurora, Michael Angelo's prophets, Raphael's sibyls, while all about were sketches, landscapes and crayon drawings, gifts from the most famous living painters, many of whom are friends of the house. A grand piano, open and covered with music, indicated recent and continual use.—DOWNS, ANNIE, 1879, *A Visit to George Eliot, The Congregationalist, May* 28.

> Dead! Is she dead?
> And all that light extinguished! . . .
> How plain I see her now,
> The twilight tresses, deepening into night,
> The brow a benediction, and the eyes
> Seat where compassion never set, and like
> That firm, fixed star, which altereth not its place
> While all the planets round it sink and swim,
> Shone with a steady guidance. O, and a voice
> Matched with whose modulations softest notes
> Of dulcimer by daintiest fingers stroked,
> Or zephyrs wafted over summer seas,
> On summer shores subsiding, sounded harsh.
> Listening whereto, steeled obduracy felt
> The need to kneel, necessity to weep,
> And craving to be comforted; a shrine
> Of music and of incense and of flowers,
> Where hearts, at length self-challenged, were content
> Still to be sad and sinful, so they might
> Feel that exonerating pity steal
> In subtle absolution on their guilt.

—AUSTIN, ALFRED, 1880, *George Eliot, Dec.* 29; *Soliloquies in Song, pp.* 100, 102.

However I may lament the circumstances, Westminster Abbey is a Christian Church and not a Pantheon, and the Dean thereof is officially a Christian priest, and we ask him to bestow exceptional Christian honours by this burial in the Abbey. George Eliot is known not only as a great writer, but as a person whose life and opinions were in notorious antagonism to Christian practice in regard to marriage, and Christian theory in regard to dogma. How am I to tell the Dean that I think he ought to read over the body of a person who did not repent of what the Church considers mortal sin, a service not one solitary proposition in which she would have accepted for truth while she was alive? How am I to urge him to do that which, if I were in his place, I should most emphatically refuse to do? You tell me that Mrs. Cross wished for the funeral in the Abbey. While I desire to entertain the greatest respect for her wishes, I am very sorry to hear it. I do not understand the feeling which could create such a desire on any personal grounds, save those of affection, and the natural yearning to be near even in death to those whom we have loved. And on public grounds the wish is still less intelligible to me. One cannot eat one's cake and have it too. Those who elect to be free in thought and deed must not hanker after the rewards, if they are to be so called, which the world offers to those who put up with its fetters. Thus, however I look at the proposal it seems to me to be a profound mistake, and I can have nothing to do with it.—HUXLEY, THOMAS HENRY, 1880, *Letter to Herbert Spencer, Dec.* 27; *Life and Letters, ed. his Son, vol.* II, *p.* 19.

> OF THESE IMMORTAL DEAD WHO STILL LIVE
> ON
> IN MINDS MADE BETTER BY THEIR PRESENCE.
> HERE LIES THE BODY
> OF
> "GEORGE ELIOT"
> MARY ANN CROSS.
> BORN 22ND NOVEMBER, 1819.
> DIED 22ND DECEMBER, 1880.

—INSCRIPTION ON MONUMENT, 1880, *Highgate Cemetery.*

George Eliot, when you saw her in repose, had a forbidding countenance. People who did not like her used to say she looked like a horse; a remark which has also been made about a celebrated living actor. It was true so far as this: that the portion of the face below the eyes was disproportionately long and narrow. She had that square fullness of brow over the eyes which Blake had, and which led Blake to affirm that the shape of his head made him a Republican. George Eliot's radicalism went much farther than mere republicanism. She never can have been a beautiful woman, either in face or figure. She was tall, gaunt, angular, without any flowing ease of motion, though with a self-possession and firmness of muscle and fibre which saved her from the shambling awkwardness often the characteristic of long and loose-jointed people. . . . Her eyes were, when she talked, luminous and beautiful, dark in colour and of that unfathomable depth and swift changefulness which are seldom to be seen in the same orbs, except in persons whose force of character and force of intellect are both remarkable. They could be very soft, and she smiled with her eyes as well as with that large mouth of hers; and the smile was full of loveliness when it did not turn to mocking or mark that contemptuous mood which was not, I gather, very infrequent with her. In conversation which did not wake this demon of scornfulness, born of conscious intellectual superiority, the face was full of vivacity and light, whether illuminated by a smile or not.—SMALLEY, GEORGE W., 1880–91, *George Eliot, Dec. 25; London Letters and Some Others*, vol. I, pp. 246, 247.

Her low, soft voice, which is now spoken of as sweet and exquisitely modulated, seemed to me wanting in that something sympathetic and endearing which such voices usually possess. It was not exactly indifferent; but it seemed to have no vibrations of human weakness, whatever later sorrow and passion may have imparted to it. Subdued as it was, it was the voice of a strong woman; of one who needed not to assert herself and cared not for recognition. —LIPPINCOTT, SARA JANE (GRACE GREENWOOD), 1881, *The Independent*.

Somewhere about 1827 a friendly neighbor lent "Waverley" to an elder sister of little Mary Evans. It was returned before the child had read to the end, and in her distress at the loss of the fascinating volume she began to write out the story as far as she had read it for herself, beginning naturally where the story begins with Waverley's adventures at Tully Veolan, and continuing until the surprised elders were moved to get her the book again. Elia divided her childish allegiance with Scott, and she remembered fastening with singular pleasure upon an extract in some stray almanac from the essay in commemoration of "Captain Jackson," and his "slender ration of single Gloucester," and proverbs in praise of cheeserind. This is an extreme example of the general rule that a wise child's taste in literature is sounder than adults generally venture to believe. Not many years later we may imagine her a growing girl at school. Almost on the outskirts of the old town of Coventry, toward the railway station, the house may still be seen, itself an old-fashioned, five-windowed Queen Anne sort of dwelling, with a shell-shaped cornice over the door, with an old timbered cottage facing it, and near adjoining a quaint brick-and-timber building, with an oriel window thrown out upon oak pillars. Between forty and fifty years ago, Methodist ladies kept the school, and the name of "little mamma," given by her schoolfellows, is a proof that already something was to be seen of the maternal air which characterised her in later years, and perhaps more especially in intercourse with her own sex. Prayer meetings were in vogue among the girls, following the example of their elders, and while taking no doubt a leading part in these, she used to suffer much self-reproach about her coldness and inability to be carried away with the same enthusiasm as others. At the same time nothing was further from her nature than any sceptical inclination, and she used to pounce with avidity upon any approach to argumentative theology within her reach, carrying Paley's "Evidences" up to her bedroom, and devouring it as she lay upon the floor alone.—SIMCOX, EDITH, 1881, *George Eliot, The Nineteenth Century*, vol. 9, p. 779.

Here [Nuneaton] she was born in November, 1820[?]; and it seems pleasant to reflect that but a few miles off in the same county of Warwick was the birthplace of Shakspere, whose place among male writers seems more nearly filled by Marian Evans or George Eliot among female writers than by any other woman, so that we have the greatest English man and the greatest English woman born, though two centuries and a half apart in time, but a few miles apart in space.—LANIER, SIDNEY, 1881, *The English Novel*, p. 164.

It is difficult for any one admitted to the great honor of friendship with either Mr. Lewes or George Eliot to speak of their home without seeming intrusive, in the same way that he would have been who, unauthorized, introduced visitors, yet something may be said to gratify a curiosity which surely is not now impertinent or ignoble. When London was full, the little drawing-room in St. John's Wood was now and then crowded to overflowing with those who were glad to give their best of conversation, of information, and sometimes of music, always to listen with eager attention to whatever their hostess might say, when all that she said was worth hearing. Without a trace of pedantry, she led the conversation to some great and lofty strain. Of herself and her works she never spoke; of the works and thoughts of others she spoke with reverence, and sometimes even too great tolerance. But those afternoons had the highest pleasure when London was empty or the day wet, and only a few friends were present, so that her conversation assumed a more sustained tone than was possible when the rooms were full of shifting groups. It was then that, without any premeditation, her sentences fell as fully formed, as wise, as weighty, as epigrammatic, as any to be found in her books. Always ready, but never rapid, her talk was not only good in itself, but it encouraged the same in others, since she was an excellent listener, and eager to hear. Yet interesting as seemed to her, as well as to those admitted to them, her afternoons in London, she was always glad to escape when summer came, either for one of the tours on the Continent in which she so delighted, or lately to the charming home she had made in Surrey. She never tired of the lovely scenery about Witley, and the great expanse of view obtainable from the tops of the many hills.—PAUL, C. KEGAN, 1881, *George Eliot, Harper's Magazine, vol.* 62, *p.* 921.

A woman of strong passions, like her own Maggie, deeply affectionate by nature, of a clinging tenderness of disposition, Marian Evans went through much inward struggle, through many painful experiences before she reached the moral self-government of her later years. Had she not, it is hardly likely that she could have entered with so deep a comprehension into the most intricate windings of the human heart. That, of course, was to a great extent due to her sympathy, sympathy being the strongest quality of her moral nature. She flung herself, as it were, into other lives, making their affairs, their hopes, their sorrows her own. And this power of identifying herself with the people she came near had the effect of a magnet in attracting her fellow-creatures.—BLIND, MATHILDE, 1883, *George Eliot (Famous Women), p.* 56.

Mrs. Lewes' manner had a grave simplicity which rose in closer converse into an almost pathetic anxiety to give of her best—to establish a genuine human relation between herself and her interlocutor—to utter words which should remain as an active influence for good in the hearts of those who heard them. . . . Mrs. Lewes' humour, though fed from a deep perception of the incongruities of human fates, had not, except in intimate moments, any buoyant or contagious quality, and in all her talk,—full of matter and wisdom and exquisitely worded as it was, —there was the same pervading air of strenuous seriousness which was more welcome to those whose object was distinctly to *learn* from her than to those who merely wished to pass an idle and brilliant hour.—MYERS, FREDERIC WILLIAM HENRY, 1883, *George Eliot, Essays Modern, p.* 257.

On Friday, December 17, 1880, she attended the presentation of the Agamemnon of Æschylus in the original Greek, with the accompaniments of the ancient theatre, by the undergraduates of Balliol College, Oxford. She was very enthusiastic about this revival of ancient art, and planned to read anew all the Greek dramatists with her husband. The next day she attended a popular concert at St. James Hall, and listened with her usual intense interest. Sitting in a draught she caught cold, but that evening she played through much of the music she had heard in the afternoon. The next day she was not so well as usual, yet she met her friends in the afternoon. On Monday her larynx was slightly affected, and a physician was called, but no danger was apprehended. Yet her malady gained rapidly. On Tuesday night she was in a dangerous condition and on Wednesday the pericardium was found to be seriously diseased. Toward midnight of that day, December 22, after a period of unconsciousness, she quietly passed away. She was buried on the 29th, in the unconsecrated portion of Highgate Cemetery, by the side of George Henry Lewes.—COOKE, GEORGE WILLIS, 1883, *George Eliot, A Critical Study of Her Life, Writings and Philosophy, p.* 101.

I may mention here that my wife told me the reason she fixed on this name was that George was Mr. Lewes' Christian name, and Eliot was a good, mouth-filling, easily pronounced word.—CROSS, JOHN W., 1884, *George Eliot's Life as related in her Letters and Journals, vol.* I, *p.* 310.

Music was an absorbing passion with her. She played brilliantly, but her technical knowledge was even better than her power of performance. She played only for a few chosen friends. Her music was so intensely part of herself, that she could not give it freely; and it had a wonderful effect upon her. After either performing, or listening to, fine music, she was frequently completely unnerved, unable to command herself, and more likely to break down into tears than to talk calmly. But she enjoyed writing about harmony. No one ever drew the musical nature better than she did in the musician of "Daniel Deronda."—LILLIE, MRS. JOHN, 1885, *A Meeting with George*

Eliot, Some Noted Princes, Authors, and Statesmen of Our Time, ed. Parton, p. 64.

Although I had known Mary Ann Evans as a child at her father's house at Griff, our real acquaintance began in 1841, when after she came with her father to reside near Coventry, my sister, who lived next door to her, brought her to call upon us one morning, thinking, amongst other natural reasons for introducing her, that the influence of this superior young lady of Evangelical opinions might be beneficial to our heretical minds. She was then about one-and-twenty, and I can well recollect her appearance and modest demeanor as she sat down on a low ottoman by the window, and I had a sort of surprised feeling when she first spoke, at the measured, highly-cultivated mode of expression, so different from the usual tones of young persons from the country. We became friends at once. We soon found that her mind was already turning toward greater freedom of thought in religious opinion, that she had even bought for herself Hennell's "Inquiry," and there was much mutual interest between the author and herself in their frequent meetings at our house.— BRAY, CHARLES, 1885, *Phases of Opinion and Experience During a Long Life*, p. 257.

The life of Marian Evans had much I never knew—a doom of fruit without the bloom, like the Niger fig:—

> Her losses make our gains ashamed—
> She bore life's empty pack
> As gallantly as if the East
> Were swinging at her back.
> Life's empty pack is heaviest,
> As every porter knows—
> In vain to punish honey,
> It only sweeter grows.

—DICKINSON, EMILY, 1885, *To Thomas Niles, Letters*, vol. II, p. 418.

As a wise, benignant soul George Eliot will still remain for all right-judging men and women.—MORLEY, JOHN, 1885, *The Life of George Eliot, Macmillan's Magazine*, vol. 51, p. 256.

It is a pleasant, substantial house [Griff House], built of warm red brick, with old-fashioned, small-paned casement windows. The walls are almost hidden by creepers, a glorious old pear-tree, roses and jessamine, and over one end a tangle of luxuriant ivy. Across the smooth green lawn and its flower beds, an old stone vase covered with golden lichen made a point of color beneath the silver stems of a great birch-tree. Outside the light iron fence a group of sheep were bleating below a gnarled and twisted oak. Behind them rose the rich purple-brown wood we had come through, and beyond the wood we caught glimpses of far-away blue distance, swelling uplands and wide-stretching valleys, with here and there a huge chimney sending up a column of black smoke or white puff of steam. On the house roof pigeons were cooing forth their satisfaction at the sunshine. From the yew-tree close by, a concert of small chirping voices told that spring was coming, while a blackbird in the bushes made violent love to his mate, and wooed her with jovial, rollicking song. Within, the house is in much the same state as in the days of Mary Ann Evans's girlhood. — KINGSLEY, ROSE G., 1885, *George Eliot's Country, Century Magazine*, vol. 30, p. 346.

Conceive, next, the tenth Muse, or Sibyl, lounging in an arm-chair and shading her face idly with a hand screen; a powerful-looking, middle-aged woman, with a noticeable nose and chin, a low forehead, a fresh complexion, and full and very mobile mouth. Dress, on this occasion, a plainly cut, tight-fitting dress of blue cashmere, fastened at the throat with a cameo brooch. This was "Mawrian Evans," as Carlyle called her, the George Eliot of the novels. She realised in face and form the description I afterward gave to her in the "Session of the Poets:"

> George Eliot gazed on the company boldly
> With the limbs of a sylph and the head of John Locke!

I had been particularly struck by her resemblance to Locke's well-known portrait, engraved as a frontispiece of the famous "Essay." At that time her figure was graceful to elegance. When I last saw her, shortly before her husband's death, she stooped painfully as she walked, and wore an old-fashioned crinoline.—BUCHANAN, ROBERT, 1886, *A Talk with George Eliot, A Look Round Literature*, p. 219.

She was not, as the world in general is aware, a handsome, or even a personable woman. Her face was long; the eyes not large, nor beautiful in color—they were, I think, of a grayish blue—the hair, which she wore in old-fashioned braids coming low down on either side of her face, of a rather light brown. It was streaked with gray when last I saw her. Her figure was of middle height, large-boned and powerful. Lewes often said that she inherited from her peasant ancestors a frame and constitution originally very robust. Her head was finely formed, with a noble and well-balanced arch from brow to crown. The lips and mouth possessed a power of infinitely varied expression. George Lewes once said to me when I made some observation to the effect that she had a sweet face (I meant that the face expressed great sweetness): "You might say what a sweet hundred faces! I look at her sometimes in amazement. Her countenance is constantly changing." The said lips and mouth were distinctly sensuous in form and fulness. . . . Her speaking voice was, I think, one of the most beautiful I ever heard, and she used it *conscientiously*, if I may say so. I mean that she availed herself of its modulations to give thrilling emphasis to what was profound in her utterances, and sweetness to what was gentle or playful. She bestowed great care, too, on her enunciation, disliking the slipshod mode of pronouncing which is so common. I have several times heard her declare with enthusiasm that ours is a beautiful language, a noble language even to the ear, when properly spoken; and imitate with disgust the short, *snappy*, inarticulate way in which many people utter it.—TROLLOPE, THOMAS ADOLPHUS, 1888, *What I Remember*, pp. 470, 471.

Her marriage with Mr. John Cross took place on May 6, 1880. It would be wrong to attempt to present any other account of this than that which Mr. Cross has himself given in the life of his wife. The marriage was severely criticised at the time by her best friends. This was due to various causes. Second marriages are absolutely forbidden by the Positivist creed, and her breach of this rule would be sure to alienate all who were of this persuasion. The world, which has forgiven her relations with Lewes on the ground that they arose from an overmastering devotion, was shocked when it found that the affection which had caused such an act of sacrifice was capable of being succeeded by another equally strong. The difference of nearly twenty years between the age of the bride and bridegroom also gave occasion for remark. On the other hand, no one can have studied the character of George Eliot, even superficially, without being convinced how necessary it was for her to have some one to depend upon, and how much her nature yearned for sympathy and support. No better companion could certainly have been found than Mr. Cross, with his strong vigorous sense, manly character, and business habits. —BROWNING, OSCAR, 1890, *Life of George Eliot (Great Writers)*, p. 134.

There is no good portrait, I believe, of her. She had long features, and would have been called plain but for her solemn, earnest eyes, which had an expression quite in keeping with her voice, which was one not easily forgotten. I never detected in her any trace of genial humour, though I doubt not that it was latent in her; and I thought her a person who had drawn her ideas far more from books and an acquaintance with certain types of humanity whom she had set herself deliberately to study—albeit with rare perception—than from an easy intuitive familiarity with all sorts and conditions of men. But she worked out *thoroughly* what she knew by the intuition of genius, though in this she was very far inferior to Scott.—LELAND, CHARLES GODFREY, 1893, *Memoirs*, p. 390.

After this first visit to "The Priory," the doors were kindly open to us on Sundays during our stay in London. Unhappily, I have no notes of those visits, nor of George Eliot's conversation, but I must always remember how the beauty of her voice impressed me. I also remarked the same quality I have mentioned in speaking of her letters—a sense of perfectness in her presentation of any scene or subject. I recall this impression especially in connection with a description she gave one afternoon of a late visit to Germany, portraying the charm of living in one of the places (was it Ilmenau?) made classic to us by association with Goethe. The whole was so clearly yet simply and vigorously said, that any listener, ignorant of her fame, must have felt her unusual qualities both of mind and heart.—FIELDS, ANNIE, 1899, *George Eliot*, *Century Magazine*, vol. 58. p. 444.

Only her intimate friends knew the exhausting labour which she bestowed on her books, and the untiring patience with which she strove to answer every call made on her attention by friendship, or her own household, or any incident of her literary life. Everything she did was carefully planned and studiously worked out; and whether it was a letter, the visit of a friend, a foreign tour, or the plot of a novel, she put into it the best she had, and the utmost pains to make it perfect. Where she failed at all, I think, was in spontaneity, verve, and *abandon*. This extreme conscientiousness to do everything as well as she could do it gave a certain air of stiffness to her letters, made some of her books overcharged and *langweilig* (this is especially true of "Romola"), and it certainly ruined her poetry.—HARRISON, FREDERIC, 1901, *George Washington and other American Addresses*, p. 210.

MARRIAGE

If there is any one action or relation of my life which is, and always has been, profoundly serious, it is my relation to Mr. Lewes. It is, however, natural enough that you should mistake me in many ways, for not only are you unacquainted with Mr. Lewes's real character and the course of his actions, but also it is several years now since you and I were much together, and it is possible that the modifications my mind has undergone may be quite in the opposite direction of what you imagine. No one can be better aware than yourself that it is possible for two people to hold different opinions on momentous subjects with equal sincerity, and an equally earnest conviction that their respective opinions are alone the truly moral ones. If we differ on the subject of the marriage laws, I at least can believe of you that you cleave to what you believe to be good; and I don't know of anything in the nature of your views that should prevent you from believing the same of me. How *far* we differ I think we neither of us know, for I am ignorant of your precise views; and, apparently, you attribute to me both feelings and opinions which are not mine. We cannot set each other quite right in this matter in letters, but one thing I can tell you in few words. Light and easily broken ties are what I neither desire theoretically nor could live for practically. Women who are satisfied with such ties do *not* act as I have done. That any unworldly, unsuperstitious person who is sufficiently acquainted with the realities of life can pronounce my relation to Mr. Lewes immoral, I can only understand by remembering how subtile and complex are the influences that mould opinion. But I *do* remember this: and I indulge in no arrogant or uncharitable thoughts about those who condemn us, even though we might have expected a somewhat different verdict. From the majority of persons, of course, we never looked for anything but condemnation. We are leading no life of self-indulgence, except, indeed, that, being happy in each other, we find everything easy. We are working hard to provide for others better than we provide for ourselves, and to fulfil every responsibility that lies upon us. Levity and pride would not be a sufficient basis for that.—ELIOT, GEORGE, 1855, *To Mrs. Bray*, Sept. 4; *George Eliot's Life as related in her Letters and Journals*, ed. Cross, vol. I, p. 235.

Of her relations to Lewes it seems to me discussion is not now possible. It is known that Lewes's wife had once left him, that he had generously condoned the offence and received her again, and that in a year she again eloped; the laws of England make such a condonation preclude divorce; Lewes was thus prevented from legally marrying again by a technicality of the law which converted his own generosity into a penalty; under these circumstances George Eliot, moved surely by pure love, took up her residence with him, and according to universal account, not only was a faithful wife to him for twenty years until his death, but was a devoted mother to his children. That her failure to go through the form of marriage was not due to any contempt for that form, as has sometimes been absurdly alleged, is conclusively shown by the fact that when she married Mr. Cross, a year and a half after Lewes's death, the ceremony was performed according to the regular rites of the Church of England.—LANIER, SIDNEY, 1881, *The English Novel*, p. 298.

Pass on, O world, and leave her to her rest!
Brothers, be silent while the drifting snow
Weaves its white pall above her, lying low
With empty hands crossed idly on her breast.
O sisters, let her sleep! while unrepressed
Your pitying tears fall silently and slow,
Washing her spotless, in their crystal flow,
Of that one stain whereof she stands confessed.
Are we so pure that we should scoff at her,
Or mock her now, low lying in her tomb?
God knows how sharp the thorn her roses wore
Even what time their petals were astir
In the warm sunshine, odorous with perfume.
Leave her with Him who weighed the cross she bore!

—DORR, JULIA C. R., 1881-85, *George Eliot, Afternoon Songs*, p. 5.

George Eliot was at heart too pure and noble as well as great to need any veil hung over her career. This is not meant in any sense to justify anything in that career that the highest laws of life will not justify. It is only to say that what George Eliot thought of it all in her own deep heart and mind, and which she has probably revealed in some of her letters, is the very divine secret of human existence that the struggling human heart everywhere longs to know. And in George Eliot's case supremely it is this aspect of her life as understood and believed in or regretted by herself that everybody wants to understand. A hundred years hence her fidelity to George Lewes and her convictions about that will outweigh a thousand Daniel Derondas. George Eliot was a martyr to a mistaken idea of life. It is a new phase of martyrdom, and all the more important because she bore it like a saint.—THORNE, WILLIAM HENRY, 1885-87, *Modern Idols*, p. 139.

Is it strange that Marion Evans was often sad? that the knowledge of her power over men and women was more fruitful of sorrow than of delight to her? I may be wrong in thinking, but I like to think, that one of the motives, which determined her to accept the love of the man, to whom she gave her hand after Mr. Lewes's death, was that she might, by the celebration of her marriage, do her best to preserve her name and fame and the story of her former life from being used to discredit an institution and a rite she venerated. Anyhow her marriage was an act, by which she publicly and impressively declared her disapproval of the great purpose of the enemies of marriage, and denied their right to speak of her as one of themselves. The act was thus interpreted by those innovators, who at the time of the marriage spoke with no little warmth of her miserable abandonment of their cause and principles. . . . She could not have proclaimed more effectually her deliberate opinion that the ordinances of marriage are salutary and sacred, and that it is the duty of women to comply with them. Instead of making for the end desired by the extreme Shelleyan Socialists, the story of the great novelist's life sets forth nothing more clearly than that she regarded the main condition of her association with Mr. Lewes, regretfully.—JEAFFRESON, JOHN CORDY, 1885, *The Real Shelley*, vol. II, p. 474.

Society was at first as stern to George Eliot after her domestic intimacy with Lewes as Mrs. Carlyle had been. I remember hearing an instance of this some years after that connection was formed. Lewes and George Eliot once thought of establishing a domicile in Kent, and a south-eastern semi-suburb of London, much tenanted by wealthy city-people. When news of the intention of the distinguished pair reached the denizens of the region a council of male and female heads of families was held to consider whether George Eliot should be "received." It was decided that she should not. As is well known, public opinion altered in course of time, and ultimately, the lady rejected by London citizens was courted and caressed by daughters of Queen Victoria herself.— ESPINASSE, FRANCIS, 1893, *Literary Recollections and Sketches*, p. 300.

George Eliot's more transcendental friends never forgave her for marrying. In a morally immoral manner they washed their virtuous hands of her. I could not help thinking it was the most natural thing for the poor woman to do. She was a heavily laden but interesting derelict, tossing among the breakers, without oars or rudder, and all at once the brave Cross arrives, throws her a rope, and gallantly tows her into harbour. I am sure that she was very sensitive, and must have had many a painful half-hour as the helpmate of Mr. Lewes. By accepting the position, she had placed herself in opposition to the moral instincts of most of those whom she held most dear. Though intellectually self-contained, I believe she was singularly dependent on the emotional side of her nature. With her, as with nearly all women, she needed a something to lean upon. Though her conduct was socially indefensible, it would have been cruel, it would be stupid, to judge her exactly as one would judge an ordinary offender. What a genius she must have had to have been able to draw so many high-minded people to her! I have an impression that she felt her position acutely, and was unhappy. George Eliot was much to be pitied. I think she knew that I felt for her . . . . for more than once, when I was taking leave, she said, "Come and see me soon, Mr. Locker; don't lose sight of us." And this to an outsider, a nobody, and not in her set!—LOCKER-LAMPSON, FREDERICK, 1895, *My Confidences*, p. 316.

Nothing can be sadder or more melancholy than the conclusion, which after events seem to have too surely proved, that the dream of these two distinguished intellects, of these two lonely hearts, was dispelled, and that their poor "house of cards" tottered and fell. It is to their credit, perhaps, that while they lived they let no human eye behold its ruins; that they bravely and valiantly enveloped them with flowers, meeting a malignant world with smiling front. We respect them as we do the man who covers, and does not flaunt his rags, who hides and does not display his infirmity. . . . It is to be supposed that whatever the end of the drama may have been which was played out between these two, at its beginning Marian Evans gauged what she was giving, knew what it would mean to her, and what it did. This liaison was at any rate a marriage; and if it wrung that tardy respect which is accorded to courage and consistency, even when ill-directed, it carried with it all the responsibilities of those ill-assorted unions to which death alone shall bring release. If others saw a certain measure of consecration in the relations of George Eliot and Mr. Lewes, in what were they to blame? They proclaimed themselves the prophets of no new freedom. Their position was rather defined by reticence and silence. . . . But if the "house of cards" crumbled at last, let it be remembered that many such frail fabrics have fallen before upon which the benediction of the Church of England has been spoken. We can hardly look upon the fatal blight which sapped at its foundation this particular edifice as the direct requital of an offended heaven.—CRUGER, JULIA GRINNELL (JULIEN GORDON), 1896, *Was George Eliot a Hypocrite? The Cosmopolitan*, vol. 20, pp. 315, 316.

Mrs. Procter declared [1884] that she "had never called on George Eliot; that she would not have taken a house-maid with such a character." This brought out Browning and Lord Houghton, who told me many hitherto unknown stories about Thornton Hunt, the supposed lover of the first Mrs. Lewes; of Lewes himself, and of George Eliot, who seemed to have been most generous and self-sacrificing in giving up fame and name for Lewes, whom they did not think deserved so much goodness.—SHERWOOD, MARY E. W., 1897, *An Epistle to Posterity*, p. 219.

Lewes was a brilliant talker of the firework school, and no mean *dilettante* in art and literature. Scholars affirm he had not the least glimmer of insight into what the Greeks of old meant by their philosophy; it was just the most dangerous mind to have control over George Eliot's brain, that much larger and more powerful machine.—PONSONBY, MARY E., 1901, *George Eliot and George Sand, The Nineteenth Century*, vol. 50, p. 610.

SCENES OF CLERICAL LIFE
1857–58

I trouble you with a MS. of "Sketches of Clerical Life" which was submitted to me by a friend who desired my good offices with you. It goes by this post. I confess that before reading the MS. I had considerable doubts of my friend's powers as a writer of fiction; but, after reading it, these doubts were changed into very high admiration. I don't know what you will think of the story, but, according to my judgment, such humor, pathos, vivid presentation, and nice observation have not been exhibited (in this style) since the "Vicar of Wakefield;" and, in consequence of that opinion, I feel quite pleased in negotiating the matter with you.—LEWES, GEORGE HENRY, 1856, *Letter to John Blackwood*, Nov. 6; *George Eliot's Life as related in her Letters and Journals*, ed. Cross. vol. I, p. 300.

The January number begins with the first of a new series by an unknown writer. I do not even know his name. If he is not a first-rate, he is the best simulation I have seen for many a day. All who have read the proof here agree in my admiration. Mr. Simpson's only fear is that "Amos Barton" being so perfectly admirable, the man must have exhausted himself in the first story of the series. What will be the effect of two first-rate series going on in the Magazine at once? (The other was Bulwer's "What will He do with It?") It has long been a dream of mine that such a combination might work wonders, and now there seems a chance of realising it. I recollect offering Warren any amount if he would set to work on a series while "My Novel" was going on.—BLACKWOOD, JOHN, 1856, *Letter to Langford*, Dec. 24; *William Blackwood and His Sons*, ed. Oliphant, vol. II, p. 436.

Sir,—Will you consider it impertinent in a brother author and old reviewer to address a few lines of earnest sympathy and admiration to you, excited by the purity of your style, originality of your thoughts, and absence of all vulgar seeking for effect in those "Scenes of Clerical Life" now appearing in *Blackwood?* If I mistake not much, your muse of invention is no hackneyed one, and your style is too peculiar to allow of your being confounded with any of the already well-known writers of the day. Your great and characteristic charm is, to my mind, Nature. . . . What I see plainly I admire honestly, and trust that more good remains behind. Will you always remain equally natural? That is the doubt. Will the fear of the critic, or the public, or the literary world, which spoils almost every one, never master you? Will you always write to please yourself, and preserve the true independence which seems to mark a real supremacy of intellect? But these questions are, I fear, impertinent. I will conclude. Pardon this word of greeting from one whom you may never see or know, and believe me your earnest admirer.—GURNEY, ARCHER, 1857, *To the author of "Mr. Gilfil's Love-Story,"* May 14; *George Eliot's Life as related in her Letters and Journals,* ed. Cross, vol. I, pp. 324, 325.

My Dear Sir,—I have been so strongly affected by the two first tales in the book you have had the kindness to send me, through Messrs. Blackwood, that I hope you will excuse my writing to you to express my admiration of their extraordinary merit. The exquisite truth and delicacy both of the humor and the pathos of these stories, I have never seen the like of; and they have impressed me in a manner that I should find it very difficult to describe to you, if I had the impertinence to try. In addressing these few words of thankfulness to the creator of the Sad Fortunes of the Rev. Amos Barton, and the sad love-story of Mr. Gilfil, I am (I presume) bound to adopt the name that it pleases that excellent writer to assume. I can suggest no better one: but I should have been strongly disposed, if I had been left to my own devices, to address the said writer as a woman. I have observed what seemed to me such womanly touches in those moving fictions, that the assurance on the title-page is insufficient to satisfy me even now. If they originated with no woman, I believe that no man ever before had the art of making himself mentally so like a woman since the world began.—DICKENS, CHARLES, 1858, *To George Eliot,* Jan. 17; *George Eliot's Life as related in her Letters and Journals,* ed. Cross, vol. II, p. 2.

You would not, I imagine, care much for flattering speeches, and to go into detail about the book would carry me farther than at present there is occasion to go. I can only thank you most sincerely for the delight which it has given me; and both I myself, and my wife, trust that the acquaintance which we seem to have made with you through your writings may improve into something more tangible. I do not know whether I am addressing a young man or an old—clergyman or a layman. Perhaps, if you answer this note, you may give us some information about yourself. But at any rate, should business or pleasure bring you into this part of the world, pray believe that you will find a warm welcome if you will accept our hospitality.—FROUDE, JAMES ANTHONY, 1858, *To George Eliot,* Jan. 17; *George Eliot's Life as related in her Letters and Journals,* ed. Cross, vol. II, p. 4.

Mr. Eliot's strength lies in the conception of female character.—MARTINEAU, JAMES, 1858, *Professional Religion.*

They are intensely realistic pictures of perfectly commonplace life and character. The style of the composition is admirable. It is admirable enough to make these sketches well worth reading for the sake of the style alone. But it is so completely admirable that it scarcely of itself attracts any attention at all.—WILKINSON, WILLIAM CLEAVER, 1874, *A Free Lance in the Field of Life and Letters,* p. 8.

If you should be wandering meditatively along the bank of some tiny brook, a brook so narrow that you can leap across it without effort, so quiet in its singing that its loudest tinkle cannot be heard in the next field, carrying upon its bosom no craft that would draw more water than the curving leaf of a wild-rose floating down stream, too small in volume to dream of a mill-wheel and turning nothing more practical than maybe a piece of violet-petal in a little eddy off somewhere,—if, I say, you should be strolling alongside such a brook and should see it suddenly expand, without the least intermediate stage, into a mighty river, turning a thousand great wheels for man's profit as it swept on to the sea, and offering broad highway and favorable currents to a thousand craft freighted with the most precious cargoes of human aspiration: you would behold the aptest physical semblance of that spiritual phenomenon which we witnessed at our last meeting, when in tracing the quiet and mentally-wayward course of demure Marian Evans among the suave pastorals of her native Warwickshire, we came suddenly upon the year 1857 when her first venture in fiction—"The Scenes of Clerical Life"—appeared in *Blackwood's Magazine* and magically enlarged the stream of her influence from the diameter of a small circle of literary people in London to the width of all England.—LANIER, SIDNEY, 1881, *The English Novel*, p. 175.

The "Scenes of Clerical Life" were to George Eliot's future works what a bold, spirited sketch is to a carefully elaborated picture. All the qualities that distinguished her genius may be discovered in this, her first essay in fiction. With all Miss Austen's matchless faculty for painting commonplace characters, George Eliot has that other nobler faculty of showing what tragedy, pathos, and humor may be lying in the experience of a human soul "that looks out through dull gray eyes, and that speaks in a voice of quite ordinary tones."—BLIND, MATHILDE, 1883, *George Eliot (Famous Women)*, p. 130.

A piece of work which in all her after life, George Eliot never surpassed. It was probably only the humourous *mise en scène*, the delightful picture of the village and the surrounding farms and their inhabitants, Mrs. Hackett, and her neighbours, which he (Mr. Lewes) read in that tremendous moment while the author stood by, not the least aware that her faltering essay was in fact, in its brevity and humility, as perfect a work of genius as ever was given to the world.—OLIPHANT, MARGARET O. W., 1892, *The Victorian Age of English Literature*, p. 465.

The work of George Eliot which first arrested attention and compelled admiration were the "Scenes of Clerical Life." There the quality most conspicuous is the intensity of emotion, the concentration of tragic feeling within the sphere of commonplace life. The canvas is small; the incident is uneventful; there is no complexity of plot, and no august dramatic picture. But what impresses us most is, nevertheless, the intense depth of tragic feeling. There is none of the delicate monotone of Jane Austen's novels, with their smoothness of movement, the subtle delicacy of description, their avoidance of any touch of tragedy. But in George Eliot the depth of feeling is portrayed with restless effort and certainty of hand, and no elaboration is spared that may heighten the effect. The commonplace, the humorous, the restful picture of everyday life, is skilfully worked in; but we never for one moment are allowed to forget that all the side touches are mere contributions to one special aim—that of increasing the intensity of the tragic chord that is to be struck. The style corresponds exactly to this central aim. Not a sentence is other than elaborately framed. Each antithesis of feeling is carefully pressed home. Each incident that is to heighten the effect is told with almost painful care. Each touch of humour is so expressed as to heighten the note of tragedy and contrast. In the very narrowing of the scene, and in the concentration with which it is focussed, we have another proof of the determination with which the author's purpose is kept in view. —CRAIK, HENRY, 1896, *English Prose, vol. v*, p. 663.

Arbury Hall was probably finished in or about 1773, as in that year Sir John Astley, of the adjoining Astley Castle, made Sir Roger Newdigate a present of the famous painting depicting the celebrated exploits of Sir John de Astley, who flourished in the early part of the fifteenth century. The outside of the house, with its castellated grey-tinted front and mullioned windows, is easily recognised by all readers of "Mr. Gilfil's Love Story." It is in the inside, however, that the descriptions of George Eliot force themselves upon the mind as the visitor looks with a curious eye upon the ecclesiastical and other adornments placed in their respective positions by the lavish hand of Sir Roger.— MORLEY, GEORGE, 1897, *In Adam Bede's Neighbourhood, The Art Journal*, vol. 49, p. 236.

ADAM BEDE
1859

When on October 29, I had written to the end of the love-scene at the Farm between Adam and Dinah, I sent the MS. to Blackwood, since the remainder of the third volume could not affect the judgment passed on what had gone before. He wrote back in warm admiration, and offered me, on the part of the firm, £800 for four years' copyright. I accepted the offer. The last words of the third volume were written and despatched on their way to Edinburgh, November the 16th, and now on the last day of the same month I have written this slight history of my book. I love it very much, and am deeply thankful to have written it, whatever the public may say to it—a result which is still in darkness, for I have at present had only four sheets of the proof.— ELIOT, GEORGE, 1858, *Journal, Nov. 16; George Eliot's Life as related in her Letters and Journals*, ed. Cross, vol. II, p. 51.

I owe the author much gratitude for some very pleasing hours. The book indeed is worthy of great admiration. There are touches of beauty in the conception of human character that are exquisite, and much wit and much poetry embedded in the "dialect," which nevertheless the author over-uses. The style is remarkably good whenever it is English and not provincial—racy, original, and nervous. I congratulate you on having found an author of such promise, and published one of the very ablest works of fiction I have read for years. —LYTTON, SIR EDWARD BULWER, 1859, *To John Blackwood, April 24; George Eliot's Life as related in her Letters and Journals*, ed. Cross, vol. II, p. 74.

I do not think that any novelist has strewed over his work wit so abundant or so varied, so fruitful in surprises, so full of sallies. Mrs. Poyser in "Adam Bede," is in this respect one of the most extraordinary creations of prose fiction.—SCHERER, EDWARD, 1861-91, *George Eliot, Essays on English Literature*, tr. Saintsbury, p. 10.

It is as a picture, or rather as a series of pictures, that I find "Adam Bede" most valuable. The author succeeds better in drawing attitudes of feeling than in drawing movements of feeling. — JAMES, HENRY, 1866, *The Novels of George Eliot, Atlantic Monthly*, vol. 18, p. 487.

Of "Dinah" we scarcely can trust ourselves to speak. The character is so eminently and heartily Christian, even in the most of its finer shades, that we do not care to point out the particulars in which it betrays the want of the entirest sympathy on the part of the author. Surely it was written from the fresh remembrances of days of warm and confiding Christian faith, now perhaps under the chill of an honest, and a temporary eclipse.—PORTER, NOAH, 1870, *Books and Reading*, p. 119.

Is always likely to remain George Eliot's most popular work. It is a story of which any English author, however great his name, could not fail to have been proud. Everything about it (if I except perhaps a touch of melodrama connected with the execution scene) is at once simple and great, and the plot is unfolded with singular simplicity, purity, and power.— HUTTON, RICHARD HOLT, 1871, *George Eliot, Essays in Literary Criticism*.

We feel inclined to call her best work.— SCHERR, J. 1874, *A History of English Literature*, tr. M. V., p. 279.

That beautiful Dinah Morris you will remember in "Adam Bede,"—solemn, fragile, strong, Dinah Morris, the woman-preacher whom I find haunting my imagination in strange but entrancing unions of the most diverse forms, as if, for instance, a snowdrop could also be St. Paul, as if a kiss could be a gospel, as if a lovely phrase of Chopin's most inward music should become suddenly an Apocalypse revealing us Christ in the flesh,—that rare, pure and marvelous Dinah Morris who would alone consecrate English literature if it had yielded no other gift to man. . . . This publication of "Adam Bede" placed George Eliot decisively at the head of English novel-writers, with only Dickens for second, even.—LANIER, SIDNEY, 1881, *The English Novel*, pp. 165, 203.

Where in modern fiction shall we find more of the exhilarating surprise that is the offspring of wit, or humour more profoundly, yet more laughingly wise, than are to be found in the pages of "Adam Bede?" Where, out of those pages, shall we find fitting counterparts to the immortal Mrs. Poyser, and her fellow-immortal, the amiable cynic, Bartle Massey. The humour of Scott never pierces into the heart of things, as does that of George Eliot; the humour of Dickens, glorious in its frolicsome extravagance, is clownish and superficial, and cannot be compared with the "ideal comedy,"—to use Shelley's expression—which we find in the prose drama of George Eliot. —CALL, W. M. W., 1881, *George Eliot, Westminster Review*, vol. 116, p. 168.

Whether, in Dinah Morris, George Eliot intended to represent Mrs. Evans or not, she did represent her faithfully and fully. . . . The only point at which the writer has deviated from fact is in the marriage of Dinah and Adam. As a matter of fact the real Dinah married Seth Bede (Samuel Evans). Adam was George Eliot's father, Robert Evans.—BULKLEY, L., 1882, *Dinah Morris and Mrs. Elizabeth Evans, Century Magazine*, vol. 24, p. 552.

Every conscience, as well as every imagination, will be clarified and invigorated by the perusal of "Adam Bede," the first work of the author that attracted wide public attention. A novel of the real school, humble in its characters, faithful in its portraiture, and beyond praise in its moral spirit. The epoch is of the eighteenth century.—WELSH, ALFRED H., 1883, *Development of English Literature and Language*, vol. II, p. 471.

George Eliot never drew a more living figure than this of Hetty, hiding such a hard little heart under that soft dimpling beauty of hers. Again, I think that only a woman would have depicted just such a Hetty as this. The personal charms of this young girl are drawn in words that have the glow of life itself; yet while intensely conscious of her beauty, we are kept aware all the time that, to use one of the famous Mrs. Poyser's epigrammatic sayings, Hetty is "no better nor a cherry wi' a hard stone inside it." George Eliot is never dazzled or led away by her own bewitching creation as a man would have been.— BLIND, MATHILDE, 1883, *George Eliot (Famous Women)*, p. 158.

The first and last master-piece of George Eliot. "Adam Bede" breaks upon the reader with all the freshness and truth of nature. Every element influencing character is expressed in the workings of the very souls of the rural, half-educated folk acting out their lives according to their conscience, their early training, and their personal character. Their beliefs are there, and their lives are colored by their beliefs. —MULLANY, PATRICK FRANCIS (BROTHER AZARIAS), 1889, *Books and Reading*, p. 39.

George Eliot, who had personally experienced the sentiment of Christianity in its purest and most intimate form, has created to prove its efficacy the sweet and admirable figure of Dinah Morris. This young and beautiful woman, borne up by religious enthusiasm, devotes her whole life, her ardent soul, her persuasive tongue, her courageous labours, to the ideal of charity taught her by the Gospel. She is above all rigidity of form, above all prejudice. A powerful movement bears her on: She overflows with love and compassion, and in the intensity of her feelings this weak girl finds a supreme force.—NEGRI, GAETANO, 1891, *George Eliot: La sua vita ed i suoi Romanzi*.

Adam Bede was a new book, and in this I had my first knowledge of that great intellect for which I had no passion, indeed, but always the deepest respect, the highest honor; and which has from time to time profoundly influenced me by its ethics. . . . The life and character I have found portrayed there have appealed always to the consciousness of right and wrong implanted in me; and from no one has this appeal been stronger than from George Eliot. Her influence continued through many years, and I can question it now only in the undue burden she seems to throw upon the individual, and her failure to account largely enough for motive from the social environment. There her work seems to me unphilosophical.—HOWELLS, WILLIAM DEAN, 1895, *My Literary Passions*, p. 185.

It is of all her books the heartiest, the wittiest, the most cheerful, or rather the least desponding. In that book it may be that she exhausted herself and her own resources of observation as an eye-witness. She wrote fine things in other veins, in different scenes, and she conceived other characters and new situations. But, for all practical purposes "Adam Bede" was the typical romance which everything she had thought or known impelled her to write, in which she told the best of what she had seen and the most important of what she had to say. Had she never written anything but "Adam Bede," she would have had a special place of her own in English romance:—and I am not sure that anything else which she produced very materially raised, enlarged, or qualified that place.—HARRISON, FREDERIC, 1895, *Studies in Early Victorian Literature*, p. 213.

The reason why she at first wrote under a *nom de plume* is plain. To the great wallowing world she was neither Miss Evans nor Mrs. Lewes, so she dropped both names as far as title pages were concerned and used a man's name instead—hoping better to elude the pack. When "Adam Bede" came out a resident of Nuneaton purchased a copy and at once discovered local earmarks. The scenes described, the flowers, the stone walls, the bridges, the barns, the people—all was Nuneaton. Who wrote it?

No one knew, but it was surely some one in Nuneaton. So they picked out a Mr. Liggins, a solemn-faced preacher, who was always about to do something great, and they said "Liggins." Soon all London said "Liggins." As for Liggins, he looked wise and smiled knowingly. Then articles began to appear in the periodicals purporting to have been written by the author of "Adam Bede." A book came out called "Adam Bede, Jr.," and to protect her publisher, the public, and herself, George Eliot had to reveal her identity.—HUBBARD, ELBERT, 1895, *Little Journeys to the Homes of Good Men and Great*, p. 20.

No one of George Eliot's novels has given to the world a larger number of clear and memorable portraits. The weakness and vanity of Hetty, the thoughtless profligacy of the not wholly evil Donnithrone, the genial common sense and humor of Parson Irwine, the rapt and mystic yet most practical piety of Dinah Morris, and the shrewd wit and caustic proverbs of Mrs. Poyser. All these are household words. Of the picture of the hero, Adam Bede himself, the present Bishop Wilkinson once said in his pulpit that it seemed to him the best presentment in modern guise and colour of the earthly circumstances which surrounded the life of the divine Founder of Christianity, as he toiled in the carpenter's shop, to supply His own, His mother's wants. That surely is no commonplace effort of fiction which throws any illustrative light, however faint or broken, on the sacred narrative of human redemption.—RUSSELL, GEORGE W. E., 1896, *George Eliot Revisited, The Contemporary Review*, vol. 65.

The work on which her reputation with the general public still mainly rests.—GRAHAM, RICHARD D., 1897, *The Masters of Victorian Literature*, p. 54.

THE MILL ON THE FLOSS
1860

This "Mill" has delighted me. It has turned out such an amount of good grist, it is so filled with heart-probings and knowledge of human life, so earnestly free from any attempt to dress up, to express, or find a vent for the author's egotism! It deals sturdily with the real stuff that life is made of, and, like life, constantly makes you wish that the characters were a little different—that this and that would not turn out just so.—SEDGWICK, CATHARINE M., 1860, *To Mrs. K. S. Minot, May 12; Life and Letters*, ed. Dewey, p. 382.

The chief defect—indeed, the only serious one—in "The Mill on the Floss" is its conclusion.—JAMES, HENRY, 1866, *The Novels of George Eliot, Atlantic Monthly*, vol. 18, p. 490.

It is a masterly fragment of fictitious biography in two volumes, followed by a second-rate one-volume novel,—the three connected into a single whole by very inadequate links. . . . Yet, "The Mill on the Floss" is a book of great genius. Its overflowing humor would alone class its author high among the humorists, and there are some sketches in it of English country life which have all the vivacity and not a little of the power of Sir Walter Scott's best works.—HUTTON, RICHARD HOLT, 1871, *George Eliot, Essays in Literary Criticism*.

Few or none, I should suppose, of the most passionate and intelligent admirers would refuse to accept "The Mill on the Floss" as on the whole at once the highest and the purest and the fullest example of her magnificent and matchless powers—for matchless altogether, as I have already insisted, they undoubtedly are in their own wide and fruitful field of work. The first two-thirds of the book suffice to compose perhaps the very noblest of tragic as well as of humorous prose idyls in the language; comprising, as they likewise do, one of the sweetest as well as saddest and tenderest as well as subtlest examples of dramatic analysis—a study in that kind as soft and true as Rousseau's, as keen and true as Browning's, as full as either of the fine and bitter sweetness of a pungent and fiery fidelity. But who can forget the horror of inward collapse, the sickness of spiritual reaction, the reluctant incredulous rage of disenchantment and disgust, with which the first came upon the thrice unhappy third part?—SWINBURNE, ALGERNON CHARLES, 1877, *A Note on Charlotte Brontë*, p. 28.

Is the most poetical of George Eliot's novels. The great Floss, hurrying between green pastures to the sea, gives a unity of its own to this story, which opens to the roar of waters, the weltering waters which accompany it at the close. It forms the elemental background which rounds the little lives of the ill-starred family group nurtured on its banks.—BLIND, MATHILDE, 1883, *George Eliot (Famous Women)*, p. 166.

Maggie, the heroine of "The Mill on the Floss," is perhaps the rarest and happiest combination in fiction of a human being living on the flat level of commonplace experiences, and yet invested with a poetic, romantic, and pathetic beauty which touches the very quick of the reader's sentiment, and allies her creator to Goldsmith and Bunyan in an artless eloquence which is irresistible.—NORRIS, MARY HARRIOTT, 1890, ed. *George Eliot's Silas Marner, Biographical Sketch*, p. 10.

I suppose it is her best book, though it may not contain her best scenes. The objection which is often made and still oftener felt to the repulsiveness of Maggie's worship of a counter-jumping cad like Stephen, is somewhat uncritical. I suspect that most women resent it, because they feel the imputation to be true: and most men out of a not wholly dissimilar feeling which acts a little differently.—SAINTSBURY, GEORGE, 1895, *Corrected Impressions*, p. 165.

A work in which passion and the tumult of the soul are not objectively analyzed but sympathetically portrayed with unsurpassed vividness and elemental power, a work which is undisputably one of the great literary epitomes of the pathos and tragedy of human existence—it is hard to reconcile one's self to the evolution in which temperament disappeared so completely in devotion to the intellect alone as to result in the jejune artificiality of "Daniel Deronda."—BROWNELL, W. C., 1900, *George Eliot, Scribner's Magazine*, vol. 28, p. 723.

If we choose Maggie Tulliver for the representative woman of George Eliot, as we chose Lucy Fountain in the case of Charles Reade, we shall at least be going no farther wrong, I think. She is at any rate typical of that order of heroine which her author most strongly imagined, not quite upon the Miltonian formula for a poem of "simple, sensuous, passionate," but upon such a variation of it as should read complex, sensuous, passionate. She is, of all the kinds of heroines, the most difficult for men justly to appreciate, and in their failure something of the ignoble slight they feel for her attaches also to her creator.—HOWELLS, WILLIAM DEAN, 1901, *Heroines of Fiction*, vol. II, p. 45.

In the "Mill on the Floss," there is a superabundance of talk, and a certain lack of perspective in the characters. When, however, she controls her pen for a supreme effect, as at the death of the brother and sister in the final chapter, then indeed she shows herself a true artist.—ENGEL, EDWARD, 1902, *A History of English Literature*, rev. Hamley Bent, p. 456.

SILAS MARNER
1861

"Silas Marner" comes to show in its turn that the author, among the other secrets of genius, possesses that of fecundity. . . . What wonderful creations are Dinah and Hetty, Maggie and Silas, old Lisbeth and the Dobson family! Every one of George Eliot's personages, however subordinate the part, however passing the appearance, has a special physiognomy and characteristic style of speaking.—SCHERER, EDMOND, 1861-91, *George Eliot, Essays on English Literature*, tr. Saintsbury, pp. 6, 8.

To a certain extent, I think "Silas Marner" holds a higher place than any of the author's works. It is more nearly a masterpiece; it has more of that simple, rounded, consummate aspect, that absence of loose ends and gaping issues, which marks a classical work.—JAMES, HENRY, 1866, *The Novels of George Eliot, Atlantic Monthly*, vol. 18, p. 482.

I call "Silas Marner" her most finished work, not only because of the symmetry with which each part is adjusted in relation to the whole, nor because of the absence of those partly satirical, partly moral reflections with which George Eliot usually accompanies the action of her stories, but chiefly on account of the simple pathos of the central motive into which all the different incidents and characters naturally converge.—BLIND, MATHILDE, 1883, *George Eliot (Famous Women)*, p. 182.

Men of letters, I believe, give the palm to "Silas Marner." They are attracted by the exquisite workmanship of the story. The plot was constructed by George Eliot out of the merest hint. The story was written in haste, at one gush. It is a perfect gem—a pure work of art, in which the demands of art have alone to be considered.—BROWNING, OSCAR, 1888, *The Art of George Eliot, Fortnightly Review*, vol. 49, p. 538.

Comes nearer to being a great success than any of the more elaborate books.—HARRISON, FREDERIC, 1895, *Studies in Early Victorian Literature*, p. 211.

"Silas Marner" is perhaps by general consent the author's most perfect work of art.

It contains many of her striking characteristics as a thinker and writer, but is free from the vein of philosophic teaching which makes her later novels rather heavy reading. In the story of the linen-weaver of Raveloe we find blended in happy proportion the homely humor and lively portrayal of country life familiar in George Eliot's earlier novels and the tragic pathos and deep moral purpose of her later work. It is noted as well for its unusual number of strong dramatic situations as for the poetic beauty of its style. It also has special merits for the student who wishes to compare the essay with the novel.—WAUCHOPE, GEORGE ARMSTRONG, 1899, *ed. George Eliot's Silas Marner, p. 17.*

"Silas Marner" is the only novel in which George Eliot deals with tense, direct action and curtails the profusion of by-play among her minor incidental personages. In all probability this is the work to which posterity will assign the position of honour.— ENGEL, EDWARD, 1902, *A History of English Literature,* rev. Hamley Bent, p. 456.

In Silas Marner George Eliot is a little tempted to fall into the error of the amiable novelists who are given to playing the part of Providence to their character. It is true that the story begins by a painful case of apparent injustice. . . . A modern "realist" would, I suppose, complain that she had omitted, or touched too slightly for his taste, a great many repulsive and brutal elements in the rustic world. The portraits, indeed, are so vivid as to convince us of their fidelity, but she has selected the less ugly, and taken the point of view from which we see mainly what was wholesome and kindly in the little village community. Silas Marner is a masterpiece in that way, and scarcely equalled in English literature, unless by Mr. Hardy's rustics in "Far From the Madding Crowd" and other early works. —STEPHEN, LESLIE, 1902, *George Eliot (English Men of Letters), pp. 107, 110.*

ROMOLA
1863

George Eliot first went astray in "Romola." All her previous works had been living products of the imagination,—"Romola" *was manufactured.* A very great piece of work, unquestionably; a piece of work that perhaps produces a higher sense of the writer's immense and diversified *force* than any of her other works; but bearing the same relation to art, when compared with Hetty or Janet, that an elaborate imitation of one of the great Italian masters does when compared with a bit of true rainy sky by Turner or one of Wilkie's dirty boy-faces.—SKELTON, JOHN, 1868, *Poetry and George Eliot, Fraser's Magazine, vol. 78, p. 470.*

Her "Romola" is one of the finest historical novels in our language, yet it was a publisher's failure. Its style was too pure, its art too refined, its pictures too clearly and faithfully drawn, for the readers of her former works. But the book lifted her instantly into a new importance in the estimate of the small class whose verdict is but another term for fame.—TAYLOR, BAYARD, 1876, *Essays and Notes, p. 339.*

A highly-finished, eloquent, artistic work, and by a select class considered the greatest intellectual effort of the author. — CHAMBERS, ROBERT, 1876, *Cyclopædia of English Literature, ed. Carruthers.*

The Lady who writes over the *nom de plume* of George Eliot is the greatest living Englishwoman,— a woman who, since Mrs. Browning died, has had no peer as a literary artist among her sex; but she carefully elaborates in her best work a high moral purpose, and, lest some fool may possibly miss or mistake it, she works it all into the last page of "Romola."—HOLLAND, JOSIAH GILBERT, 1876, *Every-day Topics, First Series, p. 57.*

I have just read through the cheap edition of "Romola," and though I have only made a few alterations of an important kind—the printing being unusually correct —it would be well for me to send this copy to be printed from. I think it must be nearly ten years since I read the book before, but there is no book of mine about which I more thoroughly feel that I could swear by every sentence as having been written with my best blood, such as it is, and with the most ardent care for veracity of which my nature is capable. It has made me often sob with a sort of painful joy as I have read the sentences which had faded from my memory. This helps one to bear false representations with patience; for I really don't love any Gentleman who undertakes to state my opinions well enough to desire that I should find myself all wrong in order to justify this statement.—ELIOT, GEORGE, 1877, *To John Blackwood, Jan. 30; George*

Eliot's Life as related in her Letters and Journals, ed. Cross, vol. III, p. 217.

Nobody who did not share the scholar's enthusiasm could have described the blind scholar in his library in the adorable fifth chapter of "Romola;" and we feel that she must have copied out with keen gusto of her own those words of Petrarch which she puts into old Bardo's mouth.—MORLEY, JOHN, 1885, *The Life of George Eliot*, *Macmillan's Magazine*, vol. 51, p. 248.

It is, perhaps, the best historical novel ever written. Replete with learning, weighted with knowledge in every page, the finish is so rare that the joints between erudition and imagination cannot be discovered. Read it when you have never been to Florence, it will make you long to go there; read it when you have learnt to love Florence, it will make you love Florence more; read it when you have studied the Renaissance which George Eliot had studied so deeply, and you will feel its beauties as those feel the beauties of a symphony of Beethoven who know the score by heart.— BROWNING, OSCAR, 1888, *The Art of George Eliot, Fortnightly Review*, vol. 49, p. 538.

To call it a complete success is to go too far. The task was too great. To frame in a complex background of historical erudition an ethical problem of even greater complexity and subtlety—this was a task which might have sorely tried even greater powers than hers—a task in which Goethe and Scott might have succeeded, but which Goethe and Scott were too truly the born artists to attempt, without ample care, and too busy with many things to devote to it the required labour. "Romola" is certainly a wonderful monument of literary accomplishments; but it remains a *tour de force*, too elaborate, too laboured, too intricate, too erudite. As the French say, it has *trop de choses*, it is too long, too full, over-costumed, too studiously mounted on the stage.—HARRISON, FREDERIC, 1895, *Studies in Early Victorian Literature*, p. 215.

In "Silas Marner," beautiful and complete in itself as it is, we have only the preface, to which "Romola" is the accomplished fact. While "Silas Marner" is perfect in its simplicity, "Romola" is great in its complexity. We must remember the stupendous historic background of the story—Florence with all her ancient grandeur, her teeming inhabitants with their cries of joy, of pain, of hope, of revenge; and above all is heard the clarion voice of Savonarola rushing through the Florentine soul like a mad river. All this gigantic background is conjured up to show—what? The evolution of one beautiful life! Great and good people always leave their souls behind them, whether it be in statuary, or books, or deeds. George Eliot has left her living soul with Romola.— DAWSON, THOMAS, 1895, *Character Development in "Romola," Four Years of Novel-Reading*, ed. Moulton, p. 93.

I read it again and again with the sense of moral enlargement which the first fiction to conceive of the true nature of evil gave all of us who were young in that day. Tito Malema was not only a lesson, he was a revelation, and I trembled before him as in the presence of a warning and a message from the only veritable perdition. His life, in which so much that was good was mixed with so much that was bad, lighted up the whole domain of egotism with its glare, and made one feel how near the best and the worst were to each other, and how they sometimes touched without absolute division in texture and color. The book was undoubtedly a favorite of mine, and I did not see then the artistic falterings in it which were afterward evident to me.— HOWELLS, WILLIAM DEAN, 1895, *My Literary Passions*, p. 218.

It is a very remarkable *tour de force*, but it is a *tour de force* executed entirely against the grain. It is not alive: it is a work of erudition not of genius, of painful manufacture not of joyous creation or even observation.— SAINTSBURY, GEORGE, 1896, *A History of Nineteenth Century Literature*, p. 324.

In Romola and in Savonarola we touch the heights. The "tall lily" is an exquisite conception and is supreme in human loveliness.—LINTON, MRS. LYNN, 1897, *Women Novelists of Queen Victoria's Reign*, p. 96.

"Romola" is unique in its way, and has hosts of admirers. There are readers to whom it introduced the Italian Renaissance, who, in its pages first read of Florence, Savonarola, the Medici. There are scholars who shared George Eliot's enthusiasm for "the City by the Arno" and "the wonderful fifteenth century," so cordially as to credit "Romola" with having successfully reproduced a moment and a *milieu* which they were only too grateful to have recalled. Besides, there is that master-piece of evolution, the character of Tito Melema.—BROWNELL, W. C., 1900, *George Eliot, Scribner's Magazine, vol.* 28, *p.* 724.

"Romola" is full of faults. The learning is too obtrusive. There is too much and too obvious an effort at minute historical accuracy, which is the mint and anise and cumin of every historical romance. Romola herself, though a portrait lovingly drawn, is hardly a creation of flesh and blood. But, in spite of Mr. Stephen, I respectfully maintain that the figure of Savonarola stands out in almost startling reality, and that Tito Melema is absolutely true to life. . . . "Romola" is not a smooth tale, chiefly of love. It is a serious attempt to depict Florentine life four-hundred years ago, and by its success or failure in achieving that object it must stand or fall.—PAUL, HERBERT, 1902, *George Eliot, The Nineteenth Century, vol.* 51, *pp.* 939, 940.

It would be absurd to speak without profound respect of a book which represents the application of an exceptionally powerful intellect carrying out a great scheme with so serious and sustained a purpose. . . . Romola is to me one of the most provoking of books. I am alternately seduced into admiration and repelled by what seems to me a most lamentable misapplication of first-rate powers. . . . If we can put aside the historical paraphernalia, forget the dates and the historical Savonarola and Machiavelli, there remains a singularly powerful representation of an interesting spiritual history; of the ordeal through which a lofty nature has to pass when brought into collision with characters of baser composition; throw into despair by the successive collapses of each of the supports to which it clings; and finding some solution in spite of its bewilderment amidst conflicting gospels, in each of which truth and falsehood are strangely mixed. There is hardly any novel, except "The Mill on the Floss," in which the stages in the inner life of a thoughtful and tender nature are set forth with so much tenderness and sympathy.—STEPHEN, LESLIE, 1902, *George Eliot (English Men of Letters), pp.* 125, 126, 141.

FELIX HOLT
1866

I have got two copies of "Felix Holt"—the last sent me by Mr. Langford. I suppose as an equivalent for the six copies of "Miss Marjoribanks,' which I ought to have; and I fear I have got them on false pretences, for I don't think I could say anything satisfactory about it. It leaves an impression on my mind as of "Hamlet" played by six sets of gravediggers. Of course it will be a successful book, but I think chiefly because "Adam Bede" and "Silas Marner" went before it. Now that I have read it, I have given up the idea of reviewing it.—OLIPHANT, MARGARET O. W., 1866, *Letter to Blackwood, Autobiography and Letters, ed. Coghill, p.* 210.

Decidedly inferior to the rest.—MCCARTHY, JUSTIN, 1872, *George Eliot and George Lewes, Modern Leaders, p.* 140.

I cannot tell you with that eagerness I devoured "Felix Holt." For perfect force-in-repose, Miss Evans (or, I should have said, Mrs. Lewes) is not excelled by any writer.—LANIER, SIDNEY, 1875, *To Gibson Peacock, March* 24; *Letters, p.* 12.

Felix is a typical conception with all the reality in it that the genius of his creator could infuse, but still only a typical conception. We question, too, whether, as the Radical workman of 1832, he is not also an anachronism. The trial scene, in which the hero is the prisoner at the bar, has two really fine passages in it—the sympathetic, spontaneous utterance of the independent minister, and the earnest and selfforgetting, yet self restraining passion which impels Esther to volunteer and give her evidence in vindication of the unlucky Felix. In humorous talk and witty repartee this novel is less affluent than "Adam Bede," the "Mill on the Floss," or "Silas Marner." The opening chapter offers, perhaps, the very finest picture of rural scenery and remote country life to be found even in the works of George Eliot.—CALL, W. M. W., 1881, *George Eliot, Westminster Review, vol.* 116, *p.* 179.

In its construction "Felix Holt" is perhaps the most unsatisfactory of all George Eliot's books. The ins and outs of Transome and Durfey and Scaddon and Bycliffe were all too intricate in the weaving and too confused in the telling to be either intelligible or interesting. In trying on the garment of Miss Braddon the author of "Felix Holt" showed both want of perception and a deplorable misfit. . . . Felix himself is one of George Eliot's masterpieces in the way of nobleness of ideal and firmness of drawing.—LINTON, MRS. LYNN, 1897, *Women Novelists of Queen Victoria's Reign*, pp. 84, 87.

"Felix Holt" contains at least the lovable Mr. Lyon, and though the wearisome wordiness of the book is a handicap from which it will always suffer, it will always remain a highly interpretative picture of a momentous epoch in English political and social history—the birth, in fact, of the modern English world engendered by the Reform Bill.—BROWNELL, W. C., 1900, *George Eliot, Scribner's Magazine*, vol. 28, p. 724.

I have in my possession about sixteen letters written to me in the months from January to May, 1866, asking for assistance in legal points relating to "Felix Holt." And during that period I had many interviews with her thereon, and read large portions of the story in MS. and in proof. The letters and my own recollections testify to the indefatigable pains that she took with every point of local color, her anxiety about scrupulous accuracy of fact, and the often feeble health under which the book was produced. . . . "Felix Holt" and "Daniel Deronda" were the only novels on which I was consulted, and then simply as to points of law and legal practice. I wrote the "opinion" of the Attorney-General, printed in italics in chapter xxxv. of "Felix Holt," as a guide to the language used in Lincoln's Inn, and she inserted it bodily in the book. I remember telling her that I should always boast of having written one sentence that was embodied in English literature. The "opinion" was little more than "common form," and she took kindly my little *mot*.—HARRISON, FREDERIC, 1901, *Reminiscences of George Eliot, Harper's Magazine*, vol. 103, p. 579.

Mr. Felix Holt would have been quite in his place at Toynbee Hall; but is much too cold-blooded for the time when revolution and confiscation were really in the air. Perhaps this indicates the want of masculine fiber in George Eliot and the deficient sympathy with rough popular passions which makes us feel that he represents the afterthought of the judicious sociologist and not the man of flesh and blood who was the product of the actual conditions. Anyhow, the novel appears to be regarded as her least interesting.—STEPHEN, LESLIE, 1902, *George Eliot (English Men of Letters)*, p. 155.

MIDDLEMARCH
1871–72

I suppose you cannot have read "Middlemarch," as you say nothing about it. It stands quite alone. As one only just moistens one's lips with an exquisite liqueur, to keep the taste as long as possible in one's mouth, I never read more than a single chapter of "Middlemarch" in the evening, dreading to come to the last, when I must wait two months for a renewal of the pleasure. The depth of humour has certainly never been surpassed in English literature. If there is ever a shade too much learning, that is Lewes's fault.—THIRLWALL, CONNOP, 1872, *Letters to a Friend, ed. Stanley*, June 4, p. 278.

The book has all the multifariousness of life; the author has, as it were, created a world in which we see the diverse feelings, passions, and interests of complicated characters without the veils of self adulation or of exaggerated distrust with which we view our own lives, or the prejudice with which we regard those of our neighbors. Ordinary terms of praise sound insipid before the excellence with which this task is done. The very truth which this writer possesses seems so like simplicity that we feel inclined to take it for granted as a *sine qua non*, which we ought to accept with as little emotion as we do the air we breathe. . . . One of the most remarkable books of one of the greatest living writers. . . . From its wonderful accuracy in depicting life, from the morality of its lesson, from the originality, keenness, and fate-like sternness of the author, we may draw the conclusion that it is a book which every one should read for a wide knowledge of the world.—PERRY, S. S., 1873, *George Eliot's Middlemarch, North American Review*, vol. 116, pp. 433, 440.

Despite the vigorous bloom, the inconsistent life of "Middlemarch," do we not feel that there is an overwrought completion about it? The persons of the story are elaborated almost to exhaustion; there appears to be a lack of proportion in the prominence so fully accorded to each individual in his or her turn, for minor characters are dwelt upon too much in detail; and there is little or no mystery of distance about any of the figures, at any time. . . . As an effort of clear intellectual penetration into life, we could hardly demand anything better than "Middlemarch." But it is still **too** much an effort, and not enough an accomplished insight; it remains, as the author has called it, a study, rather than a finished dramatic representation.—LATHROP, GEORGE PARSONS, 1874, *Growth of the Novel, Atlantic Monthly*, vol. 33, pp. 688, 689.

"Middlemarch," with its undeniable excellences, is a somewhat disjointed composition, and disperses the interest of the reader *ad infinitum*.—SCHERR, J., 1874, *A History of English Literature*, tr. M. V., p. 279.

Certainly George Eliot is no maudlin sentimentalist—no melodramatic emotion-monger like him of "Little Nell." But for high and pure pathos,—pathos conceived in the key of that magnanimity which, in a world like ours, fallen and in sore need of redemption, is always the highest and purest pathos,—I should scarcely know where to look for anything finer than "Middlemarch" supplies.—WILKINSON, WILLIAM CLEAVER, 1874, *A Free Lance in the Field of Life and Letters*, p. 33.

In "Middlemarch" the peculiar powers of the author are exhibited in the highest and widest play of their development. None of her books is so deeply thoughtful, none commands so broad a view of the human horizon, none is so rich in personal portraiture.—WELSH, ALFRED H., 1883, *Development of English Literature and Language*, vol. II, p. 477.

I know not where else in literature to look for a work which leaves such a strong impression on the reader's mind of the intertexture of human lives. Seen thus in perspective, each separate individuality, with its specialized consciousness, is yet as indissolubly connected with the collective life as that of the indistinguishable zoöphyte which is but a sentient speck necessarily moved by the same vital agency which stirs the entire organism.—BLIND, MATHILDE, 1883, *George Eliot (Famous Women)*, p. 241.

One of her works, notwithstanding, must always be the guide of those who would know the provincial England of our day. "Middlemarch" is Nature herself. If merit is to be judged by perfection of execution, this depressing work sets George Eliot higher than the mingled pathos and humour of "Adam Bede" and "The Mill on Floss," the dignity of "Romola," or the moral enthusiasm of "Daniel Deronda."—GARNETT, RICHARD, 1887, *The Reign of Queen Victoria*, ed. Ward, vol. II, p. 490.

It is a great prose epic, large in size, commanding in structure, affording an ample space for a great artist to work upon. Perhaps even more than "Adam Bede" has it become part of the ordinary furniture of our minds, of the current coin of our thoughts. Casaubon, Will Laidlaw, Mr. Brooke are types which are ever present with us, like Becky Sharp and Colonel Newcome; and if Dorothea and Lydgate are more remote, it is because they are rarer characters, not because they are less truly drawn. "Middlemarch" gives George Eliot the chiefest claim to stand by the side of Shakespere. Both drew their inspiration from the same sources, the villages and the country houses which we know so well. —BROWNING, OSCAR, 1890, *Life of George Eliot (Great Writers)*, p. 142.

The style of "Middlemarch" is so full of science, of culture, of observation, of experience, that to follow it in its development, to see how it arises from the very heart of things, to gather its meaning in the original and incisive phrases in which it is clothed, is an intense intellectual enjoyment.—NEGRI, GAETANO, 1891, *George Eliot: La sua vita ed i suoi Romanzi*.

The *girl* is real enough; it is her chances which she and her biographer seem to me to have singularly missed, probably because the very weight and worth of English Dissenters forty to fifty years ago secluded them from all society but their own.... In truth, "Middlemarch" is to me as a landscape seen in the twilight; *au teint grisâtre*. It is from first to last the plaint of a lost ideal. I do not think it even a true rendering of life as it was lived in England sixty years ago. It would be easy to account for this by saying that the writer had lost "the wider hope." I prefer not to do it. Such an explanation is, indeed, so far obviously true as that in a country town the most strenuous belief, the most unflagging work, is religious. But the scepticism of "Middlemarch" also extends to things social and human.—BELLOC, BESSIE RAYNER, 1894, *In A Walled Garden*, pp. 6, 12.

It is, indeed, a half dozen novels in one. Its scale is cyclopædic, as I said, and it is the microcosm of a community rather than a story concerned with a unified plot and set of characters. And it is perhaps the writer's fullest expression of her philosophy of life.—BROWNELL, W. C., 1900, *George Eliot, Scribner's Magazine*, vol. 28, p. 724.

"Middlemarch" is George Eliot herself, with her large, grave, earnest, tolerant view of human nature and human life.—PAUL, HERBERT, 1902, *George Eliot, The Nineteenth Century*, vol. 51, p. 943.

DANIEL DERONDA
1876

Here we have what goes a considerable way towards filling an intellectual void — faithful pictures of modern Anglo-Jewish domestic life. But the author in some respects proceeds further, and evidently possesses loftier and wider aims than the mere exercise of the romance-writer's skill among new scenes. George Eliot has thrown no hasty or superficial glance over the externals of Judaism. She has acquired an extended and profound knowledge of the rites, aspirations, hopes, fears, and desires of the Israelites of the day. She had read their books, inquired into their modes of thought, searched their traditions, accompanied them to the synagogue; nay, she had taken their very words from their lips, and, like Asmodeus, has unroofed their houses. To say that some slight errors have crept into "Daniel Deronda" is to say that no human work is perfect; and these inaccuracies are singularly few and unimportant. . . . Curiously enough the Jewish episodes in "Daniel Deronda" have been barely adverted to by the reviewers. Most of these gentlemen have slurred over some of the finest and most characteristic passages in the book, with the remark that they possessed no general interest. Possibly the critics were unable to appreciate the beauty of the scenes they deemed unworthy of attention, or perhaps they consider the Jewish body too insignificant to be worth much discussion. . . . The book is a romance. Artistic truth in literature, as in painting, is always sought for by great workmen in preference to mere realistic truth. In Daniel Deronda, George Eliot has created a type which, though scarcely likely to appeal to the masses, aught to teach more than one lesson to serious thinkers. Here is a man who lays aside entirely all purely personal considerations, all feelings of ambition or aggrandisement, to devote the best years of his existence to the loftiest national aims.—PICCIOTTO, JAMES, 1876, *Deronda the Jew, Gentleman's Magazine*, N. S., vol. 17, pp. 594, 595, 597.

"Daniel Deronda" alone (the book, not the man) is proof enough that its author has the courage to enter upon the surest road to the highest kind of popularity—that which apparently leads above it. There is not a sentence, scarcely a character, in "Daniel Deronda" that reads or looks as if she were thinking of her critics before her readers at large, or of her readers at large before the best she could give them. She has often marred a stronger or more telling effect for the sake of a truer and deeper—and this belongs to a kind of courage which most artists will be inclined to envy her. But her processes of construction open another question, too long to speak of in a few words. Apart from all considerations of such processes in detail, "Daniel Deronda" is a probably unique example of the application of the forms of romance to a rare and difficult problem in human nature, by first stating the problem—(the transformation of Gwendolen)—in its extremest form, and then, with something like scientific precision as well as philosophic insight, arranging circumstances so as to throw upon it the fullest light possible.—FRANCILLON, R. E., 1876, *George Eliot's First Romance, Gentleman's Magazine*, N. S. vol. 17, p. 427.

"Daniel Deronda" has succeeded in awaking in my somewhat worn-out mind an interest. So many stories are tramping over one's mind in every modern magazine nowadays that one is macadamized, so to speak. It takes something unusual to make a sensation. This does excite and interest me, as I wait for each number with eagerness.—STOWE, HARRIET BEECHER, 1876, *To Mrs. Lewes, March 18; Life Compiled from Her Letters and Journals*, ed. Stowe, p. 473.

It seems to us that none of George Eliot's former novels so distinctly present the quality of her intellect, as "Daniel Deronda." In it she has reached both her clearest height of achievement and the barriers of art which she is unable to scale. It is no disparagement to recognize the latter, for they equally mark the extent of her development and the intensity of her aspiration. In reviewing the first volume of the work we noticed her tendency to analyze, as well as present, her characters.

She explains, and comments upon them, their words, movements, and changes of countenance: sometimes a chapter seems to open in some realm of abstract philosophical speculation, out of which the author slowly descends to take up the thread of her story. Sometimes these disquisitions are so sound and admirably stated that we are glad to come upon them: frequently they strike us as unnecessary and not particularly important; and occasionally they are mere high-sounding platitudes.—TAYLOR, BAYARD, 1876, *Essays and Notes*, p. 340.

"Daniel Deronda" is a novel both of incident and character; and, in addition, it exhibits a wealth of subtle, deep and comprehensive thought altogether unexampled among the novels of the time. One feels in reading, rereading and studying the book that in respect to mere largeness of intellect it is unmatched among the works of the most distinguished novelists of the century. Scott, Dickens and Thackeray may excel George Eliot in their special departments of fiction; but if we apply the intellectual test, and ask which of the four has mastered most thoroughly the knowledge and advanced thought of the age, the judgment of all cultivated persons would be given unreservedly in favor of the author of "Daniel Deronda." In sobriety, breadth and massiveness of understanding, in familiar acquaintance with the latest demonstrated truths of physical, historical, economic and intellectual science, and in the capacity to use these truths as materials for a philosophy of nature, and human nature, this woman is the acknowledged peer of such men as John Stuart Mill and Herbert Spencer. Leaving out of view the peculiar powers which make the great novelist, and fastening our attention on the understanding alone, it is obvious that George Eliot might hold, in one corner of her broad brain, all that portion of Scott's intellect which dealt with the philosophy of history as distinguished from its picturesqueness; in another corner, all that part of the intellect of Dickens which, in dealing with political economy, was prone to substitute benevolent sentiments for inexorable laws; and in still another corner, all that portion of the intellect of Thackeray which penetrated beneath the social shams he pitilessly satirized to the principles which make society possible.—WHIPPLE, EDWIN PERCY, 1877, *Daniel Deronda, North American Review*, vol. 124, p. 31.

The first thing that it is natural for a Jew to say about "Daniel Deronda" is some expression of gratitude for the wonderful completeness and accuracy with which George Eliot has portrayed the Jewish nature. Hitherto the Jew in English fiction has fared unhappily; being always represented as a monstrosity, most frequently on the side of malevolence and greed, as in Marlowe's Barabbas and Dickens's Fagin, or sometimes as in Dickens's Riah, still more exasperatingly on the side of impossible benevolence. What we want is truth, not exagggeration, and truth George Eliot has given us with the large justice of the great artist. The gallery of Jewish portraits contained in "Daniel Deronda" gives in a marvelously full and accurate way all the many sides of our complex national character. . . . Perhaps the most successful of the minor portraits is that of the black sheep Lapidoth, the Jew with no redeeming love for family, race or country to preserve him from that sordid egotism (the new name for wickedness) into which he has sunk. His utter unconsciousness of good and evil is powerfully depicted in the masterly analysis of his state of mind before purloining Deronda's ring. . . . Criticism on the Mordecai part of "Daniel Deronda" has been due to lack of sympathy and want of knowledge on the part of the critics, and hence its failure is not (if we must use the word) objective. If a young lady refuses to see any pathos in Othello's fate because she dislikes dark complexions, we blame the young lady, not Shakspeare: and if the critics have refused to see the pathos of Mordecai's fate because he is a Jew of the present day —so much the worse for the critics!— JACOBS, JOSEPH, 1877, *Mordecai: a Protest against the Critics, Jewish Ideals*, pp. 61, 64. 82.

Beside the clever critics some readers of "Daniel Deronda" ought perhaps to put on record their experience, and confess what have been the dealings of this book with their spirits. Those who have heard in it "the right voice," which one follows "as the water follows the moon, silently," will have been conscious of a quickening and exaltation of their entire spiritual life. The moral atmosphere they breathed became charged with a finer and more vivifying element; the face of the world seemed to glow for them with richer tint," "a more vivid gravity of expression;" moods of *ennui* or rebellion appeared more futile and unworthy than formerly; it became natural to believe high things of man; and a certain difficulty and peril attended the necessary return to duller or at least humbler tempers of heart (as it is difficult to pass from a sonata of Beethoven to the common household sounds), until these too were touched and received a consecration. The book has done something to prevent our highest movements from making our every-day experience seem vulgar and incoherent, and something to prevent our every-day experience from making our highest moments seem spectral and unreal. To discover the central motive of "Daniel Deronda" it should be studied in connection with its immediate predecessor, "Middlemarch."— DOWDEN, EDWARD, 1877–78, *Studies in Literature*, p. 277.

I repeat that the story of Gwendolen and Grandcourt takes its place beside the author's best work: and that, if the character-drawing is not stronger, it is at any rate subtler and more scientific. Gwendolen's conversation with Klesmer on her vocation as an actress, her interview with Mirah when she wishes to ascertain the truth of the rumors she has heard about Deronda, the tragedy on board the boat in the Gulf of Genoa, the good-byes and the confessions at the moment of final separation, are among the scenes, hard to manage, or even unmanageable, where the genius of George Eliot, compact at once of tact and power, breaks out in all its supremacy.—SCHERER, EDMOND, 1877–91, *Daniel Deronda, Essays on English Literature*, tr. Saintsbury, p. 62.

If I were asked for the most significant, the most tender, the most pious and altogether the most uplifting of modern books it seems to me I should specify "Daniel Deronda." . . . No man could deny the truth of the picture; the galled jade was obliged to wince; this time it was *my* withers that were wrung. Thus the moral purpose of "Daniel Deronda," which is certainly beyond all comparison less obtrusive than that of any other book written by George Eliot, grew, by its very nearness, out of all perspective. Though a mere gnat, it sat on the very eyelash of society and seemed a monster.—LANIER, SIDNEY, 1881, *The English Novel*, pp. 264, 280.

I have always thought, for instance, that the figure of Daniel Deronda, whose portrait, blurred and uncertain as it is, has been drawn with the most amazing care and with endless touches and retouches, must have become at last to George Eliot a kind of awful veiled spectre, always in her brain, always seeming about to reveal his true features and his mind, but never doing it, so that to the end she never clearly perceived what manner of man he was, nor what was his real character—BESANT, SIR WALTER, 1884, *The Art of Fiction*, p. 21.

She made a noble picture of Florence. And, in "Daniel Deronda," a fine defence of the Jews. That, I think, was the most Christian thing she ever did.—EGAN, MAURICE FRANCIS, 1889, *Lectures on English Literature*, p. 12.

The story of Gwendolen in "Deronda," up to the moment of her marriage, is one of the most masterly of impersonations. When, however, a female perfection comes in the shape of Dorothea, and still more a male perfection in the form of Daniel Deronda, this admirable genius fails and sinks into morasses of fictitious imagination, and laboured utterance. Her true inspiration had nothing to do with these artificial and fantastic embodiments of new philosophy and a conventional ideal.—OLIPHANT, MARGARET O. W., 1892, *The Victorian Age of English Literature*, p. 469

The choice of "Adam Bede" to represent George Eliot is again evidence of the soundness of the popular instinct; but it is not surprising to find many books preferred to "Daniel Deronda."—MABIE, HAMILTON W., 1893, *The Most Popular Novels in America, The Forum*, vol 16, p. 513.

One day she told me that in order to write "Daniel Deronda," she had read through two hundred books. I longed to tell her that she had better have learned Yiddish and talked with two hundred Jews, and been taught, as I was by my friend Solomon the Sadducee, the art of distinguishing Fraülein Löwenthal of the Ashkenazim from Senorita Aguado of the Sephardim *by the corners of their eyes!*—LELAND, CHARLES GODFREY, 1893, *Memoirs*, p. 390.

A friend told me something which I think puts the matter in a nut shell. He said he had been seated next to what he described as a girl of the period. It was the period when "Daniel Deronda" was the reigning book, and so he put to her the inevitable question, "Have you read 'Daniel Deronda?'" And what do you think was the answer? "No, but I have been told it." Think; she had been told "Daniel Deronda!" You who have read "Daniel Deronda" —that compendium of a whole philosophy of life, combined with a story as intricate as Shakespeare's plots—fancy a young lady being told the whole! It was as if someone had been asked, "Have you read Herbert Spencer's 'Psychology?'" and he should answer, "Well, no; but I heard it across the dinner table." "Have you heard Mendelssohn's 'Elijah?'" And the reply would be, "Yes; that is to say, a friend hummed it over to me."—MOULTON, RICHARD G., 1894, *The Study of Literature, Journal of Proceedings and Addresses of the National Educational Association*, p. 215.

When "Daniel Deronda" is reached, there is but little left of the author of "Adam Bede."—GRAHAM, RICHARD D., 1897, *The Masters of Victorian Literature*, p. 57.

"Daniel Deronda" is the most wearisome, the least artistic, and the most unnatural of all George Eliot's books. Of course it has the masterly touch, and, for all its comparative inferiority, has also its supreme excellence. But in plot, treatment and character it is far below its predecessors.—LINTON, MRS. LYNN, 1897, *Women Novelists of Queen Victoria's Reign*, p. 106.

"Daniel Deronda" was then a work of great audacity. For it was deliberately planned to present a new heroic type. Deronda is no reminiscence nor survival: he is a hero who would never have existed till our own day.—SCUDDER, VIDA D., 1898, *Social Ideals in English Letters*, p. 190.

The chief sign of decline in George Eliot's last novel, "Daniel Deronda," is the attempt to replace these vigorous living beings with badly imagined puppets like the Meyricks. She had used up the material of her youth, and found nothing in her brilliant life of culture and travel to take its place.—MOODY, WILLIAM VAUGHN, AND LOVETT, ROBERT MORSS, 1902, *A History of English Literature*, p. 377.

I must repeat that George Eliot was intensely feminine, though more philosophical than most women. She shows it to the best purpose in the subtlety and the charm of her portraits of women, unrivalled in some ways by any writer of either sex; and shows it also, as I think, in a true perception of the more feminine aspects of her male characters. Still, she sometimes illustrates the weakness of the feminine view. Daniel Deronda is not merely a feminine but, one is inclined to say, a school-girl's hero. He is so sensitive and scrupulously delicate that he will not soil his hands by joining in the rough play of ordinary political and social reformers. He will not compromise, and yet he shares the dislikes of his creator for fanatics and the devotees of "fads."—STEPHEN, LESLIE, 1902, *George Eliot (English Men of Letters)*, p. 190.

IMPRESSIONS OF THEOPHRASTUS SUCH
1879

Her thoughts are too intense to bear crowding. We have been accustomed of old to her subtle psychological analysis; but we have never before had it given to us in the undiluted form. Narrative and dialogue have elsewhere allowed the characters to develop themselves gradually and dramatically under our eyes. In her present work, however, George Eliot allows herself to speak under a thin disguise in her own person; and the result is a series of character sketches, admirable in truthfulness, insight, and power, but almost painful in their elaborateness and weight of matter. Theophrastus Such, the eponymus of the volume, had probably for his *raison d' être* the desire of the author to avoid that possible imputation of self-consciousness which might have been raised by the critical reader, had the essays been published without the intervention of such a supposititious godfather. A bachelor of unprepossessing and awkward exterior, Theophrastus has not turned out a success in social life, and he gives us his impressions of others and of himself with a genuine frankness which is partially attributed to his expectation that nobody will read his fugitive sketches. In his first essay, "Looking Inward," he deals with that most difficult of problems, his own individuality as it seems to others.— ALLEN, GRANT, 1879, *Some New Books, Fortnightly Review*, vol. 32, p. 144.

A great authoress of our time was urged by a friend to fill up a gap in our literature by composing a volume of Thoughts: the result was that least felicitous of performances, "Theophrastus Such."—MORLEY, JOHN, 1887, *Aphorisms, Studies in Literature*, p. 71.

It contains studies of character, such as might form the rough drafts for future novels, embodying moral lessons which she desired to convey. The style is weighty and periodic, influenced by the English of the seventeenth century which she loved so well. The compact statement of arguments, the subtlety of analysis and insight are as apparent as in any of her works. The humour is sometimes admirable, at others heavy and laboured; there is little dramatic interest. "Theophrastus" does not exist as a personality, and the veil which divides him from the writer herself is of varying degrees of density. Still the book furnishes many "wise, witty, and tender sayings," and from its inherent truthfulness and absence of affectation is a most valuable source of information for the feelings and opinions which lay deepest at her heart.—BROWNING, OSCAR, 1890, *Life of George Eliot* (*Great Writers*), p. 133.

The summer of 1878 was partly occupied by George Eliot in writing "Theophrastus Such"—perhaps the only one of her books which was not a success. I have a guilty conscience as to this book, as I may have contributed to induce her to write it. I pointed out to her that our English literature, so rich and splendid in almost every field of poetry and prose, was deficient in those collections of Thoughts which the French call *Pensées*—pregnant apothegms embedded in terse and memorable phrase which would be remembered like fine lines of poetry, and be cited as readily as a familiar proverb. It seemed to me—it seems to me still—that she was eminently fitted to produce such a book, and indeed the "Wit and Wisdom of George Eliot" was a volume culled from her writings. But "Theophrastus Such"—where the queer title came from I know not—was not an adequate expression of her powers. She was in very poor health all the time, and George Lewes was then stricken with his last illness. His death delayed publication, and when she read "Theophrastus" in revise, she had serious thoughts of suppressing it. . . . Would she had done so! Her life was ebbing away when it was actually published.—HARRISON, FREDERIC, 1901, *Reminiscences of George Eliot, Harper's Magazine*, vol. 103, p. 582.

POEMS

The writing has the diffuseness of literature, rather than the condensation of poetry; and, admirable as some of it is, we wish it away: at the lowest, we say to ourselves, if a poet had had to utter this, our pleasure would have been perfect; but, as it is, what is before us is almost too good, and yet it is not good enough; it does not compel us to think, *le poëte a le frisson*, either while we read or afterward. There is too much aggregation and accumulation about it; we are set thinking, and set feeling; we are agitated; but we are not thrilled by any single sudden notes. . . . Leaving the workmanship and the intellectual conception, or interwoven moral criticism, of the poem ("Spanish Gypsy") and coming to the story, I am sure of only echoing what all the world will say when I call this in the highest degree poetic; and poetically dramatic, too.—RANDS, W. B. (MATTHEW BROWNE), 1868, *George Eliot as a Poet, Contemporary Review*, vol. 8, pp. 391, 392.

We imagine George Eliot is quite philosopher enough, having produced her poems mainly as a kind of experimental entertainment for her own mind, to let them commend themselves to the public on any grounds whatever which will help to illustrate the workings of versatile intelligence, —as interesting failures, if nothing better. She must feel they are interesting; an exaggerated modesty cannot deny that. . . . In whatever George Eliot writes, you have the comfortable certainty, infrequent in other quarters, of finding an idea, and you get the substance of her thought in the short poems, without the somewhat rigid envelope of her poetic diction. If we may say, broadly, that the supreme merit of a poem is in having warmth, and that it is less valuable in proportion as it cools by too long waiting upon either fastidious skill or inefficient skill, the little group of verses entitled "Brother and Sister" deserve our preference.—JAMES, HENRY, 1874, *George Eliot's Legend of Jubal, North American Review*, vol. 119, p. 485.

George Eliot's metrical work has special interest, coming from a woman acknowledged to be, in her realistic yet imaginative prose, at the head of living female writers. She has brought all her energies to bear, first upon the construction of a drama, which was only a *succes d'estime*, and recently upon a new volume containing "The

Legend of Jubal" and other poems. The result shows plainly that Mrs. Lewes, though possessed of great intellect and sensibility, is not, in respect to metrical expression, a poet. Nor has she a full conception of the simple strength and melody of English verse, her polysyllabic language, noticeable in the moralizing passages of "Middlemarch," being very ineffective in her poems. That wealth of thought which atones for all her deficiencies in prose does not seem to be at her command in poetry. "The Spanish Gypsy" reads like a second-rate production of the Byronic school. "The Legend of Jubal" and "How Lisa Loved the King" suffer by comparison with the narrative poems, in rhymed pentameter, of Morris, Longfellow, or Stoddard. A little poem in blank-verse, entitled "O may I join the choir invisible!" and setting forth her conception of the "religion of humanity," is worth all the rest of her poetry, for it is the outburst of an exalted soul foregoing personal immortality and compensated by a vision of the growth and happiness of the human race.—STEDMAN, EDMUND CLARENCE, 1875-87, *Victorian Poets*, p. 254.

The "Legend of Jubal" tells, in sustained language, the story of the lyre and its inventor, and the fate he met at the hands of those who loved his music. But the same volume contains four dramatic scenes—entitled "Armgart"—presenting phases in the life of a passionate proud singer who loses her exquisite voice, and these scenes are fuller of real poetry, albeit, as tragic sketches, they are not compact enough in the grouping of the figures. The artistic exultation of the singer in the earlier scenes is conveyed to us in a wondrously full manner. Here, and in a subsequent poem, "Stradivarius," the deep musician-nature of the poetess reveals itself almost uncontrollably. In "Stradivarius" we have a sombre-toned picture of the steady conscientious violin-maker pursuing his loved occupation with as great a sense of responsibility as if he had been ordained to the work by the direct command of heaven. The character is drawn in simple strong lines. But the verses that most genuinely reveal such distinctly poetic faculty as George Eliot possessed are those entitled "Brother and Sister." This short series of sonnets on child-life is autobiographical, and, even more emphatically than the description of Maggie Tulliver's girlhood, shows how keenly the novelist had lived as a child, and how lasting her impressions of her early existence were. Probably George Eliot never excelled, in prose, the extraordinary studies of child-life (boy-life as well as girl-life) in "The Mill on the Floss."—ROBERTSON, ERIC S., 1883, *English Poetesses*, p. 332.

In her poetry George Eliot is much more a doctrinaire than in her novels, all her poems, except a few of the shorter ones, are devoted to the inculcation of some moral or philosophic teaching. The very effort she was obliged to make to give herself utterance in poetry predisposed her to intellectual subjects and those of a controversial nature. For this reason her verse has a special interest for those who are attracted to her teachings. Her pen was freer, more creative, in her great novels than in her poems. In fact, her novels, especially "Adam Bede" and "The Mill on the Floss," are much more poetical than much she did in verse.—COOKE, GEORGE WILLIS, 1883, *George Eliot: A Critical Study of Her Life, Writings and Philosophy*, p. 162.

George Eliot, with brain surcharged with richest thought and choicest, carefulest culture; with heart to hold all humanity, if that could save; with tongue of men and angels to tell the knowledge of her intellect, the charity of her heart—yet, having not faith, becomes, for all of satisfaction that she gives the soul, but sounding brass and tinkling cymbal! She will not bid me hope when she herself has no assurance of the thing hoped for. She must not speak of faith in the unknown. She cannot be cruel, but she can be dumb; and so her long procession of glorious thoughts, and sweet humanities, and noblest ethics, and stern renunciations, and gracious common lots, and lofty ideal lives, with their scalding tears, and bursting laughter, and flaming passion—all that enters into mortal life and time's story—makes its matchless march before our captured vision up to—the stone-wall. . . . Her teaching takes its shape from the attitude of her own soul. To epitomize, then. George Eliot's pages are a labyrinth of wonder and beauty; crowded with ethics lofty and pure as Plato's; with human natures fine and fresh as Shakespeare's; but a labyrinth in which you lose the guiding cord! With the attitude and utterance of her spirit confronting me, I cannot allow her verse to be poetry. She is the *raconteur*, not the *vates;* the scientist not the seer.—CLEVELAND, ROSE ELIZABETH, 1885, *George Eliot's Poetry and Other Studies*, pp. 18, 22.

"The Spanish Gypsy" is the work upon which the deniers of George Eliot's poetic faculty, mainly base their judgment. In speaking of it their voice is loud and confident. "The Legend of Jubal" and "Brother and Sister" bring it down to a lower tone; and as they approach that lyric of solemn rapture, "Oh may I join the choir invisible!" it dies into a whisper. "The Spanish Gypsy" is therefore the structure brave upon which those who greatly dare, because they greatly admire, will, with courageous eagerness plant their standard as a signal that there as elsewhere they are ready to stand an assault. Nor will they fear to admit that there are passages in "The Spanish Gypsy" which lack the metrical inevitableness just referred to, —passages which might have taken the form of prose without any loss of essential weight or beauty; but then they are to be found not less in the "Iliad," the "Inferno," the "Paradise Lost." To the whole world, however, these works are indubitable poetry; and those who regard "The Spanish Gypsy" also as poetry, and poetry of a very noble order, base their regard on the fact that the final impression left by it as by them is of an imaginative conception which could only be made fully manifest in an embodiment of verse.—MILES, ALFRED H., 1892, *The Poets and the Poetry of the Century, Joanna Baillie to Mathilde Blind*, p. 298.

With all her consummate literary gifts and tastes, George Eliot never managed to write a poem, and never could be brought to see that the verses she wrote were not poems. It was an exaggeration of the defect that mars her prose; and her verses throw great light on her prose. They are overlaboured; the conception overpowers the form; they are too intensely anxious to be recognized as poems. We see not so much poetic passion, as a passionate yearning after poetic passion. We have,—not the inevitable, incalculable, inimitable, phrase of real poetry,—but the slowly distilled, calculated, and imitated effort to reach the spontaneous.—HARRISON, FREDERIC, 1895, *Studies in Early Victorian Literature*, p. 219.

Her genius was sensuous enough, and passionate enough, in all conscience; but the first note of poetry, simplicity, was signally lacking. The thought of her poems is profound, involved and highly analytical; in a word, as much as possible the reverse of simple; and the verbal medium and apparatus is rugged with the ruggedness of a violent attempt to press into poetic form that of which poetry itself is intolerant. — RUSSELL, GEORGE W. E., 1896, *George Eliot Revisited, The Contemporary Review*, vol. 69, *p*, 364.

She merely put some of the thoughtful commonplaces of her time and school into wooden verse, occasionally grandiose but never grand, and her purple passages have the purple of plush not velvet.—SAINTSBURY, GEORGE, 1896, *A History of Nineteenth Century Literature*, p. 322.

THE SPANISH GYPSY
1868

I read the "Spanish Gypsy" about a month ago, and enjoyed it very much. Perhaps, in point of form, it is an imperfection that it is neither drama nor epic, but it has the advantage of greater variety in being both.—THIRLWALL, CONNOP, 1868, *Letters to a Friend*, ed. Stanley, July 21 *p*. 158.

"The Spanish Gypsy," like "Romola," is a mistake, and a mistake in several respects. The story violates the laws of imaginative probability; the dialogue is strained and declamatory; the dramatic action, in spite of the sustained intellectual force, is feeble and flags; the characters are destitute of life. Yet on each of these details an immense amount of hard and conscientious labour has been expended, and the cleverness of the counterfeit is in places so remarkable, that it need not surprise us that even sharp-sighted critics should have been deceived. It is indeed better poetry than almost any one *except* a poet could write. . . . Brilliant with epigram though it be, is uneasy, artificial and declamatory. It manifests a ceaseless striving after effects. There is hardly a page unvexed by some verbal paradox.—SKELTON, JOHN, 1868, *Poetry and George Eliot, Fraser's Magazine*, vol. 78, pp. 471, 474.

On the whole, Zarca, the gypsy chief, is perhaps the most vividly drawn of George Eliot's purely ideal characters. . . . There is an unmistakable grandeur and power of invention in the heroic figure of Zarca, although, in spite of this power, we miss the convincing stamp of reality in him and not only in him, but more or less in all the characters of "The Spanish Gypsy." . . . For, although she here chose one of the most romantic of periods and localities, the Spain of Ferdinand and Isabella, with the mingled horror and magnificence of its national traditions, she does not really succeed in resuscitating the spirit which animated those devout, cruel, fanatical, but ultra-picturesque times. The Castilian noble, the Jewish astrologer, Zarca, and the Spanish Inquisitor, even the bright, gloriously conceived Fedalma herself, think and speak too much like sublimated modern positivists. — BLIND, MATHILDE, 1883, *George Eliot (Famous Women)*, p. 220.

The fatal objection to "The Spanish Gypsy," and to all George Eliot's poems, is that, save for a few lines here and there, they might as well, or better, have been written in prose.—PAUL, HERBERT, 1902, *George Eliot, The Nineteenth Century, vol.* 51 p. 938.

THE LEGEND OF JUBAL
1870

In the evening read "The Legend of Jubal," by Mrs. Lewes,—a poem of a good deal of power, but in parts rather confused, as the "new style" poetry often is to me.—LONGFELLOW, HENRY WADSWORTH, 1870, *Journal, April 5; Life, ed. Longfellow, vol.* III, p. 148.

In the "Legend of Jubal" (1870) the authoress found a subject which called all her most characteristic qualities into exercise—wisdom, large-heartedness, gentle irony, heartfelt compassion. The poetical form is also most happily chosen; the grand heroic couplet, laden but not overladen with noble thought, sweeps on with accumulating power to the most affecting of catastrophes.—GARNETT, RICHARD, 1887, *The Reign of Queen Victoria, ed. Ward, vol.* II, p. 488.

GENERAL

It is one of the greatest merits of the greatest living writer of fiction,—of the authoress of "Adam Bede,"— that she never brings you to anything without preparing you for it; she has no loose lumps of beauty, she puts in nothing at random: after her greatest scenes, too, a natural sequence of subordinate realities again tones down the mind to this sublunary world. Her logical style—the most logical, probably, which a woman ever wrote—aids in this matter her natural sense of due proportion; there is not a space of incoherency, not a gap. It is not natural to begin with the point of a story, and she does not begin with it; when some great marvel has been told, we all wish to know what came of it, and she tells us. Her natural way—as it seems to those who do not know its rarity— of telling what happened, produces the consummate effect of gradual enchantment and as gradual disenchantment.—BAGEHOT, WALTER, 1864, *Sterne and Thackeray, Works, ed. Morgan, vol.* II, p. 167.

From the time when the interesting "Scenes of a Clerical Life" were published, down to the issue of "Felix Holt," George Eliot has the great merit of being true to herself. . . . The corruption which a life of fiction-writing, like a life of politics, is apt to produce, has not been able to dull her moral sense, nor to rust the keenness of her sympathy for the sorrows and joys of men and women. Even the wearing effects of time she shows but little. She has neither become a cynic, nor a humorist, nor coarse, but still keeps in the path of realistic art, studying the roadside nature, and satisfied with it. She continues to receive the great reward which every true realist longs for, that she is true to nature without degenerating to the commonplace, and the old blame, that they have not enough of the ideal, which they covet too.—SEDGWICK, ARTHUR G., 1866, *Felix Holt the Radical, North American Review, vol.* 103, p. 557.

Considering George Eliot as a writer generally without having regard to her special vocation as a writer of novels, criticism cheerfully recognises many rare excellences. First among these of common consent, must be placed her style. It would be flattery to place her on a level with Thackeray. But now that we have lost Thackeray, she is in this point above all others. Trollope, indeed, has a merit of his own; but his easy naturalness is altogether on a lower level. George Eliot's style is rich in beauty and power. It is a splendid vehicle. We can often mark its effect in raising the thought to a dignity greater than its own. Her wealth of allusion is considerable, and it is indicated with becoming reserve, not ostentatiously obtruded, as is the fashion with most of our present novelists; to borrow a graceful simile from Mr. Hannay, it is like "violets hidden in the green of her prose." Above all her style is not the result of art only: it has that indescribable stamp which marks it as the result of feeling and thought. The thought may not be always deep, the feeling may not be always right, but both are uniformly original and sincere.—LANCASTER, HENRY H., 1866-76, *George Eliot's Works, Essays and Reviews*, p. 354.

If he were not so fantastic, if he were less gross and cruel, if he could believe in anything, if life were not a hideous strife of interests in which the stronger tramples on the weak, if he did not love evil for its own sake, Balzac would certainly be one of the two greatest novelists of the world, Miss Evans the other. As it is, he must always be admired with reservations, and regarded as a ruthless pathologist. The higher place of a true physiologist (such as I think Miss Evans is) cannot be claimed for him.—SYMONDS, JOHN ADDINGTON, 1868, *To his Sister Charlotte, Jan. 1; Life, ed. Brown*, vol. II, p. 20.

The novels of George Eliot are not didactic treatises. They are primarily works of art, and George Eliot herself is artist as much as she is teacher. Many good things in particular passages of her writings are detachable; admirable sayings can be cleared from their surroundings, and presented by themselves, knocked out clean as we knock out fossils from a piece of limestone. But if we separate the moral soul of any complete work of hers from its artistic medium, if we murder to dissect, we lose far more than we gain. . . . Complete in all its parts, and strong in all, the nature of George Eliot is yet not one of those rare natures which without effort are harmonious. There is no impression made more decisively upon the reader of her books than this. No books bear upon their faces more unmistakably the pain of moral conflict, and the pain of moral victory, only less bitter than that of defeat. Great forces warring with one another; a sorrowful, a pathetic victory—that is what we discern. —DOWDEN, EDWARD, 1872-78, *Studies in Literature*, pp. 241, 258.

Her writing does not soothe, because she keeps so constantly before us the stern effort she is making, not to swerve from strict analysis. The authoress presides too watchfully over the progress of our acquaintance with the imaginary beings to whom she has introduced us; and we should be more at ease, if she would omit some of the more wordy of her examinations into their mental status at each new turn of the story.—LATHROP, GEORGE PARSONS, 1874, *Growth of the Novel, Atlantic Monthly*, vol. 33, p. 688.

George Eliot is more than a brilliant novelist. She is a great writer. She is more than simply a great writer. She is a prime elemental literary power. In literature such, she is scarcely less in ethics. She is a great ethical teacher—it may be not an original, but at least a highly charged derivative, moral living force. Perhaps even thus much is still too little to have said. For George Eliot seems already securely to belong to the very small number of those choice literary names which we jealously account our greatest. . . . She loves to be sententious. She is fonder of reflection than she is of narration. Her plot is for the sake of her dialogue, her dialogue is for the sake of her character, and her character is for the sake of the wit and the wisdom that her many-sided genius is consciously capable and therefore desirous of lavishing on the world. . . . Psychological analysis is her strength and her joy. She creates character, she devises incident and situation, chiefly that she may have her occasion of indulging that almost superhuman faculty which is hers, of laying bare to its ultimate microscopic secret, the anatomy of the living human consciousness in play. . . . The knowledge of the human heart that George Eliot displays, is not an acquired knowledge. It was born with her and in her. It is genius. It is a gift which is Shakespearian in quality—one might, perhaps, as well be frankly true to himself and out with his thought—it is *finer* than Shakespeare. In quantity it is less, but in quality it is more. —WILKINSON, WILLIAM CLEAVER, 1874, *A Free Lance in the Field of Life and Letters*, pp. 1, 10, 12, 18.

What novelist has more conclusively made good her claim to rank almost with the highest, than George Eliot?—SMITH, GEORGE BARNETT, 1875, *Elizabeth Barrett Browning, Poets and Novelists*, p. 107.

Among the highest characteristics of "George Eliot" as a writer of fiction is her remarkable power in the delineation, not so much of character already formed, as of its development. Almost unconsciously the reader follows every process in the growth of those strong individual types with which her novels are filled, and sees the logical influence of every circumstance and event brought to bear upon their lives. In all of her works the physical and material difficulties to which her actors are subjected, and all those things which ordinarily constitute the "plot" of a romance, are, without losing their interest in any way, made completely subordinate to this leading design of picturing the development of the individual character under different conditions. Thus her novels form some of the best examples in the English language of the true carrying out of the highest purpose of fiction.—BURLINGAME, EDWARD L., 1875, *American Cyclopædia, vol.* x, *p.* 382.

But two women before her—Madame de Staël and George Sand—have so devoted themselves to lifelong study, in all attainable departments of knowledge, for the sake of high success in literature. She is more feminine than the former, more masculine than the latter, resembles both in her interest in physical, ethical, and social science, yet, in her style as a writer, hardly reaches either the sculptured symmetry of the one or the warmth, color, and fluent grace of the other.—TAYLOR, BAYARD, 1876, *Essays and Notes*, p. 340.

To exalt the social and abase the selfish principle, to show the futility of merely personal claims, cares and cravings, to purify the passions by exhibiting their fatal or miserable issues when they are centered in the individual alone—such are the moral purposes which we feel at work beneath all her artistic purposes. . . . The flow of George Eliot's writing, we have felt, is apt to be impeded with excess of thought; while of writing which does flow, and in flowing carry the reader delightfully along, George Sand is an incomparable mistress. But this is only the sign of deeper differences. George Sand excels in the poetical part of her art. George Eliot excels in the philosophical. Each is equally mistress of human nature and its secrets, but the one more by instinct. the other more by reflection. In everything which is properly matter of the intellect, the English writer is the superior of the French by far.— COLVIN, SIDNEY, 1876, *Daniel Deronda, Fortnightly Review, vol.* 26, pp. 602, 614.

In largeness of Christian charity, in breadth of human sympathy, in tenderness toward all human frailty that is not vitally base and self-seeking, in subtle power of finding "a soul of goodness" in things apparently evil, she has not many equals, certainly no superior, in the writers of the day. . . . Self-sacrifice is the divine law of life and its only fulfilment; self-sacrifice not in some ideal sphere sought out for ourselves in the vain spirit of self-pleasing, but wherever God has placed us, amidst homely, petty anxieties, loves and sorrows; the aiming at the highest attainable good in our own place, irrespective of all results of joy or sorrow, of apparent success or failure—such is the lesson that begins to be conveyed to us in George Eliot's "Clerical Scenes." The lesson comes to us in the quiet, unselfish love, the sweet hourly self-devotion of the "Milly" of "Amos Barton" so touchingly pure and full that it never recognizes itself as self-devotion at all.—BROWN, JOHN CROMBIE, 1879, *The Ethics of George Eliot's Works.*

But if she has failed as a novelist where novelists of less genius have succeeded, she exhibits power to which, amongst other novelists, we can hardly find a parallel, and which only very rarely have expressed themselves in prose fiction at all. She may be less than Miss Austen in art, but she is greater than Scott in insight. Indeed, to compare her even to Scott is an unfairness to her. We must go for our parallel yet a stage higher; and we must not stop short of the world's greatest poets.—MALLOCK, WILLIAM HURREL, 1879–84, *George Eliot on the Human Character, Atheism and the Value of Life,* p. 153.

George Eliot is genius and culture. Had she never written a page of fiction, she must have been regarded with admiration by all who knew her as a woman of deep thought and of a varied knowledge such as men complacently believe to be the possession only of men. It was not this, however, which made her a great novelist. Her eyes were not turned inward or kept down in metaphysical contemplation. She studied the living world around her. She had an eye for external things keen almost as that of Dickens or Balzac. George Eliot is the only novelist who can paint such English people as the Poysers and the Tullivers just as they are. She looks into the very souls of such people. She tracks out their slow, peculiar mental processes; she reproduces them fresh and firm from very life. Mere realism, mere photographing, even from the life, is not in art a great triumph. But George Eliot can make her dullest people interesting and dramatically effective. She can paint two dull people with quite different ways of dulness—a dull man and a dull woman, for example—and the reader is astonished to find how utterly distinct the two kinds of stupidity are, and how intensely amusing both can be made.—MCCARTHY, JUSTIN, 1880, *A History of Our Own Times from the Accession of Queen Victoria to the Berlin Congress*, vol. IV, ch. lxvii, p. 131.

She, of all novelists, has attacked the profound problems of our existence. She has taught that the mystery worthy of a great artist is not the shallow mystery of device, but the infinite perspective of the great, dark enigmas of human nature; that there is a deeper interest in human life seen in the modern, scientific daylight, than in life viewed through a mist of ancient and dying superstitions; that the interest of human character transcends the interest of invented circumstances; that the epic story of a hero and a heroine is not so grand as the natural history of a community. She, first of all, has made cross sections of modern life, and shown us the busy human hive in the light of a great artistic and philosophic intellect. She has not sought to see men in the dim haze of a romantic past, but to bring men into close vision, who, by difference of race, condition, or the lapse of time, were far away. George Eliot has made the typical novel of this age of scientific thought and growing unbelief in the supernatural. . . . George Eliot, more than any other, has shown that romance, so far from dying under the influence of the stern skepticism of our time, has had opened to it a new and more vigorous life.—EGGLESTON, EDWARD, 1881, *George Eliot and the Novel, The Critic*, vol. 1, p. 9.

George Eliot's novels are admirably various in their scenery. They now paint Methodist life in the days of Wesley, now Mediæval Catholicism in the days of Savonarola, now the whole range of the Jewish nationality. They are alike in their rich play of humour and pathos, in sympathy with the varieties of human character, in the spirit of humanity that is allied with every honest aspiration; they are alike also in the steadiness with which every one exalts the life that is firmly devoted to the highest aim it knows. Again and again, there is the type of the weak pleasure-loving mind, too easily misled, and of the firm spirit, capable of self-denial, true to its own highest sense of right. George Eliot's novels will cloud no true faith; they are the work of a woman of rare genius whose place is, for all time, among the greatest novelists our country has produced. — MORLEY, HENRY, 1881, *Of English Literature in the Reign of Victoria with a Glance at the Past*, p. 408.

What Lord Beaconsfield says of Lady Montford in "Endymion" is perfectly applicable to George Eliot: "Her character was singularly feminine; she never affected to be a superior woman." Though the intellectual equal of any woman who ever wrote a book, and of many men who have no intellectual superiors among their fellows, George Eliot was yet as unpretending as if she had no right to a place among the most worthy. Others of her sex, without a tithe of her abilities, are given to demanding their rights. She was satisfied to discharge to the best of her power what she regarded as her duties as a member of a civilized community. Her ideal of existence was a very different one from that which women of inferior gifts but greater pretensions set forth in writing or in speech.—RAE, W. FRASER, 1881, *George Eliot's Life and Writings, International Review*, vol. 10, p. 458.

At the present moment George Eliot is the first of English novelists, and I am disposed to place her second of those of my time. She is best known to the literary world as a writer of prose fiction, and not improbably whatever of permanent fame she may acquire will come from her novels. But the nature of her intellect is very far removed indeed from that which is common to the tellers of stories. Her imagination is, no doubt, strong, but it acts in analyzing rather than in creating. Everything that comes before her is pulled to pieces so that the inside of it shall be seen, and be seen, if possible, by her readers as clearly as by herself. This searching analysis is carried so far that in studying her later writings, one feels one's self to be in company with some philosopher rather than with a novelist. I doubt whether any young person can read with pleasure either "Felix Holt," "Middlemarch," or "Daniel Deronda." I know that they are very difficult to many that are not young. Her personifications of character have been singularly terse and graphic and from them has come her great hold on the public, though by no means the greatest effect which she has produced. The lessons which she teaches remain, though it is not for the sake of the lessons that her pages are read. Seth Bede, Adam Bede, Maggie and Tom Tulliver, old Silas Marner, and, much above all, Tito, in "Romola," are characters, which when once known, can never be forgotten. I cannot say quite so much for any of those in her later works, because in them the philosopher so greatly overtops the portrait-painter, that, in the dissection of the mind, the outward signs seem to have been forgotten. In her, as yet, there is no symptom whatever of that weariness of mind which, when felt by the reader, induces him to declare that the author has written himself out. It is not from decadence that we do not have another Mrs. Poyser, but because the author soars to things which seem to her to be higher than Mrs. Poyser.—TROLLOPE, ANTHONY, 1882–83, *Autobiography*, p. 178.

That she did teach positivism is unfortunately true, so far as her literary touch and expression is concerned. That philosophy affects all her books with its subtly insinuating flavor, and it gives meaning and bias to most of them. They thus gain in definiteness of purpose, in moral vigor, in minutely faithful study of some phases of human experience, and in a massive impression of thoughtfulness which her work creates. At the same time, they undoubtedly lose in value as studies of life; in free range of expression for her genius, her poetry and her art; and in that spiritual vision which looks forward with keen gazing eyes of hope and confident inquiry. Her teaching, like most teaching, is a mingled good and evil. . . . George Eliot's books have an interest as an attempt at an interpretation of life from its more practical and realistic side, and not less as a reaction against the influences of very near all the great literary minds of the earlier half of the century in England. . . . Her enthusiasm for altruism, her zeal for humanity, lends a delightful feature to her books. It gives a glow and a consecration to her work, and makes her as great a prophet as positivism is capable of creating. And it is no idle power she awakens in her positivist faith in man. She shames those who claim a broader and better faith.—COOKE, GEORGE WILLIS, 1883, *George Eliot: A Critical Study of Her Life, Writings and Philosophy*, pp. 413, 414, 418.

George Eliot is the greatest of the novelists in the delineation of feeling and the analysis of motives. . . . If you say the telling of a story is her forte, you put her below Wilkie Collins or Mrs. Oliphant; if you say her object is to give a picture of English society, she is surpassed by Bulwer and Trollope; if she be called a satirist of society, Thackeray is her superior; if she intends to illustrate the absurdity of behavior, she is eclipsed by Dickens; but if the analysis of human motives be her forte and art, she stands first, and it is very doubtful whether any artist in fiction is entitled to stand second. She reaches clear in and touches the most secret and the most delicate spring of human action.—SHEPPARD, NATHAN, 1883, ed. *The Essays of George Eliot*, p. 7.

If it be true that the work of every artist is but a confession of his own life and feelings, one may say that the writings of George Eliot are essentially a confession of her childhood. The most living characters of her novels, those who have a home in all our memories, are sprung from the real men and women of her early days. That is why they are so veracious and so vivid. Nothing lives and endures like the life and recollection of our very first impressions, like the heart of the child which pulses in the brain of the man. Her own child's heart is born again to us in the adorable image of Maggie Tulliver, the dear little girl, so oddly compact of day-dreams and logic, of imaginative enthusiasm and serious good feeling.—DARMESTETER, JAMES, 1883–96, *English Studies*, tr. Mrs. Darmesteter, p. 99.

I will not do Mr. Trollope such an ill turn as to compare him with George Eliot, the greatest, I suppose, of all writers of fiction till she took to theories and Jews. It was a wonderful feat to draw Romola; it was a wonderful feat to draw Mrs. Poyser; but for the same hand to draw Romola and Mrs. Poyser was something more than wonderful; if the fact were not certain, one would deem it impossible.—FREEMAN, EDWARD A., 1883, *Anthony Trollope*, Macmillan's Magazine, vol. 47, p. 240.

It would be rash to compare George Eliot with Tacitus, with Dante, with Pascal. A novelist—for as a poet, after trying hard to think otherwise, most of us find her magnificent but unreadable—as a novelist bound by the conditions of her art to deal in a thousand trivialities of human character and situation, she has none of their severity of form. But she alone of moderns has their note of sharp-cut melancholy, of sombre rumination, of brief disdain. Living in a time when humanity has been raised, whether formally or informally, into a religion, she draws a painted curtain of pity before the tragic scene. Still the attentive ear catches from time to time the accents of an unrelenting voice, that proves her kindred with those three mighty spirits and stern monitors of men. In George Eliot, a reader with a conscience may be reminded of the saying that when a man opens Tacitus he puts himself into the confessional. She was no vague dreamer over the folly and the weakness of men, and the cruelty and blindness of destiny. Hers is not the dejection of the poet who "could lie down like a tired child, and weep away this life of care," as Shelley at Naples; nor is it the despairing misery that moved Cowper in the awful verses of the "Castaway." It was not such self-pity as wrung from Burns the cry of life "Thou art a galling load, along, a rough, a weary road, to wretches such as I;" nor such general sense of the woes of the race as made Keats think of the world as a place where men sit and hear each other groan, "Where but to think is to be full of sorrow, and leaden-eyed despairs." She was as far removed from the plangent reverie of Rousseau as from the savage truculence of Swift. Intellectual training had given her the spirit of order and proportion, of definiteness and measure, and this marks her alike from the great sentimentalists and the sweeping satirists.—MORLEY, JOHN, 1885, *The Life of George Eliot, Macmillan's Magazine, vol.* 51, p. 250.

After all that has been written about George Eliot's place as an artist, it may be doubted if attention has been properly directed to her one unique quality. Whatever be her rank amongst the creators of romance (and perhaps the tendency now is to place it too high rather than too low), there can be no doubt that she stands entirely apart and above all writers of fiction, at any rate in England, by her philosophic power and general mental calibre. No other English novelist has ever stood in the foremost rank of the thinkers of his time. Or to put it the other way, no English thinker of the higher quality has ever used romance as an instrument of thought. Our greatest novelists could not be named beside her off the field of novel-writing. Though some of them have been men of wide reading, and even of special learning, they had none of them pretensions to the best philosophy and science of their age. Fielding and Goldsmith, Scott and Thackeray, with all their inexhaustible fertility of mind, were never in the higher philosophy compeers of Hume, Adam Smith, Burke, and Bentham. But George Eliot, before she wrote a tale at all, in mental equipment stood side by side with Mill, Spencer, Lewes, and Carlyle. If she produced nothing in philosophy, moral or mental, quite equal to theirs, she was of their kith and kin, of the same intellectual quality.—HARRISON, FREDERIC, 1885, *The Choice of Books and Other Literary Pieces*, p. 212.

Religion even to George Eliot is not an inner power of Divine mystery awakening the conscience. It is at best an intellectual exercise, or a scenic picture, or a beautiful memory. Her early Evangelicalism peeled off her like an outer garment, leaving behind only a rich vein of dramatic experience which she afterwards worked into her novels. There is no evidence of her great change having produced in her any spiritual anxiety. There is nothing indeed in autobiography more wonderful than the facility with which this remarkable woman parted first with her faith and then with the moral sanctions which do so much to consecrate life, while yet constantly idealizing life in her letters, and taking such a large grasp of many of its moral realities. Her scepticism and then her eclectic Humanitarianism had a certain benignancy and elevation unlike vulgar infidelity of any kind. There are gleams of a higher life everywhere in her thought. There is much self-distrust, but no self-abasement. There is a strange externality—as if the Divine had never come near to her save by outward form or picture—never pierced to any dividing asunder of soul and spirit. Amid all her sadness—and her life upon the whole is a very sad one—there are no depths of spiritual dread (of which dramatically—as in "Romola"—she had yet a vivid conception), or even of spiritual tenderness—TULLOCH, JOHN, 1885, *Movements of Religious Thought in Britain During the Nineteenth Century*, p. 162.

Her commanding position among the novelists of her time renders her the harbinger among women of that eminent achievement in the world of letters which is destined to follow a thorough and liberal training of their native gifts. But, although greater writers may hereafter appear in the domain of fiction, their most brilliant portrayals of the society around them can never supersede the pictures she has given to the world. Her novels will possess a permanent value, not only as literary masterpieces, but as glowing transcripts of such phases of women's advancement as belong to the history of our century. In their profound study of that social and intellectual progress which the author was privileged to see, they will serve as a more vivid illustration of the development of woman's mind than any mere historian could supply. But while the future will honor her imperishable work, and the transcendent powers she brought to its accomplishment, it cannot fail, from the standpoint of distance, to recognize, also, the limitations of her view. It will perceive that her interpretation of human life stopped short of the utmost truth; since a lack of spiritual insight blinded her vision to the limitless outcomes of endeavor, the final adjustments of time. Her penetrative glance, which no visible atom could escape, will appear then too weak to have discerned, below the material surface, those stable foundations upon which the universe rests in eternal poise; too sadly downcast to have turned from the passing shadows at her feet to behold the clear sunlight of heaven.— WOOLSON, ABBA GOOLD, 1886, *George Eliot and her Heroines*, p. 173.

Add Thackeray's sharp and bright perception to Trollope's nicety in detail, and supplement both with large scholarship and wide reach of philosophic insight; conceive a person who looks, not only *at* life and *into* life, but *through* it, who sympathizes with the gossip of peasants and the principles of advanced thinkers, who is as capable of reproducing Fergus O'Connor as John Stuart Mill, and is as blandly tolerant of Garrison as of Hegel—and you have the wonderful woman who called herself George Eliot, probably the largest mind among the romancers of the century, but with an incurable sadness at the depth of her nature which deprives her of the power to cheer the readers she interests and informs.—WHIPPLE, EDWIN PERCY, 1887, *In Dickens-Land*, Scribner's Magazine, vol. 2, p. 744.

Such wealth and depth of thoughtful and fruitful humour, of vital and various intelligence, no woman has ever shown—no woman perhaps has ever shown a tithe of it. In knowledge, in culture, perhaps in capacity for knowledge and for culture, Charlotte Brontë was no more comparable to George Eliot than George Eliot is comparable to Charlotte Brontë in purity of passion, in depth and ardour of feeling, in spiritual force and fervour of forthright inspiration. . . . George Eliot, as a woman of the first order of intellect, has once and again shown how much further and more steadily and more hopelessly and more irretrievably and more intolerably wrong it is possible for mere intellect to go than it ever can be possible for mere genius. Having no taste for the dissection of dolls, I shall leave Daniel Deronda in his natural place above the ragshop door; and having no ear for the melodies of a Jew's harp, I shall leave the Spanish Gipsy to perform on that instrument to such audience as she may collect.—SWINBURNE, ALGERNON CHARLES, 1887, *A Note on Charlotte Brontë*, pp. 19, 21.

George Eliot's books have also been a study for me, sometimes rather an arduous one.—HAMERTON, PHILIP GILBERT, 1887, *Books Which Have Influenced Me*, p. 59.

Her style is everywhere pure and strong, of the best and most vigorous English, not only broad in its power, but often intense in its description of character and situation, and always singularly adequate to the thought. Probably no novelist knew the English character—especially in the Midlands—so well as she, or could analyze it with so much subtlety and truth. She is entirely mistress of the country dialects. In humour, pathos, knowledge of character, power of putting a portrait firmly upon the canvas, no writer surpasses her, and few come near her. Her power is sometimes almost Shakespearian. Like Shakespeare, she gives us a large number of wise sayings, expressed in the pithiest language.— MEIKLEJOHN, J. M. D., 1887, *The English Language: Its Grammar, History and Literature*, p. 365.

He, Charles Reade, had no stomach for the fulsome eulogy piled on George Eliot, the less so because it became an open secret that this bold advertisement was the outcome of judicious wire-pulling. As an artist he conceived it the right of every member of his craft to demand a fair field and no favor. No marvel, therefore, if when, stung by a keen sense of injustice, he delivered himself rather slightingly of the idol before whom, at the bidding of her own Nebuchadnezzar behind the scenes, the entire press of England did obeisance.— READE, CHARLES L., AND REV. COMPTON, 1887, *Memoir of Charles Reade*, p. 301.

The nineteenth-century Amazon. — THOMPSON, MAURICE, 1889, *The Domain of Romance, The Forum*, vol. 8, p. 333.

George Eliot was, indisputably, a woman of genius, but her writings (the popular verdict to the contrary notwithstanding) include, at most, only one novel of the first rank. Her excellence is in her wise sayings. —LEWIN, WALTER, 1889, *The Abuse of Fiction, The Forum*, vol. 7, p. 665.

In her vast and lucid intellect, German Criticism, French Positivism, and English Rationalism, in which she was successively trained, were dominated and directed by an active spirit of tolerance, of love and of compassion, and the outcome is an individuality profoundly original. Her art, like her reason, perfectly balanced, trained to the purest realism, is as far removed from the crudeness now too bitter and again too fine-spun of the French, as it is from the formless nebulosity of the Russian writers. She also looks at life with a microscope to discover the fibres of which it is composed; but she does not use clouded glasses, and therefore she sees and reproduces perfect images. Science and poetry unite in her to teach us a moral based upon love and tolerance, a moral which, instead of repudiating modern thought, is deduced from it as a logical consequence. This is the reason of the originality of this powerful writer, the reason of her charm and her glory, and the reason also of this book, in which I have tried to trace the salient lines of this noble figure.— NEGRI, GAETANO, 1891, *George Eliot: La sua vita ed i suoi Romanzi*.

George Eliot's mental discipline and ascetic restraint in speculation does not permit her social sympathies full flow.—KAUFMAN, MORITZ, 1892, *Charles Kingsley, Christian Socialist and Social Reformer*, p. 138.

How great was the place George Eliot filled in modern literature we may measure by the impossibility of naming her successor. . . . Her fiction is wrought with a majesty and power which give it a category of its own and secure for it a noble place in English literature. It is superb fiction; but it is much more than fiction.— DAWSON, W. J., 1892, *Quest and Vision*, pp. 129, 146.

George Eliot's work fills us with an intense sense of reality. Her characters are substantial, living people, drawn with a Shakesperean truth and insight. In order to interest us in them she is not forced, as Dickens was, to rely on outward eccentricities. In Tom and Maggie Tulliver, in Dorothea Brooke, in Tito Melema, or in Gwendolen Harleth, we enter into and identify ourselves with the inner experiences of a human soul. These and the other great creations of George Eliot's genius are not set characters; like ourselves, they are subject to change, acted upon by others, acting on others in their turn; moulded by the daily pressure of things within and things without. We are made to understand the growth of the degeneration of their souls; how Tito slips half consciously down the easy slopes of self-indulgence, or Romola learns through suffering to ascend the heights of self-renunciation. The novels of George Eliot move under a heavy weight of tragic earnestness; admirable as is their art, graphic and telling as is their humor, they are weighed down with a burden of philosophic teaching, which in the later books, especially "Daniel Deronda," grows too heavy for the story, and injures the purely literary value.—PANCOAST, HENRY S., 1893, *Representative English Literature*, p. 426.

He [Edward A. Freeman] liked the reality and truth to life of George Eliot's works, but curiously failed to appreciate Dickens. "I read 'The Mill on the Floss' years ago, but not lately," he wrote in 1885. " 'Adam Bede' I read again this year. George Eliot's people are all real people. You have seen such people, or you feel you might have seen such—so utterly different from the forced wit and vulgarity of so many, I should say, of Dickens."—PORTER, DELIA LYMAN, 1893, *Mr. Freeman at Home, Scribner's Magazine*, vol. 14, p. 616.

In its averages George Eliot's style approaches that of Dickens, except that the less elaborate philosophizing of the latter keeps the word-average of his paragraph down. But the sentence of the two writers is nearly the same, and George Eliot's percentage of sentences of less than 15 words is the same, within 3 per cent. as Dickens's. Of the two writers the balance in the matter of the short sentence is in favor of the woman, who has 43 per cent. Evidently there is here quite as much variability in the female style as in the masculine. It should be noted, however, that George Eliot's short sentences tend to occur together; the same is true of her long sentences. In the dialogue the sentence is short; in the narrative it is long. We may say that George Eliot's paragraphs have unity, barring an occasional philosophical digression. We may say that they show logical coherence, excepting now and then one where a remote conclusion is introduced before it is analyzed.—LEWIS, EDWIN HERBERT, 1894, *The History of the English Paragraph*, p. 157.

George Eliot's people were never made: they were born like mortals. Personality existed in them, and their author gave them an essence, as no writer excepting Shakespeare had ever done; with the development of this strong personality, moreover, there existed also a power of expression rivalled only by that of the great dramatist himself. Her humor is inimitable; it is natural and genuine, and nowhere in her pages are we jarred by the intrusion of the grotesque or the unreal; here all is intensely human, with the unity of nature and its calm. But there is a third respect in which this woman novelist surpassed her predecessors, and won a place in the domain of story-telling which has not yet been wrested from her.—SIMONDS, W. E., 1894, *An Introduction to the Study of English Fiction*, p. 68.

Twenty years ago it required, if not a genuine strength of mind, at any rate a certain amount of "cussedness," not to be a George-Eliotite. All, or almost all, persons who had "got culture" admired George Eliot, and not to do so was to be at a best a Kenite among the chosen people, at worst an outcast, a son of Edom and Moab and Philistia. Two very different currents met and mingled among the worshippers who flocked in the flesh to St. John's Wood, or read the books in ecstasy elsewhere. There was the rising tide of the æsthetic, revering the creator of Tito. There was the agnostic herd, faithful to the translator of Strauss and the irregular partner of Mr. G. H. Lewes. I have always found myself most unfortunately indisposed to follow any fashion, and I never remember having read a single book of George Eliot's with genuine and whole-hearted admiration.—SAINTSBURY, GEORGE, 1895, *Corrected Impressions*, p. 162.

Perhaps few students adequately realise the singular service that much of George Eliot's work may be made to render to the truth. Nature meant her for a great theologian, as well as a superb interpreter of human life and character; but the Coventry Socinians, the task of translating Strauss, and the sinister influence of George Henry Lewes turned her into a nominal agnostic not altogether content with her rôle. Essentially constructive in genius, we can almost hear the sigh of pain surging in her breast when she feels compelled for the moment to be destructive. She seems never to have entirely lost the Christian sympathies of her early life, and in some attenuated sense is an illustration of the doctrine of final perseverance. The saddest and most depressing of her books have in them a lingering aroma of religion, indeed more than an aroma; for they illustrate many principles which are precise parallels and analogies to some of the fundamental principles of the faith whose historic credulity she had thought well to repudiate. In her own soul there was a subtle residuum of theology nothing could volatilize or destroy. And she was ever seeing some of the elements of this rudimentary theology verified in those manifold phases of life she studied with an almost infallible scrutiny.— SELBY, THOMAS G., 1896, *The Theology of Modern Fiction*, p. 8.

Her genius was certainly great, and her style was often eloquent, always elaborate and skilful, and, in its earlier phases, instinct with feeling and force. But as she left the simplicity of her earlier canvas, so her style lost its distinctive character, and was less closely allied to her genius. Its analytical precision wearies us; its elaboration seems to be studied in order to produce an impression upon that vague entity —the average reader; and what was at first the impulse of the eager student of human nature, seeking an outlet for emotion in delicacy and subtlety of expression, became a literary trick and an imposing pedantry. It was only the strength of her intellectual power that preserved her genius from being even more depressed by an acquired and unnatural habit.— CRAIK, HENRY, 1896, *English Prose*, vol. v, p. 666.

The creations of George Eliot,—Tito and Baldassare, Mrs. Poyser and Silas Marner, Dorothea Brooke and Gwendolen,—are not as familiar to the reading public of to-day as they were to that of ten or fifteen years ago. Of the idolatry which almost made her a prophetess of a new cult we hear nothing now. She has not maintained her position as Dickens, Thackeray, and Charlotte Brontë have maintained theirs. But if there be little of partisanship and much detraction, it is idle to deny that George Eliot's many gifts, her humour, her pathos, her remarkable intellectual endowments, give her an assured place among the writers of Victorian literature.—SHORTER, CLEMENT, 1897, *Victorian Literature*, p. 52.

Her writings always depend upon a primary postulate, and to this postulate all characters, scenes, and situations are ultimately subordinated. This postulate is: The ideal social order as a whole, the establishment of sane and sound social relations in humanity, the development and progress of human society toward such an ideal of general human life.—WALDSTEIN, CHARLES, 1897, *Library of the World's Best Literature*, ed. Warner, vol. IX, p. 5367.

In the "Mill on the Floss" and "Silas Marner" a curious phenomenon appeared —George Eliot divided into two personages. The close observer of nature, mistress of laughter and tears, exquisite in the intensity of cumulative emotion, was present still, but she receded; the mechanician, overloading her page with pretentious matter, working out her scheme as if she were building a steam-engine, came more and more to the front. In "Felix Holt" and on to "Daniel Deronda" the second personage preponderated, and our ears were deafened by the hum of the philosophical machine, the balance of scenes and sentences, the intolerable artificiality of the whole construction. George Eliot is a very curious instance of the danger of self-cultivation. No writer was ever more anxious to improve herself and conquer an absolute mastery over her material. But she did not observe, as she entertained the laborious process, that she was losing those natural accomplishments which infinitely outshone the philosophy and science which she so painfully acquired. She was born to please, but unhappily she persuaded herself, or was persuaded, that her mission was to teach the world, to lift its moral tone, and, in consequence, an agreeable rustic writer, with a charming humour and very fine sympathetic nature, found herself gradually uplifted until, about 1875, she sat enthroned on an educational tripod, an almost ludicrous pythoness. From the very first she had been weak in that quality which more than any other is needed by a novelist, imaginative invention. So long as she was humble, and was content to reproduce, with the skillful subtlety of her art, what she had personally heard and seen, her work had delightful merit. But it was an unhappy day, when she concluded that strenuous effort, references to a hundred abstruse writers, and a whole technical system of rhetoric would do the wild-wood business of native imagination. The intellectual self-sufficiency of George Eliot has suffered severe chastisement. At the present day scant justice is done to her unquestionable distinction of intellect or to the emotional intensity of much of her early work.—GOSSE, EDMUND, 1897, *A Short History of Modern English Literature*, p. 369.

Never, surely, were books more wistful than those great novels, "Romola," "Middlemarch," "Daniel Deronda." Their animus is wholly new: it is neither scorn nor laughter; it is sympathy. This sympathy, more than any other quality, gives to the work of George Eliot a depth of thoughtfulness unsounded by the shallow criticism on life of her predecessors.—SCUDDER, VIDA D., 1898, *Social Ideals in English Letters*, p. 185.

To the theologian George Eliot offers, for a variety of reasons, a most fascinating study. The bent of her mind was distinctly theological, and underlying all she wrote there was a theological conception of life and of the universe.... Singular to say, the very feature in George Eliot's works which imparts to them a supreme interest for the student of religion and theology, is that to which special exception has been taken by the critics.... It is profoundly affecting to think that before George Eliot sat down to the composition of her first novel she had ceased to be a Christian believer. Though she could not but have felt the painfulness of the wrench it cost her to part with so much that was dear, and though she did show some concern at the grief she caused her friends, yet she quailed not before consequences nor ever once exhibited any vacillation of judgment, nor any sign of recantation or retreat. She never appears to have faltered in her unbelief, never seems to have doubted the rectitude of the change which had come over her....

George Eliot's ethical system is summed up in the one word Duty. With her it was an imperial word which covered the entire territory of life, and included every relation in which men stand to each other, whether as landlord and tenant, priest and parishioner, husband and wife, parent and child, brother and sister. With her the way of Duty must ever be trodden, though it be bordered with no wayside flowers, and is strewn with cruel flints that make the traveller's feet to bleed.—WILSON, S. LAW, 1899, *The Theology of Modern Literature*, pp. 231, 232, 247, 262.

Notwithstanding all these differences between her earlier and her later work, George Eliot was from first to last a philosopher and moralist. All her novels and tales are constructed on the ethical formula of Mrs. Gaskell's "Ruth." For the way in which she thought out and applied this doctrine of the act and its train of good and ill, the only appropriate epithet is magnificent. She explained chance and circumstance, giving to these words a new content. All happenings, she showed, are but the meeting and the intermingling of courses of events that have their source in the inner history of mankind. This invisible medium in which we move is outside of time. The past is here in what was done yesterday; the future is here in what is done to-day; and "our finest hope is finest memory." Whatever may be her method of telling a story,—whether she begins at the beginning or breaks into the midst of her plot and in due time gathers up its threads,—George Eliot always comes quickly to an incident which discovers somewhat the moral quality of her characters; and then she proceeds slowly with their self-revelation.—CROSS, WILBUR L., 1899, *The Development of the English Novel*, p. 244.

As regards her style, George Eliot may be accepted as one of the safest models in our language. Her mastery of English was remarkable, her choice of words was unerring, and her vocabulary was sufficiently extensive to meet the demands of her great intellect. Her sentences, when subjected to the most acute analysis, will be found not only to conform to the laws of unity, mass, and coherence, but to possess a strength and rhythm characteristic of only our highest prose. Her style is admirably adapted to her subject, that of English provincial life; and in this branch of the novel she stands supreme.—WAUCHOPE, GEORGE ARMSTRONG, 1899, *ed. George Eliot's Silas Marner*, p. 26.

George Eliot certainly stands at the head of psychological novelists, and though within far narrower limits she has here and there been equalled—by Mr. Hardy, for example; and in highly differentiated types, in the subtleties and *nuances* of the *genre* by Mr. Henry James—it is probable that the *genre* itself will decay before any of its practitioners will, either in depth or range, surpass its master spirit.... One may speak of George Eliot's style as of the snakes in Iceland. She has no style. Her substance will be preserved for "the next ages" by its own pungency or not at all. No one will ever read her for the sensuous pleasure of the process. She is a notable contradiction of the common acceptation of Buffon's "*le style c'est l'homme.*" Her very marked individuality expresses itself in a way which may be called a characteristic manner, but which lacks the "order and movement" that Buffon defined style to be when he was defining it instead of merely saying something about it.—BROWNELL, W. C., 1900, *George Eliot, Scribner's Magazine, vol.* 28.

In spite of her detractors, in spite of the demon of depreciation raging and seeking whom in the past he may next devour, George Eliot was very great. Her moral force, her sustaining power in holding up to her contemporaries the highest ideal she could frame of what has been called the evangel of altruism, never deserted her; she loathed egotism and the worship of self. Had she seen the latest manifestations of the decadent school, she would have felt amply justified in lashing as she did the first symptoms of this malady. She believed in herself, and her disciples believed in her, with unquestioning fervour; but when we attempt to find out what in her work will live, it is doubtful if the admiration of those who are not disciples does not mean more than the enthusiasm of her worshippers. She was great and she was also original; the pathos of Silas Marner, the humour of Mrs. Poyser, the limitations of Tulliver *père*, the fascinations of Tito, the detestableness of Grandcourt, &c., have a spontaneous and vibrating ring which is of the essence of George Eliot's mind; and the ring is the ring of genius.—PONSONBY, MARY E., 1901, *George Eliot and George Sand, The Nineteenth Century, vol.* 50, p. 611.

Francis Trevelyan Buckland
1826–1880

Born 17th December 1826, at Christ Church College, Oxford, was educated at Winchester and Christ Church and after five years studying medicine at St. George's Hospital, London, was assistant surgeon to the 2nd Life Guards (1854–63). From his boyhood a zealous naturalist, he contributed largely to the *Times, Field, Queen,* and *Land and Water,* which last he started in 1866; and he was also author of "Curiosities of Natural History" (4 vols. 1857–72), "Fish-hatching" (1863), "Logbook of a Fisherman and Zoologist" (1876), "Natural History of British Fishes" (1881), and "Notes and Jottings from Animal Life" (1882). In 1867 he was appointed inspector of salmon-fisheries. In 1870 special commissioner on salmon-fisheries in Scotland, and in 1877 on the Scotch herring-fisheries. He died December 19th, 1880. See Life by G. C. Bompas (1885).—PATRICK AND GROOME, eds., 1897, *Chambers's Biographical Dictionary,* p. 148.

PERSONAL

He certainly is not at all premature; his great excellence is in his disposition, and apparently strong reasoning powers, and a most tenacious memory as to facts. He is always asking questions, and never forgets the answers he receives, if they are such as he can comprehend. If there is anything he cannot understand, or any word, he won't go on until it has been explained to him. He is always wanting to see everything made, or to know how it is done; there is no end to his questions, and he is never happy unless he sees the relations between cause and effect.—BUCKLAND, MRS. WILLIAM, 1830, *Journal, June 26; Life of Frank Buckland,* ed. Bompas, p. 3.

We first made his acquaintance in 1870, when appointed along with him to inquire into and report upon the effect of recent legislation on the Salmon Fisheries of Scotland. . . . At that time he was in the prime of life, somewhat under the middle height, and broad-shouldered and powerfully built, with a clever pleasant face, in which the most noticeable features were the large, dark, expressive eyes. He was about the most true and genuine man we ever met, without a particle of affectation, saying what he thought and felt simply and naturally. He learned to have a thorough enjoyment of life in all its phases; and it would have been difficult to say whether he was most at home in the polished society of a luxurious country house, or while engaged in demonstrating the anatomy of a salmon, a herring, or a lobster to a group of fishermen assembled round a fishing-boat on the beach. At that time he took but little care of himself, and thought nothing of wading across a river up to his waist, even though he could not change his wet clothes for hours afterwards; or minutely examining the structure and details of a salmon-ladder while up to his knees in water. At that period he seemed to have a wonderful amount of latent caloric, and never appeared to feel cold. He was a great smoker, and to him a pipe or a cigar was an absolute necessity of life. Yet his constant smoking never seemed to spoil his appetite or to lessen his natural vivacity and flow of spirits. On every subject, which bore upon his special study of natural history, whether connected with our inquiry or not, he took a lively interest.—YOUNG, ARCHIBALD, 1880, *The Scotsman.*

At school he certainly received his share of chastisement, and within a year or two of his death he showed some of his friends scars on his hands which he said were his uncle's doings. He was probably a trying pupil to an impatient school-master; yet he contrived to acquire a large share of classical knowledge. He had whole passages of Virgil at his fingers' ends. He used to say, when he could not understand an act of parliament, that he always turned it into Latin; and within a fortnight of his death he was discussing a passage of a Greek play with one of the accomplished medical men who attended him, interesting himself about the different pronunciation of ancient and modern Greek, and the merits of Greek accentuation. Mathematics were not supposed to form a necessary part of a boy's education forty years ago and it may be doubted whether even his dread of his uncle's ferule or the discipline at Winchester could have induced him to make any progress in the study. To the end of his life he always regarded it as a providential circumstance that nature had given him eight fingers and two thumbs, as the arrangement had enabled him to count as far as ten. When he was engaged on long inspections, which involved the expenditure of a good deal of money he always carried it in small paper parcels each containing ten sovereigns; and, though he was fond of quoting the figures which his secretary prepared for him in his reports, those who knew him best doubted whether they expressed any clear meaning to him. He liked, for instance, to state the number of eggs which various kinds of fish produced, but he never rounded off the calculations which his secretary made to enable him to do so. The unit at the end of the sum was, in his eyes, of equal importance to the figure, which represents millions, at the beginning of it.—WALPOLE, SPENCER, 1881, *Mr. Frank Buckland, Macmillan's Magazine, vol.* 43, *p.* 303.

His personal characteristics were most attractive. No one ever met him without longing to meet him again. His simple, earnest, humorous temperament reflected itself in all he wrote, so that no one read a book by him without also determining to read the next he should publish. Thus he had an enormous number of friends and acquaintances, from the highest in the land to the giants and dwarfs, and, lower still, to the waifs and strays, of human life in London. Fifty-four years seem a short span in which to break down the apathy of Englishmen to the life and sufferings of the lower animals, to instill a love of natural history among the people, and to set on foot some of the most important enterprises in the way of acclimatisation and fish culture in order to benefit the economical condition of this country. Yet it is Buckland's merit to have succeeded in this. He was able to die with the pleasant consciousness of having made no enemies, and of having by his teaching largely increased the happiness of his fellow-men by directing them to the practical study of nature. The life of such a man well deserved to be written. Buckland was a philanthropist of no ordinary kind. He strove to augment the sum of England's material resources, and he left men more cheerful, genial and friendly than he found them.—WATKINS, M. G., 1883, *Life of Frank Buckland, The Academy, vol.* 28, *p.* 11.

We know that he was very pious. Being so, he could accept evolution neither in its Darwinian phases nor in general. Though accepting his religion through faith and belief, he was naturally sceptical, and required strong proofs for anything out of the usual way. Firmly believing in design, he accepted only objects or effects as proof, not seeing that processes might be more conclusive evidence. The trouble his mother foresaw in his volatile disposition was obviated by earnestness, industry, and a noble purpose. Few have done more in disseminating science and in making it practical. To continue his teachings he leaves an excellent reputation, his writings and his museum casts, mounted specimens, and skeletons—mainly the work of his own hands.—GARMAN, S., 1885, *Life of Frank Buckland, The Nation, vol.* 41, *p.* 472.

Few men can now recall those unique breakfasts at Frank's rooms in the corner of Fell's Building; the host, in blue peajacket and German student's cap blowing blasts out of a tremendous wooden horn; the various pets who made it difficult to speak or move; the marmots and the dove and the monkey and the chameleon and the snakes and the guinea-pigs; the afterbreakfast visits to the eagle or the jackal or the pariah dog or Tiglath-pileser, the bear, in the little yard outside. The undergraduate was father of the man. His house in Albany Street became one of the sights of London; but to enter it presupposed iron nerves and *dura ilia.* Introduced to some five-and-twenty poor relations, free from shyness, deeply interested in your dress and person, you felt as if another flood were toward, and the animals parading for admission to the ark. You remained to dine: but, as in his father's house so in his own, the genius of experiment, supreme in all departments, was nowhere so active as at the dinner table. Panther chops, rhinoceros pie, bison steak, kangaroo ham, horse's tongue, elephant's trunk, are reported among his manifestations of hospitality; his brother-in-law quotes from the diary of a departing guest —"Tripe for dinner; don't like crocodile for breakfast." — TUCKWELL, W., 1900, *Reminiscences of Oxford, p.* 106.

GENERAL

In its now revised and improved form, with additional plates of organic remains, Buckland's "Geology and Mineralogy" is the best general work on this interesting study.—CHAMBERS, ROBERT, 1876, *Cyclopædia of English Literature*, ed. Carruthers.

Writing, indeed, seems to have been the solace and amusement as well as the business of his life. He wrote a great deal, and easily and rapidly, not only at his office and at his house, but in railway carriages, steamboats and other public conveyances. His writings, like those of most men who have written so much and so rapidly, are unequal, but the best of them are admirable. The style is thoroughly original, and wonderfully descriptive, bringing the object or scene written about clearly and vividly before the reader's eye; and it may safely be affirmed that no one has ever done more to render natural history popular and attractive.—YOUNG, ARCHIBALD, 1880, *The Scotsman.*

The love of fun and laughter, which was perceptible while he was transacting the dullest business, distinguished him equally as a writer. It was his object, so he himself thought, to make natural history practical; but it was his real mission to make natural history and self-culture popular. He popularised everything that he touched, he hated the scientific terms which other naturalists employed, and invariably used the simplest language for describing his meaning. His writings were unequal: some of them are not marked by any exceptional qualities. But others of them, such as the best parts of the "Curiosities of Natural History," and "The Royal Academy Without a Catalogue" are admirable examples of good English, keen critical observation and rich humour. . . . The more laboured compositions which Mr. Buckland undertook did not always contain equal traits of happy humour. He was at his best when he took the least pains, and a collection of his very best pieces would deserve a permanent place in any collection of English essays.—WALPOLE, SPENCER, 1881, *Mr. Frank Buckland, Macmillan's Magazine*, vol. 43, p. 307.

No more zealous, truth-loving, or painstaking man ever studied more earnestly or described more accurately the various gifts and instincts, the nature and habits of birds and beasts. A quaint vein of humour runs through his writings, which must commend them to every reader, especially to the young; and few writers have conveyed more varied and useful information. — ROOPER, GEORGE, 1883, *President's Address to Hertfordshire Natural History Society.*

To trace the power of the Creator in His works, and to increase the use of His creatures to mankind, were to Frank Buckland the chief ends of natural history, and the chief purpose of his life. He was indeed slow, nay, unwilling, to admit the truth of Darwin's teaching, and of the theory of evolution, too often represented as superseding the necessity of a Creator, and the evidence of design; and he often humourously but vehemently protested against his supposed relationship to his monkey pets. The point of this protest was against the notion that chance could produce the order of the universe, or a monkey develop itself into a man. To him, the old notion of a universe formed by a fortuitous concourse of atoms, was not more unreasonable, than the notion of the harmony of nature, or the structure of any beast or fish, being the result of a mere chance combination of circumstances. Each alike must beget chaos. . . . Those who would know Frank Buckland better should read his books, which, after all, form his best portraiture. In these, the incidents of his life, his pets, his queer companions, are made familiar, and on this thread are strung a fund of curious information and droll anecdote. These seem to talk to us in his old tones, and recall his sparkling eye and merry laugh, his restless energy, and tenderness of feeling for man and beast.—BOMPAS, GEORGE C., 1885, *Life of Frank Buckland*, pp. 425, 433.

Many naturalists have studied the habits and structure of animals with no less care and scientific judgment than he has; but, above his other qualifications, he has brought to his occupation a sympathetic insight of the feelings of dumb creatures, and has interpreted their thoughts, desires, and emotions with wonderful understanding. He has established confidential relations with monkeys, and has learned the aspirations and disappointments of the beasts of the field. When he writes about one of the creatures whose acquaintance he has made, it seems to be a revelation of private life; and the sympathy which he shows awakens similar feelings in us. The monkey is no longer a speechless brute. It becomes, through Mr. Buckland's interpretation, a genial and intelligent fellow-being. He has done more than anyone else to make the animal world intelligible to man, and yet he is a resolute opponent of the Darwinian theory.—RIDEING, WILLIAM H., 1885, *Dr. Francis Trevelyan Buckland, Some Noted Princes, Authors and Statesmen of Our Time, ed. Parton, p.* 26.

Genial, sagacious, enthusiastic, always prone to look at the humorous side of the subject, Buckland aimed rather at enlisting the sympathies of others in his favourite studies than at acquiring the name of a profound writer of science.—WATKINS, M. G., 1886, *Dictionary of National Biography, vol.* VII, *p.* 204.

His various duties and his endless private work were incessant. Never careful of his health, a constitution naturally strong soon broke down, after repeated illnesses. As a writer, Buckland was lively and graphic, and as an observer, acute without being always accurate. His knowledge was more extensive than deep, and though not a great naturalist or a great author, he was a genial, kindly man, who "loved all things, both great and small," and was himself loved in return. His enthusiasm was, moreover, infectious, and hence, by stimulating others to pursue the study of nature more scientifically than he did himself, he exerted a greater influence on the scientific world in which he moved than many more distinguished labourers.— BROWN, ROBERT, 1887, *Celebrities of the Century, ed., Sanders, p.* 187.

Tom Taylor
1817–1880

Born, at Sunderland, 1817. Early education at school there. Studied at Glasgow Univ., 1831–32, 1835–36. Matric., Trin. Coll., Camb., 1837; B. A., 1840; Fellow 1842; M. A., 1843. Prof. of English Literature, Univ. Coll., London. Called to Bar at Middle Temple, Nov. 1845. Assistant Sec. to Board of Health, 1850; Sec., 1854. Married Laura W. Barker, 19 June 1885. Sec. to Local Government Act Office, 1858–72. Wrote over 100 dramatic pieces, 1845–80. Editor of Punch, 1874–80. For some time Art Critic to "The Times" and "The Graphic." Died, at Wandsworth, 12 July 1880. *Works:* "The King's Rival" (with Charles Reade), 1854; "Masks and Faces" (with Charles Reade), 1854; "Two Loves and a Life" (with Charles Reade), 1854; "Barefaced Impostors" (anon.; with F. G. B. Ponsonby and G. C. Bentinck) [1854]; "The Local Government Act, 1858, etc.," 1858; "The Railway Station, painted by W. P. Frith, described," 1862; "Handbook of the Pictures in the International Exhibition of 1862," 1862; Text to Birket Foster's "Pictures of English Landscapes" 1863 [1862]; "A Marriage Memorial" [1863], "Catalogue of the Works of Sir Joshua Reynolds" (with C. W. Franks), 1869; "The Theatre in England" (from "The Dark Blue"), 1871; "Leicester Square," 1874; "Historical Dramas," 1877. [Also a number of separate dramatic pieces, published in Lacy's Acting Edition of Plays.] He *translated:* Vicomte Hersart de La Villemarqué's "Ballads and Songs of Brittany," 1865; and *edited:* "The Life of B. R. Haydon," 1853; C. R. Leslie's "Autobiographical Recollections," 1860; Mortimer Collins' "Pen Sketches by a Vanished Hand," 1879.—SHARP, R. FARQUHARSON, 1897, *A Dictionary of English Authors, p.* 276.

PERSONAL

Certainly the highest-toned of all the "Punch" and "Household Words" school— a Cambridge scholar, who, to maintain his mother and sisters, submitted to very distasteful literary toil, even theatrical burlesques, but who has come out of it unstained, and will be, I predict, amongst the most eminent of our new writers.— MITFORD, MARY RUSSELL, 1854, *Letter to Miss Jephson, July* 12; *The Friendships of Mary Russell Mitford, ed. L'Estrange, p.* 114.

He is a tall, slender, dark young man, not English-looking, and wearing colored spectacles, so that I should readily have taken him for an American literary man.— HAWTHORNE, NATHANIEL, 1856, *English Note-Books, vol.* II, *p.* 6.

Claude Mellot seems to have come into a fortune of late years, large enough at least for his few wants. He paints no longer, save when he chooses; and has taken a little old house in one of those back lanes of Brompton where islands of primæval nursery garden still remain undevoured by the advancing surges of the brick and mortar deluge. There he lives, happy in a green lawn and windows opening thereon, in three elms, a cork, an ilex and a mulberry, with a great standard pear, for flower and foliage the queen of all suburban trees. . . . Claude's house is arranged with his usual defiance of all conventionalities. Dining or drawing-room proper there is none. The large front room is the studio, where he and Sebina eat and drink as well as work and paint, and out of it opens a little room, the walls of which are all covered with gems of art (where the rogue finds money to buy them is a puzzle), that the eye can turn nowhere without taking in some new beauty, and wandering on from picture to statue, from portrait to landscape, dreaming and learning afresh after every glance.—KINGSLEY, CHARLES, 1857, *Two Years Ago*.

My *vis-à-vis* happened to be Tom Taylor, who was decidedly the liveliest of the company. Tom was a man of thirty-eight, [1857] or thereabouts, rather tall than short, well-built, with a strong, squarish face, black eyes, hair, and moustache, and a gay, cheerful, wide-awake air, denoting a happy mixture of the imaginative and the practical faculties. He was always ready to join in the laugh, and to crown it by provoking another. In fact, he showed so little of English reserve, so much of unembarrassed American *bonhommie*, that we ought, properly, to call him, "Our English Cousin."—TAYLOR, BAYARD, 1862, *Personal Sketches, At Home and Abroad, Second Series*, p. 418.

His everyday life was as unlike that of Claude Mellot as could be, for besides his office work, which was done most punctually and diligently, he had always a play on the stocks, and work for Punch, or the magazines, on hand. He was at his desk early every morning, often at five o'clock, for three hours' work before breakfast, after swallowing a cup of milk. And I believe it was this wealth of work of many kinds which gave such a zest to the recreation at Eagle Lodge on those summer evenings. Then, in play hours, if the company were at all sympathetic—and very little company came there which was not so—he would turn himself loose, and give the rein to those glorious and most genial high spirits, which thawed all reserves, timidities, and conventionalities, and transformed all present for the time being into a group of rollicking children at play, with our host as showman, stage manager, chief tumbler, leader of all the revels. In the power and faculty for excellent fooling, which ran through every mood, from the grotesque to the pathetic, but with no faintest taint of coarseness, or malice, or unkindliness, and of luring all kinds of people to join in it, no one in our day has come near him.—HUGHES, THOMAS, 1880, *In Memoriam, Macmillan's Magazine*, vol. 42, p. 298.

That Tom Taylor realised and did his duty with conscientiousness is certain. With those fellow-critics who were wont to meet him at the exhibitions, and to pursue with him the dusty labours of the press day, his minuteness and steadiness were proverbial. Most of us take in the side of a room at a general glance, and then proceed to the further consideration of the half-dozen pictures which for some quality or other have taken our eye; but he gave separate and deliberate attention to every one without exception. It is no exaggeration to say that he often went through the entire catalogue without missing a number, and he did his work with so much method—opera-glass in hand, and the case slung across his shoulders—that the more erratic journalists who had been excited by the premonitory whispers of the studios to make a zigzag flight through the rooms in search of excitement, were frequently but half through their work while he was serenely finishing the last of his last hundred, putting up his glass, and exchanging a serious nod with his friends, or perhaps pausing for the first time to listen to the last good thing which Mr. Sala might be saying to a little knot of less business-like emissaries of the press, on his way out.—OLDCASTLE, JOHN, 1881, *Bundles of Rue, Magazine of Art*, vol. 4, p. 66.

GENERAL

The new play at the Haymarket ["Masks and Faces"] wants the scope and proportions of a regular English comedy, being in outline and structure of a French cast; but in character it is English, in sentiment thoroughly so, and its language and expression, whether of seriousness or humour, have the tone at once easy and earnest which truth gives to scholarship and wit. —MORLEY, HENRY, 1852, *Journal of a London Playgoer*, Nov. 27, p. 56.

Why, my dear old Tom, I never *was* serious with you, even when you were among us. Indeed, I killed you, quite, as who should say, without seriousness, "A rat! A rat!" you know, rather cursorily.

Chaff, Tom, as in your present state you are beginning to perceive, was your fate here, and doubtless will be throughout the eternity before you. With ages at your disposal, this truth will dimly dawn upon you; and as you look back upon this life, perhaps many situations that you took *au sérieux* (art-critic, who knows? expounder of Velasquez, and what not) will explain themslves sadly—chaff! Go back!
—WHISTLER, J. M'NEILL, 1879, *The Gentle Art of Making Enemies*, p. 39.

He was very able in many ways, as scholar, poet, critic, dramatist; but we have had greater men than he in our generation in each one of these lines, and greater men are left among us. But where shall we turn for the man who will prove such a spring of pure, healthy, buoyant, and kindly fun for the next, as he has been to us for the last thirty years?—HUGHES, THOMAS, 1880, *In Memoriam, Macmillan's Magazine*, vol. 42, p. 298.

Tom Taylor was not a brilliant critic, but he was a sure one; he had no touch of genius to guide him in his verdicts, but he had long training and an infinite capacity for taking pains. There are many artists who can claim the greatest of living art-critics—Mr. Ruskin—as the foster-father of their art; his writing has inspired the first efforts which his criticism afterwards corrected. Tom Taylor did not inspire, because he did not create; but in his measure he did much to discover and encourage talent in the young and the obscure; and there are several artists, who can remember the delight with which they read the good word in the *Times* about their earliest exhibited productions. On the other hand, Tom Taylor was fearless, as Mr. Ruskin has been fearless, to condemn what he thought deserved to be condemned.—OLDCASTLE, JOHN, 1881, *Bundles of Rue, Magazine of Art*, vol. 4, p. 66.

That the idea of making Peg Woffington the heroine of a play was exclusively Charles Reade's; that the shaping of the play into the form in which it was finally produced was Tom Taylor's. But that the credit of the play should be equally divided between the two authors, as each brought to the work qualities and powers peculiarly his own, the ultimate result being the production of certainly one of the very best and finished comedies of modern times.—TAYLOR, ARNOLD, 1886, *Letter*, Oct. 11; *Charles Reade by Charles L., and Rev. Compton Reade*, p. 193.

Worthy to rank with Mr. Wills as a poetical dramatist, is Mr. Tom Taylor, who is at once the most successful writer of his class, with only one exception, and the *bête noir* of a large clique of critics. Mr. Taylor is less original but more diverse—less happy, but more careful, than Mr. Wills; and his dialogue, though bald like most modern dialogue, is more apt and to the purpose. I am certainly not among those gentlemen who deny Mr. Taylor the merit of originality; on the contrary, I believe his talents are underrated, simply because a foolish and erroneous idea has been circulated as to his indebtedness to foreign sources. To my mind he has seldom or never exceeded the allowable privileges of a dramatist, and almost all his success is due to dramatic faculties and instincts entirely his own. He is the author of some of the very brightest pieces of the day, and if in his historical and poetical productions he has failed to maintain a high level of literary excellence, he has merely failed in common with almost all caterers for the modern stage.—BUCHANAN, ROBERT, 1886, *The Modern Stage, A Look Round Literature*, p. 253.

Tom Taylor was a ripe, classical scholar, and an admirable playwright; he was essentially clever, just, and upright, but he was not very much gifted with either wit or humour in the true sense of the term. Beyond his exceedingly droll "Adventures of an Unprotected Female," I cannot recall any Punch contributions of his which were absolutely comic; and, being altogether bereft of an ear for music, the poetry on which he occasionally ventured was, as a rule, deplorably cacophonous.—SALA, GEORGE AUGUSTUS, 1895, *Life and Adventures*, vol. II, p. 246.

He essayed almost every department of the drama, but made his chief success in domestic comedy. His mastery of stagecraft was great, and many of his pieces still keep the boards; but he lacked dramatic genius or commanding power of expression. —KENT, CHARLES, 1898, *Dictionary of National Biography*, vol. LV, p. 473.

Original writers were perpetually snubbed and Tom Taylor, a very able writer, and as quick as lightning, was glad enough to accept £150 down for the most successful melodrama of our time, "The Ticket-of-Leave Man," because it was adapted, and very well adapted too, from a fine play by Brisebarre and Nus, called "Leonard," and went cheap for the very good reason that there was no protection for stolen goods, and any manager could employ a hack writer to give him another version of "Leonard."—SCOTT, CLEMENT, 1899, *The Drama of Yesterday and Today, vol.* I, *p.* 474.

James Robinson Planché
1796–1880

Born, in London, 27 Feb. 1796. Articled to a bookseller, 1810. Upwards of seventy dramatic pieces produced, 1818–71. Married Elizabeth St. George, 26 April, 1821. F. S. A., 24 Dec. 1829 to 1852. Rouge Croix Pursuivant at Arms, Heralds' Coll., 13 Feb. 1854; Somerset Herald, 7 June 1866. Civil List Pension, June 1871. Died, in Chelsea, 30 May, 1880. *Works:* [exclusive of a number of dramas, burlesques, and extravaganzas, mostly printed in "Lacy's Acting Edition of Plays," or in Cumberland's or Duncombe's "British Theatre"]: "Costumes of Shakespeare's King John" (5 pts.), 1823–25; "Shere Afkun," 1823; "Descent of the Danube," 1828; "History of British Costumes," 1834; "A Catalogue of the collection of Ancient Arms . . . the property of Bernard Brocas," 1834; "Continental Gleanings" [1836?]; "Regal Records," 1838; "Souvenir of the Bal Costumé . . . at Buckingham Palace," 1843; "The Pursuivant of Arms," 1852; "A Corner of Kent," 1864; "Pieces of Pleasantry for Private Performance" [1868]; "Recollections and Reflections," (2 vols.), 1872; "William with the Ring," 1873; "The Conqueror and his Companions" (2 vols.), 1874; "A Cyclopædia of Costume" (2 vols.), 1876–79; "Suggestions for establishing an English Art Theatre," 1879; "Extravanganzas," ed. by T. F. D. Croker and S. Tucker (5 vols.), 1879; "Songs and Poems," 1881. He *translated:* Hoffman's "King Nutcracker," 1853; Countess d'Aulnoy's "Fairy Tales," 1855; "Four-and-twenty Fairy Tales selected from those of Perrault, etc.," 1858; and *edited:* H. Clark's "Introduction to Heraldry," 1866.—SHARP, R. FARQUHARSON, 1897, *A Dictionary of English Authors, p.* 228.

PERSONAL

This active spirit, so varied in accomplishments, so deeply imbued with taste, so full of sweet and genial fancy, has at last passed away. The latter part of his life was unfortunately embittered by family misfortune. But he bravely took to his home a widowed daughter and eight children, for whose sake he still toiled, and struggled with manly fortitude and Christian kindliness. Suffering, also, from excruciating disease, was hard to bear in his old days. But his genial spirit still shone forth throughout all.—SIMPSON, J. PALGRAVE, 1880, *James Robinson Planché, The Theatre, vol.* 5, *p.* 99.

It is only very recently that a well-known face is missing from the tables of those who love the society of artists, and, old as he was when he passed away from the scenes of his successes, his death caused surprise, for he had looked for so many years the same, his cheery spirits never seemed to flag, and he appeared to have defied the inevitable. This was Planché. I knew him well and met him often. I suppose that in his long journey through life, although he met with great successes, he never made an enemy; and though many of his contemporaries might be named whose literary fame is greater, how few have caused more amusement! He was, moreover, fortunate in being associated with Madame Vestris, who seemed to be created to embody upon the stage, and even to give additional charm to his refined and elegant burlesques. —BALLANTINE, WILLIAM, 1882, *Some Experiences of a Barrister's Life, vol.* I, *p.* 284.

Planché was, when I first knew him, a little bent, bowed, and shrivelled old gentleman, who in a second could twist his features so as to resemble a chattering monkey. He was one of the old school of good manners, obviously a courtier, and at times a veritable "pocket Polonius."—SCOTT, CLEMENT, 1899, *The Drama of Yesterday and To-day, vol.* II, *p.* 11.

GENERAL

Whatever the origin of Planché's pieces, there can be no doubt that he exercised a considerable influence on the English stage. The two most characteristic qualities of his writings were taste and elegance. Breadth of tone in comedy—power which might in most cases have been justly looked on as fustian, and sentiment which chiefly displayed itself in maudlin clap-trap—had been the main attributes and aims of most of the dramatists of the first quarter of the century. Planché introduced into his works elements which gave a fresh direction to the comedy writers of the period. True, they were redolent of hairpowder and bedecked with patches; but they had a pleasant smack of elegance and grace; and, although not displaying the breadth of low comedy, the tendency to fine heavily-phrased writing, or the platitudes of artificial sentiment which were the prevailing characteristics of most of his immediate predecessors, they were accepted with delight by the public. In adopting and adapting French models he had imbued himself with the spirit of the French school, and almost founded a new school of his own. "The natural," somewhat heightened in colour by the stage rouge, which is more or less necessary to all dramatic doings, and the due proportions of which were well taught by his foreign prototypes, took the place of stereotyped artificiality.—SIMPSON, J. PALGRAVE, 1880, *James Robinson Planché, The Theatre, vol. 5, p.* 96.

In the first years of the reign of Victoria the stage had in Mr. James Robinson Planché, a delightful writer of brilliant extravaganzas, fairy pieces with grace of invention and treatment, and with ingenuity and beauty in the manner of presentment. . . . Mr. Planché distinguished himself as a student of ancient life and manners, whose antiquarian knowledge, joined to his good taste, made him a valuable counsellor upon all points of dramatic costume.—MORLEY, HENRY, 1881, *Of English Literature in the Reign of Victoria With a Glance at the Past, p.* 349.

He was an assiduous student of archæology . . . A great deal that Planché has written is not literature. In even his best comedies his style can hardly be called brilliant, while his characters are drawn on more or less conventional lines. But the dialogue is dramatically effective and the plots are neatly constructed. The imbroglio in "The Follies of a Night" (perhaps the most entertaining of his comedies), is managed with delightful address. It is in his extravaganzas, however, that his peculiar talent shines out most brightly. These little pieces cannot properly be described as burlesques. Their writer had a vein of poetry as well as a frolic wit; he never stooped to vulgarity or brainless buffoonery. He adhered as closely as he could to the lines of the old stories which he cast into dramatic form. His fairy plays are brimful of humour and graceful fancy, ringing with mirth and music, lightly touched here and there with the colours of romance. There blows through them a breath from the country over the hills and far away, not, it is true, from the moonlight-coloured dreamland of the olden fairy poetry, but from the powdered and perfumed and delightfully modish world of gruff, bluff kings, and bombastic chancellors, and foppish wiseacres, and shrewish queens, and machinating cooks, and charming oppressed princesses, and town-witted elves—the world into which Thackeray leads us when he introduces us to Rosalba and Bulbo.—WHYTE, WALTER, 1894, *The Poets and the Poetry of the Century, Humour, Society, Parody and Occasional Verse,* ed. Miles, *pp.* 218, 220.

From 1818 onward Planché was the author, adapter, translator, and what not, of innumerable—they certainly run to hundreds—dramatic pieces of every possible sort from regular plays to sheer extravaganzas. He was happiest perhaps in the lighter and freer kinds, having a pleasant and never vulgar style of jocularity, a fair lyrical gift, and the indefinable knowledge of what is a play. But he stands only on the verge of literature proper, and the propriety, indeed the necessity, of including him here is the strongest possible evidence of the poverty of dramatic literature in our period. It would indeed only be possible to extend this chapter much by including men who have no real claim to appear, and who would too forcibly suggest the hired guests of story, introduced in order to avoid a too obtrusive confession of the absence of guests entitled to be present.—SAINTSBURY, GEORGE, 1896, *A History of Nineteenth Century Literature, p.* 423.

More graceful extravaganzas than those written for the Lyceum by Planché were never seen on any stage. The versification was always neat and admirable, the rhyming faultless, and the puns of the very best kind.—SCOTT, CLEMENT, 1899, *The Drama of Yesterday and To-day, vol.* II, *p.* 190.

Lydia Maria Child
1802–1880

Born in Medford, Mass., 11th February, 1802. Her father was David Francis. Lydia was assisted in her early studies by her brother, Convers Francis, who was afterwards professor of theology in Harvard College. . . . She studied in the public schools and one year in a seminary. In 1814 she went to Norridgewock, Maine, to live with her married sister. She remained there several years and then returned to Watertown, Mass., to live with her brother. He encouraged her literary aspirations, and in his study she wrote her first story, "Hobomok," which was published in 1823. It proved successful, and she next published "Rebels," which ran quickly through several editions. She then brought out in rapid succession "The Mother's Book," which ran through eight American, twelve English and one German editions, "The Girl's Book," the "History of Women," and the "Frugal Housewife" which passed through thirty-five editions. In 1826 she commenced to publish her "Juvenile Miscellany." In 1828 she became the wife of David Lee Child, a lawyer, and they settled in Boston, Mass. In 1831 they became interested in the anti-slavery movement, and both took an active part in the agitation that followed. Mr. Child was one of the leaders of the anti-slavery party. In 1833 Mrs. Child published her "Appeal in Behalf of that Class of Americans Called Africans." Its appearance served to cut her off from the friends and admirers of her youth. Social and literary circles shut their doors to her. The sales of her books and subscriptions to her magazines fell off, and her life became one of battle. Through it all she bore herself with patience and courage, and she threw herself into the movement with all her powers. While engaged in that memorable battle, she found time to produce her lives of Madame Roland and Baroness de Staël, and her Greek romance "Philothea." She, with her husband, supervised editorially the *Anti-Slavery Standard*, in which she published her admirable "Letters from New York." During those troubled times she prepared her three-volume work on "The Progress of Religious Ideas." She lived in New York City with her husband from 1840 to 1844, when she removed to Wayland, Mass., where she died 20th October, 1880. Her Anti-Slavery writings aided powerfully in bringing about the overthrow of slavery, and she lived to see a reversal of the hostile opinions that greeted her first plea for the negroes. Her books are numerous. Besides those already mentioned the most important are "Flowers for Children" (3 volumes 1844–46); "Fact and Fiction" (1846); "The Power of Kindness" (1851); "Isaac T. Hopper, A True Life" (1853); "Autumnal Leaves" (1856); "Looking Towards Sunset" (1864); "The Freedman's Book" (1865); "Miria" (1867), and "Aspirations of the World" (1878). . . . A volume of her letters, with an introduction by John Greenleaf Whittier and an appendix by Wendell Phillips, was published in Boston in 1882.—MOULTON, CHARLES WELLS, 1893, *A Woman of the Century, ed. Willard and Livermore, p. 173.*

PERSONAL

Mrs. Child, casually observed, has nothing particularly striking in her personal appearance. One would pass her in the street a dozen times without notice. She is low in stature and slightly framed. Her complexion is florid; eyes and hair are dark; features in general diminutive. The expression of her countenance, when animated, is highly intellectual. Her dress is usually plain, not even neat—anything but fashionable. Her bearing needs excitement to impress it with life and dignity. She is of that order of beings who are themselves only on "great occasions."—POE, EDGAR ALLAN, 1846, *Lydia M. Child, The Literati, Works of Edgar Allan Poe, ed. Stedman and Woodberry, vol. VIII, p. 114.*

There comes Philothea, her face all aglow,
She has just been dividing some poor creature's woe,
And can't tell which pleases her more, to relieve
His want, or his story to hear and believe;
No doubt against many deep griefs she prevails,
For her ear is the refuge of destitute tales;
She knows well that silence is sorrow's best food,
And that talking draws off from the heart its black blood,
So she'll listen with patience and let you unfold
Your bundle of rags as 'twere pure cloth of gold,
Which, indeed, it all turns to as soon as she's touched it,
And (to borrow a phrase from the nursery) muched it.
—LOWELL, JAMES RUSSELL, 1848, *A Fable for Critics.*

A dear lovable woman, welcome at a sick bedside; as much in place there as when facing an angry nation; contented in the home she made; the loyal friend; such ingenuity in devising ways to help you; the stalwart fidelity of friendship, rare in these easy going, half-and-half, non-committal days; such friendship as allowed no word of disparagement, no doubt of a friend's worth, to insult her presence. A wise counsellor, one who made your troubles hers and pondered thoughtfully before she spoke her hearty word. We feel we have lost one who would have stood by us in trouble, a shield. She was the kind of woman one would choose to represent woman's entrance into broader life. Modest, womanly, simple, sincere, solid, real, loyal; to be trusted; equal to affairs and yet above them; mother-wit ripened by careful training, and enriched with the lore of ages; a companion with the pass-word of every science and all literatures; a hand ready for fire-side help and a mystic loving to wander on the edge of the actual reaching up and out into the infinite and the unfathomable; so that life was lifted to romance, to heroism and the loftiest faith. May we almost have a faith that is almost sight. How joyful to remember, dear friend, your last counsel, the words you thought spirit hands had traced for your epitaph: "You think us dead. We are not dead; we are the living."
—PHILLIPS, WENDELL, 1880, *Remarks at the Funeral of Lydia Maria Child, Oct. 23*, p. 268.

She bid fair to be the most popular authoress in America, and her recorded publications show a continuous production of books and pamphlets from 1824 to 1878, ranging from works of the imagination to cookery-books, from New England history to the history of religions, from juvenile periodicals (the first ever established) to political tracts. It is well known that her open association with the abolitionists, following her husband's example, cost her her literary popularity at one blow, and made literary ambition seem despicable to her, though it may be thought strange that the author of "Hobomok," "The Rebels," and "Philothea" was not led to produce an anti-slavery romance anticipating "Uncle Tom's Cabin."—GARRISON, W. P., 1883, *Mrs. Child's Letters, The Nation*, vol. 36, p. 88.

Thenceforth her life was a battle; a constant rowing hard against the stream of popular prejudice and hatred. And through it all—pecuniary privation, loss of friends and position, the painfulness of being suddenly thrust from "the still air of delightful studies" into the bitterest and sternest controversy of the age—she bore herself with patience, fortitude, and unshaken reliance upon the justice and ultimate triumph of the cause she had espoused. Her pen was never idle. Wherever there was a brave word to be spoken, her voice was heard, and never without effect. It is not exaggeration to say that no man or woman at that period rendered more substantial service to the cause of freedom, or made such a "great renunciation" in doing it. A practical philanthropist, she had the courage of her convictions, and from the first was no mere closet moralist, or sentimental bewailer of the woes of humanity. She was the Samaritan stooping over the wounded Jew. She calmly and unflinchingly took her place by the side of the despised slave and free man of color, and in word and act protested against the cruel prejudice which shut out its victims from the rights and privileges of American citizens. Her philanthropy had no taint of fanaticism; throughout the long struggle, in which she was a prominent actor, she kept her fine sense of humor, good taste, and sensibility to the beautiful in art and nature.—WHITTIER, JOHN GREENLEAF, 1883, *ed. Letters of Lydia Maria Child, Biographical Introduction*, p. IX.

The impulse which Miss Edgeworth gave to juvenile literature has never died out, and we pass naturally with it to the life of her who issued in America the first children's magazine. "Here comes Philothea, her face all aglow." And these half-quizzical lines give us a far better idea of Mrs. Child than the very unlike portrait to be seen in these letters. Of all beautiful women, Mrs. Child was perhaps the most beautiful to those who loved her; and this not so much on account of the exquisite form and color of the mask she wore as because the soul took such triumphant possession of her whole body. Her complexion had the delicacy and freshness of the "apple-blossoms," of which her brother, Dr. Francis, once said, as he might have said of her, that they seemed "more and more beautiful" every year of his life. Her eyes glowed with a warm fire or danced with childlike merriment; and, when her hair was as white as snow, it still reminded us of the rippling brown curls which fell from her open brow when she first became a wife. Her whole being was fired with a sacred enthusiasm, which was not only felt by herself, but was evident to others, as pervading her to her very fingers' ends.—DALL, CAROLINE H., 1883, *Lydia Maria Child, Christian Review, vol.* 19, *p.* 519.

In religious matters she did not identify herself with any local society, or anything strictly denominational. She attended Dr. Sears's preaching, because she liked the man, but was in full sympathy, we judge, with only her own standard of faith. In earlier life she was nominally a Swedenborgian. . . . Whether at home or abroad, she was plainly dressed. This may have been through a slight oddity or eccentricity, and a reluctance to appear extravagant. She was especially peculiar in what she wore on her head. The writer recently held in his hands two bonnets, the last ones worn by Mrs. Child. They were almost alike, and evidently the old was not exchanged for the new because of change in the style. . . . She received company at her house with characteristic simplicity, and with a warmth which made one feel welcome.—HUDSON, ALFRED SERENO, 1890, *The Home of Lydia Maria Child, New England Magazine, vol.* 8, *pp.* 412, 413.

She was not a beautiful girl in the ordinary sense; but her complexion was good, her eyes very bright, her mouth expressive and her teeth fine. She had a good deal of wit, liked to use it, and did use it upon Mr. Child, who was a frequent visitor, but her deportment was always maidenly and lady-like. . . . Immediately after their marriage they went to house-keeping in a very small house in Boston, most plainly furnished by the little money which Mrs. Child had saved out of her literary earnings. I dined with her once in that very humble home. She kept no servant, and did her own cooking. She had prepared a savory dish, consisting of a meat-pie, perhaps mutton, baked in a small oven, and there were roasted or baked potatoes, and a baked Indian pudding. Mr. Child came in to the two o'clock dinner, breezy, cheerful, and energetic as ever. There was no dessert, and no wine, no beverage of any kind but water, not even a cup of tea or coffee. This was the beginning of the married life of Lydia Maria Child, a woman of genius, who, in a worldly point of view, ought to have had a different lot, but who never faltered or failed in her duty to her husband, and who was, beyond all doubt, perfectly happy in her relations with him through their long lives.— CURTIS, GEORGE TICKNOR, 1890, *Reminiscences of N. P. Willis and Lydia Maria Child, Harper's Magazine, vol.* 81, *pp.* 719, 720.

I saw her only twice, but she impressed me as a strong and lofty personality, so far above the usual social human being that her solitude and the sparseness of her environment seemed to partake of the character of luxuries which most of us were unfit to share.—PHELPS, ELIZABETH STUART, 1896, *Chapters from a Life, p.* 182.

GENERAL

We are glad to see that the author of "Hobomok," whom we understand to be a lady, has resumed her pen. That interesting little tale made its way to the public favor solely by its own merits, and was scarcely noticed by our critics, till their opinions had been rendered of little consequence by the decision of the literary community. Whatever objections may be made to the mode in which the story is conducted, and the catastrophe produced, it cannot be denied, that these faults are abundantly redeemed by beauties of no ordinary value. In graphic descriptions of scenery, in forcible delineations of character, in genuine pathos, we think "Hobomok" may be safely compared with any work of fiction, which our country has produced. . . . The author has paid the usual price of an early reputation, that of being compelled to use redoubled exertions in order to prevent it from fading. We cannot venture to say, that her laurels have lost none of their freshness by the present attempt, ["The Rebels"] but on the other hand, we think that her failure is only a partial one, and that it may be ascribed to other causes than want of ability. . . . The narrative is greatly deficient in simplicity and unity, and is not so much one story as a number of separate stories, not interwoven, but loosely tied together.—GRAY, J. C., 1826, *The Rebels, North American Review, vol.* 22, *pp.* 400, 401, 402.

This lady has long been before the public as an author, with much success. And she well deserves it,—for in all her works we think that nothing can be found, which does not commend itself by its tone of healthy morality, and generally by its good sense. Few female writers, if any, have done more or better things for our literature, in its lighter or graver departments. She has continued to render herself popular in fiction and fact; to be graceful alike in telling a village story, and in giving a receipt for the kitchen; to be at home in the prose and poetry of life; in short, to be just the woman we want for the mothers and daughters of the present generation. We have long watched the course of Mrs. Child, and in general, with satisfaction. Sometimes we have been more than satisfied,—we have admired her.—MELLEN, G., 1833, *Works of Mrs. Child, North American Review, vol. 37, p. 139.*

I am fully aware of the unpopularity of the task I have undertaken; but though I expect ridicule and censure, I do not fear them. A few years hence the opinion of the world will be a matter in which I shall have not even the most transient interest; but this book will be abroad on its mission of humanity long after the hand that wrote it is mingling with the dust. Should it be the means of advancing even one single hour the inevitable progress of truth and justice, I would not exchange the consciousness for all Rothschild's wealth or Sir Walter's fame.—CHILD, LYDIA MARIA, 1833, *Appeal in behalf of that class of Americans called Africans, Preface.*

Mrs. Child has some intellectual traits, which are well suited to success in this field of literary enterprise. She has a vigorous and exuberant imagination, and an accurate eye for beauty of form. She understands the harmonious construction of language, and can describe both nature and society with liveliness and truth. Her style, in its general character, is rich and eloquent; abounding in brilliant turns and fanciful illustrations. It is generally simple, energetic, and impressive, but sometimes it is too dazzling. In fact, the copiousness of her imagination, and the ardor of her feelings, which lend such power to her enthusiastic eloquence, in a measure injure her style for classical novel-writing. —FELTON, C. C., 1837, *Philothea, North American Review, vol. 44, pp. 77, 79.*

Mrs. Child has sent me a Book, "Philothea," and a most magnanimous epistle. I have answered as I could. The Book is beautiful, but of a *hectic* beauty; to me not pleasant, even fatal-looking. Such things grow not in the ground, on mother earth's honest bosom, but in hothouses,—Sentimental-Calvinist fire traceable underneath! —CARLYLE, THOMAS, 1838, *To Emerson, June 15; Correspondence of Carlyle and Emerson, ed. Norton, vol. I, p. 169.*

There is a vivacious naturalness about the book, ["Letters from New York"] compassing even its oddities, covering up its minor defects of rhetoric, that to one like ourselves, tired with the heat and dust of this dry September, is refreshing as an April shower. At times, too, there are scattered up and down over the letters little eloquent apostrophes, which, if we liken its general vivacity to a shower, may in sequence be likened to an iced draught of the pure element. We have not even now said what we might say, that there is an extravagant tone pervading the whole, which being at once natural and graceful in the writer, we can by no means condemn; but the same being strange and unsuited to a running comment upon practical matters, and such occasionally are sublimed by the writer's touch, we cannot wholly praise. . . . One word more, and a kind one, to Mrs. Child. We wish not to lessen one iota the amount of your influence, which we believe to be considerable; and so believing, we implore you, by your hatred of formalism and cant, of ostentations and pride—by your sympathy with human want, and your hearty relish for all that is natual and noble in thought and in action, to direct that influence against the crying evils of social life. Your energies misdirected will avail less than those of a weak man; rightly directed, they will avail more than those of the strongest. —MITCHELL, DONALD G., 1845, *Letters from New York, American Review, vol. 7, p. 74.*

"Philothea," in especial, is written with great vigor, and, as a classical romance, is not far inferior to the "Anacharsis" of Barthélemy; its style is a model for purity, chastity and ease.—POE, EDGAR ALLAN, 1846, *The Literati, Works, ed. Stedman and Woodberry, vol. VIII, p. 113.*

Mrs. Child has a large acquaintance with common life, which she describes with a genial sympathy and fidelity,—a generous love of freedom, extreme susceptibility of impressions of beauty, and an imagination which bodies forth her feelings in forms of peculiar distinctness and freshness. Her works abound in bright pictures and fanciful thoughts, which seem to be of the atmosphere in which she lives. She transfuses into them something of her own spirit, which, though meditative and somewhat mystical, is always cheerful and radiant. In her revelation on music, illustrations of the doctrine of correspondence, and all the more speculative parts of her various writings, she has shown that fine perception of the mysterious analogy which exists between the physical and moral world, and of the mode in which the warp and woof of life are mingling, which is among the first attributes of the true poet.—GRISWOLD, RUFUS WILMOT, 1847, *The Prose Writers of America*, p. 427.

The design of the abolitionists, let us believe, is the improvement and happiness of the coloured race; for this end Mrs. Child devoted her noblest talents, her holiest aspirations. Seventeen years ago she consecrated her powers to this work. The result has been, that her fine genius, her soul's wealth has been wasted in the struggle which party politicians have used for their own selfish purposes. Had Mrs. Child taken the more quiet, but far more efficient mode of doing good to the coloured race by aiding to establish schools in Liberia—preparing and sending out free colored emigrants, who must there become teachers and exemplars to thousands and millions of the poor black heathen; if she had written for this mission of peace as she has poured her heart out in a cause only tending to strife, what blessed memorials of these long years would now be found to repay her disinterested exertions!—HALE, SARAH JOSEPHA, 1852, *Woman's Record*, p. 620.

Mrs. Child is a woman of strong and generous impulses, with a lively sense of beauty, especially fond of music, and of tracing fanciful analogies between its subtile suggestions and the sister arts, believing in absolute truth and justice, but somewhat too enthusiastic to preserve always the just balance of judgment. Her works apparently reflect her own nature, and bring the reader and author face to face. In the haste of composition there are occasional slips, and among so many works there is not a uniform standard of merit; still there are few authors who have added so much to the pleasure and to the moral culture of our generation. It is to be hoped that a revised edition of her works may be published, as many of them are now out of print.—UNDERWOOD, FRANCIS H., 1872, *A Hand-book of English Literature, American Authors*, p. 220.

Whose "Letters from New York" were models in their kind; whose stories for young people have not been surpassed by any writer, except Andersen; whose more labored works have a quality that entitles them to a high place among the products of mind, is a devotee of the transcendental faith.—FROTHINGHAM, OCTAVIUS BROOKS, 1876, *Transcendentalism in New England*, p. 382.

In judging of this little book, ["Hobomok"] it is to be remembered that it marked the very dawn of American imaginative literature. Irving had printed only his "Sketch Book;" Cooper only "Precaution." This new production was the hasty work of a young woman of nineteen—an Indian tale by one who had scarcely even seen an Indian. Accordingly "Hobomok" now seems very crude in execution, very improbable in plot; and is redeemed only by a certain earnestness which carries the reader along, and by a sincere attempt after local coloring. It is an Indian "Enoch Arden," with important modifications, which unfortunately all tend away from probability. . . . As the first work whose scene was laid in Puritan days, "Hobomok" will always have a historic interest, but it must be read in very early youth to give it any other attraction. . . . The "Frugal Housewife" now lies before me, after a great many years of abstinence from its appetizing pages. The words seem as familiar as when we children used to study them beside the kitchen fire, poring over them as if their very descriptions had power to allay an unquenched appetite or prolong the delights of one satiated. . . . As it ["Appeal"] was the first anti-slavery work ever printed in America in book form, so I have always thought it the ablest; that is, it covered the whole ground better than any other. I know that, on reading it for the first time, nearly ten years after its appearance, it had more formative influence on my mind in that direction than any other, although of course the eloquence of public meetings was a more exciting stimulus. It never surprised me to hear that even Dr. Channing attributed a part of his own anti-slavery awakening to this admirable book. . . . I well remember the admiration with which this romance ["Philothea"] was hailed; and for me personally it was one of those delights of boyhood which the criticism of maturity cannot disturb. . . . She was one of those prominent instances in our literature of persons born for the pursuits of pure intellect, whose intellects were yet balanced by their hearts, both being absorbed in the great moral agitations of the age. . . . She wrote better than most of her contemporaries, and well enough for her public, she did not, therefore, win that intellectual immortality which only the best writers command. . . . But she won a meed which she would value more highly, —that warmth of sympathy, that mingled gratitude of intellect and heart which men give to those who have faithfully served their day and generation.—HIGGINSON, THOMAS WENTWORTH, 1899,*Contemporaries,* pp. 114, 117, 123, 124, 140, 141.

As for the exact literary rank of this heroic woman, the critical scales must be passed to younger and cooler hands. In the homes of a few "original Garrisonians" her early books were still cherished. We learned to read, that we might not be dependent on our busy elders for daily absorption in her "Flowers for Children." Our own offspring seem to detect a moral and Edgeworthian flavor in the cherished volume, and prefers "Little Women." We first heard the very names of Pericles and Plato in her Greek romance "Philothea." "The Letters from New York" widened the visa of a village street to our boyish eyes. Though not successful in rhythmical utterance, Mrs. Child had much of the poet's nature. Her "Philothea" is almost a rhapsody. Her firm faith in thought-transference, her half-belief in metempsychosis, her mystical and ideal tendencies generally, unite with the frugality of the Yankee housewife even more grotesquely, at times, than the similar mixture in Emerson; and, like him, she is herself the first to laugh. Of all the picturesque figures among Transcendentalists and Abolitionists, there is perhaps not one so utterly lovable. Some of her books may yet regain their influence.—LAWTON, WILLIAM CRANSTON, 1902, *Introduction to the Study of American Literature,* p. 187.

George Ripley
1802–1880

American man of letters, was born at Greenfield, Mass., graduated at Hartford in 1823, and in 1826 at the Cambridge Divinity School. From 1828–31 he was a Unitarian minister at Boston, but then resigned his pastorate and went to Europe to study philosophy. On his return he edited, with Dr. Hedge, "Specimens of Foreign Standard Literature" (1838–42,) and published "Discourses on the Philosophy of Religion" (1839), which produced an animated controversy with Professor Andrews Norton. Dr. Ripley was one of the initiators of transcendentalism, wrote for the *Dial,* and in 1844 lost his fortune in the socialistic experiment of Brook Farm. In 1849 he became literary editor of the *Tribune,* and later "reader" for Harpers. In 1852 he edited a "Handbook of Literature and the Fine Arts" with Mr. Bayard Taylor, and in 1858 "Appleton's New American Cyclopædia" with Mr. C. A. Dana.—SANDERS, LLOYD, C., ed., 1887, *Celebrities of the Century,* p. 862.

PERSONAL

He was lacking in the gift of thrilling speech, his convictions did not fall glowing from his lips. His ideas, though clear, cogent, and earnestly put forth, did no execution. In a small room, among personal friends, on his own themes, and following his own impulse, he was eloquent, persuasive, enchanting; but in a meeting-house, on a formal occasion, before a mixed audience, on impersonal subjects, he was unimpassioned, almost cold. He must have his hearer within arm's length; then his full power was felt. Individually his parishioners were much attached to him. They found him delightful in their homes; a true friend, sympathetic and consoling, more than ready in all cases of need with counsel and assistance. For many years after his ministry ceased, those who had known him as a pastor spoke of him with a depth of affection which nothing but faithful service could justify or explain. A few still live to speak tender words in his memory. — FROTHINGHAM, OCTAVIUS BROOKS, 1882, *George Ripley (American Men of Letters), p. 52.*

The more the subject has been thought over, and long-buried memories of our dear friend reappear, the wider and richer the theme opens. And it would need many pages to present the least adequate portraits of George Ripley as a Christian minister, a scholar, an expounder of philosophy, a social reorganizer, a literary critic, an encyclopædist, a friend and a man. To me, in reviewing his diversified yet consistent, progressive and ascending career, he takes a front rank among the many leaders of thought whom it has been my rare privilege to know, in our own republic and in Europe. Especially would it gratify me to bear my testimony to the generous and quite heroic spirit, whereby he and his great souled wife were impelled to organize Brook Farm; and to the wise sagacity, genial good-heartedness, friendly sympathy, patience, persistency, and ideal hopefulness with which they energetically helped to carry out that romantic enterprise to the end.—CHANNING, WILLIAM HENRY, 1882, *Letter to Mr. Frothingham, April 7; George Ripley by Octavius Brooks Frothingham (American Men of Letters), p.* 302.

Although a scholar of great metaphysical and theological acuteness, and a critic of high rank exerting through the last years of his life a powerful influence as literary editor of the New York *Tribune*, George Ripley is chiefly remembered as the founder of the Brook Farm Community. Into this idea he threw all of his tremendous zeal and energy. He resigned his pulpit in Boston to devote his whole time to it, and for it he labored with earnestness and self-denial. He was the motive power of the movement.—PATTEE, FRED LEWIS, 1896, *A History of American Literature, p.* 234.

Mr. Ripley, who sat at the head of the table, [Brook Farm, 1847] talked supremely well. He was a most striking figure, and every one was so intellectual and superior that one wished, had it been less warm and more fragrant, to stay there. Mr. Ripley, who afterwards became a very dear friend of mine in New York society, often spoke of that glimpse of mine at what had been to him a painful disappointment. He told me how badly some characters "panned out," how many illusions he lost. "It all went up in smoke," he said; "and yet the theory seemed most plausible."—SHERWOOD, MARY E. W., 1897, *An Epistle to Posterity, p.* 37.

To the last there was a merry twinkle under the gold-bowed spectacles of Dr. Ripley. For all this I think the Brook-Farm failure left a sore place in his heart. Later reform projects seemed to him, I feel sure, artificial, dishonest—as compared with that first out-put of the seeds of justice and brotherhood; always (for him) there was a rhythmic beat of celestial music in that far away choir of workers and singers —brought together by his agency, bonded by his affectionate serenities — and put upon the road—amidst rural beatitudes— toward the Delectable Mountains and the heights of Beulah. . . . If an honest pure-thoughted man ever lived 'twas George Ripley; and he carried a beautiful zeal and earnestness into that Brook-Farm undertaking. Much as he enjoyed the genius of Hawthorne, I do not think he had kindly thought of the "Blithedale Romance": not indeed blind to its extraordinary merit, or counting it an ugly picture—but as one throwing a quasi pagan glamour over a holy undertaking.—MITCHELL, DONALD G., 1899, *American Lands and Letters, Leather-Stocking to Poe's "Raven," pp.* 161, 162.

Ripley discharged all the obligations resting on the Brook Farm Phalanx at the time of its dissolution. Although these did not amount to more than one thousand dollars, the last receipt was dated December 22, 1862, and was an acknowledgment of payment, partly in money and partly by a copy of the "Cyclopædia," received for groceries. No sharper comment is necessary on the deprivations of his first years in New York. It has been felt that nobody gained less from the Brook Farm experiment than did Ripley, and although that surmise must in many ways be true, it cannot, in the largest sense, be accepted by those who have followed carefully the man's after life. The blows of the hammer may harden the metal into a rail or temper it into a Damascus blade. Both the bludgeon and the blade are useful, but the latter does the finer work. So when courage becomes not defiance but fortitude; when endurance does not allow itself to sink into stoicism at the death of that in which belief has been deepest, there is good certainty that much besides a crushing impact has accrued to the victim of fate.—SWIFT, LINDSAY, 1900, *Brook Farm, Its Members, Scholars and Visitors*, p. 145.

GENERAL

He wrote from observation, reading, knowledge, not from feeling or fancy. From the first he did this. His training at school and college; his years of experience in an exacting profession; his exercise in reviews and controversies; his familiarity with the best productions of American, English, German and French genius; the severe mental and moral discipline of Brook Farm, all conspired with a remarkable firmness and moderation of temperament, to repress any impulse towards affectation or undue exhilaration of judgment, while his natural buoyancy of spirits, his inborn kindness of heart, his knowledge of intellectual difficulties, and his sympathy with even modest aspirations, saved him from moroseness, and rendered it impossible for him to ply with severity the scourage of criticism. . . . The competency of Mr. Ripley's literary judgments has often been remarked on. He did not wait till others had spoken, and then venture an opinion. He spoke at once, and he spoke with confidence, as one who had good reason for what he said. Whether the book in question was the "Scarlet Letter," the "Origin of Species," or the "Light of Asia," the verdict was equally prompt and decided. There was no dogmatism, no boasting, no claim to special insight, no affectation of patronage; simply a quiet recognition of talent and an appreciation of its value in the world of letters. That his judgments were generally confirmed by specialists is an evidence of their intrinsic worth; that they were usually ratified by the public testifies to his knowledge of the public taste. . . . His intellectual temperament aided him in his task. The absence of passion was a great advantage. The lack of ardent partisan feeling made possible the calm, clear, judicial temper so necessary to the critic. The want of what may be called the "artistic constitution" which delights in music, painting, sculpture, architecture, did something to insure the equability of his poise. His mental force was not wasted by emotion or attenuated by **distraction**. He was no dreamer, no **visionary**, no enthusiast, no creature of imagination or fancy. He was, through and through, a critic, gentle but firm, intelligent, exact, holding the interests of truth paramount to all others, always hoping that the interest of truth might be served by the effort of careful writers.—FROTHINGHAM, OCTAVIUS BROOKS, 1882, *George Ripley (American Men of Letters)*, pp. 201, 286, 292.

The wisest, most equitable, and keenly discriminating while generous critic of his nation. . . . These masterly essays, which have never been surpassed in America, for thoroughness of scholarship, massive argument and loftiness of appeal. And, indeed, it would be difficult, anywhere to find a more lucid exposition of the highest Spiritual Philosophy,—a more profound and penetrating while sympathetic interpretation of Spinoza's speculative and ethical System,—or a more touchingly reverent, while finely discriminating, analysis of Schleiermacher's inspiring doctrine, than can be found in these admirably composed "Three Letters of an Alumnus," each of which in temper, thought, and style, might serve as a model of philosophical discussion, vitalised and sanctified by religious fervour and magnanimous humanity. These "Letters" clearly indicate that, if their writer had felt free in conscience to consecrate his life to scholarship, he would have found no superior and but few peers among his countrymen, as a Philosopher, a Theologian, or a Religious Historian and Critic.—CHANNING, WILLIAM HENRY, 1883, *George Ripley, The Modern Review*, vol. 4, pp. 521, 534.

It seems to me, one can hardly assign to this veteran American critic a high or permanent place in our literary history. He was equipped with a wide knowledge, including philosophy and theology, as well as belles-lettres; contemporary European literature was familiar to him; his tastes and sympathies were, as a rule, both kindly and catholic; he had few hobbies to ride or rancors to exhibit; no trace of embittering personal dissappointment appeared in his reviews; and he did not yield, as far as I know, to individual dislikes or petty spites. But his critical work could not be compared, in merit, with that of such an essayist as Mr. Lowell, nor with the unsigned and unrecognized reviews of some less known writers. It lacked grasp; the points Dr. Ripley sought to make must be found by the readers at some cost of time and trouble. His writing was, as a rule, diffuse; terse or remarkable characterizations were lacking; nor did one often find a sentence that went straight to the heart of a book. Dr. Ripley was considered to have an unusual ability as a summarizer of the books he reviewed, but summarizing by paraphrase or by scissors-work, is the easiest kind of criticism. Again, his use of adjectives, was sometimes deemed a merit; but these adjectives were generally used to round out a style perpetually "balanced" or Johnsonian. The writer evidently sought to leave an impression of profundity and nice analytical power; but this impression was produced upon those who delighted in the literary habit of saying that, though B follows A in the alphabet, it undoubtedly precedes C. Dr. Ripley's reviews, as a rule, could have been divided into parallel columns, each sentence separated into halves by such words as, but, yet, though, notwithstanding.—RICHARDSON, CHARLES F., 1887, *American Literature, 1607–1885*, vol. I, p. 429.

Jones Very
1813–1880

Born in Salem, Mass., 28 Aug., 1813; died there, 8 May, 1880. He made voyages with his father, a cultivated sea-captain, and had schooling in Salem and New Orleans. A graduate of Harvard in 1836, he taught Greek there for two years. His first volume of essays and poems appeared in 1839. In 1843 the Cambridge Association licensed him to preach, but he was never ordained. He was the intimate friend of Emerson and Channing, and a frequent contributor to "The Christian Register" and other Unitarian journals. His friend James Freeman Clarke edited a complete posthumous edition of his poems and essays. In 1883 Very's "Poems" were reëdited by William P. Andrews, with a memoir. The sonnet, somewhat on the Shakesperean model, was the form of expression most natural to him.—STEDMAN, EDMUND CLARENCE, ed., 1900, *An American Anthology, Biographical Notes*, p. 829.

PERSONAL

Jones Very came hither two days since. His position accuses society as much as society names that false and morbid. And much of his discourse concerning society, church and college was absolutely just. He says it is with him a day of hate: that he discerns the bad element in every person whom he meets, which repels him: he even shrinks a little to give the hand, that sign of receiving. The institutions, the cities which men have built the world over, look to him like a huge ink-blot. His only guard in going to see men is, that he goes to do them good, else they would injure him spiritually. He lives in the sight that He who made him, made the things he sees. He would as soon embrace a black Egyptian mummy as Socrates. He would obey,—obey. He is not disposed to attack religions or charities, though false. The bruisëd reed he would not break, smoking flax not quench. . . . He had the manners of a man,—one, that is, to whom life was more than meat. He felt it, he said, an honour to wash his face, being, as it was, the temple of the spirit. I ought not to omit to record the astonishment which seized all the company when our brave Saint the other day fronted the presiding Preacher. The preacher began to tower and dogmatise with many words. Then I foresaw that his doom was fixed; and, as soon as he had ceased speaking, the Saint set him right, and blew away all his words in an instant,—unhorsed him, I may say, and tumbled him along the ground in utter dismay, like my angel of Heliodorus; never was discomfiture more complete. In tones of genuine pathos, he bid him wonder at the Love which suffered him to speak there in his chair of things he knew nothing of; one might expect to see the book taken from his hands and him thrust out of the room, and yet he was allowed to sit and talk, whilst every word he spoke was a step of departure from the truth; and of this he commanded himself to bear witness.—EMERSON, RALPH WALDO, 1838, *Journal*, Oct. 26.

He was good as goodness itself, true as truth. With his knowledge and wisdom he was as simple as a child—transparent and artless. He was the extremest possible distance from pomposity or pretension, and when he believed that poetry, which came to him like the breath of heaven, did actually come from heaven, it was so naturally and simply said one felt it was his profoundest conviction. It was a sacred idea—a divine reality.—WATERSON, ROBERT C., 1882, *Century Magazine, vol.* 24, *p.* 862.

In college, as in school, he was too sedate to be widely and generally popular, but all who knew him reverenced the lofty purity of his character, and he soon gathered around him a small circle of warmly attached friends. He was sensitive and reserved, but the cordiality of his tone and the sweet naturalness of his smile of welcome at once attracted whoever made his acquaintance, though the uniform gravity of his daily walk and conversation prevented the many from approaching him as an intimate. . . . "Men in General," said Dr. Channing, "have lost or never found this higher mind, their insanity is profound, Mr. Very's is only superficial. To hear him talk was like looking into the purely spiritual world, into truth itself. He had nothing of self-exaggeration, but seemed to have attained self-annihilation and become an oracle of God." Dr. Channing repeated that he had "not lost his reason," and quoted some of his sayings, identical with many parts of his sonnets, as proofs of the "iron sequence of his thoughts."—ANDREWS, WILLIAM P., 1883, *ed. Poems by Jones Very, Memoir, pp.* 7, 10.

GENERAL

His essays entitled "Epic Poetry," "Shakespere," and "Hamlet," are fine specimens of learned and sympathetic criticism; and his sonnets, and other pieces of verse, are chaste, simple, and poetical, though they have little range of subjects and illusion. They are religious, and some of them are mystical, but they will be recognised by the true poet as the overflowings of a brother's soul.—GRISWOLD, RUFUS WILMOT, 1842, *The Poets and Poetry of America, p.* 392.

Jones Very has written some of the best sonnets in our language.—PEABODY, ANDREW P., 1856, *American Poetry, North American Review, vol.* 82, *p.* 243.

Jones Very has always piped the sweet, sad notes of religious melancholy.—WARD, JULIUS HAMMOND, 1863, *Quietism in the Nineteenth Century, North American Review, vol.* 97, *p.* 400.

His verse is characterized by a remarkable purity and delicacy of thought, and great ease and simplicity of style, while it breathes the spirit of a sweet and loving trust, and is pervaded by a fine, subtle sense of the enduring realities. In very many of his poems there is the unmistakable element or master-touch that belongs to the higher order of genius.—PUTNAM, ALFRED P., 1874, *Singers and Songs of the Liberal Faith, p.* 336.

Among the minds stirred about half a century ago by the impulse of Transcendentalism, one of the least conspicuous, and since that time one of the least known, was one which now fairly promises to be foremost in the poetic interpretation of the movement. . . . Jones Very, for forty years past one of the most reserved, modest, retiring, and unknown of literary men, now slowly comes to the front, while many of the briliant and attractive men and women who were in the group in which Emerson, Alcott, and Margaret Fuller were the principal figures, begin to fade away, and, dying, leave scarcely a sign to indicate the secret of their charming influence. . . . Natural genius and the finest classical culture had given him unerring good taste and command of the Shakspearean sonnet as a means of communicating his thought to the world, and the uninstructed reader would never suspect that he was reading the words of a man "beside himself" according to the standard of what we call "common sense." His was uncommon sense as Channing thought, a higher mood of sanity, to which few men ever attained.—BATCHELOR, GEORGE, 1883, *A Poet of Transcendentalism, The Dial, vol.* 4, *pp.* 58, 59.

"Essays and Poems," by Jones Very,—a little volume, the work of an exquisite spirit. Some of the poems it contains are as if written by a George Herbert who had studied Shakespeare, read Wordsworth, and lived in America.—NORTON, CHARLES ELIOT, 1884–86, *ed. The Correspondence of Thomas Carlyle and Ralph Waldo Emerson, vol.* I, *p.* 360, *note.*

The sort of inspiration which gleams through the best of the sonnets is in the prose almost wholly lacking. Literary skill he had little or none, though, at his best, he had something far better than literary skill. . . . In all these poems we find a strenuous insistence on submission of the will to God,—submission in itself inevitable, but, if made voluntarily, a source of the highest joy. . . . Emerson exhorts, encourages, instructs; but the attitude of Very is different. There is a certain sternness in his verse, a flavor of absolutism, which carries one back a thousand, two thousand years out of modern skepticism and doubt. Emerson compares him to David and Isaiah. On this point, the comparison is just. By his passionate and wholly modern sensibility to Nature, by his broad and spiritual view of God, he stands apart from them; but he shares, if in a far less degree, their tone of austere judgment and command. He has in common with them a sense of wrath and scorn at the meanness and pettiness of men around him, a feeling of isolation in the midst of a people who have fallen off from God. . . . Jones Very is not and never can be one of the great figures of literature. His breadth is too slight in proportion to his depth. Moreover, the outward form of current religious phraseology, in which he clothed his profound spiritual life, is in a certain degree repellent to many men of this generation; and, on the other hand, his passionate idealism does not altogether please the average religious mind. With our material civilization and our democratic habit he has little in common. But that which makes the soul and inspiration of his verse—his love of Nature, with his tender mysticism—must give him a place permanent at least, if not prominent in our literature.—BRADFORD, G., JR., 1887, *Jones Very, Unitarian Review*, vol. 27, pp. 112, 113, 114, 118.

Jones Very, a sort of Unitarian monk and mystic, packed into many a sonnet or meditative hymn rich and weighty words of reverence and consecration, which he deemed inspired by ghostly power from above, and which he wrote in implicit obedience to the spiritual voice within. Some of these poems are harmed by a semi-Buddhistic Christian Quietism, as though Molinos had been incarnated anew in the Salem streets; others display the serene sure beauty of church-yard lilies.— RICHARDSON, CHARLES F., 1888, *American Literature*, 1607-1885, vol. II, p. 233.

Was a sort of slender American shadow of William Blake, with the masculine strength and the painter's genius left out; he was a mystic and a spiritist, and wrote some deep and delicate little poems under what he believed to be direct spirit guidance.—HAWTHORNE, JULIAN, AND LEMON, LEONARD, 1891, *American Literature*, p. 155.

Very has received a rarer and nobler recognition than popularity; men of genius have concurred in praising him. In respect to his poems and the voice that speaks in them, Bryant, Emerson, and Hawthorne have each paid positive tribute. The mind from which Very's poetry came was of an unusual order, and one that cannot be judged without special study, though the poetry of that mind may be enjoyed. He was one of those few Americans (perhaps the only American) for whom religious contemplation is everything; and one of those mortals to whom above others is, in spiritual things, granted the clearest vision. Such a man, as we know with regard to oriental mystics, with whom conditions are more favorable for solitary, rapt meditation than in America, naturally and rightly regards himself as a teacher of divine truth, and an exposer of worldly pretension and sin; in America less naturally but not less rightly, this was the case with Very.— SIMONDS, ARTHUR B., 1894, *American Song*, p. 57.

His sympathy with nature is profound, but his methods of expression not varied. This and the frequent repetition of his subject give his writings an impression of monotony fatal to an extended reading. He is seldom trite, though his reflections are often drawn from the commonest objects. Close to ourselves lie the wonders of nature, is the keynote of his poetry. The wind-flower, the columbine, and the snowdrop were to him as eloquent as a forest, a mountain, or an ocean. He was one of the most original as well as most unreadable of our poets. All his poems are infused with the sweetness of his own anemones and columbines, of too subtle an essence to suit the general taste.—ONDERDONK, JAMES L., 1899-1901, *History of American Verse*, p. 185.

Had in him an eccentric streak amounting almost to insanity; but his "Poems and Essays" (1839) reveal an original and intensely spiritual nature, and an unusual gift of terse, fresh, direct expression within a limited field.—BRONSON, WALTER C., 1900, *A Short History of American Literature*, p. 210.

THOMAS CARLYLE

Engraving by Walker & Boutall. From Painting
by Sir J. E. Millais, P.R.A.

EDWARD FITZGERALD.

Engraving from a Photograph.

Thomas Carlyle
1795-1881

1795, Born at Ecclefechan, Annandale, Dumfriesshire. 1800, at the Village School. 1806–1809, at the Grammar School, Annan. 1809, enters Edinburgh University. 1814–1815, Teacher of Mathematics at Annan. 1816–1818, Master at Kirkcaldy; friendship with Edward Irving. 1818–1820, at Edinburgh; divinity and law; writes first articles for Brewster's *Encyclopædia;* begins the study of German literature. 1821, his "New Birth;" visits Haddington with Irving; meets Miss Jane Welsh. 1822, tutor to the Bullers; writes "Life of Schiller" for the *London Magazine.* 1824, translates "Wilhelm Meister;" first visit to London with the Bullers; meets Coleridge at Highgate; visits Paris; correspondence with Goethe begun. 1825, at home, Hoddam Hill. 1826, marries Jane Welsh, and settles at Comely Bank, Edinburgh; meets Jeffrey; writes "Jean Paul" for the *Edinburgh Review.* 1827–1831, removes to the Welshs' Manor, Craigenputtock; "Essay on Burns" in the *Edinburgh Review;* contributes magazine articles now published under "Miscellanies;" writes "Sartor Resartus." 1831, removes to London; his father's death. 1832–1833, returns to Craigenputtock; visit from Emerson; "Sartor Resartus" published in *Fraser's Magazine;* winter in Edinburgh. 1834, settles at Cheyne Row (Chelsea), London. 1837, lectures in London on German Literature; "The French Revolution." 1839, "Chartism." 1841, lectures in London on heroes; "Heroes and Hero Worship" published. 1843, "Past and Present." 1845, "Cromwell." 1850, "Latter-Day Pamphlets." 1851, "Life of Sterling." 1858–1865, "History of Frederick the Second." 1866, elected Lord Rector of Edinburgh University; address on the Choice of Books; death of Mrs. Carlyle. 1874, order of merit from the German Emperor. 1875, "The Early Kings of Norway." 1881, death; "Reminiscences," J. A. Froude, Ed. 1882, "Thomas Carlyle," J. A. Froude, Ed. 1883, "Letters and Memorials of Jane Welsh Carlyle," J. A. Froude, Ed. 1883, "Correspondence of Carlyle and Emerson," C. E. Norton, Ed. 1886, "Early Letters of Thomas Carlyle," C. E. Norton, Ed. 1887, "Correspondence between Goethe and Carlyle," C. E. Norton, Ed.—GEORGE, ANDREW J., 1897, *ed. Carlyle's Essay on Burns, p.* 80.

PERSONAL

Carlyle breakfasted with me, and I had an interesting morning with him. He is a deep-thinking German scholar, a character, and a singular compound. His voice and manner, and even the style of his conversation, are those of a religious zealot, and he keeps up that character in his declamations against the anti-religious. And yet, if not the god of his idolatry, at least he has a priest and prophet of his church in Goethe, of whose profound wisdom he speaks like an enthusiast. But for him, Carlyle says, he should not now be alive. He owes everything to him! But in strange union with such idolatry is his admiration of Bonaparte. Another object of his eulogy is—Cobbett, whom he praises for his humanity and love of the poor! Singular, and even whimsical, combinations of love and reverence these.—ROBINSON, HENRY CRABB, 1832, *Diary,* Feb. 12; *Reminiscences, ed. Sadler, vol.* II, *p.* 168.

I found him one of the most simple and frank of men, and became acquainted with him at once. We walked over several miles of hills, and talked upon all the great questions that interested us most. The comfort of meeting a man is that he speaks sincerely; that he feels himself to be so rich, that he is above the meanness of pretending to knowledge which he has not, and Carlyle does not pretend to have solved the great problems, but rather to be an observer of their solution as it goes forward in the world. I asked him at what religious development the concluding passage in his piece in the *Edinburgh Review* upon German literature (say five years ago), and some passages in the piece called "Characteristics," pointed? He replied that he was not competent to state even to himself,—he waited rather to see. My own feeling was that I had met men of far less power who had got greater insight into religious truth. He is, as you might guess from his papers, the most catholic of philosophers; he forgives and loves everybody, and wishes each to struggle on in his own place and arrive at his own ends. . . . He talks finely, seems to love the broad Scotch, and I loved him very much at once. I am afraid he finds his entire solitude tedious, but I could not help congratulating him upon the treasure in his wife, and I hope he will not leave the moors; 'tis so much better for a man of letters to nurse himself in seclusion than to be filed down to the common level by the compliances and imitations of city society.—EMERSON, RALPH WALDO, 1833, *Letter to Alexander Ireland, Aug. 31; Ralph Waldo Emerson: Recollections of his Visits to England, ed. Ireland, p. 53.*

I found time to make a visit to Carlyle, and to hear one of his lectures. He is rather a small, spare, ugly Scotchman, with a strong accent, which I should think he takes no pains to mitigate. His manners are plain and simple, but not polished, and his conversation much of the same sort. He is now lecturing for subsistence, to about a hundred persons, who pay him, I believe, two guineas each. . . . To-day he spoke—as I think he commonly does—without notes, and therefore as nearly extempore as a man can who prepares himself carefully, as it was plain he had done. His course is on Modern Literature, and his subject to-day was that of the eighteenth century; in which he contrasted Johnson and Voltaire very well, and gave a good character of Swift. He was impressive, I think, though such lecturing could not well be very popular; and in some parts, if he were not poetical, he was picturesque. He was nowhere obscure, nor were his sentences artificially constructed, though some of them, no doubt, savored of his peculiar manner.— TICKNOR, GEORGE, 1838, *Journal, June 1; Life, Letters and Journals, vol.* II, *p. 180.*

His manners and conversation are as unformed as his style; and yet, withal, equally full of genius. In conversation, he piles thought upon thought and imagining upon imagining, till the erection seems about to topple down with its weight. He lives in great retirement,— I fear almost in poverty. To him, London and its mighty maze of society are nothing; neither he nor his writings are known.— SUMNER, CHARLES, 1838, *To George S. Hillard, Dec. 4; Memoir and Letters of Sumner, ed. Pierce, vol.* II, *p. 22.*

Attended Carlyle's lecture, "The Hero as Prophet: Mahomet," on which he descanted with a fervour and eloquence that only a conviction of truth could give. I was charmed, carried away by him.— MACREADY, W. C., 1840, *Diary, May 8; Reminiscences, ed. Pollock, p. 488.*

We had fine fun with Carlyle, who talked broad Scotch, and utter nonsense without end. His nostrums respecting law reform did not go unscathed. His presumption, his dictatorial and positive manner, combined with his utter weakness, excited in my mind contempt. Yet this is a great star in these times of darkness.— ROEBUCK, JOHN ARTHUR, 1841, *To Mrs. Roebuck, April 9; Life and Letters, ed. Leader, p. 136.*

Carlyle's conversation and general views are curiously dyspeptic, his indigestion coloring everything. There was something particularly engaging in his reprobation of a heartless caricature of the execution of poor Louis XVI., which he desired us not to look at, but introduced a beautiful one of himself smoking in his tub, which John Sterling compares to one of Michael Angelo's prophets. He stood at the window with his pipe to help us draw a comparison. —FOX, CAROLINE, 1842, *Memories of Old Friends, ed. Pym; Journal, June* 6, *p. 179.*

Some one writes about "notes for a biography" in a beggarly "Spirit of the Age" or other rubbish basket—rejected *nem. con.* What have I to do with their "Spirits of the Age?" To have my "life" surveyed and commented on by all men even wisely is no object with me, but rather the opposite; but how much less to have it done *unwisely*! The world has no business with my life; the world will never know my life, if it should write and read a hundred biographies of me. The main facts of it even are known, and are likely to be known, to myself alone of created men. The "goose goodness" which they call "Fame!" *Ach Gott!*—CARLYLE, THOMAS, 1843, *Journal, Oct.* 10; *Thomas Carlyle, A History of His Life in London, ed. Froude, vol.* I, *p. 1.*

Accustomed to the infinite wit and exuberant richness of his writings, his talk is still an amazement and a splendor scarcely to be faced with steady eyes. He does not converse: only harangues. . . . Carlyle allows no one a chance, but bears down all opposition, not only by his wit and onset of words, resistless in their sharpness as so many bayonets, but by actual physical superiority—raising his voice, and rushing on his opponent with a torrent of sound. This is not in the least from unwillingness to allow freedom to others. On the contrary, no man would more enjoy a manly resistance to his thought. But it is the habit of a mind accustomed to follow out its own impulse, as the hawk its prey, and which knows not how to stop in the chase. Carlyle, indeed, is arrogant and over-bearing; but in his arrogance there is no littleness—no self-love. It is the heroic arrogance of some old Scandinavian conqueror, it is his nature and the untameable energy that has given him power to crush the dragons. You do not love him, perhaps, nor revere; and perhaps, also, he would only laugh at you if you did; but you like him heartily, and like to see him the powerful smith, the Siegfried, melting all the old iron in his furnace till it glows to a sunset red, and burns you, if you senselessly go too near. He seems, to me, quite isolated,—lonely as the desert,—yet never was a man more fitted to prize a man, could he find one to match his mood. He finds them, but only in the past. He sings rather than talks. He pours upon you a kind of satirical, heroical, critical poem, with regular cadences, and generally, near the beginning, hits upon some singular epithet, which serves as a *refrain* when his song is full, or with which, as with a knitting needle, he catches up the stitches, if he has chanced, now and then, to let fall a row. For the higher kind of poetry he has no sense, and his talk on that subject is delightfully and gorgeously absurd. He sometimes stops a minute to laugh at it himself, then begins anew with fresh vigour.—OSSOLI, MARGARET FULLER, 1846, *Letters from Paris, Dec.; Memoirs*, vol. II, p. 188.

Carlyle seems in better health than usual and talks away lustily, and there is always something to take one's attention in his talk, and often a sort of charm in it; but less instructive talk I never listened to from any man who had read and attempted to think. His opinions are the most groundless and senseless opinions that it is possible to utter; or rather they are not opinions, for he will utter the most opposite and contradictory and incompatible opinions in the most dogmatic and violent language in the course of half an hour. The real truth is that they are not opinions, but "shams." And I think it is the great desire to have opinions and the incapacity to form them which keeps his mind in a constant struggle and gives it over to every kind of extravagance. It is wonderful that a man of no opinions should exercise such an influence in the world as he appears to do; but I suppose it is an influence of concussion and subversion rather than any other.—TAYLOR, SIR HENRY, 1848, *To his Wife, Sept. 19; Correspondence*, ed. Dowden, p. 184.

Thomas Carlyle is really a notable monster, and to be respected for the many noble thoughts he has elaborated and for the words of wisdom which he has flung abroad to bear divine fruit among foolish-hearted men; but I can't help thinking, face to face in a small parlour he is rather terrible, and I fancy prophets are best exhibited in the pulpit or in the wilderness. —BLACKIE, JOHN STUART, 1848, *Letter to Miss Augusta Wyld; John Stuart Blackie, A Biography*, ed. Stoddart, vol. I, p. 241.

What shall I say of Carlyle? Perhaps it will be childish to say anything of *him* after no more acquaintance than an hour's conversation. Of my impressions accept a few words. I confess to being very much pleased and a little disappointed. Pleased that the appearance of the man was so much more *loveable*, and disappointed that it was rather less *great* than I had expected. I was prepared for a face, manner and expression less tender but more profound. Not in the vulgar sense of mystic alchemical fakir profundity, I don't mean that. If there be any truth in his theory of "Wudtan"—if there be divinity in *movement*—then is Carlyle divine. Body, hands, eyes, lips, eyebrows—almost cheeks, for even they seem mutable—did you ever see such a personification of motion? I felt, in seeing and hearing, that I could love the man as few men can be loved; but I went away hoping and trusting less—though I never trusted much—in *the sage*. We had a long talk (he was very kind to me), and if I had been blindfolded and heard it in the street I could have sworn at once to the speaker. But it made me melancholy to see how hopeless—no affectation of despair, but heartfelt black hopelessness—he is of himself and all mankind.—DOBELL, SYDNEY, 1849, *To Rev. George Gilfillan, Dec. 12; Life and Letters of Dobell*, ed. Jolly, vol. I, p. 112.

Here, also, I became acquainted with Thomas Carlyle, one of the kindest and best, as well as most eloquent of men; though in his zeal for what is best he sometimes thinks it incumbent on him to take not the kindest tone, and in his eloquent demands of some hearty uncompromising creed on our parts, he does not quite set the example of telling us the amount of his own. Mr. Carlyle sees that there is a good deal of rough work in the operations of nature: he seems to think himself bound to consider a good deal of it devilish, after the old Covenanter fashion, in order that he may find something angelical in giving it the proper quantity of vituperation and blows; and he calls upon us to prove our energies and our benevolence by acting the part of the wind rather than the sun, of warring rather than peace-making, of frightening and forcing rather than conciliating and persuading. . . . I believe that what Mr. Carlyle loves better than his fault-finding, with all its eloquence, is the face of any human creature that looks suffering, and loving, and sincere; and I believe further, that if the fellow-creature were suffering only, and neither loving nor sincere, but had come to a pass of agony in this life, which put him at the mercies of some good man for some last help and consolation toward his grave, even at the risk of loss to repute, and a sure amount of pain and vexation, that man, if the groan reached him in its forlornness, would be Thomas Carlyle.—HUNT, LEIGH, 1850, *Autobiography*, ed. Ingpen, vol. II, pp. 209, 211.

Are you aware that Carlyle traveled with us to Paris? He left a deep impression with me. It is difficult to conceive of a more interesting human soul, I think. All the bitterness is love with the point reversed. He seems to me to have a profound sensibility—so profound and turbulent that it unsettles his general sympathies.—BROWNING, ELIZABETH BARRETT, 1851, *To Mrs. Jameson*, Oct. 21; *Letters*, ed. Kenyon, vol. II, p. 25.

Carlyle dresses so badly, and wears such a rough outside, that the flunkies are rude to him at gentlemen's doors.—HAWTHORNE, NATHANIEL, 1855, *English Note-Books*, vol. I, p. 241.

I have seen Carlyle's face under all aspects, from the deepest gloom to the most reckless or most genial mirth; and it seemed to me that each mood would make a totally different portrait. The sympathetic is by far the finest, in my eyes. His excess of sympathy has been, I believe, **the master-pain of his life**. He does not know what to do with it, and with its bitterness, seeing that human life is full of pain to those who look out for it: and the savageness which has come to be a main characteristic of this singular man is, in my opinion, a mere expression of his intolerable sympathy with the suffering. He cannot express his love and pity in natural acts, like other people; and it shows itself too often in unnatural speech. But to those who understand his eyes, his shy manner, his changing colour, his sigh, and the constitutional *pudeur* which renders him silent about everything that he feels the most deeply, his wild speech and abrupt manner are perfectly intelligible. . . . Yellow as a guinea, with downcast eyes, broken speech at the beginning, and fingers which nervously picked at the desk before him, he could not for a moment be supposed to enjoy his own effort; and the lecturer's own enjoyment is a prime element of success. The merits of Carlyle's discourses were however so great that he might probably have gone on year after year till this time, with improving success, and perhaps ease: but the struggle was too severe. From the time that his course was announced till it was finished, he scarcely slept, and he grew more dyspeptic and nervous every day; and we were at length entreated to say no more about his lecturing, as no fame and no money or other advantage could counterbalance the misery which the engagement caused him.— MARTINEAU, HARRIET, 1855–77, *Autobiography*, ed. Chapman, vol. I, pp. 287, 289.

Something was said of Carlyle the author. Thackeray said "Carlyle hates everybody that has arrived—if they are on the road, he may perhaps treat them civilly." Mackintosh praised the description in the "French Revolution" of the flight of the King and Queen (which is certainly one of the most living pictures ever painted with ink), and Thackeray agreed with him, and spoke of the passages very heartily.—MOTLEY, JOHN LOTHROP, 1858, *To his Wife*, May 28; *Correspondence*, ed. Curtis, vol. I, p. 229.

He is a Samuel Johnson, a Coleridge, and a Teufelsdröckh, in one. It is curious to listen to the strong prejudice, mixed with the lofty and noble thoughts, clothed in that weird and grotesque phrase of his, fall from his lips in high-pitched Scotch patois, full of intense energy and power.—SMILES, SAMUEL, 1860, *Brief Biographies*, p. 282.

Of Mr. Carlyle's conversation I cannot call up a more accurate idea than by describing his talk as of the same character as his writings. Always forcible, often quaint and peculiar; felicitous in his occasional touches of fancy; not unfrequently sarcastic.—KNIGHT, CHARLES, 1863, *Passages from a Working Life During half a Century*, p. 446.

In a few minutes after the doors were opened, [at Rectorial Address] the large hall was filled in every part; and when up the central passage the Principal, the Lord Rector, the Members of the Senate, and other gentlemen advanced towards the platform, the cheering was vociferous and hearty. The Principal occupied the chair, of course; the Lord Rector on his right, the Lord Provost on his left. When the platform gentlemen had taken their seats, every eye was fixed on the Rector. To all appearance, as he sat, time and labour had dealt tenderly with him. His face had not yet lost the country bronze which he brought up with him from Dumfriesshire as a student, fifty-six years ago. His long residence in London had not touched his Annandale look, nor had it—as we soon learned—touched his Annandale accent. His countenance was striking, homely, sincere, truthful—the countenance of a man on whom "the burden of the unintelligible world" had weighed more heavily than on most. His hair was yet almost dark; his mustache and short beard were iron-grey. His eyes were wide, melancholy, sorrowful; and seemed as if they had been at times a-weary of the sun. Altogether, in his aspect there was something aboriginal, as of a piece of unhewn granite, which had never been polished to any approved pattern, whose natural and original vitality had never been tampered with. In a word, there seemed no passivity about Mr. Carlyle; he was the diamond, and the world was his pane of glass; he was a graving tool, rather than a thing graven upon—a man to set his mark on the world—a man on whom the world could not set its mark. . . . Amid a tempest of cheering and hats enthusiastically waved, Mr. Carlyle, slipping off his Rectorial robe—which must have been a very shirt of Nessus to him—advanced to the table, and began to speak in low, wavering, melancholy tones, which were in accordance with the melancholy eyes, and in the Annandale accent with which his playfellows must have been familiar long ago. So self-centered was he, so impregnable to outward influences, that all his years of Edinburgh and London life could not impair, even in the slightest degree, that.—SMITH, ALEXANDER, 1866, *Sketches and Criticisms*, pp. 117, 119.

A strong-faced and strange weird-looking man of seventy-seven summers, who, notwithstanding he had passed by so many years the Psalmist's threescore and ten, still carried his medium-sized and well-knit figure erect. His face was dark, ruddy, and wrinkled, with bold brows and wonderfully bright blue eyes. I needed no one to tell me that I stood in the presence of Thomas Carlyle, certainly one of the most celebrated and original writers of the nineteenth century.—WILSON, JAMES GRANT, 1874, *Thomas Carlyle, Harper's Magazine*, vol. 48, p. 726.

I have no doubt he would have played a Brave Man's Part if called on; but, meanwhile, he has only sat pretty comfortably at Chelsea, scolding all the world for not being Heroic, and not always very precise in telling them how. He has, however, been so far heroic, as to be always independent, whether of Wealth, Rank, and Coteries of all sorts: nay, apt to fly in the face of some who courted him. I suppose he is changed, or subdued, at eighty: but up to the last ten years he seemed to me just the same as when I first knew him five and thirty years ago. What a Fortune he might have made by showing himself about as a Lecturer, as Thackeray and Dickens did; I don't mean they did it for Vanity: but to make money: and that spend generously. Carlyle did indeed lecture near forty years ago before he was a Lion to be shown, and when he had but few readers. I heard his "Heroes" which now seems to me one of his best Books. He looked very handsome then, with his black hair, fine Eyes, and a sort of crucified Expression.—FITZGERALD, EDWARD, 1876, *To C. E. Norton, Jan. 23; Letters*, ed. Wright, vol. I, p. 378.

A residence of more than forty years in London has not modified the strong Scottish enunciation which Carlyle brought with him from his native Dumfriesshire. The vowels come out broad and full; the gutturals—which are so sadly clipped in modern English speech, depriving it of all masculine vigor—have their due prominence. His manner in talking is striking and peculiar; now bursting into Titanic laughter at some odd conceit; now swelling into fierce wrath at some meanness or wrong; now sinking into low tones of the tenderest pathos; but running through all is a rhythmic flow, a sustained recitative, like that in which we may imagine old Homer to have chanted his long-resounding hexameters.—GUERNSEY, ALFRED H., 1879, *Thomas Carlyle: His Life -His Books-His Theories*, p. 20.

Those who have listened to the wonderful conversation of Carlyle know well its impressiveness and its charm: the sympathetic voice now softening to the very gentlest, tenderest tone as it searched far into some sad life, little known or regarded, or perhaps evil spoken of, and found there traits to be admired, or signs of nobleness,—then rising through all melodies in rehearsing the deeds of heroes; anon breaking out with illumined thunders against some special baseness or falsehood, till one trembled before the Sinai smoke and flame, and seemed to hear the tables break once more in his heart: all these, accompanied by the mounting, fading fires in his cheeks, the light of the eye, now serene as heaven's blue, now flashing with wrath, or presently suffused with laughter, made the outer symbols of a genius so unique that to me it had been unimaginable had I not known its presence and power. His conversation was a spell; when I had listened and gone into the darkness, the enchantment continued; sometimes I could not sleep till the vivid thoughts and narratives were noted in writing.—CONWAY, MONCURE DANIEL, 1881, *Thomas Carlyle*, p. 14.

It is not easy, it is not possible, to say the last word about Mr. Carlyle. Posterity will regard him with deep sympathy and reverence, as one of the greatest of literary forces; thwarted, like Byron, by self-will; torn, like Swift, by *sæva indignatio*; and all his life vexed, almost physically, by a fierce hunger and thirst after righteousness.—LANG, ANDREW, 1881, *Mr. Carlyle's Reminiscences, Fraser's Magazine*, vol. 103, p. 528.

Think of the simplicity and frugality of his life, the nobility of his heart, the sublimity of his purposes. I have known many good and great men. I have never known one so strong and straight, so sturdy and striking as Thomas Carlyle—strong and straight like a pyramid, a mystery to the common crowd of travellers, and certainly not to be measured in its width and breadth, in its height and depth, by the small pocket-rule of "common sense."—MÜLLER, FRIEDRICH MAX, 1881, *Letter, Life and Letters*, ed. his Wife, vol. II, p. 104.

Although in common with many others, I believe that the literary pretensions of Carlyle have been vastly overstated, and that as a thinker and philosopher he possessed no such spiritual method as is likely to make his influence either precious or permanent, I would gladly, at this juncture, think of nothing less pleasant than his rugged yet charming personality.—BUCHANAN, ROBERT, 1881, *Wylie's Life of Carlyle, The Contemporary Review*, vol. 39, p. 793.

He was constantly intolerant of those who differed from him; never by any chance imagining the possibility that they might be right and he wrong. Always proclaiming in his books the infinite virtues of patience and silence, he made no attempt whatever to practise as he preached. The least illness, the least personal inconvenience, such as getting his tea too weak or his coffee too cold, made him complain as if all the world had been going headlong to ruin, and he himself were the only righteous man left alive. His temper, which he was at no particular pains to curb, was harsh and violent. Altogether he was, as his mother well observed, "gey ill to live wi'."—NICOLL, HENRY J., 1882, *Landmarks of English Literature*, p. 425.

In the grave matters of the law he walked for eighty-five years unblemished by a single moral spot. There are no "sins of youth" to be apologised for. In no instance did he ever deviate even for a moment from the strictest lines of integrity. He had his own way to make in life, and when he had chosen his profession, he had to depend on popularity for the bread which he was to eat. But although more than once he was within sight of starvation he would never do less than his very best. He never wrote an idle word, he never wrote or spoke any single sentence which he did not with his whole heart believe to be true. Conscious though he was that he had talents above those of common men, he sought neither rank nor fortune for himself. When he became famous and moved as an equal among the best of the land, he was content to earn the wages of an artisan, and kept to the simple habits in which he had been bred in his father's house. He might have had a pension had he stooped to ask for it; but he chose to maintain himself by his own industry, and when a pension was offered him it was declined. He despised luxury; he was thrifty and even severe in the economy of his own household; but in the times of his greatest poverty he had always something to spare for those who were dear to him. When money came at last, and it came only when he was old and infirm, he added nothing to his own comforts, but was lavishly generous with it to others. Tenderhearted and affectionate he was beyond all men whom I have ever known. His faults, which in his late remorse he exaggerated, as men of noblest natures are most apt to do, his impatience, his irritability, his singular melancholy, which made him at times distressing as a companion, were the effects of temperament first, and of a peculiarly sensitive organisation; and secondly of absorption in his work and of his determination to do that work as well as it could possibly be done. Such faults as these were but as the vapours which hang about a mountain, inseparable from the nature of the man. They have to be told because without them his character cannot be understood, and because they affected others as well as himself. But they do not blemish the essential greatness of his character, and when he is fully known he will not be loved or admired the less because he had infirmities like the rest of us.—FROUDE, JAMES ANTHONY, 1884, *Thomas Carlyle, A History of his Life in London*, vol. I, p. 4.

He was not constitutionally arrogant; he was a man of real modesty; he was even, I think, constitutionally diffident. He was a man, in short, whom you could summer and winter with, without ever having your self-respect wantonly affronted as it habitually is by mere conventional men and women. He was, to be sure, a very sturdy son of earth, and capable at times of exhibiting the most helpless natural infirmity. But he would never ignore nor slight your human fellowship because your life or opinions exposed you to the reproach of the vain, the frivolous, the self-seeking. He would of course curse your gods ever and anon in a manful way, and scoff without mercy at your tenderest intellectual hopes and aspirations; but upon yourself personally, all the while,—especially if you should drink strong tea and pass sleepless nights, or suffer from tobacco, or be menaced with insanity, or have a gnawing cancer under your jacket,—he would have bestowed the finest of his wheat. He might not easily have forgiven you if you used a vegetable diet, especially if you did so on principle; and he would surely have gnashed his teeth upon you if you should have claimed any scientific knowledge or philosophic insight into the social problem,—the problem of man's coming destiny upon the earth. But within these limits you would have felt how truly human was the tie that bound you to this roaring, riotous, most benighted, yet not unbenignant brother.—JAMES, HENRY, SR., 1884, *Some Personal Recollections of Carlyle, Literary Remains*, ed. James, pp. 430, 439.

From personal intercourse, extending over many years, we, in common with all who came into close contact with him, know that Carlyle himself was truthful to the core; and, also, that he devoutly and reverently accepted the essential truths of the Christian religion. True, that, in earlier student days, unduly influenced, as he himself admitted, by his boundless admiration for Goethe, he had wavered somewhat in regard to certain outward matters of form; but, though still admiring the great German poet, he soon lived through that phase, and, looking back, wrote those verses comparing himself to a moth that had singed its wings by fluttering too near the candle-flame. The root belief in saving truth, to which he firmly clung down to the end of his days, was substantially that which his godly mother had taught him. Her strong faith was also his, though rarely, and then somewhat enigmatically, formulated by him. As he himself repeatedly and emphatically told us, he held fast by the grand old Bible truths, revealed from heaven, as the only eternal and veritable realities on which a man could safely lean with all his weight. In regard to Carlyle's religious belief, Mr. Froude did not, and, unfortunately, from different upbringing, could not, understand him.... One of the greatest thinkers and teachers of the century, Carlyle's heart was pure, loving, tender, and true; and, even had certain opinions, peculiar, personal traits, or eccentricities of temperament—which, in some form or other, would seem to be inseparable from great originality of mind —actually been the very grave faults which his traducers mistakenly try to make them, these, calmly viewed in the light of his great veracity and sterling virtues, can only be regarded as spots on the sun.—SYMINGTON, ANDREW JAMES, 1885, *Some Personal Reminiscences of Carlyle*, pp. 10, 19.

No one who knew Carlyle but must have noticed how instantaneously he was affected or even agitated by any case of difficulty or distress in which he was consulted or that was casually brought to his cognisance, and with what restless curiosity and exactitude he would inquire into all the particulars, till he had conceived the case thoroughly, and as it were, taken the whole pain of it into himself. The practical procedure, if any was possible, was sure to follow. If he could do a friendly act to any human being, it was sure to be done; if the case required exertion, or even continued and troublesome exertion, that was never wanting.... There were, I say, infinite depths of tenderness in this rugged man. Not even in the partner of his life whom he so bewailed and commemorated, woman though she was, and one of the most brilliant of her sex, and the most practically and assiduously benevolent, were there such depths and dissolutions of sheer tenderness as there were in him.—MASSON, DAVID, 1885, *Carlyle Personally and in his Writings*, pp. 39, 41.

His life, the prey of biographers and the stumbling-block of fools, had chiefly literary eventfulness.—SAINTSBURY, GEORGE, 1886, *Specimens of English Prose Style*, p. 354.

It is one of the regrets of my life that I never saw or heard Carlyle. Nature, who seems to be fond of trios, has given us three dogmatists, all of whom greatly interested their own generation, and whose personality, especially in the case of the first and last of the trio, still interests us,—Johnson, Coleridge, and Carlyle. Each was an oracle in his way, but unfortunately oracles are fallible to their descendants. ... Each oracle denies his predecessor, each magician breaks the wand of the one who went before him. There were Americans enough ready to swear by Carlyle until he broke his staff in meddling with our anti-slavery conflict, and buried it so many fathoms deep that it could never be fished out again. It is rather singular that Johnson and Carlyle should each of them have shipwrecked his sagacity and shown a terrible leak in his moral sensibilities on coming in contact with American rocks and currents, with which neither had any special occasion to concern himself, and which both had a great deal better have steared clear of. But here I stand once more before the home of the long-suffering, much-laboring, loud-complaining Heraclitus of his time, whose very smile had a grimness in it more ominous than his scowl. Poor man! Dyspeptic on a diet of oatmeal porridge; kept wide awake by crowing cocks; drummed out of his wits by long-continued piano-pounding; sharp of speech, I fear, to his high-strung wife, who gave him back as good as she got! I hope I am mistaken about their everyday relations, but again I say, poor man!— for all his complaining must have meant real discomfort, which a man of genius feels not less, certainly, than a common mortal.—HOLMES, OLIVER WENDELL, 1887-91, *Our Hundred Days in Europe*, pp. 138, 139.

We found Mr. Carlyle at home [1852]. ... We were shown into a comfortable room on the ground floor, which I suppose must have been the dining-room, and presently we heard Mr. Carlyle descending from the upper regions. He gave us a cordial welcome, and sat down at a little distance on a rather straightbacked chair. ... I remember the strong impression made on my mind by the interview was that Mr. Carlyle's conversation was very like his books, and much of it as good as almost anything I had ever read in them. The new impression derived from the slight personal intercourse was of his real kindness of heart, the deep latent sympathy of his nature. There was a peculiar gentleness in his tone, an accent of deep and sincere feeling in his voice, in speaking of Sir W. Hamilton, and especially in referring to his crippled condition arising from the serious stroke of paralysis that had partially disabled him a few years before.—BAYNES, THOMAS S., 1887, *An Evening with Carlyle, The Athenæum, April 2,* pp. 449, 450.

Doctor Pessimist Anticant, in Anthony Trollope's novel "Warden," is intended for Thomas Carlyle.—FREY, ALBERT R., 1888, *Sobriquets and Nicknames,* p. 91.

In Switzerland I live in the immediate presence of a mountain, noble alike in form and mass. A bucket or two of water, whipped into a cloud, can obscure, if not efface that lordly peak. You would almost say that no peak could be there. But the cloud passes away, and the mountain, in its solid grandeur, remains. Thus, when all temporary dust is laid, will stand out, erect and clear, the massive figure of Carlyle.—TYNDALL, JOHN, 1890, *Personal Recollections of Thomas Carlyle, New Fragments,* p. 397.

How well Kingsley understood the chief characteristics of Carlyle is evident from the life-drawing he gives of him in the person of Sandy Mackaye, though, strangely enough, Carlyle failed to recognize himself in this portrait.—KAUFMANN, MORITZ, 1892, *Charles Kingsley Socialist and Social Reformer,* p. 176.

It has been a personal pain to me in recent times to find among honourable and cultivated people a conviction that Carlyle was hard, selfish, and arrogant. I knew him intimately for more than an entire generation—as intimately as one who was twenty years his junior, and who regarded him with unaffected reverence as the man of most undoubted genius of his age, probably ever did. I saw him in all moods and under the most varied conditions, and often tried his impatient spirit by dissent from his cherished convictions, and I found him habitually serene and considerate, never, as so many have come to believe of his ordinary mood, arrogant or impatient of contradiction. I was engaged for nearly half the period in the conflict of Irish politics, which from his published writings one might suppose to be utterly intolerable to him; but the readers of these letters will find him taking a keen interest in every honest attempt to raise Ireland from her misery, reading constantly, and having sent after him, wherever he went, the journal which embodied the most determined resistance to misgovernment from Westminister, and throwing out friendly suggestions from time to time how the work, so far as he approved of it, might be more effectually done. This is the real Carlyle; a man of generous nature, sometimes disturbed on the surface by trifling troubles, but never diverted at heart from what he believed to be right and true.—DUFFY, SIR CHARLES GAVAN, 1892, *Conversations with Carlyle,* p. 6.

The opulent originality, vigour, and picturesqueness of Carlyle's talk astonished all who heard it. What he said might be wise, or only half-wise, or, as sometimes happened, wholly unwise, but it was always striking, never commonplace. It is true that both as a host and as a guest he was too fond of engrossing the conversation, that with him dialogue too often became monologue, that his prophet-like denunciations of the present, in season and out of season, were occasionally wearisome in their monotonous vehemence and iteration and reiteration long-drawn-out. But it was not always thus with him. In the society of two or three friends, if he could not help being emphatic, he could be calm, and reasonable, take as well as give, and listen patiently to the expression of opinions opposite to his own. It was in such a gathering that he was most satisfactory, if not most astonishing. There was, moreover, one gift, that of oral narration, which he possessed in a more remarkable degree than any man of his generation, and his exhibition of it was always acceptable, combining as it did epic detail with lyrical emotion. I have heard of a distinguished company at a dinner-party suspending, at an early stage of the meal, the process of deglutition, to listen with rapt attention while Carlyle, starting from some chance remark by a fellow guest, gave a vivid account of John Sobieski's defence of Vienna against the Turk. Never surely was there an eminent man of letters—not Macaulay himself, for even he had brilliant flashes of silence—to whom, as to this Apostle of Silence, seemed in so great a degree a necessity of his nature to be always either speaking or writing.—ESPINASSE, FRANCIS, 1893, *Literary Recollections and Sketches,* p. 204.

I believe that what Mr. Carlyle absolutely needed above all things on earth was somebody to put on the gloves with him metaphorically about once a day, and give and take a few thumping blows; nor do I believe that he would have shrunk from a tussle à la Choctaw, with biting, gouging, tomahawk and scalper, for he had an uncommonly *dour* look about the eyes, and must have been a magnificent fighter when once roused. — LELAND, CHARLES GODFREY, 1893, *Memoirs*, p. 432.

I never shared the admiration felt for him by so many able men who knew him personally, and therefore had means which I did not possess of estimating him aright. To me his books and himself represented an anomalous sort of human fruit. The original stock was a hard and thorny Scotch peasant-character, with a splendid intellect superadded. The graft was not wholly successful. A flavor of the old acrid sloe was always perceptible in the plum.—COBBE, FRANCES POWER, 1894, *Life by Herself*, vol. II, p. 482.

The greatest Englishman of letters of this century found it indispensable for his contentment to belittle almost every man of real importance whom he met.—DAVIDSON, JOHN, 1895, *Sentences and Paragraphs*, pp. 88, 91.

In a somewhat shabbily furnished room, (but on the walls there was a large copy of the Berlin picture of Frederick the Great dressed as a drummer-boy; and on the table a number of Frederick's snuff-boxes were strewn about) in a dingy little street in Chelsea, an old man, worn, and tired, and bent, with deeply lined, ascetic features, a firm underjaw, tufted grey hair, and tufted grey and white beard, and sunken and unutterably sorrowful eyes, returned from the fireplace, where with trembling fingers he had been lighting his long clay pipe, and resumed his place in front of the reading-desk. . . . Now, in endeavoring to place on paper, a few of Carlyle's *obiter dicta*, it is impossible to convey to the reader how immeasurably they lose in the process. Carlyle did not talk Scotch—not any dialect of it; but he spoke with a strong South-of-Scotland insistence of emphasis; then he had a fine abundance of picturesque phraseology; and, above all, he liked to wind up a sentence with something—a wild exaggeration, it might be, or a sardonic paradox, or a scornful taunt—but, anyhow, with something that sounded like the crack of a whip.—BLACK, WILLIAM, 1896, *Recollections of Carlyle's Talk, Good Words*, vol. 38.

Mr. Bancroft had given me a letter to Carlyle [1869], and we diligently drove to Cheyne Walk; but the sage was out walking. I think he always was, when Americans called.—SHERWOOD, MARY E. W., 1897, *An Epistle to Posterity*, p. 153.

Whenever a chance offered itself, we called on the Carlyles. My father would say, "Mr. and Mrs. Carlyle on the whole enjoy life together, else they would not have chaffed one another so heartily." Carlyle made a point of not unfrequently paying his respects to my mother, who he knew could not go to see him; and the last time he called my nephew, "golden-haired Ally," was brought in to the great man. Carlyle put his hands on the little fellow's head and said solemnly, "Fair fall thee, little man, in this world, and the next." Upon which my father said to me: "Carlyle is the most reverent and most irreverent man I know."—TENNYSON, HALLAM, 1897, *Alfred Lord Tennyson, A Memoir by his Son*, vol. II, p. 233.

Much has been made of his brusque manner. Truth is, he could not bear inanity or even the semblance of it. Yet he was tolerant in a high degree to honest worth. Emerson observed that "Carlyle worshipped a man that manifested any truth in him." To hold his attention one had to be thorough. He rushed at the stranger mind, and sometimes, too, by a byway, probing deeply, and all the time with flashing eyes—these small, pupiled orbs, that, although dreamy-looking in repose, seemed, in his eager questioning attitudes, to leave their places and dart meteor-like towards yours. I will ever see those eyes on their way to mine during our first tussling interview. The fancy is as strong as fact, and still felt to be as real as truth itself. I have seen him in many moods, and began to learn that his silence was at times a compliment to all about him. The silence of others, too, was a stern necessity of his supersensitive nature. Indeed, without quietude life to him was intolerable. His nature was the very antipodes of that of Gibbon, who managed to sit as a mute for eight sessions in the House of Commons! Nothing annoyed him more than noisy platitudes, no matter where or by whom they were echoed.— PATRICK, JOHN, 1898, *The Carlyles in Scotland, Century Magazine*, vol. 57, p. 323.

I did not see Carlyle until he was an old

man, after the death of his wife, living in retirement. A more dignified, courteous, and friendly senior it was impossible to imagine. He sate by his simple fireside, in the house in which he lived for forty-six years, and poured out "Latter-day Pamphlets" with great energy and strong Lowland accent. The effect was startling. He was exactly like all his portraits—the Whistler is the best both in art and in likeness—the words were strangely the same as he used in his fiercest hour, nay even exceeding this, for he wished that many people and things "might all be dawmed doun to hale"—so that it seemed an illusion, as if some wraith of Sartor had been summoned up to give a mocking presentation of the prophet. He said what he had often said, till it seemed to me as if he were repeating thoughts which were graven in his memory. His bonhommie, his fire, his friendly manners struck me deeply.—HARRISON, FREDERIC, 1901, *George Washington and Other American Addresses*, p. 201.

Thirty years afterward, in June, 1872, I felt an irrepressible desire to see the grand old man once more, and I accordingly addressed him a note requesting the favor of a few minutes' interview. . . . After we had waited some time, a feeble, stooping figure, attired in a long blue flannel gown, moved slowly into the room. His gray hair was unkempt, his blue eyes were still keen and piercing, and a bright hectic spot of red appeared on each of his hollow cheeks. His hands were tremulous, and his voice deep and husky. After a few personal inquiries the old man launched out into a most extraordinary and characteristic harangue on the wretched degeneracy of these evil days. The prophet, Jeremiah, was cheerfulness itself in comparison with him. . . . He amused us with a description of half a night's debate with John Bright on political economy, while he said, "Bright theed and thoud with me for hours, while his Quaker wife sat up hearin' us baith. I tell ye, John Bright got as gude an he gie that night;" and I have no doubt that he did. Most of his extraordinary harangue was like an eruption of Vesuvius, but the laugh he occasionally gave showed that he was talking about as much for his own amusement as for ours.—CUYLER, THEODORE L., 1902, *Recollections of a Long Life*.

JANE WELSH CARLYLE

And I sit here thinking, thinking,
How your life was one long winking
At Thomas' faults and failings, and his undue share of bile!
Won't you own, dear, just between us,
That this living with a genius
Isn't, after all, so pleasant,—is it, Jeannie Welsh Carlyle?
—CHANDLER, BESSIE, 1883, *To Mrs. Carlyle, Century Magazine*, vol. 27, p. 160.

Now we have him in his Jane's letters, as we have seen something of him before in the Reminiscences: but a yet more tragic Story; so tragic that I know not if it ought not to have been withheld from the Public: Assuredly, it seems to me, ought to have been but half of the whole that now is. But I do not the less recognize Carlyle far more admirable than before—if for no other reason than his thus furnishing the world with weapons against himself which the World in general is glad to turn against him.—FITZGERALD, EDWARD, 1883, *To C. E. Norton, May 12; Letters, ed. Wright*, vol. I, p. 494.

I suppose you have read by this time Mrs. Carlyle's "Correspondence." A very painful book in more ways than one. There are disclosures there that never should have been made, as if they had been caught up from the babblings of discharged housemaids. One blushes in reading, and feels like a person caught listening at the keyhole.—LOWELL, JAMES RUSSELL, 1883, *To C. E. Norton, April 22; Letters, ed. Norton*, vol. II, p. 273.

Had she even shared to the full, the literary interests of the man of genius whose overwhelming personality left her so lonely, she would doubtless have entered the lists as a brilliant and successful authoress. But her share seemed, for the most part, limited to the listening to Carlyle's tremendous denunciations of all people, things, and systems, since the creation of the world. On her sofa she lay, night after night, exhausted, with nerves "all shattered to pieces," and gave her word of sympathy when she could. To the casual visitor these fierce and powerful monologues of Carlyle's were fascinating—to her, they must have been almost intolerable at times. Had she been placed in a congenial companionship, with a man many degrees less intellectual than Thomas Carlyle—a man with whom the deeper sympathies of a woman's heart had met full response—we cannot doubt that the world would have known Jane Welsh Carlyle as a writer. But that career was closed to her, and all connected with literature seemed interwoven with the loneliness and disappointment of her own lot.—IRELAND, ANNIE E., 1891, *Life of Jane Welsh Carlyle*, p. 307.

Mr. Froude has been severely censured as painting in too dark colors Carlyle's grim, savage humour, his thoughtless cruelty to his wife, and her unhappiness; but the documentary evidence he has presented fully justifies him. Mrs. Carlyle said herself, not long before her death: "I married for ambition. Carlyle has exceeded all that my wildest hopes ever imagined of him; and I am miserable." Her husband, indeed, appreciated her talents and found pleasure in her society but he never seems to have experienced for her the passion of love as it is commonly understood. The pair had no children, and, as Mr. Froude tells us, when Carlyle was busy his wife rarely so much as saw him save when she would steal into his dressing-room in the morning while he was shaving. . . . Whether Mrs. Carlyle would have been happier with Irving for a husband instead of Carlyle is doubtful. That Irving would have been to her most tender, loving and considerate, his treatment of the woman he married, not from love, but from a sense of duty, compels us to believe; but whether his failure in his career, and the want of that gratification of her pride and satisfaction of her ambition which she got with Carlyle, would not have been as sore a trial to her as Carlyle's harshness is not so sure.—HITCHCOCK, THOMAS, 1891, *Unhappy Loves of Men of Genius*, pp. 209, 211.

Mrs. Carlyle did not, like her husband, write books, but in her own way she was, to use a favourite expression of his, as "articulate" as her husband. She was too bright and clever a talker not to enjoy practising her gift. Naturally she shone more in conversation when her husband was absent than when he was present. Sometimes, when the company in the little house at Chelsea was miscellaneous, the claims of the hostess to be heard conflicted with those of the host, and there was between her and one or other of their guests a cross-fire of conversation which sadly irritated Carlyle. It was better, at least if they were at home, when they talked successively rather than simultaneously, but her husband did not always allow her that alternative. She once repeated to me, with quiet glee, a remark dropped by Samuel Rogers at one of his breakfast parties, at which Carlyle and she were among the guests. When Carlyle's thunder had been followed by his wife's sparkle, their sardonic host said in a half-soliloquy which was intended to be audible: "As soon as that man's tongue stops, that woman's begins."—ESPINASSE, FRANCIS, 1893, *Literary Recollections and Sketches*, p. 205.

I do not want to speak disrespectfully of poor Carlyle; but in spirit it is somewhat hard to keep one's hand off him, as we reconstitute those scenes in the gaunt house at Craigenputtock. There is a little detail in one scene which adds a deeper horror. I have said that Mrs. Carlyle had to scrub the floors; and as she scrubbed them, Carlyle would look on smoking,—drawing in from tobacco pleasant comfortableness and easy dreams—while his poor drudge panted and sighed over the hard work, which she had never done before. Do you not feel that you would like to break the pipe in his mouth, to shake him off his chair, and pitch him on to the floor, to take a share of the physical burden which his shoulders were so much better able to bear?—O'CONNOR, T. P., 1895, *Some Old Love Stories*, p. 290.

The most important event in his life took place in 1826, when he married Miss Jane Welsh, a young lady who traced her descent to John Knox, who had some property, who had a genius of her own, and who was also the more determined to marry a man of genius. She had hesitated between Irving and Carlyle, and whatever came of it, there can be no doubt that she was right in preferring the somewhat uncouth and extremely undeveloped tutor who had taught her several things,— whether love in the proper sense was among them or not will always be a moot point. . . . It is certain that Carlyle— springing from the lower ranks of society, educated excellently as far as the intellect was concerned, but without attention to such trifles as the habit (which his future wife early remarked in him) of putting bread and butter in his tea, a martyr from very early years to dyspepsia, fostering a retiring spirit and not too social temper, thoroughly convinced that the times were out of joint and not at all thoroughly convinced that he or any one could set them right, finally possessed of an intensely religious nature which by accident or waywardness had somehow thrown itself out of gear with religion—was not a happy man himself or likely to make any one else happy who lived with him. But it is certain also that both in respect to his wife and to those men, famous or not famous, of whom he has left too often unkindly record, his bark was much worse than his bite. And it is further certain that Mrs. Carlyle was no down-trodden drudge, but a woman of brains almost as alert as her husband's and a tongue almost as sharp as his, who had deliberately made her election of the vocation of being "wife to a man of genius," and who received what she had bargained for to the uttermost farthing.—SAINTSBURY, GEORGE, 1896, *A History of Nineteenth Century Literature*, pp. 233, 235.

ESSAY ON BURNS
1828

It is one of the very best of his essays, and was composed with an evidently peculiar interest, because the outward circumstances of Burns's life, his origin, his early surroundings, his situation as a man of genius born in a farmhouse not many miles distant, among the same people and the same associations as were so familiar to himself, could not fail to make him think often of himself while he was writing about his countryman.—FROUDE, JAMES ANTHONY, 1882, *Thomas Carlyle; A History of the First Forty Years of his Life*, vol. II, p. 25.

Worth all that every one else has ever said about Burns put together.—MOULTON, LOUISE CHANDLER, 1885, *Carlyle: His Works and his Wife, Some Noted Princes, Authors and Statesmen of Our Time*, ed. Parton, p. 186.

The essay on Burns is the very voice of Scotland, expressive of all her passionate love and tragic sorrow for her darling son. It has paragraphs of massy gold, capable of being beaten out into volumes, as indeed they have been. Unlike some of Carlyle's essays, it is by no means open to the charge of mysticism, but is distinguished by the soundest good sense.—GARNETT, RICHARD, 1887, *Thomas Carlyle (Great Writers)*, p. 48.

Let no student come to the reading of this little book with the purpose merely of finding certain facts in the life of the poet; for while the facts are there, they are incidental and subsidiary to the revelation of the mind and soul of the poet. To know the mind and soul of the poet,—that should be the aim of the student. Reading thus, Carlyle will be found to be the revealer of

"The light that never was, on sea nor land;
The consecration and the Poet's dream."

And surely that should redeem the reader from slavery to a mere literary task,—a compelled service performed in slave-like fashion. It should, it must, suffuse his heart with the glow of sympathy. In such a frame, he will find Carlyle to be an *inspirer*, breathing into his soul many a sweet and pure suggestion, many a strong and purposeful sentiment; so helping him, as high literature ever should, to make his own life and action more noble.—WICKES, W. K., 1896, ed. *Thomas Carlyle's Essay on Robert Burns*, Preface, p. 3.

His first, and perhaps greatest, critical work was upon a brother Scot—Burns. By him Burns received his first sympathetic interpretation.—GEORGE, ANDREW J., 1898, *From Chaucer to Arnold, Types of Literary Art*, p. 654, *note*.

SARTOR RESARTUS
1834

The only thing about the work, tending to prove that it is what it purports to be, a commentary on a real German treatise, which is a sort of Babylonish dialect, not destitute, it is true, of richness, vigor, and at times a sort of singular felicity of expression, but very strongly tinged throughout with the peculiar idiom of the German language. This quality in the style, however, may be a mere result of a great familiarity with German literature, and we cannot, therefore, look upon it as in itself decisive, still less as outweighing so much evidence of an opposite character. . . . The work before us is a sort of philosophical romance in which the author undertakes to give, in the form of a review of a German treatise on dress, and a notice of the life of the writer, his own opinions upon Matters and Things in General. The hero, Professor Teufelsdröckh, seems to be intended for a portrait of human nature as affected by the moral influences to which, in the present state of society, a cultivated mind is naturally exposed. . . . Contains, under a quaint and singular form, a great deal of deep thought, sound principle, and fine writing. It is, we believe, no secret in England or here, that it is the work of a person to whom the public is indebted for a number of articles in the late British Reviews, which have attracted great attention by the singularity of their style, and the richness and depth of their matter. Among these may be mentioned particularly those on "Characteristics" and the "Life of Burns" in the Edinburgh Review, and on "Goethe" in the Foreign Quarterly. . . . We take pleasure in introducing to the American Public a writer, whose name is yet in a great measure unknown among us, but who is destined, we think, to occupy a large space in the literary world. We have heard it intimated, that Mr. Carlyle has it in contemplation to visit this country, and we can venture to assure him, that, should he carry his intention into effect, he will meet with a cordial welcome.— EVERETT, ALEXANDER H., 1835, *Thomas Carlyle, North American Review*, vol. 41, pp. 459, 481, 482.

This consists of two intertwisted threads, though both spun off the same distaff, and of the same crimson wool. There is a fragmentary, though, when closely examined, a complete biography of a supposed German professor, and, along with it, portions of a supposed treatise of his on the philosophy of clothes. Of the three books, the first is preparatory, and gives a portrait of the hero and his circumstances. The second is the biographical account of him. The third under the rubric of extracts from his work, presents us with his picture of human life in the nineteenth century. How so unexampled a topic as the philosophy of clothes can be made the vehicle for a philosophy of man, those will see who read the book. But they must read with the faith that, in spite of all appearances to the contrary, it is the jest which is a pretence, and that the real purport of the whole is serious, yea, serious as any religion that ever was preached, far more serious than most battles that have ever been fought since Agamemnon declared war against Priam. . . . In this book that strange style appears again before us in its highest oddity. Thunder peals, flute-music, the laugh of Pan and the nymphs, the clear disdainful whisper of cold stoicism, and the hurly-burly of a country fair, succeed and melt into each other. Again the clamour sinks into quiet, and we hear at last the grave, mild hymn of devotion, sounding from a far sanctuary, though only in faint and dying vibrations. So from high and low, from the sublime to the most merely trivial, fluctuates the feeling of the poet.— STERLING, JOHN, 1839, *Carlyle's Works, London and Westminster Review*, vol. 33, pp. 52, 53.

His soul is a shrine of the brightest and purest philanthropy, kindled by the live coal of gratitude and devotion to the Author of all things. I should observe that he is not orthodox.— ELIOT, GEORGE, 1841, *Letter, Dec. 16; Literary Anecdotes of the Nineteenth Century*, vol. II, p. 474.

We think "Sartor Resartus" the finest of Mr. Carlyle's works in conception, and as a whole. In execution he is always great; and for graphic vigour and quantity of suggestive thought, matchless: but the idea, in this book, of uncovering the world — taking off all the clothes— the cloaks and outsides — is admirable.— HORNE, RICHARD HENGIST, (ELIZABETH BARRETT BROWNING?), 1844, *A New Spirit of the Age*, p. 343.

"Sartor Resartus" appears to me to be at the same time the most profound and the most ·brilliant glance that has been thrown upon our century, upon its tendencies and its desires.— MONTÉGUT, ÉMILE, 1849, *Revue des Deux Mondes*, 6th S. vol. 2.

"Ah, Thomas Carlyle, you have much to answer for, in sending adrift upon the fog-banks such raw and inexperienced boys as I was when your mighty genius found me out. Many a day of miserable doubt and night of morbid wretchedness have you caused me. Yet, for all that, I owe you more and love you better than any author of the time. 'Sartor Resartus' first fell in my way while I was living in Washington, and I much question if Christopher Columbus was more transported by the discovery of America, than I was in entering the new realm which this book opened to me. Everything was novel, huge, grotesque or sublime: I must have read it twenty times over, until I had it all by heart. It became a sort of touchstone with me. If a man had read 'Sartor,' and enjoyed it, I was his friend; if not, we were strangers. I was as familiar with the everlasting 'nay,' the center of indifference, and the everlasting 'yea,' as with the sidewalk in front of my house. From Herr Teufelsdröckh I took the Teutonic fever, which came nigh costing me so dear." And happily the number is not few of those who can add, in the words of the same writer, "Years have passed since he lead me forth to the dance of ghosts, and I have learned to read him with a less feverish enthusiasm; but, I believe, with a more genuine appreciation of his rare and extraordinary powers. He did me harm, but he has helped me to far more good. With all his defects, to me he stands first among the men of this generation."—MILBURN, WILLIAM HENRY, 1859, *Ten Years of Preacher-Life.*

You may have the strongest conviction that you ought to like an author; you may be ashamed to confess that you don't like him; and yet you may feel that you detest him. For myself, I confess with shame, and I know the reason is in myself, I cannot for my life see anything to admire in the writings of Mr. Carlyle. His style, both of thought and language, is to me insufferably irritating. I tried to read "Sartor Resartus," and could not do it. So if all people who have learned to read English were like me, Mr. Carlyle would have no readers.—BOYD, ANDREW K. H., 1862, *Leisure Hours in Town*, p. 84.

When Carlyle's "Sartor Resartus" first appeared, as a serial in Fraser's Magazine, the publisher would have discontinued it, in despair, but for the letters of earnest appreciation received from two men, one of whom was Ralph Waldo Emerson. This was in 1835; and in 1870 the same work, in a cheap popular edition, reached a sale of 40,000 copies.—TAYLOR, BAYARD, 1879, *Studies in German Literature*, p. 395.

A work which, with all its affectations, obscurities (I do not hesitate to add, insincerities), has taken a strong hold on the imaginations of that large section of the public which does not go to the poets for its edification, but prefers the fashioners of "mystical" prose. . . . In "Sartor Resartus," the traces of literary conventionalism were kicked over altogether. The work might be called a wild hotchpotch of German mysticism, Lowland Scotch, broad caricature, and literal autobiography. In its long-windedness, in the zeal with which the one solitary idea, or "Clothes" theory, was worked to death, it was certainly very German. But with all its defects,—or rather perhaps, in consequence of its defects,—it was a work of genius.—BUCHANAN, ROBERT, 1881, *Wylie's Life of Carlyle, Contemporary Review*, vol. 39, pp. 797, 798.

Out of his discontent, out of his impatience with the hard circumstances which crossed, thwarted, and pressed him, there was growing in his mind "Sartor Resartus." He had thoughts fermenting in him struggling to be uttered. He had something real to say about the world, and man's position in it to which, could it but find fit expression, he knew that attention must be paid. The "Clothes Philosophy," which had perhaps been all which his first sketch contained, gave him the necessary form. His own history, inward and outward, furnished substance; some slight substance being all that was needed to disguise his literal individuality; and in the autumn of the year he set himself down passionately to work. Fast as he could throw his ideas upon paper the material grew upon him. The origin of the book is still traceable in the half fused, tumultuous condition in which the metal was poured into the mould. With all his efforts in calmer times to give it artistic harmony he could never fully succeed. "There are but a few pages in it," he said to me, "which are rightfully done." It is well perhaps that he did not succeed. The incompleteness of the smelting shows all the more the actual condition of his mind. If defective as a work of art, "Sartor" is for that very reason a revelation of Carlyle's individuality.—FROUDE, JAMES ANTHONY, 1882, *Thomas Carlyle: A History of the First Forty Years of His Life*, vol. II, p. 104.

The most stimulating *quasi*-philosophical book that I ever read is "Sartor Resartus." It came into my hands before I knew much about its author, and it made me greedy for several of his subsequent works, though, after the Carlylese dialect became current among the horde of imitative scioliosts, I ceased to enjoy it in its source. I must have imbibed and assimilated all that is best in "Sartor Resartus," for when I took it up anew a year or two ago, I found in it for the most part but the reflection of my own familiar thought and sentiment, and the very portions of it that I had most admired seemed to me, though true, trite and stale. This must be the fate of every book in advance of its time in the legitimate line of progress, and the surest test of the actual worth of the ethical and philosophical works that flashed fresh surprises on the last generation is that they now appear commonplace and superfluous, because their contents have become the property of the general mind.—PEABODY, ANDREW P., 1888, *Books that Have Helped Me*, p. 45.

I bought Carlyle's "Sartor Resartus," first edition, and read it through forty times ere I left college, of which I "kept count." — LELAND, CHARLES GODFREY, 1893, *Memoirs*, p. 77.

Is unquestionably the most original, the most characteristic, the deepest and most lyrical of his productions.—HARRISON, FREDERIC, 1895, *Studies in Early Victorian Literature*, p. 49.

A very large part of the book owes nothing at all to Swift. In the second portion, the story of Teufelsdröckh's life, his clothes philosophy sinks out of sight altogether; and such chapters as the fifth and eighth of the third book are too weighty and earnest to be really part and parcel of what was in the first instance a jest. The influence of Swift's thought is strongest in the first or original portion. The rest is really made up of Carlyle's own experience of life and his brooding over all problems that can engage the active brain, from the reality of the universe and the existence of God to the condition of the poor and the phenomenon of the man of fashion. The book is to be regarded as the epitome of all that Carlyle thought and felt in the course of the first thirty-five years of his residence on this planet. Many things which he wishes to say that cannot be ranged under any rubric of the philosophy of clothes, such as his criticism of duelling, are, notwithstanding, given room. This position I hope to make good.—MACMECHAN, ARCHIBALD, 1895, ed. *Sartor Resartus*, Introduction, p. xxi.

Nearly four fifths of the book, I should say, is chaff; but the other fifth is real wheat, if you are not choked in getting it. Yet I have just read the story of an educated tramp who carried the book in his blanket thousands of miles, and knew it nearly by heart.—BURROUGHS, JOHN, 1897, *On the Re-reading of Books, Century Magazine*, vol. 55, p. 148.

It is to "Sartor Resartus" we must turn for the fullest disclosure of Carlyle's religious history and beliefs. In that book, written among the solitudes of Craiggenputtock, we have a revelation of his own interior life, though to some extent veiled and symbolical. Herr Teufelsdröckh is the spiritual counterpart of Carlyle himself, and the work partakes of the nature of an autobiography. Through its pages we get a vivid insight into the mental struggles, heart sorrows, and soul-conflicts of an earnest and thoughtful man, groping his way through the thick darkness of scepticism out into the daylight of faith and liberty. Autobiographies are a species of literature in whose favour we are not much prepossessed, they are so often stilted and artificial, and so manifestly got up for effect. But no such suspicions can possibly attach to "Sartor," which is undoubtedly the product of a sincere and unaffected soul, and enjoys the reputation of being "one of the truest self-revelations ever penned."—WILSON, S. LAW, 1899, *The Theology of Modern Literature*, p. 158.

He knew that he had put into the book the best that was in him, and he knew its worth. His wife had said to him when she finished reading the last page, "It is a work of genius, dear." But neither of them knew the long and bitter struggle that must be gone through before the world would recognize its worth. What more pitiful than the thought of Carlyle, hawking about that masterpiece among the publishers, who would have none of it?—WARD, MAY ALDEN, 1900, *Prophets of the Nineteenth Century*, p. 49.

But "Sartor" is nothing if not a semi-prophetic book, as prophecy goes nowadays: it is in this aspect that it appeals to or repels us; it is its gleams and rifts of truth that focus the attention. For here also Carlyle is every way the reverse of equable and self-contained, moving by stormful and uncertain energies, with sudden swirling sunward rushes, whence he swerves with baffled and beating pinions to collect himself for another upward dart. His teaching, tempestuous and fitful, abounds in cloven profundities of gloom, and luminous interpaces of height. By these, in the main, we must gauge him. Nor must we attribute to him more than he claimed for himself, or deny his limitations.—THOMPSON, FRANCIS, 1901, *Sartor Re-read, The Academy*, vol. 61, p. 17.

Like Byron, Carlyle is in romantic revolt against convention; like Wordsworth and Shelley, though in a very different way than either, he seeks for some positive ideal upon which to construct a habitable moral world in place of the uninhabitable one he has striven to destroy. "Sartor Resartus," which is both destructive and constructive, is pre-eminent in doctrinal interest among all his books. It is also extremely ingenious in plan, and is written with a wonderful mingling of wild sardonic humor, keen pathos, and an eloquence and imaginative elevation almost biblical.—MOODY, WILLIAM VAUGHN, AND LOVETT, ROBERT MORSS, 1902, *A History of English Literature*, p. 315.

THE FRENCH REVOLUTION
1837

He left us [John Stuart Mill] in a relapsed state, one of the pitiablest. My dear wife has been very kind, and has become dearer to me. The night has been full of emotion, occasionally of sharp pain (something cutting or hard grasping me round the heart) occasionally of sweet consolation. I dreamt of my father and sister Margaret alive; yet all defaced with the sleepy stagnancy, swollen hebetude of the grave, and again dying as in some strange rude country: a horrid dream, the painfullest too when you wake first. But on the whole should I not thank the Unseen? For I was not driven out of composure, hardly for moments. "Walk humbly with thy God." How I longed for some psalm or prayer that I could have uttered, that my loved ones could have joined me in! But there was none. Silence had to be my language. This morning I have determined so far that I *can* still write *a* book on the French Revolution, and will do it. Nay, our money will still suffice. It was my last throw, my *whole* staked in the monstrosity of this life—for too monstrous, incomprehensible, it has been to me. I will not *quit* the game while faculty is given me to try playing. I have written to Fraser to buy me a "Biographie Universelle" (a kind of increasing the stake) and fresh paper: mean to huddle up the *Fête des Piques* and look farther what can be attempted.—CARLYLE, THOMAS, 1835, *Journal*, March 6; *Thomas Carlyle: A History of his Life in London*, ed. Froude, vol. I, p. 24.

This is not so much a history, as an epic poem; and notwithstanding, or even in consequence of this, the truest of histories. It is the history of the French Revolution, and the poetry of it, both in one; and on the whole no work of greater genius, either historical or poetical, has been produced in this country for many years. . . . We need not fear to prophesy that the suffrages of a large class of the very best qualified judges will be given, even enthusiastically, in favor of the volumes before us; but we will not affect to deny that the sentiment of another large class of readers (among whom are many entitled to the most respectful attention on other subjects) will be far different; a class comprehending all who are repelled by quaintness of manner. For a style more peculiar than that of Mr. Carlyle, more unlike the jog-trot characterless uniformity which distinguishes the English style of this age of periodicals, does not exist. Nor indeed can this style be wholly defended even by its admirers. Some of its peculiarities are mere mannerisms, arising from some casual association of ideas, or some habit accidentally picked up; and what is worse, many sterling thoughts are so disguised in phraseology borrowed from the spiritualist school of German poets and metaphyscians, as not only to obscure the meaning, but to raise, in the minds of most English readers, a not unnatural or inexcusable presumption of there being no meaning at all. Nevertheless, the presumption fails in this instance (as in many other instances); there is not only a meaning, but generally a true, and even a profound meaning, and, although a few dicta about the "mystery" and the "infinitude" which are in the universe and in man, and such like topics, are repeated in varied phrases greatly too often for our taste, this must be borne with, proceeding as one cannot but see, from feelings the most solemn, and the most deeply rooted which can lie in the heart of a human being. These transcendentalisms, and the accidental mannerisms excepted, we pronounce the style of this book to be not only good, but of surpassing excellence; excelled, in its kind, only by the great masters of epic poetry;

and a most suitable and glorious vesture for a work which is itself, as we have said, an epic poem.—MILL, JOHN STUART, 1837, *The French Revolution, Early Essays, ed. Gibbs, pp.* 271, 272.

After perusing the whole of this extraordinary work, we can allow, almost to their fullest extent, the high qualities with which Mr. Carlyle's idolaters endow him. — THACKERAY, WILLIAM MAKEPEACE 1837, *The Times, Aug.*

By the way, have you read Carlyle's extraordinary History of that wonderful period? Does it offend your classical taste? It finds great favour with many intelligent people here. They seem to think that the muses of History and Poetry have struck up a truce, and are henceforth to go on lovingly together. I must confess myself much interested. Carlyle seems to be an example of the old proverb of "the prophet without honour in his own country."— CHANNING, WILLIAM ELLERY, 1838, *To Miss Aikin, Feb.* 7; *Correspondence of William Ellery Channing and Miss Aikin, ed. Le Breton, p.* 304.

Carlyle *does* offend my classical taste; but the worst of it is that I have been absolutely riveted to his first volume, which I have this minute finished, and that I am hungering for the next. A very extraordinary writer certainly, and though somewhat, I must think, of a jargonist, and too wordy and full of repetition, yet sagacious, if not profound, and wonderfully candid. I think, too, that he shows an exactness and extent of knowledge of his subject which very advantageously distinguishes him from poetical historians in general. I assure you he is not without enthusiastic admirers here.— AIKIN, LUCY, 1838, *To Dr. Channing, April* 18; *Correspondence of William Ellery Channing and Lucy Aikin, ed. Le Breton, p.* 309.

People say the book is very deep: but it appears to me that the meaning *seems* deep from lying under mystical language. There is no repose, nor equable movement in it: all cut up into short sentences half reflective, half narrative; so that one labours through it as vessels do through what is called a short sea—small, contrary going waves caused by shallows, and straits, and meeting tides, etc.—FITZ-GERALD, EDWARD, 1838, *To Bernard Barton, April*; *Letters, ed. Wright, vol.* I, *p.* 42.

Of all books in the English language which the present age has given birth to, it is that which, most surprising and disheartening men at first sight, seems afterwards, so far as can be judged from the very many known experiments, the most forcibly to attract and detain them. The general result appears to be an eager, wide ebullience of the soul, issuing in manifold meditations, and in an altered and deepened feeling of all human life. The book has made no outward noise, but has echoed on and on within the hearts of men.—STERLING, JOHN, 1839, *Carlyle's Works, London and Westminster Review, vol.* 33, *pp.* 59, 60.

I commend to your notice, if it comes in your way, Carlyle on the French Revolution. A queer, tiresome, obscure, profound and original work. The writer has not very *clear* principles and views, I fear, but they are very deep.—NEWMAN, JOHN HENRY, 1839, *To Mrs. J. Mozley, Apr.* 23; *Letters and Correspondence during his Life in the English Church, ed. Mozley, vol.* II, *p.* 251.

He has done no more than give us *tableaux*, wonderful in execution, but nothing in conception, without connection, without a bearing. His book is the French Revolution *illustrated*—illustrated by the hand of a master, we know, but one from whom we expected a different labour. . . . The eternal *cursus et recursus* inexorably devours ideas, creeds, daring, and devotedness. The Infinite takes, to him, the form of Nihilation. It has a glance of pity for every set of enthusiasms, a smile, stamped with scepticism for every act of great devotedness to ideas. Generalities are odious to it; detail is its favorite occupation, and it there amuses itself as if seeking to lay at rest its inconsolable cares.— MAZZINI, JOSEPH, 1840, *Monthly Chronicle, No.* 23.

In these times there have appeared in Europe few works so worthy of attention; few so notable at once for their repulsive and attractive qualities. If your glance stops at the surface, and external singularities repel you, do not read this strange book. The mystic and obscure form chosen by Carlyle will soon fatigue you, and you will chafe at so many disguises which are not even transparent. If you are charmed by purity of diction, if you are accustomed to the Anglo-Gallic style of

Addison, to the brief, incisive, altogether British sentences of Bacon, to the energetic and robust periods of Southey, Carlyle will displease you. . . . If you are an historian of fact, and pride yourself above all on a practical study of events and circumstances, you will be still more annoyed; for facts are badly told by him, sometimes magnified as to their importance, sometimes heaped together or scattered apart, always without that clear arrangement which constitutes history. But if you are a philosopher, that is to say a sincere observer of mankind, you will re-read his work more than once. It will specially charm you, if you dare lift yourself above parties, and the prejudices of the day. It is neither a well-written book, nor an exact history of the French Revolution. It is not an eloquent dissertation,—still less a transmutation of events and men into romantic narrative. It is a philosophic study, mingled with irony and drama, nothing more. . . In writing it, the author concerned himself much more with the thought than the expression; he has thought more of the work than he has elaborated it. He has almost always seen clearly; he has often spoken badly. His narrative has all the glow of a present and actual scene. He has found himself profoundly isolated in England. This misfortune for his life is auspicious for his glory. He has sacrificed nothing to party. He has been the man of his own thought, and the expression of his own character.—CHASLES, VICTOR EUPHÉMION PHILARÈTE, 1840, *Revue des Deux Mondes*, 4th S. *vol.* 24.

Mr. Carlyle has written too well himself on the unconsciousness of man's highest faculty not to be aware that however dramatic a work should be, no showman is required to stand by and interrupt the course of the action by perpetually appearing on the stage. This is the great fault of his "French Revolution." It would be idle to complain that it is not a history; for probably (notwithstanding its title-page), it never seriously pretended to such a character. But looking on it as a series of scenes and pictures, and fragmentary sketches of remarkable events etched out in a bold, rough, Callot-like outline, they do possess this singular defect, that everywhere the shadow of the writer himself comes across and perplexes the eye. We are speaking now solely of the composition. Of the historical views contained in the work we may speak elsewhere. But this personal appearance of the writer is to be noticed, because it is unhappily too much in accordance with the general practice and a very bad practice—of our modern literature. It is egotistical. Until it ceases to be egotistical, it will achieve nothing great or good. Shakespeare painted all things but himself.—SEWELL, WILLIAM, 1840, *Carlyle's Works, Quarterly Review, vol.* 66, *p.* 456.

I prefer his history of the French Revolution to all those we have ourselves produced; I find it quite as dramatic, and I will venture to say more profound.—MONTÉGUT, ÉMILE, 1849, *Revue des Deux Mondes*, 6th. *S. vol.* 2.

The last great book published in his lifetime, wherein he recognized at once the presence of a new literary potentate, was Carlyle's "French Revolution." Never had he read a history, he declared, which interested him so much; and doubtless all the more because of the emotion which the tremendous course of events it describes had excited in him, when, in his own and Landor's youth, he read of them day by day. Not a few opinions, indeed, he found rising to the surface of that book to which he hardly knew what reception to give; but with wisdom and with feeling he found it to be full to overflowing, nor could he rest satisfied till he had seen and spoken with the author.—FORSTER, JOHN, 1869, *Walter Savage Landor*, a *Biography, p.* 562.

He saw nothing but evil in the French Revolution. He judges it as unjustly as he judges Voltaire, and for the same reasons. He understands our manner of acting no better than our manner of thinking. He looks for Puritan sentiment; and, as he does not find it, he condemns us. The idea of duty, the religious spirit, self-government, the authority of an austere conscience, can alone, in his opinion, reform a corrupt society; and none of all these are to be met with in French society. —TAINE, H. A., 1871, *History of English Literature*, tr. *Van Laun, vol.* II, *bk.* V, *ch.* IV, *p.* 472.

So overmastering is the interest of the story, that it is only by an effort that the supreme intellectual feat implied in the creation of such a work can be realised. To consult all authorities, however insignificant, which could throw light on the events, to keep the thread of narrative and chain of circumstances distinct in the mind, and weld all into one well-balanced piece of artistic work, nowhere marred by undue insistance on trivial points, or insufficient examination of important ones—this could be accomplished only by the possessor of an unexampled historic imagination. It is small wonder that such a history as this was hailed by the leading minds of England and America as the production of a great man of genius.— SHEPHERD, RICHARD HERNE, 1881, *Memoirs of the Life and Writings of Thomas Carlyle, vol.* I, *p.* 166.

That it is worthy of the position which, in England at least, is generally assigned it, of the best of its author's works, judged from all points of view, I have no doubt. . . . It is the most practically serviceable in the education of the citizen and the man of letters, and above all, it is the first sprightly running of its author's mind in the direction of practical and historical application of an original, if partial and one-sided, view of human life and human affairs.—SAINTSBURY, GEORGE, 1881, *The Literary Work of Thomas Carlyle, Scribner's Monthly, vol.* 22, *pp.* 96, 97.

Carlyle's book on the French Revolution has been called the great modern epic, and so it is—an epic as true and germane to this age, as Homer's was to his. . . . Of all Carlyle's works, his "French Revolution" is, no doubt, the greatest, that by which he will, probably, be longest remembered. It is a thoroughly artistic book, artistically conceived, and artistically executed. On it he expended his full strength, and he himself felt that he had done so.—SHAIRP, JOHN CAMPBELL, 1881, *Prose Poets, Aspects of Poetry, pp.* 429, 433.

This is truly a marvellous book. But it is not so much a history as a succession of pictures, or perhaps a succession of poems in prose. It is pervaded with Carlyle's philosophy, and is probably his most brilliant work. He finds abundance of demons to hate, and a few heroes to admire. Mirabeau and Danton seem to be his favorites, while Lafayette and Bailly are treated with a more or less obvious contempt. He gives us a picture of pandemonium, interspersing it with judgments that seem sometimes preposterous and sometimes inspired. Every student of the Revolutionary period should read the book; but he will gain his chief advantage from it after his studies have already made him master of the leading facts of the history. Though it is probably the most remarkable work ever written on the Revolution, it will prove unsatisfactory to nearly every student unless it be studied in connection with a work of more commonplace merits. —ADAMS, CHARLES KENDALL, 1882, *A Manual of Historical Literature, p.* 331.

Mr. Carlyle's Revolution is more and more felt to be a literary picture, and less and less a historical examination. It is based on an idea now recognised to be thoroughly inadequate; it is saturated with doctrines for which the author himself no longer retained any trust or hope; and it leads us to a conclusion which all that is manly and true in our generation rejects with indignation. — HARRISON, FREDERIC, 1883, *Histories of the French Revolution, The Choice of Books and Other Literary Pieces, p.* 410.

Carlyle wrote the last word of "The French Revolution" as the clock was striking ten and the supper of oatmeal porridge was coming up. He naturally felt the house too narrow, and went forth into the night. Before departing he said to his wife, "I know not whether this book is worth anything, nor what the world will do with it, or misdo, or entirely forbear to do, as is likeliest: but this I could tell the world: You have not had for a hundred years any book that comes more direct and flamingly from the heart of a living man. Do what you like with it, you." After which oration, the hall-door closed upon the most angry and desperate man of genius then in the flesh; with cause, had he known it, to have been the most thankful and hopeful.—GARNETT, RICHARD, 1887, *Thomas Carlyle (Great Writers), pp.* 81, 86.

But by-and-bye another book opened up a new world to me. Fond of historical reading, in the later years of my university life I had drenched myself with French memoirs, largely connected with the Revolution period. In those days they might be picked up on stalls, cheap, from Arthur Young's travels down to the malicious gossip of the Duchesse d'Abrantes. But they left a very confused impression on one's mind. It happened to me now, however, happily to get hold of Carlyle. Had I been a true Carlylean, of course I should have been absorbed in "Sartor

Resartus," and, from that starting point, gone on to see all things in the light of the clothes' philosophy. But I did not read "Sartor" till years after, and not then, I fear, with proper appreciation. The "French Revolution," however, I devoured eagerly, being sufficiently versed in the story already really to profit by its vivid pictures and singular insight. I found it to be *the* epic poem of our age, with the vision of a seer and the moral power of a Hebrew poet, even though I had to protest against some of its verdicts. If Coleridge gave me clear guiding lights in the realm of theology, Carlyle introduced me to deeper and broader views of human life and history. I did not, indeed, accept all his judgments; yet the book was like a revelation to me, and still remains, of all his works, the one I read oftenest, and never weary of reading. Certainly it is an era in one's life when one gets rid of Dryasdust, and comes face to face with the grand poetic justice of Providence. An epic poem, and yet a great history! But must not a great history be always an epic?—SMITH, WALTER C., 1887, *Books Which Have Influenced Me*, p. 94.

Even Carlyle, rugged and harsh in his John-Knox nature, could have been a poet, as his "Heroes and Hero Worship," Burns's "Essay," and "French Revolution" prove. In no poem ever written was there more use of what is to be felt for what is to be known than in the last-named work. As history it is, of course, a failure; but that is true of other attempts than his, and oftener because there is too little feeling than too much. The man who writes only generalizations, without giving first the facts, writes history to as little purpose as Carlyle. If we are first to know the facts before we read our history, Carlyle's volumes are as good as Green's, and, as interpretative literature, far better.—SHERMAN, L. A., 1893, *Analytics of Literature*, p. 420, *note*.

One of the first literary distinctions of Queen Victoria's reign was the publication of this book. . . . The perfection at once of that new grandiose yet rugged voice, which broke every law of composition and triumphed over them all, which shocked and bewildered all critics and authorities, yet excited and stirred the whole slumbrous world of literature, and rang into the air like a trumpet,—and of a new manner altogether of regarding the events of history, a great pictorial representation, all illuminated by the blaze, sometimes lurid, sometimes terrible, of the highest poetic genius and imagination,—were fully displayed in this astonishing work. . . . Carlyle seized the reality of the most lamentable, the most awful, the most influential of recent epochs. It is no mere record, but a great drama passing before our eyes. . . . A book more interesting than any romance, which those who took it up could not lay down, and which was far too impressive in its general character, too powerful and novel in its art, to be mistaken or overlooked.—OLIPHANT, MARGARET O. W., 1894, *The Victorian Age of English Literature*, pp. 120, 121, 123.

His "French Revolution" is not history in the proper sense of the word. It is a set of lurid pictures illustrative of that great event, by an artist of singular power, pictures which bring out its real significance in a quite unique manner.—LILLY, WILLIAM SAMUEL, 1895, *Four English Humourists of the Nineteenth Century*, p. 123.

Its passion, energy, colour, and vast prodigality of ineffaceable pictures, place it undoubtedly at the head of all the pictorial histories of modern times.—HARRISON, FREDERIC, 1895, *Studies in Early Victorian Literature*, p. 51.

Probably nowhere is there a history which in every chapter, and almost in every sentence, breathes the artistic purpose as Carlyle's "History of the French Revolution" does. It has been frequently called the "epic" of the Revolution. In point of fact, as Froude justly says, the conception is rather dramatic, and the best comparison is to Æschylus.—WALKER, HUGH, 1897, *The Age of Tennyson*, p. 27.

CHARTISM
1840

I will tell you some good things to read—though not sure they are quite in your way: viz., Carlyle's "Chartism." . . . Carlyle is a very striking writer; full of a sort of grim humour:—the grin-horribly-a-ghastly-smile kind of style; the subject, too, being one which develops such a power well. This is not an inviting or flowery description to give of an author; but for a variety he is wonderfully impressive.—MOZLEY, JAMES BOWLING, 1840, *To his Sisters, March 7*; *Letters, ed. his Sister*, p. 101.

We pass through the book as through

a journey of many ways and many objects, brilliantly illuminated and pictured in every direction, but without arriving at any clear conclusion, and without gathering any fresh information on the main subject, during the progress. By his not very clear argument about "might" and "right," he has enabled any despot to show some sort of reasoning for any violent act.—HORNE, RICHARD HENGIST (ELIZABETH BARRETT BROWNING?), 1844, *A New Spirit of the Age*, p. 343.

I prefer his little book called "Chartism" to all the descriptions of social maladies and all the statistics that have been bestowed upon us in these latter times.—MONTÉGUT, ÉMILE, 1849, *Revue des Deux Mondes*, 6th S. vol. 2.

"Chartism," Carlyle's next book, is the briefest, and also the most simple, direct, and business-like of any of his works. The splendours of diction which characterised his previous efforts were now, as in his account of Luther, rigorously laid aside, as if he had resolved that he would have practical belief or nothing. No one could read this little book with any intelligence, and think of it as a mere literary performance: it is his first distinct effort as a Social Reformer. German Transcendentalism retires into the Divine Silences, and English practically comes to the front. It must be understood that "Chartism" was published long before the Corn Laws were repealed, and that it made a very deep impression at the time of its appearance. How much of the subsequent practical legislation may have been directly or indirectly influenced by it, it is perhaps impossible now to determine. All we can say is, that from this time legislation did begin, in various directions, to take the practical tone Carlyle here strove to initiate.—LARKIN, HENRY, 1886, *Carlyle and the Open Secret of his Life*, p. 96.

A little book, but a great one. Wildly declamatory, truth without soberness, it contains some of Carlyle's finest writings, and is as fresh today as the day it was published; nor is it intolerant like its more modern representatives.—GARNETT, RICHARD, 1887, *Thomas Carlyle (Great Writers)*, p. 98.

HEROES AND HERO WORSHIP
1841

Have you read poor Carlyle's raving book about heroes? Of course you have, or I would ask you to buy my copy. I don't like to live with it in the house. It smoulders. He ought to be laughed at a little. But it is pleasant to retire to the Tale of a Tub, Tristram Shandy, and Horace Walpole, after being tossed on his canvas waves. This is blasphemy. Dibdin Pitt of the Coburg could enact one of his heroes.—FITZGERALD, EDWARD, 1841, *To W. H. Thompson, March 26*; *Letters, ed. Wright, vol.* I, p. 71.

Carlyle's "Hero-worship" trembled in my hand like a culprit before a judge; and as the book *is* very full of paradoxes, and has some questionable matter in it, this shaking seemed rather symbolical. But, oh! it is a book fit rather to shake (take it all in all) than to be shaken. It is very full of noble sentiments and wise reflections, and throws out many a suggestion which will not waste itself like a blast blown in a wilderness, but will surely rouse many a heart and mind to a right, Christian-like way of acting and of dealing with the gifted and godlike in man and of men.—COLERIDGE, SARA, 1843, *To Mrs. Farrer, Sept. 5*; *Memoir and Letters, ed. her Daughter*, p. 204.

"Heroes and Hero Worship"—was its author's chief, if not his only, bid for popularity, and has, perhaps, remained the most popular of his works.—SAINTSBURY, GEORGE, 1881, *The Literary Work of Thomas Carlyle, Scribner's Monthly*, vol. 22, p. 100.

However the matter may have stood in 1841, in 1887 "Hero Worship" is likely to be read with great admiration but little astonishment. The stars in their courses have fought for Carlyle. The influence of great or reputed great men upon politics and thought has been so enormous, the impotence of the most respectable causes without powerful representatives has been so notorious, that the personal element in history has regained all the importance of which it has been deprived by the study of general laws. The problem of harmonizing it with the truth of general laws remains without solution from Carlyle. He simply ignores these laws, and assumes that the hero appears when God pleases, and acts as pleases himself. It is also difficult to square the truth of "Hero Worship" with the truth of "Sartor Resartus." — GARNETT, RICHARD, 1887, *Thomas Carlyle (Great Writers)*, p. 101.

He was more alive than any man since Swift to the dark side of human nature. The dullness of mankind weighed upon him like a nightmare. "Mostly fools" is his pithy verdict upon the race at large. Nothing then could be more idle than the dream of the revolutionists that the voice of the people could be itself the voice of God. From millions of fools you can by no constitutional machinery extract anything but folly. Where then is the escape? The millions, he says (essay on Johnson), "roll hither and thither, whithersoever they are led;" they seem "all sightless and slavish," with little but "animal instincts." The hope is that, here and there, are scattered the men of power and of insight, the heaven-sent leaders; and it is upon loyalty to them and capacity for recognizing and obeying them that the future of the race really depends. This was the moral of the lectures on "Hero-Worship." Odin, Mahomet, Dante, Shakespeare, Luther, Cromwell, and Napoleon, are types of the great men who now and then visit the earth as prophets or rulers. They are the brilliant centers of light in the midst of the surrounding darkness; and in loyal recognition of their claims lies our security for all external progress. By what signs, do you ask, can they be recognized? There can be no sign. You can see the light if you have eyes; but no other faculty can supply the want of eyesight. And hence arise some remarkable points both of difference from and coincidence with popular beliefs.— STEPHEN, LESLIE, 1897, *Library of the World's Best Literature*, ed. Warner, vol. VI, p. 3238.

PAST AND PRESENT
1843

Father Saurteig,—Thanks to thee for thy new *work*—a real piece of work such as even thou hadst not before given us the like of—not even in "Sartor Resartus." I could wish thou hadst not put forth more of this at once than the two or three first books, and that the *first* had been placed last of these. Thou shouldst have begun assuredly with thy true revivification of the men of St. Edmundsburg. Neither can I agree with my teacher in what he more than once proclaimeth as his judgment general, touching Oliver of Tyburn; nor, indeed, am I very sure that I leap as yet contentedly to any of thy distinct conclusions, save one—namely, that we are all wrong and all like to be damned. But I thank thee for having made me conscious of life and feeling for sundry hours by thy pages, whether figurative, or narrative, or didactic. Thou hast done a book such as no other living man could do or dream of doing.— LOCKHART, JOHN GIBSON, 1843, *To Carlyle, Apr. 27; The Life and Letters of John Gibson Lockhart*, ed. Lang, vol. II, p. 238.

His finest work, as matter of political philosophy, is undoubtedly his "Past and Present." In this work he is no longer the philosopher of the circle. He allows the world a chance.— HORNE, RICHARD HENGIST (ELIZABETH BARRETT BROWNING?), 1844, *A New Spirit of the Age*, p. 343.

"Past and Present" is at once a monument of the keen practical spirit of the man and of what may be called his literary *flair*, or scent. Ecclesiological mediævalism was at its very height, and in itself Mr. Carlyle hated it, or regarded it with a partly unutterable sense of sarcastic astonishment. Yet he managed, out of a book published to interest readers who read in this spirit, to make something quite different,—to expound his own views, preach his own gospel, and illustrate his own fancies. . . . A unique book, which no one, perhaps, but its author could have written, neither the like of it will any other man write.—SAINTSBURY, GEORGE, 1881, *The Literary Work of Thomas Carlyle, Scribner's Monthly*, vol. 22, pp. 100, 101.

It is at once the most tender and pathetic picture of the Past and the most unsparing indictment of the Present that exists in modern English literature. — TOYNBEE, ARNOLD, 1883–84, *Lectures on the Industrial Revolution in England*.

With my memory of the Preston riots still vivid, I procured "Past and Present," and read it perseveringly. It was far from easy reading; but I found in it strokes of descriptive power unequalled in my experience, and thrills of electric splendour which carried me enthusiastically on. I found in it, moreover, in political matters, a morality so righteous, a radicalism so high, reasonable, and humane, as to make it clear to me that without truckling to the ape and tiger of the mob, a man might hold the views of a radical.—TYNDALL, JOHN, 1890, *Personal Recollections of Thomas Carlyle, New Fragments*, p. 349.

Of the book itself, considered as a piece

of literature and not as a message from a modern prophet, it is easy to say harsh things. Like all Carlyle's works, it is very wordy and diffuse, and there is much chaff hiding the solid grain. There is the usual exaggeration in his style of writing and speaking, and the usual striving after effect by the use of extraordinary nicknames and similes. . . . The greatest fault in the book is not its style or the want thereof, but a certain absence of any clear connexion between the world of the nineteenth century and that of Abbot Samson, even as contrasts. Only here and there is the link between them hinted at; it is the contrast that strikes us most.—GIBBINS, H. DE B., 1892, *English Social Reformers*, p. 201.

He has left us in "Past and Present" our truest and most sympathetic picture of mediæval monasticism at its high water mark, a picture which no Catholic writer can hope to rival. He understood what those monks of St. Edmundsbury felt and thought, with perfect comprehension. Yet was he a student of the Middle Ages? Far from it, but he was a student of man.—TREVELYAN, G. M., 1899, *Carlyle as a Historian, The Nineteenth Century*, vol. 46, p. 500.

No one has made mediævalism more attractive. "Past and Present" is a very notable book. The reconstitution of mediæval life in the picture he makes out of the chronicle of Jocelin of Brakelond is vivid and telling—especially telling in contrast with certain sides of modern life with its "thirty thousand distressed needlewomen in London alone" and its "cash payment the sole nexus between men." The book is, of course, inspired by the desire of exhibiting this contrast—a desire which, of course, impairs its veracity. It is in fact a pamphlet.—BROWNELL, W. C., 1901, *Victorian Prose Masters*, p. 69.

LIFE AND LETTERS OF OLIVER CROMWELL
1845

We do not quarrel with Mr. Carlyle for his enthusiasm, if he feels it; but he really must not call people "flunkeys" and "canting persons" if they do not share it with him. He has thrown himself for the present on Oliver's own account of himself, and is content to stand by in the humble posture of direction post, or, at the highest, of showman. He shows us Oliver; an engraving of his portrait, very characteristic and striking; his letters and his speeches, equally full of character. We are left alone with the great man, to form our own judgment of him. Mr. Carlyle ought not to complain if his own interjectional bursts of rapture, and orders to love Oliver, produce less effect than the sight he presents to us. We do not grudge Puritanism its great man any more than its temporary triumph. It earned what it won by good means as well as bad. . . . His book labours and struggles, and leaves only impressions which counteract one another. Its parts do not adjust themselves naturally; fact pulls against commentary; elucidation falls dead upon the latter; and between them the living image of Cromwell drops through. Mr. Carlyle's own idea does not rise of itself out of his documents; he has to protect and foster it. There is a painful effort, a monotonous, impatient bluster, to keep up the reader's heroic mood. . . . We believe that he meant to bring out a genuinely English idea of excellence, to portray a man of rude exterior and speech, doing great things in a commonplace and unromantic way. But he must match his ideal with something better than Cromwell's distorted and unreal character, his repulsive energy, his dreary and ferocious faith, his thinly veiled and mastering selfishness.—CHURCH, RICHARD WILLIAM, 1846-97, *Carlyle's Cromwell, Occasional Papers*, pp. 15, 26, 52.

The style of the book on Cromwell is occasionally a trial even to the lovers of Carlyle's picturesque and shaggy diction, and few men can pronounce some of the sentences aloud without running the risk of being throttled. To follow the course of his thought through the sudden turns, and down the abrupt declivities of his style, exposes one at times to the danger of having his eyes put out of joint.—WHIPPLE, EDWIN PERCY, 1848, *Essays and Reviews*, vol. II, p. 353.

Many will find Carlyle presumptuous, coarse; they will suspect from his theories, and also from his way of speaking, that he looks upon himself as a great man, neglected, of the race of heroes; that, in his opinion, the human race ought to put themselves in his hands, and trust him with their business. Certainly he lectures us, and with contempt. He despises his epoch; he has a sulky, sour tone; he keeps purposely on stilts. He disdains objections. In his eyes, opponents are not up to his form. He bullies his predecessors; when he speaks of Cromwell's biographers, he takes the tone of a man of genius astray amongst pedants. He has the superior smile, the resigned condescension of a hero who feels himself a martyr, and he only quits it, to shout at the top of his voice, like an ill-taught plebian. . . . Carlyle's masterpiece is but a collection of letters and speeches, commented on and united by a continuous narrative. The impression which they leave is extraordinary. Grave constitutional histories hang heavy after this compilation. The author wishes to make us comprehend a soul, the soul of Cromwell, the greatest of the Puritans, their chief, their abstract, their hero, and their model.—TAINE, H. A., 1871, *History of English Literature*, tr. Van Laun, vol. II, bk. V, ch. IV, pp. 451, 470.

This book is, in my opinion, by far the most important contribution to English history, which has been made in the present century. Carlyle was the first to break the crust which has overlaid the subject of Cromwell since the Restoration, and to make Cromwell and Cromwell's age again intelligible to mankind, Anyone who will read what was written about him before Carlyle's work appeared, and what has been written since, will perceive how great was the achievement. The enthusiast, led away by ambition, and degenerating into the hypocrite, the received figure of the established legend, is gone for ever. We may retain each our own opinion about Cromwell, we may think that he did well or that he did ill, that he was wise or unwise; but we see the real man. We can entertain no shadow of doubt about the genuineness of the portrait; and, with the clear insight of Oliver himself, we have a new conception of the Civil War and of its consequences.—FROUDE, JAMES ANTHONY, 1884, *Thomas Carlyle; A History of his Life in London*, vol. I, p. 305.

Though containing some of his finest descriptions and battle-pieces, conspicuously that of "Dunbar"—it is the least artistic of his achievements, being overladen with detail and superabounding in extract.—NICHOL, JOHN, 1892, *Thomas Carlyle (English Men of Letters)*, p. 183.

His "Cromwell" is essentially the portrait of a soul: a very skillfully constructed autobiography with connecting narrative and reflections, exhibiting its subject with a vividness never surpassed, so far as I know, in that species of composition.—LILLY, WILLIAM SAMUEL, 1895, *Four English Humorists of the Nineteenth Century*, p. 123.

On the whole, we may count the "Cromwell" as the greatest of Carlyle's effective products. With his own right hand, alone and by a single stroke, he completely reversed the judgment of the English nation about their greatest man. The whole weight of Church, monarchy, aristocracy, fashion, literature, and wit, had for two centuries combined to falsify history and distort the character of the noblest of English statesmen. And a simple man of letters, by one book, at once and forever reversed this sentence, silenced the allied forces of calumny and rancour, and placed Oliver for all future time as the greatest hero of the Protestant movement. There are few examples in the history of literature of so great and so sudden a triumph of truth and justice. At the same time, it is well to remember that the "Cromwell" is not a literary masterpiece, in the sense of being an organic work of art. It is not the "Life" of Cromwell: it was not so designed, and was never so worked out. It is his "Letters and Speeches," illustrated by notes.—HARRISON, FREDERIC, 1895, *Studies in Early Victorian Literature*, p. 48.

Carlyle's "Cromwell" is, more than either of the other histories, an illustration of his own doctrine of heroes, and less than either of the others is it a history of a nation as well as of a man. Cromwell to a great extent speaks for himself, and Carlyle expounds and comments on his uncouth and sometimes obsolete manner of expression. The commentary is free and even ample, yet there is less of Carlyle himself in this than in any other of his works. The great features of it are its delineation of the man Cromwell and the proof it presents of Carlyle's skill in the use of documents. Carlyle has not converted everybody to his own view of Cromwell, but he has at least coloured the opinion of everybody who has since studied the period.—WALKER, HUGH, 1897, *The Age of Tennyson (Handbook of English Literature)*, p. 28.

LATTER-DAY PAMPHLETS
1850

Have you read Carlyle's "Pamphlets?" The last, called "The Stump Orator," contains some good things, and the *Guardian* can not sneer it down, with all its talent at sneering. People affect to despise its *truisms*, when I believe, in fact, at heart they are galled by some of its bold, broad *truths*, expressed with a graphic force and felicitous humor which it is easier to rail at than to hide under a bushel. Put what bushel over it they may, it will shine through, and indeed burn up the designed extinguisher, as the fire eats up a scroll of paper.—COLERIDGE, SARA, 1849, *To Mrs. H. M. Jones, May 19; Memoir and Letters, ed. her Daughter,* p. 333.

When I speak of the Latter Day Prophet, I conclude you have read, or heard of, Carlyle's Pamphlets so designed. People are tired of them and of him: he only foams, snaps, and howls, and no progress, people say: this is almost true: and yet there is vital good in all he has written.—FITZGERALD, EDWARD, 1850, *To F. Tennyson, Aug. 15; More Letters,* p. 25.

It is with some consternation that I approach the subject of Carlyle's politics. One handles them as does an inspector of police a parcel reported to contain dynamite. The "Latter-Day Pamphlets" might not unfitly be labelled "Dangerous Explosives."—BIRRELL, AUGUSTINE, 1884, *Obiter Dicta, First Series,* p. 34.

As was natural, the "Latter-Day Pamphlets" were treated as a series of political ravings. For that estimate Carlyle himself was largely responsible. He deprived himself of the sympathy of intelligent readers by the violence of his invective and the lack of discrimination in his abuse. Much of what Carlyle said is to be found in Mill's "Representative Government," said, too, in a quiet, rational style, which commands attention and respect. Mill, no more than Carlyle, was a believer in mob rule. He did not think that the highest wisdom was to be had by the counting of heads. Thinkers like Mill and Spencer did not deem it necessary to pour contempt on modern tendencies. They suggested remedies on the lines of these tendencies. They did not try to put back the hands on the clock of time; they sought to remove perturbing influences. Much of the evil has arisen from men trying to do by political methods what should not be done by these methods. Carlyle's idea that Government should do this, that, and the other thing has wrought mischief, inasmuch as it has led to an undue belief in the virtues of Government interference. His writings are largely responsible for the evils he predicted.—MACPHERSON, HECTOR C., 1896, *Thomas Carlyle (Famous Scots Series),* p. 146.

In spite of their variety of subjects—"Stump Orator," "Jesuitism," "Model Prisons," etc.—leave the definite sensation of a prolonged and scarcely modulated shriek.—BROWNELL, W. C., 1901, *Victorian Prose Masters,* p. 79.

LIFE OF JOHN STERLING
1851

These bricks from Babylon convey but scanty intimation of the varied interest of the book. However the readers of it may differ from its opinions, they cannot but find, even in Mr. Carlyle's misjudgments and prejudices, ample matter for serious reflection: for if he misjudges, it is generally because he is looking too intently at a single truth, or a single side of a truth; and such misjudgments are more suggestive than the completest propositions of a less earnest, keen-sighted, and impassioned thinker.—BRIMLEY, GEORGE, 1851–58, *Carlyle's Life of Sterling, Essays, ed. Clark,* p. 251.

Well, the book has come at last, and, notwithstanding the evil animus of parts of it, a milder, more tender, and more pleasant gossiping little volume we have not read for many a day. The mountain has been in labor, and lo! a nice lively field-mouse, quite frisky and good-humored, has been brought forth. It is purely ridiculous and contemptible to speak, with some of our contemporaries, of this volume as Mr. Carlyle's best, or as, in any sense, a great work. The subject, as *he* has viewed it, was not great, and his treatment of it, while exceedingly graceful and pleasant, is by no means very powerful or very profound. —GILFILLAN, GEORGE, 1855, *A Third Gallery of Portraits,* p. 267.

Far the most pleasant as well as one of the truest of his books.—GREG, W. R., 1860, *Kingsley and Carlyle, Literary and Social Judgments,* p. 119.

I have always felt, notwithstanding a great affection and admiration for Carlyle, that his "Life of Sterling" has in it a breath of Mephistopheles, something of the mocking scornful spirit, satirically superior to all a young man's hereditary beliefs, and with a careless pleasure in pursuing and stripping him of these but weakly founded non-individual religious views which had built up the outer fabric of his life, such as hurts the moral sense, wonderful as is the almost lyrical strain of its lament and praise.—OLIPHANT, MARGARET O. W., 1897, *William Blackwood and his Sons, vol.* II, *p.* 186.

One winter night I tried to re-read Carlyle's "Past and Present" and certain of his "Latter-Day Pamphlets;" but I found I could not, and thanked my stars that I did not have to. It was like riding a spirited but bony horse bareback. There was tremendous go in the beast; but oh, the bruises from those knotty and knuckle-like sentences! But the "Life of Sterling" I have found I can re-read with delight; it has a noble music.—BURROUGHS, JOHN, 1897, *On the Re-reading of Books, Century Magazine, vol.* 55, *p.* 148.

One recoils at much of Carlyle's expression in this work, but, with all its blemish of pity and Philistinism and pessimism, it stands remarkable, a monument built by such hands,—I will not say planned by such a mind, for the mind protested; but nevertheless the hands, obedient to the spirit, built it with the best they could bring in gratitude to helpful love whose sunlight had reached an imprisoned soul.—EMERSON, EDWARD WALDO, 1897, ed. *A Correspondence Between John Sterling and Ralph Waldo Emerson, p.* 6.

HISTORY OF FRIEDRICH II
1858–64

Infinitely the wittiest book that ever was written,—a book that one would think the English people would rise up in mass and thank the author for, by cordial acclamation, and signify, by crowning him with oak-leaves, their joy that such a head existed among them, and sympathizing and much-reading America would make a new treaty or send a Minister Extraordinary to offer congratulation of honoring delight to England, in acknowledgment of this donation,—a book holding so many memorable and heroic facts, working directly on practice; with new heroes, things unvoiced before;—the German Plutarch (now that we have exhausted the Greek and Roman and British Plutarchs), with a range, too, of thought and wisdom so large and so elastic, not so much applying as inosculating to every need and sensibility of man, that we do not read a stereotype page, rather we see the eyes of the writer looking into ours, mark his behavior, humming, chuckling, with undertones and trumpet-tones and shrugs, and long-commanding glances, stereoscoping every figure that passes, and every hill, river, road, hummock, and pebble in the long perspective. With its wonderful new system of mnemonics, whereby great and insignificant men are ineffaceably ticketed and marked and modelled in memory by what they were, had, and did; and withal a book that is a Judgment Day, for its moral verdict on the men and nations and manners of modern times. And this book makes no noise; I have hardly seen a notice of it in any newspaper or journal, and you would think there was no such book. I am not aware that Mr. Buchanan has sent a special messenger to Great Cheyne Row, Chelsea, or that Mr. Dallas has been instructed to assure Mr. Carlyle of his distinguished consideration. But the secret wits and hearts of men take note of it, not the less surely. They have said nothing lately in praise of the air, or of fire, or of the blessing of love, and yet, I suppose, they are sensible of these, and not less of this book, which is like these.—EMERSON, RALPH WALDO, 1859, *Diary, Correspondence of Carlyle and Emerson, ed. Norton, vol.* II, *p.* 305.

In conclusion, after saying, as honest critics must, that "The History of Friedrich II. called Frederick the Great" is a book to be read in with more satisfaction than to be read through, after declaring that it is open to all manner of criticism, especially in point of moral purpose and tendency, we must admit with thankfulness, that it has the one prime merit of being the work of a man who has every quality of a great poet except that supreme one of rhythm which shapes both matter and manner to harmonious proportion, and that where it is good, it is good as only genius knows how to be. With the gift of song, Carlyle would have been the greatest of epic poets since Homer. Without it, to modulate and harmonize and bring parts into their proper relation, he is the most amorphous of humorists, the most shining avatar of whim the world has ever seen. . . . The figures of most historians seem like dolls stuffed with bran, whose whole substance runs out through any hole that criticism may tear in them, but Carlyle's are so real in comparison, that, if you prick them, they bleed. He seems a little wearied, here and there, in his Friedrich, with the multiplicity of detail, and does his filling-in rather shabbily; but he still remains in his own way, like his hero, the Only, and such episodes as that of Voltaire would make the fortune of any other writer. Though not the safest of guides in politics or practical philosophy, his value as an inspirer and awakener cannot be over-estimated.—LOWELL, JAMES RUSSELL, 1866–71, *Carlyle, My Study Windows,* pp. 147, 148, 149.

While Carlyle showed in this History his marvellous power at its height, there is no book of his that defines more clearly the limitations of his power, or more frequently chafes the reader by the twists and wrenches given to our mother, tongue.— MORLEY, HENRY, 1881, *Of English Literature in the Reign of Victoria, with a glance at the Past,* p. 314.

The first effect of the book in England was to weaken its author's moral influence, for the Christian conscience of the country revolted against its teaching, and was shocked by the pictures of Frederick and his father. It was only as the book receded from view, and its author's previous writings were reverted to, that the painful impression wore off. That feeling was only too well founded. Though he did not magnify Frederick, in whom Force without Righteousness was incarnate, as he had magnified Cromwell, it cannot be denied that he treats this unspeakable monster with a deference to which he was in no way entitled; and at times it would almost appear as if he loved him for his unendurable brutality, while he has actually the hardihood to charge other historians with injustice in not recognising the candour with which Frederick owned that his seizure of Silesia was one of the greatest crimes ever perpetrated.—WYLIE, WILLIAM HOWIE, 1881, *Thomas Carlyle, The Man and his Books,* p. 269.

The industry of research displayed in the ten volumes of this long history is **marvellous**. Taken as a whole, it may be called wearisome, as the writer himself confessed; though his highest powers of humourous and graphic portraiture find exercise in many passages.—GOSTWICK, JOSEPH, 1882, *German Culture and Christianity,* p. 199.

A work of superlative genius, which defies every canon of criticism and sets at nought every rule of historical composition. It is a succession of startling flashes and detonations. In no one of Carlyle's works do the peculiar qualities of his genius show themselves with more intensity. There is scarcely a paragraph that does not contain in itself either a poem or a picture. The book is founded on the most exhaustive study and the most careful observation. The author even visited the more important of Frederick's battle-fields, and had surveys made in the interests of absolute accuracy. Every scrap of German writing that would throw light upon the reign appears to have been examined and weighed. The result is one of the most remarkable books in the English language, and one which, all things considered, is unquestionably the best history of Frederick the Great in any language.—ADAMS, CHARLES KENDALL, 1882, *A Manual of Historical Literature,* p. 272.

No ancient or modern character rivalled Cromwell in Carlyle's affection. His not unmixed satisfaction in the progress of the Life of Frederick was qualified by an imperfect sympathy with his hero. The disproportionate space which is allotted to the king's rough and narrow-minded father may, perhaps, indicate a lingering reluctance to enter on the principal subject. The history of Prussia and of Germany, which occupies the greater part of the first volume, is in clearness, in skilful brevity, and in fulness of knowledge, a literary masterpiece. Voltaire himself could not have condensed the story of several centuries into happier units, nor would he have shown the same conscientious industry in collecting his materials. Carlyle's elaborate apology for Frederick William has caused great offence in England, though the paradoxes in which it abounds are explained and to a great extent modified by the incipient play of satirical and sympathetic humour. — VENABLES, G. S., 1884, *Carlyle's Life in London, Fortnightly Review, vol.* 42, *p.* 604.

Just at the time when the first instalment of Carlyle's "Life of Frederick" was published, I found him [Macaulay] engaged in the perusal of the opening chapters. His wrath—I can use no milder word—against Carlyle's style was boundless. He read aloud to me four or five of the most Carlylean sentences, and then, throwing the book on the library table, exclaimed, "I hold that no Englishman has the right to treat his mother-tongue after so unfilial a fashion." . . . Before a week had elapsed I was again at Holly Lodge, and he at once recurred to Carlyle's history. "Pray read it," he said, "as soon as you can find time. Of course I have not got, and never shall get, reconciled to his distortions and contortions of language; but there are, notwithstanding, passages of truly wonderful interest and power, and in the infinite variety of new historical facts, and in the delight and instruction they afford, if my first feeling has been that of annoyance at the strange way of telling the story, my second and permanent feeling is one of gratitude that—even in such a way—the story has been told."—STUART, JAMES MONTGOMERY, 1885, *Reminiscences and Essays.*

Although in the prophetic sight of the writer that most remarkable book may, at the moment it was written, have borne a conscious reference to events which were still future, but have since most wonderfully illustrated its great theme, the world in general recognized nothing of the sort in it. The author, if he knew himself to be a *vox clamantis* at the time, must have been astonished at the rapidity with which his Gospel of Force triumphed as soon as it had its chance. Some of us shook our heads over it, one great man amongst us, whose place I am proud to occupy, I dare not say to fill, did not hesitate to speak words of summary condemnation; but the doctrine itself was esoteric, the words, like much else of Carlyle's, were Φωνᾶντα συνέτοιν, but συνέτοισιν only; to the ears of the many they required the sacred interpreter. —STUBBS, WILLIAM, 1886-1900, *Seventeen Lectures on the Study of Mediæval and Modern History and Kindred Subjects,* p. 60.

The book oftenest in my hand of late years is certainly Carlyle's "Frederick."— RUSKIN, JOHN, 1887, *Books which Have Influenced Me,* p. 45.

His "Frederick" appeals to us chiefly as a comedy of humours, and I, for my part, always regret that its author lavished so much time over military details, now of little interest save to professional warriors. —LILLY, WILLIAM SAMUEL, 1895, *Four English Humourists of the Nineteenth Century,* p. 123.

It is not a book at all, but an encyclopædia of German biographies in the latter half of the eighteenth century. Who reads every word of these ten volumes? Who cares to know how big was the belly of some court chamberlain, or who were the lovers of some unendurable Frau? What a welter of dull garbage! In what dustheaps dost thou not smother us, Teufelsdröckh! O, Thomas, Thomas, what Titania has bewitched thee with the head of Dryasdust on thy noble shoulders?— HARRISON, FREDERIC, 1895, *Studies in Early Victorian Literature,* p. 47.

By this later work Carlyle outstripped, in the judgment of serious critics, his only possible rival, Macaulay, and took his place as the first scientific historian of the early Victorian period. His method in this class of work is characteristic of him as an individualist; he endeavours, in all conjunctions, to see the man moving, breathing, burning in the glow and flutter of adventure. This gives an extraordinary vitality to portions of Carlyle's narrative, if it also tends to disturb the reader's conception of the general progress of events. —GOSSE, EDMUND, 1897, *A Short History of Modern English Literature,* p. 346.

CORRESPONDENCE AND REMINISCENCES

The hasty and ill-advised publication of the "Reminiscences," abounding in unfortunate matter, given to the world with feminine zeal but without even the pretence of clear-headed editorial supervision, has certainly let loose the full tongue of detraction.—BUCHANAN, ROBERT, 1881, *Wylie's Life of Carlyle, Contemporary Review,* vol. 39, p. 793.

It was the lot of the present writer to read nearly all the obituary notices of him which appeared in the leading journals after his death. With not an exception they were extremely eulogistic, praising his works and applauding in the highest terms the dignity and stern conscientiousness of his life. But when, about three weeks later, the "Reminiscences" were published by Mr. Froude, the tide took a turn. They were found to be full of harsh, and, as in the case of Charles Lamb, even cruel and heartless judgments; and Carlyle's faults of temper, his malice, and his uncharitableness began to be sharply commented on. A few of the more sturdy admirers of the Seer of Chelsea protested that the "Reminiscences" did not give any idea of the real Carlyle at all; that nothing could be more unjust than to form an estimate of his character from angry passages written in his old age, when weak health and agonising sorrow had rendered him scarcely responsible for his utterances. This defence proved to be but a refuge of lies.—NICOLL, HENRY J., 1882, *Landmarks of English Literature*, p. 424.

Sweet heart, forgive me for thine own sweet sake,
Whose kind blithe soul such seas of sorrow swam,
And for my love's sake, powerless as I am
For love to praise thee, or like thee to make
Music of mirth where hearts less pure would break,
Less pure than thine, our life-unspotted Lamb.
Things hatefullest thou hadst not heart to damn,
Nor wouldst have set thine heel on this dead snake.
Let worms consume its memory with its tongue,
The fang that stabbed fair Truth, the lip that stung
Men's memories uncorroded with its breath.
Forgive me, that with bitter words like his
I mix the gentlest English name that is,
The tenderest held of all that know not death.
—SWINBURNE, ALGERNON CHARLES, 1882, *After Looking into Carlyle's Reminiscences*.

Carlyle takes his place among the first of English, among the very first of all letter-writers. All his great merits come out in this form of expression; and his defects are not felt as defects, but only as striking characteristics and as tones in the picture. Originality, nature, humor, imagination, freedom, the disposition to talk, the play of mood, the touch of confidence—these qualities, of which the letters are full, will, with the aid of an inimitable use of language, . . . preserve their life for readers even further removed from the occasion than ourselves, and for whom possibly the vogue of Carlyle's published writings in his day will be to a certain degree a subject of wonder.—JAMES, HENRY, JR., 1883, *The Correspondence of Carlyle and Emerson*, Century Magazine, vol. 26, p. 265.

Reluctantly, and only when he found that his wishes would not and could not be respected, Carlyle requested me to undertake the task which he had thus described as hopeless; and placed materials in my hands which would make the creation of a true likeness of him, if still difficult, yet no longer as impossible as he had declared it to be. Higher confidence was never placed by any man in another. I had not sought it, but I did not refuse to accept it. I felt myself only more strictly bound than men in such circumstances usually are, to discharge the duty which I was undertaking with the fidelity which I knew to be expected from me. Had I considered my own comfort or my own interest, I should have sifted out or passed lightly over the delicate features in the story. It would have been as easy as it would have been agreeable for me to construct a picture, with every detail strictly accurate, of an almost perfect character. An account so written would have been read with immediate pleasure. Carlyle would have been admired and applauded, and the biographer, if he had not shared in the praise, would at least have escaped censure. He would have followed in the track marked out for him by a custom which is all but universal. . . . Had I taken the course which the "natural man" would have recommended, I should have given no faithful account of Carlyle. I should have created a "delusion and a hallucination" of the precise kind which he who was the truest of men most deprecated and dreaded; and I should have done it not innocently and in ignorance, but with deliberate insincerity, after my attention had been specially directed by his own generous openness to the points which I should have left unnoticed. I should have been unjust first to myself—for I should have failed in what I knew to be my duty as a biographer. I should have been unjust secondly to the public.—FROUDE, JAMES ANTHONY, 1884, *Thomas Carlyle, A History of his Life in London*, vol. I, pp. 2, 3.

I hardly know, in all literature, a more pathetic book than the volume of "Reminiscences."—MOULTON, LOUISE CHANDLER, 1885, *Carlyle: his Works and his Wife, Some Noted Princes, Authors and Statesmen of Our Time*, ed. Parton, p. 184.

Every one agrees with you as to Froude and Carlyle, but there is no doubt that one of the bad effects of Froude's extraordinary proceedings has been to tire people of Carlyle, and discipline them from occupying themselves any more with him, for the present at any rate.—ARNOLD, MATTHEW, 1887, *To C. E. Norton, Aug. 31; Letters, ed. Russell, vol.* II, *p.* 430.

Mr. Froude has done his worst or his best, and it cannot be undone. Even Mr. Eliot Norton's brilliant re-editing cannot undo it. And what is the result? Simply that we must thank either Mr. Froude or his blunder for enabling us to understand how great Carlyle really was. . . . Carlyle, as we know him now, is more real, and immeasurably more impressive than the Carlyle we knew before. The literary small-talkers may say the idol is shattered; but those to whom Carlyle was never an idol, but an instructor and inspirer, must be glad and not sorry that he has become so real to them.—LEWIN, WALTER, 1887, *Garnett's Life of Carlyle, Academy, vol.* 32, *p.* 128.

He was no sooner dead—this great, universally honoured chief of literature in England, a man against whom no one had a word to say, to whom the nation itself, amid all its huge business and interests, gave a moment's pause of respectful silence to acknowledge his greatness—than the book of his fiery grief, the "Reminiscences," which had given outlet to his passion and misery, and of which he remembered only that it was to be anxiously revised or not published at all, was flung just as it was, like a red-hot stone in the face of the country which mourned for Carlyle.—OLIPHANT, MARGARET O. W., 1892, *The Victorian Age of English Literature, p.* 129.

The indiscretions of a biographer who thought it his duty to let "the many-headed beast know" everything, even the most private details of the life of one of the most whimsical and dyspeptic of men, —a biographer, I may add, who misjudged his hero, as a man without humour was sure to misjudge one who was full of it, by taking all his extravagant statements *au pied de la lettre*. Perhaps too much has been made of the indiscretion of a writer, who, so far as indiscreet publication was concerned, seems not to have gone much beyond what he was commissioned or allowed to do by Carlyle himself. But it is worth while to remark that there are many details of a man's life, which gain an undue importance by being revived after the lapse of years, and when it is no longer possible to supply the necessary explanation of the words and action that express only the feelings of the passing hour.— CAIRD, EDWARD, 1892, *The Genius of Carlyle, Essays on Literature and Philosophy, vol* I, *p.* 237.

One of the details of these Memoirs has been to make us understand that the woman whom the mighty genius and the arrogant selfishness of Carlyle so overshadowed, was almost his equal in literary gifts, and vastly his superior in courage, in unselfishness, and generally in character. —O'CONNOR, THOMAS POWER, 1895, *Some Old Love Stories, p.* 240.

Breach of trust, and breach of *such* a trust! And all to provide some readable paragraphs for a book which no mere bookseller's success could ever render other than a failure. From bewildered theologians Mr. Froude had early learned that Jesuitical "doctrine of devils" that the end justifies the means; and so, thinking no man would ever know it, and solacing his uneasy conscience with the delusion that his work would be of permanent value in elucidating the character of the noblest man of modern times, he apparently decided to act on this bad rule for once, and opened and read the love-letters which it was his duty not to read, and printed matter which it was his duty not to print. Never did Providence more swiftly and visibly refute that same "doctrine of devils" which has never in the long run profited any man. Mr. Froude's work defaced for a time the memory of Carlyle by multiplying delusions and mistakes, and the only thing likely to be permanently remembered is the breach of faith which it was hoped would never be known.—WILSON, DAVID, 1898, *Mr. Froude and Carlyle, p.* 5.

What he felt, he thought; and what he thought, he wrote. The denunciatory mood was frequent with Carlyle, and it would be easy to collect enough of his secular anathemas for a droll sort of commination service. Men, women, children, if they disturbed him, came in for his curse. All annoyances spoke to Carlyle and his wife through a megaphone, and were proclaimed by them through a still larger variety of the same instrument. Every cock that crowed near their house was a clarion out of tune, and the "demon-fowls" were equaled by dogs, of which each had to their ears the barking power of Cerberus. When Carlyle traveled, fierce imprecations upon everything viatic were wafted back from every stage to the poor "Goody" in Cheyne Row, often while she was facing alone the problem of fresh paint and paper. On the only occasion I can now recall of Carlyle himself being at home during repairs, they were to him what a convulsion of nature would be to most of us, and his outcries were of cosmic vehemence and shrillness. In these wild splutterings of genius, a maid servant was a "puddle," a "scandalous randy," or even a "sluttish harlot;" a man servant was a "flunkey;" and, if he waked Carlyle too early in the morning, he was a "flunkey of the devil." Rank, wealth, and worldly respectability were, it need not at this day be said, no defence against these grotesque indictments. — COPELAND, CHARLES TOWNSEND, 1899, *Carlyle as a Letter Writer, Letters of Thomas Carlyle to his Youngest Sister*, p. 3.

The "Reminiscences" and the volumes that succeeded them gave, in many quarters apparently, the *coup de grâce* to Carlyle's vogue. Vogue of their own they notoriously had in a true *succès de scandale*, and Carlyle's friends could only denounce his chosen executor and biographer. But this was of course extremely transient, and the result was an immense weariness with the whole subject. Carlyle's own writings fell speedily into a neglect as complete probably as has ever happened to a writer of anything like his power.— BROWNELL, W. C., 1901, *Victorian Prose Masters*, p. 50.

Carlyle preached nothing more persistently than heroism and reverence for heroes. As an author, if not as a husband, he made it manifest that he was himself a hero, great as his own Luther, Knox, or Cromwell. That quality of nobility in labour, joined almost to an unconsciousness of it, gave his reminiscences rare interest, and the fame of them after two decades has scarcely dimmed.—HALSEY, FRANCIS WHITING, 1902, *Our Literary Deluge and Some of its Deep Waters*, p. 186.

GENERAL

When I recollect how the "Edinburgh Reviewers" treated my works not many years since, and when I now consider Carlyle's merits with respect to German literature, I am astonished at the important step for the better. . . . The temper in which he works is always admirable. What an earnest man he is! and how he has studied us Germans! He is almost more at home in our literature than ourselves. At any rate, we cannot vie with him in our researches in English literature. GOETHE, JOHANN WOLFGANG, BY ECKERMANN, 1828, *Conversations, tr. Oxenford*, vol. II, p. 86.

Few writers of the present time have risen more rapidly into popularity than Mr. Carlyle, after labouring through so long a period of comparative neglect. Whatever judgment critics may be pleased to pass on him, it is certain that his works have attracted of late no common share of attention. His little school of sectaries has expanded into a tolerably wide circle of admirers. His eccentricity of style has become the parent of still greater eccentricities in others, with less genius to recommend them; and his mannerism has already infected, to a certain extent, the fugitive literature of the day. . . . The great merit of Mr. Carlyle as a writer, and the great pleasure which his writings give, arise from their *suggestive* character. He is always furnishing hints for thought; a slight sentence, a passing observation, often seem to open long vistas for reflection; but he rarely thinks out a subject for his reader: he never weighs, and reasons, and arrives at balanced conclusions. His brief outlines first arrest the attention, and then provoke objection: we feel tempted to debate and argue every point with him, proposition by proposition; but it is wonderful on how much more cordial terms we part with a companion of this description— angered though we may have felt at times by mutual contradiction—than with one of those formal and useful guides who fall under the general denomination of historian—to which, in plain truth, Mr. Carlyle has no title whatever.—MERIVALE, HERMAN, 1840, *Carlyle on the French Revolution, Edinburgh Review*, vol. 71, pp. 411, 415.

Carlyle, with all his ideality and power of words, never creates an ideal character, rather the test of a poet; he is never affected, as a prophet,—he dare not be so, it would neutralize his earnestness and reforming energy.—Fox, Caroline, 1840, *Memories of Old Friends*, ed. *Pym*; *Journal July* 18, *p.* 120.

Mr. Carlyle formerly wrote for the [Edinburgh] *Review*,—a man of talents, though, in my opinion, absurdly overpraised by some of his admirers. I believe, though I do not know, that he ceased to write because the oddities of his diction and his new words compounded *à la Teutonique* drew such strong remonstrances from Napier.—Macaulay, Thomas Babington, 1841, *Letter to Hunt, Oct.* 29; *Correspondence of Leigh Hunt*, ed. *his Eldest Son, vol.* II, *p.* 25.

Mr. Carlyle is obscure only; he is seldom, as some have imagined him, quaint. So far he is right; for although quaintness, employed by a man of judgment and genius, may be made auxiliary to a poem, whose true thesis is beauty, and beauty alone, it is grossly, and even ridiculously, out of place in a work of prose. But in his obscurity it is scarcely necessary to say that he is wrong. Either a man intends to be understood, or he does not. If he write a book which he intends not to be understood, we shall be very happy indeed not to understand it; but if he write a book which he means to be understood, and, in this book, be at all possible pains to prevent us from understanding it, we can only say that he is an ass—and this, to be brief, is our private opinion of Mr. Carlyle, which we now take the liberty of making public.—Poe, Edgar Allan, 1843, *William Ellery Channing, Works*, ed. *Stedman and Woodberry, vol.* VIII, *p.* 209.

I cannot find that Carlyle leads us directly to a centre; but I do find that he makes us despair for want of one, and that he expresses the indistinct wailings of men in search of it better than all the other writers of our day.—Maurice, Frederick Denison, 1843, *Letter to Mr. Daniel Macmillan, Aug.* 31; *Life*, ed. *Maurice, vol.* I, *p.* 348.

Who does not understand German nowadays, who is not acquainted with German literature since Lessing? Always excepting Mr. Carlyle.—Beddoes, Thomas Lovell, 1844, *To Thomas Forbes Kelsall, Nov.* 13; *Letters, p.* 243.

I never read any of his books, for though divers people profess to understand and admire them, the few passages I have looked at seem always such absurd and unintelligible rant that I feel no desire to go on further. They say that his style is formed on German writers, and that an acquaintance with the language would make me appreciate them, but I do not see what is gained by that so long as the affected ass professes to talk English.—Freeman, Edward A., 1846, *To Mrs. Eleanor Gutch, May* 16; *Life and Letters*, ed. *Stephens, vol.* I, *p.* 93.

Not one obscure line, or half-line did he ever write. His meaning lies plain as the daylight, and he who runs may read; indeed, only he who runs *can* read, and keep up with the meaning. It has the distinctness of a picture to his mind, and he tells us only what he sees printed in largest English type upon the face of things. He utters substantial English thoughts in plainest English dialects; for it must be confessed, he speaks more than one of these. . . . His felicity and power of expression surpass even his special merit as historian and critic. Therein his experience has not failed him, but furnished him with such a store of winged, ay and legged words, as only a London life, perchance, could give account of. We had not understood the wealth of the language before. Nature is ransacked, and all the resorts and purlieus of humanity are taxed, to furnish the fittest symbol for his thought. He does not go to the dictionary, the wordbook, but to the word-manufactory itself, and has made endless work for the lexicographers.—Thoreau, Henry David, 1847-66, *Thomas Carlyle and His Works, A Yankee in Canada, pp.* 218, 219.

There are persons, mole-blind to the soul's make and style,
Who insist on a likeness 'twixt him [Emerson] and Carlyle;
To compare him with Plato would be vastly fairer,
Carlyle's the more burly, but E. is the rarer;
He sees fewer objects, but clearlier, truelier,
If C.'s an original, E.'s more peculiar;
That he's more of a man you might say of the one,
Of the other he's more of an Emerson;
C.'s the Titan, as shaggy of mind as of limb,—
E. the clear-eyed Olympian, rapid and slim;
The one two thirds Norseman, the other half Greek,
Where the one's most abounding, the other's to seek;
C.'s generals require to be seen in the mass,—
E.'s specialties gain if enlarged by the glass;

C. gives nature and God his own fits of the
    blues,
And rims common-sense things with mystical
    hues,—
E. sits in a mystery calm and intense,
And looks coolly around him with sharp com-
    mon-sense;
C. shows you how every-day matters unite
With the dim transdiurnal recesses of night,—
While E., in a plain, preternatural way,
Makes mysteries matters of mere every day;
C. draws all his characters quite à la Fuseli,—
Not sketching their bundles of muscles and
    thews illy,
He paints with a brush so untamed and pro-
    fuse,
They seem nothing but bundles of muscles and
    thews.
—LOWELL, JAMES RUSSELL, 1848, *A Fable for Critics.*

I like Carlyle better and better. His style I do not like, nor do I always concur in his opinions, nor quite fall in with his hero worship; but there is a manly love of truth, an honest recognition and fearless vindication of intrinsic greatness, of intellectual and moral worth, considered apart from birth, rank, or wealth, which commands my sincere admiration.—BRONTË, CHARLOTTE, 1849, *Letter to W. S. Williams, April 16; Charlotte Brontë and Her Circle,* ed. Shorter, p. 195.

I cannot say what I personally owe to that man's writings.—KINGSLEY, CHARLES, 1850, *Letter to Thomas Cooper, Feb. 15.*

Mr. Carlyle adopted a peculiar semi-German style, from the desire of putting thoughts on his paper instead of words, and perhaps of saving himself some trouble in the process. I feel certain that he does it from no other motive; and I am sure he has a right to help himself to every diminution of trouble, seeing how many thoughts and feelings he undergoes. He also strikes an additional blow with the peculiarity, rouses man's attention by it, and helps his rare and powerful understanding to produce double its effect. It would be hard not to dispense with a few verbs and nominative cases, in consideration of so great a result. Yet, if we were to judge him by one of his own summary processes, and deny him the benefit of his notions of what is expedient and advisable, how could we exculpate this style, in which he denounces so many "shams," of being itself a sham? of being affected, unnecessary, and ostentatious? a jargon got up to confound pretension with performance, and reproduce endless German talk under the guise of novelty?—HUNT, LEIGH, 1850, *Autobiography.*

While all Europe admired only independence, Carlyle has passed his life in glorifying obedience and faith; he has understood and he has declared that docility was, under another name, the faculty of learning and of profiting by the science of others. All his works are, in a word, a homage rendered to the invisible protection that the intelligence of the wise extends to the masses, and a plea and a prayer that their kingdom may come. In his eyes the lights diffused among communities can profit them only on one condition; each one must do his business, each must exercise the aptitudes he possesses, and instead of deciding on everything, learn to leave things to the judgment of those who know more than himself.—MILSAND, M. J., 1850, *Revue des Deux Mondes,* 6th S., vol. 6.

Carlyle's "Pantheism" is not like that of Oersted or any philosopher, and is, I fear, an unmanageable object of attack. It is so wholly unsystematic, illogical, wild, and fantastic, that thought finds nothing in it to grapple with. How can one refute the utterances of an oracle or the spleen of a satirist? His power over intellectual men appears to me not unlike that of Joe Smith the prophet over the Mormons; dependent on strength of will and massive effrontery of dogma persevered in amid a universal incertitude weakening other men. The sick and anxious always like best the physician who has most assurance; they are comforted by the presence of so much *force,*—just as poor prostrate France will believe in rifles and eagles after ceasing to believe in anything else. Carlyle's influence appears to spring much less from what he says, estimated by its own persuasiveness, than from the mere consideration that such a man as he thinks all moral and religious doctrine just so much unbelievable trash. I know not how such an influence can be met, except by a positiveness as powerful and as gifted.—MARTINEAU, JAMES, 1852, *To R. H. Hutton, May 19; Life and Letters,* ed. Drummond, vol. I, p. 340.

So much for Mr. Carlyle, who has had the double misfortune of writing according to the humor—that is, the ill-humor, of the moment, without the slightest regard to consistency and truth, and to be surrounded by none but admirers, or listeners borne down by mere noise. In England his fashion is waning rapidly, and I have no doubt but that, like most overrated men, he will live to share the common fate of idols knocked down by his former worshippers in revenge of their own idolatry.—MITFORD, MARY RUSSELL, 1852, *Letter to Miss Jephson, Aug. 23; The Friendships of Mary Russell Mitford*, ed. L'Estrange.

I am a great advocate for hero-worship, and when you have looked closely into Carlyle you may discover him to be quite as much of a hero as Cromwell.—LANDOR, WALTER SAVAGE, 1852, *Letter to John Forster, Walter Savage Landor, A Biography*, p. 597.

The melancholy Polyphemus of Chelsea. —GILFILLAN, GEORGE, 1855, *A Third Gallery of Portraits*, p. 270.

There can be no doubt that Mr. Carlyle's is a somewhat peculiar style, and some few of its peculiarities may have been borrowed from the German. But his mind is a strongly original one; and he would certainly have thought and expressed himself in a way of his own if no such thing as the language or literature of Germany had ever been heard of. Let the attempt be made to re-write one of his more characteristic passages in other words and another manner, and the result will probably surprise the sceptical experimenter. It will not be easy to find anything which could be changed for the better without a loss of part of the meaning or effect designed to be conveyed. For, unquestionably, a more careful writer, one more attentive to all the minutiæ of expression, is not to be found in the language. And this rapid, elliptical, richly allusive style will be found to be, with all its startling qualities, one of the most exactly grammatical in our literature. In this respect it ranks with that of Sterne and that of Rabelais.—CRAIK, GEORGE L., 1861, *A Compendious History of English Literature and of the English Language*, vol. II, p. 561.

The young Crown Princess of Prussia (Princess Royal of England) was here for three days a little while ago. . . . She spoke of Carlyle's last work—I mean his "History of Frederick the Great." I said that Carlyle's other works seemed to me magnificent, wonderful monuments of poetry and imagination, profound research, and most original humour. But that I thought him a most immoral writer, from his exaggerated reverence for brute force, which he was so apt to confound with wisdom and genius. A world governed à la Carlyle would be a pandemonium.— MOTLEY, JOHN LOTHROP, 1862, *To his Mother, Dec. 22; Correspondence*, ed. Curtis, vol. II, p. 105.

The contradictions belong to the time: we may find them in ourselves. And they cannot be resolved, as you fancy they may, into the mere worship of might. That comes uppermost at times; often he recoils from it with the intensest horror, and affirms and feels justice to be the one ruler in heaven and earth. The infinite wail for a real and not a nominal father, for a real and not an imaginery king, comes out in Carlyle more than in any man I know, and I am shocked at myself when I feel how I have been refusing to hear it, and only interpreting it by the devil's cry, "What have I to do with thee?" which mingles in it.—MAURICE, FREDERICK DENISON, 1862, *Letter to J. M. Ludlow, May 30; Life*, ed. Maurice, vol. II, p. 404.

He writes biography like a showman. He stands in front of his heroes, as it were, with a long stick, pointing out their peculiarities with a grin and describing them in the well known language of the van. His mere diction outweighs in impertinence whatever it may win in power.—KEBBEL, THOMAS EDWARD, 1864, *Essays upon History and Politics.*

Mr. Carlyle has no artistic sense of form or rhythm, scarcely of proportion. Accordingly he looks on verse with contempt as something barbarous,—a savage ornament which a higher refinement will abolish, as it has tattooing and nose-rings. With a conceptive imagination vigorous beyond any in his generation, with a mastery of language equalled only by the greatest poets, he wants altogether the plastic imagination, the shaping faculty, which would have made him a poet in the highest sense. He is a preacher and a prophet,— anything you will,—but an artist he is not, and never can be. It is always the knots and gnarls of the oak that he admires, never the perfect and balanced tree. . . . So long as he was merely an exhorter or dehorter, we were thankful for such eloquence, such humor, such vivid or grotesque images, and such splendor of illustration as only he could give; but when he assumes to be a teacher of moral and political philosophy, when he himself takes to compounding the social panaceas he has made us laugh at so often, and advertises none as genuine but his own, we begin to inquire into his qualifications and his defects, and to ask ourselves whether his patent pill differs from others except in the larger amount of aloes, or has any better recommendation than the superior advertising powers of a mountebank of genius. . . . Mr. Carlyle seems to be in the condition of a man who uses stimulants, and must increase his dose from day to day as the senses become dulled under the spur. He began by admiring strength of character and purpose, and the manly self-denial which makes a humble fortune great by steadfast loyalty to duty. He has gone on till mere strength has become such washy weakness that there is no longer any titillation in it; and nothing short of downright violence will rouse his nerves now to the needed excitement. . . . Since "Sartor Resartus" Mr. Carlyle has done little but repeat himself with increasing emphasis and heightened shrillness. Warning has steadily heated toward denunciation, and remonstrance soured toward scolding.— LOWELL, JAMES RUSSELL, 1866–71, *Carlyle, My Study Windows*, pp. 126, 127, 130, 131.

We honestly confess that, right or wrong, we believe it would have been better for the world and for himself if Mr. Carlyle never had written a line, than that he should write as he is writing now. We flatter ourselves that, as there was much noble thinking done before he was born, there would have been enough noble thinking to carry humanity on to its goal if Mr. Carlyle had never appeared. Providence has not left the race dependent on any teacher; and Providence could hardly have furnished a better illustration of the danger of pinning our faith on any teacher, however wise or illustrious, than by permitting Thomas Carlyle to become in his old age the apostle of violence, the despiser and reviler of those whom God has left dependent for their happiness and security on the justice and humanity of their more richly gifted fellows.—GODKIN, E. L., 1867, *Thomas Carlyle, The Nation*, vol. 5, p. 194.

His books opened anywhere show him berating the wrong he sees, but seldom the means of removing. There is ever the same melancholy advocacy of work to be done under the dread master: force of strokes, the right to rule and be ruled, the dismal burden. He rides his Leviathan as fiercely as did his countryman,—Hobbes; can be as truculent and abusive. Were he not thus fatally in earnest, we should take him for the harlequin he often seems, not seeing the sorrowing sadness thus playing off its load in this grotesque mirth, this scornful irony of his; he painting in spite of himself his portraits in the warmth of admiration, the blaze of wrath, giving us mythology for history mostly.—ALCOTT, A. BRONSON, 1869, *Concord Days*, p. 161.

The Rousseau of these times for English-speaking nations is Thomas Carlyle. An apology is perhaps needed for mentioning one of such simple, veracious, disinterested, and wholly highminded life, in the same breath with one of the least sane men that ever lived. Community of method, like misery, makes men acquainted with strange bedfellows. Two men of very different degrees of moral worth may notoriously both preach the same faith and both pursue the same method, and the method of Rousseau is the method of Mr. Carlyle. With each of them thought is an inspiration, and justice a sentiment, and society a retrogression. In other words, the writer who in these days has done more than anybody else to fire men's hearts with a feeling for right and an eager desire for social activity, has with deliberate contempt thrust away from him the only instruments by which we can make sure what right is, and that our social action is wise and effective. A born poet, only wanting perhaps a clearer feeling for form and a firmer spiritual self-possession to have added another name to the noble gallery of English singers, he has been driven by the impetuosity of his sympathies to attack the scientific side of social questions in an imaginative and highly emotional manner . . . Though Mr. Carlyle has written about a large number of men of all varieties of opinion and temperament, and written with emphasis and point and strong feeling, yet there is not one of these judgments, however much we may dissent from it, which we could fairly put a finger upon as *saugrenu*, indecently absurd and unreasonable. Of how many writers of thirty volumes can we say the same?—MORLEY, JOHN, 1870, *Carlyle, The Fortnightly Review, vol.* 14, *pp.* 6, 18.

When you ask Englishmen, especially those under forty, who amongst them are the thinking men, they first mention Carlyle; but at the same time they advise you not to read him, warning you that you will not understand him at all. Then, of course, we hasten to get the twenty volumes of Carlyle—criticism, history, pamphlets, fantasies, philosophy; we read them with very strange emotions, contradicting every morning our opinion of the night before. We discover at last that we are in presence of an extraordinary animal, a relic of a lost family, a sort of mastodon, lost in a world not made for him. We rejoice in this zoological good luck, and dissect him with minute curiosity, telling ourselves that we shall probably never find another animal like him. . . . We are at first put out. All is new here—ideas, style, tone, the shape of the phrases, and the very vocabulary. He takes everything in a contrary meaning, does violence to everything, expressions and things. With him paradoxes are set down for principles; common sense takes the form of absurdity. We are, as it were, carried unto an unknown world, whose inhabitants walk head downwards, feet in the air, dressed in motley, as great lords and maniacs, with contortions, jerks, and cries; we are grievously stunned by these extravagant and discordant sounds; we want to stop our ears, we have a headache, we are obliged to decipher a new language. . . . Carlyle is a Puritan seer, before whose eyes pass scaffolds, orgies, massacres, battles, and who, besieged by furious or bloody phantoms, prophesies, encourages, or curses. If you do not throw down the book from anger or weariness, you will lose your judgment; your ideas depart, nightmare seizes you, a medley of contracted and ferocious figures whirl about in your head; you hear the howls of insurrection, cries of war; you are sick; you are like those listeners to the Covenanters, whom the preaching filled with disgust or enthusiasm, and who broke the head of their prophet, if they did not take him for their leader. . . . From the sublime to the ignoble, from the pathetic to the grotesque, is but a step with Carlyle. With the same stroke he touches the two extremes. His adorations end in sarcasms. . . . He leaps in unimpeded jerks from one end of the field of ideas to the other; he confounds all styles, jumbles all forms, heaps together pagan allusions, Bible reminiscences, German abstractions, technical terms, poetry, slang, mathematics, physiology, archaic words, neologies. . . . Carlyle takes religion in the German manner, after a symbolical fashion. This is why he is called a Pantheist, which in plain language means a madman or a rogue.—TAINE, H. A., 1871, *History of English Literature,* tr. *Van Laun, vol.* II, *bk.* V, *ch.* IV, *pp.* 436, 437, 438, 440, 463.

His command of words must be pronounced to be of the highest order. Among the few that stand next to Shakespeare he occupies a very high place. As his peculiar feelings are strongly marked, so are the special regions of his verbal copiousness. As a matter of course, he was specially awake to, and specially retained, expressions suiting his peculiar vein of strength, rugged sublimity, and every form of ridicule and contempt down to the lowest tolerable depths of coarseness. . . . He is not an exact writer. Hating close analysis, his aim always is to give the broad general features rather than the minute details. He has little of the hair-splitting, dividing and distinguishing mania of De Quincey; no desire to sift his opinions on a topic, and say distinctly what they are and what they are not.—MINTO, WILLIAM, 1872-80, *Manual of English Prose Literature, pp.* 144, 158.

I have already mentioned Carlyle's earlier writings as one of the channels through which I received the influences which enlarged my early narrow creed; but I do not think that those writings, by themselves, would ever have had any effect on my opinions. What truths they contained, though of the very kind which I was already receiving from other quarters, were presented in a form and vesture less suited than any other to give them access to a mind trained as mine had been. They seemed a haze of poetry and German metaphysics, in which almost the only clear thing was a strong animosity to most of the opinions which were the basis of my mode of thought; religious scepticism; utilitarianism, the doctrine of circumstances, and the attaching any importance to democracy, logic, or political economy. Instead of my having been taught anything, in the first instance, by Carlyle, it was only in proportion as I came to see the same truths through media more suited to my mental constitution, that I recognised them in his writings. Then, indeed, the wonderful power with which he put them forth made a deep impression upon me, and I was during a long period one of his most fervent admirers; but the good his writings did me, was not as philosophy to instruct, but as poetry to animate. . . . . I did not, however, deem myself a competent judge of Carlyle. I felt that he was a poet, and that I was not; that he was a man of intuition, which I was not; and that as such, he not only saw things long before me, which I could only when they were pointed out to me, hobble after and prove, but that it was highly probable he could see many things which were not visible to me even after they were pointed out. I knew that I could not see round him, and could never be certain that I saw over him; and I never presumed to judge him with any definiteness, until he was interpreted to me by one greatly the superior of us both—who was more a poet than he, and more a thinker than I—whose own mind and nature included his, and infinitely more.—MILL, JOHN STUART, 1873, *Autobiography*, pp. 174, 176.

Mr. Carlyle's style, which is at first repulsive, becomes in the end very attractive. His humor, although grave, is not saturnine. Some of his graver epigrams, indeed, pierce at once to the very heart of a subject. He worships the hero; yet he is in general thoroughly radical. He loves the poor worker in letters, the peasant, the farmer with his horny hand, the plain speaker, the bold speaker; yet he has no pity for the negro, who, he says, should submit to slavery because he is not fit for freedom. — PROCTER, BRYAN WALLER, 1874(?) *Recollections of Men of Letters*, p. 165.

In Mr. Carlyle's writings humour of every sort abounds; he is a great idealist and humourist; the spectacle of startling contradictions, the grotesque exaggerations, are presented side by side in too grim a form for laughter, and yet there is a dreadful Rabelaisian merriment.—HOOD, EDWIN PAXTON, 1875, *Thomas Carlyle: Philosophic Thinker, Theologian, Historian and Poet*.

In Carlyle's wit and humour there are many peculiar characteristics. His wit is a heavy, thumping kind, like the battering ram of old, hammering away with "thunderlike percussion" at some old abuse or timeworn institution. He reminds us of the heathen tradition of one of the gods, who is described as "all hands, all eyes, all feet," to seek out, overtake, and punish falsehood and wrongs. His humour is often of such a kind as makes us laugh through tears, and laughs itself in its most savage words. It has in it a wild, grim fancy, with something of the fierce, grotesque, and fiery earnestness of Hogarth, with the free, daring caricature of Cruikshank. A rough, rugged, vehement spirit is in him, as well as a hearty humour, which ever and anon breaks out, sporting with the foibles, fancies and manners of the age.—DAVEY, SAMUEL, 1876, *Darwin, Carlyle and Dickens: with Other Essays*.

It was from a man still living, Thomas Carlyle, that the English public was to learn the value of this literature which had suddenly grown up to a place near their own. He knew how dense was the English ignorance about the Germans, and he set himself busily to work to give his fellow-countrymen information which might remove their prejudices, and by means of his translations to supply them with the means of corroborating or refuting what he said in praise of these newly discovered writers.—PERRY, THOMAS SERGEANT, 1877, *German Influence in English Literature, Atlantic Monthly*, vol. 40, p. 143.

Mr. Carlyle plays with his electrical battery upon the will. . . . It is not the intellect alone, or the imagination alone, which can become sensible of the highest virtue in the writings of Mr. Carlyle. He is before all else a power with reference to conduct. . . . Mr. Carlyle is a mystic in the service of what is nobly positive, and it is easy to see how his transcendental worship of humanity, together with his reverence for duty, might condense and materialize themselves for the needs of a generation adverse to transcendental ways of thought, into the ethical doctrines of Comte. . . . Mr. Carlyle is so deeply impressed by the fact that truthfulness, virtue, rectitude of a certain kind, the faithful adaptation of means to ends, are needful in order to bring anything to effect, that where ends are successfully achieved, he assumes some of the virtuous force of the world to have been present. With this falls in his sense of the sacredness of fact; to recognize fact, to accept conditions, and thereby to conquer,—such is the part of the hero who would be a victor. Add to all this, the stoical temper, a sternness in Mr. Carlyle's nature, which finds expression in his scorn for mere happiness, and we shall understand how his transcendentalism makes us acquainted with strange heroes.—DOWDEN, EDWARD, 1877-78, *The Transcendental Movement and Literature*, Studies in Literature, pp. 73, 74, 75, 76.

From 1835 to 1860 there was not in England any more remarkable man of letters than Thomas Carlyle; none who had more influence or more power over men's minds. He was at once a writer, a historian and a thinker; the writer was admired and formed a school, the historian was read with vivacity, a circle was formed round the thinker, and his disciples took his sentences for oracles. However, if it is true that the characteristic of a great writer is to have as many different styles as he had subjects to treat, Carlyle was not a great writer. He has always had only one style, well suited, truly, to himself, that of Carlyle. Into every subject he carried the oratorical style, tone, accent, and even the gesticulation, for he gesticulates much. He was prodigal of his exclamation, he carried to excess apostrophe and prosopopœia. When one has read much of him, it is a blessing to read again three or four pages of Voltaire, without even troubling to select them; oracles are often admirable, but they disturb too much; one tires soon of dealings with them and their eloquent gesticulation. Neither was Carlyle a great historian. One can never study his commentary on Cromwell's speeches, his French Revolution, and his Frederick II. without gaining much benefit; but what makes the historian is the power of understanding everything, and the absence of *parti-pris*, and Carlyle was less solicitous to understand than to praise that which he loved, and to paint in black that which he did not like. He has not told us about Cromwell, he has celebrated him; he has not explained the French Revolution, he has chanted it on his lyre, to which, for the occasion, he added a brazen string which made the sounds truly diabolic.... If Carlyle can be reckoned neither among the great prose writers, nor among the great historians, nor among the great thinkers, it must be admitted that he had in him the stuff of a great poet, and we must accuse nature which in dowering him with the most brilliant imagination, had denied him the gift of rhythm and cadenced speech.—CHERBULIEZ, VICTOR, 1881, *Revue des Deux Mondes, March*.

As a representative author, a literary figure, no man else will bequeath to the future more significant hints of our stormy era, its fierce paradoxes, its din, and its struggling parturition periods, than Carlyle. He belongs to our own branch of the stock, too; neither Latin nor Greek, but altogether Gothic. Rugged, mountainous, volcanic, he was himself more a French Revolution than any of his volumes.... As launching into the self-complacent atmosphere of our days a rasping, questioning, dislocating agitation and shock, is Carlyle's final value.... The way to test how much he has left his country were to consider, or try to consider, for a moment, the array of British thought, the resultant *ensemble* of the last fifty years, as existing to-day, *but with Carlyle left out*. It would be like an army with no artillery. The show were still a gay rich one—Byron, Scott, Tennyson, and many more—horsemen and rapid infantry, and banners flying—but the last heavy roar so dear to the ear of the train'd soldier, and that settles fate and victory, would be lacking. — WHITMAN, WALT, 1881, *Death of Thomas Carlyle, Specimen Days and Collect*, pp. 168, 169.

I never much liked Carlyle. He seemed to me to be "carrying coals to Newcastle," as our proverb says; preaching earnestness to a nation which had plenty of it by nature, but was less abundantly supplied with several other useful things.—ARNOLD, MATTHEW, 1881, *To M. Fontanés, March 25; Letters*, ed. Russell, vol. II, p. 222.

Anything that I can do to help in raising a memorial to Carlyle shall be most willingly done. Few men can have dissented more strongly from his way of looking at things than I; but I should not yield to the most devoted of his followers in gratitude for the bracing wholesome influence of his writings when, as a very young man, I was essaying without rudder or compass to strike out a course for myself.—HUXLEY, THOMAS HENRY, 1881,

To Lord Stanley, March 9; Life and Letters, ed. Huxley, vol. II, p. 36.

To sum up, if I had to characterize the moral and intellectual influence exercised by Carlyle, I should say that he seems to me to have, above all things, helped to loosen the fetters of positive creed in which thought was imprisoned among his countrymen. Carlyle was a mystic, and mysticism here, as elsewhere, discharged the function which belongs to it in the chain of systems: to wit, that of dissolving dogma under pretence of spiritualizing it, of shattering faith under pretence of enlarging it. When men heard Carlyle speak so much of divinity and eternity, of mystery and adoration, they hailed him as the preacher of a religion higher and wider than current belief. In vain did orthodoxy, more keen-sighted, point out the negations which lay hid under the writer's formulas. It is so pleasant to free oneself without appearing to break too sharply with consecrated words and institutions. Since then speculation has made much way in England. The universal mysteries of our author have been exchanged for exact research, precise definitions, rigorous ascertainments. I do not know whether Carlyle was aware of it, but he lived long enough to see his influence exhausted, his teaching out of date. It is true that, as consolation, he could take himself to witness that he had served as the transition between the past and the present, and that this is in the long run the best glory to which a thinker can pretend here below. — SCHERER, EDMOND, 1881–91, *Thomas Carlyle, Essays on English Literature*, tr. *Saintsbury, p. 235.*

In this he was akin to all the prophets, one of their brotherhood,—that he maintained the spiritual and dynamic forces in man as against the mechanical. While so many, listening to the host of materialising teachers, are always succumbing to the visible, and selling their birthright for the mess of pottage which this world offers, Carlyle's voice appealed from these to a higher tribunal, and found a response in those deeper recesses which lie beyond the reach of argument and analysis. This he did with all his powers, and by doing so rendered a great service to his generation, whether they have listened to him or not.— SHAIRP, JOHN CAMPBELL, 1881, *Prose Poets, Aspects of Poetry, p. 422.*

In his clearer moments, when he lays aside his wrath and addresses himself to his nobler work of edifying exhortation, he commands a lofty soul-piercing language, which seems to extinguish all ignoble desires, and call forth their opposites by a sort of celestial affinity. . . . His literary faculty, if not perfect—very few are perfect—was extraordinary and magnificent in the extreme. His supreme gift is his penetrating imagination, of seeing as it were into the heart of things in a moment, and reproducing them in words which it is impossible to forget. . . . In this respect he well deserves the epithet of poet, much more than many metrical and musical persons. . . . And he sees so much and so well outside himself, because he has so much inside, because, by his own richness of thought and feeling, he comes ready prepared to observe, to note, to recognize things when they present themselves. . . . Carlyle's depth of insight into character was owing to the depth and capacity of his own nature. He had lived the lives of a dozen men before he put pen to paper, by reason of the passions with which he had become intimate in his own breast. In the next place, his hard peasant life, his education in the school of poverty, had made him acquainted with fact at first hand. He had not been shielded, like the unfortunate rich, from wholesome collision with realities. . . . The combined result of his natural endowment and his stimulating training was to make him the most figurative and imaginative prose writer in our language. All nature seems under his sway for colours and image—seems to offer him, as it were, the right suggestive thing to express his thought.—MORRISON, JAMES COTTER, 1883, *Thomas Carlyle, Macmillan's Magazine, vol. 47, pp. 210, 211.*

To say that Carlyle is not a great writer, or, more than that, a supreme literary artist, is to me like denying that Angelo and Rembrandt were great painters, or that the sea is a great body of water. His life of Herculean labor was entirely given to letters, and he undoubtedly brought to his tasks the greatest single equipment of pure literary power English prose has ever received.—BURROUGHS, JOHN, 1884, *Arnold on Emerson and Carlyle, Century Magazine, vol. 27, p. 926.*

Carlyle cannot be killed by an epigram, nor can the many influences that moulded him be referred to any single source. The rich banquet his genius has spread for us is of many courses.... Carlyle's eye was indeed a terrible organ: he saw everything. ... He may be a great philosopher, a useful editor, a profound scholar, and anything else his friends like to call him, except a great historian.... By nature he was tolerant enough; so true a humourist could never be a bigot. When his war-paint is not on, a child might lead him. His judgments are gracious, chivalrous, tinged with a kindly melancholy and divine pity. But this mood is never for long. Some gadfly stings him: he seizes his tomahawk and is off on the trail. It must sorrowfully be admitted that a long life of opposition and indigestion, of fierce warfare with cooks and Philistines, spoilt his temper, never of the best, and made him too often contemptuous, savage, unjust.—BIRRELL, AUGUSTINE, 1884, *Obiter Dicta, First Series, pp.* 5, 11, 22, 24.

The world's final judgment upon Carlyle, we feel certain, will be that he was himself above all a man of letters. He had the graphic faculty more than any other. He could not help putting pen to paper. The "pictured page" came forth from him naturally, and grew under his hand irresistibly—yet always under the impulse of a high ideal. This is the explanation of the different ways in which he speaks—or at least it is the chief explanation—for no doubt also mere mood sometimes swayed him. Literature was to him "the wine of life." It should not be converted "into daily food." Above all, it must not be confounded with the "froth ocean of printed speech, which we loosely call literature." This must be said for Carlyle—no less than for Milton—that he never ceased to claim a high ideal for literature, and to vindicate for its theme "whatsoever in religion is holy and sublime, and in virtue amiable and grave." In this respect Carlyle's influence has been good without exception.—TULLOCH, JOHN, 1885, *Movements of Religious Thought in Britain During the Nineteenth Century, p.* 121.

One of the most interesting pieces of autobiography ["Essay on Walter Scott"] and one of the worst pieces of literary criticism in the English language.—COURTHOPE, WILLIAM JOHN, 1885, *The Liberal Movement in English Literature, p.* 123.

Thomas Carlyle was a great spiritual force in his best day; but he long outlived his best day, and the objects whereon his prime force was expended. He was a great writer of history, a fiery kindler of the historical sense in men. He was a wonderful literary artist; and this is the really distinctive note of him, though his art at the best was somewhat abnormal, falling short of the serene level of perfect art. Thinker, prophet, or judge he was not. It was the long mistake of his life to imagine himself thinker, prophet and judge; to mistake literary mastery for philosophic power. And it is the same mistake in his few devoted followers which exaggerated the value of his latter-day deliverances, and has given to the world those unworthy jottings of his least heroic moods.—HARRISON, FREDERIC, 1885, *Froude's Life of Carlyle, The Choice of Books and Other Literary Pieces, pp.* 181, 191.

Thou wert a Titan, but a Titan tossed
With wild tumultuous heavings in thy breast,
And fancy-fevered, and cool judgment lost
In mighty maelstroms of divine unrest.
What souls were drugged with doubt in sceptic time
Thy cry disturbed into believing life,
And fools that raved in prose or writhed in rhyme
Were sharply surgeoned by thy needful knife:
But, if there were who in this storm of things
Sighed for sweet calm, and in this dark for light,
And in this jar for the wise Muse that sings
All wrong into the ordered ranks of right,
They thanked not thee, who didst assault their brain
With thunder-claps and water-spouts for rain.
—BLACKIE, JOHN STUART, 1886, *Messis Vitæ*.

St. Thomas Coprostom, late of Craigenputtock and Chelsea.... The Gospel according to St. Coprostom has the invaluable merit of pungent eccentricity and comparatively novel paradox. The evangelist of "golden silence"—whose own speech, it may be admitted, was "quite other" than "silvern"—is logically justified in his blatant but ineffable contempt for the dull old doctrines of mere mercy and righteousness, of liberty that knows no higher law than duty, of duty that depends for its existence on the existence of liberty.—SWINBURNE, ALGERNON CHARLES, 1886, *La Légende des Siècles, A Study of Victor Hugo, p.* 134.

The great Silence-monger.—DOYLE, SIR FRANCIS HASTINGS, 1886, *Reminiscences and Opinions, p.* 245.

His style, whether learned at home or partly acquired under the influence of Irving and Richter (see Froude, I., 396), faithfully reflects his idiosyncrasy. Though his language is always clear, and often pure and exquisite English, its habitual eccentricities offended critics, and make it the most dangerous of models. They are pardonable as the only fitting embodiment of his graphic power, his shrewd insight into human nature, and his peculiar humor, which blends sympathy for the suffering with scorn for fools. His faults of style are the result of the perpetual straining for emphasis of which he was conscious, and which must be attributed to an excessive nervous irritability seeking relief in strong language, as well as to a superabundant intellectual vitality. Conventionality was for him the deadly sin. Every sentence must be alive to its finger's end. As a thinker he judges by intuition instead of calculation. In history he tries to see the essential fact stripped of the glosses of pedants; in politics, to recognize the real forces masked by constitutional mechanism, in philosophy, to hold the living spirit untrammelled by the dead letter.—STEPHEN, LESLIE, 1887, *Dictionary of National Biography*, vol. IX.

The only influence that Carlyle ever exercised upon me was through Emerson, as I never could endure Carlyle's immense pretension and conceit.—HAMERTON, PHILIP GILBERT, 1887, *Books which Have Influenced Me*, p. 58.

What he despised, and would teach others to despise, was earth's treasures, pleasures, fashions, forms, manners, shams, cant, and all oppression and wrong. What he loved was God above all and his fellow-man, pity for distress, industry in work, sacrifice of self, honesty of purpose, truth in word and deed, purity of heart, good works anywhere and everywhere. — ARNOLD, A. S., 1888, *The Story of Thomas Carlyle*.

Carlyle always seemed to me to frame a new humbug for every humbug he plucked down, and a humbug quite as dangerous to the times present as the one demolished. It was the commonplace rather than the false which he attacked, and he substituted for it the extravagant and the grotesque. His perpetual and oftentimes petty explosives of words, phrases, thoughts, were wearisome to me: a package of crackers fired off in a barrel.—BASCOM, JOHN, 1888, *Books that Have Helped Me*, p. 32.

I came under the power of Carlyle's genius a year before I commenced Goethe. He was a great assistance to me in the way of emancipation from the spell of those earlier writings of which I have spoken. ... I read first the "Hero Worship" in 1857, finding it somewhat dull reading. Having acquired some familiarity with his style of expression and with this leading thought I took up the "Miscellanies," and the author soon became fascinating. As I grew in capacity to understand him he gained more and more power over me, until I could only pity my former self, who had found anything of Carlyle's dull. I suppose that I caught less than one in five of the ideas of the "Sartor Resartus" on first reading. I struggled with the ponderous and complex art-form of the work, and finally extracted the chief thought and many minor reflections of exceeding value to me. But I returned again and again to the book in after years, with the vain hope of discovering any affirmative significance in his "everlasting yea." In my latter years I have come to believe that Carlyle's solution of the problem of life, at least in that early work, was rendered nugatory by the very terms in which he stated it. In other words, he presupposed the impossibility of an affirmative answer.—HARRIS, WILLIAM T., 1888, *Books that Have Helped Me*, p. 22.

The young men of the days immediately before me in college had been greatly affected by Wordsworth. I have heard Henry Bellows say that his acquaintance with Wordsworth was a new life to him. But the first wave, so to speak, the fresh rush, of Wordsworth's poetry had passed, before we of my time were old enough to read poetry. And it was another wizard who was to startle us from the proprieties of our boyhood. This was Carlyle. I have an odd association with "Sartor Resartus," which serves me as an aid to memory about the first knowledge of the "Sartor" papers here. When I entered college, in 1835, I had to go to my uncle, in a real and not in a metaphorical sense. I was to ask him "to sign my bond"—the bond required by the college, that it might be sure we paid our bills. I found him reading "Sartor Resartus," in "Fraser," I think. He laid it down, showed it to me, and asked me if I knew what *sartor resartus* meant. As I had entered college with a certain distinction in Latin, I was rather mortified that I had to confess that the Latin school, Virgil, Ovid, Horace, and Cicero, had passed me by, and left me innocent of any knowledge of the meaning of either word. But we soon learned our Carlyle well, whatever we knew or did not know in Latin. It is not one man or two, in that generation, it is every one who wrote or read English, who was under his power, and the critics of future times will be able to show very accurately how and where that tide-wave struck the voyage of every man of letters who lived in the middle of this century.— HALE, EDWARD EVERETT, 1888, *Books that Have Helped Me, p.* 9.

Among the great writers who, without attempting to found sects, have profoundly influenced modern thought, Carlyle undoubtedly occupies the foremost place. With all his extravagances and eccentricities, he was essentially a Hebrew prophet in modern guise, preaching a true gospel— that of sincerity.—LAING, S., 1888, *Modern Science and Modern Thought, Sixth Ed., p.* 238.

That supremely self-conscious preacher of unconsciousness. — LEWIN, WALTER, 1889, *The Abuse of Fiction, The Forum, vol.* 7, *p.* 666.

Isaiah of the nineteenth century.— SCHULZE-GAEVERNITZ, GERHART VON, 1890, *Zum socialen Frieden.*

The man, however, whose teaching did most to rouse the age to a sense of the insufficiency of its work was Thomas Carlyle, whose "Sartor Resartus" began to appear in 1833, and who detested alike the middle-class Parliamentary government dear to Macaulay, and the Democratic government dear to Grote and Mill. He was a prophet of duty. Each individual was to set himself resolutely to despise the conventions of the world, and to conform to the utmost of his power to the divine laws of the world. Those who did this most completely were heroes, to whom and not to Parliamentary majorities or scientific deductions, reverence and obedience were due. The negative part of Carlyle's teaching — its condemnation of democracy and science—made no impression. The positive part fixed itself upon the mind of the young, thousands of whom learnt from it to follow the call of duty, and to obey her behests.—GARDINER, SAMUEL R., 1890-91, *A Student's History of England, vol.* III, *p.* 941.

Whatever else may be said about Carlyle, no one can question that he took his literary vocation most seriously. He was for a long time a very poor man, but he never sought wealth by advocating popular opinions, by pandering to common prejudices, or by veiling most unpalatable beliefs. In the vast mass of literature which he has bequeathed to us there is no scamped work, and every competent judge has recognised the untiring and conscientious accuracy with which he verified and sifted the minutest fact. His standard of truthfulness was extremely high, and one of his great quarrels with his age was that it was an age of half-beliefs and insincere professions. . . . A firm grasp of facts, he maintained, was the first characteristic of an honest mind; the main element in all honest, intellectual work. His own special talent was the gift of insight, the power of looking into the heart of things; piercing to essential facts, discerning the real characters of men, their true measure of genuine, solid worth. . . . In his writings, amid much that has imperishable value, there is, I think, much that is exaggerated, much that is one-sided, much that is unwise. But no one can be imbued with his teaching without finding it a great moral tonic, and deriving from it a nobler, braver, and more unworldly conception of life.—LECKY, WILLIAM EDWARD HARTPOLE, 1891, *Carlyle's Message to his Age, Contemporary Review, vol.* 40, *pp.* 525, 526, 528.

The grand old iron-worker in literature, the brawny blacksmith of letters.—CHENEY, JOHN VANCE, 1891, *The Golden Guess, p.* 6.

Carlyle's own brightness now makes him shine as a fixed star in our literary firmament. His radiance may be obscured; quenched it cannot be. His faults and foibles are manifest, yet is he esteemed in spite of them, and by too many because of them. His prejudices are vexatious, at least occasionally. So are those of De Quincey, at his best the best English prose-writer of this century. Amid all Carlyle's prejudices, amid all his denunciations of men and things to be condemned, we see him capable of hope; we feel he sympathizes with his fellow-creatures. Beneath a mask of ferocity love beams from his countenance. — GREENE, J. REAY, 1891, *Carlyle's Lectures on the History of Literature, Preface, p.* viii.

For the thunders and roarings of Carlyle have united with the calm delicacy of Ruskin to promote an influence for good in the discussion of social questions that is none the less real because it has not been so direct as that of men more prominent as practical social reformers. One is more inclined to look at these two as historian and art-critic; yet to ignore their reforming influence in modern England would be to fail in recognizing some of the most important factors of social amelioration in the present century. Both Carlyle and Ruskin will live in our history as true prophets, for they have been the two greatest inspirers and awakeners of the mind of England in an age in which the mental and spiritual faculties of our race have sometimes seemed in danger of succumbing to the material.—GIBBINS, H. DE B., 1892, *English Social Reformers, p.* 183.

The general verdict on Carlyle's literary career assigns to him the first place among the authors of his time. No writer of our generation, in or out of England, has combined such abundance with such power. Regarding his rank as a writer there is little or no dispute: it is admitted that the irregularities and eccentricities of this style are bound up with its richness. In estimating the value of his thought we must distinguish between instruction and inspiration. If we ask what new truths he has taught, what problems he has definitely solved, our answers must be few. This is a perhaps inevitable result of the manner of his writing, or rather of the nature of his mind.—NICHOL, JOHN, 1892, *Thomas Carlyle (English Men of Letters), p.* 249.

Certainly I remember that the finest appreciation of Carlyle—a man whom every critic among English-speaking races had picked to pieces and discussed and reconstructed a score of times—was left to be uttered by an inspired loafer in Camden, New Jersey.—QUILLER-COUCH, A. T., 1892, *Adventures in Criticism, p.* 236.

The dominant stratum of Carlyle's character was morality, hard Scotch granite, out of which the sweetest waters could break, and on whose top soil the tenderest seedlings could thrive—humor, pathos, poetry, the most subduing gentleness, all were there; but the main formation of his mind was all the same vehement sternness, with more than a touch of the Pharisaism that metes and judges, and swears by the law rather than the Gospel. He had little love of music, no love of art, and considerable contempt for any poetry but the poetry of action. To him it was inconceivable that any human creature should claim any dignity or reverence as a minister of the beautiful.—DAWSON, W. J., 1892, *Quest and Vision, p.* 28.

The demand for poetical form is to Carlyle what the vase is to the imprisoned Genie, abolish it and the mighty figure overshadows land and sea. When no longer required to write as a poet, Carlyle first becomes the poet; the ear so insensible to metrical harmony develops a fine sense for the voluminous harmonies of prose; he is not only sublime but rhythmical. Unfortunately the plan of this collection excludes Carlyle the poet; we can only exhibit Carlyle the verse writer cramped and shorn for want of the special endowment of which he denied the existence. Yet he could write nothing wholly uninteresting, and in the least successful of his metrical experiments there is a something which the world will not let die. It is significant that the most successful of his acknowledged attempts should be his rendering of Goethe's Helena in the twelve syllabled iambics of the original, in our language a stately, but stilted metre, absolutely devoid of every variety of rhythm.—GARNETT, RICHARD, 1894, *The Poets and the Poetry of the Century, John Keats to Lord Lytton, ed. Miles, p.* 120.

Carlyle's most orderly paragraphs belong to the period of his life when Goethe's influence over him was freshest and strongest. For order in the paragraph is due largely to an ascendency of the intellectual element over the emotional; and Carlyle's emotions were never so well-tempered—or least ill-tempered—as when he saw most clearly the mastery that Goethe had of his own nature. Thus the "Life of Schiller" is sequent and orderly in a degree surprising to the reader who has of late fed on the "French Revolution." In this early time Carlyle saw life steadily and achromatically. But as his egotism waxed strong with his days, as his impatience of the world increased and his hopes of reforming it decreased, he became subject to starts of the wildest incoherence. In such papers as the "Latter Day Pamphlets" he is wholly under the influence of his habitually strongest emotions; he raves. . . . In his historical writing Carlyle is a great master of the law of proportion, as concerns both the paragraph and the whole composition. He combines Hume's power of making a paragraph illustrate a given philosophical idea, and Macaulay's power of heightening that impression by pictorial means. He moulds his material, fuses his facts, emphasizes the salient, subordinates the unimportant. In elaborating large plans, he constantly reduces his macrocosm to microcosm to be sure of making his point; he reiterates his central truth; he does not disdain numerous formal but living summaries.—LEWIS, EDWIN HERBERT, 1894, *The History of the English Paragraph, pp.* 147, 150.

No sweating smith ever groaned more at his task than did this greatest of modern English literary artists. He fairly grovelled in toil, bemoaning himself and smiting his fellow-man in sheer anguish of spirit; producing his masterpieces to an accompaniment of passionate but unprofane curses on the conditions under which, and the task upon which, he worked. This, however, was the artisan, not the artist, side of the great writer; it was the toilworn, unrelenting Scotch conscience astride his art and riding it at times as Tam o' Shanter spurred his gray mare, Meg, on the ride to Kirk Alloway.—MABIE, HAMILTON WRIGHT, 1894, *My Study Fire, Second Series, p.* 17.

To me, profoundly averse to autocracy, Carlyle's political doctrines had ever been repugnant. Much as I did, and still do, admire his marvellous style and the vigour, if not the truth, of his thought—so much so that I always enjoy any writing of his, however much I disagree with it—intercourse with him soon proved impracticable. Twice or thrice, in 1851-2, I was taken to see him by Mr. G. H. Lewes; but I soon found that the alternatives were—listening in silence to his dogmas, sometimes absurd, or getting into a hot argument with him, which ended in our glaring at one another; and as I did not like either alternative I ceased to go.—SPENCER, HERBERT, 1894.

The Late Professor Tyndall, Fortnightly Review, vol. 61, *p.* 144.

Of the Power, which through thought and opinion is shaping the future of mankind in all varieties, perhaps the most forcible expression in the nineteenth Christian century is to be found in the work of Thomas Carlyle. He spoke as one having authority, and not as the Scribes: his appeal is therefore direct to the sense of truth in man, and to no other court. That sense of truth he knew to be an inheritance from the past—the product of the struggles, efforts, thoughts, and teaching of former generations. Charles Darwin did not believe more firmly that in the individual we were to look for the advance of the species; Ernst Haeckel does not declare more decisively that we are the results of the past—that in us and through us creation is still going on.—DUNCAN, ROBERT, 1895, *ed. Thoughts on Life by Thomas Carlyle, Introduction, p.* XI.

Carlyle's mission was not merely to destroy: he shattered error in order that the clogged fountain of truth might once more gush forth. Before eyes long dimmed with gazing on insincerity he would hold up shining patterns of sincerity; souls groping for guidance, he would stay and comfort by precedents of strength; hearts pursuing false idols, he would chasten by examples of truth. Men talked—and nowhere more pragmatically than in the churches—as if God, after having imparted his behests to a few Hebrews ages ago, had retired into some remote empyrean, and busied himself no more with the affairs of men. But to Carlyle the immanence of God was an ever-present reality, manifesting itself throughout all history and in every individual conscience, but nowise more clearly than in the careers of great men.—THAYER, WILLIAM ROSCOE, 1895-99, *Carlyle, Throne-Makers, p.* 174.

Carlyle was probably never at his best when he gave himself to the study of a particular author. His genius rather lay in the more general aspects of his work, and in the force with which he gave an entirely new turn to the currents of English criticism.—VAUGHAN, C. E., 1896, *ed. English Literary Criticism, p.* 200.

Carlyle, the apostle of agnostic stoicism. —PRESSENSÉ, FRANCIS DE, 1896, *Cardinal Manning.*

How far exaggeration could go, and how far unquestionable genius could find contorted diction, and every conceivable antic of phraseology, a worthy and convenient means of picturesque description or impressive moralising, can never be seen in more striking manifestation than in the style which Carlyle deliberately adopted, and as tenaciously maintained. Genius must make its own laws; and however severe the strain upon our faith or upon our sense of proportion and harmony, we must hesitate to question the validity of these laws in their personal application. We may, however, be permitted to regret that the resources of such genius were not sufficient to find expression at less expense of uncouth phrase and ejaculatory emphasis, and could not more frequently hold its course in that more serene stream of language which Carlyle can occasionally achieve, where the effect of the restraint and restfulness is perhaps not less picturesque than that of the hurtle and passion of words, and where the impression, if less startling, is certainly not less lasting.—CRAIK, HENRY, 1896, *English Prose, vol.* v, *p.* 5, *Introduction.*

Conceiving imaginations, however, are of two kinds. For the one kind the understanding serves as a lamp of guidance; upon the other the understanding acts as an electric excitant, a keen irritant. Bagehot's was evidently of the first kind; Carlyle's conspicuously of the second. There is something in common between the minds of these two men as they conceive society. Both have a capital grip upon the actual; both can conceive without confusion the complex phenomena of society; both send humourous glances of searching insight into the hearts of men. But it is the difference between them that most arrests our attention. Bagehot has the scientific imagination, Carlyle the passionate. Bagehot is the embodiment of witty common sense; all the movements of his mind illustrate that vivacious sanity which he has himself called "animated moderation." Carlyle, on the other hand, conceives men and thier motives too often with a hot intolerance; there is heat in his imagination,—a heat that sometimes scorches and consumes. Life is for him dramatic, full of fierce, imperative forces. Even when the world rings with laughter, it is laughter which, in his ears, is succeeded by an echo of mockery; laughter which is but a defiance of tears.—WILSON, WOODROW, 1897, *Mere Literature and Other Essays, p.* 96.

From the point of view, in fact, of the historian of letters, the formative work of Macaulay in prose stands side by side with that of Tennyson in poetry as the two most important phenomena of the last seventy years. As regards its effect upon expression—upon the form as distinct from the matter of English literature—the career of Macaulay reduces that of Carlyle to the proportion of a mere meteoric episode.—TRAILL, HENRY DUFF, 1897, *Social England, vol.* VI, *p.* 513.

The place which was occupied by Swift in the eighteenth century is held by Carlyle in the nineteenth, and though every line that he has written should cease to be read, he will still be remembered as the greatest of literary figures in an age of great men of letters.—SHORTER, CLEMENT, 1897, *Victorian Literature, p.* 128.

It was the greatness of Carlyle that the fiery naturalism of the Revolution, which had become prophetic in Shelley, was in him enriched by that relative and organic apprehension of life, art, and history, which had grown up among the foes of revolution. In poetry as in ethics, truth was his last word; but few of its preachers have insisted so powerfully that truth has infinitely various accents, and that the poetry which is not original is naught.—HERFORD, C. H., 1897, *The Age of Wordsworth, p.* 89.

Surely there is human interest in these sketches, "exercises" though they be. They are certainly not Carlyle's highest possible even at that time. But they are human, sympathetic, soulfully remunerative work. And doubtless the task of reading for them led him insensibly into the wider fields of the Essays, and ultimately perhaps gave us "Heroes and Hero Worship" and "The French Revolution." Also I find in most of them touches of the coming greatness. Sparks from the flint tell of the latent fire. Accents of ironic scorn come to our ears with something of the sting of that stormy Annandale voice which afterwards broke in upon so many babbling controversies, like the eagle's scream dispersing the chatter of a jay convention. And after all preface of derogation, these Essays remain fragments of honest, clear-lined, honourable workmanship. I like to think of the young author writing them in the peasant's but-and-ben, and especially of his father beginning to respect him more when he showed him one after the other good Sir David Brewster's fifteen-guinea cheques, and bought for him that pair of marvellous spectacles with the first. I have the greater fellow-feeling, that I know one man who never expects to be happier than when he threw his first hard-earned ten-pound-note into his mother's lap.—CROCKETT, S. R., 1897, ed. *Montaigne and Other Essays Chiefly Biographical by Thomas Carlyle Now First Collected, Foreword*, p. XII.

Carlyle also was God's prophet—a seer stormy indeed and impetuous, with a great hatred for lies and laziness, and a mighty passion for truth and work; lashing our shams and hypocrisies; telling our materialistic age that it was going straight to the devil, and by a vulgar road at that; pointing out the abyss into which luxury and licentiousness have always plunged. Like Elijah of old, Carlyle loved righteousness, hated cant, and did ever plead for justice, and mercy, and truth. If his every sentence was laden with intellect, it was still more heavily laden with character. To the great Scotchman God gave the prophet's vision and the seer's sympathy and scepter.—HILLIS, NEWELL DWIGHT, 1899, *Great Books as Life-Teachers*, p. 26.

In spite of all his maniloquent dreaming, Carlyle is true or means to be true to the uncompromising facts of life; he dreams only that he may the more victoriously labor; and in his Gospel of Work and his doctrine of Hero-worship he returns from the misty regions of transcendentalism and confronts the practical concerns of common life. No one is more contemptuous than Carlyle of dilettante webspinning, or of idle playing with emotion.—GATES, LEWIS E., 1900, *English Literature of the Nineteenth Century, The Critic*, vol. 36.

Carlyle, like Rousseau or Shelley, was an imaginative setter forth of abstract principles. It was only by such a writer that Rousseau could at all be combated in the long run. But there was this difference between the Frenchman and the Scot, that while the abstractions of the one were either purely fanciful inventions, with no experience whatever to support them, or at best abstractions from groups of facts looked at imperfectly, the abstractions of the other were derived from very definite facts contemplated with the utmost exactitude of rigorous observation; or, if invented in the first instance as mere theories, were verifiable and subjected to the most rigid verification of fact. One of Carlyle's favourite ideas, the danger of shams,—that is, of worn-out institutions and doctrines—and also of mere blind amiability in human affairs, was a lesson learnt directly from the Revolution. From other historical examples, studied more precisely than the "ancient classical concern" was by Rousseau, he evolved the doctrine embodied in the ringing phrase "might is right." . . . This was Carlyle's most powerful weapon, the Talus flail with which he laid about him among the shams, the new as well as the old, the deceptive but enticing ideals that floated over the world from the kingdom of the Celts, and certain sturdier ones of native growth, smashing them alike unsparingly.—LARMINIE, WILLIAM, 1900, *Carlyle and Shelley, The Contemporary Review*, vol. 77, p. 732.

The resemblance between Ruskin and Carlyle seems to me to have been purely superficial, and the frequent bracketing of their names—less frequent than it was, and growing daily rarer—is based upon a misconception of the real natures of both of these extraordinary men. . . . Ruskin did, all the same, verily believe in God; Carlyle believed only in himself. Ruskin's impatience was of a noble kind, Carlyle's of an ignoble. Ruskin was grieved that the generation with which his life was cast should deny God. Carlyle was violently angry that anybody should deny Carlyle, or should presume to think otherwise than he thought. . . . Ruskin's religion came from his heart, Carlyle's from his liver. . . . Carlyle broke his wife's heart, and I have never heard of any living soul to whom he gave a sixpence or for whose help or comfort he would have walked a mile. . . . Nobody should read Carlyle's books till he is of an age to bring his own experience of the world as a necessary counter-poison, till he can smile at their atrabilious denunciations of things in general, and relish their one truly valuable quality—literary excellence.—MURRAY, HENRY, 1901, *Ruskin and Carlyle, Robert Buchanan and Other Essays*, pp. 144, 145, 146.

As a man of letters he had the supreme faculty of vision, and was able to discern the inmost facts of a scene, an event, or of a life; and, more than all, he had the gift of the word, the genius for vivid description. ... Carlyle's literary faculty was his undoing as a sociologist; for he was wont to prophesy without data in experience. And lacking clairvoyancy, unable to see any other outcome for a society rapidly democratizing save anarchy and chaos, he was prevented from uttering the creative word that might have inaugurated a new epoch. Mistaken in nearly all points relating to political democracy, he was always right in discussing questions of industry, and his dream of "some chivalry of labor" is even now being realized—the complete democratizing of labor, which Carlyle actually feared, being reserved for a distant future.—TRIGGS, OSCAR LOVELL, 1902, *Chapters in the History of the Arts and Crafts Movement, pp.* 10, 11.

I have said all that is to be said against Carlyle's work almost designedly: for he is one of those who are so great that we rather need to blame them for the sake of our own independence than praise them for the sake of their fame. He came and spoke a word, and the chatter of rationalism stopped, and the sums would no longer work out and be ended. He was a breath of Nature turning in her sleep under the load of civilisation, a stir in the very stillness of God to tell us he was still there.— CHESTERTON, G. K., 1903, *Thomas Carlyle*.

Benjamin Disraeli
Earl of Beaconsfield
1804–1881

Born, in London, 21 Dec. 1804. Educated at school at Blackheath. Articled to solicitor 18 Nov. 1821. Entered at Lincoln's Inn, 1824. Visit to Spain, Italy, and Levant, 1828–31. Worked at literature for five years. M. P. for Maidstone, July 1837. Married Mrs. Wyndham Lewis, 23 Aug. 1839. M. P. for Shrewsbury, 1841. Visit to Germany and France, autumn of 1845. Leader of Opposition in House of Commons, Sept. 1848. Chancellor of Exchequer, Feb. 1852. Contrib. to "The Press" newspaper, 1853–58. Chancellor of Exchequer second time, 1865. Prime Minister, March to Nov., 1868. Active political life. Wife died, 15 Dec. 1872. Prime Minister second time, Jan. 1874 to March 1880. Last speech in House of Commons, 11 Aug. 1876. Created Earl of Beaconsfied, 12 Aug. 1876. Died, 19 April 1881. Buried at Hughenden. *Works:* "Vivian Grey" (anon.), pt. i., 1826; pt. ii., 1827; "The Star Chamber" (anon.; suppressed), 1826; "The Voyage of Captain Popanilla" (anon), 1828; "The Young Duke" (anon.), 1831; "Contarini Fleming" (anon.), 1832; "England and France," (anon.), 1832; "What is he?" (anon.), 1833; "The Wondrous Tale of Alroy" (anon.), 1833; "The Present Crisis Examined," 1834; "The Rise of Iskander," 1834; "The Revolutionary Epic," 1834; "Vindication of the British Constitution," 1835; "Letters of Runnymede" (anon), 1836; "The Spirit of Whigism," 1836; "Venetia" (anon.), 1837; "Henrietta Temple," (anon.), 1837; "The Tragedy of Count Alarcos" (anon.), 1839; "Coningsby," 1844; "Sybil," 1845; "Tancred," 1847; "Mr. Gladstone's Finance," 1862; "Lothair," 1870; "Novels and Tales," (collected), 1870–71; "Endymion" (anon.), 1880. *Posthumous:* "Home Letters," 1885; "Correspondence with his Sister," 1886. He *edited* the following editions of works by his father: "Curiosities of Literature," 1849; "Charles I.," 1851; "Works," 1858–59; "Amenities of Literature," 1881; "Literary Character," 1881; "Calamities of Authors," 1881. *Life:* by Kebbel, 1888; by Froude, 1890.—SHARP, R. FARQUHARSON, 1897, *A Dictionary of English Authors, p.* 81.

PERSONAL

He possesses just the qualities of the impenitent thief, whose name, I verily believe, must have been Disraeli. For aught I know, the present Disraeli is descended from him; and with the impression that he is, I now forgive the heir-at-law of the blasphemous thief who died upon the cross.— O'CONNELL, DANIEL, 1833, *In a Speech*.

Disraeli had arrived before me, and sat in the deep window, looking out upon Hyde Park, with the last rays of daylight reflected from the gorgeous gold flowers of a splendidly embroidered waistcoat. Patent leathers pumps, a white stick, with a black cord and tassel, and a quantity of chains about his neck and pockets, served to make him, even in the dim light, rather a con-

BENJAMIN DISRAELI

Engraving from a Photograph.

JOHN BRIGHT

From Original Painting by Chappel.

spicuous object. . . . Disraeli has one of the most remarkable faces I ever saw. He is lividly pale, and but for the energy of his action and the strength of his lungs, would seem to be a victim to consumption. His eye is as black as Erebus, and has the most mocking, lying-in-wait sort of expression conceivable. His mouth is alive with a kind of working and impatient nervousness, and when he has burst forth, as he does constantly, with a particularly successful cataract of expression, it assumes a curl of triumphant scorn that would be worthy of a Mephistopheles. His hair is as extraordinary as his taste in waistcoats. A thick heavy mass of jet-black ringlets falls over his left cheek almost to his collarless stock, while on the right temple it is parted and put away with the smooth carefulness of a girl's, and shines most unctuously—
"With thy incomparable oil, Macassar!"
—WILLIS, NATHANIEL PARKER, 1835, *Pencillings by the Way*.

He has a strongly marked Hebrew face, with brilliant eyes, and intensely black hair.—LEVERT, OCTAVIA WALTON, 1853, *Souvenirs of Travel*, vol. I, p. 27.

Though in general society he was habitually silent and reserved, he was closely observant. It required generally a subject of more than common interest to produce a fitting degree of enthusiasm to animate and to stimulate him into the exercise of his marvelous powers of conversation. When duly excited, however, his command of language was truly wonderful, his sarcasm unsurpassed; the readiness of his wit, the quickness of his perception, the grasp of mind that enabled him to seize on all the parts of any subject under discussion, those only would venture to call in question who had never been in his company at the period I refer to [1831].—MADDEN, RICHARD ROBERT, 1855, *Literary Life and Correspondence of the Countess of Blessington*, vol. II, p. 209.

By and by came a rather tall, slender person, in a black frock-coat, buttoned up, and black pantaloons, taking long steps, but I thought rather feebly or listlessly. His shoulders were round, or else he had a habitual stoop in them. He had a prominent nose, a thin face, and a sallow, very sallow complexion; . . . and had I seen him in America I should have taken him for a hard-worked editor of a newspaper, weary and worn with night-labor and want of exercise, —aged before his time. It was Disraeli, and I never saw any other Englishman look in the least like him; though, in America, his appearance would not attract notice as being unusual.—HAWTHORNE, NATHANIEL, 1856, *English Note-Books*, vol. II, p. 20.

Lady Dufferin made herself very agreeable all dinner-time. I told her I had just heard Disraeli speak. She said she had always known him and liked him in spite of his tergiversations and absurdities. When he was very young and had made his first appearance in London society as the author of "Vivian Grey," there was something almost incredible in his aspect. She assured me that she did not exaggerate in the slightest degree in describing to me his dress when she first met him at a dinner party. He wore a black velvet coat lined with satin, purple trousers with a gold band running down the outside seam, a scarlet waistcoat, long lace ruffles falling down to the tips of his fingers, white gloves with several brilliant rings outside them, and long black ringlets rippling down upon his shoulders. It seemed impossible that such a Guy Fawkes could have been tolerated in any society. His audacity, which has proved more perennial than brass, was always the solid foundation of his character. She told him, however, that he made a fool of himself by appearing in such fantastic shape, and he afterwards modified his costume, but he was never to be put down.—MOTLEY, JOHN LOTHROP, 1858, *To his Wife, June 13; Correspondence of John Lothrop Motley*, ed. Curtis, vol. I, p. 264.

If Mr. Disraeli had, as he once said, the "best of wives," he, on his part, proved the best of husbands. Till the last day of her life he paid to his wife those attentions which are too often associated rather with the romance of youthful intercourse than with the routine of married life. When he rose to the highest point of his ambition, the only favor he would accept of the Queen was a coronet for his wife. He was scarcely ever absent from her side until the dark day when the fast friends were to be parted. She knew that she was dying, but refrained from telling him so, in order that he might be spared the pain of bidding her farewell. He also knew that her last hour was at hand but kept silence lest he should distress her. Thus they parted, each anxious to avoid striking a blow at the other's heart. The domestic lives of public men are properly held to be beyond the range of public comment; but in an age when marriage is the theme of ridicule from "leaders of progress" it may be that this passage in Mr. Disraeli's career may be pondered with some profit by the young.—JENNINGS, L. J., 1873, *Benjamin Disraeli, Atlantic Monthly, vol. 32. p. 642.*

The enclosed letter and copy of my answer ought to go to you as a family curiosity and secret. Nobody whatever knows of it beyond our two selves here, except Lady Derby, whom I believe to have been the contriver of the whole affair. You would have been surprised, all of you, to have found unexpectedly your poor old brother converted into Sir Tom; but alas! there was no danger at any moment of such a catastrophe. I do, however, truly admire the magnanimity of Dizzy in regard to me. He is the only man I almost never spoke of except with contempt; and if there is anything of scurrility anywhere chargeable against me, he is the subject of it; and yet see, here he comes with a pan of hot coals for my guilty head. I am, on the whole, gratified a little within my own dark heart at this mark of the good-will of high people—Dizzy by no means the chief of them—which has come to me now at the very end, when I can have the additional pleasure of answering, "Alas, friends! it is of no use to me, and I will not have it." Enough, enough! Return me the official letter, and say nothing about it beyond the walls of your own house. — CARLYLE, THOMAS, 1875, *Letter to John Carlyle*, Jan. 1; *Thomas Carlyle, A History of his Life in London*, ed. Froude, vol. II, p. 369.

His portrait is everywhere, and even caricature can add little to the oddity of this strange face, with the piercing eyes, the long, Semitic nose, the lips compressed in a sad smile, the chin adorned with a Mephistophelic thin and pointed beard. I hardly ever spoke to my English friends of Disraeli in old times without hearing him abused, and I have never found myself in contact with him without finding great charm in his quiet manners, in his well-measured and pointed phrases. It always seemed to me that there was nothing ordinary or vulgar in the man; he was different from the common type. I have heard him attacked even for his excessive politeness. Somebody once told me that the author of "Lothair" was a snob and took a real delight in choosing heroes and heroines in the upper classes. He was the leader of the aristocratic party, and the aristocrats were never tired of saying that he only represented them politically, that he did not speak or move or act like the "chosen few." So it may be, but the man who has contrived, with all his disabilities, to impose his leadership on the proudest aristocracy of the world cannot be an ordinary man.— LAUGEL, A., 1878, *A French Estimate of Lord Beaconsfield, The Nation, vol. 27, p.* 209.

With Lord Beaconsfield everything is in keeping; the novelist is part of the man, and the Prime Minister of the novelist. I can never read his books or see him at work on the world's stage without recalling the Mr. Disraeli of fifty years ago, as a contemporary depicts him, dressed in velvet and satin, his wrists encircled by ruffles, his hair cunningly curled, his fingers loaded with rings, an ivory cane in his hand; with all the exterior of a dandy—a dandy of genius; a bundle of contradictions, ambition allied to scepticism, determination hiding itself under sallies and paradoxes. So much for his person: his life has followed suit. A foreigner, a Jew, he raised himself from an attorney's office to the peerage of England, and the headship of his country's government. The character of his policy—full of theatrical strokes, of new departures, whimsical or bold as the case may be—is well known. In everything that he has done, you feel the Oriental's taste for the brilliant, the adventurer's taste for the turns of Fortune's wheel, the parvenu's taste for pomp. But it is in his writings more than anywhere else that he shows himself as he is: because Lord Beaconsfield is at bottom an artist first of all. His old dandyism was already literary; and his modern policy is still romantic.—SCHERER, EDMOND, 1880-91, *Essays on English Literature*, tr. Saintsbury, p. 240.

In his private character it seems to be generally admitted that he was not only irreproachable, but graced with some ennobling qualities. His exemplary devotion to his wife has been referred to already. And that devotion derives additional merit from the fact that it was lavished on a wife much older than himself, not strikingly attractive, and not wedded chiefly in love. Few men occupying such a position as Lord Beaconsfield's would have bestowed on such a wife, during their long years of married life, all the attention and gallantry of a youthful lover. — MACCOLL, MALCOLM, 1881, *Lord Beaconsfield, Contemporary Review, vol.* 39. *p.* 1010.

> But, He, unwitting youth once flown,
> With England's greatness linked His own,
>   And steadfast to that part,
> Held praise and blame but fitful sound,
> And in the love of country found
>   Full solace for His heart.
> Now in an English grave He lies:
> With flowers that tell of English skies
>   And mind of English air,
> A grateful Sovereign decks His bed;
> And hither long with pilgrim tread
>   Will the English race repair.

—AUSTIN, ALFRED, 1881, *At his Grave, Contemporary Review, vol.* 39, *p.* 1017.

We knew Mrs. Wyndham Lewis long before she became Lady Beaconsfield. Her education must have been sound and good; her mind was of a high order; and it may be regarded as certain that by her constant companionship—nay, by her frequent counsel and her wise advice—she aided largely in directing the after-conduct of her statesman husband, and so claims a share of the gratitude due to the illustrious man, who in often consulting her, derogated in no whit from the dignity of manhood, as First Minister of the Queen and of the kingdom. It is enough to say of Lady Beaconsfield, that she was worthy to be the friend, companion, and counselor of Lord Beaconsfield, as well as his wife. She must have been a generous woman. Her splendid diamonds were always at the command of her friends—such of them as had to attend court or any stateballs; and I know her to have given a diamond ring to Letitia Landon—when she had known that the poetess was in immediate need of money—with a well-understood hint that there was no necessity for her keeping it. She was not only a handsome but a charming woman, well born and nurtured, with manners easy and selfpossessed, generous and sympathetic; and if her second husband had been born in the purple she would in no way have discredited the position to which he raised her. That when she became his wife she was dearly and devotedly loved by her great statesman-husband there is no doubt; yet the world might not have known it—perhaps would not have believed it—for she was his elder by fifteen years, and he had long passed the verge of manhood. It was in March, 1838, that Wyndham Lewis died. In August, 1839, Disraeli married his widow.—HALL, SAMUEL CARTER, 1883, *Retrospect of a Long Life, p.* 162.

In private life he is said to have been kind and constant in his friendships, liberal in his charities, and prompt to recognise and assist struggling merit wherever his attention was directed to it. In general society he was not a great talker, and few of his witticisms have been preserved which were not uttered on some public occasion. He usually had rather a preoccupied air, and though he was a great admirer of gaiety and good spirits in those who surrounded him, he was incapable of abandoning himself to the pleasures of the moment, whatever they might be, like Lord Derby or Lord Palmerston. He was no sportsman; and though he records in his letter to his sister that he once rode to hounds, and rode well, he seems to have been satisfied with that experience of the chase. Though a naturalist and a lover of nature in all her forms, he had neither game nor gamekeepers at home. He preferred peacocks to pheasants, and left it to his tenants to supply his table as they chose.—KEBBEL, T. E., 1888, *Dictionary of National Biography, vol.* XV, *p.* 116.

It will be noted that if his autobiographical sketches err on the side of exaggerated approval that is not a failing to be traced in the critical remarks of his contemporaries. In truth an adequate appreciation of the force of Disraeli's character, can be reached only after due appreciation of the difficulties by which his pathway was surrounded. . . . Those familiar with Mr. Disraeli only in the closing years will find much to marvel at in the disclosures made of his earlier life and manner. In the days when he wore the black velvet coat lined with satin, the purple trousers, the scarlet waistcoat, and the long lace ruffles, he appears to have been a youth of even dazzling personal beauty. Handsome youths not infrequently develop into comely old men. But Lord Beaconsfield's face in old age could certainly not be called handsome. Of his once luxuriant curling locks there remained a carefully-nurtured residue singularly black in hue. To the last he wore the single curl drooping over his forehead. He had abandoned all foppery of dress, though on fine spring days, as already noted, he liked to wear lavender kid gloves. Unlike Mr.

Gladstone, who regularly greets the summer array in a white hat, a light tweed suit, and a blue necktie, Lord Beaconsfield was ever soberly attired, the cut of his clothes suggesting rather the efforts of Hughenden art than the triumphs of Bond Street. He always wore a frock coat, and in the House of Commons had a curious little habit, when he sat down, of carefully arranging the skirt over his legs. Then he crossed his knees, folded his arms, and, with head hung down, sat for hours apparently immobile, but, as was shown when occasion arose, watchful and wary. Of his good looks there were left a pair of eyes remarkably luminous for one of his age, and plump, small, well-shaped white hands, of which he was pardonably proud.—LUCY, HENRY W., 1889, *Mr. Disraeli, Temple Bar, vol.* 86, *pp.* 61, 63.

The professed creed of Disraeli was that of a "complete Jew," that is to say, he believed in "Him that had come;" and "did not look for another." To use his own words, he "believed in Calvary, as well as Sinai."—FRASER, SIR WILLIAM, 1891, *Disraeli and his Day.*

There was not an English drop of blood in his veins, nor an English taste or sentiment or feeling in his nature. He was foreign, not only in race and religion, but in character and intellect and feature and manner, to the great people whom he ruled. Mazarin himself was not a parallel, for though he rose from an obscurer origin and, though an Italian, came to govern France, he at least was one in creed with the nation he controlled. But no one imagined that Disraeli believed, although he conformed. He was initiated into the Jewish communion in the ordinary way when he was eight days old, and through life he constantly avowed, in speech and writing, his sympathy for the people from whom he sprang and the faith in which he was born. He was baptized with his father's family in his youth, but he remained a circumcised Jew to the last, as alien to Christianity as to England. More even than this, his personal peculiarities were those most offensive to the English of every grade. The flashy Brummagem Hebrew had nothing in common with the solid, substantial Briton. In his youth he was gaudy in dress, pert in language, forward and conceited in manner; he always loved display and parade, and was showy in politics and meretricious in everything. Worse still, he was false to his early friends; he turned on his first political leader; he deserted the party that had brought him into public life, and betrayed the principles of the other to which he turned. Yet he remained the idol of those whom he duped; he brought the aristocracy that he satirized to his feet; the despised plebeian forced Cecils and Stanleys to do his bidding, and, long an object of aversion to the queen, he finally compelled her to become his disciple and then conferred on her a newer title and what she thought a grander crown.—BADEAU, ADAM, 1893, *Lord Beaconsfield, The Cosmopolitan, vol.* 14, *p.* 502.

What a wonder, then, that to Disraeli, a romanticist in statecraft, an idealist in politics, and a Provencal in sentiment, his chivalrous regard for the sex should have taken a deeper complexion when the personage was not only a woman but a queen? In trifles Disraeli never forgot the sex of the sovereign. In great affairs he never appeared to remember it. To this extent the charge of flattery brought against him may be true. He approached the Queen with the supreme tact of a man of the world, than which no form of flattery can be more affective and more dangerous. So far the indictment against him may be upheld. The word "subservience" is the translation of this simple fact into the language of political malice.—BRETT, REGINALD B., 1896, *The Yoke of Empire, p.* 138.

Yet after a great defeat, after a year of rayless seclusion, and fourteen years of absence altogether from this changing world, Lord Beaconsfield retains a hold upon the popular mind which has scarcely relaxed since its unsuspected strength was revealed at his death. To some that may appear an exaggerated statement, but I believe it would bear any test that could be applied to it. Test is difficult—the dead do not return; but let us imagine a pageant in the Queen's honour—20th June of this royal year—in which the greater of her old departed servants should rise and take part with these others of to-day—all in their robes of State. It is not pretended that Lord Beaconsfield would make the first figure in that noble procession—(the Great Duke! what in these days would the sight be worth of that "good grey head" moving with the rest under the dome of St. Paul's!) —but who believes that he would pass with less acclaim or less regret than attended his last days with us?—GREENWOOD, FREDERICK, 1897, *Disraeli Vindicated, Blackwood's Magazine*, vol. 161, p. 426.

Those who had observed his course from the beginning gave him no credit for settled convictions upon any subject, except the honour and interest of the race from which he had sprung; and his books, in which there was much glitter and tinsel, but little solid or genuine matter, confirmed that impression. He seemed to be an actor, in a mask which he never took off. He had courage, audacity, temper, patience, and an indomitable will; and by these qualities, and a study of men, too cynical to be deep, but useful for party management, he established his position. He had also a certain magnanimity, which made him generally impassive and unruffled, even when successfully attacked, and free from all appearance of ill-will or resentment against those who attacked him; a hard hitter himself whenever it suited his purpose, he could take hard blows, as nothing more than the regular practice of the game. He seems to have drawn his own portrait, when he said of Sidonia: "It was impossible to penetrate him. Though unreserved in his manner, his frankness was strictly limited to the surface. He observed everything, thought ever, but avoided serious discussion. If you pressed him for an opinion, he took refuge in raillery, or threw out some grave paradox, with which it was not easy to cope." Lord Beaconsfield was a man of genius, certainly; those of his writings which have most the appearance of seriousness leave the impression that he was more Radical than Conservative, with a strong sense of the hollowness of the politics of his time. As an orator, he was greatest when least serious; no man excelled him in the satirical vein. But his graver efforts were turgid and artificial; wrapping up the absence of much definite meaning in ponderous words. Even in private he did not seem (to observers like myself, who seldom met him) to talk naturally. The one really great work of his life was to raise his own race to a footing of fuller social and political equality in this country with their fellow-citizens; obliterating the last remnants of a state of feeling towards them, which had formerly been productive of much wrong.—PALMER, ROUNDELL (EARL OF SELBORNE), 1898, *Memorials, Part II., Personal and Political*, vol. I, p. 478.

Gracious is the only word which I can apply to his manner to those around him, and it had a fascination over them which I could perfectly understand, and I could easily comprehend that he should have a surrounding of devotees. The serene, absolute self-confidence he evidently felt was of a nature to inspire a corresponding confidence in his followers. It was an interesting display of the power of a magnetic nature, and gave me a higher idea of the man than all his writings had given or could give. For his intellectual powers and their printed results I never had a high opinion, but his was one of the most interesting and remarkable personalities I ever encountered.—STILLMAN, WILLIAM JAMES, 1901, *The Autobiography of a Journalist*, vol. II, p. 498.

History will not leave him without a meed of admiration. When all possible explanations of his success have been given, what a wonderful career! An adventurer foreign in race, in ideas, in temper, without money or family connections, climbs, by patient and unaided efforts, to lead a great party, master a powerful aristocracy, sway a vast empire, and make himself one of the four or five greatest personal forces in the world. His head is not turned by his elevation. He never becomes a demagogue; he never stoops to beguile the multitude by appealing to sordid instincts. He retains through life a certain amplitude of view, a due sense of the dignity of his position, a due regard for the traditions of the ancient assembly which he leads, and when at last the destinies of England fall into his hands, he feels the grandeur of the charge and seeks to secure what he believes to be her imperial place in the world. Whatever judgment history may ultimately pass upon him, she will find in the long annals of the English Parliament no more striking figure. —BRYCE, JAMES, 1903, *Studies in Contemporary Biography*, p. 68.

ORATORY AND SPEECHES

Mr. D'Israeli's appearance and manner, were very singular. His dress also was peculiar: it had much of a theatrical aspect. His black hair was long and flowing, and he had a most ample crop of it. His gestures were abundant: he often appeared as if trying with what celerity he could move his body from one side to another, and throw his hands out and draw them in again. At other times he flourished one hand before his face, and then the other. His voice, too, is of a very unusual kind: it is powerful, and had every justice done to it in the way of exercise; but there is something peculiar in it which I am at a loss to characterise. His utterance is rapid, and he never seems at a loss for words. On the whole, and notwithstanding the result of his first attempt, I am convinced he is a man who possesses many of the requisites of a good debater. That he is a man of great literary talent, few will dispute.—GRANT, JAMES, 1838, *Random Recollections of the Lords and Commons, Second Series, vol.* II, *p.* 335.

D'Israeli made a beautiful speech last night on moving certain resolutions declaratory of the unequal burthens on land. Nothing could be more eloquent, and, what is more rare in his speeches, more temperate and conciliatory. It consequently produced more solid effect than his more jeering and smart effusions.—GREVILLE, HENRY, 1849, *Leaves from His Diary, March 9; ed. Enfield, p.* 325.

D'Israeli is not a very eloquent or graceful speaker. There seems such an affluence of thought, he hesitates in the choice of words.—LEVERT, OCTAVIA WALTON, 1853, *Souvenirs of Travel, vol.* I, *p.* 47.

That Mr. Disraeli is a great orator few will deny. It is perhaps premature to assign him place with any of our most renowned classical speakers; and indeed this would be a difficult task, since his style both of thought and delivery are quite original, and partake so much of the idiosyncrasy of the man, that there are few like him in our great mass of English statesmen who are deservedly regarded as models in the forensic art.—MILL, JOHN, 1863, *Disraeli, the Author, Orator and Statesman, p.* 237.

It was curious to see the immediate change from a negligent, impatient posture in the House, to one of great eagerness at the first sound of Bright's voice; an eagerness which only Disraeli's impenetrable face was wholly free from. No man ever succeeded better than he does in the assumption of utter insensibility. While Bright flung his taunts at him not a muscle moved; there he sat with his lower jaw dropped, and his eyes glassy and stiff; maintaining the same listless look when he was described as "issuing flash political notes which would not pass at the bank, however they imposed upon the inexperienced;" and when he was pointed at by Bright's finger, directing the attention of the House to his attitude, "Look at the right honourable gentleman, the Chancellor of the Exchequer—look at him! Is he not a marvel of cleverness to have led that party so long and to mislead it at last, as he is doing now?" All eyes following this, with a great deal of laughing, had no effect in stirring the Sphinx outwardly, and I don't think so much as an eyelash gave way. It is this dead calm which lashes Gladstone into such passionate vehemence when he attacks Dizzy. It is certain that Disraeli rose with the feeling of the House against him; but the wonderful dexterity, the wit, the exquisite pleasantry, and the excellent temper of his speech turned it quite round to him and saved the Ministry.—POLLOCK, LADY, 1867, *To Henry Taylor, March 29; Correspondence of Henry Taylor, ed. Dowden, p.* 275.

It is difficult to determine whether Mr. Disraeli's work (looked at merely from a critical and literary point of view) is to be found in his speeches or in his books—whether he is a writer who has accidentally turned speaker, or a speaker who has accidentally turned writer. I have never greatly admired the early Protectionist speeches in which he assailed Sir Robert: they are splendidly impertinent and audacious, and we know that Sir Robert did not like them; but the invective is laboured, and the irony is not incisive but simply savage. The picture altogether is as black as one of Rembrandt's etchings; the delicate tints, the natural play of light and shadow having been omitted. There are many scenes and dialogues and characters in the novels that are vastly superior to this portrait of Sir Robert, much as it was applauded in its day; but I do not think there is anything, even in "Coningsby," quite equal to the airy quizzing, the refined and brilliant *chaff*, the gentlemanly and good-humoured banter of Lord Palmerston, Lord John Russell, Sir Charles Wood, and other House of Commons men whose names are passing away, which is to be found in Mr. Disraeli's later speeches. Caricatures more or less no doubt, but caricatures by a man who has a naturally fine eye for the nicest traits of character. They are wonderfully true, and yet to some extent ideal, like the cartoons that Richard Doyle used to contribute in the old days of Punch. Let any idle admirer of Mr. Disraeli collect the lightly-touched, wittily-conceived sketches which may be gleaned from the speeches delivered by the leader of the opposition between 1848 and 1858, and he will bring together a striking gallery of historical portraits, far more true to the life than historical portraits commonly are.—SKELTON, JOHN, 1870, *Mr. Disraeli's Lothair, Fraser's Magazine, vol.* 81, *p.* 793.

All the world is familiar with the sarcasms of Disraeli (Lord Beaconsfield); his hits at Peel as one who had "caught the Whigs bathing, and run away with their clothes,"—as a politician who had always "traded on the ideas of others, whose life had been one huge appropriation clause," etc. Wit is not merely the handmaid of the Premier's genius; it is the right arm of his power. Much of its point is due to his by-play,—to the subtle modulations of his voice, his peculiar shrug, and the air of icy coolness and indifference with which he utters his sneers and sarcasms. Nothing can be more polished than his irony; it is the steeled hand in the silken glove. Yet, on account of its personality and vindictiveness, it cannot be commended for imitation. As it has been well said, the adder lurks under the rose-leaves of his rhetoric; the golden arrows are tipped with poison.—MATHEWS, WILLIAM, 1878, *Oratory and Orators, p.* 123.

Last of all Lord Beaconsfield came also . . . . The whole hall rises for him the applause is deafening; the greeting such as he is rightly proud of. It was a common remark that Lord Beaconsfield was looking uncommonly well. So he was; so long as he thought people were looking at him. The condition of this great man's health is an affair of state, and is discussed very much as Louis XIV's bodily welfare was discussed when he changed his shirts in public. Lord Beaconsfield does not change his shirts in public. He finds it less embarrassing to effect from time to time an exchange of what are sometimes called his principles. He has, however, his physical peculiarities, and one who sees him from time to time is able to guess near enough at his actual health. When he made his entry into the Library of the Guildhall, I stood near the door. I could see him pull together and compose the muscles of his face till the desired expression was attained. All resemblances, says a great physiognomist, lie in the eyes and mouth. Individual expression lies there too, and the brief space during which Lord Beaconsfield was advancing up the aisle was not too brief for a good look at these features. They quite confirmed the good reports from Hatfield which I recently mentioned. A strange fire burned in his eyes. The jaw and lips were set fast. For those two minutes no man's face was more full of energy, no step firmer than his, septuagenarian as he is, with four years added to the seventy. He wore his Windsor uniform of dark blue with embroideries in gold, with pendent sword, and on his breast that matchless and priceless star of diamonds inclosing the ruby cross of the Garter which fills all meaner breasts with envy. . . . Later in the evening Lord Beaconsfield paid Sir Stafford Northcote the compliment of supposing that his speech on finance was occupying the attention of the audience. He leaned back in his chair, his mask slipped off for a moment, the light from the great chandelier above streamed full on his face, and you saw what he was like when not posing for the gallery. The cheeks grew hollow, the tint of his skin waxlike, the cavernous jaws fell slightly apart, the carefully trained curls on the left brow slid out of place, the fire sank low in his eyes, the whole face aged painfully in a minute. If ever a human countenance looked weary and bored and scornful, Lord Beaconsfield's was that countenance at that moment.—SMALLEY, GEORGE W., 1879-91, *Lord Beaconsfield as Seen at Guildhall Banquet, Nov.* 11; *London Letters and Some Others, vol.* I, *pp.* 55, 59.

The secret of his political success is to be found in his gifts as House of Commons orator, and it is as severe a reflection upon the English system of Government as could be made that these gifts should have sufficed to enable their possessor to have a large share in the Government of an empire like England during the greater portion of his life. We do not mean at all to underrate his gifts. The author of the "Political Adventures" refers to his rhetorical faculty with contempt; but it is by no means a contemptible faculty. His serious phrases are open to reproach that they are not sincere. Not so, however, with his invective, his satire, his irony, his humour, and his wit. These are all genuine. These are the weapons which have made him the invaluable ally, and finally the leader, of the Conservative party in the House of Commons. — SEDGWICK, A. G., 1880, *Brandes's Beaconsfield, The Nation*, vol. 30, p. 421.

His great triumphs were in his briefest speeches, spurts of twenty minutes' length, full of point and sparkle. In order to make a speech of two hours in length, a man must needs have a certain proportion of facts to work upon. Mr. Disraeli never displayed a constitutional liking for facts, and when of occasional necessity he came to handle them, it was not with a master-hand. In proportion as he was permitted to disregard facts, or even to distort them, so was he successful in dealing with them. But if he could get away altogether from this hard ground, giving full run to his fancy and wit, he was at his happiest, and was the cause of the greatest happiness in others.— LUCY, HENRY W., 1882, *Glimpses of Great Britons, Harper's Magazine*, vol. 65, p. 168.

As an orator Lord Beaconsfield did not greatly shine. Indeed, in the highest sense of the word, he was no orator. He lacked ease and fluency. He had no turn for the lucid exposition of complicated facts, nor for the conduct of a close and cogent argument. Sustained and fiery declamation was not in his way. And least of all had he that truest index of genuine eloquence, the power of touching the emotions. He could not make his hearers weep, but he could make them laugh; he could put them in good humour with themselves; he could dazzle them with brilliant rhetoric, and he could pour upon an opponent streams of ridicule and scorn more effective than the hottest indignation. When he sought to be profound or solemn, he was usually heavy and labored. For wealth of thought or splendor of language his speeches will not bear for a moment to be compared—I will not say with Burke's, but with those of three or four of his own contemporaries. Even in his own party, Lord Derby, Lord Ellenborough, and Lord Cairns surpassed him. . . . What he wanted in eloquence he more than made up for by tactical adroitness. No more consummate parliamentary strategist has been seen in England. He had studied the House of Commons till he knew it as a player knows his instrument. — BRYCE, JAMES, 1882, *Lord Beaconsfield, Century Magazine*, vol. 23, pp. 739, 740.

STATESMAN

He was the best representative whom the "Republic of Letters" ever had in Parliament, for he made his way by talents —especially by a fascination of words— essentially literary. And on the other hand, though he charmed Parliament, he never did anything more: he had no influence with the country; such a vast power over Englishmen as has been possessed by Lord Palmerston and by Mr. Gladstone was out of his way altogether. Between Mr. Disraeli and common Englishmen there was too broad a gulf, too great a difference; he was simply unintelligible to them. "Ten miles from London," to use the old phrase, there is scarcely any real conception of him. His mode of regarding parliamentary proceedings as a play and a game is incomprehensible to the simple and earnest English nature. Perhaps he has gained more than he has lost by the English not understanding him; at any rate, the fact remains that the special influence of this great gladiator never passed the walls of the amphitheater.—BAGEHOT, WALTER, 1876, *Mr. Disraeli as a Member of the House of Commons, Works*, ed. Morgan, vol. III, p. 450.

His premiership, like his early public career, has been a political romance. Who else, in all the long row of British statesmanship, would have produced such startling surprises, such scenic effects, such audacious transformations? To purchase a controlling share in the Suez Canal, to hail the Queen as Empress of India, to send the fleet into the waters of Constantinople, to acquire Cyprus, were acts of daring, which only a courageous and self-confident spirit, fond of striking displays of power, could have successfully executed.—TOWLE, GEORGE MAKEPEACE, 1878, *Beaconsfield*, p. 115.

That whole character is complete in its selfishness, that whole career is uniform in its dishonesty. Throughout his whole life I do not find even on a single occasion a generous emotion, one self-sacrificing act, a moment of sincere conviction—except that of the almighty perfection of himself. I find him uniform in all his dealings with his fellow man, and behind every word he utters I can only see the ever-vigilant custodian of his own interests. And it is this perfect uniformity in his character and career that most estranges me. . . .

Lord Beaconsfield is the same from the beginning; as he is in old age, as he was in middle age, so he was in youth. His maturity without virtue is the natural sequel to his youth without generous illusions. There is throughout the same selfishness—calm, patient, unhasting, unresting. Such a man the myriads of this mighty Empire accept as chief ruler; for such a man millions of pure hearts beat with genuine emotion; to such a man 't is given to sway by his single will your fortunes and mine, and even those of the countless generations yet to come. Which shall a near posterity most wonder at—the audacity of the impostor, or the blindness of the dupe? —the immensity of the worship, or the pettiness of the idol?—O'CONNOR, THOMAS POWER, 1879, *Lord Beaconsfield, A Biography*, p. 674.

Speaking generally, an imaginative man is a magnanimous man; for the larger vision of the poet is incompatible with parochial pettiness. This was eminently the case with Disraeli; his temper was sweet, and he was neither spiteful nor malignant. Yet, men who were too dense and stupid to meet him in fair fight were always harping, parrot-like, on his vindictiveness. The fine edge of his intellect scared them, and they ran away exclaiming that the blow which they could not turn was foul. But what candid friend, with the best intentions, has succeeded in producing any specific act of meanness or baseness? He hit hard; there were times when he asked no quarter and gave none; but still, upon the whole, he was a magnanimous foe, who fought above-board, who looked his enemy in the face, who was not treacherous. "He never feared the face of man;" and there are no traces in any part of his career of the *tricks* to which the coward resorts.—SKELTON, JOHN, 1881, *A Last Word on Disraeli, Contemporary Review*, vol. 39, p. 978.

On the 19th April, 1881, the mischievous and evil-minded fortune which had persecuted the Tories sent a crowning blow, and Lord Beaconsfield passed away. From that hour to this there has hardly been a Tory in or out of Parliament, high or low, rich or poor, who, observing at any particular moment the political situation, has not exclaimed, muttered, or thought, "Oh, if Lord Beaconsfield were alive!" This is really the proudest monument to the departed leader, more enduring than the bronze on Abbey Green. This is the truest testimony of his inestimable value to the party who for so long jeered, feared, flouted, followed, and following at the last greatly loved. This, too, is the criticism pointed and unanswerable at the conduct of affairs since his death, which no amount of memorials of confidence, no number of dinners in Pall Mall, no repetitions, however frequent, of gushing embraces between the lord and the commoner, can meet, modify, or gainsay.— CHURCHILL, RANDOLPH S. LORD, 1883, *Elijah's Mantle, Fortnightly Review*, vol. 39, p. 614.

Keen must be the critical faculty which nicely discerns where the novelist ended and the statesman began in Benjamin Disraeli.—BIRRELL, AUGUSTINE, 1884, *Obiter Dicta, First Series*, p. 2.

Was he a great statesman? Not as I understand the term. There is only one measure of the first rank associated with his name, the Reform Act of 1867, and in passing this he committed the very offence he charged upon Sir Robert Peel, that is, he "found the Whigs bathing, and stole their clothes." In matters of foreign policy he acquired a reputation for energy and brilliancy but acted more from haphazard than from deliberate method. He deified the lust of empire, and created the accursed spirit of Jingoism. It was as a party leader that he most shone, for he led the Tories through the wilderness and brought them out into the promised land. When he waxed grandiloquent about the constitution and the monarchy, it was not that these were really the apple of his eye, but they furnished opportunity for the use of sounding phrases and elaborate rhetoric. Probably no public man was ever guilty of so many subterfuges and tergiversations. When uttering his misrepresentations his coolness was superbly unique. Although he wielded an immense personal power over thousands of Englishmen, there never was a statesman who had less in himself of what was truly English.—SMITH, GEORGE BARNETT, 1886, *The Prime Ministers of Queen Victoria*, p. 330.

An aggregate of atoms is not a nation, which is rather an organic union and communion of individuals. Such, in brief, was also the political creed of Disraeli, who desired nothing more than the reconciliation of new ideas with ancient institutions through growth rather than through revolution, and the permanent defence of a constitution which is in fact the English character, expressed through the modulations of the national voice, and not by the shouts of numerical majorities. Faith, freedom, industry, and order: these are the great elements which make and keep a nation great, and these elements will be found always and eloquently present in the prophetic pronouncements of Disraeli.—SICHEL, WALTER, 1902, *The Prophecies of Disraeli, The Nineteenth Century, vol. 52, p. 124.*

VIVIAN GREY
1826-27

Murray was much pleased with the philip [sic] at young D'Israeli in the "Noctes" a month or two ago. This fellow has humbugged him most completely. After the tricks of which he has been guilty, he will scarcely dare show his face in London again for some time. You are aware, I dare say, that "Vivian Grey" was palmed off upon Colburn by Mrs. Austin, the wife of the Honourable Mr. Warde's [sic] lawyer, as the production of the author of "Tremaine!" and upon this understanding Colburn gave three times as much as he would otherwise have done.—WATTS, ALARIC A., 1826, *Letter to Blackwood, Oct. 7; William Blackwood and his Sons, ed. Oliphant, vol. I, p. 507.*

We are reading the second part of "Vivian Grey," which we like better than the first. There is a scene of gamesters and swindlers wonderfully well done. I know who wrote "Almack's." Lady de Ros tells me it is by Mrs. Purvis, sister to Lady Blessington; this accounts for both the knowledge of high, and the habits of low, life which appear in the book.—EDGEWORTH, MARIA, 1827, *To Mrs. Ruxton, April 8; Life and Letters, ed. Hare, vol. II, p. 150.*

This is a piquant and amusing novel, though its merits are not of a very high order. . . . The foundation of the story is extravagant. The powers, purposes, and influence of a mature man are attributed to a boy of twenty; and the work is rather a series of sketches than a regularly built story. The hero has no mistress but politics, and no adventures but political adventures. The other prominent characters are all fools or knaves, and all are more or less forced and unnatural. Their aggregate makes a strong picture, which dazzles, but does not satisfy. The style of writing is dashing and careless, occasionally rising into hasty extravagance, and at times sinking into mawkish sentimentality. The morality of the book is loose. It is, in fact, little more than a picture of the vices and follies of the great, with an active spirit in the midst of them, making their vices and follies the stepping-stones to his ambition.—BRYANT, WILLIAM CULLEN, 1827, *New York Review, Dec.*

The work was read with great avidity. It contained so many and such direct references to public men and recent events—such sarcastic views of society and character in high life—and was at once so arrogant, egotistic, and clever, that it became the book of the season and the talk of the town. Passages of glowing sentiment and happy description gave evidence of poetic feeling and imagination.—CHAMBERS, ROBERT, 1876, *Cyclopædia of English Literature, ed. Carruthers.*

One day, suddenly, "Vivian Grey" burst upon astonished society, and took it by storm. It found its way at once to every drawing-room table. It was the town talk at ministerial *soirées*, in the lobbies of the House of Commons, at the Pall Mall clubs. Great ladies asked each other if they had read it; wondered who wrote it; guessed whom the author meant to represent by the Marquis of Carabas, and Lord Courtown, and Mr. Cleveland; and who was Vivian Grey himself.—TOWLE, GEORGE MAKEPEACE, 1878, *Beaconsfield, p. 21.*

"Vivian Grey," with all its youthful faults, gives one a greater impression of purely intellectual brilliance than anything else he ever wrote or spoke.—BRYCE, JAMES, 1882, *Lord Beaconsfield, Century Magazine, vol. 23. p. 742.*

"Vivian Grey" is crude, naturally; and although it is overflowing with high spirits it lacks form and is quite unrepresentative.—LORD, WALTER FREWEN, 1899, *Lord Beaconsfield's Novels, The Nineteenth Century, vol. 45, p. 251.*

CONTARINI FLEMING
1832

In the evening we took up Disraeli's "Contarini Fleming," and got very much interested in it. It is full of life; a fresh, young vigor of style, that bears one on like a steed.—LONGFELLOW, HENRY WADSWORTH, 1852,

Journal, April 9; *Life,* ed. *Longfellow,* vol. II, p. 219.

Although the spirit of poesy, in the form of a Childe Harold, stalks rampant through the romance, there is both feeling and fidelity to nature whenever he describes the Orient and its people. Then the bizarre, brilliant *poseur* forgets his role, and reveals his highest aspirations.—CABELL, ISA CARRINGTON, 1897, *Library of The World's Best Literature,* ed. Warner, vol. III, p. 1634.

ALROY
1833

One of the finest of modern prose poems. There are, indeed, two objections which may be stated to it:—one, its form, which is too Frenchified, reminding you, in its short chapters, and abrupt transitions, and glancing hints of thought, of "Candide;" and the second (one which his biographer presses against him with all his might), the peculiar rhythm of the more ambitious passages, which makes parts of it seem hybrids between poetry and prose. But, after deducting these faults, the tale is one of uncommon interest. Some of the situations are thrilling to sublimity, and the language and imagery are intensely oriental, and in general as felicitous as they are bold.— GILFILLAN, GEORGE, 1855, *A Third Gallery of Portraits,* p. 357.

In "Alroy," Mr. Disraeli has avoided all the errors which he fell into in the "Revolutionary Epic." The style is perfectly original, the story wild and romantic, but glowing with the true oriental fire. In this work he has also laid hold of, and skilfully employed, the pre-existing supernatural machinery which was already familiar to the reader's mind. . . . Alroy's entrance into Jerusalem and his interview with the Grand Rabbi, are fine specimens of Mr. Disraeli's method of portraying the peculiarities of the Jewish character. The scene in the synagogue is also well drawn.—MILL, JOHN, 1863, *Disraeli the Author, Orator and Statesman,* pp. 279, 282.

VENETIA
1837

It must, I fear, be admitted that "Venetia" is almost the weakest of Lord Beaconsfield's novels as a work of fiction, and that such interest as it possesses is mainly biographical. It is so close a copy of reality that the structure seems loose and inartificial, and the sequence of events capricious. The really artistic novelist is an eclectic artist who chooses out of life the events susceptible of treatment in fiction, and imparts to them the logical concatenation which the ordinary littlenesses of life obstruct or obscure. Disraeli has simply copied, and except by the rather clumsy device of fixing a piece of Byron upon Shelley, has made hardly an endeavour to combine or diversify. The domestic bereavement of Lord Lyndhurst, to whom the book is dedicated, has, he says, restrained him from offering any account of "the principles which had guided me in its composition." This must have been a meagre catalogue at best; but the biographer redeems the novelist, and he is right in claiming credit for the endeavour "to shadow forth, though but in a glass darkly, two of the most renowned and refined spirits that have adorned these our latter days."—GARNETT, RICHARD, 1887-1901, *Shelley and Lord Beaconsfield, Essays of an Ex-Librarian,* p. 117.

"Venetia" is founded on the characters of Byron and Shelley, and is amusing reading. The high-flown language incrusted with the gems of rhetoric excites our risibilities, but it is not safe to laugh at Disraeli; in his most diverting aspects he has a deep sense of humor, and he who would mock at him is apt to get a whip across the face at an unguarded moment. Mr. Disraeli laughs in his sleeve at many things, but first of all at the reader.—CABELL, ISA CARRINGTON, 1897, *Library of the World's best Literature,* ed. Warner, vol. III, p. 1635.

HENRIETTA TEMPLE
1837

It is difficult to characterize this work except by calling it a diagnosis of love *à la Disraeli.* Nothing is attempted except it be a display of the tender passion. The lovers sigh like furnaces, their hearts throb, and rend, and quiver, and no—not quite break. Their souls are in burning ethereal ecstacy or in the depth of darkness and despair. The hero prays, swears, mopes, and raves. And the ladies—their tender, bursting, pining hearts, are racked—bless them. It is impossible to go on. It is an admirable book.— MILL, JOHN, 1863, *Disraeli the Author, Orator and Statesman,* p. 310.

"Henrietta Temple," a mere and sheer love story written in a dangerous style of sentimentalism, is one of the most effective things of its kind in English, and holds its ground despite all drawbacks of fashion in speech and manners, which never tell more heavily than in the case of a book of this kind.—SAINTSBURY, GEORGE, 1896, *A History of Nineteenth Century Literature*, p. 161.

CONINGSBY
1844

Ben Disraeli, the Jew scamp, has published a very blackguard novel, in which the Pusey and Young England doctrines are relieved by a full and malignant but clever enough detail of all the abominations of Lord Hertford, and Croker figures in full fig. I should not wonder if there were some row —the abuse of Crokey is so very horrid, ditto of Lord Lowther. Peel is flattered, but the Government lashed. Awful vanity of the Hebrew.—LOCKHART, JOHN GIBSON, 1844, *To Walter Scott Lockhart, May* 13; *Life and Letters*, ed. Lang, vol. II, p. 199.

Did you read "Coningsby," that very able book, without character, story, or specific teaching? It is well worth reading, and worth wondering over. D'Israeli, who is a man of genius, has written, nevertheless, books which will live longer, and move deeper. But everybody should read "Coningsby." It is a sign of the times.—BROWNING, ELIZABETH BARRETT, 1844, *To Mrs. Martin*, Oct. 5; *Letters*, ed. Kenyon, vol. I, p. 203.

In "Coningsby," the dramatic and didactic elements are not so closely interwoven with each other as not to admit of being separated, and it is perfectly possible to convey to the reader a clear idea of the chief positions which are maintained in it, without trenching on the province of the literary critic, or anticipating the remarks we have to make on the plot, the characters, and the language.—KEBBEL, T. E., 1888, *Life of Lord Beaconsfield*, p. 40.

As a tale, "Coningsby" is nothing; but it is put together with extreme skill to give opportunities for typical sketches of character, and for the expression of opinions on social and political subjects. We have pictures of fashionable society, gay and giddy, such as no writer ever described better; peers, young, middle-aged, and old, good, bad, and indifferent, the central figure a profligate old noble of immense fortune, whose person was equally recognised, and whose portrait was also preserved by Thackeray. Besides these, intriguing or fascinating ladies, political hacks, country gentlemen, mill-owners, and occasional wise outsiders, looking upon the chaos and delivering oracular interpretations or prophecies. Into the middle of such a world the hero is launched, being the grandson and possible heir of the wicked peer.—FROUDE, JAMES ANTHONY, 1890, *Lord Beaconsfield* (*Prime Ministers of Queen Victoria*), p. 109.

On no subject is he more prone to give the reins to his imagination than that of the intellectual and artistic superiority of the Jewish race, as in "Coningsby," his finest story.—GRAHAM, RICHARD D., 1897, *The Masters of Victorian Literature*, p. 69.

"Coningsby" is perhaps the best known of all his novels—by name. But for the neophyte it contains too much political dissertation.—LORD, WALTER FREWEN, 1899, *Lord Beaconsfield's Novels*, *The Nineteenth Century*, vol. 45, p. 250.

Much more than a novel; a political manifesto with a serious practical aim, to furnish a programme for a new Conservative party. —BAKER, ERNEST A., 1903, *A Descriptive Guide to the Best Fiction*, p. 25.

SYBIL
1845

"Sybil" is not an improvement upon "Coningsby." The former novel was received with marked approbation, from the apparent sympathy which it displayed with a suffering and neglected class. "Sybil" will meet with far inferior success; its pictures only show how strongly and coarsely the author can paint, and are obviously not the result of any genuine regard for the poor and afflicted. It is not as a mere work of fiction that we intend to criticise "Sybil, or the Two Nations," though even in this point of view we think it very faulty,—abrupt in its transitions—incorrect in costume—extravagant in delineation—and fantastic, and sometimes absurd in its philosophy—and far from high-minded in its conception and its plot.— GREG, W. R., 1845, *Sybil*, *The Westminster Review*, vol. 44, p. 141.

TANCRED
1847

Writing himself much more detestable stuff than ever came from a French pen, can do nothing better to bamboozle the unfortunates who are seduced into reading his "Tancred" than speak superciliously of all other men and things—an expedient much more successful in some quarters than one would expect.—ELIOT, GEORGE, 1847,

To Miss Mary Sibree, May 10; *George Eliot's Life as related in her Letters and Journals,* ed. Cross. *vol.* I, *p.* 118.

"Tancred" cannot be esteemed a work of art, even if that term may be justly applied in the limited sense of mere construction. There is in it no great living idea which pervades, moulds, and severely limits the whole. If we consider the motive, we find a young nobleman so disgusted with the artificial and hollow life around him, that he sacrifices everything for a pilgrimage to what he believes the only legitimate source of faith and inspiration. We cannot, to be sure, expect much of a youth who is obliged to travel a thousand miles after inspiration; but we might reasonably demand something more than that he should merely fall in love, a consummation not less conveniently and cheaply attainable at home. If the whole story be intended for a satire, the disproportion of motive to result is not out of proper keeping. But Mr. D'Israeli's satire is wholly of the epigrammatic kind, not of the epic, and deals always with individuals, never with representative ideas. An epigram in three volumes post octavo is out of the question. The catastrophe has no moral or æsthetic fitness. Indeed, there is no principle of cohesion about the book, if we except the covers. Nor could there be; for there is no one central thought around and toward which the rest may gravitate. All that binds the incidents together is the author's will, a somewhat inadequate substitute for a law of nature.—LOWELL, JAMES RUSSELL, 1847, *Disraeli's Tancred, North American Review, vol.* 65, *p.* 219.

"Tancred" is unquestionably one of the most interesting and original of Lord Beaconsfield's works. It is a serio-comic, ironically mystic book; on the first reading, it seems too absurd to be subjected to serious criticism, but one takes it up again, and, although it falls asunder into the two large fragments, its wit and brilliant Oriental scenes and conversations dwell in the memory. It comprises, moreover, Disraeli's whole field of vision, and ranges between the veriest frivolities of high life, an amusing gastronomic disquisition, and the highest religious pathos of which the author is capable, as well as the most far-reaching of his poetical schemes.—BRANDES, GEORGE, 1880, *Lord Beaconsfield, A Study,* tr. *Mrs. George Sturge, p.* 271.

There remains a book that is rarely mentioned, but that should take rank immediately after "Esmond" if not side by side with that masterpiece—"Tancred."— LORD, WALTER FREWEN, 1899, *Lord Beaconsfield's Novels, The Nineteenth Century, vol.* 45, *p.* 251

LOTHAIR
1870

In all "Lothair" there is but one living figure, but one that leaves an impress of reality or even of ideal truth; and this figure is one of the subordinate personages. Lothair himself is a mere name; Theodora, a stereoscopic figure, salient and striking, but as dead as plaster-of-paris. The dukes and duchesses, cardinals and monsignor are a mere supernumerary procession of puppets that walk across Mr. Disraeli's stage, uttering, as if it were no concern of theirs, his wit and sarcasm. But when St. Aldegonde appears, be it for only a moment, we see a living soul. And one proof of this firm, well-rounded individuality is that he can be looked at in a different light by different people. This is the case with Shakespeare's personages, as it is with men and women in real life. Like them, St. Aldegonde can be misconceived, misapprehended, misunderstood; because like them he is alive; that like all living things he provokes liking and disliking, and brings into the problem of his personal relation with those whom he meets their feelings toward him.—WHITE, RICHARD GRANT, 1870, *The Styles of Disraeli and of Dickens, The Galaxy, vol.* 10, *p.* 255.

"Lothair" is certainly free from the prevailing vice of the present age of novels. It is in no degree tinted with *sensationalism.* It has as distinct a purpose as a Parliamentary Blue Book, and is about as exciting as one. Its object is to expose the arts and wiles of the Catholics, clergy and laity, to entice into the fold of Rome young noblemen and gentlemen of great estates. If our indistinct recollection of Mr. Disraeli's former novels does not much mislead us, their fundamental errors as works of art, lay in their being virtually pamphlets in the disguise of stories, to prove this or that theory of politics or morals. . . . It is hard to see how a man capable of those caustic, bitter, cruel diatribes of twenty years since against Sir Robert Peel could be capable of the platitudinous dulness of "Lothair." It shows at least how very absurd a novel a very clever man can write — which is consolatory to the average stupidity of mankind.—QUINCY, EDMUND, 1870, *Lothair*, *The Nation, vol.* 10, *pp.* 372, 373.

"Lothair" is undoubtedly a really amusing and interesting book, but as a literary work it cannot be placed beside "Tancred" or "Sybil"—for two reasons. We detect, in the first place, the occasional infelicity and unfamiliarity of the pen which has been long laid aside. There have always been curiously immature passages in Mr. Disraeli's books—passages of laboured and tawdry rhetoric, which were brought into unfortunate and undeserved prominence by the airy finish and eminent exactness of the work in which they were set. But in "Lothair" the *dramatis personæ* themselves are generally unsubstantial and unreal. They are, with a few admirable exceptions, lay-figures without distinct or urgent individuality of any sort, whereas the actors in the earlier books were obviously the productions of a man whose genius was not merely mimetic but finely dramatic. . . . "Lothair" is the "Arabian Nights" translated into modern romance.—SKELTON, JOHN, 1870, *Mr. Disraeli's Lothair, Fraser's Magazine, vol.* 81, *pp.* 797, 799.

"Lothair" is not a mere novel, and its appearance is not simply a fact for Mr. Mudie. It is a political event. When a man whose life has been passed in Parliament, who for a generation has been the real head of a great party, sits down, as he approaches the age of seventy, to embody his view of modern life, it is a matter of interest to the politician, the historian, nay, almost the philosopher. The literary qualities of the book need detain no man. Premiers not uncommonly do write sad stuff; and we should be thankful if the stuff be amusing. But the mature thoughts on life of one who has governed an empire on which the sun never sets, have an inner meaning to the thoughtful mind. Marcus Aurelius, amidst his imperial eagles, thought right to give us his Reflections. The sayings of Napoleon at St. Helena have strange interest to all men. And Solomon in all his glory was induced to publish some amazing rhapsodies on human nature and the society of his own time. —HARRISON, FREDERIC, 1870-86, *The Choice of Books and Other Literary Pieces*, *p.* 148.

He [Librarian New York Mercantile Library] bought 500 copies of "Lothair," and afterward sold about 150 of them, as the public interest in the work gradually died away. There are still, however 50 or 75 copies in use all the time. More of the surplus stock might be sold; but experience has shown that the popularity of a book is subject to unforseen revivals, and if Mr. Disraeli should die, or become prime minister, or do anything else to bring himself into prominent notice, there would be a sudden call for all the copies on hand.—HASSARD, JNO. R. G., 1871, *The New York Mercantile Library, Scribner's Monthly, vol.* 1, *p.* 363.

Of Mr. Disraeli's "Lothair" 1500 copies were at first subscribed, but it was soon found necessary to increase the number to 3000. The demand was, however, as brief as it was eager, and the monumental pile of "remainders" in Mr. Mudie's cellar is the largest that has ever been erected there to the hydra of ephemeral admiration.—CURWEN, HENRY, 1873, *A History of Booksellers*, *p.* 428.

The weakest of all his novels.—CHAMBERS, ROBERT, 1876, *Cyclopædia of English Literature*, ed. Carruthers.

The novel bears the closest resemblance to the productions of his earlier days; as in them, passages of splendid diction alternate with passages of the most vapid inanity; and the book—strange to say—is characterised, too, by its admiring descriptions of the nobility—their mansions and their luxurious surroundings,—a form of mean adulation of which one would think Mr. Disraeli's attainment of one of the highest positions in England might have cured him. There are some clever sketches of contemporary characters; there are here and there bright epigrams; but the book is dreary and prolix, and the bright passages are the exception, —the dull the rule. So far as the book could be said to have any purpose at all, it was a strong attack upon the Roman Catholic Church.—O'CONNOR, THOMAS POWER, 1879, *Lord Beaconsfield, A Biography, p.* 599.

What makes "Lothair" psychologically interesting arises from the same position of affairs that has made the style official, namely, that the author stands at the summit of his wishes, and has realized his schemes, so that he no longer needs to take various circumstances into consideration. "Lothair" is a more straightforward book than the "Trilogy," so called, which preceded it. It is not only without false mysticism, but in a religious point of view, it is the most openly free-thinking work that Disraeli has written, so opposed to miracles that it might be taken for the work of a Rationalist if the fantastic author had not signed it with his fantastic doctrine, never renounced, of the sole victorious Semitic principle.—BRANDES, GEORGE, 1880, *Lord Beaconsfield,* tr. Mrs. George Sturge, p. 347.

"Lothair" came as a sort of successor to "Tancred," and its surface faults are precisely those which spoiled the earlier novels, and exposed their author to a good deal of humorous, and perhaps not altogether undeserved, satire. "Coningsby" is a caricature, but there are things in "Lothair" which are almost as absurd as anything in Thackeray's famous parody. The "ropes of pearls" which Lothair gives to Theodora; the crucifix of gold and emeralds, with its earth from the holy places covered in with "slit diamonds;" the tomb of alabaster, with its encircling railings of pure gold; Mr. Phœbus with his steam yacht "Pan," and his Ægean Island, his colossal wealth, and stupendously beautiful womankind; the extremely gorgeous society of dukes and their daughters, marquises, and merchant princes—all these things are, we venture to think, faults of taste, and are rather out of place in matter-of-fact England in the nineteenth century. But though we may dislike these things, it is impossible to contend that they justify the torrent of abuse with which "Lothair" was received. Much of it may, of course, be traced to the violent prejudice which dogged every step of Lord Beaconsfield's career—a prejudice by no means confined to his political opponents, but fully shared by many of the representatives of the old Conservative party.—HITCHMAN, FRANCIS, 1887, *Lothair and Endymion, National Review,* vol. 9, *p.* 383.

The Theodora of Disraeli's "Lothair." She is in truth one of the noblest creations of a modern novelist; she impersonates all the traits which Shelley specially valued in woman; she is a maturer Cythna, a Cythna of flesh and blood. What is equally to the point, she is her creator's ideal also. Disraeli usually deals with his characters with easy familiarity, and, except when he is depicting a personal enemy, with amiable indulgence. He sees their foibles, nevertheless, and takes care that these shall not escape the reader. In Theodora alone there is nothing of this. She has captivated her creator, as Galatea captivated Pygmalion. There is not a single touch of satire in the portrait; it plainly represents the artist's highest conception of woman, which proves to be essentially the same as Shelley's.—GARNETT, RICHARD, 1887-1901, *Shelley and Lord Beaconsfield, Essays of an Ex-Librarian, p.* 103.

ENDYMION
1880

A man's talent—an orator's, for instance—is not always in the exact ratio of his personal value; and in the same way the interest excited by a book may be out of proportion to its intrinsic merit. Lord Beaconsfield's new novel is an instance of this. As a novel it is hardly distinguished from the run of those which the English press turns out every year. It permits itself to be, rather than insists on being, read. It amuses the reader without enthralling him. And yet it has been in everybody's hand, and for the moment has been the theme of everybody's talk. People were anxious to see the present state of the talent and the opinions of a man who has for so long a time both held the political stage and plied the pen of the novelist. They were curious once more to meet this puzzling personage on whose score public opinion has not yet made itself up. I venture to think that it is Lord Beaconsfield's personality which gives the interest to his books, and even to his policy.—SCHERER, EDMOND, 1880-91, *Endymion, Essays on English Literature,* tr. Saintsbury, *p.* 240.

There is, moreover, nothing about the career of Endymion which arouses our interest or sympathies. He is from the first fatally successful. The obstacles which arise in his path we know at the outset will not prove to be real obstacles, and vanish entirely at the touch of the author's magical wand. There is no real struggle, and Endymion, whether he wants money, office, or a wife, is as certain to get what he longs for as we are to turn over the pages which advance him in his happy career. He finally marries Lady Montfort, and becomes Prime Minister of England. The plot is undeniably flat. In fact, there is no plot that deserves the name. The characters in Endymion are numerous, some of them being characters taken from contemporary politics, some the creations of the author's fancy. Myra and Endymion of course belong to the latter class, and Myra is really an extraordinary character.—SEDGWICK, A. G., 1880, *Beaconsfield's Endymion, Nation,* vol. 31, *p.* 413.

This book is called a novel by way of advertisement that it is in prose and is fictitious; but it needed no such descriptive label. If the definition of a novel is a "prose fiction" and nothing more, "Endymion" fulfils the requisition. It has in effect no plot and no characters, but is simply a narrative of things which have happened, and which have not and never can happen, constituting the political adventures, to a limited extent, of a large number of people, some of whom Lord Beaconsfield liked and some of whom he did not like. The style is diffuse, but less extravagant than has been usual with its author. The difference between this and his earlier works is the difference between the garrulity of old age and the enthusiasm of youth. What is lost in dash is gained in temperance. Otherwise the style is about the same as that of its predecessors, and relieved in the same way by epigrammatic turns and pointed sayings.—FULLER, MELVILLE W., 1881, *Beaconsfield's Novel, The Dial, vol.* 1, *p.* 188.

There will no doubt, be some reproach that this is a political novel without political principles, and a picture of success in life without ethical consideration; but the author may well say that that is his affair. He chooses to depict political life as he has found it, and he leaves it to others to invest it with graver forms, and to draw from it more solemn conclusions. He is the artist, not the political philosopher.—MILNES, RICHARD MONCKTON (LORD HOUGHTON), 1881, *Notes on Endymion, The Fortnightly Review, vol.* 35, *p.* 76.

There is nothing remarkable in "Endymion" except the intellectual vivacity, which shows no abatement.—FROUDE, JAMES ANTHONY, 1890, *Lord Beaconsfield (Prime Ministers of Queen Victoria), p.* 256.

GENERAL

Mr. D'Israeli began his literary career as an amusing writer merely. He was no unmeet Homer for a dandy Achilles, whose sublime was impertinence. His "Vivian Grey," no doubt, made some score of sophomores intolerable in the domestic circle; his "Young Duke" tempted as many freshmen to overrun their incomes. Nature is said to love a balance of qualities or properties, and to make up always for a deficiency in one place by an excess in some other. But our experience of mankind would incline us to doubt the possible existence of so large a number of modest men as would account for the intensity of Mr. Disraeli's vicarious atonement. It is painful to conceive of an amount of bashfulness demanding such a counterpoise of assurance. It would seem that he must have borrowed brass, that he must be supporting his lavish expenditures *aere alieno,* when he assumes the philosopher, and undertakes to instruct.—LOWELL, JAMES RUSSELL, 1847, *Disraeli's Tancred, North American Review, vol.* 65, *p.* 216.

He has great powers of description, an admirable talent for all dialogue, and remarkable force, as well as truth, in the delineation of character. His novels are constructed, so far as the story goes, on the true dramatic principles, and the interest sustained with true dramatic effect. His mind is essentially of a reflecting character; his novels are, in a great degree, pictures of public men or parties in political life. He has many strong opinions—perhaps some singular prepossessions—and his imaginative works are, in a great degree, the vehicle for their transmission.—ALISON, SIR ARCHIBALD, 1853, *History of Europe,* 1815–1852, *ch.* V.

Familiar with those scenes of life in which readers are the most interested, possessing a highly imaginative cast of mind and descriptive powers of no common order, it is no marvel that the author of "Vivian Grey" should be one of the most popular writers of his time.—ALLIBONE, S. AUSTIN, 1854–58, *A Critical Dictionary of English Literature, vol.* I, *p.* 505.

We pass to analyse, in a general way, Disraeli's intellectual powers. These are exceedingly varied. He has one of the sharpest and clearest of intellects, not, perhaps, of the most philosophical order, but exceedingly penetrating and acute. He has a fine fancy, soaring up at intervals into high imagination, and marking him a genuine child of that nation from whom came forth the loftiest, richest and most impassioned song which earth has ever witnessed—the nation of Isaiah, Ezekiel, Solomon and Job. He has little humor, but a vast deal of diamond-pointed wit. The whole world knows his powers of sarcasm. They have never been surpassed in the combination of savage force, and, shall we say, Satanic coolness, of energy and of point, of the fiercest *animus* within, and the utmost elegance of outward expression. He wields for his weapon a polar icicle—gigantic as a club—glittering as a star—deadly as a scimitar—and cool as eternal frost. His style and language are the faithful index of these varied and brilliant powers. His sentences are almost always short, epigrammatic, conclusive—pointed with wit and starred with imagery—and so rapid in their bickering, sparkling progress! One, while reading the better parts of his novels, seems reading a record of the conversations of Napoleon. — GILFILLAN, GEORGE, 1855, *A Third Gallery of Portraits*, p. 360.

A fantastic kind of Eastern exaggeration —the unpruned luxuriance of a Judean vine whose branches run over the wall— characterizes both the plots and the style of Mr. Disraeli's works.—COLLIER, WILLIAM FRANCIS, 1861, *A History of English Literature*, p. 515.

In descriptive power, he is hardly surpassed by any living writer, and in the exposition of politics, social theories, and the illustration of real public life by means of fictitious personages and incidents, he is without a rival.—CATHCART, GEORGE R., 1874, ed., *Literary Reader*, p. 171.

The accidents of his literary career appear to us much more interesting than those of his birth and station. It is true that his books often contain passages which reveal the force of his judgment and the excellence of his satirical abilities. But they also contain such a mass of gush, nonsense, and "talk," such an unworldly carelessness of being thought a fool, and such an apparent ignorance of what the world thinks foolish, that it is hard for us to conceive that they are the work of one who has since proved himself to be, of all the eminent people of his time and country, perhaps the most consummate man of the world. In no books is there to be found less of that sneaking caution in expressing the mind just as it is, which a very little commerce with the world teaches. The gush, the nonsense, and the "talk" come straight to the surface. He is not in the least ashamed to express his admiration of the fine houses, fine dinners and fine manners of the great. And the nonsense and the "talk" are not alone the outcome of his youth. We find him, after having been premier, writing a book full of the same kind of things which he wrote as a boy. His talents have been so commanding, the force of his will has been such, that he has been able to "carry" these immaturities.—NADAL, E. S., 1877, *Benjamin Disraeli, Scribner's Monthly*, vol. 14, p. 191.

I can even find an hour's amusement in the absurdities of that extraordinary mountebank whose remarkable fortune it now is for the moment to misgovern England.—ATKINSON, WILLIAM P., 1878, *The Right Use of Books*, p. 21.

He is, as we have endeavored to show, without any place in literature properly so called. The peculiarities of his style are chiefly defects, his characters generally libels or nonentities, his construction defective and his plot worthless, yet he has actually succeeded in making himself apparently the most popular novelist of the day. In intrinsic interest there is no sort of comparison between the novels of Lord Beaconsfield and those, we will not say of George Eliot but of Trollope. It is unsafe to predict, but in all probability Trollope's books will be taken as pictures of English life of to-day when the very names of "Endymion" and "Lothair" are lost to the world. . . . He has never been or pretended to be a scrupulous person, and he has no real reason to like or admire the aristocracy which he has fought his way into with tongue and pen. They have helped him against their will to political power; there is no reason why they should not help him to other things, even at their own expense, and it is at this expense that this clever adventurer has been all his life living. People really read such novels as "Lothair" and "Endymion" for much the same reason that they read a "society journal." If we can imagine a "society journal" edited by Lord Beaconsfield, the parallel would be complete. — SEDGWICK, A. G., 1880, *Beaconsfield's Endymion, The Nation*, vol. 31, p. 414.

We have dilated at some length on the various aspects of Lord Beaconsfield's humour, for it is to our minds far the most important feature of his writings, but after all it is for his daring and dazzling wit that he will universally be remembered. It is, as we have said, a rare quality, and it is also a gift that lives. Wit has wings. A happy phrase becomes a proverb, and the wittier half of a work, like the favourite melodies of a composition, survives the whole. The more will this be likely when the γνώμη is to repeat ourselves intellectually true, when fancy jumps with fact. This is we imagine, the secret of Lord Beaconsfield's wit. It may seem paradoxical to assert of its popular paradoxes that they are just, but we do so. He, like his Sidonia, "said many things that were strange, yet they instantly appeared to be true." Be this as it may, wit is certainly the most plentiful element of his later novels. They are confessedly novels of conversation. . . . It is in "Coningsby" and "Lothair" that perhaps the best of his apophthegms are found. . . . Whatever the divergencies of opinion on the literary merit of Lord Beaconsfield—and this rests with the best critic, posterity—it is at least unquestionable that in wit and humour he never flags.—SICHEL, WALTER SYDNEY, 1881, *The Wit and Humour of Lord Beaconsfield*, Macmillan's Magazine, vol 44. pp. 145, 146, 148.

The talent of Disraeli's novels, particularly the early ones, is that of a showy, romantic mind, which mistook flippancy for wit, which assumed cynicism for effect, and which was at all times defective in taste. They are cleverly rather than well written; are meretricious and tawdry, and they add nothing to our knowledge of life and character. If they are read twenty years hence, it will be out of curiosity respecting their writer, who will probably be said to have delineated the fashionable and political life of his time satirically, and not altogether unskilfully. Disraeli the novelist will be speedily forgotten, but Disraeli the man and the politician will be long remembered.—STODDARD, RICHARD HENRY, 1881, *The Earl of Beaconsfield, The Critic*, vol. 1, p. 111.

Heaven forbid that we should look to the England of Lord Beaconsfield for our standard of morals and manners! He does not depict our mother country, for motherhood there is none in his portraiture.—HOWE, JULIA WARD, 1881, *English Society and "Endymion," The Critic*, vol. 1, p. 31.

The characteristic note, both of his speeches and of his writings, is the combination of a few large ideas, clear, perhaps, to himself, but generally expressed in a vaguely grandiose way, and often quite out of relation to the facts as other people saw them, with a wonderfully acute discernment of small incidents of personal traits, which he used occasionally to support his ideas, but more frequently to conceal their weaknesses—that is, to make up for the absence of practical arguments, such as his hearers would understand.—BRYCE, JAMES, 1882, *Lord Beaconsfield, Century Magazine*, vol. 23, p. 738.

Lord Beaconsfield, even his most ardent admirers would admit, gave no evidence that he was possessed of the creative faculty in verse; an ardent imagination he undoubtedly had. He wrote, so far as I am aware, only two sonnets, one of which—that on Wellington—certainly deserves a place in any sonnet-anthology.—SHARP, WILLIAM, 1886, ed. *Sonnets of this Century*, p. 275, note.

The late Lord Beaconsfield, unrivalled at epigram and detached phrase, very frequently wrote and sometimes spoke below himself, and in particular committed the fault of substituting for a kind of English Voltairian style, which no one could have brought to greater perfection if he had given his mind to it, corrupt followings of the sensibility and philosophism of Diderot and the mere grandiloquence of Buffon.—SAINTSBURY, GEORGE, 1886, *Specimens of English Prose Style*, p. 34.

Mr. Disraeli, though eminent in literature, did not put his whole heart into it, as Sir Edward had done. As a way to distinction, when no other seemed open to him he was glad and proud to be an author; but his real love was to sway the listening senate; to be a leader of parties, and a ruler of men; the organizer of great schemes of policy, and to achieve not alone an English, but a European and cosmopolitan reputation. The consequence was that his literary career—bright though it seemed in the morning of his life—was a comparative failure as he advanced in years, and that he never achieved any greater success than the very moderate one which the French, when they wish to be good-natured, designate euphemistically as a "*succès d'estime.*" As an author, he never ranked and never will rank, among the "immortal few," but only as one of the crowd of mediocrities, not shining with any particular lustre during his own day, and destined to be extinguished in the blinding mists with which posterity covers the names and works of all who write for an age, or a portion of an age, and not "for all time."—MACKAY, CHARLES, 1887, *Through the Long Day*, vol. I, p. 255.

These books abound in wit and daring, in originality and shrewdness, in knowledge of the world and in knowledge of men; they contain many vivid and striking studies of character, both portrait and caricature; they sparkle with speaking phrases and happy epithets; they are aglow with the passion of youth, the love of love, the worship of physical beauty, the admiration of whatever is costly and select and splendid—from a countess to a castle, from a duke to a diamond; they are radiant with delight in whatever is powerful or personal or attractive—from a cook to a cardinal, from an agitator to an emperor. They often remind you of Voltaire, often of Balzac, often of "The Arabian Nights." You pass from an heroic drinking bout to a brilliant criticism of style; from rhapsodies on bands and ortolans that remind you of Heine to a gambling scene that for directness and intensity may vie with the bluntest and strongest work of Prosper Mérimée; from the extravagant impudence of "Popanilla" to the sentimental rodomontade of "Henrietta Temple;" from ranting romanticism in "Alroy" to vivid realism in "Sybil." Their author gives you no time to weary of him, for he is worldly and passionate, fantastic and trenchant, cynical and ambitious, flippant and sentimental, ornately rhetorical and triumphantly simple in a breath. He is imperiously egoistic, but while constantly parading his own personality he is careful never to tell you anything about it. And withal he is imperturably good tempered: he brands and gibbets with a smile, and with a smile he adores and applauds.—HENLEY, WILLIAM ERNEST, 1890, *Views and Reviews*, p. 20.

Disraeli was a phrase-maker by nature, and his fame in that direction was well deserved. He touched the height in his attacks upon Peel, when personal feeling aided native cleverness to its most epigrammatic expression. . . . Some of his epigrams have been forgotten; some will pass into history with the political circumstances which gave them birth; but no statesman of the century put so many clever things into such small compass, and Disraeli as a phrase-maker deserves study and remembrance.—ROBBINS, ALFRED F., 1894, *Lord Beaconsfield as a Phrase-maker, The Gentleman's Magazine, vol.* 276, *pp.* 311, 312.

Disraeli, with all his wit and *savoir faire*, has printed some rank fustian, and much slip-slop gossip. . . . Belongs to that very small group of real political satirists of whom Swift is the type. He is not the equal of the terrible Dean; but it may be doubted if any Englishman since Swift has had the same power of presenting vivid pictures and decisive criticisms of the political and social organism of his times. It is this Aristophanic gift which Swift had. Voltaire, Montesquieu, Rabelais, Diderot, Heine, Beaumarchais had it. Carlyle had it for other ages and in a historic spirit. There have been far greater satirists, men like Fielding and Thackeray, who have drawn far more powerful pictures of particular characters, foibles, or social maladies. But since Swift we have had no Englishman who could give us a vivid and amusing picture of our political life, as laid bare to the eye of a consummate political genius.— HARRISON, FREDERIC, 1895, *Studies in Early Victorian Literature, pp.* 18, 90.

It is easy to detect faults, which stand out on the very surface of his work, and are, indeed, an essential part of the methods by which he produced his effect. The imagination is often fantastic, the ornament is unduly lavish, the gilding is sometimes tawdry and overdone, the sentiment often inflated. Mediocrity will satisfy itself by calling this vulgarity and pretentiousness. But in truth it was only the natural result of an imagination singularly luxuriant, combined with a far-reaching sarcasm, and an undercurrent of deep thought and brooding melancholy.—CRAIK, HENRY, 1896, *English Prose, vol.* V, *p.* 486.

As literature, Disraeli's novels are not great, because, using the word in an artistic and not a moral sense, they are not pure. They are pretentious and unreal, and the rhetoric rings false. The impression of insincerity, conveyed to so many by his statesmanship, is conveyed also by his novels. But notwithstanding all defects, Disraeli's novels have that interest which must belong to the works of a man who has played a great part in history. They throw light upon his character, they mark the development of his ambition, it may even be said that they have helped to make English history. It is worth remembering that "Tancred" foretells the occupation of Cyprus; and it is quite consistent with the character of Disraeli to believe that, when the opportunity came, the desire to make his own prophecy come to pass influenced him to add to the British crown one of its most worthless possessions, and to burden it with one of its most intolerable responsibilities, the care of Armenia. Indeed, the most remarkable feature in Disraeli's novels is the way in which they reflect his life and interpret his statesmanship. The magniloquence, the flash and the glitter of the early novels seem of a piece with the tales current regarding the author's manners and character, his dress designed to attract attention, and his opinions cut after the pattern of his dress. So in the "Coningsby" group we are struck with the forecast of the writer's future political action.—WALKER, HUGH, 1897, *The Age of Tennyson*, p. 76.

At the present day, Benjamin Disraeli, as a novelist, is only a name in the history of literature, and rightly so. No descriptive style could be less artistic than his. His language is that of an unliterary beginner, either high-flown as in the story of knights and robbers, or hackneyed as in the supplement of a provincial newspaper.—ENGEL, EDWARD, 1902, *A History of English Literature*, rev. Hamley Bent, p. 459.

Arthur Penrhyn Stanley
1815–1881

Born, at Alderly, Cheshire, 13 Dec. 1815. Educated at Rugby, 1829–34. Matric., Balliol Coll., Oxford, 30 Nov. 1833; Scholar, 1833–38; Ireland Scholar, 1837; Newdigate Prize, 1837; B. A., 1837; Fellow of Univ. Coll., 1838–51; Latin Essay Prize, 1839; Ellerton Theol. Prize, 1840; M. A., 1840; Ordained Deacon, 1839; Priest, 1841; Select Preacher, Oxford Univ., 1845–46, 1872–73. Sec. Oxford Univ. Commission, 1850–52. Canon of Canterbury Cathedral, 1851–58. Travelled widely on Continent and in Palestine. Contrib., to "Quarterly Rev." 1850–73; to "Edinburgh Rev.," 1850–81; to "Fraser's Mag.," 1865–80; to "Macmillan's Mag.," 1860–81; to "Good Words," 1861–81; to "Contemporary Review," 1866–75; to "Nineteenth Century," 1878–80; Chaplain to Prince Consort, 1854–61. Exam. Chaplain to Bishop of London, 1854–64. Regius Prof. of Eccles. Hist., Oxford, 1856–64. B. D. and D. D., Oxford, 1858. Canon of Ch. Ch., Oxford, 1858–64. Mem. of Hebdomadal Council, Oxford, 1860–64. Deputy Clerk of Closet, and Hon. Chaplain in Ordinary to the Queen and Prince of Wales, 1863. Married Lady Augusta Bruce, 23 Dec. 1863. Dean of Westminister, 1864. Hon. LL. D., Camb., 1864. Hon. Fellow of Univ. Coll., Oxford, 1864–81. To Moscow, for marriage of Duke of Edinburgh, 1874. Lord Rector St. Andrews Univ., 1875. Visited U. S. A., 1878. Died at Westminster, 18 July, 1881. Buried in Westminster Abbey. *Works:* [exclusive of separate sermons]: "The Gypsies," 1837; "Do States, like Individuals inevitably tend . . . to decay?" 1840; "Life and Correspondence of T. Arnold" (2 vols.), 1844 (3rd edn. same year); "Sermons and Essays on the Apostolical Age," 1847; "The Study of Modern History," 1854; "Historical Memorials of Canterbury," 1855 (2nd edn. same year); "The Reformation," 1856; "Sinai and Palestine," 1856 (3rd edn. same year); "Three Introductory Lectures on the Study of Ecclesiastical History," 1857; "The Unity of Evangelical and Apostolical Teaching," 1859; "Freedom and Labour," 1860; "Lectures on the History of the Eastern Church," 1861; "Sermons preached before . . . the Prince of Wales during his tour in the East," 1863; "The Bible, its Form and its Substance," 1863; "Lectures on the History of the Jewish Church" (3 pts.), 1863–76; "A Letter to the Lord Bishop of London," 1863; "The South African Controversy," 1867; "An Address on the Connection of Church and State," 1868 (2nd edn. same year); "Historical Memorials of Westminster Abbey," 1868; (2nd edn. same year); "The Three Irish Churches," 1869; "Essays," 1870; "The Athanasian Creed" (from "Contemp. Rev."), 1871; "The National Thanksgiving," 1872; "Lectures on the History of the Church of Scotland," 1872; "The Early Christianity of Northumbria" (from "Good Words"), 1875; "Inaugural Address at St. Andrews," 1875; "Addresses and Sermons delivered at St. Andrews, 1877; "Addresses and Sermons delivered during a visit to the United States," 1879; "Memoirs of Edward and Catherine Stanley," 1879; "Christian Institutions, 1881. *Posthumous:* "Sermons on Special Occasions," 1882; "Sermons for Children," 1887; "Letters and Verses," ed. by R. E. Prothero, 1895. He *edited:* T. Arnold's "Miscellaneous Works," 1845; "Addresses and Charges of E. Stanley, Bishop of Norwich," 1851; T. Arnold's "Travelling Journals," 1852; "The Epistle of St. Paul to the Corinthians" (2 vols.), 1855; "The Utrecht Psalter: Reports," 1874; S. Greg's "A Layman's Legacy," 1877; Bishop Thirlwall's "Letters to a Friend," 1881. *Life:* By R. E. Prothero and Dean Bradley, 1893.—SHARP, R. FARQUHARSON, 1897, *A Dictionary of English Authors*, p. 266.

EDWARD BOUVERIE PUSEY

Engraving by Walker & Boutall. From a Portrait by Miss Rosa Corder.

ARTHUR PENRHYN STANLEY

Engraving by Francis Holl, A.R.A. Photograph by Samuel A. Walker

PERSONAL

I came up to Oxford a hard reader and a passionate High Churchman—two years of residence left me idle and irreligious. Partly from ill-health, partly from disgust at my college, I had cut myself off from society within or without it. I rebelled doggedly against the systems around me. I would not work, because work was the Oxford virtue. . . . That sermon on work was like a revelation to me. "If you cannot or will not work at the work which Oxford gives you, at any rate work at something." I took up my old boy-dreams,—history—I think I have been a steady worker ever since. And so in religion, it was not so much a creed that you taught me as fairness. You were liberal, you pointed forward, you believed in a future as other "liberals" did, but you were not like them, unjust to the present or the past. I found that old vague reverence of mine for personal goodness which alone remained to me, widened in your teaching into a live catholicity. I used to think as I left your lecture-room of how many different faiths and persons you had spoken, and how you had revealed and taught me to love the good that was in them all.—GREEN, JOHN RICHARD, 1863, *To Stanley, Dec.; Letters, ed. Stephen*, pp. 17, 18.

Stanley, when disposed to be friendly, was very delightful and attractive. And I think that what made him so was not his brilliancy and resource and knowledge, but the sense that he was sincerely longing to be in sympathy with every one for whom he could feel respect. It was the basis of a very grand character; but Stanley had intellectual defects, like his physical defects as to music, or smell, or colour, or capacity for mathematical ideas, which crippled his capacity for the sympathy he wished to spread all round him. One of these defects is indicated in what his critics say of his aversion to metaphysics and dogmatic statements. They were to his mind like the glass which the fly walks on and cannot penetrate: when he came to them his mind "would not bite." Another defect seemed to me always his incapacity for the spiritual and unearthly side of religion; the side which is so strong in the people whom he opposed, Newman and Keble, and, in a lower way, the Evangelicals. . . . He was a very earnest preacher of religious morality, though he was blind to some important parts of it, and was driven by his religious partizanship to exaggerate some other parts —as in his grotesque and vehement efforts to claim admiration for the eighteenth century type of religion, and indignation at criticisms upon it.—CHURCH, RICHARD WILLIAM, 1881, *To the Warden of Keble, July* 31; *Life and Letters of Dean Church, ed. his Daughter*, pp. 351, 353.

We must not let our friends die, and I trust Stanley will long live among us. I have never known a better man—his very weaknesses arising from the best motives. —MÜLLER, FRIEDRICH MAX, 1881, *To Lady Welby, Aug.* 2; *Life and Letters, ed. his Wife*, vol. II, p. 109.

When the tomb in Westminster Abbey closed in July over all that was mortal of its great Dean, the shock was felt wherever our language is spoken. A unique life, one of which all the English race could be proud, had ended. The longing to know more, to know all that could be known of it, has come out more strongly than in any instance probably within living memory, and justly so, for he had touched so many sides of our life, and each side with such effect, had been so near the throne and the workshop, so faithful and so simple in his relations with every class, so clear and brave in upholding his own beliefs, so tolerant of those of all other men, if only they were real and in earnest.— HUGHES, THOMAS, 1881, *A Reminiscence of Arthur Stanley, Harper's Magazine*, vol. 63, p. 911.

It was perhaps as much as by anything by his readiness to associate with the Presbyterian clergy in Scotland, and to fraternise with the representatives of all sects in England, and indeed throughout the world —it was perhaps by this as much as by anything that the late Dean Stanley became the most famous English ecclesiastic of his day. He despised in this fashion prejudices still lingering in his Church, and the obloquy which was the consequence of despising them, and it was counted to him for righteousness and common sense. When they build his sepulchre in Westminster, they should write upon it for one thing "Here lies one who supposed that other Christians than those belonging to the Church of England might be saved, and who never doubted and therefore never said that there might be 'some devout persons among the Dissenters'." . . . As regards his worth to the Church and to the world, to speak plainly, it seems to me that he was not first of all an amiable, pure, noble, highly gifted and wonderfully accomplished man, and then a Church dignitary of liberal or advanced theological views; but he was first of all a Churchman of that description, and secondly he was all that you pleased to say, all that can be said or imagined, of a Christian and a gentleman. He indeed valued goodness more than any creed—no man perhaps ever valued goodness more than he.—SERVICE, JOHN, 1881, *Dean Stanley, Macmillan's Magazine*, vol. 44, pp. 467, 468.

> Twelve hundred years and more
>   Along the holy floor
> Pageants have pass'd, and the tombs of mighty
>   kings
> Efface the humbler graves of Sebert's line,
> And, as years sped, the minster-aisles divine
> Grew used to the approach of Glory's wings.
>   Arts came, and arms, and law,
>   And majesty, and sacred form and fear;
> Only that primal guest the fisher saw,
> Light, only light, was slow to re-appear.
> . . . .
>   Yet in this latter time
>   That promise of the prime
> Seem'd to come true at last, O Abbey old!
> It seem'd a child of light did bring the dower
> Foreshown thee in thy consecration hour,
> And in thy courts his shining freight unroll'd:—
>   Bright wits, and instinct sure,
> And goodness warm, and truth without alloy,
>   And temper sweet, and love of all things pure,
> And joy in light, and power to spread the joy.

—ARNOLD, MATTHEW, 1881, *Westminster Abbey, The Nineteenth Century*, vol. 11, pp. 3, 4.

His special attraction, from a social point of view, was his unique simplicity. We seem forced to commemorate it even in mentioning him. However suitable was his position as Dean of the great Abbey in which he took so lively an interest, it is impossible to speak of him now in any other way, than as Arthur Stanley. At times it seemed as if his position as a Church dignitary took to himself the aspect of a certain masquerade. I remember well the half-comic air with which he said, "I should so much have liked to ask the Pope his opinions about himself" (in recounting an interview with him, if I remember right), and there was something inexpressibly engaging in the playfulness with which he added, "I can't quite fancy thinking myself infallible;" and then came a humorous little pause, as if he was just asking himself whether, after all, that might not be compassed, and he concluded much more decidedly. "But certainly I can't conceive thinking all the Deans of Westminster infallible."— WEDGWOOD, JULIA, 1881, *Arthur Penrhyn Stanley, The Contemporary Review*, vol. 40, p. 492.

The personal charm of Dean Stanley, in public and in private, was something which everybody felt who came into the slightest association with him. Indeed, it seems, as we have intimated, to have been felt even by those who never saw him, and who knew him only through his books and by the public record of his life. It was the charm of simple truthfulness, of perfect manliness, of a true sympathy with all forms of healthy human action, and of a perpetual picturesqueness, which was enhanced by the interesting positions which he held, but was independent of them, and had its real being in his personality itself. If he had been the humblest country parson instead of being Dean of Westminster, he would have carried about the same charm in his smaller world. It was associated with his physical frame, his small stature, his keen eye, his rapid movement, his expressive voice. The very absence of bodily vigor made the spiritual presence more distinct. And the perfect unity of the outer and inner, the public and the private life, at once precluded any chance of disappointment in those who, having been attracted by his work came by and by to know him personally, and at the same time gave to those whose only knowledge of him was from his writings and his public services the right to feel that they did really know him as he was.—BROOKS, PHILLIPS, 1881, *Dean Stanley, Essays and Addresses*, p. 358.

> His hopes were ocean-wide, and clasped mankind;
> No Levite plea his mercy turned apart,
> But wounded souls—to whom all else were blind—
> He soothed with wine and balsam of the heart.

—HAYNE, PAUL HAMILTON, 1881, *Dean Stanley.*

The death of the Dean of Westminster is not so much the loss of an ecclesiastic, as the disappearance of a whole region of life, which none but himself is likely ever to supply,—the region, I mean, in which all that is really beautiful and noble in the world received a generous and delicate spiritual appreciation, without the smallest regard to any of those straight ecclesiastical or dogmatic conditions usually required for spiritual appreciation. In Dean Stanley the human sympathies were very bright and deep, while the grasp of abstract truth was comparatively feeble.—HUTTON, RICHARD HOLT, 1881, *Dean Stanley, Criticisms on Contemporary Thoughts and Thinkers*, vol. I.

If I were to put in one word what struck me as perhaps the leading characteristic of Dean Stanley, and what made him so dear to many, I should say it was not his charity, though his charity was large—for charity has in it sometimes, perhaps often, a savor of superiority,— it was not his toleration,— for toleration, I think, is apt to make a concession of what should be simply recognized as a natural right,—but it was rather, as it seems to me, the wonderful many-sidedness of his sympathies. . . . I think no man ever lived who was so pleasant to so many people. We visited him as we visit a clearer sky and a warmer climate. . . . I think the one leading characteristic of Dean Stanley,—and I say it to his praise —was the amount of human nature there was in him. So sweet, so gracious, so cheerful, so illuminating, was it that there could not have been too much of it. It brought him nearer to all mankind, it recognized and called out the humanity that was in the other man. His sympathies were so wide that they could not be confined by the boundaries of the land in which he was born: they crossed the channel and they crossed the ocean.—LOWELL, JAMES RUSSELL, 1881, *Speech at the Meeting in the Chapter House of Westminster Abbey in Commemoration of Dean Stanley*, Dec. 13.

That Monday was a wonderful day. There was everyone in the abbey, all the great and eminent men of all parties and schools in England, round his coffin. It was all very orderly and impressive and just as he would have had it. And then by degrees I began to feel what I had lost and how much I had lived in him and how I had unconsciously referred to him on all kinds of points, and how many difficulties vanished when I thought "Oh, I will see Stanley next week and then I will ask him." It is quite curious that since his death hardly a day has passed, but something has turned up in the paper, or the Bible, or a book, to make me say before I recollected he was gone, "Oh, I will ask Stanley about this."—GROVE, SIR GEORGE, 1881, *To Miss M. E. von Glehn*, Aug. 1; *Life and Letters, ed. Graves*, p. 268.

As a speaker, . . . Dean Stanley was by no means fluent. He spoke slowly and hesitatingly. He often paused to find the right word. He often deviated into the most unadorned and colloquial English. And yet, though I have heard him speak at many gatherings which differed as widely from each other as a feast of the little choristers at Westminster differs from an agitated assembly of hostile ecclesiastics, I never heard him utter one word which was unworthy of him, or make one speech which did not leave behind it a sense of charm and satisfaction. The topics were always opposite; the observations were never commonplace; the sentiments were always noble and sincere. . . . He constantly preached old sermons on old themes. . . . Often, however, his sermons on the same text were so altered by additions and omissions that they were hardly recognizable. They were written over and under, within and without, on one side of the page and on both sides. Mysterious marks and countermarks, in pencil or in red ink, indicated what portions were, on any particular occasion, to be used or to be omitted. Sometimes two sermons were rolled into one; sometimes one sermon was expanded into two. The result, so far as the manuscript was concerned, was often a chaos, rendered yet more chaotic by the handwriting which few but the Dean's intimate friends could discipher, and which often led to the most grotesque misprints. Constantly, and especially of late years, he lost his way amongst these combined passages of variously turncoated addresses, and he would pause to turn over loose pages until he resumed the manuscript at the intended point. In these cases, too, the *junctura* was sometimes anything but *levis.* Hence those who only heard him preach an old or rehabilitated sermon were unable to judge of his powers, for the difference of manner with which he preached old and new matter was very noticeable.—FARRAR, FREDERIC WILLIAM, 1882, *Dean Stanley as a Preacher, Contemporary Review*, vol. 42, pp. 807, 808.

It may be that, in ages to come, those who tell the roll of England's worthies in the aisles of Westminster may think that Stanley's name stood higher with his contemporaries than any definite achievement of his could warrant. We cannot correct the judgments of posterity; but we may feel assured that if it had been allowed us to prolong, from generation to generation, some one man's earthly days, we could hardly have sent any pilgrim across the centuries more wholly welcome than Arthur Stanley, to whatever times are yet to be. For they, like us, would have recognised in him a spectator whose vivid interest seemed to give to this world's spectacle an added zest; an influence of such a nature as humanity, howsoever it may be perfected, will only prize the more; a life bound up and incorporated with the advance and weal of men; a presence never to be forgotten, and irreplaceable, and beloved. — MYERS, FREDERIC W. H., 1883, *Arthur Penrhyn Stanley, Century Magazine*, vol. 25, p. 383.

The Dean of Westminster he [Carlyle] liked personally, almost loved him indeed, yet he could have wished him anywhere but where he was. "There goes Stanley," he said one day as we passed the Dean in the park, "boring holes in the bottom of the Church of England!"—FROUDE, JAMES ANTHONY, 1884, *Thomas Carlyle, A History of His Life in London*, vol. II, p. 223.

Every great man who has ministered in the Church of Scotland since the days of Knox, has preached from the pulpit of that church. But among them all, never greater nor more lovable man than Stanley.—BOYD, ANDREW K. H., 1892, *Twenty-Five Years of St. Andrews*, vol. I, p. 208.

It is hardly necessary to point to him as one ready at all times to resist every attempt to narrow the freedom of the individual spirit essential, as he believed, to the existence of the Church of which he was a member; or to his readiness and promptness at every period of his life to espouse the side of those who were exposed to persecution or obloquy. Yet, though plunged, as he felt himself to be, in incessant conflicts, and though always yearning for sympathy and aid, he never harboured a resentful thought, was always ready to recognize the claim to honour, and even to reverence, of those who had felt bound to refuse him their sympathy or co-operation, or had passed the sternest judgments on his own most cherished aims. Of his ceaseless activity, of his readiness to aid by all his powers those who sought his aid, there is still a cloud of witnesses. He never spared himself: his active brain, his kindly heart, gave him no rest. He never turned away from the work for which his special gifts so singularly marked him out. And how many are there still, of those who shared his friendship, who feel that his loss has made life seem different since he was taken from them. Not in any narrow sense, but in many senses, he has had no successor—no one who has exercised the same kind of influence, alike in the circle of those who entered into the controversies which divided the religious world, and those outside that circle.— BRADLEY, GEORGE GRANVILLE, 1893, *The Life and Correspondence of Arthur Penrhyn Stanley*, ed. Prothero, Introduction, vol. I, p. 26.

One main source of the freshness which pervaded his sermons, his conversation, his travels, and his literary work, was the economy of his strength which he invariably exercised. He had most clearly recognised the extent and the limitations of his powers. In travelling, he required all arrangements to be made for him, steadily refused to see any sight which did not interest him, and consequently was never tired. In society, he never attempted to make conversation, but, talking only on those subjects which aroused his enthusiasm, spoke with a fire that glowed and warmed, yet never burned or left a scar. In preaching, he enforced, and illustrated by concrete application from past or contemporary events, only those moral and spiritual aspects of Christianity which to him were most vital, and hence his sermons were never dry, laboured, or dead, but were always picturesque, interesting, and directly bearing on human life and human conduct. As a man of letters, he only worked as his powers designed him to work, and only wrote as he loved to write, and therefore his writing is never forced, but always natural and always fresh.—PROTHERO, ROWLAND E., 1893, ed. *The Life and Correspondence of Arthur Penrhyn Stanley*, vol. II, p. 237.

Through life, the senses of smell and taste were utterly unknown to him; once only— in Switzerland—he fancied he smelt the freshness of a pine-wood. "It made the world a paradise," he said.—HARE, AUGUSTUS J. C., 1895, *Biographical Sketches*, p. 25.

He was thin, he was small, but, like Cæsar, he was not insignificant. Though his features were not strictly handsome, he had a refined, an intellectual, a most interesting countenance. He was endowed with high personal courage and a chivalrous nature, I should like to say a buoyant pluck;

and there was an eager sweetness in his address that was very winning. Occasionally he had a dreamy expression. His intellectual alertness a little reminded me of Monsieur Thiers. Arthur was pure-minded and simple-mannered; and though he happened to be curiously indifferent to what is called small talk, his powers of conversation were remarkable. We constantly met, and in divers places, and he was a valued member of every society in which I found him. Arthur was a thoroughly amiable man, and entirely destitute of personal or other vanity. He had the unmistakable air of good-breeding. He was a man of the world and a courtier, in the very best sense of that word; but he was a courtier through circumstances and not by choice.—LOCKER-LAMPSON, FREDERICK, 1895, *Arthur Penrhyn Stanley, My Confidences*, p. 344.

He was a great teacher in his own way, and a great thinker, and he held a peculiar position among the Church of England ecclesiastics of his time. He was not so much a force as an influence. He cannot be said to have originated any movement, but he helped to keep many movements in order. He was a charming writer, a most delightful talker, a man who exercised great power over his Church and over the social life of his time. His home in Dean's Yard, Westminster, gave a welcome to intellect and culture and social reforms from all over the world. He had travelled much, and had made friends everywhere, and it may be said, without exaggeration, that every distinguished man or woman from any country might be met sooner or later under Dean Stanley's roof. The world lost much by losing him, and with his death it may not unfairly be said that one of the social and literary lights of London went out, not to be relumed.—McCARTHY, JUSTIN, 1897, *A History of Our Own Times from 1880 to the Diamond Jubilee*, p. 88.

With Stanley his charm of manner and temper was no small part of his power, and this makes it difficult to dwell on—what he so strongly felt himself—an indecision of character which rendered him almost incapable of holding a positive view on any subject of importance. This, indeed had been Stanley's characteristic from his earliest years, and it continued through life, showing itself at Rugby, as I have already mentioned, by an absolute devotion to Arnold, and to all his opinions; and afterwards by his singular friendship with Ward, and his union, if not his entire agreement, with Jowett. He had plenty of opinions, but they were always of a negative character; and Dr. Pusey's view of him was in this respect just, that his object was always to support persons who in their religious belief differed from everybody else. . . . It is evident that such a person could hardly in the common sense of the word be called a leader; and, indeed, his life was a succession of changes from one leader to another—first, and above all, Arnold, then Ward, and, lastly, Jowett. He had plenty of courage in following them, but I doubt whether any one, strictly speaking, followed *him*.—LAKE, WILLIAM CHARLES, 1897-1901, *Memorials*, ed. his Widow, pp. 58, 59.

LIFE OF THOMAS ARNOLD
1844

When we left college the younger Ware advised us to read the lives of men who had really helped the world. He intimated that this is the best way to find out what religion is and what it is not. He is quite right. To that bit of advice I owe the reading of a good many biographies, worthless as literary books, but in which I found good hints in the great science of living. Foremost among many of these is Stanley's "Life of Arnold," which was published, I think, in 1844. This is another of the books which moved its time, and of which you can still trace the ripple on the ocean. We did not think, when we read it, though we should have been wise enough to do so, that the author was to fill and to deserve a place in the world's regard as large as his beloved teacher's.—HALE, EDWARD EVERETT, 1888, *Books That Have Helped Me*, p. 12.

It is certainly a work of loyal affection, written with a sole object of setting before the world the greatness and goodness of its master, the author modestly effacing himself entirely from the record. To us it certainly bears an appearance of diffuseness and verbosity resulting in part from the extremely minute analysis of Arnold's conduct and motives in every branch of life, which we are inclined to think, at the present time at least, somewhat superfluous. The arrangement, too, is faulty, the separation of the text of the biography from the very numerous letters published along with it, contributing to deprive the former of its energy and the latter of its interest. The popularity of the work, however, as we have said, has in no way decreased.—OLIPHANT, MARGARET O. W., 1892, *The Victorian Age of English Literature*, p. 198.

His sorrow, his reverence, his sympathy, found relief in devoting his best energies to that "Life of Arnold," which has translated his character to the world, and given Arnold a wider influence since his death than he ever attained in his life. Perhaps, of all Stanley's books, Arnold's life is still the one by which he is best known, and this, in his reverent love for his master, to whom he owed the building up of his mind, is as he would have wished it to be.—HARE, AUGUSTUS J. C., 1895, *Biographical Sketches*, p. 50.

The book will long remain to the student of the social, religious, and political history of the former half of the nineteenth century a treasury of valuable material, because it portrays in clear outline a central figure round which clustered some of the most remarkable personages and incidents of a stirring and eventful period. Stanley's book is a large one and deals necessarily with much ephemeral controversy, religious and political, which may possibly not excite any strong interest in the present generation of readers. It is to be feared that these facts may have the effect of concealing from those readers much that is of permanent value in Arnold's history and performance. —FITCH, SIR JOSHUA, 1897, *Thomas and Matthew Arnold*, p. 2.

What I have always considered the most effective biography of the century, Stanley's "Life of Arnold."—LAKE, WILLIAM CHARLES, 1897–1901, *Memorials*, ed. his Widow, p. 3.

HISTORY OF THE JEWISH CHURCH
1863–76

Here is a book on religious matters, which, meant for all the world to read, fulfils the indispensable duty of edifying at the same time that it informs. Here is a clergyman, who, looking at the Bible, sees its contents in their right proportion, and gives to each matter its due prominence. Here is an inquirer, who, treating Scripture history with a perfectly free spirit,—falsifying nothing, sophisticating nothing—treats it so that his freedom leaves the sacred power of that history inviolate. Who that had been reproached with denying to an honest clergyman freedom to speak the truth, who that had been misrepresented as wishing to make religious truth the property of an aristocratic few, while to the multitude is thrown the sop of any convenient fiction, could desire a better opportunity than Dr. Stanley's book affords for showing what, in religious matters, is the true freedom of a religious speaker, and what the true demand and true right of his hearers?—ARNOLD, MATTHEW, 1863, *Dr. Stanley's Lectures on the Jewish Church, Macmillan's Magazine*, vol. 7, p. 327.

These volumes embody the substance of lectures delivered in the chair of ecclesiastical history at Oxford. The work is a popular presentation of the results reached by modern scholarship. It makes no claim to the merits of original research. While the author has used the results of labors like those of Ewald, he has fully acknowledged his indebtedness. The peculiar merits of the book, therefore, are not the merits of an original authority; but rather those of an unusually attractive presentation. Clearness, grace, and fluency of style are most noteworthy characteristics of these admirable and unusually attractive volumes.— ADAMS, CHARLES KENDALL, 1882, *A Manual of Historical Literature*, p. 79.

The main difference between the two parts lies in the form into which the material is thrown. In the first period, poetry, metaphor, prophecy, and history seemed to Stanley to be so intermingled that continuous narrative was in great part abandoned. In the second period this difficulty had to a great extent disappeared. Though chronological uncertainties still remained, the substantially historical character of the whole is almost universally admitted, and the sacred history speaks for itself as a continuous narrative. In other respects the aim, the spirit, the charm, and the method of the treatment are the same. There is the same bold, yet reverent, handling of subjects which are peculiarly liable to suffer from repetitions of conventional language, and from traditional methods of treatment. There is the same effort to interpret the Bible, not by our own fancies concerning it, but by what it says of itself; to distinguish between the letter and the spirit; to extinguish "the unnatural war between faith and reason, between human science and divine." . . . The two volumes are alike in aim and spirit. They also possess the same distinctive charm—the fascination of a style which is graphic, picturesque, eloquent, and rich in pertinent illustration; the same grouping into vivid pictures of a body of small facts; the same grasp of the critical and salient features in the character of an age or of an individual. . . . Both volumes are alike in being the work of a moralist who is writing historically.—PROTHERO, ROWLAND E., 1893, *ed. The Life and Correspondence of Arthur Penrhyn Stanley, vol.* II, *pp.* 246, 248, 249.

It is unquestionably a delightful book, a book which everyone ought to read and from which no one is likely to rise without a great many new and fruitful ideas. The author, however, is always thinking too much of the edification of his hearers, too little of merely representing the facts as they seem to him to have occurred. It is the Bible History seen under a painted window and not by mere white light.—DUFF, MOUNTSTUART E. GRANT, 1894, *The Life of Arthur Stanley, National Review, vol.* 22, *p.* 754.

HISTORICAL MEMORIALS OF WESTMINSTER ABBEY
1868

Dean Stanley, the pupil and the biographer of Dr. Arnold, has made some of the most valuable contributions to ecclesiastical history which our time possesses. His "Historical Memorials of Westminster Abbey" fascinates the reader by its beauty of style and by the evidences of the loving care with which the author has approached his subject.—MCCARTHY, JUSTIN, 1880, *A History of Our Own Times from the Accession of Queen Victoria to the Berlin Congress, vol.* IV, *ch.* lxvii.

Up to the time when it was written, the tombs and the history of the abbey were comparatively little known, even by scholars so accomplished as the late Dean Milman, who for many years was one of the canons. The thousands who visited it were compelled, by lack of knowledge, to look with a blank and unintelligent eye on many a monument which is now rife with interest. The Dean left no source of information unsearched. He was greatly assisted by the magnificent publication of the abbey registers, with genealogical and other notes by the American antiquary, Colonel Chester. . . . I think that the extent, variety, and minuteness of literary and historical research which the Dean has compressed into his "Memorials" have never been duly estimated. To write this book, he was obliged to expend a vast amount of time in the study of memoirs, poems and journals belonging to every period of English History.—FARRAR, FREDERIC WILLIAM, 1885, *Reminiscences of Arthur Penrhyn Stanley; Some Noted Princes, Authors and Statesmen of Our Time, ed. Parton, pp.* 12, 13.

He became, as it were, the soul of the Abbey. To follow him through its chapels and transepts was to follow a "Christian Plutarch." His presence, as he drew out the tales imprisoned in the silent stones, and made each sepulchre surrender its dead, gave to its walls and monuments life and speech and motion. From the buried stones of the original Abbey of Edward the Confessor, to the last addition made by himself, all told the tale of continuous national history. In dealing with the Bible he had endeavored to make it a living book, so that it might the more readily become a Book of Life. In the same spirit, both with voice and pen, he laboured to reanimate the inheritance of the past, to make the Abbey an eloquent memorial of all that was greatest and most famous in national history, to keep alive its powers as the incentive to heroic action, to appeal, through its splendid associations with the past, not only to the care but to the emulation of the present. Nor was it merely with the past history of England that he linked the present life of the nation.—PROTHERO, ROWLAND E., 1893, *ed. Life and Correspondence of Arthur Penrhyn Stanley, vol.* II, *p.* 281.

GENERAL

We have embarked on a beautiful book, Arthur Stanley's "Palestine:" thou wouldst be much interested in it I think. He writes charmingly, seeing things so clearly, and seeing them in their bearings, geographical and otherwise, like a true pupil of Dr. Arnold's; and there is such a high and thoughtful tone over it all.—FOX, CAROLINE, 1856, *Letter to E. T. Carne, Aug.* 29; *Memories of Old Friends, ed. Pym.*

Apart from the beautiful simplicity of his style and the richness of illustrative allusion, the charm of his sermons was very apt to lie in a certain way which he had of treating the events of the day as parts of the history of the world, and making his hearers feel that they and what they were doing belonged as truly to the history of their race, and shared as truly in the care and government of God, as David and his wars, or Socrates and his teachings. As his lectures made all times live with the familiarity of our own day, with its petty interests, grow sacred and inspired by its identification with the great principles of all the ages. With the procession of heroism and faith and bravery and holiness always marching before his eyes, he summoned his congregation in the Abbey or in the village church to join the host. And it was his power of historical imagination that made them for an instant see the procession which he saw, and long to join it at his summons.—BROOKS, PHILLIPS, 1881, *Dean Stanley, Essays and Addresses,* p. 359.

I have said that Dean Stanley was no theologian, and, indeed, had no real hold at all of the significance of abstract thought—no grasp of what I may call the backbone of mental and moral creeds — though he could often appreciate finely the fruits which such creeds bore in actual life, without being aware that it was those systems which had borne them. Indeed, his true liberality of nature, his positive inability to ignore what was good in one whose general belief he either could not share, or positively condemned, was in some measure due to this comparative insignificance of all merely intellectual discussion in his mind. He could not, if he would, have judged the tree of belief by anything but its fruits, and its fruits in the largest sense of the term. And amongst these fruits, he could not, for the life of him, help reckoning almost everything that added to the richness and variety of life,—so that when he came to estimate the value of institutions, he found himself according the most liberal sympathy to every institution which had ennobled the civilisation of any epoch, which had sheltered men of genius and power, which had given a more historic colour to the past, or which had transmitted to the present day germs of great vitality and promise. He had the keenest possible eye for historic effect, which was quite as much at the root of his great comprehensiveness, as his large sympathies with individual goodness and greatness. But what strikes one as a little strange in a man of such a temperament as this, is his gallantry as a champion.—HUTTON, RICHARD HOLT, 1881, *Dean Stanley, Criticisms on Contemporary Thoughts and Thinkers,* vol. I, p. 133.

For the purposes of a student of general history this ["Eastern Church"] is the most useful of Dean Stanley's works. It not only has to do with a subject of very considerable importance, but it possesses the rare charm of a graceful, scholarly, and eloquent method of treatment. It is one of the few ecclesiastical histories that every genuine student of the Middle Ages will find himself interested in reading.—ADAMS, CHARLES KENDALL, 1882, *A Manual of Historical Literature,* p. 180.

Read his funeral sermon on Charles Kingsley, on Sir John Herschel, on your countryman Carlyle, or that preached on the Siege of Paris. Who else in the United Kingdom could have preached them? Read, indeed, any of his published sermons. We may say as Dr. Johnson said of Baxter's "Read any; they are all good." Read any, we may add, for they are all characteristic, all stamped with his own impress.—BRADLEY, GEORGE GRANVILLE, 1883, *Recollections of Arthur Penrhyn Stanley,* p. 113.

We can indeed hardly claim for Stanley the title of an original investigator, on any subject, save only the very difficult and interesting one of the geography of Sinai and Palestine. But it would be equally unfair to speak of such popularizations as his "Jewish Church" as though they were slight or easy productions. Crude knowledge must be digested and re-digested before it can enter vitally into the intellectual system of mankind and rightly to assimilate such nutriment may often be as difficult as to collect it. The Englishman, especially, writing, as Stanley did, for two hemispheres and some half-dozen nations, must needs feel that the form in which he gives his results to this enormous public is a matter of no slight concern.—MYERS, FREDERIC W. H., 1883, *Arthur Penrhyn Stanley, Century Magazine,* vol. 3, p. 382.

There is none ["Apostolic Age"] of his many interesting writings which more distinctly indicates the line of thought which he followed throughout. It is instinct with a rare insight into the phenomena of the Apostolic time, and the bearing of these phenomena upon the true interpretation of Christian thought for all time. Like all his historic studies, it presents at once a picture of the past, and a mirror of the future.—TULLOCH, JOHN, 1885, *Movements of Religious Thought in Britain During the Nineteenth Century,* p. 205.

It was inevitable that one who "was always writing something" should sometimes be careless and slipshod, but, as a rule, nothing could be more delightful than his style, and his references are carefully verified and weighed studiously. Stanley was a very voluminous writer; twenty-five years ago the list of his publications already filled many pages of the British Museum Catalogue. Since then his writings have been very numerous, including many contributions to reviews and magazines, besides purely theological studies. This summary does not include his historical works and lectures. At no time could he write on any subject except one which attracted him; he could write only on what he thought and felt; his works are one and all a mirror of himself. . . . Essentially a popular thinker, Dean Stanley never claimed to be otherwise than a translucent and clear medium of truth in its simplest form. Where doubt had crept into the mind, many found his books a great assistance, and were helped by his vivid and animated words as no cold reasoning could have affected them. Where a profound thinker would have failed from his very depth the works of Stanley contain exactly what the average reader requires and can assimilate. And yet it is not just to characterize the work of Stanley as slight or inferior in its conception or style. While not an original investigator, the literary skill and scholarship of the Dean is shown on every page. His tone is dignified, spirited, and picturesque, lending a charm to all he touches, while perfect simplicity and candor radiates from all his teachings. —OLIVER, GRACE A., 1885, *Arthur Penrhyn Stanley*, pp. 273, 402.

Among his contemporaries, no voice was so constantly raised in the Church of England for charity and peace as that of Arthur Penrhyn Stanley. But his influence has neither been restricted to the clergy nor to members of his own church. Over laymen everywhere he has exerted a still more powerful influence, and has spoken with cheerful inspiration to those in every land who cherish the belief in a common Christianity, and the hope that in the future it may have some outward embodiment. To the general characteristics of the leaders of the Broad Church Stanley added the special gift of an historic imagination. It was this, united to the charm of a style of singular purity and poetic beauty, which gave such life and power to his published lectures on the Jewish Church.—PITMAN, ROBERT C., 1888, *Books that have Helped Me, The Forum*, vol. 4, p. 610.

His knowledge of the world and of society, his familiarity with great historical events, his keen eye for the picturesque aspects of human life, whether under secular or religious conditions, his cultivated literary tastes, his wide sympathies, his ability to detect resemblances where others saw only contradictions, to detect a spiritual meaning under the most obscure of ritual observances—these things, combined with the brilliant qualities of his mind, gave to his writings a popularity almost unexampled when we consider the fate of most theological books. As a writer of English, Newman was alone his superior in that clearness and naturalness and exquisite simplicity,—that entire freedom from all straining after effect,—which made Newman the supreme model of English with whom no other writer could compete. But much of Stanley's power as a writer lay also in the rare finish and charm of his style, which perfectly reflected the man and was therefore in a high degree artistic: it pleased the ear, it compelled the attention, it aroused and stimulated the reader, even if at times it withdrew the mind from the matter to the form—a fault of which Newman never was guilty; but it always conveyed the thought with ease and clearness, and always with something of the grace and fascination which belonged to the man. . . . To the general reader, as well as to the theological student, no books are more familiar than his "Sinai and Palestine," his "History of the Jewish Church," or his "Christian Institutions." His defects, his limitations, are also well known. His learning was not extensive, nor his scholarship always accurate, nor had he a deep insight into the working of great principles. He had no taste for philosophy or metaphysics; only that which was concrete made any appeal to his imagination.— ALLEN, ALEXANDER V. G., 1894, *Dean Stanley and the Tractarian Movement, The New World*, vol. 3, pp. 143, 144.

Stanley's social influence, and his influence as a teacher and a preacher, live forever, though indistinguishably blended with those of other good men and Christians. His influence as a theologian and a religious philosopher, never very great, have probably ceased. In that line he made, involuntarily, much noise, but he left not much impression. His best works, it will generally be thought, apart from his "Life of Arnold," are his historical lectures and his "Sinai and Palestine." The work last mentioned, which called forth his utmost enthusiasm and gave the fullest scope for the display of his special gift, has perhaps no superior in its kind. Next to it I should venture to place the lectures on the Eastern church, in which he shows to perfection his ardent historical sympathies, his power of appreciating and delineating historical character, his comprehensiveness of view and the picturesque vivacity of his style. These lectures are particularly wholesome reading just now, when abuse is being heaped on the Russian Christians by misguided Christendom. The lectures on the Jewish Church lack a critical basis and strictness of critical treatment altogether. The lecturer too often escapes from a critical difficulty into preaching. He was too much under the dominion of Ewald, who trusts too much to his own arbitrary intuition. Oscillating between orthodoxy and rationalism, accepting miracle, yet desiring to economise it to the utmost, and renouncing supplemental miracles, Stanley is sometimes found struggling with an akward problem, and struggling in vain.—SMITH, GOLDWIN, 1894, *The Nineteenth Century, vol.* 35, *p.* 221.

Dean Stanley wrote very little verse, and that little does not display high poetic merit. Prose was clearly his natural form of expression, and in the freedom of prose he was much more poetic than when hampered by the fetters of rhyme.—MILES, ALFRED H., 1897, *The Poets and the Poetry of the Century, Social, Moral, and Religious Verse, p.* 721.

Stanley neither was, nor, apparently, cared to be exact. He trusted too much to his gift of making things interesting, and had an inadequate conception of the duty he owed to his readers of writing what was true. Other travellers who have followed his footsteps in the East have sometimes found that the scenes he describes, in charming English, are such as are visible only to those whose eyes can penetrate rocks and mountains. This constitutional inaccuracy is a blot upon nearly all his works, and his one permanent contribution to literature will probably prove to be the "Life of Dr. Arnold."—WALKER, HUGH, 1897, *The Age of Tennyson, p.* 140.

The largest part of his literary work was done in the field of ecclesiastical history, a subject naturally congenial to him, and to which he was further drawn by the professorship which he held at Oxford during a time when a great revival of historical studies was in progress. It was work which critics could easily disparage, for there were many small errors scattered through it; and the picturesque method of treatment he employed was apt to pass into scrappiness. He fixed on the points which had a special interest for his own mind as illustrating some trait of personal or national character, or some moral lesson, and passed hastily over other matters of equal or greater importance. Nevertheless his work had some distinctive merits which have not received from professional critics the whole credit they deserved. In all that Stanley wrote one finds a certain largeness and dignity of view. He had a sense of the unity of history, of the constant relation of past and present, of the similarity of human nature in one age and country to human nature in another; and he never failed to dwell upon the permanently valuable truths which history has to teach. Nothing was too small to attract him, because he discovered a meaning in everything, and he was therefore never dull, for even when he moralised he would light up his reflections by some happy anecdote. With this he possessed a keen eye, the eye of a poet, for human character, and a power of sympathy that enabled him to appreciate even those whose principles and policy he disliked.—BRYCE, JAMES, 1903, *Studies in Contemporary Biography, p.* 72.

George Henry Borrow
1803–1881

Born, at East Dereham, 5 July 1803. Educated at Norwich Grammar School, 1815–18. Family changed place of residence constantly, 1803–20. Articled to Solicitor in Norwich, 1818–23. First literary publication, 1825. To London at father's death. Assisted in compilation of "Newgate Calendar." Tour through England; through France, Germany, Russia and the East, as agent for British and Foreign Bible Society, 1833–39. Contrib. letters on his travels to "Morning Post," 1837–39. Married Mary Clarke, 1840. Tour in

S. E. Europe, 1844. Bought estate on Oulton Broad. Lived there till about 1865. Removed to Brompton. Wife died there, 1869. Died, at Oulton, 26 July, 1881. *Works:* "Romantic Ballads" (from the Danish), 1826; "Targum," 1835; "The Bible in Spain" (3 vols.), 1843; "The Zincali," (2 vols.), 1841; "Lavengro," 1851; "The Romany Rye," 1857; "Wild Wales," 1862; "Romano Lavo-Lil," 1874. He *translated:* F. M. von Klinger's "Faustus," 1825; Pushkin's "The Talisman," 1835; St. Luke's Gospel into Gitano dialect, "Embéo e Majoró Lucas," 1837; "Crixote e Majoró Lucas," 1872; Ellis Wynn's "Sleeping Bard" from the Cambrian-British, 1860; Nasr Al-Dín's "Turkish Jester" (posthumous), 1884; Ewald's "Death of Balder" (posthumous), 1889. He *edited:* "Evangelisa San Lucusan Guissan" (Basque translation of St. Luke's Gospel), 1838.—SHARP, R. FARQUHARSON, 1897, *A Dictionary of English Authors*, p. 29.

PERSONAL

Since I last wrote to you, I have received a visit from a remarkable person, with whom I should like to make you acquainted. . . . His mind is full, even to overflowing, of intelligence and original thought. It is ——, the distinguished linguist, of whom I shall speak: besides his calling upon me, I also passed an evening in his society, and he talked to me the whole time. I do not know when I have heard such a flow of varying conversation—odd—original—brilliant—animating;—*any* and *every* one of these epithets might be applied to it; it is like having a *flood of mind* poured out upon you, and that, too, evidently from the strong necessity of setting the current free, not from any design to shine or overpower. I think I was most interested in his descriptions of Spain, a country where he has lived much, and to which he is strongly attached. . . . All I had to complain of was, that, being used to a sort of steam-boat rapidity, both in bodily and mental movements,——, while gallantly handing me from one room to another, rushed into a sort of *gallopade* which nearly took my breath away. On mentioning this afterwards to a gentleman who had been of the party, he said, "What could you expect from a man who has been handing *armed Croats* instead of ladies, from one tent to another?" for I believe it is not very long since my ubiquitous friend visited Hungary.—HEMANS, FELICIA DOROTHEA, 1830, *Memorials, Correspondence, ed. Chorley*, vol. II, pp. 166, 168.

Catherine Gurney gave us a note to George Borrow, so on him we called,—a tall, ungainly, uncouth man, with great physical strength, a quick penetrating eye, a confident manner, and a disagreeable tone and pronunciation. He was sitting on one side of the fire, and his old mother on the other, his spirits always sink in wet weather, and to-day was very rainy, but he was courteous and not displeased to be a little lionized for his delicacy is not of the most susceptible.—FOX, CAROLINE, 1843, *Journal, Oct. 21; Memories of Old Friends, ed. Pym.*, p. 202.

Borrow came in the evening: now a fine man, but a most disagreeable one; a kind of character that would be most dangerous in rebellious times—one that would suffer or persecute to the utmost. His face is expressive of wrong-headed determination.—EASTLAKE, ELIZABETH LADY, 1844, *Journal, March 20; Memoirs, ed. Smith*, p. 124.

It is easy to understand how one who so valued words as symbols of thought as to spend his life in interpreting them from so many tongues, should become a perfect master of his own language: not only was Borrow such a master, but he made bold and unsparing use of his power, and by its means put on record the actions of a life unique in its sustained individuality from "the flash and triumph and glorious sweat" of his first ride, till the cloud, which overhangs all, approached him. Humour, which is given us to neutralise the worst forebodings, he largely possessed; and his, while it resembled Sterne's more than any other man's, was peculiarly his own, but mingled with a sounder sentiment of pathos than is to be found in Yorick.—HAKE, A. EGMONT, 1882, *George Borrow, Macmillan's Magazine*, vol. 45, p. 63.

He must have been, I should say, full six feet four inches in height—a very well-built man, with somewhat of a military carriage; snow-white hair; dark, strongly marked eyebrows; his countenance pleasing, betokening calm firmness, self-confidence, and a mind under control, though capable of passion. His frame was without heaviness, but evidently very powerful. His hands were small for his size, beautifully formed, and very white. He was very vain of his hands, which he used to say he derived from his mother, who was of Huguenot extraction. He was, when in the vein, a delightful talker. It will give some idea of the effect of his appearance, if I recount a circumstance which occurred on his first visit at the Vicarage. My eldest son, then between ten and eleven years of age, having been introduced, stood with eyes fixed on him for some moments, and then without speaking left the apartment. He passed into the room where his mother was engaged with some ladies, and cried out, "Well, mother, that *is* a man." He could find no other words to express his admiration. The child's enthusiasm evidently delighted Borrow, who, from all I saw of him, I should judge to have been singularly alive to, and grateful for, tokens of affection. We soon came to delight in his society. He often dropped in of an evening, when he would, after tea, sit in the centre of a group before the fire with his hands on his knees—his favourite position—pouring forth tales of the scenes he had witnessed in his wanderings—sometimes among the gypsies of Spain, sometimes among those of England. Then he would suddenly spring from his seat and walk to and fro the room in silence; anon he would clap his hands and sing a Gypsy song, or perchance would chant forth a translation of some Viking poem; after which he would sit down again and chat about his father, whose memory he revered as he did his mother's; and finally he would recount some tale of suffering or sorrow with deep pathos—his voice being capable of expressing triumphant joy or the profoundest sadness.—BERKELEY, JOHN R. P., 1887, *Reminiscences of Borrow in 1854, Life, Writings and Correspondence of George Borrow*, ed. Knapp, vol. II, p. 95.

From early youth he had a passion, and an extraordinary capacity for languages, and on reaching manhood he was appointed agent to the Bible Society, and was sent to Russia to translate and introduce the Scriptures. While there he mastered the language, and learnt besides the Sclavonian and the Gypsie dialects. He translated the Testament into the Tartar Mantchow, and published versions from English into thirty languages. He made successive visits into Russia, Norway, Turkey, Bohemia, Spain and Barbary. In fact, the sole of his foot never rested. While an agent for the Bible Society in Spain, he translated the Testament into Spanish, Portuguese, Romany, and Basque—which language, it is said, the Devil himself never could learn—and when he had learnt the Basque he acquired the name of Lavengro, or word-master. . . . He had a splendid physique, standing six feet two in his stockings, and he had brains as well as muscles, as his works sufficiently show.—SMILES, SAMUEL, 1891, *Memoir and Correspondence of John Murray*, vol. II, pp. 484, 485.

He was a tall, large, fine-looking man who must have been handsome in his youth. I knew at the time in London a Mr. Kerrison, who had been as a very young man, probably in the twenties, very intimate with Borrow. He told me that one night Borrow acted very wildly, whooping and vociferating so as to cause the police to follow him, and after a long run led them to the edge of the Thames, "and there they thought they had him." But he plunged boldly into the water and swam in his clothes to the opposite shore, and so escaped.—LELAND, CHARLES GODFREY, 1893, *Memoirs*, p. 434.

The remarkable characteristic of Borrow through all his varied career was that he could mix with all sorts of company and yet hold him aloof from the vicious and depraved. He could touch pitch and not be defiled—walk through the fire and not be burned. Woe to the weak and half-hearted who shall try to pass through such ordeals as George Borrow endured! It is not everyone who can draw Ulysses's bow.—JESSOPP, AUGUSTUS, 1893, *Lavengro, The Athenæum, No.* 3428, p. 66.

George Borrow who, if he were not a gypsy by blood *ought* to have been one, was, for some years, our near neighbor in Hereford Square. My friend was amused by his quaint stories and his (real or sham) enthusiasm for Wales, and cultivated his acquaintance. I never liked him, thinking him more or less of a hypocrite. His missions, recorded in the "Bible in Spain," and his translations of the scriptures into the out-of-the-way tongues, for which he had a gift, were by no means consonant with his real opinions concerning the veracity of the said Bible.—COBBE, FRANCES POWER, 1894, *Life by Herself*, vol. II, p. 437.

Often used to dine in Albemarle Street in times well within my memory. Tall, broad, muscular, with very heavy shoulders, and perfectly white hair—my father used to tell us that Borrow's hair was grey before he was thirty—his was a figure which no one who has seen it is likely to forget. I never remember to have seen him dressed in anything but black broadcloth, and white cotton socks were generally distinctly visible above his low shoes. I think that with Borrow the desire to attract attention to himself, to inspire a feeling of awe and mystery, must have been a ruling passion. No one will ever unravel the true from the fictitious in his charming writings; it is possible that the incidents and characters connected with his extraordinary life and adventures had become so intermingled in his own mind, that he himself could hardly have unraveled them.—MURRAY, JOHN, 1895, *Some Authors I Have Known, Good Words,* vol. 36, p. 91.

In his last years Borrow was very infirm, and the few visitors who saw him—for he was far from courting visits—have given almost distressing accounts of his *entourage;* for after his wife's death he seems to have lacked many home comforts, and to have grown more melancholy than ever, though to the last he was kind and considerate to his poorer neighbours, some of whom still live to cherish his memory. He seems to have lost all savour of life, and when he could no longer stride over heath and dene, nor rejoice in the free life of the "children of the open air," when he became housebound and caged, his spirits ebbed, his heart sank within him, and on July 26th, 1881, he died at Oulton, just three weeks after completing his 78th year.—HOOPER, JAMES, 1896, *George Borrow, The National Review,* vol. 26, p. 682.

Borrow was a man of something like genius, who went his own way in life, wherever it led him, who, like one of Browning's heroes, was ever a fighter, and who yet passed away in peaceful obscurity, almost forgotten by the public, which he had once puzzled and perturbed.—MCCARTHY, JUSTIN, 1897, *A History of Our Own Times from 1880 to the Diamond Jubilee,* p. 89.

THE BIBLE IN SPAIN
1842

I read Borrow with great delight all the way down per rail, and it shortened the rapid flight of that velocipede. You may depend upon it that the book will sell, which, after all, is the rub. It is the antipodes of Lord Carnarvon, and yet how they tally in what they have in common, and that is much—the people, the scenery of Galicia, and the suspicions and absurdities of Spanish Jack-in-Office, who yielded not in ignorance or in insolence to any kind of redtapists, hatched in the hot-beds of jobbery and utilitarian mares'-nests. . . . Borrow spares none of them. I see he hits right and left and floors his man wherever he meets him. I am pleased with his honest sincerity of purpose and his graphic abrupt style. It is like an old Spanish ballad, leaping in *res medias,* going from incident to incident, bang, bang, bang, hops, steps, and jumps like a cracker, and leaving off like one, when you wish he would give you another touch or *coup de grâce.* . . . He really sometimes puts me in mind of Gil Blas; but he has not the sneer of the Frenchman, nor does he gild the bad. He has a touch of Bunyan, and, like that enthusiastic tinker, hammers away, *à la Gitano,* whenever he thinks he can thwack the Devil or his man-of-all-work on earth—the Pope. Therein he resembles my friend and everybody's friend—Punch—who, amidst all his adventures, never spares the black one. . . . He is as full of meat as an egg, and a fresh laid one—not one of your Inglis breed, long addled by over-bookmaking. Borrow will lay you golden eggs, and hatch them after the ways of Egypt; put salt on his tail and secure him in your coop, and beware how any poacher coaxes him with "raisins" or reasons out of the Albemarle preserves.—FORD, RICHARD, 1842, *Letter to John Murray, Memoir and Correspondence of John Murray,* ed. Smiles, vol. II, p. 491.

Its literary merits were considerable—but balanced by equal demerits. Nothing more vivid and picturesque than many of its descriptions of scenery and sketches of adventure: nothing more weak and confused than every attempt either at a chain of reasoning, or even a consecutive narrative of events that it included. It was evidently the work of a man of uncommon and highly interesting character and endowments; but as clearly he was quite raw as an original author. The glimpses of a most curious and novel subject that he opened were, however, so very striking, that, on the whole, that book deserved well to make a powerful impression, and could not but excite great hopes that his more practised pen would hereafter produce many things of higher consequence. The present volumes will, we apprehend, go far to justify such anticipations. In point of composition, generally, Mr. Borrow has made a signal advance; but the grand point is, that he seems to have considered and studied himself in the interval; wisely resolved on steadily avoiding in future the species of efforts in which he had been felt to fail; and on sedulously cultivating and improving the peculiar talents which were as universally acknowledged to be brilliantly displayed in numerous detached passages of his "Gipsies."—LOCKHART, JOHN GIBSON, 1842, *The Bible in Spain, Quarterly Review*, vol. 71, p. 169.

Having real merit and universal interest, being wholly popular in its style, and yet exceedingly curious in its information, crowded with anecdote and adventure, dialogue and incident, throwing a flood of light over Spain from a wholly new point of view, carrying us into the huts of the miserable peasants, giving us the gipsey-talk by the way-side, laying open the inner heart of the land, leading into the reality or prospect of danger every step of the way—although thousands and tens of thousands have been sold already; it has not yet taken its true place in general esteem. We have passed over the peninsula with many travellers, sometimes with great pleasure; but never so agreeably or profitably before: never with one who made us so familiar with national character, or gave us such a home-bred feeling for the people at large. Others have described the cities and works of art of this famous old land; many others have acquainted us sufficiently with the life of a single class in the cities—still, a large field remained unoccupied which Mr. Borrow has tilled with great patience and success. No one has ever trodden that ill-fated soil under more manifest advantages. To say nothing of his unwearied perseverance, his heroic daring, his calmness in peril, his presence of mind in disaster, and his love of adventure—several languages, the keys to the people's heart, were at his command.— HOLLAND, F. W., 1843, *The Bible in Spain, The Christian Examiner*, vol. 34, p. 170.

If any of our readers should happen not yet to have read "The Bible in Spain," we advise them to read it forthwith. Though irregular, without plan or order, it is a thoroughly racy, graphic, and vigorous book, full of interest, honest, and straightforward, and without any cant or affectation in it; indeed the man's prominent quality is honesty, otherwise we should never have seen anything in that strong love of pugilism, horsemanship, Gypsy life and physical daring of all kinds, of which his books are full. He is a Bible Harry Lorrequer,—a missionary Bamfylde Moore Carew,—an Exeter Hall bruiser —a polyglot wandering Gypsy. Fancy these incongruities,—and yet George Borrow is the man who embodies them in his one extraordinary person!—SMILES, SAMUEL, 1860, *Brief Biographies*, p. 172.

Few books possess more vivid interest.— COLLIER, WILLIAM FRANCIS, 1861, *A History of English Literature*, p. 526.

It is, I believe, the opinion of the best critics that "The Bible in Spain" is Borrow's masterpiece.—BIRRELL, AUGUSTINE, 1892, *Res Judicatæ*, p. 135.

Perhaps the most ill-advised title that a well-written book ever labored under, giving as it does the idea that the book is a prolonged tract. . . . Good reading as the book is, and ardent as its author appears to be in the cause he has espoused, there is an undeniable ring of falsity through the book. The whole enterprise was manifestly undertaken by Borrow purely in the spirit of adventure and to make a living for himself; while it was demanded of the Bible Society's agent that, in his reports, zeal for the Protestant faith alone should seem to have been his aim when he began the work. So, like everything written to order, "The Bible in Spain" fails in spontaneity. The adventures, indeed, are written with gusto, and there are enough of them to carry off the woeful cant which fills in between scene and scene; and throughout Borrow was persuaded by the idea that he was writing for the Bible Society, and was ever artist in dire strait? There is something exquisitely ridiculous in the whole situation—the plight of Borrow, the plight of the Bible Society—it is hard to say which of the two must have been more bewildered. The story goes that "*there always was a large attendance* in the Society's room" on the days when Borrow's letters were to be read, and one can believe it. But the story does not relate that, in Spain, Borrow sat puzzling over how to dish up his adventures with the proper seasoning of zeal, and, I dare say, wrote many a line "with his tongue in his cheek," as the vulgar saying goes. Now, this may be doing Borrow an injustice, but it is certainly the impression one gets in reading "The Bible in Spain," and to read between the lines is often the best way of getting the truth out of a book. Nothing could undo Borrow's hatred of Popery. ... "The Bible in Spain" remains to this day far the most popular of Borrow's books.—FINDLATER, JANE H., 1899, *George Borrow, Cornhill Magazine, vol.* 80, pp. 602, 603.

LAVENGRO
1851

He has written a book called "Lavengro," in which he proposes to satisfy the public curiosity about himself, and to illustrate his biography as "Scholar, Gypsy, and Priest." The book, however, is not all fact; it is fact mixed liberally with fiction,—a kind of poetic rhapsody; and yet it contains many graphic pictures of real life,—life little known of, such as exists to this day among the by-lanes and on the moors of England. One thing is obvious, the book is thoroughly original, like all Mr. Borrow has written. It smells of the green lanes and breezy downs,—of the field and the tent; and his characters bear the tan of the sun and the marks of the weather upon their faces. The book is not written as a practised bookmaker would write it; it is not pruned down to suit current tastes. Borrow throws into it whatever he has picked up on the highways and by-ways, garnishing it up with his own imaginative spicery *ad libitum*, and there you have it,—"Lavengro; the Scholar, the Gypsy, the Priest!" But the work is not yet completed, seeing that he has only as yet treated us to the two former parts of the character; "The Priest" is yet to come, and then we shall see how it happened that Exeter Hall was enabled to secure the services of this gifted missionary.—SMILES, SAMUEL, 1860, *Brief Biographies*, p. 158.

Circumstantial as Defoe, rich in combinations as Lesage, and with such an instinct of the picturesque, both personal and local, as none of these possessed, this strange wild man holds on his strange wild way, and leads you captive to the end. His dialogue is copious and appropriate; you feel that like Ben Jonson he is dictating rather than reporting, that he is less faithful and exact than imaginative and determined; but you are none the less pleased with it, and suspicious though you be that the voice is Lavengro's and the hands are the hands of some one else, you are glad to surrender to the illusion, and you regret when it is dispelled.—HENLEY, WILLIAM ERNEST, 1890, *Views and Reviews*, p. 136.

The most delightful of all his books.—FINDLATER, JANE H., 1899, *George Borrow, Cornhill Magazine, vol.* 80.

GENERAL

Have you seen or heard anything of a strange man named Borrow, who has written a book called the "Gypsies in Spain," and the "Bible in Spain?" They are most interesting books, and he is a most strange man. He had a wonderful facility in gaining the confidences of the lower classes, especially the gypsies. He gives all his adventures with wonderful openness, and some of the oddest stories come out. Some of his statements about the priests have given great offence to the Dublin Review people, and they have made a fierce attack on poor Mr. Borrow, but he is a bold man, and can stand his own ground.—MACMILLAN, DANIEL, 1843, *Letter to Rev. D. Watt, Apr.* 29; *Memoir of Daniel Macmillan, ed. Hughes*, p. 111.

The "Gypsies of Spain," Mr. Borrow's former work, was a Spanish olla—a hotchpotch of the jockey tramper, philologist, and missionary. It was a thing of shreds and patches—a true book of Spain; the chapters, like her bundle of unamalgamating provinces, were just held together, and no more, by the common tie of religion, yet it was strange, and richly flavoured with genuine *borracha*. It was the first work of a diffident unexperienced man, who, mistrusting his own powers, hoped to conciliate critics by leaning on Spanish historians and gypsie poets. These corks, if such a term can be applied to the ponderous levities by which he was swamped, are now cast aside; he dashes boldly into the tide, and swims gallantly over the breakers. The Gypsies were, properly speaking, his pilot balloon. The Bible and its distribution have been *the* business of his existence; wherever moral darkness brooded, there, the Bible in his hand, he forced his way. . . . Mr. Borrow, although no tourist "in search of the picturesque," has a true perception of nature. His out-of-door existence has brought him in close contact with her, in all her changes, in all her fits of sunshine, or of storm; and well can he portray her, whatever be the expression. Always bearing in mind the solemn object of his mission, he colours like Rembrandt, and draws like Spagnoletto, rather than with the voluptuous sunniness of Claude Lorraine and Albano. His chief study is man; and therefore, as among the classics, landscape becomes an accessory.—FORD, RICHARD, 1843, *The Bible in Spain, Edinburgh Review, vol.* 77, *pp.* 105, 114.

In George Borrow's works I found a wild fascination, a vivid graphic power of description, a fresh originality, an athletic simplicity (so to speak), which give them a stamp of their own. After reading his "Bible in Spain" I felt as if I had actually traveled at his side, and seen the "wild Sil" rush from its mountain cradle; wandered in the hilly wilderness of the Sierras; encountered and conversed with Manehegan, Castillian, Andalusian, Arragonese, and, above all, with the savage Gitanos. — BRONTË, CHARLOTTE, 1849, *Letter to W. S. Williams, Feb.* 4; *Charlotte Brontë and her Circle, ed. Shorter,* p. 189.

This Borrow is a remarkable man. As agent for the British and Foreign Bible Society he has undertaken journeys into remote lands, and, acquainted from his early youth not only with many European languages, but likewise with the Romany of the English gipsies, he sought out with zest the gipsies everywhere, and became their faithful missionary. He has made himself so thoroughly master of their ways and customs that he soon passed for "one of their blood." He slept in their tents in the forests of Russia and Hungary, visited them in their robber caves in the mountainous pass-regions of Italy, lived with them five entire years in Spain, where he, for his endeavours to distribute the Gospel in that Catholic country, was imprisoned with the very worst of them for a time in the dungeons of Madrid. He at last went over to North Africa, and sought after his Tartars even there. It is true no one has taken equal pains with Borrow to introduce himself amongst this rude and barbarous people, but on that account he has been enabled better than any other to depict their many mysteries, and the frequent impressions which his book has passed through within a short period show with what interest the English public have received his graphic descriptions.—SUNDT, ELLERT, 1850, *Beretniag om Fante eller Landstriggerfolket i Norge.*

Though we do not doubt that Mr. Borrow is a good counsel in his own cause, we are yet strongly of opinion that Time in his case has some wrongs to repair, and that "Lavengro" has *not* obtained the fame which was its due. It contains passages which in their way are not surpassed by anything in English literature. The truth and vividness of the description both of scenes and persons, coupled with the purity, force, and simplicity of the language, should confer immortality upon many of its pages. . . . To this we must add that various portions of the history are known to be a faithful narrative of Mr. Borrow's career, while we ourselves can testify, as to many other parts of his volumes, that nothing can excel the fidelity with which he has described both men and things. Far from his showing any tendency to exaggeration, such of his characters as we chance to have known, and they are not a few, are rather within the truth than beyond it. However picturesquely they may be drawn, the lines are invariably those of nature. Why under these circumstances he should envelop the question in mystery is more than we can divine. There can be no doubt that the larger part, and possibly the whole, of the work is a narrative of actual occurrences, and just as little [doubt] that it would gain immensely by a plain avowal of the fact.—ELWIN, WHITWELL, 1857, *Roving Life in England, Quarterly Review, vol.* 101, *p.* 472.

No man's writing can take you into the country as Borrow's can: it makes you feel the sunshine, see the meadows, smell the flowers, hear the skylark sing and the grasshopper chirrup.—Who else can do it? I know of none.—WATTS, THEODORE, 1881, *Reminiscences of George Borrow, The Athenæum, No.* 2810, *p.* 307.

There is this difficulty in writing about him, that the audience must necessarily consist of fervent devotees on the one hand, and of complete infidels, or at least complete know-nothings, on the other. To any one who, having the faculty to understand either, has read "Lavengro" or "The Bible in Spain," or even "Wild Wales," praise bestowed on Borrow is apt to seem impertinence. To anybody else (and unfortunately the anybody else is in a large majority) praise bestowed on Borrow is apt to look like that very dubious kind of praise which is bestowed on somebody of whom no one but the praiser has ever heard. I cannot think of any single writer (Peacock himself is not an exception) who is in quite parallel case. . . . Strong and vivid as Borrow's drawing of places and persons is, he always contrives to throw in touches which somehow give the air of being rather a vision than a fact. Never was such a John-a-Dreams as this solid, pugilistic John Bull. Part of this literary effect of his is due to his quaint habit of avoiding, where he can, the mention of proper names. The description, for instance, of Old Sarum and Salisbury itself in "Lavengro," is sufficient to identify them to the most careless reader, even if the name of Stonehenge had not occurred on the page before; but they are not named. The description of Bettws-y-Coed in "Wild Wales," though less poetical is equally vivid. Yet here it would be quite possible for a reader, who did not know the place and its relation to other named places, to pass without any idea of the actual spot.—SAINTSBURY, GEORGE, 1886, *Essays in English Literature*, 1780–1860, *pp.* 404, 412.

It was by his publication of the "Gipsies in Spain," but more especially by the "Bible in Spain," that Borrow won a high place in literature. The romantic interest of these two works drew the public towards the man as much as towards the writer, and he was the wonder of a few years. But in the writings which followed he went too far. "Lavengro," which followed his first successes in 1850, and which, besides being a personal narrative, was a protest against the "kidglove" literature introduced by Bulwer and Disraeli, made him many enemies and lost him not a few friends. The book, which has been called an "epic of ale," glorified boxing, spoke up for an open-air life, and assailed the "gentility nonsense of the time." Such things were unpardonable, and Borrow, the hero of a season before, was tabooed as the high-priest of vulgar tastes. In the sequel to the book which had caused so much disfavour he chastised those who had dared to ridicule him and his work. But it was of no avail. He was passing into another age, and the critics could now afford to ignore his onslaught. "Wild Wales," published in 1862, though a desultory work, contained much of the old vigorous stuff which characterised previous writings, but it attracted small attention, and "Romano Lavo-Lil," when it appeared in 1872, was known only to the specially interested and the curious. Still Borrow remained unchanged. His strong individuality asserted itself in his narrowed circle. His love for the roadside, the heath, the gipsies' dingle, was as true as in other days. He was the same lover of strange books, the same passionate wanderer among strange people, the same champion of English manliness, and the same hater of genteel humbug and philistinism. Few men have put forth so many high qualities and maintained them untarnished throughout so long a career as did this striking figure of the nineteenth century.—HAKE, A. EGMONT, 1886, *Dictionary of National Biography*, vol. V, *p.* 407.

For invalids and delicate persons leading retired lives, there are no books like Borrow's. Lassitude and Languor, horrid hags, simply pick up their trailing skirts and scuttle out of any room into which he enters. They cannot abide him. A single chapter of Borrow is air and exercise; and, indeed, the exercise is not always gentle.—BIRRELL, AUGUSTINE, 1892, *Res Judicatæ*, *p.* 126.

Lovers of George Borrow are wont to claim that he is one of the choicest of bedside comrades. Mr. Birrell, indeed, stoutly maintains that slumber, healthy and calm, follows the reading of his books just as it follows a brisk walk or rattling drive. "A single chapter of Borrow is air and exercise." Neither need we be wide awake when we skim over his pages. We can read with half-closed eyes, and we feel his stir and animation pleasantly from without, just as we feel the motion of a carriage when we are heavy with sleep.—REPPLIER, AGNES, 1894, *In the Dozy Hours and Other Papers*, *p.* 10.

"Lavengro" is like nothing else in either biography or fiction—and it is both fictitious and biographical. It is the gradual revelation of a strange, unique being. But the revelation does not proceed in an orderly and chronological fashion; it is not begun in the first chapter, and still less is it completed in the last. After a careful perusal of the book, you will admit that though it has fascinated and impressed you, you have quite failed to understand it. . . . "Romany Rye" is the continuation of "Lavengro," but scarcely repeats its charm; its most remarkable feature is an "Appendix," in which Borrow expounds his views upon things in general, including critics and politics. It is a marvellous trenchant piece of writing, and from the literary point of view delightful; but it must have hurt a good many people's feelings at the time it was published, and even now shows the author on his harsh side only. We may agree with all he says, and yet wish he had uttered it in a less rasping tone. . . . Writing with him was spontaneous, but never heedless or unconsidered; it was always the outcome of deep thought and vehement feeling. Other writers and their books may be twain, but Borrow and his books are one. Perhaps they might be improved in art, or arrangement, or subject; but we should no longer care for them then, because they would cease to be Borrow. Borrow may not have been a beauty or a saint; but a man he was; and good or bad, we would not alter a hair of him.—HAWTHORNE, JULIAN, 1897, *Library of the World's Best Literature*, ed. Warner, vol. IV, pp. 2178, 2179.

Capricious as was Borrow's social satire, there was in it salutary truth. The public needed to be addressed with a frankness that Thackeray was unwilling to venture upon, before it could free itself from the slough of sentiment and sham. . . . Borrow carried his readers back over the romantic revivals to the adventures of Defoe. But hanging over his books is a dreamy, poetic glamour wanting in the old picaresque novel.—CROSS, WILBUR L., 1899, *The Development of the English Novel*, p. 211.

It is sometimes needful to declare the beginning from the end. George Borrow died on July 26, 1881. His literary activity covered a period of over fifty years, from 1823 to 1874. The Bibliography of his printed works is given in thirty-four numbers. The "Zincali," the account of the Gypsies of Spain, has had eight English editions and three American reprints, besides a garbled Italian Version; the "Bible in Spain," no less than twenty-seven editions and reprints and translations into German, French, and Russian; "Lavengro," the "Romany Rye," and "Wild Wales," too, have been widely read. Such an extended literary career would alone justify a formal biography, but it is the smallest part of the justification, for no literary figure of the nineteenth century has stood for a more interesting personality than the author of the "Bible in Spain."—ADLER, CYRUS, 1899, *George Borrow, Conservative Review*, vol. 2, p. 22.

No truer books were ever penned than "The Bible in Spain" and "Lavengro"—"Romany Rye." There is no mystery about them, if you have the key. And what is the key?—only Sympathy! Believe them and read and weep and feel. Believe them and *then* investigate. Investigate the times in which Borrow lived and wandered and struggled and wrought, as the First Volume of this work will show. Not in the public documents of civil history, but in out-of-the-way pamphlets, obscure handbooks, local almanacs, rural newspapers, and old magazines—all long ago obsolete and now despised, found on the twopenny shelf of country book-stalls on market days. That is where I met "Lavengro" and "Romany Rye" and rejoiced to find them *true*. There I found the author of them to be no banshee, no brownie, no mystery at all. The *brétima*—the haze of Galicia—the forerunner of corpse-candles, witches, and all the "fairy family" of Celtic mythology—fades into thin air under the microscope of honest inspection, and untiring search in letters, records, newspapers, poll-books, army lists, and all the forgotten dust-heaps of shop and attic. Of course men easily ignore the details of family gossip current only with the mothers and grandmothers of the century.— KNAPP, WILLIAM I., 1899, ed. *Life, Writings and Correspondence of George Borrow*, vol. II, p. 159.

In "Lavengro" he speaks of the choughs continually circling about the spire of Norwich cathedral, when, no doubt, he is referring to the jackdaws: he calls the planet Jupiter a star; and he writes a book descriptive of wide journeyings in Spain without telling us anything worth knowing of the wild life of that country. Humanity always interested him, more than birds and flowers; during his travels in "Wild Wales" he was always on the look-out for roadside inns, and desirous of hobnobbing with their rustic frequenters. The gipsies' horse-dealing transactions, and the philological puzzles of their ancient language, occupied his mind and pen for hours together; but he leaves it to a Romany *chal* to describe the charm of the gipsies' open-air and roving life, contenting himself with setting down the rover's words without comment. True, he would seem to imply that the sun, moon, and stars, and the wind on the heath were as much to him as to Jasper Petulengro; but when he stood on a Welsh mountain-top, where, one would think, the wide outlook would have inspired him, he only sees a fitting opportunity for pompous declamation.—DUTT, WILLIAM A., 1901, *In Lavengro's Country, Macmillan's Magazine*, vol. 84, p. 148.

John Hill Burton
1809–1881

Historian, was born at Aberdeen, 22nd August, 1809. Having graduated at Marischal College, Aberdeen, he was articled to a lawyer, but soon came to the Edinburgh bar, where, however, he mainly devoted himself to study and letters. He was in 1854 appointed Secretary to the Prison Board of Scotland, and was a Prison Commissioner, Historiographer Royal for Scotland, an LL. D. of Edinburgh, and D. C. L. of Oxford. He died near Edinburgh, 10th August 1881. From 1833 he contributed to the *Westminster Review* on law, history, and political economy; to *Blackwood's Magazine*, *The Scotsman*, etc., he furnished many literary sketches; and he published a "Life of Hume" (1846),"Lives of Simon Lord Lovat and Duncan Forbes of Culloden" (1847), "Political Economy" (1849), "Narratives from Criminal Trials in Scotland" (1852), "The Book-Hunter" (1862), "The Scot Abroad" (2 vols. 1864), "The Cairngorm Mountains" (1864), "History of Scotland" (7 vols. 1867-70; new ed. 8 vols.1873), "History of the Reign of Queen Anne" (1880), etc. See Memoir by his wife, prefixed to a new edition of "The Book-Hunter" (1882).—PATRICK AND GROOME, eds., 1897, *Chambers's Biographical Dictionary*, p. 158.

PERSONAL

There was a good deal of the Bohemian in Burton. He was ill at ease when in full dress; he liked space and air; he was an inveterate wanderer—never happier than when tramping across the country-side, or camping among the heather. He did not care to become the mouthpiece of any clique or coterie. He valued his independence and his right to think for himself. And he was a most intrepid thinker. So long as he felt he was in the right, it did not matter to him what weight of authority might be arrayed against him. . . . The alacrity and alertness of Burton's gait were characteristic of his mind. To the last he retained an almost boyish buoyancy both of body and mind. His spare and weather-beaten frame was sustained by an amazing vitality. The gaunt and attenuated figure, with the habitual stoop, which passed you at express speed, turning neither to right nor left—the hat which possibly had seen better days, thrown far back upon the head; the black surtout, which had been cut without any very close acquaintance on the part of the tailor with the angularities of the form it was to cover, streaming behind—might excite a passing smile; but we all knew that it was a fine, manly, independent, sincere, honourable soul that was lodged in this somewhat shabby tabernacle; and the incongruities were quickly forgotten. . . . Altogether he was a man whose memory will be cherished most by those who knew him best—a man without guile, generous, sweet-tempered, honourable, incapable of meanness, who hated shams and pretences of every sort, and lived with singular simplicity (in an age from which simplicity has been banished), a pure, honest, laborious, useful life.—SKELTON, JOHN, 1881, *John Hill Burton, Essays in History and Biography*, pp. 329, 330, 331.

His defect in conversation was that he was a bad listener. His own part was well sustained. His enormous store of varied information poured forth naturally and easily, and was interspersed with a wonderful stock of lively anecdotes and jokes. But he always lacked that greatest power of the conversationalist, the subtle ready sympathy which draws forth the best power of others. He was invaluable at a dull dinner-table, furnishing the whole *frais de la conversation* himself. . . . Returning from his office to dinner at five, he would, after dinner, retire to the library for twenty minutes or half-an-hour's perusal of a novel as mental rest. . . . Although he would only read those called exciting, they did not, apparently, excite him, for he read them as slowly as if he were learning them by heart. He would return to the drawing-room to drink a large cup of extremely strong tea, then retire again to the library to commence his day of literary work about eight in the evening. He would read or write without cessation, and without the least appearance of fatigue or excitement, till one or two in the morning. . . . Constitutionally irritable, energetic, and utterly persistent, Dr. Burton did not know what dulness or depression of spirits was. . . . John Hill Burton can never have been handsome, and he so determinately neglected his person, as to increase its natural defects. His greatest mental defect was an almost entire want of imagination. From this cause the characters of those nearest and dearest to him remained to his life's end a sealed book. . . . Dr. Burton was excessively kind-hearted within the limit placed by this great want. . . . He was liberal of money to a fault. He never refused any application even from a street beggar. . . . No printer's devil or other chance messenger failed to receive his sixpence or shilling, besides a comfortable meal. . . . Many of the "motley crew" along with whom Dr. Burton received his education fell into difficulties in the course of their lives. Application from one of them always met with a prompt response. To send double the amount asked on such occasions was his rule, if money was the object desired.—BURTON, MRS. JOHN HILL, 1882, ed. *The Book Hunter, Memoir.*

Many of the younger Edinburgh generation that knew nothing of him personally in his prime, must have a vivid recollection of casual glimpses of him in those still recent years, when his stooping, eccentric figure, very untidily dressed, and with the most battered and back-hanging of hats, would be seen pushing rapidly along Princes Street or some other thoroughfare, with a look that seemed to convey the decided intimation: "Don't stop me; I care for none of you." But, if you did have a meeting with Burton in circumstances that made colloquy possible, he was the most kindly of men in his rough and unsophisticated way, with a quantity of the queerest and most entertaining old lore, and no end of good Scottish stories.—MASSON, DAVID, 1882, *John Hill Burton, Edinburgh Sketches and Memories,* p. 381.

HISTORY OF SCOTLAND
1867-70

With all its faults and shortcomings, which we have not been slow to indicate, Mr. Burton's work is now, and will probably continue to be, the best history of Scotland. So far as matters ecclesiastical are concerned, it has, and need fear, no rival. So far as regards the War of Independence, it holds the same position of superiority. If on minor points he has been less successful; if his narrative sometimes fails to attract, or his argument to convince; if we can mark omissions which mar the completeness of the work; we may yet feel justly grateful to the historian who has for the first time placed before us in the light of truth those aspects of Scottish history which are most worthy of study and best calculated to reward it.—LANCASTER, HENRY H., 1867-76, *Burton's History of Scotland, Essays and Reviews,* p. 89.

It is but simple justice to say that this work has superseded in value all other histories of Scotland. As a complete record of one of the most turbulent of all histories, it is eminently successful. To the preparation of the work the author devoted many industrious years, and on several of the most disputed questions of Scottish history he has thrown a welcome light. The work is clear in style, and is arranged with an admirable regard for historical perspective.—ADAMS, CHARLES KENDALL, 1882, *A Manual of Historical Literature,* p. 434.

This work has received the approbation of Lord Macaulay and other historical readers; it is honestly and diligently executed, with passages of vigorous and picturesque eloquence.—CHAMBERS, ROBERT, 1876, *Cyclopædia of English Literature,* ed. *Carruthers.*

The last is the work of a capable and careful writer rather than of a great historian. Burton is sensible and dispassionate, and has collected and has put into shape the principal results of modern research as applied to Scotland.—WALKER, HUGH, 1897, *The Age of Tennyson,* p. 141.

GENERAL

Burton's biographies and his "Book Hunter" secure him a more than respectable rank as a man of letters; and his legal and economical works entitle him to high credit as a jurist and an investigator of social science. His historical labours are more important, and yet his claims to historical eminence are more questionable. His "History of Scotland" has, indeed, the field to itself at present, being as yet the only one composed with the accurate research which the modern standard of history demands. By complying with this peremptory condition, Burton has distanced all competitors, but must in turn give way when one shall arise who, emulating or borrowing his closeness of investigation, shall add the beauty and grandeur due to the history of a great and romantic country. Burton indeed is by no means dry; his narrative is on the contrary highly entertaining. But this animation is purchased by an entire sacrifice of dignity. His style is always below the subject; there is a total lack of harmony and unity; and the work altogether produces the impression of a series of clever and meritorious magazine articles. Possessing in perfection all the ordinary and indispensable qualities of the historian, he is devoid of all those which exalt historical composition to the sphere of poetry and drama. His place is rather that of a sagacious critic of history, and in this character his companionship will always be found invaluable.—GARNETT, RICHARD, 1886, *Dictionary of National Biography, vol.* VIII, *p.* 11.

A most dangerous work, ["The Book Hunter"] it seems to me now, certain to scatter the contagion of bibliomania wherever it may penetrate. I do not see how a man may read it and not begin loving books as he should love his fellow-man. To the perusal of Dr. Burton's pages—in the original edition, printed on a tawny paper most unpleasantly ribbed, a wrong to the eyes of every reader—I lay my own liking for books as books, for books wholly independent of their contents, for books as works of art and as objects of curiosity.—MATTHEWS, BRANDER, 1888, *Books That Have Helped Me, p.* 80.

One of those historians who write wisely but not well. The profundity of his researches no one will be inclined to dispute, but he was unfortunately deficient in the qualities required for laying the results of his learning before the world. His "History of Scotland," published in seven volumes between the years 1853 and 1870, is the most complete work of the kind we have, as it takes us from the earliest times, when the first reliable information is supplied by Tacitus' account of the repulse of Agricola, to the rebellion of 1745. We cannot call it dry, because that word represents to our mind the class of works of information which are merely devoid of literary art. Burton's history has a graver fault: it is wordy. The incidents of his narrative are buried under an avalanche of verbiage from which it is impossible to extricate them without a long and toilsome search. This defect makes it specially difficult to use his work as a book of reference, the want of clearness and connection of narrative making it almost impossible to follow the course of an episode, even if we are lucky enough to discover where it begins or ends. Oddly enough, in his lighter works, such as the "Bookhunter," a series of essays on bibliographical subjects republished from "Blackwood's Magazine," he was more successful. His biographies, especially that of Hume, obtained a fair share of praise.—OLIPHANT, MARGARET O. W., 1892, *The Victorian Age of English Literature, p.* 555.

He was not a very good writer, but displayed very great industry and learning with a sound and impartial judgment.—SAINTSBURY, GEORGE, 1896, *A History of Nineteenth Century Literature, p.* 240.

James Spedding
1808–1881

Was educated at Trinity College, Cambridge. He graduated in 1831, being placed in the second class in classics, and among the junior optimes in mathematics, and became an honorary fellow of his college. His uneventful life was devoted to research, especially to the study of Bacon's life and works. His edition of Bacon's works, projected in 1874, was undertaken in conjunction with Mr. R. L. Ellis. Mr. Ellis, however, died before the completion of the "Novum Organum," and with the exception of occasional help from Mr. D. D. Heath, Mr. Spedding was left to carry on the work alone. The edition began to appear in 1857, and was finished in seven volumes. Then followed the "Life and Letters" of Bacon, completed in 1876. Spedding's edition is the only complete edition of Bacon, and is enriched with most valuable notes. In his "Life" of this great philosopher, too, every scrap of information is collected together; it is to this source that every future biographer of Bacon must refer. Mr. Spedding met his death from injuries inflicted by a cab, the approach of which, on account of his deafness, he had not heard. His minor works include:—"Publishers and Authors" (1867);"Reviews and Discussions not Relating to Bacon" (1869); "Evenings with a Reviewer, or Macaulay and Bacon" (1882); and some "Studies in English History," written in conjunction with Mr. J. Gairdner.—SANDERS, LLOYD C., *ed.,* 1887, *Celebrities of the Century, p.* 941.

PERSONAL

Does the thought ever strike you, when looking at pictures in a house, that you are to run and jump at one, and go right through it into some behind-scene world on the other side, as Harlequins do? A steady portrait especially invites one to do so: the quietude of it ironically tempts one to outrage it: one feels it would close again over the panel, like water, as if nothing had happened. That portrait of Spedding, for instance, which Laurence has given me: not swords, nor cannon, nor all the Bulls of Bashan butting at it, could, I feel sure, discompose that venerable forehead. No wonder that no hair can grow at such an altitude: no wonder his view of Bacon's virtue is so rarefied that the common consciences of men cannot endure it. Thackeray and I occasionally amuse ourselves with the idea of Spedding's forehead: we find it somehow or other in all things, just peering out of all things: you see it in a milestone, Thackeray says. He also draws the forehead rising with a sober light over Mont Blanc, and reflected in the lake of Geneva. We have great laughing over this. The forehead is at present in Pembrokeshire, I believe: or Glamorganshire: or Monmouthshire: it is hard to say which. It has gone to spend its Christmas there.—FITZ-GERALD, EDWARD, 1841, *To Frederick Tennyson, Jan.* 16; *Letters, ed. Wright, vol.* I, *p.* 64.

His success both in his own college and in the University examinations would have been more brilliant if he had possessed the gift of rapid composition and translation. It was his nature to be in all things deliberate; and he was neither willing nor able to struggle against his characteristic temperament. At a later period of his life he gave as a reason for declining a high appointment in the public service, that he should have found it intolerable to turn his attention to ten or twenty unconnected matters in the course of a single day. His power of sustained labour has rarely been surpassed, but in his intellect and in his temperament there was no versatility. . . . No member of the well-known society of Cambridge apostles was more heartily respected and beloved by his many friends within and without that body. The manner which faithfully represented his disposition was already formed, and it never afterwards varied. Calm and unimpassioned, he contributed his full share to conversation in a musical voice which never rose above its ordinary pitch. The ready smile with which he welcomed humorous or amusing remarks was singularly winning. His imperturbable good temper might have seemed more meritorious, if it had been possible to test his equanimity by treating him with negligence or harshness. The just impression of wisdom which was produced by his voice, his manner, and the substance of his conversation, was well described in the form of humorous exaggeration by one of the acutest and most brilliant women of his time, Harriet, the second Lady Ashburton. Lord Houghton, in his "Monographs," quotes her as saying, "I always feel a kind of average between myself and any other person I am talking with—between us two, I mean; so that when I am talking to Spedding I am unutterably foolish—beyond permission."—VENABLES, G. S., 1881, *ed. Evenings With a Reviewer, Preface, vol.* I, *p.* vi.

He was the wisest man I have known: not the less so for plenty of the Boy in him; a great sense of Humour, a Socrates in Life and in Death, which he faced with all Serenity so long as Consciousness lasted.—FITZ-GERALD, EDWARD, 1881, *To C. E. Norton, March* 13; *Letters, ed. Wright, vol.* I, *p.* 464.

The admirable Spedding, who drew all good and great men unto him, but to converse with whom, in consequence of his deliberate utterance, required an ampler leisure than even I, who am neither good nor great, found always practicable.—LOCKER-LAMPSON, FREDERICK, 1895, *My Confidences, p.* 164.

LIFE AND WORKS OF BACON
1848–76

I am delighted and interested in a most high degree by the vindication of Bacon. It seems to me no less admirable for the principles of moral discrimination and truth and accuracy of statement, especially where character is concerned, which it brings out and elucidates by particular instances, which, as it were, substantiate and vitalize the abstract propositions, than for the glorious sunny light which it casts on the character of Bacon. Then how ably does it show up, not Macaulay's character individually and personally, so much as the class of thinkers of which he is the mouthpiece and representative. — COLERIDGE, SARA, 1848, *To Aubrey DeVere; Memoir and Letters of Sara Coleridge, ed. her Daughter, p.* 347.

The lie, it may be hoped, is about to pass away. An editor worthy of Bacon has risen to purge his fame. Such labors as those undertaken by Mr. Spedding demand a life, and he has not scrupled to devote the best years of an active and learned manhood to the preliminary toil. . . . The instinct, strong as virtue, to reject the spume of satire and falsehood, has sprung at the voice of Mr. Spedding into lusty life.—DIXON, WILLIAM HEPWORTH, 1861, *Personal History of Lord Bacon from Unpublished Papers*, pp. 11, 12.

It is not merely that his contribution to English history has no rival for accuracy of judgment, and for industry carried to the extreme point; or that he has taught us to know in his true character one of the greatest statesmen of a land fertile in statesmenship. His book is more than a history, more than a biography. It is a moral school, teaching historical writers to combat the sin which most easily besets them, the tendency to put their own interpretation upon doubtful facts, and their own thoughts into the minds of men of other ages.—GARDINER, SAMUEL R., 1874, *The Letters and the Life of Francis Bacon, Academy*, vol. 6, p. 394.

Mr. Spedding says his object was to enable posterity to "form a true conception of the kind of man Bacon was," and accordingly he gives an unusually full record of a more than unusually full life. The question of legal guilt Bacon himself admitted. The moral culpability Mr. Spedding does not consider so clear, considering the corrupt practices of the age, and the philosopher's carelessness as to money and household management.—CHAMBERS, ROBERT, 1876, *Cyclopœia of English Literature, ed. Carruthers*.

In the opinion of competent judges, Mr. Spedding was second to none of his contemporaries in power of reasoning, in critical sagacity, or in graceful purity of style; nor had he any superior in conscientious industry. No one has hitherto possessed so complete a knowledge of the subject to which his life was chiefly devoted; and it is improbable that future students should throw additional light on the career and character of Bacon. In the course of his indefatigable researches, Mr. Spedding deduced many independent and original conclusions from the profound familiarity which he had acquired with the history of the time. . . . No more conscientious, no more sagacious critic has employed on a not unworthy task the labour of a life. It will be well, rather for students of history and of character than for himself, if his just fame is rescued from the neglect which he regarded with unaffected indifference.—VENABLES, G. S., 1881, ed. *Evenings With a Reviewer, Preface*, vol. I, pp. v, xxvi.

To re-edit his Works, which did not want any such re-edition, and to vindicate his Character which could not be cleared, did this Spedding sacrifice forty years which he might well have given to accomplish much greater things.—FITZGERALD, EDWARD, 1881, *To C. E. Norton, March 13; Letters, ed. Wright*, vol. I, p. 464.

The work to which he gave his life is a work of great labor, a work of great love, and a work which will be a lantern unto the feet and a light unto the paths of many generations of mankind—of as many as shall care to look back to the greatest secondary cause of their being what, in the progress of science and discovery, they shall have become.—TAYLOR, SIR HENRY, 1885, *Autobiography*, vol. I, p. 198.

Spedding's great work, the result of a life's devoted research, remains the source from which all commentators must draw their information; but few will wade through such a mass of material set forth with so little art. Mr. Spedding's plan of arranging events, as in an annual register, under the years in which they happened, detracts from the interest if not from the value of his labours. He has left a quarry from which others must hew.—NICHOL, JOHN, 1888, *Francis Bacon, His Life and Philosophy, Part I*, p. vi.

The work is an unsurpassable model of thorough and scholar-like editing. Taylor reports that about 1863 Spedding showed signs of declining interest in his task, but recovered after a long rest. His unflagging industry had made him familiar with every possible source of information, and his own writing is everywhere marked by slow but sure-footed judgment, and most careful balancing of evidence. Spedding's qualities are in curious contrast with Macaulay's brilliant audacity, and yet the trenchant exposure of Macaulay's misrepresentations is accompanied by a quiet humour and a shrewd critical faculty which, to a careful reader, make the book more interesting than its rival. Critics have thought Spedding's judgment of his hero too favourable, but on one doubts that his views require the most respectful consideration.—STEPHEN, LESLIE, 1898, *Dictionary of National Biography*, vol. LIII, p. 315.

William Rathbone Greg
1809–1881

Born at Manchester, from manager of mills at Bury became a Commissioner of Customs in 1856, and was Comptroller of H. M. Stationery Office in 1864–77. In his "Rocks Ahead" (1874), he took a highly pessimistic view of the future of England, foreboding the political supremacy of the lower classes, industrial decline, and the divorce of intelligence from religion. His other works include "The Creed of Christendom" (1851), "Essays on Political and Social Science" (1854), "Literary and Social Judgments" (1869), "Political Problems" (1870), "Enigmas of Life" (1872; 18th ed. 1891, with a memoir by widow), "Mistaken Aims" (1876), and "Miscellaneous Essays" (1884).—PATRICK AND GROOME, eds., 1897, *Chambers's Biographical Dictionary*, p. 434.

PERSONAL

It fell to the present writer at one time to have one or two bouts of public controversy with Mr. Greg. In these dialects Mr. Greg was never vehement and never pressed, but he was inclined to be—or, at least, was felt by an opponent to be —dry, mordant, and almost harsh. The disagreeable prepossessions were instantly dissipated, as so often happens, by personal acquaintance. He had not only the courtesy of the good type of the man of the world, but an air of moral suavity, when one came near enough to him, that was infinitely attractive and engaging. He was urbane, essentially modest, and readily interested in ideas and subjects other than his own. There was in his manner and address something of what the French call *liant*. When the chances of residence made me his neighbour, an evening in his drawing-room, or half an hour's talk in casual meetings in afternoon walks on Wimbledon Common was always a particularly agreeable incident. Some men and women have the quality of atmosphere. The egotism of the natural man is surrounded by an elastic medium. Mr. Greg was one of these personalities with an atmosphere, elastic, stimulating, elevating, and yet composing.—MORLEY, JOHN, 1883, *W. R. Greg: A Sketch, Macmillan's Magazine* vol. 48, p. 109.

GENERAL

I do respect Greg the manufacturer, though not the reviewer.—MAURICE, FREDERICK DENISON, 1851, *Letter to Charles Kingsley, March 23; Life*, ed. his Son, vol. II, p. 60.

The essays of Mr. W. R. Greg are, in our opinion, pre-eminently distinguished by their great good sense; they are replete with judicious observations—observations which, if they may not be characterized as profound, are certainly not such as lie on the surface, within the reach of every hand; the cultivated reader cannot rise from the perusal of his writings without the consciousness of having derived profit and instruction from them. . . . We commend them most cordially to every one who is in search of clear and sound guidance, or who can appreciate manly unaffected good sense, and distinct and impartial statements, for in reading the essays of Mr. Greg, we feel we have left the narrow boundaries of party—we are neither Whig nor Tory; we are conservative in the most philosophical sense of the term, and we are liberal and progressive in the safest of all methods, being invited to advance only where there is light upon our path, and solid ground beneath our feet.—SMITH, WILLIAM, 1872, *Mr. W. R. Greg's Political Essays, Contemporary Review*, vol. 20, p. 211.

Though unorthodox in opinion, he is sound at heart, religious in feeling, and a sincere well-wisher of humanity. He is most popular on directly practical questions, with a philanthropic turn.—CHAMBERS, ROBERT, 1876, *Cyclopædia of English Literature*, ed. Carruthers, p. 247.

What gave Mr. Greg his peculiar position among journalists, was the singular lucidity and incisiveness with which he expressed and expounded that aspect of the difficulties and dangers with which he dealt, appealing most strongly to the imagination of practical men, and especially of practical men belonging to the upper section of the middle class. For the miseries of the working class Mr. Greg's pity was profound and almost passionate, but his moral and intellectual sympathy was not with them, and was often inaccessible from their points of view. Again, as to style, Mr. Greg was never in any depreciatory sense rhetorical; for verbiage of any kind he had no taste. But he was a keen logician, and took what I may call almost a rhetorical pleasure in plunging cold steel into the heart of what he regarded as a mischievious fallacy. And this he did after a fashion which especially went home to practical men. His intellectual logic was keen enough, but still keener was the logic which the late Emperor of the French called "the logic of facts." Mr. Greg loved to look facts clearly in the face, to realise as vividly as he could exactly what they meant, before he even cared to consider whether they were capable of any agreeable or even tolerable interpretation. —HUTTON, RICHARD HOLT, 1881, *William Rathbone Greg, Criticisms on Contemporary Thoughts and Thinkers*, vol. II, p. 137.

It is no small tribute that we pay to an habitual controversialist when we assert, as we do with great confidence, that the result of his labors has been to induce thousands of his countrymen to examine the burning questions of religion with the calmness, the fairness, and the good sense which most persons find it far easier to bring to the consideration of political or social problems than to the solution of theological perplexities.—DICEY, A. V., 1882, *W. R. Greg, The Nation*, vol. 34, p. 81.

Though he took great delight in the enchanted land of pure literature, apart from all utility, yet he was of those, the fibres of whose nature makes it impossible for them to find real intellectual interest outside of what is of actual and present concern to their fellows. Composition, again, had to him none of the pain and travail that it brings to most writers. The expression came with the thought. His ideas were never vague, and needed no laborious translation. Along with them came apt words and the finished sentence. Yet his fluency never ran off into the fatal channels of verbosity. Ease, clearness, precision, and a certain smooth and sure-paced consecutiveness, made his written style for all purposes of statement and exposition one of the most telling and effective of his day. This gift of expression helped him always to appear intellectually at his best. It really came from a complete grasp of his own side of the case, and that always produces the best style next after a complete grasp of both sides.—MORLEY, JOHN, 1883, *W. R. Greg: A Sketch, Macmillan's Magazine*, vol. 48, p. 122.

If an author's special faculties cut their image most sharply on his political estimates and social speculations, his nature as a whole finds its largest expression in his religion. Even if it be merely an undisturbed tradition, the fact that this suffices for him is far from insignificant. And if it be self-formed, whether spontaneously given or deliberately thought out, it not only carries in it all the traits of the personality, but presents them in magnified scale and true proportion. Hence Mr. Greg's "Creed of Christendom," quite apart from its merits as a theological treatise, possesses a high biographical interest; for it is a transparently *sincere* book, and lays bare the interior dealings of an eminently veracious, exact, and reverent mind with the supreme problems of human belief. In order to give it its true value as a chapter in history, it should be taken into view not as an isolated product, but in connection with the earlier state of mind from which it recedes, and the latter which speaks in the Preface to the third edition (1873). This Preface—perhaps the finest of his essays—contains his last word of doubt and faith, and probably marks the resting-place of his mind in its best vigour; for, though we have since heard from him both brighter and sadder things, they seemed to be, the one the sunshine of a passing mood, the other the expression of a growing languor and weariness of life.—MARTINEAU, JAMES, 1883, *The Creed of Christendom, Nineteenth Century*, vol. 13, p. 199.

In Greg ardent philanthropy and disinterested love of truth were curiously allied to an almost epicurean fastidiousness, which made him unduly distrustful of the popular element in politics. He would have wished to see public affairs controlled by an enlightened oligarchy, and did not perceive that such an oligarchy was incompatible with the principles which he had himself admitted. Little practical aid towards legislation, therefore, is to be obtained from his writings. It was Greg's especial function to discourage unreasonable expectations from political or even social reforms, to impress his readers with the infinite complexity of modern problems and in general to caution democracy against the abuse of its power. His apprehensions may sometimes appear visionary, and sometimes exaggerated, but are in general the previsions of a far-seeing man, acute in observing the tendencies of the age, though perhaps too ready to identify tendencies with accomplished facts. His style is clear and cogent, but his persuasiveness and impressiveness rather arise from moral qualities, his absolute disinterestedness, and the absence of class feeling, even when he may seem to be advocating the cause of a class.—GARNETT, RICHARD, 1890, *Dictionary of National Biography, vol.* XXIII, *p.* 88.

He was one of the chief assailants of the Christian faith in his day, and, in a work entitled the "Creed of Christendom," did what was in him to make an end of that persistent doctrine which survives so many attacks. This work is another example of the tendency of such books to drop aside into corners and be no more seen, after having, for a moment, affrighted the timid believer. Another work, "Enigmas of Life," published in 1872, had a powerful human interest in one or two occasional passages, in which the writer let his imagination go, for instance, into speculations as to what might be a logical and reasonable Hell, with curious power, and a strange, unintentional, and very striking approach to that picture of the place of despair, which represents it as a place where the worm dieth not and the fire is not quenched.—OLIPHANT, MARGARET, O. W., 1892, *The Victorian Age of English Literature, p.* 577.

Arthur William Edgar O'Shaughnessy
1844–1881

Born, in London, 14 March, 1844. Educated privately. Junr. Assistant, British Museum Library, June 1861; Assistant in Zoology Dept., Aug., 1863. Married Eleanor Marston, 1873. Died, 30 Jan. 1881. *Works:* "An Epic of Women," 1870; "Lays of France," 1872; "Music and Moonlight," 1874; "Toyland," (with his wife), 1875. *Posthumous:* "Songs of a Worker," ed. by A. W. N. Deacon, 1881. *Life:* by L. C. Moulton, with selections from his poems, 1894.—SHARP, R. FARQUHARSON, 1897, *A Dictionary of English Authors, p.* 218.

PERSONAL

Mr. O'Shaughnessy was a rapid, nervous talker, with an American earnestness of manner. He seemed quite sure of his ground, and not one to be easily diverted from it by criticism, but was an impulsive, kind-hearted gentleman, and conscientious in the treatment of his lightest work.—STEDMAN, EDMUND CLARENCE, 1882, *Some London Poets, Harper's Magazine, vol.* 64, *p.* 883.

Again returns this day, and still, my friend,
I listen for a step that comes not near,
And hearken for a voice I may not hear
Save in my dreams, where many memories blend.
Two years have passed, and still the days extend,
Void day on day. He, too, has gone away
Who loved thy lyric work; his praise a bay
For which all songs most gladly might contend.
April, that came and found him with us yet,
And took him hence, makes sad the heart of Spring,
And January days shall not forget
That then it was *thy* sweet lips ceased to sing,
And we, who loved thee, knew our feet were set
In paths where thine were no more journeying.
—MARSTON, PHILIP BOURKE, 1883, *To Arthur O'Shaughnessy, Jan.* 30; *Wind-Voices, p.* 174.

With his handsome, sensitive, clearly cut face, his bright, earnest eyes, behind the glasses which gave him a student-like aspect, his rather slight but well-knit figure, with the noticeably small feet and hands, so well-shod and gloved, in which he took an innocent pride. He was full of enthusiasm, and I think, had length of days been given him, he would always have been the youngest man in every company. What pleasure he had in things small and great! He was as simply frank in his appreciation of his own work as in that of other people, and I shall never forget the quick "Like it, eh?" and the sudden light in his eyes when he perceived that something he was reading or reciting had found its way to his listener's interest. He was half a Frenchman in his love for and mastery of the French language; and many of his closest affiliations were with the younger school of French poets.—MOULTON, LOUISE CHANDLER, 1894, *Arthur O'Shaughnessy, His Life and His Work with Selections from His Poems, p.* 18.

GENERAL

As regards the invention and use of metres the author is particularly happy. Those of his own originating are at the same time simple, musical, and individual; and it is not very often that metric ease and beauty are sacrificed to crotchets of diction and roughness of cadence throughout his book. The main fault one has to find in the miscellaneous poems is a vagueness, not of **form**, but of thought or sentiment: **the poet is** frequently obscure; and the worst of it is that those poems which demand most pains to get to the centre of are least worth the pains. To say that Mr. O'Shaughnessy's style is already absolutely individual or by any means perfect would be rash; but that it holds sufficient good qualities and few enough bad qualities to give sure token that he can, with earnest work, get himself a complete and self-sufficient manner, one need not hesitate to affirm; and it seems probable that, as years go on, he will have that to tell to men which will be well worth the garment of a perfect poetic manner of speech.—FORMAN, H. BUXTON, 1871, *Our Living Poets*, p. 512.

In the "Epic of Women" we felt some reflection of the colour of Swinburne; in the "Lays of France" a much fainter tinge of Morris was apparent to careful eyes. In "Music and Moonlight" it would be difficult to detect any foreign influence of this kind. The book belongs to a certain class of art, and runs parallel, as may be pointed out, to the work of other men, but these do not belong to a living, or even English generation, and the similitude is one more of temperament than of style. In Mr. O'Shaughnessy's earliest book, attentive eyes saw beneath the high tone of general colouring an outline of individuality that had little in common with the sensuousness of surface. . . . As revealed in this new volume, Mr. O'Shaughnessy resembles no English writer, and he no longer has much fellowship with the French Romanticists. It sounds like a paradox, and yet is true, that this most modern of modern singers approaches no one so nearly as one whom we are apt to regard as the most old-fashioned of writers, the veritable poet of moonlight, Novalis! . . . There is an atmosphere about one class of these lyrics that reminds one of the mood one falls into on a summer afternoon, lying in a low warm nook among the rushes, close to the shining level of some river. The uniform golden tone of the foreground, the monotonous blue haze behind, paralyse more than they stimulate the imagination; and if one is alone, one slips into a sad kind of trance, longing, one knows not for what, to complete what ought to be, and is not, pleasure. One would analyse the regretful sense of incompleteness, but in that enervating air any mental effort is impossible. . . . We should, however, be giving an entirely false idea of the poetic attainment reached in this volume if we led our readers to suppose that its contents were mainly vague or intangible. There is very much here that will please even those readers for whom what is merely visionary, however musical or tender, has little charm. . . . When Mr. O'Shaughnessy is thoroughly true to his individuality he is infinitely charming. One longs to quote stanza upon stanza where it is difficult to say which is the more exquisite, the technical perfection of structure and melody, or the delicate pathos of thought.— GOSSE, EDMUND, 1874, *Music and Moonlight, The Academy*, vol. 5, pp. 359, 360.

The original poems in this book ["Songs of a Worker"] are in a measure disappointing to those who looked for a richer yield from O'Shaughnessy's lyrical genius after it had lain fallow during seven years. They scarcely show that hold upon thought and imagination which a poet should gain after enjoying the full period in which he reasonably may occupy himself with the dexterities of his craft.—STEDMAN, EDMUND CLARENCE, 1882, *Some London Poets, Harper's Magazine*, vol. 64, p. 883.

It displays that fatal lack of the power of rigid self-criticism which kept him from knowing what not to include; and it therefore failed to add materially to his reputation. The ode with which it opens is so noble that, in justice to the varied powers of this man whom, so far, you have seen chiefly as the poet of love and sorrow, it must be included in my selections. . . . This volume seems to me largely the tentative work of a poet in a transition state. In the group of poems called by a singular misnomer "Thoughts in Marble," we certainly find little of the cold chastity of sculpture. The poems are, indeed, oversensuous—going beyond even the not too rigid boundaries the author set for himself in "An Epic of Women." The book, I must take leave to say, was too indulgently edited by O'Shaughnessy's cousin, the Reverend Newport Deacon, who avows, in his introduction, that of the poems evidently intended for publication left in manuscript by the poet, not one has been omitted. This too lavish inclusiveness was certainly in some instances a grave mistake. Instead of a well-pruned garden of choice flowers, we have a riotous plot of blossoms, desperately sweet, some of them, but overrun, here and there, with weeds, and with, sometimes, more thorns than roses. Still we can but be thankful for a volume that gives us the "Song of a Fellow Worker;" a poem so blood-red with humanity as "Christ Will Return," and, above all, anything so noble as the first part of "En-Soph," in which, I think, the author approaches actual sublimity more nearly than in any other of his poems.—MOULTON, LOUISE CHANDLER, 1894, *Arthur O'Shaughnessy, His Life and His Work, with Selections from his Poems, pp.* 18, 41.

For my part, I will make bold to confess that Marston himself has, if anything, been a little over-appreciated. At any rate, he has had his full share of the good things of praise; while, on the other hand, his brother-poet, Arthur O'Shaughnessy, has received a great deal less than his due. Unforgivable as I fear the remark may seem to Marston's extreme admirers, I am bound to say that, little as has been made of O'Shaughnessy, and much as has been made of Marston, O'Shaughnessy is really the finer poet of the two. Both of them suffer rather tiresomely from that lack of thought and excess of music and other sensuous qualities which are the marks of the æsthetic school to which they belong. But Marston's verbiage (his constantly beating out thin themes of sorrow into utter tenuity of thought or fancy) is less varied by verbal or metrical magic than O'Shaughnessy's. Both poets had constantly nothing or very little to say; but whereas of his nothing Marston would turn out an uninspired, uninspiring sonnet, heavy as with a very London fog of melancholy, O'Shaughnessy of his nothing would contrive a dancing, glinting little lyric—little more than words, you may say; but is not that the very secret of the lyric? —LEGALLIENNE, RICHARD, 1894, *Retrospective Reviews, vol.* II, *p.* 141.

O'Shaughnessy's temperament was that of a genuine poet. His slender frame and spiritual expression recalled Chopin, and his best poetry has the characteristics of Chopin's music—dreamy and sometimes weird, with an original, delicious, and inexhaustible melody. Some pieces, such as "Palm Flowers," display, in addition, a remarkable faculty of gorgeous word-painting; others, such as the "Daughter of Herodias," possess much dramatic intensity, others fascinate by a semi-sensuous mysticism, and "Chaitivel" and "Bisclavaret" are wildly imaginative. All these gifts, however, except that of verbal music seemed to dwindle as the poet advanced in years, and their decay was not compensated by growth in intellectual power. The range of O'Shaughnessy's ideas and sympathies was narrow, and when the original lyrical impulse had subsided, or degenerated into a merely mechanical fluency, he found himself condemned, for the most part, to the sterile repetition. He might not improbably have forsaken poetry for criticism, in which he could have performed an important part. Enthusiastically devoted to modern French belles-lettres, and writing French with the elegance and accuracy of an accomplished native, he possessed unusual qualifications for interpreting the literature of either country to the other, and might have come to exert more influence as a critic than he could have obtained as a poet.—GARNETT, RICHARD, 1895, *Dictionary of National Biography, vol.* XLII, *p.* 309.

Sometimes either of deliberate conviction or through corrupt following of others, he indulged in expressions of opinion about matters on which the poet is not called upon to express any, in a manner which was always unnecessary and sometimes offensive. But judged as a poet he has the *unum necessarium*, the individual note of song. Like Keats, he was not quite individual. . . . But the genuine and authentic contribution is sufficient, and is of the most unmistakable kind.—SAINTSBURY, GEORGE, 1896, *A History of Nineteenth Century Literature, p.* 295.

To the most modern phase of landscape in poetry, yet with a quality which brings him into a certain relation with Shelley, belongs Arthur O'Shaughnessy (1844–81); that gifted, unhappy youth, who, in delicate metrical skill and melody of words, in my eyes, stands second to Tennyson only during the last half century; whilst he is also high in pure imaginative faculty, wasted as it often was on doleful dreams and extravagant fantasies. He took Nature, if I may use the word, into his soul like a mistress; although known to him solely through books, he was intoxicated with tropical scenery. — PALGRAVE, FRANCIS TURNER, 1896, *Landscape in Poetry, p.* 228.

O'Shaughnessy emerges most distinctly from the group by reason of his very original and exquisite lyrical gift.—BEERS, HENRY A., 1901, *A History of English Romanticism in the Nineteenth Century, p.* 389.

Sidney Lanier
1842-1881

An American poet; born at Macon, Ga., Feb. 3, 1842; died at Lynn, N. C., Sept. 7, 1881. He served in the Confederate Army as a private soldier; after the war studied law, and for a while practiced it at Macon; but abandoned that profession and devoted himself to music and poetry. From 1879 till his death he was lecturer on English literature in Johns Hopkins University. The poem "Corn," one of his earliest pieces (1874), and "Clover," "The Bee," "The Dove," etc., show insight into nature. His poetic works were collected and published (1884) after his death. He wrote also several works in prose, mostly pertaining to literary criticism and to mediæval history: among the former are: "The Science of English Verse" (1880); "The English Novel and the Principles of its Development" (1883). He edited or compiled "The Boy's Froissart" (1878); "The Boy's King Arthur" (1880); "The Boy's Percy" (1882).—WARNER, CHARLES DUDLEY ed., 1897, *Library of the World's Best Literature, Biographical Dictionary, vol.* XXIX, *p.* 326.

PERSONAL

I write hurriedly, finding much correspondence awaiting me here, so can only repeat how much joy the evidence of a new true poet always gives me,—such a poet as I believe you to be. I am heartily glad to welcome you to the fellowship of authors, so far as I may dare to represent it; but, knowing the others, I venture to speak in their names also. When we meet, I hope to be able to show you, more satisfactorily than by these written words, the genuineness of the interest which each author always feels in all others; and perhaps I may be also able to extend your own acquaintance among those whom you have a right to know.—TAYLOR, BAYARD, 1875, *To Sidney Lanier, Aug.* 17; *Life and Letters, ed. Taylor and Scudder, vol.* II, *p.* 669.

For six months past, a ghastly fever has been taking possession of me every day about 12 M., and holding my head under the surface of indescribable distress for the *next twenty hours,* subsiding only enough each morning to let me get on my working-harness, but *never intermitting.* A number of tests show it to be *not* the hectic, so well known in consumption, and to this day it has baffled all the skill I could find in N. York, Philadelphia and here. I have myself been disposed to think it arose wholly from the bitterness of having to spend my time in making academic lectures and boy's books—pot-boilers—all *when a thousand songs are singing in my heart, that will certainly kill me, if I do not utter them soon.* But I don't think *this* diagnosis has found favor with my practical physicians; and meanwhile, I work day after day in such suffering as is piteous to see. I hope this does not sound like a Jeremiad. I mention these matters only in the strong rebellion against what I fear might be your thought —namely, forgetfulness of you— if you did not know the causes which keep me from sending you more frequent messages.— LANIER, SIDNEY, 1880, *Letter to Paul Hamilton Hayne, Nov.* 19; *The Critic, No.* 112.

> Life s fragile bonds united
> By fine-spun webs of breath,
> Scarce quivered 'neath the mystic stroke—
> The unsheathed sword of Death!
> O poet preen thy pinions!
> Soar through Faith's radiant pass;
> The mists of pain fade from thy soul,
> Like frost-films from a glass!
> Thy worn, white body slumbers,
> Dreamless in Death's dark keep:—
> The drawbridge crossed, thy spirit feels
> No lethargy of sleep. . . .
> O Music, mother of soft sounds,
> Let not thy tongue be mute!
> For *he,* through silver lips, evoked
> The language of the flute.
> And nature, though her voice is dumb,
> Through dew-draped blades of corn,
> Shall shed, 'mid Southern fields of grain,
> Memorial tears at morn.

—HAYNE, WILLIAM HAMILTON, 1881, *Sidney Lanier, Sept.* 9; *Sylvan Lyrics and Other Verses.*

In his hands the flute no longer remained a mere material instrument, but was transformed into a voice that set heavenly harmonies into vibration. Its tones developed colors, warmth, and a low sweetness of unspeakable poetry; they were not only true and pure, but poetic, allegoric as it were, suggestive of the depths and heights of being and of the delights which the earthly ear never hears and the earthly eye never sees. No doubt his firm faith in these lofty idealities gave him the power to present them to our imaginations, and thus by the aid of the higher language of Music to inspire others with that sense of beauty in which he constantly dwelt. "His conception of music was not reached by an analytic study of note by note, but was intuitive and spontaneous; like a woman's reason; he felt it so, because he felt it so, and his delicate preception required no more logical form of reasoning." His playing appealed alike to the musically learned and to the unlearned —for he would magnetize the listener; but the artist felt in his performance the superiority of the momentary living inspiration to all the rules and shifts of the mere technical scholarship. — HAMERIK, ASGER, 1884, *Poems of Sidney Lanier, ed. his Wife*, p. 31.

His earliest passion was for music. As a child he learned to play, almost without instruction, on every kind of instrument he could find; and while yet a boy he played the flute, organ, piano, violin, guitar, and banjo, especially devoting himself to the flute in deference to his father, who feared for him the powerful fascination of the violin. For it was the violin-voice, that above all others commanded his soul. He has related that during his college days it would sometimes so exalt him in rapture, that presently he would sink from his solitary music-worship into a deep trance, thence to awake alone, on the floor of his room, sorely shaken in nerve. In after years more than one listener remarked the strange violin effects which he conquered from the flute. His devotion to music rather alarmed than pleased his friends, and while it was here that he first discovered that he possessed decided genius, he for some time shared that early notion of his parents, that it was an unworthy pursuit, and he rather repressed his taste. He did not then know by what inheritance it had come to him, nor how worthy is the art.—WARD, WILLIAM HAYES, 1884, *Poems of Sidney Lanier, ed. his Wife, Memorial*, p. 12.

He gloried in antiquarian lore and antiquarian literature. Hardly "Old Monkbarns" himself could have pored over a black-letter volume with greater enthusiasm. Especially he loved the tales of chivalry, and thus, when the opportunity came, was fully equipped as an interpreter of Froissart and "King Arthur" for the benefit of our younger generation of students. With the great Elizabethans Lanier was equally familiar. Instead of skimming Shakspeare, he went down into his depths. Few have written so subtly of Shakspeare's mysterious sonnets. Through all Lanier's productions we trace the influence of his early literary loves; but nowhere do the pithy quaintnesses of the old bards and chroniclers display themselves more effectively—not only in the illustrations, but through the innermost warp and woof of the texture of his ideas and his style—than in some of his familiar epistles.—HAYNE, PAUL HAMILTON, 1886, *A Poet's Letters to a Friend, Letters of Sidney Lanier*, p. 220.

He was so truly a beauty lover, so responsive to every upward influence, that what he admired in those of whom he wrote soon became a living part of his own character, his large generosities in admiration returning quickly to crown him. For this reason the tersest and most comprehensive characterisation of our poet, although it was an unconscious one, is to be drawn from his own words, which continually recur to me when I would make him known to others.—TURNBULL, FRANCES L., 1891, *Younger American Poets, ed. Sladen*, Appendix II, p. 652.

From childhood the others of us felt an impression of his distinction: this may be a reflection from a light now shining, but I do not think so. It was a distinct feeling that here was not only an elder but an original personality. . . . His imperishable work is done in seven years. He *planned* enough, in addition to that which he wrought, to require seventeen or twenty-seven. As she still lives, it may not be delicate to more than speak of her, who from the trothplight of 1867 has been a perfect help-meet, and who since the dark September day of 1881, when he died, has kept alight the sacred flame upon the hearth-stone of his memory: four sons have been nurtured and educated in the best tradition of his teaching and of his name,—a fourfold chaplet worthy of any woman's wearing.—LANIER, CLIFFORD, 1895, *Reminiscences of Sidney Lanier, The Chautauquan*, vol. 21, pp. 403, 409.

Here is one whose beauty of personality is no whit inferior to the loftiness and worth of his message. He was a spotless, sunny-souled, hard-working, divinely gifted man, who had exalted ideas both of art and of life. . . The story of his personality and work, though pathetic, is one of the most interesting and inspiring in the biographical annals of men of letters.—BASKERVILLE, WILLIAM MALONE 1896, *Southern Writers*, pp. 138, 139.

The Southwind brought a voice; was it of bird?
Or faint-blown reed? or string that quivered
long?
A haunting voice that woke into a song
Sweet as a child's low laugh, or lover's word.
We listened idly till it grew and stirred
With throbbing chords of joy, of love, of wrong;
A mighty music, resonant and strong;
Our hearts beat higher for that voice far-heard.
The Southwind brought a shadow, purple-dim,
It swept across the warm smile of the sun;
A sudden shiver passed on field and wave;
The grasses grieved along the river's brim.
We knew the voice was silent, the song done;
We knew the shadow smote across a grave.
—JEWETT, SOPHIE (ELLEN BURROUGHS), 1896, *Sidney Lanier, The Pilgrim and Other Poems.*

Lanier fought a battle with death (technically, consumption) to which Keats's classic consumption was child's play. It is so easy to fight anything, even consumption, if you have nothing else to do; but if you have a home to keep going as well, and only a pen to keep it going with—well, you look upon John Keats as one of the sybarites of immortality. Fortunately, Lanier had a flute, too, and thereby hangs much of his history, as well as the explanation of his temperament and gift.—LEGALLIENNE, RICHARD, 1900, *Sidney Lanier, The Academy, vol.* 58, *p.* 147.

GENERAL

Is a spirited story of Southern life, ["Tiger Lillies"] beginning just before the war, and closing with the war. The earlier scenes are among the mountains of Tennessee; later shifting with the Southern army to Virginia; and having an echo or two of European adventure. The author disclaims making the bloody sensational his style; and yet we have a little murder and some pretty melodramatic touches. . . . The story is entertaining, and the style lively. The latter is paragraphical and exclamationary; and in a remote way—in its mingling pedantry and raillery, grotesquely together sometimes—it reminds the reader, remotely and just a little, of the "Sketch-Book of Meister Karl." Italian, French and German words and phrases abound throughout the work.—DAVIDSON, JAMES WOOD, 1869, *Living Writers of the South, p.* 321.

Because I believe that Sidney Lanier was much more than a clever artisan in rhyme and metre; because he will, I think, take his final rank with the first princes of American song, I am glad to provide this slight memorial. . . . Perhaps the most remarkable feature of his gifts was their complete symmetry. It is hard to tell what register of perception, or sensibility or wit, or will was lacking. The constructive and the critical faculties, the imaginative and the practical, balanced each other. His wit and humour played upon the soberer background of his more recognized qualities. . . But how short was his span, and how slender his opportunity! From the time he was of age he waged a constant, courageous, hopeless fight against adverse circumstance for room to live and write. Much very dear, and sweet, and most sympathetic helpfulness he met in the city of his adoption, and from friends elsewhere, but he could not command the time and leisure which might have lengthened his life and given him opportunity to write the music and the verse with which his soul was teeming. Yet short as was his literary life, and hindered though it were, its fruits will fill a large space in the garnering of the poetic art of our country.—WARD, WILLIAM HAYES, 1884, *Poems of Sydney Lanier, ed. his Wife, Memorial, pp.* xi, xli.

It is sad to think of the fate of this supremely-striving, richly-gifted man; sad that such forces as his should have been so little conserved—that an age so rich in the material things for the want of which he perished, should be so blindly prodigal of that in which it is so beggarly poor, genius. Saddest of all is it to think of what he might have done, and did not do. These poems—fragments finished at rare intervals as strength and opportunity conspired—beautiful as many of them are, show unmistakably that they do not represent their author's highest ideals or best capacity. They are rather the preliminary trying of the strings and testing of the notes of the poetic orchestra whose full harmony he never found opportunity to sound. Yet how easily might that opportunity, for which his whole life was spent in striving, have been afforded him. If in his brief career there is so rich a gain to American letters, how great may be the loss that he died so soon.—BROWNE, FRANCIS F., 1885, *Sidney Lanier, The Dial, vol.* 5, *p.* 246.

To an age assailed by the dangerous doctrines of the fleshy school in poetry, and by that unhealthy "æstheticism" and that debauching "realism" which see in vice and uncleanness only new fields for the artist's powers of description, and no call for the artist's divine powers of denunciation—to save young men into whose ears is dinned the maxim, "art for art's sake only," "a moral purpose ruins art," Lanier came, noble-souled as Milton in youthful consciousness of power, yet humble before the august conception of a moral purity higher than he could hope to utter or attain, discerning with the true poet's insight the "beauty of holiness" and the "holiness of beauty." Had he lived and died in England, how he would have been embalmed in living odes, his sepulchre how perpetually draped with insignia of national appreciation! He is *ours*. He was an American to the centre of his great, loving heart. Shall we cherish his memory any the less lovingly because his works are the first-fruits of a reunited people—the richest contribution to our national fame in letters yet made by our brothers of the South?—GATES, MERRILL EDWARDS, 1887, *Sidney Lanier, Presbyterian Review*, vol. 8, p. 701.

> That I of him should have this thing to say,
> Lads, he will pipe no more.
> And who, forsooth, could pipe as sweet as he?
> Oh, lads, lads, lads, no more, no more!
> The whole long year from white May to white May
> Of his true music now will emptied be.
> Oh, lads, lads, lads! At sunset as we lay,
> Deep in the river rushes, he and we,
> Such daring notes would come
> From that brown reed of his, till yellow day
> Died out the west we would not but keep dumb.

—REESE, LIZETTE WOODWORTH, 1887, *The Lost Shepherd, Southern Bivouac, Jan*.

Lanier's death was a loss to American literature, relatively almost equal to that which England sustained in the death of Keats. With a matchless gift of cadence, intensest humanity and sincerity, rich creative imagination, and intellectual powers of the highest order, he was advancing, I believe, to the chief place in American song, when death stayed him. As it is, he will always be among poets a stimulating force — ROBERTS, CHARLES G. D., 1888, *ed. Poems of Wild Life*, p. 233, note.

Inborn delicacy of hearing and long training fitted Lanier for the task of investigating English verse. Quietly disregarding the learned rubbish that had accumulated, he studied our verse as a set of present phenomena of the world of sound. He listened and listened to the very thing itself, the sound-groups concerning which he wished to learn. He gathered his facts carefully, he verified and arranged them, until the great laws which underlie the phenomena stood out clear and unmistakable. These laws he then set forth in language which is as severely accurate as if he had never penned a line of poetry, as if all flights of imagination were utterly distasteful to him.—TOLMAN, ALBERT H., 1888, *The Lanier Memorial*.

His were a larger mind and a stronger hand than Timrod's or even Hayne's, yet his was a fatal fault: he lacked that spontaneity which is the chief pleasure in the verse of Hayne and Timrod In the midst of the products of a genius that certainly at times seemed large, and that was bold to the extent of eccentricity, are the too-conspicuous signs of mere intellectual experiment and metrical or verbal extravaganza. Lanier theorizes in verse; the practice-hand seeks to strike chords that can only come from the impassioned and self-forgetful singer of nature and the soul. His analytical and exhaustive musical studies—applied to literature in "The Science of English Verse"— greatly harmed his creative work.—RICHARDSON, CHARLES F., 1888, *American Literature*, 1607–1885, vol. II, p. 232.

What are really the characteristics of this amazing and unparalleled poetry of Lanier? Reading it again, and with every possible inclination to be pleased, I find a painful effort, a strain and rage, the most prominent qualities in everything he wrote. Never simple, never easy, never in one single lyric natural and spontaneous for more than one stanza, always forcing the note, always concealing his barrenness and tameness by grotesque violence of image and preposterous storm of sound, Lanier appears to me to be as conclusively not a poet of genius as any ambitious man who ever lived, labored, and failed.—GOSSE, EDMUND, 1888, *Has America Produced a Poet? The Forum*, vol. 6, p. 180.

Lanier was indubitably a lyrical poet of quite exceptional faculty, though affectation and strained effect spoilt much of his verse; but here we have to do with him simply as a sonneteer. Why he wrote sonnets at all is a mystery, for he had no inevitable bias that way; on the contrary, his mannerisms became more and more obvious and distracting. Yet his sonnets have many admirers, and undoubtedly even when most obviously "manipulated" have still a certain quality of saving grace. For this reason I have represented him by several examples, though personally I admit that their lack of rhythmic strength is a vital drawback to enjoyment. "The Harlequin Dreams," the series entitled "In Absence," and the two comprised in "Acknowledgment," are his best; in the latter there is an exuberance, an exaggeration of address which is strongly suggestive of the diction of the lesser Elizabethans. "Laus Mariae" is accepted by many as his best sonnet. Yet, interesting as it is in some respects, one cannot but wonder at the critical blindness of those who called Lanier the American Keats.—SHARP, WILLIAM, 1889, ed., *American Sonnets, Introductory Note.*

Sidney Lanier endeavored to express the soul of music in words, and prosecuted the study of poetic technique with all the zeal and more than the success of Poe.—WHITE, GREENOUGH, 1890, *Sketch of the Philosophy of American Literature,* p. 65.

It is natural to mention first the name of Sidney Lanier, for his personality, if it be true that for a man to be a great poet he must also be a great personality. In Lanier, the beautiful character, the high, unrelaxed purpose shine out. In his work the conscientious workman and the artist revelling in the exercise of his art are never lost. Indeed sometimes, as in that poem of "Sunrise," written under the same sad circumstances as Raphael's "Transfiguration" was painted, he steps from conscientious to conscious, artistic to artificial. But his contribution to American poetry, and indeed to all poetry, was great. For he asked himself what was the true *Ars Poetica,* and he endeavoured to write in accordance with the answer evolved. He seems to me parallel to Dante Rossetti. Each cherished not only poetry, but a sister art. And as Rossetti's poems betray the painter, Lanier's betray the musician. Each had a pathetic loftiness of purpose. Each had original ideas as to form. Each felt the hand of death. Each had a singularly ennobling and vivifying effect on his fellows. Each was the founder of a school, some of whom anatomise, and some of whom imitate his art. . . . Lanier differs from the other dead poets included in this book in that he was not only a poet but the founder of a school of poetry.—SLADEN, DOUGLAS, 1891, ed., *Younge American Poets, To the Reader,* pp. xxvi, xxvii.

Sidney Lanier, in nervous crises, would seem to hear rich music. It was an inherited gift. Thus equipped with rhythmical sense beyond that of other poets, he turned to poetry as to the supreme art. Now, the finer and more complex the gift, the longer exercise is needful for its full mastery. He strove to make poetry do what painting has done better, and to make it do what only music hitherto has done. If he could have lived three lives, he would have adjusted the relations of these arts as far as possible to his one satisfaction. I regard his work, striking as it is, as merely tentative from his own point of view. It was as if a discoverer should sail far enough to meet the floating rockweed, the strayed birds, the changed skies, that betoken land ahead; should even catch a breath of fragrance wafted from outlying isles, and then find his bark sinking in the waves before he could have sight of the promised continent.—STEDMAN, EDMUND CLARENCE, 1892, *The Nature and Elements of Poetry, Century Magazine,* vol. 44, p. 865.

> The dewdrop holds the heaven above,
>   Wherein a lark, unseen,
> Outpours a rhapsody of love
>   That fills the space between.
> My heart a dewdrop is, and thou,
>   Dawn-spirit, far away,
> Fillest the void between us now
>   With an immortal lay.

—TABB, JOHN B., 1894, *Lanier, Poems.*

Among the American poets of the younger generation who have passed away during the last thirty years, no one deserves higher encomium than Lanier. . . . There is something about the verse of Lanier—defective as his performance is,—for it must be acknowledged that he was not always equal in clearness and literary judgment,—that inspires respect from every lover of genius. Even where he was not perfect, he showed, as in "Corn," that he had grasped firmly the distinction in poetics between the small and the great. Besides this rare attainment, or gift, whichever it was, Lanier, even in early work, had reached a power of imagination that may be compared not unfavorably with that of Longfellow between his thirty-third and thirty-seventh years; in the minor matters of verbal imagination and onomatopœia Lanier was at times greatly Longfellow's superior. Lanier's merits as a poet are numerous and considerable. A large nature like his could not express itself trivially or in narrow limits. He has done well in the treatment of love, philosophy, mysticism, socialism, in the ballad, and technically in melody and harmony of rhythm.—SIMONDS, ARTHUR B., 1894, *American Song*, pp. 122, 123.

Sidney Lanier, then, though he reminds us here and there of Emerson, of Browning, and of Swinburne, essayed to give artistic form to his own thoughts and feelings, to sing his own song. But either sufficient time was not allowed, or fortune did not permit him to arrive at that individuality by which the great poets are instantly recognized. Limited, then, as I believe he is, in regard to simplicity, to spontaneity, to individuality, to passion, and to perfection, he cannot be called "indisputably a great poet," though he does possess decided originality and a real poetic endowment.—BASKERVILLE, WILLIAM MALONE, 1895, *Some Appreciations of Sidney Lanier, The Dial*, vol. 18, p. 301.

A poet of rare promise, whose original genius was somewhat hampered by his hesitation between two arts of expression, music and verse, and by his effort to coördinate them. His "Science of English Verse," 1880, was a most suggestive, though hardly convincing, statement of that theory of their relation which he was working out in his practice. Some of his pieces, like "The Mocking Bird" and the "Song of the Chattahoochee," are the most characteristically southern poetry that has been written in America—BEERS, HENRY A., 1895, *Initial Studies in American Letters*, p. 212.

In technique he was akin to Tennyson; in love of beauty and lyric sweetness, to Keats and Shelley; in love of nature, to Wordsworth; and in spirituality, to Ruskin, the gist of whose teaching is that we are souls temporarily having bodies; to Milton, "subtlest assertor of the soul in song." To be sure, Lanier's genius is not equal to that of any one of the poets mentioned, but I venture to believe that it is of the same order, and, therefore, deserving of lasting remembrance—CALLOWAY, MORGAN, JR., 1895, *ed. Select Poems of Sidney Lanier, Introduction*, p. 301.

May we not say of Burns's Songs, as did Carlyle in his day, "the best that Britain has yet produced?" And yet, I would like to commend to the reader, just here, a modern poet of our land, who, for heart-music and fine poetic feeling is well-nigh unmatched.—WICKES, W. K., 1896, *Thomas Carlyle's Essay on Robert Burns*, p. 104, note.

Lanier's theory of verse is in accord with Poe's. Beauty and music are poetry's all in all.

"Music is Love in search of a word,"

and lyricism is hardly more articulate. But Lanier longed for the completest intellectual equipment for his work. Poe, he said, "did not know enough." The Baltimore flute-player was a born musician, walking in an enveloping cloud of harmonies, having only to turn aside from the noises of the world and listen to become aware of an unceasing "holy song." He purposed the creation of great symphonies written in a new musical notation as eagerly as he planned for the creation of great poems framed in accordance with new laws of verse. What with his intricate endeavor to bring his two arts into close technical relation, and his thirst to compass all knowledge and acquire all skill, he put away the day of actual performance even farther than the struggle for bread had already thrust it. The most liberal span of life would have been too short for Sidney Lanier, and the life that he wrested from disease and death was but a splendid fragment. Yet his poems as they stand, in their swift surprises of beauty, their secrets of sweet sound, their "Faith that smiles immortally," rank close upon the best achievements of American song.—BATES, KATHARINE LEE, 1897, *American Literature*, p. 189.

Sixteen years have elapsed since Lanier's taking-off; and he is now seen more clearly every day to be the most important native singer the Southern United States has produced, and one of the most distinctive and lovely of American singers wherever born. Enthusiastic admirers and followers he has always attracted to him; now the general opinion begins to swing round to what seemed to many, a little time ago, the extravagant encomium of partiality and prejudice. . . . Had Lanier lived longer, had he had a freer opportunity, doubtless his literary bequest would have been richer and more completely expressive of himself. But as it is, in quality and in accomplishment

Sidney Lanier takes his place as an American poet of distinction. He is one of those rare illustrations of the union, in a son of genius, of high character and artistic production in harmony therewith; a spectacle feeding the heart with tender thoughts and pure ideals:—
"His song was only living aloud,
 His work, a singing with his hand."
—BURTON, RICHARD E., 1897, *Library of the World's Best Literature*, ed. *Warner, vol.* XV, pp. 8891, 8896.

It was into his "Science of English Verse" that he was to pour his whole enthusiasm, and it was this, in connection with his own poems, that was to prove his monument. How large its circulation has been, I do not know; but the condition of the copy before me—belonging to Harvard College Library—is a sufficient proof that it has had and still holds a powerful attraction for young students. By the record of dates at the end of the copy, I find that it was taken out once in 1880, five times in 1881, twice in 1882, four times in 1883, seven times in 1884, six times in 1885, and nineteen times in 1886, being afterwards put upon the list of books to be kept only a fortnight, and being out, the librarian tells me, literally all the time. Any author might be proud to find his book so appreciated by students six years after its first appearance. This is no place for analyzing its theory, even were my technical knowledge of music sufficient to do it justice. To me it seems ingenious, suggestive, and overstrained, but it is easy to believe that to one who takes it on that middle ground where Lanier dwelt, half way between verse and music, it might seem conclusive and even become a text-book in art.—HIGGINSON, THOMAS WENTWORTH, 1899, *Contemporaries*, p. 92.

These letters not only admit us into the fellowship of a poet, but they also disclose to us a man whose life was, in Milton's phrase, "a true poem." Here is nothing to extenuate, nothing to blot: the poet and the man are one. My purpose in editing has, accordingly, been to retain whatever reveals aught, however slight, of the man, in order that the portrait of Lanier's personality, unconsciously drawn by himself, should be as complete as possible; and what ever does not refer to this will at least illustrate the conditions by which an embodied Ideal, a Poet, so recently found himself beset in this world of ours. I know not where to look for a series of letters which, in bulk equally small, relate so humanly and beautifully the story of so precious a life.—THAYER, WILLIAM R., 1899, *Letters of Sidney Lanier, Introduction*, p. ix.

Is second only to Poe among Southern poets. His versification sometimes falls into excessive intricacy and mere caprice, and his thought occasionally fades away into inarticulate dreamery. But these errors are only the defects of his virtues. A man of the finest sensitiveness without effeminacy, and a skilled musician, he has produced dreamy, floating, mist-like, musical effects that are new in English verse; and his feeling for nature, especially for wood and marsh life as seen in parts of the South, is thoroughly modern in its union of exact observation with imaginative subtlety. Lanier had also a keen intellect, as appears from his original and suggestive books on versification and the novel. Had he lived to develop his gifts fully, he might have come to be numbered with the foremost American poets; as it is he stands only a little lower and in a secure place of his own.—BRONSON, WALTER C., 1900, *A Short History of American Literature*, p. 287.

There are two geniuses who hover over the charming city of Baltimore, slumbering all rosy red beneath what is almost a Southern sun: the one more celebrated among foreigners than in his own country, the other almost absolutely unknown in Europe. Their names: Edgar Allan Poe and Sidney Lanier, the Ahriman and the Ormuzd of the place; the demon of perversity and the angel of light; the former carried away by morbid passions that conducted him to an ignominious end, the latter faithful to the purest ideal in his life as in his work; both marked by fate for the victims of a frightful poverty; both doomed to die young, at almost the same age, after having suffered from a hopeless malady. In different degrees, with their contrasts and analogies, these two poets are the glory of the South, which cannot boast of a literature so rich as the North. . . . Sidney Lanier attains often to the height of the great American poets, and, like Walt Whitman, he is much more the poet in the absolute sense of vision, divination, and invention, than are some stars which are reputed to be of first rank. The difference is that their genius burned with a fixed and unrestrained brilliance, while his gave only intermittent light. At the moment when he flies highest, one might say, an arrow suddenly arrests his movement and causes him to fall wounded. It is, indeed, just like the disease which attacked him. One knows what a struggle it fought against the power of his spirit, and nothing is so pathetic as this fall of Icarus. But there remains a diamond shower of beautiful verses, of images grandiose and gracious, of happy expressions which compose the most exquisite of anthologies.—BLANC, MME, 1900, *Revue des Deux Mondes, January 15.*

An all too-curtailed series of "Hymns of the Marshes," which Lanier had intended to make one big ambitious poem. There are four "hymns" in all, but only two are of real importance, namely, "Sunrise" and the "Marshes of Glynn." In fact, had he written all his other poems, and missed writing these (striking, suggestive, and finelined as those other poems often are), he could hardly have been said to succeed in his high poetic ambition—as by those two poems he must be allowed to succeed. In the other poems you see many of the qualities, perhaps all the qualities, which strike you in the "Hymns"—the impassioned observation of nature, the Donne-like "metaphysical" fancy, the religious and somewhat mystic elevation of feeling, expressed often in terms of a deep imaginative understanding of modern scientific conceptions; in fact, you find all save the important quality of that ecstasy which in the "Hymns" fuses all into one splendid flame of adoration upon the altar of the visible universe. The ecstasy of modern man as he stands and beholds the sunrise or the coming of the stars, or any such superb, elemental glory, has, perhaps, never been so keenly translated into verse.—LEGALLIENNE, RICHARD, 1900, *Sidney Lanier, The Academy, vol. 58, p.* 147.

His rare and beautiful temperament, which breathed itself out in melodious lines, gives him a link in the eclectic chain of American poets; and the recent bloom of French song, spanning the Atlantic with its lotus tendril to seek nurture in a foreign soil, has, in its rich redolence, the fleeting perfume of both Poe and Lanier. Lanier's claim as an American poet is certainly a just one; and our failure to recognize it speaks loudly either for our lack of poetic appreciation or our failure to give him his true proportion in every study of American literature. . . . . To insist upon the study of Lanier as an American poet might leave one open to the charge of literary chauvinism, which, I fancy, might become as deadly a sin as its political fellow-sprite; and yet I think a strong plea should be made for the patronage and study of our native poets, whose standards of taste, in mood and form, have been made through the masters. Longfellow, Aldrich, Poe and Lanier are qualified eminently for this purpose. Through the rare grace and scope of their technique and the beauty and truth of their expressed thought they are entitled to the name of poet, whether its definition be comprehensive or limited.—SWIGGETT, GLEN LEVIN, 1901, *Sidney Lanier, The Conservative Review, vol. 5, pp.* 188, 189.

A phenomenon like Lanier is a grateful indication that the olden vigor and multiform artistic energy of the race are still potentially existent and may display that titanic force in diverse spheres which marked the spacious times of great Elizabeth, as well as the preceding era which saw the matured splendor of the Italian Renaissance. If Lanier had lived under more genial auspices—if his entire life had not been an unresting struggle against the pillar of fire in the form of war and the pillar of cloud as coming over him in the guise of poverty he might have achieved an eminence that would have placed him, ranging with his peers, among the supreme masters in the history of musical interpretation.—SHEPHERD, HENRY A., 1902, *Sidney Lanier, Current Literature, vol. 32, p.* 109.

No life in our annals gives so profound an impression of rare genius never adequately revealed. There is relatively little, even in Lanier's small volume of verse, which can be of general interest. Perhaps such music as that of "Chattahoochee," compared with Tennyson's brook, will indicate that Lanier, had he lived, might have rivaled Swinburne in the harmonic and rhythmic effects of verse. "The Marshes of Glynn," we are told, can never be forgotten by a reader who knows also the actual sounds and lights of a Southern swamp. "How Love sought for Hell" is probably the clearest utterance of his lofty ethical convictions. He felt that he had, waiting for utterance, the noble truths which can alone justify the most melodious forms.—LAWTON, WILLIAM CRANSTON, 1902, *Introduction to the Study of American Literature, p.* 308.

Josiah Gilbert Holland
(Timothy Titcomb)
1819–1881

A noted American poet, novelist, and editor; born at Belchertown, Mass., July 24, 1819; died in New York, Oct. 12, 1881. He left the practice of medicine to become editor of the Springfield Republican, which position he held from 1849 to 1866. He was editor of Scribner's Monthly, later the Century Magazine, 1870–81. Among his prose works are: "Life of Abraham Lincoln;" "Letters to the Young;" "Plain Talks on Familiar Subjects;" "Gold Foil;" and the novels "Arthur Bonnicastle," "Seven Oaks," and "Nicholas Minturn." His poems are published under the titles: "Bitter-Sweet;" "Kathrina;" "The Mistress of the Manse;" "Garnered Sheaves;" and "The Puritan's Guest." Part of his poems were written under the pseudonym "Timothy Titcomb."—WARNER, CHARLES DUDLEY, ed. 1897, *Library of the World's Best Literature, Biographical Dictionary*, vol. XXIX, p. 270.

PERSONAL

A good, brave man, a blameless man,
  He lived and wrought among us;
The truth he taught, the tales he told,
  The heart-songs that he sung us,
All shine with white sincerity,
  All thrill with strong conviction;
His words were seeds of honest deeds,
  His life a benediction.

—GLADDEN, WASHINGTON, 1881, *Hail and Farewell, Century Magazine*, vol. 23, p. 307.

Doctor Holland was at his post till the very last. His last day was a busy one, and one full of interest and pleasure. He was writing his editorials; he was talking over new projects; he had time to go out to see some beautiful stained-glass windows, whose rich and exquisite tones gave him the greatest delight; but especially the day was devoted by him to thoughts of our late President, whom he knew personally. . . . Doctor Holland was engaged that day in writing an editorial (which remains unfinished) on poverty as a means of developing character; and his illustrations were taken from the lives of Lincoln and Garfield. While writing this a book was handed to him, entitled "Garfield's Words." For an hour or so he pored over its pages, reading aloud to one of his associates the passages that struck him as most telling. He laughed his approval at one bit after another of sententious humor; his voice trembled at every passage made pathetic by the President's tragic fate.—SMITH, ROSWELL, 1881, *Topics of the Time, Century Magazine*, vol. 23, p. 314.

Doctor Holland was a man of dignified and impressive presence; he had something of that talent for affairs which is indispensable to the journalist, but he was also a man of rare simplicity and transparency. He often showed his inmost thoughts to strangers, and sometimes cast the pearls of his confidence before swine who turned upon him. He loved approbation and he craved affection.—EGGLESTON, EDWARD, 1881, *Josiah Gilbert Holland, Century Magazine*, vol. 23, p. 167.

So Heaven was kind and gave him naught to
  grieve.
Among his loved he woke at morn from rest,—
One smile—one pang—and gained betimes his
  leave,
Ere Strength had lost its use, or Life its zest.

—STEDMAN, EDMUND CLARENCE, 1881, *J. G. H., Century Magazine*, vol. 23, p. 307.

Dear friend, who lovedst well this pleasant life!
One year ago it is this very day
Since thou didst take thy uncompanioned way
Into the silent land, from out the strife
And joyful tumult of the world. The knife
Wherewith that sorrow smote us, still doth stay,
And we, to whom thou daily didst betray
Thy gentle soul, with faith and worship rife,
Love thee not less but more, —as time doth go
And we too hasten toward that land unknown
Where those most dear are gathering one by one.
The power divine that here did touch thy heart,—
Hath this withdrawn from thee, where now
  thou art?
Would thou indeed couldst tell what thou dost
  know.

—GILDER, RICHARD WATSON, 1882, *To a Departed Friend, Lyrics and Other Poems*, p. 103.

Dr. Holland took the contemptuous treatment of the critics much more to heart than Mr. Roe apparently did; and the epithet, "The American Tupper" (invented, if I remember rightly, by the New York "Sun"), rankled in his gentle mind. Even though the sale of his books ran up into hundreds of thousands, the tolerant patronage or undisguised sneer of the reviewer remained the drop of gall in the cup of his happiness.

—Boyesen, Hjalmar Hjorth, 1893, *American Literary Criticism and its Value*, The Forum, vol. 15, p. 462.

Dr. Holland personally belonged to that class of persons "whose souls by nature sit on thrones," no matter by what degree of poverty or of misfortune obscured. There was not a particle of arrogance in him, but it never occurred to him that he was not the peer in respectability of any man, and in one of his books, where a discussion is going on as to the relative shades of blueness in the blood of certain families, he goes right to the heart of the matter by making the speaker say, "God makes new Adams every day." Certainly He makes some men with such an irrepressible bent toward this or that line of work, that they cannot escape this destiny of their faculties. J. G. Holland was one of these, although it took till he was thirty years old for him to make sure of his work and place in the world—to fulfil his mission and deliver his message—with what indefatigable faithfulness wrought out and delivered, let his life-story tell; for it may as well be said, first as last, that no matter what literary form—poem, story, essay—his writings took, he was essentially a preacher, and ever and always an expounder of those things that make for righteousness. If ever his sad-hearted mother had a dream for him, it was that he might be a minister; and when she once expressed a regret that her wish had not been granted, he pointed out the larger sphere of influence given him in the newspaper, though he hardly thought she was convinced.—Plunkett, Mrs. H. M., 1894, *Josiah Gilbert Holland.*

GENERAL

These "Letters" first appeared in the "Republican," under the signature of "Timothy Titcomb," and attracted universal attention for their beauty of style, purity of English, and sound common sense. The advice contained in them is excellent, entirely practical, sufficiently minute, and eminently judicious,—intended to make, not angels, but useful and happy men and women; and they richly deserve all the popularity they have received.—Cleveland, Charles D., 1859, *A Compendium of American Literature*, p. 726.

We could easily show that "Bitter-Sweet" was not this and that and t'other, but, after all said and done, it would remain an obstinately charming little book. It is not free from faults of taste, nor from a certain commonplaceness of metre; but Mr. Holland always saves himself in some expression so simply poetical, some image so fresh and natural, the harvest of his own heart and eye, that we are ready to forgive him all faults in our thankfulness at finding the soul of Theocritus transmigrated into the body of a Yankee. It would seem the simplest thing in the world to be able to help yourself to what lies all around you ready to your hand; but writers of verse commonly find it a difficult, if not impossible, thing to do. Conscious that a certain remoteness from ordinary life is essential in poetry, they aim at it by laying their scenes far away in time, and taking their images from far away in space—thus contriving to be foreign at once to their century and their country. Such self-made exiles and aliens are never repatriated by posterity. It is only here and there that a man is found like Hawthorne, Judd, and Mr. Holland, who discovers or instinctively feels that this remoteness is attained and attainable only by lifting up and transfiguring the ordinary and familiar with the *mirage* of the ideal. We mean it as very high praise when we say that "Bitter-Sweet" is one of the few books that have found the secret of drawing up and assimilating the juices of this New World of ours. —Lowell, James Russell, 1859, *Reviews and Literary Notices*, Atlantic Monthly, vol. 3, p. 652.

It is a little difficult to estimate rightly and fairly the author whose books and moral influence have given us occasion for this article. Like a true American, he has tried a good many departments of authorship. We may say of him what Johnson wrote of one of his own, and the world's, friends, *Nullum fere, scribendi genus non tetigit;* and if he has not done all things equally well, he has done many things excellently. Being a journalist, he began, it would seem, with historical sketches in his own journal, and afterward made them into an "outline history;" from history he went into the adjoining field of romance; next climbed the tempting hill of poesy; and latterly has been gathering—upon this hill elsewhere—and discoursing upon samples and principles of morals. . . . That Dr. Holland has imagination in a high degree is shown, not only by many passages in which objects, persons, and scenes are wonderfully well thrown out, but by the whole book, "Bitter-Sweet." That he has good power of reasoning, and a very good command of language and sense of the strength of words, he evinces abundantly. That he has an honest and good purpose, and is in earnest about it, he everywhere proves to us thoroughly. He writes honestly and purely, and he does not write in general, but in the plainest and strongest way rebukes particular vices; and that not like one who willingly meddles with forbidden subjects, but like one who honestly feels that men and women ought to be rebuked for wickedness known to be too common, and ought to be shamed out of it, even at the risk of shocking some false delicacy. . . . Throughout his books we everywhere find fresh and manly sense and morals. . . . "Bitter-Sweet" we consider by far his best-wrought novel, as well as his most imaginative book.—LOWELL, ROBERT TRAILL SPENCE, 1862, *Dr. Holland, North American Review, vol. 95, pp. 88, 93, 94, 96.*

As a prose writer, Dr. Holland is admitted by all to be one of our best. As a poet, he has received much adverse, and some unkind criticism. His "Kathrina" doubtless is open to criticism. Yet it is idle to deny to this poem great and distinguishing merit. The author, at all events, may console himself with the fact, that while the critics flout, the people read and buy. No American poem, with the single exception of Longfellow's Hiawatha, has had such tangible evidences of popularity.—HART, JOHN S., 1872, *A Manual of American Literature, p. 343.*

His novels are his best works, artistically considered. "The Bay Path" is a story of the first settlement of the Connecticut Valley, and the characters and events are mainly historical. The author makes no attempt to reproduce the ancient forms of speech, but he understands well and has faithfully represented the ideas and manners of the time. " Miss Gilbert's Career" has many good points. It is a novel of modern times, and is as new, and near, and devoid of romantic associations, as a pine-shingled house in the factory village it depicts. But its principal figures are exhibited with a certain stereoscope fidelity, and the characteristic virtues and meanness of a Yankee neighborhood are naturally developed in the course of its events. — UNDERWOOD, FRANCIS H., 1872, *A Hand-book of English Literature, American Authors, p. 453.*

He was preëminently a moralist. Whether he wrote poetry or prose, letters or essays, novels or editorials, the moral purpose never forsook him. It is by this that he is to be judged. His art was never merely for art's sake, but it served to give wings to his instructions.—EGGLESTON, EDWARD, 1881, *Josiah Gilbert Holland, Century Magazine, vol. 23, p. 167.*

He was a man of good gifts, consecrated by a great motive. Of clear and vigorous intellect, he was best of all, like Noah of old, a preacher of righteousness, and one of rare power and singular sweetness. Writing of plain and homely themes, he never touched one of them that he did not ennoble; and over all that he wrote there breathed the spirit of one who loved God, and who, therefore, like Ben Adhem, "loved his fellow-man." His writings found an acceptance which has often puzzled the critics, and confounded the literary prophets. But their secret was not far to seek. They helped men. They lifted them up. They rebuked meanness. They encouraged all noble aspirations. They were always a word for "God and the right," spoken with courage, but spoken most of all in a tone of manly and brotherly sympathy that could not be misunderstood.—POTTER, HENRY C., 1881, *Sermon Preached Oct. 16; Topics of the Time, Century Magazine, vol. 23, p. 316.*

The common heart of the people always kept time to his music. And his wide influence was on the right side. Practical wisdom, broad Christian charity, earnest patriotism, and crystal purity marked his writings.—WHITTIER, ·JOHN GREENLEAF, 1881, *Communications, Oct. 24; Century Magazine, vol. 23, p. 471.*

It was not merely for the sake of telling a pleasant story, not merely for the sake of describing real life, that he wrote, but also with the ulterior purpose of exposing and redressing some wrongs, of helping forward some good causes, of making social life better than it is. . . . It is enough to say that he understood what he was about, when he wrote novels with a purpose. And it must be admitted by everybody that his purposes were high and pure; that the blows he struck with this good weapon of fiction were telling blows. . . . We may not agree with him in all the lessons that he seeks to teach in these poems; I own that I do not; but we cannot deny the lofty purpose and the earnest thought that pulsate through them all. Whatever we may say of their philosophy, the spirit that breathes through them is large and free.—GLADDEN, WASHINGTON, 1881, *Topics of the Time, Century Magazine, vol.* 23, *p.* 315.

It was the special distinction of Doctor Holland that he used the newspaper's power to serve the preacher's purpose. . . . He used the daily or the monthly journal to purify and sweeten the fountains of personal and family life. He spoke continually the word that should inspire young men to be pure, and women to be strong; the word that shed poetry over the home life; the word that threw on every interest the light of conscience and the warmth of moral feeling. . . . He was faithful to the light that was in him; he was open-eyed and sensitive to the conditions of the time; he met the opportunity as it offered. And thus he did the work that was given him to do. He did a work large in itself; large in the impress it left on two great periodicals; large as an omen of the nobler work to be done by the press, an instance of the new and greater channels through which God fulfills his purposes.—MERRIAM, GEORGE S., 1881, *Topics of the Time, Century Magazine, vol.* 23, *p.* 313.

He is at once the least poetical and one of the most popular of all the American poets. He has the peculiar faculty of writing for the people what the people want to read and can understand.—BALDWIN, JAMES, 1882, *English Literature and Literary Criticism, Poetry, p.* 535.

None of our writers has better understood the average national heart.—RICHARDSON, CHARLES F., 1888, *American Literature,* 1607–1885, *vol.* II, *p.* 227.

Holland's writings fall naturally into three classes: poems, novels, and essays and papers. His fame as a poet depends on his long narrative poems, "Bitter Sweet" and "Kathrina," which, despite their moralizing tendencies and their manifest lack of poetic inspiration, were at one time highly popular with the lovers of the sentimental. . . . Holland was not a great literary artist and he has not portrayed in enduring colors this life which he understood. He was first of all a moralist. He was at his best in his lay sermons to the young and in his papers on familiar subjects. The didactic and the moralizing are in everything he wrote, even in his poems and novels. His Timothy Titcomb letters are excellent. Their style is plain and homely, their subjects are often commonplace, yet they set true ideals before the reader in such an earnest, honest way that they can hardly fail to impress and benefit.— PATTEE, FRED LEWIS, 1896, *A History of American Literature, p.* 455.

The people ["Bitter Sweet"] were natural flesh and blood creatures, of a more cultured class, perhaps, than those described in "Snow-Bound." The verse is pure and lucid, and the underlying doctrine that evil is an essential part of the divine plan, clearly and even ostentatiously set forth. The hero, it is true is a prig, whose skysoaring instincts would not descend to explanation which would have relieved his devoted wife of much of her suffering. Certain parts also might have been omitted without in the least affecting the unity of the work. But prolixity had so long been the bane of our minor singers that it might well be condoned in this instance where there was so much of merit. . . . The promise indicated in "Bitter-Sweet" was not fulfilled in the author's later works. "Kathrina," even more than its predecessor, is overweighted with didacticism. To that large class whose tastes are gratified with a liberal mixture of Tupperism, it proved a revelation, as shown by the immense sale. The impression after reading it is one of mild wonder that the author should venture to consume several thousand lines of blank verse to prove that religion is essential to happiness. All through "Bitter-Sweet" and "Kathrina" the intent is disagreeably obstrusive to write a moral poem. The diction is frequently disfigured with mannerisms, petty affectations, and strained conceits. . . . In "The Mistress of the Manse" there are fewer offences against good taste, and less a tendency to sermonizing. It is decidedly among the best narrative poems of the Civil War. A tender, grave, and patriotic spirit characterizes the work throughout. It failed of the popular success attained by the earlier poems, perhaps because there was not enough of preaching to satisfy the poet's former admirers, and not enough of poetry to please those of a more critical judgment. —ONDERDONK, JAMES L., 1899–1901, *History of American Verse, pp.* 204, 205.

John Gorham Palfrey
1796–1881

A Unitarian clergyman in Cambridge, professor of sacred literature in Harvard University, 1831–37, subsequently a member of Congress and postmaster of Boston, 1861–67. His literary reputation rests upon his "History of New England," a painstaking, accurate work, but not especially attractive in style, and marred by want of perspective. Other works by him are, "Lectures on the Jewish Scriptures;" "The Relation between Judaism and Christianity."—ADAMS, OSCAR FAY, 1897, *A Dictionary of American Authors*, p. 281.

PERSONAL

A man of singular honesty of purpose and conscientiousness of action, a thoroughly trained theologian, he ripened and enlarged the somewhat partial knowledge of mankind and their motives which falls to the lot of a clergyman by the experience of active politics and the training of practical statesmanship. Needing office neither as an addition of emolument nor of dignity, his interest in politics was the result of moral convictions, and not of personal ambition. The loss of his seat in Congress, while it was none to himself, was an irreparable one for Massachusetts, to which his integrity, his learning, and his eloquence were at once a service and an honor.—LOWELL, JAMES RUSSELL, 1865, *Palfrey's History of New England*, North American Review, vol. 100, p. 173.

Doctor Palfrey was almost distinctly of the Brahminical caste, and was long an eminent Unitarian Minister, but at the time I began to know him he had long quitted the pulpit. He was then so far a civic or public character as to be postmaster at Boston, but his officiality was probably so little in keeping with his nature that it was like a return to his truer self when he ceased to hold the place, and gave his time altogether to his history. . . . He was refined in the essential gentleness of his heart without being refined away; he kept the faith of her Puritan tradition though he no longer kept the Puritan faith. And his defence of the Puritan severity with the witches and Quakers was as impartial as it was efficient in positing the Puritans as of their time, and rather better and not worse than other people of the same time. He was himself a most tolerant man, and his tolerace was never weak or fond; it stopped well short of condoning error, which he condemned when he preferred to leave it to its own punishment. Personally he was without any flavor of harshness; his mind was as gentle as his manner, which was one of the gentlest I have ever known.—HOWELLS, WILLIAM DEAN, 1900, *Some Literary Memories of Cambridge*, Harper's Magazine, vol. 101, p. 838.

HISTORY OF NEW ENGLAND.
1859–64

Dr. Palfrey manifests rare gifts as an historian. First of all, he loves his subject. A New England man as thoroughly in character, as veritably by right of birth, he inherits the principles which presided in the inception of our republican institutions,—the fearless integrity, the persistent adherence to the right, the uncompromising independence, the tenacity of honest purpose, the ardent love of liberty, which were the germinal principles of these Northeastern Colonies, and which have been transplanted with our emigrant population through the entire breadth of our continent. His conscientious and painstaking industry was needed, not so much for the narration of actual events on this side of the ocean, as for the often obscure and difficult investigation of their Transatlantic causes and relations. His candor is signally conspicuous in dealing with matters in which varying opinions and interests have transmitted sectional and party strifes, not indeed in the form of animosity, but of fixed historical prejudice, to the descendants of the principal actors. His minuteness of narration leaves at no point a reasonable curiosity unsatisfied; and yet he has the rare art of multiplying details without magnifying them, so that the salient topics of interest are never overlaid or dwarfed by the pressure of collateral and subsidiary material. . . . The text presents an unbroken flow of easy narrative; while in the copious notes all points of controversy are elaborately discussed, discrepancies between different authorities carefully noted, and full references given.—PEABODY, ANDREW P., 1859, *Palfrey's History of New England*, North American Review, vol. 88, p. 463.

Dr. Palfrey writes, unmistakably, as a man proud of his Massachusetts lineage. He honors the men whose enterprise, constancy, persistency, and wise skill in laying foundations have, in his view, approved their methods and justified them, even where they are most exposed to a severe judgment. He wishes to tell their story as they would wish to have it told. They stand by his side as he reads their records, and supply him with a running comment as to meaning and intention. Thus he is helped to put their own construction on their own deeds,—to set their acts in the light of their motives, to give them credit for all the good that was in their purposes, and to ascribe their mistakes and errors to a limitation of their views, or to well-founded apprehensions of evil which they had reason to dread. Under such pilotage, the passengers, at least, would be safe, when their ship fell upon a place where two seas met.—ELLIS, GEORGE EDWARD, 1859, *Palfrey's and Arnold's Histories, Atlantic Monthly,* vol. 3, p. 447.

For a number of years Dr. Palfrey has been laboriously engaged upon "A History of New England," of which the first volume appeared early in December, 1858, and of which it is praise enough to say that it comes up fully to the high expectations that were entertained of it. Evincing a noble and hearty appreciation of the early settlers of New England, guided by cool, impartial reason, and exhibiting throughout extensive research and a careful collation of facts, he has given us a work which will doubtless supersede all others upon the same subject, and be the established or classical history of that portion of our country.—CLEVELAND, CHARLES D., 1859, *A Compendium of American Literature,* p. 447.

It is to the praise of his work that its merit lies more in its tone of thought and its weight of opinion, than in pictorial effects. Brilliancy is cheap; but trustworthiness of thought, and evenness of judgment, are not to be had at every booth. Dr. Palfrey combines in the temper of his mind and the variety of his experience some quite peculiar qualifications for the task he has undertaken. . . . In the maturity of his powers, he devoted himself to the composition of the History which he has now brought to the end of its third volume, and to the beginning of a new period. It is little to say that his work is the only one of its kind. He has done it so well, that it is likely to remain so. With none of that glitter of style and epigrammatic point of expression which please more than they enlighten, and tickle when they should instruct, there is a gravity and precision of thought, a sober dignity of expression, an equanimity of judgment, and a clear apprehension of characters and events, which give us the very truth of things as they are, and not as either he or his reader might wish them to be.—LOWELL, JAMES RUSSELL, 1865, *Palfrey's History of New England, North American Review,* vol. 100, p. 173.

The "History of New England," by John G. Palfrey, is distinguished by thoroughness of investigation, fairness of judgment, and clearness and temperance of style. It is one of the ablest contributions as yet made to our colonial history.—WHIPPLE, EDWIN PERCY, 1876–86, *American Literature and Other Papers, ed. Whittier,* p. 93.

Not only the most satisfactory history of New England we have, but one of the most admirable historical works ever produced in America. It shows great learning, industrious research, comprehensive views, critical acumen, and sound judgment. In addition to these great qualities, it possesses the charm of having been written in a graceful and agreeable style.—ADAMS, CHARLES KENDALL, 1882, *A Manual of Historical Literature,* p. 547.

Palfrey, plain, matter-of-fact, straightforward, interests us from the start. The "History of New England," as he prepared it, could be made the basis of a compendious work for popular reading, and also could win the applause of Mr. Lowell and other critics of high standing. Palfrey, indeed, though read by a general public, seems to me an authors' author in some such sense, *mutatis mutandis,* as Landor was a poets' poet. He wrote of a subject familiar to at least twenty scholars of high standing, living in his own community, and within reach of the authorities upon which he relied; yet the trustworthiness of his work was not impeached in important particulars. Scholarly, accurate, and terse, he made his history, in itself, almost an original authority. His field was narrower than Bancroft's, but broader and more diversified than those covered by single works of Prescott or Motley; this fact, perhaps, accounts for the comparative obscurity of his name, as set beside those of other American historians of the first rank. One thinks of Palfrey, after all, as he would think of a nineteenth-century Thomas Prince or William Stith. But that he is an historian of an honorable rank in his country's literature, can hardly be doubted. In ability of several kinds he surpasses Hildreth, and it does not seem rash to suppose that the passage of years will emphasize the fact. Like Hildreth, he left behind plenty of obscure books, of no lasting value; but the greater achievement, though it cannot redeem the lesser from their fate, will at least be prominent in itself.—RICHARDSON, CHARLES F., 1887, *American Literature, 1607-1885*, vol. I, p. 477.

Probably the best single large piece of work that has been done in America on any part of our colonial period. . . . If Dr. Palfrey was not a man of great insight into popular movements, and was too constant an apologist of the rulers of New England, his book was nevertheless admirable on account of his extensive knowledge of sources, his industry, clearness, accuracy, and skill in narration. Among its many excellences, one which deserves particular notice is the degree of attention which it bestows upon the history of England itself during the Puritan era, and upon the mutual influence of Old England and New England during that period of exceptionally close sympathy and connection. — JAMESON, JOHN FRANKLIN, 1891, *The History of Historical Writing in America*, pp. 123, 124.

GENERAL

For ourselves, we have perused them ["Sermons"] with satisfaction and thankfulness to the author. The careless, and we know not but we should add, the critical reader, will scarcely help complaining of the occasional length of the sentences, and sometimes, it must be confessed, of an involved expression, leaving him in doubt of a meaning, which upon search, he may find too good and full to be lost or obscured. But with this exception, he will not fail to profit from the discriminating, weighty, and instructive manner of the preacher; from the tone of deep seriousness, moreover, and not seldom the eloquence, with which his various topics are enforced.—PARKMAN, F., 1834, *Professor Palfrey's Sermons, Christian Examiner*, vol. 16, p. 394.

He has a reputation for scholarship; and many of the articles which are attributed to his pen evince that this reputation is well based, so far as the common notion of scholarship extends. For the rest, he seems to dwell altogether within the narrow world of his *own* conceptions; imprisoning them by the very barrier which he has erected against the conceptions of others.—POE, EDGAR ALLAN, 1841, *A Chapter of Autography, Works*, ed. Stedman and Woodberry, vol. IX, p. 213.

Without being dazzled by excessive admiration of the wisdom or the learning of the modern continental school of critics, and as little disposed as most persons to rate very highly that show of erudition, which consists in incumbering one's pages with quotations and references, we still think that more should have been done to make us acquainted with the history and present state of discussion on many of the moot points here brought under review. . . . It is a valuable and opportune contribution to the theological literature of the country, and when completed will take precedence, we doubt not, of every other general treatise on the subject, in English, which has as yet appeared.—WALKER, J., 1838, *Dr. Palfrey on the Jewish Scriptures, Christian Examiner*, vol. 25, p. 128.

Dr. Palfrey's style is clear and exact; if it is considered as lacking in vivacity, it shows conscientious care, and is free from the verbiage that sometimes passes for rhetorical ornament. — UNDERWOOD, FRANCIS H., 1872, *A Hand-Book of English Literature, American Authors*, p. 168.

His "Academical Lectures" remain as a palpable landmark in the progress of American rationalism.—WHIPPLE, EDWIN PERCY, 1876-86, *American Literature and Other Papers*, ed. Whittier, p. 59.

James Thomas Fields
1816-1881

An American publisher and author; born in Portsmouth, N. H., Dec. 31, 1816; died in Boston, Mass., April 24, 1881. The various publishing firms of which he was partner, with Ticknor, Osgood and others, were of the first rank. He edited the Atlantic Monthly in 1862–70; and was an acceptable lecturer on literary subjects and authors. He published: "Poems"(1849); "A Few Verses for a Few Friends" (1858); "Yesterdays with Authors" (1872); "Hawthorne" (1875); "Old Acquaintance: Barry Cornwall and Some of his Friends" (1875); "In and Out of Doors with Dickens" (1876); "Underbrush" (1881), essays; "Ballads and Other Verses" (1881); and (with Edwin P. Whipple) edited "The Family Library of British Poetry" (1878).— WARNER, CHARLES DUDLEY, ed. 1897, *Library of the World's Best Literature, Biographical Dictionary*, vol. XXIX, p. 187.

PERSONAL

What is there to gloss or shun?
Save with kindly voices none
Speak thy name beneath the sun.
Safe thou art on every side,
Friendship nothing finds to hide,
Love's demand is satisfied.
Over manly strength and worth,
At thy desk of toil, or hearth,
Played the lambent light of mirth,—
Mirth that lit, but never burned;
All thy blame to pity turned;
Hatred thou hadst never learned.
Every harsh and vexing thing
At thy home-fire lost its sting;
Where thou wast was always spring.
—WHITTIER, JOHN GREENLEAF, 1881, *In Memory, J. T. F.*

I have just heard of the sudden death of my friend Mr. Fields, . . . and now we all ask, What has he left of all his life's accumulations? Houses, lands, pictures, literary reputation, all that gone—dreams, things of the past. Had he any treasure laid up in Heaven? I think from my remembrance of him that *he had just what Jesus meant by treasure laid up in Heaven*. He had a habit of quiet benevolence; he did habitually and quietly more good to everybody he had to do with than common. He favored with all his powers charitable work, and such habits as these are, I think, what Christ meant by laying up treasure in Heaven. . . . I find many traces of childlike faith in his last pieces. . . . When a friend is gone to the great hereafter how glad we are that he *did* believe.—STOWE, HARRIET BEECHER, 1881, *Letter to Charles Stowe, Life and Letters*, ed. Fields, p. 380.

The conversation of Fields had, even in his boyhood, the two charms of friendliness and inventiveness. The audacities of his humor spared neither solemn respectabilities nor accredited reputations; yet in his intercourse with his friends his wildest freaks of satire never inflicted a wound. His sensitive regard for the feelings of those with whom he mingled was a marvel of that tact which is the offspring of good nature as well as good sense. When he raised a laugh at the expense of one of his companions, the laugh was always heartily enjoyed and participated in by the object of his mirth; for, indulging to the top of his bent in every variety of witty mischief, he had not in his disposition the least alloy of witty malice.— WHIPPLE, EDWIN PERCY, 1881, *Recollections of James T. Fields, Atlantic Monthly*, vol. 48, p. 254.

Into the darkest hour of my life he came giving light and hope. I can never forget it. Turning to him first because I found help in him—how much else I found! Only those who knew him nearly knew his goodness and his greatness.—ALDEN, HENRY MILLS, 1881, *In Memory of James T. Fields, Biographical Notes and Personal Sketches*, ed. Mrs. Fields, p. 265.

How much better he left this world than he found it! How many a heart was made lighter, happier, each year of his manhood all men know. This vast West world is a great deal better and wiser because he has been. Think how few can have this said of us when all is over, work with all endeavor as we may! To me Mr. Fields's life seemed the most rounded and perfect of all men's I ever met. Very beautiful he seemed to me in soul and body, and people loved him truly.—MILLER, JOAQUIN, 1881, *In Memory of James T. Fields, Biographical Notes and Personal Sketches*, ed. Mrs. Fields, p. 267.

I shall feel that I was under great obligations to him at a most important time in my life. He was the best and most sympathetic literary counselor I ever had; and I had much opportunity to observe his constant kindnesses to others.—HIGGINSON, THOMAS WENTWORTH, 1881, *In Memory of James T. Fields, Biographical Notes and Personal Sketches*, ed. Mrs. Fields, p. 266.

How many writers know, as I have known, his value as a literary counselor and friend! His mind was as hospitable as his roof, which has accepted famous visitors and quiet friends alike as if it had been their own. From a very early period in my own life of authorship, I have looked to Mr. Fields as one who would be sure to take an interest in whatever I wrote, to let me know all that he could learn about my writings which would please and encourage me, and keep me in heart for new efforts. And what I can say for myself many and many another can say with equal truth. Very rarely, if ever, has a publisher enjoyed the confidence and friendship of so wide and various a circle of authors. And so when he came to give the time to authorship, which had always for many years been devoted to literature, he found a listening and reading public waiting for him and welcoming him.—HOLMES, OLIVER WENDELL, 1881, *In Memory of James T. Fields, Biographical Notes and Personal Sketches*, ed. Mrs. Fields, p. 262.

His *No* was as the refusal of Mount Washington to slide down into Casco Bay. I never met a man whose pivot, in a life that seemed to turn so easily, lay deeper in the cup. His good-will to men, his laughter-loving heart, his quaint and curious fancies, and his faculty for glassing all the lights and shadows of a company or a day, made it easy for those who did not know him wholly to imagine he was only what he seemed. He was a man with solemn and sacred deeps of conviction and character such as one seldom finds;—a man with "A correspondence fixed wi' heaven." The kindly and sunny heart was strong and sure as the pillars of the world. I have known no man in all my life I could tie to with a more absolute conviction that the rock and ring would hold, no matter about the strain.—COLLYER, ROBERT, 1882, *James T. Fields, The Dial*, vol. 2, p. 204.

My individual debt to Mr. Fields, in respect to my own work, is one which I cannot and would not omit to acknowledge. He often helped me about my titles, and one of the best ever given to any book of mine—"Men, Women, and Ghosts"—was of his creation. In his fine literary judgment I had great confidence, and would have accepted almost any criticism from him trustfully. . . . His was a rich life, and his a rare home. There has been no other in America quite like it. Those of us who received its hospitality recall its inspiration among the treasures of our lives. We think of the peaceful library into which the sunset over the Charles looked delicately, while the "best things" of thought were given and taken by the finest and strongest minds of the day in a kind of electric interplay, which makes by contrast a pale affair of the word conversation as we are apt to use it. We recall the quiet guest-chamber, apart from the noise of the street, and lifted far above the river; that room opulent and subtle with the astral shapes of past occupants,—Longfellow, Whittier, Dickens, Thackeray, Mrs. Stowe, Kingsley, and the rest of their high order,—and always resounding softly to the fine ear with the departed tread of Hawthorne, who used to pace the floor on sleepless nights. We remember the separation from paltriness, and from superficial adjustments, which that scholarly and gentle atmosphere commanded. We remember the master of their abode of thought and graciousness, as "Dead, he lay among his books;" and wish that we had it in our power to portray him as he was.—PHELPS, ELIZABETH STUART, 1896, *Chapters from Life*, pp. 149, 151.

GENERAL

His writings are distinguished for a natural simplicity and elegance, and generally relate to rural or domestic subjects.—GRISWOLD, RUFUS WILMOT, 1842, *The Poets and Poetry of America*, p. 444.

The glimpses of private life ["Yesterday's with Authors"], the hints of conversation, and the numerous letters thus preserved, are exceedingly interesting, and Mr. Fields's introductions and narratives are written with excellent haste and judgment. The accounts of Hawthorne and Dickens, in particular, are more delightful than any elaborate biography would be. The letters of Miss Mitford, which conclude the volume, are of less real value, as the kind-hearted lady seems to have looked at everything American through a Claude Lorraine glass, and her constant gush of admiration and affection lessens the value of her opinions.—UNDERWOOD, FRANCIS H., 1872, *A Hand-Book of English Literature, American Authors*, p. 418.

In his few poems he shows a delicate fancy and a fine lyrical vein.—SARGENT, EPES, 1880–81, *Harper's Cyclopædia of British and American Poetry*, p. 748.

It is not as a literary man, but as a publisher, that Mr. Fields is likely to be remembered. As a lecturer, he was successful mainly because he had already created an audience which was ready and waiting to welcome him. In the same way, subjects were ready to his hand, and he had a gift of expression sufficient to meet the by no means lofty standard of ordinary lecture-audiences. As a publisher, he was one of the first men in this country to see what all successful publishers now recognize as a fact, that the great secret of success in the trade lies in playing the part of a benefactor to men of letters. It is only in the present century that this new type of publisher, of which Mr. Fields was a distinguished instance, has become common or even known. ... He was neither a scholar nor a genius, nor was he, as he seems himself to have thought, a humorist, although he had a keen enjoyment and appreciation of humor which brought him to the point of successful imitation; but he was in private life a thoroughly good companion — amusing, cheerful, vivacious, an excellent storyteller, with an immense fund of anecdote. He had, too, the invaluable art of making those with whom he was thrown as much at their ease as he was himself, being able to lead or follow in conversation.— SEDGWICK, A. G. 1881, *A Modern Publisher, The Nation*, vol. 33, pp. 514, 515.

My dear Mr. James Fields was noted for his goodness to authors, and to him I not only am indebted for numerous delightful letters, but also for treasured gifts of his own poems and essays, his charming "Yesterdays with Authors," and his" Letter to Leigh Hunt in Elysium," written in a style remarkably akin to the playful spirit of Leigh Hunt's own manner. — CLARKE, MARY COWDEN, 1896, *My Long Life*, p. 254.

Ralph Waldo Emerson
1803–1882

Born, in Boston, Mass. 25 May 1803. Educated at Boston Grammar School, 1811–15; Latin School, 1815–17. To Harvard University, 1817; graduated, 1821. Engaged in tuition. Kept school at Boston, 1822–25. Studied Theology in Cambridge Divinity School, 1825–28. Approbated to preach, 1826. Ordained, 11 March 1829 as joint pastor, with Rev. H. Ware, of Second Church, Boston; succeeded to Ware's position, 1830. Married Ellen Louisa Tucker, Sept. 1829. Resigned pastorate, 1832. Wife died, Feb. 1832. Tour in Europe, 1833; friendship with Carlyle begun. Returned to U. S. A., 1834; preached in New Bedford; and settled in Concord. Lectured on various subjects, 1835, 1836, 1837. Married Lidian Jackson, Sept. 1835. Finally adopted literary life. Frequently lectured. Symposium, or Transcendental Club, formed, 1836. Edited "The Dial," 1842 to April 1844. Lecturing tour in England, 1847–49. Edited "Massachusetts Quarterly Review" (3 vols.), 1847–50. Contrib. to "Atlantic Monthly," from its beginning in Nov. 1857. LL. D., Harvard, 1866; elected on Board of Overseers, 1867. Mental shock owing to partial destruction of house by fire, July 1872. To England and Egypt with daughter. Returned to Concord, 1873. Suffered from aphasia in later years. Died, at Concord, 27 April 1882. *Works:* "Right Hand of Fellowship to Rev. H. B. Goodwin," 1830; "Historical Discourse," 1835; "Nature" (anon.), 1836; (another edn., with "Lectures on the Times," 1844); "An Oration," (Dartmouth Coll.), 1838; "An Oration" (Phi Beta Kappa Soc.), 1838; (new edn. called "Man Thinking," 1844); "An Address" (Divinity Coll.), 1838; "The Method of Nature," 1841; "Essays, first series," 1841; "The Young American," 1844; "Essays, second series," 1844; "Man the Reformer," 1844; "Orations, Lectures, and Addresses," 1844; "An Address" (on Negro Emancipation), 1844; "Poems," 1847; "Essays, Lectures and Orations," 1848; "Miscellanies," 1849; "Representative Men," 1850; "Essays and Orations," 1853; "English Traits," 1856; "The Conduct of Life," 1860; "Orations, Lectures and Essays," 1866; "May-Day," 1867; "Society and Solitude," 1870; "Poetry and Criticism," 1874; "Power, Wealth, Illusions," (from "The Conduct of Life"), 1876; "Letters and Social Aims," 1876; "Culture, Behavior Beauty," (from "The Conduct of Life"), 1876; "Books, Art, Eloquence" (from "Society and Solitude"), 1877; "Success, Greatness, Immortality" (from "Society and Solitude," and "Letters and Social Aims"), 1877; "Love, Friendship, Domestic Life" (from "Essays" and "Society and Solitude"), 1877; "Fortune of the Republic," 1878; "The Preacher" (from "Unitarian Review"), 1880. *Collected Works:* "Complete Works" (2 vols.), 1866; "Prose Works" (2 vols.), 1870; "Correspondence with Carlyle" (2 vols.) 1883; "Complete Works" (Riverside edn., 11 vols.), 1883–84. He *edited:* Marchioness Ossoli's "Memoirs," 1852; Gladwin's translation of Sadi's "Gulistan," 1865; Plutarch's

RALPH WALDO EMERSON

Engraving by J. A. J. Wilcox.

HENRY WADSWORTH LONGFELLOW

From a Painting by C. P. R. Healey, 1862.

"Morals," 1870; Channing's "The Wanderer," 1871; "Parnassus," 1875; "The Hundred Greatest Men," 1879. *Life:* by Searle, 1855; by O. W. Holmes ("American Men of Letters" series), 1885; by Dr. Garnett ("Great Writers" series), 1887.—SHARP R. FARQUHARSON, 1897, *A Dictionary of English Authors,* p. 93.

PERSONAL

Our third happiness was the arrival of a certain young unknown friend, named Emerson, from Boston, in the United States, who turned aside so far from his British, French, and Italian travels to see me here! He had an introduction from Mill, and a Frenchman (Baron d'Eichtal's nephew) whom John knew at Rome. Of course we could do no other than welcome him; the rather as he seemed to be one of the most lovable creatures in himself we had ever looked on. He stayed till next day with us, and talked and heard talk to his heart's content, and left us all really sad to part with him. Jane says it is the first journey since Noah's Deluge undertaken to Craigenputtock for such a purpose. In any case, we had a cheerful day from it, and ought to be thankful.—CARLYLE, THOMAS, 1833, *Letter to his Mother, Aug. 26; The Correspondence of Carlyle and Emerson,* ed. Norton, vol. I, p. 4.

Proceeded to Cambridge, to hear the valedictory sermon by Mr. Emerson. In this he surpassed himself as much as he surpasses others in the general way. I shall give no abstract. So beautiful, so just, so true, and terribly sublime was his picture of the faults of the Church in its present position. My soul is roused, and this week I shall write the long-meditated sermons on the state of the Church and the duties of these times.—PARKER, THEODORE, 1838, *Journal, July* 15; *Life and Correspondence,* ed. Weiss, vol. I, p. 113.

I occupy, or *improve,* as we Yankees say, two acres only of God's earth; on one which is my house, my kitchen-garden, my orchard of thirty young trees, my empty barn. My house is now a very good one for comfort, and abounding in room. Besides my house, I have, I believe, $22,000, whose income in ordinary years is six per cent. I have no other tithe or glebe except the income of my winter lectures, which was last winter $800. Well, with this income, here at home, I am a rich man. I stay at home and go abroad at my own instance. I have food, warmth, leisure, books, friends. Go away from home, I am rich no longer. I never have a dollar to spend on a fancy. As no wise man, I suppose, ever was rich in the sense of *freedom to spend,* because of the inundation of claims, so neither am I, who am not wise. But at home, I am rich,—rich enough for ten brothers. My wife Lidian is an incarnation of Christianity,—I call her Asia,—and keeps my philosophy from Antinomianism; my mother, whitest, mildest, most conservative of ladies, whose only exception to her universal preference for old things is her son; my boy, a piece of love and sunshine, well worth my watching from morning to night;—these, and three domestic women, who cook and sew and run for us, make all my household. Here I sit and read and write, with very little system, and, as far as regards composition, with the most fragmentary result; paragraphs incompressible, each sentence an infinitely repellant particle. — EMERSON, RALPH WALDO, 1838, *To Carlyle, May* 10; *Correspondence of Carlyle and Emerson,* ed. Norton, vol. I, p. 160.

As a speaker in delivering his lectures, sermons, or discourses he is remarkable. His voice is good, his enunciation clear and distinct; his manner his own, but very striking. He is always self-possessed, and his strange fancies fall upon the ear in the most musical cadences. His voice is now low and then again high, like an Æolian harp; but this is natural, not affected, and I think anywhere before an educated audience he would be deemed a remarkable speaker. In person he is tall and graceful. Some people think him slightly mad (one of his brothers died insane, and the other brother had been insane before his death), others think him almost inspired. Old men are not prepared to receive or listen to or read his thoughts. The young of both classes think highly of him. He has a great influence over many of the young minds of my acquaintance, who always couple him with Carlyle. I think him neither mad nor inspired, but original, thoughtful, and peculiar, with his mind tinged with some habits of speculation that are less practical than beautiful, and with a fearless honesty that makes him speak what he thinks, counting little any worldly considerations. In other times he might have been a philosopher, or a reformer, but he would always have been tolerant and gentle, and he would have gone into uncomplaining exile if the powers that were bade him.—SUMNER, CHARLES, 1839, *Letter to Richard Monckton Milnes, March 2; Life of Lord Houghton, ed. Reid, vol.* II, *p.* 238.

It is the doom of the Christian Church to be always distracted with controversy, and where religion is most in honor, there the perversity of the human heart breeds the sharpest conflicts of the brain. The sentiment of religion is at this time, perhaps, more potent and prevailing in New England than in any other portion of the Christian world. For many years since the establishment of the theological school at Andover, the Calvinists and Unitarians have been battling with each other upon the Atonement, the Divinity of Jesus Christ, and the Trinity. This has now very much subsided; but other wandering of mind takes the place of that, and equally lets the wolf into the fold. A young man, named Ralph Waldo Emerson, a son of my once loved friend William Emerson, and a classmate of my lamented son George, after failing in the every-day avocations of a Unitarian preacher and school-master, starts a new doctrine of transcendentalism, declares all the old revelations superannuated and worn out, and announces the approach of new revelations and prophecies.—ADAMS, JOHN QUINCY, 1840, *Diary, Aug.* 2; *Memoirs, ed. Adams, vol.* X, *p.* 345.

A spiritual-looking boy in blue nankeen, . . . whose image more than any other's is still deeply stamped upon my mind as I then saw him and loved him, I knew not why, and thought him so angelic and remarkable.—DAWES, RUFUS, 1843, *Boyhood Memories, Boston Miscallany, Feb.*

Waldo Emerson called, and sat with me a short time, expressing his wish to make me acquainted with Mr. and Mrs. Ward, whom he extolled greatly. I liked him very, very much—the simplicity and kindness of his manner charmed me.—MACREADY, W. C., 1843, *Diary, Nov.* 16; *Reminiscences, ed. Pollock, p.* 535.

It was with a feeling of predetermined dislike that I had the curiosity to look at Emerson at Lord Northampton's, a fortnight ago; when, in an instant, all my dislike vanished. He has one of the most interesting countenances I ever beheld,—a combination of intelligence and sweetness that quite disarmed me. — ROBINSON, HENRY CRABB, 1848, *Letter to T. R., April* 22; *Diary, Reminiscences, and Correspondence.*

He came to Oxford just at the end of Lent term, and stayed three days. Everybody liked him, and as the orthodox had mostly never heard of him, they did not suspect him. He is the quietest, plainest, unobtrusivest man possible; will talk, but will rarely *discourse* to more than a single person, and wholly declines "roaring." He is very Yankee to look at, lank and sallow, and not quite without the twang; but his looks and voice are pleasing nevertheless, and give you the impression of perfect intellectual cultivation, as completely as would any great scientific man in England—Faraday or Owen, for instance, more in their ways perhaps than in that of Wordsworth or Carlyle. I have been with him a great deal; for he came over to Paris and was there a month, during which time we dined together daily: and since that I have seen him often in London, and finally here. One thing that struck everybody is that he is so much less Emersonian than his Essays. There is no dogmatism or arbitrariness or positiveness about him.—CLOUGH, ARTHUR HUGH, 1848; *Letter to T. Arnold, July* 16; *Prose Remains, ed. his Wife, p.* 137.

The first man I have ever seen.—ELIOT, GEORGE, 1848, *To Miss Sara Hennell, July; George Eliot's Life as related in her Letters and Journals, ed. Cross, vol.* I, *p.* 139.

The impregnator of a whole cycle of Boston mind, and the father of thousands lesser Emersons, he is the most unapproachably original and distinct monotype of our day. . . . . Emerson's voice is up to his reputation. It has a curious contradiction, which we tried in vain to analyze satisfactorily—an outwardly repellant and inwardly reverential mingling of qualities, which a musical composer would despair of blending into one. It bespeaks a life that is half contempt, half adoring recognition, and very little between. But it is noble, altogether. And what seems strange is to hear such a voice proceeding from such a body. It is a voice with shoulders in it which he has not—with lungs in it far larger than his—with a walk in it which the public never see—with a fist in it which his own hand never gave him the model for—and with a gentleman in it which his **parochial** and "bare-necessities-of-life" sort of exterior gives no other betrayal of. We can imagine nothing in nature—which seems, too, to have a type for everything like the want of correspondence between the Emerson that goes in at the eye and the Emerson that goes in at the ear. . . . The first twenty sentences, which we heard, betrayed one of the smaller levers of Emerson's power of style which we had not detected in reading him. He works with surprises. A man who should make a visit of charity, and, after expressing all proper sympathy, should bid adieu to the poor woman, leaving her very grateful for his kind feelings, but should suddenly return after shutting the door, and give her a guinea, would produce just the effect of his most electric sentences. You do not observe it in reading, because you withhold the emphasis till you come to the key-word. But, in delivery, his cadences tell you that the meaning is given, and the interest of the sentence all over, when—flash!—comes a single word or phrase, like lightning after listened-out thunder, and illuminates with astonishing vividness, the cloud you have striven to see into.—WILLIS, NATHANIEL PARKER, 1850, *Home Journal.*

I went for a moment into Emerson's study,—a large room, in which everything was simple, orderly, unstudied, comfortable. No refined feeling of beauty has converted the room into a temple, in which stand the forms of heroes of science and literature. Ornament is banished from the sanctuary of the stoic philosopher; the furniture is comfortable, but of a grave character, merely as the implements of usefulness; one large picture only is in the room, but this hangs there with a commanding power; it is a large oil-painting, a copy of Michael Angelo's glorious Parcæ, the goddess of fate.—BREMER, FREDERIKA, 1853, *Homes of the New World,* vol. II, p. 562.

Mr. Emerson's library is the room at the right of the door upon entering the house. It is a simple square room, not walled with books like the den of a literary grub, nor merely elegant like the ornamental retreat of a dilettante. The books are arranged upon plain shelves, not in architectural book-cases, and the room is hung with a few choice engravings of the greatest men. There was a fair copy of Michael Angelo's "Fates," which, properly enough, imparted that grave serenity to the ornament of the room which is always apparent in what is written there. It is the study of a scholar. All our author's published writings, the essays, orations, and poems, date from this room, as much as they date from any place or moment.—CURTIS, GEORGE WILLIAM, 1854, *Homes of American Authors.*

Last night I heard Emerson give a lecture. I pity the reporter who attempts to give it to the world. I began to listen with a determination to remember it in order, but it was without method, or order, or system. It was like a beam of light moving in the undulatory waves, meeting with occasional meteors in its path; it was exceedingly captivating. It surprised me that there was not only no commonplace thought, but there was no commonplace expression. If he quoted, he quoted from what we had not read; if he told an anecdote, it was one that had not reached us.—MITCHELL, MARIA, 1855, *Diary, Nov. 14; Life, Letters and Journals,* ed. Kendall, p. 45.

I have heard some great speakers and some accomplished orators, but never any that so moved and persuaded men as he. There is a kind of undertone in that rich baritone of his that sweeps our minds from their foothold into deeper waters with a drift we cannot and would not resist. And how artfully (for Emerson is a long-studied artist in these things) does the deliberative utterance, that seems waiting for the fit word, appear to admit us partners in the labor of thought and make us feel as if the glance of humor were a sudden suggestion, as if the perfect phrase lying written there on the desk were as unexpected to him as to us!—LOWELL, JAMES RUSSELL, 1868–71, *Emerson the Lecturer, My Study Windows,* p. 383.

Emerson seems an extraordinary mixture of genius and rusticity. Everybody seems amazed at his nomination for the Rectorship at Glasgow, and I have had to explain the position of affairs over and over again.—TULLOCH, JOHN, 1874, *Letter to Professor Baynes, April 26; A Memoir by Mrs. Oliphant,* p. 303.

One day [1834] there came into our pulpit the most gracious of mortals, with a face all benignity, who gave out the first hymn and made the first prayer as an angel might have read and prayed. Our choir was a pretty good one, but its best was coarse and discordant after Emerson's voice. I remember of the sermon only that it had an indefinite charm of simplicity and wisdom, with occasional illustrations from nature, which were about the most delicate and dainty things of the kind which I had ever heard. I could understand them, if not the fresh philosophical novelty of the discourse. — CONGDON, CHARLES T., 1879, *Reminiscences of a Journalist.*

Emerson entered—pale, thin, almost ethereal in countenance,—followed by his daughter, who sat beside him and watched every word that he uttered. On the whole, it was the same Emerson—he stumbled at a quotation as he always did; but his thoughts were such as only Emerson could have thought, and the sentences had the Emersonian pithiness. He made his frequent sentences very emphatic. It was impossible to see any thread of connection; but it always was so—the oracular sentences made the charm. — MITCHELL, MARIA, 1879, *Life, Letters and Journals*, ed. Kendall, p. 246.

Though tall, Mr. Emerson is still erect, and has the bright eye and calm grace of manner we knew when he was in England long years ago. In European eyes, his position among men of letters in America is as that of Carlyle among English writers; with the added quality, as I think, of greater braveness of thought and clearness of sympathy. The impression among many to whom I spoke in America, I found to be, that, while Carlyle inspires you to do something not clearly defined, when you have read Emerson you know what you have to do. However, Mr. Emerson would admit nothing that would challenge the completer merits of his illustrious friend at Chelsea. He showed me the later and earlier portraits of Carlyle, which he most cherished; made affectionate inquiries concerning him personally, and as to whether I knew of any thing that had proceeded from his pen which he had not in his library. Friends had told me that age seemed now a little to impair Mr. Emerson's memory, but I found his recollection of England accurate and full of detail.—HOLYOAKE, GEORGE JACOB, 1880, *Manchester Co-operative News.*

The translator of the "Upanishads," Moksha Mulara, sends greetings and best wishes to his American Guru, Amarasunu, on his seventy-seventh birthday.—MÜLLER FRIEDRICH MAX, 1880, *To Ralph Waldo Emerson, April 19; Life and Letters*, ed. his *Wife*, vol. II, p. 91.

RALPH WALDO EMERSON.
BORN IN BOSTON, MAY 25, 1803.
DIED IN CONCORD, APRIL 27, 1882.

The passive master lent his hand
To the vast soul that o'er him planned.
—INSCRIPTION ON GRAVE, 1882.

Emerson seemed to be on the lookout for whatever indicated genius and the best aspects of the inner life. In all his conversation his voice softened and played with a lingering charm over traits, and promises that make youth lovely. One felt the grace of his large, rich, amiable, childlike nature, utterly free from dogmatism and conceit. He carried this sympathy with youth to his grave.—POWERS, HORATIO NELSON, 1882, *A Day with Emerson, Lippincott's Magazine*, vol. 30, p. 478.

Although Emerson's garb was not rustic, it was plain, never smart, and, with his homely speech, and simple manners, he did not find the country-folk shy. The phenomena of the universe were going on in and around Concord, and Emerson kept up a good relation with the humblest purveyors of fact and experience. They were richly rewarded when the day came for Emerson to lecture in the town-hall, when many a farming villager saw his prosaic face risen to a star and shining in its constellation. What a day was that when Emerson's lecture came on! Remembering what Longfellow had told me about those sophisticated Bostonians whose faces were as extinguished lamps when listening to Emerson's early lectures, I have remarked the contrast when, with illumined countenances, his villagers were gathered before him at Concord. They knew his voice and followed him. All the sermons in the village churches for a year were not so well remembered as his sentences. It has seemed to me that Emerson never spoke so well elsewhere as to his Concord audience. When I first heard him there, he appeared, as he rose, to be the very type of the New England farmer, so plain in dress and so thoroughly standing on his own feet. Ere long he was unsheathed, and we were in the hall of Pericles. It was then that I first heard Emerson, and, while it is the most vivid experience of my life, I find it nearly impossible to transcribe it. I recall no gesture, only an occasional swaying forward of the body by the impulse of earnestness. Though nearly every word had been written, the manuscript did not hold his eye, which kept its magnetic play upon the audience.—CONWAY, MONCURE DANIEL, 1882, *Emerson at Home and Abroad*, p. 367.

The tall, spare figure, crowned by the small head carrying out, with its bird-like delicacy and poise, the aquiline effect of the beaked nose and piercing eyes. But no art can reproduce the luminous transparence, as it were the sun-accustomed gaze, of those unforgettable eagle eyes, nor the benign expression of smiling wisdom which in his old age transfigured his naturally rugged features. This expression revealed something brighter than resignation or even cheerfulness: it was the external sign of a spirit that had faced without shrinking the problem of existence, had suffered with the poet's two-fold suffering, as keenly through sympathy as through experience — and that none the less found only a pledge of joy in the beauty of life and the promise of death. . . . His coloring was Saxon; the effect of the inward light which tempered the austerity of his vigorously molded countenance was not a little enhanced by the freshness of complexion which he retained almost to the end, by the clear gray-blue of his eyes, and the dry, twinkling humor of his smile. His manner towards strangers, while extremely simple, was marked by an exquisite suavity and dignity which peremptorily, albeit tacitly, prohibited undue familiarity or conventional compliment.—LAZARUS, EMMA, 1882, *Emerson's Personality, Century Magazine*, vol. 24, p. 454.

The funeral ceremonies of Emerson were touching and eloquent, but nothing that was said or done on that occasion was nearly so impressive as was the face of the man himself as he lay in his coffin. . . . Few men can have had more noticeable peculiarities of face, figure, and demeanor than Emerson. Who that had once seen him could forget his appearance? Who ever spoke in his melodious measured tones? or whose smile so well expressed the self-command that does not deal in laughter? . . . His ordinary gait in walking was that of a man whose attention is so earnestly fixed upon something on the horizon that his body is conveyed forward rather by attraction than volition. It was progression in its simplest form, steady and uniform, but without the least embellishment of grace or elegance; and yet there was in it something indicative of the nature of the man, that made mere grace and elegance seem semi-civilized. In his lectures he stood before his audience in the unstudied pose of a New England farmer. He had no gestures; sufficient for him were the modulations of the voice, and the occasional lifting of the head and brightening of the visage. Nevertheless, few speakers comprehended the art and even the artifices of oratory better than he. Every word that passed his lips was so uttered and presented as to acquire its fullest force and meaning; and no one else could have delivered his lectures so effectively and captivatingly as he. The hand that he gave you in greeting was large and firm; it held yours for a few moments in a warm and steady clasp. There was no vigorous and impulsive handshaking, but the light of composed cordiality that emanated from his features made the more demonstrative forms of greeting seem vulgar, and inexpressive.— HAWTHORNE, JULIAN, 1882, *Ralph Waldo Emerson, Harper's Magazine*, vol. 65, pp. 278, 279.

It was a treat to attend the lectures of Mr. Emerson. He gave, in successive winter seasons, in Boston and other cities, beginning in 1834, for many years, some forty or fifty different lectures, and often whole courses. It was a special pleasure to listen to him year by year. At first, by his quaint, terse, and richly laden sentences, he seemed to perplex some of our wisest men. I sat, one evening, quite near the Hon. Jeremiah Mason—a man who could penetrate into the deepest depths of the law so long as the speaker or writer kept to the "dry light." But Emerson, I saw, sorely tried him. Two ladies by his side evidently enjoyed every word they heard. The next day Mr. Mason, it is said, being asked how he liked Emerson, replied: "Oh, I couldn't understand him at all. You must ask my daughters about him; they took it all in." . . . Sometimes, while listening to his lectures, they seemed almost extemporaneous. They struck one as full of thoughts entirely fresh and original, and in some passages as if the inspiration of the hour. There was sometimes, in the beginning of a sentence, a little hesitancy, as if he was waiting for a word or words to be given him for utterance at the moment. Still they must have been, we know, the result of long premeditation as well as extensive reading.—MUZZEY, A. B., 1882, *Reminiscences and Memorials of Men of the Revolution and Their Families*, pp. 344, 345.

Though I could never find in Emerson's effusions as a "Vates" so rich a vein of thought or so awakening a power as his most devoted readers were able to recognize, yet in his own personality he appeared to me almost all that is noble, lovely, and venerable.—MARTINEAU, JAMES, 1882, *To Alexander Ireland, Dec. 31; Life and Letters*, ed. Drummond, vol. II, p. 312.

Emerson is a genuine specimen of the true Yankee, that strange latest product of mankind. New England was colonized by the Puritans, and therefore the most typical New Englander would be a minister. Emerson's ancestors were ministers for eight successive generations, and he "smacks of the soil." In his tall, gaunt figure and long, sharp face he had the unmistakable characteristics of his race, a race which has become a synonym for sharp bargains, wit, and sound sense, and intellectually Emerson was as true a Yankee as ever lived. His mind was always on the alert—paradoxical as this may seem after what has been previously said—and he was abundantly blessed with what he calls "the saving grace of common sense." The majority of his illustrations are drawn from his own observation, and others from the details of many arts and sciences. His mind, in the aspect we are now considering, appreciated the supreme worth of experience. "I love facts," he says; and again, "an actually existent fly, is more important than a possibly existent angel." The second aspect of his mind may be thus briefly stated, as almost every page of his writings and every incident of his life furnishes an illustration of it. As one half of his intellectual constitution was Platonic, the other half was thus pre-eminently Yankee.—NORMAN, HENRY, 1883, *Ralph Waldo Emerson: An Ethical Study*, Fortnightly Review, vol. 40, p. 425.

Was all his days an arch traitor to our existing civilized regiment, inasmuch as he unconsciously managed to set aside its fundamental principle in doing without conscience, which was the entire secret of his very exceptional interest to men's speculation. He betrayed it to be sure without being at all aware of what he was doing; but this was really all that he distinctively did to my observation. . . . He was lineally descended to begin with, from a half-score of comatose New England clergymen, in whose behalf probably the religious instinct had been used up. Or, what to their experience had been religion, became in that of their descendant *life*. The actual truth, at any rate, was that he never felt a movement of the life of conscience from the day of his birth till that of his death. I could never see any signs of such a life in him. I remember, to be sure, that he had a great gift of friendship, and that he was very plucky in behalf of his friends whenever they felt themselves assailed—as plucky as a woman. . . . Now Emerson was seriously incapable of a subjective judgment upon himself; he did not know the inward difference between good and evil, so far as he was himself concerned. No doubt he perfectly comprehended the outward or moral difference between these things; but I insist upon it that he never so much as dreamed of any inward or spiritual difference between them. . . . On the whole I may say that at first I was greatly disappointed in him, because his intellect never kept the promise which his lovely face and manners held out to me. He was to my senses a literal divine presence in the house with me; and we cannot recognize literal divine presences in our houses without feeling sure that they will be able to say something of critical importance to one's intellect. It turned out that any average old dame in a horse-car would have satisfied my intellectual rapacity just as well as Emerson.—JAMES, HENRY, SR., 1884, *Spiritual Creation, Literary Remains*, ed. James, pp. 293, 294, 295, 297.

Emerson's personal appearance was that of a scholar, the descendant of scholars. He was tall and slender, with the complexion which is bred in the alcove and not in the open air. He used to tell his son Edward that he measured six feet in his shoes, but his son thinks he could hardly have straightened himself to that height in his later years. He was very light for a man of his stature. . . . Emerson's head was not such as Schopenhauer insists upon for a philosopher. He wore a hat measuring six and seven-eighths on the *cephalometer* used by hatters, which is equivalent to twenty-one inches and a quarter of circumference. The average size is from seven to seven and an eighth, so that his head was quite small in that dimension. It was long and narrow, but lofty, almost symmetrical, and of more nearly equal breadth in its anterior and posterior regions than many or most heads. His shoulders sloped so much as to be commented upon for this peculiarity by Mr. Gilfillan, and like "Ammon's great son," he carried one shoulder a little higher than the other. His face was thin, his nose somewhat accipitrine, casting a broad shadow; his mouth rather wide, well formed and well closed, carrying a question and an assertion in its finely finished curves; the lower lip a little prominent, the chin shapely and firm, as becomes the corner-stone of the countenance. His expression was calm, sedate, kindly, with that look of refinement, centering about the lips, which is rarely found in the male New Englander, unless the family features have been for two or three cultivated generations the battlefield and the play-ground of varied thoughts and complex emotions as well as the sensuous and nutritive port of entry. His whole look was irradiated by an ever inquiring intelligence. His manner was noble and gracious . . . Emerson's mode of living was very simple; coffee in the morning, tea in the evening, animal food by choice only once a day, wine only when with others using it, but always *pie* at breakfast. . . . He never laughed loudly. When he laughed it was under protest, as it were, with closed doors, his mouth shut, so that the explosion had to seek another respiratory channel, and found its way out quietly, while his eye-brows and nostrils and all his features betrayed the "ground swell," as Professor Thayer happily called it, of the half-suppressed convulsion. He was averse to loud laughter in others, and objected to Margaret Fuller that she made him laugh too much.—HOLMES, OLIVER WENDELL, 1884, *Ralph Waldo Emerson* (*American Men of Letters*), pp. 359, 362, 364.

A born idealist, carrying or carried by his idealism sometimes to excess, offended by the deacons' creaking boots as they bore around the consecrated elements in their hands, he forswore his clerical part in that particular ceremony as unsuited to the Occidental mind, and proposed a change in the administration of the Lord's Supper; which his parish not accepting, he resigned his place, parting with grief from his flock. . . . All the sects may well waive claim of property in a man so human and humane . . . Emerson, supposed irreligious, was pre-eminently religious, because, not bewildered or diverted like a butterfly by the multitude of gay phenomena, he clung to the noumena, the real and invisible, and his conduct corresponded to his belief. Dogma is thought to be the parent of creed; but behavior returns the compliment, and fashions the faith. Through all the spectacle and panorama of sensible impressions, coat of many colors, protean forms, he, as Plato bids, exercised his intellect. His mind and heart sought the object of worship. The atheist leaps like a grasshopper from appearance to appearance; the pantheist fails to distinguish appearance from reality. He fixed on the unity in the universe.— BARTOL, CYRUS AUGUSTUS, 1884, *Emerson's Religion, The Genius and Character of Emerson,* ed. *Sanborn, pp.* 110, 116, 121.

The portrait by David Scott recalls his expression and action in the lecture-room during that early period. The rapt expression of intense thought was emphasized by the peculiar action of the hand, which Scott has given. His voice was modulated by every shade of feeling, but had always a peculiar resonance which gave spirit and life to its tones; and it answered to that glance of the eyes which recalled Mrs. Child's comparison of light shining out from a temple. But the charm of manner was intimately connected with the thought, and was not that superficial readiness which pleases everybody. Newspaper writers and School-ship boys thought it awkward and embarrassed. He never wearied his audience; he was a perfect artist in the correspondence between the value of the thought and the beauty of the expression, and his sentences were like jewels whose brilliancy drew your attention before you knew their worth. He was very scrupulous in regard to time, never keeping his audience more than an hour, but often tantalizing them by suddenly closing his lecture when seemingly much of his manuscript remained unread.—CHENEY, EDNAH D., 1884, *Emerson and Boston, The Genius and Character of Emerson*, ed. Sanborn, p. 16.

When the book-mania fell upon me at fifteen, I used to venture into Mr. Emerson's library, and ask what I should read, never conscious of the audacity of my demand, so genial was my welcome. His kind hand opened to me the richness of Shakespeare, Dante, Goethe, and Carlyle; and I gratefully recall the sweet patience with which he led me round the book-lined room, till the "new and very interesting book" was found, or the indulgent smile he wore when I proposed something far above my comprehension. . . . Living what he wrote, his influence purified and brightened like sunshine. Many a thoughtful young man and woman owe to Emerson the spark that kindled their highest aspirations, and showed them how to make the conduct of a life a helpful lesson, not a blind struggle.— ALCOTT, LOUISA MAY, 1885, *Reminiscences of Ralph Waldo Emerson, Some Noted Princes, Authors and Statesmen of our Time*, ed. Parton, pp. 284, 285.

Emerson came into the world with an enduring constitution, so that he lived to be within one year of fourscore. He had excellent organs of digestion, and in mature life could "eat pie" like a school-boy; he slept well at night, and during sleep kept a window open, even in midwinter; but he complains more than twice of his want of power of voice and "a commanding presence;" so that the reader of his life is led to indulge in a surmise what he would have become if he had had "a commanding presence" like Webster; or if to the question, "Whose voice is music now?" he could have claimed a right to place himself by the side of Henry Clay. Whenever he exercised his mind on public affairs, he did so with judgment and courage.—BANCROFT GEORGE, 1885, *Holmes's Life of Emerson, North American Review*, vol. 140, p. 131.

As a character Emerson appears to me greater than when regarded as an author only. . . . I saw him in Florence. A tall, slender figure, with the radiant smile which is peculiar to children and men of the highest order. His daughter Ellen was his companion, and devoted to him. The noblest culture raises men above national peculiarities and makes them perfectly unaffected. Emerson had an unpretentious dignity of demeanor, and I felt as if I had always known him. At that time he was still fresh and could work. Soon after an infirmity came upon him. He wholly lost his memory. One of my former hearers wrote me an account of his last visit to him. Emerson sat there, says the letter, like an old eagle in his eyrie. He greeted me in the most kind and friendly manner, but could no longer remember men or things.—GRIMM, HERMAN, 1886, *Ralph Waldo Emerson, Literature*, tr. Adams, pp. 23, 42.

We were babies and boys together, but I can recall but one image of him as playing, and that was on the floor of my mother's chamber. I don't think he ever engaged in boys' play; not because of any physical inability, but simply because, from his earliest years, he dwelt in a higher sphere. My one deep impression is that, from his earliest childhood, our friend loved and moved and had his being in an atmosphere of letters, quite apart by himself. I can as little remember when he was not literary in his pursuits as when I first made his acquaintance. — FURNESS, WILLIAM HENRY, 1887, *Letter to James Elliot Cabot, A Memoir of Ralph Waldo Emerson*, ed. Cabot, vol. I, p. 5.

Emerson never grew old; at heart he was to the last as young as ever, his feelings as unworn, his faith as assured as in the days of his youth. Many visions he had seen pass away, but the import of them remained, only confirmed and enlarged in scope. Nor were bodily infirmities swift to come upon him. His hair remained thick, and its brown color unchanged up to rather a late period, when suddenly it began to come off in large patches. His eyesight, which sometimes failed him in his youth, and early manhood, was remarkably strong in the latter part of his life. He used no glasses in reading his lectures until he was sixty-four, when he found the need of them in a Phi Beta Kappa speech in 1867, and was thrown into some confusion, attributed by the audience to the usual disarray of his manuscript. Dr. Hedge, in his recollections of Emerson in 1828, notes the slowness of his movements; but I think most persons who saw him first in more advanced years will have been struck with the rapid step with which he moved through the Boston streets, his eye fixed on the distance. I count myself a good walker, but I used to find myself kept at a stretch when I walked with him in the Concord woods, when he was past seventy. Miss Elizabeth Hoar and one or two other persons who remembered him from his youth have told me that he seemed to them more erect in carriage, better "set up," in later years. A life so much in the open air no doubt had gradually strengthened an originally feeble habit of body. Emerson was never quite willing to acknowledge the fact of sickness or debility.— CABOT, JAMES ELLIOT, 1887, *A Memoir of Ralph Waldo Emerson*, vol. II, p. 649.

I am not aware of any material change in my estimate of Mr. Emerson's character from the time of my earliest acquaintance with him. It is possible, however, that my judgment of him may be, in some degree, unconsciously tinged by my recollections of the lovely qualities of his mother, from whom, it always seemed to me, he inherited many of his most striking traits. If I were asked to express in the fewest words what it was in Mr. Emerson that most impressed me, I should answer without hesitation, his reverent faith in God; his pure and blameless life. — HASKINS, DAVID GREENE, 1887, *Ralph Waldo Emerson, His Maternal Ancestors with Some Reminiscences of Him*, pp. 137, 139.

The great Emerson, whose discourses, as a rule, were far above the comprehension of the common multitude, was not a good speaker, and certainly made no attempts to amuse, but, on the contrary, aimed to instruct his audiences, told me himself that he once lectured to seven people at Montreal. This he did to console me for the fact that I had mentioned to him, that I had lectured to about thirty in Philadelphia. . . . Eloquent as he was with his pen, he was abnormally shy and retiring, and did not shine in conversation, or greatly care to indulge in it. Like Wordsworth, whom he visited at Rydal Mount, and of whom he spoke to me,

He did not much or oft delight,
To season his fireside with personal talk,

though he could break through his natural undemonstrativeness upon occasion, when conversing with a companion after his own heart, with whom he could exchange ideas rather than re-echo commonplaces. — MACKAY, CHARLES, 1887, *Through the Long Day*, vol. II, pp. 143, 151.

Emerson's elocution has been frequently described, and most hearers attest its magical effect. It was, or seemed, the purest natural endowment; if it owed anything to art, it was the *ars celare*. It gave the impression of utter absorption in the theme, and indifference to all rhetoric and all oratorical stratagem. Composed and undemonstrative as any listener, almost motionless, except for a slight vibration of the body, seldom even adapting his voice to his matter, he seemed to confide entirely in the justness of his thought, the felicity of his language, and the singular music of his voice.— GARNETT, RICHARD, 1888, *Life of Ralph Waldo Emerson (Great Writers)*, p. 169.

He established certain iron rules for the management of the pilgrims. No railing or wilful rudeness or uncleanness would he permit. In the autumn of 1871, some years after the arrival of the more wild and uncouth Reformers had ceased, a man short, thick, hairy, dirty, and wild-eyed came to our door and asked to see Mr. Emerson. I showed him into the parlor and went to call my father, and returned with him, the guest had so wild a look. It appeared that he came from Russia, and very possibly the distance he had had to travel may have accounted for his very late arrival. He stood with his hat on. I knew that that hat would have to come off before spiritual communication could be opened, but wondered how it could be got off, as the man looked determined. My father saluted him, asked him to be seated and offered to take his hat. He declined and began to explain his mission. My father again asked him to take his hat off, which proposition he ignored and began again to explain his advanced views. Again the host said, "Yes, but let me take your hat, sir." The Russian snorted some impatient remark about attending to such trifles, and began again, but my father firmly, yet with perfect sweetness, said, "Very well, then, we will talk in the yard," showed the guest out, and walked to and fro with him under the apple-trees, patiently hearing him for a few minutes; but the man who was a fanatic, if not insane, and specially desired that a hall be secured for him, free of charge, to address the people, soon departed, shaking off the dust of his feet against a man so bound up in slavish customs of society as Mr. Emerson.—EMERSON, EDWARD WALDO, 1888, *Emerson in Concord*, p. 209.

It now becomes my duty to unveil and present to the British public, and to the strangers within our gates who can appreciate greatness, the statue of a great man [Carlyle]. Might I append to these brief remarks the expression of a wish, personal perhaps in its warmth, but more than personal in its aim, that somewhere upon this Thames Embankment could be raised a companion memorial to a man who loved our hero, and was by him beloved to the end? I refer to the loftiest, purest, and most penetrating spirit that was ever shown in American literature—to Ralph Waldo Emerson, the life-long friend of Thomas Carlyle.—TYNDALL, JOHN, 1890, *Personal Recollections of Thomas Carlyle, New Fragments*, p. 397.

Well do I remember his tender, shrewd, wise face as I first saw it. Almost before we were alone he made me forget in whose presence I stood. He was merely an old, quiet, modest gentleman, pressing me to a seat near him, and all at once talking about college matters, the new gymnasium, the Quarterly, and from these about books and reading and writing; and all as if he continually expected as much as he gave. And so it was ever after; no circumstances so varying but, whether I saw him alone or in the presence of others, there was the ever-ready welcome shining in his eyes, the same manifest gentleness and persistent preference of others.—WOODBURY, CHARLES J., 1890, *Emerson's Talks with a College Boy, Century Magazine*, vol. 39, p. 621.

He had a penetrating, eager, questioning look. His head was thrust out as if in quest of knowledge. His gaze was steady and intense. His speech was laconic and to the purpose. His direct manner suggested a wish for closer acquaintance with the mind. His very courtesy, which was invariable and exquisite in its way, had an air of inquiry about it. There was no varnish, no studied grace of motion or demeanor, no manifest desire to please, but a kind of wistfulness as of one who took you at your best and wanted to draw it out. He accosted the soul, and with the winning persuasiveness which befits friendliness on human terms. There was a certain shyness which indicated the modesty which is born of the spirit.—FROTHINGHAM, OCTAVIUS BROOKS, 1891, *Recollections and Impressions*, p. 166.

We, who knew him, talked with him and loved him, know that he found the kingdom of heaven on earth. He found God reigning in his babe's nursery; at the post-office; when he pruned his apple-trees, and when he took the train for Boston. We want you, who have not seen him, to believe that the man of ideas was thus a human man, a man with men. He was not a dreamer. He was an actor. He taught us how to live; and he did so because he lived himself.—HALE, EDWARD EVERETT, 1893–1900, *Addresses and Essays*, p. 257.

Emerson's manner in the lecture-room, like that which distinguished him in private was one of perfect serenity. For any emotion that he displayed, there might have been no audience before him. He always read his lectures, and in a grave monotone, for the most part, with rarely any emphasis. Much in them must have been "caviare to the general," but ever and anon some striking thought, strikingly expressed, produced a ripple of response from the audience, and the close of his finely discriminating lecture on Napoleon was followed by several rounds of applause, all this confirming what he once said to me, that such lecturing triumphs as fell to him were achieved by "hits." To the public success or failure of his lectures he appeared to be profoundly indifferent, a mood to which his experience in American lecture-rooms had habituated him. He told me, with perfect equanimity, that at home he was accustomed to see hearers, after listening to him a little, walk out of the room, as much as to say that they had had enough of him. At his Manchester lectures the audiences were numerous and attentive. Whatever they might fail to understand, they evidently felt that this was a man of genius and of high and pure mind.—ESPINASSE, FRANCIS, 1893, *Literary Recollections and Sketches*, p. 157.

In his later days Emerson's voice failed him for lecturing, and still later and more entirely his memory of words. His hesitation for the right word had to be met by guesses. At Longfellow's grave, having to speak of him, very touching was the failure —"Our dear friend, whose name at this moment I cannot recall."—LINTON, WILLIAM JAMES, 1894, *Threescore and Ten Years*, p. 216.

His works have a quality like light, and a purity as of snows caught in the high Alps, but the man was still clearer and rarer,—a nature not to be reflected in print, however skilfully ordered.—MABIE, HAMILTON WRIGHT, 1894, *My Study Fire, Second Series*, p. 44.

If Emerson laughed at all, it was very quietly. Carlyle's loud roaring laugh must have been intolerable to him. But Emerson's smile was something to remember. It was the wisest smile. His lips and eyes were implicated in it about equally. It could do many things: for one, express his "cherub scorn" of what he didn't like; also his gladness in a thought which came to him he knew not whence; again his pleasure in some palpable absurdity.—CHADWICK, JOHN WHITE, 1895, *America's Seven Great Poets, The Arena*, vol. 15, p. 16.

Emerson might be seen on his way to the post-office at precisely half-past five every afternoon, after the crowd there had dispersed. His step was deliberate and dignified, and though his tall lean figure was not a symmetrical one, nor were his movements graceful, yet there was something very pleasant in the aspect of him even at a distance. The same has also been said of good statuary, even before we know what is its subject. He knew all the people old and young in the village, and had a kindly word or a smile for every one of them. His smile was better than anything he said. There is no word in the language that describes it. It was neither sweet nor saintly, but more like what a German poet called the mild radiance of a hidden sun. No picture, photograph or bust of Emerson has ever done him justice for this reason; only such a master as Giorgione could have painted his portrait. Every morning after reading the "Boston Advertiser" he would go to his study, to take up the work of the day previous and cross out every word in it that could possibly be spared. This procedure and his taste for unusual words is what gives the peculiar style to his writing. It was characteristic of him physically and mentally. He had a spare figure; was sparing of speech, sparing of praise, and sparing of time; in all things temperate and stoical. He had an aquiline face, made up of powerful features without an inch of spare territory.

"With beams December planets dart
His keen eye truth and conduct scanned."

His eyes were sometimes exceedingly brilliant; his nose was strong and aquiline; and the lower part of his face, especially the mouth, was notably like the bust of Julius Cæsar. His voice was a baritone of rapid inflections, and when he was very much in earnest it changed to a deep bass. —STEARNS, FRANK PRESTON, 1895, *Sketches from Concord and Appledore*, p. 89.

He was a poet, a genius, and had the face of an angel.—SHERWOOD, MARY E. W., 1897, *An Epistle to Posterity*, p. 120.

The impression of Emerson as dwelling in cloud-land, the central figure in a company of ethereal shapes, is removed when he is seen before other backgrounds than those of Transcendentalism. The good people of Concord began by giving him the office of hogreeve, usually bestowed upon newly married men, and always found him eager for the well-being of the place, not only in wishes, but in service. If he had given the town nothing but the lines which live with "the embattled farmer" of French's noble statue, it would have been much, but there were many local "occasions" made richer by the voice and wisdom of Emerson. There was no little significance in the words of a simple woman who brought her work to an early end one day to go to a lecture of Emerson's before the Concord Lyceum. When she was asked if she could understand him, she replied: "Not a word, but I like to go and see him stand up there and look as if he thought everyone was as good as he was." Through his friendships in Boston, especially after the foundation of the "Atlantic Monthly" and the Saturday Club in 1857, he was brought often into contact with men of the world, in the best sense of that elastic phrase. The names of the men associated with the beginnings of these two organizations are too well known to need repetition. Emerson had great pleasure in their society; and of his effect upon them, perhaps Lowell spoke for all when he wrote to Thomas Hughes: "He is as sweetly highminded as ever, and when one meets him the fall of Adam seems a false report. Afterwards we feel our throats, and are startled by the tell-tale lump there."— HOWE, M. A. DEWOLFE, 1898, *American Bookmen*, p. 193.

He was a man of angelic nature, pure, exquisite, yet refined, and human. All concede him the highest place in our literary heaven. First class in genius and in character, he was able to discern the face of the times. To him was entrusted not only the silver trump of prophecy, but also that sharp and two-edged sword of the Spirit with which the legendary archangel Michael overcomes the brute Satan. In the great victory of his day, the triumph of freedom over slavery, he has a record not to be outdone and never to be forgotten.—HOWE, JULIA WARD, 1899, *Reminisences, 1819-1899, p.* 292.

He lectured in forty successive seasons before a single "lyceum"—that of Salem, Mass. His fine delivery unquestionably did a great deal for the dissemination of his thought. After once hearing him, that sonorous oratory seemed to roll through every sentence that the student read; and his very peculiarities,—the occasional pause accompanied with a deep gaze of the eyes, or the apparent hesitation in the selection of a word, always preparing the way, like Charles Lamb's stammer, for some stroke of mother-wit, — these identified themselves with his personality, and secured his hold. He always shrank from extemporaneous speech, though sometimes most effective in its use; he wrote of himself once as "the worst known public speaker, and growing continually worse;" but his most studied remarks had the effect of off-hand conviction from the weight and beauty of his elocution.—HIGGINSON, THOMAS WENTWORTH, 1899, *Contemporaries, p.* 9.

It was my fortune to be sent to Concord, at Mr. Redpath's suggestion, to see if Mr. Emerson would come in and give us a lecture. I went out and met the dear old man at the Manse House. He greeted me very cordially and gladly accepted the invitation to come in and lecture. The date was fixed; it was advertised in the newspapers; tickets were put out at from one to three dollars, and many of the Boston ladies sold them. The afternoon for the lecture came. The Old South was filled with as choice an audience of the blue blood of Boston as has ever assembled in that old chapel. Mr. Emerson came in and was introduced by Father Neil. As he began reading his lecture the audience was very attentive. After a few moments he lost his place, and his grand-daughter, sitting in the front row of seats, gently stepped toward him and reminded him that he was lecturing. He saw at once that he was wandering, and with the most charming, characteristic, apologetic bow he resumed his place—an incident that seemed to affect the audience more than anything that could possibly have occurred. A few moments later he took a piece of manuscript in his hand, and turning around with it, laid it on a side table. Just then one of the audience said to me (I think it was Mrs. Livermore or Mrs. Howe), "Please have the audience pass right out," and rushing up to Mr. Emerson, said, "Thank you so much for that delightful lecture," then turning around, waved the audience to go out. He probably had been speaking about fifteen minutes. The audience passed out, many of them in tears. It was one of the most pathetic sights that I ever witnessed. It did not attract very much attention just then, and I never read any account of it in the newspapers. I suppose it was out of love and veneration for the dear man that the incident did not receive public mention, but there must be a great many still alive who were witnesses of that memorable scene. It was Ralph Waldo Emerson's last public appearance.—POND, JAMES BURTON, 1900, *Eccentricities of Genius, p.* 331.

There was more congruity in the presence and conversation of Emerson with the ideal one naturally formed of him than we usually find in our personal intercourse with famous writers. I think this is partly the cause of the powerful impression he made upon his contemporaries. His manner of life, the man himself, was at one with his thought; his thought at one with his expression. There were no paradoxes, none of the supposed eccentricities of genius, to furnish the intolerable ana for future literary scavengers. He spoke of Nature not to add an elegant ornament to his pages; he lived near to her. In meeting him the disappointments, if any there were, one found in himself. For he measured men so they became aware of their own stature, not oppressively, but by a flashing, inward self-illumination, because he placed something to their credit that could not stand the test of their own audit.—ALBEE, JOHN, 1901, *Remembrances of Emerson, p.* 4.

The pure, simple-minded, high-feeling man, made of the finest clay of human nature; the one man who, to Carlyle, uttered a genuine human voice, and soothed the profound glooms of dyspeptic misanthropy; a little too apt, no doubt, to fall into the illusion of taking the world to be as comfortably constituted as himself; and apt also to withdraw from the ugly drama in which the graver passions are inextricably mixed up with the heroic and the rational, to the remote mountaintop of mystical reflection. Yet nobody could be more fitted to communicate the "electric shock" to his disciples, because of his keen perception of the noble elements of life in superiority to all the vulgar motives and models of thought, which were not the less attractive because he could not see his way to any harmonious or consistent system of thought.—STEPHEN, LESLIE, 1901, *Emerson, National Review.*

That evening Mr. Sanborn took me over to Emerson's house. We awaited the poet in the large drawing room, which, in fact, was rather a sitting-room. It was not yet dark, and the lamps were not lighted. We came forward as he entered. It was, indeed, the real, the living Emerson. Where another man would hardly have been recognized in the dim light, with him everything was accented. His tall, slightly stooped figure, his long neck and sloping shoulders, his strong features and wellformed head, came out with prominence in the quiet light. But it was not this so much as it was his large but simple manner that impressed me. I felt myself in the presence of a truly great man.— EATON, WYATT, 1902, *Recollections of American Poets, Century Magazine*, vol. 64, p. 845.

Emerson was then [1853] in the vigor of middle age, just turned of fifty, in good health and fine color, with abundant dark brown hair, no beard, but a slight whisker on each cheek, and plainly dressed. His form was never other than slender, after I knew him, and his shoulders, like Thoreau's, had that peculiar slope which had attracted notice in England, where the New England type of Anglo-Norman was not so well known as it has since become. His striking features were the noble brow, from which the hair was carelessly thrown back, though not long, and the mild and penetrating blue eye, smiling, in its social mood, in the most friendly manner, but capable, on rare occasions, of much severity.— SANBORN, FRANKLIN BENJAMIN, 1903, *The Personality of Emerson*, p. 8.

POETRY

Emerson himself is a northern hyperborean genius—a winter-bird with a clear, saucy, cheery call, and not a passionate summer songster. His lines have little melody to the ear, but they have the vigor and distinctness of all pure and compact things. They are like the needles of the pine—"the snow-loving pine"—more than the emotional foliage of the deciduous trees, and the titmouse becomes them well.—BURROUGHS, JOHN, 1873, *Birds of the Poets, Scribner's Monthly*, vol. 6, p. 572.

Here was more religious inspiration than had entered into more than a very few modern volumes of poetry, with the fervor and power of the old prophets. There was, also, that rich fulness of the best of the mystics, when they most truly rise into the height of spiritual attainment. These two tendencies were wonderfully combined in some of the poems, making them unique in modern poetry. Such a volume, however, could not soon grow into popular favor, and perhaps can never have more than a limited circle of admirers. It is a book for poets and thinkers more than for the people; yet some of these poems will ever remain the admiration of all lovers of nature and of moral inspiration.—COOKE, GEORGE WILLIS, 1881, *Ralph Waldo Emerson, His Life, Writings and Philosophy*, p. 114.

I can't imagine any better luck befalling these States for a poetical beginning and initiation than has come from Emerson, Longfellow, Bryant, and Whittier. Emerson, to me, stands unmistakably at the head, but for the others I am at a loss where to give any precedence. Each illustrious, each rounded, each distinctive. Emerson for his sweet, vital-tasting melody, rhym'd philosophy, and poems as amber-clear as the honey of the wild bee he loves to sing.— WHITMAN, WALT, 1881, *Autobiographia*, April 16, p. 184.

Here we conclude what we had to say by way of setting forth and elucidating Emerson's right to be ranked among the true poets of this country and of all countries, of this age and of many ages to come. We think it indisputable. Most likely his audience at any one time will be comparatively small. In a single halfgeneration the platitudes of a Tupper found more admirers than Emerson will have found for ages. But be his auditors many or few, they will surely be "fit." If voters were to be weighed, not counted, his would be a heavy vote. And, in the long result, it will be weight, not numbers, which will decide the final issue.— GUERNSEY, ALFRED H., 1881, *Ralph Waldo Emerson, Philosopher and Poet*, p. 327.

In this book you'll find
Music of a prophet's mind.
Even when harsh the numbers be,
There's an inward melody;
And when sound is one with sense,
'Tis a bird's song—sweet, intense.
—GILDER, RICHARD WATSON, 1882, *To E. W. G. in England (With Emerson's Poems), Century Magazine*, vol. 24, p. 396.

It is remarkable enough that Carlyle and Emerson both had in them that imaginative gift which made them aim at poetry, and both that incapacity for rhythm or music which rendered their verses too rugged, and too much possessed with the sense of effort, to sink as verse should sink into the hearts of men. Carlyle's verse is like the heavy rumble of a van without springs; Emerson's, which now and then reaches something of the sweetness of poetry, much more often reminds one of the attempts of a seeress to induce in herself the ecstasy which will not spontaneously visit her. Yet the prose, both of Carlyle and of Emerson, falls at times into that poetic rhythm which indicates the highest glow of a powerful imaginative nature, though of such passages I could produce many more from Carlyle than from Emerson. I should say that a little of Emerson's verse is genuine poetry, though not of the highest order, and that none of Carlyle's is poetry at all; but that some of Carlyle's prose is as touching as any but the noblest poetry, while Emerson never reaches the same profound pathos. HUTTON, RICHARD HOLT, 1882–94, *Criticisms on Contemporary Thought and Thinkers*, vol. I, p. 46.

It is impossible not to be refreshed and gratified by Emerson's prose; but perhaps his poetry more completely carries the reader with it, as being a higher and purer production of genius. The best passages of it are indeed as unmitigated poetry as was ever written; they are poetry down to the last syllable; they are verses which, as he himself expresses it, seem to be found, not made. Their meaning is as intimately connected with their form as sound is with speech. The mystic obscurity of some of the poems, however, and the unfamiliar subjects treated by others, have discouraged or repelled many from the study of any of them.... Emerson's point of view is so far from being conventional or obvious, and is besides, so lofty and abstract, that the careless and hasty glance of the general reader can not be expected to apprehend it.— HAWTHORNE, JULIAN, 1882, *Ralph Waldo Emerson, Harper's Magazine*, vol. 65, p. 280.

I would not know where to go for a more adequate statement of the poet's means and ends in nature than Emerson's "Wood Notes."—ROBINSON, PHIL., 1883, *Our Birds and Their Poets, Harper's Magazine*, vol. 66, p. 439.

As for Emerson's verse (though he has written some as exquisite as any in the language) I suppose we must give it up. That he had a sense of the higher harmonies of language no one that ever heard him lecture can doubt. The structure of his prose, as one listened to it, was as nobly metrical as the King James version of the Old Testament, and this made it all the more puzzling that he should have been absolutely insensitive to the harmony of verse. For it was there he failed—single verses are musical enough. I never shall forget the good-humoredly puzzled smile with which he once confessed to me his inability to apprehend the value of accent in verse.—LOWELL, JAMES RUSSELL, 1883, *To James B. Thayer, Dec. 24; Letters, ed. Norton*, vol. II, p. 275.

Where in the realm of thought, whose air is
song,
Does he, the Buddha of the West, belong?
He seems a wingèd Franklin, sweetly wise,
Born to unlock the secrets of the skies;
And which the nobler calling,—if 'tis fair
Terrestrial with celestial to compare,—
To guide the storm-cloud's elemental flame,
Or walk the chambers whence the lightning
came,
Amidst the sources of its subtile fire,
And steal their effluence for his lips and lyre?
If lost at times in vague aërial flights,
None treads with firmer footstep when he lights
A soaring nature, ballasted with sense,
Wisdom without her wrinkles or pretence,
In every Bible he has faith to read,
And every altar helps to shape his creed.
Ask you what name this prisoned spirit bears
While with ourselves this fleeting breath it
shares?
Till angels greet him with a sweeter one
In heaven, on earth we call him Emerson.
—HOLMES, OLIVER WENDELL, 1884, *At the Saturday Club.*

Taken as a whole, Emerson's poetry is of that kind which springs, not from excitement of passion or feeling, but from an intellectual demand for intense and sublimated expression. We see the step that lifts him straight from prose to verse, and that step is the shortest possible. The flight is awkward and even uncouth, as if nature had intended feet rather than wings. It is hard to feel of Emerson, any more than Wordsworth could feel of Goethe, that his poetry is inevitable. The measure, the colour, the imaginative figures, are the product of search, not of spontaneous movements of sensation and reflection combining in a harmony that is delightful to the ear. They are the outcome of a discontent with prose, not of that highstrung sensibility which compels the true poet into verse. This must not be said without exception. "The Threnody," written after the death of a deeply loved child, is a beautiful and impressive lament. Pieces like "Musquetaquid," the "Adirondacs," the "Snow-storm," "The Humble-Bee," are pretty and pleasant bits of pastoral. In all we feel the pure breath of nature, and

The primal mind,
That flows in streams, that breathes in wind.

There is a certain charm of *naiveté*, that recalls the unvarnished simplicity of the Italian painters before Raphael. But who shall say that he discovers that "spontaneous overflow of powerful feeling," which a great poet has made the fundamental element of poetry?—MORLEY, JOHN, 1884, *Ralph Waldo Emerson, An Essay*, p. 26.

In truth, one of the legitimate poets, Emerson, in my opinion, is not. His poetry is interesting, it makes one think; but it is not the poetry of one of the born poets. I say it of him with reluctance, although I am sure that he would have said it himself. . . . Emerson's poetry is seldom either simple, or sensuous, or impassioned. In general it lacks directness; it lacks completeness; it lacks energy. His grammar is often embarrassed; in particular, the want of clearly marked distinction between the subject and the object of his sentence is a frequent cause of obscurity in him. A poem which shall be a plain, forcible, inevitable whole he hardly ever produces. Such good work as the noble lines graven on the Concord Monument is the exception with him; such ineffective work as the "Fourth of July Ode" or the "Boston Hymn" is the rule. Even passages and single lines of thorough plainness and commanding force are rare in his poetry. They exist, of course; but when we meet with them they give us a sense of surprise, so little has Emerson accustomed us to them.—ARNOLD, MATTHEW, 1884, *Emerson, Macmillan's Magazine*, vol. 50, pp. 3, 4.

For to me he was a poet and much more. . . . It was among his gifts that he could feel the poetic impulse not only in himself but in others; that he knew and tested high poesy, not so much by a critical faculty and by study, as by native inspiration and appreciation. . . . His vocabulary is rich and novel, and he has brought it well into acceptance. But in marshalling these words he felt his inadequacy, and in this was the "discontented poet" of whom he wrote. He lamented his imperfect use of the metrical faculty, which he felt all the more keenly in contrast with the melodious thoughts he had to utter, and the fitting words in which he could clothe these thoughts. He would have written much more in verse if he had been content with his own metrical expression as constantly as he was delighted with it sometimes. But it is also true that he purposely roughened his verse, and threw in superfluous lines and ill-matched rhymes, as a kind of protest against the smoothness and jingle of what he called "poetry to put round frosted cake."—SANBORN, FRANKLIN BENJAMIN, 1884, *Emerson Among the Poets, The Genius and Character of Emerson*, ed. Sanborn, pp. 173, 211.

Emerson's prose is full of poetry, and his poems are light as air. But this statement like so many of his own, gives only one side of a truth. His prose is just as full of everyday sense and wisdom; and something different from prose, however sublunary and imaginative, is needed to constitute a poem. His verse, often diamond-like in contrast with the feldspar of others, at times is ill-cut and beclouded. His prose, then, is that of a wise man, plus a poet; and his verse, by turns, light and twilight, air and vapor. Yet we never feel, as in reading Wordsworth, that certain of his measures are wholly prosaic. He was so careless of ordinary standards, that few of his own craft have held his verse at its worth. . . . He knew the human world, none better, and generalized the sum of its attainments, —was gracious, shrewd, and calm,—but could not hold up the mirror and show us to ourselves. He was that unique songster, a poet of fire and vision, quite above moralist, yet neither to be classed as objective; he perceived the source of all passion and wisdom, yet rendered neither the hearts of others nor his own. His love poetry is eulogized, but it wants the vital grip, wherewith his "Concord Fight" and "Boston Hymn" fastens on our sense of manhood and patriotism. It chants of Love, not of the beloved; its flame is pure and general as moonlight and as high-removed. . . . He ranks with the foremost of the second class, poets eminent for special graces, values, sudden meteors of thought. In that gift for "saying things," so notable in Pope and Tennyson, he is the chief of American poets. From what other bard have so many original lines and phrases passed into literature, —inscriptions that do not wear out, graven in bright and standard gold?—STEDMAN, E.C., 1885, *Poets of America*, pp.134,157,160.

Emerson's poetry will be interpreted differently according to the estimation held of the value of form in poetical composition. If it be held, as it surely must, that no artist can be regardless of form without forfeiting many chaplets from his poetic crown, then Emerson's laurels will present a peculiarly bare and disordered appearance. He redeems his reputation, it is true, by many happy touches and graceful thoughts, but the instructural instinct. . . . seems entirely wanting. There are many poets who run so easily in their self-imposed harness, that only criticism can detect the strict rules in accordance with which the work has been constructed. There are other poets on a lower scale, of whom we have abundant examples in contemporary literature, who obey the laws of their composition with such surprising dexterity that, though the artifice is relieved, they almost succeed in concealing their want of inspiration. Emerson is certainly not artificial, but then he is not naturally artistic in his poems. They are formless, without end, beginning, or middle; inchoate, unhewn, unpolished; only just emerging from the quarry of nature.—COURTNEY, WILLIAM LEONARD, 1885, *Ralph Waldo Emerson, Fortnightly Review*, vol. 44, p. 329.

The verses of Emerson are sometimes difficult to be understood. He finds the subjects of poetry only in nature, whereas the highest poetry leads us into the secret of the passions, relations, and actions of living men and women. Homer treats of men and women, of love and war, of heroes and demigods, and of the gods themselves, is always melodious, and is always clear even to a child. And yet Emerson, though so different from Homer, was a poet; that which he has done best, and which will live longest, is in verse.—BANCROFT, GEORGE, 1885, *Holmes's Life of Emerson, North American Review*, vol. 140, p. 138.

We must confess that the strength of his verse sometimes becomes rudeness. There is sometimes a lack of finish that jars upon the sensitive ear. No reader of Emerson can fail to regret that his lines are so often marred by imperfections. It seems a pity that some one could not have done for him what he is said to have done for Jones Very, even to the reminding him that the Holy Ghost surely writes good grammar. . . . Some of Emerson's work, however, is not appreciably affected by such faults. The Threnody, for instance, is not without imperfections, but it overpowers these by its great beauty. The Problem utters lofty thought and sublime imagery in a music that is worthy of them. Had Emerson written nothing else, his fame as a poet should rest securely on this. Like all great poets he should be judged by his best work. Upon how few of his poems does the fame of Wordsworth rest! We read the others largely in the light of these.—EVERETT, CHARLES CARROLL, 1887, *The Poems of Emerson, The Andover Review*, vol. 7, p. 235.

If Emerson had been frequently sustained at the heights he was capable of reaching, he would unquestionably have been one of the sovereign poets of the world. At its very best his phrase is so new and so magical, includes in its easy felicity such a wealth of fresh suggestion and flashes with such a multitude of side lights, that we cannot suppose that it will ever be superseded or will lose its charm. He seems to me like a very daring but purblind diver, who flings himself headlong into the ocean, and comes up bearing as a rule, nothing but sand and common shells, yet who every now and then rises grasping some wonderful and unique treasure.

In his prose, of course, Emerson was far more a master of the medium than in poetry. . . . Emerson, as a verse-writer, is so fragmentary and uncertain that we cannot place him among the great poets; and yet his best lines and stanzas seem as good as theirs. Perhaps we ought to consider him, in relation to Wordsworth and Shelley, as an asteroid among the planets. — GOSSE, EDMUND, 1888, *Has America Produced a Poet? The Forum, vol.* 6.

The genius of his verse is best characterized by a happy phrase of Dr. Holmes's — it is elemental. It stands in a closer relation to Nature than that of almost any other poet. He has an unique power of making us participate in the life of Nature as it is in Nature herself, not as Wordsworth gives it, blended with the feelings or at least coloured by the contemplations of humanity. Such intimacy with Nature has sometimes all the effect of magic; there are moments and moods in which Emerson seems to have as far outflown Wordsworth as he outflew Thomson and Collins. But the inspiration is in the highest degree fitful and fragmentary, and is but seldom found allied with beautiful and dignified Art. The poems offend continually by lame unscannable lines, and clumsiness and obscurities of expression.— GARNETT, RICHARD, 1888, *Life of Ralph Waldo Emerson (Great Writers), p.* 130.

The poetry of Emerson occupies a peculiar position. It is obedient, as a rule, to the canons of poetic art; much of it is highly lyrical and of exquisite finish; but on the whole it is simply to be considered as a medium for the expression of thought which could not so concisely be uttered in prose. When Emerson wished to speak with peculiar terseness, with unusual exaltation, with special depth of meaning, with the utmost intensity of conviction, he spoke in poetic form. He who misses this fact cannot rightly interpret Emerson the poet. . . . It was no wonder that Emerson anticipated, in half-a-dozen poems, the later conclusions of the evolutionists. He was the singer of the upward march of nature and the onward march of man. His poetic field was too broad to be tilled thoroughly in many parts. He was too proverbial to be a great constructive artist. He gives us saws, sayings, admonitions, flashes, glimpses, few broad constructed pictures. With these we are content, and do not ask him for epics, tragedies, or "Excursions."—RICHARDSON, CHARLES F., 1888, *American Literature, 1607–1885, vol.* II, *pp.* 139, 168, 169.

Potentially the greatest of American poets.—SHARP, WILLIAM, 1889, *ed. American Sonnets, Introductory Note, p.* xxiii.

Though perhaps never guilty of writing *invita Minerva,* he is naturally more grammatic than lyric. It is only in the fusion of an emotion or an ideal that he *flows.* And even then his stream is roughened and impeded by serious technical limitations. For such long elemental wavesweeps as Milton or Byron or Shelley or Keats delighted in, he was unfit. He lacked one essential element, the sensuous — and this includes the rhythmical sense. The form is slighted — the thought or the picture only prized. But every complete poet should be an artist too, and know how to wed beautiful thoughts to beautiful forms, and in the most harmonious union. Here, I think, was Emerson's deficiency. I am sure that in all times of literature, those poems will live longest that best fulfill the demand for a perfect soul in a perfect body. . . . Whatever the technical imperfections of Emerson's verse, it is beyond question that we are lifted by his rare though broken music into chambers of thought and mystical sentiment, to which few poets of our day have the key. If he is not a great poetic artist, he is a great seer and inspirer — and of prose-poets our first.—CRANCH, CHRISTOPHER PEARSE, 1889–92, *Emerson's Limitations as a Poet, The Critic, vol.* 20, *p.* 129.

Of our New England poets, I find myself taking down Emerson oftener than any other; then Bryant; occasionally Longfellow for a few poems; then Whittier for "The Playmate" or "Snow-Bound;" and least of all, Lowell. I am not so vain as to think that the measure of my appreciation of these poets is a measure of their merit; but as this writing is so largely autobiographical, I must keep to the facts. As the pathos and solemnity of life deepens with time, I think one finds only stray poems, or parts of poems, in the New England anthology that adequately voice it; and these he finds in Emerson more plentifully than anywhere else, though in certain of Longfellow's sonnets is adequacy also.— BURROUGHS, JOHN, 1897, *On the Re-reading of Books, Century Magazine. vol.* 55. *p.* 150.

These are never the impulsive record of a passing mood or incident. Herein they differ as widely as possible from the verses of his friend Holmes, which are nearly all "occasional." Each Emersonian poem is, rather, the deliberate, labored, final expression of a calm philosophical thought.— LAWTON, WILLIAM CRANSTON, 1898, *The New England Poets*, p. 29

Emerson's passion for nature was not like the passion of Keats or of Burns, of Coleridge or of Robert Browning; compared with these men he is cold. His temperature is below blood-heat, and his volume of poems stands on the shelf of English poets like the icy fish which in Caliban upon Setebos is described as finding himself thrust into the warm ooze of an ocean not his own. But Emerson is a poet, nevertheless, a very extraordinary and rare man of genius, whose verses carry a world of their own within them. . . . He is the chief poet of that school of which Emily Dickinson is a minor poet. . . . His worship of the New England landscape amounts to a religion. His poems do that most wonderful thing, make us feel that we are alone in the fields and with the trees, —not English fields nor French lanes, but New England meadows and uplands. There is no human creature in sight, not even Emerson is there, but the wind and the flowers, the wild birds, the fences, the transparent atmosphere, the breath of nature. —CHAPMAN, JOHN JAY, 1898, *Emerson and Other Essays*, pp. 84, 85.

There is something of the *vates* in Mr. Emerson. The deep intuitions, the original and startling combinations, the sometimes whimsical beauty of his illustrations,— all these belong rather to the domain of poetry than to that of philosophy. The high level of thought upon which he lived and moved and the wonderful harmony of his sympathies are his great lesson to the world at large. Despite his rather defective sense of rhythm, his poems are divine snatches of melody. I think that, in the popular affection, they may outlast his prose.— HOWE, JULIA WARD, 1899, *Reminiscences*, 1819–1899, p. 291.

Emerson's poems, for all their erratic oddity of form, prove on consideration to possess many qualities of temper for which an orthodox mind would have sought expression in hymns. They are designed not so much to set forth human emotion or to give æsthetic delight as to stimulate moral or spiritual ardour. For all his individualism, Emerson could not help being a good old inbred Yankee preacher.— WENDELL, BARRETT, 1900, *A Literary History of America*, p. 317.

There are many cultivated Americans to whom Emerson's poems seem truly great, if not the greatest produced by any of their countrymen. Others equally cultivated maintain, however, that many of his poems are only versified versions of his essays, and declare that save in rare passages he is deficient in passion, in sensuousness, in simplicity, and cramped in his use of the metrical and other technical resources of the true poet. The fact that save for a few perfect pieces, such as the clear-cut "Rhodora" and the impressive "Days," and a slightly larger number of passages, stanzas, and lines, Emerson as a poet has not made his way with English-speaking people outside the Northern and Western States, lends great support to the arguments of his unenthusiastic critics. It can scarcely be denied, furthermore, that poems like "The Dæmon in Love" deal with subjects unfitted for concrete treatment, that true poetic glow and flow are almost entirely absent from Emerson's verses, and that his ever-recurring and often faulty octosyllabic couplets soon become wearisome. That he is at times irritatingly obscure or else uncomfortably profound, that he is given to diffuseness, that he is rarely capable of sustaining himself at a high level of execution, can almost be demonstrated. Worse still, he is prone to jargon, to bathos, to lapses of taste.—TRENT, WILLIAM P., 1903, *A History of American Literature*, p. 331.

Although the range of Emerson's poetry is narrow, it is deep, and suffused with pure light of imagination, and dominated by the supreme ideality of a philosophic mind. Its keynote is Beauty. What it lacks in mere technical excellence, what occasional flaws there may be, showing the absence of the subtle touches of the master verse-builder, in rhythm, and meter, are compensated for by the depth of insight, by the soul and heart uplifting power of inspiration, which characterize his best poems, and by the profound truths which shine like virgin gold in his virile lines . . . are felt by the student and the cultured reader of Emerson's poems—by everyone who allows himself to be touched and purified by the Ithuriel spear of this rare poet. — HUBNER, CHARLES W., 1903, *Emerson the Poet, The Book-Lover, vol. 4, p. 107.*

GENERAL

We find beautiful writing and sound philosophy in this little work, but the effect is injured by occasional vagueness of expression, and by a vein of mysticism that pervades the writer's whole course of thought. The highest praise that can be accorded to it is, that it is a *suggestive* book; for no one can read it without tasking his faculties to the utmost, and relapsing into fits of severe meditation. But the effort of perusal is often painful, the thoughts excited are frequently bewildering, and the results to which they lead us uncertain and obscure. The reader feels as in a distracted dream, in which shows of surpassing beauty are around him, and he is conversant with disembodied spirits; yet all the time he is harassed by an uneasy sort of consciousness that the whole combination of phenomena is fantastic and unreal.—BOWEN, FRANCIS, 1837, *Christian Examiner, Jan.*

J. Sterling showed me Emerson's book, and drew a parallel between him and Carlyle; he was the Plato, and Carlyle the Tacitus. Emerson is the systematic thinker; Carlyle has the clearer insight, and has many deeper things than Emerson.—FOX, CAROLINE, 1841, *Journal, June 8th; Memories of Old Friends, ed. Pym, p. 140.*

Emerson's writings and speakings amount to something:—and yet hitherto, as seems to me, this Emerson is perhaps far less notable for what he has spoken or done, than for the many things he has not spoken, and has forborne to do. With uncommon interest, I have learned that this, and in such a never-resting locomotive country too, is one of those rare men who have withal the invaluable talent of sitting still! . . . What Emerson's talent is, we will not altogether estimate by this book. The utterance is abrupt, fitful; the great idea not yet embodied struggles towards an embodyment. Yet everywhere there is the true heart of a man; which is the parent of all talent; which without much talent cannot exist. A breath as of the green country,—all the welcomer that it is *New England* country, not second-hand but first-hand country,—meets us wholesomely everywhere in these "essays:" the authentic green Earth is there, with her mountains, rivers, with her mills and farms. Sharp gleams of insight arrest us by their pure intellectuality; here and there, in heroic rusticism, a tone of modest manfulness, of mild invincibility, low-voiced but lion-strong, makes us too, thrill with a noble pride.—CARLYLE, THOMAS, 1841, *Essays by R. W. Emerson, Preface.*

Belongs to a class of gentlemen with whom we have no patience whatever— the mystics for mysticism's sake. Quintilian mentions a pedant who taught obscurity, and who once said to a pupil: "This is excellent, for I do not understand it myself." How the good man would have chuckled over Mr. Emerson. His present *rôle* seems to be the out-Carlyling Carlyle. *Lycophron Tenebrosus* is a fool to him. The best answer to his twaddle is *cui bono?* —a very little Latin phrase very generally mistranslated and misunderstood — *cui bono?*—to whom is it a benefit? If not to Mr. Emerson individually, then surely to no man living.—POE, EDGAR ALLAN, 1842, *A Chapter of Autography, Works, ed. Stedman and Woodberry, vol. IX, p. 259.*

He has all the qualities of the sage,— originality, spontaneity, sagacious observation, delicate analysis, criticism, absence of dogmatism. He collects all the materials of a philosophy, without reducing it to a system; he thinks a little at random, and often meditates without finding definite limits at which this meditation ceases. His books are very remarkable, not only for the philosophy which they contain, but also for the criticism of our times. He is full of justice towards the doctrines and the society he criticises; he finds that the conservatives have legitimate principles; he thinks that the transcendentalists are probably right; he does not look with scorn upon our socialistic doctrines. He searches for his authorities through the entire history of philosophy; and thus, after having listened to all the modern doctrines with complaisance and patience, he breaks silence to give us maxims that might have issued now from the school of the Portico, and now from the gardens of the Academy.—MONTÉGUT, EMILE, 1847, *An American Thinker and Poet, Revue des Deux Mondes, Aug.*

He has not written a line which is not conceived in the interest of mankind. He never writes in the interest of a section, of a party, of a church, or a man, always in the interest of mankind. Hence comes the ennobling literature of the times; and, while his culture joins him to the history of man, his ideas and his whole life enable him to represent also the nature of man, and so to write for the future. He is one of the rare exceptions amongst our educated men, and helps redeem American literature from the charge of imitation, conformity, meanness of aim, and hostility to the powers of mankind. No faithful man is too low for his approval and encouragement; no faithless man too high and popular for his rebuke.—PARKER, THEODORE, 1849, *Massachusetts Quarterly Review*.

Emerson's "Essays" I read with much interest, and often with admiration, but they are of mixed gold and clay—deep and invigorating truth, dreary and depressing fallacy seem to me combined therein.—BRONTË, CHARLOTTE, 1849, *To W. S. Williams, Feb. 4; Charlotte Brontë and her Circle*, ed. Shorter, p. 189.

Some things he has published will live as long as the language itself; but much of his verse, constructed upon whims rather than under the influence of the spirit of poetry, will die out among the short-lived oddities of the day. Much of his prose, too, the product of imitation, unconscious perhaps of vicious foreign models, can scarcely be expected to survive the charm which hangs about his person and lingers in the magic tones of his voice. Mr. Emerson is a great writer, and an honest and independent thinker, on the whole. He is not, however, what one of the idolaters has lately called him, a Phœbus Apollo, descended from Olympus with hurtling arrows and the silver twanging bow.... His style is often musical, clear, and brilliant; words are selected with so rare a felicity that they have the shine of diamonds, and they cut their meaning on the reader's mind as the diamond's edge leaves its trace deep and sharp on the surface of glass. But by and by, we fall upon a passage which either conveys no distinct sense, or in which some very commonplace thought is made to sound with the clangor of a braying trumpet. Quaintness of thought and expression is his easily besetting sin; and here lies the secret of his sympathy with Carlyle, that highly gifted master of oddity and affectation. As a writer, Mr. Emerson is every way Carlyle's superior, would he but let the Carlylese dialect alone. He had more imagination, more refinement and subtlety of thought, more taste in style, more exquisite sense of rhythm. Perhaps his range of intellectual vision is not so broad. He has not the learning of Carlyle, nor the abundant humour, which sometimes reconciles us even to absurdity. But Mr. Emerson has a more delicate wit, a wit often quite irresistible by its unexpected turns, and the sudden introduction of effective contrasts. Carlyle has an extraordinary abundance of words, a store of epithets, good, bad, and indifferent, by which the reader is often flooded; Emerson is more temperate and artistic.—NORTON, CHARLES ELIOT, 1850, *Emerson's Representative Men, North American Review*, vol. 70, pp. 520, 521.

How little the all-important art of making meaning pellucid is studied now! Hardly any popular writer, except myself, thinks of it. Many seem to aim at being obscure. Indeed, they may be right enough in one sense; for many readers give credit for profundity to whatever is obscure, and call all that is perspicuous shallow. But coraggio! and think of A. D. 2850. Where will your Emersons be then? But Herodotus will still be read with delight.—MACAULAY, THOMAS BABINGTON, 1850, *Diary, Jan. 12; Life and Letters*, ed. Trevelyan, ch. XII.

Emerson is certainly one of the most original writers the New World has produced. He writes least like an American of any author we have read. We do not mean this disparagingly to his character as a good and true republican, but to show our opinion of his greater breadth and depth of appreciation than is generally met with in American authors.... Mr. Emerson's power has not its foundation in the human heart: the roots of his being are in the intellect. Consequently he is deficient in one of the two great elements of genius. That this narrows his scope is too evident to need anything beyond the mere statement.... Mr. Emerson possesses so many characteristics of genius that his want of universality is the more to be regretted; the leading feature of his mind is intensity; he is deficient in heart sympathy. Full to overflowing with intellectual appreciation, he is incapable of that embracing reception of impulses which gives to

Byron so large a measure of influence and fame. Emerson is elevated, but not expansive; his flight is high, but not extensive. He has a magnificent vein of the purest gold, but it is not a mine. To vary our illustration somewhat, he is not a world, but a district; a lofty and commanding eminence we admit, but only a very small portion of the true poet's universe. What, however, he has done is permanent, and America will always in after time be proud of Ralph Waldo Emerson, and consider him one of her noblest sons.—POWELL, THOMAS, 1850, *Living Writers of America*, pp. 49, 54, 77.

His poems are mostly philosophical, which is not the truest kind of poetry. They want the simple force of nature and passion, and, while they charm the ear and interest the mind, fail to wake far-off echoes in the heart. The imagery wears a symbolical air, and serves rather as illustration, than to delight us by fresh and glowing forms of life.—OSSOLI, MARGARET FULLER, 1850 (?), *American Literature; Art, Literature and the Drama*, p. 308.

Very good scattered thoughts in it ["Representative Men"]: but scarcely leaving any large impression with one, or establishing a theory.—FITZGERALD, EDWARD, 1850, *To John Allen, March 9; Letters and Literary Remains*, ed. Wright, vol. I, p. 202.

An exquisite observer and very subtle, often very profound, thinker.—HELPS, ARTHUR, 1851, *Companions of My Solitude*, ch. XI.

He is the most original man produced by the United States up to this day. . . . Some of Emerson's poems are charming. A little piece "To the Bee," delicious in its way, is almost worthy of Milton.—CHASLES, PHILARÈTE, 1852, *Anglo-American Literature and Manners*, pp. 192, 193.

Fine soul and brave!
If quaint in rhyme, if no logician gave
Laws to thy thinking, inly sweet and wise,
Long in these woodlands may thine image live!
And many a musing Briton's heart
Shall melt, as oft with moistening eyes
He lets his noisy train depart
To linger where,—O sacred art!
In yonder grave thy Druid lies.
—PARSONS, THOMAS WILLIAM, 1852, *Emerson, Poems*, p. 66.

His first slim, anonymous duodecimo, "Nature," was as fair and fascinating to the royal young minds who met it in the course of their reading, as Egeria to Numa wandering in the grove. The essays, orations, and poems followed, developing and elaborating the same spiritual and heroic philosophy, applying it to life, history, and literature, with a vigor and richness so supreme that not only do many account him our truest philosopher, but others acknowledge him as our most characteristic poet. . . . The imagination of the man who roams the solitary pastures of Concord, or floats, dreaming, down its river, will easily see its landscape upon Emerson's pages. . . . His writings, however, have no imported air. If there be something Oriental in his philosophy and tropical in his imagination, they have yet the strong flavor of his mother earth— the underived sweetness of the open Concord sky, and the spacious breadth of the Concord horizon.—CURTIS, GEORGE WILLIAM, 1854, *Homes of American Authors*.

If he cannot interpret, he can paint nature as few else can. He has watched and followed all her motions like a friendly spy. He has the deepest egotistic interest in her. He appropriates her to himself, and because he loves and clasps, imagines that he has made her. His better writings seem shaken, sifted, and cooled in the winds of the American autumn. The flush on his style is like the red hue of the Indian summer inscribed upon the leaf. One of the most inconsistent and hopelessly wrong of American thinkers, he is the greatest of American poets. We refer not to his verse —which is, in general, woven mist, involving little—but to the beautiful and abrupt utterances about nature in his prose. No finer things about the outward features, and the transient meanings of creation, have been said, since the Hebrews, than are to be found in some of his books. But he has never, like them, pierced to the grand doctrine of the Divine Personality and Fatherhood. — GILFILLAN, GEORGE, 1855, *A Third Gallery of Portraits*, p. 289.

The Emerson philosophy, for example, is grieved that one series of writing should arrogate inspiration to themselves alone. It is obvious that a ready credence given to professed inspiration in other quarters, and later times, must tend to lower the exclusive prestige of the Scriptures. Thus the mystics may be played off against the Apostles, and all that is granted to mysticism may be considered as so much taken from the Bible. A certain door has been marked with a cross. Emerson, like the sly Abagail of the Forty Thieves, proceeds to mark, in like manner, all the doors in the street. . . . Whether in prose or verse he is the chief singer of his time at the high court of Mysticism. He belongs more to the East than to the West—true brother of those Sufis with whose doctrine he has so much in common. Luxuriant in fancy, impulsive, dogmatic, darkly oracular, he does not reason. His majestic monologue may not be interrupted by a question. His inspiration disdains argument. He delights to lavish his varied and brilliant resources upon some defiant paradox—and never more than when that paradox is engaged in behalf of an optimism extreme enough to provoke another Voltaire to write another "Candide." He displays in its perfection the fantastic incoherence of the "God-intoxicated" man.—VAUGHAN, ROBERT ALFRED, 1856-60, *Hours with the Mystics*, vol. I, p. 237, vol. II, p. 7.

I have been reading this morning for my spiritual good Emerson's "Man the Reformer," which comes to me with fresh beauty and meaning. My heart goes out with venerating gratitude to that mild face, which I dare say is smiling on some one as beneficently as it one day did on me years and years ago.—ELIOT, GEORGE, 1860, *To Miss Sara Hennell, Aug. 27*; *George Eliot's Life as related in her Letters and Journals*, ed. Cross, vol. II, p. 196.

Emerson's writing has a cold cheerless glitter, like the new furniture in a warehouse, which will come of use by and by.—SMITH, ALEXANDER, 1863, *Dreamthorp*, p. 191.

Emerson stands closest of all in relation to Blake, his verse as well as his essays and lectures being little else than the expression of this mystical simplicity. Were he gifted with the singing voice we should not have to look to the future for its supreme bard. But whenever he has sung a few clear sweet notes, his voice breaks, and he has to recite and speak what he would fain chant. His studies, also, have somewhat injured his style with technicology, making him in his own despite look at Nature through the old church and school windows, often when he should be with her in the rustic air. In some of his shorter poems, however, and in the snatches of Orphic song prefixed to some of his essays (as "Compensation," "Art," "History," "Heroism"), any one with ears to hear may catch pregnant hints of what poetry possessed by this inspiration can accomplish, and therefore *will* accomplish; for no pure inspiration having once come down among men ever withdraws its influence until it has attained (humanly) perfect embodiment.—THOMSON, JAMES ("B. V."), 1864, *The Poems of William Blake, Biographical and Critical Studies*, p. 267.

The majority of the sensible, practical community regarded him [1836] as mystical, as crazy or affected, as an imitator of Carlyle, as racked and revolutionary, as a fool, as one who did not himself know what he meant. A small but determined minority, chiefly composed of young men and women, admired him and believed in him, took him for their guide, teacher, and master. I, and most of my friends, belonged to this class. Without accepting all his opinions, or indeed knowing what they were, we felt that he did us more good than any other writer or speaker among us, and chiefly in two ways,—first, by encouraging self-reliance; and, secondly, by encouraging God-reliance.—CLARKE, JAMES FREEMAN, 1865, *The Religious Philosophy of Ralph Waldo Emerson, A Lecture.*

His genius is ethical, literary; he speaks to the moral sentiments through the imagination, insinuating the virtues so, as poets and moralists of his class are wont. . . . Of Emerson's books I am not here designing to speak critically, but of his genius and personal influence rather. Yet, in passing, I may say, that his book of "Traits" deserves to be honored as one in which England, Old and New, may take honest pride, as being the liveliest portraiture of British genius and accomplishments,—a book, like Tacitus, to be quoted as a masterpiece of historical painting, and perpetuating the New Englander's fame with that of his race. 'Tis victory of eyes over hands, a triumph of ideas. . . . The consistent idealist, yet the realist none the less, he has illustrated the learning and thought of former times on the noblest themes, and comes nearest of any to emancipating the mind of his own time from the errors and dreams of past ages.—ALCOTT, A. BRONSON, 1865-82, *Ralph Waldo Emerson, An Estimate of his Character and Genius*, pp. 18, 30, 31.

There is no man living to whom, as a writer, so many of us feel and thankfully acknowledge so great an indebtedness for ennobling impulses. . . . We look upon him as one of the few men of genius whom our age has produced, and there needs no better proof of it than his masculine faculty of fecundating other minds. Search for his eloquence in his books and you will perchance miss it, but meanwhile you will find that it has kindled all your thoughts. For choice and pith of language he belongs to a better age than ours, and might rub shoulders with Fuller and Browne,—though he does use that abominable word *reliable*. His eye for a fine, telling phrase that will carry true is like that of a backwoodsman for a rifle; and he will dredge you up a choice word from the mud of Cotton Mather himself. A diction at once so rich and so homely as his I know not where to match in these days of writing by the page; it is like homespun cloth-of-gold.—LOWELL, JAMES RUSSELL, 1868–71, *Emerson the Lecturer, My Study Windows*, p. 376.

Emerson is a great master in his way. His style has an incomparable charm. Its silvery rhythm captivates the ear. The affluence of his illustrations diffuses a flavor of oriental spicery over his pages. . . . In thus renewing my acquaintance with Emerson, I am struck with certain rare combinations which may serve to explain his position. His rejection of dogmas is cool and merciless; but he shows no sympathy with vulgar and destructive radicalism. He asserts an unlimited freedom of the individual, but maintains a moral tone, rigid almost to asceticism. With the wild havoc which he makes of popular opinion, he always respects the dignity of human nature. . . . The practical shrewdness interwoven with his poetical nature is one of the secrets of his power. You attempt to follow his lofty flight among the purple clouds, almost believing that he has "hitched his wagon to a star," when he suddenly drops down to earth, and surprises you with an utterance of the homeliest wisdom. On this account, when they get over the novelty of his manner, plain men are apt to find themselves at home with him. His acquaintance with common things, all household ways and words, the processes of every-day life on the farm, in the kitchen and stable, as well as in the drawing-room and library, engages their attention, and produces a certain kindly warmth of fellowship, which would seem to be incompatible with the coldness of his nature. Emerson is not without a tincture of science. He often makes a happy use of its results, in the way of comparison and illustration. But I do not suppose that he could follow a demonstration of Euclid, or one of the fine analysis in Physics of Tyndall or Huxley. Of such a writer as Herbert Spencer he has probably no more than a faint comprehension.—RIPLEY, GEORGE, 1869, *Journal; George Ripley (American Men of Letters) by Octavius Brooks Frothingham*, pp. 266, 267, 268.

Is a zealous interpreter and proclaimer of German philosophy, and excels equally in his characteristic description of nationalities as of poets.—SCHERR, J., 1874, *A History of English Literature*, tr. M. V., p. 310.

In philosophy, the name of Emerson at once occurs to the mind; but with all his excellences—and in some respects he is the most remarkable man America has yet produced—he is unable to stand alone. It is questionable if the world would have heard of Emerson had it not first heard of Carlyle; and in this country Emerson could not have occupied that conspicuous position to which he can justly lay claim in his own country.—SMITH, GEORGE BARNETT, 1875, *Nathaniel Hawthorne, Poets and Novelists*, p. 154.

Emerson . . . gives us ["English Traits"] probably the most masterly and startling analysis of a people which has ever been offered in the same slight bulk, unsurpassed, too, in brilliancy and penetration of statement.—LATHROP, GEORGE PARSONS, 1876, *A Study of Hawthorne*, p. 252.

It is this depth of spiritual experience and subtility of spiritual insight which distinguishes Emerson from all other American authors, and makes him an elementary power as well as an elementary thinker. The singular attractiveness, however, of his writings comes from his intense perception of Beauty, both in its abstract quality as the "awful loveliness" which such poets as Shelley celebrated, and in the more concrete expression by which it fascinates ordinary minds. His imaginative faculty, both in the conception and creation of beauty, is uncorrupted by any morbid sentiment. His vision reaches to the very sources of beauty,—the beauty that cheers.—WHIPPLE, EDWIN PERCY, 1876–86, *American Literature and Other Papers, ed. Whittier*, p. 63.

Emerson, whom I have been reading all the winter, and who gives me immeasurable delight because he does not propound to me disagreeable systems and hideous creeds but simply walks along high and bright ways where one loves to go with him.—LANIER, SIDNEY, 1877, *To Bayard Taylor, May* 25; *Letters*, p. 196.

Or will I wander out 'neath summer skies,
With Concord's sage to look in Nature's eyes,
And find therein new hopes for future years,
The while she whispers in our listening ears
Weird sentences and sibylline decrees
From cave and bank of flowers, rock, fern, and trees,
And brook that, singing, through the greenwood travels,
Whose meanings he—her Priest—alone unravels.
—JOYCE, ROBERT DWYER, 1877, *Reflections, Scribner's Monthly*, vol. 14, p. 448.

It is a subject of gratulation that Emerson, who has been before New England for the past half-century, has wielded a generally beneficial influence. With his powers and opportunities he might have done incalculable harm; but the weight of his authority has been thrown upon the side of general morality and natural development of strength of character. . . . He has preached the purest gospel of naturalism, shrinking at once from the bold and impious counsellings of Goethe and from the macularity of Carlyle. He has given us, in himself, glimpses of a noble character, and his ideals have been lofty and pure. New England could not have had a better apostle, humanly and naturally speaking. Its cultivated and rational mind turned in horror and disgust from its rigid Calvinism, its *outré*, religious frenzies, and its sordid and prosaic life. They found a voice and interpreter in Emerson. He marks the recoil from unscriptural, irrational, and unnatural religion.—O'CONNOR, JOSEPH, 1878, *Ralph Waldo Emerson, Catholic World*, vol. 27, p. 95.

He was the Transcendentalist *par excellence*. . . . One certainly envies the privilege of having heard the finest of Emerson's orations poured forth in their early newness. They were the most poetical, the most beautiful productions of the American mind, and they were thoroughly local and national. They had a music and a magic, and when one remembers the remarkable charm of the speaker, the beautiful modulation of his utterance, one regrets in especial that one might not have been present on a certain occasion which made a sensation, an era—the delivery of an address to the Divinity School of Harvard University, on a summer evening in 1838.— JAMES, HENRY, JR., 1880, *Nathaniel Hawthorne (English Men of Letters)*, pp. 82, 83.

Doors hast thou opened for us, thinker, seer,
Bars let down into pastures measureless;
The air we breathe to-day, through thee, is freer
Than, buoyant with its freshness, we can guess.
—LARCOM, LUCY, 1880, *R. W. E., May* 25; *Wild Roses of Cape Ann*, p. 175.

The intellectual life of Emerson for nearly half a century has affected educated men with an influence that is immeasurable; he is "the Columbus of modern thought." Since Lord Bacon, there has not been another writer whose resources were so wholly in himself. He belongs with the three or four philosophic minds of the first order, born of the Anglo-Saxon race. . . . There was a mild Teutonic flavor in Emerson's early style; and, as the great traits of German thought were then more noticeable than now, the reflecting public at once accused our philosopher of being an imitator of Carlyle. The statement was absurd, because the native qualities of the two men have always been diverse. There was never any similarity between Carlyle and Emerson except in regard to acuteness, honesty and fearlessness. If there was at one time observable in their writing the influence of the same German masters, there has since been a growing divergence. They have been occupied with widely different themes, and have gone on, each in his own way. The one has produced essays and poems, dealing mostly with abstract ideas; the other has written voluminous histories, biographies, and reviews. The one crystallizes thought into proverbs; the other can be downright when he will, but often indulges in long periods, connected, oratorical, and rising to climaxes. Carlyle has more energy, Emerson more insight. Carlyle is planted upon the actual, in the domain of the understanding;

Emerson soars on the wings of imagination. Carlyle portrays kings, soldiers, and statesmen, with hard outlines and abundant detail; Emerson shows us the souls of poets, prophets, and philosophers, and conveys their wisdom and love. The history of a German prince, half robber and half tyrant, may not interest future ages; but the "Essays on Nature" are a part of the permanent treasures of thinking men, like the "Phædo" of Plato, and the "Essays" of Lord Bacon.— UNDERWOOD, FRANCIS H., 1880, *Ralph Waldo Emerson, North American Review, vol.* 130, *pp.* 479, 493.

There is, perhaps, no writer of the nineteenth century who will better repay a careful and prolonged perusal than Emerson. He enjoys the rare distinction of having ascended to the highest point to which the human mind can climb,—to the point where, as he says of Plato, the poles of thought are on a line with the axis on which the frame of things revolve. . . . He stations himself at the point where the ascending lines of Law pass into Unity. Once attain to that position, and every sentence becomes luminous. The connection of ideas becomes apparent; the illustrations are seen to be pertinent and exact; and the subject to be laid open on all sides by direct and penetrating insight. We can then turn to him, with the same delight, for the philosophical expression of the deep laws of human life, as we do to Shakspeare for their dramatic representation. For he is one of the profoundest of thinkers, and has that universality, serenity, and cosmopolitan breadth of comprehension, that place him among the great of all ages. He has swallowed all his predecessors, and converted them into nutriment for himself. He is as subtile and delicate, too, as he is broad and massive, and possesses a practical wisdom and keenness of observation that hold his feet fast to the solid earth when his head is striking the stars. His scientific accuracy and freedom of speculation mark him out as one of the representative men of the nineteenth century.—CROZIER, JOHN BEATTIE, 1880, *The Religion of the Future.*

"Well," said Tyndall musingly, and half to himself, "the first time I ever knew Waldo Emerson was when, years ago, a young man, I picked up on a stall a copy of his "Nature." I read it with much delight, and I have never ceased to read it; and if any one can be said to have given *the* impulse to my mind, it is Emerson. Whatever I have done, the world owes to him."—SARGENT, MRS. JOHN T., 1880, *ed. Sketches and Reminiscences of the Radical Club, p.* 300.

In his teachings and in his life he is a great moral influence, he is an awakener and stimulator of the spiritual in man, while in his intellectual convictions he is a penetrating spirit of truth. He is a lark that heralds the coming day, a sunbeam that dissipates darkness. All the more pervasive, because purely moral and spiritual, will be his influence, reaching all hearts, pervading all forms, entering all sanctuaries, sustaining all right moral considerations, and invigorating every true resolve. Life will seem more sacred, the world holier, truth more sure, man diviner, heaven nearer, whenever we love the truth in that untrammeled spirit he has sought to vindicate. Whatever flaws may be found in his philosophic methods, none will be found in those moral and spiritual truths to which he has devoted his life for half a century.—COOKE, GEORGE WILLIS, 1881, *Ralph Waldo Emerson, His Life, Writings and Philosophy, p.* 384.

> O Seer, to whose gift
> Looms large the Future's better part,
> What other prophet voice shall lift
> This burden from the people's heart!

—JOHNSON, ROBERT W., 1881, *To Ralph Waldo Emerson, Century Magazine, vol.* 23, 200.

The most original and independent thinker and greatest moral teacher that America has produced. . . . Those who have felt throughout their lives the purifying and elevating power of Emerson's writings, and who have recognised in his inspiring career the perfect sanity of true genius, can never think of him without affectionate reverence. He now rests, in that deep repose which he has so well earned, and on laurels that will never fade. —IRELAND, ALEXANDER, 1882, *Ralph Waldo Emerson, pp.* 4, 41.

Emerson's mission was to individual minds. Those who were drawn to him, or those in whom he perceived a tendency of growth, found in him a good shepherd who carried them in his arms. He did not like to deal with people on general principles, but recognized the particular talent and the state of each who sought him, and was maternal in his faithfulness no less than his tenderness to them. He was the friend of souls. For this reason few of his conversations would bear to be reported. I was just twenty-one years of age when I first met him, and often since, reflecting how crude I was, his patience and kindness have been remembered with grateful emotion. — CONWAY, MONCURE DANIEL, 1882, *Emerson at Home and Abroad*, p. 363.

Beside the ocean, wandering on the shore,
  I seek no *measure* of the infinite sea;
  Beneath the solemn stars that speak to me
I may not care to *reason out* their lore;
  Among the mountains, whose bright summits o'er
    The flush of morning brightens, there may be
      Only a sense of *might* and *mystery*,
And yet, a thrill of infinite life they pour
  Through all my being, and uplift me high
    Above my little self and weary days.
So in thy presence, Emerson, I hear
A sea-voice sounding, neath a boundless sky,
  While mountainous thoughts tower o'er life's common ways.

—SAVAGE, MINOT JUDSON, 1882, *Emerson*, The Literary World, vol. 13, p. 161.

In essays which relate to concrete affairs classification is possible, and Emerson has availed himself of it. Wherever a genesis is attempted, logical order of sequence is necessary and is attained. In "English Traits" the matter is wisely arranged. You have first the occasion of his visit; then, in order, follow considerations on the land, race, ability, manners, etc., each one lifting us to the next without confusion. Every essay of Emerson is the result of much sifting and classifying. Seeing everything in its most universal aspects, as is habitual with him, it is quite natural that each suggests all to him. Accordingly, he resolutely excludes, by successive siftings, the matter that is less directly connected with his central theme, and retains only that which best illustrates his thought, and builds it out into a solid structure. . . . In seeing and uttering ethical laws specially befitting our modified conditions, he is the prophet of our century. . . . No one has preached more solemnly to us of our duties in a free government. Trickery and cunning, demagoguery,—these have received his rebuke, but their presence has never made him despair of our civilization. His teachings have borne noble fruit in this direction, and I believe that every American has received some impulse from Emerson that gives him greater moral courage and causes him to deal with his fellow men more frankly and generously than before. Self-respect has been taught us as the foundation of free government.— HARRIS, WILLIAM TORREY, 1882, *Ralph Waldo Emerson, Atlantic Monthly*, vol. 50, pp. 247, 250.

His uncompromising devotion to Truth never hardened into dogmatism, his audacious rejection of all formalism never soured into intolerance, his hatred of sham never degenerated into a lip-protest and a literary trick, his inflexible moral purpose went hand in hand with unbounded charity. In him the intellectual keenness and profundity of a philosopher, and the imagination of a poet, were combined with that child-like simplicity and almost divine humility which made him the idol of his fellow-townsmen and the easily accessible friend of the ignorant and the poor. No discrepancy exists between his written words and the record of his life.—LAZARUS, EMMA, 1882, *Emerson's Personality*, Century Magazine, vol. 24, p. 454.

Let me say, then, that Emerson, in my judgment, stands at the head of American literature in two of its most important functions: as philosophical essayist, and as lyric poet. As philosophical essayist he is marked by absolute sincerity, independent judgment, and the freshness of original thought. . . . I place Emerson at the head of the lyric poets of America. In this judgment I anticipate wide dissent; but the dissent, I think, will be less when I explain the sense in which the affirmation is intended. I do not mean that Mr. Emerson excels his competitors in poetic art. On the contrary, the want of art in his poetry may once for all be conceded. The verses often halt, the conclusion sometimes flags, and the metrical propriety is recklessly violated. But the defect is closely connected with the characteristic merit of the poet, and springs from the same root, — his utter spontaneity. — HEDGE, FREDERIC H., 1882, *Memorial Address at the Annual Meeting of the American Unitarian Association*.

Mr. Emerson gained nothing from his interpreters. Nor does he now. The key which they offered did not fit the wards of the lock. The vagueness of the oracle seemed to be deepened when repeated by any other lips than those which gave it first utterance. In most of the recent references in the newspapers and magazines to the opening of Mr. Emerson's career in high philosophy, emphatic statements are made as to the ridicule and satire and banter evoked by the first utterances of this transcendentalism. It is not impressed upon my memory that any of this triviality was ever spent upon Mr. Emerson himself. The modest, serene, unaggressive attitude, and personal phenomena of bearing and utterance which were so winningly characteristic of his presence and speech, as he dropped the sparkles and nuggets of his fragmentary revelations, were his ample security against all such disrespect.—ELLIS, GEORGE E., 1882, *Tributes to Longfellow and Emerson by the Massachusetts Historical Society*, p. 33.

He always talked as one quite sure that the plainest speech, the most direct way of "putting things," was best liked, and he thus constantly awakened in one the feeling, that he never could be offended by the sharpest antagonism of a sincere man. This childlike simplicity, this "believing and *therefore* speaking," was of itself a life-long power, characterizing not only the casual or private talk, but also the set public address. . . The subtle affinity between Mr. Emerson's distinctive style and line of thought and the old Gnosticism, a self-asserting transcendental philosophy, is quite clearly apparent. His completed life-work presents him to the world as the first New Englander, or rather American writer, whose speculative trend of mind took sympathetically to the Gnostic ideas, and whose inherited proclivity as a born New Englander necessitated the effort to combine those Oriental elements with the shrewd common-sense of practical Yankee life. Yet, alas, there is no vital unity. The incongruity is glaring and balks all effort to naturalize the alien mysticism as an aider to home-culture. The American will live out his supreme ideas, whatsoever they may be, in religion as well as in politics. . . . While musing, as at the begining, over the works of Ralph Waldo Emerson, we recognize now as ever his imperial genius as one of the greatest of writers; at the same time, his life-work, as a whole, tested by its supreme ideal, its method and fruitage, shows also a great waste of power, verifying the saying of Jesus touching the harvest of human life: "He that gathereth not with me scattereth abroad."—HAGUE, WILLIAM, 1883–84, *Ralph Waldo Emerson, A Paper Read Before the New York Genealogical and Biographical Society, with Afterthoughts*, pp. 5, 16, 30.

I have never cared much for Emerson, he is little more to me than a clever gossip, and his egoism reiterates itself to provocation.—RUSKIN, JOHN, 1883, *Letter to Alexander Ireland*, Feb. 9; *Literary Anecdotes of the Nineteenth Century*, vol. II, p. 448.

Mentally, he is all force; his mind acts without natural impediment or friction,— a machine that runs unhindered by the contact of its parts. As he was physically lean and slender of figure, and his face but a welding together of features, so there was no adipose tissue in his thought. It is pure, clear, and accurate, and has the fault of dryness, but often moves with exquisite beauty. It is not adhesive; it sticks to nothing except to the memory, nor anything to it. After ranging through the philosophies of the world, it emerges clean and characteristic as ever. It has many affinities, but no adhesion; it is not always self-adherent. There are in many of his essays separate statements presenting no logical continuity; but though this may cause anxiety to disciples of Emerson, it never troubled him. Wandering at will in the garden of moral and religious philosophy it was his part to pluck such blossoms, as he saw were good and beautiful,— not to discover their botanical relationship. He might, for art or harmony's sake, arrange them according to their hue or fragrance; but it was not his affair to go further in their classification. . . Emerson does not solve for all time the problem of the universe. He solves nothing; but, what is more useful, he gives impetus and direction to lofty endeavor. He does not anticipate the lessons of the ages; but he teaches us so to deal with circumstances as to secure the good instead of the evil tissue. New horizons opening before us will carry us beyond the scope of Emerson's surmise; but we shall not easily improve upon his aim and attitude.—HAWTHORNE, JULIAN, 1884, *Emerson as an American, The Genius and Character of Emerson*, ed. Sanborn, pp. 74, 77.

I do not, then, place Emerson among the great poets. But I go further, and say that I do not place him among the great writers, the great men of letters. . . . Emerson cannot, I think, be called with justice a great philosophical writer. He cannot build; his arrangement of philosophical ideas has no progress in it, no evolution; he does not construct a philosophy. Emerson himself knew the defects of his method, or rather want of method, very well; indeed, he and Carlyle criticise themselves and one another in a way which leaves little for any one else to do in the way of formulating their defects. . . . We have not in Emerson a great poet, a great writer, a great philosophy-maker. His relation to us is not that of one of these personages; yet is it a relation of, I think, even superior importance. His relation to us is more like that of the Roman Emperor Marcus Aurelius. Marcus Aurelius is not a great writer, a great philosophy-maker; he is the friend and aider of those who would live in the spirit. Emerson is the same. He is the friend and aider of those who would live in the spirit. All the points in thinking which are necessary for this purpose he takes; but he does not combine them into a system, or present them as a regular philosophy. Combined in a system by a man with the requisite talent for this kind of thing, they would be less useful than as Emerson gives them to us; and the man with the talent so to systemise them would be less impressive than Emerson.—ARNOLD, MATTHEW, 1884, *Emerson, Macmillan's Magazine*, vol. 50, pp. 4, 6, 8.

Emerson lived in a pale moonlit world of ideality, in which there was little that was adapted to tame the fierce passions and appease the agonizing remorse of ordinary human nature. He was a voice to the pure intellect and the more fastidious conscience of men, not a power of salvation for their wretchedness. But his gnomic wisdom will live long, and startle many generations with its clear, high, thrilling note.—HUTTON, RICHARD HOLT, 1884–94, *Criticisms on Contemporary Thought and Thinkers*, vol. I, p. 58.

Everything Emerson wrote belongs to literature, and to literature in its highest and most serious mood. . . . All Emerson's aspirations were toward greatness of character, greatness of wisdom, nobility of soul. Hence, in all his writings and speakings the great man shines through and eclipses the great writer. The flavor of character is stronger than the flavor of letters, and dominates the pages.—BURROUGHS, JOHN, 1884, *Arnold on Emerson and Carlyle, Century Magazine*, vol. 27, p. 928.

It is too soon to say in what particular niche among the teachers of the race posterity will place him; enough that in our own generation he has already been accepted as one of the wise masters, who, being called to high thinking for generous ends, did not fall below his vocation, but, steadfastly pursuing the pure search for truth, without propounding a system or founding a school or cumbering himself overmuch about applications, lived the life of the spirit, and breathed into other men a strong desire after the right governance of the soul. All this is generally realized and understood, and men may now be left to find their way to the Emersonian doctrine without the critic's prompting. Though it is only the other day that Emerson walked the earth and was alive and among us, he is already one of the privileged few whom the reader approaches in the mood of settled respect, and whose names have surrounded themselves with an atmosphere of religion. . . . His books were for spiritual use, like maps and charts of the mind of man, and not much for "excellence of divertisement." He had the gift of bringing his reading to bear easily upon the tenor of his musings, and knew how to use books as an aid to thinking, instead of letting them take the edge off thought. There was assuredly nothing of the compiler or the erudite collegian in him. It is a graver defect that he introduces the great names of literature without regard for true historical perspective in their place, either in relation to one another, or to the special phases of social change and shifting time. Still let his admirers not forget that Emerson was in his own way Scholar no less than Sage.—MORLEY, JOHN, 1884, *Ralph Waldo Emerson, An Essay*, pp. 1, 25.

Emerson's place as a thinker is somewhat difficult to fix. He can not properly be called a psychologist. He made notes and even delivered lectures on the natural history of the intellect; but they seem to have been made up, according to his own statement, of hints and fragments rather than of the results of sympathetic study. He was a man of intuition, of insight, a seer, a poet, with a tendency to mysticism.

This tendency renders him sometimes obscure, and once in a while almost, if not quite, unintelligible. . . . But that which is mysticism to a dull listener may be the highest and most inspiring imaginative clairvoyance to a brighter one. . . . Too much has been made of Emerson's mysticism. He was an intellectual rather than an emotional mystic, and withal a cautious one. He never let go the string of his balloon. He never threw over all his ballast of common sense so as to rise above an atmosphere in which a rational being could breathe.—HOLMES, OLIVER WENDELL, 1884, *Ralph Waldo Emerson* (*American Men of Letters*), pp. 390, 396.

That gray-eyed seer
Who in pastoral Concord ways
With Plato and Häfiz walked.
—ALDRICH, THOMAS BAILEY, 1884, *Monody on the Death of Wendell Phillips*.

In his first work, "Nature," published in 1836, he revealed that vigorous idealism which has caused him to be surnamed, in the United States, the Prince of Transcendentalists. Notwithstanding the fact that the blood of eight generations of clergymen flowed in his veins, he was anything but a theologian and a controversialist. Imagination and feeling were his leading characteristics; he might almost be called an *illuminé* of Rationalism.—D'ALVIELLA, COUNT GOBLET, 1885, *The Contemporary Evolution of Religious Thought in England, America and India*, tr. Moden, p. 170.

"English Traits," which evinces more genuine insight into the real character and underlying forces of the complex English civilization than any other book of like character, will hereafter be regarded as his clearest title to fame. The noble series of essays, "Nature," is so great, that humanity must change radically if that book does not become immortal. The connection of thought in them is by a sort of mystical flight which none but he can take. To complain of a lack of unity in them would be like complaining of the lack of evolution in Isaiah.—JOHNSON, CHARLES F., 1885, *Three Americans and Three Englishmen*, p. 206.

Crystal-sighted, truth-voiced. — COUES, ELLIOTT, 1885, *The Dæmon of Darwin*, p. ix.

A good many years since, at the house of an American friend I happened to take up a volume of Emerson's Essays which was lying upon the table. I looked into it,—read a page, and was startled to find that I had understood nothing, though tolerably well acquainted with English. I inquired as to the author. In reply I was told that he was the first writer in America, an eminently gifted man, but somewhat crazed at times, and often unable to explain his own words. Notwithstanding, no one was held in such esteem for his character, and for his prose writings. In short, the opinion fell upon my ears as so strange that I re-opened the book. Some sentences, upon a second reading, shot like a beam of light into my very soul, and I was moved to put the book into my pocket, that I might read it more attentively at home. I find it is a great deal to begin with if a book so far attracts us that we resolve, without urging, to look it through; since, as a measure of self-preservation, it is necessary to stand on the defensive nowadays against books and people, if we would reserve time and inclination for our own thoughts. I took Webster's Dictionary and began to read. The construction of the sentences struck me as very extraordinary. I soon discovered the secret; they were real thoughts, an individual language, a sincere man, that I had before me; naught superficial—secondhand. Enough! I bought the book! From that time I have never ceased to read Emerson's works, and whenever I take up a volume anew it seems to me as if I were reading it for the first time. . . . We feel that Emerson never wished to say more than just what at the moment presented itself to his soul. He never set up a system; never defended himself. He is never hasty, and always impartial. He labors after no effects in style. He speaks with perfect composure, as if translating from a language understood only by himself. He always addressed the same public,—the unknown multitude of those who buy and read his works and wish to listen to him,—and ever in the same tone of manly affability.—GRIMM, HERMAN, 1886, *Ralph Waldo Emerson, Literature*, tr. *Adams*, pp. 1, 38.

One of the few higher spiritual voices of the century that have spoken in clear, unmistakable tones of hopefulness and cheer. His coming was as the breaking of the sun through the clouds to a people long living under dreary skies. The power of the man was felt by all. Not only America, but England, the world, recognized a new and telling force. . . . One thing Emerson possessed, which was to him all-indispensable, and without which, in his age, he could never have exerted the influence he unmistakably did. His mind was essentially faithful, truthful, exact. With all his tendency to idealism and rapture, to abstraction and mysticism, he never wholly forgot the necessity of clinging to the *fact.*—DANA, WILLIAM F., 1886, *The Optimism of Ralph Waldo Emerson*, pp. 40, 45.

Emerson's works, like the Bible or Shakespeare or those collections of proverbs in which in every language are summed up the wit and wisdom of unnumbered nameless poets and philosophers, might furnish texts for sermons of any color. Theist or pantheist or agnostic might bind his arguments with quotations from the many-sided Essays. Nay, at different times Emerson tells a different story to the same person,—as I have experienced in reading his essay on Fate, for instance, which has seemed to me an inspiring assertion of the freedom of the will and an unanswerable argument for fatalism. This apparent shifting is the obstacle that prevents many persons from understanding Emerson. . . . If in one place Emerson makes a half-statement, be sure that somewhere else its complement and corrective have been recorded. He can be understood only by those who seek for the spirit of all his work. To single out a paragraph or chapter as representative, generally misrepresents him. . . Emerson is the unwearied champion of Individuals. All his sentences are addressed to them. He reveals to them the possibilities lying within reach of all. Mere bigness and burly multitudes get no praise from him. The glib cant of the demagogue issues not from his lips.—THAYER, WILLIAM R., 1886, *The Influence of Emerson*, pp. 6, 8, 12.

Emerson had at one time a great influence on me that was good in some ways, but not in all. His philosophy is stimulating and encouraging, but not quite true, because it is too optimistic for real truth. He encourages young readers in the desire to be themselves and develop their own faculties, which is very good, but at the same time he encourages a degree of self-confidence which is not always good either for young people or old ones.—HAMERTON, PHILIP GILBERT, 1887, *Books which Have Influenced Me*, p. 57.

It was Emerson's experience, both in Europe and in America, so far as people gave his work serious consideration, to be regarded as one of the authors whom Goethe would have included in his world-literature. . . . He sees everything as if he were the sole person in the universe, but this is united with the capacity to grasp things as wholes, to feel atmospheres, to measure life and force through the imagination. The real and the ideal meet in him in such equal proportions as they have met in few men at any time. It is as if Plato and Aristotle had wrought at their best in imparting to him their characteristic qualities. There is no boyhood, no youthful period in Emerson; he is a man, and has the thought and expression of his ripest years almost from the start.—WARD, JULIUS H., 1887, *Emerson in New England Thought, Andover Review*, vol. 8. pp. 381, 383.

In literature, as in life, his aim was spiritual manhood, and he valued books and men mainly as he found or deemed them to conduce to it. . . Diamonds, however, are no material for statues; and Emerson's writings, some short poems excepted, prefer no claim to the yet higher grace of logical unity and symmetrical completeness. His usual method of literary work, already described, precluded the composition of an essay in the proper sense of the term. The thought that came to him today generally bore slight affinity to the thought of yesterday or tomorrow. In exploring the notebooks where these casual visitations of the Spirit lay stored like autumn leaves heaped in a forest dingle, Emerson might find numerous analogies, but to fashion these into a coherent whole were a task akin to that which Michael Scott rightly judged too hard for the devil himself. There is just enough unity of purpose and endeavour after artistic construction in each several Essay to raise it from the category of Table-Talks, the desultory record of the wisdom of an Epictetus, a Luther, a Coleridge, and to inscribe the collection upon the roll of a great unsystematic book, along with Marcus Aurelius and Thomas à Kempis, Pascal and Montaigne. . . Emerson is rarely sublime like Marcus

Aurelius, but he disposes of a wealth of varied illustration of which Marcus Aurelius knew nothing; and he has turned every page of the book of Nature, which, until these latter ages, it has been the fault of ethical writers to neglect. . . . Emerson was a connoisseur in style, and said there had never been a time when he would have refused the offer of a professorship of rhetoric at his Alma Mater. The secret of his own method is incommunicable; for it is even truer in his case than in Carlyle's that the style is the man. To write as Emerson, one must be an Emerson. His precepts, nevertheless, may be studied by artists in all literary manners. They seem especially aimed at the crying sin of nineteenth century authorship, its diffuseness. . . . More than any of the other great writers of the age, he is a Voice. He is almost impersonal. He is pure from the taint of sect, clique, or party. He does not argue, but announces; he speaks when the Spirit moves him, and not longer. Better than any contemporary, he exhibits the might of the spoken word. He helps us to understand the enigma how Confucius and Buddha and Socrates and greater teachers still should have produced such marvellous effects by mere oral utterance.—GARNETT, RICHARD, 1888, *Life of Ralph Waldo Emerson (Great Writers)*, pp. 109, 116, 170, 188.

To the prayer of all was granted—Light!
Thou hast felt life-warmth through the age's rime,
Hast pierced the mask of flesh, the veil of time,
That heart from heart and soul from soul benight.
And who so kens thy word to man aright
Finds in the world a spiritual clime,
Beholds the Present as a land sublime,
Peopled with beings of heroic height.
—LARREMORE, WILBUR, 1888, *Emerson, Mother Carey's Chickens*.

It is well that we American students of philosophy should seek to learn and to teach the doctrine of this greatest master of ours, and greatest—perhaps the only great—American philosopher,—for, much more than philosopher,—so much more that the philosopher is but one simple element in the harmonious man, in no wise monopolizing or tyrannizing over temperament and powers,—yet is Emerson truly one of the greatest philosophers of all time, and has given the deepest answers in his time to the soul's Whence? and What? and Whither? So harmonious and synthetic is he, so interfused in his philosophy with life and poetry and beauty and counsel, that it is not a wholly grateful task to discuss him in that analytic and departmental manner which our programme imposes. — MEAD, EDWIN DOAK, 1888, *Emerson's Ethics, The Genius and Character of Emerson*, ed. Sanborn, p. 233.

Mr. Emerson protested, set up human reason, and a low phase of it at that, and with varying consistency assailed revelation and exaggerated human self-sufficiency in all his writings, both verse and prose; with occasional misgivings wrung from him by the sorrows of human infirmity, which human reason had no power to console. He failed; we know it and the world knows it.—HECKER, I. T., 1888, *Two Prophets of this Age, Catholic World*, vol. 47, p. 685.

As regards Emerson, it seems to be this consideration alone which brings out his true greatness—that he discerned the universe as divine to its inmost core. We rightly call him a seer. And what did he see? God, everywhere. It is the sight of God that he helps us to,—the sense of God that he wakes in us. The truest lover of Emerson loves him best for making an access into heaven,—a heaven both present and eternal; and it is not Emerson's personality, dear though that be, on which his thought most rests, but that vision of the heavenly reality to which the poet has helped him.— MERRIAM, GEORGE S., 1888, *Emerson's Message, Open Letters, Century Magazine*, vol. 36, p. 155.

Certain men, themselves writing-masters in the highest sense, such as Henry James, the late Matthew Arnold and David A. Wasson, have criticised Mr. Emerson as having so failed of achieving a style for himself as to threaten the permanence of his literary work. But style is of many kinds, and Emerson has one of his own, lawful, memorable and characteristic. There is a style of reasoned truth like that of Plato, Socrates, Aristotle, and of authors not a few beside. There is, too—and quite legitimate—the oracular style, the style of intuition and ejaculation. Has Solomon no style in the Proverbs, and David none in the Psalms, because neither of them has any logical continuity on the page? Is Paul,—that, "double and twisted old

Calvinist" as a friend of mine affronted Mr. Lyman Beecher with calling him,—to be rather credited with a style through the labyrinth of his epistles, in which it is sometimes so hard to find the clew? In prose and in poetry there may be too much of what is called *style*, like a rocking-horse that does not get on, or a stream flowing so smooth it lulls us to sleep. Emerson's expression answers to the *stylus* once used to cut the thought into letters, not on a paper-surface but sunk into substantial and enduring form. If the style be the man, the man in this case was in his style, which will not shorten but perpetuate by so sharply marking what he had to say.—BARTOL, CYRUS AUGUSTUS, 1888, *Emerson's Style, The Critic, June 2*.

As a man grows older he cares less and less for other people's mental processes. He must, for better, for worse, rely on the tools he has. And, year by year, he comes to closer reliance on the eternities. It has been the great good-fortune of us who write more or less now, that we have been contemporaries of Mr. Emerson. Of course, we cannot say how largely we are indebted to him. If the obligation is not direct, it is none the less an obligation because the gift came from him indirectly. —HALE, EDWARD EVERETT, 1888, *Books That Have Helped Me*, p. 13.

I have listened to him with much pleasure, and have felt the genuineness of his mind. And yet, his sudden insight and prophetic anticipation have always lacked for me that clear, extended, inner coherence which no intensity of light can replace. This sufficient possession of the entire territory occupied, this extension of thought within itself, by which we lay down the bounds of our spiritual inheritance, are something far more than mere logic—a chain of fortresses stretching over a territory within easy range of each other. They may better be likened to the diffused, unequal, but marvelously united light which falls, in a moment of creation, on a landscape. Everything is coherent, interdependent, but with the most subtile interplay of a thousand variable relations. Such a landscape is far more than detached gleams of revelation; it is a complete presentation, palpitating with its own unity. The tendency of Emerson, not so much to dwell in a land of ideas as to move continually through it, made him too migratory for my intellectual household. I could hardly keep even a chamber for him, as did the Shunammite woman for Elisha. —BASCOM, JOHN, 1888, *Books That Have Helped Me*, p. 33.

There can be no greater misfortune for a sincere and truthful mind like Emerson's than to have to get a living by "orating." This was his position, however; and there can be no doubt that his mind and his writings were the worse for this necessity. His philosophy afforded him only a very narrow range of subject. In all his essays and lectures he is but ringing the changes upon three or four ideas—which are really commonplace, though his sprightly wit and imagination give them freshness; and it is impossible to read any single essay, much more several in succession, without feeling that the licence of tautology is used to its extremest limits. In a few essays—for example, "The Poet," "Character," and "Love"—the writer's heart is so much in the matter that these endless variations of one idea have the effect of music which delights us to the end with the reiteration of an exceedingly simple theme; but in many other pieces it is impossible not to detect that weariness of the task of having to coin dollars out of transcendental sentiments to which Emerson's letters and journals often bear witness. But, whether he were delighted with or weary of his labour, there is no progress in his thought, which resembles the spinning of a cockchafer on a pin rather than the flight of a bird on its way from one continent to another.—PATMORE, COVENTRY, 1889-98, *Principle in Art, etc.*, p. 118.

His soul was one with Nature everywhere;
  Her seer and prophet and interpreter,
  He waited in her courts for love of her,
And told the secrets that he gathered there,—
  What flight the wild birds dared; why flowers were fair;
  The sense of that divine, tumultuous stir
  When spring awakes, and all sweet things confer,
And youth and hope and joy are in the air.
—MOULTON, LOUISE CHANDLER, 1890, *Emerson, The Garden of Dreams*, p. 137.

From his neighbourhood, one always returned reinvigorated, with choice moods, and sometimes even ecstacies, which carried those of extreme æsthetic sympathies and deficient ratiocinative powers quite off their feet. He knew well the wearying and prostrating moments that assault and often destroy intellectual life at its very birth, the haunting longing and aspirations, the vague unrest and insurrections which characterize the passage forth from immaturity; and he condensed the vapour into rain; his presence broke the shards of the will and concentrated the man. Nothing came afterwards precisely as it had come before; and our new eyes saw that things are not entitled to respect simply because they are. It may be that too often the old become obsolete, but this could be corrected. With his coming, adolescence ended and virility began. He aroused the best elements of the soul, agitated it to its depth and precipitated all it had of intellectual principle. He first taught us to think, and who can forget the opener of that door? The dawn of life to the mind—is there a greater boon one being can receive from another? Is there one like unto it, except the dawn of love to the heart?—WOODBURY, CHARLES J., 1890, *Talks with Ralph Waldo Emerson*, p. 10.

A most winning and delightful personality on the side of the affections and conscience, he somewhat disappoints me intellectually. With deep and lovely flashes of insight, characteristic of real genius, I find mixed many dicta which, though striking in their epigrammatic form, do not speak to me as *true*. And in the failure of coherent continuity of thought, apparently commended to him by a mistaken interpretation of the Kantain distinction of *Understanding* and *Reason*, leave his fine materials in an unorganised and patternless condition. Much as I love the man, I seek in vain to *learn* from him. The fault is probably in me. I do not mean to criticise him, but only to describe my felt relation to him.—MARTINEAU, JAMES, 1890, *To R. C. Hall, Jan. 6; Life and Letters*, ed. Drummond, vol. II, p. 313.

In this country Mr. Emerson led the dance of the hours. He was our poet, our philosopher, our sage, our priest. He was the eternal man. If we could not go where he went, it was because we were weak and unworthy to follow the steps of such an emancipator. His singular genius, his wonderful serenity of disposition inherited from an exceptional ancestry and seldom ruffled by the ordinary passions of men, his curious felicity of speech, his wit, his practical wisdom raised him above all his contemporaries. His infrequent contact with the world of affairs, his seclusion in the country, his apparitions from time to time on lecture platforms or in convention halls, gave a far off sound to his voice as if it fell from the clouds. Some among his friends found fault with him for being bloodless and ethereal, but this added to the effect of his presence and his word. The mixture of Theism and Pantheism in his thoughts, of the personal and the impersonal, of the mystical and the practical, fascinated the sentiment of the generation, while the lofty moral strain of his teachings awakened to increased energy the wills of men.—FROTHINGHAM, OCTAVIUS BROOKS, 1891, *Recollections and Impressions*, p. 48.

He was sometimes superficial, but never flippant. He never argued; he never even unfolded truths; he formulated and declared *ex cathedra* dogmas, and gathered together, without sequence of system, a number of apposite apothegms in a single theme. In common with Longfellow, he was often led to say what sounded well and meant little, but unlike Longfellow he was seldom commonplace at once in manner and matter. Although no writer is in reality more provincial than Emerson, no writer has such a semblance of superiority to all prejudices of race, nation, religion, and home training as he. But if there was much that was factitious in Emerson, there was also much that was genuine. He had at times an illuminating insight into the heart. His essays are elevating and suggestive. He was gifted with great powers of imagination. His severity had its source in his innermost character, and was more effectual against the storms of life than was the stoicism of the Romans, or the light-headedness of the Greeks. He was so free from all worldliness in motives or in tastes that he seemed immaculate. He had that courage in his faiths which only purity can give. He lived as in another world. If not quite the seer he purports to be, he was unquestionably a genius.—MABIE, HAMILTON W., 1892, *The Memorial Story of America*, p. 594.

"Can you emit sparks?" said the cat to the ugly duckling in the fairy tale, and the poor abashed creature had to admit it could not. Emerson could emit sparks with the most electrical of cats. He is all sparks and shocks. If one were required to name the most non-sequacious author one had ever read, I do not see how he could help nominating Emerson. . . . The unparalleled non-sequaciousness of Emerson is as certain as the Correggiosity of Correggio. You never know what he will be at. His sentences fall over you in glittering cascades, beautiful and bright, and for the moment refreshing, but after a brief while the mind, having nothing to do on its account but to remain wide open, and see what Emerson sends it, grows quite restive and then torpid. Admiration gives way to astonishment, astonishment to bewilderment, and bewilderment to stupefaction.—BIRRELL, AUGUSTINE, 1892, *Res Judicatæ*.

Emerson, as I read him, had no self-sufficiency. He lived and felt with the minimum of personal color, reflecting nature and man; and the study of the guide, the savage man thrown out of society like a chip from a log under the ax of the chopper, returning to the status of pure individuality,—men such as our guides were,—aroused in the philosopher the enthusiasm of a new fact. He often spoke of it, and watched the men as a naturalist does the animals he classifies. I remember Longfellow's once saying of Emerson that he used his friends as he did lemons—when he could squeeze nothing more from them, he threw them away; but this, while in one sense true, does Emerson a radical injustice. He had no vanity, no self-importance; truth and philosophy were so supreme in their hold on him that neither himself or any other self was worth so much as the solution of a problem in life. To get this solution he was willing to squeeze himself like a lemon, if need were; and why should he be otherwise disposed to his neighbor?—STILLMAN, W. J., 1893, *The Philosophers' Camp, Century Magazine*, vol. 46, p. 601.

If we hold ourselves, in a definition of unity, to meaning by the word oneness of subject, we may admit Emerson's paragraphs to have unity. More than half the time, at least, every sentence bears on the point concerned. Sequence in the analytic (*i. e.*, redintegrating) sense he had none. There is no tracking him. You are conscious that he has arrived, and from a place worth coming from, for his hands are full of gems; but no other man can find out his way, nor can he. He was always complaining that he had no system; speaks of his own "impassable paragraphs, **each** sentence an infinitely repellent particle." He has little close ordering of words for coherence, few inversions, few parallelisms of structure. Out of a desperate desire to indicate relations, he uses 49 sentence-connectives to 300 periods; but not always do they catch and hold the true relation. . . . How then, without sequence, does our author make himself clear? His statements are intuitive; but we shall find that he has a curious alternating method of intuitive statement which amounts to resolution of the main idea. The paragraph contains a half-dozen intuitive sentences, each stating the main idea from a different point of view; so that perforce some of the steps omitted in one statement are supplied in another, if only by the great variety of associations. Emerson must state the point intuitively; but he does so under so many metaphors that he is sure somewhere to hit your experiences, your quickest road to apprehension.—LEWIS, EDWIN HERBERT, 1894, *The History of the English Paragraph*, pp. 152, 153.

I have had a high joy in some of the great minor poems of Emerson, where the goddess moves over Concord meadows with a gait that is Greek, and her sandaled tread expresses a high scorn of the india-rubber boots that the American muse so often gets about in.—HOWELLS, WILLIAM DEAN, 1895, *My Literary Passions*, p. 238.

Emerson was not, indeed, a man of letters in the narrowest sense. He was more than that. He was a prophet, a sage, an inspirer of other men, who used literature, sometimes a little impatiently, as an imperfect instrument for imparting the truths he felt himself destined to convey. But he had many qualities the man of letters would do well to imitate. He was essentially a modern man. He was familiar with the past and loved many things about it; but he was "up to the times" in the fullest sense, in science, in theology, in politics. He looked forward and not back; it cannot be too often emphasized.—BRADFORD, GAMALIEL, JR., 1895, *The American Man of Letters, Types of American Character*, p. 145.

Different as they are, Franklin and Emerson are both typical Americans—taken together they give us the two sides of the American character. Franklin stands for the real, and Emerson for the ideal. Franklin represents the prose of American life, and Emerson the poetry. Franklin's power is limited by the bounds of common sense, while Emerson's appeal is to the wider imagination. Where Emerson advises you to "hitch your wagon to a star," Franklin is ready with an improved axle-grease for the wheels. Franklin declares that honesty is the best policy; and Emerson insists on honesty as the only means whereby a man may be free to undertake higher things. Self-reliance was at the core of the doctrine of each of them, but one urged self-help in the material world and the other in the spiritual. Hopeful they were, both of them, and kindly, and shrewd; and in the making of the American people, in the training and in the guiding of this immense population, no two men have done more than these two sons of New England.—MATTHEWS, BRANDER, 1896, *An Introduction to the Study of American Literature*, p. 108.

Emerson stalks like a giant from mountain peak of thought to mountain peak, while the reader is often sorely puzzled to know how to cross the deep gullies between. Emerson was a genius, and prophesied so gloriously on his mountain-tops, that we struggle forward after him despite all difficulties. Those who are not geniuses cannot hope that readers will follow their lead unless the road is shown and the chasms bridged.—BATES, ARLO, 1896, *Talks on Writing English*, p. 142.

Compare for one moment the style of Emerson with that of Wendell Holmes. The style of one represents him as much as the style of the other represents that other. The style of Emerson is manly, clear, deep, and direct; full of *verve* and poetical energy: it reflects the writer. The style of Wendell Holmes is subtle, charming, full of opalescent colour, witty, brilliant, and caustic: it also reflects the author. . . . His grand work, "Representative Men," which is, for its power of intellectual stimulation, of the greatest possible value.—FORSTER, JOSEPH, 1897, *Great Teachers*, pp. 274, 293.

In Emerson, we have, if not an acknowledged master, yet a poet whose lyricism is so strange and rare as to defy the critics. They can compare him to nobody, measure him by nothing, and are sometimes driven by sheer perplexity to pronounce him not a poet at all. They accuse him, justly enough, of abstract themes, irregular rhymes and rhythms, bewildering passages and unearthly ecstasies, a passion too "thin-piercing." Yet many readers find a unique and unwithering charm in his ethereal notes. It seems to such that here, as nowhere else in American poetry, may be felt the thrill of a spiritual secret, a whisper from beyond.—BATES, KATHARINE LEE, 1897, *American Literature*, p. 167.

But, be it said, in the year of 1837, on the last day of August, Ralph Waldo Emerson spoke at Cambridge what for sixty years has been known as his Phi Beta Kappa address. Its subject was "The American Scholar." It was the first of the great addresses which the great man made. In his published works it stands next the essay on "Nature," which was his first noteworthy volume. It was a great address. Oliver Wendell Holmes calls it our "Intellectual Declaration of Independence"; we might denominate it our Declaration of Intellectual Independence. . . . For two generations this oration has been the intellectual bread for college and other folk. Like so many other first addresses and works, it seems to be a microcosm of the whole message which the great author subsequently thought or spoke. He who would be moved by the best of the early Emerson must stoop and drink of this early and steadily flowing spring.—THWING, CHARLES F., 1897, *Emerson's "The American Scholar" Sixty Years After, The Forum*, vol. 23, pp. 661, 662.

His freshness and his courage remained undamped by the failures of others, and his directness of judgment and poetical intuition had freer scope in his rhapsodies than it would have had in learned treatises. I do not wonder that philosophers by profession had nothing to say to his essays because they did not seem to advance their favorite inquiries beyond the point they had reached before. But there were many people, particularly in America, to whom these rhapsodies did more good than any learned disquisitions or carefully arranged sermons. There is in them what attracts us so much in the ancients, freshness, directness, self-confidence, unswerving loyalty to truth, as far as they could see it. He had no one to fear, no one to please. Socrates or Plato, if suddenly brought to life again in America, might have spoken like Emerson, and the effect produced by Emerson was certainly like that produced by Socrates in olden times.—MÜLLER, FRIEDERICH MAX, 1897, *Literary Recollections, Cosmopolis*, p. 629.

In 1837 he was asked to deliver the Phi Beta Kappa oration at Cambridge. This was the opportunity for which he had been waiting. The mystic and eccentric young poet-preacher now speaks his mind, and he turns out to be a man exclusively interested in real life. This recluse, too tender for contact with the rough facts of the world, whose conscience has retired him to rural Concord, pours out a vial of wrath. This cub puts forth the paw of a full-grown lion. Emerson has left behind him nothing stronger that this address, "The American Scholar." It was the first application of his views to the events of his day, written and delivered in the heat of early manhood while his extraordinary powers were at their height. It moves with a logical progression of which he soon lost the habit. The subject of it, the scholar's relation to the world, was the passion of his life. The body of his belief is to be found in this address, and in any adequate account of him the whole address ought to be given. . . . Emerson is never far from his main thought.—CHAPMAN, JOHN JAY, 1898, *Emerson and other Essays*, pp. 17, 23.

The divine spirit of gentle peace and loving faith abiding in the man is even better than any direct teachings in his books. We of to-day find it simply impossible to imagine what the spiritual air of New England was before Emerson breathed his message and lived his life.— LAWTON, WILLIAM CRANSTON, 1898, *The New England Poets*, p. 46.

But here in this same day is Emerson, the good morning shepherd of pale meadows, green with a new optimism that is natural and sensible. He does not lead us to the edge of the abyss. He does not take us away from the humble and familiar close, for the glacier, the sea, the eternal snows, the palace, the stable, the pauper's funeral pall, the invalid's pallet, are all to be found beneath the same heaven, purified by the same stars, and subject to the same infinite energies. He comes to many at the moment when he ought to come, and in the very instant when they were in mortal need of new interpretations.

Heroic moments are less obvious, those of abnegation have not yet returned; only daily life remains to us, and yet we cannot live without grandeur. He has given to life, which had lost its traditional horizon, an almost acceptable meaning, and perhaps he has even been able to show us that it is strange enough, profound enough, great enough, to need no other end than itself. He does not know any more of it than the others do; but he affirms with more courage, and he has confidence in the mystery. You must live, all you who travel through days and years, without activities, without thought, without light, because your life, despite everything, is incomprehensible and divine. You must live because no one has a right to subtract any commonplace weeks from their spiritual sequence. You must live because there is not an hour without intimate miracles and ineffable meanings. You must live because there is not an act, not a word, not a gesture, which is free from inexplicable claims in a world "where there are many things to do, and few things to know."—MAETERLINCK, MAURICE, 1898, *Emerson,* tr. *Porter and Clarke, Poet-Lore*, vol. 10, p. 82.

Emerson was pure in thought as he was high in thought, and his thought often reached spiritual altitudes where even the front rank of preachers never climbed: hence there was lacking that high fellowship which might have strengthened and stayed him, and the want of which sometimes broke over him with a blighting sense of loneliness.—MITCHELL, DONALD G., 1899, *American Lands and Letters, Leather-Stocking to Poe's "Raven,"* p. 150.

Who is not his debtor who has ever held converse with that virile and inspiring personality? Who has not gathered from his page mental booty and intellectual enrichment such as he has derived from few other masters? A profound and original thinker himself, he has set up many other thinkers. A seer, he has taught many others to see. Rich with a Californian wealth of thought and illustration, which he has dealt out with spendthrift profusion, he has supplied intellectual capital sufficient to endow a whole crowd of mediocrities. . . . When he approaches the momentous question of God's existence, he denies the validity of all the customary arguments, such as are usually formulated in theological text-books, on the ground that they all share the fatal defect of being based on logical processes. He substitutes a shorter and more expeditious method of reaching the same great conclusion. While others are climbing with slow and toilsome effort Nature's ladder up to Nature's God, or the equally tedious ladder of syllogism, Emerson sees God by immediate perception, knows Him by direct cognition. By an agile mental leap, he vaults at a single bound into a knowledge of the Divine existence, using as his only spring-board the native intuitions of his own soul. What others reach only after long and laborious courses of reasoning, he reaches by a flash of intelligence.—WILSON, S. LAW, 1899, *The Theology of Modern Literature*, pp. 97, 102.

It may be fearlessly said that, within the limits of a single sentence, no man who ever wrote the English tongue has put more meaning into words than Emerson. In his hands, to adopt Ben Jonson's phrase, words "are rammed with thought." No one has reverenced the divine art of speech more than Emerson, or practiced it more nobly. "The Greeks," he once said in an unpublished lecture, "anticipated by their very language what the best orator could say"; and neither Greek precision nor Roman vigor could produce a phrase that Emerson could not match. Who stands in all literature as the master of condensation if not Tacitus? Yet Emerson, in his speech at the anti-Kansas meeting in Cambridge, quoted that celebrated remark by Tacitus when mentioning that the effigies of Brutus and Cassius were not carried at a certain state funeral: and in translating it, bettered the original.—HIGGINSON, THOMAS WENTWORTH, 1899, *Contemporaries*, p. 16.

A veritable prophet, telling each individual that being is better than seeing; telling the orator and publicist that it is good for a man to have a hearing, but better for him to deserve the hearing; telling the reformer that the single man, who indomitably plants himself upon his divine instincts and there abides, will find the whole world coming around to him.—HILLIS, NEWELL DWIGHT, 1899, *Great Books as Life-Teachers*, p. 26.

Emerson's work is so individual that you can probably get no true impression of it without reading deeply for yourself.

To many this may be irksome. Like all powerful individualities his can hardly leave a reader indifferent; you will be either attracted or repelled, and if repelled, the repulsion will very likely make the reading demand a strenuous act of will. But any student of American letters must force himself to the task; for Emerson, thinking, talking, writing, lecturing from that Concord where he lived during the greater part of his life, produced, in less than half a century, work which as time goes on and as the things which other men were making begin to fade, seem more and more sure of survival. America produced him; and whether you like him or not, he is bound to live.—WENDELL, BARRETT, 1900, *A Literary History of America*, p. 315.

A certain disquiet mingled in the minds of Emerson's contemporaries with the admiration they felt for his purity and genius. They saw that he had forsaken the doctrines of the Church; and they were not sure whether he held quite unequivocally any doctrine whatever. We may not all of us share the concern for orthodoxy which usually caused this puzzled alarm: we may understand that it was not Emerson's vocation to be definite and dogmatic in religion any more than in philosophy, yet that disquiet will not, even for us, wholly disappear. It is produced by a defect which naturally accompanies imagination in all but the greatest minds. I mean disorganization. Emerson not only conceived things in new ways, but he seemed to think the new ways might cancel and supersede the old. His imagination was to invalidate the understanding. That inspiration which should come to fulfil seemed too often to come to destroy. If he was able so constantly to stimulate us to fresh thoughts, was it not because he demolished the labour of long ages of reflection? Was not the startling effect of much of his writing due to its contradiction to tradition and to common sense?—SANTAYANA, GEORGE, 1900, *Interpretations of Poetry and Religion*, p. 223.

Mr. Emerson's way of looking at things was certainly just the opposite of Carlyle's and of Ruskin's too. To him the universe was in good health, if some of its denizens were not. His diagnosis was always made on affirmative lines, and justified the highest hopes. His critics said that he left out of the equation the forces of evil, and brushed away from his vision the persistence and ubiquity of sin. What the Creator is reported in Genesis to have seen, that all that he had made was good, Emerson continued to believe. In his vernacular even Sheol had its benefits.—BENTON, JOEL, 1901, *Emerson's Optimism, The Outlook, vol.* 68, *p.* 407.

If you draw a mark of equality between "Representative Men" and seventy-five cents you will see how much richer I was with the book than with the money. This was the first volume that I bought with my own money, and none since has educated me so much and none now pleases me so well to see with its broken back and bent corners, its general look of shabbiness, worn with much packing and travel, and its scribblings on the wide margins made in the days when I read it with ambitious zeal and began to feel wise and melancholy, and even to think I could piece out Emerson's sentences with reflections of my own. I read this book until I had drawn out as much as there was for me at that time. It seemed to be written for me. . . . With Emerson one never sees anything less than a vision, hears no voice but that of the soul; yes, and beyond that the Over Soul. All is in the distance, a vast perspective lined with majestic figures of men and women as they would be if they but knew their own worth; and at the end a lofty temple consecrated to the moral sentiments. In reading "English Traits" I cannot divest myself of the feeling that I am reading of a people much further removed than England and in no way related to our time and country; they seem as distant and in truth as dead as Greeks or Romans, with such a cool, remote and contemplative pencil does he paint them. Is it his imagination that produces this effect or is it that he sees things never before disclosed and hence the illusion of distance and unfamiliarity? The essential, national qualities are there, but abstracted in such a manner that they stand out like a scientific diagnosis; the diagnosis is so interesting and acute that the poor patient is forgotten. . . . The "Essays" contain the harvests of Emerson's lifetime; plain food for daily life, rare fruit and dainties for life's holidays. The quality is as the products of the sun's light and warmth; the form is spontaneous and simple, and everywhere expressive of the man. He wrote when he felt inspired; when not, he sought in right living and high thinking the renewal of the sources of inspiration. The reserve of Emerson's Essays is one of their most notable and instructive characteristics. He sees more than he says. He is like a general overlooking the field of battle, determining the strategical points and concentrating his forces upon them. What he does not heed is not important for a comprehension and complete grasp of the situation.—ALBEE, JOHN, 1901, *Remembrances of Emerson, pp.* 10, 45, 152.

One charm of Emerson is due to this affable reception of all opinions. On his first appearance in a pulpit he is described as "the most gracious of mortals, with a face all benignity," and preached with an indefinite air of simplicity and wisdom. His lectures radiate benignity and simplicity. He had no dogmas to proclaim or heretics to denounce. He is simply uttering an inspiration which has come to him. He is not a mystagogue, affecting superinducal wisdom and in possession of the only clue to the secret. If you sympathize, well and good; if you cannot you may translate his truth into your own. The ascent into this serene region, above all the noise of controversy, has its disadvantages. — STEPHEN, LESLIE, 1901, *Emerson, National Review, vol.* 36, *p.* 885.

The gentle simplicity of the man, his unswerving faith in humanity, in Nature, in the unseen Powers that guide the universe, must count for more than any mere piece of literary art he has left behind him. He certainly created no philanthropic system, perhaps taught no absolutely novel truth. He had literally no dramatic power, or large constructive imagination. His utterance is always direct and personal, as it were in his own calm, natural voice. His essays are not only without rigid local cohesion, they are often mere loose series of more or less kindred thoughts, and at times justify the extravagant legends which are current as to their haphazard growth. He has no painful or scholastic accuracy. He quotes or refers offhand to authors of all ages, with some of whom he had but nodding acquaintance. Least of all men would he desire his own books to be studied critically and accepted as authoritative.—LAWTON, WILLIAM CRANSTON, 1902, *Introduction to the Study of American Literature, p.* 135.

Henry Wadsworth Longfellow
1807–1882

Born, at Portland, Maine, 27 Feb. 1807. At school there. To Bowdoin Coll., 1822; B. A., 1825. Contrib. to various periodicals while at college. Elected Prof. of Mod. Languages, Bowdoin, 1825. Travelled in Europe, June 1826 to Aug. 1829. Began professional duties at Bowdoin, Sep. 1829. Contrib., to "North American Rev.," April 1831 to Oct. 1840. Married (i.) Mary Storer Potter, Sept. 1831. Smith Prof. of Mod. Lan., Harvard Univ., Dec. 1834. Travelled in Europe, April 1835 to Dec. 1836; wife died, at Rotterdam, 29 Nov., 1835. Began professional duties at Harvard, Dec. 1836. Contrib. "The Psalm of Life" to "Knickerbocker Mag.," June 1838. In Europe, for health, autumn of 1842. Married (ii.) Frances Elizabeth Appleton, 13 July 1843. Resigned Professorship, 1854. Active literary life. Contrib., to "Atlantic Monthly," 1857–76. Wife burnt to death, 9 July 1861. Visit to Europe, May 1868 to 1869. Hon. LL. D., Camb., 16 June, 1868. Received by Queen at Windsor, July 1868. Hon. D. C. L., Oxford, 27 July 1869. Died, at Cambridge, Mass., 24 March 1882. Buried at Mount Auburn Cemetery, Cambridge. *Works:* "Syllabus de la Grammaire Italienne" (in French), 1832; "Outre-Mer" (2 vols.), 1835; "Hyperion" (2 vols.), 1839; "Voices of the Night," 1839; "Ballads and other Poems," 1841; "Poems on Slavery," 1842; "The Spanish Student," 1843; "The Belfry of Bruges," 1846; "Evangeline," 1847; "Kavanagh," 1849; "The Seaside and the Fireside," 1850; "The Golden Legend," 1851; "The Song of Hiawatha," 1855; "The Courtship of Miles Standish," 1858; "Tales of a Wayside Inn," 1863; "Flower-de-Luce," 1867; "The New England Tragedies," 1868; "The Divine Tragedy," 1871; "Christus," (consisting of: "Divine Tragedy," "Golden Legend," and "New England Tragedies"), 1872; "Three Books of Song," 1872; "Aftermath," 1873; "The Hanging of the Crane," 1874; "The Masque of Pandora," 1875; "Poems of the 'Old South' " (with Holmes, Whittier, and others), 1877; "The Skeleton in Armor," 1877; "Kéramos," 1878; "Ultima Thule," 1880. *Posthumous:* "In the Harbour," 1882; "Michael Angelo," 1884. He *translated:* L'Homond's "Elements of French Grammar," 1830; J. Manrique's "Coplas," 1833; Dante's "Divine Comedy," (3 vols.), 1867–70; and *edited:* "Manuel de Proverbes Dramatiques," 1830; "Novelas Españolas," 1830; "Cours de Langue Française, 1832; "Saggi de' Novellieri Italiani d'ogni Secola," 1832; "The Waif," 1845; "The Poets and Poetry of Europe," 1845; "The Estray," 1847; "Poems of Places," (31 vols.), 1876–79. *Collected Works:* in 11 vols., 1866. *Life:* "Life," by his brother, Samuel Longfellow, 1886; "Final Memorials," by same, 1887.—SHARP, R. FARQUHARSON, 1897, *A Dictionary of English Authors*, p. 172.

PERSONAL

Is a native of the State of Maine, and one of the Professors in Bowdoin College. He is now in Europe.—KETTELL, SAMUEL, 1829, *Specimens of American Poetry*, vol. III, p. 238.

I cannot forbear saying how much pleasure it gave me to see your few words about Longfellow. He cares not at all for politics or statistics, for the Syrian question, or the disasters of Afghanistan. But to him the magnificent world of literature and Nature is open; every beauty of sentiment and truth and language has for him a relish; and every heart that feels is sure of a response from him. I feel for his genius and worth the greatest reverence, as for him personally the warmest love.—SUMNER, CHARLES, 1842, *Letter to George Sumner, July 8; Memoirs and Letters of Sumner*, ed. Pierce, vol. II, p. 215.

I need not praise the sweetness of his song,
Where limpid verse to limpid verse succeeds
Smooth as our Charles, when, fearing lest he wrong
The new moon's mirrored skiff, he slides along,
Full without noise, and whispers in his reeds.
With loving breath of all the winds, his name
Is blows about the world; but to his friends
A sweeter secret hides behind his fame,
And Love steals shyly through the loud acclaim
To murmur a *God bless you!* and there ends.
—LOWELL, JAMES RUSSELL, 1867, *To H. W. L.; Life of Henry Wadsworth Longfellow*, ed. Longfellow, vol. III, p. 84.

I suppose you don't remember Longfellow, though he remembers you in a black velvet frock very well. He is now white-haired and white-bearded, but remarkably handsome. He still lives in his old house, where his beautiful wife was burnt to death.

I dined with him the other day, and could not get the terrific scene out of my imagination. She was in a blaze in an instant, rushed into his arms with a wild cry, and never spoke afterwards.—DICKENS, CHARLES, 1867, *To Charles Dickens, Jr., Nov. 30; Letters, ed. Hogarth and Dickens, vol.* II, *p.* 362.

In 1843 the stately mistress of the old house died, and Professor Longfellow bought the homestead of Andrew Craigie, with eight acres of land, including the meadow, which sloped down to the pretty river. There have been very few prouder or happier moments in his life than that in which he first felt that the old house under the elms was his. Yet he must have missed the stately old lady who first had admitted him to a place in it, and whom he had grown to love as a dear friend. She seemed so thoroughly a part and parcel of the place, that he must have missed the rustle of her heavy silks along the wide and echoing halls, and have listened some time for the sound of her old-fashioned spinet in the huge drawing-room below, and, entering the room where she was wont to receive her guests, he must have missed her from the old window where she was accustomed to sit, with the open book in her lap, and her eyes fixed on the far-off sky, thinking, no doubt, of the days when in her royal beauty she moved a queen through the brilliant home of Andrew Craigie. A part of the veneration which he felt for the old house had settled upon its ancient mistress, and the poet doubtless felt that the completeness of the quaint old establishment was broken up when she passed away.—McCABE, JAMES D., JR., 1870, *Great Fortunes and How They Were Made*, p. 568.

You have sent me a Christmas greeting: more than that, a Christmas gift in the shape of a very perfect flower from your own spacious garden: wherefore I exult and stick it in my cap and defy my foes. I and wife and sons salute you and thank you and wish all happiness to you and yours here and hereafter.—TENNYSON, ALFRED LORD, 1877, *Letter to Longfellow; Alfred Lord Tennyson, A Memoir by his Son*, p. 220.

If asked to describe Longfellow's appearance, I should compare him to the ideal representations of early Christian saints and prophets. There is a kind of a halo of goodness about him, a benignity in his expression, which one associates with St. John at Patmos saying to his followers and brethren, "Little children, love one another!"—GOWER, LORD RONALD, 1878–83, *My Reminiscences, vol.* II, *p.* 265.

If this be dying, fair it is to die:
Even as a garment weariness lays by,
Thou layest down life to pass, as Time hath passed,
From wintry rigors to a Springtime sky.
Are there tears left to give thee at the last,
Poet of spirits crushed and hearts down-cast,
Loved of worn women who, when work is done,
Weep o'er thy page in twilights fading fast?
Oh, tender-toned and tender-hearted one,
We give thee to the season new begun;
Lay thy white head within the arms of Spring—
Thy song had all her shower and her sun.
Nay, let us not such sorrowful tribute bring,
Now that thy lark-like soul hath taken wing:
A grateful memory fills and more endears
The silence when a bird hath ceased to sing.
—BUNNER, HENRY C., 1882, *Longfellow, Airs from Arcady and Elsewhere*, p. 96.

His natural dignity and grace, and the beautiful refinement of his countenance, together with his perfect taste in dress and the exquisite simplicity of his manners, made him the absolute ideal of what a poet should be. His voice, too, was soft, sweet, and musical, and, like his face, it had the innate charm of tranquility. His eyes were bluish gray, very bright and brave, changeable under the influence of emotion, (as, afterward, I often saw,) but mostly calm, grave, attentive, and gentle. The habitual expression of his face was not that of sadness; and yet it was sad. Perhaps it may be best described as that of serious and tender thoughtfulness.—WINTER, WILLIAM, 1882, *New York Tribune*, March 30.

The last time he was in Europe I was there with him, and I was a witness to not a few of the honors which he received from high and low. I remember particularly that when we were coming away from the House of Lords together, where we had been hearing a fine speech from his friend the Duke of Argyll, a group of the common people gathered around our carriage, calling him by name, begging to touch his hand, and at least one of them reciting aloud one of his most familiar poems. No poet of our day has touched the common heart like Longfellow. The simplicity and purity of his style were a part of his own character. He had nothing of that irritability which is one of the proverbial elements of the poetic temperament, but was always genial, generous, lovely.—WINTHROP, ROBERT C., 1882, *Letter to George E. Ellis, Tributes to Longfellow and Emerson by the Massachusetts Historical Society*, p. 10.

To my boyish fancy, the name Longfellow had a strange, unfamiliar, foreign sound as that of some inhabitant of a distant sphere; but a sight of its owner dispelled any such whimsical vagaries. It was a clear-cut figure, of middle size, handsome, erect, the countenance cheerful, the step buoyant, the manner cordial, the voice mellow and musical; a melodious voice, educated, coming from the depths of the man, with character and cultivation in it,—the voice of a gentleman and a scholar. His conversation has a jocund flavor, as if he enjoyed his thoughts about books and the men who wrote them. It was pleasant; not deep, but hearty and appreciative; flowing in a full, easy stream along the channels of literature, making music as it flowed. The great masters of song he loved without respect to their nationality, their age, or their creed; taking them on their merits, and rendering heart honor to their genius, it mattering little to him whether they wrote in English, French, German, Italian, Spanish. When the youth met, a few years later, at Harvard College, the professor of modern languages and literatures, he found the same delightful person. The ordinary lecture-rooms being occupied, Longfellow met his classes in a kind of parlor, carpeted and furnished with comfortable chairs. The comparative elegance was so completely in keeping with the teacher and his topics that the peculiarity was not noticed at the time, and for the hour seemed to be no peculiarity at all. The professor sat and read his lectures in a simple manner, showing an entire familiarity with whatever concerned the literature of the subject; never discussing the points of the philosophical difficulty, never diving into abysses of abstraction or rising to heights of speculation, but fully equipped for the task of translation and exposition, especially the former, in which he excelled. His style of writing was flowing, picturesque, abounding in literary illustration, exuberant in imagery; more than pleased the prosaic members of the class, but none too florid for the imaginative and enthusiastic. — FROTHINGHAM, OCTAVIUS BROOKS, 1882, *Henry Wadsworth Longfellow, Atlantic Monthly*, vol. 49, p. 819.

In his youth, and during middle age, our poet was noted for his remarkable taste in dress, and in the arrangement of his fine hair. Indeed, he gave to the last the impression of a perfectly dressed man. Later, when the hair whitened, it was allowed to grow and disport itself at pleasure; and it often made one think of the loosely piled crown of an ancient prophet. He was of middle height, certainly not more; but almost everyone who saw him for the first time thought him taller. . . . Rather too much emphasis is laid upon the expression of sadness. One saw in looking at Longfellow that he was a man of deep and tender feelings, but his habitual expression was far from sad. It was grave at times, but often lighted up with smiles; and the consideration for others, which always distinguishes noble natures, gave to his speech and manners an indescribable charm.—UNDERWOOD, FRANCIS H., 1882, *Henry Wadsworth Longfellow, A Biographical Sketch*, pp. 252, 255.

His face, filled with rugged lines, presents a contour of great firmness and intelligence. The nose is Roman rather than Greek, with the very slightest aquiline tendency. His eyes are clear, straightforward, almost proud, yet re-assuring. They are rather deeply set, and shaded by overhanging brows. In moments of lofty and inspired speech they have an eagle-like look; the orbs deepen and scintillate and flash; like the great bird of prey, they seem to soar off into endless space, grasping in the talons of the mental vision things unattainable to less ambitious flight. With his moods they vary, and when calm nothng could exceed the quietness of their expression. If sad, an infinite tenderness reposes in their depths; and, if merry, they sparkle and bubble over with fun. In fact, before the poet speaks, these traitorous eyes have already betrayed his humor. I must not forget the greatest of all expressions, humility. To one whose soul and mind are given to divine thought, it is in the eye that this sentiment finds its natural outcome; and the world knows that Longfellow's faith is the crowning gem in a diadem of virtues. His face is not a mask, but an open book,—a positive index to his character.—MACCHETTA, BLANCHE ROOSEVELT, 1882, *Reminiscences of a Poet's Life*.

The regret for his loss was universal; for no modern man was ever better loved or better deserved to be loved.—DAVIDSON,

Thomas, 1882, *Encyclopædia Britannica*, Ninth Ed., vol. XIV, p. 873.

Kind, soft-voiced, gentle, in his eye there shines
The ray serene that filled Evangeline's.
Modest he seems, not shy; content to wait
Amid the noisy clamor of debate
The looked-for moment when a peaceful word
Smooths the rough ripples louder tongues have stirred.
In every tone I mark his tender grace
And all his poems hinted in his face;
What tranquil joy his friendly presence gives!
How could I think him dead? He lives! He lives!

—Holmes, Oliver Wendell, 1884, *At the Saturday Club*.

The same gentle and humane spirit which characterized his writings showed itself also in the manners of the man. He had the simplicity which belongs to strong and true natures. He never remembered, and his affability made you forget that you were in the presence of one of the most eminent of living men. His fine sympathy prompted him to meet people on their own ground of thought and interest, and to anticipate their wishes. His ways with children were delightful. . . . He was hospitable and helpful to other and younger writers. How many are indebted to him for words of encouragement and cheer! The last letter I ever received from him was written during his illness in the winter, when he took the trouble to send me an exceedingly kind word regarding something of mine he had just seen in a magazine, and which had chanced to please him. He was tolerant to the last degree of other people's faults. I never heard him speak with anything like impatience of anybody, except a certain class of critics who injure reputations by sitting in judgment upon works they have not the heart to feel, or the sense to understand.—Trowbridge, John Townsend, 1885, *Henry Wadsworth Longfellow; Some Noted Poets, Authors and Statesmen of Our Time*, ed. Parton, pp. 293, 294.

He touched life at many points; and certainly he was no book-worm or dry-as-dust scholar shut up in a library. He kept the doors of his study always open, both literally and figuratively. But literature, as it was his earliest ambition, was always his most real interest; it was his constant point of view; it was his chosen refuge. His very profession was a literary one. . . . A man of letters who was a worker,—a faithful user of his powers; one who had too much respect for his art ever to permit any carelessness in the execution or unworthiness in the theme. His art he valued, not for its own sake, but as a vehicle for noble, gentle, beautiful thought and sentiment. If he spoke of things common, it was to invest them with that charm of saying, or show that poetic element in them, which should lift them above the commonplace.—Longfellow, Samuel, 1886, *Life of Henry Wadsworth Longfellow*, vol. I, pp. vii, viii.

Ere long I paced those cloisteral aisles, ere long
I moved where pale memorial shapes convene,
Where poet, warrior, statesman, king or queen
In one great elegy of sculpture throng,
When suddenly, with heart-beats glad and strong,
I saw the face of that lost friend serene
Who robed Hiawatha and Evangeline
In such benign simplicity of song!
Then, swift as light haze on a morning lea,
All history, legend, England, backward drawn,
Vanished like vision to incorporate air;
And in one sweet colonial home o'er sea
I saw the lamp shine out across the lawn,
I heard the old clock ticking on the stair!

—Fawcett, Edgar, 1886, *Longfellow in Westminster Abbey, Romance and Revery*, p. 181.

Longfellow's true life was that of a scholar and a dreamer; and everything besides was a duty, however pleasurable or beautiful the experience might become in his gentle acceptation. He was seldom stimulated to external expression by others. Such excitement as he could express again was always self-excitement; anything external rendered him at once a listener and an observer. For this reason it is peculiarly difficult to give any idea of his lovely presence and character to those who have not known him. He did not speak in epigrams. It could not be said of him:

"His mouth he could not ope,
But out there flew a trope."

Yet there was an exquisite tenderness and effluence from his presence which was more humanizing and elevating than the eloquence of many others.—Fields, Annie, 1886, *Glimpses of Longfellow in Social Life*, Century Magazine, vol. 31, p. 888.

We gained a great deal from Longfellow. He came to Cambridge in our first year. He was not so much older than we as to be distant, was always accessible, friendly, and sympathetic. All poor teachers let "the book" come between them and the pupil. Great teachers never do; Longfellow never did. When the government acted like fools, as governments do sometimes, he always smoothed us down, and, in general, kept us in good temper. We used to call him "the Head," which meant, head of the Modern Language Department. — HALE, EDWARD EVERETT, 1886, *How I was Educated, The Forum,* vol. 1, p. 61.

His interests were chiefly domestic and social; his pursuits were the labors and the pleasures of a poet and a man of letters. His hospitality was large and gracious, cordial to old friends, and genial to new acquaintances. His constantly growing fame burdened him with a crowd of visitors and a multitude of letters from "entire strangers." They broke in upon his time, and made a vast task upon his good nature. He was often wearied by the incessant demands, but he regarded them as largely a claim of humanity upon his charity, and his charity never failed. He had a kind word for all, and with ready sacrifice of himself he dispensed pleasure to thousands. . . . No poet was ever more beloved than he; none was ever more worthy of love. The expressions of the feeling toward him after death were deep, affecting, and innumerable. One of the most striking was the placing of his bust in the Poet's Corner in Westminster Abbey in March, 1884. It was the first instance of such an honor being paid to an American poet. His bust stands near the tomb of Chaucer, between the memorials to Cowley and Dryden.—NORTON, CHARLES ELIOT, 1888, *Appleton's Cyclopædia of American Biography,* vol. IV, pp. 14, 15.

Who was as dear to England as to his native land, and under whose bust, glimmering at the corner of the south transept of Westminster Abbey, thousands pause with a sigh of regret for the loss of a life stainless as that white marble.—FARRAR, FREDERIC WILLIAM, 1891. *An English Estimate of Lowell, The Forum,* vol. 12, p. 141.

Longfellow was my friend for a great many years, and one of the most amiable men I have ever known. His home being near Boston, I saw him oftenest, and always when I was there, but for two summers he took a charming old-fashioned country house on the outskirts of the beautiful village of Pittsfield, six miles from my own summer residence in Lenox, and during those seasons I saw him and his wife very frequently, and was often in that house, on the staircase landing of which stood the famous clock whose hourly song, "Never—for ever; ever—never," has long been familiar to all English speaking people. Fanny Longfellow, the charming Mary of the poet's "Hyperion," had a certain resemblance to myself, which on one occasion caused some amusement in our house, my father coming suddenly into the room and addressing her as "Fanny," which rather surprised her, as, though it was her name, they were not sufficiently intimate to warrant his so calling her. She was seated, however, otherwise he could not have made the mistake, as besides being very much handsomer than I, she had the noble stature and bearing of "a daughter of the gods divinely tall."—KEMBLE, FRANCES ANN, 1891, *Further Records,* p. 172.

The class of 1825 became distinguished in the annals of Bowdoin for those of its graduates of that year who ultimately attained high rank in literature, theology, and politics. . . . One of the youngest was Henry W. Longfellow, who entered college when only fourteen. He had decided personal beauty and most attractive manners. He was frank, courteous, and affable, while morally he was proof against the temptations that beset lads on first leaving the salutary restraints of home. He was diligent, conscientious, and most attentive to all his college duties, whether in the recitation-room, the lecture-hall, or the chapel. The word "student" best expresses his literary habit, and in his intercourse with all he was conspicuously the gentleman. His studious habits and attractive mien soon led the professors to receive him into their society almost as an equal, rather than as a pupil; but this did not prevent him from being most popular among the students. He had no enemy.—BRIDGE, HORATIO, 1893, *Personal Recollections of Nathaniel Hawthorne,* p. 16.

I met Longfellow during his last visit to England at the house of Mr. Wynne-Finch. His large, leonine head, surmounted at that date by a nimbus of white hair, was very striking indeed. I saw him standing a few moments alone, and ventured to introduce myself as a friend of his friends, the Apthorps, of Boston, and when I gave my name he took both my hands and pressed them with delightful cordiality.—COBBE, FRANCES POWER, 1894, *Life by Herself,* vol. II, p. 458.

The poet Longfellow was such a thoroughbred gentleman, that the most timid were at ease in his society, and the presumptuous were held in check. "All the vulgar and pretentious people in the world," exclaimed a young man, fascinated by the elegant simplicity of the poet's manners, "ought to be sent to see Mr. Longfellow, to learn how to behave!" The poet was gifted with rare insight into character, and always said the right word to the right person. On being introduced to the late Nicholas Longworth, of Cincinnati, a quick-witted old gentleman, who dearly loved a joke, reference was made to the similarity of the first syllables of their names. "Worth makes the man, and want of it the fellow," replied Mr. Longfellow, quoting Pope's favorite line, and making one of the best repartees on record. Probably no American, unless it was the President of the United States, received so many visitors as the poet. They came from all parts of the world, were received—even the humblest—with gracious kindness, which said "The man who wishes to see me is the man I wish to see."—MILES, ALFRED H., 1894, *ed. One Thousand and One Anecdotes*, p. 322.

His endowment of personal culture was so generous as to give one in contact with it the keenest delight. He seemed to me a man cultivated almost to the capacity of his nature. It was inconceivable that he could, under any stress, slip into rudeness of view, or do the incomplete thing. He was finished well-nigh to elaboration. Yet, as I say, he stopped this side of gold-leaf. For he had retained his sincerity almost to the point of naïveté; he had preserved the spontaneity which a lesser man under his attrition with the world would have lost. —PHELPS, ELIZABETH STUART, 1896, *Chapters from a Life*, p. 154.

If we judge from his diary, Longfellow was never subject to overmastering impulses, but always acted with foresight,— not from selfish calculations, but from a sane and temperate judgment. He was as trustworty at nineteen as if years of experience had molded his character and settled his principles of conduct. In fact, he negatives the theory of original sin,— the flower of Puritanism disproves the cherished Puritan dogma. This quality of radical goodness of heart is reflected in his verse. The ardor of soul, the deep dejection and despair, the rebellion, of the revolutionary natures are entirely unknown to him. He is the poet of the well-disposed, the virtuous and intelligent New-Englander. —JOHNSON, CHARLES F., 1897, *Library of the World's Best Literature*, ed. Warner, vol. XVI, p. 9144.

A part of Mr. Longfellow's charm was his way of listening; another charm was his beauty, which was remarkable. His kindness to young authors has passed into a proverb, and he was a natural-born gentleman.—SHERWOOD, MARY E. W., 1897, *An Epistle to Posterity*, p. 131.

His adoration of his wife was fully justified, for rarely have I seen a woman in whom a Juno-like dignity and serenity were so wedded to personal beauty and to the fine culture of brain and heart, which commanded reverence from the most ordinary acquaintance, as in her. No one who had seen her at home could ever forget the splendid vision, and the last time I ever saw her, so far as I remember, was in the summer time, when she and her two daughters, all in white muslin, like creatures of another world, evanescent, translucent, stood in the doorway to say good-by to me. In the same costume, a little later, she met death. She was making impressions in sealing-wax, to amuse her daughters, when a flaming drop fell on the inflammable stuff, and in an instant she was in flames, burned to death before help could come. It was then that they found that Longfellow was not the cold man they had generally believed him. He never recovered from the bereavement, and shortly after he became a Spiritualist, and, until he in his glad turn passed the gates of death, he lived in what he knew to be the light of her presence. And certainly if such a thing as communion across that grim threshold can be, this was the occasion which made it possible. There was something angelic about them both, even in this life,—a natural innocence and large beneficence and equanimity which, in the chance and contradiction of life, could rarely be found in wedded state.—STILLMAN, WILLIAM JAMES, 1901, *The Autobiography of a Journalist*, vol. I, p. 234.

I succeeded at my first sitting in getting what I thought to be a characteristic, if not a poetic, pose. I was struck by the great intentness, almost a stare, with which he looked at one in pauses of the conversation. His eyes were so brilliant that he really seemed to be looking one through. It was this gaze that I tried to get in my portrait. — EATON, WYATT, 1902, *Recollections of American Poets, Century Magazine, vol.* 64, p. 844.

His place of residence was so accessible and so historic, his personal demeanor so kindly, his life so open and transparent, that everything really conspired to give him the highest accessible degree of contemporary fame. There was no literary laurel that was not his, and he resolutely declined all other laureal; he had wealth and ease, children and grand children, health and stainless conscience; he had also in a peculiar degree, the blessings that belong to Shakesphere's estimate of old age,— honour, love, obedience, troops of friends. Except for two great domestic bereavements, his life would have been one of absolutely unbroken sunshine; in his whole career he never encountered any serious rebuff, while such were his personal modesty and kindliness that no one could long regard him with envy or antagonism. Among all the sons of song there has rarely been such an instance of unbroken and unstained success.—HIGGINSON, THOMAS WENTWORTH, 1902, *Henry Wadsworth Longfellow (American Men of Letters)*, p. 1.

OUTRE-MER
1834

His rich and poetical, and yet graphic description, and the true feeling with which he looks on nature and on social life, are the qualities which most attract us in his writings, because they are not precisely those in which travellers are most apt to abound.— PEABODY, W. B., O., 1834, *Outre-Mer, North American Review, vol.* 39.

It could not flourish now, nor can it flourish hereafter, but it delighted a literate and sympathetic class of readers forty years ago to whom it was a pleasant revealment of Old World places, customs, stories and literatures. It was quietly humorous, it was prettily pathetic, and it was pensive and poetical.—STODDARD, RICHARD HENRY, 1878, *Henry Wadsworth Longfellow, Scribner's Monthly, vol.* 17, p. 4.

Of the work itself I need add but little to what has already been said in this chapter. It is, confessedly, not much more than a book of travels through France, Spain, Italy, Germany, and Holland; though the last two countries named are barely noticed. Around his descriptions of scenery, and the various incidents which pleased his youthful fancy, the author throws a halo of imagination,—a sort of dreamy atmosphere which at times makes what is real seem quite the opposite. Poesy, art, romance, and life are beautifully intermingled; and the generous feeling and true philosophy evinced by the pilgrim of the Land beyond the Sea throws a mild, yet most attractive, coloring over all the objects encountered, and all the scenes passed through. Whether we walk with him through the valley of Loire, take passage by night in the stagecoach from Paris to Bordeaux, or partake of the somewhat doubtful welcome of the inn of old Castile, we feel that we are in the company of a person of talent and of cultivated taste.—AUSTIN, GEORGE LOWELL, 1883, *Henry Wadsworth Longfellow, His Life, His Works, His Friendships,* p. 186.

HYPERION
1839

Its quiet, delicate, and beautiful pictures contrast with the terrific scenes of old romance, like a soft, autumnal scene, compared with the landscape swept by the tropical hurricane. . . . The sentimental and melancholy tone that pervades it will not be listened to by many, in the throng, and pressure, and stirring practical interests of the present age. The scenery and embellishments are remote as possible from the circle of American life; and the thoughts and feelings are too ethereal to be readily grasped by minds intent upon the exciting themes of the day. The impassioned part of the romance partakes of the same general character. It is a book for minds attuned to sentiments of tenderness; minds of an imaginative turn, and willing and ready to interest themselves in reveries as gorgeous as morning dreams, and in the delicate perceptions of art and poetry;—minds tried by suffering, and sensitively alive to the influence of the beautiful.—FELTON, CORNELIUS CONWAY, 1840, *Hyperion, North American Review, vol.* 50, pp. 145, 161.

You should read Longfellow's "Hyperion," which is an imitation of Jean Paul Richter, in the same degree, perhaps, that "Evangeline" is an imitation of Voss. It is extremely refined and pleasing. It is, however, a collection of *miscellanea* strung together on a thread of a Rhine tour, with very little of a story, only an event to begin with, and an event to end with.—COLERIDGE, SARA, 1848, *To Aubrey De Vere, Sep.; Memoir and Letters, ed. her Daughter, p.* 355.

We shall never forget the circumstance of its first perusal. We took it, as our pocket companion, with us on our first walk down the Tweed, by Peebles, Inverleithen, Clovenford, Ashestiel, and Abbotsford. It was fine at any special bend of the stream, or any beautiful spot along its brink, taking it out and finding in it a conductor to our own surcharged emotions. In our solitude we felt, We are not alone, for these pages can sympathize with us! The course of Hyperion, indeed, is that of a river, winding at its own sweet will, now laughing and singing to itself in its sparkling progress, and now slumbering in still, deep pools; here laving cornfields and vineyards, and there lost in wooded and sounding glens. Interest it has much,—incident, little: its charm is partly in the "Excelsior" progress of the hero's mind, partly in the sketches of the great German authors, and principally in the sparkling imagery and waving, billowy language of the book. Longfellow in this work is Jean Paul Richter without his grotesque extravagancies, or riotous humour, or turbulent force.—GILFILLAN, GEORGE, 1849-52, *Second Gallery of Literary Portraits*.

Independently of its literary merits, which were highly considered, it had in it a personal element which awakened much discussion and interest. Prominent among the personages introduced was one whose traits suggested one of the most eminent young ladies of the time, while the care and feeling shown in the portraiture made it evident that the heart of the writer had entered deeply into his work. It was known that Mr. Longfellow had met Miss Appleton, the supposed prototype of Mary Ashburton, while travelling in Europe, and conjectures were not wanting as to the possible progress and *dénouement* of the real romance which seemed to underlie the graceful fiction. This romance indeed existed, and its hopes and aspirations were crowned in due time by a marriage which led to years of noble and serene companionship.—HOWE, JULIA WARD, 1882, *Reminiscences of Longfellow, The Critic*, vol. 2, p. 115.

A poetical account of his travels, had at the time of its publication an immense popularity, due mainly to its sentimental romanticism. At present few persons beyond their teens would care to read it through, so unnatural and stilted is its language, so thin its material, and so consciously meditated its sentiment. Nevertheless it has a certain historical importance, for two reasons—(1) because it marks that period in Longfellow's career when, though he had left nature, he had not yet found art, and (2) because it opened the sluices through which the flood of German sentimental poetry flowed into the United States—a flood whose waters, after forty years, are not yet assuaged.—DAVIDSON, THOMAS, 1882, *Encyclopædia Britannica, Ninth Ed.*, vol. XIV, p. 871.

The portrait, the feelings recorded in the story are undoubtedly true. The incidents are imaginary. Into this romance the author put the glow, the fervor, the fever of his heart. He wove into it some pages of his own travels, modified, and some pages of literary criticism, as has been said, from his lectures. This Romance has a perennial charm for those who read it in their youth, and to whom it seemed a revelation of the new world. Many a phrase and passage remain fixed in their memories. More than one of them, in afterwards visiting Europe, has taken pains to follow the very steps of Paul Flemming; has sought out the very inns where he dined or slept; the Star at Salzig, the White House at Bingen; has turned aside to rest a Sunday at St. Gilgen, and read with his own eyes the inscription on the tablet above the dead which had become a motto for his own life; has lingered with an inexplicable feeling, that seemed as if the memory of a previous existence, under the walnut-trees of Interlaken or the lindens that crown the Rent Tower of Heidelberg Castle,—looking "at all things as they are, but through a kind of glory," the glory with which poetry and romance indue a place even beyond history.—LONGFELLOW, SAMUEL, 1886, *Life of Henry Wadsworth Longfellow*, vol. I. p. 309.

The autobiographical element in "Hyperion" is unmistakable, though not to be hunted into its fastnesses. We have in these pages the record of some of the foreign travels, experiences, and musings of a thoughtful mind, touched with the gentle but irresistible lessons of an old land of romance and tender passion. The view of life here presented is optimistic, yet overhung with a purple melancholy, and affected by that feeling of sadness, not akin to pain, of which Longfellow elsewhere sings in a well-known poem. We have in this world—the book seems to remind us—the lessons of the past, the wealth of the present, and the hope of the future. Life is a rich possession, in which joy and pathos are fitly blent, and in which pure love sanctifies manly duty. —RICHARDSON, CHARLES F., 1888, *American Literature, 1607-1885, vol.* II, *p.* 55.

There is no doubt that under the sway of the simpler style now prevailing, much of the rhetoric of "Hyperion" seems turgid, some of its learning obtrusive, and a good deal of its emotion forced; it was, nevertheless, an epoch-making book.—HIGGINSON, THOMAS WENTWORTH, AND BOYNTON, HENRY WALCOTT, 1903, *A Reader's History of American Literature, p.* 141.

THE SKELETON IN ARMOR
1841

A pure and perfect thesis artistically treated.—POE, EDGAR ALLAN, 1844, *Longfellow's Ballads, Works,* ed. Stedman and Woodberry, *vol.* VI, *p.* 128.

This vigorous poem opens with a rare abruptness. The author, full of the Norseland, was inspirited by his novel theme, and threw off a ringing carol of the sea-lover's training, love, adventure. The cadences and imagery belong together, and the measure, that of Drayton's "Agincourt," is better than any new one for its purpose. —STEDMAN, EDMUND CLARENCE, 1885, *Poets of America, p.* 191.

"Skeleton in Armor" rightfully takes a high place among the finest ballads in the language.—PANCOAST, HENRY S., 1898, *An Introduction to American Literature, p.* 189.

THE SPANISH STUDENT
1843

Upon the whole, we regret that Professor Longfellow has written this work, and feel especially vexed that he has committed himself by its republication. Only when regarded as a mere poem can it be said to have merit of any kind. For, in fact, it is only when we separate the poem from the drama that the passages we have commended as beautiful can be understood to have beauty. . . . Its thesis is unoriginal; its incidents are antique; its plot is no plot; its characters have no character; in short, it is little better than a play upon words to style it "A Play" at all.—POE, EDGAR ALLAN, 1845, *The American Drama, Works,* ed. Stedman and Woodberry, *vol.* VI.

As a dramatist he has signally failed. He lacks nerve and condensation. The story is very prettily told by the actors, but beyond the dialogue form it has no pretensions to be called a Drama.—POWELL, THOMAS, 1850, *The Living Authors of America, p.* 143.

Of Longfellow's more extensive works his so-called dramas are failures. The Puritan plays in particular are commonplace in matter and bald in versification. The "Spanish Student," more graceful than impressive, is made musical by the songs, and disfigured by an absurd close.— NICHOL, JOHN, 1882-85, *American Literature, p.* 200.

I could not hold out long against the witchery of his verse. "The Spanish Student" became one of my passions; a minor passion, not a grand one, like Don Quixote and the "Conquest of Granada," but still a passion, and I should dread a little to read the piece now, less I should disturb my old ideal of its beauty. The hero's rogue servant, Chispa, seemed to me, then and long afterward, so fine a bit of Spanish character that I chose his name for my first pseudonym when I began to write for the newspapers, and signed my legislative correspondence for a Cincinnati paper with it. I was in love with the heroine, the lovely dancer whose *cachucha* turned my head, along with that of the cardinal, but whose name even I have forgotten, and I went about with the thought of her burning in my heart, as if she had been a real person.—HOWELLS, WILLIAM DEAN, 1895, *My Literary Passions, p.* 39.

EVANGELINE
1847

By this work of his maturity he has placed himself on a higher eminence than he had yet attained, and beyond the reach of envy. Let him stand, then, at the head of our list of native poets, until some one else shall break up the rude soil of our American life, as he has done, and produce from it a lovelier and nobler flower than this poem of "Evangeline."—HAWTHORNE, NATHANIEL, 1847, *Salem Advertiser.*

As it is the longest, so it is the most complete, the most artistically finished, of all your poems. I know nothing better in the language, than all the landscape painting. The Southwestern pictures are strikingly vigorous and new. The story is well handled and the interest well sustained. Some of the images are as well conceived and as statuesquely elaborated as anything you have ever turned out of your atelier,—which is saying a great deal. You must permit me, however, to regret that you have chosen hexameters,—for which I suppose you will think me a blockhead. Although yours are as good as, and probably a great deal better than, any English hexameters (of which I have, however, but small experience), yet they will not make music to my ear, nor can I carry them in my memory. There are half a dozen particular passages in which the imagery is chiselled like an intaglio, which would make a permanent impression on my memory if it were not for the length of the metre; as it is, I only remember the thought without the diction, which is losing a great deal.—MOTLEY, JOHN LOTHROP, 1847, *To Longfellow, Dec. 18; Life of Henry Wadsworth Longfellow, ed. Longfellow, vol.* II, *p.* 104.

I did not, I am sure, make any such comparison of Longfellow's "Evangeline" with other American poems as you have ascribed to me. What I said was, that it had given me altogether more pleasure in the reading than any poem which had lately appeared—than any poem which had been published within several years. And this is true. I have never made any attempt to analyze the sources of this pleasure. The poem interested and affected me strangely. Whatever may be said of the parts, they are all harmonized by a poetic feeling of great sweetness and gentleness which belongs to the author. My ear admits, nay, delights in, the melody of the hexameter as he managed it. I no doubt expressed my satisfaction with the poem in warm terms, but the idea of bringing its poetic merits into comparison with whatever had been written in America never entered into my head.—BRYANT, WILLIAM CULLEN, 1848, *Letter to Richard H. Dana; A Biography of William Cullen Bryant by Godwin, vol.* II, *p.* 26.

I have just been reading a poem by Mr. Longfellow which appears to be more replete with genuine beauties of American growth than any other production of your poets which I have seen. The story refers to Acadie, and one of the incidents is the deportation of a whole village of peaceful inhabitants (the village is called Grand Pré) by the soldiers and sailors of "King George." I am afraid that Mr. Longfellow had some historical ground for this event.
. . . Will you have the kindness to tell me —no one can do it so well—what this history is, and where I shall find it? No doubt many incidents in our treatment of our colonies have left deep memories on your side of the Atlantic which we know little about.—WHEWELL, WILLIAM, 1848, *Letter to George Bancroft, Feb.* 4; *Life of Henry Wadsworth Longfellow, ed. Longfellow, vol.* II, *p.* 108.

Is full of the beautiful, and is most deeply pathetic, as much so as the story of Margaret in the "Excursion." . . . "Evangeline" seems to be, in some sort, an imitation of Voss's "Luise," The opening, especially, would remind any one who had read the "Luise," of that remarkable idyl. It is far inferior to that, I think, both in the general conception and in the execution. Voss's hexameters are perfect. The German language admits of that metre, the English hardly does so. Some of Longfellow's lines are but quasi-metre, so utterly inharmonious and so prosaic in regard to the diction.—COLERIDGE, SARA, 1848, *To Aubery De Vere, Sep.; Memoir and Letters, ed. her Daughter, p.* 354.

Had Theocritus written in English, not Greek,
I believe that his exquisite sense would scarce
change a line
In that rare, tender, virgin-like pastoral Evangeline.
That's not ancient nor modern, its place is apart
Where time has no sway, in the realm of pure Art,
'Tis a shrine of retreat from Earth's hubbub and strife
As quiet and chaste as the author's own life.
—LOWELL, JAMES RUSSELL, 1848, *A Fable for Critics.*

Is this natural poetry? Does the narrative *require* these "dying falls?" We answer, no; the measure jars upon us; it is as though we were reading intense prose before a slowly nodding China mandarin. The face falls at the end of every line. Where was the necessity for choosing such a form? It cannot be that the idea of its appropriateness rose up spontaneously in the author's mind on his first conceiving the piece, and that he used it because he *felt it to be the best;* at least it is to be hoped it did not. . . . But it may be urged, "Evangeline" is in a walk of art to which strictness of criticism should not be applied. It is not attempted to make the characters natural, but only to make them in harmony with each other. It is raised very high into the poetic region; and the mind which approaches it must for the nonce lay aside commonsense and put on spectacles which turn all things to gold. To appreciate such constancy as Evangeline's, one must be very refined indeed. The whole work, in short, is so *fine* that it required these awkward inclined planes of lines, that perpetually carry the reader down—and down—and down-a—in order to make it sufficiently remote and strange. . . . Now to this we must answer, and this conducts us to the *general style* of the piece, the clothing is not to our taste. It is not really fine, but tawdry; not neat, but gaudy. It pains the eye for want of harmony, and for ostentatious showiness in the coloring. To read the whole book cloys the fancy. The figures and comparisons seldom come in naturally, but are the offspring of conscious choice. The poet has always left him a "conceit, a miserable conceit."—PECK, G. W., 1848, *Evangeline, The American Review, vol. 7, pp. 162, 163.*

In "Evangeline," Mr. Longfellow has managed the hexameter with wonderful skill. The homely features of Acadian life are painted with Homeric simplicity, while the luxuriance of a Southern climate is magnificently described with equal fidelity and minuteness of finish. The subject is eminently fitted for this treatment; and Mr. Longfellow's extraordinary command over the rhymatical resources of language has enabled him to handle it certainly with as perfect a mastery of the dactylic hexameter as any one has ever acquired in our language. Of the other beauties of the poem we have scarcely left ourselves space to say a word; but we cannot help calling our readers' attention to the exquisite character of Evangeline herself. As her virtues are unfolded by the patience and religious trust with which she passes through her pilgrimage of toil and disappointment she becomes invested with a beauty as of angels. Her last years are made to harmonize the discords of a life of sorrow and endurance. The closing scenes, though informed with the deepest pathos, inspire us with sadness, it is true, but at the same time leave behind a calm feeling that the highest aim of her existence has been attained.— FELTON, CORNELIUS CONWAY, 1848, *Longfellow's Evangeline, North American Review, vol. 66, p. 240.*

Next to "Excelsior" and the "Psalm of Life" we are disposed to rank "Evangeline." Indeed, as a work of art, it is superior to both, and to all that Longfellow has written in verse. . . . Nothing can be more truly conceived or more tenderly expressed than the picture of that primitive Nova Scotia and its warm-hearted, hospitable, happy and pious inhabitants. We feel the air of the fore-world around us. The light of the Golden Age—itself joy, music, and poetry—is shining above. There are evenings of summer or autumntide so exquisitely beautiful, so complete in their own charms, that the entrance of the moon is felt almost as a painful and superflous addition: it is like a candle dispelling the weird darkness of a twilight room. So we feel at first as if Evangeline, when introduced, were an excess of loveliness,—an amiable eclipser of the surrounding beauties. But even as the moon by-and-by vindicates her intrusion and creates her own "holier day" so with the delicate and lovely heroine of this simple story: she becomes the centre of the entire scene.—GILFILLAN, GEORGE, 1849-52, *Second Gallery of Literary Portraits.*

It is somewhat unfortunate for Mr. Longfellow that he has thrown by far the greatest part of his poetical treasure into the most thankless of all forms, the hexameter. A long acquaintance justifies us in the assertion, that there are few American poems where so much fine thought and tender feeling are hid as in "Evangeline." . . . The opening sketch of the tranquil lives of the French Acadians, on the Gulf of Minas, is truly idyllic; but the peculiarity of the measure—to which the English language is so little adapted—renders it very difficult to do justice in it even to the finest poetry. The hexameter is the grave of poetry. It is the crowning monotony of writing. A sort of stale prose. An author like Mr. Longfellow should not deprive himself of so much fame, by pushing to the utmost a peculiarity by which he had attained, in so many quarters, a somewhat undeserved reputation. . . . The Beautiful is his idol; his commonest thought is an anthem to her praise; and, like a true disciple, he insensibly adopts the manner of the priest he has confessed to, till he himself becomes one of the elect. . . . Into "Evangeline" Mr. Longfellow has thrown more of his own individual poetry than into any other production.—POWELL, THOMAS, 1850. *The Living Authors of America*, pp. 135, 136, 137.

"Evangeline" is a romance, written in hexameter verse and in English upon a subject historical and French, and adorned with romantic and metaphysical colors by an American of the United States. It is the end and the beginning of two literatures; the cradle and decline of two poetries; a faint new dawn above an ancient ruin.—CHASLES, PHILARÈTE, 1852, *Anglo-American Literature and Manners*, p. 195.

He must not follow the model offered by Mr. Longfellow in his pleasing and popular poem of "Evangeline;" for the merit of the manner and movement of "Evangeline," when they are at their best, is to be tenderly elegant; and their fault, when they are at their worst, is to be lumbering.—ARNOLD, MATTHEW, 1861, *Lectures on Homer*, p. 80.

One cannot read this delightful poem without feeling that the heart of the writer is in it, not less than in the "Psalm of Life." While in the delineation of natural scenery, and of the simplicity of rural life and manners, it is minutely faithful and distinct; while its characters are so well conceived, and so graphically drawn, that in the progress of the piece they become to one as familiar friends; the highest power of the story results from the fact that the author was so possessed by his theme that he wrote almost as if narrating a personal experience. Every line throbs with vitality, and the whole is suffused with a glow of genuine feeling. The result is originality, fascination, pathos. Evangeline has become as much a real person to the reading world as Joan of Arc; and the incidents of her history hold the attention, and are believed in, like those of Robinson Crusoe.—PALMER, RAY, 1875, *Henry Wadsworth Longfellow and His Writings*, International Review, vol. 2, p. 736.

It is impossible to give an idea of the genius of Longfellow without insisting on the joy with which he revels among imaginary beauties of nature. It is to him a nature of his own, not requiring the sustenance of an outside world before his eyes, as was to Hawthorne the weird mysticism of a world which was only present to him in his fancy. There was nothing special in Hawthorne's personal experiences to have produced such dread ideas; and, though Longfellow has traveled in the course of an enjoyable life through scenes of much European beauty, not to that is to be attributed the luxuriance of the charm of description by which the readers of "Evangeline" are delighted. It is not necessary to produce such description that with the poet's fancy should be combined a reality of poetic scenery. Without the fancy, the scenery would be nothing. All the Alps with all their glory do not create for us a great Swiss poet. But, without the Alps or any of their glory, the classical but not particularly beautiful town of Cambridge, and the somewhat sterile region of Massachusetts, suffice, when the man comes to whom God has given the genius of Longfellow.—TROLLOPE, ANTHONY, 1881, *Henry Wadsworth Longfellow*, North American Review, vol. 132, p. 392.

It is what the critic had been so long demanding and clamoring for—an American poem—and it is narrated with commendable simplicity, and a fluency which is not so commendable. Poetry, as poetry merely, is kept in the background; the descriptions, even when they appear redundant, are subordinated to the main purpose of the poem, out of which they rise naturally; the characters, if not clearly drawn, are distinctly indicated, and the landscapes through which they move are perfectly characteristic of the New World.—STODDARD, RICHARD HENRY, 1882, *Henry Wadsworth Longfellow, A Medley in Prose and Verse*, p. 130.

This work did more to establish Longfellow's reputation than any of his previous ones, and if, as has been said by one of the profoundest of critics, poems are to be judged by the state of mind in which they leave the reader, the high place which "Evangeline" occupies in popular esteem is justly awarded to it; for its chaste style and homely imagery, with its sympathetic and occasionally dramatic story, produce a refined and elevated impression, and present a beautiful and invigorating picture of "affection that hopes and endures, and is patient," of the beauty and strength of woman's devotion.—NORMAN, HENRY, 1883, *A Study of Longfellow*, Fortnightly Review, vol. 39, p. 106.

A beautiful, pathetic tradition of American history, remote enough to gather a poetic halo, and yet fresh with sweet humanities; tinged with provincial color which he knew and loved, and in its course taking on the changing atmospheres of his own land; pastoral at first, then broken into action, and afterward the record of shifting scenes that made life a pilgrimage and dream. There are few dramatic episodes; there is but one figure whom we follow,—that one of the most touching of all, the betrothed Evangeline searching for her lover, through weary years and over half an unknown world. There are chance pictures of Acadian fields, New World rivers, prairies, bayous, forests, by moonlight and starlight and midday; glimpses, too, of picturesque figures, artisans, farmers, soldiery, trappers, boatmen, emigrants and priests. But the poem already is a little classic, and will remain one, just as surely as "The Vicar of Wakefield," the "Deserted Village," or any other sweet and pious idyl of our English tongue; yet we find its counterpart more nearly, I think, in some faultless miniature of the purest French school.—STEDMAN, EDMUND CLARENCE, 1885, *Poets of America*, p. 200.

"Evangeline" is as interesting as a novel. Try it on those acute, unbiased critics, the children. It fascinates them, for there is just description enough to make a background, and then the incidents follow naturally, and cumulate—each succeeding picture adding to the effect, brought in at just the right time and dwelt on just long enough, with fine, unconscious art.—JOHNSON, CHARLES F., 1885, *Three Americans and Three Englishmen*, p. 230.

"Evangeline," in which he sweeps on broad cæsural, hexameter pinions, from the fir-fretted valleys of Acadia to the lazy, languorous tides, which surge silently through the bayous of Louisiana. There was an outcry at first—that this poem showed classic affectation; but the beauty and the pathos carried the heroine and the metre into all hearts and homes in all English-speaking lands.—MITCHELL, DONALD G., 1899, *American Lands and Letters, Leather-Stocking to Poe's "Raven,"* p. 294.

The instant popularity of "Evangeline" demonstrated that the form commended itself to the masses as well as to the cultured few, and that previous failures were due to unskilfulness in use rather than to any inherent obstacles in the form itself. In the hands of an unskilful versifier nothing can be more wretched. When controlled by a master, nothing can be more melodious. It is the rhythm of passion, emotion, and delicate fancy, and therefore, in this instance, best adapted to the poet's conception of his theme. . . . "Evangeline" was published October 30, 1847, one of the decisive dates in the history of American literature. It was the first narrative poem of considerable length by an American showing genuine creative power. Its purity of diction and elevated style, its beauties of description, its tenderness, pathos, and simplicity, its similes and metaphors at once true, poetic, and apt, its frequent passages betokening imaginative power, all embodied in a form unconventional yet peculiarly appropriate, stamped it as a new and individual creation. It was the highest inspiration in idyllic poetry produced in America. The impression left by a perusal of the poem is like that attributed to the passing of its heroine. It "seemed like the ceasing of exquisite music." American literature had proved its right to recognition, and in at least this one instance the world at large has not been slow to bear tribute of admiration.—ONDERDONK, JAMES L., 1899-1901, *History of American Verse*, pp. 219, 221.

KAVANAGH
1847

All who love purity of tone, tenderness, and picturesque simplicity, have incurred a new obligation to the author of "Kavanagh." . . . In "Kavanagh" as in "Evangeline," we conceive it to be a peculiar merit that the *story* is kept down with so rigid a self-denial. The brass of the orchestra is not allowed an undue prominence. . . . "Kavanagh" is, as far as it goes, an exact daguerreotype of New England life. We say *daguerreotype*, because we are conscious of a certain absence of motion and color, which detracts somewhat from the vivacity, though not from the truth, of the representation. From Mr. Pendexter with his horse and chaise, to Miss Manchester painting the front of her house, the figures are faithfully after nature. —LOWELL, JAMES RUSSELL, 1849, *Longfellow's Kavanagh, North American Review*, vol. 69, pp. 214, 215.

Those who expected a novel which would illustrate New England character and life have not been gratified. "Kavanagh" is a sketch, and not properly a rounded and completed story. The characters are outlined rather than painted, and the main interest of the book lies in its transparent moral. It teaches two things: the value to an artist of spiritual insight into common life, and the necessity of promptness and decision if we would realize our aspirations. . . . There is no tinge of unnaturalness in the incidents of the narrative. It is not toned above the key of ordinary experience. But only those who have read it, or who have vivid recollections of the author's "Hyperion," can understand the peculiar charm which the purity of style, the sweet, mellow rhythm of the sentences, affluence of fancy, felicitous exhibition of curious learning, and delicacy and healthiness of sentiment combine to throw over every page.—KING, THOMAS STARR, 1849, *Notices of Recent Publications, Christian Examiner*, vol. 47, p. 154.

It fell rather flat, and has never been talked about in America with any enthusiasm. As the Americans found less to move them in the poet's studies of slavery than we find, so it seems to be the case that the pictures he draws in "Kavanagh" of every-day life in the rural part of Massachusetts as it was about half a century ago, appeal to us here with more freshness and beauty than they do to those who are more or less familiar with the scenes and incidents he described.—ROBERTSON, ERIC S., 1887, *Life of Henry Wadsworth Longfellow (Great Writers)*, p. 130.

The brief story is pleasing throughout; its rural pictures have a mild idyllic grace, and its gentle humour approves itself to the reader, who heartily accepts its lesson: that purpose should be transmuted into action. —RICHARDSON, CHARLES F., 1888, *American Literature, 1607–1885*, vol. II, p. 53.

A rather slight and pallid novelette, generously characterized by Emerson as "the best sketch we have seen in the direction of the American Novel."—LAWTON, WILLIAM CRANSTON, 1898, *The New England Poets*, p. 128.

THE BUILDING OF THE SHIP
1850

Admiralty, July 20.—I should have been so pleased to meet, and pay my profound respects to, the author of the finest poem on ship-building that ever was, or probably ever will be, written,—a poem which I often read with the truest pleasure.—REED, E. J., 1869, *Letter, Life of Henry Wadsworth Longfellow, ed. Longfellow*, vol. III, p. 135.

One of the most powerful productions of its distinguished author.—AUSTIN, GEORGE LOWELL, 1883, *Henry Wadsworth Longfellow, His Life, His Works, His Friendships*, p. 315.

A noble piece of work, boldly handled, passing from scene to scene, and from phase to phase of reflection, in a most impassioned style. As a poem for recitation, this is probably as affective as anything Longfellow wrote. Yet in reading "The Building of the Ship," we are constantly reminded that there is no border-line between prose and poetry. Not only does the unfettered play of rhythms in the poem cause the ear to forget the distinction at times, but the general style of thought belongs almost more to oratory than to the methods of fastidious poesy. The ending of the piece has raised thousands of American audiences to frenzies of patriotic enthusiasm, and the enthusiasm does credit both to Longfellow and to the audiences; yet is not this mere oratory fitted out in rhyme? . . . Mere oratory! Yes, it is; but finer than the finest of Webster's or Sumner's. Criticising "The Building of the Ship" as a poem, we must not forget that its form is obviously borrowed from Schiller's "Lay of the Bell."—ROBERTSON, ERIC S., 1887, *Life of Henry Wadsworth Longfellow (Great Writers)*, pp. 135, 136.

"The Building of the Ship," with its magnificent ending, is without a parallel, in its line, in English Literature.—PATTEE, FRED LEWIS, 1896, *A History of American Literature*, p. 270.

THE GOLDEN LEGEND
1851

Longfellow, in the "Golden Legend," has entered more closely into the temper of the Monk, for good and for evil, than ever yet theological writer or historian, though they may have given their life's labor to the analysis.—RUSKIN, JOHN, 1856, *Modern Painters*, vol. IV.

No more exquisitely finished and harmonious poetical work has been written in this country than the "Golden Legend."— TAYLOR, BAYARD, 1879, *Studies in German Literature*, p. 74.

"The Golden Legend," however, should be judged by itself, and is an enchanting romance of the Middle Age cast in the dramatic mould. Brought out years before the "Tragedies," it finally was merged in the "Christus" by way of toning up the whole, the poet well knowing that this was his choicest distillation of Gothic mysticism and its legendary. It is composite rather than inventive; the correspondences between this work and Goethe's masterpiece, not to speak of productions earlier than either, are interesting. There is decided originality in its general effect, and in the taste wherewith the author, like a modern maker of stained glass, arranged the prismatic materials which he knew precisely where to collect.—STEDMAN, EDMUND CLARENCE, 1885, *Henry Wadsworth Longfellow, Poets of America*, p. 205.

It contains some of his best work, but its merit is rather poetic than dramatic, although Ruskin praised it for the closeness with which it entered into the temper of the monk.—BEERS, HENRY A., 1895, *Initial Studies in American Letters*, p. 135.

"Christus," with its Golden Legend, will always be valued for its scholarly ranges and for its pleasantly recurring poetic savors. It hardly seemed up to the full score of his purpose or of his ambitions; monkish ways are laid down tenderly, as they wended through mediæval wastes; and so are Christways of later and lightsomer times: but there is no careering blast of Divine wind sweeping through the highways all, and clearing them of putrescent dusts.—MITCHELL, DONALD G., 1899, *American Lands and Letters, Leather-Stockings to Poe's "Raven,"* p. 298.

Compared with the lofty ideals exemplified in Longfellow's best work, his dramatic writings seem almost puerile. It is in these that his weakest points are most conspicuous. His culture, which stands him in such good stead in his ordinary narratives, here becomes a positive hindrance. His imaginative faculties and his constructive power seem paralyzed. Properly speaking, these are not dramas at all. The strange part of it all was that the poet sincerely hoped that his trilogy of "Christus" would be the work which would carry his name through the ages. Nothing could be more majestic than the theme, nothing more disappointing than its treatment. While the poet was so absorbed with his subject, he was, as his diary shows, not without grave misgivings as to the result. The second part, "The Golden Legend," relieves the series from the imputation of literary failure.—ONDERDONK, JAMES L., 1899-1901, *History of American Verse*, p. 226.

THE SONG OF HIAWATHA
1855

I find this Indian poem very wholesome; sweet and wholesome as maize; very proper and pertinent for us to read, and showing a kind of manly sense of duty in the poet to write. The dangers of the Indians are, that they are really savage, have poor, small, sterile heads,—no thoughts; and you must deal very roundly with them, and find them in brains. And I blamed your tenderness now and then, as I read, in accepting a legend or song, when they had so little to give. I should hold you to your creative function on such occasions. But the costume and machinery, on the whole, is sweet and melancholy, and agrees with the American landscape. And you have the distinction of opening your own road. You may well call it an "Indian Edda."—EMERSON, RALPH WALDO, 1855, *To Longfellow, Nov. 25; Life of Henry Wadsworth Longfellow*, ed. *Longfellow, vol.* II, p. 294.

I like "Hiawatha;" and I think it is liked here generally, and none the worse for being Indian.—CLOUGH, ARTHUR HUGH, 1856, *Letter to F. J. Child, Jan. 16; Prose Remains*, ed. his *Wife*, p. 235.

Permit me to dedicate to you this volume of Indian myths and legends, derived from the story-telling circle of the native wigwams. That they indicate the possession, by the Vesperic tribes, of mental resources of a very characteristic kind,—furnishing, in fact, a new point from which to judge the race and to excite intellectual sympathies, —you have most felicitiously shown in your poem of "Hiawatha." Not only so, but you have demonstrated, by this pleasing series of pictures of Indian life, sentiment, and invention, that the use of the native lore reveals one of the true sources of our literary independence. Greece and Rome, England and Italy, have so long furnished, if they have not exhausted, the field of poetic culture, that it is at least refreshing to find, both in theme and metre, something new.—SCHOOLCRAFT, HENRY R., 1856, *The Myth of Hiawatha and other Oral Legends, Mythologic and Allegoric of the North American Indians*, Dedication.

Longfellow has enriched universal literature by a truely indigenous American epic, the "Song of Hiawatha." This "Indian Edda," as the poem has been rightly called, is undoubtedly the most important poetical work that has been accomplished by an

American.—SCHERR, J., 1874, *A History of English Literature*, tr. *M. V., p.* 303.

"Hiawatha," besides any number of translations into modern languages, has been turned into Latin by Professor F. W. Newman (published in 1862); it was also made the subject of musical treatment at Covent Garden in 1861.—ROSSETTI, WILLIAM MICHAEL, 1878, *Lives of Famous Poets,* p. 387.

The story of Nature has never been told with so much liquid gaiety and melancholy,—so much of the frolic of the childlike races, and so much of their sudden awe and dejection,—as in "Hiawatha" which I, at least, have never taken up without new delight in the singular simplicity and grace, the artless art and ingenuous vivacity, of that rendering of the traditions of a vanishing race.—HUTTON, RICHARD HOLT, 1882-94, *Criticisms on Contemporary Thought and Thinkers,* vol. II, p. 77.

No meritorious work was ever more severely judged than "Hiawatha" when it first appeared. But the sales were large. It quickly became the most popular of all his works, and the reviewers who had censured it joined in the later chorus of its praise.—TROWBRIDGE, JOHN TOWNSEND, 1885, *Henry Wadsworth Longfellow; Some Noted Princes, Authors, and Statesmen of Our Time,* p. 295.

It is hard to believe that "Hiawatha" will not live in the admiration of posterity as long as any poem of this age. In its time it has been often abused, and parodied as often. Abuse and parody have now ceased; and when the redskins themselves have died from off the face of the American continent, there will always be men and women ready to follow the poet into the primeval forests, see him make for himself a woodland flute, piping to the poor painted braves and making them dance, weeping with the weeping squaws, attuning his laughter to the soft babble of their streams, and giving himself, like them, such a companionship with birds and beasts and fishes, prairie, mountains, and trees, as is not likely to find similar utterance in any future century on this globe of ever-increasing populousness. It is true that in "Hiawatha's" pleasant numbers the Red Indian, with his narrow skull and small brain, is not presented to us with less enbellishment than he gains in Cooper's romances; but the fact does not diminish Longfellow's credit as a poet. After this Indian Edda had passed through the first burst of criticism, Mr. Schoolcraft brought out a book called "The Myth of Hiawatha, and other Oral Legends of the North American Indians;" and the student who consults this compilation will be astonished at the wholly unimaginative character of the material thus diligently accumulated by a competent scholar. Yet it was from this material that Longfellow produced his masterpiece.—ROBERTSON, ERIC S., 1887, *Life of Henry Wadsworth Longfellow (Great Writers),* p. 151.

To me "Hiawatha" seems by far the best of his longer efforts; it is quite full of sympathy with men and women, nature, beasts, birds, weather, and wind and snow. Everything lives with a human breath, as everything should live in a poem concerned with these wild folk, to whom all the world, and all in it, is personal as themselves.—LANG, ANDREW, 1889, *Letters on Literature,* p. 52.

Exhales the very fragrance of the broad prairie and illimitable forest, and is steeped in an atmosphere peculiarly and perfectly its own.—DAWSON, W. J., 1892, *Quest and Vision,* p. 121.

Has been called America's first contribution to world literature. In this poem, Longfellow, having perceived the poetic capabilities of the Indian legends, welded them into a whole, the life of which is quickened by invention of his own. A breath of nature passes over the pages, and the public attention hitherto paid to the mechanism and commonplace narratives of the poem may well be turned to the higher flights of fancy and imagination.—SIMONDS, ARTHUR B., 1894, *American Song,* p. 65.

This again called out the shrill salute of a great many of those critics who "shy" at any divergence from the conventionalities by which their schools are governed, and who took captious exceptions to a metre that was strange; but the laughing waters of Minnehaha and the pretty legendary texture of this Indian poem have carried its galloping trochaic measure into all cultivated American households. "Hiawatha" did not appear, however, (1855), until its author had given over his labors as a teacher, and was resting upon the laurels which had grown all round that Cambridge home. The pretty tale of "Kavanagh," of earlier date, ranked fairly with his other ventures in the field of prose fiction—all of them wearing the air of poems gone astray—bereft of their rhymatic robes, and showing a lack of the

brawn and virility which we ordinarily associate with the homely trousers of prose.
—MITCHELL, DONALD G., 1899, *American Lands and Letters, Leather-Stockings to Poe's "Raven," p. 294.*

Parodies and criticisms have long since been forgotten, but the poem itself, as the nearest approach to an American epic, continues to be a favorite with learned and unlearned alike. — ONDERDONK, JAMES L., 1899-1901, *History of American Verse, p. 225.*

Ladies: We loved your father. The memory of our people will never die as long as your father's song lives, and that will live forever. Will you and your husbands and Miss Longfellow come and see us and stay in our Royal wigwams on an island in Hiawatha's play-ground, in the land of the Ojibways? We want you to see us live over again the life of Hiawatha in his own country.—

KABAOOSA.
WABUNOSA.
Boston, Onahoaunegises,
The Month of crusts on the snow.
—KABAOOSA AND WABUNOSA, 1900, *Letter to Mr. Longfellow's Family.*

A few days before the end of the visit, the Indians were very busy building a small platform on the island, and decorating it with green boughs, doing everything with much secrecy. After sunset, when the fire was lighted on the rocks nearby, the Indians assembled together, and Kabaoosa as the spokesman announced that they wished to have the pleasure of taking some of the party into the tribes as members. First came the ladies, as their father had turned the Ojibway legends into verse. They were led in turn before Kabaoosa, who took one of their hands in his, and made a spirited discourse in Ojibway. Then striking them three times on the shoulder, he called aloud the Indian name of adoption, and all the bystanders repeated it together. Then the new member of the tribe was led around the circle, and each Indian came forward, grasping the stranger by the hand, and calling aloud the new name. The names, which were valued names in the tribe, were all chosen with care, and given as proofs of high regard; the men of the party were honored as well as the women. Odenewasenoquay, The first flash of the lightning (Miss Longfellow); Osahgahgushkodawaquay, The lady of the open plains (Mrs. J. G. Thorp); Daguagonay, The man whom people like to camp near (J. G. Thorp, Esq.), and the names of the old chiefs Singwauk, or Sagagewayosay (Richard Henry Dana), and Bukwujjinini (Henry W. L. Dana).— LONGFELLOW, ALICE M., 1901, *A Visit to Hiawatha's People, p. 323.*

THE COURTSHIP OF MILES STANDISH
1858

We are by no means solicitous to determine the merit of this as compared with Mr. Longfellow's other poems. We have enjoyed it, and thank him for it. It contains some descriptive passages of unparalleled beauty; and, if portions of it are woven from the common fabric of every-day life, the more true are they to the massive and resolute, yet quite prosaic characters of the Pilgrim Fathers and their daughters. Miles Standish was not a paladin, nor was John Alden a knight-errant, and Priscilla Mullins was a plain, outspoken girl, without a particle of romance about her; and, while we might not have chosen them for Mr. Longfellow's heroes and heroine, we are glad that he has chosen them, and has given us so life-like pictures of them. The critics who find an anachronism in the treadle of the spinning-wheel are the best vouchers for the general versimilitude of the story; for they show that that they have applied the micrometer to ever part of it.—PEABODY, ANDREW P., 1859, *Critical Notices, North American Review, vol. 88, p. 276.*

"The Courtship of Miles Standish," of which his publishers sold twenty-five thousand copies in a month from its publication. But it is in hexameter verse, and, though popular for the time from its novelty, it can never obtain a permanent hold of the hearts of the people.—CLEVELAND, CHARLES D., 1859, *A Compendium of American Literature, p. 561.*

In this poem, as in many others, we discern that Mr. Longfellow's weakness lies not far from his strength; that he felicitously expresses the feelings and thoughts common to all, but does not possess that passion by which supreme lyrists depict the high tides of emotion. He never sings under the irrepressible impulse of some burning affection, some impassioned preference.— AUSTIN, GEORGE LOWELL, 1883, *Henry Wadsworth Longfellow, His Life, His Works, His Friendships, p. 334.*

"The Courtship of Miles Standish" was an

advance upon "Evangeline," so far as concerns structure and the distinct characterization of personages. A merit of the tale is the frolicsome humor here and there, lighting up the gloom that blends with our conception of the Pilgrim inclosure, and we see that comic and poetic elements are not at odds in the scheme of a bright imagination. The verse, though stronger, is more labored than that of "Evangeline;" some of the lines are prosaic, almost inadmissible.— STEDMAN, EDMUND CLARENCE, 1885, *Poets of America*, p. 203.

Miles Standish, the Captain of Plymouth, is a character always dear to the American heart. The little, big-hearted, choleric, generous man stands out from the grim crowd of Puritans, a very human being among the saints, able to jerk out a good round oath now and then, to love and to hate too, like other men. How much of the popular conception of the character was the real Miles Standish, and how much is Longfellow's Miles Standish, were an interesting question, did one have time and place for its discussion. Perhaps more interesting than profitable; at any rate, Longfellow's little captain has the fibre of reality about him so sturdy that it is *he* whom we see always when we read the history of the Puritans.—THANET, OCTAVE, 1888, *The Courtship of Miles Standish, Book Buyer*, vol 5, p. 451.

DANTE'S DIVINE COMEDY
1867–70

There can be, I think, no doubt that you have done something astonishing. I should not have thought it possible beforehand, and do not altogether comprehend it now how you have accomplished it. I was led on, canto by canto, wondering all the time whether you would give out or stumble; but you never did, so far as I could observe, and I meant to be watchful. The movement of your verse—its cadence and rhythm, I mean—explain, perhaps, a good deal of your power, or rather conceal it; although I confess I do not, after some consideration, understand how you make us feel a sort of presence of the *teriza rima*, in a measure so different.—TICKNOR, GEORGE, 1867, *To Longfellow*, June 1; *Life of Henry Wadsworth Longfellow*, ed. Longfellow, vol. III, p. 90.

Mr. Longfellow, in rendering the substance of Dante's poem, has succeeded in giving, also—so far as art and genius could give it—the spirit of Dante's poetry.... It is a lasting addition to the choicest treasures of our literature.... The notes and illustrations which Mr. Longfellow has appended to his translation form a comment upon the poem such as is not elsewhere to be found. The notes are full of pleasant learning, set forth with that grace and beauty of style which are characteristic of Mr. Longfellow's prose; and the long extracts which he gives from Carlyle, Macaulay, Ruskin, and other eminent writers, make his comment a thesaurus of the best judgments that exist in English concerning the poet and his poems.—NORTON, CHARLES ELIOT, 1867, *Longfellow's Translation of the Divine Comedy, North American Reviews*, vol. 105, pp. 145, 146, 147.

The review does not change my opinion of Mr. Longfellow's translation—not as the best possible, by any means, but as the best probable. The fault I should find with the criticism is one whereof the author seems to be conscious himself—at least in some measure. It is laid out on too large a scale. His portico is as much too large as that of our Boston Court-House. It seems rather an attempt to show how much the critic knows (and I am heartily glad to find an American who knows so much) than to demonstrate the defects of the translation. —LOWELL, JAMES RUSSELL, 1867, *To James B. Thayer*, Oct.; *Letters*, ed. Norton, vol. I, p. 395.

Mr. Longfellow has translated Dante as a great poet should be translated. After this version, no other will be attempted until the present form of the English language shall have become obsolete, for, whether we regard fidelity to the sense, aptness in the form of expression, or the skilful transfusion of the poetic spirit of the original into the phrases of another language, we can look for nothing more perfect.—BRYANT, WILLIAM CULLEN, 1867, *Letter to James T. Fields*, Oct. 31; *William Cullen Bryant by Godwin*, vol. II, p. 265.

Here at last that much suffering reader will find Dante's greatness manifest, and not his greatness only, but his grace, his simplicity, and his affection. Here he will find strength matched with wonderful sweetness, and dignity with quaintness—Dante of the thirteenth century and Dante of eternity. There has been no attempt to add to or to take from this lofty presence. Opening the book we stand face to face with the poet, and when his voice ceases we may well marvel if he has not sung to us in his own Tuscan.—HOWELLS, WILLIAM DEAN, 1867, *Mr. Longfellow's Translation of the Divine Comedy, The Nation, vol.* 4, *p.* 494.

It is not to Mr. Longfellow's reputation only that these volumes will add, but to that of American literature. It is no little thing to be able to say, that, in a field in which some of England's great poets have signally failed, an American poet has signally succeeded; and what the scholars of the Old World asserted to be impossible, a scholar of the New World has accomplished; and that the first to tread in this new path has impressed his footprints so deeply therein, that, however numerous his followers may be, they will all unite in hailing him with Dante's own words,—

"Tu Duca, tu Signore e tu Maestro,"—

Thou Leader and thou Lord and Master thou.
—GREENE, GEORGE W., 1867, *Longfellow's Translation of the Divina Commedia, Atlantic Monthly, vol.* 20, *p.* 198.

By the resolution to translate line for line, Mr. Longfellow ties his poetic hands. The first effect of his self binding is, to oblige him to use often long Latin-English instead of short Saxon-English words, that is, words that in most cases lend themselve less readily to poetic expression. . . . By his line-for-line allegiance, Mr. Longfellow forfeits much of his freedom. He is too intent on the words; he sacrifices the spirit of the letter; he overlays the poetry with a verbal literalness; he deprives himself of scope to give a billowy motion, a heightened color, a girded vigor, to choice passages. The rhythmical languor consequent on this verbal conformity, this lineal servility, is increased by a frequent looseness in the endings of lines, some of which on every page, and many on some pages, have—contrary to all good usage—the superfluous eleventh syllable.—CALVERT, GEORGE H., 1868–75, *Dante and his Translators, Essays Æsthetical, pp.* 148, 149.

Of late I am entirely devoted to Italian history and memoirs of the early part of this century. . . . For serious reading I have a canto of Dante every morning before my bath and tea. Longfellow's translation amuses me very much. You cannot possibly understand it unless you have read the original. I dare say that at first it was very good, but that little Dante Club sat on it every week, until they quite squashed all the poetry, and even the verse out of it.
—SCHUYLER, EUGENE, 1888, *Letter from Alassio, A Memoir, ed. Schaeffer, p.* 178.

The crown of Longfellow's achievements as a translator was a great version of Dante's "Divina Commedia." . . . It is a severely literal, almost a line for line, rendering. The meter is preserved, but the rhythm sacrificed. If not the best English poem constructed from Dante, it is at all events the most faithful and scholarly paraphrase. The sonnets which accompanied it are among Longfellow's best work. He seems to have been raised by daily communion with the great Tuscan into a habit of deeper and more subtle thought than is elsewhere common in his poetry.—BEERS, HENRY A., 1895, *Initial Studies in American Letters, p.* 136.

His translation of Dante may be regarded as simply the work of a competent and cultured scholar. He aims to reproduce the terseness of the original rather than its form. Perhaps this is all that a sustained translation of a great poem can do; for poetic work lies in the relation between the group of words and the idea, and even individual poetic words—much more, groups of them—have no foreign equivalents. But Longfellow's version is one of the few great translations of literature. — JOHNSON, CHARLES F., 1897, *Library of the World's Best Literature, ed. Warner, vol.* XVI, *p.* 9147.

Longfellow's own temperament was of the gracious and conciliatory type, by no means of the domineering quality; and it is certainly a noticeable outcome of all this joint effort at constructing a version of this great world-poem, that one of the two original delegates, Professor Norton, should ultimately have published a prose translation of his own. It is also to be observed that Professor Norton, in the original preface of his version, while praising several other translators, does not so much as mention the name of Longfellow; and in his list of "Aids to the study of the 'Divine Comedy' " speaks only of Longfellow's notes and illustrations, which he praises as "admirable." Even Lowell, the other original member of the conference, while in his "Dante" essay he ranks Longfellow's as "the best" of the complete translations, applies the word "admirable" only to those fragmentary early versions, made for Longfellow's college classes twenty years before, —versions which the completed work was apparently intended to supersede. Far be it from me to imply that any disloyalty was shown on the part of these gentlemen either towards their eminent associate or toward the work on which they had shared his labors; it is only that they surprise us a little by what they do not say. It may be that they do not praise the Longfellow version because they confessedly had a share in it, yet this reason does not quite satisfy. Nothing has been more noticeable in the popular reception of the completed work than the general preference of unsophisticated readers for those earlier translations thus heartily praised by Lowell. There has been a general complaint that the later work does not possess for the English-speaking the charm exerted by the original over all who can read Italian, while those earlier and fragmentary specimens had certainly possessed something of that charm.—HIGGINSON, THOMAS WENTWORTH, 1902, *Henry Wadsworth Longfellow (American Men of Letters)*, p. 227.

THE DIVINE TRAGEDY
1871

Since it will be a satisfaction to me to express my delight in the success of your poem, you cannot well deny me the privilege. When I heard the first announcement of it as forthcoming, I said, "Well, it is the grandest of all subjects; why has it never been attempted?" And yet I said inwardly in the next breath: "What mortal power is equal to the handling of it?" The greater and the more delightful is my surprise at the result. You have managed the theme with really wonderful address. The episodes, and the hard characters, and the partly imaginery characters, you had your liberty in: and you have used them well to suffuse and flavor and poetize the story. And yet, I know not how it is, but the part which finds me most perfectly, and is, in fact, the most poetic poetry of all, is the prose-poem,—the nearly rhymatic transcription of the simple narrative matter of the gospels.—BUSHNELL, HORACE, 1871, *Letter to Longfellow*, Dec. 28; *Henry Wadsworth Longfellow*, ed. Longfellow, vol. III, p. 192.

A large portion of this drama is a deftly arranged mosaic of passages from the Evangelists, and the reader is at first quite as much struck with the rhythmical character of the King James version, which permits the words to fall so easily into the metrical order, as he is with the poet's skill in the selection and adjustment. Probably the indifference shown by people in general to this drama is due in part to the feeling that nothing very novel was offered.... He approached this dramatic representation of the Christ somewhat as a painter might propose a Crucifixion as a votive offering, only that while the painter, in a great period of religious art, would be working in a perfectly well understood and accepted mode, this poet was artistically alone, and was not merely not helped, but actually hindered, by the prevalent religious temper.—SCUDDER, HORACE E., 1887, *Longfellow's Art, Atlantic Monthly*, vol. 59, p. 407.

It would seem that for some reason the poem did not, like its predecessors, find its way to the popular heart. When one considers the enthusiasm which greeted Willis' scriptural poems in earlier days, or that which has in later days been attracted by semi-scriptural prose fictions, such as "The Prince of the House of David" and "Ben Hur," the latter appearing, moreover, in a dramatic form, there certainly seems no reason why Longfellow's attempt to grapple with the great theme should be so little successful. The book is not, like "The New England Tragedies" which completed the circle of "Christus," dull in itself. It is, on the contrary, varied and readable; not merely poetic and tender, which was a matter of course in Longfellow's hands, but strikingly varied, its composition skillful, the scripture types well handled, and the additional figures, Helen of Tyre, Simon Magus, and Menahem the Essenian, skillfully introduced and effectively managed. Yet one rarely sees the book quoted; it has not been widely read, and in all the vast list of Longfellow translations into foreign languages, there appears no version of any part of it except the comparatively modern and mediæval "Golden Legend." It has simply afforded one of the most remarkable instances in literary history of the utter ignoring of the supposed high water-mark of a favorite author.—HIGGINSON, THOMAS WENTWORTH, 1902, *Henry Wadsworth Longfellow (American Men of Letters)*, p. 246.

SONNETS

"Longfellow wrote few weak sonnets, but I think his strongest are those which embody portraitures of characterizations of illustrious men, or which revive associations connected with them.... Among them are many that are signally notable for the superlative beauty of the thoughts they enshrine, the transparent clearness of their language, and the liquid melody of their versification—if they have any defect, it is their excess of sweetness, which sometimes cloyes upon the palate." — DESHLER, CHARLES D., 1879, *Afternoons With the Poets, pp.* 286, 289.

In the "Book of Sonnets" are some of the finest things he ever wrote, especially the five sonnets entitled "Three Friends Mine." These "Three Friends" were Cornelius Felton, Louis Agassiz, and Charles Sumner.—DAVIDSON, THOMAS, 1882, *Henry Wadsworth Longfellow, p.* 10.

The sonnet was a form of poetical expression well suited to Longfellow's genius. So far as his muse bore him he was accustomed to think clearly; he had great power of imagination, and an accurate aim in literary matters. Besides these he was possessed of a characteristic which is perhaps the one most conspicuous by its absence from the school of poetry prevalent at the present day, viz., a constant self-control. A dithryamb would have been impossible to him; he never lost sight of the artistic quality of the work he had in hand, and the freest of his songs exhibits a complete subordination of the parts.—NORMAN, HENRY, 1883, *A Study of Longfellow, The Fortnightly Review, N. S. vol.* 33, *O. S. vol.* 39, *p.* 110.

In artistic finish, the numerous sonnets produced in the last twenty years of his life not only equalled anything he had previously written but easily put him at the head of all American sonneteers.—RICHARDSON, CHARLES F., 1888, *American Literature,* 1607–1885, *vol.* II, *p.* 67.

Foremost among American sonneteers stands Longfellow, the only member of the supreme group who uses this form with ease and dignity. Some score of examples —including the beautiful "Divina Commedia" series—might be selected from his works and compared with twenty by any modern English poet, save Wordsworth, nor lose thereby for nobility of sentiment and graciousness of diction. Wordsworth himself might have been proud to include "Nature," for instance, among his finest sonnets. — SHARP, WILLIAM, 1889, *ed. American Sonnets, Introductory Note, p.* xxxix.

GENERAL

Most of Mr. Longfellow's poetry—indeed, we believe nearly all that has been published—appeared during his college life in the *United States Literary Gazette*. It displays a very refined taste, and a very pure vein of poetical feeling. It possesses what has been a rare quality in the American poets—simplicity of expression, without any attempt to startle the reader, or to produce an effect by far-sought epithets. There is much sweetness in his imagery and language; and sometimes he is hardly excelled by any one for the quiet accuracy exhibited in his pictures of natural objects. His poetry will not easily be forgotten; some of it will be remembered with that of Dana and Bryant.—CHEEVER, GEORGE BARRELL, 1829, *ed. The American Commonplace Book of Poetry.*

We cannot say that he imitates the author of the "Sketch-Book;" he has a spirit of his own. But it seems to us that his mind is much of the same description. He is sprightly, and witty, and graphic; he has seen much of the world and used his opportunities well. There is an elegant ease in his style—finished but not finical; just the thing, as we say of a private gentleman whose manners and dress excite no other remark, while they satisfy all who observe them. And withal he has the genial *bonhomie* of Irving. He sees the pleasant side of things. He likes that his reader should be innocently pleased, and is content if he be so. If Longfellow, in a word, had come before Irving his fame would be that of a founder of a school (so far as America is concerned) rather than one of the scholars. As it is he may be popular, but not famous, and will hardly have credit even for what he is worth.—CHORLEY, HENRY FOTHERGILL,(?) 1838, *The Athenæum.*

I read your poems over and over, and over again, and continue to read them at all my leisure hours; and they grow upon me at every re-perusal. Nothing equal to some of them was ever written in this world,— this western world, I mean; and it would not hurt my conscience much to include the other hemisphere.—HAWTHORNE, NATHANIEL, 1839, *To Longfellow, Dec.* 26; *Life of Henry Wadsworth Longfellow, ed. Longfellow, vol.* I, *p.* 349.

In your disposition to avoid monotony, you roughen a line occasionally, after a fashion that frets me. . . . I say this just to prove my impartiality. Not being blinded altogether to such things only proves that I must have a better eye for the beauties. So I have. Some of the later poems are admirable. The earlier ones I don't like. And why? Partly because they cannot be found fault with, and partly because they are just a piece with all the respectable poetry of their day. Your last are of a newer and much deeper spirit; sanctified and sanctifying.—NEAL, JOHN, 1840, *To Longfellow, Jan.* 13; *Life of Henry Wadsworth Longfellow, ed. Longfellow, vol.* I, *p.* 356.

Henry W. Longfellow . . . is entitled to the first place among the poets of America —certainly to the first place among those who have put themselves prominently forth as poets. His good qualities are all of the highest order, while his sins are chiefly those of affectation and imitation—an imitation sometimes verging upon downright theft.— POE, EDGAR ALLAN, 1841, *A Chapter on Autography, Works, ed. Stedman and Woodberry, vol.* IX, *p.* 199.

No translations from the continental languages into the English surpass those of Longfellow, and it is questionable whether some of his versions from the Spanish, German, and Swedish, have been equalled. The rendition of "The Children of The Lord's Supper" was the most difficult task he could have undertaken, as spondaic words, so necessary in the construction of hexameters, and so common in the Greek, Latin, and Swedish, are so rare in the English language. . . . Longfellow's works are eminently picturesque, and are distinguished for nicety of epithet, and elaborate, scholarly finish. He has feeling, a rich imagination, and a cultured taste. He is one of the very small number of American poets who have "written for posterity."—GRISWOLD, RUFUS WILMOT, 1842, *The Poets and Poetry of America, p.* 297.

Longfellow's book contains some of the most beautiful gems of American poetry,— I would almost say, some of the most beautiful in English poetry. The description of the wreck in the ballad of the "Hesperus" is one of the finest things in English ballad literature. "Excelsior" is a noble poem, which cannot die; and which, as long as it lives, will fill with new energy those who read it, besides exciting the highest admiration for the writer. "Endymion" is a most poetical thought, beautifully wrought. "It is not always May" is a truly melodious composition. "The Rainy Day" is a little pearl. "Maidenhood" is a delicate, delicious, soft, hazy composition. "God's-Acre" is a very striking thought. Then, the hexameters. I do not like this measure in English. Our language has too many little words to bear this dactylic and spondaic yoke; but Longfellow has written the best that have been written in the language. —SUMNER, CHARLES, 1842, *To Francis Lieber, Feb.* 10; *Memoirs and Letters of Sumner, ed. Pierce, vol.* II, *p.* 201.

Much as we admire the genius of Mr. Longfellow, we are fully sensible of his many errors of affectation and imitation. His artistic skill is great, and his ideality high. But his conception of the aims of poesy is all wrong; and this we shall prove at some future day, to our own satisfaction, at least. His didactics are all out of place. He has written brilliant poems, by accident; that is to say, when permitting his genius to get the better of his conventional habit of thinking, a habit deduced from German study.—POE, EDGAR ALLAN, 1842, *Longfellow's Ballads, Works, ed. Stedman and Woodberry, vol.* VI, *p.* 122.

Especially happy are we to be able to count one of Mr. Longfellow's genius and celebrity among those friends of universal liberty, who are willing to speak their word in its behalf. In this little book of poems he has spoken with feeling, with truth, and eminent poetic beauty.—WARE, WILLIAM, 1843, *Poems on Slavery, Christian Examiner, vol.* 33, *p.* 354.

Longfellow has a perfect command of that expression which results from restraining rather than cultivating fluency; and his manner is adapted to his theme. He rarely, if ever, mistakes "emotions for conceptions." His words are often pictures of his thought. He selects with great delicacy and precision the exact phrase which best expresses or suggests his idea. He colors his style with the skill of a painter. The warm flush and bright tints, as well as the most evanescent hues, of language, he uses with admirable discretion. — WHIPPLE, EDWIN PERCY, 1844, *Poets and Poetry of America, Essays and Reviews, vol.* I, *p.* 58.

In this great crowd of translations ["Poets and Poetry of Europe"] by different hands, certainly very few appear equal to Professor Longfellow's in point of fidelity, elegance, and finish. The work is an honourable memorial of his great attainments as a linguist, in which character, rather than as a poet, his fame will be sustained and advanced by this publication. — BOWEN, FRANCIS, 1845, *Longfellow's Poets and Poetry of Europe, North American Review, vol.* 61, *p.* 200.

I have been looking over the collection of your poems recently published by Carey and Hart with Huntington's illustrations. They appear to me more beautiful than on former readings, much as I then admired them. The exquisite music of your verse dwells more than ever on my ear; and more than ever am I affected by their depth of feeling and spirituality, and the creative power with which they set before us passages from the great drama of life. I have been reading aloud to my wife some of the poems that pleased me most, and she would not be content till I had written to express to you something of the admiration which I could not help manifesting as I read them. I am not one of those who believe that a true poet is insensible to the excellence of his writings, and know that you can well afford to dispense with such slight corroboration as the general judgment in your favor could derive from any opinion of mine. You must allow me, however, to add my voice to the many which make up the voice of poetic fame.—BRYANT, WILLIAM CULLEN, 1846, *To Longfellow*, Jan. 31; *Life of Henry Wadsworth Longfellow,* ed. *Longfellow, vol.* II, *p.* 31.

Longfellow is artificial and imitative. He borrows incessantly, and mixes what he borrows, so that it does not appear to the best advantage. He is very faulty in using broken or mixed metaphors. The ethical part of his writing has a hollow, second-hand sound. He has, however, elegance, a love of the beautiful, and a fancy for what is large and manly, if not a full sympathy with it. His verse breathes at times much sweetness; and, if not allowed to supersede what is better may promote a taste for good poetry. Though imitative, he is not mechanical. — OSSOLI, MARGARET FULLER, 1850? *American Literature, Art, Literature, and the Drama, p.* 308.

I do not know a more enviable reputation than Professor Longfellow has won for himself in this country—won too with a rapidity seldom experienced by our own native poets. The terseness of diction and force of thought delight the old; the grace and melody enchant the young; the unaffected and all-pervading piety satisfy the serious; and a certain slight touch of mysticism carries the imaginative reader fairly off his feet. For my own part, I confess, not only to the being captivated by all these qualities (mysticism excepted), but to the farther fact of yielding to the charm of certain lines, I can not very well tell why, and walking about the house repeating to myself such fragments as this:

"I give the first watch of the night
To the red planet Mars,"

as if I were still eighteen. I am not sure that this is not as great a proof of the power of the poet as can be given.—MITFORD, MARY RUSSELL, 1851, *Recollections of a Literary Life, p.* 62.

The modern Scandinavian genius seems to have exercised great influence over his thought. Severe intellectual beauty, a peculiar sweetness of expression and rhythm distinguishes his verse, especially the "Voices of the Night." He is a "moonlight" poet, say the Americans, and attracts the soul by his sad, sweet grandeur. The effect of his verse is often strange, and the colors are so transparent that sentimental romance would willingly claim the merit of them. No one among the Anglo-Americans has soared higher into the middle air of Poesy than Longfellow, whose most touching poem we will shortly analize. Little passion, and great calm, approaching to majesty; a sensibility stirred in its very deeps are exhibited in moderated vibration and rhythm; only the Swedish poems of Tegner can give an idea of the gentle melody and thoughtful emotion. Longfellow appears to us to occupy the first rank among the poets of his country; a distinct savor characterizes him; as you read him you seem to feel the permanent mournfulness of the mighty sounds and shadows of the endless prairie and the woods which have no history.—CHASLES, PHILARÈTE, 1852, *Anglo-American Literature and Manners. p.* 194.

Trained as a verbal artist by the discipline of a poetic translator, he acquired a tact and facility in the use of words, which great natural fluency and extreme fastidiousness enabled him to use to the utmost advantage. His poems are chiefly meditative, and have that legendary significance peculiar to the German ballad. They also often embody and illustrate a moral truth. There is little or no evidence of inspiration in his verse, as that term is used to suggest the power of an overmastering passion; but there is a thoughtful, subdued feeling that seems to overflow in quiet beauty. It is, however, the manner in which this sentiment is expressed, the appropriateness of the figures, the harmony of the numbers, and the inimitable choice of words, that gives effect to the composition. He often reminds us of an excellent mosaic worker, with his smooth table of polished marble indented to receive the precious stones that are lying at hand, which he calmly, patiently, and with exquisite art, inserts in the shape of flowers and fruit.—TUCKERMAN, HENRY T., 1852, *Sketch of American Literature*.

Our hemisphere cannot claim the honor of having brought him forth; but still he belongs to us, for his works have become as household words wherever the English language is spoken. Whether we are charmed by his imagery, or soothed by his melodious versification, or elevated by the high moral teachings of his pure muse, or follow with sympathizing hearts the wanderings of Evangeline, I am sure that all who hear my voice will join with me in the tribute I desire to pay to the genius of Longfellow.—WISEMAN, NICHOLAS, 1852, *On the Home Education of the Poor*.

Thus have we seen the poet's praise chanted alike by stern reviewer and gentle lady, by lowly critic and lordly prelate.—ALLIBONE, S. AUSTIN, 1854-58, *A Critical Dictionary of English Literature*, vol. I, p. 1130.

Longfellow's hexameters generally "read themselves" easily enough, and that it is to be over-critical to complain of them in this respect; still, I don't think they are a good type of hexameter.—ARNOLD, MATTHEW, 1862, *To his Mother, April 14; Letters* ed. Russell, vol. I, p. 197.

I have been reading the "Wayside Inn" with the heartiest admiration. The introduction is masterly—so simple, clear, and strong. Let 'em put in all their *ifs* and *buts*; I don't wonder the public are hungrier and thirstier for his verse than for that of all the rest of us put together.—LOWELL, JAMES RUSSELL, 1863, *To James T. Fields, Nov. 30; Letters*, ed. Norton, vol. I, p. 334.

Mr. Longfellow's fair-mindedness and kindness make the reader also fair and kind. We are sorry for the oppressor as for the oppressed; for we see among the motives mixed in the thought of each the wish to do what is right, darkened by want of knowledge that seemed to be knowledge, and by fanaticism that seemed to be religion. He who reads "John Endicott," in the spirit in which that story is told, will be gladder for the troubled Governor at his escape by death from the bitter warfare of heart and mind than at the escape of the Quakers from merely bodily pain by the ending of the persecution.—CUTLER, E. J., 1869, *Longfellow's New England Tragedies*, *North American Review*, vol. 108, p. 670.

We might conceive of a Longfellow Gallery, better known and more fondly cherished than the picture galleries of kings. There, in the place of honor hangs Evangeline, sweetest of rustic heroines, turning her sad face away from the desolate Grand Pré. Opposite is the Puritan damsel, Priscilla, with her bashful, clerical lover, and the fiery little captain. In the next panel is the half-frozen sound, over which skims the bold Norseman. There, under the chestnut tree, stands the swart blacksmith, all the love of a father brimming in his eyes. There leans the vast glacier, gleaming in fatal beauty, along whose verge toils upwards the youth with "Excelsior" on his banner. There the airy Preciosa is dancing away the scruples of the archbishop. Here is pictured the Belfry of Bruges, and the groups of people listening to the heavenly chime of its bells. There, shivering in a wintry sea, is the Hesperus, a helpless wreck, driving upon Norman's Woe. Yonder stands Albrecht Dürer, in a street of his beloved, quaint old Nuremberg. There, on the sculptured stairway, is the Clock, ticking its eternal *Forever! never! Never! forever!* There saunters the dreamy-eyed Sicilian, with his dainty mustaches spread like a swallow's wings. Behold the busy throngs about that huge hulk, and see the proud master waving his hand as the signal for the launch! By that empty cradle sits the mother thinking of the dead lamb of her flock. Yonder looms up Strasburg spire, while spirits of the air circle round its pinnacles, and the miracle play goes on below. That is Paul Revere, galloping in the gray of the morning along the road to Concord. In that green spot, with the limitless prairie beyond, stands Hiawatha, looking gloomily westward, whither his path leads him. Lastly, we see a broad frame, on which we read in golden letters the legend, "The

Divine Tragedy." Let us not lightly raise the veil.—UNDERWOOD, FRANCIS H., 1872, *A Hand-Book of English Literature, American Authors*, p. 260.

The average Englishman knows hardly anything of any American poet but Longfellow, who receives, I venture to think, a far more wholesale and enthusiastic admiration in England than in his own country.— MCCARTHY, JUSTIN, 1872, *George Eliot and George Lewes, Modern Leaders*, p. 136.

Tennyson undoubtedly stands at the head of all living singers, and his name might well serve as the high-water mark of modern verse; but as our volume gives a liberal space to American authorship, I have ventured to let the name of the author of "Evangeline" represent, as it well may, the present poetic culture of our English-speaking people at home and abroad.— WHITTIER, JOHN GREENLEAF, 1875, ed. *Songs of Three Centuries*, Preface, p. v.

He is now beyond question the most popular of the American poets, and has also a wide circle of admirers in Europe. If none of his larger poems can be considered great, his smaller pieces are finished with taste, and all breathe a healthy moral feeling and fine tone of humanity.—CHAMBERS, ROBERT, 1876, *Cyclopædia of English Literature*, ed. Carruthers.

Perhaps no other poet of this century has written so many things which have become the companion-pictures of scholars and unlettered people alike. Mr. Longfellow is not only the most popular poet of America, but perhaps in a more marked degree, undoubtedly in as high a degree, the most popular poet in Great Britain.—JENKINS, O. L., 1876, *The Student's Handbook of British and American Literature*, p. 487.

Or give me him who called the armèd dead—
The Skeleton—from out his narrow bed
By Newport Tower; with him the blasts I'll brave,
And tell mad stories of the Norland wave
In the King's hall, and there, to test my truth,
Hold up in Alfred's face the Walrus Tooth!
I'll seek, with Hiawatha, the bright West,
The infinite Green Prairies of the Blest,
I'll wander by Atlantic's coast, and see
The lovely meadows of sweet Acadie;
In the warm forge with Gabriel blithely sing,
The bellows blow, and make the anvil ring,
See fair Evangeline in coif and tassel,
And smoke a pipe with Benedict and Basil!
—JOYCE, ROBERT DWYER, 1877, *Reflections, Scribner's Magazine*, vol. 14, p. 448.

Longfellow's was a sweet and characteristic note, but, except in a heightened enjoyment of the antique—a ruined Rhine Castle, a goblet from which dead knights had drunk, a suit of armour, or anything frankly mediæval—except in this, Longfellow is one of ourselves—an European. "Evangeline" is an European Idyl of American Life, Hermann and Dorothea having emigrated to Acadie. "Hiawatha" might have been dreamed in Kensington by a London man of letters who possessed a graceful idealizing turn of imagination, and who had studied with clear-minded and gracious sympathy the better side of Indian character and manners. Longfellow could amiably quiz, from a point of view of superior and contented refinement, his countrymen who went about blatant and blustering for a national art and literature which should correspond with the large proportion and freedom of the republic.— DOWDEN, EDWARD, 1877-78, *The Transcendental Movement and Literature, Studies in Literature*, p. 469.

He is in a high sense a literary man; and next, a literary artist; and thirdly, a literary artist in the domain of poetry. It would not be true to say that his art is of the intensest kind or most magical potency; but it is art, and imbues whatever he performs. In so far as a literary artist in poetry is a poet, Longfellow is a poet, and should (to the silencing of all debates and demurs) be freely confessed and handsomely installed as such. How far he is a poet in a further sense than this remains to be determined.— ROSSETTI, WILLIAM MICHAEL, 1878, *Lives of Famous Poets*, p. 388.

I do not see that the poetry of Mr. Longfellow has changed much in the last twenty years, except that it has become graver in its tone and more serious in its purpose. Its technical excellence has steadily increased. He has more than held his own against all English-writing poets, and in no walk of poetry so positively as that of telling a story. In an age of story-tellers he stands at their head, not only in the narrative poems I have mentioned, but in the lesser stories included in his "Tales of a Wayside Inn" for which he has laid all the literatures of the world under contribution. — STODDARD, RICHARD HENRY, 1878, *Henry Wadsworth Longfellow, Scribner's Monthly*, vol. 17, p. 18.

Of all living poets (Tennyson not excepted), Longfellow the American has made for himself the widest social popularity As Dr. Whewell, the famous master of Trinity College, Cambridge, once said in my hearing, "The sweet and homely melodies of Longfellow have touched a thousand hearts that have been unmoved by the deeper and sometimes abstruse harmonies of Tennyson." But it is Longfellow's fresh, genuine, and tender insight into the religious thoughts and feelings of ordinary human beings, which has made him the minister of hope and stay of faith in this artificial and doubt-tossed age.—HAWEIS, HUGH REGINALD, 1880, *Poets in the Pulpit*, p. 6.

Unlike some poets of the most recent school in verse, Longfellow rarely tries to convey an idea which is not clear and intelligible to his own mind. He is as honest as Shakspeare, Milton, or Burns in this respect. . . . It is in his shorter lyrical pieces, his ballads, and his fine descriptive touches that Longfellow's powers are brought out to most advantage; for it is in these that he oftenest combines the neatness and skill of the consummate artist with the curious felicity and perfect simplicity of the genuine poet.—SARGENT, EPES, 1880–81, *Harper's Cyclopædia of British and American Poetry*, pp. 628, 629.

He has never received all the praise due to him, but he has thus escaped invidious remark. He had crept up to our hearts before we had learned to think that he was mastering our judgment. In this way he has escaped all hardships of criticism, and he certainly will not receive a heavy measure of it from me.—TROLLOPE, ANTHONY, 1881, *Henry Wadsworth Longfellow, North American Review*, vol. 132, p. 383.

There cannot, I imagine, be any doubt that Professor Longfellow is in England the most widely read of living poets. Messrs. Routledge and Sons, who are his authorized publishers in this country, have on sale at the present moment eight different editions of his works, varying in price from one shilling to one guinea; while at least a dozen other houses—profiting by the absence of an international copyright law—publish unauthorized editions adapted in the like manner to the tastes and purses of all classes. Thus it is that our English versions, answering to the demand created by an unbounded popularity, are as the leaves on the trees, or the pebbles on the shore. Thus it is that at every bookseller's shop in town or country, "Longfellow's Poems" are a staple of trade. As a prize-book for schools, as a gift-book, as a drawing-room table book, as a pocket-volume for the woods and fields, our familiar and beloved friend of something like forty years meets us at every turn. Of new copies alone, it is calculated that not less than 30,000 are annually sold in the United Kingdom; and who shall estimate the average sale of copies in the second-hand market? That it should repay its English publishers, in the face of unlimited competition, to purchase a few weeks' precedence of the high rate paid by Messrs. Routledge for Professor Longfellow's early sheets, is evidence enough of the eagerness with which we welcome every line that falls from his pen. For advance proofs of the "New England Tragedies"—perhaps the poet's least successful volume—those eminent publishers gave no less a sum than one thousand pounds sterling.—EDWARDS, AMELIA B., 1881, *Longfellow's Place in England, Literary World*, vol. 12, p. 82.

Mr. Longfellow's humanity is so broad, his sympathies are so just and true, the spirit of his poetry is so penetrating and catholic, that it would be singular indeed if he failed to exert an influence on the Canadian people as intense and real as in his own country. The esteem in which his writings are everywhere held throughout the dominion is naturally enough very high and cordial. . . . For a variety of reasons Longfellow's verse has always maintained a strong hold on the Canadian public, and to-day his writings have a larger circulation in Canada than those of any four living poets combined, and the list may comprehend Tennyson and Robert Browning. . . . But while Longfellow's writings influence much of the thought which finds an outcome in the poetic efforts of what may be locally called Canadian literature, it must be conceded that his power more keenly asserts itself in the every-day lives of the people themselves, the readers of good books and the lovers of true poetry.—STEWART, GEORGE, JR., 1881, *Longfellow in Canada, Literary World*, vol. 12, p. 83.

It was a beautiful life. It was felicitous beyond ordinary lot, and yet not so far beyond. The birds sang in its branches. The pleasant streams ran through it. The sun shone and the April showers fell softly down upon it. The winds hushed it to sleep. And, while now he falls asleep, let us read his verse anew; and through the lines let us read him, and draw into our lives something of these serenities and upliftings. So for ourselves and one another, remembering this Sunday afternoon, remembering the poet's life, living hereafter with the poet's hymns in our ears, may we, like him, leave behind us footprints in the sands of time; may our sadness resemble sorrow only as the mist resembles the rain; may we know how sublime a thing it is to suffer and be strong; may we wake the better soul that slumbered to a holy, calm delight; may we never mistake heaven's distant lamps for sad funereal tapers; and may we ever hear the voice from the sky like a falling star,—Excelsior!—LONG, JOHN DAVIS, 1882, *Remarks at a Longfellow Memorial Service, Unitarian Church, East Boston, April 2.*

No puissant singer he, whose silence grieves
  To-day the great West's tender heart and strong;
No singer vast of voice: yet one who leaves
  His native air the sweeter for his song.
—WATSON, WILLIAM, 1882, *On Longfellow's Death, Poems,* p. 93.

You remember that Bryant first won fame by a hymn to death; and so, I think, the first fame of Longfellow which won recognition for him was that translation of those sounding Spanish lines which exalt the majesty of death and sing the shortness of human life. But the first song of his own which won the recognition of the world was not a song of death, it was a "psalm of life." That little volume, the "Voices of the Night," formed an epoch in our literary history. It breathed his whole spirit,—his energy, his courage, his tenderness, his faith; it formed the prelude of all which should come after; and henceforth we find his whole life imaged in his verse. I do not mean that he tore open the secrets of the heart or the home; but all is there,—transfigured, enlarged, made universal, made the common property of all. We wander with him through foreign lands; he takes us with him into his studies, and in his translations he gives us their fairest fruits. We hear with him the greetings of the new-born child; we are taken into the sacred joy of home; the merry notes of the children's hour ring upon our ears; we feel the pains of sorrow and of loss; we hear the prayer of elevated trust. And when age draws near at last, when the shadows begin to fall, then we share with him the solemnity and sublimity of the gathering darkness. — EVERETT, CHARLES CARROLL, 1882, *Funeral Service, Mar. 26; Henry Wadsworth Longfellow, ed. Longfellow, vol.* III, *p.* 329.

Was it a small thing that the dead poet should have diffused so widely the influence of his genius, helping to shape character in other lands, to ennoble the heart, to inspire just sentiments of life, and encourage the inexperienced or the afflicted with songs of hope and cheer? With the ever-increasing advance of foreign influences and education in the East it may be safely predicted that the poems of Longfellow are destined to be more widely read and appreciated there for many years to come.—BENJAMIN, S. G. W., 1882, *Letter to Mr. Stoddard, April* 10; *Henry Wadsworth Longfellow, A Medley in Prose and Verse, ed. Stoddard, p. 229.*

He took the saddest of our New England tragedies, and the sweetest of its rural home scenes, the wayside inn, the alarum of war, the Indian legend, and the hanging of the crane in the modest household, and his genius has invested them with enduring charms and morals. Wise and gentle was the heart which could thus find melodies for the harp, lyre, and the plectrum in our fields and wildernesses, wreathing them as nature does the thickets and stumps of the forest with flowers and mosses. While all his utterances came from a pure, a tender and a devout heart, addressing themselves to what is of like in other hearts, there is not in them a line of morbidness, of depression or melancholy, but only that which quickens and cheers with robust resolve and courage, with peace and aspiring trust. He has, indeed, used freely the poet's license in playful freedom with dates and facts. But the scenes and incidents and personages which most need a softening and refining touch, receive it from him without prejudice to the service of sober history.—ELLIS, GEORGE E., 1882, *Tributes to Longfellow and Emerson by the Massachusetts Historical Society, p. 12.*

Until the silence fell upon us we did not entirely appreciate how largely his voice was repeated in the echoes of our own heart. The affluence of his production so accustomed us to look for a poem from him at short intervals that we could hardly feel how precious that was which was so abundant. Not, of course, that every single poem reached the standard of the highest among them all. That could not be in Homer's time, and mortals must occasionally nod now as then. But the hand of the artist shows itself unmistakably in everything which left his desk. The O of Giotto could not help being a perfect round, and the verse of Longfellow is always perfect in construction. He worked in that simple and natural way which characterizes the master.—HOLMES, OLIVER WENDELL, 1882, *Tributes to Longfellow and Emerson by the Massachusetts Historical Society*, p. 14.

The office of the poet is, indeed, a holy one. Sometimes he is both poet and prophet in one. Such a one Longfellow was not. But always he is both poet and priest in one: priest at the sacred shrine of the feelings. . . . He was a white-robed priest —a priest clad in purity. Whatever his clean eyes saw became clean under his gaze; whatever his fine hands seized, became fine under his touch.—ADLER, FELIX, 1882, *Addresses before the Society for Ethical Culture, April 2; Henry Wadsworth Longfellow, A Medley in Prose and Verse*, ed. Stoddard, p. 216.

Longfellow, in the foreign estimation, holds the highest place among all the names of our literature. He was one of the first to catch the attention of English critics, and they have clung to him as to a sheet anchor in the overwhelming rush of American writers since. They are fond of calling him "America's greatest Literary Son," because such an attribution would restrict our literature to a certain level of excellence which without doubt has been far exceeded by others of our authors. This has occasioned a perceptible reaction among home critics, and perhaps caused them to depreciate the real merit of Longfellow. It would be agreed that he is not a poet of the first, or even of the second, order. He can not rank with Emerson, or with Tennyson or Browning. Not the exalted treasure of celestial thought, not the dramatic power of intense passions, not the mystic subtlety of refined ideals, is his. But the chords of daily human experience, the level beauty of common life, the sense of content and grief, the imaginative picturing of legend and allegory—these he knew well. He was never false in a word or form of words. His lyre sang true every note, whether in major or minor keys. All humanity responds to its music, and that music is exquisite. There is a great variety in his work, yet he has not written anything without the charm that indicates poetry. He has never been a sloven in his verse; while at the same time he has never wandered in search of mechanical elaboration, as the fashion has been since Swinburne scared the whole guild of English writers by his exhaustive gymnastics with the entire resources of the language. Without any fantastic devices of rhythm and metre, he never failed in fitting his form to his thought, and is justly to be called a master in the mechanism of poesy.—WHITING, CHARLES G., 1882, *The Poet Longfellow Dead; Henry Wadsworth Longfellow, A Medley in Prose and Verse*, ed. Stoddard, p. 187.

His heart was pure, his purpose high,
  His thoughts serene, his patience vast;
He put all strifes of passion by,
  And lived to God, from first to last.
His song was like the pine-tree's sigh,
  At midnight o'er a poet's grave,
Or like the sea-bird's distant cry,
  Borne far across the twilight wave.
There is no flower of meek delight,
  There is no star of heavenly pride,
That shines not fairer and more bright
  Because he lived, loved, sang, and died.
—WINTER, WILLIAM, 1882, *Longfellow, Wanderers*, p. 112.

And the musical soul of his burden
  Was the Voice of the Night in his ear
That banished the truculent babel
  With the whispering word, "Be of cheer."
And stalwart and stately and hearty,
  As his patriarch farmer of Pré
Was the singer of seventy winters
  Who chanted the jubilant lay.
—CAINE, HALL, 1882, *In Memoriam, The Athenæum*, No. 2840, p. 411.

Child of New England, and trained by her best influences; of a temperament singularly sweet and serene, and with the sturdy rectitude of his race; refined and softened by wide contact with other lands and many men; born in prosperity, accomplished in all literatures, and himself a literary artist of consummate elegance, he was the fine flower of the Puritan stock under its changed modern conditions. Out of strength had come forth sweetness. The grim iconoclast, "humming a surly hymn," had issued in the Christian gentleman. Captain Miles Standish had risen into Sir Philip Sidney. The austere morality that relentlessly ruled the elder New England reappeared in the genius of this singer in the most gracious and captivating form. . . . Longfellow's genius was not a great creative force. It burst into no tempest of mighty passion. It did not wrestle with the haughtily veiled problems of fate and free-will absolute. It had no dramatic movement and variety, no eccentricity and grotesqueness and unexpectedness. It was not Lear, nor Faust, nor Manfred, nor Romeo. A carnation is not a passion-flower. Indeed, no poet of so universal and sincere popularity ever sang so little of love as a passion. . . . His poems are apples of gold in pictures of silver. . . . The literary decoration of his style, the aroma and color and richness, so to speak, which it derives from his ample accomplishment in literature, are incomparable.—CURTIS, GEORGE WILLIAM, 1882-94, *Longfellow, Literary and Social Essays,* pp. 195, 197, 200, 201.

His works are not only free from the special defects, but devoid of the peculiar merits, that mark the more strictly national literature of his country. His fancy recrosses the Atlantic for the inspiration which many derive from the past. Now and then he gives us glimpses of the hoar frost silvering his native pines, or, heaping the logs on the hearth, sits down to tell us a New England tale; but the majority of his minor poems are drawn from the same experiences and memories as his "Hyperion" and "Outre-Mer." Like Irving in the variety of his culture, superior in genius, his imagination is rather Teutonic than English. Cut Germany out of his volume, and you cut out nearly half. He lingers in feudal towers or Flemish towns, and chooses for his emblem of life's river, not the Ohio, or the Hudson, or the Assabeth, but "the Moldau's rushing stream." He has given us the best existing translations from Swedish, Danish, and Spanish, and among the best from Italian. . . . He cannot create, but he cannot touch without adorning. There is nothing in his works of the world-revealing insight of the deepest penetrative imagination; but from nature, man and books he constantly throws new illuminations on homely truths. . . . His favourite virtues are endurance, calm; his confidence, gentle hearts; his pet themes the praise and love of children. . . . Longfellow is limited in his range, because he is dowered with neither hate nor scorn.—NICHOL, JOHN, 1882-85, *American Literature,* pp. 195, 196, 197, 198.

Longfellow, like all poets who had not any great originality of initiative, was singularly dependent on his subjects for his success; but when his subject suits him, he presents it with the simplicity of a really great classic, with all its points in relief, and with nothing of the self-conscious or artificial tone of one who wants to draw attention to the admirable insight with which he has grasped the situation. He can be very conventional, when the subject is conventional. When it is not, but is intrinsically poetical, no one gives us its poetry more free from the impertinences of subjective ecstasy than he. He was not a great poet, but he was a singularly restful, singularly simple-minded, and—whenever his subject suited him as in one very considerable and remarkable instance it certainly did—a singularly classical poet, who knew how to prune away every excrescence of irrelevant emotion.—HUTTON, RICHARD HOLT, 1882-94, *Criticisms on Contemporary Thought and Thinkers, vol.* II *p.* 86.

Longfellow is wonderful in these homely felicities. Reproach him as you please for excessive harmoniousness,—a swan overladen with song,—there is a spiritual sweetness that penetrates like the odor of aloewood, a richness as of ambergris, a reverence for things holy and absent that is not so much unction as awe. With all his comprehensive learning, he is as plain and pure as an ascetic; the dust of libraries has become an illumined dust, which flickers in his sunny fantasy, and moulds itself into all imaginable gracious forms. He exhales his poems as a flower does its perfume; he never writes good poetry and then spoils it by keeping it by him till old age, as Devenant said of Lord Brooke. The beauty of his youth is with us no less than the wisdom and pathos of his age,—a circle in which the two edges of the golden ring are but a span apart.—HARRISON, JAMES ALBERT, 1882, *Henry W. Longfellow, ed. Kennedy, p.* 273.

Thou wast not robbed of wonder when youth fled,
But still the bud had promise to thine eyes,
And beauty was not sundered from surprise,
And reverent, as reverend, was thy head.
Thy life was music, and thou mad'st it ours.

—CONE, HELEN GRAY, 1882, *Henry Wadsworth Longfellow, Century, vol.* 24. *p.* 176.

In the catalogue of Ditson & Co., lists of other authors' poems that have been set to music are given. Longfellow heads the list with thirty-nine poems, next comes

Tennyson with twenty-six, Byron has sixteen, Goethe eight, Holmes six, Whittier four, and Wordsworth one.—KENNEDY, W. SLOANE, 1882, *Henry W. Longfellow, Biography, Anecdote, Letters, Criticism, p* 187.

The poems of Longfellow were in all households that made the smallest pretense to literary cultivation. Young people read them. Lovers took them into the woods. Old people had the volume in their hands as they sat musing by the firelight. The bereaved repeated them over and over, and thought more tenderly of their dead. The lonely, dissappointed, tired, desponding knew them by heart. The longing, aspiring, struggling, repeated them with fervor. In hours of leisure, weariness, weakness, thoughtful men and women were soothed and uplifted by the melodious verse. It was poetry of the heart in its peaceful, not in its martial, moods, and it met those moods not lackadaisically, but hopefully, cheerily, bravely. It was customary then to say that his poetry was sentimental. So it was, but the sentiment was healthy, sweet, and true, such as the best, even the most high-souled and intellectual, know at times, or ought to know; such as the large majority of men and women rest in at their highest moments, the choice moments of their lives. — FROTHINGHAM, OCTAVIUS BROOKS, 1882, *Henry Wadsworth Longfellow, Atlantic Monthly, vol.* 49, *p.* 820.

"Not to be tuneless in old age!"
Ah! surely blest his pilgrimage,
 Who, in his winter's snow,
Still sings with note as sweet and clear
 As in the morning of the year
When the first violets blow!
Blest!—but more blest, whom summer's heat
Whom spring's impulsive stir and beat,
 Have taught no feverish lure;
Whose muse, benignant and serene,
Still keeps her autumn chaplet green
 Because his verse is pure!
Lie calm, O white and laureate head!
Lie calm, O Dead, that art not dead
 Since from the voiceless grave,
Thy voice shall speak to old and young
While song yet speaks an English tongue
 By Charles' or Thames' wave!

—DOBSON, AUSTIN, 1882, *In Memoriam, The Athenæum, No.* 2840, *p.* 411.

Nature did not come to him as to a Pythia seated on a tripod, and fill him with passion expressible only in rhythmic prophecy; she did not even call him as a private secretary, and dictate to him her secret messages of love and tenderness, justice and watchfulness, freedom and immortality. He went to Nature, sometimes as the angel of the Annunciation, revealing to her that she was pregnant with divinity, sometimes as a priest pronouncing a benediction over her. . . . The subjects of Longfellow's poetry are, for the most part, aspects of nature as influencing human feeling,—either directly or through historical association,—the tender or pathetic sides and incidents of life, or heroic deeds preserved in legend or history. He had a special fondness for records of human devotion and self-sacrifice, whether they were monkish legends, Indian tales, Norse *drapas*, or bits of American history.— DAVIDSON, THOMAS, 1882, *Henry Wadsworth Longfellow, pp.* 12, 14.

Longfellow in his voluminous works seems to me not only to be eminent in the style and forms of poetical expression that mark the present age (an idiocrasy, almost a sickness, of verbal melody), but to bring what is always dearest as poetry to the general human heart and taste, and probably must be so in the nature of things. He is certainly the kind of bard and counteractant most needed for our materialistic, self-assertive, money-worshipping, Anglo-Saxon races, and especially for the present age in America—an age tyrannically regulated with reference to the manufacturer, the merchant, the financier, the politician and the day workman—for whom and among whom he comes as the poet of melody, courtesy, deference—poet of the mellow twilight of the past in Italy, Germany, Spain, and in Northern Europe—poet of all sympathetic gentleness—and universal poet of women and young people. I should have to think long if I were asked to name the man who has done more, and in more valuable directions, for America. I doubt if there ever was before such a fine intuitive judge and selecter of poems. His translans of many German and Scandinavian pieces are said to be better than the vernaculars. He does not urge or lash. His influence is like good drink or air. He is not tepid either, but always vital, with flavor, motion, grace. He strikes a splendid average, and does not sing exceptional passions, or humanity's jagged escapades. He is not revolutionary, brings nothing offensive or new, does not deal hard blows. On the contrary his songs soothe and heal, or if they excite, it is a healthy and agreeable excitement. His very anger is gentle, is at second hand, (as in "the Quadroon Girl" and "the Witnesses").—WHITMAN, WALT, 1882, *Death of Longfellow, The Critic*, vol. 2, p. 101.

In any estimate of his genius Longfellow deserves attention first for his prose, and all the more because it is probable that of five hundred persons who are fairly familiar with all his poetry, there is not more than one that has read his prose works. . . . Longfellow's prose has four distinct characteristics: clearness and originality of style, remarkable erudition, humour, and an unbounded fertility of imagination. It is sufficient to mention the first two of these, but the second two have been generally overlooked, and they throw so much light upon Longfellow's temperament and therefore upon his poetry, that they call for special notice. He has never received due credit for his humour, which has been pronounced indifferent by the critics, who were probably among the majority who have not read the poet's prose. . . . Longfellow's poetry is very varied in character, he has tried his wine in every kind of vessel, and, as has been said, it is very unequal in quality. . . . With all deference to the great popularity of many of his poems, and after due consideration of the subtleties of American eulogy, it seems clear enough that much of Longfellow's poetry has little or no permanent value. An occasional nod may be forgiven even to Homer, but Longfellow nods too often.—NORMAN, HENRY, 1883, *A Study of Longfellow, Fortnightly Review*, vol. 39, *pp.* 103, 105.

I give him very high rank among the poets of the century, placing him, perhaps, next to Wordsworth; while of the modern poets—those of today—assuredly he is as a Triton among the Minnows.—HALL, SAMUEL CARTER, 1883, *Retrospect of a Long Life*, *p.* 419.

> He who, beside the Charles,
> Untouched of envy or hate,
> Tranced the world with his song.

—ALDRICH, THOMAS BAILEY, 1884, *Monody on the Death of Wendell Phillips*, p. 85.

To sum up Poe's strictures as urged here and in earlier and later writings, Longfellow was a plagiarist, a didactic poet, and a writer of hexameters. In this there is so much truth as is involved in the milder statement that he belonged to the poets of cultivation rather than of irresistible original genius, that he frequently wrote to illustrate or enforce morality, and that his ear was too little refined to be offended by the spondaic flatness of an English hexameter. That Poe was sincere in his opinions, though he enforced them rudely and with the malicious pleasure of an envious rival, there can be little question; that Longfellow never pilfered from Poe, and that in the unconscious adaptations natural to a poet of culture he never imitated him, there can be no doubt at all.—WOODBERRY, GEORGE E., 1885, *Edgar Allan Poe (American Men of Letters)*, p. 231.

In the few words of sympathetic criticism to which Mr. Lowell gave utterance at the Gray Memorial ceremony at Cambridge, he remarked, though in no disparaging way, on the extent to which the element of the "commonplace" in Gray's most famous poem had contributed to its world-wide popularity. It is to the lack of this quality in Mr. Lowell's own verse that it owes, one may suspect, its comparatively narrow circle of admirers. The American poet whom all Englishmen know, and than whom few Englishmen know other, was assuredly master of this, not "golden," but plain, serviceable locksmith's-metal key to the popular heart. It need not be said,—it would, indeed, be foolish to say it—in a sneering spirit, but the element of commonplace in Longfellow, the precepitate of salts insoluble in poetry which one finds at the bottom of that pellucid verse, is extraordinarily large; and the average reader who prizes his poetry, for the solid residuum it leaves behind it, after its purely poetic qualities have disappeared through the not very fine-meshed strainer of his imagination, appraises his Longfellow accordingly. TRAILL, HENRY DUFF, 1885, *Mr. J. R. Lowell, Fortnightly Review*, vol. 44, *p.* 83.

In the history of English Literature Longfellow must stand as an American, for the reason that he is a personality. Imitation is one thing, absorbing and giving out, is another, though the ideas absorbed are reproduced in the product. Longfellow was essentially a man of culture, and literary culture in his day,—much more than it does in ours,—meant trans-Atlantic culture; but Longfellow always had a manner, not a very forcible nor pronounced manner, perhaps, in his early days, but still always a graceful, felicitous manner of his own,—part of the constitution of his mind. No one can travel in England without receiving many impressions which become part of his mental resources. Many consciously endeavor to reproduce peculiarities of logical movement, or of diction, or even of bearing which have struck them as admirable in our trans-Atlantic cousins, but the imitation is the result of effort, and will betray itself.—JOHNSON, CHARLES F., 1885, *Three Americans and Three Englishmen*, p. 215.

The best-selling American poets in this country are in the order named—Longfellow, Whittier, Bryant, and Poe; while their rank would be slightly reversed by the general judgment of the present time to the following order: Bryant, Whittier, Longfellow, and Poe.—WILSON, JAMES GRANT, 1886, *Bryant and His Friends*, p. 344.

Longfellow was content to be humanity's city missionary, so long as the common people heard him gladly. Although he was not of heroic mould, he was at least twenty times a nobler man than Poe, with a fund of miscellaneous culture, and a knowledge of human nature that in the long run more than compensated for any inferiority his imagination presented in comparison with Poe's brightest inspirations. He had not the keenness of Poe's artistic sensibility, yet it can at least be said of him that he would have scorned the execrable, if rare, faults that so disfigure Poe's writings in verse. The same width of learning in matters of general culture . . . gave Longfellow an appeal to far larger audiences than those that Whittier can attract; and by his gracious choice of subjects, and his treatment of these in almost every form of verse dear to the people, Longfellow has of course laid himself out—and successfully—to win a hearing where Whitman, with all his boasted feeling for democracy, is looked upon as an intellectual Coriolanus, contemptuous and uncouth. — ROBERTSON, ERIC S., 1887, *Life of Henry Wadsworth Longfellow (Great Writers)*, p. 175.

He was a consummate translator, because the vision and faculty divine which he possessed was directed toward the reflection of the facts of nature and society, rather than toward the facts themselves. He was like one who sees a landscape in a Claude Lorraine glass; by some subtle power of the mirror everything has been composed for him. Thus, when he came to use rich material of history, of poetry, and of other arts, Longfellow saw these in forms already existing, and his art was not so much a reconstruction out of crude material as a representation, a rearrangement, in his own exquisite language, of what he found and admired. . . . Thus it is that the lyrical translations which he made in his student days are really his own poems; he rendered the foreign form in a perfect English form; his work in this regard was that of an engraver, not that of a photographer.—SCUDDER, HORACE E., 1887, *Longfellow's Art, Atlantic Monthly*, vol. 59, p. 403.

He is always careful and painstaking with his rhythm and with the cadence of his verse. It may be said with truth that Longfellow has taught more people to love poetry than any other English writer, however great.—MEIKLEJOHN, J. M. D., 1887, *The English Language: Its Grammar, History and Literature*, p. 355.

In a speedy development such as this, we should of course be surprised to find any literary production which is the result of tranquility. Thus, with the one illustrious exception of Longfellow, America has given us no poets who can enter the lists against even Byron or the Lake school.—UNDERHILL, GEORGE F., 1887, *Literary Epochs*, p. 198.

Equally at home with the *savants* and the children who thronged about him and never, in one instance, condescending, in any unworthy way, to compromise his high vocation as an author!—HUNT, THEODORE W., 1887, *Representative English Prose and Prose Writers*, p. 52.

Was, within his limitations, as true a poet as ever breathed. His skill in narrative was second only to that of Prior and of Lafontaine. His sonnets, the best of them, are among the most pleasing objective sonnets in the language. Although his early, and comparatively poor, work was exaggeratedly praised, his head was not turned, but, like a conscientious artist, he rose to better and better things, even at the risk of sacrificing his popularity.—GOSSE, EDMUND, 1888, *Has America Produced a Poet? The Forum*, vol. 6, p. 182.

He experimented so successfully with two measures unfamiliar in English—unrhymed hexameter and unrhymed trochaic tetrameter—that in their use he has virtually had neither rivals nor successors. Furthermore, he has been deemed, by thousands, preëminently the poet of sympathy and sentiment, the laureate of the common human heart; yet none has been able to class him with the slender sentimentalists, or to deny to him the possession of artistic powers of somewhat unusual range and of unquestionable effectiveness. Longfellow has aroused affection on the one hand and stimulated criticism on the other; the personality has hardly been forgotten in the product, and yet the work has made no claims not intrinsic. Like Whittier, Longfellow is beloved; like Emerson, he is honored for his poetic evangel; and like Poe, he is studied as an artist in words and metrical effects.—RICHARDSON, CHARLES F., 1888, *American Literature, 1807–1885, vol.* II, p. 51.

Has no superior among our modern poets. —EGAN, MAURICE FRANCIS, 1889, *Lectures on English Literature*, p. 139.

I have not read much in him for twenty years. I take him up to-day, and what a flood of memories his music brings with it! To me it is like a sad autumn wind blowing over the woods, blowing over the empty fields, bringing the scents of October, the song of a belated bird, and here and there a red leaf from the tree. There is that autumnal sense of things fair and far behind, in his poetry, or, if it is not there, his poetry stirs it in our forsaken lodges of the past. Yes, it comes to one out of one's boyhood: it breathes of a world very vaguely realised—a world of imitative sentiments and forebodings of hours to come. Perhaps Longfellow first woke me to that later sense of what poetry means, which comes with early manhood.—LANG, ANDREW, 1889, *Longfellow, Letters on Literature*, p. 44.

To Longfellow alone was it given to see that stately galley which Count Arnaldos saw; his only to hear the steersman singing that wild and wondrous song which none that hears it can resist, and none that has heard it may forget. Then did he learn the old monster's secret—the word of his charm, the core of his mystery, the human note in his music, the quality of his influence upon the heart and the mind of man; and then did he win himself a place apart among sea poets.—HENLEY, WILLIAM ERNEST, 1890, *Views and Reviews*, p. 152.

Longfellow has carefully marked out the frontiers of his domain, and within these he has moved with ease as undisputed lord. He is pre-eminently the poet of the household and the affections. . . . If any poet, not a hymnist, be found upon the cottage tables of our artisans, and in the humble homes of our peasantry, that poet is likelier to be Longfellow than any other; and there are probably thousands of persons, not habitual students of literature, though otherwise well-informed and intelligent, who scarcely know whether Longfellow was an Englishman or an American.— DAWSON, W. J., 1892, *Quest and Vision*, pp. 112, 114.

Though Longfellow is the favorite poet of young girlhood, womanhood and the home, there is no sentimentality and no melancholy in his personality. His pastorals are full of picturesque figures of speech, and are imbued with a love of nature and a genial love of man. The poet has done much to create among his countrymen a love of European literature and to instill the beginnings of what may prove a mellowing culture, while, in his "Hiawatha" and "Evangeline," he has given to the world two classics, distinctively American.—MABIE, HAMILTON W., 1892, *The Memorial Story of America*, p. 593.

The winds have talked with him confidingly;
  The trees have whispered to him; and the night
Hath held him gently as a mother might,
And taught him all sad tones of melody:
The mountains have bowed to him; and the sea
  In clamorous waves, and murmurs exquisite,
Hath told him all her sorrow and delight—
  Her legends fair—her darkest mystery.
His verse blooms like a flower, night and day,
Bees cluster round his rhymes; and twitterings
  Of lark and swallow, in an endless May,
Are mingling with the tender songs he sings.—
Nor shall he cease to sing—in every lay
Of Nature's voice he sings—and will alway.
—RILEY, JAMES WHITCOMB, 1892, *Longfellow, Green Fields and Running Brooks*, p. 215.

Longfellow was emphatically the poet of his native land. Though deeply imbued with the classic spirit, and reveling at his ease in all the treasures of English and European literature, the scenery and art of the old world, with its mighty monuments and ancient historic memories, his heart was yet in this New World—its wild scenes and its fresh life; and here he found a home for his muse, and he made that home illustrious.—SAUNDERS, FREDERICK, 1894, *Character Studies*, p. 121.

Mr. Longfellow was at the time of his death the most famous of Americans. For more than fifty years he had been sending forth his writings to a world that welcomed his slightest word. In both hemispheres his influence had been felt, giving a nobler cheer to the daily life, consecrating the home and sweetening the thoughts and the intercourse of men; and yet in all these years he said very little either about his own religion or that of other men....I have said that there is, in the writings of Longfellow, very little of formal utterance on the subject of religion. I have also said that this reticence was far from indicating an absence of religious thinking and feeling. He was a Unitarian by training and conviction, and though he had "no religion to speak of," he had a very definite and noble religion to live by.—SAVAGE, W. H., 1895, *The Religion of Longfellow, The Arena, vol. 11, pp.* 145, 147.

Longfellow is the most popular poet yet born in America; and if we can measure popular approval by the widespread sale of his successive volumes, he was probably the most popular poet of the English language in this century. Part of his popularity is due to his healthy mind, his calm spirit, his vigorous sympathy. His thought, though often deep, was never obscure. His lyrics had always a grace that took the ear with delight. They have a singing simplicity, caught, it may be, from the German lyrists, such as Uhland or Heine. This simplicity was the result of rare artistic repression; it was not due to any poverty of intellect. Like Victor Hugo in France, Longfellow in America was the poet of childhood. And as he understood the children, so he also sympathized with the poor, the toiling, the lowly—not looking down on them, but glorifying their labor, and declaring the necessity of it and the nobility of work. He could make the barest life seem radiant with beauty. He had acquired the culture of all lands, but he understood also the message of his own country. He thought that the best that Europe could bring was none too good for the plain people of America. He was a true American, not only in his stalwart patriotism in the hour of trial, but in his loving acceptance of the doctrine of human equality, and in his belief and trust in his fellow-man.—MATTHEWS, BRANDER, 1896, *An Introduction to the Study of American Literature, p.* 136.

The foreign flavor of Longfellow's poetry sweetened the American air. This Harvard professor was unconsciously a great forerunner of university extension. He was becoming the poetic schoolmaster of the land, not only winning it to the love of song, but accustoming his Puritan-bred, utilitarian audience to the richer lights in which Europe views the human spectacle.... A professor in his library, among many books in many tongues, he was, nevertheless, a poet of stories and feelings, so simple that the little children love him. It may be true that his imagination was moderate, his fancy sometimes forced and artificial, his passion decorously pent within the meek New England limits of trust and resignation. Notwithstanding his far range of subject, critics have styled him the Poet of the Commonplace. It is no mean title. To lift the commonplace into the bright air of poetry is to confer one of the richest of boons on dull humanity. As Bryant sublimed our thought of nature, so Longfellow hallowed our human life itself.—BATES, KATHARINE LEE, 1897, *American Literature, pp.* 145, 147.

Not in the dawning of his golden prime
  His finest songs across the world he flung,
But who could match the pathos of his rhyme,
  When that the eve of life around him hung?
As darkness neared, rarer each touching lay;
  Then, through his lyre, we heard his rapt soul pour:
As those charmed harps that but at night-time play
Æolian strains on Pascagoula's shore.
—MIFFLIN, LLOYD, 1898, *Longfellow, The Slopes of Helicon and Other Poems, p.* 122.

One has merely to glance at any detailed catalogue of the translations from Longfellow's works . . . to measure the vast extent of his fame. The list includes thirty-five versions of whole books or detached poems in German, twelve in Italian, nine each in French and Dutch, seven in Swedish, six in Danish, five in Polish, three in Portuguese, two each in Spanish, Russian, Hungarian, and Bohemian, with single translations in Latin, Hebrew, Chinese, Sanskrit, Marathi, and Judea-German—yielding one hundred versions altogether, extending into eighteen languages, apart from the original English. There is no evidence that any other English-speaking poet of the last century has been so widely appreciated. Especially is this relative superiority noticeable in that wonderful literary cyclopædia, the vast and many-volumed catalogue of the British Museum. There, under each author's name, is found not merely the record of his works in every successive edition, but every secondary or relative book, be it memoir, criticism, attack, parody, or translation; and it is always curious to consider the relative standing of American and English authors under this severe and inexorable test. The entries or items appearing in the interleaved catalogue under the name of Tennyson, for instance, up to September, 1901, were 487; under Longfellow 357; then follow, among English-writing poets, Browning (179), Emerson (158), Arnold (140), Holmes (135), Morris (117), Lowell (114), Whittier (104), Poe (103), Swinburne (99), Whitman (64). —HIGGINSON, THOMAS WENTWORTH, 1902, *Henry Wadsworth Longfellow (American Men of Letters)*, p. 246.

We get at times even an impression of excessive amiability and gentleness in Longfellow. We almost wish for one fiercer strain, to show him a good hater, if only of injustice or cruelty. But his art, at all events, if not his life, was unclouded in its serenity.—LAWTON, WILLIAM CRANSTON, 1902, *Introduction to the Study of American Literature*, p. 214.

He was always simple in thought and expression, always healthy, always sincere, always well bred. He uttered clearly and melodiously the old inherited wisdom, and if, as Colonel Higginson says "he will never be read for the profoundest stirring, or for the unlocking of the deepest mysteries, he will always be read for invigoration, for comfort, for content." He had quiet humor, gentle pathos, the power of telling a story and of suggesting an atmosphere, and these may well suffice to maintain for him an audience that does not demand the originality and profundity of the great old masters, or the subtlety and complexity of the little new ones.—NEILSON, WILLIAM ALLAN, 1902, *Higginson's Longfellow, Atlantic Monthly*, vol. 93, p. 851.

The art of Longfellow is something too precious among our heritages from the past not to be valued at its full worth. It was the hardly saving grace which Hawthorne owned in the American literature of his time, and it is the art of Longfellow which takes from the American poetry of his generation the aspect of something fragmentary and fugitive. Whatever else it had from others, from Emerson, from Bryant, from Whittier, from Holmes, from Lowell, it had standing and presence and recognition among the world literatures from the art of Longfellow. We had other poets easily more American than he, but he was above all others the American poet, and he was not the less American because he accepted the sole conditions on which American poetry could then embody itself. As far as he ever came to critical consciousness in the matter he acted upon the belief, which he declared, that we could not be really American without being in the best sense European; that unless we brought to our New World life the literature of the Old World, we should not know or say ourselves aright.—HOWELLS, WILLIAM DEAN, 1902, *Editor's Easy Chair, Harper's Magazine, vol.* 104, p. 834.

Charles Robert Darwin
1809–1882

Born, 12 Feb. 1809, at Shrewsbury. Educated at Mr. Case's dayschool at Shrewsbury, 1817; at Shrewsbury School, 1818–25. To Edinburgh University, 1825. Medical career given up in favor of clerical. Matriculated at Christ's Coll., Cambridge, Oct. 1827; entered upon residence, Lent term 1828; B. A., 1832; M. A., 1837. Sailed as "naturalist" on the "Beagle," 27 Dec. 1831. Return to England, 6 Oct. 1836. Idea of clerical career abandoned. To Cambridge, Dec. 1836. In London, 1837–42. F. R. S., 24 Jan. 1839; Royal medal, 1853; Copley medal, 1864. Married Emma Wedgwood, 29 Jan. 1839. Secretary to Geological Society, 1838–41. In consequence of ill-health, removed to Down, Kent, 1842. Lived there, engaged in scientific work, till his death. Occasional visits to friends; and to meetings of British Association, Southampton, 1846, Oxford, 1847; Birmingham, 1849; Glasgow, 1855. County Magistrate, 1857. Hon. LL. D., Cambridge, 1877. Died, 19 April 1882. Buried in Westminster Abbey. *Works:* "Letters to Prof. Henslow" (privately printed for Cambridge Philosophical Society), 1835; "Journal and Remarks, 1832–36" (being vol. iii. of "Narrative of the Surveying Voyages of H. M. Ships, 'Adventure' and 'Beagle'"), 1839 (2nd edn. published separately, 1845); "Zoology of the Voyage of H. M. S. "'Beagle,'" (edited by Darwin, with contributions to pts. i. and ii.), 1840–43;

"The Structure and Distribution of Coral Reefs: being the first part of the Geology of the Voyage of the 'Beagle,' 1842; (2nd edn. published separately, 1874); "Geological Observations on the Volcanic Islands visited during the Voyage of H. M. S., 'Beagle': being the second part of the Geology of the Voyage, etc.," 1844; "Geological Observations on South America: being the third part of the Geology of the Voyage of the 'Beagle,'" 1846 (2nd edn. of the two preceding published together as "Geological Observations on the Volcanic Islands and parts of South America visited, etc.," 1876; "Monograph of the Fossil Lepadidæ," 1851; "Monograph of the Subclass Cirrepedia," 1851; "Monograph of the Balanidæ," 1854; "Monograph of the Fossil Balanidæ and Verrucidæ of Great Britain," 1854; "On the Origin of Species by Means of Natural Selection," 1859; "On the Various Contrivances by which Orchids are fertilized by Insects," 1862; "The Movements and Habits of Climbing Plants," 1868; "The Variations of Animals and Plants under Domestication," 1868; "The Descent of Man," 1871; "The Expression of the Emotions in Man and Animals," 1872; "The Effect of Cross and Self Fertilization in the Vegetable Kingdom," 1876; "The Different Forms of Flowers on Plants of the same Species," 1877; "The Power of Movement in Plants," (with F. Darwin), 1880; "The Formation of Vegetable Mould, through the Action of Worms," 1881. Various papers communicated to scientific journals, 1835–82. *Posthumous:* "Essay on Instinct" (published in Romanes' "Mental Evolution in Animals"), 1883; "The Life and Letters of Charles Darwin, including an Autobiographical Chapter," ed. by F. Darwin, 1887.—SHARP, R. FARQUHARSON, 1897, *A Dictionary of English Authors, p.* 73.

PERSONAL

Darwin was as simple and jovial as a boy, at dinner, sitting up on a cushion in a high chair, very erect, to guard his weakness. Among other things, he said "his rule in governing his children was to give them lump-sugar!" He rallied us on our vigorous movements, and professed to be dazzled at the rapidity of our operations. He says he never moves, and though he can only work an hour or two every day, by always doing that, and having no break, he accomplishes what he does. He left us for half an hour after dinner for rest, and then returned to his throne in the parlor.—BRACE, CHARLES LORING, 1872, *Letters, p.* 320.

In the summer of 1818 I went to Dr. Butler's great school in Shrewsbury, and remained there for seven years till Midsummer 1825, when I was sixteen years old. . . . Nothing could have been worse for the development of my mind than Dr. Butler's school, as it was strictly classical, nothing else being taught, except a little ancient geography and history. The school as a means of education to me was simply a blank. During my whole life I have been singularly incapable of mastering any language. Especial attention was paid to verse-making, and this I could never do well. . . . When I left the school I was for my age neither high nor low in it; and I believe that I was considered by all my masters and by my father as a very ordinary boy, rather below the common standard in intellect. . . . Looking back as well as I can at my character during my school life, the only qualities which at this period promised well for the future, were, that I had strong and diversified tastes, much zeal for whatever interested me, and a keen pleasure in understanding any complex subject or thing. . . . With respect to diversified tastes, independently of science, I was fond of reading various books, and I used to sit for hours reading the historical plays of Shakespeare, generally in an old window in the thick walls of the school. I read also other poetry, such as Thomson's "Seasons," and the recently published poems of Byron and Scott. I mention this because later in life I wholly lost, to my great regret, all pleasure from poetry of any kind, including Shakespeare. . . . Early in my school days a boy had a copy of the "Wonders of the World," which I often read, and disputed with other boys about the veracity of some of the statements; and I believe that this book first gave me a wish to travel in remote countries, which was ultimately fulfilled by the voyage of the Beagle. In the latter part of my school life I became passionately fond of shooting; I do not believe that anyone could have shown more zeal for the most holy cause than I did for shooting birds.—DARWIN, CHARLES, 1876–87, *Autobiography, Life and Letters of Charles Darwin, vol.* I, pp. 28, 29, 30, 31.

The one great representative body

conspicuous by its absence was the Royal Family. In life, as Professor Huxley says, they had ignored Darwin, and they ignore him now that he is dead. Continents vie with each other in doing honour to the great man who is buried to-day. In England everything that is illustrious pays him a last tribute of reverence, royalty exempted. Sometimes a king or queen who cannot be present in person sends a lord-in-waiting, a goldstick, an aide-de-camp—some sort of functionary or other—to be respectful by proxy. Not even that cold civility was thought due to Darwin by the Queen, or by the Prince of Wales, or by any single member of the family which occupies the throne. It does not matter to Darwin. It matters a little to them—not perhaps very much, but it is one thing left undone the doing of which would have strengthened, as the omission of it weakens, in whatever degree, the attachment of Englishmen to their rulers.—SMALLEY, GEORGE W., 1882-91, *Darwin in Westminster Abbey, April 26; London Letters and Some Others*, vol. I, p. 73.

Darwin's funeral was a great gathering, though not so great as when Stanley was buried. It was the mourning of the mind in Darwin's case, in Stanley's the mourning of the heart.—MÜLLER, FRIEDRICH MAX, 1882, *To his Daughter, April 27; Life and Letters*, vol. II, p. 119.

> I loved him with a strength of love
> Which man to man can only bear
> When one in station far above
> The rest of men, yet deigns to share
> A friendship true with those far down
> The ranks: as though a mighty king,
> Girt with his armies of renown,
> Should call within his narrow ring
> Of councellors and chosen friends
> Some youth who scarce can understand
> How it began or how it ends
> That he should grasp the monarch's hand.

—ROMANES, GEORGE JOHN, 1882, *Charles Darwin.*

What we may call this fervid youthfulness of feeling extended through all Mr. Darwin's mind, giving, in combination with his immense knowledge and massive sagacity, an indescribable charm to his manner and conversation. Animated and fond of humour, his wit was of a singularly fascinating kind, not only because it was always brilliant and amusing, but still more because it was always hearty and good-natured. Indeed, he was so exquisitely refined in his own feelings, and so painfully sensitive to any display of questionable taste in others, that he could not help showing in his humour, as in the warp and woof of his whole nature, that in him the man of science and the philosopher were subordinate to the gentleman. His courteous consideration of others, also, which went far beyond anything that the ordinary usages of society require, was similarly prompted by his mere spontaneous instinct of benevolence. — ROMANES, GEORGE JOHN, 1882, *Personal Character, Charles Darwin Memorial Notices reprinted from "Nature,"* p. 3.

This self-restraint seems to me to have formed the climax to the most exalted nature it has ever been my happiness to encounter. Those who knew Charles Darwin most intimately, are unanimous in their appreciation of the unsurpassed nobility and beauty of his *whole* character. In him there was no "other side." Not only was he the Philosopher who has wrought a greater revolution in human thought within a quarter of a century than any man of our time—or perhaps of *any* time,—and has given what has proven the death-blow to Theological systems which had been clinging yet more tenaciously about men's shoulders because of the efforts made to shake them off; but as a Man he exemplified in his own life that true *religion*, which is deeper, wider, and loftier than any Theology. For this not only inspired him with the devotion to Truth which was the master-passion of his great nature; but made him the most admirable husband, brother, and father; the kindest friend, neighbour, and master; the genuine lover, not only of his fellow-man, but of every creature. Of no one could it be more appropriately said:—

"He prayeth best who loveth best
All things both great and small;"

for the whole attitude of his mind was that of humble reverence for the Great Power which "made and loveth all."—CARPENTER, WILLIAM B., 1882, *Charles Darwin; His Life and Work, Modern Review*, vol. 3, p. 523.

There is, now and then, a mind—perhaps one in four or five millions—which in early youth thinks the thoughts of mature manhood, and which in old age retains the flexibility, the receptiveness, the keen appetite for new impressions, that are characteristic of the first season of youth. Such a mind as this was Mr. Darwin's. To the last he was eager for new facts and suggestions, to the last he held his judgments in readiness for revision; and to this unfailing freshness of spirit was joined a sagacity which, naturally great, had been refined and strengthened by half a century most fruitful in experiences, till it had come to be almost superhuman. . . . When the extent of his work is properly estimated, it is not too much to say that among the great leaders of human thought that have ever lived there are not half a dozen who have achieved so much as he. In an age that has been richer than any preceding age in great scientific names, his name is indisputably the foremost. He has already found his place in the history of science by the side of Aristotle, Descartes, and Newton. And among thinkers of the first order of originality, he has been peculiarly fortunate in having lived to see all the fresh and powerful minds of a new generation adopting his fundamental conceptions, and pursuing their enquiries along the path which he was the first to break.—FISKE, JOHN, 1882, *Charles Darwin, Atlantic Monthly, vol. 45, p. 835.*

One could not converse with Darwin without being reminded of Socrates. There was the same desire to find some one wiser than himself; the same belief in the sovereignty of reason; the same ready humour; the same sympathetic interests in all the ways and works of men. But instead of turning away from the problems of Nature as hopelessly insoluble, our modern philosopher devoted his whole life to attacking them in the spirit of Heraclitus and of Democritus, with results which are as the substance of which their speculations were anticipatory shadows. . . . None have fought better, and none have been more fortunate, than Charles Darwin. He found a great truth trodden under foot, reviled by bigots, and ridiculed by all the world; he lived long enough to see it, chiefly by his own efforts, irrefragably established in science, inseparably incorporated with the common thoughts of men, and only hated and feared by those who would revile, but dare not. What shall a man desire more than this? Once more the image of Socrates rises unbidden, and the noble peroration of the "Apology" rings in our ears as if it were Charles Darwin's farewell: "The hour of our departure has arrived, and we go our ways—I to die and you to live. Which is the better, God only knows."—HUXLEY, THOMAS HENRY, 1882, *Charles Darwin, Darwiniana, p. 250.*

May I beg a corner for my feeble testimony to the marvellous persevering endurance in the cause of science of that great naturalist, my old and lost friend, Mr. Charles Darwin, whose remains are so very justly to be honoured with a resting-place in Westminster Abbey? Perhaps no one can better testify to his early and most trying labours than myself. We worked together for several years at the same table in the poop cabin of the *Beagle* during her celebrated voyage, he with his microscope and myself at the charts. It was often a very lively end of the little craft, and distressingly so to my old friend, who suffered greatly from sea-sickness. After perhaps an hour's work he would say to me, "Old fellow, I must take the horizontal for it," that being the best relief position from ship motion; a stretch out on one side of the table for some time would enable him to resume his labours for a while, when he had again to lie down. It was distressing to witness this early sacrifice of Mr. Darwin's health, who ever afterwards felt the ill-effects of the *Beagle's* voyage.—STOKES, ADMIRAL LORD, 1882, *Letter to the Times, April 25.*

The dwelling of the Darwin family, as I recall it, is a spacious and substantial old-fashioned house, square in form and plain in style, but pleasing in its comfortable and homelike appearance. The approach seems now to my memory to have been a long lane, as though the house stood remote from any much-travelled highway, and without near neighbors, surrounded by trees and shrubbery, and commanding a far-reaching view of green fields and gently undulating country. A portion of the house, the front, has, I believe, been built long enough to be spoken of as old even in England, to which in the rear some modern additions have been made. Entering a broad hall at the front, we passed, on the right, the door of the room the interior of which has since been made known in pictures as "Mr. Darwin's Study;" and a little further on were welcomed immediately by Mr. and Mrs. Darwin to a spacious and cheerful parlor or family room, whose broad windows and outer door opened upon a wide and partly sheltered piazza at the rear of the house, evidently a favorite sitting-place, judging from the comfortable look of easy-chairs assembled there, beyond which was a pleasing vista of fresh green lawn, bright flower beds, and blossoming shrubbery, gravel-paths, and a glass greenhouse, or perhaps botanical laboratory, and, further yet, a garden wall, with a gate leading to pleasant walks in fields beyond. . . . The interior of the room wore a delightfully comfortable every-day look, with books and pictures in profusion, and a large table in the middle covered with papers, periodicals, and literary miscellany.—HAGUE, JAMES D., 1884, *A Reminiscence of Mr. Darwin, Harper's Magazine, vol.* 69, *pp.* 760, 761.

His days, as far as the state of his health would permit, were carefully parcelled out between work and recreation, to make the best of his time. Retiring to bed at ten, he was an early riser, and often in his library at eight, after breakfast and his first morning walk. Later in the day he generally walked again, often in his own grounds, but sometimes further afield, and then generally by quiet foot paths rather than frequented roads. The walks at one time were varied by rides along the lanes on a favourite black cob; but, some years before Mr. Darwin's death, his four-footed friend fell, and died by the roadside, and from that day the habit of riding was given up. Part of his evening was devoted to his family and his friends, who delighted to gather round him, to enjoy the charm of his bright intelligence and his unrivalled stores of knowledge. To Down, occasionally, came distinguished men from many lands; and there in later years would sometimes be found the younger generation of scientific students, looking up to the great Naturalist with the reverence of disciples, who had experienced his singular modesty, his patient readiness to listen to all opinions, and the winning grace with which he informed their ignorance and corrected their mistakes. — WOODALL, EDWARD, 1884, *Charles Darwin, p.* 38.

Of Darwin's pure and exalted moral nature no Englishman of the present generation can trust himself to speak with becoming moderation. His love of truth, his singleness of heart, his sincerity, his earnestness, his modesty, his candor, his absolute sinking of self and selfishness—these, indeed, are all conspicuous to every reader, on the very face of every word he ever printed. Like his works themselves, they must long outlive him. But his sympathetic kindliness, his ready generosity, the staunchness of his friendship, the width and depth and breadth of his affections, the manner in which "he bore with those who blamed him unjustly without blaming them in return," these things can never so well be known to any other generation of men as to the three generations who walked the world with him. Many even of those who did not know him loved him like a father; to many who never saw his face, the hope of winning Charles Darwin's approbation and regard was the highest incentive to thought and action. Towards younger men, especially, his unremitting kindness was always most noteworthy; he spoke and wrote to them, not like one of the masters in Israel, but like a fellow-worker and seeker after truth, interested in their interests, pleased at their successes, sympathetic with their failures, gentle to their mistakes. . . . He had the sympathetic receptivity of all truly great minds, and when he died, thousands upon thousands who had never beheld his serene features and his fatherly eyes felt that they had lost indeed a personal friend. Greatness is not always joined with gentleness; in Charles Darwin's case, by universal consent of all who knew him, "an intellect which had no superior" was wedded to "a character even nobler than the intellect."—ALLEN, GRANT, 1885, *Charles Darwin (English Worthies), pp.* 174, 175.

The family gave up their first-formed plans, and the funeral took place in Westminster Abbey on April 26th. The pallbearers were:—

Sir JOHN LUBBOCK,
Mr. HUXLEY,
Mr. JAMES RUSSELL LOWELL,
(American Minister),
Mr. A. R. WALLACE,
The DUKE OF DEVONSHIRE,
CANON FARRAR,
Sir J. D. HOOKER,
Mr. WM. SPOTTISWOODE,
(President of the Royal Society),
The EARL OF DERBY,
The DUKE OF ARGYLL.

The funeral was attended by the representatives of France, Germany, Italy,

Spain, Russia, and by those of the Universities, and learned Societies, as well as by large numbers of personal friends and distinguished men. The grave is in the North aisle of the Nave, close to the angle of the choir-screen, and a few feet above the grave of Sir Isaac Newton. The stone bears the inscription—

CHARLES ROBERT DARWIN,
BORN 12 FEBRUARY, 1809.
DIED 19 APRIL, 1882.

—DARWIN, FRANCIS, 1887, *Life and Letters of Charles Darwin, Appendix vol.* II, *p.* 532.

Of his personal appearance (in these days of multiplied photographs) it is hardly necessary to say much. He was about six feet in height, but scarcely looked so tall, as he stooped a good deal; in later days he yielded to the stoop; but I can remember seeing him long ago swinging his arms back to open out his chest, and holding himself upright with a jerk. He gave one the idea that he had been active rather than strong; his shoulders were not broad for his height, though certainly not narrow. . . . He walked with a swinging action, using a stick heavily shod with iron, which he struck loudly against the ground, producing as he went round the "Sand Walk" at Down, a rhythmical click which is with all of us a very distinct remembrance. . . . When interested in his work he moved about quickly and easily enough, and often in the middle of dictating he went eagerly into the hall to get a pinch of snuff, leaving the study door open, and calling out the last words of his sentence as he went. . . . In spite of his strength and activity, I think he must always have had a clumsiness of movement. He was naturally awkward with his hands, and was unable to draw at all well. This he always regretted much, and he frequently urged the paramount necessity of a young naturalist making himself a good draughtsman. He could dissect well under the simple microscope, but I think it was by dint of his great patience and carefulness. . . . His beard was full and almost untrimmed, the hair being grey and white, fine rather than coarse, and wavy or frizzled. His moustache was somewhat disfigured by being cut short and square across. He became very bald, having only a fringe of dark hair behind. His face was ruddy in colour, and this perhaps made people think him less of an invalid than he was. . . . My father was wonderfully liberal and generous to all his children in the matter of money. . . . He had a great respect for pure business capacity, and often spoke with admiration of a relative who had doubled his fortune. And of himself he would often say in fun that what he really was proud of was the money he had saved. He also felt satisfaction in the money he made by his books. His anxiety to save came in a great measure from his fears that his children would not have health enough to earn their own livings, a foreboding which fairly haunted him for many years.—DARWIN, FRANCIS, 1887, *Life and Letters of Charles Darwin, vol.* I, *pp.* 87, 88, 89, 98, 99.

In spite of that refusal to accept the Hand stretched forth out of the darkness, which saddens so many of the lives of our time, he seems a very attractive and noble person. The utter absence of bigwiggedness, the simplicity and the candour, the genuine delight in taking trouble and giving help, the kindness and brightness, the unworldliness and absence of elation, seem to me very charming. — CHURCH, RICHARD WILLIAM, 1887, *To Asa Gray, Nov.* 26; *Life and Letters of Dean Church, ed. his Daughter, p.* 395.

If ever a man's ancestors transmitted to him ability to succeed in a particular field, Charles Darwin's did. If ever early surroundings calculated to call out inherited ability, Charles Darwin's were. If ever a man grew up when a ferment of thought was disturbing old convictions in the domain of knowledge for which he was adapted, Charles Darwin did. If ever a man was fitted by worldly position to undertake unbiased and long-continued investigations, Charles Darwin was such a man. And he indisputably found realms waiting for a conqueror. Yet Darwin's achievements far transcend his advantages of ancestry, surroundings, previous suggestion, position. He stands magnificently conspicuous as a genius of rare simplicity of soul, of unwearied patience of observation, of striking fertility and ingenuity of method, of unflinching devotion to and belief in the efficacy of truth. He revolutionised not merely half-a-dozen sciences, but the whole current of thinking men's mental life.—BETTANY, G. T., 1887, *Life of Charles Darwin (Great Writers), p.* 11.

There is nothing more useful to observe

in the life of Darwin than its simplicity. He was the man of science as Marlborough was the soldier, and he was only that. From boyhood he refused all other ways of life and knowledge as by instinct, and in his maturity the ill health which ends the career of ordinary men only confirmed him in his own; he was always the collector, the investigator, or the theorizer. . . . No words can be too strong to express the lovableness of Darwin's personality, or the moral beauty of his character. . . . Never was a man more alive to what is visible and tangible, or in any way matter of sensation: on the sides of his nature where an appeal could be made, never was a man more responsive; but there were parts in which he was blind and dull. Just as the boy failed to be interested in many things, the man failed too; and he disregarded what did not interest him with the same ease at sixty as at twenty. What did interest him was the immediately present, and he dealt with it admirably, both in the intellectual, and in the moral world; but what was remote was as if it were not. The spiritual element in life is not remote, but it is not matter of sensation, and Darwin lived as if there were no such thing; it belongs to the region of emotion and imagination, and those perceptions which deal with the nature of man in its contrast with the material world.—WOODBERRY, GEORGE EDWARD, 1890, *Studies in Letters and Life*, pp. 240, 253, 258.

In all his work, and in every effort of his life, Darwin underestimated his services to science. His modesty was proverbial, and even on subjects of which he was the acknowledged master, he would, with a rare and delightful sense of justice, express the opinion that some one else might have produced greater results with the matter at command. . . . . Darwin was a firm believer in a First Cause. He was in theory an agnostic, in practice an orthodox Christian of the broadest type. Honourable in the smallest things in life, thoughtful to others, doing as he would be done by, sensitive for others to an extreme that was often an injustice to himself, kind, lovable, ready to help the young, charitable, and possessed of extreme modesty,—such was the greatest naturalist of the age, a hero of heroes, a model for all men; and when we remember that for forty years of this life there was not one day without its physical suffering, we can understand the true greatness of his nature. . . . Upon introduction I was at once struck with his stature (which was much above the average, and I should say fully six feet), his ponderous brow, and long white beard—the moustache being cut on a line with the lips and slightly brown from the habit of snuff-taking. His deep-set eyes were light blue-gray. He made the impression of a powerful man reduced somewhat by sickness. The massive brow and forehead show in his later photographs, but not so conspicuously as in a life-size head of him when younger, which hung in the parlour. In the brief hours I then spent at Down the proverbial modesty and singular simplicity and sweetness of his character were apparent, while the delight he manifested in stating facts of interest was excelled only by the eagerness with which he sought them from others, whether while strolling through the greenhouse or sitting round the generously spread table. Going to him as a young entomologist with no claim on his favour, he seemed to take delight in manifesting appreciation.—HOLDER, CHARLES FREDERICK, 1891, *Charles Darwin (Leaders in Science)*, pp. 140, 147, 239.

His passion for shooting and hunting led him into a sporting, card-playing, drinking company, but science was his redemption. No pursuit gave him so much pleasure as collecting beetles, of his zeal in which the following is an example: "One day, on tearing off some old bark, I saw two rare beetles, and seized one in each hand; then I saw a third and new kind, which I could not bear to lose, so I popped the one which I held in my right hand into my mouth. Alas! it ejected some intensely acrid fluid, which burnt my tongue so that I was forced to spit the beetle out, which was lost, as was the third one."—CLODD, EDWARD, 1897, *Pioneers for Evolution from Thales to Huxley*, p. 119.

If I were asked what traits in Mr. Darwin's character appeared to me most remarkable during the many exercises of his intellect that I was privileged to bear witness to, they would be, first, his self-control and indomitable perseverance under bodily suffering, then his ready grasp of difficult problems, and, lastly, the power of turning to account the waste observations, failures, and even blunders of his predecessors in whatever subject of enquiry. It was this power of utilising the vain efforts of others which in my friend Sir James Paget's opinion afforded the best evidence of Darwin's genius. Like so many men who have been great discoverers, or whose works or writings are proofs of their having intellects indicating great originality, he was wont to attribute his success to industry rather than ability. "It is dogged that does it" was an expression he often made use of. . . . Referring to his disregard when possible of his bodily sufferings, I remember his once saying to me that his sleepless nights had their advantages, for they enabled him to forget his hours of misery when recording the movement of his beloved plants from dark to dawn and daybreak. . . . In arguing he was ever ready with repartee, as I many times experienced to my discomfiture, though never to my displeasure; it was a physic so thoughtful and kindly exhibited. . . . I was describing to him the reception at the Linnean Society, where he was unable to be present, of his now famous account of "The two forms or dimorphic condition of Primula," for which he took the common primrose as an illustration. On that occasion an enthusiastic admirer of its author got up, and in concluding his *éloge* likened British botanists who had overlooked so conspicuous and beautiful a contrivance to effect cross-fertilisation to Wordsworth's "Peter Bell," to whom

"A primrose on the river's brim
A yellow primrose was to him,
And it was nothing more."

When I told Mr. Darwin of this he roared with laughter, and, slapping his side with his hand, a rather common trick with him when excited, he said, "I would rather be the man who thought of that on the spur of the moment than have written the paper that suggested it."—HOOKER, SIR JOSEPH DALTON, 1899, *Address at the unveiling of Darwin's Statue at Oxford, June 14.*

I remember him as the most courteous, simple, and retiring of men, wholly unconscious, it would seem, of his own vast reputation, and of such painful delicacy of bodily frame and of such intense nervous sensitiveness, that he could not endure conversation even within his family circle for more than a limited time.— HARRISON, FREDERIC, 1901, *George Washington and Other American Addresses, p.* 202.

ORIGIN OF SPECIES
1859

I have just finished your volume and right glad I am that I did my best with Hooker to persuade you to publish it without waiting for a time which probably could never have arrived, though you lived to the age of a hundred, when you had prepared all your facts on which you ground so many grand generalizations. It is a splendid case of close reasoning and long-sustained arguments throughout so many pages, the condensation immense, too great, perhaps, for the uninitiated, but an effective and important preliminary statement which will admit, even before your detailed proofs appear, of some occasional useful exemplifications, such as your pigeons and cirripedes, of which you make such excellent use.—LYELL, SIR CHARLES, 1859, *Letter to Darwin, Life of Charles Lyell, vol.* II, *p.* 325.

I am a sinner not to have written you ere this, if only to thank you for your glorious book—what a mass of close reasoning on curious facts and fresh phenomena—it is capitally written, and will be very successful. I say this on the strength of two or three plunges into as many chapters, for I have not yet attempted to read it. Lyell, with whom we are staying, is perfectly enchanted, and is absolutely gloating over it. HOOKER, SIR JOSEPH DALTON, 1859, *To Darwin, Nov.* 21; *Life and Letters of Charles Darwin, ed. Darwin, vol.* II *p.* 23.

I have read your book with more pain than pleasure. Parts of it I admired greatly, parts I laughed at till my sides were almost sore; other parts I read with absolute sorrow, because I think them utterly false and grievously mischievous. You have *deserted*—after a start in that tramroad of all solid physical truth—the true method of induction, and started us in machinery as wild, I think, as Bishop Wilkins's locomotive that was to sail with us to the moon. Many of your wide conclusions are based upon assumptions which can neither be proved nor disproved, why then express them in the language and arrangement of philosophical induction?—SEDGWICK, ADAM, 1859, *To Darwin, Dec.* 24; *Life and Letters of Charles Darwin, ed. Darwin, vol.* II, *p.* 43.

We began Darwin's book on "The Origin of Species" to-night. Though full of interesting matter, it is not impressive, from want of luminous and orderly presentation. —ELIOT, GEORGE, 1859, *Journal, Nov. 23; George Eliot's Life as related in her Letters and Journals,* ed. Cross, vol. II, p. 104.

The best part, I think, is the *whole, i. e.* its *plan* and *treatment,* the vast amount of facts and acute inferences handled as if you had a perfect mastery of them. . . . Then your candour is worth everything to your cause. It is refreshing to find a person with a new theory who frankly confesses that he finds difficulties. . . . The moment I understood your premises, I felt sure you had a real foundation to hold on. . . . I am free to say that I never learnt so much from one book as I have from yours.—GRAY, ASA, 1860, *Letter to Darwin, Jan. 23.*

Even when Darwin, in a book that all the scientific world is in ecstasy over, proved the other day that we are all come from shell-fish, it didn't move me to the slightest curiosity whether we are or not. I did not feel that the slightest light would be thrown on my practical life for me, by having it ever so logically made out that my first ancestor, millions of millions of ages back, had been, or even had not been, an oyster. It remained a plain fact that I was no oyster, nor had any grandfather an oyster within my knowledge; and for the rest, there was nothing to be gained, for this world, or the next, by going into the oyster-question, till all more pressing questions were exhausted! So—if I can't read Darwin, it may be feared I shall break down in Mrs. Duncan.—CARLYLE, JANE WELSH, 1860, *To Mrs. Russell, Jan. 28; Letters and Memorials,* ed. Froude, vol. II, p. 155.

In the name of all true philosophy we protest against such a mode of dealing with nature, as utterly dishonourable to all natural sciences, as reducing it from its present lofty level of being one of the noblest trainers of man's intellect and instructors of his mind, to being a mere idle play of the fancy, without the basis of fact or the discipline of observation. In the "Arabian Nights" we are not offended as at an impossibility when Amina sprinkles her husband with water and transforms him into a dog, but we cannot open the august doors of the venerable temple of scientific truth to the genii and magicians of romance. . . . . Such assumptions as these, we once more repeat, are most dishonourable and injurious to science; and though, out of respect to Mr. Darwin's high character and to the tone of his work, we have felt it right to weigh the "argument" again set by him before us in the simple scales of logical examination, yet we must remind him that the view is not a new one, and that it has already been treated with admirable humour when propounded by another of his name and of his lineage. We do not think that, with all his matchless ingenuity, Mr. Darwin has found any instance which so well illustrates his own theory of the improved descendant under the elevating influences of natural selection exterminating the progenitor whose specialties he has exaggerated as he himself affords us in this work. For if we go back two generations we find the ingenious grandsire of the author of "The Origin of Species" speculating on the same subject, and almost in the same manner with his more daring descendant. . . . . Mr. Darwin writes as a Christian, and we doubt not that he is one. We do not for a moment believe him to be one of those who retain in some corner of their hearts a secret unbelief which they dare not vent; and we therefore pray him to consider well the grounds on which we brand his speculations with the charge of such a tendency. First, then, he not obscurely declares that he applies his scheme of the action of the principle of natural selection to MAN himself, as well as to the animals around him. Now, we must say at once, and openly, that such a notion is absolutely incompatible not only with single expressions in the word of God on that subject of natural science with which it is not immediately concerned, but, which in our judgment is of far more importance, with the whole representation of that moral and spiritual condition of man which is its proper subject-matter. — WILBERFORCE, SAMUEL, 1860, *Darwin's Origin of Species, Quarterly Review,* vol. 108, pp. 250, 254, 257.

Interesting facts and idle fancies have seldom been combined in physical researches, and when such an alliance has been formed, the value of new facts has often compensated for the errors of their application. There are many cases, indeed, in the history of science, where speculations, like those of Kepler, have led to great discoveries in the very attempts which they suggested in order to establish or to refute them. It is otherwise, however, with speculations which trench upon sacred ground, and which run counter to the universal convictions of mankind, poisoning the fountains of science, and disturbing the serenity of the Christian world. Such is doubtless the tendency of Mr. Darwin's work on the origin of species. Trained in a less severe school than that of geometry and physics, his reasonings are almost always loose and inconclusive: His generalizations seem to have been reached before he had obtained the materials upon which he rests them: His facts, though frequently new and interesting, are often little more than conjectures; and the grand phenomena of the world of life, and instinct, and reason, which other minds have woven into noble and elevating truths, have thus become in Mr. Darwin's hands the basis of a dangerous and degrading speculation. . . . . Had Mr. Darwin written a work on the change of species, as determined by observation and experiment, without any other object but that of advancing natural science, he would have obtained a high place among philosophical naturalists. But after reading his work, in which the name of the Creator is never distinctly mentioned, we can hardly believe that scientific truth was the only object the author had in view. Researches, conducted under the influence of other motives, are not likely to stand the test of a rigorous scrutiny; and some of Mr. Darwin's not unfriendly critics have produced ample evidence that the idol of speculation has been occasionally worshipped at the expense of truth.—BREWSTER, SIR DAVID, 1862, *The Facts and Fancies of Mr. Darwin, Good Words, vol. 3, pp. 3, 8.*

The "Origin of Species" made an epoch. The product of an immense series of tentative gropings, it formed the turning-point of an entirely new series; concentrating as in a focus the many isolated rays emitted by speculative ingenuity to illuminate the diversified community of organic life, it propounded an hypothesis surpassing all its predecessors in its congruity with verifiable facts, and in its wide-reaching embrace. Because it was the product of long-continued though baffled research, and thereby gave articulate expression to the thought which had been inarticulate in many minds, its influence rapidly became European; because it was both old in purpose and novel in conception, it agitated the schools with a revolutionary ferment. No work of our time has been so general in its influence.— LEWES, GEORGE HENRY, 1868, *Mr. Darwin's Hypothesis, Fortnightly Review, vol. 9, p. 353.*

The book had hardly been published when it was found that a great crisis had been reached in the history of science and of thought. The importance of Darwin's "Origin of Species," regarded as a mere historical fact, is of at least as much importance to the world as Comte's publication of his theory of historical development. In these pages we are considering Darwin's theory and his work merely as historical facts. We are dealing with them as we might deal with the fall of a dynasty or the birth of a new state. The controversy which broke out when "Origin of Species" was published has been going on ever since, without the slightest sign of diminishing ardor. It spread almost through all society. It was heard from the pulpit and from the platform; it raged in the scientific and unscientific magazines. It was trumpeted in the newspapers; it made one of the stock subjects of talk in the dining room and smoking room; it tittered over the tea-table. . . . . Dr. Darwin's work was fiercely assailed and passionately championed. It was not the scientific principle which inflamed so much commotion; it was the supposed bearing of the doctrines on revealed religion. Injustice was done to the calm examination of Darwin's theory on both sides of the controversy. Many who really had not yet given themselves time even to consider its arguments cried out in admiration of the book, merely because they assumed it was destined to deal a blow to the faith revealed in religion. On the other side, many of the believers in revealed religion were much too easily alarmed and too sensitive. Many of them did not pause to ask themselves whether, if every article of the doctrine were proved to be scientifically true, it would affect in the slightest degree the basis of their religious faith. To this writer it seems clear that Dr. Darwin's theory might be accepted by the most orthodox believer without the firmness of his faith moulting a feather. The theory is one altogether as to the process of growth and construction in the universe, and, whether accurate or inaccurate, does not seem in any wise to touch the question which is concerned with the sources of all life, movement, and being. However that may be, it is certain that the book made an era not only in science, but in scientific controversy, and not merely in scientific controversy, but in controversy expanding into all circles and among all intelligences. The scholar and the fribble, the divine and the school-girl, still talk and argue and wrangle over Darwin and the origin of species.—MCCARTHY, JUSTIN, 1880, *A History of Our Own Times from the Accession of Queen Victoria to the Berlin Congress*, vol. IV, ch. LXVII.

Many of you will be familiar with the aspect of this small green-covered book. It is a copy of the first edition of the "Origin of Species," and bears the date of its production—the 1st of October, 1859. Only a few months, therefore, are needed to complete the full tale of twenty-one years since its birthday. Those whose memories carry them back to this time will remember that the infant was remarkably lively, and that a great number of excellent persons mistook its manifestations of vigorous individuality for mere naughtiness; in fact there was a very pretty turmoil about its cradle. My recollections of the period are particularly vivid; for, having conceived a tender affection for a child of what appeared to me to be such remarkable promise, I acted for some time in the capacity of a sort of under-nurse and thus came in for my share of the storms which threatened the very life of the young creature. . . . Those who have watched the progress of science within the last ten years will bear me out to the full, when I assert that there is no field of biological inquiry in which the influence of the "Origin of Species" is not traceable; the foremost men of science in every country are either avowed champions of its leading doctrines, or at any rate abstain from opposing them; a host of young and ardent investigators seek for and find inspriation and guidance in Mr. Darwin's great work; and the general doctrine of evolution, to one side of which it gives expression, obtains, in the phenomena of biology, a firm base of operations whence it may conduct its conquest of the whole realm of Nature.—HUXLEY, THOMAS HENRY, 1880, *The Coming of Age of "The Origin of Species," Darwiniana*, pp. 227, 228.

The "Origin of Species" was published in 1859. An educated and unprejudiced reader, who has not become familiar with natural history and reads the book in leisurely fashion, must come to the conclusion that it is a conspicuously clever performance, that it abounds in facts, that the conclusions drawn from these facts are moderate, and that there is no particular reason why such a book should set the whole world on fire. From beginning to end Mr. Darwin's most famous volume does not contain one rash statement, one dazzling remark, one specially bold conclusion, and least of all an observation to which a good lawyer, a respectable theologian, or a poet could object; while even a layman cannot help observing that Mr. Darwin knew far better than do most naturalists how to look at the living organisms of nature, and how to survey a whole field of which most men cultivate but a small part and reveal nothing save fragments and isolated facts. Those who are familiar with Humboldt's writings can hardly fail to notice that Mr. Darwin is simpler, less pedantic, less obstrusively erudite, less mysterious and mystical, far less pretentious, more amiable, more attractive, more accurate, and far more poetical,—the latter because his detail is so exquisite. — ERNST, C. W., 1882, *Darwin, The Literary World*, vol. 13, p. 146.

The book itself was one of the greatest, the most learned, the most lucid, the most logical, the most crushing, the most conclusive, that the world had ever yet seen. Step by step, and principle by principle, it proved every point in its progress triumphantly before it went on to demonstrate the next. So vast an array of facts so thoroughly in hand had never before been mastered and marshalled in favor of any biological theory. Those who had insight to learn and understand were convinced at once by the cogency of the argument; those who had not were overpowered and silenced by the weight of the authority and the mass of the learning.— ALLEN, GRANT, 1885, *Charles Darwin (English Worthies)*, p. 113.

Not only gave a better account of the evidence for the development of species than had ever been given before, but showed the fallacy of the adverse argument from hybridism, and, above all, gave a lucid explanation of how progress had been brought about by means of natural selection. . . . In ten years almost all naturalists were converted; in twenty years the doctrine had spread far beyond natural science into the dominions of ethics and psychology; and, a little more than twenty-two years after the publication of his book, Darwin was buried in Westminster Abbey, near the tomb of Sir Isaac Newton, literary men and theologians uniting with philosophers and naturalists to do honour to the memory of one of the greatest observers and thinkers that the world has ever seen.—HUTTON, FREDERICK WOLLASTON, 1887-99, *Darwinism and Lamarckism Old and New*, p. 32.

The root of the error lies, indirectly rather than directly, with Mr. Darwin. In 1859, through the publication of the "Origin of Species," he offered to the world what purported to be the final clue to the course of living Nature. That clue was the principle of the Struggle for Life. After the years of storm and stress which follow the intrusion into the world of all great thoughts, this principle was universally accepted as the key to all the sciences which deal with life. So ceaseless was Mr. Darwin's emphasis upon this factor, and so masterful his influence, that, after the first sharp conflict, even the controversy died down. With scarce a challenge the Struggle for Life became accepted by the scientific world as the governing factor in development, and the drama of Evolution was made to hinge entirely upon its action. It became the "part" from which science henceforth went on "to reconstruct the whole," and biology, sociology, and theology, were built anew on this foundation.—DRUMMOND, HENRY, 1894, *The Ascent of Man*, p. 12.

Incomparably the greatest work which the biological sciences have seen.—POULTON, EDWARD B., 1896, *Charles Darwin and the Theory of Natural Selection*, p. 102.

The influence of this book ranks it with the treatises of Copernicus and of Newton, with the "Contrat Social" and the "Wealth of Nations." It is doubtful if any other book, in all the history of modern thought, has been so far-reaching in its influences, or productive of such immense intellectual results. There is a difference, not merely of degree but almost of kind, between the intellectual processes of the men who lived before Darwin and those who have grown to manhood during the period in which the evolutionary leaven has been working in men's minds.—PAYNE, WILLIAM MORTON, 1902, *Literature and Criticism, Editorial Echoes*, p. 68.

DESCENT OF MAN
1871

In the "Descent of Man" Darwin dealt at length and boldly with that subject on which he had hitherto deemed it well to be reticent. He presented man as a co-descendent with the catarhine, or "downnostrilled" monkeys, from a hairy quadruped, furnished with a tail and pointed ears, and probably a climber of trees. Nay he traced back the claim of descent until he found, as the progenitor of all the vertebrate animals, some aquatic creature provided with gills, hermaphrodite, and with brain, heart and other organs imperfectly developed. The treatise in which this view is presented falls in no respect behind Mr. Darwin's other great work in closeness of reasoning and grasp of facts. The portion of the work—more than one-half—bearing on sexual selection, if somewhat less satisfactory and conclusive, forms yet a most important contribution to the wide subject of the genesis of species.—PROCTOR, RICHARD A., 1882, *Charles R. Darwin, Knowledge*, vol. 7, p. 549.

On the moral and social side, the ultimate importance of the "Descent of Man" upon the world's history can hardly be overrated by a philosophic investigator. Vast as was the revolution affected in biology by the "Origin of Species," it was as nothing compared with the still wider, deeper, and more subtly-working revolution inaugurated by the announcement of man's purely animal origin. The main discovery, strange to say, affected a single branch of thought alone; the minor corollary drawn from it to a single species has already affected, and is destined in the future still more profoundly to affect, every possible sphere of human energy. Not only has it completely reversed our entire conception of history generally, by teaching us that man has slowly risen from a very low and humble beginning, but it has also revolutionized our whole ideas of our own position and our own destiny, it has permeated the sciences of language and of medicine, it has introduced new conceptions of ethics, and of religion, and it threatens in the future to produce immense effects upon the theory and practice of education, of politics, and of economic and social science. These wide-reaching and deep-seated results began to be felt from the first moment when the Darwinian principle was definitely promulgated in the "Origin of Species," but their final development and general acceptance was immensely accelerated by Darwin's own authoritative statement in the "Descent of Man."—ALLEN, GRANT, 1885, *Charles Darwin (English Worthies)*, p. 141.

The "Descent of Man" of which Mr. Darwin was kind enough to give me a copy before publication, inspired me with the deadliest alarm. His new theory therein set forth, respecting the nature and origin of conscience, seemed to me then, and still seems to me, of absolutely fatal import.—COBBE, FRANCES POWER, 1894, *Life by Herself*, vol. II, p. 447.

GENERAL

I first read Darwin's "Journal" three or four years back, and have lately re-read it. As the journal of a scientific traveler, it is second only to Humboldt's "Personal Narrative;" as a work of general interest, perhaps superior to it. He is an ardent admirer and most able supporter of Mr. Lyell's views. His style of writing I very much admire, so free from all labour, affectation, or egotism, yet so full of interest and original thought. — WALLACE, ALFRED RUSSEL, 1845, *Letters to Henry Walter Bates, Pioneers of Evolution*, ed. Clodd, p. 125.

Ah, that I could begin to study nature anew, now that you have made it to me a live thing, not a dead collection of means. But my work lies elsewhere now. Your work, nevertheless, helps mine at every turn. It is better that the division of labour should be complete, and that each man should do only one thing, while he looks on, as he finds time, at what others are doing, and so gets laws from other sciences which he can apply, as I do, to my own.—KINGSLEY, CHARLES, 1863, *To Charles Darwin, June 14*; *Charles Kingsley, his Letters and Memories of his Life*, ed. his *Wife*, vol. II, p. 173.

My recent studies have made me more adverse than ever to the new scientific doctrines which are flourishing now in England. This sensational zeal reminds me of what I experienced as a young man in Germany, when the physio-philosophy of Oken had invaded every centre of scientific activity; and yet, what is there left of it? I trust to outlive this mania also. As usual, I do not ask beforehand what you think of it, and I may have put my hand into a hornet's nest; but you know your old friend Agass., and will forgive him if he hits a tender spot.—AGASSIZ, LOUIS, 1867, *To Sir Philip De Grey Egerton, March 26*; *Life and Correspondence*, ed. *Agassiz*, vol. II, p. 647.

This largeness of knowledge and readiness of resource render Mr. Darwin the most terrible of antagonists. Accomplished naturalists have levelled heavy and sustained criticism against him—not always with the view of fairly weighing his theory, but with the express intention of exposing his weak points only. This does not irritate him. He treats every objection with a soberness and thoroughness which even Bishop Butler might be proud to imitate, surrounding each fact with its appropriate detail, placing it in its proper relations, and usually giving it a significance which, as long as it was kept isolated, failed to appear. This is done without a trace of ill-temper. He moves over the subject with the passionless strength of a glacier; and the grinding of the rocks is not always without a counterpart in the logical pulverization of the objector.—TYNDALL, JOHN, 1874, *Address before the British Association for the Advancement of Science at Belfast, Report*, p. lxxxvii.

I have been translating into Spanish a sketch of Mr. Darwin's life—no, not *your* Mr. Darwin, certainly, you foolish little person, but his father. Not that I like science any better than I ever did. I hate it as a savage does writing, because he fears it will hurt him somehow; but I have a great respect for Mr. Darwin as almost the only perfectly disinterested lover of truth I ever encountered. I mean, of course, in his books, for I never had the pleasure of seeing him.—LOWELL, JAMES RUSSELL, 1878, *To Mrs. W. E. Darwin, Sept. 1*; *Letters*, ed. Norton, vol. II, p. 230.

The sole innovation of Darwinism upon this doctrine of evolution consisted in attempting to strip from it all proof of the incessant creative action of a designing mind, by reducing it to a blind mechanical process, necessarily resulting from inherent mudborn energies and productive power, and this attempt, resting solely upon the two unfounded assumptions of a battle for life and of the necessary survival of the higher organisms over the lower ones in that contest, it has now been shown, must be regarded as an ignominious failure. Yet the very making of this attempt contributed much to the speedy and joyful acceptance of the Darwinian hypothesis in certain quarters. It was the pepper which made the dish palatable to Huxley, Haeckel & Co.,— that is, to those English and German naturalists whose previous bias in favor of materialism and fatalism indisposed them to recognize anywhere any proofs of the being of a God.— BOWEN, FRANCIS, 1879–80, *Malthusianism, Darwinism and Pessimism; Gleanings from a Literary Life*, p. 369.

I am not likely to take a low view of Darwin's position in the history of science, but I am disposed to think that Buffon and Lamarck would run him hard in both genius and fertility. In breadth of view and in extent of knowledge these two men were giants, though we are apt to forget their services. Von Bär was another man of the same stamp; Cuvier, in a somewhat lower rank, another; and J. Müller another. "Colossal" does not seem to me to be the right epithet for Darwin's intellect. He had a clear rapid intelligence, a great memory, a vivid imagination, and what made his greatness was the strict subordination of all these to his love of truth. —HUXLEY, THOMAS HENRY, 1882, *To G. J. Romanes, May 9; Life and Letters*, ed. Huxley, vol. II, p. 42.

Notwithstanding the extent and variety of his botanical work, Mr. Darwin always disclaimed any right to be regarded as a professed botanist. He turned his attention to plants doubtless because they were convenient objects for studying organic phenomena in their least complicated forms; and this point of view, which, if one may use the expression without disrepect, had something of the amateur about it, was in itself of the greatest importance. For, from not being, till he took up any point, familiar with the literature bearing on it, his mind was absolutely free from any prepossession. He was never afraid of his facts or of framing any hypothesis, however startling which seemed to explain them. However much weight he attributed to inheritance as a factor in organic phenomena, tradition went for nothing in studying them. In any one else such an attitude would have produced much work that was crude and rash. But Mr. Darwin—if one may venture on language which will strike no one who had conversed with him as overstrained—seemed by gentle persuasion to have penetrated that reserve of nature which baffles smaller men. In other words, his long experience had given him a kind of instinctive insight into the method of attack of any biological problem, however unfamiliar to him, while he rigidly controlled the fertility of his mind in hypothetical explanations by the no less fertility of ingeniously-devised experiment. Whatever he touched he was sure to draw from it something that it had never before yielded, and he was wholly free from that familiarity which comes to the professed student in every branch of science, and blinds the mental eye to the significance of things which are overlooked because always in view.—DYER, W. T. THISELTON, 1882, *Work in Botany, Charles Darwin Memorial Notices from "Nature,"* p. 43.

No man of his time has exercised upon the science of Geology a profounder influence than Charles Darwin. . . . In fine, the spirit of Mr. Darwin's teaching may be traced all through the literature of science, even in departments which he never himself entered. No branch of research has benefited more from the infusion of this spirit than geology. Time-honoured prejudices have been broken down, theories that seemed the most surely based have been reconsidered, and when found untenable, have been boldly discarded. That the Present must be taken as a guide to the Past, has been more fearlessly asserted than ever. And yet it has been recognized that the Present differs widely from the Past, that there has been a progress everywhere, that Evolution and not Uniformitarianism has been the law by which geological history has been governed. For the impetus with which these views have been advanced in every civilized country, we look up with reverence to the loved and immortal name of Charles Darwin.—GEIKIE, ARCHIBALD, 1882, *Work in Geology, Charles Darwin Memorial Notices reprinted from "Nature,"* pp. 15, 27.

Mr. Darwin's latest books belong to a period in which, having lived to witness the complete success of his great work, he has employed his time in recording the results of his researches on many subsidiary points, of no little interest and importance The treatises on the Expression of the Emotions in Man and Animals, on the Movements and Habits of Climbing Plants, on Insectivorous Plants, on Cross and Self Fertilization, on the Different Forms of Flowers, and on the formation of Vegetable Mould through the Action of Worms should be read as models of sound scientific method by every one who cares to learn what scientific method is. They may be counted, too, among the most entertaining books of science that have ever been written; and the points that have been established in them, taken in connection with Mr. Darwin's previous works, make up an aggregate of scientific achievement such as has rarely been equaled. . . . On the Sunday following Mr. Darwin's death, Canon Liddon, at St. Paul's Cathedral, and Canons Barry and Prothero, at Westminster Abbey, agreed in referring to the Darwinian theory as "not necessarily hostile to the fundamental truths of religion." The effect of Mr. Darwin's work has been, however, to remodel the theological conceptions of the origin and destiny of man which were current in former times. In this respect it has wrought a revolution as great as that which Copernicus inaugurated and Newton completed, and of very much the same kind.—FISKE, JOHN, 1882, *Charles Darwin, Atlantic Monthly, vol.* 49, p. 845.

Unambitious and unassuming, he has never thrust himself before the public, nor sought for honours and emoluments. He worked for the love of science and of truth, careless of his own reputation if only he could impart to others that which his own mind had grasped so firmly and analysed so accurately. As a naturalist, not even his greatest enemies will deny him the meed of praise. No other man could have drawn so much knowledge from a single scientific voyage, and the works consequent upon his connection with the expedition of the *Beagle* would have stood out as monuments of vast genius and unparalleled industry, even had he never written those better known and much criticised books which have made his name the war-cry of opposing factions.—BUCKLAND, A. W., 1882, *Charles Darwin, Knowledge, vol.* 1, p. 571.

One of the most notable men of the age—among scientific men doubtless the most notable . . . Whatever judgment posterity may pronounce upon his genius and his work, we may say that no other naturalist ever made an impression at once so deep, so wide and so immediate. The name of Linnæus most invites comparison; but the readers and pupils of Linnæus over a century ago were to those of Darwin as tens are to thousands, and the interest of the subjects discussed were somewhat in the same ratio. Humboldt, who, like Darwin, began with research in travel, and to whom the longest of lives, vigorous health, and the best of opportunities were allotted, essayed similar themes in a more ambitious spirit, enjoyed equal popularity, but left no great impression upon the thought of his own day and ours. As a measure of contemporary celebrity, one may note that no other author that we know of ever gave rise in his own active life-time to a special department of bibliography. Dante-literature and Shakespere-literature are the growth of centuries; but *Darwinismus* had filled shelves and alcoves and teeming catalogues, while the quiet but unremitting investigator was still supplying new and even novel subjects for comment. Note, also, that the terms which he chose as the catch-word of his theory and more than one of the phrases by which he illustrated it, less than twenty-five years ago, have already in their special meanings been engrafted into his mother-tongue, and even into other European languages, and are turned to use in common converse with hardly any sense of strangeness.—GRAY, ASA, 1882, *Darwin, The Literary World, vol.* 13, p. 145.

A conqueror greater than Alexander, who extended the empire of human knowledge.—CURTIS, GEORGE WILLIAM, 1882 *The Leadership of Educated Men, Orations and Addresses, vol.* I, p. 316.

In no country of the world, however, England not excepted, has the reforming doctrine of Darwin met with so much living interest or evoked such a storm of writings, for and against, as in Germany. It is therefore only a debt of honor we pay, if at this year's assembly of German Naturalists and Physicians we gratefully call to remembrance the mighty genius who has departed, and bring home to our minds the loftiness of the theory of nature to which he has elevated us. And what place in the world could be more appropriate for rendering this service of thanks than Eisenach, with its Wartburg, this stronghold of free inquiry and free opinion! As in this sacred spot 360 years ago Martin Luther, by his reform of the church in its head and members, introduced a new era in the history of civilisation, so in our days has Charles Darwin, by his reform, of the doctrine of development, conserned the whole preception, thought, and volition of mankind into new and higher courses. It is true that personally both in his character and influence, Darwin has more affinity to the meek and mild Melanchthon than to the powerful and inspired Luther. In the scope and importance, however, of their great work of reformation, the two cases were entirely parallel, and in both the success marks a new epoch in the development of human mind.—HAECKEL, ERNST HEINRICH, 1882, *Darwin, Goethe and Lamarck; Lecture given at Eisenach.*

It is well known that Mr. Darwin's theory on the Origin of Species has been accepted in Germany more widely, with more absolute faith, and with more vehement enthusiasm, than in the country of its birth. In Germany, more conspicuously than elsewhere, it has itself become the subject of developments as strange and as aberrant as any which it assumes in the history of Organic Life. The most extravagant conclusions have been drawn from it—invading every branch of human thought, in Science, in Philosophy, and in Religion. These conclusions have been preached, too, with a dogmatism as angry and as intolerant as any of the old theologies. It is the fate of every idea which is new and fruitful, that it is ridden to the death by excited novices. We cannot be surprised if this fate has overtaken the idea that all existing animal forms have had their ancestry in other forms which exist no longer, and have been derived from these by ordinary generation through countless stages of descent.— ARGYLL, DUKE OF, 1882, *The Theories of Darwin and Their relation to Philosophy, Religion and Morality by Rudolf Schmidt, tr. Zimmermann, Introduction, p. 5.*

Darwin seems to me to be the Copernicus of the organic world.—REYNOLD, E. DUBOIS, 1883, *Darwin and Copernicus, Addresses before the Berlin Academy of Sciences.*

His name has given a new word to several languages, and his genius is acknowledged wherever civilisation extends. Yet the very greatness of his fame, together with the number, variety, and scientific importance of his works has caused him to be altogether misapprehended by the bulk of the reading public. Every book of Darwin's has been reviewed or noticed in almost every newspaper and periodical, while his theories have been the subject of so much criticism and so much dispute, that most educated persons have been able to obtain some general notion of his teachings, often without having read a single chapter of his works,—and very few, indeed, except professed students of science, have read the whole series of them. It has been so easy to learn something of the Darwinian theory at second-hand that few have cared to study it as expounded by its author. It thus happens that while Darwin's name and fame are more widely known than in the case of any other modern man of science, the real character and importance of the work he did are as widely misunderstood.— WALLACE, ALFRED RUSSEL, 1883-95, *Natural Selection and Tropical Nature, p. 450.*

Darwin: Socrates?

Dæmon (Socrates): Who else should greet thee here than he whose spirit guided thee thine earth-life through? Thou knewest it not; but all men saw thy method was Socratic. Thy natal star was mine that beamed upon thee in the Abbey church. Thy Nemesis and I are one. 'Twas my familiar spirit speaking through the course of Nature's evolution from the moner to the man, pointing the way of truth through mundane matter to the substance of soul that clothes thy spirit now in brightness. This, thy Dæmon, is the Love of Truth.—COUES, ELLIOTT, 1885, *The Dæmon of Darwin, p. 48.*

Aside from their scientific value, the works of Darwin have a broad human interest, and are therefore not to be overlooked by the literary man. They add to our knowledge of nature, not after the manner of the closest naturalist, but after the manner of the great explorers and discoverers. It is mainly vital knowledge which he gives us. What a peculiar human interest attaches to the results of his observations upon the earth-worm and the formation of vegetable mould; to his work upon the power of movement in plants; to his discovery of the value of cross-fertilization in the vegetable kingdom, to say nothing of the light which he has thrown upon the origin of species and the descent of man. Of course, all kinds of knowledge are not equally valuable; all knowledge does not alike warm and enlighten us; but there is much in Darwin that warms and enlightens us. Contact with such a broad, sane, sincere spirit, is of itself of the highest value. Indeed, to ignore Darwin is not only to ignore modern science; it is to ignore one of the broadest and most helpful minds of the century. And then to object to him upon such whimsical grounds as Ruskin does—namely, "because it is every man's duty to know what he *is*, not to think of the embryo he was," and also "because Darwin has a mortal fascination for all vainly curious and idly speculative persons"—is a piece of folly that it would be hard to match even in the utterances of this prince of caprice.—BURROUGHS, JOHN, 1886, *Ruskin's Judgment of Gibbon and Darwin, The Critic*, May 1.

His style has been much praised; on the other hand, at least one good judge has remarked to me that it is not a good style. It is, above all things, direct and clear; and it is characteristic of himself in its simplicity, bordering on naïveté, and in its absence of pretence. He had the strongest disbelief in the common idea that a classical scholar must write good English; indeed, he thought that the contrary was the case. In writing, he sometimes showed the same tendency to strong expressions as he did in conversation.—DARWIN, FRANCIS, 1887, *Life and Letters of Charles Darwin, vol.* I, *p.* 131.

Never, perhaps, did a biography give such an unmixedly pleasing impression both of its hero and of his friends. In these hundreds of unstudied letters there is not a sentence which we could wish otherwise written; nor are the surrounding group of correspondents unworthy of the central figure. In this respect their various theoretical opinions seem to make little difference; but we soon feel that it is not from a chosen company of men such as these that we can argue as to the ultimate influence of any belief or disbelief upon the mass of mankind. Ignorant and prejudiced critics are the only villains in the tale, and even their howling comes to us faint as the woolfish sounds which Æneas heard across the waters as he steered safe by Circe's isle. How different from the restless bitterness of Carlyle, who makes us feel that he is struggling alone to retain reason and humanity among the crowding bears and swine!—from the sad resolve of George Eliot, who seems ever to be encountering the enchantress with the sprig of moly, herself half doubtful of its power! And linked with this peace of conscience there is a boyish yet a steadfast happiness; a total freedom from our self-questioning complexities — from the Welt-Schmerz which, in one form or other has paralysed or saddened so many of the best lives of our times. Can we get nearer to the source of this tranquility? Can we detect the prophylactic which kept the melancholy infection at bay?—MYERS, FREDERIC W. H., 1888, *Charles Darwin and Agnosticism, Fortnightly Review, vol.* 49, *p.* 105.

Evidence is not wanting that at times he had misgivings that his own intellect was not competent to judge of the facts he had collected, and that he was biased by long brooding over a certain kind of thoughts. He feared, at times, that he might be only a "crank" following an *ignis-fatuus.* "How awfully flat I shall feel," he writes, "if when I get my notes together on species, etc., the whole thing explodes like an empty puff-ball!" But he felt that competent judges were at hand, at least three of them, on whose verdict the theory could stand or fall so far as he was concerned. Darwin realized that if he could convince Lyell, Hooker, and Huxley, the battle was won. If these three great minds gave assent, the truth must be there. For the rest of the scientific world, especially for the younger and more observant of his fellow-workers, the adoption of the theory of descent would be only a question of time. Nothing in the history of science is more remarkable than the calm patience and humility with which Darwin awaited the verdict of posterity on the main question involved in his theory of the origin of species.—JORDAN, DAVID S., 1888, *Darwin's Life and Letters, The Dial, vol.* 8, *p.* 217.

What is the relation of Agassiz to Darwin--of Agassizian development to

Darwinian evolution? I answer, it is the relation of formal science to physical or casual science. Agassiz advanced biology to the *formal* stage; Darwin carried it forward, to some extent at least, to the *physical* stage.—LE CONTE, JOSEPH, 1888, *Evolution and its Relation to Religious Thought, p.* 46.

The publication of the "Life and Letters" of the late Mr. Charles Darwin by his son, has thrown light upon some points of Darwin's opinions and character which till now were obscure, and has re-awakened an interest in his well-known theory of "natural selection" which had begun somewhat to flag. . . . The influence which Mr. Darwin has exercised over men's minds with respect to this question is probably greater than that of any writer since St. Paul.—MIVART, ST. GEORGE, 1889, *Darwin's Brilliant Fallacy, The Forum, vol.* 7, *p.* 99.

The conception of evolution has penetrated every department of organic science, especially where it touches man. Darwin personally, to whom belongs the chief place of honour in the triumph of a movement which began with Aristotle, has been a transforming power by virtue of his method and spirit, his immense patience, his keen observation, his modesty and allegiance to truth; no one has done so much to make science—that is to say, all inquiry into the traceable causes or relation of things—so attractive.—ELLIS, HAVELOCK, 1890, *The New Spirit, Introduction, p.* 5.

Nobody can value more than I do the significance for the general student of the splendid achievement of Darwin; but it was a splendid achievement for humanity at large because the age was ripe for the extension of the historical conception far beyond the boundaries of humanity proper. . . . If you can conceive Darwin's knowledge of natural history, his investigations, and his marvelous induction that led to the principle of natural selection, with all its consequences, if, I say, you can conceive all this transferred to the last century, some properly informed naturalist might, no doubt, have been convinced; but the world at large could have found no place for the doctrine. It would have been to them only one oddity the more in nature, or rather in speculation. They would have called it Darwin's paradox, and would have banished it into the realm of curiosities. It was coming into an historical age, that made Darwin's book so great a prize, and the idea of natural selection so deeply suggestive to philosophy. . . . With the one exception of Newton's "Principia," no single book of empirical science has ever been of more importance to philosophy than this work of Darwin's.—ROYCE, JOSIAH, 1892, *The Spirit of Modern Philosophy, pp.* 285, 286.

One of the noblest and yet humblest of the high priests of inductive science.—VIGNOLES, O. J., 1893, *The Home of a Naturalist, Good Words, vol.* 34, *p.* 97.

The name of Charles Darwin will ever be pre-eminent among the immortal coterie of commanding thinkers who have made the nineteenth century the most notable epoch in the history of scientific thought and attainment. The influence of his careful and patient research and the logical deductions which he gave mankind in his masterly volumes have changed, to a great extent, the current of a world's thought. Not that Darwin alone accomplished this, for never was a king surrounded by more loyal knights than was this great man environed by giant thinkers who nobly fought for the thought he sought to establish, against the combined opposition of established religious and scholastic conservatism. But the important fact must not be overlooked that had it not been for the years of patient observation and research, which enabled Mr. Darwin tangibly to demonstrate the truth of many important contested questions, the splendid philosophical presentations of Spencer, the important labors of Dr. Alfred Russel Wallace, and other scarcely less vigorous thinkers would have only been sufficient to arouse a fierce war, which even a century might not have settled in favor of the bold innovators. Hence Mr. Darwin will ever stand as the great apostle of evolutionary thought, vaguely foreshadowed by Buffon, St. Hilaire, and Erasmus Darwin, and boldly outlined by Lamarck.—FLOWER, B. O., 1893, *Life of Charles Darwin, The Arena, vol.* 7, *p.* 352.

In the first place, with regard to merely historical accuracy, it appears to me undesirable that naturalists should endeavor to hide certain parts of Darwin's teaching, and give undue prominence to others. In the second pace, it appears to me still more undesirable that this should be done—as it usually is done—for the purpose of making it appear that Darwin's teaching did not really differ very much from that of Wallace and Weismann on the important points in question. I myself believe that Darwin's judgment with regard to all these points will evidently prove more sound and accurate than that of any of the recent would-be improvers upon his system; but even apart from this opinion of my own, it is undesirable that Darwin's views should be misrepresented, whether the misrepresentation be due to any unfavorable bias against one side of his teaching, or to sheer carelessness in the reading of books.—ROMANES, GEORGE JOHN, 1894, *Darwin and after Darwin, Introduction*, pt. II, p. 8.

A great merit of his writings lies in the amount of his facts, and in the moderation with which he states them. But his results, though gaining acceptance, are still matter of dispute. There is little charm in his style; the charm lies in the originality and boldness of his theories, and the interest of his subject. He is probably the most eminent man of science of the century.— ROBERTSON, J. LOGIE, 1894, *A History of English Literature*, p. 380.

His educational history, his thoroughness, his scientific honesty, his logical power, his power of minute observation and broad generalization, the greatness of the problems with which he dealt, and the profound influence of his views upon the thought of the world, all conspire to make him a model, in the study of scientific method. Some of his views have been rejected, and many may be profoundly modified by more accurate knowledge, but these things will in no way affect the value of Darwin as a type of what education should accomplish, and how it must accomplish it.—CRAMER, FRANK, 1896, *The Method of Darwin*, p. 31.

The style of Darwin attempts no ornateness, and on the other hand it is not one of those extremely simple styles which are independent of ornament and to which ornament would be simply a defacement. But it is very clear; it is not in the least slovenly; and there is about it the indefinable sense that the writer might have been a much greater writer, simply as such, than he is, if he had cared to take the trouble, and had not been almost solely intent upon his matter. Such writers are not so common that they should be neglected, and they may at least stand in the Court of the Gentiles, the "provincial band" of literature.—SAINTSBURY, GEORGE, 1896, *A History of Nineteenth Century Literature*, p. 413.

A man who has effected a greater revolution in the opinions of mankind than anyone, at least since Newton, and whose name is likely to live with honor as long as the human race moves upon the planet. — LECKY, WILLIAM EDWARD HARTPOLE, 1896, *Democracy and Liberty, vol.* I, p. 255.

The style of Darwin's writing is remarkable for the absence of all affectation, of all attempt at epigram, literary allusion, or rhetoric. In this it is admirably suited to its subject. At the same time there is no sacrifice of clearness to brevity, nor are technical terms used in place of language. The greatest pains are obviously given by the author to enable his reader to thoroughly understand the matter in hand. Further, the reader is treated not only with this courtesy of full explanation, but with extreme fairness and modesty. Darwin never slurs over a difficulty nor minimizes over it. He states objections and awkward facts prominently, and without shirking proceeds to deal with them by citation or experiment or observation carried out by him for the purpose. His modesty towards his reader is a delightful characteristic. He simply desires to persuade you as one reasonable friend may persuade another. He never thrusts a conclusion nor even a step towards a conclusion upon you, by a demand for your confidence in him as an authority, or by an unfair weighting of the arguments which he balances, or by a juggle of word-play. The consequence is that though Darwin himself thought he had no literary ability, and labored over and rewrote his sentences, we have in his works a model of clear exposition of a great argument, and the most remarkable example of persuasive style in the English language —persuasive because of its transparent honesty and scrupulous moderation.— LANKESTER, E. RAY, 1897, *Library of the World's Best Literature, ed. Warner, vol.* VIII, p. 4392.

As a philosher who regards evolutionism in some form as affording the most hopeful method of approaching the mystery of existence, I am inclined to hold that when historical perspective has cleared away the mole-hills we have made into mountains, it will be here that will be found Darwin's most momentous and enduring service to knowledge and to mankind.—SCHILLER, F. C. S., 1897, *Darwinism and Design, Contemporary Review, vol.* 71, *p.* 883.

Darwin's books owe comparatively little to the graces of style. He wrote slowly, and confesses to have found composition difficult. It was not therefore to the literary quality of his work, but to the interest attaching to the numberless observations of facts that he recorded, and the startling nature of the speculations to which they led him, that the extraordinary success of his books was due.— GRAHAM, RICHARD D., 1897, *The Masters of Victorian Literature, p.* 463.

The greatest of Victorian natural philosophers. . . . He is one of the great artificers of human thought, a noble figure destined, in utter simplicity and abnegation of self, to perform one of the most stirring and inspiring acts ever carried out by a single intelligence, and to reawaken the sources of human enthusiasm. Darwin's great suggestion, of life evolved by the process of natural selection, is so far-reaching in its effects as to cover not science only, but art and literature as well; and he had the genius to carry this suggested idea, past all objections and obstacles, up to the station of a biological system the most generally accepted of any put forth in recent times.— GOSSE, EDMUND, 1897, *A Short History of Modern English Literature, p.* 358.

Darwin, though a specialist of genius, and a specialist on a great scale, was still, after all, a specialist. And he never claimed to bring the world a new cosmical philosophy; it was enough for him to introduce one new hypothesis, linking together all forms of life, and to see this hypothesis conquering mind after mind, until the whole civilized world seemed to bow to its discoverer. Darwin dealt with the evolution of species, Spencer has dealt with the evolution of the universe.—MACKINTOSH, ROBERT, 1899, *From Comte to Benjamin Kidd, p* 67.

Gabriel Charles Dante Rossetti
1828–1882

Born in London, and early in his professional career modified his name into Dante Gabriel Rossetti. He was the brother of Christina Georgina Rossetti, and son of Gabriele Rossetti, an Italian poet-patriot, who escaped to England as a political exile after the failure of the Neapolitan insurrection in 1821. In 1835 Dante Gabriel entered King's College School, where he remained for eight years, when he studied first at an Art academy, and afterwards at the Royal Academy Antique School. He left the academy in 1848, and the following year exhibited his first picture, "The Girlhood of Mary Virgin." In 1848 he associated with Holman Hunt and Thomas Woolner in founding the Pre-Raphaelite Brotherhood, and two years later contributed "The Blessed Damozel" to *The Germ*, which had been started as the official organ of that movement. In 1856 he became one of the contributors to *The Oxford and Cambridge Magazine*, which also advocated Pre-Raphaelite principles. In 1860 he married Elizabeth Eleanor Siddal, his model and pupil; who died two years later, under tragic circumstances, being found dead in her bed from the effects of an overdose of laudanum. Under stress of deep grief, he impulsively buried in his wife's coffin the manuscript copies of both his published and unpublished poems, which he eight years later permitted to be exhumed at the earnest solicitation of his friends. The poems thus recovered were revised for publication, and appeared in 1870. It was this volume which inspired Mr. Robert Buchanan's article "The Fleshly School of Poetry," in *The Contemporary Review*. The strictures of this critic, followed by others equally harsh, served to make Rossetti, always retiring in his habits, almost a recluse. Shortly before the publication of Mr. Buchanan's criticism, he had resorted to chloral as a remedy for insomnia, and his disturbed condition of mind caused by the hostile reception given to his poems led him into such excessive use of the drug, as to ultimately cause his death. He published "The Early Italian Poets" (translation, 1861;) "Poems," 1870, and a new edition 1881; "Dante and his Circle" (translations), 1874; "Ballads and Sonnets," 1881. A collected edition of his poems and translations, edited by his brother, Mr. William Michael Rossetti, was published in 1887.—RANDOLPH, HENRY F., 1887, *ed. Fifty Years of English Song, Biographical Notes, vol.* IV, *p.* 26.

SIR HENRY JAMES SUMNER MAINE

From a Portrait by Lowes Dickinson.

DANTE GABRIEL ROSSETTI

From a Portrait by S. Hollyer.

PERSONAL.

Called on Dante Rossetti. Saw Miss Siddal, looking thinner and more deathlike and more beautiful and more ragged than ever; a real artist, a woman without parallel for many a long year. Gabriel as usual diffuse and inconsequent in his work. Drawing wonderful and lovely Guggums one after another, each one a fresh charm, each one stamped with immortality, and his picture never advancing. However, he is at the wall, and I am to get him a white calf and a cart to paint here; would he but study the golden one a little more. Poor Gabriello.—BROWN, MADOX, 1854, *Diary, Oct. 6; Ruskin, Rossetti Preraphaelitism*, ed. Rossetti, p. 19.

While I write, my heart is sore for a great calamity just befallen poor Rossetti, which I only heard of last night—his wife, who had been, as an invalid, in the habit of taking laudanum, swallowed an overdose—was found by the poor fellow on his return from the workingmen's class in the evening, under the effects of it—help was called in, the stomach-pump used; but she died in the night, about a week ago.— BROWNING, ROBERT, 1862, *To Miss Blagden, Feb. 15; Life and Letters of Robert Browning*, ed. Orr, vol. II, p. 375.

What wreath have I above thy rest to place,
What worthy song-wreath, Friend—nay, more than friend?
For so thou didst all other men transcend
That the pure, fiery worship of old days—
That of the boy, content to hear, to gaze—
Burned on most brightly, though as lamps none tend
The lights on other shrines had made an end
And darkness reigned where *was* the vestal blaze.
Far from us now thou art, and never again
Thy magic voice shall thrill me as one thrills
When noblest music storms his heart and brain.
The sea remembers thee, the woods, the hills,
Sunlight and moonlight, and the hurrying rills;
And love saith, "Surely this man leads my train!"
— MARSTON, PHILIP BOURKE, 1882, *In Memory of D. G. Rossetti, Wind-Voices*, p. 176.

During the last eight years of his life, Rossetti's whole being was clouded by the terrible curse of an excitable temperament —sleeplessness. To overcome this enemy, which interfered with his powers of work and concentration of thought, he accepted the treacherous aid of the new drug, chloral, which was then vaunted as perfectly harmless in its effect upon the health. The doses of chloral became more and more necessary to him, and I am told that at last they became so frequent and excessive that no case has been recorded in the annals of medicine in which one patient has taken so much, or even half so much chloral as Rossetti took. Under this unwholesome drug his constitution, originally a magnificent one, slipped unconsciously into decay, the more stealthily that the poison seemed to have no effect whatever on the powers of the victim's intellect. He painted until physical force failed him; he wrote brilliantly to the very last, and two sonnets dictated by him on his death-bed are described to me as being entirely worthy of his mature powers.— GOSSE, EDMUND, 1882, *Dante Gabriel Rossetti, Century Magazine*, vol. 24, p. 725.

His interest was entirely engrossed by his work; although well read and an excellent talker he shrank from general society, but he was a warm friend to his friends and there was about him that curious personal fascination so frequently found combined with creative genius.— HUEFFER, FRANCIS, 1882, *Ballads and Poems*, Tauchnitz Ed., Memoir, p. 24.

Naturally the sale of Mr. Rossetti's effects attracted a large number of persons to the gloomy old-fashioned residence in Cheyne Walk, Chelsea, and many of the articles sold went for prices very far in excess of their intrinsic value, the total sum realised being over £3,000. . . . But during the sale of these books on that fine July afternoon, in the dingy study hung round with the lovely but melancholy faces of Proserpine and Pandora, despite the noise of the throng and the witticisms of the auctioneer, a sad feeling of desecration must have crept over many of those who were present at the dispersion of the household goods and favourite books of that man who hated the vulgar crowd. Gazing through the open windows they could see the tall trees waving their heads in a sorrowful sort of way in the summer breeze, throwing their shifting shadows over the neglected grass-grown paths, once the haunt of the stately peacocks whose mediæval beauty had such a strange fascination for Rossetti, and whose feathers are now the accepted favours of his apostles and admirers. And so their gaze would wander back again to that mysterious face upon the wall, that face as some say the grandest in the world, a lovely one in truth, with its wistful, woful, passionate eyes, its masses of heavy wavy auburn hair, its sweet sad mouth with the full red lips; a face that seemed to say the sad old lines:

"'Tis better to have loved and lost,
Than never to have loved at all."

And then would come the monotonous cry of the auctioneer to disturb the reverie, and call one back to the matter of fact world which Dante Gabriel Rossetti, painter and poet, has left.

GOING! GOING! GONE!
—HAMILTON, WALTER, 1882, *The Æsthetic Movement in England, pp.* 59, 60.

The main features of his character were, in my apprehension, fearlessness, kindliness, a decision that sometimes made him seem somewhat arbitrary, and condensation or concentration. He was wonderfully self-reliant. . . . His work was great, the man was greater. His conversation had a wonderful ease, precision, and felicity of expression. He produced thoughts perfectly enunciated with a deliberate happiness that was indescribable, though it was always simple conversation, never haranguing or declamation. He was a natural leader because he was a natural teacher. When he chose to be interested in anything that was brought before him, no pains were too great for him to take. His advice was always given warmly and freely, and when he spoke of the works of others it was always in the most generous spirit of praise. It was in fact impossible to have been more free from captiousness, jealousy, envy, or any other form of pettiness than this truly noble man.—DIXON, RICHARD WATSON, 1882, *Letter to Hall Caine, Recollections of Rossetti, p.* 38.

Rossetti had buried the only complete copy of his poems with his wife at Highgate, and for a time he had been able to put by the thought of them; but as one by one of his friends, Mr. Morris, Mr. Swinburne, and others, attained to distinction as poets, he began to hanker after poetic reputation, and to reflect with pain and regret upon the hidden fruits of his best effort. Rossetti—in all love of his memory be it spoken—was after all a frail mortal; of unstable character: of variable purpose: a creature of impulse and whim, and with a plentiful lack of the backbone of volition. With less affection he would not have buried his book; with more strength of will he had not done so; or, having done so, he had never wished to undo what he had done; or having undone it, he would never have tormented himself with the memory of it as of a deed of sacrilege. But Rossetti had both affection enough to do it and weakness enough to have it undone. After an infinity of self-communions he determined to have the grave opened, and the book extracted. Endless were the preparations necessary before such a work could be begun. Mr. Home Secretary Bruce had to be consulted. At length preliminaries were complete, and one night, seven and a half years after the burial, a fire was built by the side of the grave, and then the coffin was raised and opened. The body is described as perfect upon coming to light. Whilst this painful work was being done the unhappy author of it was sitting alone and anxious and full of self-reproaches at the house of the friend who had charge of it. He was relieved and thankful when told that all was over. The volume was not much the worse for the years it had lain in the grave Deficiencies were filled in from memory, the manuscript was put in the press, and in 1870 the reclaimed work was issued under the simple title of "Poems."— CAINE, HALL, 1882, *Recollections of Dante Gabriel Rossetti, p.* 59.

As to the personality of Dante Gabriel Rossetti much has been written since his death, and it is now widely known that he was a man who exercised an almost irresistible charm over most with whom he was brought in contact. His manner could be peculiarly winning, especially with those much younger than himself, and his voice was alike notable for its sonorous beauty and for a magnetic quality that made the ear alert whether the speaker was engaged in conversation, recitation, or reading. I have heard him read, some of them over and over, all the poems in the "Ballads and Sonnets," and especially in such productions as "The Cloud Confines" was his voice as stirring as a trumpet tone; but where he excelled was in some of the pathetic portions of the "Vita Nuova," or the terrible and sonorous passages of L'Inferno, when the music of the Italian language found full expression indeed. His conversational powers I am unable adequately to describe, for during the four or five years of my intimacy with him he suffered too much from ill health to be a consistently brilliant talker, but again and again I have seen instances of those marvellous gifts that made him at one time a Sydney Smith in wit and a Coleridge in eloquence. In appearance he was if anything rather over middle height, and, especially latterly, somewhat stout; his forehead was of splendid proportions, recalling instantaneously to most strangers the Stratford bust of Shakespeare; and his gray-blue eyes were clear and piercing, and characterised by that rapid penetrative gaze so noticeable in Emerson. He seemed always to me an unmistakable Englishman, yet the Italian element was frequently recognisable; as far as his own opinion is concerned, he was wholly English. Possessing a thorough knowledge of French and Italian, he was the fortunate appreciator of many great works in their native tongue, and his sympathies in religion, as in literature, were truly catholic. To meet him even once was to be the better of it ever after; those who obtained his friendship cannot well say all it meant and means to them; but they know that they are not again in the least likely to meet with such another as Dante Gabriel Rossetti.— SHARP, WILLIAM, 1882, *Dante Gabriel Rossetti, A Record and a Study*, p. 36.

In the early spring of the present year there passed away at Birchington-on-Sea, in Kent, one of the most original painters and most gifted poets who was ever sent to lend light and leading to a perverse generation. A man unique in this particular—that he passed through good and evil report with serene indifference to mercenary reward or social successes; and that, while exercising an unusual influence on the higher culture of his age, and living in the very midst of a busy and somewhat pertinacious artistic circle, he remained personally unknown to most of his contemporaries as well as to the public at large.... Even fairer than his artistic or literary fame was the love and admiration he awakened in all who knew him.... When I remember how truly great he was—in that best greatness of modesty and meekness of soul, when I think how patiently he laboured at his beautiful art and how little golden praise men gave to him; when I contrast his gentle life with the strenuous lives of noisier and more prosperous men, it seems strange to think that, at any period of his career, any writer could be found blind enough or hard enough to criticise him adversely. Yet, that cruel things were written of him, and by one who should have looked longer and known better, we all know. He has been called a "fleshly" person, a sensuous, even sensual poet; he who, more than perhaps many of his contemporaries, was the least objective, the least earthly, and the most ideal.— BUCHANAN, ROBERT, 1882–86, *A Note on Dante Rossetti, A Look Round Literature*, pp. 152, 153.

I know not what friend of Rossetti's can assume the judicial attitude when speaking of him. I know not who shall render in words a character so fascinating, so original, and yet so self-contradictory. At one moment exhibiting, as Rossetti would, the sagacity of the most astute man of affairs, and the next the perversities and the whimsical vagaries of a schoolboy; startling us at one moment as he would startle us with the brilliance of the most accomplished wit, at the next with a spontaneous tenderness like that of a woman or else with some trait of simplicity and *naïveté* like that of a child—it is no wonder that misconceptions about a character so Protean should prevail. Nor is it any wonder that to us who loved him, the name of Rossetti was a word of music that never suggested the works but always the man. I say "to us who loved him," and the category contains all who knew him, for he was a man whom it was impossible to know without deeply loving, and I will not deny that it was necessary that he should be deeply loved before he could be fully known. Perhaps the strongest proof of this is that, notwithstanding all those "weaknesses" upon which the garish light of the public press has lately been flashing—notwithstanding the seclusion in which, of late years, he lived—"the jealous seclusion," as an illustrious painter has phrased it—which shut out at last not merely the outside world, but even the men of genius who had shared with him those youthful and noble struggles for art which have come to such a great fruition—notwithstanding all this, I say, these early friends of Rossetti's never lost their affectionate regard for him.—WATTS-DUNTON, THEODORE, 1883, *The Truth About Rossetti, Nineteenth Century*, vol. 13, p. 404.

I have neither drawing nor picture by

Rossetti. I am sorry for it, for some of his work which I have seen elsewhere I admired very much. Nor have I any letter from him, nor do I remember his being present when I was reading the proofs of "Maud." Indeed I would willingly have known so fine a spirit more intimately, but he kept himself so shut up that it was all but impossible to come at him. What you call "intimacy" never advanced much beyond acquaintance.—TENNYSON, ALFRED LORD, 1885, *Letter, Alfred Lord Tennyson, A Memoir by his Son, p.* 315.

Few brothers were more constantly together or shared one another's feelings and thoughts more intimately, in childhood, boyhood, and well on into mature manhood, than Dante Gabriel and myself. . . . He was always and essentially of a dominant turn; in intellect and in temperament a leader. He was impetuous and vehement, and necessarily, therefore, impatient; easily angered, easily appeased, although the embittered feelings of his later years obscured this amiable quality to some extent; constant and helpful as a friend where he perceived constancy to be reciprocated; free-handed and heedless of expenditure, whether for himself or for others; in family affection warm and equable, and (except in relation to our mother, for whom he had a fondling love), not demonstrative. Never on stilts in matters of the intellect or of aspiration, but steeped in the sense of beauty, and loving, if not always practising, the good; keenly alive also (though some people seem to discredit this now) to the laughable as well as the grave or solemn side of things; superstitious in grain, and anti-scientific to the marrow. Throughout his youth and early manhood I considered him to be remarkably free from vanity, though certainly well equipped in pride; the distinction between these two tendencies was less definite in his closing years. Extremely natural, and therefore totally unaffected in tone and manner, with the naturalism characteristic of Italian blood; good-natured and hearty, without being complaisant or accommodating; reserved at times, yet not haughty; desultory enough in youth, diligent and persistent in maturity; self-centred always, and brushing aside whatever traversed his purpose or his bent. He was very generally and very greatly liked by persons of extremely diverse character; indeed, I think, it can be no exaggeration to say that no one ever disliked him.—ROSSETTI, WILLIAM M., 1887, *ed. The Collected Works of Dante Gabriel Rossetti, Preface.*

Hamlin, the hero of Vernon Lee's novel "Miss Brown" (London, 1884), is said to represent Dante Gabriel Rossetti, the poet. —FREY, ALBERT R., 1888, *Sobriquets and Nicknames, p.* 148.

When I saw Rossetti in his prime, a healthy man, he was the noblest of men, and had a heart so good that I have never known a better, seldom its equal. Illness changed him, but then he was no longer himself. . . . Rossetti was a charming companion; he spoke well and freely on all subjects, literary and artistic, and with much knowledge of contemporary writings. His studio was a favourite resort of men whose names were on title pages, to whom he showed the work he had in progress; and, to his intimate friends, he would sometimes read a poem in a rich and sonorous voice. He had a very just mind. When an author was discussed, whatever might be said against him, he would insist on his merits being remembered. From rivalship and its jealousies he was absolutely free, and his hospitality was without limit. Above all, he was ready at all times to serve a friend, and to exert his influence to that end. — HAKE, GORDON, 1892, *Memoirs of Eighty Years, pp.* 215, 220.

I remember my wild delight in starting for London; and, arrived at Euston, how bewildered and amazed I was with the bustle and excitement of the station. My brother soon discovered me, and we drove off to Mr. Rossetti's house, No. 16 Cheyne Walk, Chelsea. The house seemed to my childish fancy big, heavy and dull. We passed into the hall, which was spacious but rather forbidding at least, to childish fancy—so sombre, so dark. The floor was of black and white marble. About everything there was an atmosphere of departed grandeur, so that I was not surprised to learn that the house had once been tenanted by a lady who ascended the throne of England. To the right hand as we entered was a door leading to what I learned to be the dining-room, but as Mr. Rossetti always had dinner in the studio, the dining-room was never used, and in the course of years it fell into neglect. On the left was the breakfast room, but as Mr.

Rossetti breakfasted in bed, this apartment would have similarly fallen into disuse had not my brother made it his study. Round about in the dark hall were one or two statues, but in still darker corners I could dimly discern old oak cabinets. I had never met a man so full of ideas interesting and attractive to a child. Indeed, now that I look back on it, I feel that Mr. Rossetti was wondrously sweet, tender and even playful with a child, and I am the most struck by this as I reflect that, except for his own little niece and nephew (now, like myself, no longer little), he was not very much accustomed to their troublesome ways and noisy chatter.—CAINE, LILY HALL, 1894, *A Child's Recollections of Rossetti*, New Review, vol. 11, pp. 247, 248, 249, 250.

For Rossetti I had great regard, though I saw not much of him. He seemed to me to be rather an Italian than an Englishman; an Italian of the time of the Medici, not without thoughts and superstitions of that period, a man of genius both in art and literature; one, however, hindering the other, the literary preponderating, and by which he will be best recollected.—LINTON, WILLIAM JAMES, 1894, *Threescore and Ten Years, 1820 to 1890, Recollections*, p. 171.

The life of one of Blake's greatest admirers, D. G. Rossetti, must be forgiven in the light of his achievements, but cannot be forgotten as one of the most dark and shuddering tragedies ever played upon the human stage.—BENSON, ARTHUR CHRISTOPHER, 1896, *Essays*, p. 178.

For the rest it is singular how lovable a man Rossetti appears in his letters here published, and it is not more fair to say that, in his correspondence with Madox Brown, which I have had occasion to study rather minutely, it is difficult to discover anything calculated to make an ordinary reader seriously dislike him. Of the two men who have attacked his person, the one, "Thomas Maitland," has recanted, and the other, the late W. B. Scott, has so liberally negatived the virtues of everybody with whom he came in contact that his Mephistophelean gibes would pass for little in any case. Mr W. Rossetti has, however, so amply confuted most of his allegations that their negative value is increased in a considerable degree.—HUEFFER, FORD M., 1896, *D. G. Rossetti and His Family Letters*, Longman's Magazine, vol 27, p. 469.

Deverell accompanied his mother one day to a milliner's. Through an open door he saw a girl working with her needle; he got his mother to ask her to sit to him. She was the future Mrs. Rossetti. Millais painted her for his Ophelia—wonderfully like her. She was tall and slender, with red coppery hair and bright consumptive complexion, though in these early years she had no striking signs of ill health. She was exceedingly quiet, speaking very little. She had read Tennyson, having first come to know something about him by finding one or two of his poems on a piece of paper which she brought home to her mother wrapped round a pat of butter. Rossetti taught her to draw. She used to be drawing while sitting to him. Her drawings were beautiful, but without force. They were feminine likenesses of his own.— HUGHES, ARTHUR, 1897, *Letters of Dante Gabriel Rossetti to William Allingham*, ed. Hill, p. 4.

Rossetti the man was, before all things, an artist. Many departments of human activity had no existence for him. He was superstitious in grain and anti-scientific to the marrow. His reasoning powers were harldy beyond the average; but his instincts were potent, and his perceptions keen and true. Carried away by his impulses, he frequently acted with rudeness, inconsiderateness, and selfishness. But if a thing could be presented to him from an artistic point of view, he apprehended it in the same spirit as he would have apprehended a subject for a painting or a poem. Hence, if in some respects his actions and expressions seem deficient in right feeling, he appears in other respects the most self-denying and disinterested of men. He was unsurpassed in the filial and fraternal relations; he was absolutely superior to jealousy or envy, and none felt a keener delight in noticing and aiding a youthful writer of merit. His acquaintance with literature was almost entirely confined to works of imagination. Within these limits his critical faculty was admirable, not deeply penetrative, but always embodying the soundest common-sense. His few critical essays are excellent. His memory was almost preternatural, and his knowledge of favorite writers, such as Shakespeare, Dante, Scott, Dumas, exhaustive. It is lamentable that his soundness or judgment should have deserted him in his own case, and that he should have been unable to share the man of genius's serene confidence that not all the powers of dullness and malignity combined can, in the long run, deprive him of a particle of his real due. — GARNETT, RICHARD, 1897, *Dictionary of National Biography, vol.* XLIX, *p.* 288.

Rossetti was one of the most fascinating characters I ever knew, open and expansive, and, when well, he had a vein of the most delightful talk of the things which interested him, mostly those which pertained to art and poetry, the circle of his friends and his and their poetry and painting. To him, art was the dominant interest of existence. . . and he tolerated nothing that sacrificed it to material or purely intellectual subjects. I remember his indignation at the death of Mrs. Wells, the wife of the Royal Academician, herself a talented painter, who died in childbed. "A great artist sacrificed to bringing more kids into the world, as if there were not other women just fit for that!" The artist was to him the *ultima ratio* of humanity, and he used to say frankly that artists had nothing to do with morality, and practically, but in a gentle and benevolent way, he made that the guiding principle of his conduct. Whatever was to his hand was made for his use, and when we went into the house at Robertsbridge [Stillman's own] he at once took the place of master of the house, as if he had invited me, rather than the converse, going through the rooms to select, and saying, "I will take this," of those which suited him best, and "You may have that," of those he had no fancy for. . . . He declined to put himself in comparison with any of his contemporaries, though he admitted his deficiencies as compared to the great Venetians, and repeatedly said that if he had been taught to paint in a great school he would have been a better painter, which was no doubt the truth; for, as he admitted, he had not yet learned the true method of painting. He refused to exhibit in the annual exhibitions, not because he feared the comparison with other modern painters, but because he was indifferent to it, though I have heard him say that he would be glad to exhibit his pictures with those of the old masters, and they would teach him something about his own. . . . The only painter of note I ever heard him speak of with strong dislike was Brett, whom he could not tolerate.—STILLMAN, WILLIAM JAMES, 1901, *The Autobiography of a Journalist, vol.* II, *p.* 470, 471, 472.

Rossetti's nick-name among some of his intimates at that time was the Sultan. For, as a mutual friend explained, everyone flies at the least sign to work for Rossetti. And there seemed to be a suggestion of the original in his inimitable air of easy indolence, his small, finely shaped hands, his supple diction, colloquial yet dignified, and always expressive. No one smoked; the conversation was rapid. . . . Towards the latter part of Rossetti's life he rarely left his house and garden. He depended upon a close circle of friends for society, and in his own way was a sociable man, but he preferred to see his friends and acquaintances by appointment, and woe-betide the too intrusive stranger. . . . Rossetti was an excellent man of business, who held his own with merchants and the great world, yet he seldom stirred from his hearth.—GILCHRIST, HERBERT H., 1901, *Recollections of Rossetti, Lippincott's Magazine, vol.* 68, *pp.* 573, 575, 576.

ART

One face looks out from all his canvasses,
One selfsame figure sits or walks or leans:
We found her hidden just behind those screens,
That mirror gave back all her loveliness.
A queen in opal or in ruby dress,
A nameless girl in freshest summer-greens,
A saint, an angel—every canvass means
The one same meaning, neither more nor less.
He feeds upon her face by day and night,
And she with true kind eyes looks back on him,
Fair as the moon and joyful as the light:
Not wan with waiting, not with sorrow dim;
Not as she is, but was when hope shone bright;
Not as she is, but as she fills his dream.
— ROSSETTI, CHRISTINA, 1856, *In an Artist's Studio*.

A mystic by temperament and right of birth, and steeped in the Italian literature of the middle age, his works in either art are filled with a peculiar fascination and fervour, which attracted to him, from those who enjoyed his intimacy, a rare degree of admiring devotion.—LEIGHTON, SIR FREDERICK, 1882, *Speech at a Banquet of the Royal Academy*.

On Easter-Sunday, the day of joy and resurrection, a great artist left us—one of those whose glorious task it is to create beauty, gladness, pity, and sympathy in a world that would else grow hardened in suffering. This Easter was clouded for many by reason of his death; but his works shall live when the fashion that praises them and the fashion that decries them are alike forgotten; shall live, a possession of ours that was not before our time; created for us to give perpetual pleasure, to bring new joy, and raise fresh feeling for all of us who have eyes and see, and for all who have ears and hear.—ROBINSON, A. MARY F., 1882, *Dante Gabriel Rossetti, Harper's Magazine, vol.* 65, *p.* 701.

First and foremost, then, Rossetti was not British. Whether he was born in England, or whether he visited or did not visit Italy, matters little. His nature was a transplantation, not merely from Italy, but from Mediæval Italy. He breathed time with the pulse of perhaps the most cosmopolitan city in the world, but he lived centuries away. . . . He was with us, but not of us. Without effort, almost without consciousness, we associate him with Madonnas, illumined manuscripts, altar-pieces, and cloisters where work was done not so much for earth as for heaven, where there were no such drums and trumpets and journals, where art was so much nature that it was praise and prayer, uninfluenced by private opinion made public, by the coins of a realm, a ribbon of honour, or the initials of an Academy however Royal—an example surely is the fortified *manner* of his purpose and work which many of us might follow with personal and public advantage. His devotion to his art, his abnegation, his patient waiting for that tide which did not seem to have a flood, and his endurance of what after all was but a local reputation—his whole work in short was a vitalised reproach to much of the paragraph literature and art abroad, and he had, must have had, a greatness of soul worthy the grove which harboured the much enduring Carlyle and the faintless George Eliot.—TIREBUCK, WILLIAM, 1882, *Dante Gabriel Rossetti, his Work and Influences, pp.* 6, 7.

On Thursday I managed to get to the Rossetti exhibition in Savile Row. If you care for my opinion, it is that the pictures are *horrors*, without a single merit. Layard calls them "women with cadaverous bodies and sensual mouths." I say, that part look as if they were going to be hanged, wringing their hands and poking out their chins—and others look as if they had been hanged, and were partially decomposed. It is disgraceful to hear so much nonsense talked by people who know nothing of art, but it is exactly those who are the most presumptuous. People don't talk law to lawyers, or medicine to doctors, but their conceit about art is incredible.—EASTLAKE, LADY, 1883, *Letter to her Nephew, Feb.* 17; *Journals and Correspondence, vol.* II, *p.* 277.

To summarise roughly his achievement purely as a painter, he must be said to have been a splendid but unequal colourist; draughtsman so imperfect that it is only in a few of his pictures that his failure in this respect is not painful, despite the poetry of their intention; and that his sense of composition was equally defective and painful also in his larger works, but it was to a great extent redeemed by the finely decorative arrangement of accessories.—MONKHOUSE, COSMO, 1883, *Rossetti's Paintings at the Royal Academy, The Academy, vol.* 23, *p.* 15.

It is in the earlier work of Rossetti that the true vindication of his fame will ultimately be found, work executed without reference to the public, and for the present somewhat eclipsed in importance by the more disputable achievement of later years. . . . Rossetti influenced most powerfully those who were at the time best prepared to receive his influence—men who could distinguish the newly-discovered principles of his art from its imperfections, and who, feeling deeply the worth of what he followed, knew also the difficulties which he had to encounter in the quest, and could therefore make the right allowance for all defect in the result. To his individual fame as an artist the long interval that has passed between the execution of his best work and its publication to the world has doubtless been a grave disadvantage. On a sudden, and with scarce any time for preparation, we are asked to take the measure of a man who brings a new message of beauty, and who brings it encumbered with certain imperfections of style and practice such as the least inspired members of our school can now find a way to avoid.—CARR, J. COMYNS, 1883, *Rossetti's Influence on Art, English Illustrated Magazine, vol.* 1, *pp.* 29, 30.

The Rossetti note is the note of originality, the note of artistic creation. He invented his own style in poetry as surely as

Shelley invented his; he invented his own style in painting as surely as Titian invented his; he invented his own new type of female beauty as surely as Lionardo invented his. Hence it is that, apart from his own direct personal achievements, Rossetti's reflected influence throughout the entire world of English taste has been as potent almost as the influence of Darwin throughout the entire world of English thought. Not only in our poetry and our painting, but in our decoration, our household furniture—even in our taste for blue china and in the binding of our books, may the spirit of Rossetti be traced directly or indirectly. Whether this influence is to be a permanent force or a fugitive fashion may be a disputable point, but beyond all disputation is its present potency.—WATTS-DUNTON, THEODORE, 1883, *The Truth about Rossetti, Nineteenth Century,* vol. 13, p. 408.

In the future, Rossetti will stand less as a painter-poet than as the leader of the great artistic movement of England in the nineteenth century; his work will be regarded and prized more for what it effected than for its intrinsic merit. As we get a little further removed in time from the controversies which have raged round the modern schools of poetry and painting it will be seen that this was the central figure of the combat, his hand raised the standard round which the foemen rallied.—QUILTER, HARRY, 1883, *The Art of Rossetti, Contemporary Review,* vol. 43, p. 201.

In Rossetti's pictures we find ourselves in the midst of a novel symbolism—a symbolism genuine and deeply felt as that of the fifteenth century, and using once more birds and flowers and stars, colours and lights of the evening or the dawn, to tell of beauties impalpable, spaces unfathomed, the setting and resurrection of no measurable or earthly day.—MYERS, FREDERIC W. H., 1883, *Rossetti and the Religion of Beauty, Cornhill Magazine,* vol. 47, p. 219.

He painted with the highest truth that is consistent with beauty. His is not the vulgar realism which copies just what it sees, but the artistic realism of a Greek statue as compared with the first chance model. It is affirmed, moreover, that he suggests varied thought, the only meaning I can attach to the words "symbolically **sugges**tive." Entering, then, the rooms where Mr. Rossetti's pictures hang, with these instructions as to what we ought to find there, what is it that we see? I, for my own part, see, first of all, monotony; the same face, the same stare, nearly the same attitude, on every wall. I leave aside for the moment the value of these things in themselves, and note only that they do not vary. To me that seems at once, and completely destructive to Mr. Rossetti's claim to be considered other than a most limited artist. . . . There are variations of degree according to the date of the picture, but never differences of kind. . . . Nothing in Mr. Rossetti's pictures is, however, so interesting as the enquiry why we should be called on to admire them. Not, be it observed, because they are good works, and because he painted as other artists the wholesome beauty of the world; but because, in spite of acknowledged faults, weaknesses, and affectations, he has something to say which no other man has said. What that message is nobody tells us.—HANNAY, DAVID, 1883, *The Paintings of Mr. Rossetti, National Review,* vol. 1, pp. 127, 129, 133.

His art is as remote from realism on the one hand, as it is from commonplace artistic fiction on the other; it is at once acutely original, and almost exclusively poetical and imaginative. . . . Rossetti was essentially romantic: I have even heard him express a doubt whether familiar themes and surroundings, and every-day passions and affections, were capable in the modern world of yielding effective material to art at all. At any rate his own instincts lead him irresistibly to the choice of material of an opposite kind; and if his work differs from that of other romantic artists, it is chiefly in that he was more than they were to the manner born. In the midst of the Nineteenth Century he belonged by nature rather than by effort to the Middle Age, the age when colors of life are most vivid and varied, and of the sense of supernatural agencies most alive. Dante Rossetti was thus truly and not artificially akin to the master after whom he was named. His genius resembled that of the real Dante, not indeed in strength, yet in complexion. He had the same cast and tendency of imagination as inspired the poet of the "Vita Nuova" to embody all the passions and experiences of the human heart in forms of many-coloured personification and symbol: he was moreover driven by something like the same unrelaxing stress and fervour of temperament, so that even in middle age, which he had almost reached when I first knew him, it seemed scarcely less true to say of Rossetti than of Dante himself, that

"Like flame within the naked hand,
His body bore his burning heart."

—COLVIN, SIDNEY, 1883, *Rossetti as a Painter, Magazine of Art*, vol. 6, pp. 177, 178.

The companionship of Rossetti and myself soon brought about a meeting with Millais, at whose house one night we found a book of engravings of the frescoes in the Campo Santo at Pisa. It was probably the finding of this book at this special time which caused the establishment of the Pre-Raphaelite Brotherhood. Millais, Rossetti, and myself were all seeking for some sure ground, some starting point for our art which would be secure, if it were ever so humble. As we searched through this book of engravings, we found in them, or thought we found, that freedom from corruption, pride, and disease for which we sought. Here there was at least no trace of decline, no conventionality, no arrogance. Whatever the imperfection, the whole spirit of the art was simple and sincere—was, as Ruskin afterwards said, "eternally and unalterably true." Think what a revelation it was to find such work at such a moment, and to recognize it with the triple enthusiasm of our three spirits. If Newton could say of his theory of gravitation, that his conviction of its truth increased tenfold from the moment in which he got one other person to believe in it, was it wonderful that, when we three saw, as it were, in a flash of lightning, this truth of art, it appealed to us almost with the force of a revolution? Neither then nor afterwards did we affirm that there was not much healthy and good art after the time of Raphael; but it appeared to us that afterwards art was so frequently tainted with this canker of corruption that it was only in the earlier work we could find with certainty absolute health.—HUNT, WILLIAM HOLMAN, 1886, *The Pre-Raphaelite Brotherhood, Contemporary Review*, vol. 49.

The religion of Rossetti's art lies certainly in its spirit rather than in its particular subjects. It is above all things, as Mr. Ruskin says, "romantic" art, as distinct from classical art like Leighton's or Poynter's.—FORSYTH, P. T., 1889, *Religion in Recent Art*, p. 16.

All these paintings, and many other productions, are masterpieces; but they are the fruit of a mind which always worked, and could only work, alone. No painter owes less to the influence of either contemporary or past art; and whatever they may lose by the rejection or lack of that influence, they evidence a nature strong enough to both conceive and construct an art of its own. Each is choice and rare, or splendid, in inventive colour; and, however odd the drawing sometimes is, the thought or emotion is always vividly given. —NETTLESHIP, J. T., 1889, *Dante Gabriel Rossetti as Designer and Writer, The Academy*, vol. 36, p. 363.

His inability to grapple with the technicalities of painting was especially unfortunate, inasmuch as it encouraged him to evade them by confining himself to single figures, whose charm was mainly sensuous, while his power, apart from the magic of his colour, resided principally in his representation of spiritual emotion. The more spiritual he was the higher he rose, and the highest of all in his Dante pictures, where every accessory and detail aids in producing the impression of almost supernatural pathos and purity.—GARNETT, RICHARD, 1897, *Dictionary of National Biography*, vol. XLIX, p. 288.

While the then better-known members of the Brotherhood were enduring a ruthless persecution in public, and achieving large measures of renown, Rossetti was taking his part in the strife, but in a quite different manner, and, as suited his idiosyncrasy, addressing a small but choice and potent circle of men of light and movement. It was not, in fact, until his death many years after that the true position of the artist of "The Beloved" and "Proserpine," of "Dante's Dream" and a score more pictures of the highest art and rarest inspiration was manifest to "the general," and Rossetti's unique honours as painter-poet and poet-painter were acknowledged as they are now.—STEPHENS, FREDERIC GEORGE, 1897, *Social England*, ed. Traill, vol. VI, p. 297.

Any adequate attempt to review the characteristics of Rossetti's own wonderful achievement, and his influence on art at large, would necessarily be lengthy; no brief note would suffice to convey a true appreciation of the originality and the power of this wayward and self-centered genius. The influence he exercised on contemporaries and successors was by no means inconsiderable, in spite of his life having been spent outside the world of art and letters. The position that he occupied in the Pre-Raphaelite Brotherhood has already been alluded to, and what share was actually his in their vivifying crusade may never be really known. But it is admitted that it was he who had the *penchant* for propaganda and proselytising, that his was the fiery soul that was the source of so much poetic aspiration; without him the Brotherhood as such would probably not have come into being, and the existence of the Brotherhood converted the sporadic (and possibly futile) efforts, which the others would doubtless have singly made on their own initiative, into a systematic attempt to introduce a healthier tendency into our national art, an attempt which has had the most far-reaching results. The intense activity of today, in all branches of art, as compared with the lethargy and torpidity of fifty years ago, can be traced very largely to the stand made by these young men and their associates. But, besides the effect that Rossetti had on art, through Pre-Raphaelism, and besides the school of direct followers that have arisen inspired by his work (a group to be treated of later), there is the influence of his own strange ideals and his unique achievements to be traced in the work of many and diverse artists.—BATE, PERCY H., 1899, *The English Pre-Raphaelite Painters, Their Associates and Successors, p.* 48.

The year 1848 marks his transition artistically from boyhood to adolescence, a gracious adolescence adorned by many qualities that we too often look for in vain in an age of tricky cleverness and pernicious skill; an adolescence in which depth of feeling and height of aspiration transcended the power of accomplishment, and no artificial or showy mannerisms obscured the honest endeavour and deep-set seriousness of purpose that characterized, not him alone, but the whole of the small band of workers with which he presently became associated.—MARILLIER, H. C., 1899, *Dante Gabriel Rossetti, an Illustrated Memorial of his Art and Life, p.* 13.

We may call Rossetti a genius; we cannot call him a master.... Rossetti never mastered his instrument. He had a great gift of sympathy, and great talents of expression; but for mastery he substituted an erratic handling of his material. His one settled habit as a painter was to attempt impulsively, ardently, or pertinaciously, to render whatever pleased him, without the supreme instinct for what his technique could accomplish.... One thing at least is certain. Rossetti's must have been an impressive figure, or it would not now be a topic unto the second generation.—HUEFFER, FORD MADOX, 1902, *Rossetti, a Critical Essay on his Art, pp.* 1, 192.

BLESSED DAMOZEL
1850

This paradisal poem, "sweeter than honey or the honeycomb," has found a somewhat further echo than any of its early fellows, and is perhaps known where little else is known of its author's. The sweet intense impression of it must rest for life upon all spirits that ever once received it into their depths, and hold it yet as a thing too dear and fair for praise or price.... No poem shows more plainly the strength and wealth of the workman's lavish yet studious hand.—SWINBURNE, ALGERNON CHARLES, 1870, *The Poems of Dante Gabriel Rossetti, Fortnightly Review, vol.* 13, *p* 564.

The nearest approach to a perfect whole is the "Blessed Damozel," a peculiar poem, placed first in the book, perhaps by accident, perhaps because it is a key to the poems which follow. This poem appeared in a rough shape many years ago in the *Germ,* an unwholesome periodical started by the Pre-Raphaelites, and suffered, after gasping through a few feeble numbers, to die the death of all such publications. In spite of its affected title, and of numberless affectations throughout the text, the "Blessed Damozel" has great merits of its own, and a few lines of real genius. We have heard it described as a record of actual grief and love, or, in simple words, the apotheosis of one actually lost by the writer; but, without having any private knowledge of the circumstances of its composition, we feel that such an account of the poem is inadmissible. It does not contain one single note of sorrow. It is a "composition," and a clever one.—BUCHANAN, ROBERT (THOMAS MAITLAND),

1871, *The Fleshly School of Poetry: Mr. D. G. Rossetti, Contemporary Review*, vol. 18, p. 340.

The "Blessed Damozel" is a very highly imaginative subject—as far removed indeed from "realism" in the vulgar sense as possible; and yet, in imagining it, the poet never seems to have lost sight for a moment of the colour and detail of his thought.—FORMAN, H. BUXTON, 1871, *Our Living Poets*, p. 191.

For pathos, and purity, and mediævalism of the most exquisite kind, this poem may fitly be compared with the missal-paintings of Fra Angelico.—EDWARDS, AMELIA B., 1878, ed. *A Poetry Book, Second Series, The Modern Poets*, p. 326, note.

"The Blessed Damozel" is perhaps the most complete vision of flesh and blood which ever was transported into the heavenly dominion; her arm warms the bar upon which she leans as she looks down from the sky to see her lover wandering forlorn on the earth. For this very reason, no doubt, as well as for the poetry, this poem achieved the conquest even of the general reader, to whose halting imagination so much help was given. The difficulties of framing a paradise which shall respond to the highest aspirations of the mind has been very largely acknowledged.—OLIPHANT, MARGARET O. W., 1892, *The Victorian Age of English Literature*, p. 443.

Whether considered in itself according to its qualities of intense passion, spirituality, and imaginativeness, or as the work of a youth of eighteen, may be said to stand alone in modern poetry.—DAWSON, W. J., 1892, *Quest and Vision*, p. 270.

Of Rossetti's lyrical verse one poem has had the good or ill fortune to attain something like popularity,—a popularity due, it is to be feared, to its picturesque and quaint phraseology rather than to its high and beautiful imaginative quality. "The Blessed Damozel," written at nineteen, remains one of the most captivating and original poems of the century,—a lyric full of bold and winning imagery and charged with imaginative fervour and glow; a vision upon which painter and poet seemed to have wrought with a single hand; a thing of magical beauty, whose spell is no more to be analyzed than the beauty of the night when the earliest stars crown it.—MABIE, HAMILTON WRIGHT, 1893, *Essays in Literary Interpretation*, p. 86.

Is the most spontaneous and convincing of all his shorter poems. It seems to have sprung straight from the heart of the boy-poet in a sort of prophetic rapture, ere he knew the sorrow which he sang, and which his song should ease, as the most perfect art can sometimes ease, in other souls, for generations to come. Its strength lies in the very acme of tenderness; its source in the purest strain of common human feeling—the passionate, insatiable craving of the faithful heart for the continuity of life and love beyond the tomb, and the deep sense of the poverty of celestial compromises to satisfy the mourner on either side of the gulf that Death has set between. Here again is the true romantic note—the insistence of the joy and glory of the physical world, the delight in the early manifestations of affection, and the awed, plaintive conflict of impatience with resignation under the mystery of parting and transition to an unknown state.—WOOD, ESTHER, 1894, *Dante Rossetti and the Pre-Raphaelite Movement*, p. 302.

Rossetti's "Blessed Damozel" is not based upon the scientific knowledge of his time. . . . Rossetti is not in a condition to understand, or even to see the real, because he is incapable of the necessary attention; and since he feels this weakness he persuades himself, in conformity with human habit, that he does not wish to do what in reality he cannot do. "What is it to me," he once said, "whether the earth revolves around the sun or the sun around the earth?" To him it is of no importance, because he is incapable of understanding it. It is, of course, impossible to go so deeply into all Rossetti's poems as into the "Blessed Damozel;" but it is also unnecessary, since we should everywhere meet with the same mixture of transcendentalism and sensuality, the same shadowy ideation, the same senseless combinations of mutually incompatible ideas.—NORDAU, MAX, 1895, *Degeneration*, p. 91.

Besides the touching emotion of the poem, the wonderful beauty and reach of its imagery, it has a melody sweeter and more sensitive than Rossetti ever attained afterward.—MOODY, WILLIAM VAUGHN, AND LOVETT, ROBERT MORSS, 1902, *A History of English Literature*, p. 343.

SISTER HELEN
1870

In "Sister Helen" we touch the key-note of Rossetti's creative gift. Even the superstitions which forms the basis of the ballad owes something of its individual character to the invention and poetic bias of the poet. The popular superstitions of the Middle Ages were usually of two kinds only. First, there were those that arose out of a jealous catholicism, always glancing towards heresy; and next there were those that laid their account neither with orthodoxy nor unbelief, and were purely pagan. The former were the offspring of fanaticism; the latter of an appeal to appetite or passion, or fancy, or perhaps intuitive reason directed blindly or unconsciously toward natural phenomena. The superstition involved in "Sister Helen" partakes wholly of neither character, but partly of both, with an added element of demonology.—CAINE, HALL, 1882, *Recollections of Dante Gabriel Rossetti, p. 25.*

"Sister Helen" is a poem to which no extracts can do justice. It must be read as a whole. Each verse is practically inseparable from the other, and the slow accumulation of scarcely defined horror is part of the mystery and might of the poem. Slight as are the changes of the burden, they are weighty in significance, and the answers of the heroine, with their grave acquiescence in the soul's death, which she knows is the price of her deeds, have dramatic force that is indescribable.—KNIGHT, JOSEPH, 1887, *Life of Dante Gabriel Rossetti (Great Writers), p. 111.*

In weirdness and pathos, tragic suggestion and word wizardry, this ballad is unsurpassed. Its forty-two short verses—originally only thirty-three—unfold the whole story of the wronged woman's ruthless vengeance on her false lover as she watches the melting of the "waxen man" which, according to the old superstitions, is to carry with it the destruction, body and soul, of him in whose likeness it was fashioned. The innocent prattle and the half-ignorant narrative and the questioning of the "little brother," who watches and reports the incidents attending the working of the charm that "sister Helen" has contrived, helps immensely in giving shape and strength to the poet's conception; and the dirge-like refrain makes the ballad indeed a splendid example of what Mr. Theodore Watts has aptly, if somewhat pedantically, called "the renascence of wonder."—FOX-BOURNE, H. R., 1887, *Dante Gabriel Rossetti, Gentleman's Magazine, vol. 262, p. 603.*

Of course the time must come when the poetry of England is melted down and merged into an anthology, and it is probable that the "Sister Helen," as being the strongest emotional poem, as yet, in the language, will be among the most lasting works, and escape dissolution for a long time to come; perhaps will survive all change. And here a very remarkable fact thrusts itself before the mind; a representative one, which is that if Rossetti had written not another line besides this poem, his genius would have appeared all the greater: for lesser work is a fatal commentary on greater.—HAKE, GORDON, 1892, *Memoirs of Eighty Years, p. 219.*

JENNY
1870

I just hear from mamma, with a pang of remorse, that you have ordered a copy of my Poems. You may be sure I did not fail to think of you when I inscribed copies to friends and relatives; but, to speak frankly, I was deterred from sending it to you by the fact of the book including one poem ("Jenny") of which I felt uncertain whether you would be pleased with it. I am not ashamed of having written it (indeed, I assure you that I would never have written it if I thought it unfit to be read with good results), but I feared it might startle you somewhat.—ROSSETTI, DANTE GABRIEL, 1870, *Letter to his Aunt, May 24; Letters to William Allingham, ed. Hill, p. 249.*

It is something very like morbidly gratified sexual sensuousness, too, that we discover in "Jenny," a poem in which a young man "moralizes" a young woman of the town whom he has accompanied home from a place of amusement, and comments on her way of life and probable character and fate after the manner of Mr. Browning in his analytical moods. It is the fashion to say of such things, that, although it is difficult to see how the author contrived it, he has managed with consummate skill to avoid the intrinsic indelicacy of his subject. As a matter of fact, however, it may be doubted if the inherent delicacy is not just what he has not avoided; and whether all writers who practise this sort of morbid anatomy do not do something towards debauching the minds of a certain number of their readers. Such things tend, we imagine, to confound the distinction between morality and immorality, and have much the same effect as the prurient moral novels with which M. Feuillet, or the excellent M. Dumas *fils* occasionally buttresses the foundations of society.— DENNETT, J. R., 1870, *Rossetti's Poems, North American Review*, vol. 111, p. 478.

After reading it again and again, and ever willing to think the fault must lie with myself, I have each time come to the same conclusion, that the pathos Mr. Swinburne considers its distinctive quality is *literary* pathos, and not sprung in the first instance from a sorrowful heart or a deep personal sense of "the pity of it, the pity of it," and that, in consequence, "a Divine pity" does *not* fill it. I am aware that such a judgment will seem to many absurd, nevertheless I still consider much of "Jenny" to be rather cold-blooded speculation, and the poem itself as a whole by no means entitled to rank as "great among the few greatest works of the artist." This does not prevent it from being, in my opinion, still a fine poem, only I cannot admit what I feel to be an exaggerated claim for it.—SHARP, WILLIAM, 1882, *Dante Gabriel Rossetti, A Record and a Study*, p. 331.

It is wisest to hazard at the outset all unfavorable comment by the frankest statement of the story of the poem. But the *motif* of it is a much higher thing. "Jenny" embodies an entirely distinct phase of feeling, yet the poet's root impulse is therein the same as in the case of "The Blessed Damozel." No two creatures could stand more widely apart as to outward features than the dream of the sainted maiden and the reality of the frail and fallen girl; yet the primary prompting and the ultimate outcome are the same. The ardent longing after ideal purity in womanhood, which in the one gave birth to a conception whereof the very sorrow is but excess of joy found expression in the other through a vivid presentment of the nameless misery or unwomanly dishonour.— CAINE, HALL, 1882, *Recollections of Dante Gabriel Rossetti*, p. 20.

"Jenny," perhaps, being cast in a more meditative form, lacks the poignancy and fervour of the utterance which comes, in "A Last Confession," from the lips of the sinner himself instead of from the spectator merely, but it surpasses all contemporary studies of its kind in its bold and masterly handling of a difficult theme. Both, however, are distinct from the lyric poems in that their abruptness of movement and irregularity of structure are the abruptness and irregularity of quick dramatic thought, impatient of metrical elaboration, surcharging the poetic vehicle with subject matter; an effect which must not be confused with the ruggedness of the true ballad-form, whose broken music haunts the ear by its very waywardness and variety of rhythm, and gains its end by a studied artlessness the more exquisite for its apparent unconstraint.—WOOD, ESTHER, 1894, *Dante Rossetti and the Pre-Raphaelite Movement*, p. 307.

KING'S TRAGEDY
1881

Even Rossetti's warmest admirers would hardly have given him credit for the power to grapple with a historic subject displayed in this remarkable work, perhaps his master piece in narrative poetry, even as "Cloud Confines" is the highest effort in the field of contemplative not to say philosophic verse.—HUEFFER, FRANCIS, 1882, *Ballads and Poems, Tauchnitz Ed., Memoir*, p. 23.

Perhaps, if one had to name a single composition of his to readers desiring to make acquaintance with him for the first time, one would select: "The King's Tragedy"—that poem so moving, so popularly dramatic, and lifelike.— PATER, WALTER, 1883, *Appreciations*, p. 227.

Is one of the most powerful of Rossetti's poems.—OLIPHANT, MARGARET O. W., 1892, *The Victorian Age of English Literature*, p. 444.

In "The King's Tragedy" Rossetti was poaching on Scott's own preserves, the territory of national history and legend. If we can guess how Scott would have handled the same story, we shall have an object lesson in two contrasted kinds of romanticism. Scott could not have bettered the grim ferocity of the murder scene, nor have equalled, perhaps, the tragic shadow of doom which is thrown over Rossetti's poem by the triple warning of the weird woman. But the sense of the historical environment, the sense of the actual in places and persons, would have been stronger in his version.—BEERS, HENRY A., 1901, *A History of English Romanticism in the Nineteenth Century*, p. 313.

HOUSE OF LIFE

This "House of Life" has in it so many mansions, so many halls of state and bowers of music, chapels for worship and chambers for festival, that no guest can declare on a first entrance the secret of its scheme. Spirit and sense together, eyesight and hearing and thought, are absorbed in splendor of sounds and glory of colours distinguishable only by delight. But the scheme is solid and harmonious; there is no waste in this luxury of genius: the whole is lovelier than its loveliest part. Again and again may one turn the leaves in search of some one poem or some two which may be chosen for sample and thanksgiving; but there is no choice to be made. Sonnet is poured upon sonnet, and song hands on the torch to song; and each in turn (as another poet has said of the lark's note falling from the height of dawn),

"Rings like a golden jewel down a golden stair."

There are no poems of the class in English— I doubt if there be any even in Dante's Italian—so rich at once and pure. Their golden affluence of images and jewel-coloured words never once disguises the firm outline, the justice and chastity of form. No nakedness could be more harmonious, more consummate in its fleshy sculpture, than the imperial array and ornament of this august poetry. Mailed in gold as of the morning and girdled with gems of strange water, the beautiful body as of a carven goddess gleams through them tangible and taintless, without spot or default.—SWINBURNE, ALGERNON CHARLES, 1870, *The Poems of Dante Gabriel Rossetti, Fortnightly Review,* vol. 13, p. 553.

Admirable as are his ballads, "The House of Life," recording a personal experience transmuted by the imagination, is Rossetti's highest achievement in verse. There are two other "sonnet-sequences," and only two, in English poetry which can take rank beside it, "The Sonnets of Shakespere" and "Sonnets from the Portuguese." —DOWDEN, EDWARD, 1887, *Victorian Literature, Transcripts and Studies*, p. 229.

"The House of Life," described as a sonnet-sequence, is undoubtedly the noblest contribution in this form of verse yet made to our literature. It should be studied with Shakespeare's sonnets and with Mrs. Browning's "Sonnets from the Portuguese," in order that its wealth of thought, its varied beauty of phrase, and its depth of feeling may be comprehended. It tells the same heart story, but in how different a key! The hundred and more sonnets which compose it are a revelation of the poet's nature; all its ideals, its passions, its hopes and despairs, its changeful moods, are reflected there; and there, too, a man's heart beats, in one hour with the freedom of a great joy, and in another against the iron bars of fate.—MABIE, HAMILTON WRIGHT, 1893 *Essays in Literary Interpretation*, p. 90.

We miss in "The House of Life" the spontaneity and simple charm of the early lyrics, though in recompense we gain the pleasure which comes from hearing a complex musical instrument played with mature mastership. — MOODY, WILLIAM VAUGHN, AND LOVETT, ROBERT MORSS, 1902, *A History of English Literature*, p. 346.

SONNETS

Sonnets . . . unexampled in the English language since Shakespeare's for depth of thought and skill and felicity of execution. —MORRIS, WILLIAM, 1870, *The Academy,* vol. 1, p. 199.

Undoubtedly the greatest of living sonneteers. . . . Mr. Rossetti's imaginative treatment is both spiritual and impassioned, the sensuous and the supersensuous are inextricably blended, and when love is the theme of his utterances it is for the most part a love of which we know not the body from the soul. There is a noteworthy integrity in his love sonnets which gives them a peculiar interest and value. No element is wanting, none is unduly preponderant.—NOBLE, JAMES ASHCROFT, 1880, *The Sonnet in England and Other Essays*, pp. 57, 58.

Yet, if the qualities which I have attempted to describe as characteristic of Mr. Rossetti, lead him occasionally to fatigue us, and snare him in the pitfall of Johnsonian pomposity, these same qualities are the sources of his strength. It is by right of them that he never turns out a sonnet which is not according to his own conception perfected, and which we may not with confidence accept as stamped with his approval. . . . His sonnets are unrefreshing. We rise from them without exhilaration, without that sense of liberated oxygen, which is communicated by Keats, by Wordsworth, at their best. We almost invariably miss in them the feeling of reality, the freshness of the outer air, a quick and vital correlation to actual humanity. They are the cabinet productions of an artist's intellect engrossed in self. So pungent is the aroma, so hot the colour, so loaded the design, so marked the melodies, that we long even for the wilding charm of weaker singers. . . . Those who still include Mr. Rossetti in what was called "the fleshly school," can only do so by appealing to isolated phrases in his sonnets. In these, as it seems to me, some imperfect apprehension of the right relation of aesthetic language to very natural things, some want of taste in fine, led the poet to extend in habitual *emphase* of his style to details which should have been slurred over. His defined incisive way of writing fixes the mind repulsively on physical images and "poems of privacy." The effect is vulgar and ill-bred. We shrink from it as from something nasty, from a discord to which education and good manners had rendered us uncomfortably sensible. — SYMONDS, JOHN ADDINGTON, 1882, *Notes on Mr. D. G. Rossetti's New Poems*, Macmillan's Magazine, vol. 45, pp. 324, 325, 327.

Beautiful as some of Mr. Rossetti's work is, his expression in the sonnets surely became obscure from over-involution, and excessive *fioriture* of diction. But then Rossetti's style is no doubt formed considerably upon that of the Italian poets. One is glad, however, that, this time, at all events, the right man has "got the porridge."—NOEL, RODEN, 1886, *The Poetry of Tennyson, Essay on Poetry and Poets*, p. 234.

One name, however, stands out from all others since Wordsworth and Mrs. Browning, like a pine tree out of a number of graceful larches. Dante Gabriel Rossetti is not only one of the great poets of the century, but the one English poet whose sonnet-work can genuinely be weighed in the balance with that of Shakespeare and with that of Wordsworth. No influence is at present more marked than his: its stream is narrower than that of Tennyson and Browning, but the current is deep, and its fertilizing waters have penetrated far and wide into the soil. The author of "The House of Life" thus holds a remarkable place in the literary and artistic history of the second Victorian epoch. No critic of this poet's work will have any true grasp of it who does not recognize that "Rossetti" signifies that something of greater import than the beautiful productions of one man—the historian of the brilliant period in question will work in the dark if he is unable to perceive one of the chief well-springs of the flood, if he should fail to recognize the relationship between radical characteristics of the time and the man who did so much to inaugurate or embody them.—SHARP, WILLIAM, 1886, *Sonnets of this Century, Introduction*, p. lxxi.

Upon the sonnet he lavished the wealth of his imagination and the treasures of his research. Whatever words most noble, graceful, picturesque, or significant he could, by thought and research, add to his vocabulary were reserved for his sonnets. These he polished and recast with the same earnestness that he devoted to his pictures, and his youthful work was not seldom entirely re-shapen. The principle on which he wrote was that in each sonnet a thought should be crystallized and wrought into a gem. — KNIGHT, JOSEPH, 1887, *Life of Dante Gabriel Rossetti (Great Writers)*, p. 125.

By nature and training he became possessed of great sympathy with the form and used it freely. The "Dark Glass" is one of his strongest, and in it as in many of his poems he paints love and life against a sombre background. While his sonnets are artistic, they do not linger in memory like more spontaneous utterances by Wordsworth, Milton, Keats, Mrs. Browning, etc. But it is doubtless unfair to compare him with such great poets. He was more painter than philosopher or singer, yet he felt keenly, and his lines often throb with stress and pain.—CRANDALL, CHARLES H., 1890, ed. *Representative Sonnets by American Poets*, p. 75.

Mr. Rossetti has written a larger number of noble sonnets than any other poet of our time. For this form he reserved the best of all his powers, and in it he achieved a success that will be absolutely unquestioned. —GRAHAM, RICHARD D., 1897, *The Masters of Victorian Literature*, p. 351.

These sonnets alone would suffice to

insure the immortality of the poet; for they must be ranked no lower than with the greatest in the language,—with those of Shakespeare and of Milton, of Wordsworth and of Keats.—PAYNE, WILLIAM MORTON, 1897, *Library of the World's Best Literature*, ed. Warner, vol. XXI, p. 12415.

GENERAL

I have at length had the pleasure of reading your manuscripts, but am still forced to be very brief. I hope the agreeableness of my remarks will make amends for their shortness, since you have been good enough to constitute me a judge of powers of which you ought to have no doubt. I felt perplexed, it is true, at first, by the translations, which, though containing evidences of a strong feeling of the truth and simplicity of the originals, appeared to me harsh, and want correctness in the versification. I guess indeed that you are altogether not so musical as pictorial. But, when I came to the originals of your own, I recognized an unquestionable poet, thoughtful, imaginative, and with rare powers of expression. I hailed you as such at once, without any misgiving; and, besides your Dantesque heavens (without any hell to spoil them), admired the complete and genial round of your sympathies with humanity. I know not what sort of painter you are. If you paint as well as you write, you may be a rich man; or at all events, if you do not care to be rich, may get leisure enough to cultivate your writing.—HUNT, LEIGH, 1848, *To Rossetti, March 31*; *Dante Gabriel Rossetti*, ed. Rossetti, vol. I, p. 122.

In no poems is the spontaneous and habitual interpenetration of matter and manner, which is the essence of poetry, more complete than in these. An original and subtile beauty of execution expresses the deep mysticism of thought which in some form and degree is not wanting certainly to any poets of the modern school, but which in Mr. Rossetti's work is both great in degree and passionate in kind. Nor in him has it any tendency to lose itself amid allegory or abstractions; indeed, instead of turning human life into symbols of things vague and not understood, it rather gives to the very symbols the personal life and variety of mankind. No poem in this book is without the circle of this realizing mysticism, which deals wonderingly with all real things that can have poetic life given them by passion, and refuses to have to do with any invisible things that in the wide scope of its imagination cannot be made perfectly distinct and poetically real.—MORRIS, WILLIAM, 1870, *The Academy*, vol. 1, p. 199.

Opinions must differ; but the prevailing opinion, we should say, will be that we have in Mr. Rossetti another poetical man, and a man markedly poetical, and of a kind apparently though not radically different from any other of our secondary writers of poetry, but that we have not in him a true poet of any weight. He certainly has taste, and subtlety, and skill, and sentiment in excess, and excessive sensibility, and a sort of pictorial sensuousness of conception which gives warmth and vividness to the imagery that embodies his feelings and desires. But he is all feelings and desires; and he is of the earth, earthy, though the earth is often bright and beautiful pigments; of thought and imagination he has next to nothing. At last one discovers, what has seemed probable from the first, that one has been in company with a lyrical poet of narrow range; with a man who has nothing to say but of himself; and of himself as the yearning lover, mostly a sad one, of a person of the other sex. . . . Considered as a lyrical poet pure and simple, a lyrical verse-making lover, apart from whatever praise or blame belongs to him as a Pre-Raphaelite in poetry whose Pre-Raphaelitism is its most obvious feature, it will be found that Mr. Rossetti must be credited with an intensity of feeling which is overcast almost always with a sort of morbidness, and which usually trenches on the bound of undue sensuousness of tone.—DENNETT, J. R., 1870, *Rossetti's Poems, North American Review*, vol. 111, pp. 474, 475.

He is distinctively a colourist, and of his capabilities in colour we cannot speak, though we should guess that they are great; for if there is any good quality by which his poems are specially marked, it is a great sensitiveness to hues and tints as conveyed in poetic epithet. These qualities, which impress the casual spectator of the photographs from his pictures, are to be found abundantly among his verses. There is the same thinness and transparency of design, the same combination of the simple and the grotesque, the same morbid deviation from healthy forms of life, the same sense of weary, wasting, yet exquisite sensuality; nothing virile, nothing tender, nothing completely sane; a superfluity of extreme sensibility, of delight in beautiful forms, hues, and tints, and a deep-seated indifference to all agitating forces and agencies, all tumultuous griefs and sorrows, all the thunderous stress of life, and all the straining storm of speculation. Mr. Morris is often pure, fresh, and wholesome as his own great model;. Mr. Swinburne startles us more than once by some fine flash of insight; but the mind of Mr. Rossetti is like a glassy mere, broken only by the dive of some water-bird or the hum of winged insects, and brooded over by an atmosphere of insufferable closeness, with a light blue sky above it, sultry depths mirrored within it, and a surface so thickly sown with water-lilies that it retains its glassy smoothness even in the strongest wind. . . . We question if there is anything in the unfortunate "Poems and Ballads" quite so questionable on the score of thorough nastiness as any pieces in Mr. Rossetti's collection. Mr. Swinburne was wilder, more outrageous, more blasphemous, and his subjects were more atrocious in themselves; yet the hysterical tone slew the animalism, the furiousness of epithet lowered the sensation; and the first feeling of disgust at such themes as "Laus Veneris" and "Anactoria," faded away into comic amazement. It was only a little mad boy letting off squibs; not a great strong man, who might be really dangerous to society. "I *will* be naughty!" screamed the little boy; but, after all, what did it matter? It is quite different, however, when a grown man, with the self-control and easy audacity of actual experience, comes forward to chronicle his amorous sensations, and, first proclaiming in a loud voice his literary maturity, and consequent responsibility, shamelessly prints and publishes such a piece of writing as this sonnet on "Nuptial Sleep."— BUCHANAN, ROBERT (THOMAS MAITLAND), 1871, *The Fleshly School of Poetry: Mr. D. G. Rossetti, Contemporary Review*, vol. 18, pp. 336, 338.

He is thoroughly at home among romantic themes and processes, while a feeling like that of Dante exalts the maturer portion of his emblematic verse. . . . Throughout his poetry we discern a finesse, a regard for detail, and a knowledge of color and sound, that distinguish this master of the Neo-Romantic school. His end is gained by simplicity and sure precision of touch. He knows exactly what effect he desires, and produces it by a firm stroke of color, a beam of light, a single musical note. . . . His lyrical faculty is exquisite; not often swift, but chaste, and purely English. . . . His verse is compact of tenderness, emotional ecstasy, and poetic fire. The spirit of the master whose name he bears clothes him as with a white garment. — STEDMAN, EDMUND CLARENCE, 1875-87, *Victorian Poets*, pp. 360, 361, 365, 366.

Mr. Dante G. Rossetti has written some sonnets which are probably entitled to rank with the best of their kind at any time, and one or two ballads of fierce, impassioned style, which seem as if they came straight from the heart of the old northern ballad world.—MCCARTHY, JUSTIN, 1880, *A History of our Own Times from the Accession of Queen Victoria to the Berlin Congress*, vol. IV, ch. LXVII, p. 130.

Mr. Rossetti's new volume is not versified *pseudo*-philosophy; nor rhetoric simulating passion; nor factitious simplicities; nor a mannered cleverness; nor a freshly discovered affectation. The best part of it is that rare and wonderful thing, mere poetry—clustered fruit full of the scent and colour of the sun. Such a gift of beauty brings to us for a season that audacity which a sudden accession to one's wealth or power imparts; we seem to accept life on easier and larger terms. . . . The ballads in Mr. Rossetti's volume show his craftsmanship on a larger scale than anything hitherto published.—DOWDEN, EDWARD, 1881, *Ballads and Sonnets, The Academy*, vol. 20, p. 385.

Mr. Rossetti's poetry is contained in two volumes, one published in 1870, the other in 1881. To begin with the first volume, you cannot open it without being struck by the marked individuality of manner, and also by the signs of poetic power which meet you on the surface. When you have entered a little farther into the precinct, you become aware that you have passed into an atmosphere which is strange, and certainly not bracing—the fragrances that cross your path are those of musk and incense rather than of heather and mountain thyme. It takes an effort to get into the mood which shall appreciate this poetry—you require to get acclimatized to the atmosphere that surrounds you. And, as you proceed, you meet with things which make you doubt whether you would much desire the acclimatization. At the same time you are aware of the presence of genuine poetic power, even though you may be far from admiring some of its manifestations. . . . As to the substance of the first volume, the tone of sentiment which certainly predominates is the erotic. So we call it, for it has little in common with the pure and noble devotion which the best of our older poets have immortalized. This amatory or erotic sentiment is unpleasant in the poem called "Eden Bower, or Lilith;" it is revolting in the ballad of "Troy Town." But the taint of fleshliness which runs through too many of the other poems reaches its climax in some of the twenty-eight sonnets, entitled "The House of Life." These sonnets not only express, but brood over thoughts and imaginations which should not be expressed, or even dwelt on in secret thought. Not all the subtle association or elaboration of words, nor dainty imagery in which they are dressed, can hide or remove the intrinsic earthliness that lies at the heart of them, and one cannot imagine why—one cannot but regret that—they should even have been composed by a man of so much genius.—SHAIRP, J. C., 1882, Æsthetic Poetry, Contemporary Review, vol. 42, pp. 21, 23, 24.

If Mr. Woolner's is thus a sculptor's poem, Mr. Rossetti's work is, as we have said, distinctively poet's work; his poems and his pictures are a poet's. Nevertheless, his own best art of words, has always enviously gained some beauty, some riches, some lovely power, from the habit which the use of colour and pencil must have kept alive in him—the habit which as children we all possess, and generally lose as we grow older and more literary—the indistinctive habit of making definite mental pictures. He has preserved this, and yet has foregone nothing of the literary and poetic power over thought and emotion.—MEYNELL, ALICE, 1882, The Brush, The Chisel and the Pen, Art Journal, p. 86.

Much of his best work, as we perceive without these metaphors to guide us, is chryselephantine, overwrought with jewelry. Thought and feeling do not play with him like imps imprisoned in translucent gems. He works for them a gorgeous shrine of precious wood and oriental ivory, inlays it with glossy gold, and sets it round with jewels. The limpidity which distinguishes the best Italian sonnets, the fluidity of music evolved as though by some spontaneous effort, the harmony of language produced by simple sequences of fresh uncolored words, are not his qualities, any more than is the wayward grace of the true ballad. Elaboration is everywhere apparent. Rigidity, rather than elasticity, opaque splendour rather than translucency, determine the excellence of even his noblest achievement.—SYMONDS, JOHN ADDINGTON, 1882, Notes on Mr. D. G. Rossetti's New Poems, Macmillan's Magazine, vol. 45, p. 323.

He held in all things to the essential and not to the accidental; he preferred the dry grain of musk to a diluted flood of perfume. An Italian by birth and deeply moved by all things Italian, he never visited Italy; a lover of ritual and a sympathizer with all the mysteries of the Roman creed, he never joined the Catholic Church; a poet whose form and substance alike influenced almost all the men of his generation, he was more than forty years of age before he gave his verse to the public; a painter who considered the attitude of the past with more ardor and faith than almost any artist of his time, he never chose to visit the churches or galleries of Europe.—GOSSE, EDMUND, 1882, Dante Gabriel Rossetti, Century Magazine, vol. 24, p. 719.

His work is characterised by intellectual subtlety, calm dignity of emotional reference, and pungent ideal sympathy, rather than by depth and overflow of feeling and storm and majesty of passion; while it is marked by patient elaboration and exquisite grace of finish rather than by strength of structural design and massive grandeur of form and feature. It is by the assiduous cultivation of such powers as are clearly indicated by workmanship of this kind that Mr. Rossetti has at length proved himself to be one of the finest poetical artists in our literature, and particularly one of the few really great sonneteers. . . . The "House of Life" is a standing answer to those that carp at the sonnet on the ground of its mechanical limitations and its little narrowness and general futility. We may object to Mr. Rossetti's method, we may feel that the hill air is an indispensable antidote to his moving and relaxing strains, we may say that he is simply wasting words for the sake of warm glow and rich colour; but all that will not affect the excellent structure and the undoubted vitality of these sonnets.—BAYNE, THOMAS, 1882, *The Poetry of Dante Gabriel Rossetti, Fraser's Magazine*, vol. 105, pp. 377, 381.

Oh, master of mysterious harmony!
Well hast thou proven to us the right divine
To wear thy name. The glorious Florentine
Had hailed thee comrade on the Stygian sea,—
Exiled from haunts of men, and sad as he:
And the strong angel of the inner shrine,—
Stooped he not sometimes to that soul of thine,
On messages of radiant ministry?
Thy spiritual breath was the cathedral air
Of the dead ages. Saints have with thee talked,
As with a friend. Thou knewest the sacred thrills
That moved Angelico to tears and prayer;
And thou as in a daily dream has walked
With Perugino midst his Umbrian hills.
—PRESTON, MARGARET J., 1883, *Dante Gabriel Rossetti, Literary World, March* 15.

Not only had Rossetti more genuine romantic feeling than any man of this century, but more knowledge of romance.—WATTS-DUNTON, THEODORE, 1883, *The Truth About Rossetti, Nineteenth Century*, vol. 13, p. 414.

Rossetti's luscious lines seldom fail to cast a spell.—BIRRELL, AUGUSTINE, 1884, *Mr. Browning's Poetry, Obiter Dicta*, p. 94.

With the choice of two media, in the use of both of which he was equally proficient, Rossetti made naturally frequent experiments as to which was the better adapted to his powers. To this moment the question remains unanswered. Unlike some poets, however, who have employed verse for the purpose of illustrating problems, polemical and metaphysical, with the result that they are regarded as poets among philosophers and as philosophers among poets, Rossetti has been received with enthusiasm in both capacities by both poets and painters. It may, indeed, be said that he is a painter's painter, and a poet's poet.—KNIGHT, JOSEPH, 1887, *Life of Dante Gabriel Rossetti (Great Writers)*, p. 131.

Dante Rossetti wrote as he painted, aiming by the greatest possible expenditure of labour to obtain the most purely artistic result. The end justified the means. Some, not all, of his sonnets may be censured as too pictorial, and thus deficient in the grave simplicity of thought befitting the sonnet; but as a writer of ballads, some of quite epical proportions, he is absolutely unrivalled, and his lyrics either exhibit the novel effect of an Italian graft upon English literature or are entirely without pattern or precedent. The very exquisiteness of his poetry nevertheless limited the sphere of his influence on the world at large, which he had ample power to have moved if his æsthetic conscience would have permitted.—GARNETT, RICHARD, 1887, *The Reign of Queen Victoria*, ed. Ward, vol. II, p. 486.

In endeavoring to do justice to Rossetti it must be remembered that, though born and bred in England, he was an Italian by blood and sympathy. His acquaintance with Englishmen and English books was by no means wide. Love, the constant theme of his art, is in some of his most important poems, not the English love whose stream is steady affection and only its occasional eddies passion, and which, when disappointed, does not cease to be love though it becomes sorrow: but the Italian ardour, in perennial crisis, which stabs its rival and hates its object, if she refuses its satisfaction, as ardently as it worships her so long as there is hope. The limitations, also, which characterise Rossetti's poetry belong to Italian poetry itself. There is little breadth in it, but much acuteness. It is therefore quite unfair to try an essentially Italian poet, like Rossetti, by comparing his works with the classical poetry of a nation which, for combined breadth and height, far surpasses the poetry of all other languages present and past, with the doubtful exception of the Greek. The English language itself is not made for Italian thought and passion. It has about four times as many vowel sounds as Italian and a corresponding consonantal power; that is to say, it differs from the Italian about as much as an organ differs from a flute. Rossetti uses little besides the flute-notes of our English organ; and, if he had made himself complete master of those notes, it would have been the most that could have been expected of him.—PATMORE, COVENTRY, 1889–98, *Principle in Art, etc.*, p. 101.

Such was Rossetti as he appeared to me. I am conscious of no sins of commission in what I have set down, but must plead guilty to not a few sins of omission. The responsibility of telling the world truly and fully what manner of man Rossetti was shall not be mine Nevertheless, I am sure that on the whole Rossetti would gain by the revelation. Looking back upon him over the interval since his death, with all painful feelings softened out, and nothing left to think of but the man as he lived, I seem to see him as a vivid personality, irresistible in his fascination, powerful even in his weakness, and with such light and force of genius as I have never encountered in any one else whatever.—CAINE, HALL, 1892, *The Poets and the Poetry of the Century, Kingsley to Thomson*, ed. *Miles*, p. 401.

Rossetti is the most notable of all our poet-painters, inasmuch as he was so great a master in both the arts. A point in connection with Rossetti's work may be noted, for a general misunderstanding exists concerning it. It is thought that Rossetti made poetry subservient to painting. This is erroneous. Rossetti's poems, when they are concerned with his pictures at all, are not mere adjuncts of the pictures; they may, and indeed do, help us to see deeper into his thoughts and creations; but neither is a mere auxiliary of the other, or an exponent of the other's meaning.—PARKES, KINETON, 1892, ed. *The Painter-Poets*, p. 251, note.

The trick Rossetti has in representing both mankind and material objects in a pictorial or conventional form; his unconscious assumption in his poetry that the reader is conversant with the principles and even some of the technical aspects of art, is sometimes vexatious. But we may laugh now at the petulancy of the "Quarterly Reviewer" who wrote of Rossetti's characters, "The further off they get from Nature, the more they resemble mere pictures, the better they please . . . " the poet of his school. We have at least learned to be grateful for Rossetti's picture-poems. The distance from which we look back upon his poetry is too short yet to allow us to see it in just perspective; but already his name has won an honoured place among the poets of the century.—WORSFOLD, W. BASIL, 1893, *The Poetry of D. G. Rossetti, Nineteenth Century*, vol. 34, p. 289.

Nowhere in Time's vista, where the forms of great men gather thickly, do we see many shapes of those who, as painters and as poets, have been alike illustrious. Among the few to whom, equally on both accounts, conspicuous honours have been paid, none is superior to Rossetti, of whose genius doubly exalted the artists say that in design he was pre-eminent, while, on the other hand, the most distinguished poets of our age place him in the first rank with themselves As to this prodigious, if not unique, distinction, of which the present age has not yet, perhaps, formed an adequate judgment, there can be no doubt that with regard to the constructive portion of his genius Rossetti was better equipped in verse than in design.—STEPHENS, FREDERIC GEORGE, 1894, *Dante Gabriel Rossetti*, p. 358.

He brought us a new message in his poetry; but, with all his ornate ability and technical skill, for me it has little charm, and what is poetry—or painting either—without charm? I think he might have remembered Sidney's "Look into thy heart, and write." His "I grudge Wordsworth every vote he gets" is significant.—LOCKER-LAMPSON, FREDERICK, 1895, *My Confidences*, p. 168.

Weird and spiritual are indeed often confused in Rossetti. It is easy enough to read, between the lines of his glowing emotion and intense visual imaginings, his genuine creed; and that creed is simple. A solemn sense of vast encompassing Mystery, a conviction of the unfathomable depths of human passion,—these are its factors.—SCUDDER, VIDA D., 1895, *The Life of the Spirit in the Modern English Poets*, p. 273.

In another very famous poem, "Eden Bower," which treats of the pre-Adamite woman Lilith, her lover the serpent of Eden, and her revenge on Adam, the litany refrain of "Eden Bower's in flower," and "And O the Bower and the hour," are introduced alternately after the first line in forty-nine strophes. As a matter of course, between these absolutely senseless phrases and the strophe which each interrupts, there is not the remotest connection. They are strung together without any reference to their meaning, but only because they rhyme. It is a startling example of echolalia.—NORDAU, MAX, 1895, *Degeneration*, p. 93.

Those who read them will carry away some clearly marked characteristics of his poetry, one of the most obvious being a tendency towards realism. This is only to be looked for in one whose pre-Raphaelite ideas were so pronounced with regard to painting which in him we know was so closely allied to his poetry that it has been said it is questionable whether he would not have done better to paint his poems and write his pictures, so sensuous are the former, so intellectual the latter. . . . A third feature easily recognised in his poetry is his precision of touch, power of condensation, and emphasis. This is especially remarkable in his "Sonnets," the form his verse so often took. Another of his chief characteristics in writing was his fastidiousness in the selection of words. He disliked so heartily anything slipshod or slovenly, or wanting in concentration, that he put off publishing anything till he had matured, corrected, recorrected, and altered it so that he himself in several cases never could decide as to the better of two words or expressions. In one of his longer poems, "Dante at Verona," there seems to be a faint shadow of the spirit of Browning, though Rossetti is too original to be called a disciple of any other poet.— HARPER, JANET, 1896, *Dante Gabriel Rossetti, Westminster Review*, vol. 146, pp. 314, 315.

However thick may be the mist which in places covers his poetry, when he writes in prose his thoughts and the words in which they are set forth are as clear as day. —HILL, GEORGE BIRKBECK, 1897, *Letters of Dante Gabriel Rossetti to William Allingham*, p. xxviii.

Rossetti takes his place in English literature as one of the six major poets of the later Victorian era, and as the oldest of the sub-group of three associated with the artistic revival vaguely known as Pre-Raphaelitism. . . . He possessed in an extraordinary degree both richness of imagination, and the power to pack a world of meaning into one pregnant and melodious phrase. But both his pictorial faculty and his intellectual force were tempered by a strain of mysticism, for which he has been charged with obscurity by hard-headed and dull-witted readers. He was at once the most spirited and the most material of poets; and the accusation of sensuality from which he was made to suffer could only result from inability to see more than one side of the Druid shield of his poetical personality.—PAYNE, WILLIAM MORTON, 1897, *Library of the World's Best Literature*, ed. Warner, vol. XXI, pp, 12411, 12415.

Rossetti is a poet whose work illustrates how essential breadth of view and philosophical comprehension of the world are to the highest literary worth. Here is an artist in words whose strictly artistic gifts have rarely been equalled. His ballads, notably the "Bride's Prelude" and "Rosemary," show him master of a weird, haunting verbal music. His sonnets show a phrasal power of weight and noble simplicity. His imagination pictures things in the concrete. He sees the scenes in the magic globe as distinctly as the girl who gazed into its cloudy depths. His conception of love as a spiritual energy transfused through the earthly passion, and, giving it elevation and immortality, shows that he comprehended, instinctively, at least, one great principle. But what shall we say of a man who believes that the world of Dante's day is preferable to the world of today, who has apparently never heard of the discovery of the conservation of energy nor of the main outlines of evolution, and who thinks the form of a chair or the pattern of a brocade more important and interesting than the struggle of humanity towards higher things. His world, as it ought to be, is simply a beautiful world, beautiful in form and color and old association, but without the life of conflict. It is a picturesque rather than a beautiful world which is the ideal to which he refers for commentary on the world around him.— JOHNSON, CHARLES F., 1898, *Elements of Literary Criticism*, p. 126.

In his simplicity we get a corresponding lack of simplicity and a passion for the details that render the greatest possible suggestion and association. The value of each word as an interpreter of esoteric meaning is weighed, and he had the zest of Flaubert in seeking the unique epithet to express his idea with more than Flaubert's subtlety of sense. . . . In his sonnets his wealth of imagery is most striking, and to many minds obstrusive.—CARY, ELISABETH LUTHER, 1900, *The Rossettis, Preface*, p. 223.

So far as this mysticism is genuine and heartfelt, it works upon those even who have no disposition for mysticism. But in reading Rossetti and his imitators one seldom loses the feeling that they are addressing those whose inclination will tend in that direction. They cunningly assert in their poems all kinds of seraphic allusions in which they do not believe. The real Pre-Raphaelites, that is, the painters before Raphael, believed in their pictures; but one does not receive this impression from the English Pre-Raphaelites and poets. It is artificial artlessness, the most unsatisfactory thing both in life and in all art. Another peculiarity distinguishing Rossetti is his use of the refrain so common in popular poetry. But in him we recognize at once its misuse, we see that it is mere child's play.—ENGEL, EDWARD, 1902, *A History of English Literature, rev. Hamley Bent, p. 432.*

Anthony Trollope
1815–1882

Born, in London, 1815. Educated at Harrow, 1822-25; at Sunbury, 1825-27; at Winchester, 1827-30; at Harrow again, 1830-33. Master in a school at Brussels for a short time. Held Post-Office appointment in London, 1834-41; in Ireland 1841-59; in London, 1859-67. Married Rose Heseltine, 11 June 1844. Edited "St. Paul's," 1867-71. Visit to U. S. A., 1868; to Australia and America, 1871-73. Settled in London, 1873. Active literary life. Frequent contributor to periodicals. Visit to S. Africa, 1877; to Iceland, 1878. Removed to Hastings, Sussex, 1880. Visit to Italy, 1881; to Ireland, 1882. Died, 6 Dec. 1882. *Works:* "The Macdermots of Ballycloran," 1847; "The Kellys and the O'Kellys," 1848; "La Vendée," 1850; "The Warden," 1855; "Barchester Towers," 1857; "The Three Clerks," 1858; "Doctor Thorne," 1858; "The West Indies and the Spanish Main," 1859; "The Bertrams," 1859; "Castle Richmond," 1860; "Framley Parsonage," 1861; "Tales of all Countries," 1st ser. 1861; 2nd ser. 1863; 3rd ser. 1870; "Orley Farm," 1862; "North America," (2 vols.), 1862; "Rachel Ray," 1863; "The Small House at Allington," 1864; "Can You Forgive Her?" (2 vols.), 1864-65; "Miss Mackenzie," 1865; "Hunting Sketches" (from "Pall Mall Gaz."), 1865; "Clergymen of the Church of England" (from "Pall Mall Gaz."), 1866; "Travelling Sketches" (from "Pall Mall Gaz."),1866; "The Belton Estate," 1866; "The Claverings," 1867; "The Last Chronicle of Barset," 1867 [1866], "Nina Balatka" (anon.), 1867; "Lotta Schmidt and other stories," 1867; "Linda Tressel" (anon.), 1868; "Phineas Finn," 1869; "He knew He was Right," 1869; "The Struggles of Brown, Jones, and Robinson," 1870; "The Vicar of Bullhampton," 1870; "An Editor's Tales," 1870; "Cæsar," 1870; "Sir Harry Hotspur of Humblethwaite," 1871 [1870]; "Ralph the Heir," 1871; "The Golden Lion of Granpère," 1872; "The Eustace Diamonds," 1873[1872]; "Australia and New Zealand," 1873; "Phineas Redux," 1874; "Harry Heathcote of Gangoil," 1874; "Lady Anna," 1874; "The Way We Live Now," 1875; "The Prime Minister," 1876; "The American Senator," 1877; "How the 'Mastiffs' went to Iceland" (priv. ptd.), 1878; "Is He Popenjoy?" 1878; "South Africa," 1878; "John Caldigate," 1879; "An Eye for an Eye," 1879; "Cousin Henry," 1879; "Thackeray," 1879; "The Duke's Children," 1880; "Life of Cicero," 1880; "Ayala's Angel," 1881; "Doctor Wortle's School," 1881; "Why Frau Frohmann raised her Prices, etc.," 1882 [1881]; "Lord Palmerston," 1882; "The Fixed Period," 1882; "Kept in the Dark," 1882; "Marion Fay," 1882. *Posthumous:* "Mr. Scarborough's Family," 1883; "Autobiography," ed. by H. M. Trollope (2 vols.), 1883; "The Land Leaguers," 1883; "An Old Man's Love," 1884; "Thompson Hall, etc.," 1885.—SHARP, R. FARQUHARSON, 1897, *A Dictionary of English Authors, p. 283.*

PERSONAL

Nobody could see anything of him without feeling that he was in the presence of an exceptionally high-minded as well as an exceptionally gifted man, a man of strong feelings as of strong sense, but a man who well knew how to keep his feelings in check, and a man whose practice as well as his theory was Christian. . . . To younger men his ways and manner had the special charm that, without for a moment losing dignity, he put them on an equality with himself. He happened to be older, and therefore more experienced, than they were —I do not think it ever occurred to him that he was more clever or more gifted— and whatever help might come to them from his greater experience was at their service as between comrade and comrade. . . . He loved fun; he loved laughing; he loved his kind. There was not one scrap of sentimentality about him, but there was plenty of sensibility, as well as sense.—POLLOCK, WALTER HERRIES, 1883, *Anthony Trollope, Harper's Magazine, vol. 66, pp. 911, 912.*

At the first glance, you would have taken him to be some civilized and modernized Squire Western, nourished with beef and ale, and roughly hewn out of the most robust and least refined variety of human clay. Looking at him more narrowly, however, you would have reconsidered this judgment. Though his general contour and aspect were massive and sturdy, the lines of his features were delicately cut; his complexion was remarkably pure and fine, and his face was susceptible of very subtle and sensitive changes of expression. Here was a man of abundant physical strength and vigor, no doubt, but carrying within him a nature more than commonly alert and impressible. His organization, though healthy, was both complex and high-wrought; his character was simple and straightforward to a fault, but he was abnormally conscientious, and keenly alive to others' opinion concerning him. It might be thought that he was overburdened with self-esteem, and unduly opinionated; but, in fact, he was but over-anxious to secure the good will and agreement of all with whom he came in contact. There was some peculiarity in him—some element or bias in his composition that made him different from other men; but, on the other hand, there was an ardent solicitude to annul or reconcile this difference, and to prove himself to be, in fact, of absolutely the same cut and quality as all the rest of the world. Hence he was in a demonstrative, expository or argumentative mood, he could not sit quiet in the face of a divergence between himself and his associates; he was incorrigibly strenuous to obliterate or harmonize the irreconcilable points between himself and others; and since these points remained irreconcilable, he remained in a constant state of storm and stress on the subject.—HAWTHORNE, JULIAN, 1883, *The Maker of Many Books, The Manhattan, vol. 2, p. 573.*

His life, in spite of its incessant toil, was an exceedingly happy one, and he recognized its happiness to the full. His duties offered him the opportunity of travelling extensively. Egypt, the West Indies, America, Australia, South Africa, became familiar ground to him. When at home he had his four hunters ever ready to carry him to the covert side, and (what was more difficult) to carry a rider across country who was so short-sighted that he could never form a judgment of fence or ditch, and who boldly rode straight at everything. From his habit of rising every morning at 5.30 A. M., he was able to have his literary work over in good time, and the day free for any other duty or amusement. Loving his own fireside, he yet enjoyed going into society, and seldom in his later life did he miss, when in town, the afternoon visit to the Garrick, and the afternoon rubber at whist there. Never making any very loud professions of religion, and regarding all that was innocent in life as open to his free enjoyment, all his friends knew him to be a reverent and sincere Christian.—MACLEOD, DONALD, 1884, *Anthony Trollope, Good Words, vol. 25, p. 250.*

Work to him was a necessity and a satisfaction. He used often to say that he envied me the capacity for being idle. Had he possessed it, poor fellow, I might not now be speaking of him in the past tense. And still less than of me could it be said of him that he was ever driven to literary work *deficiente crumena*. But he labored, during the whole of his manhood life, with an insatiable ardor that (taking into consideration his very efficient discharge of his duties as post-office surveyor) puts my industry into the shade.—TROLLOPE, THOMAS ADOLPHUS, 1888, *What I Remember, p. 249.*

The charming "Last Chronicle of Barset," surely as sunshiny a picture of English country life as ever was written, was then delighting us all. While preparing for dinner, I had stuck up the work where I could read it: and I glanced at several of the most beautiful passages, and at one or two of the most powerful. Filled with the enthusiasm of one who had very rarely met a popular author, I entered Strathtyrum that day. The sight of the great novelist was a blow. He was singularly unkempt, and his clothes were very wrinkled and ill-made. His manner was a further blow. We listened for the melodious accents which were due from those lips: but they did not come. Indeed, he was the only man I had heard swear in decent society for uncounted years. The swearing, which was repeated, was the most disagreeable of all: the actual asseverating, by the Holiest Name, of some trumpery statement. How could that man have written the well-remembered sentences which had charmed one through these years? Then, by way of making himself pleasant in a gathering of Scotsmen, he proceeded (the ladies being gone and we all gathered to hear him) to vilipend our beloved Sir Walter.—BOYD, ANDREW K. H., 1892, *Twenty-Five Years of St. Andrews, vol.* I, *p.* 100.

In physique, manner, and speech he might have been taken for a dragoon in mufti, or a sportsman fresh from an invigorating run in the fields; certainly not for a novelist whose forte lay in depicting the salient traits of English clergymen, the delicate shades of character among English maidens, and in composing those inimitable love-letters which so plentifully bestrew the pages of his life-like romances. During his visit to New York, Trollope was introduced to many of our literary men, and to such social gatherings as might interest a man of his pursuits. He wore spectacles, through which he seemed to inspect men and things with a quiet scrutiny, as if making perpetual mental memoranda for future use. In conversation he would sometimes ask a question, or make a suggestion respecting people to whom he had been introduced, which indicated a keen perception of the weak spots in their characters; but this was always said in a good-humoured way that left no sting behind it.—TUCKERMAN, CHARLES K., 1895, *Personal Recollections of Notable People, vol.* II, *p.* 8.

I knew him well, knew his subjects, and his stage. I have seen him at work at the "Megatherium Club," chatted with him at the "Universe," dined with him at George Eliot's, and even met him in the huntingfield. I was familiar with the political personages and crises which he describes; and much of the local colouring in which his romances were framed was for years the local colouring that I daily saw around me. . . . To re-read some of his best stories, as I have just done, is to me like looking through a photographic album of my acquaintances, companions, and familiar reminiscences of some thirty years ago. I can hear the loud voice, the honest laugh, see the keen eyes of our old friend as I turn to the admirable vignette portrait of his posthumous Autobiography, and I can almost hear him tell the anecdotes recounted in that pleasant book.—HARRISON, FREDERIC, 1895, *Studies in Early Victorian Literature, pp.* 183, 184.

Anthony Trollope, like his ancestor of old, was combative, and he was boisterous, but good-naturedly so. He was abrupt in manners and speech; he was ebullient, and therefore he sometimes offended people. I suppose he was a wilful man, and we know that such men are always in the right; but he was a good fellow. Some of Trollope's acquaintance used to wonder how so commonplace a person could have written such excellent novels; but I maintain that so honourable and interesting a man could not be commonplace. Hirsute and taurine of aspect, he would glare at you from beyond fierce spectacles. His ordinary tones had the penetrative capacity of two people quarrelling, and his voice would ring through and through you, and shake the windows in their frames, while all the time he was most amiably disposed towards you under his waistcoat. To me his *viso sciolto* and bluff geniality were very attractive, and so were his gusty denunciations, but most attractive of all was his unselfish nature. Literary men might make him their exemplar, as I make him my theme; for he may quite well have been the most generous man of letters, of mark, since Walter Scott. — LOCKER-LAMPSON, FREDERICK, 1895, *My Confidences, p.* 331.

Trollope's literary fame certainly went through the three stages of slow growth, splendid maturity, and steady decline. In his later days his readers fell off to an astonishing degreee, and time almost seemed to have come round, as in the case of Cassius, and where he did begin, there did he end, with a sadly limited circulation. He took his decaying popularity with as much composure as he had taken his early lack of popularity, as doggedly and umcomplainingly as he took his frequent falls in those hunting-fields which at one time he loved so well. He had made his name, however, in the meantime; and his best novels have a secure place in the literature of Queen Victoria's reign.—MCCARTHY, JUSTIN, 1899, *Reminiscences, vol.* I, *p.* 375.

The man, in external things, was largely the creation of his environment. He was a bluff, self-assertive, dogmatic, thoroughly aggressive Englishman, brusque, burly, money-loving, and singularly matter-of fact, so that even among his own countrymen and the men of his own set he was never generally popular. The man who dwelt within, however, and whom only his most cherished intimates ever really knew, was genial, tender-hearted, kindly, and, more than that, intensely sensitive to all the pain and all the pathos of human life. Both sides of his nature are felt in what he wrote, and both are necessary to his greatness as an author. He had power and force; he had humour and a rich vein of wholesome English fun; he had insight into character and motive; and, finally, he had a wide and accurate first-hand knowledge of men and women, gained from the circumstances of his various vocations. — PECK, HARRY THURSTON, 1900, *Anthony Trollope's Novels, Royal Ed., Introduction*.

Henry VIII, we are told—and it is one of the few statements which make that monarch attractive—"loved a man." If so, he would clearly have loved Trollope. In person, Trollope resembled the ideal beef-eater; square and sturdy, and as downright as a box on the ear. The simple, masculine character revealed itself in every lineament and gesture. His talk was as hearty and boisterous as a gust of a northeaster—a Kingsley northeaster that is, not blighting, but bracing and genial. The first time I met him was in a low room, where he was talking with a friend almost as square and sturdy as himself. It seemed as if the roof was in danger of being blown off by the vigor of the conversational blasts. And yet, if I remember rightly, they were not disputing, but simply competing in the utterance of a perfectly harmless sentiment in which they cordially agreed. A talker of feeble lungs might be unable to get his fair share in the discussion; but not because Trollope was intentionally overbearing, or even rough. His kindness and cordiality were as unmistakable as his sincerity; and if he happened to impinge upon his hearers' sore points, it was from clumsiness, not malignity. He was incapable of shyness or diffidence, and would go at any subject as gallantly as he rode at a stiff fence in the hunting-field. His audacity sprang not from conceit, but from a little over-confidence in the power of downright common sense.—STEPHEN, LESLIE, 1901, *Anthony Trollope, National Review*, vol. 38, p. 69.

Personally, Anthony Trollope was a bluff, genial, hearty, vigorous man, typically English in his face, his talk, his ideas, his tastes. His large eyes, which looked larger behind his large spectacles, were full of good-humoured life and force; and though he was neither witty nor brilliant in conversation, he was what is called very good company, having travelled widely, known all sorts of people, and formed views, usually positive views, on all the subjects of the day, views which he was prompt to declare and maintain. There was not much novelty in them—you were disappointed not to find so clever a writer more original—but they were worth listening to for their common-sense, tending rather to commonplace sense, and you enjoyed the ardour with which he threw himself into a discussion. Though boisterous and insistent in his talk, he was free from assumption or conceit, and gave the impression of liking the world he lived in, and being satisfied with his own place in it.—BRYCE, JAMES, 1903, *Studies in Contemporary Biography*, p. 118.

GENERAL

I hope you read that tale going on in the "Fortnightly"—"The Belton Estate." It is charming, like all he writes; I quite weary for the next number, for the sake of that one thing; the rest is wonderfully stupid.— CARLYLE, JANE WELSH, 1865, *To Mrs. Russel, Dec. 25; Letters and Memorials*, ed. Froude, vol. II, p. 361.

We know parsons well, and, upon the whole—though we find them men like ourselves, sometimes not too elevated, not too self-sacrificial, not too noble—we can only think the clerics drawn by Trollope are a disgrace, and almost a libel. We do not say that they are not true. They are photographically true, but they are never so from the highest and noblest sight-point. . . . If Mr. Trollope paints—and he paints firmly, consistently, and with a quiet obstinate kind of art—all that can be found in English society, the sooner that society is changed for something of a more decided pattern the better. No one can care for the faint and obscure outlines, and the colourless sort of wool, with which Mr. Trollope weaves his human and his faded tapestry.—FRISWELL, JAMES HAIN, 1870, *Modern Men of Letters Honestly Criticised*, pp. 137, 143.

I set my reader last night on beginning "The Mill on the Floss." I couldn't take to it more than to others I have tried to read by the Greatest Novelist of the Day: but I will go on a little further. Oh for some more brave Trollope; who I am sure conceals a much profounder observation than these dreadful Denners of Romance under his lightsome and sketchy touch, as Gainsboro compared to Denner.—FITZGERALD, EDWARD, 1873, *To W. F. Pollock; Letters, ed., Wright, vol.* I, *p.* 358.

He has drawn sketches, such as the portrait of Mrs. Proudie, which may stand as representatives of a class; but throughout the whole of his works there is not to be found a single character, such as Colonel Newcome, or Becky Sharp, or Jane Eyre, or Dorothea, which is a permanent addition to the world of English fiction. . . . Mr. Trollope is essentially a superficial writer and delights to deal with the outside of things. He has never successfully described the working of strong feeling. Whenever he has attempted to depict violent passion, he has always, in fact described, not strong feeling, but the most obvious outward signs of feeling. . . . The source, in fact, of Mr. Trollope's success is to be found in the satisfaction which he gives to the almost universal liking for accurate sketches of every-day life, and to the equally universal admiration for the easy optimism, which sees in English society, as it now exists, the best of all possible arrangements in the best of all possible worlds.—DICEY, A. V., 1874, *The Nation, vol.* 18, *pp.* 174, 175.

Mr. Trollope is emphatically a "man of the time," the very antipodes of imaginative writers like George Macdonald. He is a realist, a painter of men and manners of the present day, a satirist within a certain range, ready to make use of any type that may present itself, and seem characteristic as a product of the special conditions of the present century. He is rather conservative and High Church, his best portraitures being those of the clergy. Who can ever forget Mr. Slope, Dr. Grantly, Bishop Prowdie or Mrs. Prowdie? Ladies of rank, aspiring members of parliament (Irish and English), habitués of the clubs, Australian stockmen, female adventurers—all of these, and many more, he has taken up, and so set them in the midst of their surroundings, that his pictures look like photographs, and they seem to be produced as easily as the photographer throws off his scenes and portraits. Mr. Trollope is eminently practical and also public-minded, for his characters frequently refer to great public questions, and suggest politial changes. His humour is peculiar to himself, dry, direct, and with no infusion of sentiment.—CHAMBERS, ROBERT, 1876, *Cyclopædia of English Literature, ed. Carruthers.*

I can greatly enjoy Mr. Trollope's best stories, and even read his worst, for the sake of the glimpses of English life they give me.—ATKINSON, WILLIAM P., 1878, *The Right Use of Books, p.* 21.

Interesting from its author ["Cicero"] and its evident sincerity, but resting on too small a basis of scholarship for such a task. —JEANS, GEORGE EDWARD, 1880, *Life and Letters of Marcus Tullius Cicero, p.* 404.

Mr. Anthony Trollope carries to its utmost limit the realism begun by Thackeray. He has none of Thackeray's genius; none of his fancy or feeling; none of his genuine creative power. He can describe with minute photographic faithfulness the ways, the talk, and sometimes even the emotions of a Belgravian family, of a nobleman's country-house, or the "womankind" of a dean in a cathedral town. He does not trouble himself with passion or deep pathos, although he has got as far as to describe very touchingly the mental pains of a pretty girl thrown over by her lover, and has suggested with some genuine power the blended emotion, half agony of sorrow, half sense of relief, experienced by an elderly clergyman on the death of a shrewish wife. It was natural that, after the public had had a long succession of Mr. Trollope's novels, there should come a ready welcome for the school of fiction which was called the sensational.—MCCARTHY, JUSTIN, 1880, *A History of Our Own Times from the Accession of Queen Victoria to the Berlin Congress, vol.* IV, *ch.* lxvii, *p.* 131.

An exceedingly vivid portrayal of the life of the great orator. ["The Life of Cicero."] No one of the numerous biographers of Cicero has succeeded so completely in transplanting him and his surroundings into our own days. The reader is almost led to forget that the events of which he is reading were history before the advent of Christianity. They are made to seem like the events of to-day. The most essential peculiarity of the work is that it is written from what may be called Cicero's point of view. While Mommsen, Froude, Merivale, and others have looked at the condition and the necessities of the State, and have censured Cicero for not comprehending the nature of the situation, Trollope had studied the problem with a view to ascertaining and showing how it must have appeared to Cicero himself. Thus the volumes become very largely a personal rather than a political life. Whatever may be the reader's views of Cicero's political course, he cannot fail to be charmed by the picture here given of the orator's personal characteristics.—ADAMS, CHARLES KENDALL, 1882, *A Manual of Historical Literature*, p. 130.

> He was not wont, as many others use,
> The noble life of Letters to abuse;
> Its darker ways and works he did not choose.
> Nor his idle tortures of unrest—
> Blind doubts and fears that haunt th' unhealthy breast;
> Riddles that ne'er have been nor shall be guessed.
> Not on such themes his fancy loved to brood;
> He looked on life, and saw that it was good
> Or bad, according to the gazer's mood.
> And his was good. By the clear light of sense
> He drew men as they are, without pretence
> To regild virtue, or to lash offence.
> He drew the life of which his life was part;
> Drew it with faithful hand and loving heart,
> Making a friend, not tyrant, of his art.
> He writ the homely annals of his day—
> What English men and women do and say,
> The fireside story of their work and play.

—MORRIS, MOWBRAY, 1882, *Anthony Trollope, The Graphic*.

He abused his gift, overworked it, rode his horse too hard. As an artist he never took himself seriously; many people will say this was why he was so delightful. The people who take themselves seriously are prigs and bores; and Trollope, with his perpetual story, which was the only thing he cared about, his strong good sense, hearty good nature, generous appreciation of life in all its varieties, responds in perfection to a certain English ideal. According to that ideal it is rather dangerous to be definitely or consciously an artist—to have a system, a doctrine, a form. Trollope, from the first, went in, as they say, for having as little form as possible; it is probably safe to affirm that he had no "views" whatever on the subject of novel-writing. His whole manner is that of a man who regards the practice as one of the more delicate industries, but has never troubled his head nor clogged his pen with theories about the nature of his business. Fortunately he was not obliged to do so, for he had an easy road to success; and his honest, familiar, deliberate way of treating his readers as if he were one of them and shared their indifference to a general view, their limitations of knowledge, their love of a comfortable ending, endeared him to many persons in England and America.—JAMES, HENRY, 1883, *Anthony Trollope, Century Magazine*, vol. 26, p. 385.

It is exceptionally easy to read any of his best-known novels, easier to read them right through without slurring a page or a line than it is to read even Scott, and by a combination which is far from usual, it was when he had once mastered his art, as easy for him to write these novels, so far as the actual putting pen to paper went, as it is for us to read them. Thus the people who read them swiftly and easily forgot that art such as this must have been acquired with infinite pains, and did not reflect that these meant more than the actual writing down of words to the composition of a masterpiece of fiction.—POLLOCK, WALTER HERRIES, 1883, *Anthony Trollope, Harper's Magazine*, vol. 66, p. 907.

If his characters have not the depth of George Eliot's, they have equal truth. We have seen people like a great many of them, and we feel that we easily might come across people like the others. Mr. Trollope had certainly gone far to write himself out; his later work is far from being so good as his earlier. But after all, his worst work is better than a great many people's best; and, considering the way in which it was done, it is wonderful that it was done at all.—FREEMAN, EDWARD A., 1883, *Anthony Trollope, Macmillan's Magazine*, vol. 47, p. 240.

His judgments on his great contemporaries and rivals are, on the whole, sensible; but they are not marked by any profound insight, and may be thought to lean a little too hard on Dickens, whose failure in pathos is not greater than his own or Charles Lever's. His opinions on politics, on hunting, on the conduct of life in general, are not those of a philosopher, but of a hearty, healthy Englishman of far more than average abilities and experience, with no very lofty or enthusiastic views, but with a fixed preference for what is honest, cleanly, and manly, besides liking a good deal of play along with plenty of work. Accordingly, while he could not stomach Exeter Hall, as he divertingly tells us, and found himself expelled from the columns of *Good Words* because he admitted dancing into a story for its pages, his influence was always wholesomely exerted; and the future student of Victorian England who is wise enough to consult his novels for sketches of ordinary society as it was in the latter half of this century will find no one line that needs to be blotted out on ethical grounds, however he may wish, as Ben Jonson did in the case of a far greater, that he had blotted thousands in the interest of literary excellence.—LITTLEDALE, RICHARD F., 1883, *Trollope's Autobiography, The Academy*, vol. 24, p. 274.

Trollope's position in fiction is not a difficult one to fix. He was essentially a realist, but he was a realist who preferred the agreeable to the disagreeable. He was as true to nature as it is possible for a novelist to be, but he chose to study nature under the forms which please and not under those which shock the sympathies and taste of men. He had none of Scott's romantic nor of Lytton's poetical imagination. He had no social evils to expose like Dickens, no philosophical theories to expound like George Eliot. He was not a satirist like Thackeray. He may justly be described as a literary photographer of social life in the upper ranks.... While Trollope will never be studied as a master of art, the future historian will seek in his pages, as Mr. Lecky has sought in those of Fielding, for trustworthy information regarding contemporary social life. Among the novelists of the nineteenth century, the name of Anthony Trollope will be placed in the second rank. Not because the work he aimed at doing was not thoroughly well done; but because he did not aim at the highest excellence. The best photography cannot reach the plane of art.—TUCKERMAN, BAYARD, 1883, *Anthony Trollope, Princeton Review*, N. S., vol. 12, p. 27.

He would himself have been the last to claim equality with Thackeray or George Eliot. They had genius; Trollope had talent: but it was talent of rare quality. It seemed exhaustless in productive power, and capable of bringing its full strength to bear on every production, however rapidly executed.—MACLEOD, DONALD, 1884, *Anthony Trollope, Good Words*, vol. 25, p. 249.

Fantasy was a thing he abhorred; compression he knew not; and originality and ingenuity can be conceded to him only by a strong stretch of the ordinary meaning of the words. Other qualities he had in plenty, but not these. And, not having them, he was not a writer of Short-stories. Judging from his essay on Hawthorne, one may even go so far as to say that Trollope did not know a good Short-story when he saw it. —MATTHEWS, BRANDER, 1885–1901, *The Philosophy of the Short-story*, p. 24.

Introduce some art in the plot and some truth in the characterization; keep as close to actual life as a photographer; be as diffused and dogged in details as is consistent with preserving a kind of languid interest; economize material, whether of incident or emotion; realize Carlyle's sarcasm that England contains twenty millions of people, mostly bores—and you have Anthony Trollope, the most unromantic of romancers, popular in virtue of his skill in reproducing a population.—WHIPPLE, EDWIN PERCY, 1887, *In Dickens-land, Scribner's Magazine*, vol. 2, p. 743.

Next to "Middlemarch" the future student of nineteenth-century England will derive his best material from Anthony Trollope, scarcely a painter, but a matchless photographer. George Eliot exhibits the world to her reader; Trollope thrusts his reader straight into the middle of it. Unfortunately, he learned the trade of novel-writing too well, and realised Samuel Butler's ingenious fiction of the men who became the slaves of their own machines. It must be owned that the circumstances of the time were greatly against him.—GARNETT, RICHARD, 1887, *The Reign of Queen Victoria*, ed. Ward, vol. II, p. 490.

A volume ["Life of Thackeray"] neither for information nor discernment quite worthy of that excellent series.—HALES, JOHN W., 1888–93, *Victorian Literature, Folia Literaria*, p. 328.

"The Warden" established him at once in the position which he kept more or less till the end of his life. We do not think that in any of his after works Mr. Trollope ever surpassed this story, or produced anything so perfect in its subdued tones as the picture of the elderly and humbled-minded clergyman, so true, so simple and so mild, yet invulnerable in gentle resolution when his conscience had been awakened and he had perceived his position to be untenable, according to his own high yet completely unostentatious standard of right and wrong. Mr. Harding may take his place among the best and most delicately drawn of those new men and women who have been added to our spiritual acquaintance (and their name is legion) during this age, so wealthy in fiction. He does not come up to the high standard of Colonel Newcome or Esmond, but he is, in his way, as real, and even more unconsciously and gently noble-minded than they. . . . The "Last Chronicle of Barset" added a stronger note of tragedy to the varied story which began with Mr. Harding, in the person of another clergyman, Mr. Crawley, the poor, proud, learned parson with his overflowing family, and the false accusation which hung over him so long. Posterity, to which we all appeal, will find nowhere any better illustration of the Victorian age than in this series of admirable fiction—if it does not lose its way among the intolerable number of books which put forward a somewhat similar claim.—OLIPHANT, MARGARET O. W., 1892, *The Victorian Age of English Literature*, pp. 473, 476.

His exquisitely comical and conscientiously coxcombical autobiography.—SWINBUNE, ALGERNON CHARLES, 1895, *Social Verse, The Forum*, vol. 12, p. 176.

Trollope is never bombastic, or sensational, or prurient, or grotesque. Even at his worst, he writes pure, bright, graceful English; he tells us about wholesome men and women in a manly tone, and if he becomes dull, he is neither ridiculous nor odious. . . . Sometimes, but very rarely, Trollope, is vulgar—for good old Anthony had a coarse vein—it was in the family:— but as a rule his language is conspicuous for its ease, simplicity, and unity of tone. —HARRISON, FREDERIC, 1895, *Studies in Early Victorian Literature*, pp. 188, 189.

I hold that the best of Trollope's stories are excellent reading. He has admirable qualities as a writer of fiction; indeed he has helped to ameliorate the asperities of our middle-class existence. He gives enough, sometimes more than enough; but still he has a happy tact of omission. Trollope's chief excellence is in the portrayal of character; the dialogue is what people naturally use; it is even more than that—they could not well use any other. I am fond of his heroines; they are affectionate and true; one knows pretty well what they are going to do next, one always feels safe with them. His young people are not discouraged by the tedium of la grâce or bezique, or other equally mild amusements: they smile and dance and whisper themselves into each other's hearts, and, what is so very agreeable about them, they are generally content to remain there. Trollope's ideal of happiness has nothing in it of the unattainable. We know he had not the distinction of Thackeray, the exuberant genius of Dickens, or the vivid and vehement force of Charles Reade; but not seldom he is worthy of their company; and his tone can compare favourably with that of any of his illustrious contemporaries, from Bulwer and Disraeli to the Geniuses just mentioned.— LOCKER-LAMPSON, FREDERICK, 1895, *My Confidences*, p. 334.

You cannot be at perfect ease with a friend who does not joke, and I suppose this is what deprived me of a final satisfaction in the company of Anthony Trollope, who jokes heavily or not at all, and whom I should make otherwise bold to declare the greatest of English novelists; as it is, I must put before him Jane Austen, whose books, late in life, have been a youthful rapture with me. Even without much humor Trollope's books have been a vast pleasure to me through their simple truthfulness. Perhaps if they were more humorous they would not be so true to the British life and character present in them in the whole length and breadth of its expansive commonplaceness. It is their serious fidelity which gives them a value unique in literature, and which if it were carefully analysed would afford a principle of the same quality in an author who was undoubtedly one of the finest artists as well as the most Philistine of men.—HOWELLS, WILLIAM DEAN, 1895, *My Literary Passions*, p. 247.

It has been said that Trollope is a typical novelist, and the type is of sufficient importance to receive a little attention, even in space so jealously allotted as ours must be. The novel craved by and provided for the public of this second period (it has also been said) was a novel of more or less ordinary life, ranging from the lower middle to the upper class, correctly observed, diversified by sufficient incident not of an extravagant kind, and furnished with description and conversation not too epigrammatic but natural and fairly clever. This man Trollope hit with surprising justness, and till the demand altered a little or his own hand failed (perhaps there was something of both) he continued to hit it. . . . Everything that he saw he could turn into excellent novel-material. No one has touched him in depicting the humours of a public office, few in drawing those of cathedral cities and the hunting-field. If his stories, as stories, are not of enthralling interest or of very artfully constructed plots, their craftsmanship in this respect leaves very little to complain of. . . . The special kind of their excellence, the facts that they reflect their time without transcending it, and that in the way of merely reflective work each time prefers its own workmen and is never likely to find itself short of them, together with the great volume of Trollope's production, are certainly against him; and it is hard even for those who enjoyed him most, and who can still enjoy him, to declare positively that there is enough of the permanent and immortal in him to justify the hope of a resurrection.—SAINTSBURY, GEORGE, 1896, *A History of Nineteenth Century Literature*, pp. 330, 331.

Although he had had but few opportunities of knowing clergymen in actual life, and his pictures must therefore be regarded as showing his conception of what they ought to be, rather than his knowledge of what they were, his bishops, deans, archdeacons, and curates were universally recognised to be remarkably true and vivid.—GRAHAM, RICHARD D., 1897, *The Masters of Victorian Literature*, p. 77.

A writer who followed Thackeray in the systematic confinement of his studies of the "comfortable" classes of society, but who has nowhere displayed the faintest traces of Thackeray's subtle humour, his genuine though restrained pathos, his unrivalled insight into character, or his admirable prose style. Within certain narrow limits—those for instance, of the cathedral close—Trollope was not without an eye for character, and he has portrayed certain naturally humorous types to be found within these limits with a fidelity which in itself assures for them a humorous effect; but speaking generally, his art, in its mechanical realism, stands related to Thackeray's as that of the cheap photographer to the masterly portrait-painter's. It is the commonplace carried to its highest power; and the fact that for so long a series of years he stood unquestioned at the head of his branch of the literary profession and commanded a public so large that the amount of his professional earnings was for his day unprecedented, affords a phenomenon almost as discouraging in itself as the reign of Mr. Tupper in another field of literature. Indeed, if it would be unjust to the novelist to treat the two instances as precisely parallel, it is only because, vast as may be the interval which divides the third-rate in prose fiction from the first-rate, the difference between the poetaster and the poet is one not in degree but in kind.—TRAILL, HENRY DUFF, 1897, *Social England*, vol. VI, p. 517.

With many fine qualities, his nature was slightly tinged with mediocrity. So, naturally enough, he felt more interest in the kind of men and women he saw about him than in unusual characters. He loved to show people in the every-day relations of life,—acting and reacting upon each other,—and in the English setting he best knew. Thus he was a forerunner of our late realism, with its effort to fix contemporary life. Of strong yet simple emotions himself, with a satirically humorous sense of common self-deceptions and foibles, and also an optimistic belief in human nobility, he pictures the world to which most of his readers belong.—COOKE, JANE GROSVENOR, 1897, *Library of the World's Best Literature*, ed. Warner, vol. XXV, p. 15033.

All of that excellent series, "The English Men of Letters," are interesting books except Trollope's "Thackeray."—JOHNSON, CHARLES F., 1898, *Elements of Literary Criticism*, p. 21.

Dispensing for the most part with the "wearing work" and the "agonizing doubt" of the skilful plot manipulator, he sits down comfortably and writes about his cathedral folk; men and women come and go; he relates what they said and did, and draws full-length portraits of them. His main regret is "that no mental method of daguerreotype or photography has yet been discovered by which the characters of men can be reduced to writing and put into grammatical language with an unerring precision of truthful description." With his mind concentrated upon his characters, he looks them full in the face, perplexed by no ethical or philosophical medium. By virtue of this directness, he is the great chronicler of English fiction.—CROSS, WILBUR L., 1899, *The Development of the English Novel*, p. 223.

Whatever else may be said or written concerning Anthony Trollope, one thing at least must be conceded—that of all the writers of English fiction he is the most typically English.—PECK, HARRY THURSTON, 1900, *Anthony Trollope's Novels*, Royal Ed., Introduction.

Trollope's heroines are as domestic as Clarissa Harlowe. They haven't a thought beyond housekeeping or making a respectable marriage. We could hardly expect such delineations of the fair feminine qualities as could be given by feminine novelists alone. We could not ask him for a Jane Eyre, or still less for a Maggie Tulliver. . . . His are so good-natured, sensible and commonplace that he has the greatest difficulty in preventing them from at once marrying their lovers. . . . The most popular of all was Miss Lily Dale, whom Trollope himself unkindly describes as "somewhat of a French prig." She will not marry the man whom she loves because she has been cruelly jilted by a thorough snob, and makes it a point of honor not to accept consolation or admit that she can love twice. Readers, it seems, fell in love with her, and used to write to Trollope entreating him to reconcile her to making her lover happy. Posterity, I think, will make a mistake if it infers that English girls were generally of this type; but it must admit though with a certain wonder that the type commended itself to a sturdy, sensible Briton of the period, as the very ideal of Womanhood, and delighted a large circle of readers.— STEPHEN, LESLIE, 1901, *Anthony Trollope*, National Review, vol. 38, p. 81.

To begin with his value for the history of manners, he is by far our greatest realist since Fielding. Miss Austen uniformly approaches him in her own field, but that field was a very much smaller one than his. George Eliot approaches him in some passages of some of her books, but in the rest she is in no way his competitor. Lovers of Dickens are apt to attribute to that great master of sentiment and caricature the perfection of every conceivable quality; but I hardly think the well-advised of them would claim for him a literally exact portraiture of manners; and it is in that sense I am speaking of realism, putting any esoteric views there may be about a higher realism on one side. A comparison with Thackeray may perhaps help my estimate. Thackeray was by far Trollope's superior in the perception of the humours of life and in a humorous presentation of them, but in fidelity to the facts of life, or at least the facts which eye and ear tell one finally, he was by far Trollope's inferior.—STREET, G. S., 1901, *Anthony Trollope*, Cornhill Magazine, vol. 83, p. 349.

Mr. Trollope was not an artist, he was a photographer. It was only for the improvement of his style that he subjected himself to discipline. In this he persevered until he developed a narrative style which, for his purpose, could hardly be surpassed: it is lucid and easy, if somewhat commonplace. For the rest of the artist's work Trollope cared nothing. He did not devise new and startling plots, life as he knows it being sufficiently varied and interesting to satisfy ordinary people. He took pride in remaining an ordinary person himself, and in appealing to everyday emotion and narrating everyday experiences. What he saw he could tell better, perhaps, than anybody else, as Mr. Browning somewhat grudgingly said of Andrea del Sarto. What he did not see, did not exist for him. He had something of the angry impatience of the middle-class mind with all points of view not his own. In "Barchester Towers" he permitted himself to gibe at the recently published novel "Tancred," and for the author as well as the work he cherished a feeling of contemptuous dislike. There could be no finer tribute to Lord Beaconsfield's genius. "Tancred" is as far beyond anything that Mr. Trollope wrote as "Orley Farm" is superior to a Chancery pleading; and we have but to lay "Alroy" on the same table with "The Prime Minister" to see where Anthony Trollope stands. —LORD, WALTER FREWEN, 1901, *The Novels of Anthony Trollope*, Nineteenth Century, vol. 49, p. 805.

In his wide survey of social conditions in the middle and upper classes of England, he comes nearer than any other English novelist to fulfilling the vast programmes of the French realists, Balzac and Zola.— MOODY, WILLIAM VAUGHN, AND LOVETT, ROBERT MORSS, 1902. *A History of English Literature*, p. 372.

Revert in memory to such a humdrum realist as Anthony Trollope, in order vividly to realize why that fiction-maker, whose class is confessedly not the first, is likely to keep his place in the suffrages of a large, and not undistinguished, constituency. The folk of the "Barchester Chronicles" may be commonplace and unexciting; but they are verifiable and cling to the mind.—BURTON, RICHARD, 1902, *Forces in Fiction and Other Essays*, p. 15.

Certainly Trollope, like Balzac, introduced the same characters into more than one novel, which saved the trouble of inventing them; yet the creator does not trouble himself much as to what becomes of his heroes in their new embodiments. In the case of Trollope more than any other writer of a certain importance, we feel that he wrote at random without any artistic plan.—ENGEL, EDWARD, 1902, *A History of English Literature*, rev. Hamley Bent, p. 463.

Perhaps no writer represents more perfectly than Trollope the great development of social and domestic tendencies in the English novel of the middle and third quarter of the last century. A man of real genius, he yet had not genius enough to stand out from and above his time; and for that very reason he portrays it more fully, just as Ben Jonson brings us nearer to the Elizabethan Age than does Shakespeare.

. . . Trollope's novels deal almost entirely with the author's own time; no mediæval history, bravos, swordplay, moonlight romance. His people are common people; that is, they are human beings like other human beings before they are anything else. It is this constant detection of ordinary human nature under the disguises of wealth and aristocracy which misleads Mr. Saintsbury into calling Trollope a painter of middle-class life. His painting of middle-class life is good, much better than his painting of low life; but certainly his best work is on the upper classes. . . . So far as plot goes, in the stricter sense of the word, Trollope confesses that he is weak, and few will be found to differ from him.—BRADFORD, GAMALIEL, JR., 1902, *Anthony Trollope*, Atlantic Monthly, vol. 89, pp. 426, 428.

Edward Bouverie Pusey
1800–1882

Born near Oxford, 1800: died Sept. 16, 1882. An English theologian. His name was originally Edward Bouverie: the family, of Huguenot origin, became lords of the manor of Pusey, near Oxford, and from it took that name. In 1818 he entered Christ Church, Oxford, and in 1824 became a fellow of Oriel. He was associated with John Henry Newman and John Keble. In 1828 he was regius professor of Hebrew at Oxford and canon of Christ Church. In 1835 he took part in the tractarian movement, and later was suspended for three years (1843–46) from the function of preaching for publishing "The Holy Eucharist a Comfort to the Penitent." The movement thus started took the name "Puseyism." The practice of confession among the extreme ritualists of the Church of England dates from his two sermons on "the entire absolution of the penitent" (1846). Among his works are "Parochial Sermons," "Doctrines of the Real Presence," and "The Minor Prophets." He was one of the editors of the "Library of Translations from the Fathers" and the "Anglo-Catholic Library."—SMITH, BENJAMIN E., ed., 1894–97, *The Century Cyclopedia of Names*, p. 832.

PERSONAL

I have had several conversations with Pusey on religion since I last mentioned him. How can I doubt his seriousness? His very eagerness to talk of the Scriptures seems to prove it. May I lead him forward, at the same time gaining good from him! He has told me the plan of his Essay for the Chancellor's prize, and I clearly see that it is much better than mine. I cannot think I shall get it; to this day I have thought I should. . . . That Pusey is Thine, O Lord, how can I doubt? His deep views of the Pastoral Office, his high ideas of the spiritual rest of the Sabbath, his devotional spirit, his love of the Scriptures, his firmness and zeal, all testify to the operation of the Holy Ghost; yet I fear he is prejudiced against Thy children. Let me never be eager to convert him to a *party* or to a form of *opinion*. Lead us both on in the way of Thy commandments. What am I that I should be so blest in my near associates!—NEWMAN, JOHN HENRY, 1823, *Journal*, May 2 and 17; *Letters and Correspondence During his Life in the English Church*, ed. Mozley, p. 103.

I wish, my dearest mother, you could see how perfectly calm I am about my affairs. I commit them to God and feel that they do not belong to me or affect me. In many respects, it is a very good thing that I am the person it falls upon. Some things are as adverse as possible, as that the Provost of Oriel and the Warden of Wadham are among the assistants of the Vice-Chancellor; yet Jelf does not think it hopeless since he has consented to be one. I trust in my friends' prayers and that God will defend His truth; for that only have I spoken. All my friends say that good must come out of it somehow. So I am quite at rest. It seems as if something very momentous was going on, but that I had nothing to do but to wait for it, and pray and abide, as I trust under the shadow of His wings, and be at rest.—PUSEY, EDWARD BOUVERIE, 1843, *To His Mother, May 25; Life by Henry Parry Liddon, ed. Johnston and Wilson, vol.* II, *p.* 316.

You have heard, of course, of Pusey's suspension for two years, by the papers. It excites enormous indignation. All persons who are not quite with the Heads of Houses clique are disgusted. It was really a sermon which people heard and went away, thinking it fine and eloquent of course, and giving high views of the Eucharist; but as for any doctrine, the idea never entered into any one's head, till the fact came out. The Heads will find themselves in the wrong, their mode of conducting the whole business has been so desperately unfair, not to say actually arrogant and tyrannical.—MOZLEY, JAMES B., 1843, *To his Sister, June* 4; *Letters, ed. his Sister, p.* 141.

I must tell you that on arriving here I went, as in duty bound, to pay my respects to Dr. Pusey. He had been ill for a considerable period, suffering constantly from low fever. I found him lying on the sofa and apparently unable to rise, encompassed on all sides by folios. No other man have I ever seen so like a saint. The expression of holiness, humility, and charity about him makes a face, in itself ugly, a most beautiful object to contemplate. You look at him and see at once that he is a person whom it is actually impossible to offend personally, and who in the paroxysms of disease would give thanks for his sufferings, simply believing that they were sent as fatherly chastisements and would leave a benediction behind. I perceived very soon that his entire unselfishness has preserved him from all affliction as regards himself in consequence of this iniquitous and ignominious sentence with which he has been branded. There is, in fact, no drop of bitterness in his whole composition, nothing that can turn sour.—DEVERE, AUBREY, 1843, *To Henry Taylor, June* 8; *Correspondence of Henry Taylor, ed. Dowden, p.* 143.

Nothing has occurred in our own time, so pregnant with great consequences, as the late conspiracy in Oxford. . . . Men look at each other as if some wicked thing had been perpetrated, on which they could not venture to speak. In all, there is a deep feeling that it is not to end here, and a sense of love and reverence for the injured person strongly entertained. . . . There is also a very general impression, that the sermon itself is no more than a handle for a preconcerted measure; which is confirmed by the fact that they have resolutely refused to mention any one objectional proposition in the sermon, or in what way it is discordant with the Church of England. All I have met with consider the sermon very innocent and unexceptionable.— WILLIAMS, ISAAC, 1843, *Autobiography, pp.* 136, 137.

Notwithstanding an occasional difference of opinion on matters of importance, our friendship has lasted more than a quarter of a century. I feel therefore that I am not taking too great a liberty when, by dedicating this sermon to you, I avail myself of the opportunity to record my respect for the profound learning, the unimpeachable orthodoxy, and the Christian temper with which, in the midst of a faithless and pharisaical generation, you have maintained the cause of true religion, and preached the pure unadulterated word of God.—HOOK, WALTER FARQUHAR, 1845, *Mutual Forbearance Recommended in Things Indifferent, The Church and her Ordinances, vol.* II.

We have had Pusey and Manning preaching here lately, the former three times. Pusey's middle sermon, preached in the evening, was the perfection of his style. But it is wrong to talk of *style* in respect of a preacher whose very merit consists in his aiming at no style at all. He is certainly, to my feelings, more impressive than any one else in the pulpit, though he has not one of the graces of oratory. His discourse is generally a rhapsody, describing with infinite repetition and accumulativeness, the wickedness of sin, the worthlessness of earth, and the blessedness of heaven. He is as still as a statue all the time he is uttering it, looks as white as a sheet, and is as monotonous in delivery as possible. While listening to him, you do not seem to see and hear a *preacher*, but to have visible before you a most earnest and devout spirit, striving to carry out in this world a high religious theory.—COLERIDGE, SARA, 1845, *To Miss Morris, July* 7; *Memoir and Letters, ed. her Daughter, p.* 232.

Every seat, every transept, every aisle thronged to bursting; spectators or hearers wandering about the clerestories, Pusey carried up into the pulpit by a by-passage. So much for the benefits of suspension. To me, I confess, the mere sight of a vast crowd hanging on the lips of a good man is so pathetic that I would go a good way to hear it. The sermon—alas! I shuddered as I heard the text (John XX, 21) and foresaw the subject—Absolution. However, it evidently only came because it was part of his own course; the more offensive topics of which it was capable were not dwelt upon, and merely the old commonplaces and quotations reproduced in Pusey's usual confusion of style. And so, on the whole, it was like most of his sermons, a divine soul clothed in a very earthly body. The beginning very pathetic and dignified—"It will be in the memory of some that three years since," &c.—and the end, on the needs of the manufacturing towns, very earnest and solemn. I do sincerely say, "God bless him, and keep him amongst us."—STANLEY ARTHUR PENRHYN, 1846, *Letter, Life and Correspondence, ed. Prothero and Bradley, vol. I, p. 344.*

The doctor is a short man, thin, and somewhat attenuated, has a careworn look, a dim eye, a long and solemn countenance; and when I saw him, 1845, appeared dirty, unshaven, and slovenly in his attire. He approaches nearer to the *beau idéal* of a bookworm than any man I ever met with. There is a great mildness and humility of deportment about him, bordering upon nervousness and timidity; but beneath this outward shell there is evidently a kernel of ambition, and a love of notoriety. He looked like a man who was conscious he was the object of the public gaze. His conversation is sensible and erudite, but not fluent or animated. As Hebrew Professor, he expounds his views to his students with clearness and order, but without much force or originality of thought. . . . Dr. Pusey's intellectual character does not comport with those ideas which we commonly associate with men who are the founders of a mere sect, or the leaders of a party. There is little boldness or enthusiasm in him. He does not throw himself with ardour either into favourite or antagonistic theories. His intellectual genius is cold, phlegmatic, and calculating. It is the growth of long and assiduous cultivation, rather than of native vigour and strength. His mind wants the invariable and characteristic symbol of greatness.—BLAKEY, ROBERT, 1873, *Memoirs, ed. Miller, pp. 179, 180.*

I do not believe him to be open to conviction on any point in the remotest degree connected with dogma on which he has once made up his mind. . . . Dr. Pusey's remarks have a little lowered my estimate of his Hebrew scholarship, which was high, and has not raised my estimate of his judgment, which was low.— THIRLWALL, CONNOP, 1879, *To Rev. A. R. Fausset, March 25-31; Letters ed. Perowne and Stokes, pp. 315, 316.*

Dr. Pusey, as we all know, could be as intolerant as Athanasius, but, apart from what you call his theological prepossessions, he always retained through life a genuine respect for real scholarship, even for the much derided "original research." He often showed the warmest sympathy for true and earnest students in every field of Oriental philology. He took a deep interest in the discoveries of cuneiform scholars, and fully appreciated their bearing on Hebrew scholarship. He cared to know what the "Veda" and the "Avesta" had to teach us, and he was not afraid of new sciences, such as Comparative Philology and Comparative Mythology. Even when he had no time to study new subjects himself, he was always anxious to hear the latest news.—MÜLLER, FRIEDRICH MAX, 1882, *To the Editor of "The Times," Sept. 23; Life and Letters, ed. his Wife, vol. II, p. 128.*

Dr. Pusey's life had two marks especially set in it by Divine Providence: it was a life of controversy and a life of suffering. He often deplored the necessity which obliged him to spend so much of his time and thought in religious controversy. It was, he firmly believed, "the Lord's controversy," in which he was thus engaged; and he accepted a task from which much in his character would have held him back, as a duty laid on him by Providential Wisdom. . . . Certainly he did all that could be done to sweeten controversy by the charities and courtesies that were natural to his chastened temper. . . . And his life was largely a life of suffering. Assuredly it did not lack the Print of the Nails. He had his full share of home sorrows, which the affectionateness of his character sharpened to the utmost. . . . Troubles there were of another order which wounded him even more deeply. The separation which for some years followed the secession of Dr. Newman, the desertion of friends who remained, and from whose sympathy he might well have hoped for much, the coldness or active hostility of persons in high authority, the failure of younger men to answer to his reasonable expectations or to be true to themselves, above all the lacerations of the Church, to whose wellbeing and growth he was devoted heart and soul—these things cut him to the quick. . . . And this intimacy with suffering was probably one chief secret of his moral power, because it endowed him so richly, and it had endowed St. Paul, with the gift of sympathy.—LIDDON, HENRY PARRY, 1884, *Edward Bouverie Pusey, Clerical Life and Work*, pp. 368, 369.

Dr. Pusey, who used every now and then to take Newman's duties at St Mary's, was to me a much less interesting person. A learned man, no doubt, but dull and tedious as a preacher. Certainly, in spite of the name Puseyism having been given to the Oxford attempt at a new Catholic departure, he was not the Columbus of that voyage of discovery, undertaken to find a safer haven for the Church of England. I may, however, be more or less unjust to him, as I owe him a sort of grudge. His discourses were not only less attractive than those of Dr. Newman, but always much longer, and the result of this was that the learned Canon of Christ Church generally made me late for dinner at my college, a calamity never inflicted on his All Souls hearers by the terser and swifter fellow of Oriel whom he was replacing.—DOYLE, SIR FRANCIS HASTINGS, 1887, *Reminiscences and Opinions*, p. 148.

Dr. Pusey was a person with whom it was not wise to meddle, unless his assailants could make out a case without a flaw. He was without question the most venerated person in Oxford. Without an equal, in Oxford at least, in the depth and range of his learning, he stood out yet more impressively among his fellows in the lofty moral elevation and simplicity of his life, the blamelessness of his youth, and the profound devotion of his manhood, to which the family sorrows of his later years, and the habits which grew out of them, added a kind of pathetic and solemn interest. Stern and severe in his teaching at one time,—at least as he was understood,—beyond even the severity of Puritanism, he was yet overflowing with affection, tender and sympathetic to all who came near him, and, in the midst of continual controversy, he endeavoured with deep conscientiousness, to avoid the bitterness of controversy. He was the last man to attack; much more the last man to be unfair to. The men who ruled in Oxford contrived, in attacking him, to make almost every mistake which it was possible to make.—CHURCH, RICHARD WILLIAM, 1891, *The Oxford Movement*, p. 284.

Yes, here was a *good, good, real* man! And from a Patriotic point of view, what are we not to think of the patience, the firmness, the absolute confidence in his fellow-countrymen with which he waited, bestrode that fiery Pegasus, rode the great race, and won, while Newman lay sprawling on the Via Sacra? This is the unmistakable Englishman, this dogged Pusey; dogged, but did you see the tenderness! God forgive me! When I think of my blindness—BROWN, THOMAS EDWARD, 1893, *To S. T. Irwin, Oct. 9; Letters, ed. Irwin, vol.* I, p. 217.

His alms-deeds were beyond measure generous, many of them unknown till now. He built St. Saviour's Church, Leeds, in the name of a penitent, nor allowed even Dr. Hook, then Vicar of Leeds, to know whose was the hand that gave. We lay down the book [Life of Pusey] feeling sure that here was a man to whom great grace was given, and we may thank God, in Hooker's words, that "God does not tie to sacraments the grace that He gives through sacraments;" but in so far as Dr. Liddon holds up to us Pusey's life as that of a Catholic priest, perhaps the example is rather "what not to be, than what to be." It is a history of one who strove to prop up a falling building, and was wounded by many of the stones as they fell, who tried to put a new face on that which was mouldering within, who was deservedly honoured indeed in his day, but must pass and be forgotten, as are those who have given names to many other sects, foundering and to founder, while the bark of Peter rides the waves.—PAUL, C. KEGAN, 1893, *Dr. Pusey, The Month, vol.* 79, p. 534.

I was greatly impressed as an undergraduate by Dr. Pusey's preaching, as afterwards by his published writings, by his saintly life, and his loyal love, faithful unto death, for the Church, in which he received from those in authority so much opposition and distrust. His manner was in itself a sermon, and he went up to preach with a manifest humility, which no hypocrite could assume, and no actor could copy.— HOLE, S. REYNOLDS, 1893, *Memories, p.* 145.

If we were to try to describe the character of Dr. Pusey in a single sentence, we could do no better than to borrow St. Paul's expression—"Wise unto that which is good, and simple concerning evil." . . . He was wise—not with the wisdom of the world nor of the serpent—not with the wisdom which has to do with passing things —but unto that which is good; and it may be added, unto that alone. For he was simple as a child concerning evil. He could help good men, but he could never discover bad ones. Again and again he was deceived. Again and again in dealing with what seemed evil to himself, though it did not seem so to others, he signally failed in putting himself at his opponent's point of view. His greatness was the greatness of the kingdom of heaven, in patterning his life by the life of Christ.—ROGERS, ARTHUR, 1898, *Men and Movements, in the English Church, p.* 54.

He was a power in the Church of England greater than Archbishop or Bishop, for almost half a century; and for sixteen years before his death was the sole leader of his party. To the cause which that party represented he devoted, with unswerving self-sacrifice, many great gifts,—birth, high station in the University, unwearied industry, solid learning. His zeal was apostolic, his life saintly; he was a voluminous writer, a powerful preacher, not, like John Wesley, to the common people, but to learned hearers and sensitive religious minds among the clergy and educated laity. It was among these that he gathered followers; through these his influence reached the world. And upon him, as upon Wesley, the influence of his followers reacted.— PALMER, ROUNDELL, (EARL OF SELBORNE), 1898, *Memorials Part* II, *Personal and Political, vol.* II, *p.* 72.

In the pulpit to strangers his appearance was not particularly striking, nor his voice musical. His language was sometimes obscure and his sentences long and involved. But no one ever failed to be impressed by his wonderful earnestness, by the spiritual power that made itself evident, by the reverential awe towards God and gentle patient affectionateness towards man that characterized these beautiful sermons. It was felt that he was indeed a "Man of God," a prophet faithful in rebuke, uncompromising in the delivery of his message, a teacher of "all the counsel of God," the Catholic faith in its fulness. And yet there was no lack of tender human sympathy, charitable recognition of the weaknesses of men and women, and compassionate anxiety to apply every spiritual remedy to their needs.—DONALDSON, AUG. B., 1900, *Five Great Oxford Leaders, p.* 222.

To love God, to work for God—these words sum up the story of Dr. Pusey's life. Loving as he did, how could it be but a joy, shining brighter than even duty, to work for Him whom, not having seen, he loved? His eighty-second birthday found him still at that labour in the vineyard, begun in the early morning of life—labour never slackened during the few years of a great earthly love and happiness—taken up with severer self-devotion two days after all that was mortal of her who had been his love was laid in the grave. He had continued his ministrations to the Sisters at Ascot during the few days before his birthday, besides, as usual, reading for his Hebrew Lectures. . . . If it would be difficult to take a day's journey in England without seeing some even outward token of the revival in which Dr. Pusey had so large a share, his life was, notwithstanding, one of more than common trial and of wearing anxieties. Yet his own words, while still young, "One may gradually cease to know what disappointment is," came true; and, whether amid visible success, or unfulfilled hopes, he stood firm as a rock, never quailing, never changing, never ceasing to be the apostle of peace and love, while earnestly contending for the faith once delivered to the saints. And they who love him most think now of the Mercy and Love that led him all his life long, through the light affliction which is but for a moment—granting him the request of his lips, drowning him with the blessings of goodness, and the abundance of things which since the beginning of the world it hath not entered into the heart of man to conceive— which eye hath not seen nor ear heard—

Nel miro ed angelico templo
Che solo amore e luce ha per confine.

—TRENCH, MARY, 1900, *The Story of Dr. Pusey's Life, pp.* 545, 558.

He was not only the grave ascetic. My children know another side of him. Hearing that my daughter had expressed a wish to "come out," at the ball given in 1881 by our House to Prince Leopold at Commemoration, he at once sent for tickets, which were a guinea each, and gave to me. He sat up to see her dressed and start, and when we came down to breakfast next morning, his first question was whether she had had nice partners, and enjoyed herself. When my girls were growing up, he wished me to ask young men to the house, and he ordered the garden beds to be cleared away, and a tennis lawn made in the lower garden. Tennis was new at that time, and my dear father used to leave his books, and stand watching the game from his study window. He said that "it was very good exercise for the young people."—BRINE, MARY PUSEY, 1900, *The Story of Dr. Pusey's Life*, ed. Trench, p. 535.

GENERAL

To fly in the teeth of English Puseyism, and risk such shrill welcome as I am pretty sure of, is questionable: yet at bottom why not? Dost thou not as entirely reject this new Distraction of a Puseyism as man can reject a thing,—and couldst utterly abjure it and even abhor it,—were the shadow of a cobweb ever likely to become momentous, the cobweb itself being beheaded, with axe and block on Tower Hill, two centuries ago? I think it were as well to tell Puseyism that it has something of good, but also much of bad and even worst.—CARLYLE, THOMAS, 1840, *To Emerson, Dec. 9, Correspondence of Carlyle and Emerson*, ed. Norton vol. I, p. 338.

Dr. Pusey is the representative of that class of Englishmen, who, looking with reprehension and alarm upon the changes in the ecclesiastical and political system of our country which have slowly but constantly gained ground during the lapse of the last fifteen years, have ranged themselves under the freshly emblazoned banners and newly illuminated altars of the Church, have unsheathed the sword of Faith and new interpretation, earnest to restore the ancient constitution in Church and State; to stem the advancing tide of modern opinion and endeavour; to retain the strong-hold of the Divine Right of Kings and the Spiritual Supremacy of the Priesthood, and from this detached ground to say to the rising waves, "Thus far shalt thou go, and no farther," and to the troubled waters, "Peace, be still."—HORNE, RICHARD HENGIST, 1844, *A New Spirit of the Age*, p. 120.

Your judgment of the general character of Dr. Pusey's book appears to me very just, and at least very mild. Between ourselves, I find it very difficult to resist the impression that such resolute and passionate one-sidedness in a man of such extensive learning must be a reaction against inward misgivings kept under, as suggestions of the Evil one, by a violent effort of the will. His notice of Schleiermacher, however, is creditable to him, and leads one to hope that he would not now recall anything he had said of S. in former times.—THIRLWALL, CONNOP, 1865, *To Rev. J. J. Stewart Perowne, Dec. 12; Letters*, ed. Perowne and Stokes, p. 245.

We wish we could speak as favourably of the general tone and temper of Dr. Pusey's volume as we can of its learning and completeness. But unhappily, its greatest defect is the bitterness of its language,—the indiscriminate censure with which all are assailed who have ventured to entertain any doubts as to the time when the Book of Daniel was written. The charge of wilful blindness, so repeatedly brought against those whose misfortunes it is to be Dr. Pusey's opponents, is rather apt to enlist sympathy on their side than to convince us that their assailant is right. Instinctively we feel that such charges betray a weakness somewhere.... It is impossible to read such a work without the profoundest admiration for the depth and varied extent of the author's learning; but it is impossible not also to lament that the glory of this learning has been so grievously tarnished. We do not blame Dr. Pusey for ranging it all on the side of what he believes to be the truth; we do full justice to the sincerity of his convictions; we honour his piety; we even admit the force of his arguments so far as to think that he has shown, and shown far more convincingly than any one who has yet made the attempt, that the Book of Daniel is not a late production of the Maccabæan age, but belongs rightfully to the age to which it was for centuries commonly assigned. But we can express nothing but disapprobation both of the temper in which the book is written, and of the entire perversion of all critical principles by which, in our judgment, it is marked.—PEROWNE, J. J. STEWART, 1866, *Dr. Pusey on Daniel the Prophet, Contemporary Review*, vol. 1, pp. 97, 121.

A man after all to rank with religious

leaders of a high mark in all ages.—CHURCH, RICHARD WILLIAM, 1869, *To Asa Gray, Nov. 5; Life and Letters of Dean Church*, ed. his Daughter, p. 220.

The publications of Dr. Pusey are very numerous, but not one of them bids fair to take a permanent place in our literature.— CHAMBERS, ROBERT, 1876, *Cyclopædia of English Literature*, ed. Carruthers.

Dr. Pusey has been convicted so often of so many omissions, inaccuracies and mistakes in his multitudinous controversial writings, that all confidence in his fairness or capability of seeing both sides of a much disputed question is for ever lost.—SAVILE, BOURCHIER WREY, 1883, *Dr. Pusey, An Historical Sketch*, p. 6.

The motif of Dr. Pusey's book ["Historical Inquiry"] was not indeed a vindication of German Theology in its rationalistic developments. It was, however, a defence of it from the indiscriminate assaults contained in "Discourses preached before the University of Cambridge, by Hugh James Rose," and published by him, in 1825, under the title of "The State of Protestantism in Germany." . . . In contrast to Rose's book, Pusey's is an eminently fair, reasonable, and candid enquiry, liberal in the best sense of the word, as recognizing what is good no less than what is bad in German theology, and especially as setting the worst phases of German rationalism in the light of the causes which have operated in producing them. The author was no more in love with rationalism than Mr. Rose, but he understood, as the former did not do, all the phenomena which went under that name, what varying shades of truth and falsehood they presented, and by what intelligible links they were connected with one another. Nothing, indeed, is more remarkable in Dr. Pusey's work than the breadth and power of historical analysis it displays, its extreme fairness; and even to this day, when so many accounts have been given of the historical development of German theology from different points of view, it still deserves perusal.—TULLOCH, JOHN, 1885, *Movements of Religious Thought in Britain During the Nineteenth Century*, p. 60.

The Tract [No. 18] is dated St. Thomas' Day, 1833, and does not appear to have been in circulation before the beginning of January. It is longer than any of its predecessors; partly because the writer could not easily express himself otherwise than at length, but partly also because it covers more ground, and more nearly exchanges the character of a fugitive composition for that of a theological treatise. . . . It is impossible to read this tract without being profoundly impressed with the reality of the writer—of his religious convictions and life as the mainspring and warrant of his teaching. Indeed, this tract differs from its predecessors in the degree of emphasis which it lays on personal and experimental considerations. . . . Pusey's tract on Baptism was unquestionably the work in virtue of which he took his place among the leaders of the Oxford Movement. Its appearance marked an epoch, both in the history of his own religious mind and in the progress of the cause to which it contributed. —LIDDON, HENRY PARRY, 1890-93, *Life of Edward Bouverie Pusey*, ed. Johnston and Wilson, vol. I, pp. 280, 281, 343.

After all, the real key to the unpersuasiveness of Dr. Pusey's literary efforts on the subject of reunion is to be found not so much in his mistakes as in his method. As for mistakes, every writer who dares anything for the good of others makes some; and we do not envy the cold, critical nature which will wrap itself up in reserve rather than risk a blunder; we cannot feel enthusiasm for the heart that will not let its thoughts spring to other hearts and clasp them to itself in the truth, for fear its reason should have to frown on a misquotation or an unguarded expression. But it was Dr. Pusey's method that was at fault; it was wrong in theology and uninspiring in fact. *Pectus facit theologum;* the heart is the fount of true theology. *Cor cordi loquitur;* heart takes hold of heart. . . . Pusey's method was of the desk and midnight oil; he writes as one who has lost the ways of the docile, submissive child; the *abandon*, the *élan* simplicity had gone when in his later days he spoke of Rome. It was with him all analysis and weighing of difficulties on one side. But you might as well attempt to analyse the lightning-flash or the colour of the cloud as it dips into the setting sun, as analyse the fascination and the magic charm of that one city which we call eternal, and which spells one way strength and the other love. But to all this Pusey was impervious. And it was his duty to analyse and weigh objections; but it would have been his gain to have combined also, and to have seen the value of the positive witness to the truth he opposed.—RIVINGTON, W., 1898, *Dr. Pusey's "Eirenicon"—Why is it a Failure? Dublin Review, vol.* 122, *pp.* 414, 415.

His confidence in his own position and in the *via media* was tranquil. His piety was deep and sincere. While he lacks the imagination and power of luminous exposition which belong to Newman, he was a miracle of industry, his acquisitions of learning were large, and his mind was straightforward in its operations.—FISHER, GEORGE PARK, 1896, *History of Christian Doctrine, p.* 463.

Pusey's style was accused by some of bareness and by others of obscurity; but these accusations may be safely dismissed as due merely to the prevalent fancy for florid expression, and to the impatience of somewhat scholastically arranged argument which has also distinguished our times.—SAINTSBURY, GEORGE, 1896, *A History of Nineteenth Century Literature, p.* 362.

Edward Bouverie Pusey was, as regards his contributions to formal theology, superior to Newman; but both as a man and as a writer he was indefinitely smaller. . . . Pusey's writings are purely technical theology, not literature like those of Newman. Of their value diverse opinions will long be entertained. They are oracles for the High Church party; but it is well to consider what opponents think, especially such as have some grounds of sympathy. Pius IX. compared Pusey to "a bell, which always sounds to invite the faithful to Church, and itself always remains outside." In a similar spirit another great Romish ecclesiastic, when questioned as to Pusey's chance of salvation, is said to have playfully replied, "Oh, yes, he will be saved *propter magnam implicationem.*" These are just the criticisms of those who have attacked the Puseyite position from the point of view of free thought. They are also the criticisms implied in Newman's action. It is at least remarkable that critics from both extreme parties, together with the ablest of all the men who have ever maintained the views in question, should concur in the same judgment.—WALKER, HUGH, 1897, *The Age of Tennyson, pp.* 153, 154.

In his controversy with Dr. Farrar with regard to future punishment, we have the well-nigh solitary instance in this volume of a victory distinctly on his side. He succeeded in putting Dr. Farrar conspicuously in the wrong. Naturally enough, the closing years of his unselfish life brought him much beautiful appreciation, and his death many honourable testimonies from men who differed from him by the heaven's width. In so far as we are able to separate his personality from his opinions, it presents much that is engaging, and that must have endeared him immeasurably to his intimate friends. Intellectually not even Newman could surpass him in his subordination of rationality to tradition as the test of truth.—CHADWICK, JOHN WHITE, 1898, *Book Reviews, The New World, vol.* 7, *p.* 185.

We fear these Letters are destined to do harm. The bulk of them is not anti-Roman, not controversial at all. Indeed with some three quarters of their contents a Catholic would entirely concur. They are not comparable with a Saint's Letters, with the Letters of St. Francis Xavier, for instance, or those of St. Francis of Sales; but they breathe a piety earnest and venerable. Just on that account will the publication do harm. The goodness of the book will make what is evil in it tell. For there is objective evil in these pages, subtle perversion of Catholic truth, and ingenious deterrents from Catholic unity. Sad to think of the name and fame of a good man fathering upon the world a deleterious mixture of Gallicanism and Protestantism.—RICKABY, JOSEPH, 1899, *Dr. Pusey's Letters, The Month, vol.* 93, *p.* 176.

James Thomson
1834–1882

Born, at Port Glasgow, 23 Nov. 1834. Educated at Caledonian Orphan Asylum, 1843–50. At Ballincollig, near Cork, as assistant regimental schoolmaster, 1850–52; at Military Training College, Chelsea, 1852–54. Contrib., to Tait's "Edinburgh Mag.," 1858; to "National Reformer," 1860–75. Served as regimental schoolmaster till 1862. After leaving army, held various secretaryships. Visit to America, 1872; to Spain as correspondent to "New York World," 1873; Contrib., to "Cope's Tobacco Plant," 1875–81. Contrib., at various times to "Daily Telegraph," "Athenæum," "Weekly Despatch," "Fortnightly

Rev.," "Fraser's Mag.," "Cornhill Mag." Died, in London, 3 June 1882. Buried in Highgate Cemetery. *Works:* "The City of Dreadful Night," 1880; "Vane's Story," 1880; "Essays and Phantasies," 1881. *Posthumous:* "The Story of a Famous Old Jewish Firm, etc.," 1883; "A Voice from the Nile," ed. by B. Dobell, 1884 [1883]; "Shelley," (priv. ptd.), 1884; "Selections from Original Contributions by J. Thomson to 'Cope's Tobacco Plant,'" 1889; "Poetical Works," ed. by B. Dobell (2 vols.), 1895; "Biographical and Critical Studies," ed. by B. Dobell, 1896. *Life:* by H. S. Salt, 1889.—SHARP, R. FARQUHARSON, 1897, *A Dictionary of English Authors, p.* 280.

PERSONAL

It may also be said of the late James Thomson, author of "The City of Dreadful Night," that he was the English Poe. Not only in his command of measures, his weird imaginings, intellectual power and gloom, but with respect to his errant yet earnest temper, his isolation, and divergence from the ways of society as now constituted,—and very strangely also in the successive chances of his life so poor and proud, in his final decline through unfortunate habits and infirmities, even to the sad coincidence of his death in a hospital,—do the man, his genius, and career afford an almost startling parallel to what we know of our poet of "the grotesque and arabesque."—STEDMAN, EDMUND CLARENCE, 1875–87, *Victorian Poets, p.* 455.

No tears of mine shall fall upon thy face;
Whatever city thou hast reached at last,
Better it is than that where thy feet passed
So many times, such weary nights and days.
Thy journeying feet knew all its inmost ways,
Where shapes and shadows of dread things were cast:
There moved thy soul profoundly dark and vast,
There did thy voice its song of anguish raise.
Thou would'st have left that city of great night,
Yet travelled its dark mazes all in vain:
But one way leads from it, which found aright,
Who quitteth it shall not come back again.
There didst thou grope thy way through thy long pain:
Hast thou outside found any world of light?
—MARSTON, PHILIP BOURKE, 1882, *Mr. James Thomson, The Academy.*

When we come to sum up the leading points of Thomson's life and character, we are naturally met by the consideration how far his morbid despondency, which we call pessimism, was due to his misfortunes, and how far to physical causes. . . . It is the opinion of one of his biographers that Thomson inherited a constitutional melancholia, and that his early bereavement was "not the *cause* of his life-long misery, but merely the peg on which he hung his raiment of sorrow. Mr. Dobell, however, is inclined to believe that "no other affliction could have affected him as he was affected by this." One would probably be safe in concluding that the truth lies somewhere between these two theories, and that Thomson's pessimistic bent of mind was brought about partly by an inherited disposition to melancholia, and partly by the crushing misfortune of his early life. It must not be supposed, however, that, pessimist as he was, he was accustomed to make a parade of his sufferings: on the contrary, all accounts agree in representing him as a singularly cheerful companion, and one of the most brilliant of talkers. Neither did his pessimism take a cynical and misanthropic turn, as in the case of Schopenhauer, who regarded, or affected to regard, his fellow-creatures and fellow-sufferers (synonymous terms, as he thought) with aversion and dislike. Thomson's disposition, on the other hand, was always benevolent and kindly, in which respect he resembled Shelley, for whom he again and again expresses the warmest feelings of reverence and admiration, and to whom, as "the poet of poets and purest of men," "Vane's Story," with its accompanying poems, is dedicated.—SALT, H. S., 1886, *The Works of James Thomson* ("B. V."), *Gentleman's Magazine, vol.* 260, *pp.* 606, 607.

On one occasion, after he had left the hospitable house of his friends and was living alone in London lodgings, the children of his landlady (of whom, as of all children, he was fond, with a fully reciprocated affection) going to the door to admit him, closed it again in his face, and told their father that "Mr. Thomson's wicked brother was at the door;" they could not recognise their Mr. Thomson in this figure of the dipsomaniac claiming his name. Even his best friends at times found themselves forced from his society; although Mr. Foote tells us that he struggled manfully against this terrible disease. The fits were always preceded by days of blackest hypochondria, until at last, in desperation, he flew to the bottle. Except for this infirmity, he was methodical, logical, even mathematical;

and when not suffering from depression, "the most brilliant talker," says Mr. Foote, "I ever met." He was an inveterate smoker, and when he ceased to contribute to Mr. Bradlaugh's paper, his main source of income was from *Cope's Tobacco Plant*, a magazine to which he contributed some good essays, and a humourous poem about smoking, in Chaucer's vein. . . . So Thomson paced the dreary ways of that vast murky chaos called London, hardly able to keep his head above water (indeed often going under), a man of exceptional genius, quite unknown, and powerless to win hearers for his too individual strain, with an ever-growing sense of utter aloofness from his fellows, faith and hope gone, health failing, now alone in the mean dingy room, now carousing late with some acquaintance, the overwrought, unsleeping brain tortured all night, hagridden by hell-born phantoms and cruel dreams! What wonder is it that he sought momentary relief in that poison which only intensifies the suffering it promises to cure. . . . Poor Thomson had long vainly desired publication, and his first book obtained audience "fit though few," but this success came too late to serve him. Fame, long-expected, arrived; but only to look into the face of a dying man.—NOEL, RODEN, 1892, *The Poets and the Poetry of the Century, Kingsley to Thomson*, ed. Miles, pp. 634, 635, 637.

THE CITY OF DREADFUL NIGHT
1874–80

James Thomson, though his works were few and his death comparatively early, was still one of the remarkable poets of this century. Most of the poets of our time have flirted with pessimism, but through their beautifully expressed sorrow we cannot help seeing that on the whole they are less sad than they seem, or that, like Mr. Matthew Arnold, they laid hold of a stern kind of philosophic consolation. It was reserved for Thomson to write the real poem of despair; it was for him to say the ultimate word about melancholia; for, of course, it is the result of that disorder which is depicted in "The City of Dreadful Night." It was for him to gauge its horrible shapes, to understand its revelations of darkness as Shelley and others have understood revelations of light. As soon as we have read the opening pages of "The City of Dreadful Night," we feel transported to a land of infinite tragedy.—MARSTON, PHILIP BOURKE, 1883, *The English Poets* ed. Ward, New Ed. vol. IV, p. 621.

"The City of Dreadful Night" may be characterized as a sombre, darkly wrought composition toned to a minor key from which it never varies. It is a mystical allegory, the outgrowth of broodings on hopelessness and spiritual desolation. The legend of Dürer's Melancholia is marvelously transcribed, and the isometric interlude, "As I came through the Desert thus it was," is only surpassed by Browning's "Childe Roland." The cup of pessimism, with all its conjuring bitterness, is drunk to the dregs in this enshrouded, and again lurid, but always remarkable poem. — STEDMAN, EDMUND CLARENCE, 1887, *Victorian Poets*, p. 456.

The "City of Dreadful Night" published in 1874, procured him for a time considerable reputation. Those untrained, but not impotent imaginations which, like the temper of Cassius "much enforced yieldeth a single spark," are remarkable illustrations of the power of that gift amid the humblest surroundings to strike forth tragic though broken notes into the poetry of the wealthiest age.—OLIPHANT, MARGARET O. W., 1892, *The Victorian Age of English Literature*, p. 241.

"The City of Dreadful Night" is the despair of a maker of selections. It is the work by which its author's reputation must stand or fall, and from it alone can he be represented; yet to convey by means of quotation any adequate idea of its sombre and terrifying imaginative grandeur would be impossible. The poem owes its effect to the admirable art by which a powerful and peculiar impression, produced at the commencement, is unflaggingly sustained and continually heightened until the close. Examined in detail, the workmanship is by no means of an absolute perfection—the verse inclines to halt, minor flaws disfigure the surface. But if the poem be viewed broadly, as a whole, these flaws will be lost sight of; and, as I have already indicated, it is only as a whole that the Epic of Pessimism can be fairly judged.—DOUGLAS, SIR GEORGE, 1893, *ed. Contemporary Scottish Verse, Introductory Note*, p. xvii.

GENERAL

Shelley, Heine, Leopardi, Schopenhauer, —such were the writers whom Thomson valued most, and whose influence is visible in his poetry. Yet the production already mentioned, and many others, have traits which are not found elsewhere in prose or verse. — STEDMAN, EDMUND CLARENCE, 1875–87, *Victorian Poets*, p. 455.

During the last few weeks I have been studying the poetry and prose of James Thomson, a very remarkable writer, who lived at the bottom of the deep sea of oblivion, "silent and shrouded with the sense of fate." But there is no English poet now living, except Tennyson, Browning, Swinburne, and Morris, who comes near him; and he has qualities which raise him to a level at least with these, though he is not so all-round as any one of them. I will bring you acquainted with him when you come here. He is a pessimist of the deepest dye, even more poignantly pessimistic than Leopardi, not so sublime and calm.—SYMONDS, JOHN ADDINGTON, 1884, *Letter, Feb. 11; John Addington Symonds*, ed. Brown, vol. II, p. 229.

As time goes on "The City of Dreadful Night" will more and more be considered a truly remarkable poem. It has the distinction of being the most hopelessly sad poem in literature. Much of Thomson's other work is characterized by equally high qualities—one or two of the shorter poems by even greater technical skill if not exceeding it in power of sombre imagination. He stands quite by himself—following no leader, belonging to no school: to De Quincey however, he has strong affinities.—SHARP, WILLIAM, 1886, *Sonnets of this Century*, p. 325, *note*.

Leopardi and Thomson (who has been called the second Leopardi) were poets of the broken heart, as in a less degree also were Byron and Heine. But we ought also to note the immense love of which our English pessimist was capable, and the full capacity for joy. His early poetry is all idealistic, mystical, exhaling impassioned affection, and breathing the "difficult iced air" of Faith's mountain top. . . . One main character of Thomson was his love for allegory and symbol; this we find early and late in him. His pessimistic vein indeed is not to be regarded as that most proper and essential to the man merely because it came latest, when his spirit was overclouded by the dark environments of his career, co-operating with and evoking those demons of gloom and intemperate disease which lurked within, only waiting their sinister opportunity. His healthy period was surely that middle time when he worked strong and hopeful, full of human sympathy, and of trust in the great, sound, universal Heart of all, in that overruling Providence which is ever preparing man's undying spirit for larger spheres of life and labour. . . . The purport and substance of Thomson should be gauged by his earlier, quite as much as by his later work, and the manner in that is often good also. We get an exuberant exultation in life, a glad, immense embrace of all Nature (including even Death, the renovator), as characterising the true and "Happy poet." Here we have the "Lord of the Castle of Indolence," as lovely, I think, as anything Thomson wrote in his maturity, yet composed at the early age of twenty-five, where the Spenserian measure is used with the skill of his namesake in the masterpiece bearing the same title.—NOEL, RODEN, 1892, *The Poets and the Poetry of the Century, Kingsley to Thomson*, ed. Miles, pp. 629, 630, 631.

In the love of cloud-scenery, and the faithful painting of it; in all those large effects of weirdness and solemnity which make sunrises and sunsets so full of awe and mystery; in the poetry of wonder and desolation, Thomson is a master, and he has studied Shelley to good purpose. . . . He is a man who has broken down in the quest, who has sought the Holy Grail in vain, who at last, hopeless of seeing any divine light "starlight mingle with the stars," has laid himself down in the unending forest, and is choked with the thick drift of darkness which every way falls upon him like the black snow of death. He has no questions to put to the oracle of doom; he has received his answer, and here records his belief that life is

"Darkness at the core,
And dust and ashes all that is."

—DAWSON, W. J., 1892, *Quest and Vision*, pp. 268, 274.

His claims, however, must rest on a comparatively small body of work, which will no doubt one day be selected and issued alone. "The City of Dreadful Night" itself, incomparably the best of the longer poems, is a pessimist and nihilist effusion of the deepest gloom amounting to despair, but couched in stately verse of an absolute sincerity and containing some splendid passages. With this is connected one of the latest pieces, the terrible

"Insomnia." Of lighter strain, written when the poet could still be happy, are "Sunday at Hampstead" and "Sunday up the River," "The Naked Goddess," and one or two others; while other things, such as "The fire that filled my heart of old," must also be cited. Even against these the charge of a monotonous, narrow, and irrational misery has been brought. But what saves Thomson is the perfection with which he expresses the negative and hopeless side of the sense of mystery, of the Unseen; just as Miss Rossetti expresses the positive and hopeful one. No two contemporary poets perhaps ever completed each other in a more curious way than this Bohemian atheist and this devout lady.—SAINTSBURY, GEORGE, 1896, *A History of Nineteenth Century Literature*, p. 298.

The striking contrast in "B. V.'s." character—a courageous genial spirit, coupled with an intolerable melancholia; spiritual aspiration with realistic grasp of fact; ardent zeal for democracy and free thought with stubborn disbelief in human progress —is clearly marked in his writings, which are lit up here and there with flashes of brilliant joyousness, but, blackly pessimistic in the main. His masterpiece is the "City of Dreadful Night,"... next to this are "Vane's Story," an autobiographic fantasia, and the oriental narrative "Weddah and Om-el-Bonain." Many of the lyrics, grave or gay, are poignantly beautiful, and the prose essays, satires, criticisms, and translations have great qualities that deserve to be better known. Shelley, Dante, Heine, and Leopardi were his chief literary models; his mature style, in its stern conciseness is less Shelleyan than Dantesque. — SALT, H. S., 1898, *Dictionary of National Biography*, vol. LVI, p. 256.

John Brown
1810–1882

Born, at Biggar, Lanarkshire, 22 Sept. 1810. At private school in Edinburgh, 1822–24; at High School 1824–26. To Edinburgh Univ., Nov. 1826. Began to study medicine, May 1827. Apprenticed to James Syme, surgeon, 1828–33. M. D. Edinburgh, 1833. Started practice in Edinburgh, where he lived till his death. Married Catharine Scott M'Kay, 4 June 1840; she died 6 Jan. 1864. F. R. C. P., 1847. Fellow of Roy. Soc. of Edinburgh, 1859. Assessor to Rector of Edinburgh Univ., 1861–62. Hon. LL. D., Edinburgh, 22 April 1874. Crown Pension, 1874. Died, in Edinburgh, 11 May 1882. Buried in New Calton cemetery. *Works:* "Horæ Subsecivæ," ser. i., 1858; ser. ii., 1861; ser. iii., 1882; "Rab and His Friends," (extracted from preceding), 1859; "On the deaths of Rev. J. M'Gilchrist, J. Brown, J. Henderson," 1860; "With Brains, Sir!" (anon.), 1860; "Health," 1862; "Marjorie Fleming" (from "North Brit. Rev."), 1863; "Jeems, the Doorkeeper," 1864; "Minchmoor," 1864; "Thackeray," 1877; "John Leech," 1877;" Something about a Well," 1882. *Life:* by E. T. Maclaren, 1890; by A. Peddie (with selected letters), 1893.—SHARP, R. FARQUHARSON, 1897, *A Dictionary of English Authors*, p. 33.

PERSONAL

A more beautiful soul never looked out from a more beautiful face, and saw God, and lived in the light of his countenance. Of course, his piety was the reverse of sour —was as sweet, and gentle, and loving as a pure spirit could be. It was not exactly the old Scottish piety, but it was still less the English kind; and, indeed, I know not that it belonged to any age, or to any Church, but just to John Brown; and to him it was perfectly natural and real. Always serious, he was often even sad; and yet what an amount of playful, tricksy, wayward nonsense he would perpetrate, and even carry on for whole weeks on end! Some odd fancy would strike him, and being with those he could trust, it was uttered with the utmost gravity, and the fun was kept up as long as they could toss the light shuttlecock back.... Strait-laced folk never could comprehend him; thought him strangely loose, irreverent, unprofitable, though nothing would have profited them so much as to get really for once close to his mind. It would have done them no end of good to learn how much true divine reverence could be under forms of speech quite alien to theirs, and how much yearning Christian love could express itself in ways widely foreign to their lips. I wish I could remember half the quaint touching stories I have heard from him in illustration of this. He was an exquisite storyteller, quite simple, with a look in his face half-pawky, half-pathetic, which never failed to catch and keep the interest of the hearer.—SMITH, WALTER C., 1882, *Dr. John Brown, Good Words, vol.* 23, *pp.* 449, 450.

Living always in Scotland, Dr. Brown was seen but rarely by his friends who resided in England. Thus, though Dr. Brown's sweetness of disposition and charm of manner, his humour, and his unfailing sympathy and encouragement, made one feel toward him as to a familiar friend, yet, of his actual life I saw but little, and have few reminiscences to contribute. One can only speak of that singular geniality of his, that temper of goodness and natural tolerance and affection, which, as Scotchmen best know, is so rare among the Scotch. . . . I have never known any man to whom other men seemed so dear,—men dead, and men living. He gave his genius to knowing them, and to making them better known, and his unselfishness thus became not only a great personal virtue, but a great literary charm. When you met him, he had some "good story" or some story of goodness to tell,—for both came alike to him, and his humour was as unfailing as his kindness. There was in his face a singular charm, blended, as it were, of the expressions of mirth and of patience.—LANG, ANDREW, 1883, *Rab's Friend, Century Magazine, vol.* 25, *p.* 241.

A darkish-haired man, of shorter stature than his father, with fine soft eyes, spirited movement, and very benignant manner, the husband of a singularly beautiful young wife, and greatly liked and sought after in the Edinburgh social circles in which he and she appeared. This was partly from the charm of his vivid temperament and conversation, and partly because of a reputation for literary ability that had been recently gathering round him on account of occasional semi-anonymous articles of his in newspapers and periodicals, chiefly art-criticisms. . . . To the end he loved his profession; to the end he practiced it; to the end there were not a few families, in and about Edinburgh, who would have no other medical attendant, if they could help it, than their dear and trusted Dr. John.—MASSON, DAVID, 1883, *Dr. John Brown of Edinburgh, Macmillan's Magazine, vol.* 47, *pp.* 282, 283.

In his medical capacity he was remarkable for his close and accurate observation of symptoms, skill and sagacity in the treatment of his cases, and conscientious attention to his patients. It may even be said that whatever position he may be thought to have taken in literature, he was first of all a physician thoroughly devoted to his profession, and, though not writing on strictly professional subjects, yet originally diverging into authorship on what may be called medical grounds. Naturally unambitious, it is doubtful if, with all his wide culture and enthusiastic love of literature, he would ever, but for his love of his profession, have been induced to appear before the world as an author at all. It is observable that the whole of the first volume of "Horæ Subsecivæ"—perhaps, though not the most popular, yet the most substantially valuable of the whole series—is almost exclusively devoted to subjects intimately bearing on the practice of medicine.—BROWN, J. TAYLOR, 1886, *Dictionary of National Biography, vol.* VII, *p.* 20.

I knew him first in Edinburgh, among those who loved him most dearly, because they knew him best. To know him at all was to love him much. He was one of those men whom, from the moment in which you hold their hand and look into their face, you believe, and find to be, sincere. Made to be a doctor, not only for his skill as a physician, his sympathies with suffering, his kindness to the poor, but because his very presence refreshed and cheered, there was warmth in his smile, and music in his voice, to revive the hopes of the sad.— HOLE, S. REYNOLDS, 1893, *Memories, p.* 85.

Even as I sit, with the photograph before me, with his full-length figure holding his dog, and the memory of his presence clearly before that "inner eye," the pen still delays and hesitates in the attempt to describe him as he was. The fine skull, the tender in-seeing eyes, the firm mouth yet ready to break into fun with one of the earliest or latest Scottish anecdotes, all this we see and hear, and yet fail to portray him to those who knew him not.—FIELDS, MRS. JAMES T., 1894, *A Shelf of Old Books, p.* 78.

He had a very true social nature, and it was curious to observe how readily he entered into pleasant and friendly relations with anyone. If a stranger met him for the first time he seemed to have a kind of perfect tact in placing himself at once in the exactly appropriate footing with him. His way was, on being introduced, to move his spectacles up to his forehead, and some frank, cordial, original, or unexpected smiling remark, some odd touch of humor, some pleasant reference, perhaps to something the other had done or made himself famous by, broke down at once the barrier of non-acquaintance. Peace be to the memory of a true and noble soul! Brave, frank, open-hearted, steadfast, generous, unselfish—a soul which had, perchance, in its abounding energy, over-weighted itself with too much and too many things, and failed because at last it came up against the impossible.—BROWN, JOHN TAYLOR, 1901–03, *Dr. John Brown, a Biography and a Criticism*, ed. Dunlop, pp. 41, 73.

GENERAL

The *tone* of the book, its true unsectarian liberality, its scholarly taste and feeling, and the unobtrusive and unaffected piety which breathes over its pages, are exactly what we would expect from such a culture. . . . The "Horæ Subsecivæ" indeed not infrequently recalls the "Religio Medici;" there is the same quaintness, clear insight, genial heartiness, and recondite research. . . . The story of "Rab and his Friends" is a veritable gem. It is true, simple, pathetic, and touched with an antique grace which, in such vicinity, charms and surprises. If any pre-Raphaelite aspirant would learn how Doric homeliness may be united with the utmost perfection and symmetry of form, let him read this beautiful episode.— SKELTON, JOHN, 1859, *Professional Sectarianism, Fraser's Magazine*, vol. 59, pp. 448, 450.

Will you tell Dr. John Brown that when I read an account of "Rab and his Friends" in a newspaper, I wished I had the story to read at full length; and I thought to myself the writer of "Rab" would perhaps like "Adam Bede." When you have told him this, he will understand the peculiar pleasure I had on opening the little parcel with "Rab" inside, and a kind word from Rab's friend. I have read the story twice—once aloud, and once to myself, very slowly, that I might dwell on the pictures of Rab and Ailie, and carry them about with me more distinctly. I will not say any commonplace words of admiration about what has touched me so deeply; there is no adjective of that sort left undefiled by the newspapers. The writer of "Rab" *knows* that I must love the grim old mastiff with the short tail and the long dewlaps—that I must have felt present at the scenes of Ailie's last trial.— ELIOT, GEORGE, 1859, *To John Blackwood,* Feb. 13; *George Eliot's Life as related in her Letters and Journals*, ed. Cross, vol. II, p. 60.

I am much obliged to you for introducing me to Dr. Brown's book, which I like very much. There is a *soul* in it somehow that one does not find in many books, and he seems to me a remarkably good critic, where his Scoticism doesn't come in his way.—LOWELL, JAMES RUSSELL, 1862, *To James T. Fields, Aug. 2; Letters*, ed. Norton, vol. I, p. 322.

One very obvious characteristic of these papers ["John Leech and Other Papers"] is their appearance of ease and spontaneity. They impress us as the work of one full of his subject, delighted with it, and expressing quite naturally and of necessity his delight to his readers. We can believe that they were composed with something of the rapidity with which "Rab and his Friends" was written—between twelve and four of a summer morning, as the author tells us in one of his pleasantly garrulous prefaces, in which, in true essayist's fashion, he buttonholes his reader and talks with him as familiarly as with a friend.—GRAY, J. M., 1882, *John Leech and Other Papers, The Academy*, vol. 21, p. 169.

He was essentially an essayist of the type of Addison and Charles Lamb, blending humour and pathos and quiet thoughtfulness, not inferior to theirs, with a power of picturesque description which neither of them had. For though city-bred like Lamb, his delight was not "in the habitable part of the earth," but in its lonely glens and by its quiet lakes, on Minchmoor, or in the Enterkin, or where Queen Mary's "baby garden" shows its box-wood border grown into trees among the grand Spanish chestnuts in the Lake of Menteith. How it was that he came to find his right vein, I cannot tell; but its first "lode" produced the touching story of Rab and Ailie and Bob Ainslie, which at once gave him a foremost rank among our English humorists.— SMITH, WALTER C., 1882, *Dr. John Brown, Good Words*, vol. 23, p. 448.

By constitution, no less than by circumstances, Dr. John Brown was unfitted for large and continuous works, and was at home only in short occasional papers. One compensation is the spontaneity of his writings, the sense of immediate throb and impulse in each. Every paper he wrote was, as it were, a moment of himself, and we can read his own character in the collected series. . . . These Art-criticisms of Dr. John Brown, however, are hardly criticisms in the ordinary sense. No canons of art are expounded or applied in them. All that the critic does, is to stand, as it were, before the particular picture he is criticising,—a Wilkie, a Raeburn, a Turner, a Landseer, a Delaroche, a Holman Hunt, or, as it might happen, some new performance by one of his Edinburgh artist-friends, Duncan, Sir George Harvey, or Sir Noel Paton,—exclaiming, "How good this is, how true, how powerful, how pathetic!" . . . His most elaborate paper of Art-criticism is that entitled "John Leech." It is throughout a glowing eulogium on the celebrated caricaturist, with notices of some of his best cartoons, but passing into an affectionate memoir of the man, on his own account and as the friend of Thackeray, and indeed incorporating reminiscences of Leech and Thackeray that had been supplied him by a friend of both as material for a projected Memoir of Leech on a larger scale. If not in this particular paper, at least here and there in some of the others, the query may suggest itself whether the laudation is not excessive. One asks sometimes whether the good Dr. John was not carried away by the amiable fault of supposing that what happens to be present before one of a decidedly likeable kind at any moment, especially if it be recommended by private friendship, must be the very nonsuch of its kind in the whole world. —MASSON, DAVID, 1883, *Dr. John Brown, Edinburgh, Macmillan's Magazine, vol. 47, pp. 283, 288.*

Three volumes of essays are all that Dr. Brown has left in the way of compositions: a light, but imperishable literary baggage. His studies are usually derived from personal experience, which he reproduced with singular geniality and simplicity, or they are drawn from the tradition of the elders, the reminiscences of long-lived Scotch people, who, themselves, had listened attentively to those who went before them. . . . Among Dr. Brown's papers on children, that called "Pet Marjorie" holds the highest place. Perhaps certain passages are "wrote too sentimentally," as Marjorie Fleming herself remarked about the practice of many authors. But it was difficult to be perfectly composed when speaking of this **fairy-like** little girl, whose affection was as warm as her humour and genius were precocious. "Infant phenomena" are seldom agreeable, but Marjorie was so humorous, so quick-tempered, so kind, that we cease to regard her as an intellectual "phenomenon." Her memory remains sweet and blossoming in its dust, like that of little Penelope Boothby, the child in the mob cap whom Sir Joshua painted, and who died very soon after she was thus made immortal.— LANG, ANDREW, 1883, *Rab's Friend, Century Magazine, vol. 25, pp. 245, 246.*

Dr. John Brown (born in 1810) is one of the writers whose fame greatly exceeds the amount of their productions. It is built upon a few sketches—scarcely a substantial volume among them. Indeed it may be said to rest almost exclusively upon the little brochure entitled "Rab and his Friends," by which he is known almost wherever English is spoken. The tenderness and insight of that little book,—though its hero is a dog and the attendant figures those of a homely and aged pair without any beauty but of the heart, or romance save that subdued and profound and everlasting romance which attends the footsteps of devoted love even in the humblest tracks—has gained, with scarcely a dissentient voice, the interest and affection of every reader. The author had a great personal popularity wherever he went, of the same character as that gained by his book, the appreciation of all who knew him of a singularly kind and amiable nature. Of such a reputation the critic has nothing to say, books and man being equally raised above the usual measurements and balances of literary criticism. — OLIPHANT, MARGARET, O. W., 1892, *The Victorian Age of English Literature, p. 582.*

The keenest interest in his own profession was found in close alliance with the widest literary outlook; the liveliest humour, and appreciation of it in others; a poet's and a painter's eye for the loveliness of scenery, and a deeply religious and sympathetic nature. . . . His style, imitated from no one model, is the easy, unstudied style of a good letter-writer and talker, yet rising often into a singular beauty and eloquence when some deep moral emotion possesses him. Again and again we feel that with him, as with Samuel Johnson, his wisdom was "the Wisdom of the Just." John Brown is already a classic, because he has made himself loved much. He is yet one more witness that it matters little for an essayist what are his themes, if only the personality of the writer is delightful, and is diffused and discernible through all his work.—AINGER, ALFRED, 1896, *English Prose*, ed. Craik, vol. v, pp. 540, 541.

Brown wrote a style of very high merit. In the miscellaneous collection of his writings, which he entitled "Horæ Subsecivæ," there is much to remind the reader of Lamb. Yet he was guiltless of imitation and the resemblance which exists because he had the same fine humour and the same sensitiveness of perception as the earlier writer. No one has written better than Brown about dogs; and his comprehension of them and his power of depicting them are seen even better in "Our Dogs" than in the famous essays on Rab, where the human figures divide the interest with the great mastiff. Brown's critical papers are few, but they show that he knew how to get at the heart of his subject.—WALKER, HUGH, 1897, *The Age of Tennyson*, p. 210.

Never was an author more deeply or more justly loved. His many friends recall with a peculiar softening his exquisite qualities of mind and heart—his delicate infancy and frolicsome humour, his earnest pleading for downrightness and intensity of character and life, the sweetness of his charity, his unselfish thoughtfulness for others, and his childlike freshness, simplicity and honest impulsiveness. All loved him for his sunny nature; those who knew him best were still more endeared to him by the mysterious cross which this sweet and gentle spirit, in long intervals of gloom, was called upon to bear.—GRAHAM, RICHARD D., 1897, *The Masters of Victorian Literature*, p. 448.

It is difficult to characterise the "Horæ Subsecivæ" as a whole. They range over a great variety of topics, and vary not a little in tone and manner of treatment. But apart from this, there are some incidental points in them which cannot fail to strike the reader, and make him feel the charm at once of a remarkable intellect and of a very attractive personality in the writer. We discover at once that he is full of keen but quiet and measured enthusiasm, dwelling with delight on all that is beautiful and true, and best and greatest, either in human character or in inanimate nature. You recognize in him also a man of unfailing sense and intelligence, with a peculiar power of insight—a widely-read man, an accurate thinker, and possessing what I would call an original gift of style. It is curious how he throws his whole nature into his literary work—not merely his intellect, as most men do, but his tastes, his loves, his whims, his hobbies, and the pervading flavour of his humour. Perhaps I might say that the strong personal element in the book, if not to be regarded as its main characteristic, is that which first attracts the attention.—BROWN, JOHN TAYLOR, 1901-03, *Dr. John Brown, a Biography and a Criticism*, ed. Dunlop, p. 103.

William George Ward
1812-1882

Theologian, was the son of Mr. Ward, formerly director of the Bank of England and member for the City. The son was educated at Winchester College, and at Christ Church, Oxford, and took his degree in 1834. He obtained a fellowship at Balliol, where he remained for some years as mathematical tutor. Mr. Ward plunged with zeal into the Tractarian Movement inaugurated by Newman and Pusey, and in 1844 published a remarkable work, "The Ideal of a Christian Church Considered in Comparison with its Existing Practice." It commented on the Reformation in a hostile spirit, and was condemned by convocation by 776 votes against 386. Mr. Ward was further degraded from his M. A. degree. Shortly afterwards he seceded to the Church of Rome. Ward was for many years editor of the *Dublin Review*, and lectured on theology at St. Edmund's College, Herts. A collection of his able "Essays on the Philosophy of Theism," written in opposition to J. S. Mill, was published in 1884.—SANDERS, LLOYD C., ed. 1887, *Celebrities of the Century*, p. 1028.

PERSONAL

He had many stories of our dear old friend, which would have amused you, showing that he was on his death-bed what he had been throughout life, the same grotesque mixture of deep devotional feeling, with a *levity of expression* which scandalized those who did not understand him, as if, having been forced into seriousness for a minute or two, the pent-up animal spirits must have their fling, and kick up their heels a little! *Manning*, he told us, used to pull awfully long faces at the French novels he found on the shelves of the Fat Friend's study; and then the Fat Friend began to reason with him that novels and the opera were *his* way of getting his amusement, just as "you get yours by going down to the House of Commons and hearing 'debates.'" I prefer Carlotta Patti, and Trebelli to all your great statesmen and orators.— GOULBURN, EDWARD MEYRICK, 1882, *Letter to Lake, Dec. 25*; *Memorials of William Charles Lake, ed. his Widow*, p. 261

How Mr. Ward, being what he was, and beginning as he did, should have ended as he did, will be a matter of speculation to many. How a man with such justifiable confidence in his own intellectual power and professing, moreover, to trust so largely in the Shechinah of his individual conscience —"that image of God in the soul, that witness to God and to the law of God in man" —should have been the servant of so many successive masters, and at last, wearied out, should have submitted himself unreservedly to the one whom he had learned to regard as Infallible, has the puzzle of an apparent contradiction. How, delighting as he did, with exceeding delight, in dramatic literature and performances, a man of so much geniality and so humorous should have resolutely closed his eyes to the ever-changing drama of life throughout the centuries, is not easy to understand; yet perhaps therein partly lay the explanation of his life. Man, the *whole* man, with *all* his powers, must dedicate himself to the service of life, if he would avoid error and attain his highest.—TENNYSON, HALLAM, 1889, *Noticeable Books, Nineteenth Century*, vol. 26, p. 344.

There were curious gaps in Ward's character, both moral and intellectual. He was very affectionate and felt coldness, but he did not feel deaths. He asked naturally, without finding an answer, why we should have any special affection for relations. His notion of patriotism did not include any admiration for the fatherland. It was limited to special grief at national vices and special pleasure in national virtues. His intellect—which, though he thought little of it, he truly declared to be, in certain directions, almost infinite—was curiously capricious, and he never emancipated himself from its caprices. He understood pure mathematics and indulged his detestation of applied mathematics; he was a great dialectician, but he indulged his distaste for history. One effect was that he had to take his facts at second-hand, in a way which astonished Bonamy Price; another, that he had to discuss much without any clear view of the facts.—SIMCOX, G. A., 1889, *William George Ward and the Oxford Movement, The Academy*, vol. 35, p. 387.

There was something to smile at in his person, and in some of his ways—his unbusiness-like habits, his joyousness of manner, his racy stories; but few more powerful intellects passed through Oxford in his time, and he has justified his University reputation by his distinction since, both as a Roman Catholic theologian and professor, and as a profound metaphysical thinker, the equal antagonist on their own ground of J. Stuart Mill and Herbert Spencer. But his intellect at that time was as remarkable for its defects as for its powers. He used to divide his friends, and thinking people in general, into those who had facts and did not know what to do with them, and those who had in perfection the logical faculties, but wanted the facts to reason upon. He belonged himself to the latter class. He had, not unnaturally, boundless confidence in his argumentative powers; they were subtle, piercing, nimble, never at a loss, and they included a power of exposition which, if it was not always succinct and lively, was always weighty and impressive. Premises in his hands were not long in bringing forth their conclusions; and if abstractions always corresponded exactly to their concrete embodiments, and ideals were fulfilled in realities, no one could point out more perspicuously and decisively the practical judgments of them which reason must sanction.—CHURCH, RICHARD WILLIAM, 1891, *The Oxford Movement*, p. 207.

I remember well the first time that I saw your father—it was, I *think*, at the second or third meeting of the Society. He came into the room along with Manning, and the marked contrast between them added to the impressiveness. I remember thinking that I had never seen a face that seemed so clearly to indicate a strongly developed sensuous nature, and yet was at the same time so intellectual as your father's. I do not mean merely that it expressed intellectual *faculty*. . . . I mean rather the predominance of the intellectual life, of concern (as Matthew

Arnold says) for the "things of the mind." I did not then know your father's writings at all; and though from what I had heard of him I expected to find him an effective defender of the Catholic position, I certainly did not anticipate that I should come—as after two or three meetings I did come—to place him in the very first rank of our members, as judged from the point of view of the Society in respect of their aptitudes for furthering its aim. The aim of the Society was, by frank and close debate and unreserved communication of dissent and objection, to attain—not agreement, which was of course beyond hope—but a diminution of mutual misunderstanding. For this kind of discussion your father's gifts were very remarkable. The only other member of the Society who in my recollection rivals him is—curiously enough—Huxley.—SIDGWICK, HENRY, 1893, *To Wilfrid Ward, William George Ward and the Catholic Revival*, p. 313.

As a quick-witted dialectician, thoroughly acquainted with all the weak points of his antagonist's case, I have not met with Dr. Ward's match. And it all seemed to come so easily to him; searching questions, incisive, not to say pungent, replies, and trains of subtle argumentation, were poured forth, which, while sometimes passing into earnest and serious exposition, would also, when lighter topics came to the front, be accompanied by an air of genial good-humour, as if the whole business were rather a good joke. But it was no joke to reply efficiently. . . . He was before all things a chivalrous English gentleman; I would say a philosophical and theological Quixote, if it were not that our associations with the name of the knight of LaMancha are mainly derived from his adventures, and not from the noble directness and simplicity of mind which led to those misfortunes.—HUXLEY, THOMAS HENRY, 1893, *To Wilfrid Ward, William George Ward and the Catholic Revival*, pp. 314, 315.

There was a flavour of comedy in Mr. Ward's view of himself, in his almost dogmatic definitions of his own ignorance and limitations and incapacities, and in his equally dogmatic self-confidence, which it would have been bad art and worse taste to keep out of view. A large element in the engaging side of the man was the gusto with which he laughed at himself and the frankness with which he took all his friends into his confidence on that head. . . . Few people ever enjoyed a laugh at themselves as did William George Ward. Certainly in all my experience of life I have never come across another person who found a far greater spring of amusement in analysing, proclaiming to the world, and even caricaturing, his own want of knowledge, his own want of courage, and the child-like incapacities which he discerned or fancied he discerned in himself, than he ever found in doing the same disservice for anyone else. In his judgments of others he was the personification of wise and charitable agnosticism. In his judgments of himself he was not half agnostic enough. He supposed that his knowledge of his own weaknesses was absolute, whereas hardly any man knows accurately, and certainly Mr. Ward did not know at all accurately, where his weaknesses ended and suddenly passed into unique strength.—HUTTON, RICHARD HOLT, 1894, *Noticeable Books, Nineteenth Century*, vol. 35, pp. 227, 228.

Mr. Ward's Catholic life, so far as his intellectual work is concerned, divides itself naturally into the period of his teaching at St. Edmund's, his writings (especially his writings in this *Review*) on the controversy which culminated at the time of the Vatican Council, and his philosophical and metaphysical polemic against such men as Professor Huxley, John Stuart Mill, and Dr. Alexander Bain. It is when analysing these latter controversies that our author displays the striking clearness of his style. To master such subjects at all is no light task. But to state the various sides to a long and intricate controversy upon abstruse questions of speculative philosophy, and to do so with even-handed justice and temper, and at the same time with such limpid clearness that the whole reads like a simple narrative of facts, is an achievement so considerable that it raises its author far above the average level of English descriptive and analytical biographers. — WILBERFORCE, WILFRID, 1894, *William George Ward, Dublin Review*, vol. 115, p. 23.

For the next ten years, from 1835 to 1845 he was certainly the greatest conversationalist and (excepting always Newman) the greatest centre of intellectual life of that description in Oxford. There was no subject he was not ready to discuss, from politics and moral and metaphysical philosophy to music of every description, from Haydn down to the last opera, even more than theology. I ought, however, to except two subjects, history and poetry; he believed as little in history as Sir R. Walpole's famous dictum implies—"Don't read me history, for that I know is false"—and he hated all poetry, except as embodied in the hymns and ritual of the Roman Church. In fact, he was the prince of talkers, perhaps the last of the great conversationalists since Coleridge. This would have been recognised everywhere, though no doubt it was more strongly felt in Balliol than in the rest of the University. It was the few who lived with him familiarly, whether as pupils or afterwards in the common room, who most appreciated his power, though large allowance was made even by them for his insatiable passion for paradox.—LAKE, WILLIAM CHARLES, 1897–1901, *Memorials*, ed. his Widow, p. 24.

GENERAL

Since Mr. Ward laid down the office of Editor, he published two volumes of articles selected from his contributions to the [*Dublin*] *Review*. To the second of these, which is entitled, "Essays on the Church's Doctrinal Authority," he prefixed a preliminary Essay which may be described as an intellectual history and analysis of the sixteen years of his Editorship. He has traced very accurately the condition of opinion and the tendency of thought among Catholics before the year 1862, and the successive controversies in which he was involved down to the year 1873. The whole Essay is a summing up of his own words and acts, and a calm and candid justification of the whole polemical attitude in which he habitually lived. . . . He was supposed to be full of self-assertion and intolerance; exaggerated and extreme both in thought and language. Perhaps few men have ever been more docile to the Church, to traditional judgments, and to the authority of theologians; few more fearful of novelties, of his own want of various learning, and of his liability to err. It was with these dangers before him, that Mr. Ward incessantly laboured in three distinct fields. First in Philosophy, without which the intellectual conception of Theology can have no sound and precise foundation; secondly, in the relation between Religion and Politics, including the office of the Civil Power and the Civil Princedom of the Sovereign Pontiff; Thirdly, on Catholic Education, especially in its higher form. It would be impossible to give any adequate idea of these incessant labours without a history which would fill volumes, and an analysis which would require a full statement of every thesis, together with the objections of opponents and the detailed answer to each.— MANNING, HENRY EDWARD, 1882, *William George Ward*, Dublin Review, vol. 91, pp. 266, 268.

He enjoyed argument and paradox, was a remorseless antagonist, with a mischievous delight in making listeners stare. He scorned timidity and half-way opinions. He laid on his colors with the palette knife, and did little to blend the tones afterward. For him, a thing was so, or was not so; and if so, it was very much so, quite absolutely so always. He indulged himself in what has been called "inverted hypocrisy," and showed himself in the worst lights the facts would admit of. So far from putting all his goods in the shop window, he would rather display a bare counter and close his shutters if he had not a complete stock. Always mirthful and genial when most in earnest, he never lost his temper, and would transfix you with a syllogism while retaining an angelic and infantine smile. He cared nothing for facts apart from principles, and ranked meaningless historic details with village gossip.—RICHARDS, C. A. L., 1889, *A Hero of the Oxford Movement*, The Dial, vol. 10, p. 101.

If we take into account only the necessarily restricted number of men who have taken up a carefully thought out and permanent position in these difficult, complex, still largely problematical questions; and if we pass over among them such men as Father Knox in England, and Drs. Scheeben, and Von Schäzler, and Father Schneemann in Germany, perhaps also Père Ramière in France, of whom at least the first four were, on their own admission, learners on these points from your father— it will be seen how quite exceptional was the length to which he carried his theory. Take his "De Infallibilitatis Extensione" (1869) and its seventeen Theses. According to his own admission there, the very Theologians and Roman Congregations to whom he wanted to attribute quasi infallible authority, refused to endorse thesis after thesis of his. Take again his attitude on the *ex Cathedrâ* character of the *Syllabus*. He first obliges every Catholic to accept it *sub mortali;* he next takes off this obligation; he finally re-imposes it. Take, finally, the Vatican definition. He never made any secret of how much he cared for the question as to the *Object,* the range of Infallibility, and how little comparatively for that as to its *Subject,* its organ; of how backward he thought, on the first question, the opinions of the large majority of the Bishops of the Council; and how disappointed he was that the Council, whilst giving a most moderate definition as to the *Subject,* left the question of the *Object* exactly where it was before your father began insisting that it was *the* great Catholic question of the age.—HÜGEL, FRIEDRICH VON, 1893, *To Wilfrid Ward, William George Ward and the Catholic Revival,* p. 373.

The acute collision between the two extreme parties in the eventful years preceding the Vatican Council, the comparative disappearance of both since then, and the subsequent renewal, in a more permanent form, of the combination of Ultramontanism with the endeavour to find a *modus vivendi* with modern thought and modern political conditions, make undoubtedly a turning-point in the history of contemporary Christian thought. In the events surrounding this crisis Mr. W. G. Ward took, both directly and indirectly, an active share. He represented in politics and theology the unqualified opposition to the extremes of Liberal Catholicism against which Pius IX's pontificate was a constant protest; and in philosophy his tendency was towards the fusion of Ultramontane loyalty, with a sympathetic assimilation of all that is valuable in contemporary thought, as the best means of purging it of what is dangerous. The history, then, of this crisis is naturally given in the story of his life.—WARD, WILFRID, 1893, *William George Ward and the Catholic Revival,* p. ix.

W. G. Ward, commonly called "Ideal" Ward from his famous, very ill-written, very ill-digested, but important "Ideal of a Christian Church," which was the alarmbell for the flight to Rome, was a curiously constituted person of whom something has been said in reference to Clough. He had little connection with pure letters, and after his secession to Rome and his succession to a large fortune he finally devoted himself to metaphysics of a kind. His acuteness was great, and he had a scholastic subtlety and logical deftness which made him very formidable to the loose thinkers and reasoners of Utilitarianism and anti-Supernaturalism.—SAINTSBURY, GEORGE, 1896, *A History of Nineteenth Century Literature,* p. 371.

W. G. Ward lived, but only to prove by his "Ideal of a Christian Church" that the power of writing good English was not among his endowments.—WALKER, HUGH, 1897, *The Age of Tennyson,* p. 146.

His crusade was carried on chiefly in the "Dublin Review," which he raised from decadence and edited with conspicuous success from 1863 to 1878. In its pages he defended the encyclical "Quanta Cura" and "Syllabus Errorum" of 1864, and led the extreme wing of the ultramontane party in the controversy on papal infallibility. He speculated freely on the extent of infallibility, and reduced the interpretative functions of the "schola theologorum" to a minimum. His startling conclusions he enunciated with the serenity of a philosopher and defended with the vehemence of a fanatic.—RIGG, J. M., 1899, *Dictionary of National Biography, vol.* LIX, p. 346.

William Harrison Ainsworth
1805-1882

Born, in Manchester, 4 Feb. 1805. Educated at Manchester Grammar School, 1817–21 Articled in 1821 to Mr. Kay, solicitor, of Manchester. Contrib. to "Arliss's Magazine," "Manchester Iris," "Edinburgh Magazine," "London Magazine;" and started a periodical called "The Bœotian," of which only six numbers appeared. In 1824 to Inner Temple. Married Anne Frances Ebers, 11 Oct. 1826. In business as a publisher for eighteen months. Life of literary activity. Visit to Switzerland and Italy, 1830. "Rookwood" begun in 1831. Series of novels published 1834–81. Editor of "Bentley's Miscellany," March 1839 to Dec. 1841. Edited "Ainsworth's Magazine," 1842–54. Edited "New Monthly Magazine," 1845–70. Lived at Kensal Manor House. Entertained by Mayor at Banquet in Manchester Town Hall, 15 Sept. 1881. Died, at Reigate, 3 Jan. 1882.

Buried at Kensal Green. *Works:* "Considerations as to the best means of affording immediate relief to the Operative Classes in the manufacturing districts," 1826; "Rookwood" (anon.), 1834; "Crichton," 1837; "Jack Sheppard," 1839; "Tower of London," 1840; "Guy Fawkes," 1841; "Old St. Paul's," 1841; "The Miser's Daughter," 1842; "Windsor Castle," 1843; "St. James's," 1844; "Lancashire Witches," 1848; "Star Chamber," 1854; "James the Second," 1854; "The Flitch of Bacon," 1854; "Ballads," 1855; "Spendthrift," 1856; Mervyn Clitheroe" (in parts), 1857-58; "The Combat of the Thirty," 1859; "Ovingdean Grange," 1860; "Constable of the Tower," 1861; "Lord Mayor of London," 1862;" "Cardinal Pole," 1863; "John Law the Projector," 1864; "The Spanish Match," 1865; "Auriol," 1865; "Myddleton Pomfret," 1865; "The Constable de Bourbon," 1866; "Old Court," 1867; "South Sea Bubble," 1868; "Hilary St. Ives," 1869; "Talbot Harland," 1870; "Tower Hill," 1871; "Boscobel," 1872; "The Good Old Times," 1873; "Merry England," 1874; "The Goldsmith's Wife," 1875; "Preston Fight," 1875; "Chetwynd Calverly," 1876; "The Leaguer of Lathom," 1876; "The Fall of Somerset," 1877; "Beatrice Tyldesley," 1878; "Beau Nash," [1879?]; "Stanley Brereton," 1881. The greater part of "December Tales," published anonymously in 1823, was Ainsworth's work; "Sir John Chiverton" (anon.), 1826, is probably by Ainsworth and J. P. Aston. Contrib. by Ainsworth are in "Works of Cheviot Tichburn," 1822, and "A Summer Evening Tale," 1825.—SHARP, R. FARQUHARSON, 1897, *A Dictionary of English Authors, p.* 3.

PERSONAL

Mr. Ainsworth, who had been a publisher at one part of his busy life, next set up "Ainsworth's Magazine," and in it wrote certain stilted nonsense—"The Tower of London," "Old St. Paul's," "The Miser's Daughter," and so forth. Of these not one could hold the public without its illustrations. Some of Cruikshank's best work went to these rubbishy books, which are now bought at large prices *for the engravings*. . . . Mr. Ainsworth is, we believe, as Lord Lytton is, we know, a wealthy man through his literature; but if every farthing each has received from his books, pensions and all, were a hundred-pound note, and employed in building reformatories for boy-thieves, the unhappy man could not undo the evil his perverted taste, vulgar admiration, and his fatal itch of writing to pander to the savage instincts of the thief and robber, has caused, and will yet cause, in years to come.—FRISWELL, JAMES HAIN, 1870, *Modern Men of Letters Honestly Criticised, pp.* 264, 270.

This delicately drawn portrait of the novelist, just at the time that he had achieved his reputation,—hair curled and oiled as that of an Assyrian bull, the gothic arch coat-collar, the high neck-cloth and the tightly strapped trowsers,—exhibits as fine an exemplar as we could wish for, of the dandy of D'Orsay type, and pre-Victorian epoch. . . . One of Ainsworth's earliest residences was the "Elms" at Kilburn. From this he removed to Kensal Manor House, on the Harrow Road, where, for a long series of years, he dispensed his genial and liberal hospitality to a large circle of friends,—chiefly literary men and artists,—who made it a rallying point. From this he removed to Brighton, and later on, to Tunbridge Wells. Subsequently in the retirement befitting his advancing years, he resided with his eldest daughter, Fanny, at Hurstpierpoint. He had also a residence at St. Mary's Road, Reigate, Surrey; and here he died, on Sunday, January 3rd, 1882, in the seventy-seventh year, of his age. On the 9th of the same month his remains were interred at the Kensal Green Cemetery; the ceremony being of very quiet and simple character, in accordance with his express wish.—BATES, WILLIAM, 1874-98, *The Maclise Portrait-Gallery of Illustrious Literary Characters, pp.* 256, 262.

I saw little of him in later days, but when I knew him in 1826, not long after he married the daughter of Ebers, of New Bond Street, and "condescended" for a brief time to be a publisher, he was a remarkably handsome young man—tall, graceful in deportment, and in all ways a pleasant person to look upon and talk to. He was, perhaps, as thorough a gentleman as his native city of Manchester ever sent forth. Few men have lived to be more largely rewarded not only by pecuniary recompense, but by celebrity—I can hardly call it fame. His antiquarian lore was remarkable, and he made brilliant and extensive use of it in his long series of historical romances.—HALL, SAMUEL CARTER, 1883, *Retrospect of a Long Life, p.* 407.

Mr. Harrison Ainsworth, at this time in

the hey-day of his fame and popularity, was one of the four literary dandies of the period—all handsome men, and favorites of the ladies, as well for their personal graces as for their genius. These four were Mr. Benjamin Disraeli, Mr. Edward Lytton Bulwer, Mr. Charles Dickens, and Mr. Harrison Ainsworth. None could deny that Mr. Ainsworth was unquestionably the best-looking man of the four—the very Antinous of literature, in the prime of his early manhood, and in a full flush of a popularity that continued unabated until a late period of his life.—MACKAY, CHARLES, 1887, *Through the Long Day*, vol. I, p. 240.

GENERAL

I read with interest, during my journey, "Sir John Chiverton" and "Brambletye House"—novels, in what I may surely claim as the style
"Which I was born to introduce—
Refined it first, and show'd its use."
They are both clever books.—SCOTT, SIR WALTER, 1826, *Journal*, Oct. 17; *Life by Lockhart*, ch. lxxii.

With regard to the Newgate narrative of "Jack Sheppard" and the extraordinary extensive notoriety it obtained for the writer, upon the residuum of which he founded his popularity, so much just severity has already been administered from criticism and from the opinion of the intellectual portion of the public, and its position has been so fully settled, that we are glad to pass over it without farther animadversion. The present popularity of Mr. Ainsworth could not have risen out of its own materials. His so-called historical romance of "Windsor Castle" is not to be regarded as a work of literature open to serious criticism. It is a picture book, and full of very pretty pictures. Also full of catalogues of numberless suits of clothes. It would be difficult to open it anywhere without the eye falling on such words as cloth of gold, silver tissue, green Jerkin, white plumes.... "Old St. Paul's, a tale of the Plague and the Fire," is a diluted imitation of some parts of De Foe's "Plague in London," varied with libertine adventures of Lord Rochester and his associates. It is generally dull, except when it is revolting.—HORNE, RICHARD HENGIST, 1844, *A New Spirit of the Age*, pp. 314, 315.

It may appear unjust to the genius of Victor Hugo to say so, but to our minds the romances of Ainsworth possess more resemblance to the particular manner of "Notre Dame de Paris" than any other productions of English Literature.... The works of Ainsworth possess much of this fragmentary and convulsive character, and the erudition (often great) which he has lavished on his pictures of past ages, bears, like that of Victor Hugo, a painful air of effort—of having been *read up* for the purpose, and collected for the nonce. The most successful of Ainsworth's romances are "Rookwood" (the first) and "Jack Sheppard:" the former owes its success chiefly to the wonderful hurry and rapid vividness of Turpin's ride from London to York in one day, and in the latter the author has broken up what appeared to the public to be new ground—the adventures of highwaymen, prostitutes, and thieftakers. Defoe had done this before, and with astonishing power and invention and probability; but that great moralist has never confounded good and evil, and has shown his squalid ragamuffins as miserable in their lives as they were contemptible and odious in their crimes. Ainsworth, however, has looked upon the romantic side of the picture, and has represented his ruffian hero as a model of gallantry and courage. This, we know, is contrary to universal experience and probability; and while we read with breathless interest the escape of Jack from prison, we forget the monstrous inconsistencies of the story, and the mean and wolfish character of the real criminal, who is here elevated into a hero of romance. To the ignorant and uneducated, who are charmed, like everybody else, with the boldness, dexterity, and perseverance so often exhibited by the worst characters, and which are here dignified with all the artifices of description, but who cannot distinguish between the good and the evil which are mixed up even in the basest characters, this kind of reading is capable of doing, and has done, the greatest mischief; and the very talent—often undeniable—of such works, only renders them the more seductive and insidious.—SHAW, THOMAS B., 1847, *Outlines of English Literature*, pp. 375, 376.

In the interest and rapidity of his scenes and adventures, Mr. Ainsworth evinced a dramatic power and art, but no originality or felicity of humour or character.... There are rich, copious and brilliant descriptions in some of these works, but their tendency must be reprobated. To portray scenes of low successful villainy, and to paint ghastly and hideous details of human suffering, can be no elevating task for a man of genius, nor one likely to promote among novel-readers a healthy tone of moral feeling or sentiment. The story of "Jack Sheppard," illustrated by the pencil of Cruikshank, had immense success, and was dramatised.—CHAMBERS, ROBERT, 1876, *Cyclopædia of English Literature*, ed. *Carruthers*.

His novels, though readers have now turned to tales of another fashion, have never been without the merit of great skill in the shaping of a story from historical material well studied and understood. Ainsworth's strength has lain in the union of good, honest antiquarian scholarship with art in the weaving of romance that is enlivened and not burdened by his knowledge of the past.—MORLEY, HENRY, 1881, *Of English Literature in the Reign of Victoria, With a Glance at the Past*, p. 340.

It is deeply to be lamented that Cruikshank's connection with Harrison Ainsworth—a connection in which the artist found some of his finer inspirations—was marred by quarrels, and was sundered finally with a controversy, which is the counterpart of that he engaged in with the biographer and the friends of Charles Dickens. I suspect that Thackeray involuntarily led Cruikshank to claim more than his proper share in the successes he and Harrison Ainsworth had together.... Thackeray, let it be said, was always unjust to Harrison Ainsworth. He caricatured him unmercifully in *Punch*, and never lost an opportunity of being amusing at his expense. His reasoning in regard to "Jack Sheppard" is manifestly unjust and unsound. "Jack Sheppard" was the natural sequence to "Rookwood" which, in popular parlance, had taken the town by storm, and had suddenly made the young author famous. "Dick Turpin's Ride to York" became the talk of all England. Colnaghi published a separate set of illustrations, by Hall, of the principal scenes described by Ainsworth. Cruikshank was called in only to furnish some illustrations to the second edition. The success of "Rookwood" directed the mind of "Paul Clifford," and probably suggested to Dickens "Oliver Twist." Even Cruikshank himself admits that "Jack Sheppard" was "originated"
by the author. A fashion for highwaymen and burglars as heroes of romance had been set by Ainsworth; and Bulwer and Dickens dived into the haunts of thieves to get at their *argot*, or "patter flash," and their ways of thinking and acting. Both made great hits. "Paul Clifford" and "Oliver Twist" were the two books of the day. Mr. Ainsworth, irritated by the unceremonious manner in which his ground had been invaded, put forth "Jack Sheppard" (1839), on assuming the editorship of "Bentley's Miscellany." It was as natural a step from "Rookwood," especially after "Paul Clifford" and "Oliver Twist," as chapter two is from chapter one. Mr. Ainsworth had his revenge upon the trespassers, for "Jack" threw "Oliver," for the moment, into the background.—JERROLD, BLANCHARD, 1882, *The Life of George Cruikshank*, vol. I, pp. 241, 245.

The charm of Ainsworth's novels is not at all dependent upon the analysis of motives or subtle description of character. Of this he has little or nothing, but he realises vividly a scene or an incident, and conveys the impression with great force and directness to the reader's mind.—AXON, WILLIAM E. A., 1885, *Dictionary of National Biography*, vol. I, p. 198.

Equally fertile in production, but by no means comparable to Bulwer in ability. ... In 1834 he made his first success with the novel of "Rookwood," in which the praises of Dick Turpin, the highwayman, are sung with an ardour worthy of a better cause. It sprang at once into a popularity which was perhaps above its merits; it had, however, the advantage of being condemned by moralists as tending to the encouragement of vice. We are not tempted to join in the chorus of admiration, but will admit that there is some power in the description of the famous ride to York. A few years later, Ainsworth returned to the safer path of historical romance with the somewhat tedious novel of "Crichton," but in 1839 again shocked the world with the history of "Jack Sheppard," a work much inferior to "Rookwood" in literary merit. —OLIPHANT, MARGARET O. W., 1892, *The Victorian Age of English Literature*, p. 286.

In the long succession of successful novels and romances that flowed for years from Mr. Ainsworth's pen, there was an abundance of the "properties" of the historic past, but little of what is properly known as literature. Notwithstanding this, some of these fictions contain the results of a good deal of painstaking research into the past; and doubtless many young readers have received no little instruction from their pages.—RUSSELL, PERCY, 1894, *A Guide to British and American Novels*, p. 135.

First essayed felonious fiction in his interesting but unequal romance, "Rookwood," in which one of the leading characters was the notoriously coarse and crapulous highwayman and horse-thief Dick Turpin. Turpin's ride to York, as a piece of word-painting, has been rarely, if ever, surpassed in the prose of the Victorian era. It is true that more than once it has been alleged that Harrison Ainsworth was not the writer of this astonishing episode, but that it was the composition of his friend Dr. William Magınn. As to the truth or falsehood of this allegation I am wholly incompetent to pronounce; but looking at Ainsworth's marvellous pictures of the Plague and the Fire in his "Old St. Paul's," and the numerous picturesque studies of Tudor life in his "Tower of London," I should say that Turpin's ride to York was a performance altogether within compass of his capacity.—SALA, GEORGE AUGUSTUS, 1895, *Life and Adventures*, vol. I, p. 86.

Had a real knack of arresting and keeping the interest of those readers who read for mere excitement: he was decidedly skilful at gleaning from memoirs and other documents scraps of decoration suitable for his purpose, he could in his better day string incidents together with a very decided knack, and, till latterly, his books rarely languished. But his writing was very poor in strictly literary merit, his style was at best bustling prose melodrama, and his characters were scarcely ever alive.—SAINTSBURY, GEORGE, 1896, *A History of Nineteenth Century Literature*, p. 139.

Denis Florence MacCarthy
1820–1882

Born at Dublin, and a member of the Irish bar, but never practiced. His first literary work was contributed to the Irish *Nation*, and he was especially noted for his linguistic attainments; his poems including, in addition to original verse, translations from nearly all of the modern European languages. In 1881 he received from the Royal Academy of Spain a medal for his translations of the works of Calderon. He published "Ballads, Poems and Lyrics," 1850; "The Bell Founder," 1857; "Underglimpses, and Other Poems," 1857. His translations of Calderon were published 1853–1873.— RANDOLPH, HENRY F., 1887, ed. *Fifty Years of English Song, Biographical Notes*, vol. IV, p. xxi.

PERSONAL

MacCarthy, like Charles Lamb when he was the associate of Hazlitt and Hunt, loved the men more than he shared their political passions. He was a law student soon to be called to the bar, but he was essentially a poet and a man of letters, happy in his study, charming in society, where his spontaneous humour was the delight of his associates, but never thoroughly at home in the council room or on the platform.—DUFFY, SIR CHARLES GAVAN, 1880, *Young Ireland*, p. 293.

While Ireland has lost in him one of the most graceful of her lyrists, his large circle of intimates deplore a friend endeared to them, not more by his brilliant intellectual endowments than by the genial sympathies of his nature. For the gift of song was not in his case counterbalanced by the extravagance of feeling or action which too often accompanies it, and was rather the crowning harmony of a finely tuned mind, than the wild note of undisciplined fancy setting all the other strings ajar. This immunity of his nature from the flaws of the poetic temperament is shared by his writings, and the strain of morbid feeling and fantastic exaggeration of thought affected by many modern bards finds no echo in his simple and manly verse.—CLERKE, E. M., 1883, *Denis Florence MacCarthy, Dublin Review*, vol. 92, p. 261.

It cannot but be a melancholy satisfaction to me to contribute to a memorial that will commemorate, not only the lofty genius, but the social and moral worth of one of the truest poets and best men it has been my lot personally to know, esteem, regard, honor—the late Denis Florence MacCarthy.—HALL, SAMUEL CARTER, 1883, *Retrospect of a Long Life*, p. 351, note.

GENERAL

It is, ["Translation of Calderon"] I think, one of the boldest attempts ever made in

English verse. It is, too, as it seems to me, remarkably successful. Not that *asonantes* can be made fluent and graceful in English verse, or easily perceptible to an English ear, but that the Spanish air and character of Calderon are so happily and strikingly preserved. . . . In the present volume Mr. MacCarthy has far surpassed all he had previously done; for Calderon is a poet who, whenever he is translated, should have his very excesses and extravagances, both in thought and manner, fully produced in order to give a faithful idea of what is grandest and most distinctive in his genius. Mr. MacCarthy has done this, I conceive, to a degree which I had previously supposed impossible. Nothing, I think, in the English language will give us so true an impression of what is most characteristic of the Spanish drama, perhaps I ought to say of what is most characteristic of Spanish poetry generally.—TICKNOR, GEORGE, 1861, *History of Spanish Literature*, ch XXIV, note.

Mr. MacCarthy's national poetry is rather didactic than historical or dialectic, with a few exceptions, such as the very spirited ballad of "The Foray of Con O'Donnell," in which the portrait of the ancient Irish wolfdog is very admirable; and he has also some graphic descriptions of national scenery. He has a fondness for intricate and what may be termed assonanté metres, which are sometimes remarkably successful, as in "Waiting for the May."—WILLIAMS, ALFRED M., 1881, *The Poets and Poetry of Ireland*, p. 405.

Under the head of political and occasional poems may be mentioned, in conclusion, the odes for the O'Connell Centenary in 1876 and the Centenary of Moore in 1879, recited before immense audiences with great enthusiasm. As we have said before, all the above poems are buried in a few rare volumes or scattered through the pages of periodicals. The worthiest monument his much-loved countrymen could raise to his memory would be a complete edition of his original poems. In the volume of "Ballads, Poems, and Lyrics," published in 1850, appeared a number of translations from the French, Italian, Spanish and German. These were distinguished by their grace and fidelity, and showed the wide range of the poet's reading.—CRANE, T. F., 1882, *Denis Florence MacCarthy, Catholic World*, vol. 35, p. 669.

MacCarthy taught the uses of a national literature, and the noble and unselfish reward it aimed to win, with a persuasiveness that recalled Davis.—DUFFY, SIR CHARLES GAVAN, 1882, *Four Years of Irish History*, 1845–1849, p. 72.

A prose work, "Shelley's Early Life from Original Sources" brought out some highly interesting facts in reference to the great English poet, especially as to that period of his youth when he for a while threw himself into the struggles of Ireland for the amelioration of her laws. "Waiting for the May" is one of Mr. MacCarthy's best known and most admired lyrics. In the Centenary of Moore he was naturally chosen to take a leading part, and composed an ode which was fully worthy of the great occasion.— O'CONNOR, T. P., 1882, *The Cabinet of Irish Literature*, ed. Read, vol. IV, p, 154.

Despite his gift of melodious verse, it is less through his original poetry that Mr. MacCarthy is known in literature than through his successful translations from the great Spanish dramatist whom he chose for his principal subject of study, and whose works his own lyrical facility, and other mental endowments, so well qualified him for interpreting. . . . With the more mobile Celt the case is different. His quicker perceptions and more responsive temperament give him the power of merging his own individuality in that of another, and clothing his mind at will in a new language or a new habit of thought. And it was because he grafted on this typical Irish geniality of temperament the quick sensibilities of a poet, and the finely-strung perceptions of a man of letters, that Mr. MacCarthy was so admirably fitted for his part as the interpreter of foreign genius.—CLERKE, E. M., 1883, *Denis Florence MacCarthy, Dublin Review*, vol. 92, pp. 269, 270.

Was a frequent and valuable contributor to it (*The Nation*). . . . He was an industrious writer, having produced five volumes of original verse as well as numerous translations from Calderon, and his work was always on a high level. The strain of indignant satire in "Cease to do Evil" does not often recur—his imagination dwelt rather on the sweet and gracious aspects of life and Nature, and these he rendered in verse marked by sincere feeling, wide culture, and careful though unpretentious art. —BROOKE, STOPFORD A., AND ROLLESTON, T. W., 1900, eds. *A Treasury of Irish Poetry*, p. 169.

William Stanley Jevons
1835-1882

Born in Liverpool, 1st September 1835, studied there and in London. Assayer to Sydney mint 1854-59, in 1866 he became professor of Logic and Political Economy at Owens College, Manchester, and in 1876-81 held the chair of Political Economy at University College, London. He was drowned 13th August 1882 whilst bathing at Bexhill, near Hastings. Jevons popularised the mathematical methods of Boole, and wrote "Elementary Lessons in Logic" (1870); "Principles of Science" (1874), "Studies in Deductive Logic" (1880), and "Pure Logic and other Minor Works," (1890). To the science of political economy he contributed "The Coal Question" (1865), which led to the appointment of a Royal Commission, and "Theory of Political Economy" (1871; 3d ed. 1888). See his "Letters and Journals," edited by his wife (1886).—PATRICK AND GROOME, eds., 1897, Chambers's Biographical Dictionary, p. 534.

PERSONAL

A philosophic mildness irradiated his private life. His friends and all who consulted him in their difficulties experienced that the wisest was also the kindest of men. Those who know nothing of him but his books should learn that it was only in his controversial writing that the appearance of a sort of *odium logicum* might seem to overcast the serenity of his nature. After all, like Mr. Butler in the "Heart of Midlothian," he was a man and had been a teacher. The imposed necessity of using Mill's writings as text-books may have led him at once to scan minutely the faults and to estimate too extravagantly the influence of his great predecessor, till at last he burst out—"I will no longer consent to live silently under the incumbus of bad logic and bad philosophy which Mill's works have laid upon us." There may have been here an error of judgment; but there never was an unworthy feeling of jealousy in the breast of the philosopher.—EDGEWORTH, F. Y., 1882, *William Stanley Jevons, The Academy*, vol. 22, p. 151.

Jevons was distinguished by a noble simplicity of disposition. In accordance with this, the key-note to his character, he was pious in the broadest sense of the word, tender-hearted, readily interested in whatever had a real human significance, and, notwithstanding, a constitutional tendency to depression, very easily pleased and amused. Both intellectually and morally self-centred, he was entirely free from sordid ambition, and from the mere love of applause. No more honest man ever achieved fame while living laborious days, and striving from his boyhood upward to become "a powerful good in the world."—WARD, ADOLPHUS WILLIAM, 1892, *Dictionary of National Biography*, vol. XXIX, p. 378.

GENERAL

In him an antique boldness of theory was complemented by the cautious spirit of Baconian investigation. He seemed to see with equal eye the general and the particular. Of him alone it would be difficult to say that he looked on one side of truth's shield more readily than the other. . . . At the basis of his system, as the ground work of his magnificent "Principles of Science," he placed Logic. He took a mathematical pleasure in manipulating her empty forms. . . . The abstract nature of Prof. Jevons' intellect, instinctly flying to the highest generalisations, is conspicous in his daring attempt to apply mathematics to political economy. Of course the attempt stands condemned beforehand by dull routine and *littérateur* pertness—profoundly ignorant of the methods of mathematics. . . . Coming to the more ordinary level of abstraction, in the region of "Middle Axiom," we shall find more universally conspicuous monuments of genius in Prof. Jevons' splendid investigations on the "Fall in the Value of Gold," the "Coal Question," and a series of some fifty papers of the highest economical and statistical value. In such publications as formed part of educational or scientific series, the scientific primer of Political Economy, and the volume on "Money" he showed his unrivalled power of making dry subjects attractive and even amusing.—EDGEWORTH, F. Y., 1882, *William Stanley Jevons, The Academy*, vol. 22, p. 151.

Some of his equations are perhaps useful as a concise mode of expression: others appear to illustrate the impossibility of dealing with abstract ideas by mathematical processes. He is, consequently, often credited with the obviously absurd theory that the ultimate criterion of value is the current estimation of a commodity, or, to use the ill-chosen Jevonian expression, "the final degree of utility." Such a theory, like many others of a similar kind, would confound the essence or the substance of a thing with its mere phenomenal expression or manifestation. No one denies, or ever has denied, that supply and demand enter into the temporary value or the price of anything, but this is very different from confounding the mere expression of value in any particular instance with that value which constitutes the substance of every economic object, and without which that object could not be.—BAX, ERNEST BELFORT, 1887, ed., *The Wealth of Nations, Introduction, vol.* I, *p.* xxxvi.

The treatise on economics which Jevons had planned and partly written, and which he intended to make his *magnum opus*, will remain lost to the world. But he left behind him more than enough to warrant his European reputation as a statistician of vast industry and rare gifts of combination, and as an economist of high original power. In the opinion of Professor Alfred Marshall, the great body of Jevons's economic work "will probably be found to have more constructive force than any save that of Ricardo that has been done during the last hundred years." As a logician, he sought with considerable success to advance, as well as defend, the position taken up by Boole, and to establish the applicability of his theory of reasoning to all branches of scientific inquiry.—WARD, ADOLPHUS WILLIAM, 1892, *Dictionary of National Biography, vol.* XXIX, *p.* 377.

Working on Boole's system, William Stanley Jevons arrived at a more convenient symbolic method in his works "Pure Logic" (1864), "The Substitution of Similars" (1869), and "The Principles of Science" (1872). The last two of these belong chronologically to our next period, but are mentioned here because they are so closely associated with the preceding logical movement. In "The Principles of Science" Jevons does not deal merely with formal inferences, but goes over the ground traversed by Mill in his inductive logic. Competent critics are of the opinion that he displays more knowledge of actual scientific methods of investigation than Mill, but less philosophic insight.—WHITTAKER, T., 1897, *Social England, ed. Traill, vol.* VI, *p.* 327.

George Perkins Marsh
1801–1882

An American philologist; born in Woodstock, Vt., March 15, 1801; died in Vallombrosa, Italy, July 23, 1882. A graduate of Dartmouth in 1820, he practiced law in Burlington, Vt., became Member of Congress, 1842–49, minister to Turkey 1849–53, and first minister to the new kingdom of Italy 1861, holding the post until his death, a period of over twenty years. As a diplomatist he had great ability. His services to the study of language, especially the history of his own tongue, give him a distinguished place among American scholars. The "Origin and History of the English Language" remains a standard work. He translated Rask's "Icelandic Grammar" (1838); and also published "Lectures on the English Language" (1861); an edition of Wedgwood's "Etymology;" and "The Earth as Modified by Human Action" (1874). A revised edition of his complete works appeared in 1885; his "Life and Letters" compiled by his widow in 1888. A part of his fine library of Scandinavian literature was acquired by the University of Vermont.—WARNER, CHARLES DUDLEY, *ed.*, 1897, *Library of the World's Best Literature, Biographical Dictionary, vol.* XXIX, *p.* 369.

PERSONAL

A savant, and has written an excellent book on the English language. He is a tall, stout, homely-looking man of about fifty-five, redeemed from Yankeeism by his European residence and culture. I like him very much, and his wife is a handsome woman.—ARNOLD, MATTHEW, 1865, *To his Wife, June* 22; *Letters ed. Russell, vol.* I, *p.* 328.

When I recall the career of this eminent scholar, I am impressed with the harmony of his life, as well as of its ending. He left college fired with a desire to acquire knowledge from the study both of books and nature, and whether following the profession of law, or serving his country as a statesman or diplomat, he never varied from his original purpose. He first saw the light in one of the beautiful valleys of Vermont, and he died in an equally beautiful valley among the Apennines, almost within the shadow of the most ancient seats of learning. When in his early prime, his mind reveled among the historical records and wild scenery of Scandinavia; it was then his privilege to travel extensively through the countries bordering on the Mediterranean; and when the shadows of his life were lengthening, Providence gave him a pleasant home under Italian skies, where he died, and where his grave is certain to be visited with love and veneration by thousands of his countrymen in future years.—LANMAN, CHARLES, 1882, *George Perkins Marsh, Literary World, vol.* 13, *p.* 353.

It has been my fortune in a varied and adventurous life to make the acquaintance of many distinguished men, and of all I ever knew George P. Marsh was the noblest combination, *me judice*, of the noblest qualities which distinguish man—inflexible honesty, public and private; the most intelligent and purest patriotism; ideality of the highest as to his service in his official career; generosity and self-sacrifice in his personal relations; quick and liberal appreciation of all good in others, and the most singular modesty in all that concerned himself; unfaltering adherence to truth at any cost; an adamantine recognition of duty which knew no deflection from personal motive; and, binding the whole in the noblest and truest of lives, a sincere religious temperament, in which the extreme of liberality to others was united to the profoundest humility as to himself. . . . Mr. Marsh could never have been a popular man, except among students. His high, unbending sense of justice; his aversion to and contempt for anything that savored of duplicity, disingenuousness, partiality, or favoritism; his intolerance of anything that resembled corruption, unfitted him for American politics, while the same justice in personal matters, coupled with a singular want of egoistic ambition and rare humility, seemed to prevent that display of personal preferences which contributes so largely to the creation of individual enthusiasm. If anybody loved him, it was for the sake of the truth and the justice he himself so revered; he was so broad in his humanities, so uncompromising in his judgments on his own feelings, so free from vanity of any kind, or ostentation, that he seemed almost impersonal. — STILLMAN, WILLIAM JAMES, 1882, *The Late George P. Marsh, The Nation, vol.* 35, *p.* 304.

Perhaps the most remarkable feature in Mr. Marsh's linguistic attainment was his ability to speak and write a language as soon as he could read it fluently. His ear was extremely acute in distinguishing vocal sounds, and his power of reproducing them was not less remarkable. He never lost an opportunity of listening to the conversation of those to whom the language he was studying was native, and always joined in it when possible. His memory, naturally very tenacious, and strengthened by the necessity of trusting to it rather than to his eyes, served him for the rest. . . . His physical powers were now (1839) in their fullest vigor, and he had little the appearance of a close student. The tall and slender aspect, which his six feet of stature gave him in his early youth, had disappeared in the development of full, strong muscles, and his firm step and erect bearing conveyed the impression of great bodily strength, which, in fact, he possessed. His habitual expression was grave; the firm-set mouth might even be called stern; and his earnest gray eyes always seemed to look through the object they were resting upon. There was, in short, an intense personality about him, which inspired all who knew him with respect, and many who did not know him with something very like fear.—MARSH, CAROLINE C., 1888, ed. *Life and Letters of George Perkins Marsh, vol.* I, *pp.* 22, 29.

Mr. Marsh was always an early riser. His working time was between five and nine in the morning. He struck an average when he was a lawyer by sleeping in his office while his partner listened to bores; in the House of Representatives it was a standing pleasantry to predict when J. Q. Adams and G. P. Marsh would go to sleep. He read as fast as another man would turn the leaves of a book, and his habit was to begin in the middle and read both ways. He read many books at once, changing from one to another every hour or so.—MARCH, FRANCIS ANDREW, 1888, *George Perkins Marsh, The Nation, vol.* 47, *p.* 214.

During the later portion of my life at Florence, and subsequently at Rome, Mr. G. P. Marsh and his very charming wife were among our most valued friends for many years. . . . Mr. Marsh was a man of very large and varied culture. A thorough classical scholar and excellent modern linguist, philology was, perhaps, his most favourite pursuit. . . . Mr. Marsh died, full of years and honors, at a ripe old age. But the closing scene of his life was remarkable from the locality of it. He had gone to pass the hot season at Vallombrosa, where a comfortable hotel replaces the old *forestieria* of the monastery, while a school of forestry has been established by the government within its walls. Amid those secular shades the old diplomatist and scholar breathed his last, and could not have done so in a more peaceful spot. But the very inaccessible nature of the place made it a question of some difficulty how the body should be transported in properly decorous fashion to the railway station in the valley below—a difficulty which was solved by the young scholars of the school of forestry, who turned out in a body to have the honor of bearing on their shoulders the remains of the man whose writings had done so much to awaken the government to the necessity of establishing the institution to which they belonged. — TROLLOPE, THOMAS ADOLPHUS, 1888, *What I Remember*, pp. 448, 450.

Physically, he represented a more stalwart bit of New England manhood than Bancroft. . . . His father was a large landowner, magistrate, and sturdy Puritan. The Puritan sturdiness the son inherited, with many yeoman-like qualities, and quite unusual bookish aptitudes. As a boy he regaled himself with stolen readings of an early Encyclopædia Britannica; nor did he at any age or under any circumstances outgrow an insatiate greed for "knowing things." He had never any patience with dabblers or with those who "half knew" things. This touch of portraiture, will, I am sure, be recognized by anyone who ever encountered the stalwart presence and the questioning attitude which always belonged to George P. Marsh. . . . We know that his appetite for the beautiful, whether in art or nature, never abated; we know that the old Cromwellian Puritanism in him always growled (though under breath) at any invasion upon popular rights; we know that tiaras and mitres always had a pasteboard look to him; we know that courtesy and friendliness and *bonhomie* always touched him, whether in kings or paupers; we know that he greatly loved to inoculate all open-minded, cultivated American travellers with his own abounding love for Italian art and Italian hopes; we know that the water-flashes of Tivoli or Terni, or all the blues by Capri, never wiped from his memory the summer murmurs of the Queechee at Woodstock, or the play of the steely surface of Champlain, under its backing of Adirondack Mountains.—MITCHELL, DONALD G., 1899, *American Lands and Letters, Leather Stocking to Poe's "Raven,"* pp. 59, 60, 72.

GENERAL

Mr. Marsh is known as a scholar of profound and various erudition, as a writer of strongly marked individuality and nationality. His sympathies are with the Goths, whose presence he recognizes in whatever is grand and peculiar in the characters of the founders of New England, and in whatever gives promise of her integrity, greatness, and permanence. He is undoubtedly better versed than any American in the fresh and vigorous literature of the north of Europe, and perhaps is so also in that fruit of a new birth of genius and virtue, the Puritan literature of Great Britain, and continental Europe. In the "Goths in New England," (published in 1836), he has contrasted in a striking manner the characters of the Goths and the Romans, and traced the presence and influence of the former in the origin and growth of this republic; and in a discourse recently delivered before the New England Society of the city of New York, he enters again upon the subject, and points to the growth among us, of the Roman element which is as antagonistical to freedom as it is to Gothicism.—GRISWOLD, RUFUS WILMOT, 1847-70, *The Prose Writers of America*, ed. Dillingham, p. 414.

Mr. Marsh's articles are admirably solid. His style is his weak point. It is apt to be what I should call "congregational." But he is much better than usual in the *Nation* thus far. As an editor, I should find fault with his articles as being too palpably parts of a book. He does not get under way quite rapidly enough for a newspaper. But all he says is worth reading for its matter.—LOWELL, JAMES RUSSELL, 1866, *To E. L. Godkin*, Oct. 19; *Letters*, ed. Norton, vol. I, p. 372.

Prof. Marsh's two volumes on the English Language entitle him to a prominent place in literature. They are the fruits of original reading and study, and are marked by breadth of view and soundness of judgment. —HART, JOHN S., 1872, *A Manual of American Literature*, p. 254.

Mr. Marsh is an eminent scholar in the northern languages of Europe, and holds a high place among philologists. His principal work, entitled "Lectures on the English Language," is a treatise of great value, and possesses an unusual degree of interest.—UNDERWOOD, FRANCIS H., 1872, *A Handbook of English Literature, American Authors*, p. 206.

The subject of it ["Man in Nature"] is the modifications and alterations which this planet has undergone at the hands of man. His subject leads him to consider much at large the denudation of mountains, which has caused and is causing such calamitous mischief in Italy and the south of France. He shows very convincingly and interestingly that the destruction of forests causes not only floods in winter and spring, but drought in summer and autumn. And the efforts which have recently been made in Italy to take some steps towards the reclothing of the mountain-sides have in great measure been due to his work, which has been largely circulated in an Italian translation.—TROLLOPE, THOMAS ADOLPHUS, 1888, *What I Remember*, p. 448.

In 1838 he printed an Icelandic grammar. He collected the rarest books in these northern languages and read them. He also wrote articles about them, and delivered orations —or, at least, an oration, a great one, delivered before the Philomathesian Society of Middlebury, Vermont, in 1843. At that time these languages and literatures, the Anglo-Saxon and Icelandic, were as remote from common scholarly knowledge as Algonkin or Choctaw. The swarm of German scholars had not yet lighted upon them. Grimm's knowledge of "Beowulf" was talked of much as Mr. Trumbull's knowledge of Eliot's Bible is now. Four or five Englishmen were working with Grimm or after him. The Kembles were lamenting that John Mitchell Kemble was nothing better than the chief of Anglo-Saxonists in England. No one of them was to be compared for a moment with Mr. Marsh in general mental vigor or special linguistic genius. His published works are eminently fresh and original, not of any school, not discussions of other students' views but clear statements of what he saw with his own eyes in his own copies of the original works, with the comments of an American thinker. His "Lectures on the English Language," delivered before the post-graduates of Columbia College in 1859, and "Lectures on the Origin and History of the English Language and Its Early Literature," delivered before the Lowell Institute in 1860, were almost extemporaneous utterances from the stores of his earlier studies, but they were everywhere recognised as the best books of their kind, and they are still counted among the books which no gentleman's library can be without.—MARCH, FRANCIS ANDREW, 1888, *George Perkins Marsh, The Nation*, vol. 47, p. 214.

Those lectures for Harvard and Columbia resulting in his scholarly books upon early English literature and language; scholarly and interesting, but lacking the careful synthesis which is apt to be lacking in works written swiftly, out of whatever fulness of knowledge, for a special and pressing occasion. He himself was never quite satisfied with these "chips" hewed away from the tree of his knowledge. In "Man and Nature," there was enough of wise observation, sound reasoning, cumulated knowledge for a half-dozen treatises; but there was also that unstudied assemblage of parts which did not invite the lazy companionship and easy perusal of the average book-reader.—MITCHELL, DONALD G., 1899, *American Lands and Letters, Leather Stocking to Poe's "Raven*," p. 67.

Orville Dewey
1794–1882

An American Unitarian clergyman. He was born in Massachusetts, graduated at Williams College, and later became a divinity student at Andover. He preached in Boston for two years, as assistant to Dr. Channing, forming a friendship which was only broken by death. In 1823 he became pastor of the Unitarian Church in New Bedford. He went to New York in 1835, and while pastor there secured the erection of the Church of the Messiah. About 1844 he quitted the pulpit and lectured in various parts of the country. Among his works are: "Letters on Revivals;" "Discourses on Human Nature;" "Discourses on Human Life" (1841); "Discourses on the Nature of Religion;" and "The Unitarian Belief." A collected edition of his works appeared in New York

(1847). Consult his "Autobiography and Letters," edited by his daughter (Boston, 1884).—GILMAN, PECK AND COLBY, *eds.*, 1903, *The New International Encyclopædia, vol.* VI, *p.* 29.

PERSONAL

In conversation, a person of Dr. Dewey's thought and culture cannot but be attractive, if he gives freedom to his thoughts and play to his fancy. This he does to an unusual degree. He is one of the best conversationists, maintaining lively chat of anecdote, illustration, and repartee, with a vein of sound sense constantly revealing itself, and an underlying strata of philosophical and religious thought ever cropping out. In person, Mr. Dewey is of medium height, with a well-compacted body, surmounted by a head quite too large to be proportioned; with a full, high, and broad forehead; with dark, short, undirected hair; and a large, flexible, expressive, and homely mouth. Dr. Dewey's style is the result of severe discipline, and one difficult of attainment. It is both ornate and chaste. It is not so likely to win the applause of the many; but it finds its way to an aristocracy of mind on terms of confidence. It has a nobility of air, which marks it as of a privileged order.... The orator must possess dignity, yet without pomposity; ease, without slovenliness; richness of style, without inflation; simplicity, without abruptness; power, without commotion; earnestness, without haste; he must be impassioned, but not passionate; roused, but not vehement; on-going, but not impetuous. Such an orator is Dr. Dewey. His periods are perfectly complete and rounded, yet filled by the thought; the variety is great, yet a symmetry prevails; and in general we find that harmony between the thoughts and their form, which should always obtain. Some excel in style, but lack thought; others are rich in thought, but fail in style; some use words to please the ear merely; others discard all grace and melody. Dr. Dewey combines the two. It is doubtful whether the name of Saxon or Roman would apply to his style. Artistic and scholarly it certainly is. His imagination is rich, but not superfluous; ready, but not obtrusive. It takes not the lead of truth, but waits on her as a handmaid. It flies, but not to weariness; soars, but does not strain its flight.... When Dr. Dewey appears in the pulpit, one feels that an earnest, devout, thoughtful man is to speak. There is no restlessness, no unnecessary shifting and arranging, no sudden angular movements, no commotion, no hurry.—FOWLER, HENRY, 1856, *The American Pulpit, pp.* 282, 286, 287.

Dewey, reared in the country, among plain but not common people, squarely built, and in the enjoyment of what seemed robust health, had, when I first saw him, at forty years of age, a massive dignity of person; strong features, a magnificent height of head, a carriage almost royal; a voice deep and solemn; a face capable of the utmost expression, and an action which the greatest tragedian could not have much improved. These were not arts and attainments, but native gifts of person and temperament. An intellect of the first class had fallen upon a spiritual nature tenderly alive to the sense of divine realities. His awe and reverence were native, and they have proved indestructible. He did not so much seek religion as religion sought him. His nature was characterized from early youth by a union of massive intellectual power with an almost feminine sensibility; a poetic imagination with a rare dramatic faculty of representation. Diligent as a scholar, a careful thinker, accustomed to test his own impressions by patient meditation, a reasoner of the most cautious kind; capable of holding doubtful conclusions, however inviting, in suspense; devout and reverent by nature,—he had every qualification for a great preacher, in a time when the old foundations were broken up and men's minds were demanding guidance and support in the critical transition from the days of pure authority to the days of personal conviction by rational evidence. Dewey has from the beginning been the most truly human of our preachers. Nobody has felt so fully the providential variety of mortal passions, exposures, the beauty and happiness of our earthly life, the lawfulness of our ordinary pursuits, the significance of home, of business, of pleasure, of society, of politics. He has made himself the attorney of human nature, defending and justifying it in all the hostile suits brought against it by imperfect sympathy, by theological acrimony, by false dogmas. Yet he never was for a moment the apologist of selfishness, vice, or folly; no stricter moralist than he is to be found;

no worshipper of veracity more faithful; no wiser or more tender pleader of the claims of reverence and self-consecration.—BELLOWS, HENRY W., 1879, *Address at the Fifty-fourth Anniversary of the Founding of the Church of the Messiah, New York; Autobiography and Letters of Orville Dewey, ed. Dewey, p. 358.*

Here and there one remains, to listen with interest to a fresh account of persons and things once familiar; while the story will find its chief audience among those who remember Mr. Dewey as among the lights of their own youth. Those also who love the study of human nature may follow with pleasure the development of a New England boy, with a character of great strength, simplicity, reverence, and honesty, with scanty opportunities for culture, and heavily handicapped in his earlier running, by both poverty and Calvinism, but possessed from the first by the love of truth and knowledge, and by a generous sympathy which made him long to impart whatever treasures he obtained. To trace the growth of such a life to a high point of usefulness and power, to see it unspoiled by honor and admiration, and to watch its retirement, under the pressure of nervous disease, from active service, while never losing its concern for the public good, its quickness of personal sympathy, nor its interest in the solution of the mightiest problems of humanity, cannot be an altogether unprofitable use of time to the reader, while to the writer it is a work of consecration.—DEWEY, MARY E., 1883, ed. *Autobiography and Letters of Orville Dewey, p. 8.*

Miss Mary Dewey, in the admirable memoir of her father, lays great stress on his affectionate qualities. These cannot be too emphatically asserted; yet they probably had more scope than even she suspected. Indeed, unless I am much mistaken, they formed the basis of his character. He was a most deep-feeling man. He loved his friends in and out of the profession, with a loyal, hearty, obliging, warm, and even tender emotion, expressing itself in word and deed. It was overflowing, not in any sentimental manner, but in a manly, sincere way. He was a man of infinite good-will, of a quite boundless kindness. His voice, his expression of face, his smile, the grasp of his hand,—all gave signs of it. He felt things keenly; his sensibilities were most acute; even his thoughts were suffused with emotion. He could not discuss speculative themes as if they were cold or dry. Nothing was arid to his mind. In prayer it was not unusual for his audience to discern tears rolling down his cheeks. . . . In him, heart was uppermost; intellect, conscience, were of subordinate value when taken alone; in fact, they were incomplete by themselves, and wanted their proper substance. He said once that his skin was so delicate that the least soil on his hands was felt all through his system and prevented him from working. The excessive sensibility, which could not be understood by the world at large, was at the bottom of his likes and dislikes, and of his personal fears and hopes. Excitement drained off his strength. He exhausted himself physically, and fell into ill-health by exertions that would not have taxed an ordinary constitution. It cost him a great deal to write sermons, to visit the sick and sorrowing, to conduct public services. At the same time, he was disqualified, by a certain want of steel in his blood, for any but the clerical profession, where qualities like his are of inestimable value, and of the rarest kind.—FROTHINGHAM, OCTAVIUS BROOKS, 1891, *Recollections and Impressions, p. 176.*

GENERAL

The distinguishing peculiarity of these "Discourses," is, in fact, that they aim to persuade and convince men, with an earnestness and power from which there is no escaping, of their spiritual and immortal nature,—of the exceeding and eternal worth of that nature,—of the primary obligation to value and cultivate it,—of the inexpressible sin of neglecting, abusing, perverting it. The title-page announces Discourses on *various subjects,*—and they are various in the common sense of the word,—but still they are only different points of view from which the attention is directed to one central prospect. Whatever be the name of the discourse, its great end and aim is to bring men to knowledge,—not coldly and theoretically, but earnestly and abidingly,—that they are responsible creatures, living under the eye and government of an infinite God, and having far higher trusts and interests than any which belong to this world alone. . . . We need say nothing of Mr. Dewey's style. . . . It exactly befits the thought. It is the spontaneous language of an earnest and eloquent spirit. It has starts, and breaks, and parentheses within parentheses,—but no confusion, no obscurity. We see how it might be criticized; but we shall not criticize it, and we would not have it other than it is;—or, if different in some few respects, not so different as to change its character.—GREENWOOD, F. W. P., 1835, *Dewey's Discourses, Christian Examiner, vol.* 18, *pp.* 390, 396.

The views which he presents, ["Discourses"] on subjects so various, and singly of such wide relations, it is to be supposed will be found, in different places, more or less striking and weighty. But this is apparent throughout, that he is speaking his own observations and convictions; that he is uttering himself; that, however he may have been indebted to books for excitements and illustrations, he owes to them none of his processes of inquiry, and none of his conclusions. Often his views, while they are novel, are sagacious and satisfactory; his appeals are often strongly exciting. But this charm is never absent from what he writes, that it is evidently fresh from the author's own mind. And, as to style, there is often a grace and gorgeousness, and often a condensed force of diction, which makes ample amends for the somewhat characteristic infelicities, to which we have referred.—PALFREY, JOHN GORHAM, 1838, *Dewey's Discourses, North American Review, vol,* 47, *p.* 473.

Believing that the philosophy of the filial heart is higher and of infinitely more worth than that of the doubting head, we rejoice in the expression of simple, childlike, faith, by one whom the world will not easily suspect of either having been awed into the popular belief, or of believing one, and preaching and printing another. We have been refreshed and strengthened by reading these sermons. It gladdens us to know that one, who has stood so prominent among the champions of liberty and progress in religion, retains so firm an attachment to that basis of miracle and inspiration, on which alone, as we think, Christianity can rest. These Discourses recognise the distinction between Natural and Revealed Religion, the insufficiency of the former of itself both as to doctrine and evidence, and man's deep need of an express and authoritative revelation from the Author of his being. They are so rich in just and striking thought, that to give a fair analysis of them would be to reprint them entire.—PEABODY, ANDREW P., 1842, *Dewey's Two Discourses, Christian Examiner, vol.* 31, *p.* 72.

He is admired by those who are capable of appreciating the philosophy of morals, without reference to his peculiar theological belief. His reasoning is generally comprehensive, and his illustrations often poetical. There is a happy mixture of ease and finish in his style, and he is remarkable for interesting the hearer in themes which would be trite if treated with less earnestness. Perhaps the pathos of his rhetoric is its most effective characteristic.—GRISWOLD, RUFUS WILMOT, 1847-70, *The Prose Writers of America,* ed. *Dillingham, p.* 303.

The author of these discourses ["Discourses and Reviews"] stands in the very first rank of Unitarian literature. As a pulpit orator, his reputation is distinguished. . . . These essays are not chargeable with the usual offensiveness of controversial writing. Dr. Dewey possesses all the qualifications which are needed to give seemliness and polish to the form of his opinions. He shines more to our apprehension, in the gentle glow of sentiment, than in the conflict of reasoning. Nothing is more characteristic of the whole work, than a disposition to avoid bold statement of positions, sharp cutting of defining lines, and penetrating analysis of philosophical difficulties. The shudder with which the author sometimes flies back from metaphysical methods is more amiable in the saloon, than dignified in the field of disputation. Yet he is not a common man, and where he is in the right, as he frequently is, we admire the perspicuity and scholarlike elegance, with which he can express a familiar truth.—ALEXANDER, J. W., 1847, *Dewey's Controversial Discourses, Princeton Review, vol.* 19, *pp.* 1, 2.

There is a great beauty of style—much force, and much felicity, of language about them. They display a rich and vigorous imagination, a fine and cultivated taste, and for the most part an elevated and courteous spirit; to all which we regret that, by the hostile bearing of the work upon our orthodox faith, we are obliged to render but the scanty justice of this paragraph.—MARTIN, B. N., 1848, *Dewey's Controversial Writings, The New Englander, vol.* 6, *p.* 67.

The discourses of Dr. Dewey are full of

profound thought, of strong religious convictions, and are written in a solidly attractive style.—UNDERWOOD, FRANCIS H., 1872, *A Hand-Book of English Literature, American Authors*, p. 144.

The theologian and preacher who came nearest to Channing in the geniality and largeness of his nature, and the persuasiveness with which he enforced what may be called the conservative tenets of Unitarianism, was Orville Dewey, a man whose mind was fertile, whose religious experience was deep, and who brought from the Calvinism in which he had been trained an interior knowledge of the system which he early rejected. He had a profound sense not only of the dignity of human nature, but of the dignity of human life. In idealizing human life he must still be considered as giving some fresh and new interpretations of it, and his discourses form, like Channing's, an addition to American literature, as well as contribution to the theology of Unitarianism. He defended men from the assaults of Calvinists, as Channing had defended Man. Carlyle speaks somewhere of "this doghole of a world;" Dewey considered it, with all its errors and horrors, as a good world on the whole, and as worthy of the Divine beneficence. — WHIPPLE, EDWIN PERCY, 1876-86, *American Literature and Other Papers*, ed. *Whittier*, p. 58.

Everywhere in this volume ["Sermons"] there is great felicity of diction, and a happy faculty of illustration, a sense of what is great and beautiful, a shrewd insight into the ways of the world and into our human nature. But these are not what make up its special charm and power. Here is a man thoroughly in earnest, who, with a powerful intellect and a great soul, has been reverently looking into the greatest and most vital of all subjects for nearly fourscore years. In the opening dawn of childhood, treading "unconsciously on the hidden springs of wisdom and mystery," through all the succeeding years, he has been grappling with these momentous problems, and here we have the maturest processes and results of all his thinking and of his life's experience. Here are marks of the conscientious and laborious workings of a strong and thoroughly trained mind. Great subjects, carefully examined and thought out, are brought before us.—MORISON, J. H., 1877, *Dr. Dewey's Sermons, Unitarian Review*, vol. 7, p. 55

His creed, his method, and his intellectual and spiritual nature closely resembled those of his friend Channing, to whom in youth he had been assistant minister; but the distinctly literary ability of his sermons and other writings was less; and, unlike Channing, he was not a power in philanthropy, nor did he make his influence felt in literary criticism. Upon his thoughtful and reverent lectures on "The Problem of Human Destiny" his present literary reputation chiefly rests. But it is the misfortune (in one sense) of the minister, however earnest and able, that his books and sermons, unless of striking and significant force, or of literary ability so high as to give them a renown aside from that due to their moral mission, are not widely remembered or often read. We think of what clergymen *did*, or perhaps of what they *were*, but not of what they *are* in literature.—RICHARDSON, CHARLES F., 1887, *American Literature*, 1607-1885, vol. I, p. 293.

One of the profoundest thinkers of his generation.—PATTEE, FRED LEWIS, 1896, *A History of American Literature*, p. 207.

Richard Henry Dana, Jr.
1815-1882

A distinguished American publicist, son of R. H. the Elder; born at Cambridge, Mass., Aug. 1, 1815; died Jan. 6, 1882. Obliged to suspend college studies because of an affection of the eyes, he shipped as a seaman on board a whaling vessel. His observations during the two years of his life as a common sailor are contained in his celebrated narrative "Two Years before the Mast" (1837). Returning to Boston, he studied law and was admitted to the bar. In 1841 he published "The Seaman's Friend," often afterwards republished under the title "The Seaman's Manual." He details his experiences and observations during a visit to Cuba, in the little volume "To Cuba and Back" (1859). He edited Wheaton's "Elements of International law" (1866), and wrote a series of "Letters on Italian Unity" (1871).—WARNER, CHARLES DUDLEY, ed. 1897, *Library of the World's Best Literature, Biographical Dictionary*, vol. XXIX, p. 130.

PERSONAL

One lovely afternoon in the spring of the preceding year Mr. Dana had visited, with his wife and daughter, the old Protestant cemetery where stands the pyramid of Caius Cestius, and where Shelley and Keats are buried; a spot than which none is more familiar to English-speaking visitors in Rome. As they stood there under the tall cypress-trees by the ruins of the old walls, looking across them to the city beyond, the air filled with the fragrance of flowers and resounding with the song of nightingales, Mrs. Dana said to her husband: "Is not this the spot where one would wish to lie for ever?" and he answered, "Yes, it is indeed!" And this spot his wife now selected for her husband's grave. . . . The stone that now marks it is of rough white marble, on the polished face of which, surmounted by a leaning cross, is cut this inscription:—

RICHARD HENRY DANA
of Boston,
United States of America.
Born August 1, 1815,
Died in Rome
January 6, 1882.

—ADAMS, CHARLES FRANCIS, 1890, *Richard Henry Dana, A Biography, vol.* II, *p.* 386.

Did ever a man suffer more than Dana from his mental peculiarities, perversities or obliquities, or whatever you choose to call them? He thought anybody could collect authorities, and that to do this was a day laborer's task; he used Lawrence's collections, and then despised his notes because they were mere collections of authorities, and at last thought himself under no obligation to him, because the notes were what anybody could have done, and so would not say the soft word that might have turned away wrath, but wrote instead what almost rendered a lawsuit inevitable; —and then Lawrence pursued him with a personal and political vindictiveness which ruined Dana's career, lost him his only chance, and was to Lawrence, whatever became of his lawsuit, a perfectly satisfactory vindication. Two hundred and fifty dollars paid —— —— —— or some other equally accurate man would have rendered any suit impossible; and a little harmless and truthful flattery would have removed all desire for a controversy from Lawrence's mind. But, the whole thing was very characteristic of one side of Dana's mind.—LOTHROP, THORNTON K., 1890, *Letter to Charles Francis Adams, Aug.* 25; *Richard Henry Dana, A Biography, ed. Adams, vol.* II, *p.* 417.

There were unique combinations in Dana: he was an aristocrat before-the-mast, a haughty and humble Christian. In England he rejoiced in the abandonment of "the aristocratic distinction of the manor pew" (Adams, ii, 76, 91); yet he practically spent his life in such a pew, and never could quite find his way to the handle of the door. In Washington he records with delight the information that the Unitarian church near by has a very thin congregation (i., 109); yet he heartily admired Theodore Parker, thought his sermon on Webster the best tribute paid to that great man (i., 226), and favored Parker's selection as an honorary member of the Harvard Phi Beta Kappa . . . on the ground that he was no further from the truth than most of the members of the society, or than Dr. Franklin, its supposed founder. No man of his time could state with equal lucidity or equal compactness, either before a popular audience or in a court-room, any argument involving a principle; and he kept himself in touch with his audience, although, it must be owned, with the very tips of his fingers.— HIGGINSON, THOMAS WENTWORTH, 1891, *Adams's Dana, The Nation, vol.* 52, *p.* 53.

He was a man of absolute nobility and simplicity of character,—devoted to principle, to duty, to friendship, to his country. One could hardly help criticising and finding fault with him; but the criticisms could only fall on his head and his temper; they could never touch his heart and his conscience, with any one who really knew him. Undoubtedly, he was not in line with the ordinary front of his country's thought; but the qualities he took away with him can ill be spared, be they popular or unpopular.—EVERETT, WILLIAM, 1896, *Two Friends of California, Overland Monthly, N. S., vol.* 28, *p.* 582.

TWO YEARS BEFORE THE MAST
1837

This is, in many respects, a remarkable book. It is a successful attempt to describe a class of men, and a course of life, which, though familiarly spoken of by most people, and considered as within the limits of civilization, will appear to them now almost as just discovered. To find a new subject in so old a sphere of humanity is something; and scarcely second to this are the spirit and skill with which it is handled. It seems as if the writer must have been favored with a special gift for his novel enterprise. It is a young sailor's narrative at the end of his only voyage. It is his first attempt as an author, and certainly the last which, considering his previous condition and pursuits, he could ever have dreamed of making. Though it was written from a desire and purpose to enlighten people as to the state and evils of a seafaring life, though it constantly offers matter for serious reflection, and is necessarily occupied, a large part of the time, with very humble materials, yet it is as entertaining as a well-contrived fiction, it is as luminous as poetry, and its interest never flags. Thus it is likely to be a standard work in its particular line, at least till it instructs some other adventurer to surpass it. We think we can see, in the good reception it has had, much more than sudden admiration of a novelty; and in the book itself, much more than the rapid fruit of youthful spirits and fancy. Hard labor is necessary to effect any thing considerable in literature; and probably few works ever cost more, if we may reckon the toils, sacrifices, and temptations of a common sailor, as a part of his preparation for a memorable narrative of sea life.—CHANNING, EDWARD T., 1841, *Two Years Before the Mast, North American Review, vol.* 52, *p.* 56.

About the best sea-book in the English tongue.—DICKENS, CHARLES, 1869, *Speeches and Sayings, p.* 80.

There are some books which it is difficult to class. Thus, Richard H. Dana, Jr., published some thirty years ago a volume called "Two Years Before the Mast," which became instantly popular, and is popular now, and promises to be popular for many years to come. In reading it anybody can see that it is more than an ordinary record of a voyage, for there runs through the simple and lucid narrative an element of beauty and power which gives it the artistic charm of romance. — WHIPPLE, EDWIN PERCY, 1876-86, *American Literature and Other Papers, ed. Whittier, p.* 135.

Dana, by way of restoring his infirm health, shipped as a common seaman, and wrote this story of his experiences several years after his return to Boston. It is one of the best, if not the best, true narrative of sea-life ever published: the style is quiet and simple, the descriptions vivid and stirring, and the record of facts so manifestly accurate and impartial, and, at the same time, so thoughtful and intelligent, that the reader feels as if he himself were a participant in the author's adventures. A hitherto unknown side of life is revealed in all its details: and its veracity and importance are evidenced by the fact that the book is still in print, and is probably read by as many persons to day as at the time of its first appearance.—HAWTHORNE, JULIAN, AND LEMMON, LEONARD, 1891, *American Literature, p.* 20.

"Two Years Before The Mast" is still so much read that it may be called, without Macaulay's exaggeration, a book that every schoolboy knows. . . . I need not here speak of its racy idiomatic English, its spice of youthful adventure, its wholesome atmosphere redolent of sea-spray flung up by the breezes. Here was an American author who gave to his facts so much of the charm of Defoe's fictions that a writer in the "Encyclopædia Britannica" calls him "The Author of the Popular Novel 'Two Years Before the Mast,'" which is founded on personal experience."—ANDERSON, EDWARD PLAYFAIR, 1891, *The Sequel of "Two Years Before The Mast," The Dial, vol.* 77, *p.* 380.

Until Richard H. Dana and Herman Melville wrote, the commercial sailor of Great Britain and the United States was without representation in literature. Dana and Melville were Americans. They were the first to lift the hatch and show the world what passes in a ship's forecastle; how men live down in that gloomy cave, how and what they eat, and where they sleep; what pleasures they take, what their sorrows and wrongs are; how they are used when they quit their black sea-parlors in response to the boatswain's silver summons to work on deck by day or by night. . . . Dana lifted the curtain and showed you the sort of life hundreds and thousands of those fellow creatures of ours called "sailors" were living in his day, and had been living long prior to his day, and will go on living whilst there remains a ship afloat. No Englishman had done this. Marryat makes his Newton Foster a merchant sailor; but Marryat knew nothing of the hidden life of the merchant service. . . . Fenimore Cooper came very near to the truth in his Ned Myers, but the revelation there is that of the individual. Ned is one man. He is a drunken, swearing, bragging Yankee *only* sailor; very brutal, always disgusting.

Cooper's book is true of Ned Myers; Dana's of all sailors, American and English. . . . When you talk of sailors, you do not think of steamers. If you inquire for a seaman, you are conducted to a ship that is not impelled by machinery, but by the wind. You will find the seaman you want, the seaman Dana wrote about, the generic seaman whose interpretation I count among the glories of literature, seeing how hidden he has been, how darkly obscure in his toil and hourly doings,—*this* seaman you will find in the deck-house or the forecastle of the sailing ship. He is not thrashed across the Atlantic in six days. He is not swept from the Thames to the uttermost ends of the earth in a month. He is afloat for weeks and weeks at a spell, and his life is that of the crew of the "Pilgrim." Do you ask what manner of life it is? Read "Two Years Before the Mast," and recognize the claim I make for American literature by witnessing in that book the faultless picture of a scene of existence on whose wide face Richard Dana was the first to fling a light.—RUSSELL, WILLIAM CLARK, 1892, *A Claim for American Literature, North American Review*, vol. 154, pp. 138, 139, 140.

The only class of men who ever found "Two Years Before The Mast" uninteresting was that in which aristocratic feeling is developed more highly than in any other Americans,—namely, the officers of the Navy. To them, the author was a common sailor, and his experiences in the forecastle and on the jibboom were as dull and low as the cook's in the galley. And perhaps Mr. Dana's own set in Boston was the only community in history who, feeling themselves gentlemen all over, entertained a positive repulsion to the Army and Navy as professions.—EVERETT, WILLIAM, 1896, *Two Friends of California, Overland Monthly*, N. S., vol. 28, p. 582.

John William Draper
1811–1882

An American physiologist, chemist, historical and miscellaneous prose-writer; born near Liverpool, England, May 5, 1811; died at Hastings-on-the-Hudson, N. Y., Jan. 4, 1882. He came to this country in 1833, and took his degree as M. D. at the University of Pennsylvania in 1836. He became professor of chemistry in the University of New York in 1841, and in 1850 professor of physiology. Among his works are: "Human Physiology" (1856); "History of the Intellectual Development of Europe" (1862), a work of great importance and very widely read: "History of the American Civil War" (1867-70); "History of the Conflict between Religion and Science" (1875), which ran through many editions and was translated into nearly all the languages of Europe.—WARNER, CHARLES DUDLEY, ed., 1897, *Library of the World's Best Literature, Biographical Dictionary*, vol. XXIX, p. 151.

GENERAL

Professor Draper's works have had, and are having, a very rapid sale, and are evidently very highly esteemed by that class of readers who take an interest, without being very profoundly versed, in the grave subjects which he treats. He is, we believe, a good chemist and a respectable physiologist. His work on Human Physiology, we have been assured by those whose judgment in such matters we prefer to our own, is a work of real merit, and was, when first published, up to the level of the science to which it is devoted. . . . He writes in a clear, easy, graceful, and pleasing style, but we have found nothing new or profound in his works. His theories are almost as old as the hills, and even older, if the hills are no older than he pretends. His work on the "Intellectual Development of Europe," is in substance, taken from the positivists, and the positivist philosophy is only a reproduction, with no scientific advance on that of the old physiologists or hylozoists, as Cudworth calls them. He agrees perfectly with the positivists in the recognition of three ages or epochs, we should rather say stages, in human development; the theological, the metaphysical, and the scientific or positivist. . . . We own we have treated Professor Draper's work with very little respect, for we have felt very little. His "Intellectual Development of Europe" is full of crudities from beginning to end, and for the most part below criticism, or would be were it not that it is levelled at all the principles of individual and social life and progress. The book belongs to the age of Leucippus and Democritus, and *ignores*, if we may use an expressive term, though hardly English, Christian civilization and all the progress man and nations have effected since the opening of the Christian era. It is a monument not of science, but of gross ignorance.— BROWNSON, ORESTES A., 1868, *Professor Draper's Books, Works*, ed. *Brownson, vol.* IX, *pp.* 292, 297, 318.

But he has not confined his studies to the sciences. He has aspired to co-ordinate the results of all modern learning into a broad philosophical view of the progress of mankind. This is the theme of his principal work, the " History of the Intellectual Development of Europe." It may be likened in a measure, to Buckle's " History of Civilization," and to the recent works of Lecky; but the author has made an original plan, and has developed his own ideas in the view of the world's history. His style is sententious and dignified; his works will be read for their ideas, and will command respect from all thoughtful men.—UNDERWOOD, FRANCIS H., 1872, *A Hand-Book of English Literature, American Authors*, p. 366.

John William Draper had undertaken to write and to publish a "History of the Intellectual Development of Europe," on the so-called inductive method recommended by Buckle. But the author has made the great mistake of utterly disregarding and ignoring art in her various forms. How is the intellectual development possible without the element of the Beautiful? And what would the world and the existence of man be without Beauty?—SCHERR, J., 1874, *A History of English Literature*, tr. *M. V.*

This is a work ["Intellectual Development of Europe"] written with unquestionable ability. The most striking feature of the book is its attitude towards Christianity. It maintains that the rise of Christianity in Europe has been a misfortune; that the age of faith was the age of barbarism; and that civilization has advanced only as faith has declined. Though the work presents only one side of a great question, that side is presented with unusual skill. The author's philosophy of history, if it may be called such, is essentially that of Buckle. The book has been, and will continue to be, much admired and very severely criticised. . . . This book ["History of the American Civil War"] is pervaded with Dr. Draper's peculiar views of the causes of national de elopment. It is introduced by a long dissertation, which occupies nearly the whole of the first volume, and in which the author elaborates his peculiar theories. His beliefs are essentially those of Buckle. At bottom, he has no faith in other causes than those which can be traced directly to Nature. Climate is the great controlling force. . . . As an attempt to build a history on a philosophical foundation, the work cannot be called a very signal success. Until it can be shown that an isothermal has something to do with such blunders as those at Fredericksburg and Chickamauga, most men will regard Dr. Draper's theories as not proved.—ADAMS, CHARLES KENDALL 1882, *A Manual of Historical Literature*, pp. 538, 539.

Draper's "Intellectual Development of Europe" must take its place among the valuable contributions of the age to the philosophy of history. It is intended to demonstrate *a posteriori* that human life, collective and individual, is subject to the dominion of law. Varieties of antecedent and concomitant conditions determine social advancement: and its stages—the same for a miniature man as for a nation—are the Age of Credulity, the Age of Inquiry, the Age of Faith, the Age of Reason, and the Age of Decrepitude. We are thus reminded of Buckle and Comte, with their one-sided accumulation of facts, and their fatalistic views of causation.—WELSH, ALFRED H., 1883, *Development of English Literature and Language*, vol. II, p. 422.

John W. Draper's "History of the American Civil War," is the most impartial work so far written upon the question of slavery and its final results.—BALDWIN, JAMES, 1883, *English Literature and Literary Criticism, Prose*, p. 83.

Of literary character are the books of John W. Draper, who wrote a dry "History of the American Civil War," and a weighty but unsympathetic "History of the Intellectual Development of Europe."—RICHARDSON, CHARLES F., 1887, *American Literature*, 1607–1885, *vol.* I, p. 518.

Dr. Draper's lasting contributions to physiology and to pure chemistry were few and relatively unimportant. On the other hand, his name is associated with a number of results of the greatest value in physical chemistry, especially in photochemistry. The chemical action of light early attracted his attention and for many years formed his favorite subject of investigation.—GILMAN, PECK, AND COLBY, 1903, *The New International Encyclopædia*, vol. VI, p. 285.

John Richard Green
1837-1883

Born, at Oxford, 12 Dec. 1837. At Magdalen Coll. School, 1845-51; with private tutors, 1851-53. Matric. Jesus Coll., Oxford, 7 Dec. 1855; Scholar, 1855-60; B. A., 1860; M. A., 1862; Ordained Deacon, 1860. Curate of St. Barnabas, King Square, London, 1860-63. Curate of Holy Trinity, Hoxton, 1863-66; perpetual curate of St. Philip's, Stepney, 1866-69. Contrib. to "Saturday Rev.," 1862. Prosecuted historical studies. Librarian of Lambeth Palace, 1869-83. Gave up clerical life, 1869. Married Alice Stopford, June 1877. Hon. Fellow Jesus Coll., Oxford, 1877-83. Hon. LL. D., Edinburgh, 1878. Visit to Egypt, 1881. Increasing ill-health. Died, at Mentone, 7 March, 1883. *Works:* "Short History of the English People," 1874; "Stray Studies from England and Italy," 1876; "A History of the English People" (4 vols., expanded from preceding), 1877-80; "Readings from English History," 1879; "A Short Geography of the British Islands" (with his wife), 1880; "The Making of England," 1881. *Posthumous:* "The Conquest of England" (completed by his wife), 1883. He *edited:* "Literature Primers," 1875-79; "History Primers," 1875-84; "Classical Writers," 1879-82; Addison's "Essays," 1880.—SHARP, R. FARQUHARSON, 1897, *A Dictionary of English Authors, p.* 118.

PERSONAL

I recall little or nothing of childhood beyond a morbid shyness, a love of books, a habit of singing about the house, a sense of being weaker and smaller than other boys. Our home was not a happy one—the only gleam of light in it was my father's love for and pride in me. He was always very gentle and considerate; he brought me up by love and not by fear, and always hated to hear of punishment and blows. I was fourteen when he died, but I recall little of him save this vague tenderness; a walk when he encouraged me to question him "about everything;" his love of my voice—a clear, weak, musical child's voice—and of my musical ear and faculty for catching tunes; and his pride in my quickness and the mass of odd things which I knew. . . . All was not fun or poetry in these early schooldays. The old brutal flogging was still in favour, and the old stupid system of forcing boys to learn by rote. I was set to learn Latin grammar from a grammar in Latin! and a flogging every week did little to help me. I was simply stupefied,—for my father had never struck me, and at first the cane hurt me like a blow,—but the "stupid stage" soon came, and I used to fling away my grammar into old churchyards and go up for my "spinning" as doggedly as the rest. Everything had to be learned by memory, and by memory then, as now, I could learn nothing. How I picked up Latin Heaven knows; but somehow I did pick it up, and when we got to books where head went for something, I began to rise fast among my fellow-schoolboys. But I really hated my work, and my mind gained what it gained not from my grammars and construing, but from an old school library which opened to me pleasures I had never dreamed of.—GREEN, JOHN RICHARD, 1873, *Letter, Nov.* 4; *Letters, ed. Stephen, pp.* 3, 6.

My first acquaintance with the late J. R. Green was made at Oxford in the autumn of 1859, when he was a senior man, about to pass his first school in greats, and I was in my freshman's term. . . . When I first met him I was at once struck with his bright, speaking eyes, and his remarkably sparkling conversation, the like of which I have never heard since. I was once able to identify him by his conversation. A country clergyman mentioned to me his having met at a dinner in a friend's house a most wonderful person, who made himself exceedingly pleasant, and enchanted everyone by the racy way in which he said whatever he had to say. My friend did not know who he was, but there was no mistaking the description; only one man in Oxford answered to it; that was J. R. Green. . . . To those whom he liked no one could make himself so delightful, but no one in his younger days made himself more enemies. He had a terrible gift of sarcasm; he knew it, it gave him a sense of power, and he may possibly have used it sometimes for the pleasure of using it. He was a most awkward opponent in any wordy debate, his repartee was instantaneous and decisive, never spiteful nor malicious. He was not popular with his contemporaries; such persons seldom are; the fault was probably more often theirs than his. To his intimates his singular individuality of character, his tender love, his perpetual wit, and his great power of sympathy rendered him the most fascinating of friends. Half-hours in his company were never dull; and, when the need arose, no one could show more delicate or more helpful sympathy than such as I have known him to bestow on those whom he had made his friends.—BROWNE, H. L., 1883, *Some Personal Reminiscences of J. R. Green, The Academy, vol. 23, p.* 187.

Incomplete as his life seems, maimed and saddened by the sense of powers which ill health would not suffer to produce their due results, it was not an unhappy one, for he had the immense power of enjoyment which so often belongs to a vivacious intelligence. He delighted in books, in travel, in his friends' company, in the constant changes and movements of the world. Society never dulled his taste for these things, nor was his spirit, except for passing moments, darkened by the shadows which to others seemed to lie so thick around his path. He enjoyed, though he never boasted of it, the fame his books had won, and the splendid sense of creative power. And the last six years of his life were brightened by the society and affection of one who entered into all his tastes and pursuits with the most perfect sympathy, and enabled him, by her industry and vigour, to prosecute labours which physical weakness must otherwise have checked before the best of all his works had been accomplished.—BRYCE, JAMES, 1883, *John Richard Green, Macmillan's Magazine, vol.* 48, *p.* 65.

There was probably no man whose writings and whose personality had a closer connexion with one another than those of John Richard Green. A singular mixture of strength and weakness distinguished him; but neither strength nor weakness could have been spared; both went to make up a character in which even the weaker elements became a kind of strength. And both his character and his writings were deeply impressed by the special circumstances of his life. Nothing perhaps tended more to make Green and his writings what they were than his birth as an Oxford citizen. It told more to the advantage of the readers of his writings than it did to the advantage of his own personal career; but, on the whole, it was a strengthening and ennobling element. His native city and its history were ever near to his heart. Those who knew him best in the days when his mind and character were forming were struck, and were sometimes annoyed, by a kind of dislike which he often expressed towards the University of Oxford. This is a feeling which is certainly not common among its members, at any rate not among such members of it as Green. Now in this there was something of that waywardness and capriciousness which was so apt to come out in all that he did and wrote, something too of that love of saying startling things in a startling way which was perhaps natural in one of the very best of talkers.— FREEMAN, EDWARD A., 1883, *John Richard Green, British Quarterly Review, vol.* 78 *p.* 120.

His was a nature which could not take rest whilst any work remained to be done, and in the East-end the work of a parson of genius was no less than infinite. Into each position to which he was appointed—St. Barnabas, Holy Trinity, Hoxton, a missioncuracy at St. Peter's, Stepney, and finally the neighbouring vicarage of St. Philip's— he threw himself with the whole energy of his nature, and from each in turn, after an effort more or less prolonged, he withdrew with shattered health. . . . But he retired from the post he had so bravely held, a broken man. The seeds of consumption had been sown unsuspected by himself in those arduous years, and almost immediately declared themselves. Henceforward he was doomed, as he said, to the life of the student and the invalid, flitting winter by winter to those southern shores, whence came back to his friends in England the sheaves of charming letters he has left behind him. Of those days, the days of his travel, the days of his best historic work, the days of perfect happiness in married life, the days over which hung always the close shadow of the end which now at last has come, there is no space to speak. Despite the depression of illness and of waning strength, they were perhaps his happiest days, not only on account of the dear companionship in which he dwelt, but because he was giving what remained of life undividedly to the work he held to be his duty. Indeed, he never ceased working. Years before he had truly, though half-lightly, forecast his own epitaph, "*He died learning.*" When he was too weak to sit, his toil went forward on the sofa, and when he could not rise, it still went forward on his bed. Amidst all the vivacity and the merriment which no inroads of disease impaired, he felt, like his favourite Bede, the responsibility of knowledge, and would fain have passed it on before the end came.—GELL, PHILIP LYTTLETON, 1883, *John Richard Green, Fortnightly Review, vol.* 39, *pp.* 741, 747.

That slight nervous figure, below the medium height; that tall forehead, with the head prematurely bald; the quick but small eyes, rather close together; the thin mouth, with lips seldom at rest, but often closed tightly as though the teeth were clenched with an odd kind of latent energy beneath them; the slight, almost feminine hands; the little stoop; the quick alert step; the flashing exuberance of spirits; the sunny smile; the torrent of quick invective, scorn, or badinage, exchanged in a moment for a burst of sympathy or a delightful and prolonged flow of narrative—all this comes back to me, vividly! And what narrative, what anecdote, what glancing wit! What a talker! A man who shrank from society, and yet was so fitted to adorn and instruct every company he approached, from a parochial assembly to a statesman's reception! . . . Green was an omnivorous reader even in those busy days. No new book escaped him, and he seemed to master its contents with a bewildering rapidity. He was full of quick discernment; and I remember one night his reading out some passages of Swinburne's then new book of "Poems and Ballads," selected by the *Athenæum* for scathing ridicule, and saying, "This is the greatest master of poetical language since Shelley; but he can't think."—HAWEIS, HUGH REGINALD, 1883, *John Richard Green, Contemporary Review, vol.* 43, *pp.* 734, 739.

It was in 1863 that we met; I was not yet a professor, he had not begun to wear the air of an ascetic. We were invited to Wells, to a meeting of the Somerset Archæological Society, to stay with a common friend whom you will have no difficulty in identifying. I was told, "if you leave the station at two you will meet Green, and possibly Dimock," the biographer of St. Hugh whom I knew already. I knew by description the sort of man I was to meet; I recognised him as he got into the Wells carriage, holding in his hand a volume of Renan. I said to myself, "if I can hinder, he shall not read that book." We sat opposite and fell immediately into conversation. I dare say that I aired my erudition so far as to tell him that I was going to the Archæological meeting and to stay at Somerleaze. "Oh, then," he said, "you must be either Stubbs or Dimock." I replied, "I am not Dimock." He came to me at Navestock afterwards, and that volume of Renan found its way uncut into my wastepaper basket. That is all; a matter of confusion and inversion, and so, they say, history is written. Well, perhaps a friendship between two historical workers may be called a historic friendship and, to be historical, should gather some of the mist of fable about its beginning: anyhow it was a friendship that lasted for his life, and the loss of which I shall never cease regretting.—STUBBS, WILLIAM, 1884, *A Last Statutory Public Lecture, May* 8; *The Study of Medieval and Modern History and Kindred Subjects, p.* 377.

It is now just twenty years since I made Green's acquaintance, and my recollections of what speedily ripened into a warm friendship are still fresh. He had reluctantly decided to retire from the East-end parish on account of failing health. He still wore the clerical costume and the white tie, and I remember well the impression his appearance made upon me. His figure was slight and below middle height, but, once you had seen him, your gaze was concentrated on his face and head. Mr. Sandys's portrait, prefixed to the "Conquest of England," is very like in the intensity of the expression, but not so much so in the features. The nose was very small, and was overshadowed by the brow of the highly-developed forehead. In a cloak-room you could always recognize his hat by its extraordinary diameter. The eyes were rather sunk, and were not, I think, quite straight; but no one who ever encountered them could forget their keenness—their appearance of being able to see through anything. He was very conscious of his own bodily insignificance, and I think, of all the countless anecdotes he knew, none pleased him more than that which represents Wilkes as saying, "Give me half an hour's start, and I can beat the handsomest man in England." He was a great admirer of physical beauty, both in men and women, and especially of tallness.—LOFTIE, W. J., 1888, *John Richard Green, New Princeton Review, vol.* 6, *p.* 370.

I remember that that night I renewed my acquaintance with Mr. J. R. Green, of Jesus College, who has become widely known by his "History of the English People," and other historical writings of great value. Green died at Mentone, after residing there several winters, and on his grave in the Mentone Cemetery there is the striking inscription, "he died learning." He rather scandalized some of the brethren by saying that he looked upon the prophecies of Israel in much the same way as upon the prophecies of Merlin. He had a countenance of singular charm, beautiful eyes and a beaming look. Singularly enough, his first curacy had been in connection with the Pastoral Aid Society; next he was drafted off to one of those East London livings which Dr. Tait would give to his clever young men, not perhaps very much to the advantage of the East Enders, and he was afterwards transferred to the Librarianship of Lambeth, than which a more appropriate appointment could not have been made.—ANON., 1889, *Reminiscences of a Literary and Clerical Life.*

Another remarkable man I saw but once [in 1881], but that once made a great impression on me—J. R. Green. , . . He was in a very far stage of consumption when I paid him a visit in Kensington Square. He only could speak in a whisper, but his talk was full of fire, ideas, and interests in the ideas of others; and his pretty, gentle wife sat by and treasured every word he spoke, till his coughing became violent; then she took us away, telling us how she was beginning to write quite easily with her left hand to his dictation, her right being paralysed after long years of incessant work. He dictated sometimes eleven hours in the day.—NORTH, MARIANNE, 1892, *Recollections of a Happy Life*, ed. Mrs. Symonds, vol. II, p. 216.

During our walks Mr. Freeman also talked much of his special friends. For Mr. J. R. Green, whom he always called "Johnny," he had a strong affection. Mr. Freeman was fourteen years his senior, and had known him ever since his boyhood, when he carried him on his shoulders. I remember the day in May, 1882, when he took me to lunch at Mr. Green's house in London, and there I saw for myself how much the elder and the younger writer w ›re to each other. It was only the year before Mr. Green's death, and he looked very frail. He wore a little black skull-cap. His eyes were bright and his manner and talk particularly charming. That he shared Mr. Freeman's vivid sense of the ludicrous, was shown by the frequent laughter at that lunch-table. Among other things which amused him, was Mr. Freeman's declaration that he never let a man die at the end of a chapter in the "Norman Conquest," because Johnny told him not to.—PORTER, DELIA LYMAN, 1893, *Mr. Freeman at Home, Scribner's Magazine*, vol. 14, p. 620.

All his friends speak of the singular brilliancy of his conversation, and attribute it partly to the vivacity and alertness of his intellect, and the readiness with which mere statements of fact grouped themselves in his mind into vivid pictures. But it also implied the quick sympathy of an exquisitely sensitive nature. If he could appreciate Freeman's historical dissertations, he could enjoy the charm of naïve simplicity in women and children.—STEPHEN, LESLIE, 1901, ed. *Letters of John Richard Green*, p. 67.

This distaste for the routine methods of education debarred him from high university distinctions, but was in reality, as the event proved, his scholarly and artistic salvation. His genius was too original to suffer compression into the academic mould, which would have deadened his most vital intellectual impulses.—PAYNE, WILLIAM MORTON, 1901, *John Richard Green, The Dial*, vol. 31, p. 430.

Green, born in Oxford, and spending many of his happiest years there, knew and loved both town and University. He went to Magdalen Grammar School at the age of eight, and he won an Open Fellowship at Jesus at sixteen, before he was old enough to go into residence. His biographers tell us that he entered college a friendless, homeless boy, and that he continued, as an undergraduate, to lead a solitary life. His Welsh co-students, with their close home-associations, looked upon him as an English interloper, and left him much to himself. But he found books in the Library, sermons in the stones of Oxford, and good in everything. He read enormously; and he wandered, in his solitary, studious way, among the spots and the buildings which were rich in their associations of ancient times, recalling, as he went, the memories of the past, and in his own mind combining them and putting together in coherent form. . . . His rooms at Jesus are unknown; and the Hall-porter, in 1899, had never heard his name.—HUTTON, LAURENCE. 1903, *Literary Landmarks of Oxford*, pp. 116, 117.

SHORT HISTORY OF THE ENGLISH PEOPLE
1874

Mr. Green's style is eminently readable and attractive. A lively imagination, not always under the most rigid control, imparts its own colors to the dry details of history, where a more scrupulous or conscientious writer would have wearied himself, and fatigued his readers, unwilling to venture beyond the arid region of facts. . . . Upon inaccuracies in detail we have not insisted, prejudicial as such inaccuracies must be in a manual intended for schools, for it is not to be expected that in so wide a subject they could be altogether avoided. Our objections are of a graver and more general kind. It is against the whole tone and teaching of the book that we feel ourselves called upon most emphatically to protest. Under the disguise of a school history, Mr. Green has disseminated some very violent opinions in politics and religion. His design is not the less subtle and dangerous because, in accomplishing this object, he has been misled into ingenious perversions of facts, and in the ardour of his temperament has misrepresented the conduct and motives of men— of those especially who have upheld the Church and the Monarchy. His sympathies seem not with order, but with disorder; not with established Government, but with those who have attempted to overthrow it. In the most ardent and furious of the leaders of the French Revolution he finds "a real nobleness of aim and temper," which he denies to the champions of good government, or the peaceful upholders of religion and morality. To him the aristocracy, in conjunction with the Monarchy, seem the plagues of mankind, united in a dire conspiracy against popular freedom, progress, and development. Is this a history, we ask, to be put into the hands of the young and incautious? Is it from this they are to learn wisdom and moderation, to form just and equitable judgments of past events, or of the great actors of times that are gone? Is this the teaching by which they are to estimate rightly the deeds of kings, the worth of an aristocracy, the beneficial effects of order and religion? We think not. We have warned our readers against the errors and tendencies of Mr. Green's book. It is for them to exercise the necessary precautions, both for themselves and for those who are committed to their care and guidance.—BREWER, J. S., 1876-81, *A Short History of the English People, English Studies*, ed. Wace, pp. 50, 102.

This book has extraordinary merits. It is rather a commentary on the history of England than a history itself, and therefore those who already have some knowledge of the subject are likely to be most profited by its use. The qualities which have given to the work its great popularity are the brilliancy of its style, the breadth of its generalizations, the vividness with which it portrays the general drift of events, the clearness with which it shows the relations of cause and effect, the prominence which it gives to the literary and social progress of the people, and the skill with which the author has made his selections and exclusions. The book has been shown to be somewhat inaccurate in matters of minor detail; but the inaccuracies are, for the most part, such as may easily be remedied by careful revision, without disturbing the general arrangement of the work. For the purposes of the general reader it is superior to all other works in a single volume. Its value is also increased by a carefully drawn list of authorities at the beginning of each subject. These lists afford a somewhat comprehensive and very valuable bibliography of English history.—ADAMS, CHARLES KENDALL, 1882, *A Manual of Historical Literature*, p. 467.

His accuracy has been much disputed. When the first burst of applause that welcomed the "Short History" had subsided, several critics began to attack it on the score of minor errors. They pointed out a number of statements of fact which were doubtful, and others which were incorrect, and spread in some quarters the impression that he was on the whole a careless and untrustworthy writer. I do not deny that there are in the first editions of the "Short History" some assertions made more positively than the evidence warrants, but this often arises from the summary method of treatment. A writer who compresses the whole history of England into eight hundred pages of small octavo, making his narrative not a bare narrative but a picture full of colour and incident, but incident which, for brevity's sake, must often be given by allusion, cannot be always interrupting the current of the story to indicate doubts or quote authorities for every statement in which there may be an element of conjecture; and it is probable that in some instances when the authorities are examined their result will appear different from that which the author has given them. On this head the "Short History," if not perfect, is open to no grave censure. Of mistakes, strictly so called—*i. e.*, statements demonstrably incorrect and therefore ascribable to haste or carelessness—there are enough to make a considerable show under the hands of a hostile critic, yet not more than one who has read a good deal of history will be prepared to expect. The book falls far short of the accuracy of Bishop Thirlwall or Ranke, short even of the accuracy of Gibbon or Carlyle; but it is not much below the standard of Mr. Grote's care, it is up to that of Macaulay or Robertson, and decidedly above Dean Milman or David Hume. I take famous names, and could easily put a better face on the matter by choosing for comparison contemporary writers whose literary eminence is higher than their historical.—BRYCE, JAMES, 1883, *John Richard Green, Macmillan's Magazine*, vol. 48, p. 70.

It views events in their just proportions, and places them in their true perspective; and estimates with commendable judgment and impartiality the various forces and movements that have given to the English people a value and significance. He has taken his conception of history mainly from Professor Freeman, but has brought to its consideration a vividness, a brilliance of style, and a picturesque human interest that entitle the author to rank with the romantic historians of English literature.—GRAHAM, RICHARD D., 1897, *The Masters of Victorian Literature*, p. 227.

He is best known by his historical work on English subjects, especially the famous "Short History of the English People," perhaps the most popular work of its class and kind ever written. Mr. Green professed, on a principle which has been growing in favour for some time, to extend the usual conception of historical dealing to social, literary, and other matters. These, however, had never as a fact been overlooked by historians, and the popularity of the book was chiefly due to its judicious selection of interesting facts, to the spirit of the narrative, and to the style, based partly on Macaulay, but infused with modernness which exactly hit the taste of the readers of our time.—SAINTSBURY, GEORGE, 1898, *A History of Nineteenth Century Literature*, p. 245.

It has often been said that Mr. Green taught us to write history. No similar book has ever been so successful, and the method and execution are admirable, but it was meant to be, and is, an historical narrative, and for that very reason some may prefer the "Student's History" of Professor Gardiner.—RAFFETY, FRANK W., 1899 *Books Worth Reading*, p. 148.

The strong sense of literary form, which is conspicuous in all his work, led him to bring together topics which, if treated at all, are broken up and become discontinuous on the old system. He wished to bring out the unity and continuity of great religious or literary movements or of economic changes, such as the growth of town life, in which the leading moments are not defined by the accession of kings or the event of battles. The narrative had, to a great extent, to be reorganised and the stress laid upon a different series of events. It was impossible, therefore, that Green should fully satisfy critics who desiderated a manual on the old model. Green had, in fact, written something quite different, and something which, as Freeman cordially admitted, was admirable from his own point of view. He had written, within a brief compass, nothing less than the first history of England which would enable his countrymen to gain a vivid and continuous perception of the great processes by which the nation had been built up, and which had been overlooked or incidentally noticed in the histories which adhere rigidly to sequences of outward political fact.—STEPHEN, LESLIE, 1901, *ed. Letters of John Richard Green*, p. 211.

A HISTORY OF THE ENGLISH PEOPLE
1877-80

By far the most important general history of England that has ever been written. It not only covers the whole period of English history down to the close of the Napoleonic wars, but it also embodies the results of those researches into special periods which of late have been so characteristic of English historical activity. To these merits must be added several others of scarcely less importance. The author writes in an unusually vigorous and interesting style. His pages are not encumbered with notes, but at the beginning of the history of each period is to be found a very complete and valuable account of the sources from which information on the subject treated is to be drawn. These bibliographical instructions will be found of the greatest use to the special student of English history.—ADAMS, CHARLES KENDALL, 1882, *Manual of Historical Literature*, p. 436.

THE MAKING OF ENGLAND
1881

Mr. Green's new book possesses all the well-known charms of his fascinating style, and combines with them a great many other excellences in a far higher degree than usual. . . . Where the subject demands it, his colours are as bright and as vivid as ever; but, where logical argument or grave philosophical reflection is needed, Mr. Green rises to the situation, and the weightier passages thus interspersed between his glowing word-pictures certainly whet the reader's appetite far better than the uninterrupted feast which he used to spread so much too lavishly before us. Moreover his present book is a piece of real original research. We do not say that it probes very deep into the fundamental question. As far as scholarship goes, it cannot compare with Mr. Elton's profoundly learned and broadly scientific work just published, which deals with much the same period; but, looking at it as an essay written wholly within the narrow bounds of Mr. Freeman's Teutonic school, and based almost entirely upon the documentary evidence, it deserves high praise for its thoroughness and its general ability. It marks Mr. Green as a competent original historian, not a mere clever adapter and literary confectioner of other men's solid material. . . . Taking it all in all, Mr. Green's new book is a most useful contribution to our knowledge of a very dark period, and it stamps his place as a far higher one than that secured by his more captivating, but far less original, "Short History of the English People." It will probably long represent the last word of the Teutonists on the nature and extent of the primitive English settlement.—ALLEN, GRANT, 1881, *The Making of England, The Academy*, vol. 21, pp. 111, 112.

In the early spring of 1881, he was seized by a violent attack of illness, and it needed but a little time to show that there could never be any return to hope. The days that might still be left to him must henceforth be conquered day by day from death. In the extremity of ruin and defeat he found a higher fidelity and a perfect strength. The way of success was closed, the way of courageous effort still lay open. Touched with the spirit of that impressioned patriotism which animated all his powers, he believed that before he died some faithful work might yet be accomplished for those who should come after him. At the moment of his greatest bodily weakness, when fear had deepened into the conviction that he had scarcely a few weeks to live, his decision was made. The old plans for work were taken out, and from these a new scheme was rapidly drawn up in such a form that if strength lasted it might be wrought into a continuous narrative, while if life failed some finished part of it might be embodied in the earlier "History." Thus, under the shadow of death, the "Making of England" was begun. During the five summer months in which it was written that shadow never lifted. It was the opinion of his doctors that life was only prolonged from day to day throughout that time by the astonishing force of his own will, by the constancy of a resolve that had wholly set aside all personal aims. His courage took no touch of gloom or disappointment; every moment of comparative ease was given to his task; when such moments failed, hours of langour and distress were given with the same unfaltering patience. As he lay worn with sickness, in his extreme weakness unable to write a line with his own hand, he was forced for the first time to learn how to dictate; he had not even strength himself to mark the corrections of his printer's proofs, and these, too, were dictated by him, while the references for the volume were drawn up as books were carried one by one to his bedside, and the notes from them entered by his directions. With such sustained zeal, such eager conscientiousness was his work done that much of it was wholly rewritten five times, other parts three times; till as autumn drew on he was driven from England and it became needful to bring the book rapidly to an end which fell short of his original scheme, and to close the last chapters with less finish and fulness of labor.—GREEN, ALICE STOPFORD, 1883, ed. *The Conquest of England by John Richard Green, Preface*, p. v.

This book, published in 1882, brought down English history to the consolidation of the kingdoms under Egbert, and showed Green's qualities as a critical historian. His rare power of dealing with fragmentary evidence, his quick eye for what was essential, his firm hold of the main points, his ripe knowledge of all that could illustrate his subject, above all, his feeling for reality, and his insight into probabilities, enabled him to give life and movement to the earliest period of our national life. Apart from its other merits this book exercised a wide influence, which is still growing, as an example of the methods by which archæology can be turned into history. It gave a stimulus to the pursuit of local archæology, and showed archæologists the full importance of their work. It proved not merely that the merits of the "Short History" were those of literary style and brilliancy of presentation, but that the whole book was the fruit of patient research and thorough knowledge, which only needed longer time and a larger scale to establish its conclusions.—CREIGHTON, MANDELL, 1890, *Dictionary of National Biography, vol.* XXIII, *p.* 48.

THE CONQUEST OF ENGLAND
1883

J. R. Green once said of himself: "I know what men will say of me—'He died learning.'" Nothing in the whole of his works affords a more striking instance of his penetrating insight than this casual remark, recorded in the prefatory memoir which precedes the "Conquest of England." "He died learning." These three words, like all true sayings, have a profound application; they hit exactly the most noteworthy, and yet perhaps the least noted, feature of Green's rare and admirable genius. We may indeed doubt whether, like all men of vivid imagination, he did not overrate the intelligence of others. It is quite possible that critics might not of themselves have said of our author what he has said of himself. But the words, once uttered, are a revelation. Any person of ordinary acumen can see their truth. The true source of all that was best in J. R. Green's work was that he died, and one must also add lived, learning. . . . He is so brilliant as a writer, his skill in presenting to our view the most striking aspect of his subject is so obvious, that even intelligent students overlook, even if they do not deny, the compass of his knowledge. He never plays the pedant, and therefore he never gets with the public full credit for learning. But whoever reads Green's notes on the condition and history of English towns—notes which, as we understand the matter, have not received the last touches that would have been given them by their writer if he had lived—will easily see that he was, in spite of the brilliancy of his style, something much better and greater than a striking writer, and that he died learning because he had lived the studious, concentrated life of a learned man devoted to learning.—DICEY, A. V., 1884, *Green's Conquest of England, The Nation, vol.* 38, *pp.* 213, 214.

GENERAL

I can assure you that hardly any enterprise we have ever been engaged in has been more satisfactory to me personally, and not less to other members of the firm, than your Primers. Believe me, my dear Green, that you are loved, and honoured, and trusted among us all in a very high degree, and we count all that you do with and for us as among our most precious work.—MACMILLAN, DANIEL, 1877, *Letter to Green; Letters of John Richard Green, ed. Stephen, p.* 218.

No one who really wishes to learn can read his "Short History of the English People" without being impressed by the power of the writer to impart knowledge in a fresh and original form; nor can he compare that book with the subsequent larger History without being struck with the writer's conscientious desire to abandon pre-conceived notions which we look in vain for in many authors of high repute. In estimating, as far as it is possible to do, the value of Mr. Green's work, it is first necessary to ask what we expect from a historian. If it is to give us a thoroughly accurate account of events which have happened, no doubt Mr. Green has often been found wanting. It is mere panegyric, and nothing else, to speak of him as here and there substituting one name for another, or one date for another. He was often incorrect on matters of much higher importance than these. Readers who have a special acquaintance with any part of his vast subject can easily suggest sources of information which he has neglected and arguments to which he has paid no attention. But is not fulness of knowledge incompatible with the undertaking of so vast a work as a complete History of England, and would he not have himself delayed his undertaking if it had been possible for him to do so? . . . If Mr. Green had been able to defer his work for twenty years there is no reason to suppose that he would ever have attained anything like the accuracy, say, of Mr. Freeman. It was not in his nature to do so, though it was in his nature to aim at it. But, for all that, it is not impossible that he may have been able to impart to us something that Mr. Freeman does not give us. Both these writers have the invaluable power of making the past live before us, but they do it in a very different way. Mr. Freeman fixes on concrete facts, on geographical positions, acts recorded to have been done, or laws issued by authority. At these he gazes till he makes them tell their secret and the secret of the men among whom these things were done. Mr. Green proceeded in a precisely opposite way. That which impressed him most in men was that they were alive. That which he saw in history was the continuous life of the race, the change of thought which makes each generation differ from the last. —GARDINER, SAMUEL R., 1883, *J. R. Green, The Academy*, vol. 23, p. 186.

The "Short History" is wonderful; in many respects it is admirable. It did not indeed fill up the particular hole which it was meant to fill up; but it revealed the existence of another hole and filled that up most happily. The "Making of England" was needful for his reputation; it has high merits in itself; it is amazing as the work of one whose strength had already given way. But the Green of twenty years back both promised and had begun greater things than these. I cannot regret that he has made so brilliant an introduction to my own work; but it was not an introduction for which I looked, but a continuation. The times to which I must ever look back are the days when he and I walked together over so many of the most stirring sites of English, Norman, and Angevin history, when he was planning what we now never can have, the tale of the second Making of England told in full as perhaps he alone could have told it.—FREEMAN, EDWARD A., 1883, *John Richard Green, British Quarterly Review*, vol. 78, p. 133.

Green writes the story of his England as a keenly observant American traveller might record the impressions of a journey through the dear old home of his fathers. He himself realizes the England of the past, its topography, and the features, forms, and characters of its successive swarms of invaders, as if he had been an onlooker of the whole series of transactions. With his keenness of imagination, combined with his intensely sympathetic admiration for the race which laid the foundations of England's greatness, Green could not choose but overflow in graphic eloquence that is almost epic. But his was no mere outburst of uninformed exuberance. He was nearly forty years of age when he published his "Short History," and he had been amassing materials for it all his life. How exhaustive and painstaking was his investigation into the materials of our early history is seen in the abundant notes to his "Making of England," which may be taken as an example of the thoroughness with which he went to work throughout in mastering the authorities on which he based his structure. His eager eloquence of style is simply the reflection of his clearness of conception and his enthusiasm for his subject.—KELTIE, J. SCOTT, 1883, *Some Characteristics of Mr. Green's Histories, British Quarterly Review*, vol. 78, p. 137.

Attempting a schoolbook, produced a literary masterpiece, though his "Short History" had both to be expanded and to be purged of many errors before, as "The History of the English People," it became a model of what condensation can effect. In his "Making of England," Green showed remarkable power of painting the external conditions that influence the life of a people. — GARNETT, RICHARD, 1887, *The Reign of Queen Victoria*, ed. Ward, vol. II, p. 475.

The animated and poetical style, the independent and original judgment, as well as the novel conception of the whole, at once attracted the admiration of the great majority of its readers. It is not, perhaps, a work of faultless accuracy, but that is hardly to be expected from a book which is written up to a theory; for facts as looked upon by the spectator, whose mind is already made up on the subject, show the most obliging readiness to assume any form he chooses. The literary power of Green is undeniable; in some passages, as in his account of the last uprising of Wales before its conquest by Edward I., his naturally picturesque style develops into genuine poetry, while his narrative is usually spirited and his delineation of character striking, if perhaps a little too imaginative. Yet we think that those have formed too high an estimate of his qualities who would rank him with Macaulay. His narrative power is confined to occasional episodes, between which we find intervals, where the interest languishes, if it does not die altogether; if we are tempted to go on beyond a period which has pleased us, it is not because the enchantment of the narrative carries us on, but because we hope to find in a new chapter another unconnected passage as spirited as that we have been reading; and this expectation is often disappointed. Having once gained the attention of his audience by a masterly summary of English history, Green hoped to retain it for the larger work, into which the "Short History" was expanded. This attempt, however, was not so successful. The larger history may have gained in value as a class-book by its more elaborate form; as a literary effort it lost in terseness and force more than it gained by higher elaboration.—OLIPHANT, MARGARET O. W., 1892, *The Victorian Age of English Literature, p.* 539.

The sentence is much longer than Macaulay's, the paragraph very much longer than Macaulay's. The single-sentence paragraph is abolished. The variety that Macaulay secured by varying the length of the paragraph and its structure is lacking here. The paragraphs are not well massed. The element of variety being made little of, an attempt is made to supply its place with that of intensity and weight. There are no waste sentences. The short sentences are sententious, and the long ones, while admirable in accuracy, are sometimes a little heavy. The coherence is good, but it is the coherence of severe method, and depends neither on connectives nor on transitional clauses. After all, it is a noble style, though not an easy one.—LEWIS, EDWIN HERBERT, 1894, *The History of the English Paragraph, p.* 167.

It is not difficult to point out the defects of his picturesque method. The interest of his style lies to a great extent in his power of illustration, but at times he uses it in excess. The elaboration of analogy and the extravagant quotation of the memorable sayings of his characters interrupt the flow of his paragraphs; and by his favourite device of a succession of short jerky sentences he often signally fails in his endeavour to be vivid. There is a suggestion that the writer has not assimilated his material, and is only feeling his way to a complete description through a multitude of notes. The well-known passages on the character of Elizabeth . . . illustrate this: it is too long and too miscellaneous in style. The result is little else than a bare summation of the details, not that artistic whole which should be something more than the total of the contributing facts. This flaw in individual passages is the more striking as in the general conception of his subject, especially in the "Short History," he shows the sublimating power of a writer of high order. Green's habit of work, moreover, was too hurried for a perfect style. His constitutional keenness, increased rather than diminished by ill-health, made his style at times immature, as at others it made it vivacious. It was not from lack of revision—for he recast his more important books—that a certain restlessness remains in his more finished work. . . . In his best passages his art is impressionist, fresh, and suggestive; when he seems to fail it is by excess of colour and crudeness of composition. The shortcomings of his technique, however, can never make us forget that he is essentially an artist in prose.—SMITH, G. GREGORY, 1896, *English Prose, ed. Craik, vol.* v, *pp.* 736, 737.

In John Richard Green a poet in history combined the picturesqueness of Froude with something of the exactitude and breadth of Freeman. The "Short History of the English People," in 1874, produced a sensation such as is rarely effected in these days by any book that is not a masterpiece of imaginative art. It treated history in a new vein, easily, brightly, keenly, sometimes with an almost jaunty vivacity. The danger of Green lay in his excess of poetic sensibility, his tendency to be carried away by his flow of animal spirits, to confound what was with what must or should have been; but he was a delightful populariser of history, a man of strongly emphasised character who contrived to fascinate a world of readers by charging his work with evidences of his own gay subjectivity.—GOSSE, EDMUND, 1897, *A Short History of Modern English Literature, p.* 376.

The extraordinary imaginative power which enabled Green to throw himself into the life of the distant past. This is his supreme merit as a historian, and in this quality he has never been surpassed.—LODGE, RICHARD, 1904, *Chambers's Cyclopædia of English Literature, ed. Patrick, vol.* III, *p.* 653.

Edward FitzGerald
1809-1883

Born, at Bredfield House, Woodbridge, Suffolk, 31 March 1809. At King Edward VI.'s Grammar School, Bury St. Edmunds, 1821-26. To Trinity Coll., Camb., Oct. 1826; B. A., 1830. Visit to Paris, 1830. Family removed to Ipswich, 1825; to Boulge Hall, near Bredfield, 1835. Intimate friendship with Thackeray and Carlyle. Married Lucy Barton, 1856 [?]. Lived at Farlingay Hall, near Woodbridge, 1853–60; in Woodbridge, 1860–74; at Little Grange, 1874–83. Died, suddenly, at Merton Rectory, Norfolk, 14 June 1883. Buried at Boulge. *Works:* "Euphranor," (anon.), 1851; "Polonius" (anon.), 1852; Trans. of "Six Dramas" of Calderon, 1853; Trans. of the "Salámán and Absál" of Jánú (anon.), 1856; Trans., of the "Rubáiyát of Omar Khayyám" (anon.), 1859; Trans. of Æschylus' "Agamemnon" (anon.), 1876; Trans. of Calderon's "Mighty Magician" (anon.), 1877. *Posthumous:* "Works" (2 vols.), 1887; "Letters and Literary Remains," ed. by W. Aldis Wright (3 vols.), 1889; "Letters," ed. by W. A. Wright (2 vols.), 1894; "Letters to Fanny Kemble, 1871–1883;" ed. by W. A. Wright, 1895. He *edited:* "Selections from the Poems and Letters of Bernard Barton," 1842; "Readings in Crabbe," 1882.—SHARP, R. FARQUHARSON, 1897, *A Dictionary of English Authors, p.* 100.

PERSONAL

Old Fitz who from your suburb grange,
   Where once I tarried for a while,
Glance at the wheeling Orb of change,
   And greet it with a kindly smile;
Whom yet I see as there you sit
   Beneath your sheltering garden-tree,
And while your doves about you flit,
   And plant on shoulder, hand, and knee,
Or on your head their rosy feet,
   As if they knew your diet spares
Whatever moved in that full sheet
   Let down to Peter at his prayers;
Who live on milk and meal, and grass.
—TENNYSON, ALFRED LORD, 1883–85, *To E. Fitzgerald, Tiresias and Other Poems.*

The Poet-Laureate, on hearing of his death, wrote to the late Sir Frederic Pollock: "I had no truer friend: he was one of the kindliest of men, and I have never known one of so fine and delicate a wit. I had written a poem to him the last week, a dedication, which he will never see." When Thackeray, not long before he died, was asked by his daughter which of his old friends he had loved most, he replied, "Why, dear old Fitz, to be sure; and Brookfield." And Carlyle, quick of eye to discern the faults and weaknesses of others, had nothing but kindliness, with perhaps a touch of condescension, "for the peaceable, affectionate, and ultra-modest man, and his innocent *far niente* life." It was something to have been intimate with three such friends, and one can only regret that more of his letters addressed to them have not been preserved. Of those written to the earliest and dearest friend of all, James Spedding, not one is left. One of his few surviving contemporaries, speaking from a life-long experience, described him with perfect truth as an eccentric man of genius, who took more pains to avoid fame than others do to seek it.—WRIGHT, WILLIAM, ALDIS, 1889-1902, *ed., Letters and Literary Remains of Edward FitzGerald, Preface, vol.* I, *p.* viii.

FitzGerald, though shy and retired, was no weakling, and with him taste was no mere capacity for enjoying the graces and refinements of letters. He loved with a constant and ardent affection what is great, noble, and heroic. His friendships with living men were not seldom friendships with the strong—and together with Thackeray, Tennyson, Spedding, Carlyle, we must reckon among the strong his dear lugger captain "who looks," he says, "in his cottage like King Alfred in the Story." So, too, in books, in music, in painting, in religion, he was especially attracted by all that is simple, lofty, and heroic.—DOWDEN, EDWARD, 1889, *Letters and Literary Remains of Edward FitzGerald, The Academy, vol.* 36, *p.* 63.

FitzGerald's charities are probably forgotten, unless by the recipients; and how many of them must be dead, old soldiers as they mostly were, and suchlike! But this I have heard, that one man borrowed £200 of him. Three times he regularly paid the interest, and the third time FitzGerald put his note of hand in the fire, just saying he thought that would do. His simplicity dated from very early times. For when he was at Trinity, his mother called on him in her coach-and-four, and sent a gyp to ask him to step down to the college-gate, but he could not come—his only pair of shoes was at the cobbler's. And down to the last he was always perfectly careless as to dress. I can see him now, walking down into Woodbridge, with an old Inverness cape, slippers on feet, and a handkerchief, very likely, tied over his hat. Yet one always recognised in him the Hidalgo. Never was there a more perfect gentleman. His courtesy came out even in his rebukes. A lady one day was sitting in a Woodbridge shop, gossiping to a friend about the eccentricities of the Squire of Boulge, when a gentleman, who was sitting with his back to them, turned round, and, gravely bowing, gravely said, "Madam, he is my brother." They were eccentric, certainly, the FitzGeralds. FitzGerald himself remarked of the family: "We are all mad, but with this difference —*I* know that I am."—GROOME, F. H., 1889, *Edward FitzGerald: An Aftermath*, *Blackwood's Magazine*, vol. 146, p. 616.

I chanced upon a new book yesterday: I opened it, and, where my finger lay 'Twixt page and uncut page, these words I read—
Some six or seven at most—and learned thereby
That you, Fitzgerald, whom by ear and eye
She never knew, "thanked God my wife was dead."
Ay, dead! and were yourself alive, good Fitz,
How to return you thanks would task my wits:
Kicking you seems the common lot of curs—
While more appropriate greeting lends you grace:
Surely to spit there glorifies your face—
Spitting—from lips once sanctified by Hers.
—BROWNING, ROBERT, 1889, *To Edward Fitzgerald*, *July 8*; *The Athenæum*, *No.* 3220.

For many years before his death he made his home at Woodbridge, and when I did read there, his friendly devotion to me and my family was an occasion of some embarrassment to me, for when I came on the platform and courtseyed to my audience, Mr. Fitzgerald got up and bowed to me, and his example being immediately followed by the whole room, I was not a little surprised, amused, and confused by this general courtesy on the part of my hearers, who, I suppose, supposed I was accustomed to be received standing by my listeners. Mr. Aldis Wright, Edward Fitzgerald's intimate friend, has long promised the reading public his memoirs, in which, if justice is done to him, he will appear not only as one of the ripest English scholars, but as a fine critic of musical and pictorial art, as well as literature.—KEMBLE, FRANCES ANN, 1891, *Further Records*, 1848–1883, p. 297.

(On the planting (October 7, 1893) at the head of Fitzgerald's grave at Boulge two rose-trees, whose ancestors had "strowed roses" over the grave of Omar Khayyám: "My tomb shall be in a spot where the North-wind may strow roses upon it" (Omar Khayyám to Khwajah Nizami).)

Hear us, ye winds! From where the North-wind strows
Blossoms that crown the "King of Wisdom's" tomb,
The trees here planted bring remembered bloom
Dreaming in seed of Love's ancestral rose
To meadows where a braver North-wind blows
O'er greener grass, o'er hedge-rose may and broom,
And all that makes East England's field-perfume
Dearer than any fragrance Persia knows.
Hear us, ye winds, North, East, and West and South!
This granite covers him whose golden mouth
Made wiser ev'n the Word of Wisdom's King.
Blow softly o'er the grave of Omar's herald
Till roses rich of Omar's dust shall spring
From richer dust of Suffolk's rare Fitzgerald.
—WATTS-DUNTON, THEODORE, 1893, *Prayer to the Winds.*

His neighbors and dependents knew that under eccentricities of dress and manner, and occasional petulance, there beat the kindliest heart, full of sympathy, of paternal interest in their cares, expressing these in charities wayward, but genuinely helpful, with no sound of trumpet to herald the almsgiving. . . . A tall, sea-bronzed man, as I remember him, wearing a slouch hat, often tied on with a handkerchief, and wrapped in a big cloak, walking with shuffling gait, hob-nobbing with the beachmen, among whom he had his favorites, recipients of his bounty in boats and gear—everybody knew old Fitz by sight, and many called him "dotty." . . . On the death of his mother he married Barton's only daughter, but, after a short experience of conjugal life, for which he was wholly unsuited, a separation was agreed upon, FitzGerald behaving in the matter of alimony with his usual liberality.—CLODD, EDWARD, 1894, *Edward FitzGerald, English Illustrated Magazine*, vol. 11, pp. 529, 530, 532.

Our description of his appearance is drawn from recollections of him after he was sixty years of age, and when he began to stoop; but even then he was in height above the medium, and gave the impression of having been a fine, good-looking man in his younger days. He had a melancholy cast of countenance—a mist of despondent sadness hung over his face; a complexion bronzed by exposure to sun and sea air, large nose, deep upper lip, sunken, pale blue eyes and bushy eyebrows, large, firmly closed mouth, dimpled chin, and fine head. About his half-bald head was a comely grace, whilst the fringe of hair on the outskirts was touched by a softened grey, which helped to add to the dignity of his appearance. The expression was severe, that of a man whom you could hardly expect a child to question as to the time of day. Generally he had a dreamy look. His voice, though soft and gentle, was not musical; his manner generally was placid and mild; but when walking along road or street, he was so absorbed in thought, that if addressed, he would answer in a querulous, impatient tone, as though annoyed by impertinent interruption. . . . He was extremely careless as to his personal appearance, never knowing when to cast off an "old acquaintance," as he described it, in the shape of hat, coat, or shoes. In texture his clothes resembled that worn by pilots, and presented the appearance of being crumpled and untidy. They were put on anyhow, and made to fit him, he used to say, like a sack. Though so meanly clad, plenty of good apparel was found in his wardrobe after his decease. In walking he slouched awkwardly, always taking the least frequented footpath. He generally carried a stick, very rarely using an umbrella. In cold or wet weather he wore a large grey plaid shawl round his neck and shoulders. His trousers, which were short, by the aid of low shoes exhibited either white or grey stockings. Perhaps the most noticeable part of his apparel during his later years was an old battered black-banded tall hat, the greasy look of which indicated long service.—GLYDE, JOHN, 1900, *The Life of Edward FitzGerald*, pp. 83, 86.

RUBÁIYÁT OF OMAR KHAYYÁM
1859

He is to be called "translator" only in default of a better word, one which should express the poetic transfusion of a poetic spirit from one language to another, and the re-presentation of the ideas and images of the original in a form not altogether diverse from their own, but perfectly adapted to the new conditions of time, place, custom, and habit of mind in which they reappear. In the whole range of our literature there is hardly to be found a more admirable example of the most skilful poetic rendering of remote foreign poetry than this work of an anonymous author affords. It has all the merit of a remarkable original production, and its excellence is the highest testimony that could be given, to the essential impressiveness and worth of the Persian poet. It is the work of a poet inspired by the work of a poet; not a copy, but a reproduction, not a translation, but the redelivery of a poetic inspiration.—NORTON, CHARLES ELIOT, 1869, *Nicholas's Quatrains de Khèyam, North American Review*, vol. 109, p. 575.

If Fitzgerald's accuracy had equalled his ingenuity, he might claim the very first place amongst modern translators.—HARRISON, FREDERIC, 1879, *The Choice of Books and Other Literary Pieces*, p. 57.

None can say that Lenten fare makes Lenten thought
  Who reads your golden Eastern lay,
Than which I know no version done
  In English more divinely well;
A planet equal to the sun
  Which cast it, that large infidel
Your Omar; and your Omar drew
  Full-handed plaudits from our best
In modern letters.
—TENNYSON, ALFRED LORD, 1883–85, *To E. Fitzgerald, Tiresias and Other Poems.*

These pearls of thought in Persian gulfs were bred,
Each softly lucent as a rounded moon;
The diver Omar plucked them from their bed,
FitzGerald strung them on an English thread.
—LOWELL, JAMES RUSSELL, 1888, *In a Copy of Omar Khayyám, Heartsease and Rue*, p. 26.

The little pamphlet of immortal music called "The Rubáiyát of Omar Khayyám." . . . FitzGerald's versions are so free, he is so little bound by the details of his original, he is so indifferent to the timid pedantry of the ordinary writer who empties verse out of the cup of one large language into that of another, that we may attempt with him what would be a futile task with almost every other English translator—we may estimate from his versions alone what manner of poet he was. In attempting to form such an estimate we are bound to recognise that his best-known work is also his best. The "Omar Khayyám" of FitzGerald takes its place in the third period of Victorian poetry, as an original force wholly in sympathy with other forces, of which its author took no personal cognisance. Whether it accurately represents or not the sentiment of a Persian astronomer of the eleventh century is a question which fades into insignificance beside the fact that it stimulated and delighted a generation of young readers, to whom it appealed in the same manner, and along parallel lines with, the poetry of Morris, Swinburne, and the Rossettis. After the lapse of thirty years we are able to perceive that in the series of poetical publications of capital importance which marked the close of the fifties it takes its natural place.—GOSSE, EDMUND, 1889, *Edward FitzGerald, Fortnightly Review*, vol. 52, pp. 63, 65.

"Omar Khayyám" is a celebrated work in his version, but it is largely his own work, and it may be hoped that the other translations will become better known, for, without having the commanding qualities of Omar, they are studded with charming stories in verse, and not encumbered with Eastern moods of thought so much as to disturb a Western mind; to us they are more pleasing. The two poetical speeches of the English and Roman generals, with their fine movement, are also a kind of translation—from prose to verse, though nearer to original composition.—WOODBERRY, GEORGE E., 1889, *The Translator of Omar Khayyám, The Nation*, vol. 49, p. 114.

The man whose shy audacity of diffident and daring genius has given Omar Khayyám a place for ever among the greatest of English poets. That the very best of his exquisite poetry, the strongest and serenest wisdom, the sanest and most serious irony, the most piercing and the profoundest radiance of his gentle and sublime philosophy, belong as much or more to Suffolk than to Shiraz, has been, if I mistake not, an open secret for many years—"and," as Dogberry says, "it will go near to be thought so shortly." Every quatrain, tho' it is something so much more than graceful or distinguished or elegant, is also, one may say, the sublimation of elegance, the apotheosis of distinction, the transfiguration of grace.—SWINBURNE, ALGERNON CHARLES, 1891, *Social Verse, The Forum*, vol. 12, p. 183.

As a translator he stands almost alone, his peculiar virtue, noticeable alike in his versions from the Spanish and Greek, being so capitally and once for all illustrated in that of "Omar Khayyám" that in narrow space it is not necessary to go beyond this. From the purist and pedantic point of view FitzGerald, no doubt, is wildly unfaithful. He scarcely ever renders word for word, and will insert, omit, alter, with perfect freedom; yet the total effect is reproduced as perhaps no other translator has ever reproduced it. Whether his version of the "Rubáiyát," with its sensuous fatalism, its ridicule of asceticism and renunciation, and its bewildering kaleidoscope of mysticism that becomes materialist and materialism that becomes mystical, has not indirectly had influences, practical and literary, the results of which would have been more abhorrent to FitzGerald than to almost anyone else, may be suggested. But the beauty of the poem as a poem is unmistakable and altogether astounding. The melancholy richness of the rolling quatrain with its unicorn rhymes, the quaint mixture of farce and solemnity, passion and playfulness, the abundance of the imagery, the power of the thought, the seduction of the rhetoric, make the poem actually, though not original or English, one of the greatest of English poems.—SAINTSBURY, GEORGE, 1896, *A History of Nineteenth Century Literature*, p. 209.

Among the works which he published in his lifetime his fame must principally rest on his rendering of the "Rubáiyát." The great unbelieving astronomer-poet of Persia possesses a special interest for children of the modern world, but did not attract readers at once on the appearance of an English version. According to an account which has been published, the accident of a stray copy falling into the hands of Rossetti, Swinburne, and Burton, first saved it from neglect. If it is fair to argue from the free manner in which he handled the text of "Æschylus," his version of "Omar" is probably far from literal. The first stanza was entirely his own, and two grand lines at the beginning of the thirty-third were borrowed from Hafiz:

"Earth could not answer; nor the seas that mourn

In flowing purple of their Lord forlorn."

The editor of his remains and his friend Professor Cowell admit that he allowed himself great liberties. But a free rendering may sometimes be more faithful than an accurate one, and FitzGerald was especially qualified to penetrate his poet's meaning.—TODHUNTER, MAURICE, 1896, *Edward FitzGerald, The Westminster Review*, vol. 145, p. 257.

His edition of the "Rubáiyát" of Omar Khayyám was published anonymously by Bernard Quaritch in 1859, after it had lain neglected for two years in the office of Fraser's Magazine. It was equally neglected by the public; and the publisher, to whom he made a gift of the work, exposed the pamphlets for sale at a penny each. They were gradually picked up, and the germs of the Omar Khayyám cult were planted. It was almost ten years before a second edition was called for; in this the number of quatrains was increased from seventy-five to one hundred and ten. . . . In June 1883 he went to visit his old friend Mr. Crabbe at Merton Rectory. In the morning he was found "as if sleeping peacefully, but quite dead." . . . Since then, FitzGerald's fame has been continually growing, and the world recognizes that he added at least one classic to universal literature. — DOLE, NATHAN HASKELL, 1897, *Library of the World's Best Literature*, ed. Warner, vol. X, p. 5799.

I can never forget my emotion when I first saw Fitz-Gerald's translation of the Quatrains. Keats, in his sublime ode on Chapman's Homer, has described the sensation once for all:—

"Then felt I like some watcher of the skies,
When a new planet swims into his ken."

The exquisite beauty, the faultless, the singular grace of those amazing stanzas, were not more wonderful than the depth and breadth of their profound philosophy, their knowledge of life, their dauntless courage, their serene facing of the ultimate problems of life and of death. Of course the doubt arose, which has assailed many as ignorant as I was of the literature of the East, whether it was the poet or his translator to whom was due this splendid result. Could it be possible that in the Eleventh Century, so far away as Khorassan, so accomplished a man of letters lived, with such distinction, such breadth, and such insight, such calm disillusion, such cheerful and jocund despair? My doubt lasted only till I came upon a literal translation of the Rubáiyát, and I saw that not the least remarkable quality of Fitz-Gerald's poem was its fidelity to the original. In short, Omar was an earlier Fitz-Gerald, or Fitz-Gerald was a re-incarnation of Omar.—HAY, JOHN, 1897, *Address Before the Omar Kháyyám Club, Dec.*

Why is it that, from the moment the genius of Fitz-Gerald made him known to all who speak the English language, he had taken rank with the immortals, whom no change of taste or fashion can dethrone? I do not pretend to give a full answer to this question, but there are one or two considerations which are obvious. First, as regards form; apart from the strange fascination of the metre, there is within a narrow compass, in point of actual bulk, a wholeness and completeness in Omar, which belongs only to the highest art. . . . There is nothing in Omar's work that could be added or taken away without injuring its perfection. Then as regards substance, where else in literature has the littleness of man, as contrasted with the trifling infinitude of his environment, the direct result of serenity and acquiescence, been more brilliantly or more powerfully enforced?—ASQUITH, HERBERT HENRY, 1898, *Address Before the Omar Kháyyám Club, April.*

He stands as one more example of men who have done good work and have died unrewarded, leaving behind them an ever-widening circle of fame.—DOLE, NATHAN HASKELL, 1899, ed. *Rubáiyát of Omar Khayyám*, Preface, p. xxiii.

Of Edward FitzGerald's quatrains, forty-nine are faithful and beautiful paraphrases of single quatrains to be found in the Ouseley or Calcutta MSS., or both. Forty-four are traceable to more than one quatrain, and may therefore be termed the "composite" quatrains. Two are inspired by quatrains found by FitzGerald only in Nicholas' text. Two are quatrains reflecting the whole spirit of the original poem. Two are traceable exclusively to the influence of the Mantik ut-tair of Ferid ud din Attār. Two quatrains primarily inspired by Omar were influenced by the Odes of Hafiz. And three, which appeared only in the first and second editions and were afterwards suppressed by Edward FitzGerald himself, are not—so far as a careful search enables me to judge—attributable to any lines of the original texts. Other authors may have inspired them, but their identification is not useful in this case.—HERON-ALLEN, EDWARD, 1899, *Edward FitzGerald's Rubá'iyát of Omar*

Khayyám with their Original Persian Sources Collated from his own MSS., and Literally Translated, p. xi.

If Dante Gabriel Rossetti, the artist-poet and mystic, had not been lounging one day about the book-stalls of Piccadilly, dipping now into the "farthing" and now into the "penny box," in seach of treasure, the "Rubáiyát of Omar Khayyám" would doubtless have sunk still deeper under the dusty piles of unsalable old books and waited another decade for a discoverer. It was already wearing on to a decade since the little quarto pamphlet in its brown paper wrappers—"Beggarly disguise as to paper and print, but magnificent vesture of verse"—had been issued from the press of Mr. Bernard Quaritch at the sum of five shillings, and, failing of buyers, had fallen by natural stages to the ignominy of the "penny box." . . . Whether or not the pamphlet that Rossetti bore home from Piccadilly was the first that had been rescued from the penny box, it was at least the first that had made a personal appeal to its buyer. All the imagination of the poet, and his circle of dream-sown spirits, was quickened by it, and in that brotherhood of artists and mystics, styled the "Pre-Raphaelites," the study of the "Rubáiyát" grew into a cult and Omar came at last into his own.—RITTENHOUSE, JESSIE B., 1900, ed., *The Rubáiyát of Omar Khayyám, Introduction,* pp. vii, viii.

LETTERS

FitzGerald's letters have the charm of many felicities of description, reminiscence, confession, criticism, rising naturally out of pages which have the rare charm of ease. He touches the keys gently and soothingly, and glides into passages of unlaboured beauty. What, for example, can be more delightful than this record of the pleasant idleness of a day in spring?—DOWDEN, EDWARD, 1889, *Letters and Literary Remains of Edward FitzGerald, The Academy,* vol. 36, p. 63.

His correspondence now reveals him, unless I am much mistaken, as one of the most pungent, individual, and picturesque of English letter-writers. Rarely do we discover a temperament so mobile under a surface so serene and sedentary; rarely so feminine a sensibility side by side with so virile an intelligence. He is moved by every breath of nature; every change of hue in earth or air affects him; and all these are reflected, as in a camera obscura, in the richly coloured moving mirror of his letters. It will not surprise one reader of this correspondence if the name of its author should grow to be set, in common parlance, beside those of Gray and Cowper for the fidelity and humanity of his addresses to his private friends. Meanwhile, we ought, perhaps, to have remembered what beautiful pages there were in *Euphranor,* and in particular to have recalled that passage about the University boat-races which Lord Tennyson, no easy critic to satisfy, has pronounced to be one of the most beautiful fragments of English prose extant.—GOSSE, EDMUND, 1889, *Edward Fitzgerald, Fortnightly Review,* vol. 52, p. 70.

I also read "Fitzgerald's Correspondence" with great interest and satisfaction. I quite agree with you that they are among the best we have. I fancy he took enough pains with them to make them as easy as they are. They were his only means of communication with the outward world, of *translating* himself as it were into the vulgar tongue. He was a scholar and a gentleman—I change the order of the words because I fancy a distinction and a pleasing one. I agree with you as to the general sanity of his literary judgments—though he would not have been so agreeable as he is without a few honest prejudices too. We are so hustled about by fortune that I found solace as I read in thinking that here was a man who insisted on having his life to himself, and largely had it accordingly. A hermit, by the bye, as he was, has a great advantage in forming secure conclusions. Another charm of the book to me was that it so often reminded me of J. H.—LOWELL, JAMES RUSSELL, 1889, *To C. E. Norton,* ed. *Norton,* vol. II, p. 385.

Among the letters too charming to be lost, yet too personal and frankly confiding to be read without some twinges of conscience, are those of Edward FitzGerald, the last man in all England to have coveted such posthumous publicity. They reveal truthfully that kind, shy, proud, indolent, indifferent, and intensely conservative nature; a scholar without the prick of ambition, a critic with no desire to be judicial, an unwearied mind turned aside from healthy and normal currents of activity. Yet the indiscreet publishing of a private opinion, a harmless bit of criticism such as any man has a right to express to a friend, drew down upon this least aggressive of authors abuse too coarse to be quoted. It is easy to say that Browning dishonored himself rather than FitzGerald by the brutality of his language. This is true; but, nevertheless, it is not pleasant to go down to posterity branded with Billingsgate by a great poet; and it is doubly hard to bear such a weight of vituperation because a word said in a letter has been ruthlessly given to the world.—REPPLIER, AGNES, 1893, *Essays in Idleness*, p. 215.

The premier translator is always admirable, whether in verse or prose, and his good wine needs no bush.... Edward FitzGerald ranks easily with the best half-dozen of our later letter-writers.—JOHNSON, W. G., 1895, *More FitzGerald Letters, The Dial*, vol. 19, pp. 174, 175.

He is still the most independent of critics, who cannot admire Goethe's "Faust" as a work of construction or imagination, or "doat on George Eliot," or take any satisfaction in Tennyson's later productions (least of all, in the "dramas"), or join a Browning Society, or find Irving endurable as an actor. His "famous Lyceum Hamlet... was incomparably the worst I had ever witnessed, from Covent Garden down to a Country Barn.... When he got to 'Something too much of this,' I called out from the Pit door where I stood, 'A good deal too much,' and not long after returned to my solitary inn."—GARRISON, W. P., 1895, *FitzGerald and Mrs. Kemble, The Nation*, vol. 61, p. 298.

On the whole, of volumes of letters very recently given to the world, those of Edward Fitzgerald, the translator of Omar Khayyám, seem to have most of the genuine epistolary spirit in them, in association with a true feeling for good books, and the things that good books bring into the mind, with an easy view of human nature; with a kindly eye for the ups and downs of human life, and a clear perception that one of the prime secrets is not to expect more from life than life is capable of giving.—MORLEY, JOHN, 1895, *Matthew Arnold, Nineteenth Century*, vol. 38, p. 1043.

During his lifetime the translator of "Omar Khayyám," who cared very little for fame, was comparatively unknown beyond a small circle of cultured friends and admirers. But his peculiarly charming letters, published since his death, seem likely to give him a permanent position not so very far removed from that which Horace Walpole or even Charles Lamb enjoy by consent. The mere fact that he did not write for the world, but for his friends, gives his remains a greater charm in an age of babble and advertisement. They are, indeed, a striking instance of, what has been happily termed, "the value of reserve in literature." —TODHUNTER, MAURICE, 1896, *Edward FitzGerald, The Westminster Review*, vol. 145, p. 255.

His correspondence, by which mainly the world knows him, is full of interesting revelations. His whims and foibles, and his own gentle amusement over them; his bookish likes and dislikes, one as hearty as the other; his affection for his friends, whose weak points he could sometimes lay a pretty sharp finger on, notwithstanding, frankness being almost always one of an odd man's virtues; his delight in the sea and in his garden ("Don't you love the oleander? I rather worship mine," he writes to Mrs. Kemble); his pottering over translations from Spanish, the Persian, and the Greek ("all very well; only very little affairs:" he feels "ashamed" when his friend Thompson inquires about them); his music, wherein his taste was simple but difficult (he played without technique and sang without a voice, loving to "recollect some of Fidelio on the pianoforte," and counting it more enjoyable "to perform in one's head one of Handel's choruses" than to hear most Exeter Hall performances),—all these things, and many more, come out in his letters, which are never anything *but* letters, written to please his friends,—and himself,—with no thought of anything beyond that. In them we see his life passing.—TORREY, BRADFORD, 1900, *Edward FitzGerald, Atlantic Monthly*, vol. 86, p. 621.

GENERAL

Whatever deductions may have to be made by the student, who feels that in the "Agamemnon" Mr. FitzGerald has done less than a more sustained effort of his singular powers might have produced, it will be acknowledged by all competent judges that his translation separates itself at once from merely meritorious work, and takes a place apart among English versions of Greek poetry. It is almost trivial to say that the diction of a modern author is Shakespearean. The phrase seems to mean much; but, when analysed, it conveys an indistinct impression. Yet Mr. FitzGerald's style in the finest passages of this great torso has a weight, a compactness and a picturesqueness, to find the proper parallel for which we must look back to Shakespeare's age. The strong sonorous verse has the richness and the elasticity, of Marlowe's line; and for the first time, after so many attempts, the English reader catches in his translation a true echo of the pompous Aeschylean manner. . . . Convinced of the impossibility of presenting the Greek play in its integrity to English readers, and doubtful of his power to succeed where "as good versifiers and better scholars," had seemed to him to fail, he determined to recast the "Agamemnon" of the Attic poet, adhering in parts to the original, and in parts diverging from it, according to his sense of fitness. The result is that, while the whole poem is profoundly penetrated with the Aeschylean spirit, which it reproduces with wonderful vividness, and while certain portions are accurate transcripts from the original, the Greek student will find many of the most impressive passages suppressed, and some most carefully prepared effects omitted.—SYMONDS, JOHN ADDINGTON, 1877, *Agamemnon, The Academy*, vol. 12, pp, 4, 5.

His life, taken altogether, was a gratification of refined tastes and a simple exercise of unpretending virtues among his friends and acquaintances. . . . Original genius he did not possess, but his appreciativeness of excellence was sound and true; whenever he praises, one is compelled to assent. He spent the most of his energy in endeavouring to render foreign classics into English in such a way as to make them effective to modern taste. He did not write for those who could read the originals. He professed only to make adaptations rather than translations, and he cut and modified with a free hand. Scholars have praised his work for what it strove to accomplish, accepting the limitations which his taste imposed upon it. Taste, however developed and refined, is still not genius, and it must be frankly acknowledged that he has not given us just what Calderon, Æschylus, and Sophocles created. His Persian translations vary even more widely from the originals.—WOODBERRY, GEORGE EDWARD, 1889, *The Translator of Omar Khayyám, The Nation*, vol. 49, p. 114.

Judging from the pure wine of poetry which, in the capacity of a translator, he has added to our literature, and from the sanity, the sense of style, the vigor of intellect, and the large imaginative grasp of his thought everywhere apparent in his versions, one may fairly doubt whether his self-supposed inferiority to the Tennysons, and Carlyle and Thackeray was not a matter of ambition rather than of native capacity. At all events, the translator who, by the fine originality and daring creativeness of his renderings of such various poets, has fairly earned a right to the title of prince of translators since old Chapman, may safely be said to have deserved better of his language and of future memory than any secondary poet of his time. It is only when we consider that really great translators are even rarer than poets who can pass awhile for great, that we are capable of doing justice to the modest genius of him who made great Sophocles, mighty Æschylus, sad Omar, and impassioned Calderon, clasp hands across the centuries and speak with living force in English words. He has made these masters speak upon his page, perhaps not just as they would have spoken had they been Englishmen, but with a music and a power scarcely inferior to their own. He has done for them in short, what Chaucer did for Boccaccio, what Coleridge did for Schiller. The quatrains from Omar seem to be little less original with FitzGerald than is the Elegy with Gray, and perhaps the one poem will live as eternally as the other. If this be true, or even half true, then "dear old Fitz," with his "innocent *far niente* life," . . . has after all left his countrymen a legacy which they will prize when Swinburnes and Morrises and Mrs. Brownings shall be remembered, if at all, like Waller and Marvell and Donne, by a few tuneful lines in old anthologies.—ANDERSON, MELVILLE B., 1889, *The Translator of Khayyám, The Dial*, vol. 10, p. 164.

Who is rashly to decide what place may not finally be awarded to a man capable of such admirable feats in English prose and verse? There can be little doubt that when much contemporary clamour has died out for ever, the clear note of the Nightingale of Woodbridge will still be heard from the alleys of his Persian garden.—GOSSE, EDMUND, 1889, *Edward Fitzgerald, Fortnightly Review*, vol. 52, p. 70.

What Fitzgerald might have done with his gifts and his opportunities, his talents, his scholarship, and his competence, if he had devoted his days to literature, we may conjecture, but we cannot know. But he did not devote his days to literature, wherein he had no ambition to excel. He read and read, he thought and thought; but he was averse from writing books, and of the three which he published he prefixed his name to but one. This was his second book, Six Dramas from Calderon (1853); his first one, Euphranor (1851), stealing into the world anonymously, and dying silently—a fate which nearly overtook his last one, the Rubáiyát of Omar Khayyám (1861), which, also published anonymously, and at his expense, was luckily preserved by one of those miracles which sometimes illuminate the history of literature. Fitzgerald kept a few copies for himself, and gave the rest of the edition to the publisher, who derived no profit from it, since it would not sell, and could scarcely be given away. Still there was something in it that made its way, a force that would be recognized, an imperishable vitality, the vitality of the master, Omar Khayyám, and the scholar, Edward Fitzgerald.—STODDARD, RICHARD HENRY, 1892, *Under the Evening Lamp*, p. 261.

John William Colenso
1814–1883

Bishop of Natal, was born at St. Austell, January 24, 1814, and graduating in 1836 from St. John's College, Cambridge, as second wrangler, was elected a fellow. In 1838 he became an assistant-master at Harrow, in 1842 a tutor at Cambridge, and in 1846 rector of Forncett St. Mary in Norfolk. He published "Miscellaneous Examples in Algebra" in 1848, "Plane Trigonometry" in 1851, and "Village Sermons" in 1853, in which same year he was appointed first Bishop of Natal. He soon mastered the Zulu language, prepared a grammar and dictionary, and translated the Prayer-book and part of the Bible. In a Commentary on the Epistle to the Romans (1861) he objected to the doctrine of eternal punishment. He became convinced of the improbability of many statements of facts and numbers in the Bible; and "The Pentateuch and the Book of Joshua Critically Examined" (seven parts, 1862–79) brought down upon its writer an avalanche of criticism, and was condemned in both Houses of Convocation. In 1864 he was deposed from his see by his Metropolitan, Bishop Gray of Capetown; but on appeal the Privy-council declared the deposition "null and void" (1865); and in 1866 the Court of Chancery ordered the payment of his income, with arrears. Bishop Gray next publicly excommunicated him, and consecrated a new bishop with nearly the same diocese. In 1874 Colenso visited England, conferred with the Archbishop of Canterbury, and pleaded the cause of Langalibalele, a dispossessed Zulu chief. He was author of "Ten Weeks in Natal" (1855); "The New Bible Commentary Literally Examined" (1871-74); "Lectures on the Pentateuch and the Moabite Stone" (1873); and a volume of "Sermons" (1873). His works in algebra and arithmetic are still standard school-books. He died at Durban, Natal, June 20, 1883. See "Life" by Sir G. W. Cox (2 vols. 1888).—PATRICK AND GROOME, *eds.* 1897, *Chambers's Biographical Dictionary*, p. 230.

PERSONAL

Oh, my dear Mr. Froude, I surely couldn't have looked so bored as that. I couldn't because I wasn't. I own to feeling rather antipathetic to that anomalous bishop. A man arrived at the years of discretion wearing an absurd little black silk apron, disturbs my artistic feelings to begin with. Then consider whom I am descended from, the woman who when King James offered to make her husband a bishop if she would persuade him to return to this country and be a peaceable subject, held up her apron and answered, "*I would rather keep his head in there.*" Add to all this that I strongly believe with a German friend of mine, that it is *the mixing up of things* which is *the Great Bad!* and that this particular bishop mixes up a black silk apron with arithmetical confutation of the Bible, and you will allow that I have better reason than a woman usually has for first impressions, why I should not *take to* Colenso.—CARLYLE, JANE WELSH, 1864, *Letter to James Anthony Froude*; Thomas Carlyle, *A History of His Life in London*, ed. Froude, vol. II, p. 223.

Five years after his first departure, Dr. Colenso, with his wife and family, came home to England; and, as soon as possible, put through the press the first volume of his "Pentateuch and Book of Joshua critically examined." . . . It was at this time the writer first saw him, at the table of a distinguished man of science. The first impression he gave was that of a most courteous and high-bred gentleman; the second that of a man powerful physically and by strength of will; the third, that of extreme sincerity, simplicity, and sweetness of character. A tall, strong man, some six feet one or two inches in height, with gray eyes, iron-gray hair, regular features, and a jaw, not coarse, but so strong and firm as to suggest to every beholder the idea of indomitable resolution; a man who could wrestle with a marauding Caffre, or contend with an Archbishop of Canterbury, equally readily at any time.—COBBE, FRANCES POWER, 1867, *Bishop Colenso, Christian Examiner, vol.* 83, *pp.* 12, 13.

Among the figures who acted in his drama, he will not pass, as Gray or Wilberforce may do, into the legends of the saints, but he will have a niche in history beside Thirlwall and Stanley. It will be remembered that his dignity and temper in controversy never failed, though the most abusive language was poured out on him; that he loved the truth, and was willing to trust to it; and that his heart burnt with the fire of humanity and justice. One who experienced his kindness must also place on record how he could devote time and thought to the service of a friend. We shall not easily see his like.—WESTLAKE, J., 1883, *Bishop Colenso, The Academy, vol.* 23, *p.* 456.

I knew Colenso; we met him [1864] in one of our walks. He joined us, and talked of what he had done with some slight elation. "Poor fellow!" said Carlyle, as he went away; "he mistakes it for fame. He does not see that it is only an extended pillory that he is standing on." I thought and think this judgment a harsh one. No one had been once more anxious than Carlyle for the "Exodus." No one had done more to bring it about than Colenso, or more bravely faced the storm which he had raised, or, I may add, more nobly vindicated, in later life, his general courage and honesty when he stood out to defend the Zulus in South Africa. Stanley spoke more truly, or more to his own and Colenso's honour, when he told the infuriated Convocation to its face, that the Bishop of Natal was the only English prelate whose name would be remembered in the next century. —FROUDE, JAMES ANTHONY, 1884, *Thomas Carlyle, A History of His Life in London, vol.* II, *p.* 223.

He had done a great work, and he had done it with singular sweetness and serenity of temper. Those who knew him will remember the charm and dignity of his manner, and for those who never saw him, his writings will attest at the least his unswerving and incorruptible veracity.—COX, SIR G. W., 1887, *Dictionary of National Biography, vol.* XI, *p.* 293.

He faced this tornado of abuse, and these hurricanes of universal anathema, with the calmest dignity. He never once lost his temper; he never returned so much as one angry word to men who had heaped on him every species of abuse and contempt, and of whom many were incomparably his inferiors, not only in learning, but in every grace. . . . Future times will remember Bishop Colenso with honor and gratitude, when the names of nineteen-twentieths of his accusers have been buried in merciful oblivion. They will remember how, almost alone among colonial bishops, he not only devoted nearly the whole of his years to the duties of his see until his death, but also "with intense, indefatigable labor," mastered the Zulu language; produced a Zulu grammar and dictionary; translated into Zulu much of the Bible (correcting inconceivably frightful errors in some small previous attempts); and, in the cause of the oppressed, braving all hostile combinations, came home only to plead the wrongs of Langalibalele, and did his best to obtain justice for King Cetshwayo.—FARRAR, FREDERIC WILLIAM, 1897, *Men I Have Known, pp.* 223, 226.

GENERAL

Have you heard of that wonderful Bishop Colenso? Such a talk about him too. And he isn't worth talking about for five minutes, except for the absurdity of a man making arithmetical onslaughts on the Pentateuch, with a bishop's little black silk apron on!— CARLYLE, JANE WELSH, 1863, *To Miss Grace Welsh, March* 2; *Letters and Memorials, ed. Froude, vol.* II, *p.* 256.

I think it a pity that he commits himself in his books to so much speculative and precarious criticism. His analysis of the Psalms and argument from them struck me as forced and weak; and I find Russell is painfully impressed with its untenable character, though in most respects satisfied with his volumes.—MARTINEAU, JAMES, 1863, *To Mr. Tayler, Sept. 4; Life and Letters,* ed. Drummond, vol. I, p. 404.

We have not seen that, among the half-hundred books and half-thousand pamphlets which it has called out, any new views as to the Pentateuch or the Book of Joshua have been elicited, which we need present at any length to our readers, or with any great care discuss. What is new in Bishop Colenso's own suggestions of detail is perhaps curious, but it seems to us certainly trivial. The greater part of his suggestions are not new, as he himself says. They are household words to every intelligent Christian in America, in France, or in Germany. We believe we might add, they are the familiar speculations of all the enlightened men not bound by the strictest ties of the Church in Spain, in Italy, and in Russia. England is the only country in Christendom where at this moment, the promulgation of these views could be welcomed with such a howl of indignation and surprise. . . . The handful of illustrations which Bishop Colenso presents, where he might have presented thousands, are painfully and sedulously discussed, as if the whole case were wrapped up in them. Eyerything in the controversy shows to us, that to the great majority of the English clergy, of the higher orders as well as of the lower, the discovery that the Pentateuch is self-contradictory, or that any statement in it is untenable, is not simply painful, but a surprise.—HALE, EDWARD EVERETT, 1863, *The Colenso Controversy, Christian Examiner,* vol. 75, pp. 99, 103.

If the Bishop desired a sudden immortality, he has secured his wish. If he sought to put his thoughts in such a form that those for whom he wrote might thoughtlessly receive his opinion as law with regard to the gravest questions that have ever commanded the attention of man, he has been successful. There is a baldness and a boldness in the style of his book, a lowness and, if we may use the term, a filthiness of mind, as if gorging himself with details bordering upon obscenity, which caters to a class of readers who are ever too eager to catch at anything which may foster and strengthen their prejudices against the stern and pure spirit of revelation. Sometimes, as we have read page after page, it seemed as if we could see in the eye of the consecrated Bishop the leer of the Arch-deceiver himself, as looking up at us he said, "Yea! hath God said this?" . . . It was begotten like a house-plant. It will die like a mushroom.—STEARNS, O. S., 1863, *Bishop Colenso, The Christian Review,* vol. 28, pp. 466, 479.

Literary criticism, however, must not blame the Bishop of Natal because his personal position is false, nor praise Spinoza because his personal position is sound. But, as it must deny to the Bishop's book the right of existing, when it can justify its existence neither by edifying the many nor informing the few, it must concede that right to Spinoza's for the sake of its unquestionably philosophic scope. . . . There are alleged contradictions in Scripture; and the question which the general culture of Europe, informed of this, asks with real interest is, as I have said,—*What then?* To this question Spinoza returns an answer, and the Bishop of Natal returns none. The Bishop of Natal keeps going round forever within the barren sphere of these contradictions themselves; he treats them as if they were supremely interesting in themselves, as if we had never heard of them before, and could never hear enough of them now. Spinoza touches these verbal matters with all possible brevity, and presses on to the more important. It is enough for him to give us what is indispensably necessary of them. . . . He, too, like the Bishop of Natal, touches on the family of Judah; but he devotes one page to this topic, and the Bishop of Natal devotes thirteen. To the sums in Ezra—with which the Bishop of Natal, "should God, in His providence, call him to continue the work," will assuredly fill folios —Spinoza devotes barely a page. He is anxious to escape from the region of these verbal matters, which to the Bishop of Natal are a sort of intellectual land of Beulah.—ARNOLD, MATTHEW, 1863, *The Bishop and the Philosopher, Macmillan's Magazine,* vol. 7, pp. 252, 253.

So sincere is my dislike to all personal attack and controversy, that I abstain from reprinting, at this distance of time from the occasion which called them forth, the essays in which I criticised the Bishop of Natal's book; I feel bound, however, after all that has passed, to make here a final declaration of my sincere impenitence for having published them. The Bishop of Natal's subsequent volumes are in great measure free from the crying fault of his first; he has at length succeeded in more clearly separating, in his own thoughts, the idea of science from the idea of religion; his mind appears to be opening as he goes along, and he may perhaps end by becoming a useful biblical critic, though never, I think, of the first order. Still, in here taking leave of him at the moment when he is publishing, for popular use, a cheap edition of his work, I cannot forbear repeating yet once more, for his benefit and that of his readers, this sentence from my original remarks upon him: *There is truth of science and truth of religion; truth of science does not become truth of religion till it is made religious.* And I will add: Let us have all the science there is from the men of science; from the men of religion let us have religion.—ARNOLD, MATTHEW, 1865, *The Function of Criticism at the Present Time, Essays in Criticism*, p. 26, note.

There are two Bishops, and two only, among all the Bishops of the Colonial Churches, who won for themselves the glory of having endeavored to translate the truths of the Scriptures into the uncouth tongues of the people whose pastors they have become. The one is Bishop Patteson of Melanesia, and the other is Bishop Colenso of Natal. If, in pursuance of this investigation, he was led to take too minute care of the words and letters of the Sacred Volume, as I fully think he was, still one would have thought that the sacredness and the value of the labour in which he was employed ought to have procured for him something different from the vast vocabulary of abuse which, as a general rule, is the only response his labours have met with in this country.—STANLEY, ARTHUR PENRHYN, 1865-67, *The South African Controversy, Essays Chiefly on Church and State*, p. 313.

He has recently published a volume of the sermons he has preached since his return to his bishopric,—sermons in which many of the theological questions of the day are dealt with in an able and thoroughly original manner. But the peculiar merit of these discourses is one above their learning and originality. It consists in that warm and simple piety, that strong, clear faith in the LIVING GOD, which has been from first to last the characteristic of the man whom his enemies proclaim as the most dangerous infidel of the day. Well will it be for England, if, fifty years or a century hence, her clergy, with all their cowardly tampering with truth, have left in the hearts of the masses of her people such real manly faith, faith in God and duty and immortality, as breathes through every word and deed of the heretic Bishop of Natal.—COBBE, FRANCES POWER, 1867, *Bishop Colenso, Christian Examiner*, vol. 83, p. 15.

I return the Bishop's paper. If I formed my opinion of Colenso from such statements alone, I should have but a low estimate of his knowledge and powers of reasoning. They are, in my judgment, puerile, hardly ingenius, hardly ingenuous. He does not seem to me to understand the bearing and importance of the subject. But I do not judge Colenso on such grounds. I honour him as a bold, honest, single-minded man, with a deep and sincere love of truth. He is a man, too, of remarkably acute intellect and indefatigable industry. But he entered on these enquiries late in life, struck boldly into one track, in which he marches with fearless intrepidity, looking neither to the right nor to the left. Moreover, he wants wide and general knowledge. He rides his hobby with consummate skill, but he rides it to death. Everything must give way before his Jehovistic and Elohistic theory. Now, I fully believe that to a certain limit, but not in its application to all the writings of the Old Testament (as we have them); for I am a worse sceptic than Colenso, doubting whether we have them in unaltered, unimpeachable integrity. I believe the whole of Colenso's theory about the development of the Jewish religion to be all pure conjecture and from (to me) most unsatisfactory premises. As history, much of the German criticism, as well as his, is purely arbitrary: doubtful conclusions from more doubtful facts. None of this, however, in the least lowers my respect for Colenso, and my sense of his ill usage by persons to whom his knowledge is comparatively the widest, his ignorance much more trustworthy than their knowledge. As for his piety, I have read some, and intend to read more of his sermons. None of his adversaries, of course, read them. If they did, it might put even them to shame, especially as contrasted with their cold, dry dogmatism.—MILMAN, HENRY

HART, 1867, *Letter to Sir Charles Lyell, June 23; Henry Hart Milman, by his Son,* p. 284.

The examination of the Pentateuch soon resolved itself into an examination of all the Hebrew scriptures. The book of Deuteronomy contained many passages which could not have been written until long after the settlement of the Jews in Canaan. He was struck by its resemblance to the prophecies of Jeremiah. Now the historical books showed that the so-called Mosaic law was never carried out before the Babylonish captivity. The popular religion down to the time of the great prophets was a debased idolatry, according to the writing of the prophets themselves. But in the time of Josiah occurred the discovery of the Book of the Law in the Temple. This book, whatever it was, had been utterly forgotten. He inferred that the book discovered was the book of Deuteronomy, and this book is identical in feelings, style, purpose, and language with the book of the prophecies of Jeremiah. The conclusion followed that it was written by Jeremiah and placed in the Temple in order that its discovery should lead to a resolution on the part of the king to put down the abominations which were eating out the spiritual life of his people. This conclusion, the bishop insisted, threw light on many difficulties, and proved the books of Chronicles to be a narrative deliberately falsified with the set purpose of exalting the priests and Levites.

—Cox, SIR G. W., 1887, *Dictionary of National Biography,* vol. XI, p. 291.

It would be unjust to pass over this brave man, who in the teeth of opposition made himself a genuine critic, and who won his battle more completely for others than for himself. . . . Though by no means a negative critic, he was not qualified to do thoroughly sound constructive work either in historical criticism or in theoretic theology. Let us be thankful for all that he did in breaking up the hard soil, and not quarrel with him for his limitations.—CHEYNE, T. K., 1893, *Founders of Old Testament Criticism, pp.* 196, 203.

Colenso's avowed object was to destroy what he called the idol of Bibliolatry. The letter of the Bible he compared to the law as understood by St. Paul, which was to be put aside as a thing dead and of the past, while the spirit lives and could never die. The accuracy of the Pentateuch may go, but the Sermon on the Mount abideth ever. —HUNT, JOHN, 1896, *Religious Thought in England in the Nineteenth Century,* p. 240.

In 1862 the excitement was renewed by the publication of Colenso's book on the Pentateuch. It seems arid, now, for there is nothing attractive in the application of arithmetical formulas to Noah's Ark; but it was just the kind of argument needed at the time and for the audience addressed.— WALKER, HUGH, 1897, *The Age of Tennyson,* p. 159.

Charles Reade
1814–1884

Born, at Ipsden, Oxfordshire, 8 June 1814. Privately educated, 1822–27; at school at Staines, 1827–29. At home 1829–31. Matric., Magdalen Coll., Oxford, 26 July 1831; Demy, 1831–35; B. A., 18 June 1835; Vinerian Scholar, 1835; Fellow of Magdalen Coll., July 1835; M. A., 1838; Vinerian Fellow, 1842; D. C. L., 1 July 1847; Vice-Pres., Magdalen Coll., 1851. Student of Lincoln's Inn, Nov. 1836; called to Bar, 16 Jan. 1843; Friendship with Mrs. Seymour begun, 1852. Play "The Ladies' Battle" (adapted from Scribe and Legouvé), produced at Olympic Theatre, 7 May 1851; "Angelo," Olympic, 11 Aug. 1851; "A Village Tale," Strand, 12 April, 1852; "The Lost Husband," Strand, 26 April 1852; "Masks and Faces," Haymarket, 20 Nov. 1852; "Gold," Drury Lane, 10 Jan. 1853; "Two Loves and a Life," (with Tom Taylor), Adelphi, 20 March, 1854; "The Courier of Lyons," (afterwards called "The Lyons Mail"), Princess's, 26 June 1854; "The King's Rival" (with Tom Taylor), St. James's, Oct. 1854; "Honour before Titles," St. James's, 3 Oct. 1854; "Peregrine Pickle," St. James's, Nov. 1854; "Art," (afterwards called "Nance Oldfield"), St. James's, 17 April 1855; "The First Printer," (with Tom Taylor), Princess's, 3 March 1856; "Never Too Late to Mend," (dramatized from his novel), Princess's, 4 Oct. 1865; "The Double Marriage" (dramatized from novel "White Lies"), Queen's Theatre, 24 Oct. 1867; adaptation of Tennyson's "Dora," Adelphi, 1 June 1867; "Foul Play" (with Dion Boucicault; dramatized from novel), Holborn Theatre, 1868 (revised version, called "The Scuttled Ship," by Reade alone, Olympic, 1877); "Free Labour" (dramatized from novel, "Put Yourself in His Place"), 28 May 1870; "The Robust Invalid," (adapted from Molière), Adelphi, 15 June 1870; "Shilly Shally," Gaiety, 1 April 1872; "Kate Peyton's Lovers" (dramatized from novel "Griffith Gaunt,"), Queen's Theatre, 1 Oct. 1875; "Drink," (dramatized from Zola), Princess's, 2 June 1879; "Love and Money," (with H. Pettitt), 18 Nov. 1882; "Single Heart and Double Face," Edinburgh, Nov. 1883. Died, in London, 11 April 1884. Buried in Willesden Churchyard. *Works:* "Peg Woffington," 1853; "Christie Johnstone," 1853; "Two Loves and a Life" (with Tom Taylor), 1854; "The King's Rival" (with Tom Taylor), 1854; "Masks and Faces" (with Tom Taylor), 1854; "It is Never Too Late to Mend," 1856; "White Lies," 1857; "The Course of True Love never did run Smooth," 1857; "Jack of all Trades," 1858; "Autobiography of a Thief," 1858; "Love me Little, Love me Long," 1859; "The Eighth Commandment," 1860; "The Cloister and the Hearth," 1861; "Hard Cash," 1863; "Griffith Gaunt," 1866; "Foul Play," (with Dion Boucicault), 1868; "Put Yourself in his Place," 1870; "A Terrible Temptation," 1871; "The Wandering Heir," 1872; "A Simpleton," 1873; "A Lost Art Revived," 1873; "A Hero and a Martyr," 1874; "Trade Malice," 1875; "A Woman Hater," 1877; "Readiana," 1883. *Posthumous:* "The Perilous Secret," 1884; "Singleheart and Doubleface," 1884; "The Jilt, and Other Tales," 1884; "Good Stories of Man and other Animals," 1884; "Bible Characters," 1888. *Life:* by C. L. and C. Reade, 1887.—SHARP, R. FARQUHARSON, 1897, *A Dictionary of English Authors,* p. 237.

PERSONAL

A tall man, more than thirty, fair-haired, and of agreeable talk and demeanor.—HAWTHORNE, NATHANIEL, 1856, *English Note-Books, April* 8, *vol.* II, *p.* 14.

I am quite sure that you—who loved and reverenced him [Charles Dickens] as he deserved—will be glad to have something that belonged to him familiarly, even though the thing is of no value in itself. Therefore I venture to send you this little pen-tray as a relic. It belonged to our little sitting-room at the office—a place that he was very fond of—and used very much, so that this little article was constantly under his eye, and associated with his familiar every-day life. Will you accept it from me with my love and regard? You don't need to be told by me—still I think it will be pleasant to you—now—to have a fresh assurance of the affection and esteem in which he held you. You did not meet very often; but I never heard him speak of you except with the heartiest and most cordial expressions of admiration, respect, and personal affection.—HOGARTH, GEORGINA, 1870, *Letter to Charles Reade, Memoir of Charles Reade, ed. Reade and Reade, p.* 391.

To a wonderful energy and virility of genius and temperament Charles Reade adds a more than feminine susceptibility and impatience when criticism attempts to touch him. With a faith in his own capacity and an admiration for his own works such as never were surpassed in literary history, he can yet be rendered almost beside himself by a disparaging remark from the obscurest critic in the corner of the poorest provincial newspaper. There is no pen so feeble anywhere but it can sting Charles Reade into something like delirium. He replies to every attack, and he discovers a personal enemy in every critic. Therefore he is always in quarrels, always assailing this man and being assailed by that, and to the very utmost of his power trying to prevent the public from appreciating or even recognizing the wealth of genuine manhood, truth, and feeling, which is bestowed everywhere in the rugged ore of his strange and paradoxical character. I am not myself one of Mr. Reade's friends, or even acquaintances; but from those who are, and whom I know, I have always heard the one opinion of the sterling integrity, kindness, and trueheartedness of the man who so often runs counter to all principles of social amenity, and whose bursts of impulsive ill-humor have offended many who would fain have admired.—MCCARTHY, JUSTIN, 1872, *Charles Reade, Modern Leaders, p.* 193.

Mrs. Seymour and I were old people, you know. During the nineteen years I lived in the same house with her she led an innocent life, a self-denying life, and a singularly charitable life. In the exercise of this grace there was scarcely a Scriptural prescript she did not fulfil to the letter. She was merciful to all God's creatures; she took the stranger into her house for months; she cared for the orphan; she visited and nursed the sick; she comforted the afflicted in mind; she relieved the poor in various classes of life, constantly hiding her bounty from others, and sometimes from its very objects. Those charities are still continued out of her funds, and through the influence of her example. God drew her nearer to Him by five months of acute suffering. She bore her agonies (from cancer of the liver) with meek resignation, and sorrow for me, who was to lose her, but none for herself. . . . My grief for her is selfish. You know what I have lost—a peerless creature, wise, just, and full of genius, yet devoted to me. She alone sustained me in the hard battle of my life, and now, old and broken, I must totter on without her, sick, sad, and lonely. My remorse is for this. I had lived entirely for the world, and so disquieted her with my cares, instead of leading her on the path of peace, and robbed God of a saint, though not of a believer.—READE, CHARLES, 1880, *Letter to Joseph Hatton, June* 14; *Memoir of Charles Reade*, ed. Reade and Reade, pp. 445, 446.

In his undergraduate days the future novelist seems to have been rather Byronic. A tall graceful youngster, with a splendidly-proportioned figure and muscles to match, he attracted attention by his long flowing curls. Abhorring alcohol in every form as well as tobacco, he did not assimilate largely with his junior common-room, though he was far from unpopular. He read—in his own fashion—and at the age of twenty-one figured in the third class, and was at once elected fellow. His fellowship rendered him independent, and for the best part of twenty years he lived a life of incessant action, mostly in the open air. Nevertheless, unlike Lord Beaconsfield's fine young English gentleman, he was devoted to books, and in effect was storing up material which afterwards enabled him to construct situations, not only stagey but real. At the time the man was very much a Guy Livingstone. He was a dead shot; he knocked Alfred Mynn round the field at Liverpool; he excelled as an archer and as a pedestrian; few if any could beat him in throwing a castnet, and among other accomplishments he reckoned theatrical dancing. — READE, COMPTON, 1884, *Charles Reade, Contemporary Review*, vol. 45, p. 709.

My acquaintance with him did not begin till his infirmity of deafness had grown to be a source of much inconvenience to him; but it certainly had not the effect, often attributed to it, of making him impatient or morose. His hollowed hand, and smiling, attentive face are always present in the picture which my memory draws of him. He expressed himself very strongly upon matters in which his feelings were moved, but they were always moved in the right direction, and though, when contending with an adversary on paper, he did not use the feather end of his pen, his heart was as soft as a woman's. He was never moved by those petty jealousies which (with little reason, so far as my experience goes) are attributed to his craft, and the last time he spoke to me on literary subjects was in praise of one who might well have been considered a rival—Wilkie Collins.—PAYN, JAMES, 1884, *Some Literary Recollections*, p. 164.

It was in the summer of 1876 that I first made the acquaintance of Charles Reade, at a little dinner given by Mr. John Coleman, then manager of the Queen's Theatre. . . . Pleasant beyond measure was that night's meeting; pleasanter still the friendly intimacy which followed, and lasted for years; for all the many distinguished men that I have met, Charles Reade, when you knew him thoroughly, was one of the gentlest, sincerest, and most sympathetic. With the intellectual strength and bodily height of an Anak, he possessed the quiddit and animal spirits of Tom Thumb. He was learned, but wore his wisdom lightly, as became a true English gentleman of the old school. His manners had the stateliness of the last generation, such manners as I had known in the scholar Peacock, himself a prince of taletellers; and, to women especially, he had the grace and gallantry of the good old band of literary knights. Yet with all his courtly dignity he was as frank-hearted as a boy, and utterly without pretence. What struck me at once in him was his supreme veracity. Above all shams and pretences, he talked only of what he knew; and his knowledge, though limited in range, was large and memorable. . . . A magnificent whist and chess player, he would condescend to spend whole evenings at the primitive game of "squales." In these and all other respects, he was the least bookish, the least literary person that ever used a pen.—BUCHANAN, ROBERT, 1884, *Recollections, of Charles Reade, Pall Mall Gazette.*

My first interview with the eminent author, in 1863, left upon me an impression of breadth and amplitude which, though in a measure due to accident and artificial circumstances, remained undisturbed throughout the course of a long and unbroken friendship. The house he lived in, No. 6 Bolton Row, was of unusual magnitude, and the room in which he received his guests was of corresponding dimensions. A table which in point of size might have served for billiards was strewn with enormous sheets of tinted paper, upon which he was writing, in a bold and heavy hand, a forthcoming installment of "Hard Cash." His portly frame completely filled an exceptionally spacious armchair, and as he rose to give greeting he was easily able to look down upon the visitors, though one of them was above the average stature. His manner, dignified, gracious, and extremely gentle, was in thorough harmony with the largeness of the surroundings, and in the conversation which ensued there was certainly nothing that indicated a narrow side to his character.—HOUSE, E. H., 1887, *Charles Reade, Atlantic, vol.* 60, *p.* 525.

Magdalen College, Oxford, is one of the those almshouses for the rich which abound in England. . . . From this charity fund, Reade drew not less than $2,000 a year for the remaining fifty years of his life—$100,000 in all—for which he never rendered one particle of service of any kind, unless we except assistance in defeating parliamentary efforts to abolish the whole thieving job and use the money as the donor has directed. What wonder is it that he shared the disgusting English view of the relation of *meum* and *tuum* as far as the rights of debtor and creditor were concerned? A debt is a misfortune and a dun is a bore. If, when I hold another man's money, he asks for it, he insults me. . . . It may be well to look at the story of his relations with Mrs. Seymour. His Fellowship would be forfeited by marriage. Mrs. Seymour was an actress at the Haymarket, "above mediocrity," and "well-looking off the stage." Reade moved to her house, and afterward took her to his; introduced her to everybody as his housekeeper; was never separated from her for the remaining nineteen years of her life; mourned her death as a fatal blow to his happiness; called her his "lost darling;" was never really himself after he lost her, and was buried by her side. The biographer (Rev. Compton Reade) says everything in his power to prove that their relations were purely platonic. He fails signally.—KIRKLAND, JOSEPH, 1887, *Charles Reade, Novelist, The Dial, vol.* 8, *pp.* 36, 37.

Reade was through life of a litigious and somewhat vain disposition, and, convinced that he was receiving inadequate remuneration alike from his plays and his two novels, he embarked on a series of lawsuits, which proved very disastrous to his pecuniary position. From Bentley, the publisher of his two novels, he received only 30 *l.* apiece. An action at law resulted in his being mulcted in costs to the amount of 220*l.* No more successful were six suits which he brought in vindication of what he alleged to be his rights in his dramatic work. In 1860 he attacked in a pamphlet called "The Eighth Commandment" such thefts of the products of the brain as those from which he imagined himself to be a sufferer. In the same work he advocated a wider scheme of international copyright, and denounced the system of wholesale piratical "adaptation" from the French dramatists. — KENT, CHARLES, 1896, *Dictionary of National Biography, vol.* XLVII, *p.* 355.

THE CLOISTER AND THE HEARTH
1861

I do not say that the whole of life, as it was at the end of the fourteenth century, is in "The Cloister and the Hearth." But I do say, that there is portrayed so vigorous, lifelike, and truthful a picture of a time long gone by, and differing in almost every particular from our own, that the world has never seen its like. To me it is a picture of the past more faithful than anything in the works of Scott. As one reads it, one feels in the very atmosphere of the century; one breathes the air just before the Great Dawn of Learning and Religion; it is still twilight, but the birds are twittering already on the boughs; it is a time when men are weary of the past; there is no freshness or vigour in the poetry; all the tunes are old tunes. . . . Comparison between "The Cloister and the Hearth" and "Romola" is forced upon one. Both books treat of the same period; similar pictures should be presented in the pages of both. Yet—what a difference! In the man's work we find action, life, movement, surprise, reality. In the woman's work we find languor, tedium, and the talk of nineteenth-century puppets dressed in fifteenth century clothes.—BESANT, WALTER, 1882, *Charles Reade's Novels, Gentleman's Magazine, vol.* 253, *pp.* 212, 214.

For my own part, I would rather have written "The Cloister and the Hearth" than half-a-dozen "Romolas," and I would rather have been Charles Reade, great, neglected, and misunderstood in his generation, than the pretentious and pedagogic Talent which earned the tinsel crown of contemporary homage, too speedily dethroned, and, in the good time that is coming for Genius, justly forgotten.—BUCHANAN, ROBERT, 1884, *Recollections of Charles Reade, Pall Mall Gazette.*

A story better conceived or better composed, better constructed or better related, than "The Cloister and the Hearth," it would be difficult to find anywhere.... The variety of life, the vigour of action, the straightforward and easy mastery displayed at every step in every stage of the fiction, would of themselves be enough to place "The Cloister and the Hearth" among the very greatest masterpieces of narrative; while its tender truthfulness of sympathy, its ardour and depth of feeling, the constant sweetness of its humour, the frequent passion of its pathos, are qualities in which no other tale of adventure so stirring and incident so inexhaustible can pretend to a moment's comparison with it—unless we are foolish enough to risk a reference to the name by which no contemporary name can hope to stand higher, or shine brighter, for prose or for verse, than does that of Shakespeare's greatest contemporary by the name of Shakespeare.—SWINBURNE, ALGERNON CHARLES, 1884, *Charles Reade, Nineteenth Century, vol. 46, p. 556.*

Can scarcely be spoken of with praise too high. It is like one of those mediæval pictures in which we see in a succession of scenes, which occupy what in a more artificial piece would be simply background, the whole life and progress of the man whose picture, whether a portrait or a leading incident in his life, is the chief subject. The wonderful romance of Gerard and his companion, with its hundred episodes which are not archaic, and bear no mark of the midnight oil, but fresh as the breath of the primitive country with all its fierce little walled towns and noble castles and hospitable convents, rolls out before us in endless detail, without ever withdrawing our attention from the noble young figure, all ardour, purity and faith which is the chief interest. "The Cloister and the Hearth" is one of the books which we should put into our list for the furnishing and endowment of that desert island, for which we are so often asked to choose an imaginary library.—OLIPHANT, MARGARET O. W., 1892, *The Victorian Age of English Literature, p. 478.*

I think I must have worn out more copies of this book than of any other.... No novel of Scott's approaches the "Cloister" in lofty humanity, in sublimity of pathos. The last fifty pages of the tale reach an elevation of feeling that Scott never touched or dreamed of touching. And the sentiment is sane and honest, too: the author reaches to the height of his great argument easily and without strain. It seems to me that, as an appeal to the feelings, the page that tells of Margaret's death is the finest thing in fiction. It appeals for a score of reasons, and each reason is a noble one.... Reade wrote some twenty novels beside "The Cloister and the Hearth," and not one of the twenty approaches it. One only—"Griffith Gaunt"—is fit to be named in the same day with it; and "Griffith Gaunt" is marred by an insincerity in the plot which vitiates, and is at once felt to vitiate, the whole work. On everything he wrote before and after "The Cloister" Reade's essential vulgarity of mind is written large. That he shook it off in that great instance is one of the miracles of literary history.—QUILLER-COUCH, A. T., 1894, *Adventures in Criticism, pp. 129, 131, 133.*

Reade's greatest novel, the mediæval romance, in four volumes, entitled "The Cloister and the Hearth," was published in 1861. About one-fifth had originally appeared in 1859 under the title of "A good Fight" in "Once a Week," and the circulation of the periodical was consequently increased by twenty thousand. The tale was gradually expanded in the two following years. The scene is laid in Holland, Germany, France, and Italy of the fifteenth century, and the manners, customs, politics, and familiar conversation of the epoch are successfully realised. There are incidentally introduced, along with the imaginary characters, historical personages like Froissart, Gringoire, Villon, Deschamps, Coquillart, Luther, and Erasmus, the last being portrayed as a fascinating child. Sir Walter Besant, in his introduction to the cheap edition of 1894, characterised the work as the greatest historical novel in the language. According to Mr. Swinburne, "a story better conceived, better constructed, or better related, it would be difficult to find anywhere."—KENT, CHARLES, 1896, *Dictionary of National Biography*, vol. XLVII, p. 356.

Is universally admitted to be Reade's masterpiece, and well deserves to be ranked among the best historical novels of the century. There are many who go further, and maintain that it is the finest single fiction of the Victorian era. It is a tale of the fifteenth century, and brings before the reader with startling vividness the cruelty and sordidness, the heroisms and the consecrations of life in the deep darkness that preceded the dawn of the Reformation of Europe. The knowledge displayed is immense. There are humour and pathos in abundance. The canvas is crowded with all kinds of figures — beggar and thief, adventurer and peasant, priest and noble, grouped with admirable effect, and taking part in a series of intensely dramatic scenes and adventures. The whole tale moves at a singular elevation, and conveys a sense of unwonted power. As to its main part, the story is of the rare constancy and pure affection of two sorely-tried hearts sent to an early grave by a combination of fateful circumstances such as could only have arisen in these far-off times.—GRAHAM, RICHARD D., 1897, *The Masters of Victorian Literature*, p. 80.

Reade's masterpiece is a historical novel, "The Cloister and the Hearth" (1860), a story of the early Reformation and of the life of Erasmus. To the construction of this work Reade brought his laborious method of getting up his facts, but in spite of its learning the book is one of the three or four best historical novels since Scott. — MOODY, WILLIAM VAUGHN, AND LOVETT, ROBERT MORSS, 1902, *A History of English Literature*, p. 313.

GRIFFITH GAUNT
1866

I have been sickened to see and hear the things vented against your noble piece of work; I found in it what, let me say, I always find in you, a sincere and loyal love of that which renders beauty beautiful and manhood best. I found in it Nature, too, who does not read the weekly journals enough to forget why Moses wrote the Decalogue, nor what reason She gave him first of all to do it. I am no novel reader, and in morals they call me a Puritan—but I admire and marvel at your exquisite and most healthy and excellent story, which teaches the force of a true love over an unspiritual temperament, and paints a lady that is indeed every inch a lady. To be brief, I lent the book to my sister when I had read it: and will defend it as an enrichment of the best English literature with hearty good will, at any place and time.— ARNOLD, SIR EDWIN, 1866, *Letter to Charles Reade, Memorial of Charles Reade*, ed. Reade and Reade, p. 333.

If such a story as "Griffith Gaunt," . . . be compared with almost any ordinary novel of the day, the first note of difference will be found in the overwhelming amount of incident in the former as compared with the latter; the second, that the descriptions of persons, scenery, place, voice, gesture, &c., necessary in every novel, are much shorter in "Griffith Gaunt" than the other. The third, that the conversations do not drag and seem too long or discursive, but that they carry on the action and develop the characters.—BESANT, WALTER, 1882, *Charles Reade's Novels, Gentleman's Magazine*, vol. 253, p. 201.

But for tragic power, for unfaltering command over all the springs and secrets of terror and pity, it is not comparable with the book which would beyond all question be generally acknowledged by all competent judges, as his masterpiece, if its magnificent mechanism were not vitiated by a moral flaw in the very mainspring of the action. This mainspring, if we may believe the sub-title of "Griffith Gaunt," is supplied by the passion of jealousy. But the vile crime on which the whole action of the latter part of the story depends, and but for which the book would want its very finest effects of pathos and interest, is not prompted by jealousy at all: it is prompted by envy. A man tied by law to a wife whom he believes unfaithful has inadvertently, by no fault of his, won the heart of a woman who believes him free, and has nursed him back from death to life. Unable to offer her marriage, and aware of her innocent regard for him, he loyally determines to withdraw from her society. An old suitor of hers meets and taunts him in the hour of his leave-taking. Instantly, rather than face the likelihood of a rival's triumph, the coward turns back and offers his hand to the girl, whose good offices he requites by deliberate betrayal of her trust and innocence to secret and incurable dishonour. This is no more an act of jealousy than murder by slow poison is an act of impatience. It is an act of envy; and one of the basest on record in fiction or in fact. . . . Great as was usually the care displayed in the composition of Mr. Reade's other works, and great as was sometimes the skill which ensured success to this ungrudging and conscientious labour of love, there is not another of his books which as an all but absolute and consummate work of art can be set beside or near this masterpiece.—SWINBURNE, ALGERNON CHARLES, 1884, *Charles Reade, Nineteenth Century*, vol. 16, pp. 558, 561.

He found his material anywhere, in the village, in the country town, in London, at sea, with a knowledge and acquaintance with all which was always broad and full of light wherever he chose to place the centre, and with an indifference to time as well as place which was a high test of his wonderful power. For though he was essentially a writer of the nineteenth century, and his books a record of the manners and morals of his day, yet his greatest work is a historical romance of the fifteenth century —and one of the most powerful of his lesser romances, "Griffith Gaunt," contains an admirable and living picture of English life a hundred years ago, no book of costumes as so many are, but a most animated transcript of a time which is entirely past. This work is not to be compared with "Esmond" as a work of art, but it has a strength and swiftness and power of rapid realisation which is as remarkable in its way. It is, however, what is called a disagreeable book, and therefore has never had the popularity it deserves.—OLIPHANT, MARGARET O. W., 1892, *The Victorian Age of English Literature*, p. 477.

GENERAL

Mr. Reade's scenes are too limited to make us at home in them; his characters are too sketchy for us to feel familiarly conversant with them. His men and women do not seem to us as life-companions, but rather as passing acquaintances, whom we have met at a dinner-party, in a rail-car, or at a watering-place; with whom we have passed a pleasant hour or two, but of whom we do not know enough to put them upon our list of assured friends; nor have they that innate power of fascination which enables them, as a transient acquaintance sometimes will, to cling to the memory *nolens volens*. Instead of this, we perceive that they will soon yield place to successive visitors of nearly the same calibre, and we think no more about them. Even Christie Johnstone, the freshest and least hackneyed character, appears, after the interval of a week, not as a whole and well-defined woman; but we see in the retrospect only a strong arm, linked to a voice with a singular local *patois*, with now and then a whiff of not over-fresh herrings; while brilliant Peg Woffington, sweet Mable Vane, and sorrow-bleached Rachael, have all become airy phantoms, undistinguishable amid the numerous successors to public favor that have appeared since their advent, from the English and American press.— SMITH, MRS. E. V., 1856, *Reade's Novels, North American Review*, vol. 82, p. 370.

Charles Reade is not a clever writer merely, but a great one, —how great, only a careful *résumé* of his productions can tell us. We know too well that no one can take the place of him who has just left us, and who touched so truly the chords of every passion; but out of the ranks some one must step now to the leadership so deserted, —for Dickens reigns in another region,— and whether or not it shall be Charles Reade depends solely upon his own election: no one else is so competent, and nothing but wilfulness or vanity need prevent him,—the wilfulness of persisting in certain errors, or the vanity of assuming that he has no farther to go. He needs to learn the calmness of a less variable temperature and a truer equilibrium, less positive sharpness and more philosophy; he will be a thorough master, when the subject glows in his forge and he himself remains unheated. . . . Charles Reade's style, which, after the current inanities, is as inspiring as a fine breeze on the upland; it tingles with vitality; he seems to bring to his work a superb physical strength, which he employs impartially in the statement of a trifle or the storming of a city; and if on this page he handles a ship in a sea-fight with the skill and force of a Viking, on the other he picks up a pin cleaner of the adjacent dust than weaker fingers would do it. . . . Charles Reade is the prose for Browning. The temperament of the two in their works is almost identical, having first allowed for the delicate femininity proper to every poet and the richness that Browning lavishes, till it strikes the world no more than the lavish gold of the sun, the lavish blue of the sky, Reade, taking warning, hoards and lets out only by glimpses. Yet such glimpses! for beauty and brilliancy and strength, when they do occur, unrivalled.—SPOFFORD, HARRIET PRESCOTT, 1864, *Charles Reade, Atlantic Monthly, vol.* 14, *pp.* 137, 138.

I have—read—through—"Very Hard Cash;" and very hard it is to read. Reade has some pretty remarkable powers,— powers of description and of characterization; but the moment he touches the social relations, and should be dramatic, he is struck with total incapacity.—DEWEY, ORVILLE, 1867, *To his Daughter, Mary, Sep.* 10; *Autobiography and Letters, ed. Dewey, p.* 298.

Charles Reade is, as an author, very well worth studying. He is so thorough in what he does, so determined and so intense, that he falls into exaggeration, and yet it is doubtful whether he over-paints the truth. It is the languid age that is in fault, and *not* the vivid author.—FRISWELL, JAMES HAIN, 1870, *Modern Men of Letters Honestly Criticised, p.* 84.

Those who have any knowledge of English classics need not be reminded of the broad, practical Christianity which pervades the writings of Charles Reade, whom Dr. Stanton evidently heard of for the first time the other day. All his works bear witness against this charge of rationalism. "Peg Woffington," "Christie Johnstone," "Put Yourself in His Place," "The Cloister and the Hearth"—where are we to find nobler lessons of life or a more refreshing Christianity than in these models of masculine fancy and sterling Anglo-Saxon literature?—HATTON, JOSEPH, 1870, *Letter to The New York Times.*

We do not know if we are prurient and prudish, which is what Mr. Reade has called some of his critics; it shall be as he likes about that; but we feel it laid upon us, as they say, to give it as our judgment that in this last book of Mr. Reade's there is an amount of gestation and parturition, and wet-nursing, not to mention life with the *demi-monde,* that makes "A Terrible Temptation" rather disagreeable to us, and, we fear, a book of dubious tendency. . . . Usually Mr. Reade is—we had almost said, a pure writer. We should hesitate, however, to apply to him just that word, for while he certainly is not an impure writer, yet purity is a word not very precisely descriptive of him. The passion of love is what he has always dealt with; and with him love is always the flesh-and-blood love of entirely human lovers. It is clearly the love of the sexes. As we say, however, Mr. Reade usually treats of it without coarseness, although rarely without a warmth which, to speak within bounds, is not always marked by delicacy. And in the case of Lady Bassett and Mr. Angelo he passes over the boundary, and becomes coarse to the point of indecency. . . . It is, however, as we have said, very interesting and very clever, and although Mr. Reade appears to have only too little respect for himself, and not enough for his readers either, it is certain that in losing the power or the will to delight he has not diminished in the least his power to amuse; and, moreover, might, if he would, keep us all pleased and excited, without hovering on the perilous verge of forbidden regions, or going over the border.—DENNETT, J. R., 1871, "*A Terrible Temptation,*" *The Nation, vol.* 13, *pp.* 107, 108.

He is a magnificent specimen of the modern special correspondent, endowed with the additional and unique gift of a faculty for throwing his report into the form of a thrilling story. But it requires something more than this, something higher than this, to make a great novelist whom the world will always remember. Mr. Reade is unsurpassed in the second class of English novelists, but he does not belong to the front rank. His success has been great in its way, but it is for an age and not for time.— McCARTHY, JUSTIN, 1872, *Charles Reade, Modern Leaders, p.* 201.

After nine years of nominal connection with the bar, he produced the first of the romances by which he is known—the sprightly and charming little story of "Peg Woffington." There are not wanting those who regard this as Reade's most artistic and finished work. It is certainly free from many of those eccentricities and obtrusive mannerisms which too frequently mar the effect of his later books; while it has all the dramatic power of his imagination, and all the raciness which he is able to impart to the dialogues of his characters. An even simpler and more touching story was that of "Christie Johnstone," published in 1853; a story more popular than "Peg Woffington," and which refutes the frequent critical assertion that Reade is lacking in tenderness and sympathy. . . . If popularity be the test of literary rank, Charles Reade has perhaps assumed the place left vacant by Charles Dickens; for the works of no living novelist are seized, read, and noticed, with more avidity.—TOWLE, GEORGE M., 1873, *Charles Reade, Appleton's Journal, vol. 9, pp. 620, 621.*

There is no one I admire so much. There is a swing of easy power about him which is beyond praise.—OLIPHANT, MARGARET O. W., 1876, *To Mr. Blackwood, June 7; Autobiography and Letters, ed. Mrs. Coghill, p. 259.*

Charles Reade in his novel work resembles the old dramatists. If he takes his reader to a North Country fishing village, he does not make up an elaborate picture of the houses, the boats, the nets spread out upon the seashore, the smell of the fish, the narrow streets, the reek and the dirt of it. I do not say that in some hands such a description is not pleasing, but it is not part of Reade's method. He is not a painter of scenery nor of houses; he does not care for picturesque "bits" and effects of light unless they help his story; he is a painter of men and women. Therefore, in the space of half a page or thereabouts, he introduces us briefly to the kind of folks we are to meet, and then sets them to talk for themselves. Not a bit of furniture; not an inch of tapestry; no blue china; no cabinets; yet, when all is told and the curtain drops we know the place where the people live better than if we had read pages of description. This is the art of the dramatist. . . . He resembles no other writer living or dead. His merits are his own, and they are those of the first order of writers. He cannot be classified: In order to be classified, a man must be either a leader or one of a following. . . . In fine, he paints women as they are, men as they are, things as they are. What we call genius is first the power of seeing men, women, and things as they are—most of us, being without genius, are purblind—and then the power of showing them by means of "invention"—by the grafting of "invention" upon fact. No living man has shown greater power of grasping fact and of weaving invention upon it than Charles Reade.—BESANT, WALTER, 1882, *Charles Reade's Novels, Gentleman's Magazine, vol. 253, pp. 201, 214.*

He does not seem to have been born an artist in language. . . . The burnished and incisive style of Mr. Reade, his sedulous and sustained literary workmanship, ought to commend him strongly to French readers, who have been taught to exact a like merit from their own novelists. Another characteristic trait would be better appreciated on the other side of the Channel than at home, and that is the dramatic quality of his narratives. Many of them have been, and all might be, adapted for the stage. . . . There is, it seems to us, a tendency to underrate Mr. Reade's skill in characterization. It is true that none of his conceptions have niched themselves in our remembrance in the sense that Little Nell, Dick Swiveller, Colonel Newcome and Major Pendennis are household denizens; yet we venture to predict that Christie Johnstone and Peg Woffington, Triplet and David Dodd will be found to have a firm hold upon the next, as well as the present generation. We do not recall one book of Mr. Reade's whose chief actors are not individualized, and whose features, physical and mental, are not deeply printed on the mind, being almost always self-betrayed in action or dialogue, and very seldom catalogued by the author. . . . Mr. Reade is always a realist, as much so as was Mr. Trollope, although his realism is of an artistic, not a mechanical sort.—HAZELTINE, MAYO WILLIAMSON, 1883, *Chats About Books, pp. 328, 330, 331, 333.*

On the question of prison reform, of the lunacy laws, of copyright in plays and books, of criminal procedure, he appealed to the great English people, and invariably triumphed. But the works in which he made his immortal appeals are not pamphlets; they are masterpieces of realistic imagination. It is as true to say of him that he was only a "copious pamphleteer" as it was to say of Thackeray that he was no gentleman, of Dickens that he was only a cockney humorist, or Shelley that he was merely a transcendentalist, of Wordsworth that he had no "form," and of Shakespeare that he had no "style," all which weighty assertions have been made within man's memory by the criticism that is contemporary, or by the perversity which is "not for an age, but for all time."—BUCHANAN, ROBERT, 1884, *Charles Reade, Harper's Magazine, vol. 69. p. 606.*

Charles Reade, as a lover of justice and mercy, a hater of atrocity and foul play, may claim a place in the noble army of which Voltaire was in the last century, as

Hugo is in this, the indefatigable and lifelong leader; the great company of witnesses, by right of articulate genius and might of intelligent appeal, against all tenets and all theories of sophists and of saints which tend directly or indirectly to pamper or to stimulate, to fortify or to excuse, the tyrannous instinct or appetite for cruelty innate and latent alike in peoples of every race and every creed. . . . In the power of realising and vivifying what he could only have known by research or by report, Reade is second only to Defoe; while in liveliness and fluency of narrative he is generally as superior alike to Defoe and to Balzac as he is inferior to the one in depth and grasp of intellect, to the other in simplicity and purity of self-forgetting and self-effacing imagination. . . . In Reade the properties and functions of the playright were much less thoroughly fused and harmonised with the properties and functions of the narrator. The work of Dumas as a novelist is never the worse and sometimes the better for his experience of the stage; that of Reade is sometimes the better and sometimes the worse for his less distinguished experiences in the same line. In this respect he stands midway between Dumas and Scott, who was hampered as a dramatist either by his habit of narrative writing or by his sense of a necessity to be on his guard against the influence of that habit.—SWINBURNE, ALGERNON CHARLES, 1884, *Charles Reade*, *Nineteenth Century*, vol. 16, pp. 551, 552.

All his sympathies were with the class from which he originally sprang. He was never able, as has been said over and over again, to draw ladies and gentlemen, and was fond of representing them as awful examples of cold-blooded selfishness. . . . His interest was in characters and situations, and the distinctions of classes counted for very little with him, except for dramatic purposes. At the time of his death his reputation had suffered a serious decline, owing to the fact, among others, that he appeared to have done his best work, and to have become reckless as to his position. He was not content with the natural vigor of a thoroughly masculine style, but he continually attempted to reinforce it by tricks and devices which were sometimes amusing, sometimes contemptible, and always weak and trivial. . . . His range was perhaps not very great; his heroines all bore a strong family resemblance to each other; his men were not characters taken from life, like Thackeray's, but they were made of flesh and blood, and hoped and feared and loved and struggled, so that their life was for the time our own.—SEDGWICK, A. G., 1884, *Charles Reade*, *The Nation*, vol. 38, pp. 335, 336.

There can be little doubt that "Griffith Gaunt" is Reade's masterpiece. . . . A strain of health and manliness runs through all Reade's work: it is not all meant for babes, but it is always on the side of morality. No more unfair charge was ever uttered than that which denounced "Griffith Gaunt" and "A Terrible Temptation" as indecent books. Reade is never afraid to handle themes which to delicate susceptibilities may savour of indelicacy; but it is only the prurient prude who could condemn his manner of treatment. For his own part, he is an enthusiastic defender of Faith and Religion: the "last words to mankind" which he had placed on his tombstone breathe a spirit of the simplest Christianity. A vigorous writer, a clear-headed thinker, untroubled by metaphysical mirage or philosophic doubt, with a rare eye for picturesque effects and a rare appreciation for the subtler details of character, Charles Reade was almost, if not quite, a genius, and only just failed in being an artist.—COURTNEY, W. L., 1884, *Charles Reade's Novels*, *Fortnightly Review*, vol. 42, pp. 463, 471.

The death of Charles Reade, at the age of seventy, withdraws from among us another of that very small group of writers who can lay claim to genius as distinguished from mere talent. Granted that it was not genius of one of the higher types, yet genius is to be seen unmistakably in all his best work, marking it with *verve*, originality, and vigorous action, and in particular exhibiting so much ingenuity in construction of plots and the invention of telling situations that it seems strange that it is as novelist rather than as dramatist (though he essayed both careers) that his reputation was made and is likely to rest.—LITTLEDALE, RICHARD F., 1884, *Charles Reade*, *The Academy*, vol. 25, p. 277.

"Never Too Late to Mend" was far from being his last story. It was his first great ship launched out into the sea of novel-writing. His brain was teeming with plans, and it was only necessary for him to watch the retreating figures of one drama, to behold another company entering by the opposite wing upon the theatre of his mind. . . . A book ["The Eighth Commandment"] which stands among the first of Charles Reade's works in dramatic power. His sketch of the life of M. Maquet is unrivaled, and if novel-readers fail to read the book for lack of a love-story, no author should fail to read it as an example of vigorous wit infused into a dry subject.—FIELDS, ANNIE, 1884, *An Acquaintance with Charles Reade, Century Magazine*, vol. 29, pp. 72, 74.

Into the merits of our author's quarrel with the publishers it would be superfluous to enter, if, indeed, such a quarrel existed outside the region of his sensitive imagination. That he benefited is most improbable. Mrs. Seymour gave him practical assistance of a very valuable kind, but he belonged to the class of penny-wise gentry who leave the pounds to shift for themselves; and it is a fact that he omitted to square accounts with the late Mr. Trübner for so many years that his claim was actually statute-run. Fortunately for him, he had to deal with a man of scrupulous integrity, and thus obtained his own. But it is none the less true that he was totally unconscious of Trübner being in his debt, just as sometimes he would forget for twelve or eighteen months to draw the check for his Fellowship from the Bursar of Magdalen. From a business point of view, nevertheless, he was fully justified in rescuing his copyrights from Messrs. Bentley. At present these books are a genuine literary property, and have a steady sale. In short, if at the moment penalized to the extent of £150, and put to the excitement and trouble of two lawsuits, he amply recouped himself. Moreover, his victory was a memorable one, since, whereas in the first action, which failed, he employed as his counsel, Mr., afterwards Mr. Justice, Lush, a lawyer second only to Cockburn, who, nevertheless, broke down, in the second action he trusted solely to the forensic genius of Charles Reade, barrister at law of Lincoln's Inn, who never before had held a brief, but who none the less triumphed where Lush had failed.—READE, CHARLES L., AND READE COMPTON, 1887, *Charles Reade, A Memoir*, p. 227.

Vitalize this dull reality by vivid feeling; put passion into everything; eliminate all that does not stimulate; be as fruitful in incidents as Trollope is in commonplaces; envelope the reader in a whirl of events; drag him violently on through a series of minor unexpected catastrophes to the grand unexpected catastrophe at the end; heap stimulants on him until he feels like a mad Malay running amuck through the streets—and you have Charles Reade, the great master of melodramatic effect.—WHIPPLE, EDWIN PERCY, 1887, *In Dickens-Land, Scribner's Magazine*, vol. 2, p. 743.

In "Griffith Gaunt" and still more markedly in "A Terrible Temptation," Reade overstepped the boundaries which separate the fiction of our tongue from the license of continental writers. The main objection made to the first named book at the time of its publication was its deliberate portrayal, with the utmost detail, of the life of the hero as the husband of two women at once; loving them both in different fashions, but to an equal degree; and the final winning of him by one of the women on her bearing him a child. This Reade defended with characteristic fierceness, on the score of dramatic necessity—inventing the alliteration of "Prurient Prudes" to fit his assailants. Good men accepted his plea of dramatic necessity. Edward Arnold wrote to him: "I found it in Nature. . . . I am no novel-reader, and in morals they call me a Puritan—but I admire and marvel at your exquisite and most healthy story, which teaches the force of a true love over an unspiritual temperament." But even if we admit his plea on the general issue, what can be said in defence of the particular offence of putting indelicate words into the delicate lips of maidenhood? What motive could there have been save the suggesting of impure thoughts to the reader? 'Tis but a straw, but it marks the drift of the current.—KIRKLAND, JOSEPH, 1887, *Charles Reade, Novelist, The Dial*, vol. 8, p. 38.

Charles Reade collected incident as Herbert Spencer collected sociological data, and his study was almost like the counting-room of a man of affairs, with its pigeon-holed papers and array of scrap-books. —BOWKER, R. R., 1888, *London as a Literary Center, Harper's Magazine*, vol. 77, p. 3.

Mr. Charles Reade's incorporation of fragments of the "dialogues" of Erasmus in the "Cloister and the Hearth," and of Swift's "Polite Conversation" in the "Wandering Heir," was a proper and even a praiseworthy use of preëxisting material. But Mr. Reade did not always remain within his rights, and it is impossible to doubt that his "Portrait" was first hung in the private gallery of Mme. Reybaud, and that some of his "Hard Cash" was filched from the coffers of the "Pauvres de Paris" of MM. Brisebarre and Nus. Mme. Reybaud's picture was not a Duchess of Devonshire which a man might so fall in love with that he could not help stealing it—indeed, it is not easy to discover why Mr. Reade wanted it; but the drama of MM. Brisebarre and Nus is ingeniously pathetic, and although no one has made as skilful use of its fable as Mr. Reade, has served to suggest also Miss Braddon's "Rupert Godwin, Banker," Mr. Sterling Coyne's "Fraud and its Victims," and Mr. Dion Boucicault's "Streets of New-York."—MATTHEWS, BRANDER, 1888, Pen and Ink, p. 39.

It ["Christie Johnstone"] seems to me still —allowing for a deal of irrelevant matter that is now out of date, if attractive at any time—one of the most beautiful and dramatic stories ever written. I do not find it easy to read it without a quickened pulse, and a ready response to its touches of humanity. One of its finest scenes is that in which the heroine Christie, the Newhaven fish-wife, sets sail on the Firth of Forth to save a young artist, who, while bathing, has been carried away by the tide and in danger of losing his life. The motives that prompt her to the rescue are purely human. She effects her purpose, but is not aware that the man she rescues is her own temporarily estranged lover. The treatment of the incident is praiseworthy in the extreme, but unsuited, except in a mutilated form, for presenting on the boards of a theatre. On the other hand it contains scenes that would act admirably.—ARCHER, FRANK, 1892, How to Write a Good Play, p. 74.

It may be noted that in nearly all of Reade's exceedingly fine fictions, crime is the pivot on which the action turns, as in the case of the "Double Marriage," "Hard Cash," and many others. But crime, treated as Reade treats it, is made to yield its most salutary lessons; and, as crime unhappily exists, novels of this type may be justly regarded as fulfilling an ethical as well as a recreative purpose.—RUSSELL, PERCY, 1894, A Guide to British and American Novels, p. 113.

I ought not to omit from the list of these favorites an author who was then beginning to have his greatest vogue, and who somehow just missed of being a very great one. We were all reading his jaunty, nervy, knowing books, and some of us were questioning whether we ought not to set him above Thackeray and Dickens and George Eliot, *tutti quanti*, so great was the effect that Charles Reade had with our generation. He was a man who stood at the parting of the ways between realism and romanticism, and if he had been somewhat more of a man he might have been the master of a great school of English realism; but, as it was, he remained content to use the materials of realism and produce the effect of romanticism. He saw that life itself infinitely outvalued anything that could be feigned about it, but its richness seemed to corrupt him, and he had not the clear ethical conscience which forced George Eliot to be realistic when probably her artistic prepossessions were romantic. As yet, however, there was no reasoning of the matter, and Charles Reade was writing books of tremendous adventure and exaggerated character, which he prided himself on deriving from the facts of the world around him. He was intoxicated with the discovery he made that the truth was beyond invention, but he did not know what to do with the truth in art after he had found it in life, and to this day the English mostly do not. We young people were easily taken with his glittering error, and we read him with much the same fury that he wrote. "Never Too Late To Mend;" "Love Me Little, Love Me Long;" "Christie Johnstone;" "Peg Woffington;" and then, later, "Hard Cash," "The Cloister and the Hearth," "Foul Play," "Put Yourself in His Place"—how much they all meant once, or seemed to mean!—HOWELLS, WILLIAM DEAN, 1895, My Literary Passions, p. 193.

In passing we may remark that Reade's humour is not of a high order, being for the most part of a very commonplace burlesque type. He has comic passages, it is true, such as the death-bed scene of Jane Hardie; but these flashes of fun are not produced intentionally, and owe their piquancy principally to their delightful incongruity. . . . He does elevate the banners of purity, truth, and love—and then blinds us by flapping them in our faces. He advocates district-visiting; but in two of his books he tells us what a thankless office it is, and how little sympathy the objects of our charity have for any woes but their own. . . .

He makes goodness generally, save in the case of Gerard and Christie Johnstone, a spiritless, colorless thing. We feel, with Mark Twain, that moral excellence is petrefication, and religious sensibility a disease; and "we don't want to be like any of his good people, we prefer a little healthy wickedness." . . . One of Reade's books, "The Cloister and the Hearth," has the vital spark in it that will live; the others will not.—CUMPSTON, ELLEN, 1895, *Is Dickens More Famous than Reade? Four Years of Novel-Reading*, ed. Moulton, pp. 52, 54, 55.

It ["Hard Cash"] is the most severe, relentless, inspiring exposition of the potentiality of oppression which may exist in a private lunatic asylum that has ever been written. It ended the irresponsible private asylum in England, and it made the treatment of the insane by severity well-nigh an impossibility in any asylum.—STODDARD, F. H., 1900, *The Evolution of the English Novel*.

Mark Pattison
1813–1884

Born, at Hornby, Yorks, 10 Oct. 1813. Educated by his father. Matric., Oriel Coll., Oxford, 2 April 1832; B. A., 1836; M. A., 1840; Fellow of Lincoln Coll., 8 Nov. 1839 to 1860; Tutor, 1842–55. Ordained Deacon, 1841; Priest, 1843. Denyer Theological Prize, Oxford, 1841 and 1842; B. D., 1851. Frequent contributor to periodicals, 1842–83. Rector of Lincoln Coll., Oxford, 1861–84. Married Emilia Frances Strong, 10 Sept. 1861. Mem. of Athenæum Club, 1862. Died, at Harrowgate, 30 July 1884. Buried in Harlow Hill Churchyard. *Works:* "Casauboniana" (anon.), 1840; "Tendencies of Religious Thought in England, 1688–1750," in "Essays and Reviews," 1860; "Suggestions on Academical Organization," 1868 [1867]; "Isaac Casaubon," 1875; "Milton," 1879. *Posthumous:* "Memoirs," ed. by his wife, 1885; "Sermons," 1885; "Essays," ed. by H. Nettleship (2 vols.), 1889. He *edited:* Pope's "Essay on Man," 1869; Pope's "Satires and Epistles," 1872; Milton's "Sonnets," 1883.—SHARP, R. FARQUHARSON, 1897, *A Dictionary of English Authors*, p. 223.

PERSONAL

I have really no history but a mental history. When I read other person's autobiographies I feel that they were justified in writing them by the variety of experiences they have gone through, and the number of interesting persons they have known. Harriet Martineau, *e. g.*, or Leigh Hunt, were in the way of seeing historic names, and can tell one much about them. I have seen no one, known none of the celebrities of my own time intimately, or at all, and have only an inaccurate memory for what I hear. All my energy was directed upon one end—to improve myself, to form my own mind, to sound things thoroughly, to free myself from the bondage of unreason, and the traditional prejudices which, when I began first to think, constituted the whole of my intellectual fabric. I have nothing beyond trivial personalities to tell in the way of incident. If there is anything of interest in my story, it is as a story of mental development.—PATTISON, MARK, 1884 (?), *Memoirs*, p. 1.

I always considered him the best-read man at Oxford. Anywhere, but at Oxford he would have grown into a Lessing.—MÜLLER, FRIEDRICH MAX, 1884, *To T. Althaus, Dec. 21; Life and Letters*, ed. his Wife, vol. II, p. 176.

Measured by any standard commensurate to his remarkable faculties, Pattison's life would be generally regarded as pale, negative, and ineffectual. Nevertheless, it is undeniable that he had a certain singular quality about him that made his society more interesting, more piquant, and more rapid than that of many men of a far wider importance and more commanding achievement. . . . The result of culture in Pattison's actual life was not by any means ideal. For instance, he was head of a college for nearly a quarter of a century, and except as a decorative figurehead with a high literary reputation, he did little more to advance the working interests of his college during these five-and-twenty years, than if he had been one of the venerable academic abuses of the worst days before reform. But his temperament, his reading, his recoil from Catholicism, combined with the strong reflective powers bestowed upon him by nature to produce a personality that was unlike other people, and infinitely more curious and salient than many who had a firmer grasp of the art of right living. In an age of effusion to be reserved, and in days of universal professions of sympathy to show a saturnine front, was to be an original. There was nobody in whose company one felt so much of the ineffable comfort of being quite safe against an attack of platitude. There was nobody on whom one might so surely count in the course of an hour's talk for some stroke of irony or pungent suggestion, or, at the worst, some significant, admonitory, and almost luminous manifestation of the great *ars tacendi*. In spite of his copious and ordered knowledge, Pattison could hardly be said to have an affluent mind. He did not impart intellectual direction like Mill, nor morally impress himself like George Eliot. Even in pithy humour he was inferior to Bagehot, who was certainly one of the most remarkable of the secondary figures of our generation. But he made everyone aware of contact with the reality of a living intelligence. It was evident that he had no designs upon you. He was not thinking of shaking a conviction, nor even of surprising admiration.—MORLEY, JOHN, 1885, *On Pattison's Memoirs, Macmillan's Magazine*, vol. 51, p. 446.

If we attempt to judge the life of Mark Pattison from an ideal standpoint, we must pronounce it a failure—a magnificent failure perhaps, but still a failure. This it was because he not only did not succeed in fully realising the aim he put before himself, but also because he showed in his own character and career the inadequacy of that aim. His conceptions of an elevated philosophic education, of the functions of a University, of the obligations and attractions of the scholar's life, will always be found inspiring by those who are fit to appreciate them; but he only partially succeeded in illustrating by his example what he had illuminated by his learning; and the impression which his "Memoirs" give us of a life of misery, the intensity of which is only brought into relief by the brilliancy of his attainments, shows us the inadequacy as a guide to life of purely intellectual aspirations.—NETTLESHIP, HENRY, 1889, *Mark Pattison, Church Quarterly Review*, vol. 28, p. 371.

Pattison was by no means a recluse. For some years after his marriage in 1861 his house was a centre of all that was best in Oxford society. Under a singularly stiff and freezing manner to strangers and to those whom he disliked, he concealed a most kindly nature, full of geniality and sympathy, and a great love of congenial, and especially of female, society. But it was in his intercourse with his pupils, and generally with those younger than himself, that he was seen to most advantage. His conversation was marked by a delicate irony. His words were few and deliberate, but pregnant with meaning, and above all stimulating, and their effect was heightened by perhaps too frequent and, especially to undergraduates, somewhat embarrassing flashes of silence. His aim was always to draw out by the Socratic method what was best in the mind of the person he conversed with, and he seemed to be seeking information and suggestions for his own use. To the last he was open to new personal impressions, was most grateful for information on subjects which were of interest to him, and was always full of generous admiration for good work, or even for work which, if not really good, was painstaking or marked by promise.—CHRISTIE, RICHARD COPLEY, 1895, *Dictionary of National Biography*, vol. XLIV, p. 62.

There is no history of mental growth and struggles which is to me more touching and interesting, though it is impossible not to feel that the results were very painful.—LAKE, WILLIAM CHARLES, 1897–1901, *Memorials*, ed. his Widow, p. 58.

From Jowett to Mark Pattison is a transition popular but unphilosophic: to bracket the two men, as is often done, shows superficial knowledge of both. Both, no doubt, were clergymen, both missed disappointingly and afterwards exultingly obtained the Headship of their Colleges, both wrote in "Essays and Reviews." Behind these accidents are life equipment, experiences, characters, temperaments, standing in phenomenal contrast. Pattison's mind was the more comprehensive, instructed, idealistic, its evolution as intermittent and self-torturing as Jowett's was continuous and tranquil. Pattison's life, in its abrupt precipitations and untoward straits, resembled the mountain brook of Wordsworth's solitary; Jowett's floated even, strong, and full, from the winning of the Balliol scholarship by the little white-haired lad with shrill voice and cherub face, until the Sunday afternoon at Headley Park, when the old man, shrill, white-haired and cherubic still bade "farewell to the College," turned his face to the wall, and died.—TUCKWELL, W., 1900, *Reminiscences of Oxford, p.* 216.

GENERAL

It may suit Mr. Pattison's ["Essays and Reviews"] purpose, and fill out his trial of antitheses, to sneer at the philosophy of this period as "without insight." But it shows bad taste and defective knowledge to include in this sneer such men as Butler, the father of modern ethical science, not only in England, but for all Europe; Berkeley, the pure and refined spiritualist, and one of the most elegant writers and original philosophical thinkers that England has produced; Samuel Clarke, a co-worker with Newton, the well-matched opponent of Leibnitz, and one of the greatest masters of abstract metaphysical reasoning that the world has ever seen; and even Warburton, who, with all his defects of temper, has been well called "the last of our really *great* divines."—BOWEN, FRANCIS, 1861, *Essays and Reviews, Gleanings from a Literary Life, p.* 452.

As an author Pattison has not made the impression which his great powers and unusual attainments might have been expected to produce. He had, indeed, within him so many impediments to large and successful authorship that the wonder is not that he wrote so little as that he wrote as much as he did. First of all he was a victim of curiosity, of his wide and sleepless interests in all manner of subjects about which he cared and read simply for themselves, without any after thought of working up his reading into a salable literary form. With a tithe of his acquisitions an expert young penman would have produced shelves of smooth readable volumes, and gained a reputation in letters, as reputations now go. He had none of the business author about him, who has one eye for his subject, and the other—the wider open of the two—on the market values of his wares in publishers' offices. He valued knowledge too highly to make a trade of it, even if paid only in fame. In the next place he was fastidious to a fault; his taste was superior to his power of production. He was too severe a critic of his own writings. Then, his scrupulous conscientiousness was extreme, and he never felt sufficiently prepared for literary work. . . . And yet with all these drawbacks he has produced valuable works which the world would be unwise to neglect. . . . They all bear on the one theme on which his whole heart was set—the praise and commendation of learning. No one need fear that in reading the slightest thing of Pattison's he will waste his time. He never wrote because he had to say something, but always because he had something to say.—MORISON, JAMES COTTER, 1884, *Mark Pattison, Macmillan's Magazine, vol.* 50, *pp.* 406, 407.

He was full of the passion for knowledge; he was very learned, very acute in his judgment on what his learning brought before him, very versatile, very shrewd, very subtle; too full of the truth of his subject to care about seeming to be original; but, especially in his poetical criticisms, often full of that best kind of originality which consists in seeing and pointing out novelty in what is most familiar and trite. But, not merely as a practical but as a speculative writer, he was apt to be too much under the empire and pressure of the one idea which at that moment occupied and interested his mind. He could not resist it; it came to him with exclusive and overmastering force; he did not care to attend to what limited it or conflicted with it. . . . Though every competent reader must do justice to Pattison's distinction as a man of letters, as a writer of English prose, and as a critic of what is noble and excellent and what is base and poor in literature, there is a curious want of completeness, a frequent crudity and hardness, a want, which is sometimes a surprising want, of good sense and good taste, which form unwelcome blemishes in his work, and just put it down below the line of first-rate excellence which it ought to occupy.—CHURCH, RICHARD WILLIAM, 1884, *Mark Pattison, Occasional Papers, vol.* II, *pp.* 354, 355.

Mark Pattison's highest praise is, perhaps, that he was able, so long ago, to look at such things as we see them now. He kept an open mind, and so he looked towards the future, and was able to take in new ideas, to be touched by the Zeit-geist. . . . Workers like Mark Pattison are rare; few men have the strength and clearness to make for the ends he was striving for—for self-culture, for perfection, for such truth as he could attain. And still fewer have the restraint and unselfishness to be satisfied with wisdom as its own exceeding great reward. Among these rare and gifted beings,

Mark Pattison, in spite of all that can be said, must take his place; by doing so he becomes in some sense a benefactor to his kind. The lesson he teaches those who are willing to learn it is expressed in those words of his with which this essay began: "The highest life is the art to live." That he solved the problem of living we need not think; but at least he set a noble example to those who wish to solve it. He did his best.—GALTON, ARTHUR, 1885, *Urbana Scripta, pp.* 201, 208.

As you read his "Memoirs," you hardly know whether he meant to give a picture of himself or a picture of the Oxford he had known. The two are blended together, and they ought not to be separated. To understand Pattison you must take account of the university environment in which he moved, and there is no better way in entering Oxford as it was, or of understanding how it has become what it is, than to try to appreciate the character of one of the most noteworthy among its teachers. The most salient peculiarity in the character painted with such painful care by Pattison himself, is the astonishing combination of a certain intellectual strength and greatness with a quality which one cannot call by any other name than weakness. For the proper understanding of the "Memoirs," the primary requisite is to appreciate the great and even noble side of their author's character. There is the more reason for insisting upon this because Pattison has not really done himself justice.—DICEY, A. V., 1885, *Pattison's Memoirs, The Nation, vol.* 41, *p.* 176.

Whatever were the effects of Pattison's arguments, ["Sermons"] whether put aside as fatal snares or followed out to extravagant conclusions, most young men must have caught from them something of his moral force and mental clearness. His lofty tone was indeed intellectual, but singularly in sympathy with, and adaptable to, spiritual aspirations; in that unity of the ascetic and philosophical life on which he always insisted. He disarmed clerical criticism by his loyal advocacy of our English Church, "a Church which has never yet broken with reasons or proscribed education"—surely the noblest praise a son of hers has ever offered her—and by the echoes which it often awakened of the golden age of English homiletics. This not only by his dignified, weighty, and truly theological handling, but by the unconscious use of quaint but perfectly exact phrases.—PURCELL, E., 1885, *Sermons by Mark Pattison, The Academy, vol.* 8, *p.* 283.

Mark Pattison was too fastidious a scholar, and too indifferent to the charms of notoriety, to produce much, but what he did is the best of its kind. His life of Milton in the admirable series entitled "English Men of Letters" is certainly second to none. His edition of some of Pope's poems in the Clarendon Press Series are models of annotation. His original inquiry into the causes of the rise and extinction of Deism in the eighteenth century, published in the famous volume of "Essays and Reviews," has been accepted as a substantial contribution to religious history.—ANDERSON, MELVILLE B., 1885, *Mark Pattison, The Dial, vol.* 6, *p.* 72.

For his true portrait we must look into his "Essays" and his "Life of Casaubon." His own personality is evident in whatever he writes.—CHRISTIE, RICHARD COPLEY, 1895, *Dictionary of National Biography, vol.* XLIV, *p.* 63.

Had a less amiable character than Stanley's, but a greater intellect and far nicer, profounder, and wider scholarship, though he actually did very little. . . . It would be entirely unjust to regard him as merely a man who was "going to do something." His actual work though not large is admirable, and his style is the perfection of academic correctness, not destitute of either vigour or grace.—SAINTSBURY GEORGE, 1896, *A History of Nineteenth Century Literature, pp.* 373, 374.

Charles Stuart Calverley
1831-1884

Born (Charles Stuart Blayds), at Martley, Worcestershire, 22 Dec. 1831. Father assumed name of Calverley, 1852. Educated by private tutors; then at Marlborough. At Harrow, Sept. 1846 to July 1850. To Balliol Coll., Oxford, as scholar, Nov. 1850; Chancellor's Prize, 1851. Resumed family name of Calverley, 1852. Removed to Christ's Coll., Camb., Oct. 1852; Craven Scholarship, 1854; Camden Medal, 1853 and 1855; Browne

Medal, 1855; Latin Essay Prize, 1856; B. A., 1856; M. A., 1859; Fellow of Christ's Coll., 14 Dec. 1857 to 24 June, 1863. Married Ellen Calverley, 1863. Called to Bar at Inner Temple, 1 May 1865. Severe accident, winter of 1866; obliged to relinquish profession. Died at Folkestone, 17 Feb. 1884; buried there. *Works:* "Verses and Translations" (under initials: C. S. C), 1862; "Translations into English and Latin," 1866; "Theocritus, translated into English Verse," 1869; "Fly Leaves" (under initials: C. S. G.), 1872. *Collected Works:* "Literary Remains," with *memoir* by W. J. Sendall, 1885.—SHARP, R. FARQUHARSON, 1897, *A Dictionary of English Authors,* p. 46.

PERSONAL

He was the best runner and jumper I ever knew.... Whenever I think of Calverley I think of fun and good-fellowship; of the "wild joys of living; the leaping from rock up to rock; the cool silver shock of the plunge in the pool's living water;" of health and youth and strength. Alas, alas!—PAYN, JAMES, 1884, *Some Literary Recollections,* pp. 138, 139.

Most of Blayds' Harrow contemporaries who went to Cambridge entered at Trinity, and there was in those days but little communications between Trinity and Christ's. At Christ's he was cock of the roost, and a true Bohemian, he liked to take his ease at his inn, and had a horror of general society. Only some admirable skit like his Tripos verses, some practical joke worthy of Theodore Hook, or some brilliant success like the Craven Scholarship, kept his name alive with Harrow men.—TOLLEMACHE, LIONEL A., 1884, *C. S. Calverley, Character Sketches,* p. 308.

A bright, sunny boyhood, fearless and careless; a youth full of brilliant promise, and studded with intellectual triumphs; a manhood marked by no striking incidents, no ambitious struggles, no alternations of failure and success—darkened, alas! in later years, and brought to an untimely close by the ravages of a fatal and insidious malady —such are, in brief, the outlines of a career which in itself would seem to possess but scanty claims upon the attention of the general observer. But if the incidents of Calverley's life were thus trite even to commonplace, yet his own bearing amongst them, and the physical and intellectual personality which marked each successive stage, would be found, if accurately and adequately portrayed, to present a striking and an interesting picture. From childhood up there never was a time when he failed to impress in some enduring manner those amongst whom he moved.—SENDALL, WALTER J., 1884, *Charles Stuart Calverley, Fortnightly Review,* vol. 35, p. 736.

On the testimony of those who knew him best, Calverley's published writings convey only a very imperfect idea of his powers. At Oxford and at Cambridge he was justly regarded as a prodigy of versatility and intellectual brilliance. He excelled in scholarship and athletics; his wit, his sunny humour, his musical talents, his gifts as a conversationalist, a caricaturist and a comic rhymer, the ease with which he carried off University honours as if in play made him the idol and delight of his fellows. At Cambridge his jests went the round of the University. The Latin poem with which he won the Chancellor's Prize at Oxford is said to have been composed so rapidly that it might almost be termed an improvisation. His appearance in his college days is thus described by Mr. Sendall; "Short of stature, with a powerful head of the Greek type, covered thickly with crisp curling masses of dark hair, and closely set upon a frame whose supple joints and well-built proportions betokened both speed and endurance—he presented a picture of health, strength, and activity." He was a fascinating companion from his sparkling gaiety, his modesty and kindness. He was the most loyal and generous of friends; he was a favourite everywhere;—when he visited Cumberland he won the hearts of the dalesmen as readily as he had captivated the Cambridge undergraduates. But he seems to have had no ambition.—WHYTE, WALTER, 1894, *The Poets and the Poetry of the Century, Humour, Society, Parody, and Occasional Verse,* ed. Miles, p. 434.

Charles Stuart Calverley is by common consent the king of metrical parodists. All who went before merely adumbrated him and led up to him; all who have come since are descended from him and reflect him. Of course he was infinitely more than a mere imitator of rhymes and rhythms. He was a true poet; he was one of the most graceful scholars that Cambridge ever produced; and all his exuberant fun was based on a broad and strong foundation of Greek, Latin, and English literature.—RUSSELL, G. W. E., 1898, *Collections and Recollections.*

Among these men—I mean of my own time—incomparably the most brilliant, the finest scholar, the most remarkable man from every point of view, was Calverley. He was the hero of a hundred tales; all the audacious things, all the witty things, all the clever things, were fathered upon him. It is forty years since his time, and no doubt the same audacities, repartees, and things of unexpectedness which never die have been fathered upon others, his successors in brilliant talk and scholarship. But consider, to a lad like myself, the delight of knowing a man who was not only the finest scholar of his year—writing Latin verses which even to eyes like mine were charming—but a man who could play and sing with a grace and sweetness quite divine as it seemed to me; who could make parodies the most ridiculous and burlesques the most absurd; who kept a kind of open-house for his intimates, with abundance of port and claret—he was the only man in college who kept claret; whose English verses were as delightful as his Latin; who was always sympathetic, always helpful, always considerate.—BESANT, SIR WALTER, 1902, *Autobiography*, p. 86.

GENERAL

Calverley and Dobson are the best of the new *farceurs*. "Fly-Leaves," by the former, contains several burlesques and seriocomic translations that are excellent in their way, with most agreeable qualities of fancy and thought.—STEDMAN, EDMUND CLARENCE, 1875-87, *Victorian Poets*, p. 273.

Assuming that all competent judges are agreed as to the the superlative goodness of his classical compositions and translations, I will only observe in this place, that in all such work his professed aim and object were faithfully to represent, not the sense merely of his author, but also the form and expression. It is not sufficient, in his view, that the thoughts and ideas of the original should be reproduced, in language of itself however appropriate and idiomatic, by the copy; this is indeed indispensable, but this is not enough; there must in addition to a wholly faithful *sense*-rendering, be also to some extent a *word*-rendering, and even if possible a *form*-rendering. . . . Calverley's own measure of success in translating upon his own method is, I venture to think, almost if not quite unrivalled, and constitutes the distinctive mark of his performances in this department. . . . His own clearness and, so to speak, point-blank directness of mental vision, rendered him especially impatient of all the crooked and nebulous antics and vagaries of thought or speech in which writers of the modern transcendental school are pleased to indulge; and his parodies of this class must be regarded as a genuine and out-spoken expression of resentment that so much genius should seem to take so much pains to be unintelligible.—SENDALL, WALTER, J., 1885, ed. *The Literary Remains of Charles Stuart Calverley, Memoir*, pp. 80, 83, 89.

Calverley wrote a small amount of verse that, merely as verse, is absolutely faultless. To compare great things with little, you might as well try to alter a line of Virgil's as one of Calverley's. Forget a single epithet and substitute another, and the result is certain disaster. He has the perfection of the phrase,—and there it ends. I cannot remember a single line of Calverley's that contains a spark of human feeling. —QUILLER-COUCH, A. T., 1891, *Adventures in Criticism*, p. 156.

The monstrously overrated and preposterously overpraised C. S. Calverley: a jester, graduate or undergraduate, may be fit enough to hop, skip and tumble before university audiences, without capacity to claim an enduring or even a passing station among even the humblest of English humourists.—SWINBURNE, ALGERNON CHARLES, 1891, *Social Verse, The Forum*, vol. 12, p. 182.

Oh, when the grey courts of Christ's College glowed
With all the rapture of thy frequent lay,
When printers' devils chuckled as they strode,
And blithe compositors grew loudly gay:
Did Granta realise that here abode,
Here in the home of Milton, Wordsworth, Gray,
A poet not unfit to cope with any
That ever wore the bays or turned a penny?
The wit of smooth delicious Matthew Prior,
The rhythmic grace which Hookham Frere displayed,
The summer lightning wreathing Byron's lyre,
The neat inevitable turns of Praed,
Rhymes to which Hudibras could scarce aspire,
Such metric pranks as Gilbert oft has played,
All these good gifts and others far sublimer
Are found in thee, beloved Cambridge rhymer.

—STEPHEN, JAMES KENNETH, 1891, *To C. S. C., Lapsus Calami and Other Verses*, p. 1.

He was, like Yorick, "a fellow of infinite jest, a most excellent fancy," gifted with an extraordinary ingenuity in producing and manipulating his little tricks of verse and scholarly *jeux d'esprit*, which, together with the wild pranks that he played when an undergraduate, have secured him an undying memory at both universities. Those who were at Harrow, or at Oxford, or Cambridge with him, still regard with some of the wondering admiration of old days the extraordinary powers which seemed to make any degree of future fame possible to the brilliant young writer. But the hopes thus aroused were never destined to be fulfilled. Perhaps he never could have done anything greater than the graceful and witty trifles, of which we are sometimes tempted to say in the midst of our admiration that this man was doing for work what others do—not so well, certainly,—for play. . . . His translations from the classics and his Greek and Latin verse have deservedly given him a place among scholars quite as high as the immortal "Ode to Beer" or any other of the great little efforts of his youth entitled him to.—OLIPHANT, MARGARET O. W., 1892, *The Victorian Age of English Literature*, pp. 455, 456,

Calverley had a wonderful sense of rhythm and of the power and beauty of words. He was a student of style from his boyhood. With his imagination and deep human sympathy, his sensitiveness, his exquisite appreciation of verbal music, and his mastery of poetic *technique*, he seemed to possess in unusual completeness the equipment of a serious lyrical artist; but his powers, by a charming perversity of genius, were enlisted in the service of an elvish irrepressible humour and a satiric wit equally whimsical and keen. His satire was guided by severe good taste. He derided outworn rhymes, and sham sentiment, obscure and contorted phrases, and lackadaisical refrains. His humour gains a peculiar pungency from the classic terseness and finish of his clear-cut verse. In certain of his pieces the air of mock gravity is so well maintained that the lines when first read might be taken for serious poetry, until a sharp deft change from the florid to the familiar, from the sentimental to the burlesque, an ingeniously incongruous phrase, a rhyme of ludicrous felicity, betrays their satiric intent. His exquisite literary sense enabled him to produce broadly humorous effects by subtle and singularly terse conjunctions of ornate with prosaic diction. And the succinctness of the expression, the severity of the literary form never embarrassed the play of his wit nor retarded the current of his humour.—WHYTE, WALTER, 1894, *The Poets and the Poetry of the Century, Humour, Society, Parody and Occasional Verse*, ed. *Miles*, p. 435.

So far is Calverley superior in this and other particulars to all the servile herd who have followed him, that, according to the principles we have laid down, the "cream" of "Fly-leaves" should have occupied a third of our volume.—POWELL, G. H., 1894, ed. *Musa Jocosa*, p. 16.

Partly from indifference, partly because of the accident which made great effort in his later years impossible, he never wrote anything worthy of his talents. What he has left however is the very best of its kind. He is one of the most skilful of translators; and his parodies and satiric verse are excellent.—WALKER, HUGH, 1897, *The Age of Tennyson*, p. 257.

Richard Hengist Horne
1803–1884

Born, in London, 1 Jan. 1803. Educated at Sandhurst. Midshipman in Mexican Navy, served in War against Spain, 1829. At conclusion of War went to U. S. A. Returned to England. Contrib., to "Monthly Repository," under initials: M. I. D. Contrib. poem to "Athenæum," 1828. Edited "Monthly Repository," July 1836 to June 1837. Sub-commissioner to report on Employment of Children in Mines, 1843. Contrib., to "Howitt's Journal;" to "Household Words," June 1851. Married Miss Foggs, 1847. To Australia with W. Howitt, 1852; Commander of Gold Escort, Victoria, 1852. Commissioner of Crown Lands for Gold Fields, 1853–54; Territorial Magistrate, 1855. Returned to England, 1869. Substituted Christian name "Hengist" for "Henry." Civil List Pension, 1874. Contrib., to "Harper's Mag.;" "New Quarterly Mag.," "Fraser's Mag.," "Longman's Mag.," and other periodicals. Died at Margate, 13 March 1884. Buried there. *Works:* "Exposition of the . . . Barriers excluding Men of Genius from the Public" (anon.), 1833; "Spirit of Peers and People," 1834; "Cosmo de Medici," 1837; "The

Death of Marlowe," 1837; "The Russian Catechism" [1837?]; "Life of Van Amburgh," (under pseud. "Ephraim Watts"), [1838]; "Gregory VII.," 1840; "The History of Napoleon," (2 vols.), 1841; "Orion," 1843 (6th edn. same year); "A New Spirit of the Age," (with Mrs. Browning and R. Bell), 1844 (2nd edn. same year); "The Goodnatured Bear," 1846; "Memoirs of a London Doll," 1846; "Ballad Romances," 1846; "Judas Iscariot," 1848; "The Poor Artist" (anon.), 1850; "The Dreamer and the Worker," (2 vols.), 1851; "Australian Facts and Prospects," 1859; "Prometheus the Fire-bringer," 1864; "The South-Sea Sisters," [1866]; "The Lady Jocelyn's Weekly Mail," 1869; "The Great Peacemaker" (from "Household Words"), 1872; "The Countess Von Labanoff" (from "New Quarterly Mag."), 1877; "Laura Dibalzo," 1880; "King Nihil's Round Table," 1881; "Bible Tragedies" [1881]; "Soliloquium Fratris Rogeri Baconis" (from "Fraser's Mag."), 1882; "The Last Words of Cleanthes" (from "Longman's Mag."), [1883]; "Sithron" (anon.), 1883. He *edited:* Black's trans. of Schlegel's "Lectures," 1840; "Poems of Geoffrey Chaucer Modernised," 1841; "Shakespeare's Works," 1857; L. Marie's "Notes . . . on . . . Prize Essays on the Vine," 1860.—SHARP, R. FARQUHARSON, 1897, *A Dictionary of English Authors*, p. 137.

PERSONAL

The late R. Hengist Horne passed away in a very faint adumbration of that high reputation he once enjoyed. From the early days of "the farthing Epic"—"Orion" —to the publication of the "Bible Tragedies," is changes! No poet of this generation more lived his life than did "Orion:" he seems to have dwelt in, or at any rate visited all the habitable (and several of the unhabitable) parts of the globe.—SHARP, WILLIAM, 1886, *ed. Sonnets of this Century*, p. 293, *note*.

He was a good musician, he played excellently on the guitar, sang well and was a marvellous whistler. He was an expert swimmer. Horne had his affectations. When he went out to Australia he was "Richard *Henry*," but he came back "Richard *Hengist*." In the bush he had met a Mr. Hengist, whose name he took.—BULLEN, A. H., 1891, *Dictionary of National Biography*, vol. XXVII, p. 359.

I was in England at the end of 1882, and during the following year, and half of 1884; and, our acquaintanceship resumed, spent many evenings with the old man at his lodgings in Northumberland Street, Marylebone. Through the two winters he would cook our dinner at the stove in his sitting-room, priding himself on his cooking (he was very much of an epicure, an epicurean in his life), and we ate on what room was left by books and letters on a little round table before the fire. He had always good wine, supplied by an admiring friend, and we sat and talked of books or of his Australian life. He was proud of showing how strong, in spite of his years (his dated with the century), his physique still was; and one evening he showed me his bare foot, that I might see he was really web-footed. He had taken several prizes for swimming. . . . After reaching the "threescore years and ten," he leaped from the pier at Eastbourne to give a lesson in swimming.—LINTON, WILLIAM JAMES, 1894, *Threescore and Ten Years*, p. 22.

In the last year or two of his life the veteran man of letters found his eyesight becoming defective; and finally he was almost blind; but in all other respects he was in great bodily and mental vigor up to the summer of 1883, when he contracted the illness of which he died. This mental vigor indeed caused him to chafe at the younger generation or two of readers who knew not "Orion," or knew it but as a "farthing tradition;" and the old athlete was ever ready to back with a powerful body any quarrel into which a powerful but impatient intellect might lead him. There were but few among his intimates with whom he had not quarreled more or less; but one or two remain who cherish his memory for what was strong and noble and generous in the wayward old Titan. — FORMAN, HENRY BUXTON, 1895, *Literary Anecdotes of the Nineteenth Century*, ed. Nicoll and Wise, p. 243.

It was very characteristic of him that, during his lengthened stay in Australia, he sent nothing over to his wife, whom he had left behind, and who had to go back to her own family, but portraits of himself.—HAZLITT, W. CAREW, 1897, *Four Generations of a Literary Family*, vol. I, p. 249.

He himself, with his incredible mixture of affectation and fierceness, humor and absurdity, enthusiasm and ignorance, with his incoherency of appearance, at once so effeminate and so muscular, was better than all his tales. He was a combination of the troubadour and the prize-fighter, on a miniature scale. It was impossible not to think of a curly white poodle when one looked at him, especially when he would throw his fat little person on a sofa and roll about, with gestures less dignified than were, perhaps, ever before seen in a poet of between seventy and eighty years. And yet he had a fine, buoyant spirit, and a generous imagination with it all. But the oddity of it, alas! is what lingers in the memory—those milky ringlets, the extraordinary turn of the head, the embrace of the beribboned guitar! . . . Horne's physical strength was very extraordinary in old age. It was strangely incompatible with the appearance of the little man, with his ringletted locks and mincing ways. But he was past seventy before he ceased to challenge powerful young swimmers to feats of natation, and he very often beat them, carrying off from them cups and medals, to their deep disgust. He was nearly eighty when he filled us, one evening, with alarm by bending the drawing-room poker to an angle in striking it upon the strained muscles of his fore-arm. He was very vain of his physical accomplishments, and he used to declare that he was in training to be a centenarian.—GOSSE, EDMUND, 1899, *Recollections of "Orion" Horne, North American Review*, vol. 168, pp. 491, 497.

ORION
1843

"Orion" will be admitted, by every man of genius, to be one of the noblest, if not the very noblest poetical work of the age. Its defects are trivial and conventional—its beauties intrinsic and *supreme*.—POE, EDGAR ALLAN, 1844, *Horne's "Orion," Works*, ed. Stedman and Woodberry, vol. VI, p. 287.

From some cause, which to me has ever been a mystery, "Orion" has not become popular. It contains passages to which, for description, it is difficult to find anything superior; and the thought or idea carried through the whole never flags.—TROLLOPE, ANTHONY, 1881, *Henry Wadsworth Longfellow, North American Review*, vol. 132, p. 395.

His masterpiece, "Orion," is a great poem, characterised by a severe majesty and an admirable breadth of effect.—ROBERTS, CHARLES G. D., 1888, ed. *Poems of Wild Life*, p. 233, note.

It is not true that "Orion" is Horne's only work of value; but it is so much better than anything else of his, and so characteristic of him, that by all but students the rest may be neglected. And it is an example of the melancholy but frequently exemplified truth, that few things are so dangerous, nay, so fatal to enduring literary fame, as the production of some very good work among a mass of, if not exactly rubbish, yet inferior stuff. I do not think it extravagant to say that if Horne had written nothing but "Orion" and had died comparatively young after writing it, he would have enjoyed very high rank among English poets. For, though doubtless a little weighted with "purpose," it is a very fine poem indeed, couched in a strain of stately and not second-hand blank verse, abounding in finished and effective passages, by no means destitute of force and meaning as a whole, and mixing some passion with more than some real satire. But the rather childish freak of its first publication probably did it no good, and it is quite certain that the author's long life and unflagging production did it much harm.—SAINTSBURY, GEORGE, 1896, *A History of Nineteenth Century Literature*, p. 117.

I confess that I have often tried to appreciate his *Farthing Epic* and other effusions, but I have laid the books down, wondering that such works should meet with appreciation, save on some principle of mutual insurance.—HAZLITT, W. CAREW, 1897, *Four Generations of a Literary Family*, vol. I, p. 162.

"Orion" is Horne's masterpiece. The philosophic thought clogs the epic movement, but the thought is weighty enough, and expressed with sufficient terseness and force, to be worthy of attention for its own sake. The verse is almost always good and sometimes excellent. Horne is indebted more to Keats than to anyone else. Sometimes he appears to echo him consciously; at other times the reminiscence is probably unconscious. But as Horne was always a bold and original thinker his discipleship was altogether good for him. The sonorous quality of his verse is partly due to his model; the meaning remains his own.—WALKER, HUGH, 1897, *The Age of Tennyson*, p. 65.

GENERAL

With an eager wish to do justice to his "Gregory the Seventh," we have never yet found exactly that opportunity we desired. Meantime, we looked, with curiosity, for what the British critics would say of a work which, in the boldness of its conception, and in the fresh originality of its management, would necessarily fall beyond the routine of their customary verbiage. We saw nothing, however, that either could or should be understood—nothing, certainly, that was worth understanding. The tragedy itself was, unhappily, not devoid of the ruling cant of the day, and its critics (that cant incarnate) took their cue from some of its infected passages, and proceeded forthwith to rhapsody and æsthetics, by way of giving a common-sense public an intelligible idea of the book.—POE, EDGAR ALLAN, 1844, *Horne's "Orion," Works*, ed. Stedman and Woodberry, vol. VI, p. 262.

When you get Mr. Horne's book you will understand how, after reading just the first and the last poems, I could not help speaking a little coldly of it—and in fact, estimating his power as much as you can do, I did think and do, that the last was unworthy of him, and that the first might have been written by a writer of one tenth of his faculty. But last night I read the "Monk of Swineshead Abbey" and the "Three Knights of Camelott" and "Bedd Gelert" and found them all of different stuff, better, stronger, more consistent, and read them with pleasure and admiration. . . . Mr. Horne succeeds better on a larger canvass, and with weightier material; with blank verse rather than lyrics. He cannot make a fine stroke. He wants subtlety and elasticity in the thought and expression. Remember, I admire him honestly and earnestly. No one has admired more than I the "Death of Marlowe," scenes in "Cosmo," and "Orion" in much of it. But now tell me if you can accept with the same stretched out hand all these lyrical poems? I am going to write to him as much homage as can come truly.—BROWNING, ELIZABETH BARRETT, 1846, *To Robert Browning*, Jan. 6; *The Letters of Robert Browning and Elizabeth Barrett Browning*, vol. I, pp. 370, 371.

I am not sure that in natural gifts he is inferior to his most famous contemporaries. That he here receives brief attention is due to the disproportion between the sum of his productions and the length of his career,—for he still is an occasional and eccentric contributor to letters. There is something Elizabethan in Horne's writings, and no less in a restless love of adventure which has borne him wandering and fighting around the world, and breaks out in the robust and virile, though uneven, character of his poems and plays. He has not only, it would seem, dreamed of life, but lived it. Taken together, his poetry exhibits carelessness, want of tact and wise method, but often the highest beauty and power. A fine erratic genius, in temperament not unlike Beddoes and Landor, he has not properly utilized his birthright. His verse is not improved by a certain transcendentalism which pervaded the talk and writings of a set in which he used to move.—STEDMAN, EDMUND CLARENCE, 1875-87, *Victorian Poets*, p. 248.

Perhaps it can be said that the name of the late Richard Hengist Horne is more widely known, in this country, than his works. But, however this may be, it certainly is a fact that he is more particularly remembered by the lovers of Mrs. Browning as having been the one to first introduce her to the literary world. He lived to see that that was an honor indeed.—GOULD, ELIZABETH PORTER, 1884, *Mrs. Browning and "Orion" Horne, The Critic*, vol. 4, p. 245.

I have always felt that R. H. Horne is one of the few modern poets likely to be remembered by future generations—at all events by the students of our literature—as having written really good and memorable poetry. I have never myself, indeed, been able thoroughly to sympathize with the almost unqualified eulogium which (if I remember rightly) Edgar Poe once passed upon "Orion," although there is assuredly very much to admire in it. But in an age singularly unfruitful in English dramatic poetry of a high order, Horne's "Cosmo de Medici" and "The Death of Marlowe" stand out as not unworthy of a place beside "Colombe's Birthday," "The Blot in the 'Scutcheon," and "Pippa Passes."— NOEL, RODEN, 1884, *Letter, March 24; Literary Anecdotes of the Nineteenth Century*, ed. Nicoll and Wise, p. 246.

Horne was a talented, energetic, and versatile writer. His epic and his early tragedies have much force and fire, but they are not born for immortality.—BULLEN, A. H., 1891, *Dictionary of National Biography*, vol. XXVII, p. 359.

Horne, in 1885, had already published his fine tragedy of "Cosmo de Medici," in five acts, and "The Death of Marlowe," in one act, works with more of the vigorous character and high poetic quality of the Elizabethan dramatist than anything that has been written since the Elizabethan days. . . . A man of indubitable genius he yet wanted that one element of genius, humour. Still he merited far more than he had of contemporary appreciation, and very much of his verse may rank with the very best of that of the nineteenth century poets. . . . I always think of Horne as one who ought to have been great, he came so near to it in his work, in the greatness and nobility of his best writings. — LINTON, WILLIAM JAMES, 1894, *Three Score and Ten Years, pp.* 20, 21, 23.

It was a misfortune both for himself and for literature that his circumstances were not such as to take him out of the turmoil of earning his livelihood by the exercise of his really extraordinary talents. His ingenuity and inventiveness, which were almost without limit, were constantly in requisition to produce something remarkable. Had he been able to sit apart "out of the hurley-burley" and contemplate his best subjects in a philosophic spirit, concentrating his energies of mind on the production of the best result, we might have had greater work from him. As it is, it may be doubted whether he would not stand better with posterity if he had left, instead of a vast mass of varied and clever literature, only some dozen or so of lyrical poems, "Orion," "Cosmo de Medici," "The Death of Marlowe," and "Judas Iscariot;" for these are in their own way masterly productions, and strong enough to bear each its burden of conscious instructiveness.—FORMAN, HARRY BUXTON, 1894, *The Poets and the Poetry of the Century, John Keats to Lord Lytton*, ed. Miles, p. 493.

He was a very remarkable poet for seven or eight years, and a tiresome and uninspired scribbler for the rest of his life. His period of good work began in 1837, when he published "Cosmo de Medici" and "The Death of Marlowe;" it closed in 1843, with the publication of "Orion," and the composition of all that was best in the "Ballad Romances." If any one wished to do honor to the *name* of poor old Horne — and in these days far less distinguished poets than he receive the honors of rediscovery — the way to do it would be to publish in one volume the very best of his writings, and nothing more. The badness of the bulk of his later verse is outside all calculation. How a man who had once written so well as he, could ever come to write, for instance, "Bible Tragedies" (1881), is beyond all skill of the literary historian to comprehend.—GOSSE, EDMUND, 1899, *Recollections of "Orion" Horne, North American Review, vol.* 168, *p.* 492.

Henry Fawcett
1833–1884

Born, at Salisbury, 26 Aug. 1833. Educated at school at Alderbury, 1841 (?)–47; at Queenwood Agricultural Coll., 3 Aug. 1847–49; at King's Coll. School, London, 1849–52. To Peterhouse, Cambridge, Oct. 1852; migrated to Trinity Hall, Oct. 1853; B. A., 1856; M. A., 1859. Fellowship at Trinity Hall, Dec. 1856. Entered at Lincoln's Inn, 26 Oct. 1854; settled there as student, Nov. 1856. Visit to Paris, 1857. Accidentally blinded while shooting, 17 Sept. 1858. Returned to Trinity Hall. Read papers on Political Economy at British Assoc., Sept. 1859; Member of Polit. Econ. Club, 1861. Prof. of Polit. Econ., Cambridge, 27 Nov. 1863 to 1884. Resigned Fellowship, 1866, to be re-elected same year under new statutes permitting marriage. Married Millicent Garrett, 23 April, 1867. Life spent in London, except during lectures at Cambridge. Read paper on "Proportional Representation" at Social Science Assoc., 1859. M. P. for Brighton, 12 July 1865; re-elected, Nov. 1868. M. P. for Hackney, 24 April 1874; re-elected, 31 March 1880, as Postmaster-General. Contrib., at various times to "Macmillan's Magazine," and "Fortnightly Review" (List of articles is given in Leslie Stephen's "Life" of Fawcett). Severe illness in Nov. 1882. Doctor of Polit. Econ. Würzburg, 1882. F. R. S., 1882. Lord Rector of Glasgow Univ., and Hon. LL. D., degree, 1883. Corresponding member of Institute of France, 1884. Died, at Cambridge, 6 Nov. 1884; buried at Trumpington. *Works:* "Mr. Hare's Reform Bill, simplified and explained," 1860; "The Leading Clauses of a new Reform Bill," 1860; "Manual of Political Economy," 1863; "The Economic Position of the British Labourer," 1865; "Pauperism," 1871; "Essays and Lectures," (with **Mrs.**

Fawcett), 1872; "The Present Position of the Government" (from "Fortnightly Review"), 1872; "Speeches on Some Current Political Questions," 1873; "Free Trade and Protection," 1878; "Indian Finance" (from "Nineteenth Century"), 1880; "State Socialism" (from his "Manual of Polit. Econ."), 1883; "Labour and Wages" (from "Manual of Polit. Econ."), 1884. *Life:* by Leslie Stephen, 1885.—SHARP R. FARQUHARSON, 1897, *A Dictionary of English Authors, p.* 97.

PERSONAL

No one can look upon him but he will see on his face the characters of courage, frankness, and intelligence. He is six feet two inches in height, very blonde, his light hair and complexion and his smooth beardless face giving him something of the air of a boy. His features are at once strongly marked and regular. He narrowly escaped being handsome, and his expression is very winning. His countenance is habitually serene, and no cloud or frown ever passes over it. His smile is gentle and winning. It is probable that no blind man has ever before been able to enter upon so important a political career as Professor Fawcett, who, yet under forty years of age, is the most influential of the independent Liberals in Parliament. From the moment that he took his seat in that body he has been able—and this is unusual—to command the close attention of the House. He has a clear fine voice, speaks with the utmost fluency, has none of the university intonation and none of the hesitation or uneasy attitudes of the average Parliamentary speaker. He scorns all subterfuges, speaks honestly his whole mind, and comes to the point. At times he is eloquent, and he is always interesting.—CONWAY, MONCURE DANIEL, 1875, *Professor Fawcett, Harper's Magazine, vol.* 50, *p.* 353.

I have made a new Acquaintance here. Professor Fawcett. . . . when Wright was gone called on me, and also came and smoked a Pipe one night here. A thoroughly unaffected, unpretending man; so modest indeed that I was ashamed afterwards to think how I had harangued him all the Evening, instead of getting him to instruct me. But I would not ask him about his Parliamentary Shop: and I should not have understood his Political Economy: and I believe he was very glad to be talked to instead, about some of those he knew, and some whom I had known.—FITZGERALD, EDWARD, 1882, *Letters to Fanny Kemble, Sep.* 1, *pp.* 238, 239.

There were two or three questions on the papers this evening to Mr. Fawcett. Among others one by Mr. Sexton in reference to the negotiations between the Post Office and the Midland Great Western Railway. Mr. Shaw Lefevre announced that Mr. Fawcett was ill with pleurisy, and that probably he would not be able to resume his duties for some time. There was immediately a murmur of sympathy throughout the House, where Mr. Fawcett was the most popular of men and of Ministers. Within two hours after this announcement it was known that he was dead. The regret for this sudden and unexpected termination of a picturesque, useful, and manly career struck everybody with sorrow, and one could see how faces changed their expression as the information was passed from one member to another.—O'CONNOR, T. P., 1884, *Gladstone's House of Commons, Nov.* 6, *p.* 465.

A momentary silence 'mid the strife
Of tongues, and thro' the land a deeper hush
Than broods o'er autum woodlands all aflush
With glory eloquent of fading life,
Bespeak a common loss and sorrow rife
In English hearts and homes, for one who sought
No selfish ends, but ever planned and wrought
For all men's good. Now fall'n upon the wife,
Whose love illumined his darkness, is the Night;
And he who, dutiful and undismayed,
Confronted adverse Fate, and, in despite
Of his own blindness, evermore essayed
To win for others larger hope and light,
Beholds the splendor that shall never fade.
—ROLPH, JOHN L. F., 1884, *Henry Fawcett: In Memoriam, National Review, vol.* 4, *p.* 568.

Fawcett's friends always spoke of him as a man to be loved, and no doubt they were right, but to those outside of that circle he seemed pre-eminently a man to be respected. What has been said of him since his death proves how universal the respect was, and how high was the opinion the world had formed of his character and abilities. It is sometimes said the world takes a man at his own valuation, and this is perhaps true enough in Fawcett's case. It would he hard to name a man who had a more complete confidence in himself. This confidence was not a vain egotism. It sprang from a reasoned conviction. **He had** a habit of judging by the dry light of reason, and he applied this process to himself as to other subjects of interest. He had no doubts about anything. He was as sure of himself as of a proposition in geometry. His mind had a mathematical cast which to a certain extent unfitted him for politics. He argued in straight lines, and lacked the flexibility which is in most cases a condition of success in English public life. When he had demonstrated that a thing ought to be on principle, he became impatient of those who would have shown him it was impossible in the circumstances, or premature.—SMALLEY, GEORGE W., 1884-91, *Mr. Fawcett, London Letters and Some Others*, vol. I, p. 81.

Various proposals were immediately made to honour Fawcett's memory. A statue is to be erected in the market-place of Salisbury, near a statue previously erected to Sydney Herbert, on the spot where he took his first childish steps, and to which he always returned with fresh affection. In Cambridge there is to be a portrait by Mr. Herkomer of the figure so familiar for a generation. Measures are still in progress for some appropriate memorial in India to the man who showed so unique a power of sympathy with a strange race. A national memorial is in preparation, which is to consist of a scholarship for the blind at Cambridge, some additional endowment for the Royal Normal College for the Blind at Norwood, and a tablet is to be erected in Westminster Abbey. A memorial is also to be erected in recognition of his services to women; and the inhabitants of Trumpington are placing a window to his memory in their church. Such monuments are but the outward symbols of the living influence still exercised upon the hearts of his countrymen by a character equally remarkable for masculine independence and generous sympathy.—STEPHEN, LESLIE, 1885, *Life of Henry Fawcett*, p. 468.

His commanding form would have been noticeable under any circumstances. . . . Not less familiar was his well-known form to boaters on the Cam, or to skaters on the Fens in times of frost. His marvellous courage was seen in things small as well as great. Swimming, rowing, and skating, as well as riding, were amongst his accomplishments, and whatever skill he possessed was pardonably exaggerated by the admiration of sympathising beholders. When to this general familiarity with his stalwart figure is added the unfailing kindliness and cheerfulness of his manner to every one, whether high or low, it becomes easy to understand why in his case the public loss has been mourned with something of the tenderness of private sorrow. His memory for the tones of a voice was remarkable, and people who had only spoken to him once or twice were astonished, as well as gratified, to find that when they addressed him again they had no need to remind him of their names, for scarcely had a word been spoken before the hearty response showed the readiness of his recognition.—PICTON, J. ALLANSON, 1885, *Professor Fawcett, Good Words*, vol. 26, p. 31.

The member for Brighton was soon a popular member. The tall, manly figure, led about by an attendant, was gazed at with reverence in the House of Commons. His political creed gave an emphasis of individuality to a man who could so completely master himself. Nor were his politics—such as he put before the House—calculated to give offence to honest adversaries. Perhaps his views upon India—a subject which was so dear to him, that he got the sobriquet of the "Member for India"—were more likely to stir party hostility than his views upon toleration or upon Reform. . . . It is, however, to Fawcett's management of the Post Office that we naturally turn with the greatest interest; for it was as Post Master General that he won the highest laurels which were bestowed on him by the national gratitude.—MARSHALL, A. F., 1886, *A Blind Worker, The Month*, vol. 56, pp. 246, 247.

Mr. Henry Fawcett, the blind spectacled Postmaster-General, is one of the tallest and most sinewy looking men in the House. He is a man of great intellectual vigor, tenacity of purpose, and courage mingled with caution, and a trenchant parliamentary debater as well as an admirable platform-speaker. On account of his profound knowledge of Indian affairs and sympathy with the people of that country, he is sometimes called "the member for India;" and when, with little money, he was trying to force the portals of "the rich man's club" at Westminster, a great number of very poor Hindoos subscribed a sum sufficient to defray the cost of his return for Hackney.—MATHEWS, WILLIAM, 1887, *The House of Commons; Men, Places and Things*, p. 197.

GENERAL

True heart! We feel in England and o'er sea
The whole of thy great life-work nobly planned
Not only for thyself the victory,
But in thy triumph triumphs all thy land,
Which, sad from end to end for loss of thee,
Of civic heroes counts no life more grand.
—MARSTON, PHILIP BOURKE, 1884, *In Memory of Right Hon. H. Fawcett, M. P.*

O strenuous spirit, darkling hast thou shined!
O light unto thy country, who hast lent
Eyes to the dim hope of the ignorant!
Why the great form of Justice standeth blind
Thou dost make plain. From thy immur'd mind
Thou, as from prison-walls, thy voice has sent
Forceful for faculty's enfranchisement,
And free commerce of sympathies that bind
Men into nations; even thy harsh divorce
From the familiar gossip of the eyes
Moved thee to speed sweet human intercourse
By art's most swift and kindly embassies:
So didst thou bless all life, thyself being free
Of faction, that last bond of liberty.
—FIELD, MICHAEL, 1884(?) *Henry Fawcett.*

The language was lucid, the arrangement good, the ideas just. You read with pleasure, because you felt yourself in the hands of a man who thoroughly understood his subject and instructed you; but the light had little warmth, and seemed to shine with equal monotony on every part. There was even in his way of applying economic doctrines to practical problems a touch of what people called pedantry, but which might be better described as an extreme rigidity, a disposition to see only the blacks and whites of a question, and not to appreciate the subtler considerations which come in, and must be allowed to modify the broader conclusions of economic science.—BRYCE, JAMES, 1884, *The Late Mr. Fawcett, The Nation, vol. 39. p. 457.*

Fawcett's writings display a keen and powerful, if rather narrow, intellect. He adhered through life to the radicalism of J. S. Mill; he was a staunch free-trader in economic questions, an earnest supporter of co-operation, but strongly opposed to socialism, and a strenuous advocate of the political and social equality of the sexes. His animating principle was a desire to raise the position of the poor. He objected to all such interference as would weaken their independence or energy, and though generally favourable on this account to the *laissez-faire* principle, disavowed it when, as in the case of the Factory Acts, he held that interference could protect without enervating.—STEPHEN, LESLIE, 1885, *Dictionary of National Biography, vol. XVIII.*

Certainly, nobody has less rubbish in his mind than Fawcett. But he did not escape the dangers which attend an exclusive devotion to work which promises to yield a directly useful result. As his biographer frankly admits, he had some of that narrowness and rigidity from which the practical man seldom escapes. He was not an original thinker. Even in political economy he did no more than illustrate and spread the ideas of minds broader and subtler than his own. But he had a healthy love of facts, and a power of using them which made him, wherever a calm judgment was needed, a man to lean upon. If, moreover, his intellectual interests were comparatively few, there was no trace of narrowness in his moral nature.—MACDONELL, G. P., 1885, *Life of Henry Fawcett, The Academy, vol. 28, p. 385.*

This book ["Manual of Political Economy"] probably did more to popularise the study than almost any other that has been published.—PICTON, J. ALLANSON, 1885, *Professor Fawcett, Good Words, p. 33.*

With great thinkers of the eighteenth century Fawcett firmly believed in Reason, and was prepared to make Reason, as far as she would carry him, the guide of his life. This earnest desire to follow out in practice the truths which his mind grasped, is visible both in his dealings with others and in his conduct of his own life, and it is this simple acting upon simple convictions which so greatly distinguishes him from the crowd who have neither definite beliefs nor fixed courses of action. . . . It is curious to see, as one follows Fawcett's political career, what simplicity and vigor the genuine adherence to very elementary economical or moral axioms could give to the conduct of a member of Parliament.—DICEY, A.V., 1886, *Stephen's Fawcett, The Nation, vol. 42, p. 15.*

He published, besides his manual, "Pauperism: Its Causes and Remedies," "Speeches on Some Current Political Questions," and "Free Trade and Protection," etc. In his economic writings Professor Fawcett was an uncompromising advocate of free trade and the individualistic economic doctrines with which that party is associated; in politics he was a Liberal.—GILMAN, PECK, AND COLBY, 1903, *The New International Encyclopædia, vol. VII, p. 256.*

Wendell Phillips
1811–1884

American Abolitionist, was the descendant of a Boston family of aristocratic leanings. Educated at Harvard University, he was called to the bar in 1834; but in 1837 joined the movement for the abolition of slavery, and two years later retired from his profession because he could no longer abide by the oath of fidelity to the United States Constitution. His speeches on behalf of the movement were full of inspiration and mastery of the resources of oratory, notably that uttered over the grave of Brown, the Harper's Ferry insurrectionist, in 1859. He spoke with equal eloquence on temperance and the emancipation of women. When, after the Civil War, Garrison ceased to be president of the Anti-Slavery Society, on the ground that the cause was won, Phillips took his place, and succeeded in winning for the negro full citizenship. In 1870 he resigned his office, and his organ, "The Anti-Slavery Standard," was converted into a monthly magazine. Wendell Phillips continued until a few years before his death to advocate social and moral reforms upon the platform. "Speeches, Letters, and Lectures" (1863); "A Memorial of W. Phillips from the City of Boston" (1884).—SANDERS, LLOYD C., ed., 1887, *Celebrities of the Century*, p. 827.

PERSONAL

He stood upon the world's broad threshold; wide
The din of battle and of slaughter rose;
He saw God stand upon the weaker side,
That sank in seeming loss before its foes:
Many there were who made great haste and sold
Unto the cunning enemy their swords,
He scorned their gifts of fame, and power, and gold,
And, underneath their soft and flowery words,
Heard the cold serpent hiss; therefore he went
And humbly joined him to the weaker part,
Fanatic named, and fool, yet well content
So he could be the nearer to God's heart,
And feel its solemn pulses sending blood
Through all the widespread veins of endless good.
—LOWELL, JAMES RUSSELL, 1843, *Wendell Phillips*.

May we not think now that the task of binding up the wounds of a bruised and shattered country, of reconciling jarring interests thrown into new and delicate relationships, of bringing peace to sore and wearied nerves, and abiding quiet to those who are fated to dwell side by side in close proximity, may require faculties of a wider and more varied adaptation, and a spirit breathing more of Calvary and less of Sinai? It is no discredit to the good sword gapped with the blows of a hundred battle fields, to hang it up in all honor, as having done its work. It has made place for a thousand other forces and influences each powerless without it, but each now more powerful and more efficient in their own field. Those who are so happy as to know Mr. Phillips personally, are fully aware how entirely this unflinching austerity of judgment, this vigorous severity of exaction, belong to the public character alone, how full of genial urbanity they find the private individual. We may be pardoned for expressing the hope that the time may yet come when he shall see his way clear to take counsel in public matters with his own kindly impulses, and that those genial traits which render his private intercourse so agreeable, may be allowed to modify at least his public declarations.—STOWE, HARRIET BEECHER, 1868, *Men of Our Times*, p. 501.

The aid which Mr. Phillips gave to the cause of woman was characterized like all his work, by a great strength of purpose, and solidity of moral conviction. There was nothing airy, fanciful, or voluntary in his advocacy of woman suffrage. The solidity of Mr. Phillip's belief was matched by the extension of his views. Some have spoken of him as having shown a failure of judgment in his later years. He was not infallible. But his view of justice was infallible, for it was founded upon the truth of God himself. . . . Wendell Phillips would have thrown open to women the doors of every opportunity, of every career. He would have had them free as air in the streets, which he wished to see pure enough for the presence of angels, and which, we know, would only attain that purity when the angels of humanity should walk in them. But let no one think or say that this heart's desire of his involved the desertion of home and the neglect of its duties. His own devotion to the woman who was home to him shows us that he knew the value of the fireside, and its dear and sacred intimacy.—HOWE, JULIA WARD, 1884, *Commemoration, Faneuil Hall*, Feb. 9.

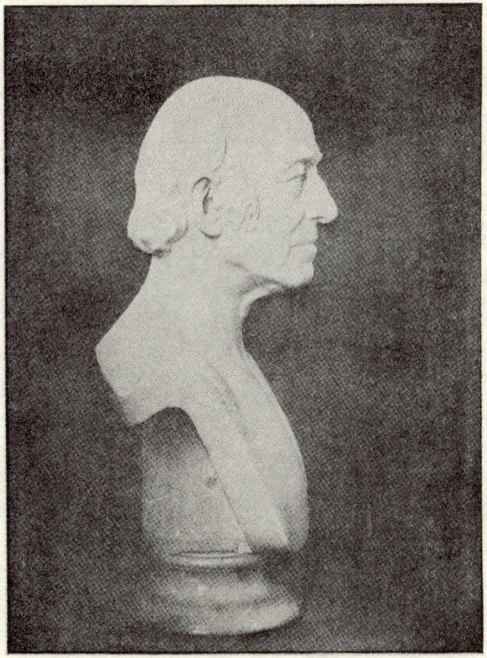

WENDELL PHILLIPS

Engraving by F. T. Stuart.

WILLIAM LLOYD GARRISON

From the Bust by Anne Whitney

Few names that the history of the commonwealth of Massachusetts has underscored are more worthy of being cherished than that of the Phillips family; and it is a matter for public congratulation, that there exist to-day such worthy monuments for its perpetuation as the two academies of Andover, Mass., and of Exeter, N. H. We have intimated that these two institutions are monuments to a family. They are so, because they were built up, not by the wisdom and self-denial of one individual of that family, but by the very remarkable unanimity of aim and coincidence of judgment of six members of it, representing three generations. Still more essentially are they so, because they were the outcome of a marked nobleness of spirit and elevation of character, that have not ceased to distinguish representatives of the Phillips family through nine generations.—AUSTIN, GEORGE LOWELL, 1884, *The Life and Times of Wendell Phillips*, p. 17.

I pass from conversations in the privacy of his study and library, to say a word or two of what Mr. Phillips was in his still more private affections. I never saw his wife; though in his conversations and his correspondence with me he often spoke of her, and it was my privilege to exchange many communications with her. He was a lover all his life.... She was, as he wrote once "his council, his guide, his inspiration." Within a year or two, in correspondence with him, I ventured to call her his Egeria; and I think they were both greatly pleased with her being so called.... So the wife of Mr. Phillips was his Egeria, his councillor, his guide, and his inspiration.—BUCKINGHAM, EDGAR, 1884, *The Life and Times of Wendell Phillips*, ed. Austin, p. 89.

Since then we have lost Wendell Phillips, and all the town has been debating whether he was the noblest or the basest man that ever lived, and we discriminating souls have decided that he was a mixture of the two.—BROOKS, PHILLIPS, 1884, *To Mr. Cooper*, Feb. 12; *Life and Letters*, ed. Allen, vol. II, p. 54.

His comprehensive philanthropy had made him, even during the anti-slavery contest, the untiring advocate of other great reforms. His powerful presentation of the justice and reason of the political equality of women, at Worcester, in 1851, more than any other single impulse, launched the question upon the sea of popular controversy. In the general statement of principle nothing has been added to that discourse; in vivid and effective eloquence of advocacy it has never been surpassed. All the arguments for independence echoed John Adams in the Continental Congress. All the pleas for applying the American principle of representation to the wives and mothers of American citizens echo the eloquence of Wendell Phillips at Worcester.—CURTIS, GEORGE WILLIAM, 1884, *Wendell Phillips, A Eulogy Delivered Before the Municipal Authorities of Boston, Mass., April 18*, p. 32.

After a long and stormy life his sun went down in glory. All the English-speaking people on the globe have written among the names that shall never die, the name of that scoffed, detested, mob-beaten Wendell Phillips.... He has taught a lesson that the young will do well to take heed to—the lesson that the most splendid gifts and opportunities and ambitions may be best used for the dumb and the lowly.... He belongs to the race of giants, not simply because he was in and of himself a great soul, but because he bathed in the providence of God, and came forth scarcely less than a god; because he gave himself to the work of God upon earth, and inherited thereby, or had reflected upon him, some of the majesty of his master. When the pigmies are all dead, the noble countenance of Wendell Phillips will still look forth, radiant as a rising sun—a sun that will never set. He has become to us a lesson, his death an example, his whole history an encouragement to manhood—to heroic manhood.—BEECHER, HENRY WARD, 1884, *Wendell Phillips, Plymouth Pulpit, Sunday Morning*, Feb. 10.

In his outward man, Wendell Phillips was cast in classic mold. His oratorical mother was Mâyâ the Eloquent, and his father was Jupiter the Thunderer. Above the middle height, his form was patterned after the best models of manhood, and closely resembled, by actual measurements, the Apollo Belvedere. He was neither stout nor thin, but retained from youth to age his suppleness and grace of proportion. Of nervous sanguine temperament, his complexion was ruddy, and gave him the appearance of one whose soul looked through and glorified the body; hence that singular radiance which was often startling. The head was finely set upon broad shoulders and a deep chest. The chin was full and strong; the lips red and somewhat compressed; the nose aquiline; the eyes blue, small but piercing; the brow both broad and high. . . . In middle life he lost a large part of his hair; but this only served the more clearly to reveal the superb contour of the skull. His profile was fine-cut as a cameo. In expression the face was at once intellectual and serene; it wore a look of resolute goodness. His pose was easy and natural, every change of attitude being a new revelation of manly grace. No nobler physique ever confronted an audience.—MARTYN, CARLOS, 1889, *Wendell Phillips as an Orator, The Forum Magazine, vol. 8, pp. 305, 306.*

> Short-stemmed and curt
> His wreath should be, and braided by strong hands,
> Hindered with sword-hilt, while the braider stands
> With loin upgirt.
> Too late to urge
> Thy tardy crown. Draw back, O Northern blond!
> Let black hands take, to bind the Southern frond,
> A severed scou:ge!
> Haughty and high,
> And deaf to all the thunders of the throng,
> He heard the lowest whisper of his wrong
> The slave could sigh.
> In some pent street,
> O prophet-slaying city of his care,
> Pour out thine eyes, loose thy repentant hair,
> And kiss his feet!
> . . . .
> Last from the fight,
> So moves the lion, with unhasting stride,
> Dragging the slant spear, broken in his side—
> And gains the height!

—STAFFORD, WENDELL PHILLIPS, 1890, *Wendell Phillips, Atlantic Monthly, vol. 66, pp. 35, 36.*

> No fetter but galled his wrist,
> No wrong that was not his own.
> What if those eloquent lips
> Curled with the old-time scorn?
> What if in needless hours
> His quick hand closed on the hilt?
> 'T was the smoke from the well-won fields
> That clouded the veteran's eyes.
> A fighter this to the end!

—ALDRICH, THOMAS BAILEY, 1891, *A Monody on the Death of Wendell Phillips, Century Magazine, vol. 41, p. 579.*

One could but speak of him after all and preëminently as "a gentleman!" His true, enfleshed democracy was born of that exquisite courtesy towards all humankind which was the breath of his very being. His scholarship and eloquence were its natural attributes as much as were his beauty of person and grace of manner. I recall him clearly, dressed simply with a loose short robe in place of a coat, spotless linen, no jewelry of any kind—stud, chain, or ring—well-worn trousers, a light vest, and, as I recall, slippered feet. He was when standing, a figure of graceful model and height, five feet eleven, of fair complexion, with soft reddish-gold hair, clean-shaven cheeks and jaw, a face that always seemed to me to be illumined from within. The eyes were rather small and deep-set, but penetrative, a light-blue gray in hue; the head was large well proportioned and balanced. Except as to the height of the imperial forehead and the rounded coronal beyond and above, its size, breadth, and height would not strike one at first. The full face was very kindly yet grave and quiet in expression. The eyes held you firmly and at once. The profile was noble and exquisite in line, effect, and proportion. The nose, at roots broad, at nostrils full, yet fine and even delicate in shape, was a well-moulded Roman, approaching the aquiline in form. Below was a longish upper lip, a mouth of strength and repressed lines, drawn down slightly at the ends—a touch of the lion's character; lips well-rounded but not full; below, a strongly defined chin, not large or heavy, but fully indicative of will-power and firmness. The curving eyebrows were large and wide apart, approaching the antique in shape. But it was a noble forehead, the height above the brows, and the depth from the ears forward and upward, that commanded attention. He was possessed and moulded of grace. His pose was always statuesque. His garb was simple, refined, neutral, yet it became his own and was part of his personality. In conversation, Mr. Phillips' voice was simply delicious—low, even-toned, softly modulated, and yet possessing a clear, easy distinctness of enunciation which was a great delight to listeners.—HINTON, RICHARD J., 1895, *Wendell Phillips, The Arena, vol. 13, p. 230.*

While Mr. Phillips was a raging lion in denouncing iniquity wherever he found it, among his friends and in his family he was the most gentle and affectionate of men.—HALE, EDWARD EVERETT, 1899, ed. *Autobiography, Diary and Correspondence of James Freeman Clarke, p. 141.*

ORATORY

Some of us remember the Lovejoy meeting held in Faneuil Hall in '37, and the speech of the State's Attorney, casting scorn and ridicule upon the martyr, and how a young man, seizing his chance, sprang to his feet, held fast the chairman's eye till he reached the platform, and, amid mingled applause and hisses, poured forth such a flood of indignant invective, such royal reason, that his victim never recovered from the stroke. It was the first intimation of the young orator's gifts. And from that time to the present, his name and fame have made way throughout the country; the rumour of him has crossed the seas, and he stands now the first of American orators, with honors yet to be won in new fields for which his genius has been fitted by wide acquaintance with the people, and by past controversies with powerful opponents. — ALCOTT, A. BRONSON, 1867, *Wendell Phillips, The Radical, vol. 3, p. 105.*

None who have heard Wendell Phillips can be satisfied with any description of the charm with which these things have been uttered. Standing before the people with the ease of one born for his task, with the authority that comes of lowliness before a great idea, relying absolutely upon the eloquence of his truth, simple almost to coldness even amid his most scathing rebukes, his gestures few and natural, his voice clear and flexible, his serene, high forehead, fair hair, and light blue eye modifying the severity of his low features, he is listened to with alternations of breathless silence and wild outbursts of enthusiasm. He has never made a failure, never lost an opportunity. . . . His foes have never dared listen to him. Mobs sent to break up his meetings have been known to return to their employers, saying, "Never man spake like this man." I have sat under his voice for more than an hour, and it always seemed to have been only a few minutes. Consecrated to "one idea," as the sneerers said, he called about that a wealth of illustration, anecdote, lighting up with it long tracks of history, until one could only regret that his critics did not exchange all their so-called ideas for this one. "Let no one despise the negro any more," said a man of letters who heard him; "he gave us Wendell Phillips."—CONWAY, MONCURE DANIEL, 1871, *Wendell Phillips, Fortnightly Review, vol. 14, p. 71.*

So simple, pure, and direct is the oratory of Mr. Phillips that it evades description. We can dwell upon the manifold beauties of a picture by a great artist; but it is difficult to dilate upon Giotto's O. There it stands. It is without a flaw. It completely answers the purpose for which it was intended. There is nothing more to be said about it. So it is with the eloquence of Mr. Phillips. . . . The orator culls none of the flowers of rhetoric as he goes: you may search in vain through his volume of published speeches for one beautiful metaphor, one brilliant antithesis, one elaborately constructed period. He has no peroration. But, on the other hand, he never utters a sentence that a child might not comprehend; he uses no illustration the force of which would not be apparent to the group about the stove in a country store; he discusses political issues in such a way that the young girl who has come to the lecture with her lover, who never read a debate in Congress in her life, and does not know the names of the Senators from her own State, understands what he says, and is interested. . . . We have said little, after all, of the eloquence of Wendell Phillips, except that it cannot be described. No man who has heard it has ever denied its marvellous power; no man has ever imitated it, or conveyed a conception of its fascination to another; no man who has not heard it will ever know what makes it great.—WOODS, GEORGE BRYANT, 1871(?), *Wendell Phillips as an Orator; Essays, Sketches and Stories, pp. 92, 93, 96.*

As an orator, Mr. Phillips has few equals, and no superiors. His fellow citizens justly look upon him as a most distinguished man, and wherever he speaks he is always greeted with a full house, and an appreciative audience. It is to be regretted that time has made such inroads upon his health as to partially prevent him from appearing upon the lecture platform. His public utterances will always occupy a prominent place among the best thoughts of the age.—WHITMAN, C. M., 1883, *American Orators and Oratory, p. 348.*

The keynote to the oratory of Wendell Phillips lay in this: that it was essentially conversational—the conversational raised to its highest power. Perhaps no orator ever spoke with so little apparent effort, or began so entirely on the plane of his average hearers. It was as if he simply repeated, in a little louder tone, what he had just been saying to some familiar friend at his elbow. The effect was absolutely disarming. Those accustomed to spread-eagle eloquence felt, perhaps, a slight sense of disappointment. Could this easy, effortless man be Wendell Phillips? But he held them by his very quietness; it did not seem to have occurred to him to doubt his power to hold them. The poise of his manly figure, the easy grace of his attitude, the thrilling modulation of his perfectly-trained voice, the dignity of his gesture, the keen penetration of his eye, all aided to keep his hearers in hand. The colloquialism was never relaxed, but it was familiar without loss of dignity. When he said "isn't" and "wasn't" or even, like an Englishman, dropped his g's, it did not seem inelegant; he might almost have been ungrammatical and it would not have impaired the finer air of the man. Then, as the argument went on, the voice grew deeper, the action more animated, and the sentences came in a long sonorous swell, still easy and graceful, but powerful as the soft stretching of a tiger's paw. He could be as terse as Carlyle, or his periods could be as prolonged and cumulative as those of Choate or Evarts; no matter; they carried in either case the same charm.—HIGGINSON, THOMAS WENTWORTH, 1884, *Obituary Notice of Wendell Phillips.*

Eloquent as Mr. Phillips was as a lecturer he was far more effective as a debater. Debate was to him the flint and steel which brought out all his fire. His memory was wonderful. He would listen to an elaborate speech for hours, and, without a single note in writing of what had been said, reply to every part of it as fully and completely as if the speech were written out before him. Those who heard him when not confronted by an opponent, have a very limited comprehension of his amazing resources as a speaker.—DOUGLASS, FREDERICK, 1884, *Address on Wendell Phillips.*

Our glorious summer days sometimes breed, even in the very rankness of their opulence, enervating and unhealthy weaknesses. The air is heavy. Its breath poisons the blood; the pulse of nature is sluggish and mean. Then come the tempest and the thunder. So was it in the body politic, whether the plague was slavery or whatever wrong; whether it was weakness in men of high degree or tyranny over men of low estate; whether it was the curse of the grogshop, or the iron hand of the despot at home or abroad,—so it was that like the lightning Phillips flashed and struck. The scorching, hissing bolt rent the air, now here, now there. From heaven to earth, now wild at random, now straight it shot. It streamed across the sky. It leaped in broken links to a chain of fire. It sometimes fell with reckless indiscrimination alike on the just and on the unjust. It sometimes smote the innocent as well as blasted the guilty. But when the tempest was over, there was a purer and a fresher spirit in the air, and a sweeter health. Louder than the thunder, mightier than the wind, the earthquake, or the fire, a still small voice spake in the public heart, and the public conscience woke.—LONG, JOHN D., 1884–95, *Wendell Phillips, After-Dinner and Other Speeches*, p. 10.

The Phi Beta Kappa Society of Harvard College, which consists of the fifteen or twenty best scholars in each college class, and a few other people whom these choose on the ground of scholarship or intellectual note, is probably in temper as conservative a body as is to be found in New England. It is their custom every year to have a public oration, to which they march in solemn procession, headed by the oldest living members. Toward the end of Mr. Wendell Phillips's life, he was invited to deliver one of these orations, a little to the disquiet of prudent Phi Beta Kappa men, who were aware that his temper was not precisely of a conservative order. A good many went to hear him with much curiosity as to what he might say, and apprehension that they might have to disapprove it by silence at moments which to less balanced minds might seem to call for applause. In the earlier parts of his oration they found themselves agreeably surprised: he said nothing to which they were unprepared to assent, and what he said, he said beautifully. They listened with relief and satisfaction; when the moment for applause came, they cordially applauded. So the oration went on with increasing interest on the part of the audience. Finally, when some fresh moment for applause came, they applauded, as a matter of course; and it was not until they had done so that they stopped to think that what the cleverest of our oratorical tricksters had betrayed them into applauding was no less revolutionary an incident than the then recent assassination of the Emperor Alexander of Russia. Now, this result was attained simply by a skilful use of words: in this case very probably by a deliberately malicious use of words that should make a theatre full of people do a thing which not one of them really wished to do. It was not what he said that they applauded; it was what he implied,—not dynamite and dagger, but that not very clearly defined notion of liberty and freedom and the rights of man, which still appeals to the American heart.—WENDELL, BARRETT, 1891, *English Composition*, p. 243.

It is surprising that so thorough an historian as Von Holst has omitted to make mention of his speech [Lovejoy Speech] which really struck the key-note of the antislavery movement from first to last. As we have it now, revised by its author from the newspaper reports of the time, it is one of the purest, most spontaneous and magnetic pieces of oratory in existence. It deserves a place beside those two famous speeches of James Otis and Patrick Henry which ushered in the war of separation from England. It possesses even a certain advantage, in the fact that it never has been nor is likely to be made use of for school declamations. It will always remain fresh, vigorous, and original as when it was first delivered. — STEARNS, FRANK PRESTON, 1895, *Sketches from Concord and Appledore*, p. 187.

This austere and irreconcilable enthusiast with the blood of the martyr in his veins, was in oratory a pure opportunist. He was a general who went into battle with a force of all arms, but used infantry or artillery or cavalry as each seemed most apt to the moment. He formed his plan, as Napoleon did, on the field and in presence of the enemy. For Phillips—and the fact is vital to all criticism of his oratory—spoke almost always, during twenty-five years of his oratorical life, to a hostile audience. His audiences were often mobs; they often sought to drive him from the platform, sometimes to kill him. He needed all his resources merely to hold his ground and to get a hearing. You cannot compare oratory in those circumstances with oratory in a dress debate, or even with the oratory of a great parliamentary contest. On this last has often hung, no doubt, the life of a ministry. On Phillips's mastery over his hearers depended sometimes his own life, sometimes that of the antislavery cause—with which,

as we now all see and as then hardly anybody saw, was bound up the life of the nation. It was, in my judgment, the oratory of Phillips which insured the maintenance of that great antislavery struggle during the last ten years or more which preceded the War. His oratory must be judged with reference to that—to its object as well as to its rhetorical qualities. He had and kept the ear of the people. To have silenced that silver trumpet would have been to wreck the cause. I speak of the Abolitionist cause by itself—that which relied solely on moral forces and stood completely outside of politics.—SMALLEY, GEORGE W., 1897, *Library of the World's Best Literature*, ed. Warner, vol. XX, p. 11409.

He was the most polished and graceful orator our country ever produced. He spoke as quietly as if he were talking in his own parlor, and almost entirely without gestures, yet he had as great a power over all kinds of audiences as any American of whom we have any record. . . . Eloquent as he was as a lecturer, he was far more effective as a debater. Debate was for him the flint and steel which brought out all his fire. . . . In his style as a debater he resembled Sir Robert Peel, in grace and courtliness of manner and in fluency and copiousness of diction. He never hesitated for a word, or failed to employ the word best fitted to express his thought on the point under discussion. . . . No speaker of his day ever treated a greater variety of topics, nor with more even excellence, than Wendell Phillips. . . . Now that Phillips and Garrison and the era in which they flourished have passed into history, it is common for writers who treat on that period to talk of these two champions of freedom as if they were equals, or of Phillips, even, as if he were Garrison's inferior. Those who knew both men smile at such absurdities. Phillips and Garrison were equals in one respect only—in moral courage and unselfish devotion to the slave. Garrison was a commonplace man in respect to intellectual ability, whereas Phillips was a man of genius of the rarest culture. Garrison was a strong platform speaker. Phillips was one of the greatest orators of the century. Only three men of his time could contest the palm of eloquence with him—Webster, Clay, and Beecher.— POND, J. B., 1900, *Eccentricities of Genius*, pp. 7, 8, 11, 13.

GENERAL

Those who have listened to his perfect utterances, whether in fervid denunciation, indignant protest, or pathetic appeal, seldom have the opportunity to examine in cool blood the true character of the rhetoric that fascinated them. While they watched the magnificent stream of eloquence, it seemed like the course of a river of molten lava. Let them to-day walk over the cooled and hardened surface, and they will find how rough and full of scoriæ the track is. Mr. Phillips's speeches have been collected in a handsome volume, with a portrait. Apart from its relations to the topics it deals with, and viewed simply as a specimen of composition, there is hardly any modern book so disappointing. The apt illustration, the witty anecdote, the emphatic statement, the traces of strong feeling, are to be seen in every discourse. But there are also slang phrases and vituperative epithets, which might be tolerated in an off-hand speech, but which when seen on the printed page debase the style and weaken its force.—UNDERWOOD, FRANCIS H., 1872, *A Hand-Book of English Literature, American Authors*, p. 357.

From the midst of the flock he defended, the
    brave one has gone to his rest;
And the tears of the poor he befriended, their
    wealth of affliction attest.
From the midst of the people is stricken a sym-
    bol they daily saw
Set over against the law-books, of a higher than
    human law;
For his life was a ceaseless protest, and his voice
    was a prophet's cry,
To be true to the truth, and faithful, though the
    world were arrayed for the lie.
—O'REILLY, JOHN BOYLE, 1884, *Wendell Phillips*.

He raised his voice—the scornful smiled,
    A jeering rabble came to hear;
The statesman mocked, the mob reviled,
    Pulpit and press gave little cheer.
He raised his voice—the scoffer frowned,
    Disciples gathered day by day;
In him the living Word was found,
    The light, the life, the truth, the way.
He raised his voice—the crowded hall
    Answered to eloquence and right;
And statesmen heard at last the call
    Of freemen rising in their might.
He raised his voice—the shackles fell,
    And all beneath the stars were free.
Ring out! ring out, centennial bell,
    The living fact of liberty.
—BRUCE, WALLACE, 1887, *Wendell Phillips, Old Homestead Poems*, p. 97.

Phillips spoke always for the poor man, for the downtrodden man, for the underdog in the fight, for the man who could not speak for himself. He spoke violently often. He was not afraid of collision, though he loved peace and the battles of ideas alone. "Peace, if possible," he wrote in the boys' albums, "but justice at any rate." No man must suffer injustice in order that I may be convenienced—the state is not safe so. This Phillips never failed to see, and this enabled him to deal with every problem radically. He knew that there was nothing anarchic in the real fibre of the American people—and he dreaded no temporary or sporadic violences in readjustment; he only dreaded injustice and gout.—MEAD, EDWIN D., 1890, *A Monument to Wendell Phillips, New England Magazine*, vol. 9, p. 539.

Phillips' was the literary or rhetorical temperament, not the scholar's. He had an admirable memory for odds and ends, for available scraps or telling incidents, and he spent his life in training his resources in this direction; but there is no reason to suppose that he had ever in his life studied anything with scholarly thoroughness, except possibly, as he claimed, the English Revolution. This is no reproach to him—he had a great admiration for even the semblance of scholarship in others; but no man can combine everything, and it is a wrong to our young people when we assume that such a thing as universal genius is now practicable. . . . His judgments of men were prompt, fearless, independent, but the judicial quality rarely belonged to them.—HIGGINSON, THOMAS WENTWORTH, 1890, *Martyn's Life of Phillips, Nation*, vol. 51, pp. 328, 329.

As an orator Phillips was what Henry Clay would have been with a Harvard education. To Clay's fire and magnetism he joined Everett's rhetorical art and marvellous vocabulary. As a master of sarcasm and invective he can be compared only to John Randolph of Roanoke, and as a fierce delighter in opposition he may be compared to Webster. But Phillips' orations, like those of Clay, are hard to read. Examined in cold blood, his sentences often seem harsh and even coarse. The fire of his invective was fed at times with unseemly material and he often depended upon his consummate oratorical skill to carry sentences that will hardly pass the searching criticism of the reader.—PATTEE, FRED LEWIS, 1896, *A History of American Literature*, p. 327.

His speeches were true speeches. In print, lacking the magic of his delivery, they are like the words of songs which for lyric excellence need the melodies to which they have once been wedded. Who ever heard him speak remembers his performance with admiration. As the years pass, however, this admiration often proves qualified by suspicion that, with the light which was his, he might have refrained from those denunciations of established order, which, to conservative thinking, still do mischief.—WENDELL, BARRETT, 1900, *A Literary History of American, p.* 350.

Richard Monckton Milnes
Lord Houghton
1809—1885

Born, in London, 19 June, 1809. Educated at Hundhill Hall School, and privately. Matric. Trin. Coll., Camb., Oct. 1827; M. A. 1831; Travelled on Continent, 1832–35. M. P. for Pontefract, 1837–63. Married Hon. Annabel Crewe, 30 July 1851. One of founders of Philobiblon Soc., 1853. Hon. D. C. L., Oxford, 20 June, 1855. Created Baron Houghton, July 1863. F. R. S., 1868. Visit to Canada and U. S. A., 1875. Hon. Fellow, Trinity Coll., Camb., 1875–85. Secretary for Foreign Correspondence, Royal Acad., 1878; Hon. LL. D., Edinburgh, 1878. Trustee of British Museum, 6 May 1881. Pres. London Library, 1882. Died, at Vichy, 11 Aug., 1885. Buried at Fryston. *Works:* "Memorials of a Tour in Some Parts of Greece," 1834; "Poems of Many Years," 1838; "Memorials of a Residence on the Continent, and Historical Poems," 1838 (another edn. called: "Memorials of Many Scenes," 1844); "A Speech on the Ballot," 1839; "Poetry for the People," 1840; "One Tract More" (anon.), 1841; "Thoughts on Purity of Election," 1842; "Palm-Leaves," 1844; "Poems legendary and historical," 1844; "Real Union of England and Ireland," 1845; "Life, Letters, and Literary Remains of John Keats" (2 vols.), 1848; "The Events of 1848," 1849; "Answer to R. Baxter," 1852; "On the Apologies for the Massacre of St. Bartholomew" [1856]; "A Discourse of Witchcraft," 1858; "Good Night and Good Morning," 1859; "Address on Social Economy," 1862; "Monographs," 1873; "Poetical Works" (collected; 2 vols.), 1876. He *edited:* "The Tribute" (with Lord Northampton), 1836; Keats' "Poetical Works," 1854; "Boswelliana," 1856 and 1874; "Another Version of Keats' 'Hyperion'" [1856]; D. Gray's "The Luggie," 1862; Peacock's Works, 1875; Bishop Cranmer's "Recantacyons" (with J. Gairdner), 1885. *Life:* by Sir T. Wemyss Reid, 1890.—SHARP, R. FARQUHARSON, 1897, *A Dictionary of English Authors, p.* 138.

PERSONAL

Milnes, a member of Parliament, a poet, and a man of fashion, a Tory who does not forget the people, and a man of fashion with sensibilities, love of virtue and merit among the simple, the poor, and the lowly.—SUMNER, CHARLES, 1838, *Letter, Life of Lord Houghton*, ed. Reid, vol. I, p. 223.

Never lose your good temper, which is one of your best qualities, and which has carried you hitherto safely through your startling eccentricities. If you turn cross and touchy, you are a lost man. No man can combine the defects of opposite characters. The names of "Cool of the evening," "London Assurance," and "In-I-go Jones" are, I give you my word, not mine. They are of no sort of importance; they are safety valves, and if you could by paying sixpence get rid of them, you had better keep your money. You do me but justice in acknowledging that I have spoken much good of you. I have laughed at you for those follies which I have told you of to your face; but nobody has more readily and more earnestly asserted that you are a very agreeable, clever man, with a very good heart, unimpeachable in all the relations of life, and that you amply deserve to be retained in the place to which you have too hastily elevated yourself by manners unknown to our cold and phlegmatic people.—SMITH, SYDNEY, 1842, *Letter to Richard Monckton Milnes, Apr.* 22; *Life of Lord Houghton,* ed. Reid, vol. I, p. 214.

Mr. Vavasour was a social favourite, a poet, and a real poet, quite a troubadour, as a member of Parliament; travelled, sweet tempered and good hearted, very amusing and very clever. With catholic sympathies and an eclectic turn of mind, Mr. Vavasour saw something good in everybody and everything, which is certainly amiable, and perhaps just, but disqualified, a man in some degree for the business of life, which requires for its conduct a certain degree of prejudice. Mr. Vavasour's breakfasts were renowned. Whatever your creed, class, or merit—one might almost add, your character—you were a welcome guest at his matutinal meal, provided you were celebrated. That qualification, however, was rigidly enforced. Individuals met at his hospitable house who had never met before, but who for years had been cherishing in solitude mutual detestation with all the irritable exaggeration of the literary character. He prided himself on figuring as the social medium by which rival reputations became acquainted, and paid each other in his presence the compliments which veiled their ineffable disgust. All this was very well in the Albany, and only funny; but when he collected his menageries at his ancestral hall in a distant county, the sport sometimes became tragic.—DISRAELI, BENJAMIN (LORD BEACONSFIELD), 1847, *Tancred.*

See him if you have opportunity: a man very easy to *see* and get into flowing talk with; a man of much sharpness of faculty, well tempered by several inches of "Christian *fat*" he has upon his ribs for covering. One of the idlest, cheeriest, most gifted of, fat little men.—CARLYLE, THOMAS, 1847, *To Emerson, Dec. 30; Correspondence of Carlyle and Emerson,* ed. Norton, vol. II, p. 188.

Tell Miss Martineau it is said here that Monckton Milnes refused to be sworn in a special constable that he might be free to assume the post of President of the Republic at a moment's notice.—ARNOLD, MATTHEW, 1848, *To his Mother, April; Letters* ed. Russell, vol. I, p. 8.

He has a beautiful forehead, and most expressive eyes.—LEVERT, OCTAVIA WALTON, 1853, *Souvenirs of Travel,* vol. I, p. 79.

The most interesting feature of his character, as it stands before the world, is his catholicity of sentiment and manner,—his ability to sympathize with all manner of thinkers and speakers, and his superiority to all appearance of exclusiveness, while, on the one hand, rather enjoying the reputation of having access to all houses, and, on the other, being serious and earnest in the deepest recesses of his character.—MARTINEAU, HARRIET, 1855-77, *Autobiography,* ed. Chapman, vol. I, p. 259.

Milnes is a good speaker in Parliament, a good writer of poems, which have been praised by critics who have roosted on his mahogany tree, a man of fashion, and altogether a swell of the first class.—MOTLEY, JOHN LOTHROP, 1858, *To his Wife, May 28; Correspondence,* ed. Curtis, vol. I, p. 228.

> He enters from the common air
> Into that temple dim;
> He learns among those ermined peers
> The diplomatic hymn.
> His peers? Alas! when will they learn
> To grow up peers to him?

—PROCTER, MRS. BRYAN WALLER, 1863, *On Richard Monckton Milnes becoming Baron Houghton.*

I have known him ever since I was a girl, but only as a friendly acquaintance that met frequently upon cordial terms. He was everywhere in London society at the time when I was living very much in it, and I therefore saw him almost wherever I went. He has always been kind and good-natured to me, but, beyond thinking him so, I never felt any great interest in his society, or special desire for his intercourse. He is clever, liberal-minded, extremely good-natured, and good-tempered, and with his very considerable abilities and genuine amiable qualities a valuable and agreeable acquaintance. . . . I had no conversation of any particular interest with him, for he is very deaf, and having lost his teeth, speaks so indistinctly that I, who am also very deaf, could hardly understand half he said; so you see his visit was no particular satisfaction or gratification to me, nor could it possibly have been either to him.—KEMBLE, FRANCES ANN, 1875, *Letter to H——, Nov.* 30; *Further Records,* p. 134.

Monckton Milnes had made his [Carlyle] acquaintance, and invited him to breakfast. He used to say that, if Christ was again on earth, Milnes would ask Him to breakfast, and the Clubs would all be talking of the "good things" that Christ had said. But Milnes, then as always, had open eyes for genius, and reverence for it truer and deeper than most of his contemporaries.—FROUDE, JAMES ANTHONY, 1884, *Thomas Carlyle: A History of his Life in London,* vol. I, p. 133.

> Adieu, dear Yorkshire Milnes! we think not now
> Of coronet or laurel on thy brow;
> The kindest, faithfullest of friends wast thou.

—ALLINGHAM, WILLIAM, 1885, *Lord Houghton, Aug. 11.*

He was famous for the interest he took in notorieties, and especially in notorious sinners, always finding some good reason for taking an indulgent view of their misdeeds. I have heard that, on the occasion of some murderer being hung, his sister, Lady Galway, expressed her satisfaction, saying that if he had been acquitted she would have been sure to have met him next week at one of her brother's Thursday-morning breakfasts.—TAYLOR, SIR HENRY, 1885, *Autobiography, vol. I, p. 273.*

I next met Lord Houghton at dinner in Albany in the winter of 1876–7, where he was the guest of Lieutenant Governor Dorsheimer. The ten intervening years had told upon his personal appearance, but more upon his manner. He seemed very fidgety and nervous. He was constantly doing something that did not then need doing; he was either pulling at his wristbands, or at the sleeves of his under-garments, or trying to get some new effect from his shirt collar. His head struck me as too low on the top to answer the purposes of a man of a very high order of character, or to win love and respect in any great degree, but his pure blue eyes were as striking and attractive as ever. No one could look into them a second time and not see that they were the eyes of no ordinary or commonplace man. He laughed frequently and explosively, apparently as a matter of politeness, rather than because he was amused. His talk was agreeable, and his manner that of a man who had no concern about the impression he was producing—the perfection of high breeding.—BIGELOW, JOHN, 1885, *Some Recollections of Lord Houghton, Harper's Magazine, vol. 71, p. 955.*

His brilliancy and talents in tongue or pen —whether political, social, or literary— were inspired chiefly by goodwill towards man; but he had the same voice and manners for the dirty brat as he had for a duchess, the same desire to give pleasure and good: for both were his wits and his kindness. Once, at Redhill (the Reformatory), where we were with a party, and the chiefs were explaining to us the system in the courtyard, a mean, stunted, villainous-looking little fellow crept across the yard (quite out of order, and by himself), and stole a dirty paw into Mr. Milnes's hand. Not a word passed; the boy stayed quite quiet and quite contented if he could but touch his benefactor who had placed him there. He was evidently not only his benefactor, but his friend.—NIGHTINGALE, FLORENCE, 1889, *Letter to Miss Jane Milnes, Life of Lord Houghton, ed. Reid, vol. II, p. 7.*

I knew Lord Houghton for thirty years or more, and had a warm regard for him. He was kind-hearted and affectionate, keen to discover and eager to proclaim the merit of the unrecognized. He had a reverence for genius wherever he met with it, and few people showed a sounder judgment in literary matters when he was seriously called upon to exercise it. Then with his great ability, wide reading, and knowledge of the world, and his air—half romantic, half satirical— he was very attractive. Lord Houghton was whimsical in his wit, and sometimes more than whimsical in his offhand opinions, which those who understood him received as he intended they should be. He was not unduly taken up with his poetry; he was modest about it.— LOCKER-LAMPSON, FREDERICK, 1889, *Letter to T. Wemyss Reid, Life of Lord Houghton, ed. Reid, vol. II, p. 453.*

The man who had known Wordsworth and Landor and Sydney Smith; who during the greater part of his life had been the friend, trusted and well-beloved, of Tennyson, Carlyle, and Thackeray, was also one of the first to hail the rising genius of Swinburne, and to lend a helping hand to other great writers of a still younger generation. Nor were his friendships confined to the literary world. The Miss Berrys, who had known Horace Walpole in their youth, knew and loved Monckton Milnes in their old age. Among statesmen he had been the friend of Vassal Holland, Melbourne, Peel and Palmerston, in the heyday of their fame; he had first seen Mr. Gladstone as an undergraduate at Oxford; and been the associate of Mr. Disraeli when he was still only the social aspirant of Gore House; had been the confidant of Louis Napoleon before he was a prisoner at Ham, and had known Louis Philippe, Thiers, Guizot, and Lamartine, alike in their days of triumph and defeat. Lamennais, Wiseman, Edward Irving, Connop Thirlwall, and Frederick Maurice had all influenced his mind in youth; he had "laid the first plank of a kind of pulpit" from which Emerson could preach "throughout all Saxondom," and he had recognised the noble character and brilliant qualities of Miss Nightingale long before the world had heard her name. These were but a few of the friendships of Monckton Milnes. —REID, T. WEMYSS, 1891, *The Life, Letters, and Friendships of Richard Monckton Milnes, First Lord Houghton, Preface, p.* xii.

One of the best after-dinner speakers in the kingdom, Milnes's natural ease failed him when he addressed the House of Commons, and he gave his audience an impression of affectation. His parliamentary career, however, was not barren; and, in the passing of his Bill for establishing reformatories for juvenile offenders, he accomplished a reform the importance of which can hardly be exaggerated. Milnes's disappointment at missing the coveted prize of office, even if keen, which may be doubted, can only have been transient. In his large nature there was scant lodgment for any mean regret. His intense delight in life, his joyous spirit and unfailing good humour, were a source of constant happiness alike to himself and to those with whom he came in contact.—ROLPH, JOHN F., 1891, *Reid's Houghton, The Academy, vol.* 39, *p.* 6.

His genuine goodness, his devotedness to those whom he called his friends, his love of humanity, won for him a place in many hearts. The very essence of his nature was kindness; and though he had some foibles which were calculated to make the thoughtful smile, he must be forgiven much, because of his sensibility as a man and his staunchness as a friend.—HANNIGAN, D. F., 1891, *Lord Houghton, Westminster Review, vol.* 135, *p.* 157.

Were we asked what were the features in Lord Houghton's character which made the deepest impression on ourselves, we should say his extreme tolerance, his great kindliness, and his entire absence of egotism. It was a common subject of remark among his friends that it was almost impossible to induce Lord Houghton to talk on any subject whatever which in any way reflected credit on himself. — PEACOCK, EDWARD, 1891, *Richard Monckton Milnes, Lord Houghton, Dublin Review, vol.* 108, *p.* 34.

For social success . . . he had a rare combination of gifts—a quick intelligence, a lively wit, a kindly temper, infinite curiosity, especially about his fellowmen; a great power of making himself pleasant, yet with sarcasm enough to be able to diffuse a slight sense of alarm—the whole coupled with just so much of singularity in his manners as gave a flavor of originality to everything he did. For fifty years he was a conspicuous figure in London society, knowing everybody worth knowing, and full of recollections of everybody who had been eminent in the generation next before his own. This social fame not only interfered with his success in politics, but with his literary reputation.—BRYCE, JAMES, 1891, *Reid's Life of Lord Houghton, The Nation, vol.* 52, *p.* 119.

He loved and lived for his friends, and was never weary in doing good. To need his help was to have it, whether it was deserved or not. His life was a round of generous acts, performed in secret and out of pure kindness. — STODDARD, RICHARD HENRY, 1892, *Under the Evening Lamp, p.* 275.

It was his delight to assemble around him men of the most varied pursuits, and often those more or less antagonistic to each other, in order to bring about, under the congenial influences of the table, a reconciliation. His sister, Lady Galway, assured me that, opposed as she and her brother were in politics, which occasioned no little good-natured sparring between the two, never a word had affected their close and enduring mutual love from the time they were children till death parted them at a ripe old age, and that never did she hear from his lips a word of unkindness towards a human being.—TUCKERMAN, CHARLES K., 1895, *Personal Recollections of Notable People, vol.* II, *p.* 17.

GENERAL

From the midmost fountain of his delightful thoughts, there ever and anon springs up an unpleasant remembrance of other writers, which detracts from the gratification our taste would otherwise experience. Of this the reader will judge for himself; but making all allowance for such defect or drawback, we are sure that he will be surprised and delighted by such specimens of rare and admirable genius in a poet still extremely young, and known to the world at present in an arena usually held to be very uncongenial to similar exercises of the imagination.—LYTTON, SIR EDWARD LYTTON BULWER, 1838, *Present State of Poetry.*

His poetry, while possessing unusual merits of a certain kind, is yet defective and ineffectual from the want of the poetic soul. It wants impulse and glow. It is elaborate, elegant, stately, and sonorous in form and movement, generous, moral, and devout in sentiment, bearing with it an air of philosophical pretension, and shaded by a gentle touch of melancholy. But there is a frequent want of ease, and a straining after what is original and striking both in sentiment and diction, which turn the pleasure of perusal into laborious effort. The reader is not borne on by the current, but is obliged to bend his mind with an effort and make a study of the verses.—WARE, HENRY, JR., 1839, *Milnes's Poems, North American Review*, vol. 49, p. 349.

His poetry is the poetry of reflection and not of passion, and is a transcript of trains of thought rather than of moods of feeling; nor does it abound with the element of the purely picturesque. It commends itself by a certain thoughtful elegance, a pure and correct tone of feeling, a delicate spirit of observation, and a scholarlike grace of style. To the endowments of a great poet, the life-giving breath of inspiration, the creative power of genius that soars into the highest heaven of invention, and subdues, melts, and moulds the heart at will, he can hardly lay claim; but he may justly aspire to no mean rank among those poets, whose aim it has been to make men happier and wiser by their thoughts and their affections; who have drawn "that wisdom, which is love," from many-coloured scenes of life, and who have found the seeds of poetry springing in the furrows of the common heart and mind. He is fully as much of a philosopher as of a poet, and the interest and value of his poetry are derived as much from the thoughtful spirit, which breathes through it, as from the more strictly poetical element. Nor does he escape the faults to which poetry of this class is exposed. He is sometimes tame and monotonous, dwelling too much upon particulars and details, and giving to his subject an injudicious expansion; and sometimes he clothes in the form and body of verse what is essentially prosaic, and what, by no change of garb, can be made otherwise.—HILLARD, GEORGE STILLMAN, 1842, *Recent English Poetry, North American Review*, vol. 55, p. 218.

Mr. Milnes does not appear to possess the least *dramatic* passion, nor does he display much impulse or energy in his poetry. There is no momentum in the progress of his lines; and the want is conspicuously betrayed in his blank verse. . . . He thinks the truth boldly, and feels generously the use of speaking it; but the medium of expression between him and the public, is somewhat conventionally philosophical in its character, and too fine and recondite in its peculiarities, to be appreciated by the people popularly so called.—HORNE, RICHARD HENGIST, 1844, *A New Spirit of the Age*, pp. 154, 156.

Mr. Monckton Milnes has presented to the world several volumes of poems abounding in such brilliant imagery, and containing such refined sentiments, that they have secured for him a very high place in the estimation of all to whom the beautiful or interesting in art or nature possess any charms.—ALISON, SIR ARCHIBALD, 1853, *History of Europe*, 1815–1852, *ch.* v.

Music and thought are what he gives us rather than point and dashing description. In his quiet strains we come sometimes upon reflections of considerable depth, and the shadow of the literary devotee always falls athwart his pages. We like his utter freedom from artificiality; his range of poetic powers is not of the highest order, but there is scarcely a poet who could be named who has done so uniformly well in all themes selected for treatment.—SMITH, GEORGE BARNETT, 1875, *English Fugitive Poets, Poets and Novelists*, p. 406.

The poetry of Lord Houghton is of a modern contemplative type, very pure, and often sweetly lyrical. Emotion and intellect blend harmoniously in his delicate, suggestive verse, and a few of his songs—among which "I wandered by the brookside" at once recurs to the memory—have a deserved and lasting place in English anthology. This beloved writer has kept within his limitations. He has the sincere affection of men of letters, who all honor his free thought, his catholic taste, and his generous devotion to authors and the literary life. To the friend and biographer of Keats, the thoughtful patron of David Gray, and the progressive enthusiast in poetry and art, I venture to pay this cordial tribute, knowing that I but feebly repeat the sentiments of a multitude of authors on either side of the Atlantic.—STEDMAN, EDMUND CLARENCE, 1875–87, *Victorian Poets*, p. 244.

No one can deny an inborn voice of song to Lord Houghton. His poetical activity began when Wordsworth was first recognized as a great English poet, when there was a growing reaction against the adoration of Byron, and when the most popular lyrist in England was —Mrs. Hemans! Yet in his earliest verse we find but very faint reflections of two of these authors. If, in his graver and more thoughtful poems, he seems to have caught an occasional tone from Wordsworth, or in his sentiment a softer cadence from Mrs. Hemans, we shall find, on explaining the complete poetical records of his life, that such resemblances are inevitable, because springing from congenital features of his own poetic nature. He seems to stand—if on a lower plane—somewhere between Byron and Wordsworth: that is, in making a specific classification of poets, we must refer him to an intermediate variety. The simple, frank, unambitious character of most of his poetry is a feature which must not be overlooked in these days. — TAYLOR, BAYARD, 1877–80, *Lord Houghton, Critical Essays and Literary Notes*, ed. Taylor, p. 327.

The merit and beauty of Lord Houghton's poetic performances are in an inverse ratio to their length. He is seen at his best, his thought is most felicitous and his diction most polished, in his shorter pieces. He was, as Lord Beaconsfield described him, under the guise of Mr. Vavasour in "Tancred"—a description so admirable that it practically exhausts the man—"a poet and a real poet." . . . Intense sympathy is, perhaps, the key-note of Houghton's poetry as it is of his character. He did not describe so much as interpret. Instead of drawing a mere picture of Oriental personalities, or of the heroes of the old Greek mythology, he identified himself with them, and told the world what they felt.—ESCOTT, T. H. S., 1885, *Lord Houghton, Fortnightly Review*, vol. 44, pp. 433, 434.

Houghton was a Wordsworthian, and nothing else. He differed from Wordsworth, in that he manifested no marked predilection for description, no individual observation of woods or waters, trees or flowers—no mysterious sympathy with, and no inexplicable worship of, nature, either for what it is or what it symbolizes; but he resembled him in that he reverenced his own personality as an exceptional one, which it was not, and that he magnified everything that pertained to himself in the shape of an outward event, or the shadow of an inward experience. We wonder while we read him what it was that induced him to write many of the things that we are reading. They lack the interest which attaches to actions, with which, by the way, he seldom grapples, and they lack the more recondite interest which attaches to speculative trains of thought. We find fault with them, and rightly, but in spite of all our fault-finding there is a charm about them which we are unable to resist, and equally unable to define. It may be in the atmosphere in which they live, move, and have their being, though nothing that is clothed in flesh and blood could exist there for a moment; or it may be in the vibration of some chord in our souls which answers to their music.—STODDARD, RICHARD HENRY, 1885, *Lord Houghton's Poetry, The Critic*, Aug. 22.

Richard Monckton Milnes, whom Carlyle once described as "a pretty little Robin Redbreast of a man," and who certainly could sing, in the days in which that description was applied to him, a very taking little song of his own. . . . It is curious that the poem which has certainly been more popular than any other in all Lord Houghton's works, and which almost every one connects with Monckton Milnes' name, was the little love poem called "The Brookside." That is happily expressed, no doubt, but it is wholly without the brand of Lord Houghton's personal character,—and in a poet who has usually so little of the magic of form as Lord Houghton, one needs the impress of character even more than in a poet who adorns everything that he touches, and transfigures it merely by passing it through the medium of his thought. We should, indeed, find few of Lord Houghton's poems so little characteristic of him as "The Brookside," though it may have been that poem, or a poem of that kind, which suggested to Carlyle the comparison to "a pretty little Robin Redbreast." On the whole, Monckton Milnes' genius was embodied in a certain determination to blend the insight of the man of the world with the sentiment of the poet, and not to allow the sentiment of the poet to run away with the insight of the man of the world.—HUTTON, RICHARD HOLT, 1885, *The Late Lord Houghton, Criticisms on Contemporary Thought and Thinkers*, vol. II, pp. 190, 194.

"It is twenty years," wrote the late Matthew Browne, "since I heard a bundle of rags in a gutter singing, 'I wandered by the brook-side, I wandered by the mill;' and it is not three years since I heard the same bundle of rags, scarcely changed in face, voice, coat, trousers, spatter-dashes, or otherwise, sing the same song in another gutter." This was written in 1872. Another sixteen years have passed away, and there has been no diminution in the popularity of Lord Houghton's beautiful and tender song. There have been greater poets who have stirred fewer hearts. Who would not be glad to have written "Strangers Yet," which has within it the promise of immortality, being one of the most cherished of English ballads? . . . Lord Houghton was so much the patron and encourager of poets that for that very reason he missed something of the poetic distinction to which he was himself entitled. Critics have thought more of how he helped poor David Gray than of how he now and then wrote poems which found their way to an immeasurably wider audience than any which the author of "The Luggie, and Other Poems," ever contrived to reach. Perhaps a further reason why his genius has been underrated is to be found in the fact that he always, and as if by design, gave the impression of being in everything an amateur. He was serious, but not quite earnest, an apparent contradiction in terms which will be intelligible enough to those who knew him.—WATSON, AARON, 1888, *North Country Poets*, ed. Andrews, p. 226.

Some time or other the world will discover, with much pleasure and surprise, what a true poet there lived in a man whom it regarded chiefly as a pleasant companion with odd ways and manifold accomplishments. . . . His poetry did not assert itself; it had a modesty about it which the poet himself did not claim. It shunned the sensational, and the refinement which so marks it presented probably the greatest obstacle to its popularity. Though rich in fancy, it is grave-hearted, and in an unusual degree thoughtful; it is full of pathos, and that pathos often rests gently, like Wordsworth's "lenient cloud," on scenes and incidents not only of modern but of conventional life.—DEVERE, AUBREY, 1889, *Letter to T. Wemyss Reid*, Nov. 4; *Life of Lord Houghton*, ed. Reid, vol. I, p. 119.

Milnes's poetry was not in 1843 very highly appreciated, even in his own country. At that time I was stupefied at the thought of how much poetical genius must be scattered, so to say, broadcast over the breadth and length of Great Britain, for one so elegant, so observant, so evidently the Muses' favourite, not to be praised to the very skies. This wonderment, in its general bearing, has increased, I need hardly say, rather than diminished, during the years that have escaped us since. But as regards the poet Milnes, it must be acknowledged that full justice is being done, both in England and abroad, to the genius, the felicity of diction, the gentle plaintiveness of him to whom I will gratefully apply the words of one of his favourite German poets, Friedrich Rückert:—

"Dein Blick hat mich mir werth gemacht."
—BUNSEN, GEORGE VON, 1889, *Letter to T. Wemyss Reid*, *Life of Lord Houghton*, ed. Reid, vol. II, p. 69.

A wit and writer who tried to legitimize bad grammar on the liberal principle that every one had a right to do what he liked with his own language. He, too, like the brewers, could not do without being a lord, though already a patrician, which is greater, and which a king cannot create.—HAKE, GORDON, 1892, *Memoirs of Eighty Years*.

Restraint and sobriety with great elegance characterise all he writes; but Milnes was not untouched by the Doubt and Despair of his time.—GIBBS, H. J., 1892, *The Poets and the Poetry of the Century, Frederick Tennyson to Clough*, ed. Miles, p. 191.

Lord Houghton undoubtedly had no strong vein of poetry. But it was always an entire mistake to represent him as either a fribble or a sentimentalist, while with more inducements to write he would probably have been one of the very best critics of his age.—SAINTSBURY, GEORGE, 1896, *A History of Nineteenth Century Literature*, p. 302.

Though he shines as a writer of what may be called, without disparagement, poetical trifles, there is also a serious strain by no means contemptible in his verse. "Strangers Yet" is a fine specimen of pathos. In "Poems, Legendary and Historical," however, Houghton is less successful, and the best of them do not bear comparison with Aytoun's "Lays of the Scottish Cavaliers," which belong to the same class. Houghton's critical work in prose is on the whole more valuable than his verse, for there his culture told, and the lack of high imagination is less felt.—WALKER, HUGH, 1897, *The Age of Tennyson*, p. 58.

Georgiana Charlotte Lady Fullerton
1812–1885

Born September 23, 1812, the second daughter of the First Earl of Granville, for some years Ambassador Extraordinary and Plenipotentiary to the Court of Russia, and subsequently Ambassador to the Court of France. In 1833 she married Captain Alexander George Fullerton, eldest son of George A. Fullerton, Esq., of Ballintoy Castle, Ireland. She commenced her career as an authoress with a novel entitled "Ellen Middleton," published in 1844, and which caused a great sensation. "Grantley Manor," a novel bearing on the war of creeds, appeared in 1847; "The Old Highlander," 1849; "Lady Bird," 1852; "The Life of St. Frances of Rome," 1855; "La Comtesse de Bonneval, histoire du temps de Louis XIV.," 1857; "The Countess Bonneval; her Life and Letters," 1858; "Apostleship in Humble Life; a sketch of the life of Elizabeth Twiddy," 1860; "Laurentia, a tale of Japan," 1861; "Rose Leblanc," 1861; "Too Strange not to be True," 1864; "Constance Sherwood; an autobiography of the sixteenth century," 1865; "A Stormy Life," 1867; "The Helpers of the Holy Souls," 1868; "Mrs. Gerald's Niece," 1869; "The Gold-digger and other Verses," 1872; "Dramas from the Lives of the Saints—Germaine Cousin, the Shepherdess of Pibrac," 1872; "Seven Stories," and "The Life of Louisa de Carvajal," 1873; "A Sketch of the Life of the late Father H. Young," 1874; "The Life of Mère Marie de la Providence," 1875; "The Miraculous Medal," 1880; "A Will and a Way," 1881. She has also translated "The Life, Virtues, and Miracles of the Blessed John Berchmans," by F. Deynoodt (1866); "The Miracle at Metz," by Verdenal, (1866); "The Life of the Marchesa G. Faletti di Barolo," by S. Pellico, 1866; "Natalie Narischkin, Sister of Charity of St. Vincent de Paul" by Mrs. Craven, 1877; "The Notary's Daughter," by Mdme. d'Aulnoy, and "The House of Penarvan," by Jules Sandeau, 1878; "The Life of Mère Duchesne," 1879, and "Life of the Ven. Madeleine Barat," 1880; both by the Abbé Baunard; and "Elaine," by Mrs. Augustus Craven, 1882. In 1846 Lady Georgiana Fullerton became a convert to Roman Catholicism.—HAYS, FRANCES, 1885, *Women of the Day*, p. 73.

PERSONAL

Like those who are not only of the highest birth but the highest breeding, Georgiana Leveson was distinguished throughout her life by the utmost modesty and simplicity of character and manners. —BOWLES, EMILY, 1888, *Lady Georgiana Fullerton, Dublin Review*, vol. 103, p. 313.

She loved the poor. She begged for them, she worked for them, she economized for them. She deprived herself of luxuries constantly for their sake. A friend tells how she walked long distances rather than hire a cab, that she might add to her insatiable purse for the poor. She was not unmindful of the duties of her state in life. She played her part as hostess in her husband's house with grace and elegance. She wrote for the poor, not for the public. The money paid her by the publishers found its way to the poor.— EGAN, MAURICE FRANCIS, 1889, *Lectures on English Literature*, p. 153.

She was tall and largely built, her face was plain, but full of bright intelligence and gentle humour, naturally a merry face; she always dressed in black, wearing a shawl across her shoulders, and no gloves. She said that gloves cost too much money, and that she had much rather give the half-crown to the poor. Having had many occasions of speaking with her, I would describe the impression she made on her contemporaries as so marked that in entering even a crowded room Lady Georgiana would have been one of the first people to be noticed, from her majestic figure and the plain severity of her dress. She was very nobly born. Her father, Lord Granville, served his country for a long series of years as Ambassador to France. Her mother, an excellent, conscientious woman, was daughter to that beautiful Duchess of Devonshire, of whom so many anecdotes survive, and whose life-size portrait by Gainsborough disappeared so mysteriously some years ago. Sir Joshua Reynolds also repeatedly painted the Duchess, the best known portrait being the one wherein she is playing with her child. It was after this lovely grandmother that the little girl was named Georgiana. . . . Of her manifold charities one knows not how to speak. She was the kindest and most industrious of women. The charge of orphans, sick people, and schools was a daily matter of course to her, as to many another; but in touching ever so slightly upon her sphere of activity, one became aware of the odds and ends which were, so to speak, stuffed into the crevices from year's end to year's end.—BELLOC, BESSIE RAYNER, 1894, *In a Walled Garden*, pp. 100, 110.

ELLEN MIDDLETON
1844

While I was there Lady Georgiana Fullerton gave me to read so much as she has written of the novel she has been for sometime about. It is a very extraordinary performance, and if the second part of it is as good as the first, it will be excellent; as it is, it is deeply interesting. — GREVILLE, CHARLES C. F., 1843, *A Journal of the Reign of Queen Victoria from 1837 to 1852*, ed. Reeve, Oct. 16, vol. I, p. 519.

Who is Lady Georgiana Fullerton? Who is that Countess of Dacre, who edited "Ellen Wareham,"—the most passionate of fictions—approached only in some particulars of passion by this? The great defect of "Ellen Middleton" lies in the disgusting sternness, captiousness, and bullet headedness of her husband. We cannot sympathize with her love for him. And the intense selfishness of a rejected lover precludes that compassion which is designed. Alice is a *creation* of true genius. The imagination, throughout, is of a lofty order, and the snatches of original verse would do honor to any poet living. But the chief merit, after all, is that of the *style*—about which it is difficult to say too much in the way of praise, although it has, now and then, an odd Gallicism—such as "she lost her head," meaning she grew crazy. There is much, in the whole manner of this book, which puts me in mind of "Caleb Williams."—POE, EDGAR ALLAN, 1844, "*Ellen Middleton*," *Marginalia, Works*, ed. Stedman and Woodberry, vol. VII, p. 251.

The tale is very well told, with no exaggeration of style, or attempt at studied effect, the authoress trusting to arrest the reader's interest rather by the pathetic character of her incidents, and the apparent nature and probability with which they follow each other, than by any elaborate overworking. . . . Still, with all these merits, our verdict on it is not in her favour. The interest she excites is a false one. . . . The book is further disfigured by a tinge of that Anglo-Catholic semi-religious tone, which is rapidly degenerating into a kind of sentimental mysticism, and desecrates high and holy things into the mere make-weights of a questionable tale.—MONCRIEFF, J., 1844, *Recent Novels, North British Review*, vol. 1, pp. 560, 561,

In that novel, for the first time, her full character was unveiled to the world, and probably to herself. The charm, the interest, the refined beauty, the fervent imagination; above all, the vivid colouring of latent passion, gave it a vitality which is still felt after a lapse of four and forty years. —BOWLES, EMILY, 1888, *Lady Georgiana Fullerton, Dublin Review*, vol. 103, p. 321.

The tale on which her chief fame rests was the product of the heart-searchings that she underwent, at the very time when the thoughts and studies of good men were tending to discover neglected truths in the Church of England.—YONGE, CHARLOTTE M., 1897, *Women Novelists of Queen Victoria's Reign*, p. 197.

GRANTLEY MANOR
1847

I know not whether the pleasures of your country life allow you any leisure for reading. If they do, let me recommend to you Lady Georgiana Fullerton's last novel, "Grantley Manor." I have reached only as far as the seventeenth page, in which I find a piece of eloquence such as I never found in any other novel for the sublimity of the thought and for the purity of the expression.—LANDOR, WALTER SAVAGE, 1847, *To Mrs. Graves-Sawle, June 2; Letters*, ed. Wheeler, p. 157.

We cannot pass from Bulwer to Lady Georgiana Fullerton without taking a perilous leap. "Grantley Manor" is a novel having the rose-color of Young England and the purple light of Puseyism on its pages, and doubtless presents a very one-sided view of many important matters with which it deals; but it evinces talent of a very high order, and is one of the most pleasing novels of the season. The author is perhaps too elaborate in her diction, and is stirred too often by an ambition for the superfine, to catch that flowing felicity of style which should be the aim of the novelist—a style in which sentences should only represent thought or fact, and never dazzle away attention from the matter they convey. But with some faults of manner and some blunder in plot, the novel evinces considerable dramatic power, and has a number of striking characters. The interest is well sustained, though rapidity of movement in the story is ever subsidiary to completeness of delineation in the characters.

No one can criticise the novel with any justice to the writer, without keeping constantly in mind that her object is not so much a consistent or even probable story, as a forcible and subtle representation of character, as influenced by events best calculated to bring out all its hidden virtues or vices.—WHIPPLE, EDWIN PERCY, 1848, *Novels of the Season, Essays and Reviews, vol.* II, *p.* 367.

It possesses more than ordinary interest, and bears the mark of genius and power. We have rarely read a novel written by a lady which indicated more ability or contained less that was extravagant or offensive. . . . Judging from the work before us Lady Georgiana Fullerton is a gifted and highly cultivated woman, endowed with fine powers of observation, and possessing very considerable knowledge of the human heart, and mastery over its passions. Her characters are drawn with freedom and delicacy, within the bounds of nature, and with a nearer approach to individuality, as in Margaret and old Mrs. Thornton, than is common save in authors of the very highest rank. She intersperses her work with many wise and just, if not profound and original, remarks, and hits off many of the petty vices, annoyances, and foibles of conventional and every-day life not unsuccessfully. In a purely literary point of view, we may object, however, to a too visible effort at intense writing, a want of calmness and repose, and the attempt to give us a vivid impression of the exquisite beauty of her heroines by dissecting and lining it feature by feature, instead of leaving it to be depicted by the imagination of her readers from the effects it is seen to produce on those within the sphere of its influence.—BROWNSON, ORESTES A., 1848, *Grantley Manor, or Popular Literature, Works, ed. Brownson, vol.* XIX, *p.* 244.

GENERAL

She stands, for her rare ability, rich and chaste imagination, high culture, and varied knowledge, elevation and delicacy of sentiment, purity, strength, and gracefulness of style, and the moral and religious tendency of her writings, at the head of contemporary female writers. She lives and writes for her religion, and seeks, through rare knowledge of the human heart and of the teachings of the church, combined with the graces and charms of fiction, to win souls to the truth, or at least to disarm the prejudices and disperse the mists of ignorance which prevent them from seeing and loving it. Her works have done much in this direction, and deserve the warm gratitude of Catholics.—BROWNSON, ORESTES A., 1871, *Mrs. Gerald's Niece, Works, ed. Brownson, vol.* XIX, *p.* 544.

"A Will and A Way" has the moving elements of a great historical tragedy. It gives us truer glimpses of that time of tragedies than we get anywhere outside the more honest parts of Carlyle. Lady Georgiana Fullerton fills each inch of her great canvas so carefully, giving no hasty blotches of crimson merely for effect, that she interprets even the philosophy of the Revolution by means of her social sketches better than many pretentious writers. The reader who has not the time to collate the memoirs of the period may yield himself to the guidance of Lady Georgiana Fullerton for a knowledge of France in the throes of the Terror. She does not exaggerate even the smallest incident for her purpose. Each touch, as we said before, has the true color of truth. There is enough matter in this book to fill a dozen novels and make them absorbingly interesting, and enough suggestion for many months of high thinking. —EGAN, MAURICE FRANCIS, 1889, *Lectures on English Literature, p.* 162.

As to literary fame, she may be described as having written one first-rate book and a number fairly above the average.—YONGE, CHARLOTTE MARY, 1897, *Women Novelists of Queen Victoria's Reing, ed. Yonge, p.* 203.

John Campbell Shairp
1819–1885

Born, at Houston, Linlithgowshire, 30 July 1819. Early education at Houston. At Edinburgh Academy, Oct. 1829 to 1834. At Glasgow Univ., autumn of 1836 to 1839; Snell Exhibitioner, April 1840. Matric., Balliol Coll., Oxford, 3 June 1840; Newdigate Prize Poem, 1842; B. A., 1844; M. A., 1877. Assistant Master at Rugby, 1846–57. Married Eliza Douglas, 23 June 1853. Assistant to Prof. of Latin at St. Andrews Univ., Oct. 1857;

Professor, 1868-72. Contrib. to "Good Words," and "North British Review." Principal of United Coll. of St. Salvator and St. Leonard, 1868-85. Pres. of Educational Institute of Scotland, Prof. of Poetry, Oxford, June 1877 to 1885. Died at Oronsay, Argyll, 18 Sept. 1885. Buried in Houston Church. *Works:* "Charles the Twelfth," 1842; "The Wants of the Scottish Universities," 1856; "The Uses of the Study of Latin Literature," 1858; "Kilmahoe," 1864; "John Keble," 1866; "Studies in Poetry and Philosophy,"1868; "Culture and Religion," 1870; "Life and Letters of J. D. Forbes" (with P. G. Tait and A. A. Reilly), 1873; "Address" [on Missions], 1874; "On Poetic Interpretation of Nature," 1877 (2nd edn. same year); "Robert Burns," 1879; "Aspects of Poetry," 1881. *Posthumous:* "Sketches in History and Poetry," ed. by G. J. Veitch, 1887; "Glen Dessaray, and other Poems," ed. by F. T. Palgrave, 1888; "Portraits of Friends," 1889. He *edited:* Dorthy Wordsworth's "Recollections of a Tour Made in Scotland," 1874. *Life:* by Prof. W. Knight, 1888.—SHARP, R. FARQUHARSON, 1897, *A Dictionary of English Authors, p.* 253.

PERSONAL

I can recall the room in which I first saw him, and his appearance as he stood on the hearth-rug in front of the fire. He was a little older than most undergraduates are, and he looked perhaps a little older than he was,—I mean more manly-looking and more fully developed. He received me, as a new-comer from Scotland and Glasgow, with that frank, kindly greeting—"the smile in the eye as well as on the lip," as in the young shepherd in "Theocritus"—which was never absent in our meetings after longer or shorter separation in later years. I retain the impression rather of the high spirit and animation, and of a kind of generous pride characteristic of him, than of the milder, far-away, contemplative look which became familiar to one in later years. Except that he became bald and somewhat gray, he never seemed to change much in other ways during all the subsequent years that I knew him; and if he looked a little older than he was in youth, he retained much of fresh youthfulness in his appearance when he was nearly an old man. . . . He received from Nature a combination of the courage and independent spirit of a man, with the refinement and ready spirit of a woman. And this natural endowment was tempered into a consistent character by constant watchfulness against any assertion of self, in the way either of indulgence, or interest, or vanity. . . . As he had a quick sense of personal dignity, and a generous impetuosity of spirit, it was possible that he might sometimes take, and sometimes, though rarely, give offense; but if this happened, he was always prompt to receive or to make acknowledgment, and the matter was never afterwards remembered. At no time of his life would any one have said in his presence anything essentially coarse or irreverent; or if he had done so once, he would not have repeated the experiment. — SELLARS, WILLIAM YOUNG, 1889, *Portraits of Friends by Shairp, pp.* 37, 56, 58.

It was not his erudition as a scholar which gained for him the high place he occupied among his contemporaries, for although a fair classic, he was not distinguished as such, the art of writing Greek and Latin verse never having received the attention in the "grounding" of boys in Scotch schools which it does in England. It was Shairp's personality, his enthusiasm, his appreciativeness, and his general vigour of thought and varied accomplishments, which won the hearts of the best men of his time. . . . His influence as a teacher was more intense in the case of a few than general. Many a man now doing noble work can trace the first stirrings of those higher thoughts and aims that have dominated his life to the tender, penetrating power which Shairp exercised. But there was one kind of student whom he failed to reach, and who was repelled rather than attracted by him. The boisterous lads, coarse in manners and in nature, however clever they might be, who were untouched and apparently untouchable by the finer aspects of religion and poetry, had little appreciation of the man who sometimes stung them with an appropriate epithet or restrained them by a discipline more commonly experienced at a public school than a Scottish university, where the freedom resembles the German rather than English type. . . . The impression which one chiefly cherishes of him is an exquisite combination of the highest culture with the most devout religious spirit. . . . Of splendid physique, he knew no fatigue, and would breast a corrie or face a summit with the elastic step and sound "wind" of a ghillie. There was scarce a solitude from Eskdale to

Minchmoor he had not visited. He knew each "water" from Liddesdale to Manor. Yarrow and Ettrick were a part of himself. He had gazed from every chief range from Broadlaw to the Criffel, and from Tinto to the Cheviots, and had dwelt with loving eye on each historic scene from Enterkine to Otterbourne. The shepherds of Tala and Teviot knew him well.—MACLEOD, DONALD, 1889, *Principal Shairp, Goods Words, vol.* 30, *pp.* 84, 85, 86.

Principal Shairp had a genius for friendship, was a lover of his fellow-men, not in any vague philanthropic fashion, but with an alert interest and sympathy for individuals. His heart, always open to a true man, found not a few worthy of entering it. It was said to a certain clever contemporary, by one who knew him in his youth, that he could not go down to the front gate without meeting a lion, so happy and adventurous were his chance encounters. It would seem true of Principal Shairp that he could not enter any company without finding a friend. He had a remarkable discernment of what it was in each new comrade that won his attachment. As he survived a good many of his famous friends, he recorded his impressions of them; and when he departed, a fitting hand was found to do the same kind office, sympathetically and discerningly, for him.—RICHARDS, C. A. L., 1893, *A Man of Many Friends, The Dial, vol.* 10, *p.* 306.

As a professor he was earnest and stimulating, never overlooking the importance of sound scholarship, but grappling also with the thought of his author, and expounding comparative literature. He advocated a higher standard for entrants to the universities, and warmly encouraged a residential college hall at St. Andrews, which, however, had only a brief existence. In 1868 Shairp succeded James David Forbes as principal of the United College, St. Andrews, occupying the Latin chair at the same time till 1872. He was a vigorous head, and interested himself in university extension, specially favouring a union of interests between St. Andrews and Dundee.—BAYNE, THOMAS, 1897, *Dictionary of National Biography, vol.* LI, *p.* 344.

GENERAL

The volume ["Culture and Religion"] is a valuable contribution to the discussion of a question which has not yet received from the religious point of view the exhaustive treatment it deserves. The aim and spirit of Mr. Shairp's book are excellent and his lectures cannot fail to be both interesting and serviceable to young men. I shall take great pleasure in directing the attention of my students to it.—ANGELL, JAMES BURRILL, 1872, *Letter to the Publishers.*

His past writings are not voluminous; but in all of them there is the clear tone of a man who seeks the best truth he can find, and does not spend thought upon trifles. . . . In 1864 Mr. Shairp published "Kilmahoe, a Highland Pastoral, with other Poems," and if he did not in that book prove himself a master-poet, he proved the fellowship of feeling that entitles him to tell students at Oxford what a master-poet is. . . . If this book on the poetic interpretation of Nature has a few weaknesses, it has essential strength. It comes of an earnest mind. It deals justly with an important movement in the literature of our century as something more than a slight question of taste. Professor Shairp works with a high aim, looks to the heart of his subject, and what he has written must win for him the respect of all his readers.—MORLEY, HENRY, 1877, *Recent Literature, Nineteenth Century, vol.* 2, *pp.* 693, 703.

His essays make no pretensions to be elaborate works of art in themselves. They are the simple overflowings of a full and refined mind, saturated with poetical feeling and lucid thought on the various topics which such a Professorship as his suggests. What he has to say he says in pure and delightful English, and often with very great point and effect, though without the almost sculpturesque unity of impression which Mr. Arnold's lectures on translating Homer, on Heine, and on the Celtic genius, produced upon their readers. Mr. Shairp talks to us as an accomplished man, with a great store of central heat in him, and a passionate love for poetry, would talk of the various aspects of his favourite study.—HUTTON, RICHARD HOLT, 1882, *Professor Shairp's "Aspects of Poetry," Criticisms on Contemporary Thought and Thinkers, vol.* II, *p.* 159.

As he strode across the heather or bent he was for ever crooning to himself old songs that kept time to his steps, or went pondering lines he was composing, selecting the aptest words to utter what his eye beheld. This is the charm of his poetry. It is the direct expression of nature as he beheld her, the sincere and pure utterance of a spirit that loved her every aspect.—MACLEOD, DONALD, 1889, *Principal Shairp, Good Words*, vol. 30, p. 86.

Than whom, of Scotland's many faithful sons, none was more devoted to her,—nay, perhaps, almost too exclusively. No one, if we put aside Ossian, known to me, has felt or rendered so deeply the gloom, the sublime desolation of the Highland region. That overpowering sense of weight and grandeur which calls forth the inward cry to the mountains to cover us, as we pass beneath some vast precipice, in truth, was always with Shairp. He has not his beloved Wordsworth's mastery, his brightness of soul, his large philosophy of Nature; nor, in the region of art, Wordsworth's fine finish, his happiness of phrase: the minor key dominates.—But, united with great delicacy of sentiment and touch, he had the never-failing charm of perfect high-hearted sincerity; and if we reflect on the long-lasting hatred or indifference which mountain lands have met from poetry, Shairp, so far as his skill served, merits a high place in characteristically modern verse. — PALGRAVE, FRANCIS TURNER, 1896, *Landscape in Poetry*, p. 255.

Helen Hunt Jackson
H. H.
1831–1885

Author, poet and philanthropist, born in Amherst, Mass., 18th October, 1831, and died in San Francisco, Cal., 12th August, 1885. She was the daughter of Professor Nathan W. Fiske, of Amherst College. She was educated in the female seminary in Ipswich, Mass. In 1852 she became the wife of Captain Edward B. Hunt, of the United States Navy. She lived with him in various military posts until his death, in October, 1863. In 1866 she removed to Newport, R. I., where she lived until 1872. Her children died, and she was left desolate. Alone in the world, she turned to literature. In early life she had published some verses in a Boston newspaper, and aside from that she had shown no signs of literary development up to 1865. In that year she began to contribute poems to the New York "Nation." Then she sent poems and prose articles to the New York "Independent" and the "Hearth and Home." She signed the initials "H. H." to her work, and its quality attracted wide and critical attention. In 1873 and 1874 she lived in Colorado for her health. In 1875 she became the wife of William S. Jackson, a merchant of Colorado Springs. In that town she made her home until her death. She traveled in New Mexico and California, and spent one winter in New York City, gathering facts for her book in behalf of the Indians, "A Century of Dishonor," which was published in 1881. Her Indian novel, "Ramona," was published in 1884. That is her most powerful work, written virtually under inspiration. Her interest in the Indians was profound, and she instituted important reforms in the treatment of the Red Men by the Government. Her other published works are: "Verses by H. H." (1870, enlarged in 1874), "Bits of Travel" (1873), "Bits of Talk About Home Matters" (1873), "Sonnets and Lyrics" (1876), several juvenile books and two novels in the "No Name" series, "Mercy Philbrick's Choice" (1876), and "Hetty's Strange History" (1877).—MOULTON, CHARLES WELLS, 1893, *A Woman of the Century*, ed. Willard and Livermore, p. 414.

PERSONAL

Five hundred feet above the level of the top of Mt. Washington is Mrs. Jackson's home. Its driveway is a steep but excellent carriage road, several miles in length, at whose entrance you will pay toll of admiration and wonder to a little brook that deliberately runs up hill before you. . . . On Cheyenne, high as you are, you still seem on level ground, beautiful with green grass and trees and brooks and flowers; while mountains on which, perhaps, the snow is lying in August, range around you, and you gaze down, not on lower mountains, but down, down to the very plains, stretching miles upon miles, level as a parlor floor, away to an almost limitless horizon. It is no wonder that we linger. But an hour before sunset our host re-harnesses the horses; for Mrs. Jackson, though most "at home" on Cheyenne Mt., where she has been known to picnic thirteen Sundays in succession, has a House Beautiful in the little town of Colorado Springs which contains her kitchen, dining-room and sleeping apartments. And it is a house well worth description as the home of a poet; not because it is one of the æsthetic palaces such as have recently been described as the homes of London poets and artists, in whose majestic halls and apartments we are told that "the silence is like a throne;" but because it is a wonderful illustration of what the poetic and artistic instinct can make of the average American house.—ROLLINS, ALICE WELLINGTON, 1885, *Authors at Home, The Critic.*

I cannot find her type: in her were blent
Each varied and each fortunate element
Which souls combine, with something all her own—
Sadness and mirthfulness, a chorded strain,
The tender heart, the keen and searching brain,
The social zest, the power to live alone.
Comrade of comrades—giving man the slip
To seek in Nature truest comradeship,
Tenacity and impulse ruled her fate,
This grasping firmly what that flashed to feel—
The velvet scabbard and the sword of steel,
The gift to strongly love, to frankly hate!
Patience as strong as was her hopefulness;
A joy in living which grew never less
As years went on and age drew gravely nigh;
Vision which pierced the veiling mists of pain,
And saw beyond the mortal shadows plain
The eternal day-dawn broadening in the sky;
The love of Doing, and the scorn of Done;
The playful fancy, which, like glinting sun,
No chill could daunt, no loneliness could smother.
—COOLIDGE, SUSAN, 1885, *H. H., Christian Union, Sep. 17.*

Whoever knew her beautiful personality, whoever saw her fair and still youthful face —a face that would never have grown old, —heard her winning voice, or felt the warm charm of her cordial, sincere, unaffected manner, has something to be glad of, and to remember always. The writer of this met her but once, but that once can never be forgotten. To the great multitude who knew her as "H. H." only, whatever relates to her is interesting. Few women of this generation, or any other, have gone down to the grave followed by truer or more grateful love from countless hearts that their written words have inspired or comforted.—DORR, JULIA C. R., 1885, *Emerson's Admiration of "H. H.," The Critic, Aug. 29.*

If it be the supreme achievement of a life to grow into larger and larger mastery of itself and of the materials with which it works, to match increasing and widening opportunities with true vision and more adequate performance, Helen Jackson was surely near the goal when she vanished from the race. The eager intentness of eye and ear, the wide and ever widening applause, sweet with that recognition of what is best in one which all earnest workers crave, were hers, also, the consciousness of having wrought with no uncertain hand for those whose hands are bound, and spoken with no uncertain voice for those who are dumb. . . . Of her generous friendship, her noble faculty of recognizing and admiring purpose and gifts in others, her deep, full sympathy with men and women in all their trials and aspirations, her apt and often glowing speech, the charm and quality of her striking personality, one has no heart to speak while the sense of loss is so deep and immediate. Among the letters which came from the deathbed there were several, sent in the writer's care, to women who are striving with high purpose in the field which she has left. In every instance these brief and painfully written notes were words of generous praise, of unstinted admiration, of stimulus and hope for the future.—MABIE, HAMILTON W., 1885, *Helen Jackson, Christian Union, Aug. 20.*

Great heart of many loves! while earth was thine
Thou didst love Nature and her very mood:
Beneath thine eye the frail flower of the wood
Uplifted not in vain its fleeting sign,
And on thy hearth the mast-tree's blaze benign,
With all its sylvan lore, was understood!
Seems homely Nature's mother-face less good,
Spirit down-gazing from the Fields Divine?
Oh, let me bring these gathered leaves of mine,
Praising the common earth, the rural year,
And consecrate them to thy memory dear—
Thought's pilgrim to thy mortal body's shrine,
Beneath soft sheddings of the mountain pine
And trailing mountain heath untouched with sere!
—THOMAS, EDITH M., 1886, *To The Memory of Helen Jackson, Atlantic Monthly, vol. 58, p. 195.*

She was the author to the many—a woman to only a few, and this few of mixed constituency. For conventional people, people of the polite world who become rigid by conformity, she cared very little; they bored her, though her sense of courtesy probably checked any expression of it. On the other hand, with people in humble life, with eccentric personages or strong individualities, with artists, with earnest workers in any department, she was always in a pleased and eager sympathy. . . . Her demeanor towards strangers was that of an amiable woman of the world, fenced with a certain reserve, which thawed in an instant under the assurance of sympathy, and became something finer than cordiality. No one could have had a greater dislike of being remarked or lionized, and perhaps the apprehension of such a result had made her more than commonly shy and guarded; but her surrender to a favorable impression was immediate and complete.—SWINBURNE, LOUIS, 1886, *Reminiscences of Helen Jackson, New Princeton Review, vol. 2, pp.* 76, 77.

RAMONA
1884

The story of two decaying civilizations seen in the light of a fresher and stronger social, political, and religious development which tramples them ruthlessly, because unconsciously, into the dust of a new but half-appreciated realm. Hitherto fiction had treated California only as the seat of a new civilization. It had been delineated as the gold-digger's paradise, the adventurer's Eden, the speculator's El Dorado. "Ramona" pictures it as the Indian's lost inheritance and the Spaniard's desolated home.—TOURGÉE, ALBION WINEGAR, 1884, *Ramona.*

I have often thought that no one enjoyed the sensation of living more than Mrs. Jackson, or was more alive to all the influences of nature and the contact of mind with mind, more responsive to all that was exquisite and subtle either in nature or in society, or more sensitive to the disagreeable. This is merely saying that she was a poet; but when she became interested in the Indians and especially in the hard fate of the Mission Indians in California, all her nature was fused for the time in a lofty enthusiasm of pity and indignation, and all her powers seemed to her consecrated to one purpose. Enthusiasm and sympathy will not make a novel, but all the same they are necessary to the production of a work that has in it real vital quality; and in this case all previous experience and artistic training became the unconscious servants of Mrs. Jackson's heart. I know she had very little conceit about her performance; but she had a simple consciousness that she was doing her best work, and that if the world should care much for anything she had done, after she was gone, it would be for "Ramona." She had put herself into it. And yet I am certain that she could have had no idea what the novel would be to the people of Southern California, or how it would identify her name with all that region and make so many scenes in it places of pilgrimage and romantic interest for her sake.—WARNER, CHARLES DUDLEY, 1887, *"H. H." in Southern California, The Critic, p.* 237.

A book instinct with passionate purpose, intensely alive and involving the reader in its movement, it yet contains an idyl of singular loveliness, the perfection of which lends the force of contrast to the pathetic close. A novel of reform, into which a great and generous soul poured its gathered strength, it none the less possesses artistic distinction. Something is, of course, due to the charm of atmosphere, the beauty of the background against which the plot naturally placed itself; more, to the trained hand, the pen pliant with long and free exercise; most, to the poet-heart. "Ramona" stands as the most finished, though not the most striking, example that what American women have done notably in literature they have done nobly.—CONE, HELEN GRAY, 1890, *Woman in American Literature, Century Magazine, vol.* 40, *p.* 927.

This was the expiring effort of her genius, and is by far its most powerful and memorable illustration. The story is deeply interesting, the literary skill is adequate, and the burning purpose of the book does not lead the writer to forget the obligations of art. It marks the worthy close of a noble career, and insures Mrs. Jackson a place in the literature of our country which few of her sex can be held to have attained.—HAWTHORNE, JULIAN, AND LEMMON, LEONARD, 1891, *American Literature, p.* 287.

The name of Helen Hunt Jackson deservedly stands first in the literary world as connected with modern effort by women for the deliverance of our native American Indians from oppression and injustice, as shameful as have been endured in any civilized land or by any race under the guardianship or power of any civilized government. ... To this resolve her facile pen, her poetic fire, and her genius for graphic delineation and clear, strong statement were given, and the story of "Ramona," the data of which were procured among the Indians of California while she was a government inspector among them, was given to idyllic, classic romance, to the American conscience, and to the humane of all civilized society. She poured her heart into the story and her heart's blood out through its pages. She put the labor of the working years of an average life-time into that half-decade of toil for a hunted race, and so it was again, as not infrequently in this world's story, that the righteous zeal and the intense compassion of a quick spirit "ate up" the life, and another consecrated genius fell, another great heart broke.—QUINTON, AMELIA STONE, 1891, *Care of the Indian, Woman's Work in America, pp.* 374, 375.

Pathetic romance is best typified by the "Ramona" of Mrs. Helen Hunt Jackson—a tale full of poetic insight as well as of poetic beauty, in behalf of the Indian. Its author is the greatest representative of a large school of modern writers, characterized by extreme sensitiveness, artistic perception, poetic aspirations, and a somewhat sentimental but a very genuine love for the suffering and the oppressed. Their chief fault is, that while they soften the heart they never invigorate the will.—MABIE, HAMILTON W., 1892, *The Memorial Story of America, p.* 596.

The most original and picturesque novel of American life with the exception of Hawthorne's two greatest romances. . . . She was too true an artist to intrude herself into her picture.—COOLIDGE, SUSAN, 1900, *Ramona, Monterey Ed., Introduction, pp.* v, vi.

There was no need to employ "artistic license" in working up the sketches for publication, fact, in this particular instance, being so much richer than fiction; and in this shaping and assorting of material gathered so long ago, I have merely tried to follow the path laid out by the author herself; which was to handle all detail in such manner as would best conduce to the artistic unison of the whole. As for the characters themselves, I have now in my possession sketches and studies made from life at the time of my meeting the originals, —a meeting that was often as much fraught with meaning for me as it was for Mrs. Jackson. All the dramatic incidents of the story were familiar to me long before I saw the book, as they are either literal descriptions of events which took place in the course of our travels, or they are recollections of anecdotes told when I, as well as Mrs. Jackson, was among the group of listeners.—SANDHAM, HENRY, 1900, *Ramona, Monterey Ed., Notes on Illustrations, p.* xxxii.

POEMS

The selections from American writers are necessarily confined to the present century; but some of them have secured a wide fame. Some of them are recent, and have yet to earn their laurels. . . . The poems of a lady who contents herself with the initials H. H. in her book published in Boston (1874) have rare merit of thought and expression, and will reward the reader for the careful attention which they require.— EMERSON, RALPH WALDO, 1875, ed., *Parnassus, p.* x.

Mrs. Hunt's poems are stronger than any written by women since Mrs. Browning, with the exception of Mrs. Lewes's.—DICKINSON, EMILY, 1875, *Letters, vol.* II, *p.* 320.

Perhaps the finest recent examples of exquisitely subtle imagination working under the impulse of profound sentiment are to be found in the little volume entitled "Poems by H. H."—WHIPPLE, EDWIN PERCY, 1876-86, *American Literature and Other Papers, ed. Whittier, p.* 131.

The woman who has come nearest in our day and tongue to the genius of Elizabeth Barrett Browning, and who has made Christina Rossetti and Jean Ingelow appear but second-rate celebrities. When some one asked Emerson a few years since whether he did not think "H. H." the best womanpoet on this continent, he answered in his meditative way, "Perhaps we might as well omit the *woman;*" thus placing her, at least in that moment's impulse, at the head of all. . . . As the most artistic among her verses I should class the "Gondoliers," in which all Venice seems reflected in the movement and cadence, while the thought is fresh and new and strong. Then there are poems which seem to hold all secrets of passion trembling on the lips, yet forbear to tell them; and others, on a larger scale, which have a grander rhythmical movement than most of our poets have dared even to attempt. Of these the finest, to my ear, is "Resurgam;" but I remember that Charlotte Cushman preferred the "Funeral March," and loved to read it in public. . . . "H. H." reaches the popular heart best in a class of poems easy to comprehend, thoroughly human in sympathy; poems of love, of motherhood, of bereavement; poems such as are repeated and preserved in many a Western cabin, cheering and strengthening many a heart.— HIGGINSON, THOMAS WENTWORTH, 1879,

Short Studies of American Authors, pp. 41, 44, 45.

I would that in the verse she loved some word
Not all unfit I to her praise might frame:
Some word wherein the memory of her name
Should through long years its incense still afford.
But no; her spirit smote with its own sword;
Herself has lit the fire whose blood-red flame
Shall not be quenched;—this is her living fame
Who struck so well the sonnet's subtle chord.
—GILDER, RICHARD WATSON, 1885,"*H. H.*," *The Critic*, Aug. 29.

The verse of the brilliant and devoted "H. H." (the sense of whose loss is fresh upon us) is more carefully finished, though perhaps it sings the less for its union of intellectuality with a subtile feeling whose intenseness is realized only by degrees. Her pieces, mostly in a single key, and that grave and earnest, have won the just encomiums of select critics, but certainly lack the variety of mood which betokens an inborn and always dominant poetic faculty.—STEDMAN, EDMUND CLARENCE, 1885, *Poets of America*, p. 445.

Mrs. Jackson had the characteristics of the "Dial" group at its best; deep and sincere thought, uttered for its own sake in verse not untinged by the poetic inspiration and touch. In her poems the influence of the mind is felt before that of the heart; they are reflective and suggestive, sometimes concisely argumentative. Certain phases and senses of spirit, brain, and nature lay long in the poet's thought, and at length found deliberate and apt expression in word and metre. The character of H. H.'s product is explained by the frequency with which she chose single words—often abstract nouns—as titles. It is meditative not lyrical; it lacks spontaneity and outbursts; the utter joyance of the poetry of nature and humanity, that will sing itself, is seldom present, even when nature and man are the themes. Large creative impulse is also absent. It is therefore poetry that never rises above the second class, but its place in that class is high.—RICHARDSON, CHARLES F., 1888, *American Literature, 1607–1885*, vol. II, p. 238.

"H. H." were long while familiar and welcome initials with the Transatlantic reading public, and both as a woman and a writer Mrs. Helen Hunt Jackson exercised a widespread and beneficent influence. Her "Freedom" is an especially noble sonnet, though its rhythmic strength unfortunately flags somewhat in the last line. The greatest charm of her work, both in prose and verse, is her keen sense of colour. For flowers she had what could not be called other than a passion, and her friends have delighted in recalling her eagerness and joy over every bloom and blossom in the neighbourhood of her home, near Cheyenne Mountain, in Colorado. In personality she was the most poetic of poets, and in her love of physical beauty more "Greek than the Greeks." It is probable that no woman of her time exercised such a sway over the admiration and sympathies of the younger American writers. Her "Ramona" is a prose idyl which deserves a place among the memorable works of imaginative fiction. Much of Mrs. Jackson's poetry, however, is void of its subtlest charm to those who never met her; it has the common fault of Transatlantic verse, a too nervous facility, a diffuseness which palls rather than attracts. When, a few years hence, some sympathetic but sternly critical hand shall give us a selection of all that is best in the writings of "H. H.," her name will rest on a surer basis.—SHARP, WILLIAM, 1889, ed., *American Sonnets, Introductory Note*, p. xliii.

Nature was bountiful to her. She was what is called a natural poet, human in sympathies, and with a fine lyric touch. . . . The broad human heart shows itself from one end of her writing to the other. She is essentially human, and she has eminently the faculty of creating an interest for she chooses bright, picturesque metres, and uses picturesque expressions. It was said of Longfellow that no one will deny that the world is better for his having been born. This is true also of "H. H." She was a sort of feminine Longfellow, inferior to him, as one would expect a woman to be, in scholarship and learning,— like him in striking the keynote of *home*.—SLADEN, DOUGLAS, 1891, ed., *Younger American Poets, To the Reader*, p. 28.

As a poet Mrs. Jackson's range was not a wide one, but within her limits she sang surpassingly well. She was not a creator; she simply read her own heart. The awfulness of her affliction cut her off for a time from the world, and like a great storm it cleared the atmosphere about her so that she looked far into the mysteries that encompass mortal life. It was her raptness, her mysticism, that appealed so strongly to Emerson. An intensity of feeling and expression characterizes all of her lyrics. Some of her conceits are almost startling in their vividness and originality. . . . Mrs Jackson ranks with the four or five Americans who have succeeded with the sonnet. Nearly half of her poems are written in this difficult measure.—PATTEE, FRED LEWIS, 1896, *A History of American Literature*, pp. 406, 407.

GENERAL

Mrs. Jackson soars to your estimate lawfully as a bird.—DICKINSON, EMILY, 1879, *Letters*, vol. II, p. 329.

O soul of fire within a woman's clay!
Lifting with slender hands a race's wrong,
Whose mute appeal hushed all thine early song,
And taught thy passionate heart the loftier way.
—HIGGINSON, THOMAS WENTWORTH, 1886, *To the Memory of H. H., Century Magazine*, vol. 32, p. 47.

Up to the time when she espoused the cause of the Indians all her productions sprang from a purely artistic impulse, independent of any extrinsic force; afterwards, the plastic sense was subordinated to the larger interest she had come to find in humanity. Thenceforward her simple delight in form and color and cadence are regulated by her moral convictions. It is all the difference there is between her volume of poems and "Ramona." Upon the latter, her maturest production, in spite of the spontaneity of its birth, there seems to me the seal of deliberation and effort. Yet even here I hesitate for fear of overstating; for it was when examining the proof-sheets of that charming Indian pastoral, I remember, the present writer ventured to praise the purity of its literary workmanship, to the author's evident distress. With a writer who was already a veteran, she said, that was a matter of course, and she proceeded to rebuke him gently for his insensibility to the sad reality which the picture nearly reflected. It was impossible to reply at that moment that the whole tragedy was made what it was only by her exquisitely simple and lucid art of narration, which she had come to count second to her ultimate purpose. No doubt if she had lived her art and her philanthropy would have come more into equilibrium, and mingled to produce a more perfect work than "Ramona" even.— SWINBURNE, LOUIS, 1886, *Reminiscences of Helen Jackson, New Princeton Review*, vol. 2, p. 80.

The winning and humorous side of her character appeared in her prose descriptions of travel and phases of existence, collected under the title of "Bits of Travel." It would be difficult to speak too highly of the style and spirit of these narrations. The humor is all-pervading, and carries pathos with it: a lovely, human light irradiates the pages, and makes the foibles of the characters as charming as their virtues. A broad, charitable, human mind is at work, with the delicate insight of a woman, and a steady healthfulness of mood that we are more accustomed to expect from the masculine genius.—HAWTHORNE, JULIAN, AND LEMMON, LEONARD, 1891, *American Literature*, p. 286.

Essential charm of womanhood, frank, generous, passionate, clings to the poems of Helen Hunt Jackson. The daughter of an Amherst professor, she poured forth in song the heart-break and the healing of her widowed youth. The new interests of the new life that came to her beneath the majestic beauty of the Rockies are largely expressed in prose,—in her burning pleas for the Indian, "A Century of Dishonor" and "Ramona."—BATES, KATHARINE LEE, 1897, *American Literature*, p. 178.

Richard Grant White
1822-1885

An American journalist, critic and Shakespearean scholar; born in New York city, May 22, 1822; died there, April 8, 1885. His journalistic work was in connection with the New York Courier and Enquirer (1851-58), and World (1860-61); and the London Spectator (1863-67), for which he wrote "Yankee Letters." Among his published books are: "Biographical and Critical Hand-Book of Christian Art" (1853); "Shakespeare's Scholar" (1854); "National Hymns: A Lyrical and National Study for the Times" (1861); "Memoirs of the Life of William Shakespeare, with an Essay towards the Expression of His Genius," etc. (1865); "Poetry of the Civil War" (1866); "Words and their Uses" (1870); "England Without and Within" (1881); "The Riverside Shakespeare," with biography, introduction, and notes (1883, 3 vols.); an annotated edition of Shakespeare (1857-65, 12 vols.). He published one novel, "The Fate of Mansfield Humphreys" (1884).—WARNER, CHARLES DUDLEY, ed. 1897, *Library of the World's Best Literature, Biographical Dictionary*, vol. XXIX, p. 571.

PERSONAL

A very tall young man, with a strong and not markedly handsome face, known as Richard Grant White. He talked well, [1840] and had a marked tendency to allude to the writings of one Shakespeare, of whom he appeared to be a "Scholar." He had also some very pronounced ideas connected with philology, giving promise that some day he might be heard from with reference to spellings, derivations, the morals of literature, etc.—MORFORD, HENRY, 1880, *John Keese, His Intimates, Morford's Magazine*, June.

His life was retired, and his intimates were not numerous. At concerts and at the opera his tall, erect, and striking figure (he was six feet and three inches), resembling that of an English guardsman, was very familiar to *habitués*. He was a man of many accomplishments and achievements, but almost exclusively devoted to literary and artistic pursuits.—WILSON, JAMES GRANT, 1885, *Bryant and His Friends*, p. 427.

There was a certain whimsicality in his temperament, as there was in the temperament of Mr. Charles Astor Bristed, which amused his friends and enraged his enemies. A ripe scholar, he was contemptuous toward the crass ignorance (for it could be nothing less) which questioned his *dicta*, either in regard to music, of which he was a student and a proficient; or language, in which he was acute rather than learned; or art, of which he was a skilful connoisseur; or, worse than all, the niceties of Elizabethan erudition. Courtly and polished in his personal address, his pen was apt to run away with him when once he put it on paper. His composure was exasperating,—exasperating to his equals, and maddening to his inferiors, which most of his assailants assuredly were. If he could have shut his eyes to some of the foibles of his countrymen, as the best of his countrymen shut their eyes to some of his foibles, he would have had a pleasanter time of it; and he liked a pleasant time. But he was like Iago—"nothing if not critical." . . . I can hardly say that I knew this accomplished man-of-letters, though I was acquainted with him for a quarter of a century and upwards. . . . The world is said to be a very small place, we meet the same people so often; but I have not found it so. The last time I met Mr. White was at the Authors' Club a year and a half ago. We lived within hailing distance of each other, only two streets apart, he with a southern exposure in his rooms, I with a northern one in mine. There was no reason why we should not have met often, or only the reason that the world is very, very large,—in a busy crowded city like this.—STODDARD, RICHARD HENRY, 1885, *Richard Grant White, The Critic*, vol. 6, pp. 181, 182.

The whole life of Richard Grant White was passed in New York. He was born there and he died there, and in all the intervening years his absences from the town were few and brief. . . . His knowledge of his own country from personal observation was also unusually limited for an American of any condition. Yet, long as he lived in New York, he never conceived any real affection for the great commercial capital. He was a stranger in a strange city. . . . From first to last he had no intimates among the writers of his day. Until the establishment of the Authors' Club, a short time before his death, he belonged to none of the associations of his craft. . . . He lived wholly apart from the ways and the sympathies of the literary class around him. He went to them neither for applause nor for intellectual stimulus. . . . He was keenly sensitive about the dignity of his profession and the conduct becoming a gentleman. He prided himself on never having been an applicant for any place or favor. He would not elbow his way to a superior seat; for, of all God's creatures, the being now described as a "hustler" was most odious in his eyes. . . . Mr. White was looked upon, by the younger writers more especially, as an arrogant and conventional man, starched, affected, and supercilious, incapable of other emotion than self-admiration,—vain, conceited, and a coxcomb. This impression was strengthened by the formality of his manners, the precision of his speech, and the suggestion in the cut of his garments and the character of his utterance that he was an Anglomaniac, who felt himself above his calling and his colleagues. As he was two inches upward of six feet in height, and carried himself with remarkable erectness, he did overtop them physically. . . . He was incapable of malice himself,—as incapable as he was of jealousy,—and though he had a keen sense of humor, as he demonstrated very conspicuously, he never resorted to its use as a cloak for envy and malignity. He could not accuse himself of any lack of courtesy to those with whom he came in contact, for he was always courteous and considerate to the last degree. If he never permitted obtrusive familiarity, neither did he himself fail in showing due regard for others.—CHURCH, FRANCIS P., 1891, *Richard Grant White, Atlantic Monthly, vol. 67.*

GENERAL

He has, for years, been recognized as a thinker and scholar of singular independence of character. He has shown, in treating every object he has discussed, so confident a mastery of the subject matter relating to it, and has been so bold in rigidly following out to their logical conclusions the novel, and occasionally somewhat eccentric, trains of thought he has started, that he has become a constantly questioned although still a palpable force in our literature. Perhaps he is most eagerly read by those who most vehemently disagree with him in opinion. On the whole, it may be said that no other American man of letters has had his great merits more grudgingly allowed, and his minor defects more assiduously magnified. . . . What most attracts us in his career as a professional American man of letters is the courage with which he has expressed his opinions, whether popular or unpopular; the patience with which he has investigated the materials of literary and social history on which just opinions regarding such matters are founded; and the acuteness, independence, force, and fertility of thought he has brought to the discussion of every debatable question which has attracted his attention as a critic and a scholar. We might clamorously demur to many of his most confident judgments, but the spirit which animates him as a thinker and seeker after truth appears to us pure, wise, and unselfish.—WHIPPLE, EDWIN PERCY, 1882, *Richard Grant White, Atlantic Monthly, vol. 49, pp. 214, 222.*

The death of Mr. White has left a blank in American letters which only one writer, Mr. Horace Howard Furness, can be said to fill. He was our foremost Shakespearean scholar, and was recognised as such by all competent judges abroad, even by those who dissented from many of his conclusions. . . . If I am any judge of English prose, the prose of Mr. White, when at its best, is frank, lucid, direct, and manly.—STODDARD, RICHARD HENRY, 1885, *Richard Grant White, The Critic, vol. 6, p. 181.*

The satirical power which the late Richard Grant White possessed was little known to the public, because he studiously avoided the presentation of his claims on that score. . . . By his scholarly attitude and work, as well as by his frequent anonymous contributions to press criticisms of books, he rendered good service to the cause of American letters.—LATHROP, GEORGE PARSONS, 1886, *The Literary Movement in New York, Harper's Magazine, vol. 73, p. 814.*

White's faults as a critic were a severity sometimes amounting to ill-nature; an egotistic self-assertion that was unjust to his opponents; an inability to state fairly the other side of a question; a fondness for petty discussions; and an occasional prolixity. As a writer on Shakespeare and an editor of his works, he dwelt with increasing and one-sided force upon the defects of Shakespeare's personality, until the puzzled reader wondered how Hamlet or Juliet could be evoked from the brain of so mean a man. But White exposed and shamed many pretentious ignoramuses, Shakespearean and other; he ridiculed and routed the wretched crew of annotators, "conjectural" readers, and forgers of text; and he made very clear (especially in "The Life and Genius of Shakespeare," vol. I, of the twelve-volume edition) the true and the false in the Shakespeare life-legend. Not a philologist himself, he promoted the study of the forms and uses of words; and in general he performed a sound service to American criticism by his very cynicism and coldness. Here was a writer who could sharply challenge sentimentality and half-knowledge, within his particular field. His notes on England are much inferior to Hawthorne's or Emerson's both in description and in analysis; and his one novel, portentously called "The Fate of Mansfield Humphreys; with the Episode of Mr. Washington Adams in England, and an Apology," is a laughable failure.—RICHARDSON, CHARLES F., 1887, *American Literature, 1607–1885, vol. I, p. 442.*

His "Words and their Uses," an admirable and unhackneyed guide to sound prose composition, was published in 1870; his "Every Day English," about ten years later. During this period he also wrote monthly papers for "The Galaxy" magazine, and articles, sometimes critical, sometimes controversial. In the latter, he was especially felicitous; few men were better able to annihilate an opponent, while maintaining thorough good-humor. . . . White's musical criticisms have not been rescued from the periodicals in which they originally appeared, yet they are the best that have been written in this country.—HAWTHORNE, JULIAN, AND LEMMON, LEONARD, 1891, *American Literature*, pp. 305, 306.

Sir Henry Taylor
1800–1886

Born, at Bishop Middleham, Durham, 1800. Served in Navy as Midshipman, 1814. To London, 1816. In Civil employment for some years, in London; at Barbados for few months in 1820. Settled in London, 1823. Held post in Colonial Office, 1824–72. Married the Hon. Theodosia Alicia Ellen Frances Charlotte Spring-Rice, 1839. Hon. D. C. L., Oxford, 2 July 1862, K. C. M. G., 30 June 1869. Died, at Bournemouth, 27 March, 1886. *Works:* "Isaac Comnenus" (anon.), 1827; "Philip Van Artevelde," 1834; "The Statesman," 1836; "Edwin the Fair," 1842; "The Eve of the Conquest," 1847; "Notes from Life," 1847; "Notes from Books," 1849; "The Virgin Widow," 1850; "St. Clement's Eve," 1862; "Poetical Works" (3 vols.), 1864 [1863]; "A Sicilian Summer," 1868; "Crime considered, in a letter to the Rt. Hon. W. E. Gladstone," 1868; "Autobiography . . . 1800–1875" (2 vols.), 1885 (priv. ptd. 1874–77); "Works" (5 vols.), 1877–78. *Posthumous:* "Correspondence," ed. E. Dowden, 1888.—SHARP, R. FARQUHARSON, 1897, *A Dictionary of English Authors*, p. 275.

PERSONAL

The two volumes that I send you are making a rumour, and are highly and I believe justly extolled. They are written by a friend of mine, a remarkably handsome young man whom you may have seen on one of our latest Thursday evening conversazioni.—COLERIDGE, SAMUEL TAYLOR, 1834, *To Miss Eliza Nixon, July 9; Letters*, ed. E. H. Coleridge, vol. II, p. 774.

I breakfasted in the morning at Rogers's, to meet the new poet, Mr. Taylor, the author of "Van Artevelde:" our company, besides, being Sydney Smith and Southey. Van Artevelde, a tall, handsome young fellow.—MOORE, THOMAS, 1835, *Diary, March 28; Memoirs, Journal and Correspondence*, ed. Russell, vol. VII, p. 76.

Went to breakfast with Rogers. Met Lyon, Aubrey de Vere, and to my great delight, Henry Taylor, author of "Philip Van Artevelde." He talked much, and talked well; his knowledge of our poets is very extensive indeed; he quoted much, and excellently well.—MACREADY, W. C., 1846, *Diary, July 2; Reminiscences*, ed. Pollock, p. 584.

Taylor himself, a solid, sound-headed, faithful, but not a well-read or wide-minded man, though of marked veracity, in all senses of that deep-reaching word, and with a fine readiness to apprehend new truth, and stand by it.—CARLYLE, THOMAS, 1867, *Southey, Reminiscences*, ed. Norton, vol. II, p. 278.

Though thus intoxicated by solitude, Sir Henry Taylor has had little of the Wordsworthian passion for nature. He seeks refreshment and restoration from the beauty of the world, and has a peculiar delight in sylvan recesses, the haunts of meditation; but external nature has not been for him a sibyl, a maenad, a bride, or an awful mother. His wisdom and power have been drawn from human life, from human life in certain concrete forms, leading up to generalisations which are *axiomata media*, of invaluable service to the dramatic poet, but hardly attaining the rank of first principles. . . . Sir Henry Taylor for a long time cared less for the society of men of letters than for that of wits, and less for that of wits than for the society of bright, refined, and accomplished women. Half his pleasure in their presence was social, and half was the poet's pleasure of the imagination. For sometimes it was enough that they should be seen, and should set his fancy at play. Here is a gleam of poetry in the reception-room, an oasis in the social wilderness, a solitude, a refuge, a delight amid the monstrous regiment of dowagers and damozels.—DOWDEN, EDWARD, 1885, *Autobiography of Henry Taylor, The Academy, vol.* 27, *p.* 268.

Fourscore and five times has the gradual year
Risen and fulfilled its days of youth and eld
Since first the child's eyes opening first beheld
Light, who now leaves behind to help us here
Light shed from song as starlight from a sphere
Serene as summer; song whose charm compelled
The sovereign soul made flesh in Artevelde
To stand august before us and austere,
Half sad with mortal Knowledge, all sublime
With trust that takes no taint from change or time,
Trust in man's might of manhood. Strong and sage,
Clothed round with reverence of remembering hearts,
He, twin-born with our nigh departing age,
Into the light of peace and fame departs.
—SWINBURNE, ALGERNON CHARLES, 1886, *On the Death of Sir Henry Taylor, The Athenæum, No.* 3050, *p.* 488.

His life was full of honour, and the close of it thoroughly to be envied. In the midst of a loving family he went, without a pang or a struggle, into the rest of death. His reputation as a man of letters, though perhaps of slow growth, is destined, I think, to endure. Though a zealous interest in literature was the ruling passion of his nature, I know no one, since Walter Scott, who rose above the ordinary defects of the literary character, more thoroughly and nobly. Jealousy and vanity were unknown to him, and if a man cannot be a poet without belonging to the "genus irritable," a poet he was not. His genius, in truth, if not of the highest order, had nothing in common with the genius of disease; on the contrary, it was braced and strengthened by great general ability, a sound judgment, and a masculine good sense. . . . He cared a great deal for many things, but what he did not care a great deal for, he put aside as if it had no existence. He therefore allowed sundry subjects, which might have brought him, a dramatic poet, into closer and more cordial intercourse with varieties of men, to lie outside his ken, and this limited in some degree his reach of imagination, and his powers of thought. He has spoken for himself in his memoirs, so that these remarks are perhaps superfluous, but I could not pass over the loss of so dear a friend in silence.—DOYLE, SIR FRANCIS HASTINGS, 1886, *Reminiscences and Opinions, pp.* 408, 409.

After an intimacy with him extending much over forty years, I never saw him once out of temper or once made anxious about trifles. He lived in a large world, built up by justice and truth, and in him there was no small world. . . . He was not only free from morbidness, but without a touch of sensitiveness. No criticism pained him, and no friend feared to speak to him with entire frankness. In his young days he was said to be a severe censor; but as life advanced, his judgments became more indulgent without becoming less just. He judged deeds as before; but not always those who did them. . . . It may be well to add that by no virtue was he more signally marked than by humility.—DE VERE, AUBREY, 1897, *Recollections, pp.* 177, 178.

PHILIP VAN ARTEVELDE
1834

I have been really *cheered* and delighted by some passages of a new work—"Philip Van Artevelde"—and more particularly by parts of its noble preface contained in the Athenæum of to-day. I feel assured that you will greet as gladly as myself the rising up of what appears to be a majestic mind amongst us; and the putting forth of strengthening and elevating views respecting the high purposes of intellectual power. I have already sent to order the book, feeling that it will be quite an addition to the riches of *my mental estate.*—HEMANS, FELICIA DOROTHEA, 1834, *Letter, May; Memorials, ed. Chorley, vol.* II, *p.* 311.

Years and years have passed since it came in the way of our office to call attention to the appearance of a new English poem at once of such pretensions and such execution. If Mr. Taylor should devote himself to dramatic composition with a view to *the stage*, he must learn to brace his dialogue somewhat more tightly, and to indulge less in discursive reflection; but he has already done enough to secure himself a place among the real artists of his time.—LOCKHART, JOHN GIBSON, 1834, *Philip Van Artevelde, The Quarterly Review, vol.* 51, *p.* 391.

I have heard the word "washy" applied to the superficial style of painting, where the figures have no depth, massiveness, substance, and the epithet seems to me to suit a good deal of the fashionable poetry and fiction. One admirable exception I lately met with in "Philip Van Artevelde."

Here I found myself amidst real beings, breathing the breath of life, and, in spite of some affectation of style, speaking and acting from their own souls, and not graceful or sentimental puppets, through whom the author shows you his skill and fine thoughts. —CHANNING, WILLIAM ELLERY, 1835, *To Miss Aikin, Jan. 5; Correspondence of William Ellery Channing and Lucy Aikin, ed. Le Breton*, p. 234.

The publication of his poem in this country was preceded by such high encomiums from the leading Reviews of Great Britain, that it was impossible that its reception amongst us should be unprejudiced and impartial; and if, notwithstanding the first feeling of disappointment from this cause and the detection of some faults in the work which we were not prepared to see, we have yet risen from its perusal with a conviction that it is a work of rare beauty and power, there can be no doubt that it well deserves this character. It is a very daring work, and risks failure in every way by attempting to unite every variety of composition in one piece. It passes from the stern to the tender, from the lofty to the pathetic, and strikes all the changes of the heroic, the lyric, the dramatic, and the descriptive, the didactic, and the familiar. No young author ever made his beginning in a bolder and more venturesome enterprise, or by his first attempt secured a more decided claim to be esteemed a writer of high and diversified talents, whose fame is already sure.—WARE, HENRY, JR., 1835, *Taylor's Philip Van Artevelde, Christian Examiner*, vol. 19, p. 245.

The arguments of Mr. Taylor lead us directly to the question of why does he not write in prose? Certainly "Philip Van Artevelde" would have been as dramatic and romantic in prose as in its present form. Its rhythm appears unnecessary, and he evidently feels it. After writing a romance in about ten thousand lines of verse, which ought to have been three volumes of elegant prose, he then composes a Preface to justify the proceeding. He says, "My critical views have rather resulted from composition than directed it." Finding he could rise no higher, he strives to show that rising higher would argue a loss "of the equipoise of reason."—HORNE, RICHARD HENGIST, 1844, *A New Spirit of the Age*, p. 354.

First and highest in this list comes "Philip Van Artevelde," of which we can say that it bears new fruit at the twentieth reading. At first it fell rather coldly on the mind, coming as it did, not as the flower of full flushed being, but with the air of an experiment made to verify a theory. It came with wrinkled critic's brow, consciously antagonistic to a tendency of the age, and we looked on it with cold critic's eye, unapt to weep or glow at its bidding. But, on closer acquaintance, we see that this way of looking, though induced by the author, is quite unjust. It is really a noble work that teaches us, a genuine growth that makes us grow, a reflex of nature from the calm depths of a large soul. The grave and comprehensive character of the ripened man, of him whom fire, and light, and earth have tempered to an intelligent delegate of humanity, has never been more justly felt, rarely more life-like painted, than by this author. — OSSOLI, MARGARET FULLER, 1850(?), *The Modern Drama; Art, Literature, and the Drama*, p. 124.

Though the motion is often quick and always progressive in Mr. Taylor's plays, though there is much of humour in them and much also of pathos, he does not depend on action only for his effect; but lays bare and examines the sources of action, and shows the early, underground springs of the mind from which the rivers of thought well up to the light with admirable success. I do not know that we have a clearer idea of the inward working of Hamlet's mind than we have of that of Van Artevelde, as he rises through patriotism from the contented philosophy of private life to be the saviour of his city and dictator of his countrymen; and afterwards falls through too close a contact with worldly greatness and worldly ways into sin, violence, and destruction.—TROLLOPE, ANTHONY, 1865, *Henry Taylor's Poems, Fortnightly Review*, vol. 1, p. 131.

The author of the finest dramatic poem of our time.—HOLLAND, SIR HENRY, 1871, *Recollections of Past Life*, p. 11.

There are those, the writer is one, in whose life the first reading and re-reading of "Philip Van Artevelde" was an epoch. The other writings of Sir Henry Taylor, both in prose and verse, left their impression, but the great "Dramatic Romance" has always stood alone. It was not merely the wonderful thoughtfulness and beauty of passages beyond number: and not many readers know how many lines from "Philip

Van Artevelde" have passed into stock quotations: *The world knows nothing of its greatest men* has been said by numbers who never read a play of Sir Henry Taylor's. But there was a strange and awe-inspiring influence exerted upon youthful readers by the stern sobriety, the restrained good sense, combined with the bright gleam of something very near to the highest poetic genius. One thought the author must be sixty at least: we find he was only thirty-four: though in the days of the first enthusiastic study of the drama that would have appeared as advanced middle age. Good sense, in combination with brilliancy, overawes readers of twenty-two: impresses them with the sense of an infinite elevation above their own standpoint.—BOYD, ANDREW K. H., 1885, *Sir Henry Taylor's Autobiography*, *Longman's Magazine*, vol. 5, *p.* 624.

The poem is remarkable throughout for its metre, which cannot be surpassed in force, variety, harmony, and dramatic significance. . . . His is not the poetry which contents itself with raking superficially the loose soil of the affections. He ploughs deeply, and turns up a substratum of human feeling not often revealed to light in the merely descriptive drama so common in modern times. . . . Were a critic to describe "Philip Van Artevelde" in one word, he might say it was a solid work. In its extreme thoughtfulness it preserves the better characteristics of our age; but those who have only been in the habit of reading poetry as a trivial amusement, or a relaxation from study, and who are only familiar with works produced to gratify the taste of the moment, to stimulate the jaded appetite, to flatter an abject love of the mere ornaments of poetry, or an effeminate dependence on its sensual part,—all those persons must have at first felt surprised at finding themselves confronted with a work so substantial in its materials, so manly in its structure, so severe in its style, and so gravely impressive in spirit and general tendency, as this remarkable work. It is full of the philosophy of practical life; and in this respect it is analogous to many productions of an age which has occupied itself with the philosophy of all subjects.—DE VERE, AUBREY, 1887, *Essays Chiefly on Poetry*, vol. I, pp. 288, 293.

As a study of a group of characters, "Philip Van Artevelde" stands almost alone.—JAPP, ALEXANDER H., 1894, *The Poets and the Poetry of the Century*, Keats to Lytton, ed. Milnes, p. 314.

"Philip Van Artevelde" is so clearly Taylor's best work that his literary faculty may be judged, certainly without danger of depreciation, from it alone. It is a historical drama, and the title sufficiently indicates the age and country in which the scene is laid. The whole drama is long, and the slow movement adapts it rather for reading than for representation. It is composed of two parts, separated by "The Lay of Elena," a lyrical piece in which may be detected echoes both of Wordsworth and Coleridge, with an occasional suggestion of Scott. . . . A man of talent with a touch of genius, Taylor saw clearly what the poetry of his time needed, but for want of the "passion of thought" he failed to supply it. —WALKER, HUGH, 1897, *The Age of Tennyson*, pp. 62, 63.

GENERAL

Henry Taylor's Tragedies are of the very best kind.—SOUTHEY, ROBERT, 1834, *To C. C. Bedford, July 3*; *Life and Correspondence*, ch. xxxv.

I think, or hope, that he will yet write things worthy of ungrudging praise; and I much approve his manly style, as an antidote to the sentimental jargon of which we have so much; but he must cultivate moral refinement, to give pleasure where he must wish to please. Above all, he must never again make his hero exclaim, "How little flattering is a woman's love!"—AIKIN, LUCY, 1835, *To Dr. Channing, March 10*; *Correspondence of William Ellery Channing and Lucy Aikin*, ed. Le Breton, p. 241.

The diligent students and cultivated admirers of poetry will assign to the author of "Edwin the Fair" a rank second to none of the competitors for the laurel in his own generation. They will celebrate the rich and complex harmony of his metre, the masculine force of his understanding, the wide range of his survey of life and manners, and the profusion with which he can afford to lavish his intellectual resources. The mere lovers of his art will complain, that in the consciousness of his own mental wealth, he forgets the prevailing poverty; that he levies too severe a tribute of attention, and exacts from a thoughtless world meditations more deep, and abstractions more prolonged, than they are able or willing to command. . . They will admit that the author of "Edwin the Fair" can both judge as a philosopher, and feel as a poet; but will wish that his poetry had been less philosophical, or his philosophy less poetical. It is a wish that will be seconded by those who revere his wisdom, and delight in his genius; and who, therefore, regret to anticipate that his labours will hardly be rewarded by an early or an extensive popularity.—STEPHEN, SIR JAMES, 1842, *Taylor's Edwin the Fair, Edinburgh Review, vol.* 76, *p.* 120.

No educated person can read the works of Mr. Taylor without a consciousness that he is communing with a mind of high order. They are reflective and dignified, and are written in pure and nervous English. The dialogue is frequently terse and impressive, and sometimes highly dramatic. Mr. Taylor has no sickly sentiment, and scarcely any pathos or passion; but in his writings there are pleasant shows of feeling, fancy, and imagination which remind us that he might have been a poet of a different sort had he been governed by a different theory. His principal faults, so far as style is concerned, are occasional coarseness of expression, and inappropriate or disagreeable imagery. He exhibits also a want of that delicacy and refinement of conduct and feeling in some of his characters which would have resulted from a nicer sense of the beautiful and a more loving spirit in himself.—GRISWOLD, RUFUS W., 1844, *The Poets and Poetry of England in the Nineteenth Century, p.* 408.

Taylor, whose noble intellect and fine constructive powers were early affected by the teachings of Wordsworth, entered a grand protest against the sentimentalism into which the Byronic passion now had degenerated. He would, I believe, have done even better work, if this very influence of Wordsworth had not deadened his genuine dramatic power. He saw the current evils, but could not substitute a potential excellence or found an original school. As it is, "Philip Van Artevelde" and "Edwin the Fair" have gained a place for him in English literature more enduring than the honors awarded to many popular authors of his time. — STEDMAN, EDMUND CLARENCE, 1875–87, *Victorian Poets, p.* 237.

His success in characterisation seems to be limited to the cases in which he has drawn upon his observation, or in which ample data for the construction of types have lain at his disposal. Where he has failed it is evident that he has transcended the range of sight, or been inadequately furnished with historical and biographical material. The students of his plays must be content to miss the shaping forethought, the definite analysis, the vivid energy, and intense passion of the great dramatists; but, in lieu of these, they will be rewarded with a discriminating selection of dramatic subjects, many truthful portraits and representations of historical scenery, much ripe scholarship and sound wisdom, habitual dignity and occasional grace of style, and a uniformly high-minded and healthy tone.— HEWLETT, HENRY G., 1880, *The Works of Sir Henry Taylor, Nineteenth Century, vol.* 8, *p.* 811.

The subject of this Saxon drama abounds in variety of interests, political, ecclesiastical, personal, and romantic; and not less various are the modes of treatment.... Throughout it we find one spirit; the spirit, namely, of England in the time of that struggle which raged with such violence between the "men of arms and the men of thought." Throughout the whole play we trace this spirit working its way in different characters according to their constitution, varying with their varieties, but everywhere active.—DEVERE, AUBREY, 1887, *Essays Chiefly on Poetry, vol.* II, *pp.* 3, 14.

Sir Henry Taylor was a man of sterling moral worth, intellectual power, sound wisdom, refined taste, and mature judgment; a man of thought and scholarship; and, more especially, a dramatic poet of great and peculiar ability, whose works, thoroughly English in character, have deservedly given him an enduring reputation among all thoughtful readers.—SYMINGTON, ANDREW JAMES, 1888, *North Country Poets, ed. Andrews, p.* 238.

His chief dramatic poem, "Philip Van Artevelde," has had the good fortune to please the critics, and has been greatly applauded and admired in those circles where applause is the most sweet, but it cannot be said ever to have caught the general ear. It has not sufficient force either of life or of poetry to secure that wider audience, yet the place of the author among contemporary poets has always been high, though without this essential basis of fame. His other works—"Edwin the Fair," the "Virgin Widow," and "St. Clement's Eve"— have not, we think, gained even this *succès d'estime.*—OLIPHANT, MARGARET O. W., 1892, *The Victorian Age of English Literature*, p. 242.

Sir Henry Taylor, though the bulk of his poems are in the form of dramas, was not *par excellence* a dramatic poet. He had more regard for the delicacies of character, and the *nuances* of thought in relation to them, than for incident, situation, and what would go towards effect in representation. In truth, his dramas are overweighted with thought and reflection—"too full of good things," as has been said. . . . Sir Henry Taylor was generally too inclined to brood and meditate over his "men and women" to present them with that force of sustained and convincing reality needful for the stage. . . . He was a wonderful restorer of historical episodes; a romancer born out of due time, seeking to accommodate himself to a form hardly in keeping with his spirit and temper. Many bright droplets of lyrical verse are scattered through the plays, full of light and natural naïveté and brightness. The same has to be said of the short poems printed at the end of the plays.—JAPP, ALEXANDER H., 1894, *The Poets and The Poetry of the Century, Keats to Lytton*, ed. Milnes, pp. 313, 316.

There is always a public for what is called "thoughtful" poetry, and Taylor's is more than merely thoughtful. But it may be suspected by observers that when Robert Browning came into fashion Henry Taylor went out.—SAINTSBURY, GEORGE, 1896, *A History of Nineteenth Century Literature*.

His work is like his life, smooth, calm, unchargeable with faults; but it is not the kind that animates mankind.—WALKER, HUGH, 1897, *The Age of Tennyson*, p. 62.

William Barnes
1801–1886

Born, near Pentridge, Dorsetshire [22 Feb. ?] 1801; baptized 20 March. At school at Sturminster; entered Solicitor's office there, 1814 or 1815; to another at Dorchester, 1818. Contrib., verses to "Weekly Entertainer," 1820. Took Mastership of School, at Mere, Wiltshire, 1823; settled at Chantry House, Mere, 1827; Married Julia Miles, [summer of 1827?]. Contrib. to "Dorset County Chronicle," 1827–35; to "Gentleman's Mag.," 1831–41. Two farces by him performed by travelling dramatic company, 1832; contrib. to "Hone's Year Book," 1832. Wrote first poems in Dorsetshire dialect, 1833. Gave up school at Mere and opened one in Dorchester, 1835. Entered name on books of St. John's Coll., Cambridge, 1837. Intimacy with Sheridan begun, 1844. Visit to London, June, 1844. Sec. of Dorset County Museum at its foundation, 1845. Ordained Deacon, 28 Feb. 1847; Priest, 14 March 1848; Pastor of Whitcombe, near Dorchester, Feb., 1847 to Jan. 1852. Resided three terms at St. John's College, Cambridge, 1847, 1848, 1850; B. D. degree, Oct., 1850. Visit to London, 1851. Wife died, 21 June, 1852. Contrib. to "Retrospective Review," 1853–54. Civil List Pension, April 1861; contrib., to "Macmillan's Magazine," 1861–67. Presented with Rectorship of Came, Jan. 1862. Gave up school and removed to Came, July 1862. Friendship with Tennyson and Coventry Patmore begun, 1862. Contrib. to "Fraser's Magazine," 1863; to "Ladies' Treasury," 1863–67. Gave reading of his poems, 1863-65. Active literary life. Severe illness, 1884. Died, at Came, 11 Oct. 1886; buried there. *Works:* "Orra," 1822; "The Etymological Glossary," 1829; "A Catechism of Government in General," 1833; "The Mnemonic Manual," 1833; "A Few Words on the Advantages of a more common adoption of Mathematics as a branch of Education," 1834; "A Mathematical Investigation of the principle of Hanging Doors," 1835; "An Investigation of the Laws of Case," 1840; "An Arithmetical and Commercial Dictionary," 1841; "A Pronouncing Dictionary of Geographical Names," 1841; "The Elements of Grammar," 1842; "The Elements of Linear Perspective," 1842; "Exercises in Practical Science," 1844; "Sabbath Days," 1844; "Poems of Rural Life, in the Dorset Dialect," 1844; "Poems, partly of Rural Life, in national English," 1846; "Outlines of Geography," 1847; "Se Gefylsta," 1849; "Humilis Domus," 1849; "A Philological Grammar," 1854; "Notes on Ancient Britain and the Britons," 1858; "Hwomely Rhymes: a second collection of poems in the Dorset dialect," 1859; "Views of Labour and Gold," 1859; "The Song of Solomon, in the Dorset Dialect" (privately printed), 1859; "Tiw," 1862; "A Grammar and Glossary of the Dorset Dialect," 1864; "Poems of Rural Life in the Dorset Dialect: third collection," 1862; "A Guide to

Dorchester," 1864; "Poems of Rural Life in Common English," 1868; "Early England and the Saxon English," 1869; "A Paper on Somerset," 1869; "An Outline of English Speech-craft," 1878; "Poems of Rural Life in the Dorset Dialect" (collections i.-iii. together), 1879; "An Outline of Redecraft," 1880; "A Glossary of the Dorset Dialect," 1886. He *edited:* J. Poole's "Glossary and Some Pieces of Verse of the Old Dialect, etc.," 1867. *Life:* by his daughter, Lucy Baxter, 1887.—SHARP, R. FARQUHARSON, 1897, *A Dictionary of English Authors, p.* 18.

PERSONAL

Mr. Barnes has a face of the finest Saxon type, its natural strength filtered, so to say, and refined through generations of pure and thoughtful life. His features are regular, his forehead high, broad, and serene, his mouth wears a kindly smile, and his snow-white hair and beard—the latter falling almost to his breast—form a fit frame for a countenance at once venerable and vivacious. He wears an antique Dorset gentleman's dress, with black silk stockings fastened at the knee with buckles, a costume decidedly quaint, and at first seeming to be the Episcopal costume. What most struck me about him was the look of spiritual and intellectual health, and the expression of these in his soft blue eyes, and in his clear flexible voice. I could not help feeling some surprise that he should be a clergyman, as the traits and tone of the literary man seemed to be so preponderant in him.—CONWAY, MONCURE DANIEL, 1874, *South-Coast Saunterings in England, Harper's Magazine, vol.* 48, *p.* 188.

If a Dorset man, who loves his country, cannot write of William Barnes without affectionate bias, fellow-natives will easily forgive him; and the kind alien reader will add the needful grain of salt to this brief notice of the poet who has just closed a long and honoured life, spent wholly in the county of his birth, of his heart, and of his song. Among my earliest memories are his face and figure, when he was master of a school in Dorchester, which he left some twenty-four years since for the care of a neighbouring village. There, in quiet activity, he passed the rest of his days; a delightful neighbour and friend, a pious, wise, and kindly clergyman (not unlike him that Chaucer drew). None who knew him can forget the charm of his society and conversation. He was enthusiastic on matters philological and antiquarian, and brought to bear on them abundant originality and varied and curious learning. But no subject of human interest came amiss to him; only of his own poetry he did not care to talk. Talk of it or not, however, he could not talk *it*. His habitual cast of thought and sentiment seemed to be just what one sees, heightened and rhythmic, in his poems.—MOULE, C. W., 1886, *William Barnes, The Academy, vol.* 30, *p.* 277.

Notwithstanding the wide appreciation of his verse both here and in America, so largely local were the poet's interests that it may be questioned if the enthusiasm which accompanied his own readings of his works in the town-halls of the shire was not more grateful to him than the admiration of a public he had never seen. The effect, indeed, of his recitations upon an audience well acquainted with the *nuances* of the dialect—impossible to impart to outsiders by any kind of translation—can hardly be imagined by readers of his lines acquainted only with English in its customary form. The poet's own mild smile at the boisterous merriment provoked by his droll delivery of such pieces as "The Shy Man," "A Bit o' Sly Coorten," and "Dick and I" returns upon the memory as one of the most characteristic aspects of a man who was nothing if not genial; albeit that, while the tyranny of his audience demanded these broadly humorous productions, his own preferences were for the finer and more pathetic poems, such as "Wife a-lost," "Woak Hill," and "Jaäy a-past." . . . Few young people who have seen him only in latter life, since the pallor and stoop of old age overcame him, can realize the robust, upright form of his middle life, the ruddy cheek, and the bright quick eye. The last, indeed, dimmed but slightly, and even on his death-bed his zest for the subject of speech-form was strong as ever. In one of his latest conversations he became quite indignant at the word "bicycle." "Why didn't they call it 'wheel-saddle'?" he exclaimed. Though not averse to social intercourse, his friendships extended over but a small area of society.—HARDY, THOMAS, 1886, *The Rev. William Barnes, The Athenæum, No.* 3077, *p.* 502.

So uniformly mild were his manners and language that he was often suspected of being deficient in determination and spirit; a suspicion which in reality had no very solid justification; but Barnes was such a decided advocate of peace at any price that he would never, except when driven by sheer necessity, enter any arena as a probable disputant. . . . Barnes was of medium height, stoutly built, and his face, though instinct with profound and, as it were, quiet intelligence, was composed of somewhat heavy features. It is noticeable that in very early manhood his head was as bald as it was at the latest period of his life. . . . Not only whilst he was in the schoolroom, but throughout the day, Barnes usually—constantly, I was about to say—wore, in all seasons, clement or inclement, a long, light-blue, rough-faced, flannel-textured dressing gown. In fact, during the whole time—four or five years—that I was numbered among his pupils, I rarely saw him otherwise attired: and now, whenever he presents himself to my imagination, he invariably wears the well-remembered garment: to me that long-flowing gown is inseparably associated with the man.—WALLIS, C. J.,1888, *Early Manhood of William Barnes, Gentleman's Magazine, vol. 265, pp. 26, 28, 30.*

GENERAL

Mr. Barnes, with an accurate estimate, I think, not so much of his own powers, as of the powers and resources of his Dorsetshire Doric, has confined himself to the lyrical interpretation of such simple emotions as arise out of the simple drama of an average country life. I refer this absence of ambitious aim, in his little odes, to the nature of his dialect, rather than to any deficiency in himself; because I do not choose to believe, though some such assumption is constantly made, that the art of doing one thing very well implies that you are to do everything else particularly ill. . . . As a rule, his little pieces exhibit a delicate grace and a completeness not unworthy of Horace. . . . At the time, moreover, when I began to turn this lecture over in my mind several laudatory articles referring to him, which have recently appeared, were still unwritten. I do not, however, regret the labour which I have given to the subject; he deserves, unless I deceive myself, all and more than all, the notice which he has obtained; and I am happy to find the conclusions, at which I had arrived in this matter, fortified by the unanimous concurrence of so many able critics. It is surely no light praise for an author, by one and the same work, to render valuable services to philology, and to secure, without requiring a particle of indulgence on any ground of dialect, the renown of a distinguished poet.—DOYLE, SIR FRANCIS HASTINGS, 1868, *Lectures Delivered Before the University of Oxford, pp. 63, 66, 75.*

His poems seldom exhibit a very striking thought, or perhaps even a very original expression; but they all have a sort of atmosphere of homely romance which renders them genuinely poetical. Yet the reader cannot help regretting their faintness, while he acknowledges their delicacy.—JOHNSON, ROSSITER, 1875, *Little Classics, Authors, p. 18.*

To this primary claim to an abiding place among such minor classics as Herbert, Suckling, Herrick, Burns, and Blake, William Barnes adds that of a sustained perfection of art with which none of them can compare. His language has the continual slight novelty which Aristotle inculcates as proper to true poetic expression, and something much higher than the *curiosa felicitas*, which has been absurdly rendered "curious felicity," but which means the "careful luck" of him who tries many words, and has the wit to know when memory, or the necessity of metre or rhyme, has supplied him unexpectedly with those which are perhaps even better than he knew how to desire. The words of Barnes are not the carefully made clothes, but the body of his thoughts and feelings. Another still rarer praise of his work is that he never stops in it till he has said all that should be said, and never exceeds that measure by a syllable; and about this art there is not the slightest apparent consciousness either of its abundant fulness or its delicate reticence. He seems, in fact, never to have written except under the sense of a subject that makes its own form, and of feelings which form their own words—that is to say, he is always classic both in form and substance.—PATMORE, COVENTRY, 1886-98, *Principle in Art, p. 138.*

With the exception of a few pieces by Tennyson, and the more disputable exception of one or two songs in the Lancashire dialect, Mr. Barnes's "Poems of Rural Life" are the only compositions in any English "folk-speech" that have won an acknowledged place in the national literature. There is little danger in predicting that these charming idylls will continue to be read with admiration and delight when many a more conspicuous poetic reputation of the present day has long been forgotten.—BRADLEY, HENRY, 1886, *A Glossary of the Dorset Dialect*, The Academy, vol. 29, p. 214.

Unlike Burns, Béranger, and other poets of the people, Mr. Barnes never assumed the high conventional style; and he entirely leaves alone ambition, pride, despair, defiance, and other of the grander passions which move mankind great and small. His rustics are, as a rule, happy people, and very seldom feel the sting of the rest of modern mankind—the disproportion between the desire for serenity and the power of obtaining it. One naturally thinks of Crabbe in this connection; but though they touch at points, Crabbe goes much further than Barnes in questioning the justice of circumstance. Their pathos, after all, is the attribute upon which the poems must depend for their endurance; and the incidents which embody it are those of everyday cottage life, tinged throughout with that "light that never was," which the emotional art of the lyrist can project upon the commonest things. It is impossible to prophesy, but surely much English literature will be forgotten when "Woak Hill" is still read for its intense pathos, "Blackmore Maidens," for its blitheness, and "In the Spring" for its Arcadian ecstasy.—HARDY, THOMAS, 1886, *The Rev. William Barnes*, The Athenæum, No. 3077, p. 502.

By far the best rural poet South Britain ever had, followed no model but nature.—GARNETT, RICHARD, 1887, *The Reign of Queen Victoria*, ed. Ward, vol. II, p. 464.

We have in English nothing equal to them. Mr. Barnes's Lancaster Ballads are admirable, but they have not the easy truth to nature of these sonnets of Belli.—STORY, WILLIAM WETMORE, 1890, *Conversations in a Studio*, vol. II, p. 550.

The verses of Barnes, like his studies, bear all the marks of the English character. No English poet, of first rank, has ever been so free from foreign influence in any age. "I do not want," he said, "to be trammelled with the thoughts and style of other poets, and I take none as my model, except the Persian and Italian, on which I have framed some, as regards only metre and rhyme." This is notable. Barnes never gets beyond his Dorsetshire fields. Many, since another English poet as he, Nicholas of Guilford, six hundred years before, wrote, also in Dorsetshire, his "Owl and the Nightingale," have written out of the pure love of their native country, but none have written so singly. Barnes is like one of our forest oaks, so typical of English landscape. His verse, like Langland's, is full of righteousness; like Chaucer's, it is filled with the joy of life.—More rustic than Crabbe, more literary than Clare, there are no eclogues in the English language which can compare, in perfection of touch, with the protypes of Theocritus and Virgil, save only those which are to be found in the poetry of William Barnes.—SAYLE, CHARLES, 1894, *The Poets and the Poetry of the Century, Keats to Lytton*, ed. Miles, p. 402.

The landscape of this admirable poet in all its details is presented to us simply as it presented itself to his eye and heart—simply as a pleasure to the mind; perfectly truthful, yet not itself dwelt on or moralised. It is with him the fit, the ever-present background to human life in the country, for Dorset to Barnes forms his England. Wholly modern, almost wholly devoted to his simple neighbours; purely Christian as was his work in song—yet its truest parallels may be found in many lyrics of Horace and the Greek "Anthology." They are alike in admirably accurate and appropriate glimpses of Nature, in the variety of characters exhibited, in tenderness of feeling, in exquisite simplicity, in perfect poetical unity. . . . We have no one, Crabbe excepted, who has approached him in the multitude of his scenes and characters, taken almost wholly from the village life of his birth-county—pictures which, though not excluding its darker aspects, yet often display healthy labour and healthy happiness; whilst, turning to their qualities as art, these endless lyrics never fail in sweet simple words, set to sweet simple music, in metres most skilfully handled or invented; never fail, lastly, in a unity and felicity of treatment which has been justly compared to the exquisite skill of Horace. Various tests have been proposed of genuine feeling for poetry. As one, I would venture to add —a true appreciation of William Barnes.—PALGRAVE, FRANCIS TURNER, 1896, *Landscape in Poetry*, pp. 269, 272.

The great charm of his poetry is its perfect freshness. The Dorset poems are eclogues, wholly free from the artificiality which commonly mars compositions of that class; they are clear, simple, rapid and natural. There is no affectation of profound thought, and no straining after passion, but a wholly unaffected love for the country and all that lives and grows there. The vital importance of language to poetry is nowhere more clearly seen than in Barnes, for all the spirit of the Dorset poems evaporates, and all the colour fades from the specimens the poet was induced to publish in literary English.—WALKER, HUGH, 1897, *The Age of Tennyson, p.* 66.

Richard Chenevix Trench
1807–1886

Born, in Dublin, 9 Sept. 1807. Early education at Twyford; at Harrow, 1819–25. Matric. Trin Coll., Camb. 1825; B. A., 1829; M. A., 1833; B. D., 1850; D. D., 1856. Travelled on Continent, 1829. Married Hon. Frances Mary Trench, 31 May 1832. Ordained Deacon, 1832; Priest, 1833. Curate of Curdridge, 1835–40; of Alverstoke, 1840–45. Rector of Itchinstoke, 1845–46. Hulsean Lecturer, Camb., 1845–46; Chaplain to Bp. of Oxford, 1847–64. Professor of Divinity, King's Coll., London, 1847–58. Dean of Westminster, Oct., 1856 to 1863, Dean of Order of Bath, 1856–64. Archbishop of Dublin and Bishop of Glendalough and Kildare, Jan. 1864; resigned, Nov. 1884. Chancellor of Order of St. Patrick, 1864–84. D. D., Dublin, 1864. Died, in London, 28 March 1886. Buried in Westminster Abbey. *Works* [exclusive of separate sermons, ecclesiastical charges, etc.]: "The Story of Justin Martyr," 1835; "Sabbation," 1838; "Notes on the Parables of Our Lord," 1841; "Poems from Eastern Scources," 1842; "Genoveva," 1842; "Five Sermons," 1843; "Exposition of the Sermon on the Mount," 1844; "Hulsean Lectures for 1845," 1845; "Hulsean Lectures for 1846," 1846; "Sacred Poems for Mourners," 1846; "Notes on the Miracles of Our Lord," 1846; "The Star of the Wise Men," 1850; "On the Study of Words," 1851; "On the Lessons in Proverbs," 1853; "Synonyms of the New Testament," 1854 (2nd edn. same year); "Alma," 1855; "English, Past and Present," 1855; "Five Sermons," 1856; "On some Deficiencies in our English Dictionaries," 1857; "On the Authorized Version of the New Testament," 1858; "A Select Glossary of English Words used formerly in Senses different from their Present," 1859; "Sermons Preached in Westminster Abbey," 1860; "Commentary on the Epistles to the Seven Churches in Asia," 1861; "The Subjection of the Creature to Vanity," 1863; "The Salt of the Earth, etc.," 1864; "Gustavus Adolphus, etc.," 1865; "Poems," 1865; "Studies on the Gospels," 1867; "Shipwrecks of Faith," 1867; "Plutarch," 1873; "Sermons, preached for the most part in Dublin," 1873; "Lectures on Mediæval Church History," 1877; "Brief Thoughts and Meditations on some passages in Holy Scripture," 1884; "Sermons, New and Old," 1886. *Posthumous:* "Letters and Memorials," ed. by M. M. F. Trench (2 vols.), 1888; "Westminster and other Sermons," 1888. He *translated:* "Life's a Dream, etc.," from the Spanish of Calderon, 1856; and *edited:* "Sacred Latin Poetry," 1849; his mother's "Journal" [1861] and "Remains," 1862; "A Household Book of English Poetry," 1868.—SHARP, R. FARQUHARSON, *A Dictionary of English Authors, p.* 282.

PERSONAL

Went to South Place to luncheon, and met Dean Trench there,—a large melancholy face, full of earnestness and capacity for woe.—FOX, CAROLINE, 1846, *Memories of Old Friends,* ed. *Pym.; Journal, May* 18, *p.* 224.

At "Dublin's" breakfast, I met Robert Browning, Dean Stanley, Lady Augusta, a lot more ladies, and a duke or two, and, after breakfast, "Dublin" read to me—with his five beautiful daughters grouped about —from Browning, Arnold, Rossetti, and others, till the day was far spent. When I went away he promised to send me his books. He did so, I put them in my trunk, and did not open them till I got to America. Fancy my consternation as well as amazement and delight to find that this "Dublin" was Trench, the author of "Trench on Words." Ah! Why didn't he sign his name Trench? for I knew the book almost by heart.—MILLER, JOAQUIN, 1870, *Memorie and Rime, p.* 28.

I found his grace to be all that I had pictured him, and more. In person he was large, though not tall, with a massive head, dark, expressive eyes, and deep toned but pleasant voice. His manner was quiet and unaffected. There was no show or pretension about him, no assumption of superior dignity, no display of vast attainments; but in reality he was as plain and simple in speech as if he were not, what I knew him to be, a profoundly learned scholar and divine, and one able to pronounce definitive judgement on numerous questions in theological, classical, and historical lore.—SPENCER, JESSE AMES, 1890, *Memorabilia of Sixty-Five Years, p.* 203.

Once upon a time on that spot, Richard Trench and I fell out over a game of quoits. He lost his temper, flew into an Irish rage, took up a quoit and threw it at my head. Such an outrage called for instant chastisement, and I am afraid it must be said that I administered it, as boys are wont to do, rather too savagely; for the next day he had to go to London to see a dentist, in order to have his teeth, which had suffered in the fray, put to rights. Who would have supposed that such an encounter could ever have taken place between the future sedate and amiable Archbishop and the future advocate of reconciliation among Christians? Perhaps it was desirable for the formation and development of both our characters. It may be that the former, considering the temper that he often showed as a boy, had need to undergo some such experience ere he could attain to the perfection of mildness and equanimity which he displayed in after life.—WORDSWORTH, CHARLES, 1891, *Annals of My Early Life,* 1806–1846, *p.* 30.

GENERAL

From his "Justin Martyr," through his "Elegiac Poems," down to those from Eastern sources, his course towards compositional excellence has been steady and evident. In the last-mentioned volume especially there are several poems of exquisite beauty, whose music lingers on the memory and refuses to be forgotten.—MOIR, D. M., 1851–52, *Poetical Literature of the Past Half-Century.*

Order into your Book Club "Trench on the Study of Words;" a delightful, good book, not at all dry (unless to fools); one I am sure you will like. Price but three and sixpence and well worth a guinea at least.—FITZGERALD, EDWARD, 1852, *To George Crabbe,* June 2; *Letters,* ed. Wright, vol. I, *p.* 217.

I know of no books on language better calculated to excite curiosity and stimulate inquiry into the proper meaning and use of the English tongue, than those interesting volumes, "The Study of Words," "English, Past and Present," "The Lessons contained in Proverbs," and the essay on the English New Testament.—MARSH, GEORGE PERKINS, 1860, *Lectures on the English Language, Lecture XII, p.* 278, *note.*

Trench, in his exegetical writings, so blends the offices of interpreter and preacher, that it is not always easy to know in which sense to take him. He is so intent on the multitude of lessons that may be drawn from any given word, clause, or sentence, that he not unfrequently fails to designate the particular sense intended by the writer. But he is always entertaining and instructive. His is one of those rich minds, which cannot enter into communion with other minds without enriching them. No matter what his professed subject is, it will be found either to contain or to suggest materials for which his reader will thank him.—PEABODY, ANDREW P., 1862, *Critical Notices, North American Review, vol.* 94, *p.* 277.

Besides being a star of the first magnitude in the literary and ecclesiastical world, Archbishop Trench has an honoured name amongst modern poets and hymn-writers. —MILLER, JOSIAH, 1866–69, *Singers and Songs of the Church, p.* 490.

Dr. Trench's poems have in no wise depended upon his status as an ecclesiastic; they have appealed to no party in the Church; they have made their way by no organised praise or factitious diffusion, but by slow pervasive contact with earnest and lonely minds. His public has been gradually won, and is gradually increasing; there are many for whom his words have mingled themselves with Tennyson's in hours of bereavement, with Wordsworth's in hours of meditative calm. . . . It is by his "Elegiac Poems" that Dr. Trench has won his almost unique position in many hearts. . . . A nature like Dr. Trench's, full of clinging affections, profound religious faith, and constitutional sadness, was likely to feel in extreme measure both these bereavements and these consolations. The loss of beloved children taught him the lessons of sorrow and of hope, and the words in which that sorrow and that hope found utterance have led many a mourner in his most desolate hour to feel that this great writer is his closest and most consoling friend.—MYERS, FREDERIC WILLIAM

HENRY, 1883, *Archbishop Trench's Poems, Essays Modern*, pp. 235, 247, 249.

Whether a place be conceded to Archbishop Trench among the great men of the past half century or not, it must at least be allowed that he was largely mixed up with great minds and great matters. The influence which he exerted over those who had control in church and state was considerable; but we think the unconscious influence of his writings, his example and—if one may use the expression—his presence was even more considerable. . . . The whole cast of his mind was reflective. He was a man of thought rather than of action; and probably nothing but a strong sense of duty compelled him to turn from the studies in which he delighted and the society which delighted in him to the throne of Dublin, around which clouds of threatening storms had begun to gather. But danger never made him hesitate to take any step he thought right; and if his intense Anglicanism coloured his views in an unmistakable way, his courage, his patience, his innate sense of justice, and his purity of motive combined to keep him out of the doubtful paths of mere expediency. . . . We have here as elsewhere evidence of that sad, foreboding nature which left its impress upon his poetry, and showed itself outwardly in his somewhat gloomy features. They were often lit up with the fire of enthusiasm, just as his habitual gravity was tempered by a keen appreciation of wit and humour; but, both in his looks and his conversation, sombreness predominated. Perhaps his association with Ireland may have deepened it in him; but the tendency to gloom was probably inherited from his Huguenot ancestors.—ROBINSON, CHARLES J., 1888, *R. C. Trench, The Academy*, vol. 34, pp. 411, 412.

It was in 1851 that Trench published the first fruits of his researches into language. Delivered originally to the students in an obscure normal school for elementary teachers, these lectures have been over and over again reprinted; they have become a classbook wherever English is studied, and together with those other volumes, "English Past and Present," "A Select Glossary of English Words," and "On Some Deficiencies in our English Dictionaries," are to be found in every philological library. It is in these linguistic studies that Trench is seen at his best, and when engaged in the etymology, the history, the morality, or the poetry in words he shows distinct signs of a gift almost akin to genius. . . . His poetry is penetrated by the high purity and nobility of his character.—PALGRAVE, FRANCIS T., 1889, *ed. The Treasury of Sacred Song*, p. 356, note.

Dr. Trench's poems fill a considerable volume, and possess many merits. They manifest true culture and large command of language. They are full of noble aspiration, breathing deep and sincere piety; but do not evidence any strongly marked originality. His verse, beautiful and attractive as it is, is more that of a devout mind, and a rare and fine scholar with much music in his soul, than of a poet by Divine decree.—GIBBS, H. J., 1892, *The Poets and the Poetry of the Century, Frederick Tennyson to Clough*, ed. Miles, p. 137, 139.

The most popular ["Study of Words"] of scholarly and the most scholarly of popular works on the subject.— SAINTSBURY, GEORGE, 1896, *A History of Nineteenth Century, Literature*, p. 300.

Did great service to the study of the English language. His "Study of Words" and "English Past and Present" have done more to popularise philology than, probably, any other books we possess.—WALKER, HUGH, 1897, *The Age of Tennyson*, p. 211.

Paul Hamilton Hayne
1831–1886

Born Charleston, S. C., 1 Jan. 1830; died "Copse Hill," Grovetown, Ga., 6 July 1886. He was graduated at the University of South Carolina, gave up the practice of law for literature, and edited successively, "Russell's Magazine," the Charleston "Literary Gazette" and "Evening News." He was a colonel in the Confederate army, and wrote several popular Confederate songs. The war undermining his health and destroying his home, he retired with his family to a cottage, "Copse Hill," at Grovetown, in the pine barrens near Augusta, Ga. Hayne was long our representative Southern poet, honored and beloved by his colleagues in all portions of the United States, and by not a few of the Motherland. He issued "Poems," 1855; "Sonnets and Other Poems," 1857; "Avolio, a Legend

JOSIAH GILBER HOLLAND

Engraving by H. B. Hall & Sons.

PAUL HAMILTON HAYNE

Engraving by H. B. Hall & Sons.
From a Photograph.

of Cos," 1859; "Legends and Lyrics," 1872; "The Mountain of the Lovers, and Other Poems," 1873. He wrote a memoir of Henry Timrod, 1873; and lives of Hugh S. Legaré and of his uncle, Robert Y. Hayne, 1878. An elegant edition of his complete poems appeared in 1882.—STEDMAN, EDMUND CLARENCE, ed., 1900, *An American Anthology, Biographical Notes*, p. 798.

PERSONAL

No poet was ever more blessed in a wife, and she it is, who, by her self-renunciation, her exquisite sympathy, her positive, material help, her bright hopefulness, has made endurable the losses and trials that have crowded Mr. Hayne's life. Those who know how to read between the lines can see everywhere the influence of this irradiating and stimulating presence.—PRESTON, MARGARET J., 1882, *Poems of Paul Hamilton Hayne, Biographical Sketch*, p. vii.

Though round him shone the singer's aureole,
His mighty heart was simple as a boy's.
His pine woods felt him, and his loved winds blow,
For requiem, round his more than palace home.
Dumb the King's mortal lips, for aye; but, lo!
Through what he wrote the soul is never dumb,
Though the stars, wheeling proudly, seem to know
That he who loved them to his own is come.
—MARSTON, PHILIP BOURKE, 1886, *On the Death of Paul Hamilton Hayne*.

In the earlier years of his literary career he would frequently awake at night, get out of bed, light a candle, and compose many lines upon some poem which he said had "forced itself upon his mind." He was more systematic in writing prose than verse, although many characteristic specimens of the former may be found in the fly-leaves of all kinds of books. When engaged in preparing an essay, a book-review, a story, the copying of manuscript for the printer, or the claims of a large correspondence, he would usually go to his standing-desk in the morning, soon after breakfast, and write for hours. In reading a book he often made marginal comments with his pencil, and always marked the passages that impressed him most. These proved aids to reflection, and sometimes from the simplest of them the suggestion for a poem would be utilized. As a rule, perhaps, my father wrote prose more rapidly and satisfactorily under pressure, and the same may be said of some of his elaborate poems. He became alert "when he could hear the printing-press clattering behind him," and would have agreed with Sir Walter Scott in saying, "I cannot pull well in long traces, when the draught is too far behind me!" My father said more than once, when pressed to finish proof-sheets, "I will make it up at the last heat."—HAYNE, WILLIAM H., 1892, *Paul H. Hayne's Methods of Composition, Lippincott's Magazine*, vol. 50, p. 794.

Hayne, though at times a partisan where his friends were concerned, was essentially a noble spirit; the noblest and most charming character, with the exception of Simms, to be found among Southern writers, one is almost tempted to say, among Southern gentlemen. He wrote the most delightful letters of all of Simms's correspondents. He was always loyal, always frank, always the gentle lover of what seemed to him to be true and beautiful. When he travelled from home his genial nature won the love of men like Fields and Longfellow. No more simple and refined gentleman was ever nurtured in the old South. If he lacked Simms's vigor and powers of varied accomplishment, or Timrod's artistic self-control, his genius was, nevertheless, more receptive, more keenly alive to the beauties of nature and of art. Without lacking virility, he charms chiefly by his possession of traits of character distinctively feminine. His gentleness, his receptivity, his delicacy of feeling, his facility in surrendering himself to the dominion of master minds, are all feminine traits, some of which have impaired the value of his poetry, but which have combined to give a unique charm to his personality.—TRENT, WILLIAM P., 1892, *William Gilmore Simms (American Men of Letters)*, p. 230.

I shall always hold pleasant memory of a visit I made to Hayne's lonely home, amid the arid pine hills of Georgia, in November, 1881. . . . He was neither short nor tall, five feet eight I should say, slender, straight, with a well-poised head, a long face, brown eyes of an Oriental cast slightly lifted at the outer corners, dark hair and moustache, rather thick lips, a well-turned chin, straight nose, high, narrowish forehead and bronzed cheeks barely tinged with a network of fine red veins. There was a strong resemblance between his face and that of the late Robert

Louis Stevenson. I was surprised that he did not look like an invalid; for he had often written me about his hopeless physical condition. Later, upon closer observation, some constitutional lesion became vaguely apparent. — THOMPSON, MAURICE, 1901, *The Last Literary Cavalier, The Critic, vol.* 38, *pp.* 352, 353.

GENERAL

There are several that Tennyson might have written without damage to his reputation as the first artist among English poets. ... Mr. Hayne has written sonnets very much as clever as any in English. I neither except Stoddard, who has done well; nor Boker, whose success is marked; nor even Wordsworth, the Magnus Apollo of British sonneteers. Nor do I mean any very great compliment to Mr. Hayne, in these comparisons. ... Mr. Hayne has an intense love of Nature; a rich imagination, quick and bold; limited power of narrative structure, and a true sense of the music of words. His study of Tennyson has been in the spirit of the true artist. In the glowing sensuousness of his imagery one is sometimes reminded of Alexander Smith; but he has a refinement and an art-finish that Smith could never have attained. His poetry is alive with pent passion, glowing yet repressed; a tropical wealth of emotion, touched here and there with a dash of quaintness or a flaw of affectation. He is fervent, but sometimes feeble; musical and dainty in phraseology; full of earnestness, tenderness, and delicacy. Over some of his exquisite ideal poems there hangs a veil of mourning so vivid and startling, that in the complex beauty of sorrow one is puzzled, while charmed.—DAVIDSON, JAMES WOOD, 1869, *The Living Writers of the South, pp.* 243, 247.

Hayne exhibits in all his pieces a rich sensuousness of nature, a seemingly exhaustless fertility of fancy, an uncommon felicity of poetic description, and an easy command of the harmonies of verse.— WHIPPLE, EDWIN PERCY, 1876–86, *American Literature and Other Papers, ed. Whittier, p.* 131.

A poem ("Fire Pictures") which in point of variety and delicacy of fancy is quite the best of his collection, and in point of pure music should be placed beside Edgar Poe's "Bells." ... It is a poem to be read aloud; a true *recitativo*. The energy of its movements, the melody of its metres, the changes of its rhythm, the variety of its fancies, the artistic advance to its climax, particularly the management of its close, where at one and the same time, by the devices of onomatopeia and of rhythmical imitation, are doubly interpreted the sob of a man and the flicker of a flame so perfectly that sob, flicker, word, rhythm, each appears to represent the other, and to be used convertibly with the other in such will-o'-wisp transfigurations as quite vanish in mere description,—all these elements require for full enjoyment that the actual music of the poem should fall upon the ear.—LANIER, SIDNEY, 1881 (?), *Paul H. Hayne's Poetry, Music and Poetry, p.* 204.

Hayne's vitality, courage, and native lyrical impulse have kept him in voice, and his people regard him with a tenderness which, if a commensurate largesse were added, should make him feel less solitary among his pines.—STEDMAN, EDMUND CLARENCE, 1885, *Poets of America, p.* 451.

The man is dead; the bard shall never die;
Though clay lie cold and eloquent voice be stilled,
The poet lingers; wood and field and sky
And the far spaces by his soul are filled.
For him all times and seasons shall remain,
And thy best name, O South! shall still be Hayne.

—PARKER, BENJAMIN S., 1886, *Paul Hamilton Hayne, The Cabin in the Clearing and Other Poems.*

Pure was the fount of song from which he drew
Rare pearls of thought, as clear as morning dew;
His was the heritage of Orphic fires!
The clarion note his lyric lips out-blew
Was one of noble deeds and high desires.

—SCOLLARD, CLINTON, 1886, *Threnody in Memory of Paul Hamilton Hayne.*

As the earlier dews of Spring will throng
Bright on some flower that gives to breeze or bee
Its delicate symmetries and fragrant breath,
Even so, for years, clung shining round your song
The certitude of immortality,
The faith in resurrection after death!

—FAWCETT, EDGAR, 1886, *Paul Hamilton Hayne, Songs of Doubt and Dream, p.* 116.

In estimating Hayne's permanent worth as a poet, it is impossible not to compare him with other typical Southern poets. He is certainly not the equal of Lanier in shaping imagination, nor of Pinkney in lyric charm; it would be saying a great deal in either case, if he were. When we compare him with his friend Timrod, whose claims Hayne so chivalrously preferred to his own, it is evident that Timrod was the superior in fire, lyric force, and a certain wealth of utterance; and Hayne in sweetness, dignity, and self-control. . . . Hayne's was certainly the higher nature; when his songs were most nearly red-hot, they did not, like Timrod's, call the Union armies Goths and Huns, and they were free from the almost brutal tone of wrath and revenge with which Timrod rejoices over the imagined desolation of New York. . . . This great fineness of temperament undoubtedly helped Hayne's later career; it made it easy for him to strike hands with old foes; and nothing can be more generous or impassioned than his verses of thanks for the Northern aid given at a later time to the Southern cities. His longer poems are, like the longer poems of most bards, unsuccessful; and the reader turns gladly from these to his verses upon the two themes where he is strong—home affections and the enjoyments derived from external nature. The beauty and delicate tenderness of the former have been already mentioned; and the outdoor poems have the merit of using material unhackneyed and often untouched . . . Above all special merits of description, there is in these outdoor poems a charm which comes from a certain wild note, something akin to the delicate song of the blue-bird and to all soft spring scents; the expression of a lonely life amidst virgin woods and unspoiled solitudes. One may detect something of the same note in some of Bryant's earlier poems, but in Hayne's it is softer, richer, sweeter.—HIGGINSON, THOMAS WENTWORTH, 1887, *Paul Hamilton Hayne, The Chautauquan*, vol. 7, p. 231.

"The Mountain of the Lovers," the "Macrobian Bow," "Macdonald's Raid," "Unveiled," the "Vengeance of the Goddess Diana," and the "Solitary Lake," are works worth the crown of an academy. As a sonnetteer, Hayne was strong, ranking well with the best in America, and his descriptive verse is often very melodious and full of warm, harmonious color. His muse never was quite Southern, though the man was; and we feel as we read, that Keats and Shelley and Tennyson and Wordsworth have influenced him almost as much as the blue skies, the fiery sun, and the moaning pines of the sub-tropic. And yet what intensely radical Southern sentiment he sometimes voiced! On the other hand, too, what luxury of Southern sights, sounds, tastes, perfumes, and colors we enjoy in his poem, "Muscadines," than which no lesser genius than Shelley or Keats ever penned a better or a richer.—THOMPSON, MAURICE, 1888, *Literature, Sept. 22*.

His verse displays the wealth and warmth of the landscape of South Carolina and Georgia, the loneliness of the "pine barrens" where nature seems unmolested, or the swish of the wild Southern sea. As a sonnetteer, too, his place is not far below Longfellow's; American achievements in this important division of verse have not been inconsiderable. When Hayne, for a short period in his life, fell under the influence of Morris-mediævalism, the merit of his verse dwindled to that of occasional lines or passages; but when he sang his own song in his own land it was that of a true poet, who heard
'Low words of alien music, softly sung,
And rhythmic sighs in some sweet unknown tongue."

Far from the distributing centres of literature, and unaided by the stimulus or the criticism that come alone from association with brother authors, Hayne wrote too much, nor polished with sufficiently painstaking art.—RICHARDSON, CHARLES F., 1888, *American Literature, 1607–1885*, vol. II, p. 230.

The impassioned but too impetuous, too regardlessly profuse singer of the south.—SHARP, WILLIAM, 1889, ed., *American Sonnets, Introductory Note*, p. xxiv.

Hayne's poems are not all of equal interest, but every now and then one comes upon something very striking. Where he felt strongly he had stirring eloquence; what he knew familiarly he could paint vividly. — SLADEN, DOUGLAS, 1891, ed. *Younger American Poets, To the Reader*, p. xxx.

Hayne has written war lyrics, but he excelled in domestic sketches and in short pieces of quiet reflection on the subject of natural landscape, having the feeling of contentment that must precede repose in poetry. — SIMONDS, ARTHUR B., 1894, *American Song*, p. 252.

His prose works, some of which are idyllic in beauty, have not been collected in any form. These things ought not to be, since his works are part of the heritage, the treasure, and the heroism of a people. In his prose more than in his poetry he touches the transient and current, sometimes impaling follies with a sharp pen, and other times with the touch of a painter turning out sketches of persons and places aglow with life and dramatic power—sketches which shall ever be of increasing interest to the historian as well as to the lover of the beautiful. . . . "Poet laureate of the South!" Yes, that title by divine right belongs to Hayne. If the earliest and most constant loyalty to the Muse, a steady flame of poetic fervor, and the production of the largest amount of good poetry be the test, then the honor of that uncrowned preëminence goes easily to the poet of "Copse Hill."—LINK, SAMUEL ALBERT, 1896, *Pioneers of Southern Literature*, pp. 47, 50.

Hayne belongs distinctively to the artistic imaginative school of lyrists. Had he removed to New York, he would without doubt have become one of that select circle whose leaders are now Stedman and Stoddard. His ability as a literary craftsman is shown by his marked success with the sonnet, that unfailing indicator of poetic skill; his true lyric power appears in his songs of the war. He did for the South what Whittier did for the North. The lyrics "My Motherland," "Stonewall Jackson," "The Little White Glove," and above all "Beyond the Potomac," indicate the high-water mark of the Southern poetry of the Rebellion. Hayne also had great success as a narrative poet, ranking in this department only second to Bayard Taylor.—PATTEE, FRED LEWIS, 1896, *A History of American Literature*, p. 388.

Paul Hamilton Hayne, a gentleman of South Carolina, his house burned in the bombardment of Charleston, his library scattered, his store of family silver lost, started life anew, with enfeebled health, in a shanty among the Georgia pines. Overcoming a thousand obstacles, the faithful poet "beat his music out," but apart from the trumpet tone of his war-songs, it was a music in the minor key.—BATES, KATHARINE LEE, 1897, *American Literature*, p. 187.

He was not the high-priest of nature in the broadest sense. He does not disclose the range of imagination, the loftiness of conception, the profound meditativeness of the Northern masters, but he sings his notes as naturally as a bird carolling in the tree tops. So genuine is his voice, so true in tone, so musical, that it is questionable if he should be classed among our minor poets. In the silvery melody of his verse he forcibly recalls Poe, of whom he was evidently a sympathetic student. It would be difficult to find in literature a more appropriate picture of Southern scenery than in his "Aspects of the Pines."—ONDERDONK, JAMES L., 1899-1901, *History of American Verse*, p. 187.

He has left ten times as much verse as Timrod, not all valuable, nor even natural and strong. But in him too there is much real poetry, much true local color.—LAWTON, WILLIAM CRANSTON, 1902, *Introduction to the Study of American Literature*, p. 306.

Edwin Percy Whipple
1819–1886

Born at Gloucester, Mass., March 8, 1819; died at Boston, June 16, 1886. An American critic and essayist. He was employed in a bank and in a broker's office at Boston; and 1837-60 was superintendent of the reading-room of the Merchant's Exchange. He became noted as a lecturer. His works include "Essays and Reviews" (2 vols., 1848–49), "Literature and Life" (1849), "Character and Characteristic Men" (1866), "Literature of the Age of Elizabeth" (1869), "Success and its Conditions" (1871), "American Literature and Other Papers" (1887), "Recollections of Eminent Men" (1887), "Outlooks on Society, Literature, and Politics" (1888).—SMITH, BENJAMIN E., *ed.* 1894-97, *Century Cyclopedia of Names*, p. 1058.

PERSONAL

He was an essential part of the literary life of Boston at a time when that city probably furnished a larger proportion of the literary life of the nation than it will ever again supply. He was unique among the authors of that time and place in his training, tastes, and mental habit; the element that he contributed was special and valuable; he duplicated nobody, while at the same time he antagonized nobody, and the controversial history of that period will find no place for his name.—HIGGINSON, THOMAS WENTWORTH, 1886, *Edwin Percy Whipple, Atlantic Monthly*, vol. 58, p. 345.

Mr. Whipple was an intellectual sympathy incarnate. He lived to do honor to others, and to forget himself in awarding to everybody else the meed of desert. No dramatic poet, novelist, painter of likenesses on the canvas could be in his subjects and sitters more absorbed, himself unconscious of having any claim or winning a morsel of regard. . . . He was meek and lowly like his Master, and the almost more than a woman's delicacy in his robust manly mind was a sort of continual hint of the Holy spirit. A strong thinker in a slender frame, he had also the sensibility which is not unveiled, and the sentiment which cannot be sentimental or weak. Nobody would enter a more displeased protest against whoever would set him forth as a model of perfection, in any way. . . . This rarely modest disposition was well suited in the custom of his plain and quiet demeanor, in his withdrawal from appearing abroad as his bodily strength abated, and in the peculiarly placid circumstances of his lamented yet cheerful demise. . . . He had an eminent magnanimity. Did others crowd and push in the grasp for riches or race for fame?—he stood aside, he fell back, he relinquished to those who craved it the prize. I never heard a word of envy from his lips; I never saw a spark of malice in his eye. He rejoiced in his comrade's superiority and success.—BARTOL, CYRUS AUGUSTUS, 1886, *Recollections of Eminent Men, Introduction,* pp. x, xi, xii.

Whipple, with two-storied head, and bulbous spectacles; keen critic, good talker. —UNDERWOOD, FRANCIS H., 1893. *Recollections and Appreciations of James Russell Lowell.*

GENERAL

As chief among his mental characteristics we are disposed to place the rectitude which marks his critical judgments, and which is seen in the patience and thoroughness of his investigation and in the precision of his analysis, not less than in the results at which he arrives. With the utmost skill he penetrates to the heart of his subject, and lays it bare for the inspection of the curious that they may verify for themselves the correctness of the views which he presents. . . . Closely allied with this quality of mental rectitude is his power of analytical criticism, as shown in his delineations of both intellectual and moral character. He rarely fails of reaching the prime motive of a man's acts, and the principles which give a direction to his thoughts, in this peculiar psychological development. . . . Another distinguishing feature of Mr. Whipple's mind is his fondness for what he has denominated, in one of his lectures, "the ludicrous side of life." This quality, so rarely found among the descendants of the Puritans, enters deeply into his intellectual constitution, and may to a greater or less extent be detected in nearly all his essays.— SMITH, C. C., 1849, *Whipple's Essays and Reviews, Christian Examiner*, vol. 46, pp. 190, 191.

In fact, he has been infected with that unmeaning and transparent heresy—the cant of critical Boswellism, by dint of which we are to shut our eyes tightly to all authorial blemishes, and open them, like owls, to all authorial merits.—POE, EDGAR ALLAN, 1850, *Edwin Percy Whipple and Other Critics, Works,* ed. Stedman and Woodberry, vol. VII, p. 128.

To a large acquaintance with English literature, a prompt and retentive memory, a lively fancy, and considerable wit, he joins the brisk and smart exuberance of style which is the most agreeable quality of the essayist, and the most essential to his success. His command of expression is almost marvellous; he showers words upon the page with a prodigality that astonished the lean and bare scribblers who, after painful search and with many contortions, clothe their shivering thoughts in scant and inappropriate garments. He revels in the abundance of his wealth, and changes his rich costume so frequently and swiftly, that the reader begins to think he is playing tricks with dress, or is substituting words for thought. Yet the suspicion would be groundless. The expression, though lavish and ornate, is almost invariably clear, pointed, and precise. Because he has a large store to choose from, the word selected is just the appropriate word, conveying the precise idea that the writer wishes to impart, without distortion or indistinctness. Mr. Whipple's essays, therefore, form easy and luxurious reading. . . . Of all the later English essayists, Mr. Whipple may most properly be compared with Hazlitt, whom he closely resembles except in this very point of his imperturbable good humor. — BOWEN, FRANCIS, 1850, *Whipple's Lectures on Literature and Life, North American Review,* vol. 70, *pp.* 153, 156.

There is hardly a writer in the country so capable of such a series of subjects as the author of "Character and Characteristic Men;" and it may safely be said that through this book more real insight may be had into the spirit of that time than can be obtained by means of the works of any one other critical author.—WHITE, RICHARD GRANT, 1869, *The Galaxy, Oct.*

Mr. Whipple's mind is acute and analytic, and his mode of dealing with a subject shows his mastery of principles, his sincerity of character, and his power of lucid statement. His style is not uniformly easy, although his vocabulary is ample, and his choice of words is often very felicitous. At times he inclines to be epigrammatic and sparkling, and when this is the case he is apt to restrain his naturally ample utterance, and to establish a formal balance of terse phrases in short, pungent sentences, in place of the longer sweep of the older and more melodious style of English prose. Like most writers who have had their early discipline in debate, and have maintained an oratorical style by long practice in lecturing, he sometimes swells his periods into sonorous measure, and writes *at* his reader, as if in the midst of a brilliant peroration before an excited audience.— UNDERWOOD, FRANCIS H., 1872, *A Hand-Book of English Literature, American Authors, p.* 445.

With the possible exception of Lowell and Matthew Arnold, he was the ablest critical essayist of his time; and the place he has left will not be readily filled. Scarcely inferior to Macaulay in brilliance of diction and graphic portraiture, he was freer from prejudice and passion, and more loyal to the truth of fact and history. He was a thoroughly honest man. He wrote with conscience always at his elbow, and never sacrificed his real convictions for the sake of epigram and anthesis. He instinctively took the right side of the questions that came before him for decision, even when by so doing he ranked himself with the unpopular minority. He had the manliest hatred of hypocrisy and meanness; but if his language had at times the severity of justice, it was never merciless. He "set down naught in malice."—WHITTIER, JOHN GREENLEAF, 1886, *American Literature and Other Papers by Whipple, Introduction, p.* xiii.

By the mere exercise of these moral qualities, combined with great keenness of insight, he doubtless did a great deal for the American criticism of his day, and must rank with Margaret Fuller Ossoli and far above Poe in the total value of his work. It is certainly saying a great deal in his praise to admit that up to a certain time in his life there was probably no other literary man in America who had so thoroughly made the best of himself, —extracted so thoroughly from his own natural gifts their utmost resources. His memory was great, his reading constant, his acquaintance large, his apprehension ready and clear. . . . In a time and place which had produced Emerson, this narrowness of range was a defect almost fatal. It did not harm his immediate success, and he is said, in those palmy days of lecturing, to have appeared a thousand times before audiences. But now that his lectures—or his essays which might have been lectures—are read critically, many years later, we can see that the same shrinkage which has overtaken the work of Bayard Taylor and Dr. Holland, his compeers upon the lecture platform, has also overtaken his. Whether it was that this platform, by its direct influence, restricted these men, or whether it was that a certain limitation of intellect was best fitted for producing the article precisely available for this particular market, it is clear that these three illustrate alike the success and the drawbacks of the lecturing profession. —HIGGINSON, THOMAS WENTWORTH, 1886, *Edwin Percy Whipple, Atlantic Monthly,* vol. 58, *p.* 346.

Great and exceptional as were Whipple's early achievements in letters, it is easy to note why he did not accomplish more, and to see why he missed the points of excellence which a more generous culture would have given him. He had not a creative mind, but his purely critical abilities, though of the first order, needed the discipline of exact and long-continued study, and the widening of intellectual view, to make his later work something more substantial than it is. He came just short of being a great critic of literature. His vital defect is illustrated by comparing his critical writing with that of Emerson. Both have much in common—the same feeling for vitality in the works of others, the same regard for good form—but Emerson had the survey of the world, though the horizon was that of Concord, while Whipple seldom saw beyond the author or subject which he had in hand. . . . Taking up Whipple's essays today, one is surprised at the maturity and strength of his youthful work. . . . In literary knowledge Whipple had no superior among Americans, but when he undertook the entertainment of an audience the temptation drove all serious ideas out of his head, and the result is a display of rhetorical pyrotechnics which has no more present interest than a bundle of sticks. When he sat down to the dissection of an author or to the critical discussion of a subject he was another man; what he lacked in moral purpose and breadth of view was made up in vigor of style and in acuteness of probing. . . . Dear as he was to his friends, and delightful as are our memories of his overflowing wit and his brilliant conversations, his writings entirely lack the elements of perpetuity. His essays and criticisms delight for the moment, but are related neither to philosophy nor religion, nor to the interpretation of the life of humanity. They entertain one, like the feats of the athlete, but make no permanent impression, and carry no one forward in any direction.—WARD, JULIUS H., 1887, *Edwin P. Whipple as Critic, New Princeton Review*, vol. 3, pp. 98, 99, 102, 105.

Whipple began his active work as a writer, in an article on Macaulay. As a reviewer and a lecturer, Whipple reached a public which Emerson never fully influenced; though his service in emphasizing the value and strength of true character was in Emerson's own vein. Whipple showed his Americanism by the emphasis laid upon that element of character he called grit; and he displayed his Saxon temper in his unmitigated contempt for sham and shoddy.—RICHARDSON, CHARLES F., 1887, *American Literature*, 1607–1885, vol. I, p. 436.

Whipple was not only a critic; he was also a critic of first-rate ability. His literary judgments were as just as they were acute, and have been confirmed by the verdict of later years. His mind was both penetrating and comprehensive; he took the philosophical view, and showed the sources and relations of existing conditions. The range of his reading was extensive and its subjects well-chosen; he was familiar with the field of European literature, as well as with American: only Lowell rivalled him in this respect, and he gave himself, as Lowell did not, wholly to the critical function. He may fairly be classed with such men as Matthew Arnold in England, and Taine in France; for though his scope was less pretentious than theirs, the actual value of his achievements will probably not be found inferior. His gift of interpretation and expression was commensurate with his insight; so that his essays are not merely instructive to students, but delightful to the general reader. Humor he possesses in abundance; eloquence; and the faculty of giving charm and lucidity to subjects apparently dry and intricate. His merits have been acknowledged by competent foreign judges, and many an English scholar's library contains his books. No one who wishes to acquire a vivid and trustworthy conception of eminent American books and men, and of the conditions of recent American existence, can do better than to consult the writings of Whipple.—HAWTHORNE, JULIAN, AND LEMMON, LEONARD, 1891, *American Literature*, p. 208.

His best essays are still read by the student of literature for their keen analysis and fine literary sense; but he was not a great critic, and his books lack that charm of manner and richness of thought which make Lowell's and Arnold's critical essays literature.—BRONSON, WALTER C., 1900, *A Short History of American Literature*, p. 175.

It is almost impossible to understand the extravagant praise he received, but we can recognize his earnestness, his insistence —perhaps his overinsistence—upon the moral element in literature, his enthusiasm for his favourite writers, such as Wordsworth, his wide reading, his not infrequent felicity of phrase, and his ability, somewhat rare at the time, to express his dislikes in a hearty fashion. We can understand also how his apt illustrations and his anecdotes about famous men delighted his audiences. On the other hand, many of his pages suggest that he drew upon his commonplace book oftener than upon his brains, that his knowledge was frequently defective and his judgment still more so, that his criticism was lacking in subtlety, and that his style was at times far from pleasing.—TRENT, WILLIAM P., 1903, *A History of American Literature*, p. 563.

Abram Joseph Ryan
1839–1886

An American priest and verse-writer; born at Norfolk, Va., Aug. 15, 1839; died at Louisville, Ky., April 22, 1886. It was while chaplain in the Confederate army that he wrote his well-known poem "The Conquered Banner," composed shortly after Lee's surrender. Later he went North for the purpose of lecturing and publishing his works, which have appeared as "The Conquered Banner, and Other Poems" (1880); "Poems, Patriotic, Religious, and Miscellaneous" (1880); and "A Crown for Our Queen." Other poems of his which are popular are: "The Lost Cause," "The Sword of Lee," "The Flag of Erin," and the epic "Their Story Runneth Thus." At the time of his death he was engaged upon a "Life of Christ."—WARNER, CHARLES DUDLEY, ed. 1897, *Library of the World's Best Literature, Biographical Dictionary, vol.* XXIX, *p.* 473.

PERSONAL

Father Ryan's was an open, manly character, in which there was no dissimulation. His generous nature and warm heart were ever moved by kind impulses and influenced by charitable feelings, as became his priestly calling. We may readily believe him when he tells us that he never wrote a line for hate's sake. He shrank instinctively from all that was mean and sordid. Generosity was a marked trait of his character, an ennobling principle of his nature, the motive power of his actions, and the mainspring of his life. Friendship was likewise congenial to his taste, if not a necessity of his nature; and with him it meant more than a name. It was a sacred union formed between kindred spirits—a chain of affection whose binding link was fidelity. Never was he false to its claims, nor known to have violated its obligations. Hence he was highly esteemed during life by numerous persons of all classes and denominations; for his sympathies were as broad as humanity, and as far-reaching as its wants and its miseries. Yet he was a man of deep conviction and a strict adherent to principle, or what he conceived to be principle; for we find him long after the war still clinging to its memories, and slow to accept its results which he believed were fraught with disaster to the people of his section. A Southerner of the most pronounced kind, he was unwilling to make any concession to his victorious opponents of the North which could be withheld from them.—MORAN, JOHN, 1886, *Poems: Patriotic, Religious, Miscellaneous by Abram J. Ryan, Memoir of Father Ryan, p.* 30.

GENERAL

"The Conquered Banner" may fairly take its place at the top of the list of the several exquisite wails that have gone up in verse-utterance from the crushed hearts of a conquered people for a lost cause.... "Sentinel Songs" breathes the same spirit, as does, however, everything that emanates from the same pen. This wants some of the fire of the former, but its truthfulness and earnestness are unmistakable.... All the poems I have seen from Father Ryan's pen are pitched in the same key.... They all breathe the same spirit, and the same fire flashes through all.—DAVIDSON, JAMES WOOD, 1869, *The Living Writers of the South, pp.* 491, 493, 494.

His "Poems," written "off and on, always in a hurry," are, in fact, of unequal merit. The author gives a fair estimate of them when he tells us in his Preface that "they are incomplete in finish," but, as he thinks "true in tone." Patriotic or religious, they actually mirror the fervid feelings of the Southerner, and the pious aspirations of the priest. They cannot but exert a happy influence on the reader.—JENKINS, O. L., 1876, *The Student's Handbook of British and American Literature, p.* 500.

Father Ryan's fame is the inheritance of a great and enlightened nation, and his writings have passed into history to emblazon its pages and enrich the literature of the present and succeeeding ages, since it is confidently believed that, with the lapse of time, his fame and his merits will grow brighter and more enduring.—MORAN, JOHN, 1886, *Poems: Patriotic, Religious, Miscellaneous by Abram J. Ryan, Memoir of Father Ryan, p.* 25.

Seldom has a poet been so identified with a cause as this priest-Tyrtæus. In his poem one sees the whole terrible drama, founded on the brave old theme of Cavalier and Roundhead, acted afresh—the grim, old story of high hopes shattered, high blood poured out like water, romance and chivalry subjected to reality. Ryan has created a monument more beautiful and more enduring than marble over the grave of the gallant but ill-fated Gray. The "Conquered Banner," "Sentinel Songs," and the lines on his brother, are among the finest war poems in our language.—SLADEN, DOUGLAS, 1891, ed., *Younger American Poets, To the Reader*, p. 29.

His poems are the simplest of songs, and their chief quality is that they touch the heart. An atmosphere of melancholy and longing, of weariness and suffering veils their meaning from the gaze of the practical mind. Religious feeling is dominant. The reader seems to be moving about in cathedral glooms, by dimly-lighted altars, with sad processions of ghostly penitents and mourners fading into the darkness to the sad music of lamenting choirs. But the light which falls upon the gloom is the light of heaven, and amid tears and sighs over farewells and crushed happinesses hope sings a vigorous though subdued strain. The religious and melancholy tone of these poems is one reason of their general popularity. . . . His poems as a whole show rather what he was capable of than any particular excellence. . . . Father Ryan had greater poetic genius than Lowell; but the art of the latter was masterly, his talents were cultivated to the utmost, and his achievement is so great that comparison is impossible. . . . To distinguish between his artistic success and his popularity must not be forgotten. The elements of his popularity are not difficult to name. Religious feeling is the first. Devotion to Christ and Mary, His mother, the priest's awe, wonder, and love for the mass and the sacraments, the enthusiasm of the mystic for the mysteries of religion, are the most fruitful sources of his inspirations. His choice of subjects is mostly personal, peculiar to the priest, the missionary, the patriot, the pilgrim weary of the world, broken in health and spirit, eager for the perfect life. . . . He speaks from his own heart to the hearts of others. Behind these elements is the true poetic genius upon which his worth and his popularity rest together.—SMITH, JOHN TALBOT, 1894, *Father Ryan's Poems, Thirteenth Ed., Introduction*, pp. xiii, xvi.

Henry Ward Beecher
1813-1887

Born at Litchfield, Conn., June 24, 1813: died at Brooklyn, N. Y., March 8, 1887. A noted American Congregational clergyman, lecturer, reformer, and author, son of Lyman Beecher. He was graduated at Amherst College in 1834; studied theology at Lane Theological Seminary; and was pastor in Lawrenceburg, Indiana (1837–39), of a Presbyterian church in Indianapolis (1839–47), and of the Plymouth Congregational church in Brooklyn (1847–87). He was one of the founders and early editors of the "Independent," the founder of the "Christian Union" and its editor 1870–81; and one of the most prominent of anti-slavery orators. He delivered Union addresses in Great Britain on subjects relating to the Civil War in the United States in 1863. He published "Lectures to Young Men" (1844), "Star Papers" (1855), "Freedom and War" (1863), "Eyes and Ears" (1864), "Aids to Prayer" (1864), "Norwood" (1867), "Earlier Scenes," "Lecture Room Talks," "Yale Lectures on Preaching," "A Summer Parish," "Evolution and Preaching" (1885), etc.—SMITH, BENJAMIN E., ed. 1894–97, *Century Cyclopedia of Names*, p. 137.

PERSONAL

The forehead is high rather than broad; his cheeks bare; his mouth compressed and firm, with humor lurking and almost laughing in the corners: his collar turned over *à la* Byron, more perhaps for the comfort of his ears (as he is exceedingly short-necked) than for any love for that peculiar fashion. His voice is full of music, in which, by the way, he is a great proficient. His body is well developed, and his great maxim is to keep it in first-rate working order, for he considers health to be a Christian duty, and rightly deems it impossible for any man to do justice to his mental faculties without at the same time attending to his physical. His motions are quick and elastic, and his manners frank, cordial, and kind, such as to attract rather than repel the advances of others. With children he is an especial favorite; they love to run up to him and offer him little bundles of flowers, of which they know him to be passionately fond, and they deem themselves more than rewarded by the hearty "Thank you," and the tender look of loving interest that accompanies his acceptance of their gift. Add to this that his benevolence is limited only by his means, and our readers will have a pretty good idea of his general character and personal appearance.—TAYLOR, WILLIAM M. 1859, *Scottish Review*, Oct.

I finished at my church to-night. It is Mrs. Stowe's brother's, and a most wonderful place to speak in. We had it enormously full last night (*Marigold* and *Trial*), but it scarcely required an effort. Mr. Ward Beecher being present in his pew, I sent to invite him to come round before he left. I found him to be an unostentatious, evidently able, straightforward, and agreeable man; extremely well-informed, and with a good knowledge of art.—DICKENS, CHARLES, 1868, *Letter, The Life of Charles Dickens*, ed. *Forster, vol.* III, *p.* 416.

My little room is quiet enough. Lizzie is at Seabrook, and I am all alone. The sweet calm face of the pagan philosopher and emperor, Marcus Antonnus, looks down upon me on one hand, and on the other the bold, generous, and humane countenance of the Christian man of action, Henry Ward Beecher; and I sit between them as sort of compromise. — WHITTIER, JOHN GREENLEAF, 1870, *To Celia Thaxter, July* 28; *Life and Letters,* ed. Pickard, *vol.* II, *p.* 566.

I spent some hours with the famous authoress's famous brother, Henry Ward Beecher, and heard him preach at Plymouth Church on Thanksgiving Day. Logic, humour, passionate declamation, poetry, tender pathos, were marvelously blended, and I joined with the eagerly listening crowd both in laughter and tears.—HALL, NEWMAN, 1871, *An Autobiography, p.* 181.

It would be no compliment to call Henry Ward Beecher the American Spurgeon. He may be that, but he is more. If we can imagine Mr. Spurgeon and Mr. John Bright with a cautious touch of Mr. Maurice and a strong tincture of the late F. W. Robertson —if, I say, it is possible to imagine such a compound being brought up in New England and at last securely fixed in a New York pulpit, we shall get a product not unlike Henry Ward Beecher.—HAWEIS, HUGH REGINALD, 1872, *Henry Ward Beecher, Contemporary Review, vol.* 19, *p.* 317.

In all my communications with him, in five years of the encyclopædic work of an editor, I have never touched a subject of current interest of which he appeared to be ignorant. When he was unacquainted with the subject, he could suggest a direction—a book or a living authority—to go to for information. This largeness of his nature, coupled with its quickness, its mobility, makes his serious moods seem an affectation or assumption to narrow, sluggish natures. He will pass instantly, by a transition inexplicable to men of slow mental movement, from hilarity to reverence and from reverence back to hilarity again; in a conversation about diamonds he will flash on you a magnificent picture of the apocalyptic revelation of the jewelled walls of the New Jerusalem, and before his auditor has fully recovered his breath from the sudden flight, he is back upon the earth again, telling some experience with a salesman at Tiffany's or Howard's. He is catholic, broad, of universal sympathies, of mercurial temperament, of instantaneous and lightning-like rapidity of mental action. —ABBOTT, LYMAN, 1882, *Henry Ward Beecher, A Sketch of his Career, p.* 190.

This morning I have been to hear Ward Beecher. Places were kept, and his management of his voice and hold on his vast audience struck me wonderfully, but the sermon was poor. They said he knew I was coming, and was on his good behaviour, and therefore constrained. At the end of the service he came down into the area to see me, gave me the notes of his sermon, said that I had taught him much, that he had read my rebukes of him too, and that they were just and had done him good. Nothing could be more gracious and in better taste than what he said.—ARNOLD, MATTHEW, 1883, *To Miss Arnold, Oct.* 28; *Letters,* ed. Russell, *vol.* II, *p.* 263.

His face and form and motion were as individual as his mind. For those who knew him well they seemed its inevitable expression.

"His eloquent blood
Spoke in his cheeks, and so distinctly wrought
That you might almost say his body thought."

His humor twinkled in his eye. One had but to see his mouth to know his nature's tenderness; and equally his enjoyment of all things purely sensuous—all lovely colors, all beauteous forms, and all delightful sounds. The physical volume of the man was necessary to his intellectual energy and to his stormy eloquence. His impassioned outbursts would have been ridiculous in a man of slighter mould. His appearance during the last years of his life, if it did not gain in fineness, acquired greater impressiveness from his ruddy face and flowing silver hair. A stranger could not meet him on the street without knowing him to be no ordinary man; without wondering if he were not quite extraordinary.—CHADWICK, JOHN WHITE, 1887, *Henry Ward Beecher, The Nation, vol.* 44, *p.* 225.

What strikes us in Beecher, as in Webster, is the native fashion, the way he was hewn, the part God had in him,—not his volition, but his constitution. "A splendid animal" he was called by the examiner of his body and his bumps,—his hair, a mane; his head and features reminding us, though with total absence of the cruel mien, of that great king and lion, or royal beast, Henry VIII. But, like the former Henry, Beecher was a synonym for forward, aggressive motion,—his hand everywhere, with a word which was a blow. He said, "I am positive," to one who wanted him to spare an unpleasant passage or pass evasively over some delicate point in his speech. As civilian, politician, or theologian, he was nothing, if not on the jump. Never neutral, he provoked opposite opinions at his death, yet possessed in his traits the unquestionable excellence without which no man can attach to himself such warm and so many friends, hold a million watchers, in spirit with the actual crowd near his sick-bed, and draw, as sun and moon do the tides, abounding praises over his unshrouded remains.—BARTOL, CYRUS AUGUSTUS, 1887, *Henry Ward Beecher, Unitarian Review, vol.* 27, *p.* 345.

Aside from his face, Mr. Beecher would not have attracted marked attention in a crowd. His figure was short and compact. Although but five feet eight inches in height, his weight for several years had averaged about two hundred and twenty-five pounds. But his flesh was so well distributed that he did not appear clumsy nor obese. His carriage was erect and noble. His complexion was florid, and his smoothly-shaven face and white locks contrasted finely with it. His hair was somewhat thin, but to the last it fully covered his head. It was allowed to grow to the collar, and was swept behind his ears. His head was not extraordinary in size, measuring only twenty-three inches in circumference, but his massive face and features gave it an appearance of great bulk. His forehead was rather retreating than bold, except that the brow was full. His eyes were prominent and seemed large. They were grayish blue in color, and so perfect were these organs as to require no artificial aid, even for protracted work. The upper lids were full and overhanging—a formation which has been noted as characteristic of many distinguished orators and actors. His nose bore a fair proportion to the rest of his features, and presented no remarked peculiarity of form. His mouth was large, and the lips neither full nor thin. They closed firmly. The cheeks were full, quite remarkably so beneath the ears, which latter organs were well formed, and set far back upon the head. The chin was somewhat square, and gave a determined look to his face. His expression was exceedingly varied. Never was there a more mobile countenance, nor one that more quickly and decisively responded to every emotion.—SEARLE, W. S., 1887, *Beecher's Personality, North American Review, vol.* 144, *p.* 488.

I attended Mr. Beecher's funeral to-day at his church in Brooklyn, which was turned into a flower garden. No funeral just like it has taken place since the world began. I looked upon the dead body with the closed mouth, once so eloquent, and the eyes once flashing with genius. There were and there are preachers more profound and more spiritual, and orators more weighty and more polished than Mr. Beecher, but it is doubtful if any generation has produced a more powerful popular speaker who had such complete command and magnetic hold of his audience. His imagination was as fertile as that of a poet, though he never wrote a poem, or quoted poetry. His mind was a flower garden in perpetual bloom, enlivened by running brooks and singing birds. He was in profound sympathy with nature and with man, especially with the common people.—SCHAFF, PHILIP, 1888, *Journal, March; Life, ed. Schaff, p.* 404.

It is amusing to the men and women of this day to read that the most famous of modern preachers and his wife who was about to be, on their wedding-day, made their own wedding-cake, he picking over and stoning the raisins, beating the eggs and keeping the whole family in good spirits while the hurried preparations went on. But the simplicities and homeliness of life in a Massachusetts village, a half century and more ago, are very enchanting compared with the hardships on which Mr. and Mrs. Beecher were soon to enter in their Western parish. Beginning housekeeping on a meager salary, in two rooms upstairs over a stable; calling in the assistance of the paternal household on Walnut Hills, securing a cooking-stove from a brother, and dishes from a Seminary classmate, and a variety of things from "Father Beecher and Mrs. Stowe;" cleaning out the dirty rooms with their own hands, with indomitable pluck and the merriest good nature—such were the preparations made by this loving couple for their first home.—BARROWS, JOHN HENRY, 1893, *Henry Ward Beecher the Shakespeare of the Pulpit*, p. 73.

Good-by, my best beloved friend. I shall never have another like you. Mr. Beecher died of apoplexy at his residence in Brooklyn on Tuesday, March 8, 1887, at 9:40 A. M. The private funeral was held at 9:30 A. M. on the following Thursday at his late home, where none but the members of the family were present. The public funeral took place at Plymouth Church at 10:30 A. M. on Friday, the 11th. . . . Surging crowds thronged the neighboring thoroughfares. Business was suspended by proclamation of the mayor of Brooklyn. The streets in all directions were filled with the sorrowing multitude, who stood in line for hours with a hope of viewing once more the face of their departed friend. When the funeral pageant entered Plymouth Church the interior of the great structure was blooming like an immense bower of flowers and living things. Evergreens and roses, smilax and blossoming vines, greeted those who entered. It seemed, indeed, the ushering of the dead into the realm of life. Lying in state during an entire day, the body was viewed by thousands. The crush to gain one glimpse of the remains was terrible, although the interior arrangements were perfect to secure an orderly passing of the long lines of people. The Thirteenth Regiment were the guard of honor; and hour after hour, from 10 in the morning until 10 in the evening, while the great organ gave forth subdued and solemn music, the people entered, looked, and passed. It was estimated in this slow but constantly moving. stream over fifty thousand persons—men, women, and children—had come to see his face for the last time.—POND, JAMES BURTON, 1900, *Eccentricities of Genius*, p. 74.

TRIAL

I love Beecher and believe in him. He has done good to thousands. If he has fallen into temptation I shall feel grieved, but would be ashamed of myself were I less his friend. — WHITTIER, JOHN GREENLEAF, 1874, *To Elizabeth Stuart Phelps, July 14; Life and Letters*, ed. Pickard, vol. II, p. 595.

Mr. Henry Ward Beecher is so far from suffering any diminution of his popularity as a preacher or lecturer from the defamatory accusations brought against him that he is now paid double what he formerly received for either preaching or lecturing—the great attraction of his eloquence being enhanced in public estimation by his position as a martyr to an infamous slander, or the hero of a scandalous intrigue. I have been assured that he will be supported and maintained in spite of everything in his own church, as a mere matter of money interest. The church was built upon speculation by a body of gentlemen, who engaged Mr. Beecher to preach there, expecting an immense sale of their pews at a very high price, as the result of his popularity as a preacher. Hitherto their speculation has answered admirably, and the present scandal has added to their profits by cramming the church fuller than ever, and in the interest of their pew-rents they will contrive to keep their preacher's popularity undiminished with the public, as I am assured. The whole thing exhibits a moral tone in the community where it is taking place so incredibly degraded and so vulgarly vicious, that I think the lapse from virtue imputed to one individual, clergyman though he be, far less shocking and revolting than the whole religious tone and condition of his congregation and the society of which they form a part.—KEMBLE, FRANCES ANN, 1874, *Letter to H——, Dec. 6; Further Records*, p. 54.

Here is the most popular Protestant preacher, I think, that ever lived, a man whose church would be filled, if there was a bull-fight in the next street,—who gets a salary of twenty thousand dollars and is worth it to his church,—who, as a lecturer, is handled by his impresario as if he were a prima donna,—who has done more sensible, effective, good-natured talking and writing to the great middle class and the "unknown public" than any man we ever had in this country,—with a good deal of Franklin's sense and humor, with a power of holding great assemblies like Whitefield,—the best known and most popular private citizen, I suppose, we have ever had,—a saint by inheritance and connections of every kind, and yet as human as King David or Robert Burns, so that his inherited theology hangs about him in rags, and shows the flesh of honest manhood in a way to frighten all his co-religionists,— here is this wonderful creature, popular idol, the hope of liberal orthodoxy, accused of reading the seventh commandment according to the version that left out the negative. There is no doubt that he has compromised himself with unsafe persons and brought grave suspicions on himself, but the hope is universal that his defence, yet to come, will show that he has been slandered, and that his own assertions of innocence will be made good by a thorough sifting of the testimony that is brought against him. His accuser, Theodore Tilton, appears as badly as a man can, in every point of view, but it is pretended that other witnesses are to be called, and sick as everybody is of the monster scandal, it is felt that all must be known, since so much has already been made public. I am afraid you will turn away with something like disgust from the pages that I have filled with this matter, but the truth is, nothing ever made such a talk, and if it had been a settled fact that the comet was to hit the earth on the 22nd of July, late on the evening of the 21st, people would have been talking of the great "Beecher-Tilton scandal."—HOLMES, OLIVER WENDELL, 1874, *To John Lothrop Motley, July 26; Life and Letters,* ed. Morse, vol. II, p. 209.

My brother is hopelessly generous and confiding. His inability to believe evil is something incredible, and so has come all this suffering. You said you hoped I should be at rest when the first investigating committee and Plymouth Church cleared my brother almost by acclamation. Not so. The enemy have so committed themselves that either they or he must die, and there has followed two years of the most dreadful struggle. First, a legal trial of six months, the expenses of which on his side were one hundred and eighteen thousand dollars, and in which he and his brave wife sat side by side in the court-room and heard all that these plotters, who had been weaving their webs for three years, could bring. The foreman of the jury was offered a bribe of ten thousand dollars to decide against my brother. He sent the letter containing the proposition to the judge. But with all their plotting, three fourths of the jury decided against them, and their case was lost. . . . Never have I known a nature of such strength, and such almost child-like innocence. He is of a nature so sweet and perfect that, though I have seen him thunderously indignant at moments, I never saw him fretful or irritable,—a man who continuously, in every little act of life, is thinking of others, a man that all the children in the street run after, and that every sorrowful, weak, or distressed person looks to as a natural helper. In all this long history there has been no circumstance of his relation to any woman that has not been worthy of himself,—pure, delicate, and proper; and I know all sides of it, and certainly should not say this if there were even a misgiving. Thank God, there is none, and I can read my New Testament and feel that by all the beatitudes my brother is blessed. His calmness, serenity, and cheerfulness through all this time has uplifted us all.—STOWE, HARRIET BEECHER, 1876, *Letter to George Eliot, March 18; Life,* ed. Stowe, pp. 478, 480.

PREACHER AND ORATOR

Among the many consecrated edifices which distinguish Brooklyn as "the City of Churches," is included one, individualized by its unusual capacity and its modest architecture. . . . Here gather, twice on every Sabbath of the year, except during the summer solstice, about twenty-five hundred people, and the audience sometimes numbers three thousand. It is not unusual for the capacious body of the church, the broad galleries, the second elevated gallery, the several aisles, and all vacancies about pulpit and doors, to be occupied by eager listeners, and sometimes hundreds turn aside, unable to find footing within the audience-room. And this is no novel fact. It has been a fact for six years. Its persistence imparts to it the dignity of a moral phenomenon. It is unprecedented in the history of audiences, whether religious, literary, political, or artistical. What in truth is it? It is not that an orator attracts a crowd. That is often done. But it is, that twice on each Sabbath for six years, from two to three thousand people centre to an *unchanged* attraction. No dramatic genius, no melodious voice, no popular eloquence has ever done so much as that. Neither Macready, nor Garrick, nor Jenny Lind, nor Rachel, nor Gough, nor Clay, nor Choate has done it. The theatre must change its "Star" monthly, the singer must migrate often, the orator must make "angel visits" to concentrate three thousand people. And the phenomenon is the more remarkable, in that this gathering is around the Pulpit, where no Art wins, and no Pleasure stimulates; and, furthermore, it occurs when hundreds of other audience-rooms are opened for the same purpose, with pulpits suitably supplied; while competition must be banished, before the Stars of Art can fill three thousand seats for a single evening. And though a difference of expense has its effect, yet it is far from explaining the difference of fact.—FOWLER, HENRY, 1856, *The American Pulpit*, p. 141.

We cross the ferry to Brooklyn, and hear Ward Beecher at the Plymouth Church. It was a spectacle,—and himself the Preacher, if preacher there be anywhere now in pulpits. His auditors had to weep, had to laugh, under his potent magnetism, while his doctrine of justice to all men, bond and free, was grand. House, entries, aisles, galleries, all were crowded. Thoreau called it pagan, but I pronounced it good, very good,—the best I had witnessed for many a day, and hopeful for the coming time.— ALCOTT, AMOS BRONSON, 1856, *Letter*, Nov. 9; *Familiar Letters of Henry David Thoreau*, ed. Sanborn, p. 348.

Beecher preached the most dramatic and, in one sense, most effective sermon I ever heard from him, but in all the philosophy of it unspeakably crude and naturalistic; and yet I was greatly moved notwithstanding, and, I trust, profited. The close was eloquent enough to be a sermon by itself.— BUSHNELL, HORACE, 1858, *Letter to his Wife, Life and Letters*, ed. Cheney, p. 413.

No minister in the United States is so well known, none so widely beloved. He is as well known in Ottawa as in Broadway. He has the largest Protestant congregation in America, and an ungathered parish which no man attempts to number. He has church members in Maine, Wisconsin, Georgia, Texas, California, and all the way between. Men look on him as a national institution, a part of the public property. Not a Sunday in the year but representative men from every State in the Union fix their eyes on him, are instructed by his sermons and uplifted by his prayers. He is the most popular of American lecturers. In the celestial sphere of theological journals, his papers are the bright particular star in that constellation called the "Independent:" men look up to and bless the useful light, and learn therefrom the signs of the times. . . . He speaks for the ear which takes in at once and understands. He never makes attention painful. He illustrates his subject from daily life; the fields, the streets, stars, flowers, music, and babies are his favorite emblems. He remembers that he does not speak to scholars, to minds disciplined by long habit of thought, but to men with common education, careful and troubled about many things; and they keep his words and ponder them in their hearts. . . . His dramatic power makes his sermon also a life in the pulpit; his *auditorium* is also a *theatrum*, for he acts to the eye what he addresses to the ear, and at once wisdom enters at the two gates.—PARKER, THEODORE, 1858, *Henry Ward Beecher*, *Atlantic Monthly*, vol. 1, pp. 865, 869.

It may be safely said, indeed, that as a pulpit and a platform orator he has no superior. Nothing is studied, nothing artificial, about his oratory: all is natural, frank, cordial, hearty, fearless. One great secret of his power is, that he feels deeply himself the great truths that he utters, and therefore makes his audience feel them too. —CLEVELAND, CHARLES D., 1859, *A Compendium of American Literature*, p. 679.

It is not clear to the distant spectator by what aperture Mr. Beecher enters the church. He is suddenly discovered to be present, seated in his place on the platform, —an under-sized gentleman in a black stock. His hair combed behind his ears, and worn a little longer than usual, imparts to his appearance something of the Puritan, and calls to mind his father, the champion of orthodoxy in heretical Boston. In conducting the opening exercises, and, indeed, on all occasions of ceremony, Mr. Beecher shows himself an artist,—both his language and his demeanor being marked by the most refined decorum. An elegant, finished simplicity, characterizes all he does and says: not a word too much, nor a word misused, nor a word waited for, nor unharmonious movement, mars the satisfaction of the auditor. The habit of living for thirty years in the view of a multitude together with a natural sense of the becoming, and a quick sympathy with men and circumstances, has wrought up his public demeanor to a point near perfection. A candidate for public honors could not study a better model. This is the more remarkable, because it is a purely spiritual triumph. Mr. Beecher's person is not imposing, nor his natural manner graceful. It is his complete extirpation of the desire of producing an illegitimate effect; it is his sincerity and genuineness as a human being; it is the dignity of his character, and his command of his powers,—which give him this easy mastery over every situation in which he finds himself.—PARTON, JAMES, 1867, *Henry Ward Beecher's Church, Atlantic Monthly,* vol. 19, p. 42.

The sermon entitled "Sin against the Holy Ghost," is one of the most powerful and instructive doctrinal discourses upon that solemn and mysterious theme that we have read; and few sermons that have ever been written have less of the husk of dogma and more of the sweet fruit of spiritual doctrine in them, than his discourse on "The Comforting God." But it is not as a doctrinal, it is as a moral preacher, that he excels. As a moral pathologist he is wonderfully subtle in his perception of purpose and motive, understanding the bad tendencies as well as the nobler instincts of the human heart, following out a moral truth that another preacher would give in some dry formalistic husk of statement into its living issues in character, enlarging, developing, showing how it works in real life, in the family, the street, the church, tracking meanness to its hiding places, unearthing concealed selfishness, rousing the indolent and sensual, encouraging the meek heart, helping the doubting, seeing good where others would see only evil, and striving to build up a true manhood in the erring, imperfect, and lost.—HOPPIN, J. H., 1870, *Henry Ward Beecher, New Englander,* vol. 29, p. 430.

Of all the living pulpit orators of America, Henry Ward Beecher is confessedly one of the most brilliant. The son of a great pulpit orator, endowed with the rarest and most versatile abilities, he, if any man could do so, might dispense, one would suppose, with a tedious and protracted training in the art of speaking. But what do we find to have been his education? Did he shun the professors of elocution, believing, as do many of his brethren, that oratory, like Dogberry's reading and writing, comes by nature? No, he placed himself, when at college, under a skillful teacher, and for three years was drilled incessantly, he says, in posturing, gesture, and voice-culture. . . . Later, at the theological seminary, Mr. Beecher continued his drill. There was a large grove between the seminary and his father's house, and it was the habit, he tells us, of his brother Charles and himself, with one or two others, to make the night, and even the day, hideous with their voices, as they passed backward and forward through the wood, exploding all the vowels from the bottom to the very top of their voices.—MATHEWS, WILLIAM, 1878, *Oratory and Orators,* pp. 442, 443.

Personally I have no doubt that Mr. Beecher's power is not a little enhanced by his almost unique gift of language. He could fill two octavo pages with the description of a cobweb, and yet there would be much more than mere words in the description. There is a subtle *color* in his words, so that they mass up into very striking impressiveness, however poor or contracted the subject itself may be. Mr. Beecher would be as unquotable a speaker as Mr. Gladstone but for the innumerable figures which crowd to his help. Mr. Gladstone has no rhetorical imagination; he expounds—unravels—and anatomizes his subjects with a precision and fulness truly amazing, and with an eloquence as pellucid as it is massive and forceful, but there are no flowers, no figures, no hints of an infinite background. Mr. Beecher is just as copious in mere language, but then how tropical is the luxuriance of his imagination! When he concludes it is rather out of deference to custom or convenience than because the subject is exhausted. My sober impression is that Mr. Beecher could preach every Sunday in the year from the first verse in Genesis, without giving any sign of intellectual exhaustion, or any failure of imaginative fire.—PARKER, JOSEPH, 1882, *Henry Ward Beecher, A Sketch of his Career,* ed. Abbott, p. 299.

Mr. Beecher has been one of the most popular platform orators and lecturers of his time. He has taken an active part and exerted his great influence in behalf of all the great moral reform movements of the past forty years. He was one of the boldest and most advanced public thinkers and speakers on the anti-slavery question.

During the dark days of the war he made a journey to Europe. He found the popular sentiment in England running strongly against the North. He undertook to stop that current, and in a course of public addresses in the larger cities of that country, he corrected the popular misapprehension of the questions at stake, and turned the tide to flowing strongly in favor of his cause. He has done noble work for the temperance cause, and has given his mite towards advancing the cause of woman suffrage.—WHITMAN, C. M., 1883, *American Orators and Oratory*, p. 1095.

I know that you are still thinking as I speak of the great soul that has passed away, of the great preacher, for he was the greatest preacher in America, and the greatest preacher means the greatest power in the land. To make a great preacher, two things are necessary, the love of truth and the love of souls; and surely no man had greater love of truth or love of souls than Henry Ward Beecher. Great services, too, did he render to theology, which is making great progress now. It is not that we are discovering new truths, but that what lay dead and dry in men's souls has awakened. The Spirit of the Lord has been poured into humanity, and no one more than Mr. Beecher has helped to this, pouring his great insight and sympathy and courage out upon the truths which God gave him to deliver. A great leader in the theological world, believing in the Divine Christ and in eternal hope for mankind, foremost in every great work and in all progress, one of that noble band of men whose hands clutched the throat of slavery, and never relaxed their hold till the last shackle fell off; inspiring men to war, speaking words of love and reconciliation when peace had come, standing by the poor and oppressed, bringing a slave girl into his pulpit and making his people pay her ransom. A true American like Webster, a great preacher, a great leader, a great patriot, a great man.—BROOKS, PHILLIPS, 1887, *Sermon; Life and Letters*, ed. Allen, vol. II, p. 645.

He regarded preaching as specially his vocation, and in his judgment it ranked highest of all earthly pursuits. Nowhere else was he so happy as in this chosen work. As a preacher he was most widely known, and for his labors in this sphere, we doubt not, he will be the longest remembered. His field was broader than was ever before given to any preacher, and no man that ever lived preached continuously to so large and influential audiences. During his forty years in Plymouth pulpit men from every part of the civilized world came to hear him, and to every part of the civilized world did his published sermons find their way, bringing instruction, inspiration, and comfort to multitudes. Of his rank as a preacher, it is not for us to speak dogmatically. We stood too near him—perhaps all men of the present time stand too near him —to be impartial judges. Many letters and reports of sermons have come to us in which he is given the first place among the preachers of this age, and a few, among them some men who themselves hold the first rank, place him before all preachers since the Apostle Paul. Which of these, or whether either, is the true estimate or not, it does not belong to us nor to any living man to decide; but we believe that the latter judgment will in time largely prevail.—BEECHER, WILLIAM C., AND SCOVILLE, SAMUEL, 1888, *A Biography of Henry Ward Beecher*, p. 588.

Mr. Beecher was not only the most popular but the most influential preacher that this country has produced. He did more than any other man to liberalize religious sentiment—to lift orthodox theology out of the ruts in which it had been running from the days of the Puritans. His sermons were very rarely doctrinal. He was in no respect a theologian. He cared little for creeds. Belief with him was a matter of secondary importance; conduct was everything.—McCULLOCH, HUGH, 1888, *Memories of Some Contemporaries, Scribner's Magazine*, vol. 4, p. 281.

Henry Ward Beecher was a great man— one of the greatest and most remarkable men of his day. His personality was so large, his gifts so varied, his mental and moral composition so multiform, that a volume would be needed to give a complete character sketch of the man. . . . His heart was as great as his brain. He was intensely human. Artificiality he hated, and dissembling and deception he could not understand. He was sometimes called a great actor, but sincerity was his very breath of life. . . . Of the wonderful powers that made his preaching so remarkable in its effectiveness and so world wide in its fame it is hard to give a precise analysis. Among the component elements were a vividly creative imagination, a mind richly stocked by reading and observation, a ripe judgment, a deep sympathy, a remarkable adaptability to occasions and situations, and an unfailing earnestness and enthusiasm. He was an accomplished elocutionist with the natural advantages of a commanding presence and a voice of great power and flexibility.—TITHERINGTON, R. H., 1891, *Brooklyn's Statue of Beecher, Munsey's Magazine, vol. 6, pp. 30, 31.*

One minister I have known, who, though always preaching, was always fresh, was Henry Ward Beecher. His ideas were inexhaustible. The Rev. Hugh Price Hughes' definition of the essential requisites of modern preaching are "simplicity, flexibility, spontaneity and earnestness"—qualities of his own preaching, aided by a voice which travels like a bird over the audience and along the galleries. Ward Beecher had the four qualities above named, with the addition of imagination; always bright and often poetical, when every sentence was tinted with a hue of its own.—HOLYOAKE, GEORGE JACOB, 1897, *Public Speaking and Debate, p. 193.*

GENERAL

The author of "Norwood" is less of an artist than his sister, Mrs. Stowe, and under the relation of art his novel is below criticism. It contains many just observations on various topics, but by no means original or profound; it seizes some few of the traits of New England village life; but its characters, with the exception of Judge Bacon, Agate Bissell, and Hiram Beers are the abstractions or impersonations of the author's theories. The author has little dramatic power, and not much wit or humor. The persons or personages of his book are only so many points in the argument which he is carrying on against Calvinistic orthodoxy for pure naturalism. The substance of his volume seems to be made up of the fag-ends of his sermons and lectures. He preaches and lectures all through it, and rather prosily into the bargain. His Dr. Wentworth is a bore, and his daughter Rose, the heroine of the story, is a species of blue-stocking, and neither lovely nor lovable. As a type of the New England cultivated and accomplished lady she is a failure, and is hardly up to the level of the New England school-ma'am. The sensational incidents of the story are old and worn out, and the speculations on love indicate very little depth of feeling or knowledge of life, or of the human heart. The author proceeds on a theory and so far shows his New England birth and breeding, but he seldom touches reality. As a picture of New England village life it is singularly unfortunate, and still more so as a picture of village life in the valley of the Connecticut, some twenty miles above Springfield, in Massachusetts, where the scene is laid, and where the tone and manners of society in a village of five thousand inhabitants, the number Norwood is said to contain, hardly differ in refinement and polish from the tone and manners of the better classes in Boston and its vicinity.—BROWNSON, ORESTES A., 1869, *Beecher's Norwood, Works,* ed. Brownson, vol. XIX, p. 534.

As a theological scholar, or, indeed, as a trained and accurate writer, nobody would think of comparing him with Francis Wayland, or Leonard Bacon, or Edwards A. Park, or Frederick H. Hedge. In depth of spiritual insight, though not in depth of spiritual emotion, he is inferior to Horace Bushnell, Cyrus A. Bartol, and many other American divines. He feels spiritual facts intensely; he beholds them with wavering vision. But his distinction is that he is a formidable, almost irresistible, moral force. . . . An impartial student of character, accustomed to penetrate into the souls of those he desires inwardly to know, to look at things from their point of view, and to interpret external evidence by the internal knowledge he has thus obtained, would say that Mr. Beecher was exactly the heedless, indiscreet man of religious genius likely to become the subject of such a scandal as has recently disgusted the country, and yet to be perfectly innocent of the atrocious crimes with which he was charged.—WHIPPLE, EDWIN PERCY, 1876–86, *American Literature and Other Papers,* ed. Whittier, pp. 134, 135.

Suppose that Mr. Beecher had been confined to the city during all his young life. The result would have been that we should not have had Mr. Beecher at all. We should have had a strong, dramatic man, notable in many respects—but he would have been so shorn of his wonderful power of illustration, that his pulpit would have been but a common one. It is quite safe for us to say that he has learned more of that which has been of use to him, as a public teacher, from nature, than from his theological schools and books. He has recognized the word which God speaks to us in nature as truly divine—just as divine as that which he speaks in revelation. His quick apprehension of the analogies that exist between nature and the spiritual world has been the key by which he has opened the door into his wonderful success.—HOLLAND, JOSIAH GILBERT, 1876, *Every-Day Topics, p. 29.*

In his death the pulpit has lost one of its most gifted orators, and the country its best-known citizen. Mr. Beecher's place in history is that of a fixed star of the first magnitude. His genius, his character, and his career will form notable and instructive studies in all the future. He was many-sided, with a vigorous, keen, versatile intellect, most gigantic in his attainments, magnetic in power and influence, progressive in thought and action, a grand, genial, large-hearted, manly man. The chief element of his marvelous success, however, was his devotion to study. With all his rare endowments he would never trust himself to speak on any subject that he had not previously made his own through the closest analysis. In his Christian work he was a careful student of ministerial helps. He studied other preachers, he studied men, he studied himself. In his lectures on varied topics he was thoroughly informed, his mind a perfect store-house of exact knowledge, not accidentally so, but through careful, painstaking research and observation. His brain was never idle, and he esteemed it an imperative duty to keep abreast with all themes of current interest. Thus critics have rarely been able to prove him at fault in any important fact, whether stated as an argument or used as an illustration wherever he has spoken even though a combatant in the most heated controversies.—LAMB, MARTHA J., 1887, *Henry Ward Beecher, Magazine of American History, vol. 17, p. 307.*

Beecher's "Life Thoughts," when I was fourteen, tended to mellow the Calvinism of North Country Congregationalism, and Spurgeon's Sermons acted as an astringent in the opposite direction.—STEAD, W. T., 1887, *Books which Have Influenced Me, p. 37.*

Mr. Beecher's place as a writer falls below his oratorical rank. The man's presence was so mighty, and his passions even overwhelming. that, being gone, he is like Talbot in Shakespeare's play without his troops, and leaves but a remnant of himself on the printed page behind. What but genius suffers no privation in the cold types? Predominant talent, transcendent faculty for an occasion, and apt fancy to illustrate a point are published at a loss. Nothing save power of original thought or a divine vision, with command of beautiful expression, can constitute literature,—books that will endure. There are infinite wit and resource, but lack of whole and vital organism, in all the volumes Beecher has put forth. Every essay or sermon of his is a fragment, with the glitter in it as of crushed crystal or broken spar. He spoke or wrote to serve a purpose, well and bravely, but not for all time.—BARTOL, CYRUS AUGUSTUS, 1887, *Henry Ward Beecher, Unitarian Review, vol. 27, p. 355.*

"Norwood" showed him in no new light. There was nothing in it which was not in his sermons in a better form. His "Life of Christ" is without any critical value, and its discontinuance is not a matter for regret. It was a brilliant paraphrase of the New Testament narration, in which Mr. Beecher spoke ten times from his emotion to once from his reason. That he did not sooner resolve to write his autobiography, and carry out his purpose, is a great pity.—CHADWICK, JOHN WHITE, 1887, *Henry Ward Beecher, The Nation, vol. 44, pp. 225, 226.*

Henry Ward Beecher will be remembered as a preacher, and not as a writer. He wrote much, but he was not in any measure a man of letters. Most of his pieces are fugitive; some at least would hardly have been printed if a less famous man had written them. His heart was in his ministerial work, especially in his preaching; for he does not appear to have been an ideal pastor. His powers were not very various, but he was too strong a man in his own place to need any excessive eulogy. Admitting his limitations, we cannot fail to recognise and to admire the excellent service he rendered within them. He was a parson of this world, concerned with this world's movements, and, at heart, more eager about fitting people for citizenship of the United States than for citizenship of the New Jerusalem.—LEWIN, WALTER, 1889, *Biography of Henry Ward Beecher, The Academy, vol. 35, pp. 215, 216.*

How much of Mr. Beecher's literary work will survive? A great deal of it has that peculiar quality, imagination, which Lowell calls "the great antiseptic." He is one of the most quotable of men, as quotable as Marcus Aurelius, Montaigne, Bacon, or Emerson. Five or six volumes from his sermons, speeches, and essays, would contain too much wit and wisdom for posterity to willingly let die. He had Franklin's and Lincoln's homely way of saying things, and much of Thomas à Kempis's spirituality and power of bringing consolation to bruised hearts. Poet, moralist, humorist, and master of pithy proverbs, why should not Mr. Beecher be among the immortals in literature? A hundred years hence, when the Republic has become "the most powerful and prosperous community ever devised or developed by man," and the historian reviews the critical years of the nineteenth century, in which Mr. Beecher had so conspicuous a part, he will then be a larger and loftier figure than now.—BARROWS, JOHN HENRY, 1893, *Henry Ward Beecher the Shakespeare of the Pulpit*, p. 527.

Mr. Beecher was too busy a man to give more than his spare moments to general literature. His sermons, lectures, and addresses were reported for the daily papers and printed in part in book form; but these lose greatly when divorced from the large, warm, and benignant personality of the man. His volumes made up of articles in the *Independent* and *Ledger*, such as "Star Papers," 1855, and "Eyes and Ears," 1862, contain many delightful *morceaux* upon country life and similar topics, though they are hardly wrought with sufficient closeness and care to take a permanent place in letters.—BEERS, HENRY A., 1895, *Initial Studies in American Letters*, p. 182.

Mr. Beecher's style was not artificial; its faults as well as its excellences were those of extreme naturalnesss. He always wrote with fury; rarely did he correct with phlegm. His sermons were published as they fell from his lips,—correct and revise he would not. The too few editorials which he wrote, on the eve of the Civil War, were written while the press was impatiently waiting for them, were often taken page by page from his hand, and were habitually left unread by him to be corrected in proof by others. ... But while his style was wholly unartificial, it was no product of mere careless genius; carelessness never gives a product worth possessing. The excellences of Mr. Beecher's style were due to a careful study of the great English writers; its defects to a temperament too eager to endure the dull work of correction. ... In any estimate of Mr. Beecher's style, it must be remembered that he was both by temperament and training a preacher. He was brought up not in a literary, but in a didactic atmosphere. If it were as true as it is false that art exists only for art's sake, Mr. Beecher would not have been an artist. His art always had a purpose; generally a distinct moral purpose. An overwhelming proportion of his contributions to literature consists of sermons or extracts from sermons, or addresses not less distinctively didactic. His one novel was written avowedly to rectify some common misapprehensions as to New England life and character. Even his lighter papers, products of the mere exuberance of a nature too full of every phase of life to be quiescent, indicated the intensity of a purposeful soul, much as the sparks in a blacksmith's shop come from the very vigor with which the artisan is shaping on the anvil the nail or the shoe.—ABBOTT, LYMAN, 1897, *Library of the World's Best Literature*, ed. *Warner*, vol, III, pp. 1714, 1715, 1716.

The style of Henry Ward Beecher, for example, is remarkable for the number, aptness, and beauty of the figures of speech he uses. ... His oratory is distinguished by the qualities of fervid eloquence, great abundance and variety of illustration, startling independence of statement, and brilliant humor. He was an original thinker, and many of his sermons are models of persuasive argument, combining close logical thought with beautiful imagery.—NOBLE, CHARLES, 1898, *Studies in American Literature*, pp. 26, 341.

For years his printed sermons were the main source of my instruction and delight. His range and variety in all that kind of observation and subtlety of which I have just spoken; his width of sympathy; his natural and spontaneous pathos; the wealth of illustration and metaphor with which his sermons were adorned, and which were drawn chiefly from natural objects, from his orchard, his farm, his garden, as well as from machinery and from all kinds of natural processes; his naturalism and absence of theological bias; his knowledge of average men and their ways of looking at things; in a word his general fertility of thought, filling up as it did the full horizon of my mind, and running over and beyond it on all sides, so that wherever I looked he had been there before me,—all this delighted and enchanted me, and made him for some years my ideal of intellectual greatness.—CROZIER, JOHN BEATTIE, 1898, *My Inner Life, p. 183.*

For many years he poured forth from the pulpit of "Plymouth Church" sermons brilliant in thought, full of poetic beauty, rich and warm with the love of God and man.—BRONSON, WALTER C., 1900, *A Short History of American Literature, p. 274.*

For almost half a century Henry Ward Beecher was one of the most conspicuous persons in American life. The product of his brain during all that time was enormous and exceedingly varied. That he moulded the opinions of men there is no doubt; that he urged an intelligent and devoted adherence to Christianity, there can be no question; that he entered deeply into the politics of his time is evident; and through all his activity he was unfailing in the use of his voice and pen for what he considered the advancement of human society.—ADDISON, DANIEL DULANEY, 1900, *The Clergy in American Life and Letters.*

Emma Lazarus
1849–1887

A Hebrew-American poet; born in New York city, July 22, 1849, died there Nov. 19, 1887. She labored diligently in behalf of her race and devoted her pen largely to Hebrew subjects, publishing a much-discussed article in *The Century* on "Russian Christianity versus Modern Judaism." Her first volume was composed of "Poems and Translations" (1866), written between the ages of fourteen and seventeen. This was followed by "Admetus" (1871); "Alide: an Episode of Goethe's Life" (1874); "Songs of a Semite" (1882), all of which are marked by naturalness of sentiment, vivid effect, and artistic reserve of expression.—WARNER, CHARLES DUDLEY, ed. 1897, *Library of the World's Best Literature, Biographical Dictionary, vol.* XXIX, *p. 330.*

PERSONAL

When on thy bed of pain thou layest low
Daily we saw thy body fade away,
Nor could the love wherewith we loved thee stay
For one dear hour the flesh born down by woe;
But as the mortal sank, with that white glow
Flamed thy eternal spirit, night and day,—
Untouched, unwasted, though the crumbling clay
Lay wrecked and ruined! Ah, is it not so,
Dear poet-comrade, who from sight hast gone,—
Is it not so that spirit hath a life
Death may not conquer? But, O dauntless one!
Still must we sorrow. Heavy is the strife
And thou not with us,—thou of the old race
That with Jehovah parleyed, face to face.
—GILDER, RICHARD WATSON, 1887, *Century Magazine, vol.* 35, *p. 581.*

During the last fifteen years it has been my good fortune to meet her often, and to have opportunities of conversation with her upon subjects of every kind, especially those relating to literature, philosophy and universal religion. These conversations were always deeply interesting to me, and often exceedingly instructive. Her knowledge was extensive, her appreciation unhackneyed and sympathetic, her wit and humor delightful, her taste catholic, and her judgment substantial and impressive. Narrowness and bigotry were unknown to her nature, and her friendships were most valuable to those on whom she conferred them. To the courage and logic of a man she added the delicate and varying subtlety of a womanly intelligence. To have possessed in any degree the friendship of such a person is a consolation in the struggles and disappointments of life, and the sense of loss which comes from her death is amply repaid by the consciousness that she has lived.—DANA, CHARLES ANDERSON, 1887, *Emma Lazarus Memorial, The American Hebrew, vol.* 33, *p. 70.*

I think no one could see her casually without being strongly impressed by her personality. Immediately I knew that here was a woman of pure mind, sincere heart, capacity for friendship and of unselfish enthusiasm—if one were worthy of her friendship he might trust her to the end. Interesting as was the fine play of her intellectual faculties in society, I am not sure but her greater charm was in the sincerity and goodness which everyone felt in her. Her literary work bore the stamp of her absolutely unaffected character. It was all genuine, she never posed. But besides all this her poems wore the indefinable note of genius, the quality which one instantly recognized, which makes the world-wide difference between verse and poetry.—WARNER, CHARLES DUDLEY, 1887, *Emma Lazarus Memorial, The American Hebrew*, vol. 33, p. 68.

While thoroughly feminine, and a mistress of the social art and charm, she was—though without the slightest trace of pedantry—the natural companion of scholars and thinkers. Her emotional nature kept pace with her intellect; as she grew in learning and mental power, she became still more earnest, devoted, impassioned. . . . That she was aglow with the Jewish spirit, proud of her race's history and characteristics, and consecrated to its freedom from oppression throughout the world,—all this was finely manifest; yet her intellectual outlook was so broad that I took her to be a modern Theist in religion, and one who would not stipulate for absolute maintenance of the barriers with which the Mosaic law isolated the Jewish race, in certain respects, from the rest of mankind. Taking into account, however, the forces of birth and training, I could understand how our Miriam of to-day, filled with the passion of her cause, should return to the Pentateuchal faith—to the Mosaic ritual in its hereditary and most uncompromising form. Nor would any lover of the heroic in life or literature, if such had been her course, desire to have it otherwise.—STEDMAN, EDMUND CLARENCE, 1887, *Emma Lazarus Memorial, The American Hebrew*, vol. 33, p. 68.

The personality of Emma Lazarus is one that has done much to ennoble womanhood. . . . The home in which Emma Lazarus grew up was remarkable for its atmosphere of culture and refinement. All the aids to social interchange, all the accomplishments which can give a charm to daily life, softening little anxieties and turning the thoughts to constant aspiration, were present there in a very marked degree. One felt the influence of the fine picture, the choice book, the elegant instrument, not as an outside addition to the furniture, but as an inner factor in determining the elevation of taste, the trend of thought, the entrance of the spirit into pure harmony. Her life as a woman was comparatively retired. Her quiet, unpretentious manner gave strangers very little indication of the mind contained within that unobtrusive figure. She had many devoted friends, was passionately fond of Nature, and almost equally allured by art. Mr. Emerson corresponded with her for a number of years; and Miss Lazarus probably drew from this friendship as much benefit in the womanly part of her nature as she derived stimulus from the mental contact with the distinguished author. She was fond of the theatre, and particularly appreciated the splendid impersonations of Salvini. She was much sought after in cultured society in New York.—COHEN, MARY M., 1893, *Emma Lazarus: Woman, Poet, Patriot, Poetlore*, vol. 5, pp. 320, 321.

GENERAL

Down the strange past you saw the flashing sword
Of Maccabæus, and your slender hand
Brandished the Banner of the Jew; your wand
On selfish Greeks a magic numbness poured:—
Sibyl Judaica! from out our land
You scourged that beast by lofty souls abhorred.
—DEKAY, CHARLES, 1887, *To Emma Lazarus, The Critic*, vol. 2, p. 293.

Her songs of the Divine unity, repeated on the lips of her own people in all zones and continents, have been heard round the world. With no lack of rhythmic sweetness, she has often the rugged strength and verbal audacity of Browning. Since Miriam sang of deliverance and triumph by the Red Sea, the Semitic race has had no braver singer. — WHITTIER, JOHN GREENLEAF, 1887, *Emma Lazarus Memorial, The American Hebrew*, vol. 33, p. 67.

Nowhere among our writers was there a talent more genuine and substantial, a devotion to art for its own sake and for the sake of high principles, more earnest and singleminded. From the very beginning of her literary life, her poetic faculty showed a constant and regular growth in strength and depth; her last writings were the richest and most attractive fruits of her genius.—HAY, JOHN, 1887, *Emma Lazarus Memorial, The American Hebrew*, vol. 33, p. 70.

To me Emma Lazarus seemed one of the most notable of women. Her genius combined in a rare way a capacity for largeness of view with intensity of illumination and emotion. She was capable of high enthusiasm, without any alloy of religious bigotry; and it was the good fortune of her mental constitution that she was also free from moral intolerance to a degree not often found in one so wholly earnest.—EGGLESTON, EDWARD, 1887, *Emma Lazarus Memorial, The American Hebrew*, vol. 33, p. 70.

It will not be questioned that Emma Lazarus represented the most intellectual type of Jewish womanhood in this country. Her latter years were marked by a lofty, noble, religious spirit, which was full of love for her race, and which breathed the life of a Judaism higher and more elevating than that which passes current with many as Judaism. Her later writings such as the "Epistle to the Hebrews," published in *The American Hebrew*, certainly had a marked effect upon many young men and women in our community, who thereby became inspired in working in the cause of their unfortunate brethren, and strongly encouraged others in the same direction. This effort powerfully exhibited the intense Jewish feeling of this noble woman in Israel, and the keen desire which animated her to arouse the apathy existing among many of our coreligionists in communal work. Emma Lazarus, in a few of her Jewish writings, was a preacher to the intellectual Jewish young men and women, whose eloquence and sentiments touched the hearts of her flock much more powerfully and effectively than scores of sermons delivered to listless audiences in chilly temples and synagogues. —GREENBAUM, SAMUEL, 1887, *Emma Lazarus Memorial, The American Hebrew*, vol. 33, p. 71.

How shall her memory best be honored by the Jewish world and the literary world to each of which she belonged? The Jewish world may do her honor by active encouragement of those purposes which were dear to her—the technical education of immigrants, the establishment and assistance of agricultural colonies, and such other methods as are acknowledged to be the remedy of the disagreeable sociological phase of the Jewish question. And if the literary world in fact honors her memory and would keep it green, there can certainly be no better way than by continuing the work she undertook. Literature makes public sentiment and the makers of literature can pay no higher tribute to Emma Lazarus than if each in his way, following the path trodden by her and by George Eliot, will add his quota to make anti-Semitism hateful and despised among men.—SULZBERGER, CYRUS L., 1887, *Emma Lazarus as a Jew, The American Hebrew*, vol. 33, p. 79.

How Jewish patriotism was a passion that thrilled her can be judged by her writings. No aimless or vague emotion was it with her. To her, Jewish patriotism meant a response to the highest and noblest calls that can wake the Jewish heart, and wake it to love, not the Jew, but the world. . . . Her epistles to the Hebrews will remain a monument to her deep Jewish sentiment, and her suggestions therein prove her far-reaching wisdom; for she accentuated technical education as a feature in the American Jewish system, and proposed to carry American Jewish energy to attack the evil at the root by working among the East European Jews who are to-day counted by millions. For them she suggested "internal reform based on higher education," "emigration to more enlightened and progressive countries," and "repatriation and auto-emancipation in Palestine."—MENDES, PEREIRA, 1887, *Emma Lazarus, The Critic*, vol. 11, p. 295.

In dead, dull days I heard a ringing cry
Borne on the careless winds—a nation's pain
A woman's sorrow in a poet's strain
Of noblest lamentation. Clear and high
It rang above our lowlands to a sky
Of purest psalmody, till hearts are fain
To say: "In this sweet singer once again
The powers of prophet and of psalmist lie."
Rachel of Judah! ever mournful, sad
Must be the heart which thy lamenting hears;
Singer of Israel! ever proud and glad
We hail a nation's hope that thus appears;
Sad mourners by the waters! ye have had
A poet's sweetest solace for your tears.
—CROSS, ALLEN EASTMAN, 1887, *To Emma Lazarus, The Critic*, May 14.

Has the distinction of being the foremost latter-day poet of Israel. Her poetry has a singular loftiness and, if the seeming paradox be permitted, a passionate serenity, which distinguish it from the great bulk of contemporary minor verse. It is by such lyrics as "The Banner of the Jew" that she will no doubt be longest remembered, but her poetic dramas, particularly "The Dance to Death," are remarkable in the best sense. Perhaps to the majority of readers she appeals most by her renderings from the mediæval Hebrew poets of Spain, . . . by those from Petrarch and Dante, and from Heine and A. de Musset. For translation she had a faculty scarce short of genius. Miss Lazarus is not always at her ease in the sonnet, but her "Success," "Venus of the Louvre," and "Love's Protagonist," are fine examples of this form.—SHARP, WILLIAM, 1889, *ed., American Sonnets, Introductory Note*, p. xlv.

Echoes thou didst thy noble verses name,
The Legacy thou leav'st to time and fame.
Not so: O sated, modern mind, rejoice!
Here sound no echoes, but a living voice.
—CROSBY, MARGARET, 1890, *The Poems of Emma Lazarus, Century Magazine*, vol. 39, p. 522.

Was a woman of the Hebrew faith, of great sweetness and depth of character, and of lofty imaginative genius. She made it her theme and mission to appeal through the medium of verse to the highest instincts of her race, to recall to them their sublime history, and to foreshadow a glorious future. The bulk of her writings was not great; but before she died she was recognized as a poet of the first rank.—HAWTHORNE, JULIAN, AND LEMONN, LEONARD, 1891, *American Literature*, p. 282.

Our women poets of the century usually have written from the heart; none more so than Emma Lazarus, whose early verse had been that of an art-pupil, and who died young—but not before she seized the harp of Judah and made it give out strains that all too briefly renewed the ancient fervor and inspiration.—STEDMAN, EDMUND CLARENCE, 1892, *The Nature and Elements of Poetry: Imagination, Century Magazine*, vol. 44, p. 861.

Mark Hopkins
1802–1887

An American educator, grandnephew of the theologian Samuel Hopkins, and brother of the astronomer Albert Hopkins. He was born at Stockbridge, Mass., was educated at Williams College, was tutor there for two years, and after studying medicine and practicing for a short time in New York, became professor of moral philosophy in Williams in 1830, and president of the institution in 1836. He resigned the position in 1872, but remained college preacher and incumbent of the chair of moral philosophy. In 1857 he had become president of the American Board of Foreign Missions. Undoubtedly one of the greatest of American educators of his day, Hopkins did much to build up the prestige of Williams College and much more to develop the individual student. He was a powerful preacher and a successful lecturer. He published: "The Influence of the Gospel in Liberalizing the Mind" (1831); "The Connexion Between Taste and Morals" (1841); his Lowell Lectures, "The Evidences of Christianity" (3d ed. 1875); "Miscellaneous Essays and Reviews" (1847); a second series of Lowell Lectures, "Moral Science" (1862); "The Law of Love and Love as a Law" (last ed. 1881); "An Outline Study of Man" (last ed. 1893); "Strength and Beauty" (1874; in 1884 under the title "Teachings and Counsels") and "The Scriptural Idea of Man" (1883).—GILMAN, PECK, AND COLBY, eds., 1903, *The New International Encyclopædia*, vol. IX, p. 547.

PERSONAL

It is becoming customary for the head of a college to do little or no work of instruction, but it is doubtful whether the office of president, important and honorable as it is, would have had much attraction for Dr. Hopkins separated from the duties of the class-room. For the general administrative duties he had no special taste. During the first year of his presidency he said he would willingly give up half his salary if he had nothing to do but teach. Teaching was his great work. He could, indeed, do all things well. His quickness of perception, his excellent judgment, his conscientious fidelity, enabled him to succeed in all the work of college administration; but he felt that his place was in the class-room. He was truly a prince among teachers. Probably no college president, no college teacher, has ever impressed young men more strongly.

. . . In all respects he was a large man. He was formed in a large mold. In person he was tall and of imposing presence. His mind was large and strong. He took broad views of every subject. His mind was philosophical and yet practical. He grasped a subject in its principles. Hence he was never a partisan. There was nothing small or petty about him. Blended with his breath and greatness there was the charm of simplicity. In all his writings, in all his addresses, there is no striving after effect.
. . . In no great man has there been a finer blending of traits. With great virtues there are sometimes great faults. Strength in some points is counterbalanced by weakness in others. Dr. Hopkins was symmetrical, and that on a large scale. With all his ability, he trusted nothing to genius. He believed in discipline and culture, and his life was devoted to helping young men

prepare themselves for the most efficient service for God and for man.—ANDREWS, I. W., 1887, *President Mark Hopkins, Education, vol. 8, pp.* 119, 120, 121.

To the last hour of his life Dr. Hopkins was eagerly seeking for truth, and in the search was finding larger tolerance and deeper faith. His works have long been in the hands of students who have found his "Moral Philosophy," his "Outline Study of Man," his "Law of Love, and Love as a Law," and his "Strength and Beauty" full of a deep and adequate philosophy of life. And yet these books give but a faint impression of the greatness of a man whose personality was his source of power and who illustrated in his own ample and elevated life the range and inspiration of his thought. . . . Dr. Hopkins was preëminently a teacher and, therefore, a great ethical force. No truth was really mastered in his view until it had been carried to its consummation in character. It was the constant appeal to obligation which gave his teaching such immediate and final effect on all who sat in his class-room. Clear, open-minded, impatient of obscurity and pretense of all kinds, he seemed instinctively to find the heart of the question and to set it in large and right relation to the whole of things.—MABIE, HAMILTON WRIGHT, 1887, *Mark Hopkins, The Book Buyer, vol.* 4, p. 220.

President Hopkins was an exceptionally tall man, and rather thin, but he was wiry and quick in motion. His shoulders were broad, but slightly bent, and his forehead ample, rising above a pair of mild hazel eyes. He spoke with reasonable deliberation, in clear, full tones, which commanded instant respect; every one felt at once that some word of wisdom which he would not willingly lose was about to fall from those eloquent lips. He did not gesticulate much; it was unnecessary to the expression of his thought. He did not grow excited. Each thought carried its own weight. Gently but powerfully his own mind was working, and well he knew it would leave an indelible impression upon the mind of each hearer.— KASSON, FRANK H., 1890, *Mark Hopkins, New England Magazine, N. S., vol.* 3, *p.* 6.

It was the peculiarity of this teacher that he gave this stamp of universal relations in conditions largely provincial, and thus struck the keynote for many noble careers. For, whatever was provincial in any feature of our college life when I was a student at Williams, there was nothing provincial about Dr. Hopkins. Wherever he went, he was and he looked a citizen of the world, one might rather say a king of men, and this was preëminently true in the classroom. Whether he spoke, or prayed, or was silent, the observer knew that that massive head carried wisdom; and those eyes had looked into secrets of the widest range and application.—CARTER, FRANKLIN, 1892, *Mark Hopkins (American Religious Leaders), p.* 147.

Mark Hopkins is by general consent regarded as the typical American college president. James A. Garfield, the second martyr President of the United States, and at one time a pupil of Mark Hopkins, is reported to have said that a student on one end of a log and Mark Hopkins on the other would make a university anywhere. . . . President Hopkins was an accurate scholar, a great thinker, a remarkably able administrator, a noble man. As a writer, as an orator, as a teacher, he was eminently successful. In character and influence he was as nearly ideal as can be expected of a man.—WINSHIP, ALBERT EDWARD, 1900, *Great American Educators, pp.* 187, 188.

GENERAL

In treating of natural religion, we are highly gratified to observe that Dr. Hopkins pursues ["Evidences of Christianity"] a happy line between the extremes of those on the one hand who almost deify reason, and those on the other hand who deny that any thing is discoverable in morals and religion without the Bible. So, in respect to ethics, we equally rejoice in his clear assertion, that "the utility of an action is one thing, and its rightness another," and in his teaching that "the affections are not under the immediate control of the will." Indeed, we cannot recall an instance in which this profound thinker and accomplished scholar has vented a paradox, or given forth a single oracle which can be relished by the recent boastful improvers of our philosophy. In such a station as that which he adorns, a severe reserve of this nature is of good augury for the coming race of scholars. . . . Every page bespeaks the thinker and the scholar. Dr. Hopkins is altogether full of the thought, which is let alone; and the result is a translucent style, such as one admires in Southey's histories. If we were desired to characterize the work in a single word, that word should be *clearness*. We have never hesitated for an instant as to the meaning of a single sentence. In saying this, we say enough to condemn the book with a certain school. . . . The author has so cultivated the habit of looking at things in broad daylight, that his representations offer nothing to divert or distract the mind. The necessary result is beauty of diction; the style is achromatic. . . . In the true acceptation of the term, he is an original writer.—ALEXANDER, J. W., 1846, *Lectures on the Evidences of Christianity*, Princeton Review, vol. 18, pp. 368, 374, 375.

It ["Evidences of Christianity"] possesses great merits. The style is clear, forcible, not infrequently rising into eloquence and always marked by a business-like character, proceeding by the shortest way towards the main point, as if the writer were too much in earnest to waste either his own or other's time on matters of secondary importance. Having at the outset stated, with the good sense that characterises the whole volume, the precise object which he purposes to accomplish, he examines the question of the antecedent improbability of miraculous communication from God, and then shows how far miracles are susceptible of proof, and how far they are the fitting evidence of a Divine revelation.—PEABODY, E., 1846, *Hopkins's Lectures*, Christian Examiner, vol. 41, p. 218.

His peculiar tact in imparting instruction,—his powerful influence over young men, exciting both their reverence and their love,—his dignified yet affable manners, his kind and sympathizing heart, make him peculiarly fitted for the position he occupies. And when to these characteristics is added an intellect of great strength, as well as great breadth of view, combined with a rare fertility of illustration, we can readily conceive what an influence he must exert in giving "form and pressure" to hundreds of minds that are, in their turn, to take a leading part in moulding and directing public opinion.—CLEVELAND, CHARLES D., 1859, *A Compendium of American Literature*, p. 491.

Through and through Hopkins is a transcendentalist and anti-agnostic. His teachings illustrate the yielding, in America, of Reid and "common-sense" philosophy to the influence of Germany and spiritual intuitions. In Hopkins, a Trinitarian Congregational minister, in many ways a conservative, and sometimes following the Edwardsian statements, appears an optimism not less serene than that of Emerson himself.—RICHARDSON, CHARLES F., 1887, *American Literature*, 1607-1885, vol. I, p. 316.

There have been few Americans worthier of praise than Mark Hopkins. He built himself into the mental fabric of two generations of men. They hold him in gentle, loving and grateful remembrance. He erected in their hearts the "monument more enduring than brass." . . . Many great eulogiums will yet be pronounced upon the work and character of President Hopkins; touching pictures will be drawn of his person, his manner and his inspiring companionship; historians will dwell upon his gentle but mighty influence in helping forward and upward the intellectual activities of the nineteenth century.—KASSON, FRANK H., 1890, *Mark Hopkins*, New England Magazine, N. S. vol. 3, p. 3.

The lectures on the "Evidences of Christianity" delivered in January, 1844, the first important book of Dr. Hopkins, bear clear marks of the great influence that Bishop Butler had exercised upon his mind. It seems at first thought singular that the "Analogy," which was written with special reference to the unbelief of the last century, and had been published over a hundred years when Dr. Hopkins delivered these lectures, should have kept so firm a grasp on religious thought, and should leave its indelible marks on minds so different as, for instance, that of Cardinal Newman and that of Dr. Hopkins. . . . The one was indeed a Puritan, the other a Romanist. The one believed in the smallest amount of machinery in religious things and in the fullest liberty for a local church. The other was carried by his processes of thought to the acceptance of authority, to a profound hatred of schism, and to a fervent attachment to what he held as the one original Christian church. When Dr. Hopkins in conversation with one of the college professors regarding Robert Browning said, "I too am a mystic," he expressed the affinity that he had with all the great spiritual teachers of the age; and though he would have rejected with disdain much of Newman's sacramentalism, he accepted him as a brother in the higher region of spiritual thought, and with him emphasized always the immediate relation of the soul to the things unseen. No work of Newman's shows more plainly or more beautifully the far-reaching effect of the great "Analogy" than these lectures by Dr. Hopkins on the "Evidences of Christianity." — CARTER, FRANKLIN, 1892, *Mark Hopkins (American Religious Leaders)*, pp. 136, 137.

He wrote eighty-two books, pamphlets, and articles of very considerable merit, but the two which were most widely used and most influential were the "Outline Study of Man" and "The Law of Love and Love as a Law." These are great works.—WINSHIP, A. E., 1900, *Great American Educators*, p. 200.

John Godfrey Saxe
1816–1887

Poet and humorist; born at Highgate, Vt., June 2, 1816; graduated at Middlebury College 1839; was admitted to the bar at St Albans 1843; practiced law in Franklin County 1843–50; was editor of the Burlington *Sentinel* 1850–56; was State's attorney of Vermont one year, after which he devoted himself chiefly to literature and to popular lecturing; was Democratic candidate for Governor 1859 and 1860. Author of several volumes of humorous poems, the longest of which were delivered at college commencements and other anniversary occasions. His published works include "Progress" (1846); "New Rape of the Lock;" "The Proud Miss McBride;" "The Money King" (1859); "Clever Stories of Many Nations;" "The Masquerade" (1866); and "Leisure Day Rhymes" (1875). More than forty editions of his collected poems have been issued in the U. S. and in England. Died at Albany, N. Y., Mar. 31, 1887.—BEERS, HENRY A., *rev.*, 1897, *Johnson's Universal Encyclopædia, vol.* VII, p. 330.

PERSONAL

O genial Saxe, whose radiant wit
  Flashed like the lightning from the sky,
But, though each flash as keenly hit,
  Wounded but what deserved to die—
Alas! the cloud that shrouds thy day
  In gathering darkness, fold on fold,
Serves not as background for the play
  Of those bright gleams that charmed of old.
. . . .
Yet charms not now his blithesome lay,
  Nor flowery mead "in verdure clad."
The world that laughed when thou wast gay,
  Now weeps to know that thou art sad.
—PERCIVAL, C. S., 1886, *To John G. Saxe, Century Magazine, vol.* 32, p. 248.

One of the first things he did after moving to Brooklyn was to purchase a lot for family burial. At that time he was surrounded by an interesting family—a loving wife, one of the noblest women that ever lived, two sons, and three daughters. His fame was fast increasing and he was everywhere lionized and courted. Life to him then was all sunshine and smiles, but the shadows settled fast over that happy home, and to-day the mother and her three daughters sleep side by side in that Greenwood lot, and a son rests in our own Rural Cemetery. Sorrowing and suffering did their work, and the loved poet is now ending his days apart from the world, a broken-hearted man. He came back to this city alone, in 1881, shortly after his wife's death, and is now living with his son on State Street, though few of the good people of Albany know of his presence in their midst. Sickness has bowed the rugged frame and enfeebled his step. Lines of care are furrowed across his brow, and age has sprinkled the silver in his hair. He sees no visitors and rarely leaves his room. Longfellow, Emerson, and other of the writers of his day lived to a ripe age and died in the midst of their work, but Saxe still lives on at the age of seventy, though dead to the world, dead to literature, and dead to the thousands of friends whose hearts yearn to comfort and cheer the man whose genius and wit have lightened so may homes as, in his declining years, he nears the evening sunset.—HOWE, JOHN A., JR., 1886, *John G. Saxe, Fort Orange Monthly, July.*

Saxe was the author of some poems as witty as any ever written by Dr. Holmes, and some of his punning pieces are not excelled even by anything of Tom Hood's. In his younger days, as he began to be appreciated in society, he not infrequently exhibited something of natural conceit. A friend met him one morning as he was coming from the sanctum of the "Boston Post," to which paper he was a frequent contributor as well as to the "Knickerbocker," and upon asking him as to what he was doing, got this reply: "I have just left with Colonel Greene the finest sonnet that has been written since the days of Sir John Suckling."—MORRILL, JUSTIN S., 1887, *Self-Consciousness of Noted Persons*, p. 42.

GENERAL

The two principal poems ["The Money King and Other Poems"] . . . have the characteristic merits and faults of the class of poems to which they belong. Their versification is smooth and easy, their humor is genial, and is good-natured. If they unfold only simple and obvious truths, they enforce those truths by well-chosen illustrations, and their tone is always healthful.—SMITH, C. C., 1860, *Critical Notices, North American Review*, vol. 90, p. 273.

Mr. Saxe writes with facility, is intent mainly on jests and epigrams, and amuses himself and his readers by clever hits at the fashions and follies of the time. His good-natured satire does not cleave to the depths, nor is his humor of that quality which reaches to the sources of feeling, and which gives us the surprises of an April day. But he is level with the popular apprehension, and has made his name more familiarly known, in all parts of the country, than that of any of our comic versifiers.—UNDERWOOD, FRANCIS H., 1872, *A Hand-Book of English Literature, American Authors*, p. 406.

Until his fame was somewhat overshadowed by Artemus Ward, he might have been called the most popular humorous writer of America. . . . Mr. Saxe excels in light, easy verse, and in unexpected, if not absolutely punning, turns of expression. His more elaborate productions are not so successful. In the general style and effect of certain of his comic pieces he strongly reminds one of Thomas Hood. Saxe, it must be observed, is one of the very few thoroughly national poets, in this sense, that his themes and the atmosphere of his verse are almost exclusively American.—HART, JOHN S., 1872, *A Manual of American Literature*, p. 341.

John G. Saxe owes his wide acceptance with the public not merely to the elasticity of his verse, the sparkle of his wit, and the familiarity of his topics, but to his power of diffusing the spirit of his own good humor. The unctuous satisfaction he feels in putting his mood of merriment into rhyme is communicated to his reader, so that, as it were, they laugh joyously together.—WHIPPLE, EDWIN P., 1876–86, *American Literature and Other Papers*, ed. Whittier, p. 131.

The abundant verse of Mr. Saxe belongs almost exclusively to the least poetical of the several orders into which poetry is sometimes classified—*viz.*, the satirical and homiletic, which is made palatable only by natural lyric flow and grace, and by the frolic and gentle humor of its begetter. He ranked below Tom Hood and Dr. Holmes as a maker of light, often comic, ballads, pentameter satires, etc., and he had no claims as their rival in the more serious and imaginative composition of higher moods, on which something more than a passing reputation is founded. A few of his ditties, such as the "Rhyme of the Rail" and "The Briefless Barrister," will long be found in the collections. For the most part he was a popular specimen of the college-society, lecture-room, dinner-table rhymster, that may be set down as a peculiarly American type and of a generation now almost passed away. His unsophisticated wit, wisdom, and verse, were understood and broadly relished by his audiences; his mellow personality made him justly a favorite; and his printed poems obtained a large and prolonged sale among American readers. That this should have been the case, when poetry of a higher class—like Dr. Parsons's for example—failed of a general market, shows that, while good wine in the end may need no bush, its dispenser often must wait till the crowd have filled up the hostel that has the gayest sign.—STEDMAN, EDMUND CLARENCE, 1887, *John Godfrey Saxe, The Critic*, April 9, p. 79.

John Godfrey Saxe is a genius by himself. . . . The verses by Saxe excel by virtue of plain, honest statement, and are even sometimes wanting in literary finish.—SIMONDS, ARTHUR B., 1894, *American Song*, p. 171.

A poet who wrote society verse of not a little sparkle, although not equal to the best in that kind by Halleck and by Holmes.—MATTHEWS, BRANDER, 1896, *An Introduction to the Study of American Literature*, p. 224.

He came far behind Hood and his other British models, but it was not discreditable to his countrymen that they should have bought and laughed over his numerous volumes. "The Proud Miss McBride," "Rhyme of the Rail," and "The Blind Men and the Elephant" have not lost their sprightliness.—TRENT, WILLIAM P., 1903, *A History of American Literature*, p. 531.

Richard Jefferies
1848-1887

Born, at Coate Farm, Wilts, 6 Nov. 1848. Educated at schools at Sydenham and Swindon. Ran away from home, 11 Nov. 1864, but was soon afterwards sent back. Contrib. to "North Wilts Advertiser" and "Wilts and Gloucester Herald." On staff of "North Wilts Herald" as reporter, March 1866 to 1867. Ill-health 1867-68. Visit to Belgium, 1870. Contrib. to "Fraser's Mag.," and other periodicals, from 1873. Married Miss Baden, July 1874. Lived first at Coate; afterwards at Swindon till Feb. 1877. Removed to Surbiton, 1877. Contrib. to "Pall Mall Gaz.," "Graphic," "St. James's Gaz.," "Standard," "World," etc. Severe ill-health began, 1881. Removed to West Brighton, 1882; to Eltham, 1884; afterwards lived at Crowborough; and at Goring, Sussex. Died, at Goring, 14 Aug. 1887. Buried at Broadwater, Sussex. *Works:* "Reporting, Editing, and Authorship" [1873]; "A Memoir of the Goddards of North Wilts" [1873]; "Jack Brass, Emperor of England," 1873; "The Scarlet Shawl" 1874; "Restless Human Hearts" (3 vols.), 1875; "Suez-cide," 1876; "World's End," (3 vols.), 1877; "The Gamekeeper at Home" (under initials, R. J.; from "Pall Mall Gaz."), 1878; "Wild Life in a Southern County" (under initials, R. J.; from "Pall Mall Gaz."), 1879; "The Amateur Poacher" (under initials, R. J.), 1879; "Greene Ferne Farm," 1880; "Round about a Great Estate," 1880; "Hodge and his Masters," (2 vols.), 1880; "Wood Magic," 1881; "The Story of My Heart," 1883; "Nature Near London" (from "Standard"), 1883; "The Dewy Morn" (2 vols.), 1884; "Red Deer," 1884; "The Life of the Fields," 1884; "After London," 1885; "The Open Air," 1885; "Amaryllis at the Fair," 1887. *Posthumous:* "Field and Hedgerow," ed. by his wife, 1889; "History of Swindon," ed. by G. Toplis, 1897; "Early Fiction," ed. by G. Toplis, 1897. He *edited:* Gilbert White's "Natural History of Selborne," 1887. *Life:* "The Eulogy of Richard Jefferies," by Sir W. Besant, 1888.—SHARP, R. FARQUHARSON, 1897, *A Dictionary of English Authors, p.* 148.

PERSONAL

Do you know Goring churchyard? It is one of those dreary, over-crowded, dark spots where the once-gravelled paths are green with slimy moss, and it was a horror to poor Jefferies. More than once he repeated the hope that he might not be laid there, and he chose the place where his widow at last left him—amongst the brighter grass and flowers at Broadwater. He died at Goring at half-past two on Sunday morning, August 14, 1887. His soul was released from a body wasted to a skeleton by six long weary years of illness. For nearly two years he has been too weak to write, and all his delightful work, during that period, was written by his wife from his dictation. Who can picture the torture of these long years to him, denied as he was the strength to walk so much as one hundred yards in the world he loved so well? What hero like this, fighting with Death face to face so long, fearing and knowing, alas! too well, that no struggles could avail, and, worse than all, that his dear ones would be left friendless and penniless. Thus died a man whose name will be first, perhaps for ever, in his own special work.—NORTH, J. W., 1888, *The Eulogy of Richard Jefferies by Sir Walter Besant, p.* 359.

At the last, during the long communings of the night when he lay sleepless, happy to be free, if only for a few moments, from pain, the simple old faith came back to him. He had arrived long before as we have seen, at the grand discovery: that the perfect soul wants the perfect body, and that the perfect body must be inhabited by the perfect soul. To this conclusion, you have seen, he was led by Nature herself. Now he beheld clearly—perhaps more clearly than ever—the way from this imperfect and fragmentary life to a fuller, happier life beyond the grave. He had no need of priest; he wanted no other assurance than the voice and words of Him who swept away all priests. The man who wrote the "Story of My Heart;" the man who was filled to overflowing with the beauty and order of God's handiwork; the man who felt so deeply the shortness, and imperfections, and disappointments of life that he was fain to cry aloud that all happens by chance; the man who had the vision of the Fuller Soul, died listening with faith and love to the words contained in the Old Book.—BESANT, SIR WALTER, 1888, *The Eulogy of Richard Jefferies, p.* 355.

There is that most striking fact about Jefferies—the reserve and solitude in which he shrouded his life; a man of retired habits, of few friends, he stood outside and apart from the whole circle of literary society. This aloofness is fully reflected in his writings, for in his general manner of thought and expression he resembles no other author, and appears to be indebted to no other; his faults and his merits are equally peculiar and distinctive.—SALT, H. S., 1891, *Richard Jefferies, Temple Bar, vol.* 92, *p.* 223.

Reposing in one of the double transcepts of the most symmetrical of English cathedrals, the ancient fane at Salisbury, is a marble bust typifying a face remarkable for its strength and charm in repose,—at once the effigy of a poet, artist, and thinker, in whom the perceptive quality of beauty and inherent love for the beautiful are revealed by every feature. Calm and majestic, thoughtful and serene, it is a countenance that arrests the beholder, and haunts him, like some sweetly cadenced strain, long after the richly dight spire and hallowed Close of Sailsbury have receded from the view. Upon the pedestal is graven this inscription:—

To the Memory of Richard Jefferies.
Born at Coate in the Parish of Chiselden and
County of Wilts, 6th November, 1848.
Died at Goring in the County of Sussex,
14th August, 1887.
Who Observing the Work of Almighty God
with a Poet's Eye,
Has Enriched the Literature of His Country,
And won for Himself a Place Amongst
Those who have Made Men
Happier and Wiser.

To those who know his work and the character and history of the man, this tribute must appear as touching as the epitaph of "The Elegy." And perhaps its modest sentiment, reflecting his own modest nature, is sufficient,—his work lives after him and speaks more potently than any memorial that man may frame. — ELLWANGER, GEORGE H., 1896, *Idyllists of the Country Side, p.* 124.

GENERAL

It is not many weeks since one of the most fascinating of all the writers who have ever set themselves to describe the sights, sounds, and occupations, the "Works and Days" of the English country-side was removed from us by death. The remarkable merits of Mr. Richard Jefferies, both as an observer of Nature and as a literary artist, have received many tributes since his decease. He has been praised, in fact, like *probitas* in the well-known line of Juvenal, and unhappily it would seem with much the same result. . . . Of the real meaning and the real charm of "The Gamekeeper" and "Wild Life" it appears to me that the class of readers I am speaking of have never got so much as an inkling. To make anything of these books than mere collections of "Stories about Animals" or "Wonders of the Woods," or, at any rate, to get their full value out of them, and to recognize them as books to be kept by us, and read again and again, as we keep and read, or are supposed to keep and read, the works of our favourite poets, it is necessary that the reader should study them in that peculiar posture of the mind and will which . . . is the sole, the indispensable, condition of finding an enduring charm in the country. —TRAILL, HENRY DUFF, 1887, *In Praise of the Country, Contemporary Review, vol.* 52, *pp.* 477, 480.

In Jefferies' later books the whole of the country life of the nineteenth century will be found displayed down to every detail. The life of the farmer is there; the life of the labourer; the life of the gamekeeper; the life of the women who work in the fields, and of those who work at home. . . . He revealed Nature in her works and ways; the flowers and the fields; the wild English creatures; the hedges and the streams; the wood and coppice. . . . But this is not all. For next he took the step—the vast step—across the chasm which separates the poetic from the vulgar mind, and began to clothe the real with the colours and glamour of the unreal; to write down the response of the soul to the phenomena of nature: to interpret the voice of Nature speaking to the soul. Unto this last. And then he died; his work, which might have gone on forever, cut off almost at the commencement.— BESANT, SIR WALTER, 1888, *The Eulogy of Richard Jefferies, pp.* 228, 229.

The truth is that Richard Jefferies's work, his wonderful descriptive faculty, his minute and sympathetic observation of nature, can only appeal to a small circle. The general public will probably continue to hurry past him. But his place in English literature may be considered assured; and, of the small band of English writers who have laboured in the same field, he not only understood but can teach, above all others, the wisdom of the field and of the forest. Mr. Besant associated him with Thoreau and Gilbert White. But Jefferies was not so conscious a mystic—to use a much abused word—as the American recluse, though he wanders into mystic reveries in the "Story of my Heart;" and he is less primarily a naturalist, and also a far greater literary artist, than the simpler historian of Selborne. The author of "The Pageant of Summer" lived in a different literary tradition. He became a great master of that art of word-painting which is at once the distinctive excellence and principal danger of modern English style. Jefferies's accurate observation kept him free from the danger.—DAWKINS, C. E., 1888, *The Eulogy of Richard Jefferies by Walter Besant, The Academy*, vol. 34, p. 316.

I love to think of Jefferies as a kind of literary Leather-stocking. His style, his mental qualities, the field he worked in, the chase he followed, were peculiar to himself, and as he was without a rival, so was he without a second. Reduced to its simplest expression, his was a mind compact of observation and of memory. He writes as one who watches always, who sees everything, who forgets nothing. As his lot was cast in country places, among wood and pasturage and corn, by coverts teeming with game and quick with insect life, and as withal he had the hunter's patience and quick-sightedness, his faculty of looking and listening and of noting and remembering, his readiness of deduction and insistence of pursuit—there entered gradually into his mind a greater quantity of natural England, her leaves and flowers, her winds and skies, her wild things and tame, her beauties and humours and discomforts, than was ever, perhaps, the possession of writing Briton.—HENLEY, WILLIAM ERNEST, 1890, *Views and Reviews*, p. 177.

Jefferies, above all other writers, was the high-priest of Summer; his warm, sensuous, southern nature breathed intense reverence for the "alchemic, intangible, mysterious power, which cannot be supplied in any other form but the sun's rays." Who else could have described as he has described, the glare, the glamour, the multitudinous hum, the immense prodigality of a high summer noon? . . . The volumes which furnish the most notable instances of this side of Jefferies' genius are perhaps the four by which he is at present very generally known—the "Gamekeeper at Home," the "Amateur Poacher," "Wild Life in a Southern County," and "Round About a Great Estate," in all of which he manifests the same extraordinary knowledge of the fauna and flora of his native district, a knowledge based on an exceptionally keen habit of observation, and strengthened by a powerful memory and a diligent course of journal-keeping. . . . That a permanent historical value will attach to writings of this kind can hardly be doubted; they will be studied, centuries hence, along with White's Selborne and a few similar works, as a chronicle of natural history—a museum to which artist and scientists will repair for instruction and entertainment. I cannot, however, at all agree with those of Jefferies' admirers who consider these volumes (to wit, the "Gamekeeper at Home," and the rest of the same class) to be his literary masterpieces, and who speak of them as exhibiting, in contrast with his later books, what they call his "simpler and better style;" I believe, with Mr. Walter Besant, that Jefferies' word-pictures of the country life are "far from being the most considerable part of his work." . . . An innate distrust of all the precepts of custom and tradition was one of Jefferies' most noticeable characteristics; Thoreau himself was scarcely more contemptuous of conventional usages and restraints.—SALT, H. S., 1891, *Richard Jefferies, Temple Bar*, vol. 92, pp. 215, 216, 217, 219.

Still as the page was writ
'Twas nature held his hand and guided it:
Broadcast and free the lines were sown as meadows kingcup lit.
Vague longings found a tongue;
Things dim and ancient into speech were wrung;
The epic of the rolling wheat, the lyric hedge-row sung!
He showed the soul within
The veil of matter luminous and thin,
He heard the old earth's undersong piercing the modern din.
He opened wide to space
The iron portals of the commonplace:
Wonder on wonder crowded through as star on star we trace.
Others might dully plod
Purblind with custom, deaf as any clod—
He knew the highest heights of heaven bent o'er the path he trod.

—GEOGHEGAN, MARY, 1892, *Richard Jefferies, Temple Bar*, vol. 94, p. 28.

Since Gilbert White wrote of his beloved Selborne, there has perhaps hardly been a more delightful writer on natural history than Richard Jefferies, author of the "Gamekeeper at Home," and of other charming works, such as have made the town-bred boy bewail the fortune that did not cast his lines among those pleasant places, and the careless country lad curse the negligence which has made him overlook the beautiful things that others can find everywhere to see.—OLIPHANT, MARGARET O. W., 1892, *The Victorian Age of English Literature*, p. 389.

This is a book ["The Toilers of the Field"] to be deplored and deprecated, a desperate attempt to make hay while the sun shines, out of weeds, rushes, and rubbish, old and new. The only scrap of fresh matter we find is a "True Tale of the Wiltshire Labourer," written years ago for a local newspaper, but somehow never printed. It is a powerful, one-sided sketch, after the manner of *La Terre*, but frequent imitation of this manner has since reduced its directness to a suspicion of brutality. With this exception the book is entirely made up of reprints, or reprints of reprints, under a capital fancy title "The Toilers of the Field," which suggested a separate, authentic, homogeneous book. The work has, however, a certain curious value. It is in two parts. . . . Jefferies in his prime is to me as yet but a name; free from the glamour of his genius, I am therefore able to judge calmly these bye-blows of his pen. The sole notice they call for, the sole feeling they rouse, is one of astonishment that their writer ever became famous. In themselves they are just the harmless, amateur, ordinary stuff to which one is indulgently indifferent. —PURCELL, E., 1892, *Literature, The Academy*, vol. 42, p. 599.

If the critics really enjoy, as they profess to, all this trivial country lore, why on earth don't they come into the fresh air and find it out for themselves? There is no imperative call for their presence in London. Ink will stain paper in the country as well as in town, and the Post will convey their articles to their editors. As it is, they do but overheat already overheated clubs. . . . These books are already supplying the club-novelist with his open-air effects; and, therefore, the club-novelist worships them. From them he gathers that "wild apple-trees, too, are not uncommon in the hedges," and straightway he informs his public of this wonder. But it is hard on the poor countryman who, for the benefit of a street-bred reading public, must cram his books with solemn recitals of his A, B, C, and impressive announcements that two and two make four and that a hedge-sparrow's egg is blue.—QUILLER-COUCH, A. T., 1893, *Richard Jefferies, The Speaker*.

But for a certain repugnance to using the literary slang of the day I would call him an impressionist; although, by those who misname themselves impressionists, he is persistently misrepresented as addicted to catalogue-making. Yet it need hardly be pointed out that he never made a systematic study, never a complete list of anything. From the scientific student's point of view he was an idler in the land, sensuous, and therefore sensitive to nature's choicest colours and sounds and fragrancies; passionate, and so given to dreams and musings and speculations. When he one by one enumerates the birds and flowers and weeds of an English hedgerow, you feel, in the end, that his object has been neither botanical nor ornithological, but poetical. It is not into the study of a zoologist you have gone, but to the presence of an artist who has transferred a mood from his own mind into yours. The reader carries away little new knowledge, but many pleasant memories. . . . He is an enchanter who, at will, transports you into the midst of a green English landscape, where the swallows skim the cornfields, and the butterflies flutter among the wildflowers, where the chaffinch chirps from the expanding oak-leaves, and the water sparkles to the sunshine. The result differs from that produced by Gilbert White as night differs from day. One man pleases by his love of facts, and by ministering to our thirst for knowledge; the other by adding to our æsthetic pleasures.—GRAHAM, P. ANDERSON, 1893, *Round About Coate, Art Journal*, vol. 45, p. 16.

Few people have a reputation at once so limited and so wide. When his bust was unveiled in Salisbury Cathedral not long ago, there was enough stir in the papers to make one imagine his celebrity to be wider than it really is. One has only to read how he lived in penury through his latter troublous days, because his books would not sell, to get a truer insight into the extent of his popularity; and even now, when he is better known and appreciated than ever before, those to whom he is but the shadow of a name are sufficiently numerous to make all mention of him as a celebrity savour of irony. It is, in fact, with the few and not with the many that Jefferies must be content to hold the place that he deserves; to those to whom he appeals he is of such value, that were reputation judged by depth of admiration rather than by number of admirers, he were famous beyond measure already. . . . His power of expression is not connected with an easy and polished literary style. His constructions are often loose and his sentences bald and unfinished. The more one reads his essays, the more obvious it becomes that he could write only because he could feel, because Earth was his passion; and one is tempted to think that this passion which was the cause of his unique power of delineating her features, was due in turn to an acute sensitiveness of perception, a certain intense æstheticism that is visible in all his works.— MUNTZ, IRVING, 1894, *Richard Jefferies as a Descriptive Writer*, Gentleman's Magazine, N. S. vol. 53, pp. 516, 519.

Speaking generally, the language is perfectly simple and direct; there is no savour of bookishness; upon everything is the stamp of sincerity—a sincerity born of loving intercourse with the objects described. The chief defect is a sense of discontinuity, occasionally felt in some essays in which Jefferies, contrary to his usual practice, presents us with "bushel baskets full of facts," the whole not being fused together by any unifying power of the imagination. But when at his best, his style is impassioned and throbs with emotion; it is imaginative as only fine poetry can be. He displays, too, a *curiosa felicitas* in the choice of apt words and images which condense for us the life and movement of a whole scene. . . . Of Jefferies' style at its best the "Pageant of Summer" is the most sustained example. Taken as a whole, it may be said to form one grand hymn in praise of the fulness and beauty of life which culminates in the crowning glory of the summer. There is a purely human quality, too, about this essay which imparts to it the imaginative charm in which it is steeped.—FISHER, CHARLES, 1896, *A Study of Richard Jefferies, Temple Bar, vol. 109, pp.* 504, 505.

His talent, though rare and exquisite, was neither rich nor versatile. It consisted in a power of observing nature more than Wordsworthian in delicacy, and almost Wordsworthian in the presence of a sentimental philosophic background of thought. Unluckily for Jefferies, his philosophic background was not like Wordsworth's, clear and cheerful, but wholly vague and partly gloomy. Writing, too, in prose not verse, and after Mr. Ruskin, he attempted an exceedingly florid style, which at its happiest was happy enough, but which was not always at that point, and which when it was not, was apt to become trivial or tawdry, or both. It is therefore certain that his importance for posterity will dwindle, if it has not already dwindled, to that given by a bundle of descriptive selections. But these will occupy a foremost place on their particular shelf, the shelf at the head of which stand Gilbert White and Gray.—SAINTSBURY, GEORGE, 1896, *A History of Nineteenth Century Literature,* p. 397.

Jefferies' special place in literature, and his rank as a sympathising interpreter of Nature, it is safe to assume, could never have fallen to any one other than himself. There can be no second "Life of the Fields." Other Idyls may instruct and please, but in a different degree. A finer literarian may arise to hymn the pæan of the open-air; but the combinative qualities that speak from Jefferies' later work must remain to him alone. . . . Incontestably, he wrote too much; he lacked the margin of leisure, and was constantly under the goad of providing for his livelihood, for which he depended solely upon his pen. Owing to his peculiar artistic temperament, as well as to various individual characteristics, it is difficult to compare him with some other Nature-observers who were equally as painstaking as he. His work may not be appropriately classed with that of the learned Selborne rector, than whom none had a more watchful eye; nor with that of the Walden recluse, whose powers of observation in all that appertained to Nature's sights and sounds could not be surpassed. . . . Jefferies was an essayist; and, above all, the idyllist and painter of country-life as it exists in England.—ELLWANGER, GEORGE H., 1896, *Idyllists of the Country Side, pp.* 132, 133.

The early books of Richard Jefferies, those by which he won his fame, those, no doubt, on which his fame will rest, "The Gamekeeper at Home" and its immediate successors, owe but little of their charm to purely literary merits; they may almost be said to owe their charm to the very absence of the literary element. They are bundles of jottings, notes taken direct from life in a reporter's note-book, observations recorded because they are observed, and in just the words in which they presented themselves, hasty impressions of life on the wing. . . . Quickness of eye and faithfulness of hand are his two great qualities, as shown in these early books; and it is, I think, in the impression of absolute veracity, not coloured with prepossessions, not distorted by an artistic presentment, that he has the advantage over Thoreau, so much his superior as a writer. . . . In "Hodge and his Masters" there are many clever sketches of village life, and they are generally true as far as they go; but set a chapter on the habits of birds against a chapter on the habits of men, and how much more insight you will find in the former than the latter! Jefferies will give you the flora and fauna of the village with incomparable accuracy; but for the villager, go to Mr. Hardy or Dr. Jessopp.—SYMONS, ARTHUR, 1897, *Studies in Two Literatures.*

Dinah Maria Mulock Craik
1826–1887

Born [Dinah Maria Mulock], at Stoke-upon-Trent, 20 April 1826. To London, 1846 [?]. First novel produced, 1849. Settled at North End, Hampstead, 1855 [?]. Civil List Pension, 1864. Married to George Lillie Craik, 29 April 1865. Settled soon afterwards at Shortlands, Kent, where she lived till her death. Died suddenly, 12 Oct. 1887. *Works:* [all anon.], "Cola Monti," 1849; "The Ogilvies," 1849; "Olive," 1850; "The Head of a Family," 1851; "Alice Learmont," 1852; "Agatha's Husband," 1852; "Bread upon the Waters," 1852; "A Hero," 1853; "Avillon," 1853; "John Halifax, Gentleman," 1856; "Nothing New," 1857; "A Woman's Thoughts about Women," 1858; "Poems," 1859; "Romantic Tales," 1859; "A Life for a Life," 1859; "Domestic Stories," 1860; "Our Year," 1860; "Studies from Life," 1861; "Mistress and Maid," 1862; "The Fairy-Book," 1863; "A New Year's Gift to Sick Children," 1865; "Home Thoughts and Home Scenes," 1865; "A Noble Life," 1866; "Christian's Mistake," 1866; "Two Marriages," 1867; "Woman's Kingdom," 1868; "The Unkind Word," 1869; "A Brave Lady," 1870; "Fair France," 1871; "Hannah," 1871; "Little Sunshine's Holiday," 1871; "Twenty Years Ago," 1871; "Adventures of a Brownie," 1872; "Songs of Our Youth," 1874; "My Mother and I," 1874; "Sermons out of Church," 1875; "The Little Lame Prince," 1875; "The Laurel Bush," 1877; "Will Denbigh," 1877; "A Legacy," 1878; "Young Mrs. Jardine," 1879; "Thirty Years," 1880; "Children's Poetry," 1881; "His Little Mother," 1881; "Plain Speaking," 1882; "An Unsentimental Journey" 1884; "Miss Tommy," 1884; "About Money," 1886; "King Arthur," 1886; "Fifty Golden Years," 1887; "An Unknown Country," 1887. *Posthumous:* "Concerning Man," 1888. She *translated:* Guizot's "M. de Barante," 1867; Mme. de Witt's "A French Country Family," 1867; "A Parisian Family," 1870; and "An Only Sister," 1873; and *edited:* "Is it True?" 1872.—SHARP, R. FARQUHARSON, 1897, *A Dictionary of English Authors,* p. 68.

PERSONAL

Miss Mulock lived in a small house in a street a little farther down even in the wilds than ours [1853]. She was a tall young woman with a slim pliant figure, and eyes that had a way of fixing the eyes of her interlocutor in a manner which did not please my shy fastidiousness. It was embarasing as if she meant to read the other upon whom she gazed,—a pretension which one resented. It was merely, no doubt, a fashion of what was the intense school of the time. Mrs. Browning did the same thing the only time I met her, and this to one quite indisposed to be read. But Dinah was always kind, enthusiastic, somewhat didactic and apt to teach, and much looked up to by her little band of young women.—OLIPHANT, MARGARET O. W., 1885, *Autobiography,* p. 38.

Who that knew her can ever forget the tall, gray-eyed, silver-haired, motherly woman, gentle and pleasant in speech, yet firm withal and of wholesome resoluteness of purpose, who made her home in the pleasant Kentish country, ten miles southeast of London, a place of pleasant pilgrimage for so many loving friends.—BOWKER,

RICHARD ROGERS, 1888, *London as a Literary Centre, Harper's Magazine*, vol. 77, p. 20.

Mrs. Craik was quite small, had soft, loving gray eyes and silvery gray hair. Her voice was low and gentle, and her manners pretty and natural. She always dressed in quiet colors, brown or steel, and very plainly. She was noted as a good neighbor, and was never so happy as when making others happy. Her home was built in the old Elizabethan style, and the wooden beams of the ceiling could be seen in every room. Over the fire-place in the dining-room was carved the motto, "East or west, home is best." Miss Mulock was greatly interested in all charities, but one particularly occupied her heart and hand; this was the Royal College for the Blind in London. She would send out invitations to the children to come to a strawberry party in the groves and hayfields around her house, and then she would make them delightfully happy. Mr. Craik would meet them with carriages and wagons, for their home was ten or twelve miles from the station, and then the three, Mr. and Mrs. Craik and Dorothy, would try to crowd into this one day enjoyment enough to last the children for many days.—RUTHERFORD, M., 1890, *English Authors*, p. 584.

One evening in 1843, Mrs. Hall brought up to me to introduce a tall slender girl of seventeen, with graceful mien and fine grey eyes that, once seen, were not to be forgotten. They always seemed to be looking out on objects more serene than those before her. This was Dinah Maria Mulock, then a young aspirant, full of hero-worship of the great and good of every order, and destined to be known as the author of "John Halifax, Gentleman," and one of the most successful novelists of her day. I lost sight of her for a time, but some two or three years later we became very intimate. She consulted me about adopting literature as an earnest pursuit, and I had seen such indications of her genius that I gave her the warmest encouragement. There was something very interesting about her, and she had the faculty of quickly making friends.—CROSLAND, MRS. NEWTON (CAMILLA TOULMIN), 1893, *Landmarks of a Literary Life*, p. 127.

An over-tall and in younger days somewhat spindly woman, not beautiful, but good, the goodness flavouring all her writings. — LINTON, WILLIAM JAMES, 1894, *Threescore and Ten Years, 1820 to 1890, Recollections*, p. 171.

After lunch Mrs. Craik made me walk in the garden with her, and inquired more closely into the particulars of this strange illness; she encouraged and comforted me greatly. She was tall, and though white-haired, very beautiful still [1868], I thought. As we walked she bent her head (covered with the Highland blue bonnet) over mine, and as she clasped my shoulders within her arm, I could see her hand laid upon my breast, as if to soothe it; it was the loveliest hand I ever saw; the shape so perfect, the skin so white and soft. We spoke French together; she was interested about France, and liked talking of its people and customs. Before we left she asked me to write to her, and offered to render me any service I might require.—HAMERTON, MRS. PHILIP GILBERT, 1896, *Philip Gilbert Hamerton, An Autobiography and a Memoir*, p. 332.

JOHN HALIFAX, GENTLEMAN
1856

Time has not aged it; it still wears the smile of youth; and I for one believe that its mission will not be fulfilled until youths and maidens of our day and nation read it with as much relish and feel it with as much intensity as did our English cousins some thirty years or more ago.—NOURSE, ROBERT, 1883, *An Old Book for New Readers, The Dial*, vol. 4, p. 37.

Well may this strong soul rest at length; well may
This woman's earnest hand in sleep relax,
Having wrought and raised up, for all Time to view,
Among its gilded gods and dolls of clay,
The granite figure of John Halifax.
—BOYNTON, JULIA P., 1887, *Dinah Mulock Craik*.

That Dinah Maria Mulock Craik has been known for thirty years as "the author of 'John Halifax'" does not imply that she was a woman of one book, or even of only one book that was popular. After her first great effort, she gave us in swift succession novels, stories, verses and essays, full of sense and strength and often of great charm. . . . A strong desire seizes us to read the book again, to try to discover once more the great charm it held at one time for so large a world of readers. And yet we hesitate. What book is great enough to stand the test of thirty years? The strong impression is pretty sure to be weakened, and we don't want it to be weakened. Let us remember it always as we do now, vaguely; but tenderly; for "the author of 'John Halifax'" is dead. And yet curiosity overmasters tenderness. With irresistible impulse we seek out the little dusty old-fashioned volume, and turn its pages reverently but curiously. Yes, it suffers necessarily a little from the lapse of time: it is not quite realistic enough to satisfy us now; the excellent John has too few faults, the admirable Ursula, seems, alas! a little of a prig; the disputed governess, Miss Silver, does not live or move or have any being at all, certainly she fails to charm; and one need only compare the brothers' quarrel with that described by Mrs. Oliphant, and now raging in the pages of *The Atlantic*, to feel that the more modern style, in becoming more realistic, has only gained in strength and flavor, and is actually less tame than the more imaginative efforts of thirty years ago. There is a *falsetto* tone in the book, of sentiment not exactly morbid, and yet to the more modern taste not exactly healthful. But still it remains what ladies call "a beautiful story."—ROLLINS, ALICE WELLINGTON, 1887, *The Author of "John Halifax," The Critic*, vol. 11, p. 214.

She did not, however, assume her true place in fiction until the publication of "John Halifax, Gentleman," a work which attained instant and great popularity, and which has had many imitators, the sincerest flattery according to the proverb, which can be bestowed. This work, which relates the history of a good man's life and love, has but little incident, and no meretricious attractions, but attained the higher triumph of securing the public attention and sympathy by its pure and elevated feeling, fine perception of character, and subdued but admirable literary power. Miss Mulock has placed herself at the head of one division of the army of novelists. She has also added attraction to more than one landscape, throwing an interest to many readers over the little town of Tewkesbury for instance, with which the scene of John Halifax was identified, which has brought many pilgrims, we believe, to that place, not only from other parts of England, but from the other great continent across the seas where fiction has even more importance and its scenes more interest than among ourselves.—OLIPHANT, MARGARET O. W., 1892, *The Victorian Age of English Literature*, p. 485.

The enormous hold which, ever since its first appearance in 1857, "John Halifax" has had on a great portion of the English-speaking public, is due to the lofty elevation of its tone, its unsullied purity and goodness, combined with a great freshness, which appeals to the young and seems to put them and the book in touch with each other.—PARR, LOUISA, 1897, *Women Novelists of Queen Victoria's Reign*, p. 229.

It is one of the most agreeable specimens of improved puritanism in modern England, and holds its ground as one of the productions of a more refined and entertaining literature. The sincere piety that it breathed is not obtrusive, and some of the characters give evidence of real literary talent. In the distant future her name will perhaps be mentioned by the side of George Eliot.—ENGLE, EDWARD, 1902, *A History of English Literature*, rev. Hamley Bent, p. 464.

GENERAL

A young Irish authoress of great promise. She has already given to the world several novels that have obtained decided success. The best of these is "Olive," a very charming work. . . . The author of "Olive" holds a warm place in the heart of young lady novel-readers, and she has an opportunity of holding a very high rank among popular writers.—HALE, SARAH JOSEPHA, 1852, *Woman's Record*, p. 896.

Her traits as a writer are intensely feminine; the scenes and characters she describes are minutely, faithfully depicted, but in a diffuse style. Her poems have genuine religious feeling, and are graceful and refined in expression.—UNDERWOOD, FRANCIS H., 1871, *A Hand-Book of English Literature, British Authors*, p. 577.

Faith in God and faith in man were the secret of her influence. She made no parade of this, but the reader will easily discover that she holds him by all that is good in himself and by her own faith in goodness. She has left many pictures of the struggle against poverty, error, and misconception, of truth that is great and must prevail, of goodness that stands fast for ever and ever. Then, again, she wrote plain, simple English. She never used a long word if a short one would do as well, and she never took a foreign word that has an equivalent in her own language. Clearness, directness, simplicity, counted for much in her success as an author. It would be a fruitless task to say what she has not, and what she is not. Deficiencies, easily detected, are all atoned for by direct insight, which some would not hesitate to call genius. The books upon which Mrs. Craik's fame will rest were written many years ago, but she has always been able and willing to say an influential word in a good cause, and to write for a large circle of readers.—MARTIN, FRANCES, 1887, *Mrs. Craik, Athenæum, No.* 3130, *p.* 539.

Though lacking in the higher qualities of true poetry, imagination, passion, breadth of experience, and depth of emotion, there is enough true feeling and human interest in many of her poems to entitle them to recognition in these pages, and give her a true if not a very exalted place in any representative anthology of the verse of her countrywomen. "Philip, My King," the first high poem in either volume, ranked among her own favourites, and has, perhaps, been the most often quoted of her verses. "A Silly Song," too, and "A Christmas Carol" are given in an anthology for which her own selection of her own work was asked.

The ballad "In Swanage Bay," which is not included in her last volume, has none the less been very popular as a recitation, and shows ability to write a simple and touching story in verse.—MILES, ALFRED H., 1892, *The Poets and the Poetry of the Century, Joanna Baillie to Mathilde Blind, p.* 377.

She never posed as a brilliant, impassioned writer of stories which tell of wrongs, or crimes, or great mental conflicts. In her novels there is no dissection of character, no probing into the moral struggles of the human creature. Her teaching holds high the standard of duty, patience, and the unquestioning belief that all that God wills is well. . . . She was by no means what is termed a literary woman. She was not a great reader; and although much praise is due to the efforts she made to improve herself, judged by the present standard, her education remained very defective. That she lacked the fire of genius is true, but it is no less true that she was gifted with great imaginative ability and the power of depicting ordinary men and women leading upright, often noble lives.—PARR, LOUISA, 1897, *Women Novelists of Queen Victoria's Reign, pp.* 228, 247.

Philip Bourke Marston
1850–1887

Only son of Dr. Westland Marston, and godson of Dinah Maria Mulock (Mrs. Craik). It was to him she addressed her poem "Philip, My King." Notwithstanding his blindness caused by an injury to his eyes when he was a young child, he began to dictate verses from his early youth. The loss through death of his betrothed (Miss Nesbit), his two sisters, his brother-in-law, Arthur O'Shaughnessy, and his friend, Oliver Madox Brown, all occurred within the space of a few years. Rossetti encouraged his genius, and said of some of his verse that it was "worthy of Shakespeare in his subtlest lyrical moods." "Song-Tide and Other Poems" was issued in 1871, and was followed by "All in All" in 1875, and "Wind Voices," 1883. A collection of all his poems was edited with a memoir by his devoted friend, Mrs. Louise Chandler Moulton, in 1892.—STEDMAN, EDMUND CLARENCE, *ed.* 1895, *A Victorian Anthology, p.* 697.

PERSONAL

A wreath, not of gold, but palm. One day,
    Philip, my King,
Thou too must tread, as we trod, a way
Thorny, and cruel, and cold, and gray:
Rebels within thee, and foes without
Will snatch at thy crown. But go on glorious,
Martyr, yet monarch! till angels shout,
    As thou sittest at the feet of God victorious.
        "Philip, the King!"
—CRAIK, DINAH M., 1852, *Philip, My King.*

Have ye no singers in your courts of gold,
Ye gods, that ye must take his voice away
From us poor dwellers in these realms of clay?
Most like (for gods were seldom pitiful)

The chastened vision of his darkened eyes
Had too clear gaze of your deep mysteries,
And death the seal of that dread knowledge is.
—LE GALLIENNE, RICHARD, 1887, *Philip Bourke Marston.*

Thy song may soothe full many a soul hereafter,
    As tears, if tears will come, dissolve despair;
As here but late, with smile more bright than
        laughter,
Thy sweet strange yearning eyes would seem
    to bear
Witness that joy might cleave the clouds of
    care.
—SWINBURNE, ALGERNON CHARLES, 1887, *Light: An Epicede, Fortnightly Review.*

HENRY WARD BEECHER

Engraving from a Photograph.

MATTHEW ARNOLD

From a Portrait by P. Sandys, 1881.

I, myself, first met him in 1876, on the first day of July—just six weeks before his twenty-sixth birthday. He was tall, slight, and in spite of his blindness, graceful. He seemed to me young-looking even for his twenty-six years. He had a noble and beautiful forehead. His brown eyes were perfect in shape, and even in colour, save for a dimness like a white mist that obscured the pupil, but which you perceived only when you were quite near to him. His hair and beard were dark brown, with warm glints of chestnut; and the colour came and went in his cheeks as in those of a sensitive girl. His face was singularly refined, but his lips were full and pleasure-loving, and suggested dumbly how cruel must be the limitations of blindness to a nature hungry for love and for beauty. I had been greatly interested, before seeing him, in his poems, and to meet him was a memorable delight. —MOULTON, LOUISE CHANDLER, 1891, *A Last Harvest by Philip Bourke Marston, Biographical Sketch, p. 12.*

GENERAL

Philip Bourke Marston's verse is chiefly of a subjective nature, the outcome of his own emotions and experiences. He, too, resides in London, where he was born in 1850. To few poets so young have the extreme tests of life been applied more directly; he has borne the loss of his nearest and dearest, and is debarred from the sweet comfort of the light of day, in which the artist soul finds most relief. But no poet ever received more sympathy and care from those attached to him. . . . Mr. Marston has the poetic temperament, with extreme impressibility of feeling, and the imagination and wonderful memory often noted in the blind. These traits are seen in his poetry, of which the sentiment and insight are genuine, and they affect his essays and tales. — STEDMAN, EDMUND CLARENCE, 1882, *Some London Poets, Harper's Magazine, vol. 64, pp. 881, 882.*

Mr. Marston's chief drawback—from the point of view of the general reader—is monotony of theme, though in his latest volume he has done much to obviate this objection. This, and his undoubted over-shadowing by the genius of the greatest sonnet-writer of our day, are probably the reasons for his comparatively restricted reputation. Curiously enough, Mr. Marston is much better known and more widely read in America than here; indeed he is undoubtedly the most popular of all our younger men oversea. Throughout all his poetry—for the most part very beautiful—there is exquisite sensitiveness to the delicate hues and gradations of colour in sky and on earth, all the more noteworthy from the fact of the author's misfortune of blindness. —SHARP, WILLIAM, 1886, *ed. Sonnets of this Century, p. 306, note.*

The world will not let his work die out of remembrance, or cease to be grateful for the rich gifts his too short life bequeathed.— MOULTON, LOUISE CHANDLER, 1887, *Philip Bourke Marston, Critic, March 26; p. 149.*

O thou who seeing not with thy mortal eyes
Yet hast the sacred spirit of sight to see
The soul of beauty in Nature more than we;
Yea, thou who seest indeed the sunset skies
And all the blue wild billows as they rise
And summer sweetness of each bower and tree,—
Who seest the pink glad thyme-tuft kiss the bee—
The silver wing that o'er the grey wave flies:
We hail thee, singer who hast sight indeed
If to see Beauty and Truth and Love be sight;
For whom the soul of the white rose is white,
And fiery-red the fierce-souled red sea-weed;
We hail thee, —thee whom all things love and heed,
Pouring through thee their music and their might.
—BARLOW, GEORGE, 1890, *To Philip Bourke Marston, From Dawn to Sunset, p. 187.*

Ah! memory to him
Grew all-in-all,—
His noblest songs contain
The heart's rainfall.
—HAYNE, WILLIAM HAMILTON, 1893, *To the Memory of Philip Bourke Marston, Sylvan Lyrics and Other Verses.*

Matthew Arnold
1822–1888

Born, at Laleham, 24 Dec. 1822. Educated till 1836 at Laleham; at Winchester 1836–37; at Rugby, 1837–41. Family removed to Rugby (where his father was headmaster) in 1828. Scholarship at Balliol Coll., Oxford, Nov. 1840. To Balliol, Oct. 1841. Hertford Scholarship, 1842; Newdigate Prize, 1843; B. A., Dec. 1844; M. A., 1853; Fellow of Oriel Coll., 28 March 1845 to 6 April 1852. Private Sec. to Lord Lansdowne, 1847–51.

Married Fanny Lucy Wightman, 10 June 1851. For a short time Assistant Master at Rugby, 1851. Appointed Lay Inspector of Schools, 1851. Prof. of Poetry at Oxford, 1857–67. Visits to France, Germany, and Holland on education business, 1859, 1865 and 1866. Hon. LL. D., Edinburgh, 1869; Hon. D. C. L., Oxford, 21 June 1870; Order of Commander of Crown of Italy (in recognition of his tutorship of the Duke of Genoa), 1871. Rede Lecturer at Cambridge, 1882. Hon LL. D., Cambridge, 1883. Visits to America, 1883, and 1886. Died, 15 April 1888. Buried at Laleham. *Works:* "Alaric at Rome," 1840; "Cromwell," 1843; "The Strayed Reveller," by A., 1849; "Empedocles on Etna," 1852; "Poems" (1st series), 1853; "Poems" (2nd series), 1855; "Merope," 1858; "England and the Italian Question," 1859; "Popular Education in France," 1861; "On Translating Homer," 1861; "Last Words on Translating Homer," 1862; "A French Eton," 1864; "Essays in Criticism" (1st series), 1865; "New Poems," 1867; "On the Study of Celtic Literature," 1867; "Saint Brandan" (from "Fraser's Magazine"), 1867; "Schools and Universities on the Continent," 1868; "Poems" (collected), 1869; "Culture and Anarchy," 1869; "St. Paul and Protestantism," 1870; "Friendship's Garland," 1871; "A Bible Reading for Schools," 1872; "Literature and Dogma," 1873; "Higher Schools and Universities in Germany" (part of "Schools and Universities on the Continent," reprinted), 1874; "God and the Bible," 1875; "The Great Prophecy of Israel's Restoration," 1875; "Last Essays on Church and Religion," 1877; "Mixed Essays," 1879; "Geist's Grave" (from "Fortnightly Review") 1881; "Irish Essays," 1882; "Isaiah of Jerusalem," 1883; "Discourses in America," 1885; "Essays in Criticism" (2nd series), 1888; "Special Report on Elementary Education Abroad," 1888; "Civilization in the United States," 1888. *Posthumous:* "Reports on Elementary Schools," 1889; "On Home Rule for Ireland" (two letters to the "Times;" priv. ptd.), 1891; "Letters," ed. by G. W. E. Russell (2 vols.), 1895. He *edited:* selections from Johnson's "Lives of the Poets," 1878; Wordsworth's Poems (in "Golden Treasury Series"), 1879; Byron's Poems (in "Golden Treasury Series"), 1881; "Burke's Letters, Speeches, and Tracts on Irish Affairs," 1881. He contributed: an introduction to "The Hundred Greatest Men," 1879; three essays to T. H. Ward's "English Poets," 1880; an introduction to J. Smith's "Natural Truth of Christianity," 1882; "Sainte-Beuve" to "Encyclopædia Britannica," 1886; on "Schools" to T. H. Ward's "Reign of Queen Victoria," 1887.—SHARP, R. FARQUHARSON, 1897, *A Dictionary of English Authors,* p. 9.

PERSONAL

Matt does not know what it is to work because he so little knows what it is to think. But I am hopeful about him more than I was: his amiableness of temper seems very great, and some of his faults appear to me less; and he is so loving to me that it ought to make me not only hopeful, but very patient and long-suffering towards him. Besides, I think that he is not so idle as he was, and that there is a better prospect of his beginning to read in earnest. Alas! that we should have to talk of prospects only, and of no performance as yet which deserves the name of "earnest reading."—ARNOLD, THOMAS, 1840, *Letter to Lake,* Aug. 17; *Memorials of William Charles Lake, ed. his Widow,* p. 161.

It is observable that Matthew Arnold, the eldest son, and the author of the volume of poems to which you allude, inherits his mother's defect. Striking and prepossessing in appearance, his manner displeases from its seeming foppery. I own it caused me at first to regard him with regretful surprise; the shade of Dr. Arnold seemed to me to frown on his young representative. I was told, however, that "Mr. Arnold improved upon acquaintance." So it was: ere long a real modesty appeared under his assumed conceit, and some genuine intellectual aspirations, as well as high educational requirements, displaced superficial affectations. I was given to understand that his theological opinions were very vague and unsettled, and indeed he betrayed as much in the course of conversation. Most unfortunate for him, doubtless, has been the untimely loss of his father.—BRONTË, CHARLOTTE, 1851, *To James Taylor, Jan.* 15; *Charlotte Brontë and her Circle, ed. Shorter,* p. 458.

Soon after reaching London, I called on dear old Barry Cornwall, who has taken a great liking to Lorry Graham. Mrs. Procter invited both of us and our wives to a literary *soirée* at their house. In the meantime Lorry took me with him to call on Matthew Arnold. He is a man to like, if not love, at first sight. His resemblance to

George Curtis struck both of us. A little more stoutly built, more irregularly masculine features, but the same general character of man, with the same full, mellow voice. After Thackeray, I think I should soon come to like him better than any other Englishman. His eyes sparkled when I told him that I always kept his poems on my library table.—TAYLOR, BAYARD, 1867, *To E. C. Stedman, March 11; Life and Letters,* ed. Taylor and Scudder, vol. II, p. 473.

Matthew Arnold has just come in, and we have had a talk. I thought at first he looked a little as if he did not approve of my pitching into him, but then he said very nicely that he had seen a speech of mine, which he liked very much. . . . Arnold's manner is very ha-ha; but I have no doubt he is a very good fellow.—TULLOCH, JOHN, 1874, *Letter; A Memoir of the Life of John Tulloch,* ed. Oliphant, p. 287.

Mr. Matthew Arnold has been to the college, and has given his lecture on Emerson. . . . Never was a man listened to with so much attention. Whether he is right in his judgment or not, he held his audience by his manly way, his kindly dissection, and his graceful English. Socially, he charmed us all. He chatted with every one, he smiled on all. . . . We have not had such an awakening for years. It was like a new volume of old English poetry.— MITCHELL, MARIA, 1884, *Life, Letters and Journals,* pp. 195, 196.

Thou, that didst bear my Name, and deck it so
That—coming thus behind—hardly I know
If I shall hold it worthily, and be
Meet to be mentioned in one Age with thee—
Take, Brother! to the Land, where no strifes are,
This praise thou wilt not need! Before the Star
Is kindled for thee, let my funeral torch
Light thee, dear Namesake! to th' Elysian Porch!
Dead Poet! let a poet of thy House
Lay, unreproved, these bay-leaves on thy brow,
We, that seemed only friends, were lovers: Now
Death knows it! and Love knows! and I! and Thou!
—ARNOLD, SIR EDWIN, 1888, *To Matthew Arnold, April 15; Pall Mall Gazette.*

I believe that a more blameless, nay, a more admirable, man in every relation never lived. He was one of the noblest and most perfect characters I have ever known, and I have known him sixty years. I would not withdraw one word of what I said at the Union [League] Club at New York. It was not generous, it was *true*. I think him the most distinguished person in the old and right sense of that word that we had among us. To think we shall never have such papers any more, never hear him talk to us, never see that bright, manly, beautiful face any more!—COLERIDGE, JOHN DUKE LORD, 1888, *Letter to Mr. Ellis Yarnall, Century Magazine,* vol. 37, p. 532.

Mr. Arnold was not, I believe, a collector of anything. He certainly was not of books. I once told him I had been reading a pamphlet, written by him in 1859, on the Italian Question. He inquired how I came across it. I said I had picked it up in a shop. "Oh, yes," said he, "some old curiosity shop, I suppose." Nor was he joking. He seemed quite to suppose that old books, and old clothes, and old chairs were huddled together for sale in the same resort of the curious. He did not care about such things. The prices given for the early editions of his own poems seemed to tease him. His literary taste was broadly democratic. He had no mind for fished-up authors, nor did he ever indulge in swaggering rhapsodies over second-rate poets.—BIRRELL, AUGUSTUS, 1892, *Res Judicatæ,* p. 191.

I knew Arnold personally, though I cannot boast of having known him so intimately as to be provided with reminiscences. . . . Though our acquaintance was not so close as I could have wished, it left me with a singularly strong impression of Arnold's personal charm. Though the objects of my worship were to him mere wooden idols; though I once satisfactorily confuted him in an article, now happily forgotten by myself and everybody else; though I was once his Editor, and forced in that capacity to reject certain articles, on grounds, of course, quite apart from literary merit; yet he was always not only courteous but cordial, and, I may almost say, affectionate. He had that obvious sweetness of nature, which it is impossible not to recognize and not to love. Though in controversy he took and gave many shrewd blows, he always received them with a courtesy, indicative not of mere policy or literary tact, but of dislike to inflicting pain and of incapacity for having any tolerably decent antagonist in flesh and blood.—STEPHEN, LESLIE, 1893, *Matthew Arnold, National Review,* vol. 22. p. 458.

In reproduction, the defects of his face were easily exaggerated, while its finer and more characteristic qualities were of the kind which no photograph can more than suggest. Of his features the mouth was at first disappointing, being unusually large; but the lines were firm, and in conversation the early unfavourable impression was quickly lost. It was the kind of mouth which we associate with generous and sensitive natures, and its smiles were of a winning and whimsical attractiveness. . . . His look was altogether noble. . . . His unusual height and erect bearing, the thick brown hair, scarcely changed, despite his sixty years, and growing in lines of perfect grace about a brow of peculiar breadth and beauty, the clear, benignant gaze of the blue-gray eyes—these alone must have given him always and everywhere an air of preëminent distinction. . . . Certain it is that Mr. Arnold's superiority of mien gave offense in some directions, appearing to be regarded as a kind of involuntary criticism. In addition to this, his lofty mental attitude and gravity of demeanor were by some felt to be oppressive, and were misconstrued as pride. Yet proud, in a narrow and selfish sense, Arnold was not. His nature, full of dignity, was yet gentle and singularly sweet, and his interest in the masses was sympathetic and sincere. . . . Lycidas is dead, and hath not left his peer!—COATES, FLORENCE EARL, 1894, *Matthew Arnold, Century Magazine,* vol. 47, p. 932, 937.

Qualified by nature and training for the highest honours and successes which the world can give, he spent his life in a long round of unremunerative drudgery, working even beyond the limits of his strength for those whom he loved, and never by word or sign betraying even a consciousness of that dull indifference to his gifts and services which stirred the fruitless indignation of his friends. His theology, once the subject of some just criticism, seems now a matter of comparatively little moment; for, indeed, his nature was essentially religious. He was loyal to truth as he knew it, loved the light and sought it earnestly, and by his daily and hourly practice gave sweet and winning illustration of his own doctrine that conduct is three-fourths of human life. —RUSSELL, GEORGE W. E., 1895, *ed. Letters of Matthew Arnold, Prefatory Note,* vol. I, p. ix.

He was not the least of an egotist, in the common ugly and odious sense of that terrible word. He was incapable of sacrificing the smallest interest of anybody else to his own; he had not a spark of envy or jealousy; he stood well aloof from all the hustlings and jostlings by which selfish men push on; he bore life's disappointments, and he was disappointed in some reasonable hopes and anticipations, with good nature and fortitude; he cast no burden upon others, and never shrank from bearing his own share of the daily load to the last ounce of it; he took the deepest, sincerest, and most active interest in the well-being of his country and his countrymen. Is it not absurd to think of such a man as an egotist, simply because he took a child's pleasure in his own performance, and liked to know that somebody thought well of his poetry, or praised his lecture, or laughed at his wit?—MORLEY, JOHN, 1895, *Matthew Arnold, Nineteenth Century,* vol. 38, p. 1053.

He was a man of rare gifts. But he was likewise a model son, a model husband, model citizen. Genius, though not an every day phenomenon, is, I suppose, as frequent in these days as others; and, perhaps, there never was, before, so much cleverness as is now to be observed in almost every walk of life. But character—character that shows itself in filial piety, in conjugal tenderness, in good and conscientious citizenship—is perhaps not too conspicuous, especially in persons exceptionally endowed. One looks in vain for a serious blemish in Matthew Arnold's character. — AUSTIN, ALFRED, 1895, *Matthew Arnold in his Letters, The National Review,* vol. 26, p. 483.

With a satirical smile and a tone of commiseration, he would make a thrust, keen as a steel rapier, at the vulnerable point in the character of one whom he disliked, and then heal the wound by expatiating upon his good qualities.—TUCKERMAN, CHARLES K., 1895, *Personal Recollections of Notable People,* vol. II, p. 29.

The latter, with his brother Thomas, had been sent to me by their father as private pupils in a small Long Vacation party in the summer before Matthew was elected scholar at Balliol, and it is needless to say that, from my intimate connection with his family, we were very close friends during the whole of his Balliol days. He showed us both the strong and the weak sides of his character as a scholar, for he was certainly equally brilliant, desultory, and idle, and his want of knowledge of his books lost him his "first," when he was obliged, by the strictness of the college rule, to go into the Schools at the end of his third year, his examiners and his tutors being equally disappointed. I remember Liddell in particular expressing his annoyance that so able a man should have excluded himself from the highest honours.—LAKE, WILLIAM CHARLES, 1897–1901, *Memorials, ed. his Widow, p. 72.*

He was beautiful as a young man, strong and manly, yet full of dreams and schemes. His Olympian manners began even at Oxford; there was no harm in them, they were natural, not put on. The very sound of his voice and the wave of his arm were Jovelike.—MÜLLER, FRIEDRICH MAX, 1898, *Auld Lang Syne, p. 128.*

Matthew Arnold came to this country and gave one hundred lectures. Nobody ever heard any of them, not even those sitting in the front row. At his first appearance in Chickering Hall every seat was sold at a high price. Chauncey M. Depew introduced the speaker. I was looking after the business in the front of the house. There was not a seat to be had excepting a few that were held by speculators on the sidewalk. As Mr. Depew and Matthew Arnold appeared before the audience, somebody told me that General and Mrs. Grant had just arrived and had seats in the gallery, but some other people were occupying them. I immediately got a policeman, and working through the standing crowd, found that they were the last two seats on the aisle in the gallery. We had no difficulty in getting the occupants to vacate as soon as they discovered who held the tickets. We had just heard the last few sentences of Mr. Depew's introduction when Matthew Arnold stepped forward, opened out his manuscript, laid it on the desk, and his lips began to move. There was not the slightest sound audible from where I stood. After a few minutes General Grant said to Mrs. Grant, "Well, wife, we have paid to see the British lion; we cannot hear him roar, so we had better go home." They left the hall. A few minutes later there was a stream of people leaving the place. All those standing went away very early. Later on, the others who could not endure the silence moved away as quietly as they could.—POND, JAMES BURTON, 1900, *Eccentricities of Genius, p. 323.*

Judging from the many evidences of his early devotion and unflagging regard for his family, one is tempted to doubt the piece of gossip told about the way he received his family when they went to see him after he had been three months at the University—that when they were inside his lodgings, he said: "Thank God, you're all in," and when they were gone; "Thank God, you're all out." Though indeed Thomas Arnold admits that that young gownsman "welcomed his rustic *geschwister* with an amused and superior graciousness." Matthew's alert intellect, his charming waggery, and, his brother adds, his fashionable dressing, soon made him popular at Oxford where he was first welcomed for his father's fame. Max Müller's portrait of him, more graceful and authentic than one may hope to rival, declares: "He was beautiful, strong and manly, full of dreams and schemes. . . . His Olympian manners began even at Oxford . . . the very sound of his voice and the wave of his arms were Jovelike."—McGILL, ANNA BLANCHE, 1901, *The Arnolds, The Book Buyer, vol. 22, p. 380.*

Matthew Arnold was always to me, whether in the whirl of London society or in a quiet corner at the Athenæum, or in his modest Surrey home at Cobham, one of the most delightful of men to listen to. He was so cordial, so full of kindly simplicity, that I never once detected in the genial flow of his conversation that academic note which some have objected to.—MCCABE, W. GORDON, 1902, *Personal Recollections of Alfred Lord Tennyson, Century Magazine, vol. 63, p. 726.*

LITERATURE AND DOGMA
1873

It is a book of rare moral and intellectual force, original in the greatness and directness of its aim as well as in its style and diction. Mr. Arnold has felt that the time has come for him to speak out; and the creed which he here expounds and commends has a good claim to be regarded as one of the three or four leading "Gospels" of this speculative age. He proposes to guide the thought of the coming time in a channel different from any other that has yet been cut for it. Once again the much shaken mind of this generation has a promise of certainty and peace offered to it; another standard has been raised for dissatisfied intellects to follow; and there are characteristics of Mr. Arnold's creed, which are likely to make it, to a large section of

Englishmen, more attractive than any rival. . . . Few books, I believe that most of his readers will feel, have ever more urgently challenged the attention of those who believe in the God and the Christ of Christendom. It is of no use to complain of the dangerousness of Mr. Arnold's treatise. Its out-spoken plainness marks it as the product of an age in which it is settled that, at whatever risk and with whatever consequences, all beliefs shall be openly called in question and searched and sifted without mercy.—DAVIES, J. LLEWELYN, 1872, *Mr. Arnold's New Religion, Contemporary Review, vol.* 21, *pp.* 842, 855.

It is hard to understand how a man who talks so much of sweetness can have managed to steep his pen in such monotonous sourness; how one who extols seriousness can mix such excess of flippancy with the gravest topics; how one who surveys the field of thought from a loftier plane can descend into such pettinesses of jangling. It is not wonderful that in so doing he should become often unjust to his opponents. But for this, we would gladly have passed by this disagreeable side of the book unnoticed.—NEWMAN, FRANCIS W., 1873, *Literature and Dogma, Fraser's Magazine, vol.* 88. *p.* 115.

Mr. Arnold's "Literature and Dogma" is a most noteworthy and even startling production, on several accounts. In one respect it resembles "Ecce Homo," but differs from it in many more. Like that work it is (in the later portion at least) an attempt to conceive the precise purpose and mission of Christ, as well as the essentials of his character. But the conclusion arrived at is singularly discrepant. . . . It cannot for a moment be doubted by any one who reads "Literature and Dogma" in an appreciative and unprejudiced temper, that Mr. Arnold's religious instincts and intuitions are often remarkably penetrating, and nearly always beautiful and touching, even if habitually too much coloured by his own inherent preferences; and where they are erroneous and fanciful, the error arises not so much from any defect of intellectual—we might almost say spiritual—perception, as from a sort of naïve and confident audacity which enables him to deal with his materials rather as a creative poet than a conjecturing and investigating critic. He does not so much *guess* or infer. —he *knows* what each writer meant, even where that writer's words do not exactly tally with his reasoning.—GREG, WILLIAM RATHBONE, 1878, *The Creed of Christendom, Introduction to the Third Ed., pp.* 18, 19.

It is part of Mr. Arnold's inimitable manner— a point in his graceful and captivating tactics—to make it appear that he is not really asking much of even the most startled of his hearers; that those who seem furthest from him are really not so very far removed; and that the path that leads from one to the other is a great deal smoother and easier than it looks. That is, as it has always been, Mr. Arnold's urbane and dexterous method of procedure; and, of course, it is apt, despite its dialectical merits, to beget a twofold misconception. It leads some people into the error just referred to —that, namely, of supposing that their instructor is unconscious of the immense demand which he is really making upon them, the vast spiritual effort he is exacting from them, as reasoners and thinkers about religion; while in other minds it encourages the precisely converse mistake of fancying that the undertaking to which he has devoted himself is as simple a matter as his air of confident composure would appear to imply. It is, however, almost needless to add that in view of Mr. Arnold's high repute for sagacity and penetration, the latter of these misconceptions is likely to be much the more common of the two. One does not lightly suspect so clear an intelligence of having underrated the difficulties of its task; and most people, therefore, will be more ready to believe that the task itself is easier, and his handling of it more successful than is actually the case.— TRAILL, HENRY DUFF, 1884, *Neo-Christianity and Mr. Matthew Arnold, Contemporary Review, vol.* 45, *p.* 565.

For my own part I rejoice in this opportunity to say that to no book in the world do I owe so much as to "Literature and Dogma," unless it be to the great Book with which it so largely deals.— VAN RENSSELAER, M. G., 1888, *Mr. Arnold and American Art, Open Letters, Century Magazine, vol.* 36, *p.* 314.

It is full of repetitions and wearisome recapitulations, well enough in a magazine where each issue is sure to be read by many who will never see another number, but which disfigure a book. The style is likewise too jaunty. Bantering the Trinity is not yet a recognised English pastime.

Bishop-baiting is, but this notwithstanding, most readers of "Literature and Dogma" grew tired of the Bishop of Gloucester and Bristol and of his alleged desire to do something for the honour of the Godhead, long before Mr. Arnold showed any signs of weariness.—BIRRELL, AUGUSTINE, 1892, *Res Judicatæ, p.* 202.

LETTERS

These letters are a gift of sunshine to the world, not, like certain posthumous publications, a chill drizzle of rain, not, like others, a tempest with dangerous flashes of lightening. Of all eminent men, lately lost, Matthew Arnold perhaps best deserves to be loved. In his published writings there were at times a not unbecoming *hauteur*, a happy malice of the pen, and even something which, while really dexterity in saying things difficult to utter, might be mistaken for affectation. In these letters a more intimate side of his character is revealed to the public; they are absolutely simple and real; wholly free from strain; rich in the temper of enjoyment; unfailing in the spirit of genuine affection; and behind their kindness and their brightness we can discern strength, and even something of unostentatious heroism—loyalty to duty, loyalty to truth, loyalty an ideal of life.— DOWDEN, EDWARD, 1895, *Matthew Arnold's Letters, Saturday Review, vol.* 80, *p.* 757.

To me they have been absolutely fascinating. Those who hold, with Arnold himself, that he was capable of teaching England lessons of which England stood in special need; who are conscious that, however imperfectly they may have learnt his lesson, their own lives are richer and mellower because he lived and wrote; and who feel that, though they may know him only through his books, still to know him even so is "part of our life's unalterable good" —all these may join in the earnest hope that these volumes may be widely read, and may do much to spread a knowledge of one of the greatest of our nineteenth-century poets.—WALKER, HUGH, 1895, *Literature, The Academy, vol.* 48, *p.* 539.

Arnold's style expresses all variety of matter with clearness, ease, and grace, never running into rhetoric or the formal rhythm of literary prose. One might expect some flights of this sort in the description of the Alps or of Italy. One remembers that Shelley could never write in his dressing-gown even to his wife; he could never lay aside his splendor of diction and his beautiful rhythm. Mr. Arnold, while never slipshod, uses prose as clear and transparent as those Alpine streams in which he delighted. From these letters we gradually learn his taste, his passion for flowers, combining the learning of a botanist with the enthusiasm of a poet; his fondness for the "bright comradeship" of some mountain brook, and his real sympathy with birds and domestic animals. One letter narrates the virtues and graces of his Persian cat Atossa; another is an obituary of the pony Lola, who died suddenly in an honored old age. But, most of all, the playfulness and tenderness of his nature are revealed in his allusions to his children. They continually come up in this correspondence, and are never in the way, though we know that children are often *de trop* in books as well as in the drawing-room.— DANIELS, J. H., 1895, *Matthew Arnold's Letters, The Nation, vol.* 61, *p.* 452.

It is instructive to find that Mr. Arnold's literary income was rated at two hundred pounds, that he said he would need to write more essays to cover that sum, and that the tax commissioners courteously congratulated themselves on his promised industry. One of the foremost of our men of letters made two hundred pounds a year, while, look at the half-educated and quite uninspired novelists! Mr. Arnold thought but poorly of Tennyson's intellect, he had no high opinion of Thackeray, he called Burns "a beast with magnificent gleams," but he admired Miss Ingelow—and very properly. I remember no mention of Rossetti, or Mr. William Morris, or of any contemporary almost, in England. Perhaps the less said about his contemporary judgments, the better. His political ideas are more worthy of him, his affection and kindness are the essence of the man, and they shine unobscured. But, like George Eliot, Mr. Arnold did not appear at his best as a letter-writer.—LANG, ANDREW, 1896, *The Month in England, The Cosmopolitan, vol.* 20, *p.* 673.

He surely was a religious man. If his books do not show it, his letters reveal him as simply, unaffectedly, but ardently religious; and however much the daring of some of his modes of speech and the flippancy of some of his utterances may have shocked minds accustomed only to reverent treatment of religious themes, and may have disposed superficial readers to consider him an opponent of Christianity, it is impossible to read his books in the light of this interpretation without feeling that not without pain and sorrow, and in obedience to an imperative inward command, he had broken away from the faith of his fathers.—HOUGHTON, LOUISE SEYMOUR, 1897, *Matthew Arnold and Orthodoxy, The New World,* vol. 6, p. 629.

They are dissapointing in various respects; they scarcely seem worthy of his great reputation; and especially in his literary judgments does he seem to come short of what we should expect; but, on the other hand, they show the native simplicity, kindliness, and warmth of the man's character, and how admirable he was in all the domestic and ordinary relations of life.—GRAHAM, RICHARD D., 1897, *The Masters of Victorian Literature,* p. 327.

POETRY

In the morning, Dante xxviii. Clough came to dinner and brought me young (Matthew) Arnold's poems. Very clever; with a little of the Tennysonian leaven in them.—LONGFELLOW, HENRY WADSWORTH, 1853, *Journal, Feb. 23; Life, ed. Longfellow,* vol. II, p. 233.

Mr. Arnold and Mr. Swinburne are both ardently and consciously polemical. Mr. Arnold is a more dignified and composed partisan than Mr. Swinburne, but he too fights for a side. He does the gentlemanly and quiet work in the committee-room; Mr. Swinburne rushes into the street, calls names, puts his hands to his sides, and shouts till he is hoarse; but both are for their party. Mr. Swinburne makes "Atalanta in Calydon" the vehicle of a vociferous atheism, obtrusively blasphemous, than which nothing can be conceived more alien to the reverent and thoughtful spirit of Greek poetry. His crashing atheistic odes would have startled the hunters and huntresses of the Calydonian boar more than the most terrific charges of that dangerous beast. . . . Mr. Arnold does not offend so glaringly against the spirit of Greek poetry as Mr. Swinburne; but he too, in his "Empedocles on Etna," is modern and polemical, and summons the old Greek from the caverns of Etna to put into his mouth a dialect which neither he nor his fathers knew, a dialect compounded from the writings of Comte, Carlyle, and M. de Sainte Beuve.—BAYNE, PETER, 1867, *Mr. Arnold and Mr. Swinburne, Contemporary Review,* vol. 6, pp. 341, 342.

The supreme charm of Mr. Arnold's work is a sense of right resulting in a spontaneous temperance which bears no mark of curb or snaffle, but obeys the hand with imperceptible submission and gracious reserve. Other and older poets are to the full as vivid, as incisive and impressive; others have a more pungent colour, a more trenchant outline; others as deep knowledge and as fervid enjoyment of natural things. But no one has in like measure that tender and final quality of touch which tempers the excessive light and suffuses the refluent shades; which as it were washes with soft air the sides of the earth, steeps with dew of quiet and dyes with colours of repose the ambient ardour of noon, the fiery affluence of evening. His verse bathes us with fresh radiance and light rain, when weary of the violence of summer and winter in which others dazzle and detain us; his spring wears here and there a golden waif of autumn, his autumn a rosy spray of spring. His tones and effects are pure, lucid, aërial; he knows by some fine impulse of temperance all rules of distance, of reference, of proportion; nothing is thrust or pressed upon our eyes, driven or beaten into our ears. For the instinctive selection of simple and effectual detail he is unmatched among English poets of the time, unless by Mr. Morris, whose landscape has much of the same quality, as clear, as noble, and as memorable.—SWINBURNE, ALGERNON CHARLES, 1867, *Mr. Arnold's New Poems, Fortnightly Review,* vol. 8, p. 420.

"Merope" was a failure, as every poem must be where the author forgets that it is the wide human feeling, and not the local (Greek or other) expression which is the permanent thing. And the failure in "Merope" was more conspicuous for two reasons: (1), by reason of the severity of the form, and (2), by reason of its unsuitableness to the artistic temperament of the author. "Powerful thought and emotion flowing in strongly marked channels make a stronger impression:" which is true: but then the deep lines and furrows must be *filled*. A mere rivulet flowing through a gigantic arch does not produce a strong impression; a rivulet and a slight rustic arch, being more in keeping, produce a much stronger. And, moreover, this classic severity of form was quite unsuited to Mr. Arnold's genius. Mr. Arnold, if one of the most sensitive, flexible and tender, is at the same time one of the most fitful and wayward of critics. The necessity of adhering closely to a rigid model must have been a veritable bondage to a man whose own excellence and whose estimate of excellence in others depends so entirely upon the mood of the moment.—SKELTON, JOHN, 1869, *William Morris and Matthew Arnold, Fraser's Magazine*, vol. 79, p. 231.

Sharing with the Preraphaelite order of poets the practice of Wordsworthian naturalism, Mr. Arnold also shares with Wordsworth such repute as a poet may get from dry sententiousness; while, in place of the medievalism that lends so much beauty to Preraphaelite poetry, he has taken to himself classic stock, and has thus earned for much of his work a high place in the Neo-Greek division of *renaissance* poetry. But to say that he is *narrowly* neo-classic would be false; for, while he has produced no poems more replete with the higher elements of poetry than many inspired by Greek themes and wrought more or less after Greek models, he has yet given us some gems that are beautiful among the most beautiful poetry of our day, and which have been caught up by his imagination in searching the great store-houses of Scandinavian and Asiatic myth and legend. —FORMAN, HENRY BUXTON, 1871, *Our Living Poets*, p. 312.

"Merope" has that one fault against which the very gods, we are told, strive in vain. It is dull, and the seed of this dulness lay in the system on which it was written.—LOWELL, JAMES RUSSELL, 1871, *Swinburne's Tragedies, My Study Windows*, p. 222.

Arnold's circumstances have been more favorable than Hood's, and in youth his mental discipline was thorough; yet the humorist was the truer poet, although three fourths of his productions never should have been written, and although there scarcely is a line of Arnold's which is not richly worth preserving. It may be said of Hood that he was naturally a better poet than circumstances permitted him to prove himself; of Arnold, that through culture and good fortune he has achieved greater poetical successes than one should expect from his native gifts. His verse often is the result, not of "the first intention," but of determination and judgment; yet his taste is so cultivated, and his mind so clear, that, between the two, he has o'erleapt the bounds of nature, and almost falsified the adage that a poet is born, not made. . . . Through the whole course of Arnold's verse one searches in vain for a blithe, musical, gay, or serious off-hand poem. . . . Arnold has little quality or lightness of touch. His hand is stiff, his voice rough by nature, yet both are refined by practice and thorough study of the best models. His shorter metres, used as the framework of songs and lyrics, rarely are successful; but through youthful familiarity with the Greek choruses he has caught something of their irregular beauty.—STEDMAN, EDMUND CLARENCE, 1875–87, *Victorian Poets*, pp. 90, 92, 93.

How to make a Poem like Mr. Matthew Arnold. Take one soulful of involuntary unbelief, which has been previously well flavored with self-satisfied despair. Add to this one beautiful text of Scripture. Mix these well together; and as soon as ebullition commences, grate in finely a few regretful allusions to the New Testament and the lake Tiberias, one constellation of stars, half-a-dozen allusions to the nineteenth century, one to Goethe, one to Mont Blanc, or the Lake of Geneva; and one also if possible, to some personal bereavement. Flavor the whole with a mouthful of "faiths" and "infinites," and a mixed mouthful of "passions," "finites," and "yearnings." This class of poem is concluded, usually, with some question, about which we have to observe only that it shall be impossible to answer.—MALLOCK, W. H., 1878, *Every Man his Own Poet, or the Inspired Singer's Recipe Book*, p. 19.

He is a maker of such exquisite and thoughtful verse that it is hard sometimes to question his title to be considered a genuine poet. On the other hand, it is likely that the very grace and culture and thoughtfulness of his style inspires in many the first doubt of his claim to the name of poet. Where the art is evident and elaborate, we are all too apt to assume that it is all art and not genius. Mr. Arnold is a sort of miniature Goethe; we do not know that his most ardent admirers could demand a higher praise for him, while it is probable that the description will suggest exactly the intellectual peculiarities which lead so many to deny him a place with the really inspired singers of his day.—McCarthy, Justin, 1879, *A History of Our Own Times from the Accession of Queen Victoria to the Berlin Congress*, ch. xxix.

Have a simple austerity of style [Sonnets] which may almost be called ascetic.—Noble, James Ashcroft, 1880, *The Sonnet in England and Other Essays*, p. 55.

The volumes which contain the poems of Matthew Arnold are one of the priceless possessions of the English-speaking people. The critical perversity which causes their writer to see in Byron a greater poet than Shelley and in Wordsworth a greater than Hugo has not prevented him from making verse of his own, which, were not such comparisons of necessity futile, might fairly be compared with the nobler strains of Shelley and of Hugo. We have, indeed, the high authority of Mr. Swinburne for assigning to the "Thyrsis" the rank of the "Adonais," and it might not be rash to say that such poems as "Dover Beach" and "Obermann" would not be unworthy of the author of "Contemplations" and the "Legende des Siècles."—Payne, William Morton, 1884, *The Poetry of Matthew Arnold, The Dial*, vol. 4, p. 221.

Perhaps, when all is said, it remains the most noteworthy feature of Mr. Arnold's poetical work that that work was never immature. And yet the poems were all, in some sort, early poems. Before their author had fully come to middle life he had virtually abandoned metrical expression. But the earliest among them, those distinctly marked as such, have none of the special faults of youth. There is no passion in them, as we have seen,—or next to none,—no hurry, no excess. They are grave, concise, philosophical, unsparingly pruned from the beginning, and untiringly polished. Such precocity is usually thought to foretell an early decline of mental vigor. It is all the more wonderful, therefore, as measuring Mr. Arnold's vitality and versatility, that he should deliberately have unstrung his lyre only to enter with unsuspected energy into a new career, and win equal if not greater distinction as a writer of critical and didactic prose.—Preston, Harriet Waters, 1884, *Matthew Arnold as a Poet, Atlantic Monthly*, vol. 53, p. 650.

In running one's eye down the tables of contents of Mr. Arnold's poetry, one is struck with the apparent tameness of them; the titles of the early and lyrical poems have the sobriety of the "Christian Year," and in the narrative and dramatic poems, wide as is the range from sick Bokhara's king to Balder dead, from the doomed Mycernius to the wounded Tristram "famous in Arthur's court of old," we find no choice of subjects where the thrilling and romantic are the leading *motif*. Supreme artist as he is, master of a style pure, chaste, and well-nigh as faultless as work of man can be, severe in its simplicity, simple also in the main are the materials. Even where they have a studied commonplace look, as in an early poem, "Lines Written in Kensington Gardens," there the presence of genius is manifest in the uplifting of the simple and familiar to a higher level, in the suggestiveness which is never exhausted, in the hiding of power within restfulness. In truth the first impression which the poems themselves, sober in their colouring, scarce a ripple in their movement, playing on no passion, scorning all tricks and catches, frugal of metaphor and imagery, give, is one of disappointment. . . . A closer study of Mr. Arnold's poetry deepens appreciation, and we are in the end held by an irresistible charm easy neither to describe nor to define. . . . No surer test of Mr. Arnold's range and greatness and right assessment of men is supplied than in his elegiac poems. That on his friend Arthur Clough, entitled "Thyrsis," is placed by Mr. Swinburne, in which estimate most readers will agree, in equal rank with the "Lycidas" of Milton and the "Adonais" of Shelley.—Clodd, Edward, 1886, *Matthew Arnold's Poetry, Gentleman's Magazine*, N. S., vol. 36, pp. 347, 348, 349.

In passing from the thinker to the poet, I am passing from a writer whose curious earnestness and ability in attempting the impossible, will soon, I believe, be a mere curiosity of literature, to one of the most considerable of English poets, whose place will probably be above any poet of the eighteenth century, excepting Burns, and not excepting Dryden, or Pope, or Cowper, or Goldsmith, or Gray; and who, even amongst the great poets of the nineteenth century, may very probably be accorded the sixth or fifth, or even by some the fourth place. He has a power of vision as great as Tennyson's, though its magic depends less on the rich tints of association, and more on the liquid colours of pure natural beauty, a power of criticism and selection as fastidious as Gray's, with infinitely more creative genius; and a power of meditative reflection which, though it never mounts to Wordsworth's higher levels of genuine rapture, never sinks to his wastes and flats of commonplace. Arnold is a great elegiac poet, but there is a buoyancy in his elegy which we rarely find in the best elegy, and which certainly adds greatly to its charm. And though I cannot call him a dramatic poet, his permanent attitude being too reflective for any kind of action, he shows in such poems as the "Memorial Verses" on Byron, Goethe, and Wordsworth, in the "Sick King of Bokhara," and "Tristram and Iseult," great precision in the delineation of character, and not a little power even of forcing character to delineate itself.—HUTTON, RICHARD HOLT, 1886, *Newman and Arnold, Contemporary Review,* vol. 49, p. 528.

The chief qualities of his verse are clearness, simplicity, strong directness, noble and musical rhythm, and a certain intense calm.—MEIKLEJOHN, J. M. D., 1887, *The English Language: Its Grammar, History and Literature,* p. 359.

He is an academical poet, reflecting the mental attitude of the most cultured minds of his time, and also their obligations to antiquity and such moderns as Wordsworth and Goethe.—GARNETT, RICHARD, 1887, *The Reign of Queen Victoria,* ed. Ward, vol. II, p. 463.

Ah, winning, ample-browed,
Benignant minstrel!—dost our moods o'er cloud,
As one presageful destiny hath bowed.
Idle the hope that thou, condemned to break
With fond tradition for the spirit's sake,
A resonant, unfaltering chaunt couldst wake
To marshal and subdue; yet dear thy strain,
Low, elegiac, falling as the rain
Upon us in our hours of heat and pain.
—FIELD, MICHAEL, 1888, *The Rest of Immortals, Contemporary Review,* vol. 53, p. 884.

Gone! they have called our shepherd from the hill,
Passed in the sunny sadness of his song,
That song that sang of sight and yet was brave
To lay the ghosts of seeing, subtly strong
To wean from tears and from the troughs to save;
And who shall teach us now that he is still!
—LEGALLIENNE, RICHARD, 1888, *Matthew Arnold.*

Arnold's verse resembles a crystal cup of some choice liquor, fit for the banquets of Olympus, one sip of which delights, but which never cloys or intoxicates, drink we never so deep. The secret of his style is after all its purity and simplicity. Clearness without literal precision is the effect for which he strives. The transparency is that of running water, rather than that of clear air. His words are well chosen, and chosen so as to produce an immediate and definite impression, avoiding the diffuseness and repetition which now and again disfigure his prose writings. Indeed, his verse appeals to a distinctly higher audience. His ideal of the dignity of his art impose upon him a self-restraint to which he adhered with singular fidelity. In his eyes poesy is too fine an instrument to be employed on trifles.—HARDING, EDWARD J., 1888, *Matthew Arnold's Paralipomena, The Critic,* Oct. 6, p. 161.

Poet, in our poor flurried time,
Of fine completeness and of lucid ease;
Fair Master of old songs' superbest keys,
Magician of the fetterless chime,
Free from the fatal sweets of rhyme,
In Sophoclèan form and cadences,—
Poet of exquisite regret;
Of lines that aye on Time's confusèd height
Out of the storm shall stand in stars of white;
Of thoughts in deepening distance set
Perfect in pictured epithet
Touch'd with a pencil-tip of deathless light.
—ALEXANDER, WILLIAM, 1888, *Matthew Arnold.*

If one were to write out of mere personal preference, and praise most that which best fits one's private moods, I suppose I should place Mr. Matthew Arnold at the head of contemporary English poets. Reason and reflection, discussion and critical judgment, tell one that he is not quite there. . . . He has not that inspired greatness of Wordsworth, when nature does for him what his "*lutin*" did for Corneille, "takes the pen from his hand and writes for him." But he has none of the creeping prose which, to my poor mind, invades even "Tintern Abbey." He is, as Mr. Swinburne says, "The surest-footed" of our poets. He can give a natural and lovely life even to the wildest of ancient imaginings, as to "these bright and aged snakes, that once were Cadmus and Harmonia."—LANG, ANDREW, 1889. *Letters on Literature,* pp. 11, 13.

In matters of form this poet is no romancist but a classic to the marrow. He adores his Shakespeare, but he will none of his Shakespeare's fashion. For him the essentials are dignity of thought and sentiment and distinction of manner and utterance. It is no aim of his to talk for talking's sake, to express what is but half felt and half understood, to embody vague emotions and nebulous fancies in language no amount of richness can redeem from the reproach of being nebulous and vague. In his scheme of art there is no place for excess, however magnificent and Shakespearean—for exuberance, however overpowering and Hugoesque. Human and interesting in themselves, the ideas apparelled in his verse are completely apprehended; natural in themselves, the experiences he pictures are intimately felt and thoroughly perceived. They have been resolved into their elements by the operation of an almost Sophoclean faculty of selection, and the effect of their presentation is akin to that of a gallery of Greek marbles. . . . To me this last ["Balder Dead"] stands alone in modern art for simple majesty of conception, sober directness and potency of expression, sustained dignity of thought and sentiment and style, the complete presentation of whatever is essential, the stern avoidance of whatever is merely decorative, indeed, for every Homeric quality save rhythmical vitality and rapidity of movement.—HENLEY, WILLIAM ERNEST, 1890, *Views and Reviews, pp.* 84, 86.

He was a poet when he wrote "Thyrsis" and "The Strayed Reveller." He was no longer a poet when he perpetrated his verses in unrhymed Heinesque; when he compared the receding tide at Dover to the receding Sea of Faith, and could find nothing better to say of a sublime Humourist than that "the World smiled, and *the smile was Heine.*" This may be criticsm of life, but it is neither poetry nor even decent imagery. *Au reste,* Mr. Arnold forgot that Poetry, so far from being a dilettante's opinion or "criticism" of life, is the very Spirit of Life itself.—BUCHANAN, ROBERT, 1891, *The Coming Terror and Other Essays and Letters, p.* 246.

It was Arnold's work to find beauty and truth in life, to apprehend the meaning and moral worth of things, to discriminate the trivial from the grave, and to show how the serene and ardent life is better than the mean and restless.—JOHNSON, LIONEL, 1891, *Poetical Works of Matthew Arnold, The Academy, vol.* 39, *p.* 31.

In the poetry of Matthew Arnold faith is but an artistic freak. . . . The English mind will never yield a wide attention to any modern Lucretius in the person of a Matthew Arnold, singing his despairing ode concerning "The Nature of Things."—DAWSON, W. J., 1892, *Quest and Vision, pp.* 86, 90.

Mr. Arnold is the last man in the world anybody would wish to shove out of his place. A poet at all points, armed *cap-a-pie* against criticism, like Lord Tennyson, he certainly was not. Nor had his verse any share of the boundless vitality, the fierce pulsation so nobly characteristic of Mr. Browning. But these admissions made, we decline to parley any further with the enemy. We cast him behind us. Mr. Arnold, to those who cared for him at all, was the most *useful* poet of his day. He lived much nearer us than poets of his distinction usually do. He was neither a prophet nor a recluse. He lived neither above us, nor away from us. . . . His verse tells and tingles. . . . His readers feel that he bore the same yoke as themselves. Theirs is a common bondage with his. Beautiful surpassingly beautiful some of Mr. Arnold's poetry is, but we seize upon the *thought* first and, delight in the *form* afterwards. . . . What gives Arnold's verse its especial charm is his grave and manly sincerity. He is a poet without artifice or sham. He does not pretend to find all sorts of meanings in all sorts of things. He does not manipulate the universe and present his readers with any bottled elixir.—BIRRELL, AUGUSTINE, 1892, *Res Judicatæ, pp.* 192, 193, 217.

Arnold is a classic, but is he not at the foot of his class? Did ever poet before cast his thought into such perfect mould with so little fire to fuse his materials?—MOORE, CHARLES LEONARD, 1893, *The Future of Poetry, The Forum, vol.* 14, *p.* 774.

The inspiration of Matthew Arnold's verse is emotional and intellectual rather than spiritual.—BRADFIELD, THOMAS, 1894, *Ethical Tendency of Matthew Arnold's Poetry, Westminster Review, vol.* 142, *p.* 661.

Not irony, however, but sighs and lamentations, would be the proper commentary on the gradual subsidence in him of the poetic impulse, were one forced to believe that it had ever been the one imperative force in his character and genius. A born poet he unquestionably was. But he was a born critic likewise. If the critical faculty could have been kept in the abeyance till his powers as a poet had reached maturity, it would have helped him to introduce criticism of life into his verse, without any injury to the latter. Unfortunately, the critical impulse was, from the very beginning, more powerful in him than the poetic impulse, the disposition to analyze and to teach more imperious than the promptness to feel and the tendency to sing. The consequence was he began to criticize life before he had lived, and to do that most difficult of all things, viz., give utterance to the Imaginative Reason before he had become master of the instrument of verse. I have heard a sincere admirer of him affirm that he never became quite master of that instrument, and though, if one may say so, one would endorse without qualification the unflattering estimate he invariably expressed of poetry which is all sound and colour, and conspicuously deficient in subject matter, one could hardly controvert the opinion that attributes to him, as a writer of verse, a frequent disregard of sensuous beauty. Moreover, it was because of this early development in him of the reasoning and moralizing faculty that his mastery over the instrument of verse was not unoften unsatisfactory. He laid too heavy a burden on his young muse, which never recovered from this premature forcing of its powers.—AUSTIN, ALFRED, 1895, *Matthew Arnold in his Letters, National Review*, vol. 26, p. 478.

The doctrine of Stoicism modified by a doctrine of culture is nobly preached in Matthew Arnold's verse.—DOWDEN, EDWARD, 1895, *New Studies in Literature*, p. 37.

I hear of a *Penny Mat. Arnold* published by *Stead* (!!). Is that possible? And to be followed by a *Penny Clough!* Did you ever? Is he publishing them in penny numbers? the whole to cost a lot? Or, positively, can we have Mat. — the whole unmutilated Mat.—for a penny? And by STEAD? Wonders will never cease. Fancy Mat., from that fair heaven which now holds his dainty ghost, stooping to sniff at this κνίση! *sniff at*—sniff is ambiguous, is it not? It is to be observed that men like Mat. have an odd way of generating bastards. On some raid into Philistia he must have captured a Dalilah and taken her to his tent. And this is characteristic of our time; the frontiers get blurred, our choicest and best, whose very defects, if they be defects, we might have imagined would save them from such unions, are occasionally to be seen surrounded by hangers-on, who are absolutely unworthy. What is it? Some kindly looseness in the great man? or merely impudence in the small one? However this may be, I never can get a clear view of a modern writer, especially an eminent one, by reason of the admirers and imitators who are his own spurious offspring. What a *nimbus* for a celebrity! The old men are full-orbed, serene, "fixed in their everlasting seats." Now that is surely a glorious thing. There they are, the Classics. No one dreams of associating them with the feculent vulgar. No doubt we may impute a good deal of this ragamuffin salvage to the "spread of education," to the smug conviction which every man seems to cherish that he is in the secret, or that there is no secret. And the pestilent error is encouraged by the reduction of genius to "the infinite capacity of taking pains," by the insane idea that you can teach the "trick," that literature is a trade, a kapelistic art, that "the all is in us all," that there is no intellectual hierarchy, that the venerable *Poeta nascitur non fit* is venerable bosh—and a thousand and one heresies of the same "mak." Hence it comes to pass that even a εὔζωνος like Mat. gets swaddled and swathed with these terrible integuments, the fine Greek limbs of him impeded by Barbarian *braccae*. Still one has the consolation of thinking that he must be amused when he beholds waving a censer in his temple such a high-priest as Stead—amused—yes, and note the shrinking nostril, how it curves!— BROWN, THOMAS EDWARD, 1895, *To S. T. Irwin, Dec. 15; Letters*, vol. II, p. 148.

There is no Victorian poet, perhaps there is no Victorian thinker, more significant in position than Matthew Arnold. Agnosticism of thought and feeling, with all its vagueness, finds in him an exquisitely accurate exponent. No other poet has been so clear in his understanding of confusion, so positive in an unstable equilibrium. In the union of definiteness of technique with vagueness of theme the charm of his work resides. Unsatisfied desire, evasive regret, indecision, doubt, all that has not yet translated itself from the dim twilight of the feeling to the daylight world of the deed, —this Arnold gives us with delicate precision of touch. His poems are like gray shadows cast along some temple-floor, shadowy alike in clean purity of outline, and in dim uncertainty of content.—SCUDDER, VIDA D., 1895, *The Life of the Spirit in the Modern English Poets*, p. 247.

His poetry had the classical spirit in a very peculiar and rare degree; and we can have little doubt now, when so much of Arnold's prose work in criticism has been accepted as standard opinion, and so much of his prose work in controversy has lost its interest and savour, that it is his poetry which will be longest remembered, and there his finest vein was reached. It may be said that no poet in the roll of our literature, unless it be Milton has been so essentially saturated to the very bone with the classical genius. . . . His poetry, however, is "classical" only in a general sense, not that all of it is imitative of ancient models or has any affectation of archaism. It is essentially modern in thought, and has all that fetishistic worship of natural objects which is the true note of our Wordsworthian school. . . . Almost alone amongst our poets since Milton, Arnold is never incoherent, spasmodic, careless, washy, or *banal*. He never flies up into a region where the sun melts his wings; he strikes no discords, and he never tries a mood for which he has no gift. He has more general insight into the intellectual world of our age, and he sees into it more deeply and more surely than any contemporary poet. . . . As a poet, Arnold belongs to an order very rare with us, in which Greece was singularly rich, the order of *gnomic* poets, who condensed in metrical aphorisms their thoughts on human destiny and the moral problems of life. The type is found in the extant fragments of Solon, of Xenophanes, and above all of Theognis.—HARRISON, FREDERIC, 1896, *Matthew Arnold, Nineteenth Century*, vol. 39, pp. 434, 435.

His verse has everywhere the characteristic Greek signs—lucidity of thought, unity in design, reserve, fine taste, with propriety in choice of metre, crystal clearness in diction. If a certain coldness be sometimes felt, it is due to that over-didactic tendency, that want of disinterested feeling, which Arnold, in most ways so opposed, shares with Browning; nor was his overstrained value for criticism, of all pure literary forms the most transient, without a dampening effect on his own poetry. These conditions, of course, colour Arnold's landscape. It is limited in range, reaching its admirable successes almost always in the idyllic style. His conception of the scene is transparently accurate; the pictures presented have much variety, and are always in due harmony with the subject.—PALGRAVE, FRANCIS TURNER, 1896, *Landscape in Poetry*, p. 265.

Mr. Arnold is on one side a poet of "correctness"—a new correctness as different from that of Pope as his own time, character, and cultivation were from Pope's, but still correctness, that is to say a scheme of literature which picks and chooses according to standards, precedents, systems, rather than one which, given an abundant stream of original music and representation, limits the criticising province in the main to making the thing given the best possible of its kind. . . . And it is not a little curious that his own work, by no means always the best of its kind—that it would often be not a little the better for a stricter application of critical rules to itself. But when it is at its best it has a wonderful charm—a charm nowhere else to be matched among our dead poets of this century. Coleridge was perhaps, allowing for the fifty years between them, as good a scholar as Mr. Arnold, and he was a greater poet; but save for a limited time he never had his faculties under due command, or gave the best of his work. Scott, Byron, Keats, were not scholars at all; Shelley and Tennyson not critical scholars; Rossetti a scholar only in modern languages. And none of these except Coleridge, whatever their mere knowledge or instruction, had the critical vein, the knack of comparing and adjusting, at all strongly developed. Many attempts have been made at a formula of which the following words, are certainly not a perfect expression, that a poet without criticism is a failure, and that a critic who is a poet is a miracle. Mr. Arnold is beyond all doubt the writer who has most nearly combined the two gifts.—SAINTSBURY, GEORGE, 1896, *A History of Nineteenth Century Literature*, p. 283.

Arnold's permanent fame will rest rather on his poems than on his prose writings. In the coming generations, when the educational politics of our day shall have become obsolete and have ceased to interest men; when the ephemeral literature, the sociology, and the personal controversies have passed out of view, his name will stand out conspicuously with those of Tennyson and Browning, the three representative poets of the latter half of the nineteenth century. The future historian of literature who seeks a key to the moral condition of the England of our time, to its intellectual unrest, and to its spiritual aims and tendencies, will find it here.—FITCH, SIR JOSHUA, 1897, *Thomas and Matthew Arnold and their Influence on English Education*, p. 261.

As a great elegiac poet, Matthew Arnold is the clearest exponent of the subjective aspect of the religious conflict of the Victorian era. He has helped the thinkers of his generation to find an utterance for their sadness; he has interpreted their feelings. This sadness, this conflict, he has said, is natural, it is not beyond explanation; and he has, in his later poems, expressed his hope of ultimate reconciliation between doubt and belief. No one has laid bare the "malady of the century" with keener insight than he.—WORSFOLD, W. BASIL, 1897, *The Principles of Criticism*, p. 200.

To-day his poetry is all of him that remains, and its charm is likely to soothe the more strenuous minds among us for at least another generation, and perhaps for all time.—SHORTER, CLEMENT, 1897, *Victorian Literature*, p. 20.

It may be said, indeed, that in Matthew Arnold we have, perhaps, the most perfect specimen of the classic style that the essentially Romantic bent of nineteenth-century English poetry could allow to exist and flourish in our literature. It is a style which as its judicious admirers admit, has, in modern hands at any rate, its weakness as well as its strength; and in the hands of Mr. Arnold the former quality was now and then more conspicuous than the latter. It betrayed him sometimes into a stiffness with which another and greater classic, Milton, is himself on occasion justly chargeable, and sometimes into a frigidity of which Milton is much more rarely guilty.—TRAILL, HENRY DUFF, 1897, *Social England*, vol. VI, p. 277.

On the whole, patience rather than hope or action was Arnold's attitude; the tendency of his verse is certainly to depress, to banish hope, to benumb action.—WHITE, GREENOUGH, 1898, *Arnold's Poetry, Matthew Arnold and the Spirit of the Age*, p. 27.

A narrative poem ["Sohrab and Rustum"] second in dignity to none produced in the nineteenth century. — ALDRICH, THOMAS BAILEY, 1900, *Poems of Robert Herrick, Introduction*, p. xlvii.

It is frequently and truly remarked of Arnold's poetry that it never can be popular. But this is not because there is anything particularly esoteric about it, and the assumption that it appeals particularly to the elect, is largely unfounded. It is, at all events, better than *that*. It is not in the exclusive sense that Mr. Lang and Mr. Augustine Birrell find it intimately consoling. Others enjoy it in the same way, though, of course, whether or no in the same degree it would be impossible to determine. But it is poetry that never can be popular because it appeals to moods that are infrequent. It is intimately consoling if you are in a mood that needs consolation, and consolation of a severely stoic strain. Otherwise it is not. — BROWNELL, W. C., 1901; *Matthew Arnold, Scribner's Magazine*, vol. 30, p. 116.

GENERAL

No one can charge Mr. Arnold with being the slave of a system. No one can say that he is fighting for an institution which has trained him into a prejudice in its own favor. No one can say that he has travelled so long in one deep-worn lane that he can only see what happens to be at its two ends. This is what people say or think when the clergy speak in enthusiastic terms of the Bible and of religion. But Mr. Arnold is a free lance, if anybody is. Mr. Arnold represents criticism and the critical school of thought, with a prominence at present which no other Englishman has gained. What man dares, he dares; and no fear of unpopularity, of present wrath, or of future punishment will deter him from saying what he thinks. He holds a pen, too, sharp as a bee's sting, and wields it with wit, not to say humor, which most people call ill-natured, but which seems to us only the exuberance of a vigorous life.—HALE, EDWARD EVERETT, 1873, *Literature and Dogma, Old and New*, vol. 8, p. 497.

Our most brilliant literary critic. — KNIGHT, WILLIAM, 1874, *Studies in Philosophy and Literature*, p. 71.

Mr. Arnold is a true poet, but he is intensely and profoundly ethical. He is seeking always the highest truth. He is bent on the wisest and most successful conduct of life. This is the sentiment and purpose which give unity to his poetry and prose more than the acuteness, the grace, the imagination, which are common to them both. But his work is far too large and varied to be summed in any formula.—MERRIAM, GEORGE S., 1879, *Some Aspects of Matthew Arnold's Poetry, Scribner's Monthly, vol.* 18, *p.* 282.

A large familiarity with foreign literature and Continental criticism has enabled Mr. Arnold to widen the scope of contemporary English literature. . . . He tried to raise criticism from its low estate—described by Wordsworth as "an inglorious employment." It can hardly be denied that his efforts have been successful, and that we have now a more studious, learned, disinterested, and careful sort of reviewers than of old. Mr. Arnold tried his best to make critics feel that their duty is to see things as they are. A poet is now rarely reviled because his opinions, as a private citizen, are Radical, or Tory; because he lives at Hampstead, or in Westmoreland; because he goes to church, or stays away. A somewhat higher standard has been set, even for journey-men-work, and, as far as an English looker-on can judge, American literature, too, has benefited by this increased earnestness of purpose, and this growing desire for wider and clearer knowledge.— LANG, ANDREW, 1882, *Matthew Arnold, Century Magazine, vol.* 23, *p.* 860.

While so much that is effective in Mr. Arnold's writings is generally attributed to his culture, I am confident that without his rare *nature*—what is it but genius?—mere culture would have left him mechanical, brassy, insipid, where he is now vital, sweet, profound. He always has something to say, which is Carlyle's first requisite for good writing. But his literary art is masterly. His sentences are clear-cut, statuesque in their elaboration, not a word in them can be changed but to their detriment,—and yet they are limpid, crisp, graceful, strong, charged to the full with thought. And then, too, with his positive convictions and robust vigor, how delicately he handles the subtlest themes! How large and sustained his movement; how sure his grip; how imperial, without bluster or arrogance, his authority! I cannot express my admiration of his fluent, virile, precise style, his scope and insight, his wisdom, moderation, catholicity, and illuminating interpretation, without seeming to exaggerate his quality as a writer and his virtues as a man. Amid a Babel of noises and factions, he stands calm, judicial, self-contained; and minds that hate shams and love truth and beauty are reassured by his example and inspiration.—POWERS, HORATIO N., 1883, *Matthew Arnold, The Dial, vol.* 4, *p.* 122.

I have wished to praise, to express the high appreciation of all those who in England and America have in any degree attempted to care for literature. They owe Matthew Arnold a debt of gratitude for his admirable example, for having placed the standard of successful expression, of literary feeling and good manners, so high. They never tire of him—they read him again and again. They think the wit and humour of "Friendship's Garland" the most delicate possible, the luminosity of "Culture and Anarchy" almost dazzling, the eloquence of such a paper as the article on Lord Falkland in the "Mixed Essay" irresistible. They find him, in a word, more than any one else, the happily-proportioned, the truly distinguished man of letters. When there is a question of his efficacy, his influence, it seems to me enough to ask one's self what we should have done without him, to think how much we should have missed him, and how he has salted and seasoned our public conversation. In his absence the whole tone of discussion would have seemed more stupid, more literal. Without his irony to play over its surface, to clip it here and there of its occasional fustiness, the life of our Anglo-Saxon race would present a much greater appearance of insensibility. — JAMES, HENRY, 1883, *Matthew Arnold, English Illustrated Magazine, vol.* 1, *p.* 246.

Mr. Matthew Arnold is indeed a writer who speaks with a great deal of authority. He has a strong positive spirit. The strength of that positive spirit is all the more evident from the fact that it has been hindered by that sympathetic discouragement of which he so often speaks. His mind has been very open to impressions from certain authors, and indeed from men in general. And it appears to have been his disposition to regard others as more enviable than himself. . . . This constitutional confidence was of great artistic use to him in his younger days. The charming poems which he wrote at that period appear, many of them, and some of the best, to have been regarded by the poet himself quite as much as statements of truth as expressions of art.

He will not write unless he has a substantial poetical thought to express. It would be well if all poets knew equally well when not to speak. . . . In his writings upon other than literary subjects Mr. Arnold is better the nearer he keeps to the description of human nature. . . . Mr. Arnold's writings have been widely read here. They have a natural relationship to this country. He is an admirer of democracy, and has thought a great deal about the future of human character and society. His interest in the future is indeed one of his peculiarities.—NADAL, E. S., 1884, *Matthew Arnold, The Critic*, vol. 2, p. 135.

No injustice is done to Mr. Arnold in saying that condescension in the form of superciliousness more or less infects his ablest writings. He is very careful to abstain from every kind of that passionate invective, of that righteous wrath, in which vehement minds are apt to indulge when their souls are excited by the contemplation of some great wrong; there is hardly a trace in his works of the nobler age so dominant in Milton, Chatham, or Burke; but on the other hand, there is no recent English writer who excels or even equals him in the exquisitely polished poison with which he deliberately tips the light and shining arrows of his sarcasm. The wounds he inflicts may seem to be a mere scratch on the surface; but they fester; they eat into the flesh, which they hardly seem to touch; and the dull and prolonged pain they cause is as hard to bear as the sting of a scorpion or the bite of a centipede. . . . The prose of Mr. Arnold, when he is in his best mood, almost realizes his ideal of what he calls the Attic style, having its "warm glow, blithe movement, and soft pliancy of life." Take such an essay as that on "Religious Sentiment," and it seems, as we read, that it cannot be improved. In some of his theological and political discussions his style, it must be confessed, loses much of its charm. It is important, however, to discriminate between listening to Mr. Arnold and reading him.—WHIPPLE, EDWIN PERCY, 1884, *Matthew Arnold, North American Review*, vol. 138, pp. 433, 441.

To speak with perfect frankness, it seems to me that Mr. Arnold's one weak point as critic is a tendency to over-fastidiousness.—DOYLE, SIR FRANCIS HASTINGS, 1886, *Reminiscences and Opinions*, p. 182.

Matthew Arnold was a polished scholar, but as a heathen might be so. He was a heathen, and he knew the heathen. He was more at home among the heathen than in Christian society; and this is a trait of his class. Knowing the heathen better than the Christian and having more affection for him, and knowing his difficulties better than the Christian's, he could but say in answer to the question, What is highest good? "A stream of tendency which makes for righteousness." An easy way to let a man down, who wants to go down, by a pretty phrase.—HECKER, I. T., 1888, *Two Prophets of this Age, Catholic World*, vol. 47, p. 689.

Past in a moment; passed away,
The finest spirit of the day;
Past in the full meridian sense
Of masterful intelligence:
The thought that struck—the wit that played
With measured aim—with tempered blade—
The hand that with new laurels hung
The Temple of the Mother-Tongue,
The soul that nursed the inner fire
Which radiates from Apollo's lyre,
And crowns his favourites, now as then,
Among the foremost sons of men. . . .
Far beyond, and far behind,
Shall live his legacy of Mind,
A throbbing pulse of English thought,
Quick with the lessons that he taught.
Thrice happy he, whose buoyant youth
In light of Beauty sought for Truth,
Showed stars that guide to eyes that shine,
High-priest of Beauty's inmost shrine,
And, wheresoe'er new worships tend—
Ensued his goddess to the end!
—MERIVALE, HERMAN, 1888, *Matthew Arnold*.

Few men, if any, whom death could have taken from us would have been more perceptibly missed by a wider range of friends and readers than Mr. Matthew Arnold. Other men survive who command a more eager enthusiasm, or who are more actively important to the work of the world. But hardly any man was present in so many cultivated minds as an element of interest in life, an abiding possibility of stimulating and fruitful thought. His criticism of books and of life found wider acceptance in the English-speaking world than that offered by any other writer; and even the slight affectations or idiosyncrasies of his pellucid style have become so associated with the sense of intellectual enjoyment that few readers wished them away. . . . His business and achievements, indeed, were widely spread. He was an inspector of schools, a literary, social, and political essayist, a religious reformer, and a poet. To the *first* of these pursuits, widening into the study of state education generally, he probably gave the largest proportion of his time, and he became one of the most accomplished specialists in that direction whom England possessed; in the *second* pursuit he was the most brilliantly successful; to the *third*, as I believe, he devoted the most anxious and persistent thought; and by the *fourth* pursuit, as a poet, he will, we cannot doubt, be the longest remembered.—MYERS, FREDERIC W. H., 1888, *Matthew Arnold, Fortnightly Review*, vol. 49, p. 719.

Arnold is preëminently a critical force, a force of clear reason and of steady discernment. He is not an author whom we read for the man's sake or for the flavor of his personality, for this is not always agreeable, but for his unfailing intelligence and critical acumen; and because, to borrow a sentence of Goethe, he helps us to "attain certainty and security in the appreciation of things exactly as they are." Everywhere in his books we are brought under the influence of a mind which indeed does not fill and dilate us, but which clears our vision, which sets going a process of crystallization in our thoughts, and brings our knowledge, on a certain range of subjects, to a higher state of clearness and purity.—BURROUGHS, JOHN, 1888, *Matthew Arnold's Criticism, Century Magazine*, vol. 36, p. 185.

Mr. Matthew Arnold, indeed, master of all literary arts, was highly skilful in the use of the Preface, which, in his hands, served to drive home the bolt of his argument, and to rivet it firmly on the other side. Those who have read one of Mr. Arnold's prefaces know what to expect, and fall to, with increased appetite, on the book itself. — MATTHEWS, BRANDER, 1888, *Pen and Ink*, p. 50.

He did more to inculcate in the minds of English-speaking people a love for Literature for the sake of itself than any other man living or dead. He was a poet, but not a great one. He cultivated the art of using words to the utmost extent possible in a man of his temperament. He wrote at times exquisitely. He was an intellectual aristocrat, and we cannot but admire the position he took above all low, vulgar and common things. But, nevertheless, his lifelong cultivation of the art of literature led to nothing, because it did not lead to God. —EGAN, MAURICE FRANCIS, 1889, *Lectures on English Literature*, p. 1.

Mr. Arnold justly earned the thanks of this generation for the soundness of his judgments on questions of taste and for the clearness with which he delivered them. It is not to be denied, however, that his powers of lucid and felicitous expression frequently led him into the dangerous habit of substituting phrases for reasoning; and this tendency is nowhere more manifest than in the Preface which he contributed to Mr. Humphry Ward's "English Poets" published in 1880.—COURTHOPE, WILLIAM JOHN, 1889, *The Life of Alexander Pope, Pope's Works*, ed. Elwin and Courthope, vol. V, p. 377.

When all has been said, there is not to be found in modern time such a body of literary criticism as that which Mr. Arnold has left us. In no other writer of our time is there to be found so much strong sense, keen insight, subtle yet lucid analysis, calm unimpassioned judgment, feeling for humour, for pathos, for noble poetry, and high imagination clothed in a style which needed only an occasional rise into the eloquence of passionate and ringing oratory to be quite perfect. The absence of this swing and fervour has been noted as a defect; perhaps it is so; perhaps its presence would have been inconsistent with the graceful quiet playful flow of his limpid sentences. Yet his quiet was not the quiet of weakness or indecision. When he condemns these passages in the life of Shelley and his friends which no one but an infatuated idolater can defend, or speaks of the coarse brutalities of Milton's polemics as any one who has read them (except Lord Macaulay) must in his heart admit that they deserve, he does so in stinging language, which leaves no doubt as to his own stern disapprobation and unqualified dislike. Where all is excellent it is difficult to select, and of the literary papers of Mr. Arnold there is not one which should remain unread.— COLERIDGE, JOHN DUKE LORD, 1889, *Matthew Arnold, New Review*, vol. 1, p. 218.

As a critic Mr. Arnold has been compared to Sainte-Beuve, for whom he had a great admiration, and who spoke of him to me with much respect, and no doubt he had some of the merits of that eminent man, with a total absence of his moral defects. Mr. Arnold's method, however, was very different, and to my thinking not so good.

The method indeed of Sainte-Beuve seems to me quite perfect, and he gave to criticism the kind of continuous and all-engrossing toil which a Q. C. in immense practice gives to his profession. Towards the latter part of his life indeed, before he became a senator, I have reason to think that he gave more, and that he found his labours terribly wearing. Mr. Arnold's critical papers were merely essays written in the intervals of business, and, excellent as they are, would probably have been better, as well as more numerous, if he had been able to devote a larger part of his energies to them.—DUFF, MOUNTSTUART E. GRANT, 1890, *Matthew Arnold's Writings, Murray's Magazine, vol. 7, p.* 301.

Arnold intended to designate, or at least to convey, something peculiar to his own conception,—not strictly related to literature at all, it may be, but more closely tied to society in its general mental activity. In other words, Arnold was a critic of civilization more than of books, and aimed at illumination by means of ideas. With this goes his manner—that habitual air of telling you something which you did not know before, and doing it for your good, which stamps him as a preacher born. Under the mask of the critic is the long English face of the gospeler; that type whose persistent physiognomy was never absent from the conventicle of English thought.—WOODBERRY, GEORGE EDWARD, 1890–1900, *Makers of Literature, p.* 3.

> Rather, it may be, over-much
> He shunned the common stain and smutch,
> From soilure of ignoble touch
>   Too grandly free,
> Too loftily secure in such
>   Cold purity.
>
> But he preserved from chance control
> The fortress of his 'stablisht soul;
> In all things sought to see the Whole;
>   Brooked no disguise;
> And set his heart upon the goal,
>   Not on the prize.
>
> With those Elect he shall survive
> Who seem not to compete or strive,
> Yet with the foremost still arrive,
>   Prevailing still:
> Spirits with whom the stars connive
>   To work their will.

—WATSON, WILLIAM, 1890, *In Laleham Churchyard, Aug.* 18.

Insight, appreciation, patience—these are the qualities that stamp the born critic, and so intrinsically was Arnold a critic, that he seized not only the livery but the secret of the creators, and advanced himself far along their own lines. . . . Much of Arnold's poetry is but thrice-refined criticism, trebly refined pessimistic criticism; and the portion of it that is pure poetry is not song. The born critic could not learn the born poet's lay; but he could rise to noble verse, indeed to as noble verse of the kind as we have in the language. . . . If Arnold does not greatly impress us as a poet, the moment we meet him as a critic we are in the presence of a master.—CHENEY, JOHN VANCE, 1891, *The Golden Guess, pp.* 80, 81, 83.

This book, ["Friendship's Garland"] published when Arnold was filling the mouths of men with his paradoxical utterances, lighted up all through with such wit and charm of style as can hardly, of its kind, be paralleled in recent prose; a masterpiece, not dealing with remote or abstruse questions, but with burning matters of the day —this entertaining and admirably modern volume enjoyed a sale which would mean deplorable failure in the case of a female novelist of a perfectly subterranean order. —GOSSE, EDMUND, 1891, *The Influence of Democracy, Questions at Issue, p.* 60.

No recent English critic, I think, has approached him in the art of giving delicate portraits of literary leaders; he has spoken, for example, precisely the right word about Byron and Wordsworth. Many of us who cannot rival him may gain, from Arnold's writings a higher conception of what is our true function. He did, I think, more than any man to impress upon his countrymen that the critic could not be a mere combatant in a series of faction fights, puffing friends and saying to an enemy, "This will never do." The weak side, however, of the poetical criticism is its tendency to be "subjective," that is, to reflect too strongly the personal prejudices of the author.— STEPHEN, LESLIE, 1893, *Matthew Arnold, National Review, vol.* 22, *p.* 465.

Arnold's paragraphs, while they have not the very highest variety in unity, do have admirable measure and proportion. The paragraph is usually loose, with an introductory sentence of transition. A large proportion are deductive: Arnold loved to regard the paragraph as a means of illustrating a general rule—he was not particular to advance a large body of particulars and base an induction upon these. . . . The coherence of Arnold's paragraphs is well-nigh perfect in its way. It arises primarily from an oral structure—a close logical method, redintegrating in idea, slightly aggregating in sentence.—LEWIS, EDWIN HERBERT, 1894, *The History of the English Paragraph*, pp. 163, 164.

Arnold may have differed from his father about Celt and Saxon, and about a hundred other things, and some of them were important things in the eyes of both of them; but to his father he did no doubt owe that point of fundamental resemblance which made them both take the social view of human life and duty. That Matthew will live by his verse, and not by his prose, does not affect the fact that the mainspring of his activity was his sense of the use and necessity of England as a great force in the world, and his conviction that she could not exert this force effectively or wisely until her educational system had been vivified, her ideas of conduct and character clarified and widened, and all her standards of enlightment raised. For this literature was to be the great instrument. But along with literature, organisation.—MORLEY, JOHN, 1895, *Matthew Arnold, Nineteenth Century*, vol. 38, p. 1049.

Nature, for instance, plainly intended that Matthew Arnold should not write elegant prose, and she absolutely forbade him to write poetry, yet he succeeded in doing both.—BATES, ARLO, 1896, *Talks on Writing English*, p. 88.

Few Englishmen of the nineteenth century have been so sincere and so outspoken in their critisicm of their contemporaries. Matthew Arnold was often wrong, both in his premises and his conclusions; but he was always truthful and conscientious. Of some subjects he had a profound knowledge; for example, he had made a thorough study of Homer, and of Greek literature generally. He also devoted much attention to the literary aspect of the Bible. Not only was he a true apostle of culture, but the most catholic-minded and cosmopolitan of English writers. . . . He was a man of childlike and affectionate nature, and yet the possessor of an intellect which could appreciate the literatures of all nations. He was entirely free from Anglo-Saxon insularity. He lashed with refined sarcasm the smug self-complacency of the British Philistine, and made the "vulgar-mindedness" of the middle-class so odious that the best amongst them have, by this time, learned to be ashamed of their own sordid vices and almost equally sordid virtues. In many respects he was, perhaps, hypercritical. He always loved to praise the French, and to declare that they are superior to the English. . . . Matthew Arnold, classical as his poetry is in form and in its ideals, is, as a critic, the most modern of moderns. He was rather an interpreter of the spirit of the age than a prophet or a leader. If he lacked Carlyle's colossal force, he was free from that great writer's gloomy pessimism and love of vituperation. As a poet he may rank after Tennyson and Browning, and in some respects his poetry is more inspiring than that of his two illustrious contemporaries. Misunderstood and censured by the champions of orthodox literality, he was really one of the most religious-minded of men. He taught his fellow-countrymen to associate happiness, and not misery, with righteousness. It was a lesson which England had need to learn.—HANNIGAN, D. F., 1896, *Matthew Arnold's Letters, Westminster Review*, vol. 145, pp. 40, 42.

The amount of direct information that we derive from Matthew Arnold, for instance, is usually small; his opinions often miss our acceptance; and yet no student can follow his thought through many pages without a distinct gain in that which Arnold so strenuously battled for, genuine culture.—KOOPMAN, HARRY LYMAN, 1896, *The Mastery of Books*, p. 33.

Arnold's influence upon the religious views of English-speaking Protestants it would be difficult to exaggerate. We live too near his day, perhaps, to gauge the force of that influence with accuracy, but that it was a wide-spread and destructive influence cannot be denied. He was undoubtedly one of the most insidious enemies of "Orthodox" Protestantism—that is, the school of Protestant Christianity which has clung to a more or less vague notion of the Incarnation—that the century has produced. A champion of the Established Church of England as against the dissenting sects, the manner and grounds of that defence were of a nature to horrify all except the haziest minds among Broad-church Anglicans. His conception of the Christian religion bore the same relation to the dogmatic faith of the historic church that the light of the moon bears to the sun's brilliancy and heat. Clear, pale, cold—it was a reflected light, as wanting in warmth as the moon's rays; the best it may accomplish is to illumine the wayfarer's pathway enough to aid him in avoiding the pitfalls of ignorance and lust; but its faint glimmer guides his steps to the brink of blank infidelity, and then the pale rays fade into blackest night. His religion was the logical outcome of the latitudinarian views of his father. . . . He was of too fine a cultivation, and of too cosmopolitan a type, to fall into the vulgarisms regarding the church so rife in the published thought of otherwise scholarly American non-Catholics —men whose Rome-hating, Reformation-lauding traditions lead them into strangely narrow and crooked pathways of vilification.—MORSE, CHARLES A. L., 1896, *Matthew Arnold's Letters, Catholic World, vol. 63, pp. 491, 493.*

While Matthew Arnold travelled a long way beyond his father's theological ceremonies, and was certainly not opposed to the emancipation of the Jews, he inherited and adopted Dr. Arnold's invincible faith in truth, righteousness, and innocence. No line of his poetry suggests anything but what is lovely and of good report. No act of his life would have been condemned by the puritan rigor of his father. From his father also he derived much of his inbred taste and literary sense. Dr. Arnold's style is always lucid, dignified, and impressive. His mind was steeped in that standard and touchstone of perfection, the literature of Athens. Plato and Thucydides were the favorites of the father; Homer and Sophocles of the son. Greece is justified of her children.—PAUL, HERBERT WOODFIELD, 1896, *Matthew Arnold's Letters, The Forum, vol. 20, p. 630.*

It was through his writings alone that he wished all biographical hints to be made accessible to the great reading public, and so left it on record that no life of him should be written. And yet, in reading the works of a favourite author, we wish at times to have some more commonplace account of his everyday life and character with which to compare the ideal biography of him which has been insensibly forming itself in our minds. His works, especially his poetry —if he be a poet—are the outcome of some rare moments of spiritual insight; of some mood of suspense, or joy, or sorrow; of some delicate handling of a pressing intellectual problem; and our indebtedness to them for the furtherance of our deepest and truest life only serves to increase the personal interest felt for the author, and makes us wish for a more detailed account of his life than those indirect hints which his literary productions can suggest. And of such an account, in spite of the fact that no regular biography is to be written, we are not deprived in the case of Matthew Arnold, whose letters, published in two volumes, exhibit the writer in an admirable light as a most devoted son and brother, husband and father, and a perfectly charming friend to those whose correspondence with him has found a place in these volumes.—FISHER, CHARLES, 1897, *Matthew Arnold as seen through his Letters, Gentleman's Magazine, vol. 283, pp. 492, 495.*

There are probably few readers of the critical literature of the times who do not recur again and again to Matthew Arnold's criticism, not only for the charm of the style, but for the currents of vital thought which it holds. One may not always agree with him, but for that very reason he will go back to see how it is possible to differ from a man who sees so clearly and feels so justly. Of course Arnold's view is not final, any more than is that of any other man; but it is always fit, and challenges your common sense. After the muddle and puddle of most literary criticism, the reader of Arnold feels like a traveler who has got out of the confusion of brush and bog into clean and clear open spaces, where the ground is firm, and where he can see his course. "Where trees grow biggest," says Emerson, "the huntsman finds the easiest way;" and for a similar reason the way is always easy and inviting through Arnold's pages.—BURROUGHS, JOHN, 1897, *On the Re-reading of Books, Century Magazine, vol. 55, p. 149.*

He had given vogue to modes of thought and judgment which were once rare amongst Englishmen. He would have disclaimed, with some repugnance, the suggestion that he had a method. But if he had not a method, he had a mystery, an open secret, the habit of seeing every object before him in a perspective of wide culture and observation.—TOVEY, DUNCAN C., 1897, *Reviews and Essays in English Literature, p. 71.*

As a writer upon morals and politics, he is characterized by the spirit of "sweetness and light," with a purpose to make reason and the will of God prevail. The results of his work are exceedingly great.—GEORGE, ANDREW J., 1898, *From Chaucer to Arnold, Types of Literary Art*, p. 662, note.

We admit fairly and freely that Mr. Arnold is a teacher, if not of truth, at least of half truths, and those of a very valuable kind. Indeed, could we but once convince ourselves, or become convinced, that the other half were already adequately taught and acted on, and that there is much danger of there being really too much taught, as Mr. Arnold maintains, we should be happy to adopt his theory, if not his application of it. His real fault is that in his laudable anxiety to propagate "Hellenism," "spontaneity of consciousness," "the desirability of a free play of thought on our stock notions," and so forth, he lamentably under-rates the value of the other great means towards the attainment of perfection which he calls "Hebraism," and which consists mainly in the development of the moral side of man's nature and the striving to reduce at once to practice whatever of light a man may have.—OAKESHOTT, B. N., 1898, *Matthew Arnold as a Poetical and Social Critic, Westminster Review*, vol. 149, pp. 161, 162.

Perhaps the most important utterance ["Essay in Criticism"] upon criticism in modern times.—GAYLEY, CHARLES MILLS, AND SCOTT, FRED NEWTON, 1899, *An Introduction to the Methods and Materials of Literary Criticism*, p. 10.

Some ten years ago, a band of self-appointed defenders of America and its institutions undertook to drive Matthew Arnold out of court with clubs and tomahawks. He was a snob, an aristocrat, an ignoramus, knowing nothing of American institutions and not much of anything else, without the ability even to use the English language correctly, on the hypothesis that he had anything to say. But such attacks really did more good than harm, since they convinced the judicious that the critic's verdict, "Thou ailest here, and here," was timely and well-grounded; and an increasing number of Americans went on reading Mr. Arnold's works with profit and enjoyment. . . . One who reads him with care can see that he has no quarrel with those who can base upon the data at hand a more comprehensive belief than his. He is to be read, then, not for detailed information as to what one should believe and what reject in religious matters, but to place the curb of intelligent discrimination upon one's belief, and especially to check the habit of demanding of them that are weak in the faith tests that are not fundamentally necessary and are sure to repel.—JOHNSON, W. H., 1899, *The "Passing" of Matthew Arnold, The Dial*, vol. 27, pp. 351, 353.

If a single word could resume him, it would be "academic;" but, although this perfectly describes his habitual attitude even as a poet, it leaves aside his chaste diction, his pictorial vividness, and his overwhelming pathos. The better, which is also the larger, part of his poetry is without doubt immortal. His position is distinctly independent, while this is perhaps less owing to innate originality than to the balance of competing influences. Wordsworth saves him from being a mere disciple of Goethe, and Goethe from being a mere follower of Wordsworth. As a critic he repeatedly evinced a happy instinct for doing the right thing at the right time. Apart from their high intellectual merits, the seasonableness of the preface to the poems of 1853, of the lectures on Homer, and those on the Celtic spirit, renders these monumental in English literature. His great defect as a critic is the absence of a lively æsthetic sense; the more exquisite beauties of literature do not greatly impress him unless as vehicles for the communication of ideas.—GARNETT, RICHARD, 1901, *Dictionary of National Biography, Supplement*, vol. I, p. 74.

Doubtless in spite of having been perhaps prematurely disseminated he will be preserved and handed on to Bacon's "next ages." There is certainly enough pollen in his essays to flower successively in many seasons and as long as the considerations to which he consecrated his powers interest readers who care also for clear and charming and truly classic prose. . . . He had, it is true, a remarkable gift for analysis—witness his Emerson, his clairvoyant separation of the strains of Celtic, Greek, Teutonic inspiration in English poetry, his study of Homeric translation, his essays on Keats and Gray. But in spite of his own advocacy of criticism as the art of "seeing the object as in itself it really is," and his assertion that "the main thing is to get one's self out of the way and let humanity judge," he was himself never content with this. He is always concerned with the significance of the object once clearly perceived and determined. And though he never confuses the judgment of humanity (to use his rather magniloquent expression) by argumentation and special pleading, his treatment of his theme is to the last degree idiosyncratic. . . . It is obvious, therefore, that his criticism differs in kind from that of other writers. It differs especially from that most in vogue at the present time. It is eminently the antithesis of impressionist criticism. It has behind it what may fairly pass for a body of doctrine, though a body of doctrine as far as possible removed from system and pedantry.— BROWNELL, W. C., 1901, *Matthew Arnold, Scribner's Magazine*, vol. 30, pp. 105, 107, 108.

Arnold's prose has little trace of the wistful melancholy of his verse. It is almost always urbane, vivacious, light-hearted. The classical bent of his mind shows itself here, unmixed with the inheritance of romantic feeling which colors his poetry. Not only is his prose classical in quality, by virtue of its restraint, of its definite aim, and of the dry white light of intellect which suffuses it; but the doctrine which he spent his life in preaching is based upon a classical ideal, the ideal of symmetry, wholeness, or, as he daringly called it, *perfection*.—MOODY, WILLIAM VAUGHN, AND LOVETT, ROBERT MORSS, 1902, *A History of English Literature*, p. 335.

If he had never written prose the world would never have known him as a humorist. And that would have been an intellectual loss not easily estimated. How pure, how delicate, yet how natural and spontaneous his humour was, his friends and associates knew well; and . . . the humour of his writings was of exactly the same tone and quality as the humour of his conversation. It lost nothing in the process of transplantation. As he himself was fond of saying, he was not a popular writer, and he was never less popular than in his humorous vein. In his fun there is no grinning through a horse-collar, no standing on one's head, none of the guffaws, and antics, and "full-bodied gaiety of our English Cider-Cellar." But there is a keen eye for subtle absurdity, a glance which unveils affectation and penetrates bombast, the most delicate sense of incongruity, the liveliest disrelish for all the moral and intellectual qualities which constitute the Bore, and a vein of personal raillery as refined as it is pungent. Sydney Smith spoke of Sir James Mackintosh as "abating and dissolving pompous gentlemen with the most successful ridicule." The words not inaptly describe Arnold's method of handling personal and literary pretentiousness. — RUSSELL, GEORGE W. E., 1904, *Matthew Arnold (Literary Lives)*, p. 13.

Sir Francis Hastings Charles Doyle
1810–1888

Born, at Nunappleton, Yorkshire, 22 Aug. 1810. Educated at Eton till 1828. Matric., Ch. Ch., Oxford, 6 June 1828; B. A., 1832; B. C. L., 1843; M. A., 1847; Fellow of All Souls Coll., 1835–45. Student of Inner Temple, 11 Oct. 1832; called to Bar, 17 Nov. 1837. Succeeded to Baronetcy on his father's death, 6 Nov. 1839. Married Sidney Williams-Wynn, 12 Dec. 1844. Prof. of Poetry, Oxford, and Fellowship (for second time) at All Souls' Coll., 1867–77; created D. C. L., 11 Dec. 1877. Receiver-General of Customs, 1846–69; Commissioner of Customs, 1869–83. Died, 8 June 1888. *Works:* "Miscellaneous Verses," 1834; "The Two Destinies," 1844; "The Duke's Funeral" [1852]; "The Return of the Guards, and other Poems," 1886; "Lectures delivered before the University of Oxford, 1868," 1869; "Lectures on Poetry. . . . Second series," 1877; "Robin Hood's Bay," 1878; "Reminiscences and Opinions," 1886. He *translated:* Sophocles' "Œdipus Tyrannus," 1849.—SHARP, R. FARQUHARSON, 1897, *A Dictionary of English Authors*, p. 86.

PERSONAL

The "reminiscences" of Sir Francis are much pleasanter reading than his political "opinions." As might have been surmised from the martial enthusiasm which inspires the best of his poems, he is born of a race of soldiers.—OSBORN, R. D., 1886, *Sir Francis Doyle, The Nation*, vol. 43, p. 505.

Doyle was naturally indolent, but at times he could be very industrious. . . . As a young man he had the character of being somewhat eccentric, which, however, amounted to nothing more than this, that with undoubted gifts of genius, he was apt to betray an innocent superiority to conventional forms and usages, so that on occasions when it was necessary for him to appear in a strictly proper and becoming dress he was fain to call in the aid of his friend Hope to tie his neckcloth, just as my uncle the poet was wont to have recourse to his wife and daughter for similar purposes.—WORDSWORTH, CHARLES, 1891, *Annals of My Early Life*, 1806–1846, pp. 96, 98.

GENERAL

He too is of the reflective and not the impassioned school of poetry, and has evidently sat, an admiring disciple, at the feet of Wordsworth, whom he has commemorated in a graceful and pleasing sonnet. The reader will not find in his pages that marked originality and creative power which are the indications of a great poet, but he will not turn aside from them, if he will be content to derive pleasure from communing with a mind, that is accustomed to reflect and observe, that thinks always correctly and sometimes vigorously, that is not unfruitful in images of gentle beauty and delicate grace, and which utters its sentiments in flowing verse and in the language of a scholar. He does not appear to have written poetry from an irresistible impulse, but to have cultivated the accomplishment of verse as a graceful appendage to other intellectual employments and exercises, and an agreeable relaxation from graver and severer studies. Consequently his poems have no marked individuality, and no peculiar characteristics to distinguish them from others of the same class; but they please us by a more than common proportion of those poetical conceptions and capacities which are found, in a greater or less degree, in every person of refined taste and cultivated habits of thought. Perhaps their most distinctive attributes are a certain delicacy of sentiment showing a mind of uncommon fineness of organization, and with a more than common proportion of feminine elements, a taste for ideal forms of beauty, and an instinctive repugnance to every thing low, unhandsome, and debasing. His poetry is of that kind, which inspires us with much respect for the personal character of the author.—HILLARD, GEORGE S., 1842, *Recent English Poetry*, North American Review, vol. 55, p. 237.

No reader of Sir Francis Doyle's poems will need to be told that he is an enthusiastic lover of horses. His poem on the "Doncaster St. Leger" is not only a most spirited and exciting presentation of the incidents of a great race, but, so far as we know, it is unique of its kind in English literature. It shows how much stirring poetry can be elicited from the most prosaic occurrences when there is a poet's eye present to discern it.—OSBORN, R. D., 1886, *Sir Francis Doyle*, The Nation, vol. 43, p. 506.

His gifts were so great and varied, one almost fancies greater than his use of them, and he gave this same impression from his Eton days, as the letters of Arthur Hallam, Mr. Gladstone, and my father-in-law seem to me to show. He leaves some lyrics which will, I think, live long.—PALGRAVE, FRANCIS TURNER, 1888, *Journal, June; Francis Turner Palgrave, His Journals and Memoirs of his Life*, ed. Palgrave, p. 215.

Amongst modern poets Sir Francis Hastings Doyle, Bart., gained an important place, and made some lasting contributions to English poetry. Several of his poems are familiar to readers in the North of England, having special local interest. His best known productions are "The Private of the Buffs," "The Loss of the Birkenhead," and "The Spanish Mother."—ANDREWS, WILLIAM, 1888, *North Country Poets*, p. 57.

Author of some interesting reminiscences in prose, and in verse of some of the best songs and poems on military subjects to be found in the language.—SAINTSBURY, GEORGE, 1896, *A History of Nineteenth Century Literature*, p. 206.

Doyle is distinguished for the spirit and the martial ring of the ballads in which he celebrates deeds of daring. "The Red Thread of Honour," "The Private of the Buffs," and "Mehrab Khan" are pieces that take high rank among poems inspired by sympathy with the heroism of the soldier.—WALKER, HUGH, 1897, *The Age of Tennyson*, p. 258.

Sprung from a family many of whom had been famous as men of action, Doyle cherished a supreme admiration of heroism as well as a strong love of country. His poetic work is chiefly remarkable for his treatment of the ballad, a form of expression used by many English poets, and particularly by his favourite author, Sir Walter Scott. While these, however, had made the ballad archaic both in subject and expression, Doyle employed it for the treatment of contemporary events, and showed that modern deeds of national bravery were "as susceptible as any in the far past of free ballad treatment, with all the old freshness directness, and simplicty." His method has been successfully followed by subsequent writers. . . . At the same time it would convey a false impression not to observe that most of his work was commonplace pedestrian, and that though he often showed genuine poetic feeling he seldom found for it adequate expression. His verse is generally mechanical, rarely instinct with life or transfused with emotion.—CARLYLE, E. IRVING, 1901, *Dictionary of National Biography, Supplement*, vol. II, pp. 153, 154.

Sir Henry James Sumner Maine
1822–1888

Born 15th August 1822, from Christ's Hospital passed in 1840 to Pembroke College, Cambridge, where he won the Craven, and graduated in 1844 as senior classic and Chancellor's medalist. In 1845 he became a tutor of Trinity Hall, in 1847 regius professor of Civil Law, and in 1852 Reader on Jurisprudence to the Inns of Court. He was called to the bar in 1850, and went to India in 1862 as Legal Member of Council. In 1869 he was appointed professor of Comparative Jurisprudence at Oxford, and in 1871 to the Council of the Secretary of State for India, when he was created K. C. S. I. In 1877 he was elected Master of Trinity Hall at Cambridge, and in 1877 Whewell professor of International Law. He died at Cannes, February 3, 1888. It is by his work on the origin and growth of legal and social institutions that Maine will be best remembered. His books were "Ancient Law" (1861), "Village Communities in the East and West" (1871), "The Early History of Institutions" (1875), "Early Law and Custom" (1883), "Popular Government" (1885), and "International Law" (1888). A fundamental idea of Maine's was to make patriarchal power the germ of society. *See* Memoir by Sir M. E. Grant Duff (1892).—PATRICK AND GROOME, *eds.*, 1897, *Chambers's Biographical Dictionary*, p. 621.

PERSONAL

His method, his writings, and his speeches at the Indian Council Board have had a strong and lasting effect upon all subsequent ways of examining and dealing with these subjects, whether in science or practical politics. He possessed an extraordinary power of appreciating unfamiliar facts and apparently irrational beliefs, of extracting their essence and the principle of their vitality, of separating what still has life and use from what is harmful or obsolete, and of stating the result of the whole operation in some clear and convincing sentence.—LYALL, SIR ALFRED, 1887, *Law Quarterly Review*.

A man whose writings have been an honour to his age, and who did admirable service to the State; who had no enemies, and who has left on the minds of all those who had the privilege of knowing him well, an absolutely unclouded memory.—DUFF, SIR M. E. GRANT, 1892, *Sir Henry Maine, A Brief Memoir of His Life*, p. 1.

The delicacy of Maine's constitution must be remembered in all estimates of his career. It disqualified him from taking a part in the rougher warfare of life. He often appeared to be rather a spectator than an actor in affairs, and a certain reserve was the natural guard of an acute sensibility. To casual observers he might appear as somewhat cold and sarcastic, but closer friends recognised both the sweetness of his temper and the tenderness of his nature. His refinement of understanding made him alive to the weak side of many popular opinions, and he neither shared nor encouraged any unqualified enthusiasm. His inability for drudgery shows itself by one weakness of his books, the almost complete absence of any reference to authorities. He extracted the pith of a large book, it is said, as rapidly as another man could read one hundred pages, and the singular accuracy of his judgments was often admitted by the most thorough students; but he gave his conclusions without producing, or perhaps remembering, the evidence upon which they rested. It is a proof of the astonishing quickness, as well as of the clearness and concentration of his intellect, that, in spite of physical feebleness, he did so much work of such high qualities.—STEPHEN, LESLIE, 1893, *Dictionary of National Biography*, vol. XXXV, p. 345.

His friends thought, when he was gone, not of the great writer whom the world had lost, but the genial, sweet-spirited, enlightened gentleman who would never again make their gatherings bright with his presence. The general world of society and affairs had never known Sir Henry Maine. He gave the best energies of his life to public duty,—to the administration of India; but he rendered his service at quiet council boards, whose debates were of business, not of questions of politics, and did not find their way into the public prints. He had no taste for publicity; preferred the secluded groups that gathered about him in the little hall of Corpus Christi, to any assembly of the people. He did not have strong sympathies, indeed, and disdained to attempt the general ear. He loved knowledge, and was indifferent to opinion. It perhaps went along with his delicate physique and sensitive temperament that he should shrink from crowds and distrust the populace.—WILSON, WOODROW, 1898, *A Lawyer with a Style, Atlantic Monthly, vol.* 82, p. 374.

GENERAL

In his "Ancient Law" Mr. Maine has shown that the inductive method is the only way to attain clear notions as to the origin of those elementary legal conceptions which are incorporated into our social systems; and the primeval institutions and customs of India which have been handed down, almost unchanged, to the present generation—such as the village community, the undivided family, the practice of adoption taking the place of testation—furnished him with admirable subjects for the application of that method.—STRACHEY, SIR JOHN, 1868, *Speech.*

Probably no more accurate and profound researches and generalization in the field of jurisprudence have ever been made than those incorporated in this ["Ancient Law"] volume. . . . For the general student this ["Village Communities"] is one of the most valuable, and quite the most interesting of Sir Henry Maine's works. It is not only written in the judicious spirit always characteristic of the author, but it is also the fruit of special study and observation. The author has availed himself of the profound and minute researches of Von Maurer, and has turned to good account his own extensive observations and studies in India.— ADAMS, CHARLES KENDALL, 1882, *A Manual of Historical Literature*, pp. 83, 84.

Some, at least, of these essays were, on their anonymous appearance, attributed to Lord Salisbury; but what was then high praise now seems like the bitterest satire. . . . More ingenious than profound, more epigrammatic than original, more dazzling than persuasive, this work would be worthier of the present Prime Minister than of the author of "Ancient Law." . . . The history of government is studied apart from the more general history of society and general civilization, with the result that the whole subject is thrown into uncertainty and confusion.—BENN, ALFRED W., 1885, *Popular Government, The Academy, vol.* 28, p. 300.

It is hardly possible that he should discuss any subject within the publicist's range, without bringing into light some of its less superficial aspects, and adding observations of originality and value to the stock of political thought. To set people thinking at all on the more general and abstract truths of that great subject which is commonly left to be handled lightly, unsystematically, fragmentarily, in obedience to the transitory necessities of the day, by Ministers, members of Parliament, journalists, electors, and the whole host who live intellectually and politically from hand to mouth, is in itself a service of all but the first order. Service of the very first order is not merely to propound objections, but to devise working answers, and this is exactly what Sir Henry Maine abstains from doing.—MORLEY, JOHN, 1886, *Maine on Popular Government, Studies in Literature,* p. 105.

For the present we may at least say, looking to our own science of law, that the impulse given by Maine to its intelligent study in England and America can hardly be overrated. Within living memory the Common Law was treated merely as a dogmatic and technical system. Historical explanation, beyond the dates and facts which were manifestly necessary, was regarded as at best an idle ornament, and all singularities and anomalies had to be taken as they stood, either without any reason or (perhaps oftener) with a bad one. . . . A certain amount of awakening was no doubt affected by the analytical school, as Maine taught us to call it. . . . But the scientific study of legal phenomena such as we really find them had no place among us. . . . Maine not only showed that this was a possible study, but showed that it was not less interesting and fruitful than any in the whole range of the moral sciences. At one master-stroke he forged a new and lasting bond between law, history, and anthropology. Jurisprudence itself has become a study of the living growth of human society through all its stages, and it is no longer possible for law to be dealt with as a collection of rules imposed on societies as it were by accident, nor for the resemblances and differences of the laws of different societies to be regarded as casual. — POLLOCK, SIR FREDERICK, 1888-90, *Sir Henry Maine and his Work, Oxford Lectures and Other Discourses*, pp. 158, 159.

The slow irresistible pressure of Law is the strongest British influence now working in India, and Maine, from 1862 to his death, had more to do than any other single man, I will not say with making Indian law, but with determining what Indian law should be. That and the new spirit which he breathed into juridical studies in England, and to some extent in other countries of the West, are his chief titles to the remembrance of posterity. His published works are in the hands of all who care for the studies which he cultivated, and the remainder of this volume will be devoted to giving some idea of the nature and extent of his work during the years when he acted directly upon Indian legislation and government, at Calcutta and Simla.—DUFF, SIR MOUNTSTUART ELPHINSTONE GRANT, 1892, *Sir Henry Maine, A Brief Memoir of His Life*, p. 83.

Maine treated his great subject not only with similar learning and logic, but with the advantages of a lucid style and much fine literary power,—making a very abstruse subject, handled in a new and unusual method, a book as agreeable to read as it was valuable and important in historical science. If it is too much to say that he "created a new method for the study of legal ideas and the institutions founded upon them," it is yet certain that no one of his time had used that method so powerfully.—OLIPHANT, MARGARET O. W., 1892, *The Victorian Age of English Literature*, p. 551.

Few writers of our time could claim the phrase "mitis sapientia" as Maine could, though it is possible that he was a little too much given to theories.—SAINTSBURY, GEORGE, 1896, *A History of Nineteenth Century Literature*, p. 358.

It ["Ancient Law"] has two great merits. It is written in a most lucid, pleasant style, and it is decidedly original in substance. Maine's design is far less ambitious than Buckle's; but for that very reason his performance is more adequate. The most conspicuous distinction between the two is that the later writer shows in far greater measure than his predecessor the modern sense of the importance of origins. It was this that gave his work importance. To a great extent the task of recent historians has been to trace institutions to their source, and explain their later development by means of the germs out of which they have grown. In this respect Maine was a pioneer, and his later work was just a fuller exposition of the principles at the root of "Ancient Law." His "Village Communities" and his "Early History of Institutions" are both inspired by the same idea. In his "Popular Government" he may be said to break new ground; but it is easy to see the influence on that book of the author's prolonged study of early forms of society. These later books are not perhaps intrinsically inferior to "Ancient Law," but they are less suggestive, just because so much of the work had been already done by it.— WALKER, HUGH, 1897, *The Age of Tennyson*, p. 135.

I heard Maine deliver in the hall of my college at Oxford the lectures which were published in his book entitled "Village Communities in the East and West;" and his pregnant suggestions have constantly guided my work in India, and throughout my life have chiefly inspired my studies, whenever I have been able to find time for any studies at all. For his far-reaching, penetrating, and illuminating genius I have a profound admiration. . . . I pass from Maine the Law Member of Council to Maine the writer of books. He never constructed a complete science of jurisprudence, still less a complete science of sociology. His works have been described as groups of essays rather than systematic treatises; but they appear to me to possess a certain unity. He never published a revised edition of "Ancient Law," but that book contains the germinal ideas out of which all else he wrote was unfolded. . . . I remember being told at Oxford, in the year 1870 or thereabouts, that Maine was anxious to write his "Village Communities" before he forgot what he had to say. It was delightful to hear of something so entirely human in one I regarded as so great. The first chapter of that book is, I think, from an Indian point of view, one of the most important that he ever wrote. . . . The achievement known to the learned world is Maine's account of the early history of property, the process of feudalisation, and the decay of feudal property in France and England. This includes his description of the Irish tribe, and his discussions of village communities in the East and West. The subject, in fact, is nothing less than his view of the general history of property in land. In one section of this extensive field of research a whole literature has sprung up chiefly, though not exclusively, from seed of his sowing. Phear, Seebohm, Gomme, and Baden-Powell, amongst others have all written on the village community, and all acknowledge their obligations to Maine. One effect in India of Maine's teaching here is that we can never again confound Indian and English ideas of landed property.—TUPPER, CHARLES LEWIS, 1898, *India and Sir Henry Maine, Journal of the Society of Arts*, vol. 46, pp. 390, 391, 394, 395, 397.

Sir Henry Maine was a lawyer with a style, and belongs, by method and genius, among men of letters. The literary world looks askance upon a lawyer, and is slow to believe that the grim and formal matter of his studies can by any alchemy of style be transmuted into literature. Calfskin seems to it the most unlikely of all bindings to contain anything engaging to read. Lawyers, in their turn, are apt to associate the word "literature" almost exclusively with works of the imagination, and to think "style" a thing wholly misleading and unscientific. . . . He moves in a large region, where it is refreshing to be of his company, where wide prospects open with every comment, and you seem, as he talks, to be upon a tour of the world. . . . Maine disliked what is called "fine" writing, as every man of taste must; and he was no coiner of striking phrases. . . . The work which has since held the attention of the world. . . . His now celebrated volume on "Ancient Law," his first book, and unquestionably his greatest. It was the condensed and perfected substance of his lectures at the Inn of Court. It was in one sense not an original work: it was not founded on original research. Its author had broken no new ground and made no discoveries. He had simply taken the best historians of Roman law,—great German scholars chiefly—had united and vivified, extended and illustrated, their conclusions in his own comprehensive way; had drawn, with that singularly firm hand of his, the long lines that connected antique states of mind with unquestioned but otherwise inexplicable modern principles of law; had made obscure things luminous, and released a great body of cloistered learning into the world, where common students read and plod and seek to understand. . . . The book ["Popular Government"] abounds in good things. Its examination of the abstract doctrines which underlie democracy is in his best manner,—every sentence of it tells. The style is pointed, too, and animated beyond his wont,—hurried here and there into a quick pace by force of feeling, by ardour against an adversary. He finds, besides, with his unerring instinct for the heart of a question, just where the whole theory and practice of democracy show the elements that will make it last or fail. . . . Maine's style in "Popular Government" is, as I have said, much more spirited than his style elsewhere, and smacks sometimes with a very racy flavor.—WILSON, WOODROW, 1898, *A Lawyer with a Style, Atlantic Monthly*, vol. 82, pp. 363, 364, 367, 372.

Laurence Oliphant
1829–1888

Born, at Capetown, 1829. At school near Salisbury till 1841. In Ceylon (where his father was Chief Justice) with private tutor, 1841–46. Travelled on Continent with his parents, 1846–48. Returned with them to Ceylon and became private sec. to his father. To England with his mother, 1851. Student at Lincoln's Inn, 1851. Began to study law at Edinburgh, 1852. Tour in Russia, winter of 1852–53. On staff of "Daily News," 1853. In Canada, as Sec. to Lord Elgin, 1853–54. In Crimea during the War, 1855, as correspondent to the "Times." In America, 1856. Sec. to Lord Elgin on the latter's mission to China and Japan, 1857–59. Visit to Italy, 1860. First Sec. to Legation at Yeddo, June 1861; returned to England, wounded, same year. Started "The Owl," with Sir A.

Borthwick and others, 1864; contrib. to nos. 1–10. Frequent contributor to "Blackwood's Mag.," from 1865. M. P. for Stirling Burghs, 1865; resigned, 1867. To America, to join Thomas Lake Harris's community at Brocton, 1867. His mother joined him there, 1868. Returned to England, 1870. Correspondent for "The Times" during Franco-Prussian War, 1870–72. Married (i.) Alice Le Strange, June, 1872. Returned to Brocton with wife and mother, 1873. Employed by Harris in commercial and financial business; his wife sent to California. In Palestine in connection with Jewish colonization there, 1879–80. Joined by his wife in England, 1880. Visit to Egypt with her, winter of 1880–81. To Brocton on account of illness of his mother, May 1881; she died soon afterwards. Rupture of relations with Harris. To Palestine with his wife, 1882; settled at Haifa. Wife died, 2 Jan. 1887. Visit to America, 1888. Married (ii.) Rosamond Dale Owen, 16 Aug. 1888. Died at Twickenham, 23 Dec. 1888. *Works:* "A Journey to Katmandu," 1852; "The Russian Shores of the Black Sea," 1853 (2nd edn. same year); "Minnesota and the Far West," 1855; "The Transcaucasian Provinces the proper field of operation for a Christian Army," 1855; "The Transcaucasian Campaign," 1856; "Narrative of the Earl of Elgin's Mission to China and Japan" (2 vols.), 1859; "Patriots and Filibusters," 1860; "Universal Suffrage and Napoleon the Third," 1860; "On the Present State of Political Parties in America," 1866; "Piccadilly," 1870 (2nd edn. same year); "The Land of Gilead," 1880; "The Land of Khemi," 1882; "Traits and Travesties," 1882; "Altiora Peto," 1883; "Sympneumata," 1885; "Massollam," 1886; "Episodes in a Life of Adventure," 1887; "Haifa," 1887; "Fashionable Philosophy," 1887; "The Star in the East," 1887; "Scientific Religion," 1888. *Life:* by Mrs. Oliphant, 1891.—SHARP, R. FARQUHARSON, 1897, *A Dictionary of English Authors*, p. 216.

PERSONAL

New and unlooked-for developments have been vouchsafed to us since our marriage, chief among them a realization of the exquisite union awaiting humanity when all jealousies and divisions shall have been merged in the supreme desire to become one with our fellow-creatures, and through them with our God. We realize that our union, instead of separating my husband from the sainted wife whose influence overshadowed him as he wrote the pages of his book, has, in truth, bound him only the more closely, for she has become so atomically welded with me, that we, the wife in the unseen and the wife in the seen, have become as one; her life is poured through me as an instrument doubling my own affectional consciousness. Truly, when we come to realize that all sense of division between the fragments of God, called human beings, is an utterly false sense, then shall we be prepared for the in-pouring of the perfect, the universal life.—OLIPHANT, ROSAMOND, 1888, *Scientific Religion*, Preface to the American Ed., p. ii.

He was one of the men who are never young. His spirit was indomitable, and even his bodily frame, though shaken by illness, still so elastic and capable of sudden recoveries, that to associate the idea of death with his wonderful personality was the most difficult thing in the world. . . . This man, by whose loss the world is so much the poorer, was an adventurer, traveller, a born statesman, a trained diplomatist, a keen and shrewd man of business. No man was keener to see an opportunity or an advantage, or more intent upon work and production; no man ever loved action and movement more completely, or had a more cordial, almost boyish, pleasure in being in the heart of all that was going on. Yet above all, and in the midst of all his perpetual business, his pleasures, his love of society, he was a visionary—one of the race to which the unseen is always more present than the palpable.—OLIPHANT, MARGARET O. W., 1889, *Laurence Oliphant, Blackwood's Magazine*, vol. 145, p. 280.

He had held great employments, he had also been a day-labourer and a pedlar. Himself a gentleman of good Scottish descent, and finding his natural place in good society, he had friends alike among princes and beggars. To most people he appeared as a charming element in society, to many as a keen practical man of business, to some as a visionary fanatic, to a select few as an inspired prophet of the Lord, the founder of a new development of Christianity. But in whatever guise he might appear, no one could fail to feel that he was interesting. To him had been given, in unusually full measure, that mysterious indefinable charm the presence of which condones such serious faults, the absence of which goes so far towards neutralizing even transcendent virtues.— DUFF, LADY A. J. GRANT, 1889, *Laurence Oliphant, Contemporary Review*, vol. 55, p. 179.

Oliphant's life seems a lost one, save as a beacon to warn others.—LEISCHING, LOUIS, 1891, *Personal Reminiscences of Laurence Oliphant.*

If we are to consider his life a failure, so also must we consider the lives of all men and women who faithfully follow the light they have, unless that light should chance to guide them where they can lounge in easy chairs and sleep on beds of down.— LEWIN, WALTER, 1891, *Laurence Oliphant, The Academy*, vol. 40, p. 30.

Though of British parentage, Laurence Oliphant was born in Africa, spent more than two-thirds of his life out of England, and never remained more than a year or two at a time in the land of his fathers. Travel was his education, travel was his livelihood, travel was his heaven, and to be kept from travel was his hell. . . . From thirty years on to nearly three-score, he remained the same rolling stone. . . . He appears to have been incapable of a generous enthusiasm for the great literary men of his age. His reading was always limited, and he had no correspondence with writers of note. We see, indeed, in his case the strange phenomenon of a prolific and much vaunted writer without any taste or appreciation for poetry or *belles lettres*. It was this lack of taste that made it possible for Oliphant to pin his faith to such an impostor as the author of "The Great Republic: A Poem of the Sun," Thomas Lake Harris, whom he styled "the greatest poet of the age, as yet, alas! unknown to fame." It was this same lack that enabled him to accept as poetry some doggerel rhymes he had himself produced, during his separation from his wife, under the alleged influence of a spiritual "counterpart" in Heaven. Nor was his taste in other departments of art superior to his taste in literature, as is proved by his excessive admiration for Russian architecture. ANDERSON, EDWARD PLAYFAIR, 1891, *Laurence Oliphant, The Dial*, vol. 12, pp. 138, 140.

His observations were sharp and severe, but his political doctrines were of unswerving rectitude, and his judgments on men and things were both caustic and infallible. . . . He was a man who could not submit to discipline in the ordinary business of life. He lost his temper if he received any orders, and he resigned at the first remark that interfered with his arrangements.— BLOWITZ, HENRI GEORGES ADOLPHE OPPERDE, 1891, *Another Chapter of My Memoirs, Harper's Magazine*, vol. 82. pp. 292, 299.

His career as a whole, though brilliant in parts, was a melancholy waste of grand opportunities and a misuse of splendid talents . . . . At all stages of his career, Oliphant was a profoundly religious man; but his religion was not that of the majority; the system which he adopted for his own use did not wholly satisfy him, and he suffered from an abnormal development of one side of his nature. Even when under the baneful domination of Mr. Harris, he engaged in enterprises requiring a cool head and in adventures requiring a brave heart. He was a peculiar compound of mysticism as beautiful but as barren as moonshine, and of practical good sense; indeed, his business capacity was higher than his talent for philosophising. His most useful books are those telling of his explorations in the Holy Land; the most sensible of his actions were those which related to restoring its former prosperity and populousness to Palestine.—RAE, W. FRASER, 1891, *A Modern Mystic, Temple Bar*, vol. 93, pp. 413, 427.

Brilliant, versatile, and accomplished we all knew Oliphant to be, and yet there was some deep defect in his composition which prevented him from reaching the distinction to which his natural abilities, had they been accompanied with steadfastness of purpose, would undoubtedly have carried him. Whatever he undertook to do he did well, but when he had done it he had a tendency to fly off from that particular field of effort, and to take up something new. He was the very man, one might have supposed, to succeed in the diplomatic service; but somehow or other he allowed all his chances to slip through his fingers. He had not the requisite concentration of mind or sustained industry to bring him to the front at the bar, to which he once thought of devoting himself, and even the pursuit of literature he followed in an uncertain, irregular, spasmodic fashion.— JENNINGS, L. J., 1891, *Laurence Oliphant, Macmillan's Magazine*, vol. 64, p. 176.

The charm of Oliphant's alert and versatile intellect and sympathetic character was recognised by a wide circle of friends. It was felt not least by those who most regretted the strange religious developments which led to the waste of his powers and his enslavement to such a prophet as Harris. He was beloved for his boyish simplicity and the warmth of heart which appeared through all his illusions. Suggestions of insanity were, of course, made, but apparently without definite reasons. Remarkable talents without thorough training have thrown many minds off their balance, and Oliphant's case is only exceptional for the singular combination of two apparently inconsistent careers. Till his last years, at any rate, his religious mysticism did not disqualify him for being also a shrewd financier, a charming man of the world, and a brilliant writer.—STEPHEN, LESLIE, 1895, *Dictionary of National Biography*, vol. XLII, p. 137.

GENERAL

"Piccadilly" has just enough of sketchy carelessness and improbability to pass for originality, and to lead many people into thinking that the author could do much greater things if he liked. How far "Altiora Peto" has complicated or dispelled this notion it is impossible to say, though it is said to have been favourably received. We are, therefore, the more bound to confess at once that we have found it entirely dull and uninteresting, both in detail and as a whole. . . . After searching diligently and anxiously we really cannot find a single thing to praise in this book, unless it be the grammar and spelling, and the big print and thick paper; but all that is a poor compliment. Of course, one feels that Mr. Oliphant is a practised writer, and a man of ability and culture, and that there is nothing to reprobate or make game of in his work. All the same, it is as clear as his print that he has no more idea of what a novel should be than a mummy, and that he never can and never will write a novel worth yawning over.—PURCELL, E., 1883, *Altiora Peto, The Academy*, vol. 24, p. 240.

He has taken little or no pains; he has insufficient knowledge of many subjects of which he treats; the book ["Haifa"] is scrappy, careless, and unconnected, being a mere series of hasty letters scribbled off for the columns of a New York newspaper, and reprinted without arrangement, condensation, or due revision; and yet, in spite of all these defects, it possesses the delightful and indescribable flavour of genius.—TAYLOR, ISAAC, 1887, *Haifa, The Academy*, vol. 31, p. 319.

By an obvious law of its evolutionary progress physical science has of late years passed into the region of the infinitesimally minute. . . . It is a field in which Mr. Oliphant's imagination runs riot to an excess which I at least have never seen surpassed. . . . He explores the world of spirits with a self assurance which no materialist investigating the laws of matter could possibly rival.—OWEN, JOHN, 1888, *Scientific Religion, The Academy*, vol. 34, p. 81.

In 1888 he published "Scientific Religion," perhaps the least read of his works, though it was the one which he valued himself the most. It contains the history of the opinions he finally reached. The style is difficult and somewhat repellent, and the ideas extremely hard of comprehension to ordinary readers, while it is difficult to understand the union of belief in the verbal inspiration of the canon, with profound distrust of the Churches which fixed that canon. Still there are passages of great beauty, and in many points the differences between his ideas and those of the Christian Churches are rather matters of phraseology than of dogma.—DUFF, LADY A. J. GRANT, 1889, *Laurence Oliphant, Contemporary Review*, vol. 55, p. 187.

But the generation, not only of his contemporaries but of their children, must be exhausted indeed before the name of Laurence Oliphant will cease to conjure up memories of all that was most brilliant in intellect, most tender in heart, most trenchant in attack, most eager to succour in life. There has been no such bold satirist, no such cynic philosopher, no such devoted enthusiast, no adventurer so daring and gay, no religious teacher so absolute and visionary, in this Victorian age, now beginning to round towards its end, and which holds in its long and brilliant roll no more attractive and interesting name.—OLIPHANT, MARGARET O. W., 1891, *Memoir of the Life of Laurence Oliphant and of Alice Oliphant his Wife*, vol. II, p. 374.

Oliphant's failures, however, as a son, as a student, as a husband, as a lawyer, as a diplomatist, as a parliamentarian, as a religionist, as a business man, and as a colonizer did not prevent him from being an agreeable talker and a clever writer of travels and social satire. Doctor O. W. Holmes is said to have thought him the most interesting man in England. "The Tender Recollections of Irene Macgillicuddy" and "The Autobiography of a Joint Stock Company" are humorously exaggerated sketches of traits popularly supposed by the English to be characteristically American. "Fashionable Philosophy" and "Piccadilly" treat British idols in the same spirit. It would be a mistake to suppose that any of Oliphant's writings are destined to live, or to be read by posterity. The contemporary interest attaching to some of them was largely due to the fact that they were opportune, and of the nature of news touching localities such as the Crimea, to which the popular attention was turned. The interest was thus largely factitious, not inherent. Except in so far as they are bound up with "Blackwood's Magazine," copies of his works are seldom to be found in the bookstores or libraries.—ANDERSON, EDWARD PLAYFAIR, 1891, *Laurence Oliphant, The Dial, vol.* 12, *p.* 140.

This extraordinary book ["Sympneumata"] was dictated by Alice, written out by Laurence—revealed to the woman, but communicated by the man. It was their confession of faith, but more perplexing than enlightening. General Gordon read the MS. on his way to Khartoum, and wished it written from a more Biblical point of view, as, though, he said, "it contained nothing that was not to be found in the Bible, yet few would recognise it, and it would frighten the majority." ... In his writings sometimes the one nature is in full possession, sometimes the other. In "The Autobiography of a Joint-Stock Company," "The Tender Recollections of Irene Macgillicuddy," "The Episodes of a Wandering Life," "The Land of Gilead," "Haifa," &c., we have the bold satirist, the cynical philosopher, the boyish fun of the young *attaché,* or the observing traveller. In others, such as, "The Turkish Effendi," "Sympneumata," "Scientific Religion," &c., we have the opposite side—the dreamer, the mystic, who can find no use for life but to "cast it before the feet of the human brotherhood in ceaseless and organic service." Then we have "Piccadilly," "The Reconstruction of the Sheepfolds," "The Land of Khemi," "Altiora Peto," in which both natures intermingle. In "Piccadilly" we have keen satire mixed with the most serious exposition of the duty of living "the inner life." In "The Sheepfolds," he is in his most flippant mood, and yet the purport of it is to prove that there is "a dead silence on the part of the Church on the intricate problem of human life." "The Land of Khemi" is a rather bald description of the country in which he was travelling, not written in his usual fascinating style, but towards the end bringing forward his peculiar views on the Egyptians and Buddhism.—FAIRBAIRN, EVELINA, 1892, *Laurence Oliphant, Westminster Review, vol.* 137, *pp.* 508, 510.

Oliphant was a man of brilliant literary ability, and he proved that his brain was a keen, and a true, and a cultured one, not only by the books he produced but by the intelligence he displayed in that most difficult of tasks, a newspaper war-correspondent. We have, of course, only to read his novel of "Piccadilly" to see that a strong religious vein ran through his mind, but one would have thought that in his pious moods he would have looked at religion from a very high standard, and have treated it in the most dignified fashion.—ANGUS, J. KEITH, 1893, *The Booth-ism in the Life of Laurence Oliphant, Belgravia, vol.* 80, *p.* 305.

His "Piccadilly," very brightly written, is not a novel proper, but a satire directed against the various hypocrisies and corruptions of society. He had come, he says, to think that the world at large was a "lunatic asylum," a common opinion among persons not themselves conspicuous for sanity. He mentions in it "the greatest poet of the age," "Thomas Lake Harris," author of "The Great Republic: a Poem of the Sun." Harris is also typified as a mysterious prophet who meets the hero, and was, in fact, the head of a community in America. The creed appears to have been the usual mixture of scraps of misunderstood philosophy and science, with peculiar views about "physical sensations" caused by the life of Christ in man, and a theory that marriage should be a Platonic relation. Oliphant had also some belief in "spiritualism," though he came to regard it as rather diabolical than divine.—STEPHEN, LESLIE, 1895, *Dictionary of National Biography, vol.* XLII, *p.* 135.

Among the various later-day mystics who have laid claim to supernatural revelations in regard to the life and being of man, that brilliant and energetic Englishman, Laurence Oliphant, holds conspicuous place by reason of his many gifts, his position in society, the superb self-sacrifice he showed in the pursuit of occult knowledge, and his devotion to high spiritual ideals. In his beautiful and accomplished wife, Alice L'Estrange, he found a devoted co-worker. Through them was given to the world the singular work so strangely entitled "Sympneumata." . . . Through all his adventurous life, despite his literary ambitions, and beneath the polished exterior of a society man, Laurence Oliphant was ever of a deeply spiritual nature, finding no real happiness or solid satisfaction in either society, adventure, or gratified ambitions. . . . There is much in the book somewhat reasonable and truly inspiring and uplifting, especially in its portrayal of a grander humanity, strong, unselfish, pure, and intellectually great, filled with divinely tender love towards all in God's universe.—UNDERWOOD, SARA A., 1898, *Laurence Oliphant's "Sympneumata," The Arena*, vol. 20, pp. 526, 527, 534.

Richard Anthony Proctor
1837-1888

Astronomer, born at Chelsea, 23rd March 1837, graduated from St. John's, Cambridge, in 1860. Devoting himself from 1863 to astronomy, in 1866 he was elected F. R. A. S., and in 1873 made a lecturing tour in America. About this time he communicated to the R. A. S. some important papers on "The Milky Way," "The Transit of Venus," "Star Distribution," &c.; and his name is associated with the determination of the rotation of Mars, the theory of the solar corona, and stellar distribution. He charted the 324,198 stars contained in Argelander's great catalogue. His magazine *Knowledge* was founded in 1881, in which year he settled in the States; and he died at New York, 12th Sept. 1888.—PATRICK AND GROOME, *eds.* 1897, *Chambers's Biographical Dictionary*, p. 764.

PERSONAL

Personally, Proctor was a lovable man, endeared to his friends by a transparent simplicity of life and manners. His very faults were the faults of a noble nature. His pugnacity proceeded from a strong sense of justice and an earnest love of right; his frank self-assertion from a modest consciousness of his own true worth and the ridiculous disparity of native endowment between himself and his critics.—ALLEN, GRANT, 1888, *Richard Proctor, The Academy*, vol. 34, p. 193.

Proctor mixed very little in what is called "society;" he belonged to no club; it is surprising how few of his eminent contemporaries he knew personally. His delight was in his work, his appetite for knowledge was omnivorous, and he was happy in the companionship of wife and children, and of a chosen friend or two with whom to wind up the day over a rubber. He was a good oarsman, an excellent fencer, a doughty champion at chess; last, and not least he loved a romp with the children. It was within the social circle—narrow only in number—that the lovableness and simplicity of his character came out; he who, because he hated shams and quacks, of whatever profession, and all their works, was regarded by many outsiders as a querulous and agressive man, "never at peace unless he was fighting," was seen to be full of kindly considerateness and deference to men of smaller calibre and narrower culture; willing to learn of them, and fretfully anxious if he thought he had said anything that might hurt or vex them. . . . Proctor, let me add, was a man of deep religious feeling, looking with no glib complacency upon, or ready with cut-and-dried panaceas for, the sin and sorrow of the world. As with Epicurus, his quarrel was not with the gods, but with men's theories about them.—CLODD, EDWARD, 1888, *Richard Anthony Proctor, Knowledge*, vol. 11, p. 265.

In a series of papers communicated to the Royal Astronomical Society, he examined into the conditions of observation for the transits of 1874 and 1882 with great thoroughness and at much detail, and his opinions may be read in "Old and New Astronomy." . . . One of Mr. Proctor's greatest undertakings was the charting of the three hundred and twenty-four thousand stars contained in Argelander's Catalogue, showing the relation of stars down to the eleventh magnitude, with the Milky Way and its subsidiary branches. In a series of papers on "Star Distribution,"

"The Construction of the Milky Way," "The Distribution of Nebulæ and Star Clusters," and on "The Proper Motions of the Stars," etc., he completely disposed of the artificial theories which had been previously held regarding the Stellar universe. . . . Amid all this scientific activity Mr. Proctor found time for the lighter accomplishments. He was passionately fond of music, and played the piano with much delicacy of touch and feeling. He was an authority on whist, and was the author of a book on the subject; and he was at one time president of the British Chess Society in London.—MACQUEARY, HOWARD, 1893, *Richard Anthony Proctor, Astronomer, The Arena, vol.* 8, *p.* 566.

In 1884, at the close of a long lecture season in the United States, he purchased a home in St. Joseph, Missouri, and a winter residence at Lake Lawn, Florida. In social life Mr. Proctor was a genial, entertaining companion and a firm friend. As a conversationalist he had exceptional gifts. On the eighth of September, 1888, Mr. Proctor left his winter home, intending to sail for Europe a week later. In New York he was taken violently ill, and two days after his arrival died of yellow fever in one of the hospitals of that city.—WILLARD, CHARLOTTE R., 1894, *Richard A. Proctor, Popular Astronomy, vol.* I, *p.* 321.

His success on the lecture platform was from the first assured, and greatly increased his popularity. . . . His papers on the coming "Transit of Venus," in the same journal ["Knowledge"], involved him in an acrimonious controversy with the astronomer royal, Sir George Airy, as to the time and place for observing the transit. Proctor's views ultimately prevailed. Among his many gifts that of lucid exposition was the chief, and his main work was that of popularising science as a writer and lecturer. Yet he was no mere exponent. The highest value attaches to his researches into the rotation period of Mars, and to his demonstration of the existence of a resisting medium in the sun's surroundings by its effect on the trajectory of the prominences. His grasp of higher mathematics was proved by his treatise on the Cycloid, and his ability as a celestial draughtsman by his charting 324,198 stars from Argelander's "Survey of the Northern Heavens" on an equal surface projection. Many of his works were illustrated with maps drawn by himself with admirable clearness and accuracy. Versatile as profound, he wrote in "Knowledge" on miscellaneous subjects under several pseudonyms, and was a proficient in chess, whist, and on the pianoforte.— CLERKE, MISS E. M., 1896, *Dictionary of National Biography, vol.* XLVI, *p.* 420.

GENERAL

As an Astronomer and Mathematician he stands in the front rank of scientists, and to the most assiduous application and untiring industry he adds a brilliancy of imagination, lucidity of style, and a daring originality of purpose that give him a distinct and honorable place among the select and illustrious few who have widened the boundaries of exact knowledge, and devoted great intellectual power to the elucidation of some of the grandest themes in the arcana of the sciences.—FRASER, JOHN, 1873, *Richard Anthony Proctor, Scribner's Monthly, vol.* 7, *p.* 175.

It has been a favourite charge against him by a few ignorant and self-interested people, that he was simply a wonderfully clever expositor of other men's ideas and discoveries. This charge, I have noted, being made by men whose entire books are the merest paste-and-scissors compilations from the works of their predecessors, and whose worn illustrative woodcuts have done duty in text-books over and over and over again. Never was there a greater mistake, or (when deliberately uttered) a greater falsehood. Admitting that Proctor was unrivalled as a popular expositor of the most abstruse discoveries of others; he was very much more than this. He was a born mathematician, and most fertile in expedients, geometrical and analytical, in the solution of problems. I have spoken previously of his "Geometry and Cycloids," and the first edition of his "Moon," and may further advert to his papers scattered through the *Monthly Notices* of the Royal Astronomical Society, as indicative of his capacity for dealing with mathematical questions in an original manner. He applied the differential calculus to the solution of the most ludicrously diverse questions. He devoted great attention to cartography, and many of his maps, both celestial and terrestrial, are unsurpassed for their legibility, convenience, accuracy, and adaptability to the purposes for which they were designed. No existing maps of the stars visible to the naked eye can compare for efficiency with those in his

"Larger Star Atlas," with its ingenious projection of his own devising, whereby distortion is sensibly eliminated; while among his latest works his large charts for great circle sailing, and his maps of the world on the equidistant projection, are conspicuous for their beauty and accuracy.—NOBLE, WILLIAM, 1888, *Richard Anthony Proctor, Knowledge, vol.* 11, *p.* 266.

In 1881 he founded "Knowledge," a weekly scientific journal, but changed it to a monthly in 1885, and continued its editor until his death. His productiveness and versatility were remarkable. In the same issue of his journal he would appear in several *rôles* at once: as the editor and as Richard A. Proctor, writing on astronomy and mathematics; as Thomas Foster, criticising and carrying to its logical conclusions Dickens' unfinished novel of "Edwin Drood;" and then anonymously criticising and refuting the said Thomas Foster; as the whist editor and the chess editor and every other sort of editor demanded by the occasion. At the same time he was writing articles for other periodicals and newspapers, and he wrote well on every subject he handled.—BENJAMIN, MARCUS, 1888, *Appleton's Annual Cyclopædia, p.* 707.

I will not speak here of his astronomical work. Astronomers of a certain dry-as-dust school have long been in the habit of gauging that by their own measure. But those who knew him knew that for width of grasp and breadth of vision Proctor had few equals among modern thinkers. What he saw he saw with a philosophical clearness and a cosmical profundity only to be found within a very small and select circle. He could be properly judged by his peers alone. That his performance unhappily somehow fell short of his natural powers was due to the fact that the necessity for earning a living by the work of his brains compelled him to waste upon popularizing results and upon magazine articles a genius capable of the highest efforts. For myself, I do not remember to have met among contemporaries three other men who so impressed me with a consciousness of intellectual greatness.—ALLEN, GRANT, 1888, *The Academy, vol.* 34, *p.* 193.

No writer of this generation has done more to interest people in the high science of astronomy than the man whose name appears at the head of this article. Both by original investigation and by numerous popular treatises on the subject, Professor Proctor strove to promote a knowledge of astronomy. . . . His first book was on "Saturn and its System," and was published in 1865, at his own expense; its preparation occupied four years. It was very favorably received by astronomers, who recognized that a writer of exceptional ability had appeared. Geometrical conceptions were expounded with great clearness, and astronomical and historical details were explained with an ease and enthusiasm which attracted the reader. But though the book was well received by the reviewers, the public did not buy it, and he found, to his great disappointment, that its publication was a source of loss instead of profit. . . . Professor Proctor was the author of fifty-seven volumes on astronomy, the most popular of which is perhaps "Other Worlds than Ours." His last work, however, is his most important and complete production. It is entitled "Old and New Astronomy," and has been finished and published since his death by his friend Mr. Arthur C. Ranyard of England.—MACQUEARY, HOWARD, 1893, *Richard Anthony Proctor, Astronomer, The Arena, vol.* 8, *pp.* 562, 564, 565.

At a time when men of affairs as well as men of science turn with increasing interest to the subject of Astronomy, no small importance attaches to the character and work of the man of whom Professor Young could say, "As an expounder and popularizer of science he stands, I think, unrivaled in English literature." . . . The first work which Mr. Proctor published was a paper on "The Colors of Double Stars," which appeared in the Cornhill Magazine, in 1863, and for which the author received fifty dollars. This short paper of nine pages represented six weeks' labor, sometimes not more than four or five lines having been completed in a day. His first book, "Saturn and its System," was favorably received by scientific men, but proved a financial burden at a time when he especially needed remuneration. The years which followed were full of varied activities. One of his greatest undertakings was the "Charting of 324,000 stars contained in Argelander's Great Catalogue showing the relation of stars down to the 11th magnitude with the Milky Way and its subsidiary branches.—WILLARD, CHARLOTTE R., 1894, *Richard A. Proctor, Popular Astronomy, vol.* I.

Amos Bronson Alcott
1799–1888

An American philosophical writer and educator, one of the founders of the transcendental school of philosophy in New England; born at Wolcott, Conn., Nov. 29, 1799; died at Boston, March 4, 1888. From 1834–37 his private school in Boston, conducted on the plan of adapting the instruction to the individuality of each pupil, attracted attention. He was on terms of friendship with Emerson, Hawthorne, Channing, Thoreau, Margaret Fuller, and many other noted persons. After 1840 he lived in Concord, Mass., and was the projector and dean of the Concord school of philosophy. Lectures on speculative and practical subjects occupied his later years. His chief works are: "Orphic Sayings," contributed to the Dial (1840); "Tablets" (1868); "Concord Days" (1872); "Table Talk" (1877); "Sonnets and Canzonets" (1882); "Ralph Waldo Emerson, his Character and Genius" (1882;) "New Connecticut" (1886).—WARNER, CHARLES DUDLEY, ed. 1897, *Library of the World's Best Literature, Biographical Dictionary*, vol. XXIX, p. 10.

PERSONAL

He has been twice here, at considerable length; the second time, all night. He is a genial, innocent, simple-hearted man, of much natural intelligence and goodness, with an air of rusticity, veracity, and dignity withal, which in many ways appeals to one. The good Alcott: with his long, lean face and figure, with his gray worn temples and mild radiant eyes; all bent on saving the world by a return to acorns and the golden age; he comes before one like a kind of venerable Don Quixote, whom nobody can even laugh at without loving!—CARLYLE, THOMAS, 1842, *To Emerson, July 19; Correspondence of Carlyle and Emerson*, ed. Norton, vol. II, p. 8.

He is a great man and was made for what is greatest, but I now fear that he has already touched what best he can, and through his more than a prophet's egotism, and the absence of all useful reconciling talents, will bring nothing to pass, and be but a voice in the wilderness. As you do not seem to have seen him in his pure and noble intellect, I fear that it lies under some new and denser clouds.—EMERSON, RALPH WALDO, 1842, *To Carlyle, Oct. 15; Correspondence of Carlyle and Emerson*, ed. Norton, vol. II, p. 14.

Yonder, calm as a cloud, Alcott stalks in a dream,
And fancies himself in the groves Academe,
With the Parthenon nigh, and his olive-trees o'er him,
And never a fact to perplex or bore him,
With a snug room at Plato's, when night comes, to walk to,
And people from morning till midnight to talk to.

—LOWELL, JAMES RUSSELL, 1848, *A Fable for Critics*.

I had a good talk with Alcott this afternoon. He is certainly the youngest man of his age we have seen,—just on the threshold of life. When I looked at his gray hairs, his conversation sounded pathetic; but I looked again, and they reminded me of the gray dawn. He is getting better acquainted with Channing, though he says that if they were to live in the same house, they would soon sit with their backs to each other.—THOREAU, HENRY DAVID, 1848, *Letter to Emerson, Feb.*

To establish a school of philosophy had been the dream of Alcott's life; and there he sat as I entered the vestry of a church on one of the hottest days in August. He looked full as young as he did twenty years ago, when he gave us a "conversation" in Lynn.—MITCHELL, MARIA, 1879, *Life, Letters and Journals*, p. 246.

I remember one morning that Mr. Alcott spent with my husband and myself, many years ago, when his swift fancy, and slow speech, his uplifting habit of mind, his large charity, his beautiful benignity, all brought into play by the brilliant and chivalric spirit that met him, made it seem as if we had been visited by an angel in our Eden; and I have often thought since then what it was to her to have been bred and taught by such a being as that, to have lived in the daily receipt of such high thoughts, to have inherited something of such a nature. Possibly Louisa was indebted to her father in quite another fashion also; since she may have made the rebound into the practical and the successful through the pressure of exigencies arising from his life in the impractical.—SPOFFORD, HARRIET PRESCOTT, 1888, *Louisa May Alcott, The Chautauquan*, vol. 9, p. 160.

He was in some aspects at the level of Plato; yet in others hardly more than a crank: singular gifted in speculative insight, in ethical refinement and in flawless integrity, but as empty of practical sense, as destitute of practical energy, and as wild in fantastic whims and worthless in every day work, as any mere tramp on the high road of modern culture. . . . Of his fine spirit, his beautiful simplicity and purity of character, his deep wisdom in things of the spirit, and his measurably conservative temper among radical thinkers who regarded him as a leader, there could be no doubt. But very much that he said rose so far into the air of vague speculation as to lose all value and even lack all interest, and there remains little result of his long and singular life, except a name as perhaps a Yankee Pythagoras, who, for some rare thoughts and fine words, will have the fame of a philosopher with very little philosophy to show for it. His practical daughter did a work and made a mark a hundred fold better and deeper than that of her speculative and unpractical father.—TOWNE, E. C., 1888, *A Yankee Pythagoras, North American Review*, vol. 147, pp. 345, 346.

The most adroit soliloquizer I ever listened to, who delivered in a vestry-room a series of those remarkable "conversations"—versations with the *con* left out—for which he was celebrated.—FROTHINGHAM, OCTAVIUS BROOKS, 1891, *Recollections and Impressions*, p. 52.

At Concord I saw and spoke with Bronson Alcott, a strange, mystical, gentle old philosopher, very gracious, very wordy, rather incomprehensible.—LINTON, WILLIAM JAMES, 1894, *Threescore and Ten Years, 1820 to 1890, Recollections*, p. 216.

I clearly understood that Mr. Alcott was admirable; but he sometimes brought manuscript poetry with him, the dear child of his own Muse, and a guest more unwelcome than the *enfant terrible* of the drawing-room. There was one particularly long poem which he had read aloud to my mother and father; a seemingly harmless thing, from which they never recovered. Out of the mentions made of this effusion I gathered that it was like a moonlit expanse, quiet, somnolent, cool, and flat as a month of prairies. Rapture, conviction, tenderness, often glowed upon Alcott's features and trembled in his voice. I believe he was never once startled from the dream of illusive joy which pictured to him all high aims as possible of realization through talk.

Often he was so happy that he could have danced like a child; and he laughed merrily like one; and the quick, upward lift of his head, which his great height induced him to hold as a rule, slightly bent forward,— this rapid, playful *lift*, and the glance, bright and eager though not deep, which sparkled upon you, were sweet and good to see. Yet I have noticed his condition as pale and dolorous enough, before the event of his noble daughter's splendid success. But such was not his character; circumstances had enslaved him, and he appeared thin and forlorn by incongruous accident, like a lamb in chains. He might have been taken for a centenarian when I beheld him one day slowly and pathetically constructing a pretty rustic fence before his gabled brown house, as if at the unreasonable command of some latter-day Pharaoh. Ten years afterward he was, on the contrary, a Titan: gay, silvery-locked, elegant, ready to begin his life over again.—LATHROP, ROSE HAWTHORNE, 1897, *Memories of Hawthorne*, p. 415.

Although Emerson had a high opinion of Alcott, he seemed to me a shallow and illogical thinker, and I have always felt that the good opinion of Emerson was due rather to the fact that Alcott presented him with his own ideas served up in forms in which he no longer recognized them, and so appeared to Emerson as original. Such originality as he had was rather an oracular and often incomprehensible verbiage than a profundity of thought, but, as no one attempted to bring him to book, bewildered as his audience generally was by the novelty of the propositions he made or by their absurdity, he used to go on until suggestion, or breath, failed him. . . . Alcott was a drawing-room philosopher, the justice of whose lucubrations had no importance whatever, while his manner and his individuality gave to wiser people than I, the pleasure which belongs to the study of such a specimen of human nature. He amused and superficially interested, and he no doubt enjoyed his distorted reflections of the wisdom of wiser men as much as if he had been an original seeker.—STILLMAN, WILLIAM JAMES, 1901, *The Autobiography of a Journalist*, vol. I, pp. 219, 221.

GENERAL

Mr. Alcott is the great man, and Miss Fuller has not seen him. His book does him no justice, and I do not like to see it. I had not fronted him for a good while, and was willing to revise my opinion. But he has more of the god-like than any man I have ever seen, and his presence rebukes, and threatens, and raises. He *is* a teacher. I shall dismiss for the future all anxiety about his success. If he cannot make intelligent men feel the presence of a superior nature, the worse for them; I can never doubt him. His ideal is beheld with such unrivalled distinctness that he is not only justified but necessitated to condemn and to seek to upheave the vast actual, and cleanse the world.—EMERSON, RALPH WALDO, 1837, *To Margaret Fuller, May* 19; *A Memoir of Ralph Waldo Emerson*, ed. Cabot, vol. I, p. 279.

While he talks he is great, but goes out like a taper,
If you shut him up closely with pen, ink, and paper;
Yet his fingers itch for 'em from morning till night,
And he thinks he does wrong if he don't always write;
In this, as in all things, a lamb among men,
He goes to sure death when he goes to his pen.
—LOWELL, JAMES RUSSELL, 1848, *A Fable for Critics*.

He is a Yankee seer, who has suppressed every tendency in his Yankee nature toward "argufying" a point.—WHIPPLE, EDWIN PERCY, 1876–86, *American Literature and Other Papers*, ed. Whittier, p. 112.

Mr. Alcott was a teacher more than a man of letters. There is little system in his writings. They are mainly notes of thought but of such a kind as to charm and also stimulate to a high degree. . . . His was an original nature and self-poised. He sought for guidance within himself, not from his fellow men. He was not a disciple or follower of any one. At one time he was regarded as the leader of the "Transcendental" movement, but he lacked the practical qualities of which Emerson had so large a measure; yet he received and needed less influence from Emerson than, perhaps, any other member of that circle.—LEWIN, WALTER, 1888, *Amos Bronson Alcott and Louisa May Alcott*, The Academy, vol. 33, p. 206.

The "Orphic Sayings," which he contributed to "The Dial" (under Miss Fuller's administration) are perhaps most characteristic of him; he was rather mystical than profound; he delighted in forays into regions of the unknown—with whatever tentative or timid steps—and although he may have put a vehemence into his expression that would seem to imply that he was drifting in deep waters—one cannot forbear the conviction that 'twould be easy for this man of the explorative mentalities to touch ground with his feet (if he chose) —in all the bays where he swims.— MITCHELL, DONALD G., 1889, *American Lands and Letters, Leather-Stocking to Poe's "Raven,"* p. 188.

In Alcott's "Tablets" and "Concord Days" and papers reminiscent of "The Dial" period may be found interesting records—and echoes—of his great friend and spiritual master.—HAWTHORNE, JULIAN, AND LEMMON, LEONARD, 1891, *American Literature*, p. 147.

Alcott, as we have seen, attempted education for his profession, but found the world unready where his capacity lay, and himself incapable where the world's readiness was. Like Channing, although not quite so willing to accept the unobserved pathway of life, Alcott yielded to his lot with tolerable patience, and constantly sought that career of studious leisure and friendly companionship which should be the ideal of scholars. His gift of expression was not so much for writing as for speech, and conversation was his fine art; but at intervals during his whole life, he had written verses worthy of notice; and when his career was closing, he stood forth, at the age of eighty, as a poet of no mean rank. His theme was friendship; and his best skill was to draw the portraits of his friends in a series of sonnets.—SANBORN, FRANKLIN BENJAMIN, 1893, *A. Bronson Alcott, his Life and Philosophy*, vol. II, p. 514.

Lately it has come to me that Alcott's style is not literary because it continually harps on one string, that of genesis. All remarks are made, all reflections initiated, with the doctrine of Lapse in the background; a constant spectacle needed by the reader if he will interpret aright the most trivial of Alcott's utterances. He is a theological idealist intoxicated with the One, as every good theologian must be. Hence all his utterances have the form of philosophemes, and he has furnished them of the best quality both in prose and poetry. . . . But if we deny him the merit of literary art, we are yet compelled to concede rare philosophical merit. In the days of his earlier conversations, and before he had printed his works, Mr. Alcott used to read, in the course of the evening, from a red-covered book that he carried, certain poems which had his character of philosophemes. They puzzled one at first, resembling in this respect, indeed, the most of Emerson's poems as well as Browning's. But on getting familiar with them, they seemed to be very felicitous in expression, and to have an infinite depth of suggestion, as all true philosophemes should have. . . . I think, therefore, that Mr. Alcott's books wherein he has recorded his deepest and sincerest convictions are to be resorted to and studied along with the works of Plotinus and Proclus, inasmuch as they present this world-historic theory as a "survival" in a person born in our own age.—HARRIS, WILLIAM TORREY, 1893, *A. Bronson Alcott, his Life and Philosophy*, ed. Sanborn, pp. 618, 620, 664.

He was a beautiful and inspiring presence in the community where he lived, and his influence was broadening and uplifting always.—NOBLE, CHARLES, 1898, *Studies in American Literature*, p. 322.

Tradition has remembered about it ["Dial"] chiefly such oddities as the "Orphic Sayings" of Bronson Alcott,—"awful sayings," they have since been called, in days when the adjective "awful" had attained its cant meaning. There is room for grave doubt whether Alcott ever knew what some of them meant; certainly no one else ever knew, and for many years no one has wanted to know.—WENDELL, BARRETT, 1900, *A Literary History of America*, p. 303.

Whether in his capacity of philosopher or religious idealist he was much more than an aspiring soul is a question that need not be discussed here. As an educational reformer he was a good deal more, and he was probably something more as a writer, although this is not the usual opinion. His "Orphic Sayings" contributed to *The Dial* brought him harsh criticism and ridicule, at which his admirers have expressed a not justifiable indignation. Orphic literature is to-day best adapted to private circulation, as Emerson, who was sometimes scarcely less guilty than Alcott, seems to have thought when he advised against the publication of his friend's philosophical romance entitled "Psyche." Emerson, indeed, was constantly regretting that a man who talked so well wrote so ill, and taking their cue from Emerson, Lowell and other critics have treated Alcott the author with scant courtesy. Yet while it would be absurd to attribute great power or charm to Alcott's scraps of speculation or to his jottings upon social and literary topics gathered in his "Tablets" and his "Table Talk," or even to his reminiscential "Concord Days," it would be unjust to deny that these books contain suggestive pages worthy of the attention of those who do not read as they run.—TRENT, WILLIAM P., 1903, *A History of American Literature*, p. 312.

Louisa May Alcott
1832-1888

Author, born in Germantown, Penn., 29th November, 1832. Her birth was the anniversary of the birth of her father. Her first published book was "Flower Fables" (Boston, 1855). It was not successful. She continued to write for her own amusement in her spare hours, but devoted herself to helping her father and mother by teaching school, serving as nursery governess, and even at times sewing for a living. . . . In 1862 she became a nurse in the Washington Hospitals and devoted herself to her duties there with consciencious zeal. In consequence, she became ill herself and narrowly escaped death by typhoid fever. While in Washington she wrote to her mother and sisters letters describing hospital life and experience, which were revised and published in book-form as "Hospital Sketches" (Boston, 1863). In that year she went to Europe as companion to an invalid woman, spending the year in Germany, Switzerland, Paris, and London. Then followed "Moods" (1864); "Morning Glories, and Other Tales" (1867); "Proverb Stories" (1868). She then published "Little Women," 2 volumes, (1868), a story founded largely on incidents in the lives of her three sisters and herself at Concord. This book made its author famous. From its appearance until her death she was constantly held in public esteem, and the sale of her books has passed into many hundred thousands. Most of her stories were written while she resided in Concord, though she penned the manuscript in Boston, declaring that she could do her writing better in that city, so favorable to her genius and success. Following "Little Women" came "An Old-Fashioned Girl" (1870); "Little Men" (1871), the mere announcement of which brought an advance order from the dealers for 50,000 copies; the "Aunt Jo's Scrap-Bag" (1871), 6 volumes; "Work" (1873); "Eight Cousins" (1875); "A Rose in Bloom" (1876); "Silver Pitchers and Independence" (1876); "Modern Mephistopheles," anonymously in the "No Name Series" (1877); "Under The Lilacs" (1878); "Jack and Jill" (1880); "Proverb Stories" a new edition revised (1882); "Moods" a revised edition (1884); "Spinning-Wheel Stories" (1884); "Jo's Boys" (1886). This latest story was a sequel to "Little Men." "A Garland for Girls" (1887).—MOULTON, CHARLES WELLS, 1893, *A Woman of the Century*, ed. Willard and Livermore, pp. 12, 13.

PERSONAL

She never had a study—any corner will answer to write in. She is not particular as to pen and paper, and an old atlas on her knee is all she cares for. She has the wonderful power to carry a dozen plots in her head at a time, thinking them over whenever she is in the mood. Sometimes she carries a plot thus for years, and suddenly finds it all ready to be written. Often, in the dead waste and middle of the night, she lies awake and plans whole chapters, word for word, and when daylight comes has only to write them off as if she were copying. In her hardest-working days she used to write fourteen hours in the twenty-four, sitting steadily at her work, and scarcely tasting food till her daily task was done.—MOULTON, LOUISE CHANDLER, 1883, *Our Famous Women*, p. 52.

A singular combination of opposing influences dominated the youth of Louisa Alcott. It is to be doubted if any woman ever before achieved literary fame and fortune under more discouraging material circumstanes,—or what would have been discouraging to any one placed in the neighborhood of less noble natures,—or was ever led up to her attempt under more fortunate inheritance and training; and a great part of her excellence consists in the way in which she conquered one with the other.—SPOFFORD, HARRIET PRESCOTT, 1888, *Louisa May Alcott, The Chautauquan*, vol. 9, p. 160.

A girl, whose earliest teacher was Margaret Fuller; who at ten years of age, learned to know the seasons in their varied dress and nature in its deepest meanings under Thoreau's guidance; to whom men like Emerson, Channing, Ripley, and Hawthorne were every-day company, yet who was brought up almost in poverty, and with the necessity of work at home if not abroad; who had a fund of downright common sense and keen humor underlying all transcendental influence,—is one who, as a woman, might be expected to have made her mark, and she did it by the simplest, kindliest, cheeriest of writing, and the sweetest of companionship and kindness toward others.—LILLIE, LUCY C., 1888, *Louisa May Alcott, The Cosmopolitan*, vol. 5, p. 156.

On her birthday, twenty years after her first story was written, and while the whole country was enjoying her last, she writes in her diary: "Spent alone, working hard. No presents, but father's "Tablets" (recently published). I never seem to have many presents, though I give a good many. That is best, perhaps, and makes a gift very precious when it does come." Six months later, when her name was in every one's mouth, she wrote: "Very poorly; feel quite used up. Don't care much for myself, as rest is heavenly even with pain, but the family seems so panic-stricken and helpless when I break down that I try to keep the mill going." So she plods along and writes four short stories, which together bring her seventy dollars—barely as much as a writer of equal prominence nowadays would demand for one little tale. Even after she had received many thousands of dollars for "Little Women" she continued to work hard, for she always saw new ways of using money for her dear ones.—HABBERTON, JOHN, 1889, *In the Library, The Cosmopolitan*, vol. 8, p. 255.

The happy, guileless world of children claims her for its own. She comes freely among them—a child herself in her simplicity and *camaraderie*, with that undefinable "something" which means sympathy, comprehension, and, above all, appreciation. We have all been under the spell, whether we can fairly conjure it up anew or not. But now that the story of her life has been told, with its unswerving purpose and will, its gentle and absolutely disinterested affections, her works seem to fade into insignificance, while her fame lifts itself upon a broader basis, and takes ampler scope and proportions. It is the woman who rises before us, —single-minded and single-hearted, with no distraction, no bewilderment, no vagaries, and always a master-voice in her life to be obeyed,—and who comes freely among us, children no more, but struggling men and women less well trained and equipped than she, but all the more grateful to be helped, to be sustained, and even to be rebuked by so valiant an example as hers.—LAZARUS, JOSEPHINE, 1891, *Louisa May Alcott, Century Magazine, vol.* 42, *p.* 59.

Finding she had a talent for writing stories, she employed that to the best of her powers, and for the same ends. She often thought out stories while busy with sewing. Whatever her hands found to do she did cheerfully. If a sad, this is also an inspiring story: few more notable have come to public knowledge in the lives of women in our day. Its splendour and nobility should long survive, and many thousands who read her books have been grateful for knowing how cheerful, brave, and beautiful her own life was. She might have married advantageously. She had more than one offer and many attentions she did not care for; but her heart was bound up in her family. She could not contemplate her own interests as something separate from theirs. She died Louisa Alcott, and honoured be her name. —HALSEY, FRANCIS WHITING, 1902, *Our Literary Deluge and Some of its Deep Waters,* p. 124.

GENERAL

In the absence of knowledge, our authoress has derived her figures, as the German derived his camel, from the depths of her moral consciousness. If they are on this account the less real, they are also on this account the more unmistakably instinct with a certain beauty and grace. If Miss Alcott's experience of human nature has been small, as we should suppose, her admiration for it is nevertheless great. Putting aside Adam's treatment of Ottila, she sympathises throughout her book ["Moods"] with none but great things. She has the rare merit, accordingly, of being very seldom puerile. For inanimate nature, too, she has a genuine love, together with a very pretty way of describing it. With these qualities there is no reason why Miss Alcott should not write a very good novel, provided she will be satisfied to describe only that which she has seen. When such a novel comes, as we doubt not it eventually shall, we shall be among the first to welcome it. With the exception of two or three celebrated names, we know not, indeed, to whom, in this country, unless to Miss Alcott, we are to look for a novel above the average.—JAMES, HENRY, 1865, *Miss Alcott's Moods, North American Review, vol.* 101, *p.* 281.

Miss Louisa M. Alcott, in her "Little Women" and "Little Men," has almost revolutionized juvenile literature by the audacity of her innovations. She thoroughly understands that peculiar element in practical youthful character which makes romps of so many girls and "roughs" of so many boys. Real little women and real little men look into her stories as into mirrors in order to get an accurate reflection of their inward selves. She has also a tart, quaint, racy, witty good sense, which acts on the mind like a tonic. Her success has been as great as her rejection of conventionality in depicting lads and lasses deserved.—WHIPPLE, EDWIN PERCY, 1876-86, *American Literature and Other Papers, ed. Whittier,* p. 126.

It has been said that one of Mr. Alcott's best contributions to literature was his daughter, Louisa; and readers of all ages, here and in America, will give their cordial assent to that. Few writers are more popular, and none more deservedly so.—LEWIN, WALTER, 1888, *Amos Bronson Alcott and Louisa May Alcott, The Academy, vol.* 33, *p.* 206.

I fancy that all the reading world must know the story of the phenomenal furor which this book ["Little Women"] created. Twenty years have elapsed since its publication, and, looking back to the days of my own childhood, I can recall the wild delight with which "we girls" read, imitated, rehearsed, laughed, and cried over it, and how we all longed to know Miss Alcott, wondered who and what she was; and my own experience in regard to the excitement created during the first five years of its life is worth recording, merely because it proves the permanent successful quality in the work, since I see young people to-day reading it in the fashion that we did fifteen years ago, repeating all of the sentiments it elicited and all the enthusiasm which girls of our time delighted to express. We read it in much the same fashion, I think, that

Thackeray said his daughter did "Nicholas Nickleby," which was by day and by night, when she was sick or well, sleepy or wakeful, even walking or riding. We picked out our "favourites," as what girl of to-day does not?—LILLIE, LUCY C., 1888, *Louisa May Alcott, The Cosmopolitan, vol. 5, p. 162.*

Miss Alcott addressed herself to children, and no author's name is more endeared to the young than hers. Although there is little in her writing that is not drawn from personal experience, this is so colored by her imagination, and so strong through her sympathy with life, that her books represent the universal world of childhood and youth. But while they are characterized by humor, cheerfulness, good morals, and natural action, their healthfulness may be somewhat questionable on account of the sentimentality that is woven into her work and breaks the natural grace of childhood by introducing the romantic element, and a hint of self-importance and independence that tends to create a restless and rebellious spirit.—SINGLETON, ESTHER, 1888, *Appleton's Annual Cyclopædia, p. 112.*

Louisa May Alcott is universally recognized as the greatest and most popular story-teller for children in her generation. She has known the way to the hearts of young people, not only in her own class, or even country, but in every condition of life, and in many foreign lands. . . . Of no author can it be more truly said than of Louisa Alcott that her works are a revelation of herself. She rarely sought for the material of her stories in the old chronicles, or foreign adventures. Her capital was her own life and experiences and those of others directly about her; and her own well-remembered girlish frolics and fancies were sure to find responsive enjoyment in the minds of other girls.— CHENEY, EDNAH D., 1889, *Louisa May Alcott, her Life, Letters, and Journals, Introduction, pp. iii, iv.*

What was it in Miss Alcott's books that surprised and delighted the children of a score of years ago, and that still holds its charm for the childhood of to-day? Was it a new world that she discovered—a fairyland of imagination and romance, peopled by heroes and enchanted beings? Far from it. It was the literal homespun, child's world of to-day; the common air and skies, the common life of every New England boy and girl, such as she knew it; the daily joys and cares, the games and romps and jolly companions—all the actuality and detail of familiar and accustomed things which children love. For children are born realists, who delight in the marvelous simply because for them the marvelous is no less real than the commonplace, and is accepted just as unconditionally. Miss Alcott met the children on their own plane, gravely discussed their problems, and adopted their point of view, drawing in no wise upon her invention or imagination, but upon the facts of her own memory and experience. Whether or not the picture, so true to the life, as she had lived it, will remain true and vital for all times cannot now be determined. For the literature of children, no less than for our own, a higher gift may be needed; more finish, and less of the "rough-and-ready" of every-day habit and existence; above all, perhaps, a larger generalization and suggestion, and the touch of things unseen as well as things familiar.—LAZARUS, JOSEPHINE, 1891, *Louisa May Alcott, Century Magazine, vol. 42, p. 67.*

No name in American literature has more thrilled the hearts of the young people of this generation than that of Louisa May Alcott.—PORTER, MARIA S., 1892, *Recollections of Louisa May Alcott, New England Magazine, N. S., vol. 6, pp. 3, 5.*

It has been truly said that Miss Alcott's fictions have imparted genuine happiness to thousands and thousands of the young, and those thrice happy elders who have kept young in heart and feeling.—RUSSELL, PERCY, 1894, *A Guide to British and American Novels, p. 287.*

Adeline D. T. Whitney and eminently Louisa Alcott have the secret of laughter as well as of tears, but their abiding charm for girlhood is less in the story told than in the tenderness of the telling.—BATES, KATHARINE LEE, 1897, *American Literature, p. 288.*

Among the great multitude of writers of Juvenile Literature, I select for special mention here Louisa May Alcott, as on the whole the best representative of the tendencies of this form of literature.—NOBLE, CHARLES, 1898, *Studies in American Literature, p. 306.*

Her stories are transcriptions rather than creations, and if the Alcott family life had not been what it was, the "Little Women" and "Little Men" and the other delightful stories could never have been written.

For they were the literary flowering of outward and actual experiences. Coming directly out of life, Miss Alcott's books appeal *to* life. . . . Some of the more artificial writers or critics of writers who do not sufficiently relate literature to life assert that Miss Alcott's stories lack this or that, and are not "literature." Yet her books are translated into more than half a dozen languages; they are widely read in half a dozen countries, and her name is a household word where the names of some of these superfine critics will never be dreamed of, or heard. Miss Alcott appealed to the higher qualities of the spirit in our common humanity, and the response was universal. She had an infinite capacity for affection, great love for the people, an exquisite tenderness, keen, practical good sense, and a fund of humour that enlivened daily life.—WHITING, LILIAN, 1899, *Louisa May Alcott, The Chautauquan*, vol. 29, p. 281.

Just thirty years ago "Little Men" was published, and, from then until now, probably no other book excepting "Little Women" has been so much read by children. Other writers for young people have come and gone, or have come and stayed, but their popularity has never been so great in any direction as Miss Alcott's. She is less exquisitely charming than Mrs. Ewing and no more delightful than Susan Coolidge, but her appeal to the heart of most children is unfailing. She preaches them innumerable little sermons in the most barefaced way; her grown-up characters remind her little folks of their faults with a faithfulness which one sometimes feels would defeat its own end, but there is frankness about it all, and confidence that every nature has plenty of good in it to be appealed to; frankness and confidence are always winning cards, and year after year the old stories are read again. Year after year, too, the worn old copies give way after long and faithful service, and, if their original owners do not replace them, new copies must be obtained for younger children. They are read and re-read and lent and carried on journeys. They are just as popular now as they used to be, and there seems no reason why their vogue should not continue indefinitely.—EARLE, MARY TRACY, 1901, *The Book Buyer*, vol. 23, p. 381.

Asa Gray
1810–1888

An eminent American botanist; born at Paris, N. Y., Nov. 18, 1810; died at Cambridge Mass., Jan. 30, 1888. He was Professor at Harvard from 1842 to 1873, when he resigned to take charge of the herbarium of Harvard. In 1874 he was chosen a regent of the Smithsonian Institution. He was recognized throughout the world as one of the leading botanists of the age. Besides contributions to scientific journals, his numerous works include: "Elements of Botany" (1836); "Manual of the Botany of the Northern United States" (1848); "Botany of the United States Pacific Exploring Expedition" (1854); "School and Field Book of Botany" (1869); "Natural Science and Religion" (1880).—WARNER, CHARLES DUDLEY, ed. 1897, *Library of the World's Best Literature, Biographical Dictionary*, vol. XXIX, p. 230.

PERSONAL

I wish we could find a place for my friend Gray in the college. . . . He has no superior in botany, considering his age, and any subject that he takes up he handles in a masterly manner. . . . He is an uncommonly fine fellow, and will make a great noise in the scientific world one of these days. It is good policy for the college to secure the services and affections of young men of talent, and let them grow up with the institution. . . . He would do great credit to the college; and he will be continually publishing. He has just prepared for publication in the Annals of the Lyceum two capital botanical papers. . . . Gray has a capital herbarium and collection of minerals. He understands most of the branches of natural history well, and in botany he has few superiors.—TORREY, JOHN, 1835, *Letter to Prof. Henry of Princeton, Letters of Asa Gray*, ed. Gray, vol. I. p. 31.

> Just Fate! prolong his life, well spent,
> Whose indefatigable hours
> Have been as gaily innocent
> And fragrant as his flowers.

—LOWELL, JAMES RUSSELL, 1885, *To Asa Gray on his Seventy-fifth Birthday*.

Gray's work as a teacher extended over a period of more than fifty years, dating from the first lectures on botany at the Fairfield

Medical School, in 1831 and 1832, and the publication of his "Elements of Botany," in 1836. During that period he trained up a whole race of botanists, now scattered through all parts of the United States, so that wherever he went he was greeted by those who remembered his instruction with pleasure. When at Santa Barbara in 1885, an elderly man, who seemed to be about his own age, introduced himself as a former pupil in his first class at Harvard. As a college lecturer he was not seen at his best, for his somewhat hesitating manner when he spoke extemporaneously was unfavourably contrasted with the fervid, almost impetuous utterance of Agassiz, and the clear exposition and dignified address of Jeffries Wyman, his two great contemporaries at Harvard. In his public addresses he always spoke from notes, and, especially in his later years, his striking expressive face commanded the attention of his hearers from the start. In the class-room he was personally much liked, and he made a strong impression on the majority of students, although, in the days when every student was forced to study botany, there were of course some who would not have cared for the subject under any circumstances. The instruction, as was natural, bearing in mind his own early training and the state of botany in this country at the time when he became professor at Harvard, was confined mainly to the morphological study of flowering plants; for he recognized that, until some advance had been made in that direction, it was out of the question dealing adequately with the more technically complicated subjects of histology, embryology, and physiology.—FARLOW, WILLIAM G., 1888, *Memoir of Asa Gray, Address Before the American Academy of Arts and Sciences, June 13; Smithsonian Report*, p. 770.

He was most genial, [1881] and crammed with useful information, and had the rare art of adapting himself at once to any new acquaintance, seeming to know and enter into their particular hobbies. He set them galloping away easily on them, and showing themselves off to their best advantage, perfectly convinced that they were instructing Asa Gray, not Asa Gray them. His wife was very pretty and energetic, and left few sights of London unseen.—NORTH, MARIANNE, 1892, *Recollections of a Happy Life*, vol. II, p. 213.

GENERAL

Asa Gray and Dr. Torrey are known wherever the study of botany is pursued. Gray, with his indefatigable zeal, will gain upon his competitors.—AGASSIZ, LOUIS, 1847, *To Milne Edwards, May 31; Life and Correspondence*, ed. Agassiz, vol. II, p. 437.

But, after all, the mainspring and central fact about the garden is Dr. Gray himself. Though now in his 75th year, this kindly professor and wise investigator possesses to an admirable degree the activity and alertness of his younger days, when an expedition with him was a pedestrian feat to be proud of; and he has added to his quick wit and keen perception such breadth and ripeness of judgment, such fruit of large experience as make him not only *facile princeps* among our botanists, but give him foremost rank among the critics of all branches of biological science. From the beginning of his career his name has been associated with the progress of botany in the United States. —INGERSOLL, ERNEST, 1886, *Harvard's Botanic Garden and its Botanists, Century Magazine*, vol. 32, p. 246.

The greatest botanist—may we not say the greatest naturalist?—that America has yet produced.—BENNETT, ALFRED W., 1888, *Asa Gray, The Academy*, vol. 33, p. 100.

By the death of Asa Gray this academy has lost a member whose activity and zeal were unceasing, and whose brilliant talents as a scientific writer, not surpassed by those of any of the illustrious names on our roll, added much to the reputation of the society at home and abroad. . . . Dr. Gray had the rare faculty of being able to adapt himself to all classes of readers. With the scientific he was learned, to the student he was instructive and suggestive, and he charmed the general reader by the graceful beauty of his style, while to the children he was simplicity itself. The little books, "How Plants Grow," and "How Plants Behave," found their way where botany as botany could not have gained an entrance, and they set in motion a current which moved in the general direction of a higher science with a force which can hardly be estimated. . . . As a reviewer he was certainly extraordinary. Some of his reviews were in reality elaborate essays, in which, taking the work of another as a text, he presented his own views on important topics in a masterly manner. Others were technically critical, while some were simply concise and very clear summaries of lengthy works. Taken collectively, they show better than any other of his writings the literary excellence of his style, as well as his great fertility and his fairness and acuteness as a critic. Never unfair, never ill-natured, his sharp criticism, like the surgeon's knife, aimed not to wound, but to cure; and if he sometimes felt it his duty to be severe, he never failed to praise what was worthy.—FARLOW, WILLIAM G., 1888, *Memoir of Asa Gray Before the American Academy of Arts and Sciences, June* 13; *Smithsonian Report, pp.* 767, 773.

I did not follow Gray into his later comments on Darwinism, and I never read his "Darwiniana." My recollection of his attitude after acceptance of the doctrine, and during the first few years of his active promulgation of it, is that he understood it clearly, but sought to harmonise it with his prepossessions, without disturbing its physical principles in any way. He certainly showed far more knowledge and appreciation of the contents of the "Origin" than any of the reviewers and than any of the commentators, yourself excepted. Latterly he got deeper and deeper into theological and metaphysical wanderings, and finally formulated his ideas in an illogical fashion.—HOOKER, SIR J. D., 1888, *Letter to Huxley, March* 27; *Life and Letters of Thomas Henry Huxley, ed. Huxley, vol.* II, *p.* 205.

No student of natural theology can afford to neglect the original store-houses of argument and illustration which Dr. Gray has placed within reach. . . . To the late lovable, devout, and profoundly philosophical botanist of Harvard College the church owes more than it yet appreciates for its deliverance from such another mistake as was made in the time of Galileo.—WRIGHT, G. FREDERICK, 1888, *The Debt of the Church to Asa Gray, Bibliotheca Sacra, vol.* 45, *p.* 530.

Gray's comprehensive knowledge of the plants of the world, of their distribution, and specifically of the relations of North American species, genera and orders to those of the other continents, and the precision of his knowledge, enabled him to be of much service to Darwin in the preparation of the first edition of the "Origin of Species," and afterward, also, in the elaboration of Darwin's other publications. His mind was not very strongly bound to opinions about species, partly because of his natural openness to facts, his conclusions seeming always to have only a reasonable prominence in his philosophical mind, rarely enough to exclude the free entrance of the new, whatever the source, and to a considerable extent from the difficulties he had experienced in defining species and genera amidst the wide diversities and approximate blendings which variation had introduced.—DANA, JAMES D., 1888, *Asa Gray, American Journal of Science, vol.* 135, *p.* 195.

There is a special *cachet* in all Dr. Gray's papers, great and small, which is his own, and which seems to me to distinguish him from even his more famous contemporaries. There is the scientific spirit in its best form, imaginative, fearless, cautious, with large horizons, and very attentive and careful to objections and qualifications; and there is besides, what is so often wanting in scientific writing, the human spirit always remembering that besides facts and laws, however wonderful or minute, there are souls and characters over against them of as great account as they, in whose mirrors they are reflected, whom they excite and delight, and without whose interest they would be blanks.—CHURCH, RICHARD WILLIAM, 1889, *To Mrs. Gray, Oct.* 18; *Life and Letters of Dean Church, ed. his Daughter, p.* 409.

Of course, the letters give special prominence to the nature and scope of the botanical researches and discoveries on which his fame securely rests, but these letters have been chosen so skilfully that they can be read even by a layman with pleasure and profit. . . . They show that from the very outset he became not merely the correspondent but the intimate and affectionate friend of the leading botanists in all countries. The only interruptions of his toil were his occasional journeys, but these were all made tributary to his work. In these journeys, as soon as he had fairly thrown off the vexations of administrative service, he entered on new scenes with the glee of a boy, and records his impressions of delight without restraint or reserve. We shall be mistaken if the charming journals of travel only lightly freighted with botanical lore but rich in friendly gossip, botanical and other, do not prove welcome to many a reader who does not know one plant from another. —GOODALE, G. L., 1893, *Letters of Asa Gray, The Nation, vol.* 57, *p.* 377.

James Freeman Clarke
1810-1888

An American Unitarian clergyman. He was born in Hanover, N. H., and graduated at Harvard in 1829, and at the Cambridge Divinity School in 1833. He was then called to become pastor of a Unitarian church in Louisville, Ky. In 1841 he assisted in founding the Church of the Disciples, Boston, of which he was pastor from 1841 to 1850, and from 1853 until his death. He was a friend of Emerson and Channing, a supporter of the anti-slavery movement, and secretary of the American Unitarian Association in 1859-62. He was also for many years one of the overseers of Harvard, where he was professor of natural religion and Christian doctrine (1867-71), and lecturer on ethnic religions (1876-77). Besides a vast number of articles contributed to current journals and magazines, Dr. Clarke published many works, including: "Theodore" (1841), a translation from the German of De Wette; "Campaign of 1812" (1848); "Eleven Weeks in Europe" (1852); "Christian Doctrine of Prayer" (1854, new ed. 1874); "The Hour Which Cometh and Now Is" (1864, 3d ed. 1877); "Orthodoxy: Its Truths and Errors" (8th ed. 1885); "Steps of Belief" (1870); "The Ten Great Religions" (2 vols., 1871-83; vol. i., 22d ed. 1886; vol. ii., 5th ed. 1886); "Common Sense in Religion" (1874); "Essentials and Non-Essentials in Religion" (1878); "Manual of Unitarian Belief" (1884); "Anti-Slavery Days" (1884); and "Vexed Questions" (1886).—GILMAN, PECK, AND COLBY, eds., 1902, *The New International Encyclopædia, vol.* IV, *p.* 695.

PERSONAL

The heights are gained. Ah, say not so
  For him who smiles at time,
Leaves his tired comrades down below,
  And only lives to climb!
His labors,—will they ever cease,—
  With hand and tongue and pen?
Shall wearied Nature ask release
  At threescore years and ten?
Our strength the clustered seasons tax,—
  For his new life they mean;
Like rods around the lictor's axe
  They keep him bright and keen.

. . . .

With truth's bold cohorts, or alone,
  He strides through error's field;
His lance is ever manhood's own,
  His breast is woman's shield.
Count not his years while earth has need
  Of souls that Heaven inflames
With sacred zeal to save, to lead,—
  Long live our dear Saint James!
—HOLMES, OLIVER WENDELL, 1880, *To James Freeman Clarke, April* 4.

Dr. Clarke's name is intimately linked with the Transcendentalists of New England; for, although he can hardly be described as one of the leaders in that movement, he was in many ways so closely connected with its leaders, and was so imbued with its spirit that, when its history comes to be fully written, it will be found that his influence, though quiet, was far from insignificant.—LEWIN, WALTER, 1888, *James Freeman Clarke, The Academy, vol.* 33, *p.* 431.

He was well-nigh a perfect teacher. His Bible-classes, and his classes of history and literature, which in the work of his church he regularly carried on, were stimulating and suggestive. He was so fond of young people that they could hardly fail to learn from him. "Everything I know of the Norse mythology," said a young student, who will one day be teaching others in the same line, "I learned from him as we sat together, summer evenings, on the piazza."—HALE, EDWARD EVERETT, 1891, *ed. James Freeman Clarke, Autobiography, Diary and Correspondence, p.* 305.

Mr. Clarke's preaching was as unlike as possible to that of Theodore Parker. While not wanting in the critical spirit, and characterized by very definite views of the questions which at that time were foremost in the mind of the community, there ran through the whole course of his ministrations an exquisite tone of charity and good-will. He had not the philosophic and militant genius of Parker, but he had a genius of his own, poetical, harmonizing. In after years I esteemed myself fortunate in having passed from the drastic discipline of the one to the tender and reconciling ministry of the other. . . . Our minister was a man of much impulse, but of more judgment. In his character were blended the best traits of the conservative and of the liberal. His ardent temperament and sanguine disposition bred in him that natural hopefulness which is so important an element in all attempted reform. His sound mind, well disciplined by culture, held fast to the inherited treasures of society, while a fortunate power of apprehending principles rendered him very steadfast, both in advance and reserve. In the agitated period which preceded the civil war and in that which followed it, he in his modest pulpit became one of the leaders, not of his own flock alone, but of the community to which he belonged.—HOWE, JULIA WARD, 1899, *Reminiscences, 1819–1899, p.* 247.

GENERAL

James Freeman Clarke, a grandson, through his mother, of the first avowed Unitarian minister in the United States, is, if not the most gifted, at least among the most earnest, industrious, energetic, and influential of contemporary Unitarian ministers. He has a mind of singular comprehensiveness, and as open to the reception of error as to the reception of truth. He is an eclectic, or, rather, a syncretist, and holds it his duty to accept all opinions, whether true or false, as equally respectable. As a Unitarian, he comprehends both wings of the denomination, accepts both extremes, without troubling himself about the middle term that unites them. He is rarely impressed with the importance of logical consistency, and feels no difficulty in maintaining that, of two contradictory propositions, both are true, or both are false.—BROWNSON, ORESTES AUGUSTUS, 1870, *Steps to Belief, Catholic World, vol.* 12, *p.* 289.

Through all his active life Dr. Clarke has been a prominent advocate of freedom and friend of humanity, and has been distinguished for his broad and genial sympathies with sects and parties of the most varied or antagonistic views, while yet holding firmly to his own clear and well-defined opinions. This strength of conviction and catholicity of spirit, taken in connection with his large resources of thought and illustration, his keenness and cogency of argument, his ample range of knowledge and inquiry, and his simplicity and force of expression, have gained him a commanding influence among men.—PUTNAM, ALFRED P., 1874, *Singers and Songs of the Liberal Faith, p.* 284.

An attractive and scholarly account ["Ten Great Religions"] of the most important religious systems that have appeared.—ADAMS, CHARLES KENDALL, 1882, *A Manual of Historical Literature, p.* 80.

Allied to the "Channing Unitarians" by his reverential spirit and non-iconoclastic temper, and yet willing to study and to get benefit from advanced and novel schools of thought, within and without his own denomination. . . . In his books,—"The Christian Doctrine of Forgiveness," "The Christian Doctrine of Prayer," "Steps of Belief," "Orthodoxy, its Truths and Errors," and "Common-Sense in Religion," we find a distinct Christian sentiment by no means universally prevalent in the Transscendental movement. Dr. Clarke, while sharing in most of the intellectual movements which affected New England thought after 1830, left . . . no original, formative literary work of the first class, his labor having been chiefly in the constant exercise of preaching. Clarke's "Ten Great Religions" (two series), though interesting, is rather an industrious gleaning in previously tilled fields, than a force such as one feels at first-hand in Max Müller's lectures on comparative religion.—RICHARDSON, CHARLES F., 1887, *American Literature,* 1607—1885, *vol.* I, *p.* 309.

"The Doctrine of Prayer" was circulated widely among thoughtful people of all communions, and was read with such interest that many were moved to write personally to the author. This gave to him the position he was well adapted to fill, of mediating between different communions, and of showing to each what were the merits of the other. It was a good thing for us (of the Unitarian Church) that we had a man who brought us and the Orthodox people nearer to each other, and there were few among us in whom the Orthodox had the same confidence that they had in him. . . . "The Truths and Errors of Orthodoxy" was a second book which did great good in showing to earnest persons, on both sides of the imagined gulf between the Liberal and the Evangelical Churches, that it was not very much of a gulf after all. Indeed, wherever people read his books, they found out, what may be regarded as a general truth, that most intelligent Christians, so far as their everyday religion goes, are in practical agreement, though probably without knowing it. When they come to state occasions, and to the full-dress uniform of established creeds and confessions, they appear, of course, in a different array.—HALE, EDWARD EVERETT, 1891, *ed., James Freeman Clarke, Autobiography, Diary and Correspondence, p.* 256.

He deliberately accepted the tendency to

good or evil in a doctrine as a test of truth and all the doctrines appealed to him pre-eminently as calculated to increase the amount of goodness in the world and soothe its sorrow and distress. He was not a profound thinker nor a careful scholar, and he did not win the audience of those who care a great deal for serious thinking and for careful study. Of this he was aware, and by it he was not troubled, for he had great compensations. He spoke to hundreds once a week, he wrote for many thousands every day. The circulation of his writings was immense, and it answered the prayer of his youth, for it brought into the communion of his invisible church thousands who were not of the Unitarian fold. No other has done so much to commend Unitarianism to orthodox believers, and few, if any, have done more to break down the sectarian divisions of our American life.—CHADWICK, JOHN WHITE, 1891, *Nation, vol.* 52, *p.* 365.

Edward Payson Roe
1838-1888

An American novelist; born in Orange County, N. Y., March 7, 1838; died at Cornwall, N. Y., July 19, 1888. He has written a great number of very popular novels, which have been republished in England and other countries. His first novel, "Barriers Burned Away" (1872), met with immediate success, and was followed by "What Can She Do?" (1873); "The Opening of a Chestnut Burr" (1874); "From Jest to Earnest" (1875); "Near to Nature's Heart" (1876); "A Knight of the Nineteenth Century" (1877); "A Face Illumined" (1878); "A Day of Fate" (1880); "Without a Home" (1880); "His London Rivals" (1883); "A Young Girl's Wooing" (1884); "Nature's Serial Story" (1884); "An Original Belle" (1885); "Driven Back to Eden" (1885); "He Fell in Love with his Wife" (1886); "The Earth Trembled" (1887); "A Hornet's Nest" (1887); "Found, Yet Lost" (1888); "Miss Lou" (1888); and "Taken Alive, and Other Stories."—WARNER, CHARLES DUDLEY, *ed.* 1897, *Library of the World's Best Literature, Biographical Dictionary, vol.* XXIX, *p.* 463.

PERSONAL

None . . . could have loved him more than I did. The telegram which to-day told me of his death, has made my own life less interesting to me. He was so good a man that no one can take his place with those who knew him. It is the simple truth that he cared for his friends more than for himself: that his greatest happiness was to see others happy: that he would have more rejoiced in the literary fame of one of his friends than in any such fame of his own winning. All his leisure was spent in making plans for the pleasure and profit of other people. I have seen him laugh with delight at the success of these plans. As I write, so many generous, sweet, noble deeds of his throng in my memory,—deeds done so unobtrusively, delicately and heartily,—that I feel the uselessness of trying to express his value and our loss. He was at once manly and childlike: manly in honor, truth and tenderness; childlike in the simplicity that suspects no guile and practices none. He had in him that rare quality of loving sympathy that prompted sinners to bring their confessions to him, and ask help and counsel of him,—which he gave, and human love into the bargain. Among his million readers, thousands wrote to thank him for good that his books had awakened in their souls and stimulated in their lives. He knew the human heart, his own was so human and so great; and the vast success of his stories, however technical critics may have questioned it, was within his deserts, because it was based on this fact. No one could have had a humbler opinion of Roe's "art" than he had: but an author who believes that good is stronger than evil, and that a sinner may turn from his wickedness and live, and who embodies these convictions in his stories, without a trace of cant or taint of insincerity,—such an author and man deserves a success infinitely wider and more permanent than that of the skilfullest literary mechanic: and it is to the credit of our nation that he has it.—HAWTHORNE, JULIAN, 1888, *Edward Payson Roe, The Critic, vol.* 13, *p.* 43.

One need not go abroad for an estimate of his character. At Cornwall-on-the-Hudson you will find friends who delight to praise. Mr. Roe was loved there because he deserved to be. It may not be generally known that all profits from his earlier novels and writings were given to the payment of debts contracted by another. And yet such is the fact. Mr. Roe was not a rich man, though he might have been. While yet unknown to fame his endorsement of certain notes threw him into bankruptcy. Soon after, his reputation was made; but every dollar earned was given to the creditors who legally could not have collected a cent. The money was given cheerfully; and it amounted to a large sum. . . . In his family Mr. Roe was the ideal husband and father,—the very personification of kindness and generosity. . . . Next to his love of Nature was his love of mankind. I never heard from his lips an unkind word concerning the many men of whom he spoke. If he ever felt resentment I failed to know it. He enjoyed visiting and receiving friends, and was never so happy as when in their company. Those who so lately passed the day at Cornwall will remember the welcome extended them; and the openhanded and open-hearted hospitality.—ROBERTS, EDWARD, 1888, *How Mr. Roe Impressed his Friends, The Critic, Aug. 4, p. 49.*

Financially he is a giant among lilliputians as to manuscript-making. It sounds incredible; but I am authoritatively informed that the royalty from his works for the last fiscal year reached forty thousand dollars. . . . Not since Cooper, probably, has any native author's works found such a host of readers.—CLEVELAND, PAUL R., 1888, *Is Literature Bread-Winning? The Cosmopolitan, vol. 5, p. 319.*

He was methodical in his work. He had his hours for labor, and never changed them while at his home. The early morning was given to farming, the bulk of the day to writing, and the evenings to recreation. It was his custom to write out the chapters of his novels on slips and then have them copied on typewriters. The original slips look much like the slips on which Dickens wrote his copy. They are almost illegible owing to the great number of erasions, corrections, etc. Mr. Roe was a believer in Ben Jonson's saying: "Easy writing makes hard reading." He carried his corrections even into the composing department of his publisher, often taking the proof-reader's place and making changes just before the type was sent to the press-room.—WALKER, E. D., 1888, *Edward P. Roe, The Cosmopolitan, vol. 5, p. 401.*

The relations between Mr. Roe and myself were those of intimate friendship. Originally associated with him in his papers on "Small Fruits," I first met him at his home and was charmed, as all were, by his winning personality. Beneath this mere kindliness I soon found the tender, noble heart, the beautiful Christian manhood, the sympathetic and truly lovable friend. In our later collaboration on "Nature's Serial Story," I reaped my richest harvest from his friendship. The happy memories crowd thick and fast upon me as I write, and yet I am helplesss to convey by words what that companionship was to me. . . . His noble manhood has brought me many lessons for which I am grateful. I have seen him patient and sweet and courageous and equitable under circumstances which would have soured most men. I have seen him dignified, tolerant and forgiving at sharp critical censure which I knew cut more deeply into his heart than he would admit, and to which his forbearing reply would be, "Why find fault with the songsparrow because it can not sing like a thrush? Each has its appointed place and does its duty."—GIBSON, WILLIAM HAMILTON, 1888, *Letter to E. D. Walker, The Cosmopolitan, vol. 5, p. 403.*

GENERAL

I had little idea then how long the story would be. We all supposed that a few more chapters would finish it; but it grew from week to week and from month to month. Sometimes I would make a "spurt" in writing, and get well ahead of the journal, and again interruptions and various duties would prevent my touching the work for weeks, and the paper would catch up and be close at my very heels. The evolution of the story in my mind, and the task of writing out the pages, occupied about a year, and just fifty-two installments appeared in the "Evangelist." The serial publication was of much assistance in procuring a publisher for this novel in book form, for the story gradually began to attract attention and secure friends. At some period during the summer of 1872, Messrs. Dodd & Mead (Mr. Van Wagener had not yet become a member of the firm) offered to publish the story, and a 12mo edition at one dollar seventy-five cents per volume was issued about the 1st of December. Much to the surprise of others, and more to me than to any one else, the thirteenth thousand was reached by the following March. Of late years the sale of this book has been steadily increasing, and my publishers have already paid royalty on over one hundred and thirty thousand copies, including a cheap edition.—ROE, E. P., 1887, *My First Novel, The Cosmopolitan, vol.* 3, *p.* 329.

Mr. Roe accomplished the first elementary duty of an author—he secured a hearing. He was like the great popular orators, Beecher, Gough, and the rest, in that there was no trouble about collecting his audiences. But his books, like their speeches, have a vast service to render—the translation into simple language for a million readers of the first principles of social ethics, of personal rectitude, of an industrious and innocent life. These they render into plain words without any harmful influence, and with no alloy but commonplaceness: indeed, commonplaceness is not an alloy, it is only a dilution. Every manufacturing town is the better, for instance, for having a set of Roe's novels on the shelves of its public library; they may not be a literary diet so good as Scott or Thackeray, but the advantage is that the factory girls will read Roe, while they will leave Thackeray and Scott upon the shelves.—HIGGINSON, THOMAS WENTWORTH, 1888, *E. P. Roe, Harper's Bazaar.*

He never tried to reach men and women of great intellect, and wisely refused to change his style and work from that which appealed to the mass of struggling men and women. But the underlying motive with him was always the desire to help people. There are many instances of severe literary critics, who have violently censured his writings, being completely captivated by him upon personal acquaintance. The charm of simple great-heartedness was eminently his. No one could charge him with sensationalism or affectation. His modesty admitted deficiencies in his work, but the bushels of letters that poured into his hands from total strangers and the unprecedented sale of his books proved that he was vitally in accord with the heart of his fellow-men, and that he knew how to minister to them as no other American writer has done.—WALKER, E. D., 1888, *Edward P. Roe, The Cosmopolitan, vol.* 5, *p.* 399.

As to the value of his literary work, Mr. Roe would from the very first have been content to leave the verdict to the critics and to the American public. But the critics differed so widely that their judgment was merely confusing, and the American public took him to its heart. When critics like George Ripley and Julian Hawthorne praised his books, when men and women all over the United States found comfort and guidance in them, it was difficult for the humblest-minded author to believe they were the trash that they were often proclaimed to be by young people addicted to being clever,—especially as Mr. Roe's good sense helped him to see that this proclamation was often due to the fact that the clever people in question had never read his books, and often to the fact that the books had run through a provokingly large number of editions. Of course it was also true that many unprejudiced critics honestly believed the books to be trash, and said so, and that their opinions were not lightly to be set aside. But, again, it showed no conceit in an author to recognize that critics always differ, that they are often wrong, that if the people at large liked his books the critics who praised them were at least as likely to be right as the critics who condemned them, and that at all events he was giving innocent amusement if not something higher and better, to the large number of American and English readers, who constituted his audience.—WALSH, WILLIAM S., 1888, *Some Words about E. P. Roe, Lippincott's Magazine, vol.* 42, *p.* 497.

I have no close acquaintance with Mr. Roe's novels, but I know them well enough to despair of discovering why they were found to to be so eminently welcome to thousands of readers. So far as I have examined them, they have appeared to me to be—if I may speak frankly—neither good enough nor bad enough to account for their popularity. It is not that I am such a prig as to disdain Mr. Roe's honourable industry; far from it. But his books are lukewarm; they have neither the heat of a rich insight into character, nor the deathly coldness of false or insincere fiction. They are not ill-constructed, although they certainly are not well-constructed. It is their lack of salient character that makes me wonder what enabled them to float where scores and scores of works not appreciably worse or better than they have sunk.—GOSSE, EDMUND, 1889, *Making a Name in Literature, Questions at Issue, p.* 125.

So the Rev. E. P. Roe is your favourite novelist there; a thousand of his books are sold for every two copies of the works of

ROBERT BROWNING

Engraving from a Photograph.

SIR HENRY TAYLOR

From a Photograph by Mr. Hawker.

Henry Fielding? This appears to me to speak but oddly for taste in the Upper Mississippi Valley.—LANG, ANDREW, 1889, *Letters on Literature,* p. 29.

The late Rev. E. P. Roe never attracted much attention from the newspapers (and the more authoritative journals ignored him altogether); and yet he rejoiced in a popularity which threw all his competitors into the shade.— BOYESEN, HJALMAR HJORTH, 1893, *American Literary Criticism and its Value, The Forum,* vol. 15, p. 461.

Roe is the novelist of the great middle class which constitutes the reading majority. His novels are singularly fitted to appeal to the class for which they were written. Their author was a clergyman who wrote his books with a moral almost a religious purpose, a fact that disarmed the suspicious; he dwelt with domestic scenes and with characters in humble life, and he mingled sentiment and sensation with a judicious hand. His novels have no high literary merit; their style is labored, often pretentious, and their plots and situations are conventional to a degree. "Through struggle to victory" might be given as the motto of them all, the victory in each being celebrated with the chiming of wedding bells. But despite their artistic defects these novels cannot be overlooked by the literary historian. They have retained their popularity to a wonderful degree, and they have exerted no small influence for good on a large audience that cares little for more classic literature.—PATTEE, FRED LEWIS, 1896, *A History of American Literature,* p. 443.

Robert Browning
1812–1889

Born, at Camberwell, 7 May 1812. Educated at school at Peckham, till 1826. Father printed for him volume of poems, "Incondita,"1824. Educated by private tutor, 1826–29; attended lectures at University Coll., London, 1829–30. Literary career decided on. Published first poem, 1833. Resided at Camberwell. Started on tour to Russia and Italy, autumn of 1833; returned to Camberwell, summer of 1834. Contrib. poems to "Monthly Repository" (under signature "Z."), 1834. First met Macready, Nov. 1835. "Strafford" produced at Covent Garden, 1 May 1837. Married Elizabeth Barrett Moulton-Barrett, 12 Sep. 1846. To Paris and Italy. Settled in Florence, winter of 1847. Son born, 9 March 1849. Visit to Rome, 1850; to England, 1851; winter and spring in Paris; to London, summer of 1852; return to Florence in autumn. In Rome, winter 1853–54. To Normandy, July 1858. In Rome, winter of 1859–60 and 1860–61. Wife died, 29 June 1861. Left Florence, July 1861. Returned to London, Sept. 1861. Settled in Warwick Crescent. Hon. M. A., Oxford, June 1867; Hon. Fellow of Balliol Coll., Oct. 1867. Declined Lord Rectorship of St. Andrews Univ., 1868, 1877, and 1884; declined Lord Rectorship of Glasgow Univ., 1875. First revisited Italy, Aug. 1878. Autumns subsequently frequently spent in Venice. Hon. LL. D., Cambridge, 1879. Browning Society established, Oct. 1881. Hon. D. C. L., Oxford, 1882. Hon. LL. D., Edinburgh, 17 April 1884. Hon. Pres. Associated Societies of Edinburgh, 1885. Foreign Correspondent to Royal Academy, 1886. Son married, 4 Oct. 1887. Removed to De Vere Gardens. To Italy Aug. 1888. In England, winter 1888–89. Return to Italy, Aug. 1889. To Asolo. Joined son at Venice, Nov. 1889; died there, 12 Dec. 1889. Buried in Poet's Corner, Westminster Abbey, 31 Dec. *Works:* "Incondita" (priv. ptd.), 1824; "Pauline," 1833; "Paracelsus," 1835; "Strafford," 1837; "Sordello," 1840; "Bells and Pomegranates (8 pts.: i. "Pippa Passes," 1841; ii. "King Victor and King Charles," 1842; iii. "Dramatic Lyrics," 1842; iv. "The Return of the Druses," 1843; v. "A Blot in the 'Scutcheon, 1843; vi. "Colombe's Birthday," 1844; vii. "Dramatic Romances and Lyrics," 1845; viii. "Luria: and a Soul's Tragedy," 1846), 1841–46; "Christmas Eve and Easter Day," 1850; "Two Poems by E. Barrett and R. Browning," 1854; "Men and Women" (2 vols.), 1855; "Dramatis Personæ," 1864 (2nd edn. same year); "The Ring and the Book" (4 vols.), 1868–69; "Balaustion's Adventure," 1871; "Prince Hohenstiel-Schwangau," 1871; "Fifine at the Fair," 1872; "Red Cotton Night-Cap Country," 1873; "Aristophanes' Apology," 1875; "The Inn Album," 1875; "Pacchiarotto," 1876; "La Saisiaz: and the Two Poets of Croisic," 1878; "Dramatic Idylls" (2 series), 1879–80; "Jocoseria," 1883; "Ferishtah's Fancies," 1884; "Parleyings with Certain People," 1887; "Asolando," 1890

[1889]. He *translated:* Æschylus' "Agamemnon," 1877; and *edited:* the forged "Letters of Shelley," 1852; Selections from his wife's Poems, 1866 and 1880; "The Divine Order," by Rev. T. Jones, 1884; his wife's Poetical Works, 1889 and 1890. *Collected Poems:* in 2 vols., 1849; and 3 vols., 1863; in 6 vols., 1868; in 16 vols., 1888–89. *Life:* by William Sharp (Great Writers' series), 1890; "Life and Letters," by Mrs. Orr, 1891.—SHARP, R. FARQUHARSON, 1897, *A Dictionary of English Authors*, p. 34.

PERSONAL

Mr. Browning was very popular with the whole party; his simple and enthusiastic manner engaged attention and won opinion from all present; he looks and speaks more like a youthful poet than any man I ever saw.—MACREADY, WILLIAM CHARLES, 1835, *Diary, Dec. 31; Reminiscences, ed. Pollock.*

Browning's conversation is like the poetry of Chaucer, or like his own, simplified and made transparent. His countenance is so full of vigor, freshness, and refined power, that it seems impossible to think that he can ever grow old. His poetry is subtle, passionate and profound; but he himself is simple, natural, and playful. He has the repose of a man who has lived much in the open air; with no nervous uneasiness and no unhealthy self-consciousness.—HILLARD, GEORGE STILLMAN, 1853-55, *Six Months in Italy*, p. 114.

Robert Browning is an admirable man, frank, cheerful, and charming. He is said to be the most captivating conversationalist on the Continent; (however, I think there are some in America quite equal to him). There is a genial warmth, and a sparkling merriment in his words, which made us friends at once.—LEVERT, OCTAVIA WALTON, 1855, *Souvenirs of Travel*, vol. II, p. 229.

A younger man than I expected to see, handsome, with brown hair. He is very simple and agreeable in manner, gently impulsive, talking as if his heart were uppermost. He spoke of his pleasure in meeting me, and his appreciation of my books; and —which has not often happened to me— mentioned that "The Blithedale Romance" was the one he admired most.—HAWTHORNE, NATHANIEL, 1856, *English Note-Books*, vol. II, p. 106.

At Paris I met his father, and in London an uncle of his and his sister, who, it appears, performed the singular female feat of copying "Sordello" for him, to which some of its eccentricities may possibly be referred. . . . The father and uncle— father especially—show just that submissive yet highly cheerful and capable simplicity of character which often, I think, appears in the family of a great man who uses at last what the others have kept for him. The father is a complete oddity— with a real genius for drawing—but caring for nothing in the least except Dutch boors,—fancy the father of Browning!— and as innocent as a child. In the New Volumes, the only thing he seemed to care for much was that about the Sermon to the Jews.—ROSSETTI, DANTE GABRIEL, 1856, *Letters to William Allingham*, p. 161.

I thought I was getting too old to make new friends. But I believe that I have made one—Mr. Browning, the poet, who has been staying with me during the past few days. It is impossible to speak without enthusiasm of his open, generous nature and his great ability and knowledge. I had no idea that there was a perfectly sensible poet in the world, entirely free from vanity, jealousy, or any other littleness, and thinking no more of himself than if he were an ordinary man. His great energy is very remarkable, and his determination to make the most of the remainder of life. —JOWETT, BENJAMIN, 1865, *Letters*, June 12; *Life and Letters*, vol. I, p. 400.

At that dinner I sat opposite to Browning, and found that in private life he was much like another man. I had thought that his *Comitatus*, the Browning Society, would follow him everywhere to explain what he said. But if a man can talk to be understood, why can't he write to be understood? But those things are not in my line —Homer and Macaulay for me—them I can understand.—FREEMAN, EDWARD AUGUSTUS, 1884, *Mr. Freeman at Home, by Delia Lyman Porter, Scribner's Magazine*, vol. 14, p. 616.

<blockquote>
To my good friend
Robert Browning,
Whose genius and geniality
Will best appreciate what is best,
And make allowance for what may be worst,
This volume
Is
Affectionately inscribed.
</blockquote>

—TENNYSON, ALFRED LORD, 1885, *Tiresias and Other Poems, Dedication.*

Of course, in the recollections of an Englishman living during those years in Florence, Robert Browning must necessarily stand out in high relief and in the foremost line. But very obviously this is neither the time nor the place, nor is my dose of presumption sufficient, for any attempt at a delineation of the man. To speak of the poet, since I write for Englishmen, would be very superfluous. It may be readily imagined that the "tag-rag and bob-tail" of the men who mainly constituted that very pleasant, but not very intellectual society, were not likely to be such as Mr. Browning would readily make intimates of. And I think I see, in memory's magic glass that the men used to be rather afraid of him. Not that I ever saw him rough or uncourteous with the most exasperating fool that ever rubbed a man's nervous system the wrong way, but there was a quiet, lurking smile which, supported by very few words, used to seem to have the singular property of making the utterers of platitudes and the mistakers of *non-sequiturs* for *sequiturs* uncomfortably aware of the nature of their words within a very few minutes after they had uttered them. I may say, however, that I believe that, in any dispute on any sort of subject between any two men in the place, if it had been proposed to submit the matter in dispute for adjudication to Mr. Browning, the proposal would have been jumped at with a greater readiness of *consensus* than in the case of any other man there.—TROLLOPE, THOMAS ADOLPHUS, 1888, *What I Remember*, p. 403.

Is one of the most familiar figures of the metropolis, and he is also one of the few men of letters who do their work within London. A thorough Londoner, born in that commonplace part called Camberwell seventy-six years ago; his father a clerk in the Bank of England—though from his four grandparents, Scotch, creole, German, and English blood meet in his veins; educated at the University of London; living, since his wife's death exiled him from Italy, for many years in Maida Vale, and now in Kensington—he is perhaps the last person one would select in a London throng as the author of Browning's poetry. He looks rather like a bank president, a brisk and successful merchant, than a poet, with his well-set figure, his frank and pleasant face, with trim white beard and wonderfully bright eyes, his *bonhomie* of manner—altogether an agreeable gentleman, much of the world one would say, and by no means a dreamer of dreams.—BOWKER, RICHARD ROGERS, 1888, *London as a Literary Centre*, *Harper's Magazine*, vol. 76, p. 817.

Slowly we disarray,
Our leaves grow few,
Few on the bough, and many on the sod:
Round him no ruining autumn tempest blew,
Gathered on genial day,
He fills, fresh as Apollo's bay,
The Hand of God.

—FIELD, MICHAEL, 1889, *In Memoriam, Robert Browning*, *The Academy*, vol. 36, p. 405.

When I first knew him, twenty-six years ago, he was living in Delamere Crescent with his father, sister, and son. The father was a notable man. Dante Rossetti always contended that there was something Semitic on Robert Browning's handsome countenance, and the fact that his father had been a clerk of the Rothschilds added plausibility to the supposition. The family were, of old, Congregationalists in creed, but the elder Browning, as I remember, did have a slightly Jewish complexion. It was an old family; the original name, Browning told me, being DeBruni. . . . No American who knew Browning can write of him without remembering his cordiality for Americans. He met those who brought him letters of introduction with open arms. He enjoyed many of our writers, admired our ladies, and liked our sparkling Catawba—to which I had the pleasure of introducing him in the old days when Longworth made wine fit for any poet's palate. Not even memories of book-piracy could induce him to abuse America.—CONWAY, MONCURE DANIEL, 1889, *Recollections of Robert Browning*, *The Nation*, vol. 50, pp. 27, 28.

In the centre of the lofty ceiling of the room occupied by him, in the Palazzo Rezzonico, in which he slept and wrote, and in which he died, is the painting by his son of an eagle struggling with a serpent, illustrative of a passage in Shelley's "Revolt of Islam." . . . No more appropriate painting could have been over the poet, in his last days than this. It is a fitting symbol of his voluminous poetry, in which, from the earliest to the latest, his soaring spirit holds and maintains the mastery over what strives ever to overthrow man in his weakness, as the eagle, in the picture, with beak and talons, holds and maintains the mastery over the struggling serpent.—CORSON, HIRAM, 1889, *Recollections of Robert Browning, The Nation, vol.* 50, *p.* 28.

Gone from our eyes, a loss for evermore,
Gone to pursue within an ampler sphere
The aims that wing'd thy soaring spirit here!
Gone where she waits thee, who when living bore
A heart, like thine, vein'd with love's purest ore!
Gone to behold with eyes serene and clear
The world, that to thy life was ever near
In gleams, now perfect dawn, of heavenly lore!
Gone from our eyes that noble gracious head,
The quick, keen glance, the welcoming frank smile,
Hush'd, too, the voice with its strong manly ring,
But not the strains in which our souls are fed
With thoughts that life of half its pain beguile,
And hopes of what the great Beyond shall bring!
—MARTIN, SIR THEODORE, 1889, *Robert Browning.*

The formation of these Browning societies undoubtedly pleased Browning. . . . It came at a critical period, and he was a more important figure in literature by reason of the existence of these societies. He was quite aware of the ludicrous side of the business, and the effusive enthusiasms of his least wise admirers annoyed him more than he chose to own. One or two American societies seemed to have been founded and worked with little regard to that American sense of humor which so often saves people from ridicule. He was patient with them, accepted their tributes of admiration, took the will for the deed when the expression of it was absurd, and rejoiced to know that beneath all the nonsense on the surface there was a basis of real appreciation for what he himself most valued in his own writings. When appealed to, he no more professed always to know what he had meant than Rufus Choate to decipher his own handwriting after a lapse of time.—SMALLEY, GEORGE W., 1889, *London Letter, New York Tribune.*

Well do I remember that evening in 1855, at the temporary home of Mr. and Mrs. Browning near Marylebone Church, when Tennyson read aloud his recently published poem of "Maud," and my brother took a sketch of him as he sat on the sofa with the volume held high up to suit his short sight. When Tennyson had concluded, Browning was implored to read out his "Fra Lippo Lippi," which, with some little pressing, he consented to do. The contrast between the two readers was interesting and highly characteristic. Tennyson, in his introduction to his "Morte d'Arthur," has well described his own elocution—"mouthing out his hollow o's and a's " (except that "mouthing," as a term of disparagement, should be altered into some milder word)—his grand deep voice sways onward with a long-drawn chaunt, which some hearers might deem monotonous, but which gives noble value and emphasis to the metrical structure and pauses. Browning's voice, which was at once rich and peculiar, took much less account of the poem as a rhythmical whole; his delivery had more affinity to that of an actor, laying stress on all the light and shade of the composition—its touches of character, its conversational points, its dramatic give-and-take. In those qualities of elocution in which Tennyson was strong, and aimed to be strong, Browning was contentedly weak; and *vice versâ.* To which of the two modes of reading the preference should be accorded will remain a matter of taste; in the very small audience on that occasion, most were, I think, in favour of Tennyson.—ROSSETTI, WILLIAM MICHAEL, 1890, *Portraits of Robert Browning, Magazine of Art, vol.* 13, *p.* 182.

Next morning betimes the note was despatched, and a half-hour had not passed when there was a brisk rap at the Easy Chair's door. He opened it, and saw a young man, who briskly inquired, "Is Mr. Easy Chair here?" "That is my name." "I am Robert Browning." Browning shook hands heartily with his young American admirer, and thanked him for his note. The poet was then about thirty-five. His figure was not large, but compact, erect, and active; the face smooth, the hair dark; the aspect that of active intelligence, and of a man of the world. He was in no way eccentric, either in manner or appearance. He talked freely, with great vivacity, and delightfully, rising and walking about the room as his talk sparkled on. He heard, with evident pleasure, but with entire simplicity and manliness, of the American interest in his works and in those of Mrs. Browning, and the Easy Chair gave him a copy of Miss Fuller's paper in the *Tribune.* It was a bright and, to the Easy Chair, a wonderfully happy hour. As he went, the poet said that Mrs. Browning would certainly expect to give

Mr. Easy Chair a cup of tea in the evening, and with a brisk and gay good-by, Browning was gone. . . . It was not in the Casa Guidi that the Brownings were then living, but in an apartment in the Via della Scala, not far from the place or square most familiar to strangers in Florence, the Piazza Trinita. Through several rooms the Easy Chair passed, Browning leading the way, until at the end they entered a smaller room arranged with an air of English comfort, where at a table, bending over a tea-urn, sat a slight lady, her long curls drooping forward. "Here," said Browning, addressing her with a tender diminutive, "here is Mr. Easy Chair." . . . The most kindly welcome and pleasant chat followed, Browning's gayety dashing and flashing in, with a sense of profuse and bubbling vitality, glancing at a hundred topics; and when there was some allusion to his "Sordello," he asked quickly, with an amused smile, "Have you read it?" The Easy Chair pleaded that he had not seen it. "So much the better. Nobody understands it. Don't read it, except in the revised form which is coming." The revised form has come long ago, and the Easy Chair has read, and probably supposes that he understands. But Thackeray used to say that he did not read Browning because he could not comprehend him, adding, ruefully, "I have no head above my eyes."—CURTIS, GEORGE WILLIAM, 1890, *The Easy Chair, Harper's Magazine, vol. 80, p. 637.*

The poet was, personally and to a great extent in his genius, Anglo-Saxon. Though there are plausible grounds for the assumption, I can find nothing to substantiate the common assertion that, immediately, or remotely, his people were Jews. As to Browning's physiognomy and personal traits, this much may be granted: if those who knew him were told he was a Jew they would not be much surprised. In his exuberant vitality, in his sensuous love of music and the other arts, in his combined imaginativeness and shrewdness of common sense, in his superficial expansiveness and actual reticence he would have been typical enough of the potent and artistic race for whom he has so often of late been claimed. . . . What, however, is most to the point is that neither to curious acquaintances nor to intimate friends, neither to Jews nor Gentiles, did he ever admit more than that he was a good Protestant, and sprung of a Puritan stock. He was tolerant of all religious forms, but with a natural bias towards Anglican Evangelicalism.—SHARP, WILLIAM, 1890, *Life of Robert Browning (Great Writers), p. 15.*

It was the writer's good fortune, a few years ago, to meet Robert Browning at St. Moritz, in the Engadine, and later at his home in Warwick Crescent, London. . . . Mr. Browning was short and stout, and plainly enough the original of his photographs. His face was ruddy, his hair very white, his manner animated. He was noticeably well dressed, there was a comfortable and easy elegance about him. It has long been a matter of common report that Mr. Browning looked like a business man, rather than a poet and scholar. He might have been a banker, a lawyer, a physician, so far as his appearance was concerned. But if a physician, certainly a well-to-do one; if a lawyer, then a lawyer accustomed to good fees; if a banker, connected with an institution which is not going to give its depositors cause for anxiety. But while markedly "stylish," he wore his good clothes with an air of one who had never worn anything else. In his youth I fancy that he might have been something of a dandy. There was a pleasant atmosphere of large prosperity about him. His manner was simple, kind, cheery. He made one feel at home, and time went rapidly. That blessed saint of American literature, Henry W. Longfellow, made each of his chance visitors happy by his cordial and unaffected manner. But Longfellow's sweetness was the sweetness of resignation. A young woman who had called upon him told me that he was so amiable that she felt actually guilty! Browning, fascinating hypocrite that he was, made the stranger feel that his visit was not only agreeable, but positively opportune. If visitors stayed longer than they ought, the fault was quite as much his as theirs.—VINCENT, LEON H., 1890-95, *A Few Words on Robert Browning, pp. 47, 48.*

Here, in this old York Street Dissenting chapel, on the 14th of June, 1812, he was brought to be baptised, and no more valiant soldier was enlisted in the army of things spiritual, at any of the altars of Christianity, on that 14th of June, than Robert Browning. He has been what we call dead for eight years. The loss is great for those who knew him. In my memory he will always live as the most cordial man I ever knew. Never can I forget how on your entrance he would rise from his chair, advance to meet you with both arms outstretched, and cover you with the rich bounty of his welcome.—BIRRELL, AUGUSTINE, 1891-1901, *Robert Browning, Essays and Addresses*, p. 195.

We are told by Mr. Sharp that a new star appeared in Orion on the night on which Mr. Browning died. The alleged fact is disproved by the statement of the Astronomer Royal, to whom it has been submitted; but it would have been a beautiful symbol of translation, such as affectionate fancy might gladly cherish if it were true. It is indeed true that on that 12th of December a vivid centre of light and warmth was extinguished upon our earth. The clouded brightness of many lives bears witness to the poet spirit which has departed, the glowing human presence which has passed away. We mourn the poet whom we have lost far less than we regret the man: for he had done his appointed work; and that work remains to us. But the two beings were in truth inseparable. The man is always present in the poet; the poet was dominant in the man. This fact can never be absent from our loving remembrance of him. No just estimate of his life and character will fail to give it weight. —ORR, MRS. SUTHERLAND, 1891, *ed. Life and Letters of Robert Browning*, vol. II, p. 633.

He was true and tender and simple in heart to the end. My wonder has always been that a man moving among all ranks in the fashionable world for more than thirty years should have remained so untainted, and kept his soul and his art so clear. He lived in Gaza, Ekron, and all the cities of the Philistines, yet he never served their lords and never made sport for them. Moreover, he was just as pleased, as happy, as interested, gave himself just as much trouble, and was just as much carried away in talk when he was with a few unknown men and women, quite out of the fashion, as he was among persons of great fame or of high rank.—BROOKE, STOPFORD A., 1892, *Impressions of Browning and His Art, Century Magazine*, vol. 45, p. 241.

Always full of spirits, full of interest in everything from politics to hedge-flowers, cordial and utterly unaffected, he was at all times a charming member of society; but I confess that in those days (1860) I had no adequate sense of his greatness as a poet. I could not read his poetry though he had not then writtten his most difficult pieces, and his conversation was so playful and light that it never occurred to me that I was wasting precious time chatting frivolously with him when I might have been gaining high thoughts and instruction. There was always a ripple of laughter round the sofa where he used to seat himself, generally beside some lady of the company, towards whom, in his eagerness, he would push nearer and nearer till she frequently rose to avoid falling off at the end! When he drove out in parties he would discuss every tree and weed, and get excited about the difference between eglantine and eglatere (if there be any), and between either of them and honey-suckle.—COBBE, FRANCES POWER, 1894, *Life by Herself*, vol. II, p. 342.

I met Robert Browning at a party, when he happened to be surrounded by many who were congenial to him. He took me in to dinner, and my first impression of him was that he resembled one of our old-school Southern country gentlemen more than my ideal of England's mystic poet. There was a kind of friendly chattiness in his conversation, more agreeable, I thought, than distinguished. I should have named any of the men at table sooner than he as the author of "Rabbi Ben-Ezra" and "Pippa Passes." . . . Browning was always charming, often amusing in conversation, but personally he never appealed to me as much as either Longfellow or Tennyson. Perhaps this was because I frequently saw the last two in their own homes, whereas my acquaintance with Browning was a society one, which least of all reveals the deep, earnest, or best side of any character.— ANDERSON, MARY, (MADAME DE NAVARRO) 1896, *A Few Memories*, pp. 152, 154.

As I entered the parlor of Madame Milsand one day, I saw comfortably seated near the fireplace, a square, solidly built man, with white hair and beard, dressed in rough gray cloth, and wearing an air of bourgeoise dignity and pleasant *bonhomie* which betrayed nothing to me at first sight of the author of "The Ring and the Book." When we were introduced to each other my heart leaped, and it is useless to add that my imagination helped me to recognize immediately the signs of genius in the broad forehead and penetrating eyes under their heavy brows. But what really impressed me in Browning's look and in his talk was kindness; simple, open, and buoyant kindness. All the chords of sympathy vibrated in his strong voice.—BENTZON, TH., (MME. BLANC), 1896, *A French Friend of Browning, Scribner's Magazine*, vol. 20, p. 116.

His [Rossetti's] friendship with Mr. Browning came to an end through a wild suspicion that in some lines in "Fifine at the Fair" he was attacked. "On one or two occasions," writes Mr. W. M. Rossetti, "when the great poet, the object of my brother's early and unbounded homage, kindly inquired of me concerning him, and expressed a wish to look him up, I was compelled to fence with the suggestion, lest worse should ensue."—HILL, GEORGE BIRKBECK, 1897, *Letters of Dante Gabriel Rossetti to William Allingham*, p. 196.

Mr. Browning was a great disappointment at first. He looked [1884] like a retired ship-captain, was short, rather stout, red-faced, with a large nose and white hair, but he was so simple and kindly and polite that I forgave him for not looking the poet. —SHERWOOD, MARY E. W., 1897, *An Epistle to Posterity*, p. 218.

A fine-looking man [1882] of seventy years, with white hair and mustache. He was frank, easy, playful, and brilliant in conversation.—STANTON, ELIZABETH CADY, 1898, *Eighty Years and More*, p. 360.

He was a man with men, mixing with the life of his fellows; friendly and manly, taking his part in conversation frankly, and in fit circles an able and interesting talker. In a certain way he was a man of the world, measuring men and their affairs at their due value in the world, yet independent and unworldly at the heart of him. Observant, practical, common-sensible, but with a core of passion and ideality. His nature was, in fact, richly passioned, on a ground of strong intellect, with manly control and even reserve of emotion. But in his love for his mother and for his wife, and in the disturbance of feeling roused by the deaths of these, or by whatever touched the memory of the latter, we see the depth and force, we feel the fire and tenderness of his mind. His strong sensibility to music is another test of his emotional quality. He had, owing to this, a marked tenacity and constancy of affection. He had a keen memory for suffering, and a certain shrinking from it. He was thus an optimist by temper and habit, forced by bias and energy of the brain, and by dramatic observation and sympathy, to weigh his optimism, yet inclined to make the best of things.—FOTHERINGHAM, JAMES, 1898, *Studies of the Mind and Art of Robert Browning*, Third Ed., p. 42.

Robert Browning was a strong, glowing, whole-souled human being, who enjoyed life more intensely than any Englishman since Walter Scott. . . . . . Indeed, only great poets are known so intimately as we know Robert Browning. . . . Everything that was hopeful his spirit accepted; everything that was sunny and joyful and good for the brave soul he embraced. . . . Never was there a man who in the course of a long life changed less.—CHAPMAN, JOHN JAY, 1898, *Emerson and Other Essays*, pp. 187, 190.

In his methods of work he became increasingly methodical. He wrote on an average so much a day, and his work was finished at the date he set for himself. In building up his plots he was rapid and definite. The story of "The Inn Album" was decided upon and constructed in a single morning, to be carried out precisely as it was planned; and many anecdotes are told of him showing how vividly and instantly the scheme of his poem, long or short, sprang up in his mind. . . . His manuscript showed few corrections, and twenty or thirty lines a day seemed to him a good rate of production. His habit was to rise early and read or write before breakfast; after breakfast to give an hour to the newspapers, then to retire to his study for the remainder of the morning, much of which must have been occupied with his oppressive correspondence, as he never willingly wrote even a note after luncheon. Like Tennyson and Landor he was a great walker and preferred the crowded street to a park or suburb.—CARY, ELISABETH LUTHER, 1899, *Browning Poet and Man*, pp. 204, 205.

A man of the world to his finger tips, who knew every one, went everywhere, and had seen everything, he might pass as a social lion, but not as a poet, or a genius. His animal spirits, his *bonhomie*, his curious versatility and experience, made him the autocrat of the London dinner table, of which he was never the tyrant—or the bore. Dear old Browning! how we all loved him;

how we listened to his anecdotes; how we enjoyed his improvised "epitaphs of country churchyards," till we broke into shouts of laughter as we detected the amusing forgery. At home in the smoking room of a club, in a lady's literary tea-party, in a drawing-room concert, or in a river picnic, he might have passed for a retired diplomat, but for his buoyancy of mind and brilliancy of talk. His heart was as warm, his moral judgment as sound as his genius was original.—HARRISON, FREDERIC, 1901, *George Washington and other American Addresses*, p. 207.

At Cortina I met and first knew Browning, who, with his sister Sariana, our old and dear friend, came to stay at the inn where we were. I am not much inclined to reckon intellectual greatness as a personal charm, for experience has shown me that the relation is very remote; but Browning always impressed me—and then and after I saw a good deal of him—as one of the healthiest and most robust minds I have ever known, sound to the core, and with an almost unlimited intellectual vitality and an individuality which nothing could infringe on, but which a singular sensitiveness towards others prevented from ever wounding even the most morbid sensibility; a strong man armed in the completest defensive armor, but with no aggressive quality. His was a nature of utter sincerity, and what had seemed to me, reading his poetry before knowing him, to be more or less an affection of obscurity, a cultivation of the critic sense, I found to be the pure expression of his individuality. He made short cuts to the heart of his theme, perhaps more unconscious than uncaring that his line of approach could not be followed by his general readers, as a mathematican leaves a large hiatus in his demonstration, seeing the result the less experienced must work out step by step.—STILLMAN, WILLIAM JAMES, 1901, *The Autobiography of a Journalist*, vol. II, p. 627.

His physical conditions were in harmony with his spiritual characteristics. He was robust, active, loud in speech, cordial in manner, gracious and conciliatory in address, but subject to sudden fits of indignation which were like thunderstorms. In all these respects it seems probable that his character altered very little as the years went on. What he was as a boy, in these respects, it is believed that he continued to be as an old man.—GOSSE, EDMUND, 1901, *Dictionary of National Biography, Supplement*, vol. I, p. 317.

PAULINE
1833

Though evidently a hasty and imperfect sketch, has truth and life in it, which gave us the thrill, and laid hold of us with the power, the sensation of which has never failed us as a test of genius. Whoever the anonymous author may be, he is a poet. A pretender to science cannot always be safely judged by a brief publication, for the knowledge of some facts does not imply the knowledge of other facts; but the claimant of poetic honors may generally be appreciated by a few pages, often but a few lines, for if they be poetry, he is a poet. We cannot judge of the house by the brick, but we can judge of the statue of Hercules by its foot. We felt certain of Tennyson, before we saw the book, by a few verses which had straggled into a newspaper; we are not less certain of the author of "Pauline."—FOX, W. J., 1833, *The Monthly Repository*, vol. 7, p. 252.

At Richmond, whither the family had gone to live,—on the 22d of October, 1832, —Mr. Browning finished a poem which he named, from the object, not the subject, "Pauline." This piece was read and admired at home, and one day his aunt said to the young man: "I hear, Robert, that you have written a poem; here is the money to print it." Accordingly, in January, 1833, there went to press, annoyamously, a little book of seventy pages, which remained virtually unrecognized until the author, to preserve it from piracy, unwillingly received it among the acknowledged children of his muse, in 1867.—GOSSE, EDMUND, 1881, *The Early Writings of Robert Browning*, Century Magazine, vol. 23, p. 191.

The poem is defective in construction and hazy in outline. It shows little of that intimate and masterly knowledge of human passion which the author's mature works display. He seems to be labouring at a work too great for him, while he shows by strokes here and there that he may some day be great enough for any work.— WALKER, HUGH, 1895, *The Greater Victorian Poets*, p. 35.

Browning, as was natural to his peculiarly fixed temperament, his powerful overruling idiosyncrasy, remained singularly unchanged throughout his long career. Yet it is singular that "Pauline," the remarkable poem which he wrote at twenty (1832), has a freedom of touch, a breadth, in its landscape, a "joy in the world's loveliness," which, it has been truly said, never returned to him. With this also is a certain simplicity in style, too infrequent in his work, due, perhaps, to his deep early devotion to Keats and Shelley.—PALGRAVE, FRANCIS TURNER, 1896, *Landscape in Poetry*, p. 258.

"Pauline, a Fragment of a Confession," Browning's first published poem, was a psychological self-analysis, perfectly characteristic of the time of life at which he wrote it,—very young, full of excesses of mood, of real exultation, and somewhat less real depression—the "confession" of a poet of twenty-one, intensely interested in the ever-new discovery of his own nature, its possibilities, and its relations.—BURLINGAME, E. L., 1897, *Library of the World's Best Literature*, ed. Warner, vol. v, p. 2559.

As for "Pauline," that work was less connected with Sarah Flower than with her sister Eliza. Mrs. Sutherland Orr asserts that if, in spite of Browning's denials, any woman inspired the poem, it can have been no other than she. On the same authority, Robert not only conceived a warm admiration for Eliza's talents, but a boyish love for herself, notwithstanding that she was nine years his senior. It is certain that he had no ordinary feeling of tenderness and admiration for the lady.—HADDEN, J. CUTHBERT, 1898, *Some Friends of Browning, Macmillan's Magazine*, vol. 77, p. 198.

Of the eleven or twelve copies known to exist of the first edition of "Pauline," three at least are in the United States, and all in private collections. Mr. Foote's copy, in the original boards, uncut, was sold in New York in January, 1895, for $210. Mr. Maxwell's copy, bound in brown levant morocco by Mercier, of Paris, brought $260 in Boston in April of the same year.—LIVINGSTON, LUTHER S., 1899, *The First Books of Some English Authors, The Bookman*, vol. 10, p. 79.

PARACELSUS
1835

This is the simple and unaffected title of a small volume which was published some half-dozen months ago, and which opens a deeper vein of thought, of feeling, and of passion, than any poet has attempted for years. Without the slightest hesitation we name Mr. Robert Browning at once with Shelley, Coleridge, Wordsworth. He has entitled himself to a place among the acknowledged poets of the age. This opinion will possibly startle many persons; but it is most sincere.—FORSTER, JOHN, 1836, *Evidences of a New Genius for Dramatic Poetry, New Monthly Magazine*, vol. 46, p. 289.

The historical P. was a complete charlatan, seldom sober, clever, and cunning, living on the appetite of his contemporaneous public for the philosopher's stone and the universal medicine; castrated as a child by the jaws of a pig, all his life a vagabond, who at last died drunk in his single shirt at Salsburg. — BEDDOES, THOMAS LOVELL, 1844, *Letters*, p. 236.

A Promethean character pervades the poem throughout; in the main design, as well as the varied aspirations and struggles to attain knowledge, and power, and happiness for mankind. But at the same time there is an intense craving after the forbidden secrets of creation, and eternity, and power, which place "Paracelsus" in the same class as "Faust," and in close affinity with all those works, the object of which is an attempt to penetrate the mysteries of existence—the infinity within us and without us. Need it be said, that the result is in all the same?—and the baffled magic—the sublime occult—the impassioned poetry—all display the same ashes which were once wings.—HORNE, RICHARD HENGIST, 1844, *A New Spirit of the Age*, p. 282.

It was a wonderful event to me,—my first acquaintance with his poetry.—Mr. Macready put "Paracelsus" into my hand, when I was staying at his house; and I read a canto before going to bed. For the first time in my life, I passed a whole night without sleeping a wink. The unbounded expectation I formed from that poem was sadly disappointed when "Sordello" came out. I was so wholly unable to understand it that I supposed myself ill.—MARTINEAU, HARRIET, 1855-77, *Autobiography*, ed. Chapman, vol. I, p. 314.

The drama is well worth preserving, and even now a curious and highly suggestive study. Its lyrical interludes seem out of place. As an author's first drama, it promised more for his future than if it had been a finished production, and in any other case but that of the capricious, tongue-tied

Browning, the promise might have been abundantly fulfilled.—STEDMAN, EDMUND CLARENCE, 1875–87, *Victorian Poets*, p. 308.

Browning's "Paracelsus" is founded upon Marlowe; he labors for some ideal future; he revives many of the Elizabethan strains—LAWRENCE, EUGENE, 1879, *English Literature Primers, Modern Period*, p. 71.

In "Paracelsus" we have united the two great principles which lie at the basis of all Browning's work; one, which has for its end, knowledge; the other, which has for its end, conduct. The first is Browning's philosophy; the second Browning's art.—GEORGE, ANDREW J., 1895, *Optimism of Wordsworth and Browning in Relation to Modern Philosophy, The Boston Browning Society Papers*, p. 323.

"Paracelsus" lives, and will continue to live, not so much through the subtlety of its metaphysical speculations, and through certain scattered passages of the narrative, which are instinct with the highest kind of imaginative beauty, nor even through the rich and haunting music of the superb song, "Over the sea our galleys went;" but because in it the youth of twenty-three discovered his own distinctive and surpassing gift,—the divination of individual human character as an organic whole. Nobody had known for several hundred years, nor cared particularly to know, what manner of man Paracelsus was. The callow youth at Camberwell resuscitated and evoked him out of the past; not without patient research, to be sure, yet still by a species of magic.—PRESTON, HARRIET WATERS, 1899, *Robert and Elizabeth Browning, Atlantic Monthly*, vol. 83, p. 814.

In it, Browning's wonderful endowments are already manifest. His knowledge of the causes of spiritual growth and decay, his subtle analysis of motive and countermotive, his eloquence in pleading a cause, the enkindled power and beauty, of his language when blown upon by noble passion, all appear in full process of development. The hindrances from which he suffered are also only too clear, especially his tendency to lose himself in tangled thought, and to grow harsh and obscure in pursuing the secondary suggestions of his theme.—MOODY, WILLIAM VAUGHN, AND LOVETT, ROBERT MORSS, 1902, *A History of English Literature*, p. 324.

STRAFFORD
1837

Read "Strafford" in the evening, which I fear is too historical; it is the policy of the man, and its consequence upon him—not the heart, temper, feelings, that work on this policy, which Browning has portrayed.—MACREADY, WILLIAM CHARLES, 1837, *Diary*, March 19; *Reminiscences*, ed. Pollock, p. 413.

"Strafford" was a piece of passionate action with the bones of poetry. It was a maimed thing, all over patches and dashes, with the light showing through its ribs, and the wind whistling through its arms and legs; while in its head and echoing in its heart, was sung its passion for a king. It was printed as "acted." What it might have been originally is impossible to say, but we have some difficulty in conceiving how it could have been put together with so many disjointed pieces in the first instance. The number of dashes and gaps of omission made its pages often resemble a Canadian field in winter, after a considerable thoroughfare of snowshoes. It appeared, however, to please Mr. Macready, and it was played by him appropriately during several nights.—HORNE, RICHARD HENGIST, 1844, *A New Spirit of the Age*, p. 286.

So completely does the drama proceed irrespectively of historical truth, that the critic may dispense with the thankless task of pointing out discrepancies. He will be better employed in asking what ends those discrepancies were intended to serve, and whether the neglect of truth of fact has resulted in the highest truth of character.—GARDINER, SAMUEL R., 1884, *Strafford*, ed. Emily H. Hickey, Introduction, p. 408.

The play has its faults, but scarcely those of language, where the diction is noble and rhythmic, because it is, so to speak, the genuine rind of the fruit it envelops. But there are dramatic faults—primarily, in the extreme economy of the author in the presentment of his *dramatis personæ*, who are embodied abstractions—monomaniacs of ideas, as some one has said of Hugo's personages—rather than men as we are, with manifold complexities in endless friction or fusion. One cardinal fault is the lack of humour, which to my mind is the paramount objection to its popular acceptance. Another, is the misproportionate length of some of the speeches. Once again, there is, as in the greater portion of Browning's longer poems and dramas, a baneful equality of emphasis.—SHARP, WILLIAM, 1890, *Life of Robert Browning (Great Writers), p.* 82.

"Strafford" rests under this adverse cloud of pre-conceived opinion as to the capabilities of art. Yet, in the light which Browning's genius has shed upon these "possibilities of future evil," I believe a new fact in the development of dramatic craft may be described which promises to show that they are not necessarily undramatic.—PORTER, CHARLOTTE, 1893, *Dramatic Motive in Browning's "Strafford," The Boston Browning Society Papers, p.* 191.

Contains fine things; but the involution and unexpectedness of the poet's thoughts now and always showed themselves least engagingly when they were even imagined as being spoken not read.—SAINTSBURY, GEORGE, 1896, *A History of Nineteenth Century Literature, p.* 270.

SORDELLO
1840

After a silence of four years, the poet published "Sordello," which has proved, and will inevitably continue to prove, the richest puzzle to all lovers of poetry which was ever given to the world. Never was extraordinary wealth squandered in so extraordinary a manner by any prodigal son of Apollo. Its reception, if not already known to the reader, may be guessed without much difficulty; but the poem has certainly never been fairly estimated.—HORNE, RICHARD HENGIST, 1844, *A New Spirit of the Age, p.* 280.

Douglas Jerrold was recruiting himself at Brighton after a long illness. In the progress of his convalescence a parcel arrived from London, which contained, among other things, this new volume of "Sordello;" the medical attendant had forbidden Mr. Jerrold the luxury of reading, but owing to the absence of his conjugal "life guards" he indulged in the illicit enjoyment. A few lines put Jerrold in a state of alarm. Sentence after sentence brought no constructive thought to his brain. At last the idea crossed his mind that in his illness his mental faculties had been wrecked. The perspiration rolled from his forehead, and smiting his head, he sat down in his sofa, crying, "O, God, I *am* an idiot!" When his wife and sister came, they were amused by his pushing the volume into their hands, and demanding what they thought of it. He watched them intently while they read—at last his wife said: "I don't understand what the man means; it is gibberish." The delighted humorist sank in his seat again: "Thank God, I am *not* an idiot." Mr. Browning, to whom we told this, has often laughed over it, and then endeavored to show that "Sordello" was the clearest and most simple poem in the English language. — POWELL, THOMAS, 1849, *Living Authors of England, p.* 368.

Who *wills* may hear Sordello's story told
By Robert Browning; warm? (you ask) or cold?
But just so much as seemeth to enhance—
The start being granted, onward goes the dance
To its own music—the poem's inward sense;
So, by its verity . . . nay, no pretense
Avails your self-created bards, and thus
By just the chance of half a hair to us,
If understood—but what's the odds to you,
Who with no obligation to pursue
Scant tracks of thought, if such, indeed, there be
In this one poem . . . stay, my friend, and see
Whether you note that creamy tint of flesh
Softer than bivalve pink, impearled and fresh,
Just where the small o'th' back goes curving down
To the full buttock—ay, but that's the crown
Protos, incumbered, cast before the feet
Of Grecian women . . . ah! you hear me, sweet!

—TAYLOR, BAYARD, 1864, *To James T. Fields, Sept.* 26; *Life and Letters, ed. Taylor and Scudder, vol.* II, *p.* 423.

This constant demand exhausts the power of attention in a short time, and the mind is unable to sustain its watchfulness and sureness of action, so that if we read much at a sitting we often find the first few pages clear and admirable, while the last three or four over which the eye passes before we close the book leave us bewildered and jaded; and we say, "*Sordello* is so dreadfully obscure." The truth is, Mr. Browning has given too much in his couple of hundred pages; there is not a line of the poem which is not as full of matter as a line can be; so that if the ten syllables sometimes seem to start and give way under the strain, we need not wonder. We come to no places in "Sordello" where we can rest and dream or look up at the sky. Ideas, emotions, analyses, descriptions, still come crowding on. There is too much of everything; we cannot see the wood for the trees. Towards the end of the third book Mr.

Browning interrupts the story that he may "pause and breathe," that is an apt expression; but Mr. Browning seems unable to slacken the motion of his mind, and during his breathing-space, heart and brain perceptive and reflective powers, are almost more busily at work than ever.—DOWDEN, EDWARD, 1867, *Mr. Browning's Sordello, Fraser's Magazine, vol.* 76, *p.* 518.

In point of method no importance can be attached to "Sordello;" but the book is full enough of exquisite beauties and nice discriminations of the elements of character to support a considerable essay; and there is in it a luxuriant wealth of sonorous expression, suggestive of joy in a newly-discovered faculty. It is to be noted on the way that the Shelley flavour goes through "Paracelsus" and comes out with great strength in "Sordello," reinvigorated by the magnificent originality of style developed by Browning in the meantime.—FORMAN, HENRY BUXTON, 1871, *Our Living Poets, p.* 109.

"Sordello" offers jewels of great price to the diligent searcher, but none other will discover them. It is very illogical for those who have never discovered the treasure to say that it does not exist; yet this charge has frequently been laid against the poet, and critics, irritated and discouraged by the manifest application required of them, have endorsed the popular verdict, so that it has now become the fashion to say that Mr. Browning is totally unintelligible. But when any person of average intelligence devotes himself to the study of the poet's works he is invariably astonished at discovering how fallacious is this hasty general verdict.—SMITH, GEORGE BARNETT, 1879, *International Review, vol.* 6, *p.* 180.

One half of "Sordello," and that, with Mr. Browning's usual ill-luck, the first half, is undoubtedly obscure. It is as difficult to read as "Endymion" or the "Revolt of Islam," and for the same reason—the author's lack of experience in the art of composition. We have all heard of the young architect who forgot to put a staircase in his house, which contained fine rooms, but no way of getting into them. "Sordello" is a poem without a staircase. The author, still in his twenties, essayed a high thing. For his subject—

"He singled out
Sordello compassed murkily about
With ravage of six long sad hundred years."

He partially failed; and the British public, with its accustomed generosity, and in order, I suppose, to encourage the others, has never ceased girding at him, because forty-two years ago he published, at his own charges, a little book of two hundred and fifty pages, which even such of them as were then able to read could not understand.—BIRRELL, AUGUSTINE, 1884, *Obiter Dicta, p.* 90.

"Who will," says Browning, "may hear Sordello's story told." As from the mountain-top Don Quixote beheld, amid the dust and din of multitudes, the great king, Pentapolin of the Iron Arm, struggling bravely in the press, so the poet has singled out a fellow-singer, seen dimly through the gloom of "six long sad hundred years," and presents him to us.—WALL, ANNIE, 1886, *Sordello's Story Retold in Prose, p.* 45.

I recall, in about my eighteenth year, discrediting the statements I had heard relative to "Sordello's" unintelligibility, and attempting to read the book with confidence in my own anti-Philistine comprehension of it. But a few pages convinced me that report had not falsified its odious "toughness." Beautiful gleams occur in it, but they are like flying lights over a surface of heavy darkness. Now and then, for twenty lines or so, you feel as if you had smoothly mastered its meaning; again, all is disarray and density. It is like seeing a fine statue reflected in a cracked mirror: here is the curve of a symmetric arm, but you follow it only to meet an abortive bulge of elbow; there is the outline of a sculpturesque cheek, but you trace below it a repellent deformity of throat; once more you light with joy upon a thigh of faultless moulding, but lower down you are shocked by obese distortion. The whole "poem" resembles a caricature of some Gothic cathedral, in planning which some demented architect has treated his own madness to a riot of gargoyles. The *ensemble* is monstrous, inexcusable. But, like many of Mr. Browning's later, modern poems, it strikes you as more of a wilful failure than a feeble one. —FAWCETT, EDGAR, 1888, *The Browning Craze, Lippincott's Magazine, vol.* 41, *p.* 84.

"Sordello" is by common consent the most difficult of Browning's poems. . . . A poem so constructed, with such a hero and such a background, could hardly fail to be obscure, and when we add to all this the subject-matter of the poem—the inner life of a Soul—and that Soul a Poet-Soul—the many digressions and parentheses,—and Mr. Browning's instinct to write *from* the consciousness of his actors,—which his penetrating poetic insight often renders a subtle and unlooked-for consciousness—rather than *to* the consciousness of his readers,—we need not greatly wonder that many even of his most ardent disciples have given up "Sordello" as a hopeless problem—too hard a nut to crack, however valuable the kernel it contains. But hard as it is, we believe the nut to be crackable, and the kernel well worth the trouble.—MORRISON, JEANIE, 1889, *Sordello, an Outline Analysis of Mr. Browning's Poems*, pp. 1, 4.

There is a story of two clever girls who set out to peruse "Sordello," and corresponded with each other about their progress, "Somebody is dead in 'Sordello,'" one of them wrote to her friend. "I don't quite know *who* it is, but it must make things a little clearer in the long run." Alas! a copious use of the guillotine would scarcely clear the stage of "Sordello."—LANG, ANDREW, 1889, *Letters on Literature*, p. 9.

In brief the way *not* to read Browning is by means of the commentary and the annotation. One should naturally begin with the simpler poems. He who begins with "Sordello" is not likely to make great progress. Let the non-reader beware of getting his introduction to Browning through "Sordello!" That poem may wait until the last. Then it may wait a little longer; for the time that is needed to extract poetic gold from the ore of "Sordello" may be put to better use on the "Ring and the Book."—VINCENT, LEON H., 1890-95, *A Few Words on Robert Browning*, p. 19.

Picturesque detail, intellectual interest, moral meaning, struggle in vain in that tale to make themselves felt and discerned through the tangle of words and the labyrinth of act and reflection.—WOODBERRY, GEORGE EDWARD, 1890, *Studies in Letters and Life*, p. 278.

So I thought I would try myself on him in earnest, and I got "Sordello." Well, it was very hard and difficult—hard in making out what the story meant, hard in grammar and construction, hard in the learning exacted from the reader. But it was plain that it was written for a reader not afraid of trouble, and I accepted the condition. I did take a good deal of trouble, and read it many times, in many moods, in many ways, beginning at the end, or the middle, trying on it various theories, reserving what I could not make out, which was much, treasuring what I saw to be purpose, and meaning, and beauty, and insight. And so I began to feel as if the cloud was lifting, and though I do not pretend to know all that was in the poet's mind in writing, I got to feel that I had something, and something worth having. And it was an introduction to the poet's method, to his unflinching view of life, to his ever present sense (in which he is like Shakespeare, and in a lower degree like our modern *Punch*), of how much there is of tragic in the most comic, and of comic in the most tragic.—CHURCH, RICHARD WILLIAM, 1890, *To Stanley Withers, Feb. 9; Life and Letters of Dean Church*, ed. his Daughter, p. 414.

As when we watch a landscape in a mist,
　See here the cross of a great spire break through,
Note there a coil of silver river twist,
　Mark yonder, half revealed, a mountain blue
Struggle above the wind-blown vapors gray,
　Hear lowing kine in many an unseen field,
And soft-toned bells in the dim distance swung,
　And, baffled sense to fancy giving way,
We fall to muse on what may lie concealed
　Where the thick fleeces of the air are flung;—
So that who reads Sordello's story, sees
Through misty chaos of the song, arise
Dim Alps, dim Apennines, dim olive trees,
　And phantom spires thrust up to purple skies
From river-girdled cities, with the din
Of all the Middle Ages echoing,—
The clash of arms, the slaughtered women's screams,
The war cries of the Guelph and Ghibelin,
The strife of mind and force, of Pope and King;
And on the fruitful gloom intent, he dreams.
—O'CONOR, JOSEPH, 1895, *After Reading Sordello, Poems*, p. 81.

His labours gradually concentrated themselves on a long narrative poem, historical and philosophical, in which he recounted the entire life of a mediæval minstrel. He had become terrified at what he thought a tendency to diffuseness in his expression, and consequently "Sordello" is the most tightly compressed and abstrusely dark of all his writings. He was partly aware himself of its excessive density; the present writer (in 1875) saw him take up a copy of the first edition, and say with a grimace, "Ah! the entirely unintelligible 'Sordello.'"—GOSSE, EDMUND, 1901, *Dictionary of National Biography, Supplement*, vol. I, p. 308.

PIPPA PASSES
1841

"Pippa Passes" is the title of the first of these little two shilling volumes, which seem to contain just about as much as a man who lives wisely, might, after a good summer of mingled work, business and pleasure, have to offer to the world, as the honey he could spare from his hive.—OSSOLI, MARGARET FULLER, 1846, (?), *Browning's Poems; Art, Literature, and the Drama*, p. 210.

His "Bells and Pomegranates" furnish us with a series of poems almost unexampled in their strength and variety, considering the rapidity with which they were produced. The first dramatic poem of the series, "Pippa Passes," ranks amongst the best of these efforts. All the qualities which have justly earned distinction for Mr. Browning are present in this drama, which he has never surpassed for its exquisite delineation of passion and intensity of emotion, though he has subsequently worked upon broader conceptions. There is a thorough human interest attaching to the career of Pippa, the lovely peasant maid; and in this instance at least the simplicity of the characters in the poem has its counterpart in the simplicity of the poet's eloquence. In this drama we find beauty, tenderness, grace, and passion combined in an unusual degree.—SMITH, GEORGE BARNETT, 1879, *Robert Browning, International Review*, vol. 6, p. 181.

There had been nothing in the pastoral kind written so delightfully as "Pippa Passes" since the days of the Jacobean dramatists. It was inspired by the same feeling as gave charm and freshness to the masques of Day and Nabbes, but it was carried out with a mastery of execution and fullness of knowledge such as those unequal writers could not dream of exercising.—GOSSE, EDMUND, 1881, *The Early Writings of Robert Browning, Century Magazine*, vol. 23, p. 197.

"Pippa Passes" is but a series of dramatic scenes, linked together as by God's own sunshine, sweet child-Pippa, the innocent bird-song of whose young heart falls, without her knowledge, though with momentous effect, upon the ears of guilty worldly souls who hear. The episode of Ottima and Sebald with their adulterous loves, after the murder by Ottima of her old husband, is one of the most tremendous things in English drama, as, in a livid flash of lightning, the whole ghastly scene starts out upon you; you hear the bloodstained couple talk, and see them move. It is of Shakespearian power.—NOEL, RODEN, 1883, *Robert Browning, Contemporary Review*, vol. 44, p. 705.

The least dramatic in form of all his plays . . . remains, owing to the capriciousness of its form, a poem to be read in the study rather than a play to be seen on the stage.—COURTNEY, W. L., 1883, "*Robert Browning, Writer of Plays,*" *Fortnightly Review*, vol. 33, pp. 892, 893.

"Pippa Passes" is Mr. Browning's most perfect work. As a whole, he has never written anything to equal it in artistic symmetry; while a single scene—that between Ottima and Sebald—reaches the highest level of tragic utterance which he has ever attained.—SYMONS, ARTHUR, 1886, *An Introduction to the Study of Browning*, p. 47.

It has even more of the dramatic spirit than Browning's poems generally have, yet it is not a drama. It is rather a series of dramatic sketches loosely strung together by the movements of Pippa. The plan suited Browning and set him free from some of the difficulties which prevented him from ever attaining complete success in the regular drama. Each sketch represents one dramatic situation, and depicts a person or a group at a crisis of life. There is no need to follow them through various developments. The critical method, which Browning seems to have followed, suffices. —WALKER, HUGH, 1895, *The Greater Victorian Poets*, p. 56.

That lovely and powerful and tragic dramatic poem, "Pippa Passes," which alone marks with triumphant certainty Robert Browning as a poet for all time.—FORSTER, JOSEPH, 1898, *Great Teachers*, p. 311.

These songs of the wandering Pippa are the most poetical pieces that Browning ever produced, their brevity proving that he could have reached the highest point by placing a master's restriction on his words. —ENGEL, EDWARD, 1902, *A History of English Literature*, rev. Hamley Bent, p. 429.

A BLOT IN THE 'SCUTCHEON
1843

Browning's play has thrown me into a perfect passion of sorrow. To say that there is anything in its subject save what is lovely, true, deeply affecting, full of the best emotion, the most earnest feeling, and the most true and tender source of interest, is to say that there is no light in the sun, and no heat in blood. It is full of genius, natural and great thoughts, profound and yet simple and beautiful in its vigor. I know nothing that is so affecting, nothing in any book I have ever read, as Mildred's recurrence to that "I was so young—I had no mother." I know no love like it, no passion like it, no moulding of a splendid thing after its conception, like it. And I swear it is a tragedy that MUST be played; and must be played, moreover, by Macready. There are some things I would have changed if I could (they are very slight, mostly broken lines); and I assuredly would have had the old servant *begin his tale upon the scene;* and be taken by the throat, or drawn upon, by his master in its commencement. But the tragedy I never shall forget, or less vividly remember than I do now. And if you tell Browning that I have seen it, tell him that I believe from my soul there is no man living (and not many dead) who could produce such a work.—DICKENS, CHARLES, 1842, *Letter to Forster, Nov. 25; Life of Dickens, vol.* II, *p.* 46.

"Luria" is a lesson; "A Blot in the 'Scutcheon" is an experience; the one is a drama; the other is a heart's or home's interior. Luria is stately and inspiring; but Mildred and Guendolen are of us—women kiss them; all sit and weep with them.— WEISS, JOHN, 1850, *Browning, Massachusetts Quarterly Review, vol.* 4.

It is full of poetry and pathos, but there is little in it to relieve the human spirit,— which cannot bear too much of earnestness and woe added to the mystery and burden of our daily lives. Yet the piece has such tragic strength as to stamp the author as a great poet, though in a narrow range. One almost forgets the singular improbabilities of the story, the *blasé* talk of the child-lovers (an English Juliet of fourteen is against nature), the stiff language of the retainers, and various other blemishes.—STEDMAN, EDMUND CLARENCE, 1875–87, *Victorian Poets, p.* 314.

It seems but yesterday that I sat by his side in the green-room at the reading of Robert Browning's beautiful drama "A Blot in the 'Scutcheon." As a rule, Mr. Macready always read the new plays. But owing, I suppose, to some press of business, the task was intrusted on this occasion to the head prompter,—a clever man in his way, but wholly unfitted to bring out, or even to understand, Mr. Browning's meaning. Consequently, the delicate, subtle lines were twisted, perverted, and sometimes even made ridiculous in his hands. My "cruel father" was a warm admirer of the poet. He sat writhing and indignant, and tried by gentle asides to make me see the real meaning of the verse. But somehow the mischief proved irreparable, for a few of the actors during the rehearsals chose to continue to misunderstand the text, and never took the interest in the play which they would have done had Mr. Macready read it,—for he had great power as a reader. I always thought it was chiefly because of this *contretemps* that a play, so thoroughly dramatic, failed, despite its painful story, to make the great success which was justly its due.—FAUCIT, HELENA (LADY MARTIN), 1881, *Blackwood's Magazine, March.*

Neither on its first appearance, nor when Phelps revived it at Sadler's Wells, was "The Blot in the 'Scutcheon" received by the public otherwise than with warm applause.—GOSSE, EDMUND, 1881, *The Early Writings of Robert Browning, Century Magazine, vol.* 23, *p.* 199.

I had heard "My Last Duchess" and "In a Gondola" read most eloquently by Mr. Boker, and I then turned to the poet's works to find for myself the greatest of dramas in "A Blot in the 'Scutcheon." While I was at once arrested by the majesty of the verse, my mind was more attracted by the dramatic quality of the story, which stamped the author at once as a master of theatric form of narration—the oldest and the greatest of all forms. I saw in Thorold a clear and perfectly outlined character suited to stage purposes; in Mildred and Mertoun a pair of lovers whose counterparts may be found only in the immortal lovers of Verona, Juliet and Romeo, while they are as distinctly original as those of Shakespeare; and in Guendolen a revival of Imogen herself. I saw that the play, like many plays of the earlier dramatists as well as those contemporary with this production, was written for an age when the ear of the auditor was more attentive than the eye, and when the appliances of the stage were less ample than now; and I saw that, with a treatment of the text such as all stage managers have freely given even to the plays of the greatest of all dramatists, the "Blot in the 'Scutcheon" would take a front rank as an acting play.—BARRETT, LAWRENCE, 1887, *A Blot in the 'Scutcheon and Other Dramas*, ed. Rolfe and Hersey, p. 13.

The "Athenæum" (Feb. 18, 1843) spoke of "A Blot in the 'Scutcheon" as a "poetic melodrama," and called it "a very puzzling and unpleasant piece of business." It does not seem to have had very fair treatment, if we may believe the statements that have been made. It was produced on the same night that a new farce was given—"A Thumping Legacy"—and the opera of "Der Freischütz," and it is said without Browning's name. It was played only three nights. It might have consoled the poet had he known that the "pit audience," some yet unborn, would be found eventually outside the walls of the theatre. Their commendation, if less noisy, has been more lasting. The play was revived by Phelps at Sadler's Wells in 1848. The late Mr. Lawrence Barrett is said to have obtained in America success with the play in a modified and altered form.—ARCHER, FRANK, 1892, *How to Write a Good Play*, p. 37.

We are so carried along by the fervor and fire and passion which he puts into his production that we pay no heed to its failure to fulfill the first conditions of dramatic propriety. But a play as a literary product must stand, not upon the excellence of detailed scenes, but upon its perfection as an artistic whole; not upon the beauty of its poetry, but upon its adequate representation of life. The necessities of the drama at times exact, or at least permit, an occasional neglect of probability in the conduct of the characters; but they certainly do not require a persistent defiance of it, as is exhibited throughout this tragedy, which is in no sense a picture of any life that was ever lived. We are in a world of unreal beings, powerfully portrayed; for the situations are exciting, and the pathos of the piece is harrowing. But the action constantly lies out of the realm of the reality it purports to represent, and therefore out of the realm of the highest art.—LOUNSBURY, THOMAS R., 1899, *A Philistine View, Atlantic Monthly*, vol. 84, p. 773.

SAUL
1845–55

If there is one poem into which Browning has thrown all his artistic power, I think it is "Saul." How grand is the stage on which we see the suffering Titan! the black tent in the midst of the sand "burnt to powder;" the blinding glare without, darkness within. There he endures in the desert, through which flow no refreshing streams to quench the thirst of his soul; he who once had "heard the words of God, had seen the vision of the Almighty," is now blinded by the glory, and he knows not the love which his own heart has cast out.—BEALE, DOROTHEA, 1882, *The Religious Teaching of Browning, Browning Studies*, ed. Berdoe, p. 81.

"Saul" is probably the finest poem Browning ever wrote, and it has the note of immortality. I know not any modern poem more glorious for substance and form both; here they interpenetrate; they are one as soul and body, character and deed, of lofty aim and heroic countenance.—NOEL, RODEN, 1883, *Robert Browning, Contemporary Review*, vol. 44, p. 712.

This is, in every respect, one of Browning's grandest poems; and in all that is included in the idea of *expression*, is quite perfect.—CORSON, HIRAM, 1886, *An Introduction to the Study of Robert Browning's Poetry*, p. 140.

Browning's "Saul" is one of those superb outbursts of poetic force which have for modern ears, accustomed to overmuch smooth, careful, and uninspired versification, not only the charm of beauty and energy in high degree, but of contrasts as well. It sweeps along, eager, impetuous, resistless as the streams which descend the Alps and rush seaward with the joy of mountain torrents. — MABIE, HAMILTON WRIGHT, 1896, *My Study Fire, Second Series*, p. 51.

MEN AND WOMEN
1854

I fancy we shall agree pretty well on *favourites*, though one's mind has no right to be quite made up so soon on such a subject. For my own part, I don't reckon I've read them at all yet, as I only got them the day before leaving town, and couldn't possibly read them then,—the best proof to you how hard at work I was for once,—so heard them read by William; since then read them on the journey again, and some a third time at intervals; but they'll bear lots of squeezing yet. My prime favourites hitherto (without the book by me) are "Childe Roland," "B͏ᴾ. Blougram," "Karshish," "the Contemporary" (How it Strikes a Contemporary), "Lippo Lippi," "Cleon," and "Popularity;" about the other lyrical ones I can't quite speak yet, and their names don't stick in my head: but I'm afraid "The Heretic's Tragedy" rather gave me the gripes at first, though I've tried since to think it didn't, on finding the *Athenæum* similarly affected.—ROSSETTI, DANTE GABRIEL, 1855, *Letters to William Allingham*, p. 156.

Elizabeth has been reading Browning's poem, and she tells me it is great. I have only dipped into it, here and there, but it is not exactly comfortable reading. It seemed to me like a galvanic battery in full play—its spasmodic utterances and intense passion make me feel as if I had been taking a bath among electric eels. — WHITTIER, JOHN GREENLEAF, 1855, *To Lucy Larcom, Life and Letters*, ed, Pickard, vol. I, p. 370.

"Men and Women" . . . is the most finished and comprehensive of the author's works, and the one his readers least could spare. — STEDMAN, EDMUND CLARENCE, 1875–87, *Victorian Poets*, p. 322.

The series of "Men and Women," fifty-one poems in number, represents Mr. Browning's genius at its ripe maturity, its highest uniform level. In this central work of his career, every element of his genius is equally developed, and the whole brought into perfection of harmony never before or since attained. There is no lack, there is no excess. I do not say that the poet has not touched higher heights since, or perhaps before; but that he has never since nor before maintained himself so long on so high a height, never exhibited the rounded perfection, the imagination, thought, passion, melody, variety, all fused in one, never produced a single work or group at once so great and so various, admits, I think, of little doubt. Here are fifty poems, every one of which, in its way, is a masterpiece: and the range is such as no other English poet has perhaps ever covered in a single book of miscellaneous poems.—SYMONS, ARTHUR, 1886, *An Introduction to the Study of Browning*, p. 91.

"Men and Women" is a series which, for clearness and balance of matter and style, it would be impossible to surpass in the list of his poems, whether it was owing to the period of his mind, then reached, or to circumstances. — FOTHERINGHAM, JAMES, 1887–98, *Studies of the Mind and Art of Robert Browning*, p. 40.

The book by which Mr. Browning was best known was the two green volumes of "Men and Women." In these, I still think, is the heart of his genius beating most strenuously and with an immortal vitality. Perhaps this, for its compass, is the collection of poetry the most various and rich of modern English times, almost of any English times. But just as Mr. Fitzgerald cared little for what Lord Tennyson wrote after 1842, so I have never been able to feel quite the same enthusiasm for Mr. Browning's work after "Men and Women." —LANG, ANDREW, 1891, *Adventures Among Books, Scribner's Magazine*, vol. 10, p. 652.

These wonderful poems might still afford a roughness here and there, a measure broken by the very wealth of metaphor and thought, in which the poet's mind luxuriated, but they could no longer be kept back, even by a thousand parentheses and digressions, from the common intelligence, which by this time also had been trained to receive them. From that period at least, if not before, the name of Browning assumed its place by the side of Tennyson.—OLIPHANT, MARGARET O. W., 1892, *The Victorian Age of English Literature*, p. 220.

THE RING AND THE BOOK
1868–69

It is full of wonderful work, but it seems to me that, whereas other poets are the more liable to get incoherent the more fanciful their starting-point happens to be, the thing that makes Browning drunk is to give him a dram of prosaic reality, and unluckily this time the "gum-tickler" is less like pure Cognac than 7 Dials gin. Whether the consequent evolutions will be bearable to their proposed extent without the intervening walls of the station-house to tone down their exuberance may be dubious.— ROSSETTI, DANTE GABRIEL, 1868, *Letters to William Allingham*, p. 284.

"The Ring and the Book," if completed as successfully as it is begun, will certainly be an extraordinary achievement—a poem of some 20,000 lines on a great human subject, darkened too often by subtleties and wilful obscurities, but filled with the flashes of Mr. Browning's genius. We know nothing in the writer's former poems which so completely represents his peculiarities as this instalment of "The Ring and the Book," which is so marked by picture and characterization, so rich in pleading and debating, so full of those verbal touches in which Browning has no equal, and of those verbal involutions in which he has fortunately no rival. Everything Browningish is found here,—the legal jauntiness, the knitted argumentation, the cunning prying into detail, the suppressed tenderness, the humanity,—the salt intellectual humour.—BUCHANAN, ROBERT, 1868, *The Ring and the Book, The Athenæum*, Dec. 26, p. 875.

The book, as it stands, though solid truth and fact, is not by itself sufficient for the artist's needs. Some alloy must be added, in order to render it fit for use. That alloy is fancy. Dwelling and pondering upon the facts stated in the book, Mr. Browning makes exercise of his imagination, and reanimates with the creative faculty that man inherits in a second degree from his Maker the inert and dead, but yet genuine and once vital, matter of the book. . . . Not the least remarkable thing about this poem is that there is no attempt at concealment in it, no reserve of secrecy until the end. The conjurer lays his cards upon the table, and shows you all the passes in his trick. He depends upon the ingenuity of his movements, upon the intrinsic interest of his game, to rouse and rivet and retain the interest of his spectators.—SYMONDS, JOHN ADDINGTON, 1869, *"The Ring and the Book," Macmillan's Magazine*, vol. 19, pp. 259, 261.

"I grant," says Lessing, "that there is also a beauty in drapery, but can it be compared with that of the human form? And shall he who can attain the greater, rest content with the less? I much fear that the most perfect master in drapery shows by that very talent wherein his weakness lies." This was spoken of plastic art, but it has a yet deeper meaning in poetic criticism. There, too, the master is he who presents the natural shape, the curves, the thews of men, and does not labor and seek praise for faithful reproduction of the mere moral drapery of the hour, this or another; who gives you Hercules at strife with Antaeus, Laocoön writhing in the coils of the divine serpents, the wrestle with circumstance or passion, with outward destiny or inner character, in the free outlines of nature and reality, and not in the outlines of a dress-coat either of Victorian or Arthurian time.

The capacity which it has for this presentation, at once so varied and so direct, is one reason why the dramatic form ranks as the highest expression and measure of the creative power of the poet; and the extraordinary grasp with which Mr. Browning has availed himself of this double capacity, is one reason why we should reckon "The Ring and the Book" as his masterpiece.—MORLEY, JOHN, 1869, *The Ring and the Book, Fortnightly Review*, March.

"The Ring and the Book" is a wonderful production, the extreme of realistic art and considered, not without reason, by the poet's admirers, to be his greatest work.—STEDMAN, EDMUND CLARENCE, 1875–87, *Victorian Poets*, p. 334.

One of the noblest books of this century.—STEVENSON, ROBERT LOUIS, 1881, *Virginibus Puerisque and Other Papers*, p. 26

Certain rare works of literature, like others of art and philosophy, appear too gigantic to have been wholly wrought out each by the one man who we yet know did accomplish it unaided. Such a work reminds us of a great cathedral, which, even if ultimately finished in accordance with the plans of the supreme architect who designed it, could not be completed under his own supervision or during his own lifetime, being too vast and elaborate for fulfillment in a single generation. And as such a colossal work "The Ring and the Book" has always impressed me. And, indeed, without straining comparison, one may pursue with regard to it the suggestion of a great Gothic cathedral.—THOMSON, JAMES, 1881, *"The Ring and the Book," Gentleman's Magazine*, vol. 251, p. 682.

Mr. Browning was strolling one day through a square in Florence, the Piazza San Lorenzo, which is a standing market for old clothes, old furniture, and old curiosities of every kind, when a parchment-covered book attracted his eye, from amidst the artistic or nondescript rubbish of one of the stalls. It was the record of a murder which had taken place in Rome. . . . The book proved, on examination, to contain the whole history of the case, as carried on in writing, after the fashion of those days: pleadings and counter-pleadings, the depositions of defendants and witnesses; manuscript letters announcing the execution of the murderer; and the "instrument of the Definitive Sentence" which established the perfect innocence of the murdered wife:

these various documents having been collected and bound together by some person interested in the trial, possibly the very Cancini, friend of the Franceschini family to whom the manuscript letters are addressed. Mr. Browning bought the whole for the value of eightpence, and it became the raw material of what appeared four years later as "The Ring and the Book."— ORR, MRS. SUTHERLAND, 1885-96, *A Handbook to the Works of Robert Browning*, p. 76.

The greatest of his works, as a whole, is "The Ring and The Book," in which is told the story of a Roman trial for murder, in the seventeenth century. Mr. Browning shows us the most intimate feelings and motives of the murderer, the victim, the judges, the advocates on either side; the arguments of partisans, the prejudices of the people; all these are expressed with a master-hand. Such pictures of the workings of many minds, from different standpoints, and on so large a scale, are marvellous for their subtlety and force. The work is more than a narrative, but we cannot call it either a drama or an epic, though it inclines to be both, with a leaning towards the epic. Still, it is chiefly a series of wonderful sketches of character; and we are always, in Mr. Browning's work, driven back to our definition; he is a master of mental anatomy. — GALTON, ARTHUR, 1885, *Urbana Scripta*, p. 61.

His greatest work in point of size and in the sense it gives us, of his sustained power. But the whole impression is one of power misdirected. Not to speak of the irritating *bizarreries* of the advocates and of the factions of Rome, the whole method of the book is anti-poetical. Poetic truth does not consist in displaying the facts of truth disconnectedly: the poet sees life singly and sees it whole, and should enable us so to see it. But if the experiment of trying to give the totality of truth by presenting its dislocated parts in small doses is a failure, what gigantic powers are displayed in the failure!—JACOBS, JOSEPH, 1889, *Robert Browning, Literary Studies*, p. 108.

All things considered, the greatest achievement of the century in blank verse, is Robert Browning's "The Ring and the Book." I don't mean the greatest in bulk (although it *is* that, having 21,134 verses, double the number of the "Paradise Lost"); I mean the greatest achievement in the effective use of blank verse in the treatment of a great subject—really the greatest subject, when viewed aright, which has been treated in English poetry—vastly greater in its bearings upon the highest education of man than that of the "Paradise Lost." Its blank verse, while having a most complex variety of character, is the most dramatic blank verse since the Elizabethan era. Having read the entire poem aloud to classes every year for several years, I feel prepared to speak of the transcendent merits of the verse. One reads it without a sense almost of there being anything artificial in the construction of the language and by artificial I mean *put consciously into a certain shape*. Of course, it *was* put consciously into shape; but one gets the impression that the poet thought and felt spontaneously in blank verse. And it is always *verse*—though the reader has but a minimum of metre consciousness. And the *method* of the thought is always poetic. This is saying much, but not too much. All moods of the mind are in the poem, expressed in Protean verse.— CORSON, HIRAM, 1892, *A Primer of English Verse*, p. 224.

I did not mean to make even this slight departure from the main business of these papers, which is to confide my literary passions to the reader; he probably has had a great many of his own. I think I may class the "Ring and the Book" among them, though I have never been otherwise a devotee of Browning. But I was still newly home from Italy, or away from home, when that poem appeared, and whether or not it was because it took me so with the old enchantment of the land, I gave my heart promptly to it. Of course, there are terrible *longueurs* in it, and you do get tired of the same story told over and over from the different points of view, and yet it is such a great story, and unfolded with such a magnificent breadth and noble fulness, that one who blames it lightly blames himself heavily. There are certain books of it— Caponsacchi's story, Pompilia's story, and Count Guido's story—that I think ought to rank with the greatest poetry ever written, and that have a direct, dramatic expression of the fact and character, which is without rival. There is a noble and lofty pathos in the close of Caponsacchi's statement, an artless and manly break from his self-control throughout, that seems to me the last possible effect in its kind; and Pompilia's story holds all of womanhood in it, the purity, the passion, the tenderness, the helplessness. But if I begin to praise this or any of the things I have liked, I do not know when I should stop. Yes, as I think it over, the "Ring and the Book" appears to me one of the great few poems whose splendor can never suffer lasting eclipse, however it may have presently fallen into abeyance.—HOWELLS, WILLIAM DEAN, 1895, *My Literary Passions*, p. 236.

A summer vacation devoted to "The Ring and the Book" converted me to a qualified admirer of the poet. Now, after further study of his writings, I regard this poem as the greatest work of creative imagination that has appeared since the time of Shakespeare. . . . I know of no poem in all literature in which the greatness of human nature so looms up before you, or which so convinces you that a whole heaven or a whole hell may be wrapped up in the compass of a single soul. . . . I am persuaded that the generations to come will regard "The Ring and the Book," in the mere matter of creative genius, as the greatest poetical work of this generation.— STRONG, AUGUSTUS HOPKINS, 1897, *The Great Poets and Their Theology*, pp. 384, 386, 387.

Despite the great beauty of certain portions, and the chivalrous and noble defence of the wronged child, Pompilia, the whole unutterably vulgar tragedy belongs to the bad days of Italy, when crime alone seemed universally interesting.—CARY, ELISABETH LUTHER, 1899, *Browning Poet and Man*, p. 142.

The career of Guido is Browning's greatest study in the progress of evil. This creature has been called "the subtlest and most powerful compound of vice in our literature;" he is put among companions congenial to his nature,—mother, mistress, brothers,—himself
> The midmost blotch of black
> Discernible in the group of clustered crimes
>   they call
> Their palace.

The poet's genius has given us in one word an illustration of how in the vilest there still remains the possibility of reverence for truth and reality.—MELLONE, SYDNEY HERBERT, 1902, *Leaders of Religious Thought in the Nineteenth Century*, p. 270.

THE INN ALBUM
1875

The raw material of a penny dreadful, such as the theme here is, requires more artistic manipulation than Mr. Browning has given it before it can be called a poem. Beauty of any kind is what he has carefully excluded. Vulgarity, therefore, is stamped upon "The Inn Album," in spite of the ingenuity with which, by suppressing name and place and superfluous circumstances, the writer succeeds in presenting only the spiritual actions of his characters upon each other in spite of the marvelous scalpel-exercise of analysis which bears the most recondite motives, in spite of the intellectual brilliancy which gives a value to everything he has to say.—SYMONDS, JAMES ADDINGTON, 1875, *The Inn Album*, *The Athenæum*.

Now it is both incorrect and unjust to say that the "Inn Album" appeals to those tastes which are gratified by a police-report. Not only is there an entire absence of anything like offensive detail, but there is really no *description* whatever of any of the "criminal" incidents. More than that, they are in some degree connected with the persons in the manner to which we have alluded. And yet they fail to become tragic and do remain, we think, melodramatic, confronting us almost in their native ugliness, because this connection or fusion is incomplete. . . . With all its power, we are not refreshed, nor awed, nor uplifted by the "Inn Album;" it has no form to charm us, little brightness to relieve its gloom, and except for the dramatic touches we have tried to indicate, the human nature it shows us is too mean, or too commonplace, or too repellent, to excite more than the pleasure of following a psychological revelation.— BRADLEY, ANDREW CECIL, 1876, *Mr. Browning's "Inn Album," Macmillan's Magazine*, vol. 33, pp. 348, 354.

This is a decidedly irritating and displeasing performance. . . . "The Inn Album" reads like a series of rough notes for a poem—of hasty hieroglyphics and symbols, decipherable only to the author himself. A great poem might perhaps have been made of it, but assuredly it is not a great poem, nor any poem whatsoever. It is hard to say very coherently what it is. Up to a certain point, like everything of Mr. Browning's, it is highly dramatic and vivid, and beyond that point, like all its companions, it is as little dramatic as possible. It is not narrative, for there is not a line of comprehensible, consecutive statement in the two hundred and eleven pages of the volume. It is not lyrical, for there is not a phrase which in any degree does the office of the poetry that comes lawfully into the world—chants itself, images itself, or lingers in the memory. "That bard's a Browning; he neglects the form!" one of the characters exclaims with irresponsible frankness. That Mr. Browning knows he "Neglects the form," and does not particularly care, does not very much help matters; it only deepens the reader's sense of the graceless and thankless and altogether unavailable character of the poem. . . . He deals with human character as a chemist with his acids and alkalies, and while he mixes his colored fluids in a way that surprises the profane, knows perfectly well what he is about. But there is too apt to be in his style that sputter and evil aroma which characterize the proceedings of the laboratory.—JAMES, HENRY, 1876, *Browning's Inn Album, The Nation*, vol. 22, pp. 49, 50.

It is difficult to discover much beyond the mere willfulness of genius in his last volume. It is evident, from the English reviews which have already appeared, that even the most indulgent of his literary friends found it difficult to persuade themselves into admiration. This poem is neither so dull as "Fifine," so obscure as "Sordello," nor so provoking as the first half of "Aristophanes' Apology," but it is not relieved as at least the last two are, by passages that shine and burn with strong poetic flame.—TAYLOR, BAYARD, 1876, *Three Old and Three New Poets, International Review*, vol. 3, p. 402.

Seldom is there a work more inwrought with characterization, fateful gathering, intense human passion, tragic action to which the realistic scene and manners serve as heightening foils, than this thrilling epic of men and women whose destinies are compressed within a single day. . . . No one of Browning's works is better proportioned, or less sophisticated in diction.—STEDMAN, EDMUND CLARENCE, 1887, *Twelve Years of British Song, Century Magazine*, vol. 34, p. 902

GENERAL

. . . from Browning some "Pomegranate,"
   which, if cut deep, down the middle,
Shows a heart within blood-tinctured, of a
   veined humanity.
—BROWNING, ELIZABETH BARRETT, 1844, *Lady Geraldine's Courtship*.

His writings have, till lately, been clouded by obscurities, his riches having seemed to accumulate beyond his mastery of them. So beautiful are the picture gleams, so full of meaning the little thoughts that are always twisting their parasites over his main purpose, that we hardly can bear to wish them away, even when we know their excess to be a defect. They seem, each and all, too good to be lopped away, and we cannot wonder the mind from which they grew was at a loss which to reject. Yet, a higher mastery in the poetic art must give him skill and resolution to reject them. Then, all true life being condensed into the main growth, instead of being so much scattered in tendrils, off-shoots and flower-bunches, the effect would be more grand and simple; nor should we be any loser as to the spirit; it would all be there, only more concentrated as to the form, more full, if less subtle, in its emanations. The tendency to variety and delicacy, rather than to a grasp of the subject and concentration of interest, are not so obvious in Browning's minor works as in "Paracelsus," and in his tragedy of "Strafford."—OSSOLI, MARGARET FULLER, 1846, *Browning's Poems; Art, Literature, and The Drama*, p. 209.

There is delight in singing, tho' none hear
Beside the singer; and there is delight
In praising, tho' the praiser sit alone
And see the prais'd far off him, far above;
Shakespeare is not our poet, but the world's,
Therefore on him no speech! and brief for thee,
Browning! Since Chaucer was alive and hale
No man hath walkt along our roads with step
So active, so inquiring eye, or tongue
So varied in discourse. But warmer climes
Give brighter plumage, stronger wing: the breeze
Of Alpine heights thou playest with, borne on
Beyond Sorrento and Amalfi, where
The Siren waits thee, singing song for song.
—LANDOR, WALTER SAVAGE, 1846, *To Robert Browning, Works*, vol. VIII, p. 152.

Browning's Dramas are not made up of a number of beauties, distinct and isolate as pearls, threaded upon the string of the plot. Each has a permeating life and spirit of its own. When we would break off any fragment, we cannot find one which would by iteslf approach completeness. It is like tearing away a limb from a living body. For these are works of art in the truest sense. They are not aggregations of dissonant beauties, like some modern sculptures, against which the Apollo might bring an action of trover for an arm, and the Antinoüs for a leg, but pure statues, in which everything superfluous has been sternly chiselled away, and whose wonderful balance might seem tameness to the ordinary observer; who demands *strain* as the evidence of strength. . . . His men and women *are* men and women, and not Mr. Browning masquerading in different-colored dominoes. . . . If we could be sure that our readers would read Mr. Browning's poems with the respect and attentive study they deserve, what would hinder us from saying that we think him a great poet? However, as the world feels uncomfortably somewhere, it can hardly tell how or why, at hearing people called great, before it can claim a share in their greatness by erecting to them a monument with a monk-Latin inscription on it which nine-tenths of their countrymen cannot construe, and as Mr. Browning must be as yet comparatively a young man, we will content ourselves with saying that he has in him the elements of greatness. To us he appears to have a wider range and greater freedom of movement than any other of the younger English poets.—LOWELL, JAMES RUSSELL, 1848, *Browning's Plays and Poems, North American Review, April.*

Mr. Browning seems to take his poems, after writing them, and crush them together at both ends, till he gets the well-knit symmetry and consistency of a Bedouin; he succeeds in making a sort of intellectual and spiritual pemmican. Sometimes, indeed, the desire to produce something dense and nervous gets only obscurity for its result instead of an effective vivacity. When Mr. Browning began to write, we say with deference, that this was his besetting sin. . . . The fancies throng to the pen's point, throwing dashes and commas behind them, till they get out of sight of their arch instigator in the first lines. We love to linger over such passages, grudging no time, till we tie the two ends together; then we can enjoy the picture so munificently grouped. It is no condemnation of these pages to say that few people will consent to bestow so much time and labor upon them. The lovers of a smooth poetry, which can be caught at a glance, or of an easy flow of didactic talk which does not harass the average intellect, cannot sit in judgment upon Mr. Browning's involutions and lengthy crescendoes, for they are not the persons who wait to see whether the picture, at first so confused and apparently destitute of a leading group or idea, is worth the contemplation which may finally reproduce the poet's point of view, and thus call a beautiful order out of the prodigal chaos.—WEISS, JOHN, 1850, *Browning, Massachusetts Quarterly Review, vol.* 4.

What Mr. Browning has produced is great as it stands, but he suggests a power even greater than his achievement. He speaks like a spirit who is able to do that which has been almost impossible in past centuries. . . . Above every other, Mr. Browning's poetry is that of a new human species, which can now distinguish words and construe phrases. He has the sort of insight whose peculiar characteristic it is to recognize everywhere, not only forms and facts, but their mutual connections and methods of action. This philosophical power which he possesses of seizing subtle and exact relations is met with in more than one thinker, it is true; but he is one of the first, if not the first, in whom it has reached such development, without becoming the dominant faculty which subordinates all the others. For, strong as it is, it has found in his poetic imagination another faculty still stronger, which has forced it to work as its purveyor and servant. In this lies the essential originality of Mr. Browning.—MILSAND, J., 1851, *La Poésie Anglaise depuis Byron, Revue des Deux Mondes, vol,* XI, *p.* 661.

Besides "The Blot in the 'Scutcheon" which has been successfully produced at two metropolitan theatres, "Colombe's Birthday" and "Luria" show not only what he has done, but what with the hope of a great triumph before him he might yet do as a dramatist. I could show what I mean by transcribing the last act of "Colombe's Birthday." I could make my meaning clearer still by transcribing the whole play. But as these huge borrowings are out of the question, I must limit myself to a couple of dramatic lyrics, each of which tells its own story.—MITFORD, MARY RUSSELL, 1851, *Recollections of a Literary Life, p.* 181.

One of the most wonderful things in the poem ["Christmas Eve"] is, that so much of argument is expressed in a species of verse, which one might be inclined, at first sight, to think the least fitted for embodying it. But, in fact, the same amount of argument in any other kind of verse would, in all likelihood, have been intolerably dull as a work of art. Here the verse is full of life and vigour, flagging never. Where, in several parts, the exact meaning is difficult to reach, this results chiefly from the dramatic rapidity and condensation of the thoughts. The argumentative power is indeed wonderful; the arguments themselves powerful in their simplicity, and embodied in words of admirable force. The poem is full of pathos and humour; full of beauty and grandeur, earnestness and truth.—MACDONALD, GEORGE, 1853, *The Imagination and Other Essays*, p. 217.

A wonderful thing it [his poetry] is, in many points and parts; but, as a whole, it is a book of puzzles — a vast enigma — a tissue of hopeless obscurity in thought, and of perplexed, barbarous, affected jargon in language.—GILFILLAN, GEORGE, 1855, *A Third Gallery of Portraits*, p. 147.

Well, any how, here the story stays,
So far at least as I understand;
And, Robert Browning, you writer of plays,
Here's a subject made to your hand!
—BROWNING, ROBERT, 1855, *A Light Woman*.

I suppose, reader, that you see whereabouts among the poets I place Robert Browning; high among the poets of all time, and I scarce know whether first, or second, in our own: and it is a bitter thing to me to see the way in which he has been received by almost everybody.—MORRIS, WILLIAM, 1856, *Oxford and Cambridge Magazine*, March.

Robert Browning is unerring in every sentence he writes of the Middle Ages; always vital, right, and profound; so that in the matter of art . . . there is hardly a principle connected with the mediæval temper, that he has not struck upon in those seemingly careless and too rugged rhymes of his. There is a curious instance, by the way, in a short poem referring to this very subject of tomb and image sculpture; and illustrating just one of those phases of local human character which, though belonging to Shakespeare's own age, he never noticed, because it was specially Italian and un-English. . . . I know no other piece of modern English prose or poetry, in which there is so much told, as in these lines, of the Renaissance spirit,—its worldliness, inconsistency, pride, hypocrisy, ignorance of itself, love of art, of luxury, and of good Latin. It is nearly all that I said of the central Renaissance in thirty pages of the "Stones of Venice" put into as many lines, Browning's being also the antecedent work. The worst of it is that this kind of concentrated writing needs so much *solution* before the reader can fairly get the good of it, that people's patience fails them, and they give the thing up as insoluble; though, truly, it ought to be to the current of common thought like Saladin's talisman, dipped in clear water, not soluble altogether, but making the element medicinal.—RUSKIN, JOHN, 1856, *Modern Painters*, vol. IV, pp. 367, 369.

One of the greatest dramatic poets since Shakespeare's day. . . . We are confident that Mr. Browning's dramas and lyrics will long continue to find appreciative readers, and that, as culture and taste and love of pure art make progress, the number of his constant admirers will steadily increase.—SMILES, SAMUEL, 1860, *Brief Biographies*, pp. 379, 385.

He has many of the qualities which recommend a poet to the people. He is a master of the passions. His humour is bright and keen. He has a fine eye for colour. There is a rich and daring melody in his verse. He observes with minute and absolute fidelity. He is a philosophical poet; but the direct human element is always strong in his philosophy. Tennyson (our popular poet) is essentially an intellectual poet, but Browning is at once a more masculine and a more intricate and subtle thinker than the laureate. . . . The grotesque rhymes of Browning, like the poetic conceits of Shakespeare, are merely the holiday frolic of a rich and vivacious imagination. Healthy masculine vigor is apt to run riot at times. It is very significant also, that Browning, who has tried his hand at almost every kind of verse, has never written a sonnet.—SKELTON, JOHN, 1863, *Robert Browning, Fraser's Magazine*, vol. 67, pp. 240, 245.

Robert Browning, a really great thinker, a true and splendid genius, though his vigorous and restless talents often overpower and run away with his genius so that some of his creations are left but half redeemed from chaos, has this simplicity in abundant measure. In the best poems of his last two works, "Men and Women" and "Dramatis Personæ," its light burns so clear and steadfast through the hurrying clouds of his language (Tennyson's style is the polished reflector of a lamp) that one can only wonder that people in general have not yet recognised it. I cannot recommend a finer study of a man possessed by the spirit of which I am writing than the sketch of Lazarus in Browning's "Epistle of Karshish, an Arab Physician."—THOMSON, JAMES ("B. V."), 1864, *The Poems of William Blake, Biographical and Critical Sketches,* p. 266.

He is at once a student of mysticisms and a citizen of the world. He brings to the club sofa distinct visions of the old creeds, intense images of strange thoughts; he takes to the bookish student tidings of wild Bohemia and little traces of the *demi-monde.* He puts down what is good for the naughty, and what is naughty for the good. Over women his easier writings exercise that imperious power which belongs to the writings of a great man of the world upon such matters. ... He is the most of a realist, and the least of an idealist, of any poet we know. He evidently sympathizes with some part at least of "Bishop Blougram's Apology." Anyhow this world exists. There *is* good wine; there *are* pretty women; there *are* comfortable beneficies; there *is* money, and it is pleasant to spend it. Accept the creed of your age and you get these, reject that creed and you lose them. And for what do you lose them? For a fancy creed of your own, which no one else will accept, which hardly any one will call a "creed," which most people will consider a sort of unbelief. Again, Mr. Browning evidently loves what we may call the "realism," the grotesque realism, of orthodox Christianity. Many parts of it in which great divines have felt keen difficulties are quite pleasant to him. He must *see* his religion, he must have an "object-lesson" in believing. He must have a creed that will *take,* which wins and holds the miscellaneous world, which stout men will heed, which nice women will adore. —BAGEHOT, WALTER, 1864, *Wordsworth, Tennyson, and Browning; Works,* ed. Morgan, *vol.* I, *pp.* 239, 246.

I have been thinking of you so much for the last two or three days, while the first volume of Browning's "Poems" has been on my table, and I have been trying in vain to read it, and yet the *Athenæum* tells me it is wonderfully fine. . . . I never could read Browning. If Browning only gave a few pence for the book he drew from, what will posterity give for his version of it, if posterity ever find it on a stall? If Shakespeare, Milton, Dryden, Pope and Tennyson survive, what *could* their readers make out of this Browning a hundred years hence? Anything so utterly unlike the *Ring* too which he considers he has wrought out of the old gold—this shapeless thing.—FITZGERALD, EDWARD, 1869, *Letter to Tennyson, A Memoir of Tennyson,* ed. Tennyson, *vol.* II, *p.* 64.

In the general matter of its style "Balaustion's Adventure" perhaps represents the personality of its author with less accent and caprice than most of his work. The characteristic of Mr. Browning's versification is that lines or passages of which the stately march or concentrated sweetness declares him among the foremost masters of English metre, alternate with other lines or passages which seem to disavow in him the sense of metre at all—stubby or zigzag combinations of syllables not to be rolled smooth by any steam-power yet invented. He would not be himself in a work not presenting this alternation in some degree; but Balaustion presents it in a less degree than usual; the fluency of the Attic verse is catching, and scholars have long ago remarked how, at the date of the Alkestis, Euripides retains it at the full, writing with a metrical regularity and smoothness which he afterwards abandons in favour of a more careless and scuttling line charged with resolved syllables.—COLVIN, SIDNEY, 1871, *"Balaustion's Adventure," Fortnightly Review, vol.* 16, *p.* 487.

The characteristics of Mr. Browning are so marked, that but little critical sagacity is required to detect them. Indeed, they force themselves upon his readers, who cannot escape them, except by refusing to read him. He compels attention, even when he excites dislike. The two qualities which strike me most in his poetry are: first, an intensification of the dramatic faculty; and, second, the singularity of the method by which it is evolved. Mr. Browning is the greatest dramatic poet since Shakespeare, and, like Shakespeare's, his art is unique. It is to him that we must pay homage for whatever is good, great, and profound in the second period of the Poetic Drama of England. It is not what his predecessors sought to find; it is not what Shakespeare found without seeking; it is something never found, and never sought before. That so strange a flower should spring from such roots is marvellous. It is the Body blossoming into Soul. Such I conceive is Robert Browning and his work.—STODDARD, RICHARD HENRY, 1871, *Robert Browning*, *Appleton's Journal*, vol. 6.

Robert Browning is a poet who does not understand that the drama is a poetical form which does not suit his genius. He possesses a great mind and much imagination, but he has no idea of dramatic technicalities. He is a philosophical poet; but on the stage philosophy must be translated into action, and that is what Browning has not been able to do. His poetry much resembles Shelley's, but he has never succeeded, as the latter has in the "Cenci," in replacing his visionary ideas by plastic forms.—SCHERR, J., 1874, *A History of English Literature*, tr. M. V., p. 268.

If there is any great quality more perceptible than another in Mr. Browning's intellect, it is his decisive and incisive faculty of thought, his sureness and intensity of perception, his rapid and trenchant resolution of aim. To charge him with obscurity is about as accurate as to call Lynceus purblind or complain of the sluggish action of the telegraph wire. He is something too much the reverse of obscure; he is too brilliant and subtle for the ready reader of a ready writer to follow with any certainty the track of an intelligence which moves with such incessant rapidity, or even to realise with what spider-like swiftness and sagacity his building spirit leaps and lightens to and fro and backward and forward as it lives along the animated line of its labour, springs from thread to thread and darts from centre to circumference of the glittering and quivering web of living thought woven from the inexhaustible stores of his perception and kindled from the inexhaustible fire of his imagination.—SWINBURNE, ALGERNON CHARLES, 1875, *George Chapman, a Critical Essay*.

It was Procter who first in my hearing, twenty-five years ago, put such an estimate on the poetry of Robert Browning that I could not delay any longer to make acquaintance with his writings. I remember to have been startled at hearing the man who in his day had known so many poets declare that Browning was the peer of any one who had written in this century, and that, on the whole, his genius had not been excelled in his (Procter's) time. "Mind what I say," insisted Procter: "Browning will make an enduring name, and give another supreme great poet to England."—FIELDS, JAMES T., 1875, *"Barry Cornwall" and some of his Friends*, *Harper's Magazine*, vol. 51, p. 782.

While Browning's earlier poems are in the dramatic form, his own personality is manifest in the speech and movement of almost every character of each piece. His spirit is infused, as if by metempsychosis, within them all, and forces each to assume a strange Pentecostal tone, which we discover to be that of the poet himself. Bass, treble, or recitative,—whether in pleading, invective, or banter,—the voice still is there. But while his characters have a common manner and diction, we become so wonted to the latter that it seems like a new dialect which we have mastered for the sake of its literature. This feeling is acquired after some acquaintance with his poems, and not upon a first or casual reading of them. . . . His style is that of a man caught in a morass of ideas through which he has to travel,— wearily floundering, grasping here and there, and often sinking deeper until there seems no prospect of getting through. . . . One whose verse is a metrical paradox. I have called him the most original and the most unequal of living poets; he continually descends to a prosaic level, but at times is elevated to the Laureate's highest flights.— STEDMAN, EDMUND CLARENCE, 1875–87, *Victorian Poets*, pp. 296, 301, 338.

He has shown us, in his earlier works, that he *can* write with a noble simplicity and clearness. Let us, however, grant all the scope demanded by his manner of conceiving and representing characters, all the freedom necessary to an ideal of the dramatic art so severe that it scorns introduction, explanation, or expected sequence;— still, with the exercise of the friendliest tolerance, we cannot excuse the reckless disregard of all true poetic art in his later works. At the line where the ethical element enters into the best composition of an author's nature, he seems to fail us. We find personal whim set above impersonal laws of beauty; the defiance of self-assertion in place of loving obedience to an ideal beyond and above self; and even petulant exaggeration of faults, simply because others have detected and properly condemned them.—TAYLOR, BAYARD, 1876, *Three Old and Three New Poets*, *The International Review*, vol. 3, p. 403.

Nothing is straight, and simple, and easy with that poet. Everything is doubled, and twisted, and knotted at both ends, and the mere mechanical effort of the mind, so to speak, in getting at his meaning, is very great.—BURROUGHS, JOHN, 1876, *What Makes the Poet, The Galaxy*, vol. 22, p. 56.

How to make an Imitation of Mr. Browning. Take rather a coarse view of things in general. In the midst of this place a man and a woman, her and her ankles, tastefully arranged on a slice of Italy, or the country about Pornic. Cut an opening across the breast of each, until the soul becomes visible, but be very careful that none of the body be lost during the operation. Pour into each breast as much as it will hold of the new strong wine of love; and, for fear they should take cold by exposure, cover them quickly up with a quantity of obscure classical quotations, a few familiar allusions to an unknown period of history, and a half destroyed fresco by an early master, varied every now and then with a reference to the fugues or toccatas of a quite-forgotten composer. If the poem be still intelligible, take a pen and remove carefully all the necessary particles.—MALLOCK, W. H., 1878, *Every Man his own Poet, or the Inspired Singer's Recipe Book*, p. 20.

Browning is the very reverse of Shelley in this respect; both have written one fine play and several fine dramatic compositions; but throughout Shelley's poetry the dramatic spirit is deficient, while in Browning's it reveals itself so powerfully that one wonders how he has escaped writing many good plays besides the "Blot in the 'Scutcheon" and that fine fragmentary succession of scenes, "Pippa Passes."—KEMBLE, FRANCES ANN, 1879, *Records of a Girlhood*, p. 384.

In strength and depth of passion and pathos, in wild humor, in emotion of every kind, Mr. Browning is much superior to Mr. Tennyson. The Poet Laureate is the completer man. Mr. Tennyson is beyond doubt the most complete of the poets of Queen Victoria's time. No one else has the same combination of melody, beauty of description, culture and intellectual power. He has sweetness and strength in exquisite combination. If a just balance of poetic powers were to be the crown of a poet, then undoubtedly Mr. Tennyson must be proclaimed the greatest English poet of our time. The reader's estimate of Browning and Tennyson will probably be decided by his predilection for the higher effort or for the more perfect art. Browning's is surely the higher aim in poetic art; but of the art which he essays Tennyson is by far the completer master.—MCCARTHY, JUSTIN, 1879, *A History of Our Own Times from the Accession of Queen Victoria to the Berlin Congress*, ch. xxix.

On Mr. Browning's new volume, ["Dramatic Idyls"] criticism can find little to remark. Since "The Ring and the Book," the poet's style and spirit have crystallized themselves, and every fresh installment can only give us a little more of the well-known matter and manner. We have all made up our minds upon the subject beforehand, and are hardly likely to form any new opinion at this time of day. Those who admire Mr. Browning will admire the present idyls; those who find him incomprehensible will find the latest addition to his incomprehensibles more incomprehensible than ever. Probably no poem which he has ever written will prove a sorer stumbling-block to bewildered spellers-out of his meaning than the all but inarticulate story of "Ned Bratts."—ALLEN, GRANT, 1879, *Some New Books, Fortnightly Review*, vol. 32, p. 149.

In knowledge of many things he is necessarily superior to Shakespeare; as being the all-receptive child of the century of science and travel. In carefulness of construction, and especially in the genius of constructing *drama*, he claims not comparison with Shakespeare. But his truly Shakespearian genius pre-eminently shines in his power to throw his whole intellect and sympathies into the most diverse individualities; to think and feel as one of them would, although undoubtedly glorified by Browning's genius within. Goethe's canon is; "The Poet should seize the particular, and he should, if there be anything sound, thus represent the universal." In this Browning is infallible: but he is, as Shakespeare often is, perceptible through the visor of his assumed individuality. Notice the great number of persons, the wide range of characters and specialities, through which he speaks.—KIRKMAN, REV. J., 1881, *Introductory Address to the Browning Society, Browning Studies*, ed. Berdoe, p. 2.

Robert Browning in his "Paracelsus" showed the failure of one who desired at a bound to reach the far ideal; in "Sordello," showed the poet before Dante, seeking his true place in life, and finding it only when he became leader of men in the real battle of life, and poet all the more.—MORLEY, HENRY, 1881, *Of English Literature in the Reign of Victoria*.

Browning's prose and poetry are alike in this. He writes like a man who has a simple thought and a simple end in view, but every step he takes suggests some associated thought and he is perpetually sweeping these side thoughts into the path he is making. The main thought is so clear to him, and the end in view so distinct, that he is hardly aware how much he confuses his expression by catching at everything on one side and the other as he goes.—SCUDDER, HORACE E., 1882, *Browning as an Interpreter of Browning, Literary World,* vol. 13, p. 78.

It is this love of mankind, even in its meanest and most degraded forms, that accounts for the almost entire absence of bitterness and cynicism in Mr. Browning's works. Blame and rebuke he can, and that in no measured terms; but sneer he cannot. Sin and suffering are serious things to him, and he is lovingly tender to weakness. He knows nothing of the craving for telling paradoxes, and stinging hits, which besets the inferior writers who make pertness and smartness supply their want of finer qualities. Humour he possesses in no small degree, but he employs it on legitimate subjects. Ruined lives are grievous to him, sore hearts are sacred, pettiness and vanity are deplorable; he has no wish to transfix them on pins' points, and hold them up to the world's ridicule.—LEWIS, MARY A., 1882, *Some Thoughts on Browning, Macmillan's Magazine,* vol. 46, p. 210.

These early poems owe much of their fascination to a trait which is characteristic of all Browning's works and rather puzzling at first sight, namely, that preference for giving any one's thoughts and feelings rather than his own which makes him one of the least subjective poets of the century. He almost always begins by setting the reader face to face with some total stranger, but previous to 1861 it is sure to be some one well worth being known. . . . His earliest works will always be most read; but even what seems only a tangled mass of briars will be found to have its rose-buds, and to form the hedge around a fairy palace where beauty slumbers, ready to bless him who dares achieve the entrance.—HOLLAND, FREDERIC MAY, 1882, *Browning Before and After 1861, Literary World,* vol. 13, p. 79.

You ask me to "describe the Browning Society, and set forth its work to date." . . . Our main reasons for starting the Society were, that the manliest, strongest, deepest, and thoughtfullest Poet of our time had had nothing like due study and honour given him; that he needed interpreting and bringing home to folk, including ourselves; that this interpretation must be done during his life-time, or the key to it might be lost; and that we could not get together the workers that we wanted, except by forming a "Browning Society."—FURNIVALL, FREDERICK JAMES, 1882, *The Browning Society, Literary World,* vol. 13, p. 77.

Robert Browning is the poet of Psychology.—CARPENTER, H. BERNARD, 1882, *Robert Browning, Literary World,* vol. 13, p. 79.

Browning's first principle or absolute Truth is Love: that which abideth one and the same, the subject and substance of all change, the permanence by which alone change is possible, whose sum ever "remains what it was before," in short, God or Truth; for, as he tells us in "Fifine," "falsehood is change," and "truth is permanence." In the whole realm of thought, including the laws of nature, and the course of history, and especially the lots of souls, Browning has essayed to pierce through the phenomenal exterior, and the abiding reality that he reaches and brings back tidings of is Love; Love is the Truth.—BURY, JOHN, 1882, *Browning's Philosophy, Browning Studies,* ed. Berdoe, p. 31.

The obscurity of Browning does not proceed, as with Hugo and Tennyson, in their latest period, from the vague immensity of the subjects considered, from the indefiniteness of his ideas, from the predominance of metaphysical abstractions, but, on the contrary, from the very precision of the ideas and sentiments, studied in their remotest ramifications, in all their varied complications, and then presented in a mass of abstractions and metaphors, now with the infinite minuteness of scholastic argument, now with sudden leaps over abysses of deeper significance. Browning is, *par excellence,* the psychological poet.—DARMESTETER, JAMES, 1883, *Essais de Littérature Anglaise.*

A poet real and strong is always phenomenal, but Browning is the intellectual phenomenon of the last half-century, even if he is not the poetical aloe of modern English literature. His like we have never seen before. He is not what he is by mere excelling. No writer that ever wrought out his fretted fancies in English verse is the model of him, either in large, or in one trait or trick of style. Of the poets of the day we can easily see, for example, that William Morris is a modern Chaucer; that Tennyson has kindred with all the great English verse-makers, and is the ideal maker of correct, high-class English poetry of the Victorian era, having about him something of the regularity and formality and conventional properness of an unexceptional model—a beauty like that of a drawing-master's head of a young woman, but informed and molded by the expression of noble thoughts; that pagan Swinburne is Greek in feeling and Gothic in form, and so forth; but we cannot thus compass or classify Browning. Were his breadth and his blaze very much less than they are, we should still be obliged to look at him as we look at a new comet, and set ourselves to considering whence he came and whither he is going amid the immensities and the eternities. . . . In purpose and in style Browning was at the very first the Browning he has been these twenty years. He has matured in thought, grown richer in experience, and obtained by practice a greater mastery over his materials, without, however, as I think, using them of late in so pleasing or even so impressive a manner as of old; but otherwise he is now as a poet, and it would seem as a man, much the same Robert Browning whose first writings were received with little praise and much scoffing and were pronounced harsh, uncouth, affected, and obscure.—WHITE, RICHARD GRANT, 1883, *Selections from the Poetry of Robert Browning*, Introduction.

To read Landor one must exert himself, and the exertion is to some purpose. The same is true, in even a higher degree, of Browning, subtle and penetrating, eminently a thinker, exercising our thought rather than our emotion; concrete in presentation, and, when most felicitous, dramatic, but capricious in expression, and greatly deficient in warmth and music; original and unequal; an eclectic, not to be restricted in his themes, with a prosaic regard for details, and a barbaric sense of color and form.—WELSH, ALFRED H., 1883, *Development of English Literature and Language*, vol. II, p. 368.

Browning is a dramatist for the one and sufficient reason that he is, above all, the student of humanity. Humanity he draws with a loving and patient hand, but on the one condition that it shall be humanity in active and passionate exercise. Not for him the beauty of repose; the still quiet lights of meditation, removed from the slough and welter of actual struggle, make no appeal to him; the apathetic calm of a moral human being, exercised on daily uninteresting tasks, is to him well-nigh incomprehensible; storms and thunder, wind and lightning, passion and fury, and masterful strength, something on which he can set the seal of his own rugged, eloquent, amorphous verse; something which he can probe and analyse and wrap up in the twists and turns of his most idiomatic, most ungrammatical style—these are the subjects which he loves to handle. And so those whose eyes are dazzled by this excess of light, or who lose their breath in this whirl of hurrying ideas, call him unintelligible; while those quiet souls who look for form and measure and control in verse deny that such uncouth and turgid lines are poetry at all. That Browning should have essayed two transcripts from Euripides is a fact not without significance for the critic, for he has thereby opened to us the secrets of his own dramatic aptitudes.—COURTNEY, W. L., 1883, "Robert Browning, Writer of Plays," *Fortnightly Review*, vol. 33, p. 888.

It is not too much to say that Mr. Browning has not only ignored the general practice of the great poets, but has designedly inverted it. The pleasure which we derive from poetry in general arises from the beauty of its form; we forget the workman in his work. But the prevailing impression created by "Jocoseria" is formlessness, together with the constant presence of Mr. Browning. Several of the poems in the volume are so obscure that it is impossible to discover the poet's intention. In others, if the track of his idea is momentarily visible, it is almost immediately withdrawn behind a cloud of words; he sets us down in the middle of a monologue, from which, if we surrender our imagination to him, will construct us a drama; or he plunges us into a labyrinth of metaphysics in which

"panting thought toils after him in vain."
—COURTHOPE, WILLIAM JOHN, 1883, *"Jocoseria," National Review, vol.* 1, *p.* 552.

No other English poet, living or dead, Shakespeare excepted, has so heaped up human interest for his readers as has Robert Browning. . . . No poet has such a gallery as Shakespeare, but of our modern poets Browning comes nearest him. . . . The last quotation shall be from the veritable Browning—of one of those poetical audacities none ever dared but the Danton of modern poetry. Audacious in its familiar realism, in its total disregard of poetical environment, in its rugged abruptness: but supremely successful, and alive with emotion. . . . It is therefore idle to arraign Mr. Browning's later method and style for possessing difficulties and intricacies which are inherent to it. The method, at all events, has an interest of its own, a strength of its own, a grandeur of its own. If you do not like it, you must leave it alone. You are fond, you say, of romantic poetry; well, then, take down your Spenser and qualify yourself to join "the small transfigured band" of those who are able to take their Bible-oaths they have read their "Faerie Queen" all through. The company, though small, is delightful.—BIRRELL, AUGUSTINE, 1884, *Obiter Dicta, pp.* 70, 71, 81, 88.

The wide range of his work is one of his strongest characteristics, and he is remarkable for the depth and versatility of his knowledge of human nature. No poet was ever more learned, more exact, and more thorough. Ruskin has said that he is simply unerring in every line. Of all the poets, except Shakspeare, he is the most subjective—a thinker, a student, and an anatomist of the soul. This is the chief reason why he has not been more recognized. Both he and Wordsworth see the infinite—the latter in nature, the former in the soul. Browning looks into the soul, and loves to see it as God sees it. No poet has more completely merged his own individuality in his work. . . . It is not from any lack of power of melody that the poet lays himself open to the charge of harshness, nor is his roughness due to carelessness nor defiance. He can use melody both varied and exquisite. The strength of his poetry, however, is in its sense, and not in its form. As to the charge of obscurity, this may be explained by the fact that his thoughts are deep and he deals often with the terrible and grotesque. He is full of strange phrases and recondite allusions, but he is a writer on obscure subjects, not an obscure writer. He does not write down to the level of the society journal or the fashionable romance. Many of his pieces of word-painting, on the other hand, stand comparatively with those of Tennyson himself. . . . He is essentially the poet of humanity. . . . In all of Browning's poems there is something, as Mr. Lowell has said, that makes for religion, devotion, and self-sacrifice. His teaching is better, braver, manlier, more cheerful, more healthy and more religious than all that has ever before passed for poetry. He is preeminently a poet of conscience, a poet of love, and a poet of true religion.—FARRAR, FREDERIC WILLIAM, 1885, *Lecture on Robert Browning.*

Mr. Browning can construct a mind, as the geologist does a skeleton. And this simile gives us the clue to all his poetry; he is a mental anatomist. His power and his skill, in his own peculiar province, are undeniable; and among his English contemporaries unequalled. Though, in spite of his unrivalled power of describing character, we cannot call him a great dramatist; that is, if we mean by dramas, complete plays, because Mr. Browning's anatomical instincts, the minuteness of his dissection of individual characters, spoil his plays as wholes. His dramas, like most of his lyrics, are revelations of individual minds; and his searching power of showing single characters prevents him from completing his plays; he is a subtle dramatic poet, then, but not a great dramatist. . . . His admirers cannot, in much of his work, call him beautiful; the wildest of them cannot, in much of his work, call him musical; so that two important qualities of good poetry are not found always in his. It is undoubtedly far better to have thought like Mr. Browning's, than the most exquisite wording if it is empty of meaning; and it takes a greater man to give us such thought. But when we concede this to the enthusiasts of the Browning Society we should remind ourselves that those poets whom the world considers the greatest are conspicuous for their form, for their splendid workmanship. All their mental powers might remain, but had they expressed their minds less well, we should certainly not rank them so high as artists.—GALTON, ARTHUR, 1885, *Urbana Scripta, pp.* 59, 66.

Browning, however, follows out all the complexities and sinuosities of reflection in his characters. Every important action, in the human being, proceeds from innumerable little turnings and twistings of the mind, flashes of revery, conflicting sentiments and impulses. All these Browning interprets better than the actual creatures could; for, although we are sometimes aware that our motives are subtle and intricate, we are seldom able to analyze them. The very copiousness of his illustrations, his wealth of simile, his tangle of clause within clause, are the means of art which make it possible for Browning to trace the complexities and mirror them so wonderfully. He does not present them literally, any more than the purely objective dramatists do. He merely employs another kind of symbol. His is diffuse; theirs is succinct. But his way is equally truthful, and it is new. It not only presents the figure and the action, but also presents the mind, irradiated by a mysterious and vivid interior light.—LATHROP, GEORGE PARSONS, 1886, *Representative Poems of Living Poets*, ed. Gilder, Introduction, p. xix.

Archdeacon Farrar thinks Mr. Browning "obscure only in the sense that his thoughts are profound," and that his obscurity is "simply verbal, the result of an idiosyncrasy which has become a habit." I suppose the meaning of this to be that Mr. Browning's thought is never clouded, and that any difficulty in his writings arises from the inadequacy of the poet's expression. I think the latter is a very great injustice to Mr. Browning, who may have written some things hard to understand, but never fails to say—if in his own manner—just what he means to say. The only real difficulty is to arrive at his meaning when the expression is merely the husk of the thought. This is not often a difficulty. Mr. Browning is a lucid thinker, and his drift is almost always plain. Caliban, Karshish and his other monologists leave nothing in doubt; but to this lucidity I find a notable exception in some verses in "Men and Women."
—COOKE, J. ESTEN, 1886, *Mr. Browning's Great Puzzle, The Critic, vol.* 8. *p.* 201.

"Childe Roland to the Dark Tower Came," a poem for which I have a deeper and keener personal affection than for any other poem in the language, and to which individually I owe more moral inspiration than to any other product of modern literature. . . . To me "Childe Roland" is the most supreme expression of noble allegiance to an ideal—the most absolute faithfulness to a principle regardless of all else; perhaps I cannot better express what I mean than by saying the most thrilling crystallization of that most noble of human sentiments, of which a bright flower is the motto *Noblesse oblige.*—BATES, ARLO, 1886, *Mr. Browning's Great Puzzle Again, The Critic, vol.* 8, *pp.* 231, 232.

It may as well be confessed at the outset of any study of Browning that he does not observe the methods which have been evolved by the years as most effective for the embodiment of thought. We must grant also that this is a conscious and deliberate act. A man who can command music like that in the *Song* from "A Blot in the 'Scutcheon," or vigor like that in "Cavalier Tunes," is not forced to express himself so blindly as in the last ten lines of the *Invocation* from "The Ring and the Book," or so harshly as in "Red Cotton Night-Cap Country." He chooses so to express himself. . . . Browning knows English poetry as few of his critics know it. He knows, also, how to make smooth verse which shall tell its story to him who runs. Granting these facts, it is no more than fair that we treat with respect both the poet and his large following, and ask if our notions about art may not need reconstruction.—HERSEY, HELOISE E., 1886, *Select Poems of Robert Browning, Introduction.*

In an age when on every wind comes borne the cry of realism, he remains faithful to the spirit of idealism. He finds the soul to be that which transcends all other facts and laws. To him it is the one supreme fact. That is the one phenomenon he desires to study. To an investigation of it, in all its many phases, he has devoted his life. He has been as eager to look into the history of a soul as the scientist is to investigate the history of a star or earth-worm. He has felt that the individual man is worth more than any other fact or law, that he is the one unique phenomenon the world presents, and that he alone gives the inquirer an adequate object of thought. There are in the soul heights, and depths, and glories, and expanses of out-reaching mystery, which Browning has seen with eyes wonder-set and a mind zealous to know the truth. Browning has exerted an influence on literature as fresh and suggestive as that of Carlyle or Emerson. He has the same unique power, he has the same subtle gift of insight, and he has the same intensity of conviction which those men possessed. He is an original force in literature, never an imitator, but one to arouse and to stimulate all who come after him. He stands apart by himself as a poet. He had no forerunner, and he is likely to have no successor.—COOKE, GEORGE WILLIS, 1886, *Poets and Problems*, p. 277.

> To him, whose craft, so subtly terse,
> (While lesser minds, for music's sake,
> From single thoughts whole cantos make),
> Includes a poem in a verse;—
> To him, whose penetrative art,
> With spheric knowledge only his,
> Dissects by keen analysis
> The wiliest secrets of the heart;—
> To him, who rounds us perfect wholes,
> Where wisdom, wit, and love combine;
> Chief praise be this:—he wrote no line
> That could cause pain in childlike souls.

—FLEAY, FREDERICK GARD, 1886, *A Chronicle History of the Life and Work of William Shakespeare*, p. 5.

> O strong-soul'd singer of high themes and wide—
> Thrice noble in thy work and life alike—
> Thy genius glides upon a sea whose tide
> Heaves with a pain and passion infinite!
> Men's hearts laid bare beneath thy pitying touch;
> Strong words that comfort all o'er-wearied much;
> Thoughts whose calm cadence moulds our spirit-life,
> Gives strength to bravely bear amid world-strife;
> And one large Hope, full orb'd as summer sun,
> That souls shall surely meet when LIFE is won!
> So round thy heart our grateful thanks entwine;
> Men are the better for these songs of thine!
> At eve thy muse doth o'er us mellower swell,
> Strong with the strength of life lived long and well.

—KINGSLAND, WILLIAM G., 1886, *Robert Browning: Chief Poet of the Age*, p. 3.

One other book I must mention, for it affected at least the form of any work I have done in letters more than any other. In a bookseller's shop here one day—I dare hardly say how many years ago, but I was still in my teens, still in the stage when books fashion us, and are not merely used by us—I picked up some pamphlets, in yellow paper covers, and printed in double columns. I had never before heard the author's name, and his form of publication was very unusual for poetry. There was but one copy in the shop, and no one had even asked the price of it. The name of the yellow pamphlet I first picked up was curious. "Bells and Pomegranates, by Robert Browning"—what could it mean? One glance, however, discovered to me that here was a true singer. Of course, I had read all that Tennyson had then published with the delight and admiration which it could not fail to give. But something in these fresh, rough dramatic lyrics seized on me in that book-shop, and I became the possessor, I believe, of the only copy of Browning then in Edinburgh. Very soon I was pestering all my friends to read them, or to hear me read them, successfully in some cases, but to other people they were *caviare*. I do not know that any of his works since published, except, perhaps, "Men and Women" and (in parts) "The Ring and the Book," have given me anything like the same pleasure as I got from those early yellow-paper pamphlets. Sorry I am that they have somehow vanished, among the comelier editions that now occupy my shelves, for the sight of them again might revive some of the glory of those old nights when friends—all gone now—gathered in my lodging, and, amid clouds of smoke, I recited "How I brought the Good News from Aix to Ghent," or "The Flight of the Duchess," or "What's become of Waring?" These poems were not only a joy to me; they were also a power. They helped me, at least, to find what little vein might be in me.—SMITH, WALTER C., 1887, *Books which Have Influenced Me*, p. 95.

Browning's language is almost always very hard to understand; but the meaning, when we have got at it, is well worth all the trouble that may have been taken to reach it. His poems are more full of thought and more rich in experience than those of any other English writer except Shakespeare. The thoughts and emotions which throng his mind at the same moment so crowd upon and jostle each other, become so inextricably intermingled, that it is very often extremely difficult for us to make out any meaning at all. Then many of his thoughts are so subtle and so profound that they cannot easily be drawn up from the depths in which they lie. No man can write with greater directness, greater lyric vigour, fire, and impulse, than Browning when he chooses—write more clearly and forcibly about such subjects as love and war;

but it is very seldom that he does choose. The infinite complexity of human life and its manifold experiences have seized and imprisoned his imagination; and it is not often that he speaks in a clear, free voice.—MEIKLEJOHN, J. M. D., 1887, *The English Language: Its Grammar, History and Literature*, p. 358.

If the varied and sometimes conflicting tendencies of the time are reflected by the Laureate, its master-passion is incarnated in Robert Browning. Browning is essentially the poet of man. He can make poetry of anything, so long as it concerns a human being. In a dramatic age he would have been a great dramatic poet, but the conditions of his time, unfavourable to this kind of excellence, have led him to devise dramatic situations rather than complete plays, and to cast his best thought into intense, impassioned monologues.—GARNETT, RICHARD, 1887, *The Reign of Queen Victoria*, ed. Ward, vol. II, p. 461.

In the natural order of things, he who is susceptible in youth to the influence of Foster will one day find himself led captive by Robert Browning. Many-sided as this most masculine and thought-laden of our poets is, he will find many readers who have not graduated in Foster's school. But he who has relished the independence, the rugged originality, the fruitfulness of the one, can scarcely fail to be strongly attracted by the other. It was said of Crabbe that he was "Pope in worsted stockings:" it is quite as true to say that Foster is Browning in worsted stockings. There is the same robust fibre of thought, the same pioneering fearlessness, but family likeness to the lecturer and essayist is scarcely recognisable in the travelled poet who has lived in every human condition, and by the marvellous power of poetic genius read from the inside the thoughts and the life of every age. Shakespeare is more simply human, and in normal human life has a wider range. Browning has no women so lovable, no fools so motley, no clowns so irresistible; nor have the bulk of his characters that inexplicable touch which makes them live and walk as real persons. But could Shakespeare himself have entered into a Ned Bratts, or a Bishop Blougram, or a Fra Lippo Lippi, as Browning has done? For what Browning lacks in universality he has made up for by culture, by that enlargement and enlightenment which the religious problems of our own day have brought, and by confronting the Christian faith with every phase of individual experience and of the general progress of thought among men. But of Browning others can better speak, though few can have found in him so unfailing a stimulus.—DODS, MARCUS, 1887, *Books which Have Influenced Me*, p. 109.

"A Death in the Desert," can be only partly understood by itself. It must be studied with its whole environment. The circumstances of its production must be considered; knowledge of the poet's principles and methods, acquired by study of his other works, must be brought to bear on it. It needs that freedom of interpretation which he always seems to demand. For while he is lavish in suggestion, he is very chary of information. Very rarely does he give his readers ready-made opinions. His teaching stimulates, it does not forestall, thought.—GLAZEBROOK, MRS. M. G., 1887, "*A Death in the Desert*," *Browning Studies*, ed. Berdoe, p. 225.

Here was, again, a poet whose thoughts fell at once into the dramatic form, whose characters unfolded themselves by act and speech, whose treatment of subject involved a rising interest and a progressive movement, terminating in an adequate denouement, while the verse bore the impress which lives in Shakespeare and his contemporaries, and in "Marlowe's mighty line," an heir to the fellowship of those writers who have made the drama's history sublime and achieved the highest fame. A little familiarity with the mechanism of the theatre, such as Shakespeare, Alfieri, or Goldoni had, such as all the successful dramatists have had, and we should possess great plays as well as great poems from the pen of Robert Browning. Then the grand traits of his two heroines in the dramatic poem "In a Balcony" would have shone in the theatrical frame resplendent with the Antoinette of Giacometti or the Ophelia and Portia of Shakespeare; while the "Flight of the Duchesss" and other remarkable poems would have obeyed the grand laws of the dramatic form, and gone into line with the creations of those great poets with whom only Browning may be classed—"the immortal names that were not born to die."—BARRETT, LAWRENCE, 1887, *A Blot in the 'Scutcheon and Other Dramas*, ed. Rolfe and Hersey, p. 14.

Then I came in contact with the robust genius of Robert Browning. His sensuous carnations glorified my wilderness; amid them moved actual man and woman, naked and not ashamed. The pale, bloodless figures of my Oxonian romances were dismissed; in their place moved Pippa, Colombe, Valence, Mildred, the gypsy duchess. — CONWAY, MONCURE DANIEL, 1888, *Books That Have Helped Me*, p. 95.

The clearest eyes in all the world they read
With sense more keen and spirit of sight more true
Than burns and thrills in sunrise, when the dew
Flames, and absorbs the glory round it shed,
As they the light of ages quick and dead,
Closed now, forsake us: yet the shaft that slew
Can slay not one of all the works we knew,
Nor death discrown that many-laurelled head.
The works of words whose life seems lightning wrought,
And moulded of unconquerable thought,
And quickened with imperishable flame,
Stand fast and shine and smile, assured that nought
May fade of all their myriad-moulded fame,
Nor England's memory clasp not Browning's name.
—SWINBURNE, ALGERNON CHARLES, 1889, *A Sequence of Sonnets on the Death of Robert Browning, Fortnightly Review*, vol. 55, p. 1.

If aspirations were indeed achievement, Robert Browning would have been the greatest name in the roll of English poets; and even as it is, his work will rank among the greatest spiritual forces of England.— JACOBS, JOSEPH, 1889, *Robert Browning, Literary Studies*, p. 115.

The truth is that, from a fortunate fusion of several races and characters, we find united in Browning the poet's sensuous love of all earthly beauty, keen ear for rhythm and turn of speech, pregnant eloquence and high range of thought and image, run through by a steel fibre of unflinching probity and courage, high mystic and religious tendencies, philosophic insight, plastic and perceptive gifts, and virile stability. But he is necessarily, by this very fusion, a poet of a unique growth. It is waste of time to compare or associate him with other poets, English or not—to draw parallels as to style or cast of thought; and, though you may parody, you can never imitate him. It has taken the English people nearly half-a-century to make up their minds about him in any large numbers; an even now a great majority of his admirers seek philosophy where they might easily find live men and women. To Browning, from the minutest detail of gesture or habit to the most thrilling psychological crisis, all humanity has been welcome material; while in actual poetic construction the manner of a phrase or even a grotesque rhyme have, when needful, been as carefully studied in producing and finishing a mental portrait or scene as have his most resonant and majestic passages of poetic eloquence. —NETTLESHIP, JOHN T., 1889, *Robert Browning, The Academy*, vol. 36, p. 406.

The radical cause for the want of dramatic life in most of Mr. Browning's characters lies in his novel dramatic form; but whether the age or the author is at fault, it must be plain to any careful reader that Mr. Browning is incapable of using a better form. There is just enough of the dramatic tincture to body forth the man thinking, not the man acting. The end in view, I maintain, does not always seem to be thoroughly poetical or artistic; but for the portrayal of a single creature, careless of his surroundings and embodiment,—yet with perhaps the utmost fidelity to the phases of mental life,—to draw a supposititious being whose every thought and purpose, whose very soul shall be as nature plans, no more effective process could be devised. Were the author to have less of the dramatic form, there would be an entire absence of human interest; were he to introduce more, the characters drawn would be objective ones. We have the mental man all but stripped of his bodily mould.— MORRIS, HARRISON S., 1889, *Browning versus Browning, Poet-lore*, vol. 1, p. 411.

A mother's love! And that mother divine! I cannot conceive of any higher effort of religious ideality. Yet nowhere in Browning have I found any just appreciation of this supreme ideal of love. He touches it rarely and coldly. Would you know the reason? I will tell you. Browning is not simply a Christian; he is a Protestant Christian, a Protestant Anglican Christian, at times an intolerant and polemical Christian, as we see displayed in some unpleasant passages in "Christmas Eve and Easter Day," in the "Story of Pornic," and elsewhere. Hence his lack of poetic sympathy with other forms of belief.—BRINTON, DANIEL G., 1889, *Facettes of Love, from Browning, Poet-lore*, vol. 1, p. 26.

There is no poet of our time more original, be that originality good or bad, than

Browning. . . . There is no poetry on which opinions are so much divided, none so at variance with preconceived ideas, none, therefore, which it is so difficult fairly to appreciate. There is no poet of our time so uneven, none so voluminous, none so obscure. . . . His poetry, then, is for Browning, but a form of activity, a means of realizing his own individuality. He is not an Eglamour; his poetry is not the end of his existence; he does not submit to his art, nor sacrifice his perfection as a man to the perfection of his work. Like Goethe, he writes not so much to produce a great work,—to please others, as to afford play to his own individuality. Necessarily, then, as he points out in "Sordello," his work is imperfect. He has himself rather than his reader in view. He is seeking to give complete and accurate expression to what is within him, rather than to give beauty and artistic completeness to his work. Accordingly, the incongruous and non-essential from the artistic point of view, he does not prune away; these are needful for the true and complete expression of his own mind.—ALEXANDER, WILLIAM JOHN, 1889, *An Introduction to the Poetry of Robert Browning*, pp. 2, 210.

Gone from us! that strong singer of late days—
Sweet singer should be strong—who, tarrying here,
Chose still rough music for his themes austere,
Hard-headed, aye but tender-hearted lays,
Carefully careless, garden half, half maze.
His thoughts he sang, deep thoughts to thinkers dear,
Now flashing under gleam of smile or tear,
Now veiled in language like a breezy haze
Chance-pierced by sunbeams from the lake it covers.
He sang man's ways—not heights of sage or saint,
Not highways broad, not haunts endeared to lovers;
He sang life's byways, sang its angles quaint,
Its Runic lore inscribed on stave or stone;
Song's short-hand strain —its key oft his alone.
—DEVERE, AUBREY, 1890, *Robert Browning, Macmillan's Magazine*, vol. 61, p. 258.

It is as hard to explain how one got to like Browning, as it would be (to me) to explain why I put Beethoven above Mozart; and why I cannot help confessing Bach to be of higher order than Handel, though Handel has written things that seem to me Divine. I can only tell you my experience. Of course I have known Browning, in a way, for years; but I never took to him. I had not laughed at him, because I instinctively felt that he was a person to stand in awe of; and I hold it wrong to laugh where there are evidences of truth and greatness. But I am afraid I sometimes smiled at Browningites. . . . Oddness was not the word for much of all this; the poet was writing, not in a grand robe, but in his shirt-sleeves, and making faces at you. But through it all was the deep sense of truth, lighted up with gleams of beauty, such as did not belong to any poetry I knew.—CHURCH, RICHARD WILLIAM, 1890, *To Stanley Withers*, Feb. 9; *Life and Letters of Dean Church*, ed. his Daughter, pp. 413, 414.

His verse is subtle, for he wrote of the springs of human action as revealed in a thousand situations. Shakespeare summoned all the world to act upon his stage. Browning tested each individual soul in his crucible and compelled it to deliver up such secrets of the inner life as no previous analysis had disclosed. His verse is so strong that he may well be called the poet of energy. Though he wrote some stanzas of surpassing grace, the quality of strength has made his fame, which will be lasting, for his theme was high. That the spirit of man is great and immortal, because always capable of effort towards an ideal beyond, is the truth to which he was constant. Such was his philosophy.—BIGELOW, WALTER STORRS, 1890, *Robert Browning, The Magazine of Poetry*, vol. 2, p. 204.

Browning lived to realise the myth of the Inexhaustible Bottle.—HENLEY, WILLIAM ERNEST, 1890, *Views and Reviews*, p. 84.

No poet ever had more perfect opportunity to study woman's character in its sweetest and noblest aspects than Mr. Browning, and nowhere does this great artist show more consummate power, or more delicate intuition, than in his portraiture of women. Independently of all mere conventional claim on our sympathy, relying by no means exclusively upon slender forms, taper fingers, ruby lips, or the like, Mr. Browning's women step out of shadow-land into the atmosphere of breathing humanity. They have their adorable perfections and imperfections; they are feminine to the very core. Each word-painting of physical beauty has its spiritual counterpart in characters whose every outward trait bespeaks a corresponding moral quality.—IRELAND, ANNIE E., 1890, *Browning's Types of Womanhood, The Woman's World*.

Browning is animated by a robust optimism, turning fearless somersaults upon the brink of the abyss. . . . And then Browning loomed on the horizon, surely the brawniest neo-Elizabethan Titan whom our age has seen, and whom it has latterly chosen to adore.—SYMONDS, JOHN ADDINGTON, 1890, *Essays, Speculative and Suggestive*, vol. II, pp. 246, 262.

When Browning's enormous influence upon the spiritual and mental life of our day—an influence ever shaping itself to wise and beautiful issues—shall have lost much of its immediate import, there will still surely be discerned in his work a formative energy whose resultant is pure poetic gain.—SHARP, WILLIAM, 1890, *Life of Robert Browning (Great Writers)*, p. 200.

If his creations were ill-clothed in their bodies of clay, the breath that he blew into their nostrils was life of the most concentrated and passionate sort. As works of art his poems are abnormal and altogether unclassifiable; but as emanations they are strangely and superbly influential with the imagination of a sympathetic reader (that is whenever they are comprehensible at all), and there is that in them which leaves no question of the man's uncommon genius. All through, from first to last, the optimism of a sane and hopeful soul shines with fascinating intensity. . . . He was surcharged with song, but his vocal organ was not of the singing sort. In this he and Emerson were alike to a degree; they forgot the tune in the tremendous struggle with the meaning of the words, and they lost the words too often in the overwhelming rush of the thought. Minds thus constituted can create dramas, but they cannot limit the creations so as to bring them within a unit of expression. . . . A great man he was, with an imagination and a poetic vision of absolute power; this must, I think, be the final word; but he lacked the supreme gift of artistic expression through verse, an expression which, first of all, is luminous, direct and simple.—THOMPSON, MAURICE, 1890, *Browning as a Poet, America*, Jan. 2.

His work is related to the ideal life of the nation as Carlyle's is related to its practical life; and if his influence has not been wielded over quite so long a period as was that of the author of "Sartor Resartus" it has, on the other hand, extended over a more feverishly active time. . . . That he was a real poet in the sense of having written real poetry will be admitted by every competent critic. But it will have, I fear, to be added that no poet so eminent as Mr. Browning has ever left behind him so large a body of brilliant, profound, inspiring literature, wherein the essential characteristics of poetry will be sought in vain.—TRAILL, HENRY DUFF, 1890, *Robert Browning, National Review*, vol. 14, pp. 593, 597.

Nay, when he died the most fashionable of the London daily papers wrote of him in a tone of supercilious patronage, with a sort of apology to its butterfly readers for asking their attention to a writer so remote from their world as Browning. That is behind the time and foolish, yet I suspect that Browning's poetry was far less known to the world of London than Browning himself. So far as he was read in society—which reads little—he was read by the younger generation of fashionable people; to the older he was, I might almost say, unknown. He was literally unknown to some. I have heard the mention of his name followed by the remark: "Browning? Is he not an American novelist." The lady who put that question is an ornament of society, full of every kind of social intelligence, and it was not many years ago. I doubt whether he has ever been the poet of the classes. The masses, or some of them, were probably those who read him most. The critics have praised him with very large reservations. But there was a class of readers neither literary or smart who found in Browning something they wanted, and who for the sake of the kernel were willing to prick their fingers with the husk or bruise their joints over the shell. They are the people to whom the problems of life are everything, and what drew them to Browning was his penetration and power in handling these problems. — SMALLEY, GEORGE W., 1890, *London Letter, New York Tribune*.

Robert Browning wrote the sonnet rarely, possibly because he disliked its restraints; possibly he purposed to let no lesser light of his shine by the side of the "Sonnets from the Portuguese." The "Helen's Tower" is graceful complimentary and occasional verse, but would not be quoted save for its personal interest. Any one, however, who studies Browning's poetry will see how inapt the sonnet form is for the wilful, eccentric orbits in which his genius loved to move.—CRANDALL, CHARLES H., 1890, *ed.*

Representative Sonnets by American Poets, p. 77.

Of almost any one of Emerson's essays you can remember some notable phrases, a general atmosphere of that peculiar purity which we find only in New England, but no such thing as organic unity. In fact, I take it, Emerson himself could often have been found at fault, had he tried to explain exactly what he meant. Emerson's obscurity comes, I think, from want of coherently systematic thought. Browning's, on the other hand, as some recent critic has eagerly maintained, is only an "alleged obscurity." What he meant he always knew. The trouble is that, like Shakspere now and then, he generally meant so much and took so few words to say it in, that the ordinary reader, familiar with the simple diffuseness of contemporary style, does not pause over each word long enough to appreciate its full significance. What reading I have done in Browning inclines me to believe this opinion pretty well based. He had an inexhaustible fancy, too, for arranging his words in such order as no other human being would have thought of. Generally, I fancy, Browning could have told you what he meant by almost any passage, and what relation that passage bore to the composition of which it formed a part; but it is not often that you can open a volume of Browning and explain, without a great deal of study, what the meaning of any whole page is. Emerson's indubitable obscurity to ordinary readers I take to be a matter of actual thought; Browning's seems rather to be a matter of what seems—even though it really were not—deliberate perversity of phrase.—WENDELL, BARRETT, 1891, *English Composition,* p. 208.

Browning's writing goes best in the bulk—it is the general result that we enjoy, being oftener rather distracted than attracted by the component parts. . . . Browning's work is shut out, not only from the presence of poetry but, from the precincts of "good utterance." Browning need follow no predecessor in the application of the fixed laws of poetic utterance, but he must apply these laws in some way; he must establish the kinship. Where he does this, he is a poet; where he does not do this, whatever else he may be, he is not a poet. The judgment here formed is, that he often fails in this particular; hence, that only a part, the smaller part, of his writing can be called "just," "legitimate," poetry.—CHENEY, JOHN VANCE, 1891, *The Golden Guess,* pp. 133, 148.

Browning is obscure, undoubtedly, if a poem is read for the first time without any hint as to its main purport: the meaning in almost every case lies more or less below the surface; the superficial idea which a careless perusal of the poem would afford is pretty sure to be the wrong one. Browning's poetry is intended to make people think, and without thought the fullest commentary will not help the reader much.—BERDOE, EDWARD, 1891-98, *The Browning Cyclopædia, Preface,* p. vii.

The most marked literary characteristic of the poetry of Browning is its intellectuality. This gives it a twofold recommendation. It invites the study of the thoughtful. It rewards them with that for which they seek, their object being not to gain the passing pleasure of a pious sentiment, but the permanent possession of a spiritual conviction. There are other religious poets who have written psalms of life, songs of devotion, hymns of aspiration, which men have made the channels of their prayers and the marching music of their lives. There are none who can surpass or even rival Browning in the chastened beauty, the restrained but earnest enthusiasm, the catholic and genuine sympathy of those of his poems which deal directly or indirectly with the religious life.—EALAND, F., 1892, *Sermons from Browning,* p. 3.

He is a stronger and deeper man than Tennyson; an incompleter artist, but a greater poet; and his method of approaching doubt wholly differs from Tennyson's. He loves to assault it with sardonic humor, to undermine it with subtle suggestion, even to break out into grim laughter as it slowly disintegrates and falls into a cloud of dust before his victorious analysis. But not the less does he sympathize with whatever there may be of spiritual yearning, of earnest but baffled purpose in it; and no poet has ever been quicker than he to place in the fullest light of tender recognition the one redeeming quality there may be latent in the thing he hates. For faith, in Robert Browning, is a spiritual fire that never burns low. Through whatever labyrinth of guilt or passion he may lead his readers, God is ever the attending presence.—DAWSON, W. J., 1892, *Quest and Vision,* p. 96.

His best work, the work which will last

when the noises are done, is as simple as it is sensuous and passionate; and it is entirely original. It stands more alone and distinct than the work of any other English poet of the same wide range. There is a trace of Shelley in "Pauline," but for the rest Browning is like Melchizedek: he has neither father nor mother in poetry; he is without descent; and he will be—but this belongs to all great poets—without end of days. "Whole in himself and owed to none" may well be said of him, and it is a great deal to say.—BROOKE, STOPFORD A., 1892, *Impressions of Browning and his Art, Century Magazine*, vol. 45, p. 244.

Mr. Browning had a style, a very remarkable one, but of Style he is absolutely destitute, for his literary manner is one of rapid volubility and constant eagerness—qualities eternally opposed to dignity, to Style, whose very essence is its proud way of never pressing itself upon you.—WATSON, WILLIAM, 1893, *Excursions in Criticism*, p. 106.

Here at last was the second Shakespeare, but with no audience yet prepared.... Thus forty years after Browning seemed to himself and the world to have been forgotten, he is rediscovered as one of the world's great seers, hailed as the prophet of a new era, and vindicated as the chief poet of the century. No man longer calls in question his greatness or his mission. As fast as men and women attain the capacity to interpret his concentrative figures and appreciate his types, they are drawn to him. Until eye and ear have been prepared, Raphael and Mozart mean less than their inferiors. Each mind must overtake in its own development the progress of the race at large, or it will declare the best thought and sentiment of its times meaningless—though it thereby but publish its own inchoate and arrested culture. Not so very long ago it was popular to decry the symphonies of Beethoven, but little by little the presumption has become general, even among those unversed in music, that the fault is not with Beethoven, but with the undiscerning hearer. Similarly, within the last five years the once frequent girds at Browning have disappeared from public print. What with clubs, societies, and college study, what with the ever-increasing output of primers, handbooks, and commentaries, the persuasion is abroad that this poet evinces the loftiest ideals yet revealed in our literature, as well as fulfills its long delayed and often repeated prophecy of power.—SHERMAN, L. A., 1893, *Analytics of Literature*, pp. 101, 102.

If Browning's genius has remained long unrecognized and unhonoured among his contemporaries, the frequent harshness and obscurity of his expression must not bear the whole responsibility. His thought holds so much that is novel, so much that is as yet unadjusted to knowledge, art, and actual living, that its complete apprehension even by the most open-minded must be slow and long delayed. No English poet ever demanded more of his readers, and none has ever had more to give them. Since Shakespeare no maker of English verse has seen life on so many sides, entered into it with such intensity of sympathy and imagination, and pierced it to so many centres of its energy and motivity. No other has so completely mastered the larger movement of modern thought on the constructive side, or so deeply felt and so adequately interpreted the modern spirit. . . . Of all English poets he is the most difficult to classify, and his originality as a thinker is no less striking. It is true of him, as of most great thinkers, that his real contribution to our common fund of thought lies not so much in the disclosure of entirely new truths as in fresh and fruitful application of truths already known; in a survey of life complete, adequate, and altogether novel in the clearness and harmony with which a few fundamental conceptions are shown to be sovereign throughout the whole sphere of being. It is not too much to say of Browning that of all English poets he has rationalized life most thoroughly. In the range of his interests and the scope of his thought he is a man of Shakespearian mould. — MABIE, HAMILTON WRIGHT, 1893, *Essays in Literary Interpretation*, pp. 103, 110.

He is less thoroughly an artist than Tennyson, but not necessarily on that account less a poet. I recall only one poem of Browning which is absolutely without thought. I may raise a clamor of protest when I say that this one is "Childe Roland to the Dark Tower came." In this we have simply a picture. We may put a meaning into it, but to ask what the poet meant by it is to apeal to the fancy. I do not say that the poet had not an allegory in his mind when he wrote; I simply say that the allegory is not in the poem.—EVERETT, CHARLES CARROLL, 1893, *Tennyson and*

Browning as Spiritual Forces, New World, vol. 2, p. 241.

Browning seems destined to take the place of Pope and to vex the minds of future generations (for a very different reason, however) with the query, "Is he a poet?" Whatever Pope's deficiency in matter may be, no one ever questioned his supremacy in words. He sent his verbal shafts with the accuracy of Ulysses through all the rings of opinion until they fastened firmly in his target, the human mind. But it would take an order of the King to put any of Browning's phrases into general circulation.—MOORE, CHARLES LEONARD, 1893, *The Future of Poetry, The Forum*, vol. 14, p. 774.

Browning, though never popular, was an indefatigable writer, who bore the neglect of his countrymen with serene good-humour, and persisted in the choice of recondite subjects, an eccentric method of treatment, a style of versification generally harsh and abrupt, and a style of language now pedantic and now familiar, and frequently obscure. His rhymes, too, are often Hudibrastic, without being effective. His philosophical reasonings, and even his narratives, are difficult to follow; the reader arises from several perusals with only a vague idea of the author's plan or meaning. One who runs cannot read Browning; he demands the study of a specialist. Yet specialists assure us that if he is difficult to understand, the delight of understanding him is ample compensation for all the toil which the difficulties he interposes entail, and that he is inferior only to Shakespeare in the richness, subtlety, and suggestiveness of his thought. That he could be intelligible and forcible on a first reading when he chose is well proved by such pieces as "The Pied Piper," "Hervé Riel," "How they Brought the Good News from Ghent to Aix," etc.—ROBERTSON, J. LOGIE, 1894, *A History of English Literature*, p. 315.

The humour of Robert Browning was not a dominating constituent in his intellectual endowment, but it was certainly an essential one. Were we to remove from his work the passages in which its presence is obvious, even to the hasty, careless reader, and those still more numerous passages where it eludes the pointing finger or the frame of quotation marks, and yet, like the onion in Sydney Smith's salad, "unsuspected, animates the whole," the result would be, not merely impoverishment, but transformation. We should feel not merely that something had gone, but that what remained had lost a certain indefinable quality of interest and charm. . . . A large proportion of Browning's humour—witness such characteristic poems as "Bishop Blougram's Apology" and "Sludge, the Medium"—takes the form of delicate irony, where the something *said* is delicately poised against the something *implied*, and we are made to feel the attraction of both. Browning's satirical irony always preserves the geniality which is of the essence of true humour; it may be mordant, but it is never scarifying; like summer lightning it illuminates, yet does not burn.—NOBLE, JAMES ASHCROFT, 1894, *The Poets and the Poetry of the Century, Humour, Society, Parody, and Occasional Verse*, ed. Miles, pp. 337, 339.

Browning's style may be compared to a Swiss pasture, where the green meadows which form the foreground of a sublime landscape are yet combered with awkward blocks and boulders—things not without a certain rough dignity of their own, but essentially out of place.—BENSON, ARTHUR CHRISTOPHER, 1894, *Essays*, p. 298.

Robert Browning is the one poet who has taken human life for his exclusive province; and his method has for its very soul the tracing of development. . . . The vigorous spirit of Browning roams over all the world, scanning the island off the coasts of Lebanon as the wolf-haunted forests of Russia. From "Paracelsus," more full of the spirit of Luther's Germany than the casual reader dreams, and "Sordello," more full of the spirit and facts of pre-Dantean Italy than the casual reader likes, on through dramas and monologues and epics to the mobile and vivid Hellenic studies of his later years, Browning shows a more frankly human and unæsthetic interest in the past and a wider sympathy than any other poet. . . . The immense vitality and wide productiveness of Browning demand classification, but the classification is not yet found. Optimist, realist, mystic we may call him if we will, yet all the while we know that the epithet touches only one side of his great and placid nature. His robust versatility serenely defies compression into a phrase. Yet if, with the fatuous affection of mortal man for labels, we insist on knowing by whose side he is to be put, we shall find, I believe, his truest abiding-place if we name him with the great masters of Ionic Art. Humor, and humor tinged with irony, is the most distinctive, if not the most important, element in his genius. Its bitter aroma is never long absent. We believe that we breathe the pure air of the sublime, and a gust of satire slaps us sharply in the face. We feel ourselves wrapt in religious ecstasy; hey! presto! We are in the coarsest region of grotesque.—SCUDDER, VIDA D., 1895, *The Life of the Spirit in the Modern English Poets, pp.* 25, 148, 202.

It is almost too hackneyed to call Browning a Gothic man, but it is irresistibly true. The typical Greek loved life for its own sweet sake, fully enjoyed it, wished it no other, only unending. Browning, as another great Englishman has frankly confessed, could not have endured heaven itself under such conditions. Struggles, ascent, growth, were sweet to him. To be still learning was better than to know.— LAWTON, WILLIAM CRANSTON, 1895, *The Classical Element in Browning's Poetry, The Boston Browning Society Papers, p.* 336.

It is impossible for any intelligent admirer to maintain, except as a paradox, that his strange modulations, his cacophonies of rhythm and rhyme, his occasional adoption of the foreshortened language of the telegraph or the comic stage, and many other peculiarities of his, were not things which a more perfect art would have either absorbed and transformed, or at least have indulged in with far less luxuriance. Nor does it seem much more reasonable for anybody to contend that his fashion of soul-dissection at a hard-gallop, in drama, in monologue, in lay sermon, was not largely, even grossly, abused. . . . Even his longer poems, in which his faults were most apparent, possessed an individuality of the first order, combined the intellectual with no small part of the sensual attraction of poetry after a fashion not otherwise paralleled in England since Dryden, and provided an ordinary body of poetical exercise and amusement. The pathos, the power, at times the humor, of the singular soul-studies which he was so fond of projecting with little accessory of background upon his canvas, could not be denied, and have not often been excelled.—SAINTSBURY, GEORGE, 1896, *A History of Nineteenth Century Literature, pp.* 273, 274.

Browning is a poet who very frequently mentions God, and who a number of times has elaborately written concerning his nature and his relations to man. The arguments in question are frequently stated in dramatic form, and not as Browning's own utterances. Paracelsus, Caliban, David in the poem "Saul," both Count Guido and the Pope in "The Ring and the Book," Fust in the "Parleyings," and Ferishtah, are all permitted to expound their theology at considerable length. Karshish, Abt Vogler, Rabbi Ben Ezra, Ixion, and a number of others, define views about God which are more briefly stated, but not necessarily less comprehensible. On the other hand, there are the two poems, "Christmas Eve," and "Easter Day," which, without abandoning the dramatic method, approach nearer to indicating, although they do *not* directly express, Browning's personal views of the theistic problem. These poems are important, although they must not be taken too literally. Finally, in "La Saisiaz," and in the "Reverie" in "Asolando," Browning has entirely laid aside the dramatic form, and has spoken in his own person concerning his attitude towards theology.—ROYCE, JOSIAH, 1896, *Browning's Theism, The Boston Browning Society Papers, p.* 15.

From first to last Browning portrayed life either developing or at some crucial moment, the outcome of past development, or the determinative influence for future growth or decay. His interest in the phenomena of life as a whole, freed him from the trammels of any literary cult. He steps out from under the yoke of the classicist, where only gods and heroes have leave to breathe; and, equally, from that of the romanticist, where kings and persons of quality alone flourish. Wherever he found latent possibilities of character, which might be made to expand under the glare of his brilliant imagination, whether in hero, king, or knave, that being he chose to set before his readers as a living individuality to show whereof he was made, either through his own ruminations or through the force of circumstances.—PORTER, CHARLOTTE, AND CLARKE, HELEN A., 1896, *ed. Poems of Robert Browning, p.* 26.

To sum up our imperfect sketch of this strangely interesting poet, perplexing, disappointing, and fascinating, Browning is confessedly and above all a teacher, whether directly, or when he offers us his superb gallery of semi-dramatic characters and situations—semi-dramatic, or rather, perhaps, intended to be such. For, everywhere, among all sorts and conditions of men and things, how seldom does Browning—despite his disclaimers—escape from Browning! Often, one might say, if he has one eye upon his subject, the other is on himself. Hence, I suppose, many as are the scenes of passion which he has given, one note, last and sweetest—the note of disinterested love—is found all too rarely. These idiosyncrasies inevitably more or less suffuse his landscape. With its many peculiar merits, it rarely seems able to touch the inner soul of Nature herself; it lacks charm; hardly ever is the verse musical, never enchanted:—unique, indeed, to the core; yet not leaving the heart wholly satisfied.—PALGRAVE, FRANCIS TURNER, 1896, *Landscape in Poetry*, p. 264.

Of all poets none was more intensely hostile to Parody than Robert Browning. This may have been the result of his disappointment at not being generally recognized as his own parodist, since many of his lines might well pass for parodies of those that precede them. His ramshackle blank verse, with its jagged, jolting lines bristling with prepositions, conjunctions, and interjections, its contractions and elisions, its intrusive parentheses, its smallest of jokes and poorest of puns, its pedantic display of untimely erudition, and aimless wandering from the subject in hand, render it the despair of the would-be parodist. Before Browning exaggeration stands appalled: the master himself wallows in such obscurity and mazy verbiage that when Parody has done its best it finds itself after all only imitation.—MARTIN, A. S., 1896, *On Parody*, p. 109.

Browning himself was the son of one classical scholar—and the husband of another. He was lulled to sleep as a child in his father's library with the Greek verses of Anacreon (or rather the Anacreontics, we suspect). If we interpret the poem "Development" literally, he began Greek by his eighth year, and read Homer through as soon as he had "ripened somewhat," which would hardly point beyond his twelfth summer. Certainly Browning as a student must have been fully acquainted with the best Greek and Roman poets in their own speech. Balaustion, however, his first important essay in translation, appeared in the poet's *sixtieth* year. If we examine the whole body of his work up to that time, we shall find surprisingly little of direct allusion, even, to classical themes and persons. . . . In choice of subjects, in the point of view from which he studied them, and in the mass and measure of treatment, Browning was pre-eminently un-Greek, unclassical.—LAWTON, W. C., 1896, *The Classical Element in Browning's Poetry, American Journal of Philology*, vol. 17, pp. 197, 200.

Browning's relation to Christianity and to all that is involved in a belief in Christianity is undoubtedly one of the chief points of interest in his writings, and accounts, I suspect, for the extraordinary popularity which during late years they have attained. . . . The gist and nucleus of Browning's philosophy of life, may be said to be summed up in that couplet in the "Ring and the Book," "Life is probation, and the earth no goal but starting point for man."—COLLINS, JOHN CHURTON, 1896, *Browning and Christianity, Saturday Review*, vol. 81, pp. 343, 344.

The "Dramatic Lyrics," and "Men and Women," seem to our mind the most characteristically valuable of this virile poet's contributions to English literature. Though his whole occupation is with problems of the inner nature, and problems, moreover (as a previous critic has noted), less deep than devious, yet his sane and impartial voice, sometimes, in them, trembles with pathos all the more effective because it is so sudden, restrained, and brief.—THOMPSON, FRANCIS, 1897, *Academy Portraits, The Academy*, vol. 51, p. 500.

He never caught the popular ear—he has never tried to catch it. His productions have had to make their way against storms of criticism, but they have been read by a continually increasing number of thoughtful people. Whatever the student of literature may think of Browning, he must take account of the fact that never before was there a writer of verse for the study of whose writings during his lifetime clubs were formed in every large city of both hemispheres—the proceedings of some of these clubs being regularly published, like the transactions of learned societies. . . . He cares not so much for the result as for the process—he describes, not so much incidents, as people's impressions of them. . . . Rarely, if ever, has this writer's verse any tinge of the objective, much less of the epic.

... Browning is greatest as a creative genius; less great as an idealizer; least great as a literary artist. ... Emotion, music, grace—these are not so native to Robert Browning as thought. The philosopher often overtops the poet.—STRONG, AUGUSTUS HOPKINS, 1897, *The Great Poets and their Theology*, pp. 378, 382, 400, 409.

What is called the "roughness" of Browning's verse is at all events never the roughness that comes from mismanagement or disregard of the form chosen. He has an unerring ear for time and quantity; and his subordination to the laws of his metre is extraordinary in its minuteness. Of ringing lines there are many; of broadly sonorous or softly melodious ones but few; and especially (if one chooses to go into details of technic) he seems curiously without that use of the broad vowels which underlies the melody of so many great passages of English poetry. Except in the one remarkable instance of "How We Carried the Good News from Ghent to Aix," there is little onomatopœia, and almost no note of the flute; no "moan of doves in immemorial elms" or "lucent sirops tinct with cinnamon." On the other hand, in his management of metres like that of "Love Among the Ruins," for instance, he shows a different side; the pure lyrics in "Pippa Passes" and elsewhere sing themselves; and there are memorable cadences in some of the more meditative poems, like "By the Fireside."—BURLINGAME, E. L., 1897, *Library of the World's Best Literature*, ed. Warner, vol. V, p. 2564.

I began to read the two poets about the same period, 1841, when I was not quite eighteen, and long before the collected poems of either had been brought together. I then read them both constantly and knew by heart most of those of Tennyson, in particular, before I was twenty years old. To my amazement I now find that I can read these last but little; the charm of the versification remains, but they seem to yield me nothing new; whereas the earlier poems of Browning, "Paracelsus," "Sordello," "Bells and Pomegranates"—to which last I was among the original subscribers—appear just as rich a mine as ever; I read them over and over, never quite reaching the end of them. In case I were going to prison and could have but one book, I should think it a calamity to have Tennyson offered me instead of Browning, simply because Browning has proved himself to possess, for me at least, so much more staying power. — HIGGINSON, THOMAS WENTWORTH, 1897, *The Biography of Browning's Fame*, The Boston Browning Society Papers, p. 5.

He could not quote Greek verses, but he was steeped in the Greek tragedians and lyric poets. Of course this classical sympathy was but one side of his poetry. Browning was full of sympathy, nay, of worship, for anything noble and true in literature, ancient or modern. And what was most delightful in him was his ready response, his generosity in pouring out his own thoughts before anybody who shared his sympathies.—MÜLLER, FRIEDRICH MAX, 1898, *Auld Lang Syne*, p. 159.

These Renaissance poems, then,—aside from their abstract virtue as intensely felt and virily wrought verse, — perform one of the great and rare services possible to literature. They make us to know past beliefs and feelings, people and actions, so that all becomes veritable and explicable: to know them not formally and by effort and intention, but spontaneously, through the dynamic communication of heat and light. Instead of the statics of knowledge we are given the dynamics of life.—BURTON, RICHARD, 1898, *Renaissance Pictures in Robert Browning's Poetry*, Poet-lore, vol. 10, p. 76.

The joyous, fearless activity of Browning, the noble aspirations of his intellect and the mighty passions of his heart, the steady certainty that God and man are one in kind, render him the most distinctly helpful to those who have been vexed with the subtle speculations which have abounded in our scientific age. More than any poet of modern times he has that intellectual fearlessness which is thoroughly Greek; he looks unflinchingly upon all that meets him, and he apparently cares not for consequences. His is "a mind forever voyaging through strange seas of thought, alone." In many of his poems we find united the two great principles which lie at the basis of all his best work: one, which has for its end, knowledge; the other, which has for its end, conduct. The first is Browning's philosophy; the second Browning's art. There are many who delight in Browning's intricate thought,—pure exercise of the mind,—but we must believe that he contributed more to the spiritual movement of the age by his "Saul," "Apparent Failure," "Prospice," "Abt Vogler," etc., than by all his argumentative verse. These are indeed veritable fountain-heads of spiritual power.—GEORGE, ANDREW J., 1898, *From Chaucer to Arnold, Types of Literary Art*, p. 658.

Robert Browning had the keenest and subtlest intellect, the deepest and broadest human sympathy, of any English poet of his generation. He stands apart from his poetic contemporaries by the originality of his methods and by the unconventionality and power of his style.—PANCOAST, HENRY S., 1899, *Standard English Poems, Spenser to Tennyson*, p.728, note.

He very often seems to search laboriously for language that is "fit and fair and simple and sufficient," as he himself admirably expresses it, and the effort is writ large over the whole. And some of his greatest and noblest thoughts are expressed in language which fails in all four points. In "Christmas Eve," for instance, there are passages, which approach very near to the sublime, but which stop short of it, because suddenly one feels a great jolt in the metre, or a grotesque rhyme comes in which only provokes a smile, where a smile is out of place. . . . And then there is that crying sin against style, not so easily defined, but which all readers of Browning know and feel, the introduction of language which belongs by right to the sphere of logical argument into passages which where otherwise the language is that of pure poetry. And we feel that this is deliberately done; for so close is the connection between beauty of thought and beauty of form, that they never would have come of themselves into so alien a country. It seems as if Browning either lacked that fine instinctive feeling for form which preserves many a worse poet from such incongruities, or that, in his anxiety to express himself, he despairingly resorts to any means rather than leave the thing unsaid. . . . Browning's supreme title of honour is that he is in the lives of many something distinctive and unique. Many people, looking back, can say that he has spoken to them as no one else has spoken; and that life and death and all things wear a different aspect for his handling. This is saying much; but many will bear me out that these are the words of truth and sobriety.—LITTLE, MARION, 1899, *Essays on Robert Browning*, pp. 18, 19, 30.

That Robert Browning is the greatest dramatic poet of England since Shakespeare we regard as indisputable; that he belongs in the first rank of poets of any description, in spite of some uncouth mannerism, we judge also certain, though not undisputed.—ABBOTT, LYMAN, 1899, *The Love Letters of Two Poets, The Outlook*, vol. 62, p. 485.

The elements to which Browning reduces experience are still passions, characters, persons; Whitman carries the disintegration further and knows nothing but moods and particular images. The world of Browning is a world of history with civilization for its setting and with the conventiona passions for its motive forces. The world of Whitman is innocent of these things and contains only far simpler and more chaotic elements. In him the barbarism is much more pronounced; it is, indeed, avowed, and the "barbaric yawp" is sent "over the roofs of the world" in full consciousness of its inarticulate character; but in Browning the barbarism is no less real though disguised by a literary and scientific language, since the passions of civilized life with which he deals are treated as so many "barbaric yawps," complex indeed in their conditions, puffings of an intricate engine, but aimless in their vehemence and mere ebullitions of lustiness in adventurous and profoundly ungoverned souls.—SANTAYANA, GEORGE, 1900, *Interpretations of Poetry and Religion*, p. 175.

It is true, indeed, that Browning was at no time a "topical" poet; and much of his long unpopularity was, no doubt, due to his disinclination to come down into the market-place, with his singing robes about him, and make great ballads of the day to the chorus of the crowd. But there is a higher part even than that of a national poet; and Browning is, in a very real sense, the poet, not of England alone, but of the world. His attitude to men and life was never distraught by petty interests of blood or party; the one claim upon him was the claim of humanity. He was a man, and nothing that pertained to man was foreign to himself.—WAUGH, ARTHUR, 1900, *Robert Browning*, p. 150.

Browning, perhaps more than any other poet, demands that he shall be kept out of the hand of the theological anatomist; for Browning is the poet of life, of simple human life, of its anguish, its search, its doubt, its despair, its triumph. He does not find life through theology; he finds theology, so far as he finds it at all, through life. He plunges into the midst of man's life—the life that he, and you and I, and all must live, the life that is so enchanting, so bewildering, so stimulating to effort, so provoking to ambition, so disappointing to desire, so heart-breaking, so hope-raising, so killing, so rejuvenating; plunging into this perplexing, moving, mighty ocean of life, he asks what it means. Will the waves that are around lift us to the height of our desire, or will they overwhelm us and beat out our lives? Will the currents sweep us outward to death in midocean? Or is there some friendly tide which will gently but strongly bear us to some safe and happy shore? Are our struggles in the great sea vain and void? Are we the sport of forces mightier than ourselves? Or do human efforts, strong, manly resolve, and high, trusting courage count for something in the interplay of environing powers? He asks questions such as these, interrogating life with frank and open mind, and he shouts out to us across the storm the answer which he hears.—CARPENTER, W. BOYD, 1901, *The Religious Spirit in the Poets*, p. 204.

No poet ever comprehended his own character better, or comprised the expression of it in better language. This note of militant optimism was the ruling one in Browning's character, and nothing that he wrote or said or did in his long career ever belied it. This optimism was not discouraged by the results of an impassioned curiosity as to the conditions and movements in the soul in other people. He was, as a writer, largely a psychological monologuist—that is to say, he loved to enter into the nature of persons widely different from himself, and push his study, or construction, of their experiences to the furthest limit of exploration. In these adventures he constantly met with evidences of baseness, frailty, and inconsistency; but his tolerance was apostolic, and the only thing which ever disturbed his moral equanimity was the evidence of selfishness. He could forgive anything but cruelty. His optimism accompanied his curiosity on these adventures into the souls of others, and prevented him from falling into cynicism or indignation. He kept his temper and was a benevolent observer. This characteristic in his writings was noted in his life as well.—GOSSE, EDMUND 1901, *Dictionary of National Biography, Supplement*, vol. I, p. 317.

Many of Browning's characters express opinions which he cannot be supposed to share, and occasionally, as in "Prince Hohenstiel-Schwangau" and "Fifine at the Fair," it is difficult to discover the exact point at which he and his hero diverge. But taking the whole range of his work into account, few poets can be said to have revealed themselves so completely as he has done. His writings are dramatic in form, rather than in principle; his own scheme of thought can be traced through them; and this is definite enough to be systematically expounded. As far as the broad outlines of the scheme are concerned, there is no room for differences of opinion.—PIGOU, ARTHUR CECIL, 1901, *Robert Browning as a Religious Teacher*, p. 7.

Though the love of Nature was always less in him than his love of human nature, yet for the first half of his work it was so interwoven with his human poetry that Nature suggested to him humanity and humanity Nature. And these two, as subjects for thought and feeling, were each uplifted and impassioned, illustrated and developed by this inter communion. That was a true and high position. Humanity was first, Nature second in Browning's poetry, but both were linked together in a noble marriage; and at that time he wrote his best poetry.—BROOKE, STOPFORD A., 1902, *Browning's Treatment of Nature, The Critic*, vol. 41, p. 74.

Now that his life and his life's work are ended, there is no more to be said than what the calm-minded critics declared twenty years ago and more; in Browning, the philosopher and literary man stifled the poet. His head poetised and did not suffer his great and noble heart to speak, except in artificial language, difficult to understand. Despite all the "Browning Societies," he is accounted by his own countrymen as the least intelligible of their poets; and he of whom that is said must bear the blame. All great art is simple and intelligible; moderation and clearness are indispensable to it. Both these are wanting in Browning. He possessed a superabundance of imagination and an astonishing, positively acrobatic skill in versemaking and rhyming; yet he has not succeeded in producing a single lasting work of art.—ENGLE, EDWARD, 1902, *A History of English Literature*, rev. Bent, p. 428.

In leading up to this statement of the problem of Belief, I have led up to the great lesson of Browning's poetry, which so many of his interpreters have failed to bring out. Belief arises from an experience together with its intellectual interpretation; hence the worth of the belief depends on the range and depth of the experience as well as on the thoroughness of the interpretation. Browning's main thought is, the value of work—that is, effort and energy of spirit—in deepening experience and so affording new data for knowledge. His appeal is to the completest possible human experience tested and interpreted by Work,—active productive energy of spirit is the way to the meaning of things.—MELLONE, SYDNEY HERBERT, 1902, *Leaders of Religious Thought in the Nineteenh Century*, p. 254.

John Bright
1811–1889

John Bright, son of Jacob Bright, a Quaker cotton-spinner at Rochdale, was born there November 16, 1811, and educated at a Friends' school at Ackworth, and afterwards at York and Newton. While in his father's factory he took a great interest in public questions; and after a foreign tour (1835), which took in Palestine, he lectured at Rochdale on his travels, as well as on commerce and political economy. When the Anti-Corn-Law League was formed in 1839 he was a leading member, and, with Cobden, engaged in Free-trade agitation throughout the kingdom. In 1843 he became M. P. for Durham, and strongly opposed the Corn Laws until they were repealed. In 1845 he obtained the appointment of select committees on the Game Laws, and on cotton cultivation in India. In 1847 he was elected a member for Manchester; in 1852 aided in the temporary reorganisation of the Corn Law League. Like Cobden a member of the Peace Society, he energetically denounced the Crimean war (1854). In his absence on the Continent through illness, he was rejected by Manchester. Elected in 1857 for Birmingham, he seconded the motion (against the Conspiracy Bill) which led to the overthrow of Palmerston's government; and he advocated the transference of India to the direct government of the crown. During the civil war in America he warmly supported the cause of the North. His name was closely associated with the Reform Act of 1867. In 1868 he accepted office as President of the Board of Trade, but in 1870 retired through illness. He supported the disestablishing of the Irish Church (1869), and the Irish Land Act of 1870. He took office in 1873, and again in 1881, as Chancellor of the Duchy of Lancaster, but retired from the Gladstone ministry in 1882, being unable to support the government in its Egyptian policy. In 1886–88 he strenuously opposed the Home Rule policy of Mr. Gladstone, and was a great power in the Unionist party, being then as always recognised as one of the most eloquent public speakers of his time. He was Lord Rector of Glasgow University in 1883. He died March 27, 1889. See his "Speeches" (1868) and "Letters" (with memoir, by Leech, 1885; new ed. 1895), and Lives by Robertson (1877) and Barnett Smith (1881).—PATRICK AND GROOME, eds., 1897, *Chambers's Biographical Dictionary*, p. 133.

PERSONAL

I will tell you about Bright and Brightdom, and the Rochdale Bright mill some other day. Jacob Bright, the younger man, and actual manager at Rochdale, rather pleased me—a kind of delicacy in his features when you saw them by daylight—at all events, a decided element of "hero-worship," which of course went for much. But John Bright, the Anti-Cornlaw member, who had come across to meet me, with his cock nose and pugnacious eyes and Barclay-Fox-Quaker collar—John and I discorded in our views not a little. And, in fact, the result was that I got to talking occasionally in the Annandale accent, and communicated large masses of my views to the Brights and Brightesses, and shook peaceable Brightdom as with a passing earthquake; and, I doubt, left a very questionable impression of myself there!—CARLYLE, THOMAS, 1847, *Letter to His Wife*, Sept. 13; *Thomas Carlyle, A History of his Life in London*, ed. Froude, vol. I, p. 352.

Bright has certainly a magnificent face, square-jawed, resolute, commanding, with a short straight nose, a broad forehead, and a grey eye which kindles and glows, and a stern but well-cut mouth. I had forgotten how fine his head really was.—MOTLEY,

JOHN LOTHROP, 1867, *Letter to his Eldest Daughter, July 20; Correspondence*, ed. Curtis, vol. II, p. 272.

John Bright looks a hale fifty-five years. In stature he is about the height of Henry Ward Beecher, though considerably stouter. He has a face of the finest English type, full and open, with gray side-whisker, and a healthy, ruddy complexion. The mouth, chin and lower jaw, express great firmness and vigor. The nose is full, nostrils broad, while the space is broad between the clear, full, gray eyes, which appear capable of great expression. In repose they are mild and kindly. Both brow and head are broad, full and arched high in the coronal region. The whole figure is cast in a massive mould. He looks the orator and leader of men, even when silent; and there is in his presence itself a pervading sense of power. His manner is pleasant, grave and cordial, yet not unmixed with a dash of *hauteur* and brusqueness that one can readily trace to his business and public life.—HINTON, RICHARD J., 1868, *John Bright at Home, The Galaxy*, vol. 5, p. 291.

There was nothing rugged about him, nothing coarse. Occasionally, indeed, he was brusque and peremptory in his conversation, as well as in his speeches; and, if he was provoked to political discussion, he was strenuous and sometimes stern. But he did not care to be always fighting, and when he had taken off his armour he could be as playful as a child and as charming as a woman. On the platform the volcano might have been fiercely active; an hour after he had done speaking, the mountain which had poured forth streams of angry fire was covered to the very crater with vines and flowers. . . . He had a robust conscience. He cared for plain and homely virtues. He had an intellectual and moral scorn for the subtleties of casuistry. For him the line between right and wrong was strongly and firmly marked; on one side there was light, and on the other darkness. —DALE, R. W., 1889, *Mr. Bright, Contemporary Review*, vol. 55, pp. 637, 638.

In physical appearance so different from Mr. Gladstone, John Bright possessed striking characteristics of his own. A somewhat broad-shouldered figure of middle height; a large head with thick white hair and a powerful brow; the beard limited, in the older English manner, to a fringe; well-cut features; the face of roseate hue, and of true John Bullish type, but with delicately-shaped nose; a clear and open glance; the mouth finely curved, with downward lines seemingly indicating the inward pride of a man of masterful temper, who had gone through contests which cannot but leave traces of bitterness: such was the aspect of the Tribune of the People.— BLIND, KARL, 1889, *John Bright, Fortnightly Review*, vol. 45, p. 653.

Bright was essentially what has been styled a theopathic man; conversing, when in his graver moods, as though he was in the presence of the Deity, the undercurrent of his thoughts was fundamentally religious; and though there were many who denied the wisdom and the justice of his methods, there were few, indeed, who questioned his honesty of purpose.—KENT, C. B. ROYLANCE, 1899, *The English Radicals*, p. 379.

I have heard some of his finest speeches, and to my mind, he was far the grandest orator of our time. The power of his oratory lay not in eloquence or splendour of diction, in the vulgar sense, but in the touching simplicity with which he went home to the right sense and generous sympathy of true men. . . . I was at times associated with him in committees, meetings, and social and political movements, where his sterling judgment and his manly spirit guided many a cause. And I had frequent opportunities of talking to him at clubs and social gatherings, where he was conspicuous for genial humour and keen insight. John Bright was hardly surpassed as a *causeur* in his time. He retained to the last the tone and manner of the simple provincial Quaker.—HARRISON, FREDERIC, 1901, *George Washington and Other American Addresses*, p. 195.

Of the duumvirate which he formed with Cobden, Cobden was the inspiring spirit. He first directed Bright's concentration upon the corn law, and so long as he lived struck the keynote of Bright's political action. Himself a master of luminous exposition, he utilised Bright's power of trenchant analysis. When the two spoke on the same platform the order of proceeding was for Cobden to state the case and for Bright to pulverise opponents. Like Cobden, Bright was largely a self-taught man, and the circumstance no doubt contributed to form his bias to individualism. But in his address to the students of Glasgow, upon his installation as lord rector (21 March, 1883), he expressed his regret at his want of a university training. He was a constant reader, especially of poetry, history, biography, economics, and the Bible. Upon the Bible and Milton, whose "Paradise Lost" he frequently carried in his pocket, his English was fashioned. Its directness and force saved him from the Johnsonian declamation which had long done duty for oratory. He was steeped in poetry; scarcely a speech was delivered by him without a felicitous quotation. Dante (in English), Chaucer, Spenser, Shakespeare, Milton, Shenstone, Gray, "Rejected Addresses," Byron, Lewis Morris, Lowell, and many others, find place there. The Bible, read aloud by him to his family every morning and evening, was drawn upon by him both for illustration and argument.—LEADAM, I. S., 1901, *Dictionary of National Biography, Supplement, vol.* I, *p.* 289.

ORATORY

Mr. Bright is very attractive as an orator. When it is known that he is to speak, the galleries are insufficient to hold the multitude which gathers to hear him. His delivery is prompt and easy. He has none of that hesitation and apparent timidity which mark the address of many English orators; but neither, on the other hand, does he possess that rich and fascinating intonation which forces us to concede the forensic palm to Mr. Gladstone of all contemporary Englishmen. He expresses himself with boldness, sometimes almost with rudeness. His declamation is fresh, vigorous, and almost always even. At times he is unable to preserve the moderation of language and manner which retains the mastery over impulse; his indignation carries him away; his denunciation becomes overwhelming; his full voice rings out, trembling with agitation, as he exposes some wrongful or defends some good measure: then his vigorous nature appears, unadorned by cultivated graces, but admirable for its manliness and strength.—TOWLE, G. M., 1865, *John Bright and the English Radicals, Atlantic Monthly, vol.* 16, *p.* 183.

When the name of Mr. Bright is mentioned, one of our first reflections is occupied with his oratory. And in this respect, as regards its power and influence, there is but one other public man comparable with him, namely, Mr. Gladstone. . . . Robust in figure, and with a fine, genial, Saxon face, his very glance has been sufficient to fix his audience. Like Coleridge's Ancient Mariner, "he holds us with his glittering eye;" and that eye, which is of a deep blue, can now flash with indignation, and now beam with the soft light of sympathy. His broad face, high, full forehead, and mobile mouth are all in keeping with the oratory which is so characteristic of him. His voice is—or was in its meridian strength—remarkably clear and of great compass, reaching a mass of fifteen thousand persons almost as easily as it could address itself to a hundred and fifty. The speech itself is always singularly clear and vivid, now rippling with humour, now impregnated with earnestness and pathos. As one critic has observed, "his diction is drawn exclusively from the pure wells of English undefiled." Milton and the Bible are his unceasing study. There was a time when it was rare to find him without "Paradise Lost" in his hand or in his pocket. The use of Scriptural imagery is a marked feature of his orations, and no imagery can be more appropriately employed to illustrate his views; for Mr. Bright, in all his grand efforts rises far above the loaded, unwholesome atmosphere of party politics into the purer air and brighter skies of patriotism, of philanthropy.—SMITH, GEORGE BARNETT, 1881, *The Life and Speeches of John Bright, p.* 364.

"There came up a lion out of Judah," was Charlotte Brontë's exclamation when she was present at one of Thackeray's lectures. The same remark will have suggested itself to many persons who have witnessed John Bright on the occasion of one of his great oratorical efforts. The massive, well-set head, the lofty brow, the white hair, the clear blue eye, as Saxon in its expression as the language of the speaker, have immediately arrested the attention of all spectators. Yet, in the House of Commons, the visitor may have failed to recognize immediately the voice and the presence of its greatest orator. . . . His eloquence may be compared to the glow of a clear fire steadily burning almost at a white heat. There is nothing fitful or spasmodic about it. The solemn and the sportive are interwoven as naturally as the serious and comic scenes in one of Shakespeare's masterpieces. Mr. Bright has probably coined as many concise and adhesive phrases as Disraeli himself. It is he who invented the words "fancy franchise," who first employed "the cave of Adullam" as a metaphor for the refuge of the disaffected, and who compared the Adullamites themselves to the Scotch terrier of which it was difficult to say what portion formed the head and what the tail. His humour has always been of the quiet, cutting, and sarcastic style.—ESCOTT, T. H. S., 1884, *John Bright, Century Magazine*, vol. 28, p. 445.

Bright was a man of less catholic temper, less comprehensive gifts [than Cobden]. But his singleness of air, his combative spirit—it was wittily said of him that if he had not been a Quaker he must have been a prizefighter—his superb eloquence—unsurpassed for purity and nobility of language, for spontaneous grace of gesture and native majesty of intonation, for pathos, for humour, and for a command of imagery at once simple and direct, and withal profoundly appropriate and impressive,—his sympathetic insight into the sober, serious, righteous gravity of the English character, his noble scorn of wrong and his inflexible love of right, made him an irresistible advocate and an indispensable ally.—THURSFIELD, J. R., 1891-98, *Life of Peel*, p. 224.

John Bright seldom made an unsuccessful speech. Like other artists, however, he was nervous, anxious and irritable until his work was done. When his speech was over, he was as happy and sympathetic as a child. If it was a speech in the House of Commons he would retire to the members' smoking room, or stand with his back to the fire in the division lobby, and, surrounded by a group of parliamentary friends run over the debate with trenchant humour. If it was a public meeting, he would fall into his host's easy chair with a cigar, and talk far into the night on a thousand trivial topics to which his language lent a thousand charms.—MCLAREN, CHARLES, 1892, *Reminiscences of John Bright, North American Review*, vol. 155, p. 318.

It is as an orator rather than as a statesman that Bright takes highest rank. Lord Salisbury has said of him, "He was the greatest master of English oratory that this generation has produced, or I may perhaps say several generations back. I have met men who have heard Pitt and Fox, and in whose judgment their eloquence at its best was inferior to the finest efforts of John Bright." Unlike the other great orators of the queen's reign, notably Gladstone, Bright did not have a classical education. His style was formed largely upon the English Bible, and his language was the language native to the soil. His speeches are characterized by a homely simplicity which appeals especially to the popular heart and which was the secret of much of his power.—BOYD, CARL EVANS, 1899, *John Bright, The Chautauquan*, vol. 28, p. 544.

GENERAL

The speeches which have been selected for publication in this volume possess a value, as examples of the art of public speaking, which no person will be likely to underrate. Those who may differ from Mr. Bright's theory of the public good will have no difficulty in acknowledging the clearness of his diction, the skill with which he arranges his arguments, the vigour of his style, the persuasiveness of his reasoning, and above all, the perfect candour and sincerity with which he expresses his political convictions. . . . This is not the occasion on which to point out the causes which confer so great an artistic value on these compositions; which give them now, and will give them hereafter, so high a place in English literature. At the present time nearly a hundred millions of the earth's inhabitants speak the English tongue. A century hence, and it will probably be the speech of nearly half the inhabitants of the globe. I think that no master of that language will occupy a loftier position than Mr. Bright; that no speaker will teach with greater exactness the noblest and rarest of the social arts, the art of clear and persuasive exposition. But before this art can be attained (so said the greatest critic that the world has known), it is necessary that the speaker should secure the sympathies of his audience, should convince them of his statesmanship, should know that he is free from any taint of self-interest or dissimulation. These conditions of public trust still form, as heretofore, in every country of free thought and free speech, the foundation of a good reputation and of personal influence. It is with the fact that such are the characteristics of my friend's eloquence, that I have been strongly impressed in collecting and editing the materials of this volume.—ROGERS, JAMES E. THOROLD, 1868, ed. *Speeches on Questions of Public Policy by John Bright, Preface*, p. v.

He is gifted beyond any Englishman now living with rare and admirable faculty of seeing right into the heart of a subject, and discerning what it means and what it is worth. Nor is this ever a lucky jump at a conclusion. Bright never gives an opinion at random or offhand.—McCarthy, Justin, 1869, *The Liberal Triumvirate of England, The Galaxy, vol.* 7, *p.* 39.

Respected, admired, trusted, believed in as he is by thousands, I shall be astonished if a close and careful study of these beautiful speeches in the light that I have indicated does not convince other thousands that, whether for power of pathos, foresight of feeling, simplicity or sincerity, earnestness, truth, or eloquence, these volumes are hard to match in the English language.—Page, S. Flood, 1872, *The Right Honorable John Bright, M. P., Macmillan's Magazine, vol.* 25, *p.* 352.

It is impossible to study his speeches, or to listen to any one of them, without perceiving that the speaker is a well-read man, able to illustrate any and every topic from the stores of his memory. In English poetry, especially, his quotations are frequently recondite and curious, and very much to the point. The book from which he quotes most constantly is the Bible; but he rarely makes use of a verse of Scripture unless it has a close and manifest application to the subject in hand.—Apjohn, Lewis, 1881, *John Bright and the Party of Peace, Retrenchment and Reform, p.* 297.

Mr. Bright's teaching has its weak side, which it were mere flattery for any admirer to keep out of sight. But it were the grossest injustice toward a great teacher to deny that he has, by his acts no less than by his words, produced a most beneficial effect on the tone of English politics. . . . If Mr. Bright has raised the tone of politics by separating democratic agitation from the vices generally displayed by demagogues, this is not the only service, great though it be, which he has rendered to his country. His life-long labors have increased, if they have not created, a new sense of responsibility not only as regards peace and war, but as regards every matter connected with the treatment of foreign nations or the government of countries which are, in any sense whatever, dependencies.—Dicey, A. V., 1882, *The Influence of John Bright, The Nation, vol.* 35, *pp.* 305, 306.

He is as unacademical a personage as a really eminent and cultivated man can be, for his cultivation is entirely of the modern and domestic English type. He never was at a university, and at school learned little of Latin and of Greek—mere scraps, which have long since perished. He has not given evidence of having studied the literature of any Continental country, while for physical science he seems to have no interest or knowledge beyond what every intelligent man who lives in an age of inventions must have. What he does care for and has diligently and lovingly studied is modern English literature, and especially Milton and the poets who have followed him down to our own time. They are no mean instrument of training, and their influence is often felt in the correct and finished diction of his speeches. . . . His opposition to the Crimean war in 1854 made him very unpopular. His opposition to Lord Palmerston's Chinese war in 1857 cost him his seat for Manchester. He was denounced as a man thoroughly unpatriotic, devoid of a sense of the honour and dignity of England; a manufacturer, who, to sell his goods, would have the country submit to any humiliation. He was also represented as the enemy of property and education; the man who sought to hand over all political power to the ignorant masses. In fact, he had become the typical demagogue, against whose designs the *Saturday Review*, then rather a Liberal than Conservative organ, and by no means the organ of Toryism which it has now become, used every week to warn its readers.—Bryce, James, 1883, *Mr. Bright at Glasgow University, The Nation, vol.* 36, *p.* 336.

Great Tribune of the people, storms may rise,
They will not shake the pillars of thy throne,
Seeing thy rule was selflessness sincere.
And praise did never blind those patient eyes
That looked beyond State discord to the year
When golden Love shall bind all hearts in one.
—Rawnsley, H. D., 1889, *John Bright, Murray's Magazine, vol.* 5, *p.* 660.

The advantages Mr. Bright possessed for engaging in public life were at once discernible, and especially in the cause that had been launched just as he was ready to enter upon a public career. He had not occupied himself much with the economical mischiefs connected with this question, but he saw in it one of injustice, of disturbance of trade, and of periodical suffering on the part of those who earned their bread by labour, and, as he thought, one redounding to the exclusive advantage of the class he viewed with no favour. It was, therefore, precisely the question in which his energy, his fearlessness, and his most telling style of speech were sure to be available, and one in which his thorough belief in his own convictions induced him to give full play to his grand oratorical and combative powers.— VILLIERS, CHARLES PELHAM, 1889, *John Bright, Universal Review, vol. 3. p. 429.*

If his vocabulary was limited, his choice of words within those limits was singularly just and delicate. In his popular addresses, —the conditions of which admitted a more accurate preparation than his speeches in Parliament, where any speaker is partly at the mercy of the course of debate,—there are few sentences in which the boldest critic would venture to suggest the replacement of a single word. He had a most delicate sense of rhythm. In this respect not one of our most admired orators has excelled him.—VINCE, C. A., 1898, *John Bright, p. 211.*

William Wilkie Collins
1824–1889

Born, in London, Jan. 1824. Educated at private school. Tour with his parents in Italy, 1837–38. Articled to a firm of tea merchants [1838?]. Student at Lincoln's Inn, 18 May 1846; called to Bar, 21 Nov. 1851. Began to devote himself to literature, 1848. Contrib. to "Household Words," 1856; and to "All the Year Round." "The Lighthouse," produced at the Olympic theatre, Aug. 1857; "The Red Vial," at Olympic, Oct. 1858; "The Frozen Deep," at Olympic, 27 Oct. 1866; "No Thoroughfare" (dramatized from novel), at Adelphi, Dec. 1867; "Black and White" (written with Fechter), at Adelphi, March, 1868; "The Woman in White" (dramatized from novel), 9 Oct. 1871; "Man and Wife," at Prince of Wales's, 22 Feb. 1873. Visit to United States, 1873–74. "The Moonstone" (dramatized from novel), produced at Olympic, Sept. 1877; "The New Magdalen," at Olympic; "Rank and Riches," at Adelphi, 9 June 1883. Died, in London, 23 Sept. 1889. Buried at Kensal Green. *Works:* "Memoir of the Life of William Collins," 1848; "Antonina," 1850; "Rambles beyond Railways," 1851; "Basil," 1852; "Mr. Wray's Cash Box," 1852; "Hide and Seek," 1854; "After Dark," 1856; "Dead Secret," 1857; "The Queen of Hearts," 1859; "The Woman in White," 1860; "A Message from the Sea" (with Dickens), 1861 [1860]; "No Name," 1862; "My Miscellanies," 1862; "The Frozen Deep" (with Dickens; privately printed), 1866; "Armadale," 1866; "No Thoroughfare" (with Dickens), 1867; "The Moonstone," 1868; "Man and Wife," 1870; "No Name," dramatized (privately printed), 1870; "The Woman in White," dramatized (privately printed), 1871; "Poor Miss Finch," 1872; "The New Magdalen," 1873; "Miss or Mrs.?," 1873; "The New Magdalen," dramatized (privately printed), 1873; "Readings and Writings in America," 1874; "Miss Gwilt," drama adapted from "Armadale" (privately printed), 1875; "The Law and the Lady," 1875; "Alicia Warlock," 1875; "The Two Destinies," 1876; "The Moonstone," dramatized (privately printed), 1877; "The Haunted Hotel," 1879 [1878]; "The Fallen Leaves," 1879; "A Rogue's Life," 1879; "Jezebel's Daughter," 1880; "Considerations on the Copyright Question," 1880; "The Black Robe," 1881; "Heart and Science," 1883; "I say No," 1884; "The Evil Genius," 1886; "The Guilty River," 1886; "Little Novels," 1887; "The Legacy of Cain," 1888. *Posthumous:* "Blind Love," ed. by W. Besant, 1890.—SHARP, R. FARQUHARSON, 1897, *A Dictionary of English Authors, p. 62.*

PERSONAL

I forgot to say that another of Foster's guests was Wilkie Collins (the "Woman in White's" author). He is a little man, with black hair, a large white forehead, large spectacles, and small features. He is very unaffected, vivacious, and agreeable.— MOTLEY, JOHN LOTHROP, 1861, *To His Mother, March 15; Correspondence, ed. Curtis, vol. I, p. 365.*

An invalid much of the time, with that enemy of Englishmen, the gout, threatening his eyes, Mr. Collins is nowadays little seen in London society; but for many years he has kept strictly at work in London, at his house in Gloucester Place, not far from the busy turmoil of Baker Street, though he is now leaving this house for new quarters. Here the great drawing-rooms were given up for his desk-work when he was writing a novel, or for striding up and down the floor, reciting speeches and acting out scenes, if it were a play he was at work upon. One finds him a man still of striking appearance, but much aged by illness since he was seen in America, with a leonine head, the plentiful hair and flowing beard nearly white, contrasting with a short and smallish though once powerful body, and tiny white hands. The stoop of his shoulders suggests long application to his work, but his manner and speech have the vigor and crispness of an unexhausted spirit of youth.—BOWKER, RICHARD ROGERS, 1888, *London as a Literary Centre, Harper's Magazine, vol.* 77, *p.* 3.

GENERAL

At the Olympic we have had, during the week, the opening of Mr. Wilkie Collins's "Red Vial." Intent upon the course of his narrative, the author has in this instance forgotten that in a drama characters are not less essential than a plot. There is not a character in the "Red Vial." One person is, indeed, benevolent; another rigid in the sense of probity; another, represented by Mrs. Stirling, weak in the same, and wicked; and another, represented by Mr. Robson, a maniac, with wits of dimensions varying according to the convenience of the story; but they are all shadows for a tale that should be read in ten minutes, not characters to be offered bodily to our senses, for a two hours' study. Still with the same exclusive care about the story, it happens also that the author of the "Red Vial" has taken no pains to secure pithiness of expression; there is no effort to say good things pointedly, and sometimes even a tendency to say even commonplace things tediously, as if they were worth elaborating into speeches.—MORLEY, HENRY, 1858, *Journal of a London Playgoer, Oct.* 16,*p.* 223.

I must say I think the "Woman in White" a marvel of workmanship. I found it bears a second reading very well, and indeed it was having it thrown in my way for a second time which attracted so strongly my technical admiration.—OLIPHANT, MARGARET O. W., 1862, *To Mr. Blackwood, Autobiography and Letters, ed.* Coghill, *p.* 186.

Wilkie Collins collects all the remarkable police cases and other judicial narratives he can find, and makes what Jean Paul Richter called "quarry" of them—a vast accumulation of materials in which to go digging for subjects and illustrations at leisure. Charles Reade does the same with bluebooks and the reports of official inquiries. The author of the "Dead Secret" is looking for perplexing little mysteries of human crime; the author of "Hard Cash" for stories of legal or social wrong to be redressed. I need hardly say, perhaps, that I rank Charles Reade high above Wilkie Collins. The latter can string his dry bones on wires with remarkable ingenuity; the former can, as he fairly boasts, make the dry bones live.—MCCARTHY, JUSTIN, 1872, *Modern Leaders, p.* 195.

Next to Dickens, however, he ranked, *qualis inter viburna cupressus*, his very dear friend, Mr. Wilkie Collins, "an artist of the pen, there are terribly few among writers," was his terse eulogium, the plain fact being that this past master in the art of dramatic construction excels all competitors just where most English authors fail. His plots resemble nothing so much as the intricate arabesques of an Oriental designer. Their complexity dazzles, yet they are always simple, never obscure. Moreover—and here they commanded Charles Reade's most earnest enthusiasm—they, or rather some of them, lend themselves intuitively to the stage. They dramatize easily and naturally; indeed "The New Magdalen" may be fairly termed one of the most effective of modern dramas. Mr. Wilkie Collins, therefore, if we may put it so, hit Charles Reade's ideal, and secured in consequence, that sort of genuine admiration which an author offers his brother in art when he esteems him greater than himself.—READE, CHARLES L., AND REV. COMPTON, 1887, *Memoir of Charles Reade, p.* 392.

He was certainly a giant among novelists, and far above the pinchbeck sensationalists and the rocket-stick romancers of the present day. In his particular line there is no one who can come anywhere near him. —ASHBY-STERRY, J., 1889, *English Notes, The Book Buyer, vol.* 6. *p.* 361.

Exit the novelist; enter the characters; that is Collins's idea. One never sees him, never thinks of him, from first page to last. What he wishes you to know he makes his characters, his incidents tell for him; the purpose of the book always advancing, gradually reveals itself, and grows slowly into shape we hardly know how, as incident follows incident. And in all the books this purpose is sustained, consistent, and worthy. Occasionally in the preface to the story he tells us himself what this intention has been, tells it plainly, simply, manfully, and leaves the reader to say whether or no it has been achieved. . . . That Wilkie Collins was a great (one of the greatest) novelists we *know;* we, who have studied his works, have marked their range and power, their sincerity of purpose, their perfection of expression; but we know more than this, we know that in an age of self-advertisement, jealousy, and pretence, he was a type—not without faults, but still a type—of a genuine, kind-hearted, helpful-to-others *man.* He had blood, as well as brains, generosity, as well as intelligence, artistic pride and purpose in his work, as well as popular success.—QUILTER, HARRY, 1889, *In Memoriam Amici, Universal Review, vol.* 5, *pp.* 207, 224.

All the works of Wilkie Collins which we remember with pleasure are works of art as true as his godfather's pictures, and in their own line as complete. His excellent sense, his perfect self-command, his modest devotion to his art, are qualities not more praiseworthy than they are obvious. And if it were but for their rarity they should command no less attention than respect. His most illustrious friend and contemporary did not always show himself at once so loyal and so rational in observance of intellectual or æsthetic propriety. Collins never ventured to fling down among his readers so shapeless or misshapen a piece of work, though doubtless he could not furnish them with a piece of work so excellent in parts and sections, as "Little Dorrit.". . . It is apparently the general opinion—an opinion which seems to me incontestable—that no third book of their author's can be ranked as equal with "The Woman in White" and "The Moonstone:" two works of not more indisputable than incomparable ability. "No Name" is an only less excellent example of as curious and original a talent. . . . "The New Magdalen" is merely feeble, false, and silly in its sentimental cleverness; but in "The Fallen Leaves" there is something too ludicrously loathsome for comment or endurance. The extreme clumsiness and infelicity of Wilkie Collins as a dramatic teacher or preacher may be tested by comparison with the exquisite skill and tact displayed by M. Alexandre Dumas in his studies of the same or of similar subjects. To the revoltingly ridiculous book just mentioned I am loth to refer again: all readers who feel any gratitude or goodwill towards its author must desire to efface its miserable memory from the record of his works.—SWINBURNE, ALGERNON CHARLES, 1889, *Wilkie Collins, Fortnightly Review, vol.* 52, *pp.* 591, 593, 596.

Mr Collins's method is that of Mr. Browning in "The Ring and the Book." His characters view the same set of circumstances, but with very different eyes. The method has its obvious advantages and disadvantages; perhaps it is most artfully worked in "The Woman in White." Again, after reading and re-reading, one keeps one's old opinion—that for a writer so conscientious and careful, Mr. Wilkie Collins was but rarely successful in the full measure of his success. A few of his short stories, his "Woman in White," his "No Name," and, above all, doubtless, "The Moonstone"—reach a level of ingenuity and of interest which the many others fall very far short of. The humorous passages, for example, in "Armadale" and "Hide and Seek" are very laboured and melancholy.—LANG, ANDREW, 1890, *Mr. Wilkie Collins's Novels, Contemporary Review, vol.* 57, *p.* 21.

Was an author of special power. There is moral tonic in his books, stimulating thought, fine and persuasive appeals to the imagination, as well as marvellous plot and weird incidents. His strikingly dramatic stories clothed in language as simple and direct as it is strong and beautiful. The uniform fascinating grace and ease of his diction ceases to surprise us when we read with what minute and painstaking care it is produced.—BAINTON, GEORGE, 1890, *ed. The Art of Authorship, p.* 89.

The work of all novelists, except those perhaps in the very first rank, has a tendency to age; and the author of "The Woman in White," "No Name," "Armadale," does certainly not now hold in the world's esteem the place that he held twenty-five or thirty years ago. Ingenious plot-puzzles were his forte; and though a good mystery still has its charm for the modern reader, yet to produce its full effect the mystery must be surrounded by something of exotic circumstance—the scene must be laid in the South Seas, India, America. Then Collins's characters have no permanent vitality, and his general reflections on men and things can hardly be called valuable.—MARZIALS, FRANK T., 1892, *Letters of Charles Dickens to Wilkie Collins, The Academy, vol.* 42, *p.* 304.

The special power of Mr. Wilkie Collins,

as afterwards developed, was for the construction of plots, and the use of all the most elaborate machinery of the story. His was the art which keeps the reader breathless, not through a scene or act of adventure, but during the long and elaborate following out of intrigue and incident, those tangles of the web of fate, or intricate combinations of circumstance, conducting certainly to an often unsuspected end,—which never lose their effect so long as they are skilfully and powerfully done, as was the case in the earlier works of this novelist. He did not possess the still more interesting and far higher gift of creation. There is no character, no living being in his works, with the exception, perhaps, of Count Fosco, of whom the reader will probably at this distance remember even the name; but, notwithstanding this, his power of holding his audience spellbound, and of rousing the same kind of curiosity and eager interest with which we watch day by day the gradual unfolding of the links of evidence in a great trial, was unsurpassed, we might say unequalled, in his day. The sensation produced by the "Woman in White," the first and consequently most striking of the series of stories in which he has displayed this power, and which came out in a serial form in "Household Words," thus doubling the excitement of those who had to wait from week to week for a fresh instalment of the story—was prodigious. It was the subject of conversation and speculation everywhere, and the reader followed every turn, and commented upon every incident, as if some personal interest of his own hung upon the identification of the gentle, witless creature who was the shadow heroine, and the unhappy lady who was the real object of all those highly wrought and intricate snares.—OLIPHANT, MARGARET O. W., 1892, *The Victorian Age of English Literature, p.* 482.

Great as was the vogue of Collins's works for a time, the seal of permanency is scarcely to be looked for in them. They are conspicuously wanting in the higher literary and artistic qualities. His characters are mechanically drawn: they do not live, or convey to the reader an impression of reality. His style, too, lacks distinction. His supreme quality is seen in his clever handling of sensational narrative, and especially in his ingenious construction of a plot, so woven around a mystery as to hold the reader's attention and curiosity enchained to the last.—GRAHAM, RICHARD D., 1897, *The Masters of Victorian Literature, p.* 92.

Collins's descriptions have the effect of a nightmare; his power of the consistent development, even of the most improbable plot and characters, forces us under his spell. The character of Count Fosco is, besides, a real work of art.—ENGEL, EDWARD, 1902, *A History of English Literature, rev. Hamley Bent, p.* 462.

Richard William Church
1815–1889

An English author, and a clergyman of the Established Church. He was born in Lisbon, studied in Oxford, was appointed a Fellow of Oriel, and was Dean of Saint Paul's from 1871 until his death. He is chiefly known as a scholar and writer. His long list of publications includes: "Essays and Reviews" (1854); "Civilization and Religion" (1860); "University Sermons" (1868); "The Beginning of the Middle Ages" (1877); an able volume on "Bacon" (1879) and "Spenser" (1879), in the "English Men of Letters" series. A uniform editon of many of his works appeared in 1888, and a posthumous work on "The Oxford Movement" was published in 1891.—GILMAN, PECK, AND COLBY, eds., 1902, *Inernational Encyclopædia vol.* IV, *p.* 612.

PERSONAL

By this time I hope the E. Talbots will have met Dean Church. They are certainly to be envied for the opportunity of seeing so much more of so interesting a man than can be managed in London. . . . There is something of singular charm about him, and I fancy one sees it also in his writing. At least the essay on Dante has some exquisite passages "halfway between beauty and goodness," if I may so parody one of his quotations.—PALGRAVE, FRANCIS TURNER, 1878, *Letter to Lady Frederick Cavendish, Journals and Memoirs, ed. Palgrave, p.* 129.

How significant is it that Dean Church should write the history of events in which he was a prominent actor, and never once mention his own name! He does not avoid the first person singular, for it appears in the Preface and also in the body of the book—but for the first time, if I mistake not, on the last page! May I be forgiven for asking if a Scotchman or an Irishman ever performed a feat like this, or an Englishman, for that matter, outside this charmed circle.—SANDAY, W., 1891, *Dean Church, The Critical Review, vol. 1, p. 237.*

On the 10th of December, early in the morning and quite quietly, the end came. The Dean's love of Whatley had led him years before to choose a spot in the quiet country churchyard there for his last resting-place. And thither he was carried from St. Paul's after the early Communion in the northwest chapel of the cathedral, where his coffin lay in the midst, and the later funeral service, with its long procession, and solemn music, and gathering of many friends and colleagues. And there, in the snow-covered churchyard, beside the chancel of the village church, and amid the farewell gathering of old friends and parishioners, he was laid at rest. He had left a strict charge that no memorial should be raised to him. Only one thing he had asked;—that a stone like that which he had chosen to mark his son's grave at Hyères—and which, though he was spared the sorrow of knowing it, was also, within three years' time, to mark the grave of his youngest daughter there—should mark his own grave at Whatley, and that it should bear upon it the same lines from the *Dies Iræ*—

Rex tremendæ majestatis
Qui salvandos salvas gratis,
Salva me, fons pietatis.
Quærens me sedisti lassus,
Redemisti crucem passus,
Tantus labor non sit cassus.

—CHURCH, MARY C., 1894, *ed. Life and Letters of Dean Church, p. 421.*

The preaching of Dean Church was over the heads of the less cultivated. It is truly said by Canon Scott Holland: "There were no physical effects to aid the impression. The voice, though pure toned, was far from strong; and in delivery he held fast to the earlier traditions so characteristic of Newman and the Tractarian chiefs. Gesture, action, were all rigidly discarded: and the voice retained its even measured monotone throughout."—BOYD, ANDREW K. H., 1895, *Dean Church of St. Paul's, Longman's Magazine, vol. 25, p. 617.*

As parish priest and as Dean of St. Paul's he displayed the character of an English priest—learned, judicious, tolerant, saintly—in its most beautiful aspect. Firm in his convictions and great in his quietness, no man ever represented more perfectly the characteristic excellences of the Anglican Church.—HUTTON, W. H., 1897, *Social England, ed. Traill, vol. II, p. 274.*

Soon after his election at Oriel I became and always continued to be, on very close terms of friendship with Church, whose character is so universally appreciated that it is needless for me to speak of his beautiful and attractive qualities. I believe we were always entirely agreed in opinions, both at Oxford and afterwards during his life at St. Paul's.—LAKE, WILLIAM CHARLES, 1897-1901, *Memorials, ed. his Widow, p. 72.*

It was not only in his writing that he possessed so great a charm, but in his conversation at home and in society. He had a very keen and delicate sense of humour, and yet maintained perfect dignity without the loss of simplicity and ease. "Austerity and sympathy" have been described as two great notes in his character, and he was able, as Canon Scott Holland has said, to be in favour with all men, and yet never to swerve from the line of duty, and never to submit to the taint of compromise. . . . Though not gifted with great vocal powers for preaching, his reading was always a treat to those who heard him, whether it was one of Scott's novels, or a poem of Tennyson, in his drawing-room at Whatley in the evening, or his clear and impressive readings of the lessons in St. Paul's, at the great special services, when his perfect pronunciation and intonation made him easily heard. He was an untiring and industrious student, and never dropped any of his early studies. Homer and Virgil, Sophocles and Lucretius, were never put away on his shelves after Oxford days. But he was also an indefatigable correspondent, and wrote from abroad delightfully fresh accounts of the places he visited—DONALDSON, AUG. B., 1900, *Five Great Oxford Leaders, pp. 375, 376.*

GENERAL

His Essay on Dante alone stamps him as one of the first critics of any age; and his volumes on Anselm, Bacon, and "The Beginnings of the Middle Ages," his singularly brilliant and comprehensive sketch of "The Early Ottomans," must make every one who has read them sigh that a mind so powerful, so discriminating, so amply furnished with knowledge, and in command of a style at once so dignified and attractive, did not find time to leave behind him some monumental work on history, in addition to the fragmentary monographs which show how well equipped he was for the task.—MACCOLL, MALCOLM, 1891, *Dean Church, Contemporary Review, vol.* 59, *p.* 146.

It is what you feel in all his writings—the moral beauty of the man, a measure and charm which are no tricks of a well-trained pen, but the natural outcome of characters. It is not the beauty of flexible weakness, but of polished strength; the beauty not of a fragile carving but of a columnar shaft finely proportioned to bear its burden to the best advantage. Large intelligence, thorough scholarship, rare and delicate taste, simple and earnest devotion, were all combined with a certain judicial poise, a just measure in thought and conduct. . . . His silences were speeches; his suppressions were verdicts. Wisely bold at need, he had no love of figuring at the front of the stage. He had greatness thrust upon him. He could be generous and expect no recognition. You cannot think of his taking an unfair advantage or attempting to hold untenable ground. He knew how to handle hot coals without fanning them into a blaze. He could write history from one side of a controverted position, and remain impartial —just to opponents, and no more than just to friends.—RICHARDS, C. A. L., 1895, *The Story of Dean Church's Life, The Dial vol.* 18, *p.* 176.

Upon the whole, the letters do give the impression that the writer took only a transient interest in transitory things. Arnold's letters, for instance, come much nearer to a continuous commentary on the life of the time. Another impression is a sort of aloofness, of irony, of reserve. The letter in which he announces his first article on St. Anselm to his mother is really remarkable in its way. Of course he had to allow for her Protestantism; but, viewed from inside, St. Anselm is not without attractions to Protestants. It was Church's own choice to present his subject from the outside as a picture of the cat-and-dog life an archbishop had to live in the eleventh century. He wrote in the same detached way about his children, almost as a neutral observer might. He found his son odd and his daughters interesting: when the former was dying he appears to have discovered, for the first time, that he had been an affectionate son.—SIMCOX, G. A., 1895, *Life and Letters of Dean Church, The Academy, vol.* 47, *p.* 27.

There seem to be two Churches in the field—one secular, scientific, historical, literary, human; the other traditional, ecclesiastical, apologetic. And there are not wanting intimations that the basis of his mind was sceptical, and that he clung to the traditional opinion the more resolutely because he dared not trust himself to his own strength in the wide stream of modern thought. . . . His letters have the apparently inevitable felicity of style that marks his various books, and it is interesting to find one of them written at the request of some one who would learn the secret of his charm. He can only say that he has watched against the temptation to use *unreal* and *fine* words, and read good English, Newman's in particular, with Shakespere's, Wordsworth's, and the rest. It is eloquent for his catholicity that Lucretius was his favorite classic, and Matthew Arnold's books an indispensable resource. But the evidences of this quality are many.—CHADWICK, JOHN WHITE, 1895, *Dean Church, The Nation, vol.* 60, *pp.* 348, 349.

Of no modern writer is the saying so obviously true as of Church, that the style is the man. What interests us far more than any particular page in his writings is the personality behind them, a personality concealed rather than obtruded, but plainly individual and full of charm. His peculiar note is a melancholy compounded of many simples, and including those of the scholar, the divine, the traveller, and the accomplished gentleman. He was a student at once of books and of men. . . . His style, properly so called, may be defined as in the best sense academic; it is periodic in structure, correct in syntax, and harmonious in flow and cadence. It is not hard to trace in it the influence of Newman; the qualities which Church had in common or by contact with Newman; candour, lucidity, and precision, are reflected in his style; amongst smaller points of resemblance may be noted the occasional startling use of very familiar phrases; but it lacks Newman's extraordinary flexibility and ease. Its defect is the defect of the academic style, a tendency to become dry; and the defect of excessive moderation, a tendency to become tame. Further, the periods are not always well managed, the principle of suspense is too freely used. or, on the other hand, the paragraphs run to seed. But when at its best, the style is vigorous and vivid, and at no time is it without dignity.—BEECHING, H. C., 1896, *English Prose, ed. Craik, vol.* V, *pp.* 617, 618.

Well versed in theology, philosophy, and history, both ecclesiastical and secular, the author combined the power of looking at large questions largely with the critic's nice sense of detail. That he writes, however, from the orthodox and high-church standpoint is always apparent; and this could hardly be otherwise, for the greater number of the essays were contributed to "The Guardian," a professedly high-church journal. Such being his point of view, anything like entirely unprejudiced criticism, in most of the subjects treated by him, is out of the question; nor are we surprised by the writer's occasional slight tendency to digress along certain familiar or favorite lines of thought and study.—BICKNELL, PERCY F., 1897, *Dean Church's Occasional Papers, The Dial, vol.* 22, *p.* 360.

Martin Farquhar Tupper
1810–1889

Born, in London, 17 July, 1810. Early education at Charterhouse School. Matric. Ch. Ch., Oxford, 21 May 1828; B. A., 1832; M. A., 1835; D. C. L., 1847. Student of Lincoln's Inn, 18 Jan. 1832; called to Bar, 24 Nov. 1835. Married Isabella Devis, 26 Nov. 1835. F. R. S., 1845. Visited America, 1851, and 1876. Resided greater part of life at Albury House, near Guildford. Died there, 29 Nov. 1889. *Works:* "Poems" (anon.), 1832; "Proverbial Philosophy," 1838; 2nd series, 1842; 3rd series, 1867; series 1-4, 1871; "Geraldine," 1838; "A Modern Pyramid," 1839; "An Author's Mind," 1841; "St. Martha's" (priv. ptd.), 1841; "The Crock of Gold," 1844; "Heart," 1844; "The Twins," 1844; "A Thousand Lines" (anon.), 1845; "Probabilities" (anon.), 1847; "Hactenus," 1848; "Surrey," 1849; "Ballads for the Times" [1850]; "Farley Heath," 1850; "King Alfred's Poems in English Metres," 1851; "Half a Dozen No Popery Ballads" [1851]; "Hymns for All Nations," 1851; "St Martha's" (with J. Tudor), 1851; "Dirge for Wellington," 1852; "Half-a-Dozen Ballads for Australian Emigrants," 1853; "A Batch of War Ballads," 1854; "A Dozen Ballads for the Times" (anon.), 1854; "Lyrics of the Heart and Mind," 1855; "Paterfamilias's Diary of Everybody's Tour" (anon.), 1856; "Rides and Reveries of the late Mr. Æsop Smith" (anon.), 1858 [1857]; "Stephen Langton," 1858; "Some Verse and Prose about National Rifle Clubs," 1858; "Alfred" (priv. ptd.), 1858; "Three Hundred Sonnets," 1860; "Our Greeting to the Princess Alexandra," 1863; "Ode for the 300th Birthday of Shakespeare," 1864; "Plan of the Ritualistic Campaign" (priv. ptd.), [1865]; "Selections . . . Together with some Poems never before published," 1866; "Raleigh," 1866; "Tupper's Directorium," 1868; "Our Canadian Dominion," 1868; "Twenty-one Protestant Ballads" (from "The Rock"), 1868; "A Creed and Hymns," 1870; "Fifty Protestant Ballads," 1874; "Washington," 1876; "Three Five-Act Plays, and Twelve Dramatic Scenes," 1882; "Jubilate," [1886]; "My Life as an Author," 1886. He *edited:* W. G. Tupper's "Out and Home," 1856.—SHARP, R. FARQUHARSON, 1897, *A Dictionary of English Authors, p.* 285.

PERSONAL

Met the author of "Proverbial Philosophy," and heard him expatiate on the beautiful scene before him, and not in hexameters. He is a happy, little, blue-eyed man, who evidently enjoys talking, but does not approach the dignity of his didactic poem.—FOX, CAROLINE, 1856, *Memoirs of Old Friends, ed. Pym.; Journal, June* 20, *p.* 331.

For the matter, then, of autobiography, I decline its higher and its deeper aspects; as also I wish not to obtrude on the public eye mere domesticities and privacies of life. But mainly lest others less acquainted with the petty incidents of my career should hereafter take up the task, I accede with all frankness and humility to what seems to me like a present call to duty, having little time to spare at seventy-six, so near the end of my tether,—and protesting, as I well may, against the charge of selfish egotism in a book necessarily spotted on every page with the insignificant letter I; and while, of course on human-nature principles, willing enough to exhibit myself at the best, promising also not to hide the second best, or worse than that, where I can perceive it.—TUPPER, MARTIN FARQUHAR, 1886, *My Life as an Author*, p. 3.

Some of us may decline to accept Mr. Tupper's evident estimate of the poetical and intellectual value of his work; but the general verdict upon the man will be that he is a good fellow. He hints as much himself, for he says with a charming *naiveté*—"If I am not true, simple, and sincere, I am worse than I hope I am." And though he also says very truly that it is only in human nature to be willing to exhibit itself at the best, still human nature, when it is garrulous, is apt unconsciously to give us a poet at the worst also; so, as Mr. Tupper's worst, so far as it can be discerned in these pages, is a very harmless egotism—not in the least aggressive—his self-characterisation is probably not far wrong.—NOBLE, JAMES ASHCROFT, 1886, *M. F. Tupper, The Academy*, vol. 29, p. 390.

The "Autobiography" he has just published is very full of his ever-prominent and harmless egotism. Some of it is interesting. He can hardly be blamed for remembering that when he was at Christ Church, Oxford, he "had the honor of being prize-taker of Dr. Burton's theological essay, 'The Reconciliation of Matthew and John,' when Gladstone, who had also contested it, stood second;" "and when Dr. Burton," he says, "had me before him to give me the £25 worth of books, he requested me to allow Mr. Gladstone to have £5 worth of them, as he was so good a second."—MORRILL, JUSTIN S., 1887, *Self-Consciousness of Noted Persons*, p. 175.

When I knew him he was of a cheerful and agreeable presence, fond of reading his own poetry and telling his own life; and with his ruddy face and white beard he reminded me always of an English Santa Claus.—BOWKER, RICHARD ROGERS, 1888, *London as a Literary Centre, Harper's Monthly Magazine*, vol. 76, p. 819.

I would rather have written "Proverbial Philosophy"—though I never admired more than two lines in it—than have shared in the common baseness of incessantly heaping insult on a defenseless and amiable man, who, like the rest of us, may have had his foibles, but who had done his little best in life.—FARRAR, FREDERIC WILLIAM, 1890, *Literary Criticism, The Forum*, vol. 9, p. 28?

Among successful authors who dealt with Hatchard, Martin Tupper must not be altogether omitted, for Tupper's books had an enormous, though, if merit be considered, a most unaccountable sale. Rickerby, a printer in the City, had produced the first series of "Proverbial Philosophy" in 1838, but as Rickerby was more a printer than a publisher, Tupper sought a better-known man, and for the second series of the book and many subsequent editions he had dealings with Hatchard, receiving annually as he himself tells us, 500*l* to 800*l* a-year, "and in the aggregate having benefited both them and myself—for we shared equally—by something like 10,000*l* a-piece," Tupper seems to have got on very well with both John Hatchard and his son Thomas; but when they were dead his lines seem not to have fallen in such pleasant places, and a little quarrel, such as publisher and authors had in the past, and still engage in, ensued. Tupper withdrew his books from the house to Moxon. The fact was that Tupper thought that by going to Moxon his pedestrian lines might break into a trot if placed in Moxon's Catalogue beside those of Alfred Tennyson, for whom he was then publishing. Tupper, as is pretty well known, could not—or would not—disguise his love of praise and his inability to brook any adverse criticism.—HUMPHREYS, ARTHUR L., 1893, *Piccadilly Bookmen: Memorials of the House of Hatchard*, p. 69.

Whom I might have passed as a most respectable grocer and possible church warden. —LINTON, WILLIAM JAMES, 1894, *Threescore and Ten Years*, p. 172.

PROVERBIAL PHILOSOPHY
1838–71

Tupper and his "Proverbial Philosophy" are old familiar acquaintance of mine. There is good stuff in the book, but it strikes me as too wordy and inflated in its diction; and is of a nondescript class in literature—neither prose nor poetry.—BARTON, BERNARD, 1847, *To Mrs. Sutton, Oct. 23; Memoir, Letters and Poems*, ed. his Daughter, p. 85.

Mr. Tupper is one of a class whom we may call the commonplace eccentrics. They write both in verse and prose, but it is in verse that their peculiarities are most fully exhibited. If they essayed to write as other people write, they would attract no notice; — by writing strangely, they obtain attention,— as a man whose head is fit for nothing else, may still collect a crowd by standing on it. . . . Probably Mr. Tupper's most distinguished talent is a certain judicious knowingness which enables him to turn his labours to good pecuniary account. So, at least, it would appear from an advertisement at the end of his "eighteenth edition," where a French version of it is "highly recommended for schools in conjunction with the English edition!" Mr. Tupper in the frenzies of his inspiration, has still, it seems, an eye to the oven; and mounts the tripod to heave in coals at the kitchen-window!—HANNAY, JAMES, 1854, *Proverbial Philosophy, The Athenæum*, pp. 1583, 1585.

Did you see Hannay's pill for M. F. Tupper in the *Athenæum?*—ROSSETTI, DANTE GABRIEL, 1855, *Letters to William Allingham*, Jan. 23, p. 102.

It was unwontedly popular; and Tupper's name was on every tongue. Suddenly, the world reversed its decision and discarded its favorite; so that, without having done anything to warrant the desertion, Tupper finds himself with but very few admirers, or even readers: so capricious is the *vox populi*. The poetry is not without merit; but the world cannot forgive itself for having rated it too high.—COPPÉE, HENRY, 1872, *English Literature*, p. 438.

"Proverbial Philosophy" remains as one of the bright and shining examples of the absolute want of connection between literary merit and popular success.—SAINTSBURY, GEORGE, 1896, *A History of Nineteenth Century Literature*, p. 299.

Mr. Tupper could, and did, occasionally, acquit himself respectably as a writer of ballads and other kinds of minor verse, but it was not to these he owed his popularity. This was due to the extraordinary collection of rhymeless and, indeed, rhythmless platitudes which he published under the name of "Proverbial Philosophy," which was eagerly taken up by the public, and was in immense demand as a "giftbook" for a long series of years. There were those, indeed, who declared, and not wholly in an ironical spirit, that its purely material and external attractions, its conveniences in shape and size, combined with the unimpeachable propriety of its contents—that these and not any popular delusion as to its literary merits were the operative causes of its truly astonishing, and its yet more astonishingly prolonged vogue. . . . The vast and steady popularity of the author of "Proverbial Philosophy" during the greater part, if not the whole, of Tennyson's prime, and, still more, the unquestionably immense numerical preponderance of the poetaster's public over the poet's, is one of the most singular phenomena of that literary era.—TRAILL, HENRY DUFF, 1897, *Social England*, vol. VI, p. 515.

GENERAL

Our wonder is, how, with his feeling of the beauty of "Christabel," he could have so blurred and marred it in his unfortunate sequel. — WILSON, JOHN, 1838, *Blackwood's Magazine*, Dec.

Martin Tupper, a singularly good-natured man, though I cannot read his books.—MITFORD, MARY RUSSELL, 1853, *Letter to Mr. Starkey*, Aug. 18; *Friendships*, ed. L'Estrange, p. 112.

In spite of the popular theory, that nothing is so fallacious as circumstantial evidence, there is no man of observation who would not deem it more trustworthy than any human testimony, however honest, which was made up from personal recollection. The actors in great affairs are seldom to be depended on as witnesses either to the order of events or their bearing upon results; for even where selfish interest is not to be taken into account, the mythic instinct ere long begins to shape things as they ought to have been, rather than as they were. This is true even of subjects in which we have no personal interest, and not only do no two men describe the same street-scene in the same way, but the same man, unless prosaic to a degree below the freezing-point of Tupper, will never do it twice in the same way.—LOWELL, JAMES RUSSELL, 1864, *The Rebellion, its Causes and Consequences, North American Review*, vol. 99, p. 246.

Nearly every review, magazine, and critical journal, published in his time, had its say about this famous writer, but his friends have certainly outnumbered his enemies, and have carried the day. The motive which prompted his "Proverbial Philosophy" was creditable and Christian-like; it was not equal to Shakespeare, nor did it aspire to such a position; it carried pure and comforting thoughts into thousands of domestic circles, without leaving behind it the poisonous slime which emanates from the popular or fashionable press; and I have thought that I would much prefer to be shut up from the world with that curious book than with a thousand and one of the novels and scientific dissertations which flood the bookstalls and libraries of the present day.—LANMAN, CHARLES, 1883, *Haphazard Personalities, p.* 341.

It is difficult to know how to characterize Martin Tupper, whose strange productions have perhaps called forth more ridicule and sold more copies than those of all the rest of our poets put together. His "Proverbial Philosophy" was the most remarkable instance we know of a large assumption, which so imposed for a time upon the rank and file of readers that he was taken on his own estimate as a poet. The tamest and most commonplace sentiment and platitudes, in the form of dull aphorisms, filling a succession of large and dreary volumes, are the last things we should think of as likely to attract the enthusiasm of the crowd—yet they did so in the most astonishing way; and it was only the storms of laughter and ridicule which swept over him, from all whose opinion was worth having, that detached from him, with some resistance and great unwillingness, the devotion of the multitude. Of the countless editions which were produced of his works during the short period of their popularity, scarcely any are now to be seen, and it would be curious to inquire what has become of the volumes which lay on so many drawing-room tables, which were presented by anxious parents to good young people, and were held by gentle dulness as a sort of new revelation, in 1852, and the succeeding years.—OLIPHANT, MARGARET O. W., 1892, *The Victorian Age of English Literature, p.* 241.

William Allingham
1824-1889

An Irish poet; born at Ballyshannon, March 19, 1828 (?); died at Hampstead, near London, Nov. 18, 1889. Having for some years been an officer in the Customs, he became assistant editor of Fraser's Magazine in 1871 and succeeded Froude as editor in 1874, when he also married Helen Paterson, the illustrator and water-color artist. His graceful poems excel in descriptions of Irish scenery and life; some of them were illustrated by Rossetti, Kate Greenway, and other distinguished artists. Prominent among his works is "Lawrence Bloomfield in Ireland" (1864), a narrative poem on contemporary Irish life.—WARNER, CHARLES DUDLEY, ed. 1897, *Library of the World's Best Literature, Biographical Dictionary, vol.* XXIX, *p.* 15.

PERSONAL

D. G. R., and I think W. A. himself, told me, in the early days of our acquaintance, how, in remote Ballyshannon, where he was a clerk in the customs, in evening walks he would hear the Irish girls at their cottage doors singing old ballads, which he would pick up. If they were broken or incomplete, he would add to them or finish them; if they were improper, he would refine them. He could not get them sung till he got the Dublin "Catnach" of that day to print them, on long strips of blue paper, like old songs; and if about the sea, with the old rough woodcut of a ship on the top. He either gave them away or they were sold in the neighbourhood. Then, in his evening walks, he had at last the pleasure of hearing some of his own ballads sung at the cottage doors by the crooning lasses, who were quite unaware that it was the author who was passing by.—HUGHES, ARTHUR, 1897, *Letter to George Birkbeck Hill, Letters of Dante Gabriel Rossetti to William Allingham, Introduction, p.* xxiii.

"He had," as Mr. W. M. Rossetti tells me, "a good critical judgment; he was a man who could pounce on defects in a poem." Madox Brown described him as "keen and cutting." It will be seen in the course of these letters that Rossetti not only sought his criticism of his poetry, but often acknowledged its justice. Coventry Patmore was scarcely less eager to have his opinion, but was not so willing to submit to it.—HILL, GEORGE BIRKBECK, 1897, *Letters of Rossetti to Allingham, p.* xxvii.

GENERAL

What do you think of the gratuitous slight put upon you and me in Kingsley's notice of "Maud?" I would not change "Tamerton Church Tower," a poem by Patmore, nor, if I was the author of it, "The Music Master" for fifty "Mauds."—PATMORE, COVENTRY, 1855, *Letter to Allingham.*

The man has a true spirit of song in him, I have no doubt of it; and my opinion, I am happy to say, is confirmed by Carlyle in his letter to A. which I only do not forward because, from his letter, it does not appear that I am at liberty so to do. Carlyle also mentions some work of Allingham's (I have not seen it myself—it is possibly some preface to his projected work on Ireland) in these following terms—"Your pleasant and excellent historical introduction might, if modesty would permit, boast itself to be the very best ever written perhaps anywhere for such a purpose. I have read it with real entertainment and instruction on my own behoof, and with real satisfaction on yours—so clear, so brief, definite, graphic; and a fine genially human tone in it."—TENNYSON, ALFRED LORD, 1865, *Letter to William Ewart Gladstone, A Memoir of Alfred Lord Tennyson*, ed. *His Son, vol.* II, p. 31.

We find spontaneity in the rhymes of Allingham, whose "Mary Donnelly" and "The Fairies" have that intuitive grace called quality,—a grace which no amount of artifice can ever hope to produce, and for whose absence mere talent can never compensate us.—STEDMAN, EDMUND CLARENCE, 1875-87, *Victorian Poets*, p. 258.

Mr. Allingham says his "works" claim to be "genuine in their way." They are free from all obscurity and mysticism, and evince a fine feeling for nature, as well as graceful fancy and poetic diction.—CHAMBERS, ROBERT, 1876, *Cyclopædia of English Literature*, ed. *Carruthers*.

Mr. Allingham is a poet of an "equal mind," to whom verse is, indeed, a natural mode of expression, but whose emotion does not generally find utterance until it has been nursed by musing and mellowed by reflection. He is, nevertheless, one of the most spontaneous of singers determining to err on the side of nature rather than on that of art, and more careful to keep his gift pure than to cultivate it to the utmost. If he excels at all, it is in modesty. He is not the only poet who has shone in "his place" and been "content;" but he is surely the first who has been satisfied to compare himself to a gooseberry. . . . Of Mr. Allingham's essay as a dramatist, after the pathetic appeal of its Prologue that the audience should *try* to like it, we would not say harsh things if we could; but, in truth, it is not easy to like or dislike it very much.

. . . As to his lyrics, so in his play, Mr. Allingham shows no great ambition, flying low and falling light.—MONKHOUSE, COSMO, 1883, *Allingham's New Poems, The Academy*, vol. 23, pp. 72, 73.

To feel the entire fascination of his poetry, it is perhaps necessary to have spent one's childhood, like the present writer, in one of those little seaboard Connaught towns. He has expressed that curious devotion of the people for the earth under their feet, a devotion that is not national, but local, a thing at once more narrow and more idyllic. He sang Ballyshannon and not Ireland. Neither his emotions nor his thoughts took any wide sweep over the world of man and nature. He was the poet of little things and little moments, and of that vague melancholy Lord Palmerston considered peculiar to the peasantry of the wild seaboard where he lived. . . . The charm of his work is everywhere the charm of stray moments and detached scenes that have moved him; the pilot's daughter in her Sunday frock; the wake with the candles round the corpse, and a cloth under the chin; the ruined Abbey of Asaroe, an old man who was of the blood of those who founded it, watching sadly the crumbling walls; girls sewing and singing under a thorn tree; the hauling in of the salmon nets; the sound of a clarionet through the open and ruddy shutter of a forge; the piano from some larger house, and so on, a rubble of old memories and impressions made beautiful by pensive feeling. Exquisite in short lyrics, this method of his was quite inadequate to keep the interest alive through a long poem. —YEATS, WILLIAM BUTLER, 1892, *The Poets and the Poetry of the Century, Kingsley to Thomson*, ed. *Miles*, p. 211.

Was an Irish poet, of much taste, but of no great power. His inspiration is strangely fitful and uncertain, and after his removal to London, in consequence of the success of his earlier verses, it seemed almost wholly to desert him.—WALKER, HUGH, 1897, *The Age of Tennyson*, p. 256.

Though not ranking among the foremost of his generation, Allingham, when at his best, is an excellent poet, simple, clear and graceful, with a distinct though not obtrusive individuality. His best work is concentrated in his "Day and Night Songs" (1854), which, whether pathetic or sportive, whether expressing feeling or depicting scenery, whether upborne by simple melody or embodying truth in symbol, always fulfil the intention of the author and achieve the character of works of art. The employment of colloquial Irish without conventional hibernicisms was at the time a noteworthy novelty. "The Music Master" (1855), though of no absorbing interest, is extremely pretty, and although "Laurence Bloomfield" will mainly survive as a special document, the reader for instruction's sake will often be delighted by the poet's graphic felicity. The rest of Allingham's poetical work is on a lower level; there is, nevertheless, much point in most of his aphorisms, though few may attain the absolute perfection which absolute isolation demands.— GARNETT, RICHARD, 1901, *Dictionary of National Biography, Supplement, vol. I, p. 39.*

Theodore Dwight Woolsey
1801-1889

Born at New York City, Oct. 31, 1801: died at New Haven, Conn., July 1, 1889. An American educator and eminent political and legal writer. He graduated at Yale in 1820, studied law, and, later, theology; was tutor in Yale 1823-25; was licensed to preach in 1825; studied in Europe 1827-30; was professor of Greek at Yale 1831-46; and was President of Yale 1846-71. He edited the "New Englander" for a few years after 1843; and was chairman of the American company of New Testament revisers 1871-81. His works include editions of the "Alcestis" (1834), "Antigone" (1835), "Electra" (1837), "Prometheus" (1837), and "Gorgias" (1843); an "Introduction to the Study of National Law" (1860: 5th ed. 1879); "Divorce and Divorce Legislation" (1869); "Religion of the Past and of the Future" (1871); "Political Science, etc." (2 vols. 1871); "Communism and Socialism" (1880). He also edited Lieber's "Civil Liberty and Self-Government" (1871), and a "Manual of Political Ethics" (1871).—SMITH, BENJAMIN E., ed., 1894-97, *The Century Cyclopedia of Names, p. 1070.*

PERSONAL

I consider Woolsey by far the most prominent of presidents of American colleges. He is a faithful scholar and pure man, and modest withal.—LIEBER, FRANCIS, 1860, *To S. A. Allibone, July 12; Life and Letters,* ed. Perry, p. 315.

It is not too much to say, that of the academic spirit, in the best conception of it, Dr. Woolsey has been a living illustration. . . . Dr. Woolsey has afforded a signal example of the dignity, as well as the usefulness, of a purely academic career. His calling has been that of a teacher of youth. Without turning aside from that function or growing cold in his esteem for it, he has acted in other spheres, not obtrusively or of his own motion, but when his services were required or the public need imperatively invoked his aid. His opinion has been sought and given to the National Government on important points in controversy with foreign powers; but he has declined flattering offers of public office. It must be a gratification to this venerable man—a man who has never stepped out of his path to conciliate any person's favor—to receive, from his former colleagues and their associates, ten years after he has withdrawn from official labor in college, the spontaneous tribute of honor and affection of which the gold medal was the token. — FISHER, GEORGE P., 1882, *The Academic Career of President Woolsey, Century Magazine, vol. 24, p. 717.*

His person, indeed, though slight, was shapely, and his whole bearing and air expressive of courtesy and refinement; but not until the casual observer noticed his finely-formed head and clear-cut features, and looked into his full-orbed, soulful eyes, did he come to a recognition of the fact that he was in the presence of no common man. Who that has ever felt it can forget that direct, thoughtful, kindly look of his? The Franklin glasses which he wore lent his gaze a semi-mysterious power, as though he scanned alike the distant and the near in you, your lineaments and the recesses of your inner being. For an acquaintance, the look was the precursor of a quiet smile, full of sympathy and good-will; not the smile of good breeding merely, but the expression of the hidden man of the heart. By the men of New Haven of the last decade or so, he is remembered as a slight figure, passing with short, quick steps to and from the postoffice; more often as one who, with head bowed low and thoughtful mien, his right hand perhaps passed behind his back and locked in the bend of the left elbow, brought to mind the college witticism that "President Woolsey and"—another highly esteemed university dignitary "are the *stoopedest* men in New Haven."—THAYER, JOSEPH HENRY, 1889, *Theodore Dwight Woolsey, Atlantic Monthly, vol.* 64, *p.* 557.

GENERAL

Mr. Woolsey's labors will be highly appreciated by all who are engaged in classical instruction, and by those who continue their acquaintance with the great authors of Greece after leaving the walls of a college. The Prefaces, Notes, and metrical Tables, which accompany these Tragedies, form a body of critical learning, tasteful exposition and metrical science, which would do honor to a much older professor than Mr. Woolsey. . . . It is an uncommon thing in any country, for a mind of nice poetical sensibilities, to be engaged in critical labors, or to have the necessary patience in the acquisition of exact knowledge, to qualify it for such a task; but so fortunate a conjunction between profound and accurate learning, and delicate taste, when it does take place, brings out something which men will not willingly let die. With such a beginning as Mr. Woolsey has made in classical scholarship, what may we not expect from the rich studies and ripened experience of future years?—FELTON, CORNELIUS CONWAY, 1837, *Greek Tragedies, North American Review, vol.* 44, *p.* 555.

Dr. Woolsey has long been conspicuous among American scholars for the extent and thoroughness of his learning, his power of thought, and his clear and admirable style. The moral elevation of his character gives great and almost authoritative weight to his opinions, especially upon questions of public law.—UNDERWOOD, FRANCIS H., 1872, *A Hand-Book of English Literature, American Authors, p.* 209.

The unpretending form in which this work ["Introductions to the Study of International Law"] was put forth did not prevent the legal profession, as well as historical students, from at once discerning the solid learning at the basis of it, as well as the soundness and sagacity of the comments which were interspersed in the course of the exposition. This work spread his reputation as a publicist. The successive editions which have been called for since its first publication, testify to the esteem in which it is held by competent judges in this country. Its use at Oxford is one proof of the appreciation of it abroad. In this book the author does not content himself with a bare recital of the actual state of public law, or a description of international jurisprudence as a fact; he points out the relation of agreement or antagonism in which the law of nations, as recognized and acted upon, stands to the immutable principles of justice, and suggests modifications which ought to be made in existing usages.—FISHER, GEORGE P., 1882, *The Academic Career of President Woolsey, Century Magazine, vol.* 24, *p.* 713.

His scholarship combined, to a degree quite exceptional, breadth and thoroughness. His early professional training, first in law, then in theology, then in philological and general studies abroad, fostered a largeness of outlook and variety of interest which he retained to the last, and which his conscientiousness kept from superficiality. In classical philology and epigraphy this pupil of Hermann and Boeckh and Bopp did for American students the work of a pioneer; while in practical ethics and political science, the thoroughness, good sense, and, above all, the noble tone of his discussions have given them a salutary power over young men unequalled, unless perhaps by those of his friend Professor Lieber, whose fertilizing works Dr. Woolsey's editorial labors have recently helped to perpetuate. The revival of learning and comparative religion were among the special topics which he handled with evident mastery; while poetry and botany, as avocations, were subjects in which he took delight. He owned the best books, and he knew how to use them. Patient research, caution, sobriety of judgment, characterized all his work.—THAYER, JOSEPH HENRY, 1889, *Theodore Dwight Woolsey, Atlantic Monthly, vol.* 64, *p.* 559.

To President Woolsey belongs the rare honor of taking the lead in two great intellectual movements. He laid the foundations of American scholarship; he taught men to apply that scholarship to the social and political problems of the day. In each of these departments of his life work he was preëminent; in the combination of the two he stood alone and unrivalled. . . . His modesty alone prevented the world from knowing the vastness of his range of information. At a time when breadth of education was far rarer than it now is, he had read both law and theology, and had pursued a course of classical and philological study in Europe lasting several years. Nor did he allow the duties of his college office to narrow his range of subsequent work. Let one instance suffice. In the year 1864 the *New Englander* published a series of articles on the revival of learning in the fourteenth and fifteenth centuries. Knowledge of the Italian Renaissance was not at that time so easy to acquire as it has been since the appearance of Mr. Symonds' work. Such articles as these could only be the result of hard individual study at first hand. Yet the author was none other than President Woolsey himself, who, in the midst of his classics and his politics, his interest in the duties of his office, and his equally absorbing interest in public affairs, had found time to carry out, almost as a diversion, what would have exhausted another man as a specialty by itself.— HADLEY, ARTHUR T., 1889, *Theodore Dwight Woolsey, The Nation, vol.* 49, *p.* 27.

John Henry Newman
1801-1890

Born, in London, 21 Feb. 1801. At School at Ealing, 1808–16. Matric., Trin. Coll., Oxford, 14 Dec. 1816; Scholar, 1819–22; B. A., 1820. Student of Lincoln's Inn, 1819. Fellow of Oriel Coll., Oxford, April 1822 to 1845; Tutor, 1826–31. Friendship with Pusey begun, 1823. Ordained, 13 June 1824; Curate of St. Clement's, Oxford. Contrib. to "Encycl. Met.," 1824–29. Vice-Principal of Alban Hall, March 1825 to 1826. Preacher at Whitehall, 1827. Vicar of St. Mary's, Oxford, 1828 to Sept. 1843. Select Preacher, 1831–32. Travelled on Continent, winter 1832-33. Contrib. to "Brit. Mag.," 1833–36; to "British Critic," 1837–42. One of the promoters of the "Oxford Movement," 1833. Editor of "British Critic," 1838–41. Retired from Oxford, 1842; lived life of seclusion at Littlemore till 1845. Received into Roman Catholic Church, at Littlemore, 9 Oct. 1845. To Rome, Oct., 1846; ordained Priest there, and received degree of D. D. Returned to England, Dec. 1847. Founded Oratory at Birmingham, 1848; founded Oratory in London, 1850. Lost libel action brought against him by Dr. Achilli, 1853. Rector of Catholic Univ., Dublin, 1854–58. Returned to Birmingham, 1858; contrib. to "Atlantis," 1858–70; to "Rambler," 1859–60; to "The Month," 1864–66. Founded Catholic school at Edgbaston, 1859. Hon. Fellow, Trin. Coll., Oxford, 1877. Created Cardinal, 12 May 1879. Returned to Edgbaston, July 1879. Resided there till his death, 11 Aug. 1890. Buried at Rednall. *Works:* "St. Bartholomew's Eve" (anon.; with J. W. Bowden), 1821; "Suggestions on behalf of the Church Missionary Society," 1830; "The Arians of the Fourth Century," 1833; "Five Letters on Church Reform" (from "The Record"), 1833; Tracts nos. 1–3, 6–8, 10, 11, 15, 19–21, 31, 33, 34, 38, 41, 45, 47, 71, 73–75, 79, 82, 83, 85, 88, 90 in "Tracts for the Times," 1834–41; "Parochial Sermons" (6 vols.), 1834–42; "The Restoration of Suffragan Bishops," 1835; "Letter to Parishioners," 1835; "Elucidations of Dr. Hampden's Theological Statements" (anon.), 1836; "Lyra Apostolica" (anon.), 1836; "Letter to the Margaret Professor of Divinity," 1836; "Make Ventures for Christ's Sake," 1836; "Lectures on the Prophetical Office of the Church," 1837; "Letter to the Rev. G. Faussett," 1838; "Lectures on Justification," 1838; "Plain Sermons" (with others), 1839; etc.; "The Church of the Fathers" (anon.), 1840; "The Tamworth Reading Room" (under pseud.: "Catholicus," from "The Times"), 1841; "Letter . . . to the Rev. K. W. Jelf" (with initials: J. H. N.), 1841; "Letter to Richard, Bishop of Oxford," 1841; "Sermons bearing on Subjects of the Day," 1843; "Sermons . . . preached before the University of Oxford," 1843; "Essay on the Development of Christian Doctrine," 1845; "The proposed Decree on the subject of No. XC." (anon.), 1845; "Dissertatiunculæ quædam critico-theologicæ," 1847; "Loss and Gain" (anon.), 1848; "Discourses Addressed to Mixed Congregations," 1849; "Lectures on certain difficulties felt by Anglicans in submitting to the Catholic Church," 1850; "Christ upon the Waters" [1850]; "Lectures on the present position of Catholics in England," 1851; "Discourses on the Scope and Nature of University Education," 1852; "The Second Spring," 1852; "Verses on Religious Subjects" (under initials—J. H. N.), 1853; "Hymns," 1854; "Lectures on the History of the Turks" (anon.), 1854; "Who's to Blame?" (from "Catholic Standard"), 1855; "Remarks on the Oratorian Vocation" (priv. ptd.), 1856; "Callista" (anon.), [1856];

JOHN HENRY NEWMAN

From a drawing by G. Richmond, 1844.

JOHN RICHARD GREEN

Engraving by G. J. Stodart.

"The Office and Work of the Universities," 1856; "Sermons Preached on Various Occasions," 1857; "Lectures and Essays on University Subjects," 1858; "Hymn Tunes of the Oratory" (anon.; priv. ptd.), 1860; "The Tree beside the Waters" [1860]; "Verses for Penitents" (anon.; priv. ptd.), 1860; "Mr. Kingsley and Dr. Newman: a correspondence," 1864; "Apologia pro Vitâ Suâ," 1864; "Letter to the Rev. E. B. Pusey," 1866 (2d edn. same year); "The Pope and the Revolution," 1866; "The Dream of Gerontius" (under initials: J. H. N.), 1866; "Verses on Various Occasions," 1868; "Works" (36 vols.), 1868-81; "Essay in Aid of a Grammar of Assent," 1870; "Essays, critical and historical" (2 vols.), 1872; "The Trials of Theodoret," 1873; "Causes of the Rise and Success of Arianism," 1872; "The Heresy of Apollinaris," 1874; "Tracts, theological and ecclesiastical," 1874; "Letter . . . to . . . the Duke of Norfolk," 1875; "The Via Media of the English Church," 1877; "Two Sermons" (priv. ptd.), 1880; "Prologue to the Andria of Terence" (priv, ptd.), 1882; "What is of obligation for a Catholic to believe concerning the Inspiration of the Canonical Scriptures" [1884]; "Meditations and Evolutions," 1893. *Posthumous:* "Letters and Correspondence" (2 vols.), ed, by Miss Mozley, 1891 [1890]. He *translated* Fleury's "Ecclesiastical History," 1842; "Select Treatises of St. Athanasius," 1842-44; and *edited:* R. H. Froude's "Remains" (with Keble), 1838; Sutton's "Godly Meditations," 1838; "Hymni Ecclesiæ," 1838; "Bibliotheca Patrum" (with Pusey and others), 1838, etc.; Bishop Sparrow's "Rationale upon the Book of Common Prayer," 1839; Dr. Wells' "The Rich Man's Duty," 1840; "Catena Aurea," 1841; "The Cistercian Saints," pts. i., ii., 1844; "Maxims of the Kingdom of Heaven," 1860; Terence's "Phormio," 1864, and "Eunuchus," 1866; W. Palmer's "Notes of a Visit to the Russian Church," 1882; Plautus' "Aululari a," 1883; Terence's "Andria," 1883. [He also contributed prefaces to a number of theological publications, 1838-82] *Life:* by Wilfred Meynell, 1890. —SHARP, R. FARQUHARSON, 1897, *A Dictionary of English Authors, p.* 211.

PERSONAL

I was in London for a couple of days last week at Rogers' and met Newman, who was staying there. He had come for Manning's consecration. It was the first time I had seen him for twenty years nearly. He was very little changed in look or general manner or way of talking, except that he seemed almost stronger in body. He was in good spirits, very hearty, and talked very freely about all sorts of things; reminding us every now and then that he was across the border, but without embarrassment, and without any attempt to flaunt anything in our faces. It was a much more easy meeting than I could have supposed possible. We seemed to fall into the old ways of talking.—CHURCH, RICHARD WILLIAM, 1865, *To Rev. J. B. Mozley, Feb. 3; Life and Letters of Dean Church, ed. his Daughter, p.* 203.

In all the arts that make an orator or a great preacher he is strikingly deficient. His manner is constrained, awkward, and even ungainly; his voice is thin and weak. His bearing is not impressive. His gaunt, emaciated figure, his sharp, eagle face, his cold, meditative eyes, rather repel than attract those who see him for the first time. The matter of his discourse, whether sermon, speech, or lecture, is always admirable, and the language is concise, scholarly, expressive—perhaps a little overweighted with thought; but there is nothing there of the orator. — MCCARTHY, JUSTIN, 1872, *Par Nobile Fratrum—The Two Newmans, Modern Leaders, p.* 170.

This gentleman bears in his bodily appearance a considerable degree of resemblance to Dr. Pusey [1845]. Mr. Newman is a shade taller than the Doctor; but he presents the same general outline of what men of the world call monkish austerity. There is a peacefulness and gentleness of demeanour about Newman, an unobtrusive and humble deportment; a deep sense of religious obligation; a desire to withdraw from everything rude and boisterous, gay and fashionable; and outward visible sign of a constant habit of inward reflection; and a total absence of even the most distant approach to anything like literary arrogance and conceit. He likes to hear everything, but he parts with his own thoughts sparingly. In an ordinary routine of literary intercourse he would be considered but a very dull and uninteresting person; but among his own friends, and with a fireside companion, his conversation is instructive and delightful. His peculiar pursuits, his course of reading, his power of inward reflection and discrimination, place him far beyond the reach of the general run of literary men; and on this account there are but very few qualified to enter into his views, and form a right conception of his character and acquirements. Hence it is that you hear among nearly all his University friends, those who have for years been in perpetual intercourse with him, a desire to exalt his moral and religious deportment and sentiments, at the expense of his intellectual attainments. The fact is, that he shoots over the heads of his academical companions. He displays a power of thought, an acuteness of perception, and a strength of judgment to which they are strangers; and hence it is that he finds so little intellectual sympathy within the walls of the University of Oxford.—BLAKEY, ROBERT, 1873, *Memoirs, ed. Miller, p. 181.*

Mark him as he walks toward the pulpit along the narrow lane between the serried rows of "doctors of divinity," and "doctors of canon law," and "doctors of civil law," and "deans," and "tutors," and "professors," and "masters of art," while every eye of the rising generation in the galleries is fixed upon him. A slender, square figure, whose academical robes are either so made —or, from the indefinable influence that a man's nature has on the appearance of his garments, so hang in close clinging folds— as to produce, one knows not how, the impression of asceticism, he advances with swift, silent steps and eyes fixed on the ground. In the pulpit the time occupied by the preacher in silent prayer is rather long. Then, rising, his face is for the first time seen by the congregation—a face not readily to be forgotten, with slender, finely-cut features, and an appearance of emaciation, from which the attention of his hearers is drawn off by the eye beaming with intellectual power and the noble and lofty but not broad forehead above it.—TROLLOPE, THOMAS ADOLPHUS, 1874, *Recollections of Archbishop Whately, Lippincott's Magazine, vol. 14, p. 105.*

When I entered at Oxford, John Henry Newman was beginning to be famous. The responsible authorities were watching him with anxiety; clever men were looking with interest and curiosity on the apparition among them of one of those persons of indisputable genius who was likely to make a mark upon his time. His appearance was striking. He was above the middle height, slight and spare. His head was large, his face remarkably like that of Julius Cæsar. The forehead, the shape of the ears and nose were almost the same. The lines of the mouth were very peculiar, and I should say exactly the same. I have often thought of the resemblance, and believed that it extended to the temperament. In both there was an original force of character which refused to be moulded by circumstances, which was to make its own way, and become a power in the world; a clearness of intellectual perception, a disdain for conventionalities, a temper imperious and wilful, but along with it a most attaching gentleness, sweetness, singleness of heart and purpose. Both were formed by nature to command others; both had the faculty of attracting to themselves the passionate devotion of their friends and followers; and in both cases, too, perhaps the devotion was rather due to the personal ascendency of the leader than to the cause which he represented. It was Cæsar, not the principle of the empire, which overthrew Pompey and the constitution. *Credo in Newmannum* was a common phrase at Oxford, and is still unconsciously the faith of nine-tenths of the converts of Rome.—FROUDE, JAMES ANTHONY, 1881, *The Oxford Counter-Reformation, Short Studies on Great Subjects, vol. IV, p. 179.*

The foremost man in the English Church was content to send for the humble Italian monk, Father Dominic, the Passionist, and, falling at his feet, to ask reception into the Roman Church. At the call of conscience he had already resigned preferment and leadership; he now abandoned home and nearly all his friends; for ease he accepted comparative poverty; for rule over others he took on him obedience; "*et exiit nesciens quo iret.*"—PAUL, C. KEGAN, 1882, *John Henry, Cardinal Newman, Century Magazine, vol. 24, p. 280.*

The most interesting part of my visit to Birmingham was a call I made by appointment on Cardinal Newman. He was benignly courteous, and we excellencied and eminenced each other by turns. A more gracious senescence I never saw. There was no "monumental pomp," but a serene decay, like that of some ruined abbey in a woodland dell, consolingly forlorn. I was surprised to find his head and features smaller than I expected—modelled on lines of great vigor, but reduced and softened by a certain weakness, as if a powerfully masculine face had been painted in miniature by

Malbone. He was very kindly and sympathetic—his benignity as well as his lineaments reminding me of the old age of Emerson.—LOWELL, JAMES RUSSELL, 1884, *To C. E. Norton*, Oct. 17; *Letters*, ed. Norton, vol. II, p. 281.

With a keenly inquisitive mind disposed to search to the root of religious problems, he was too logical, too dogmatic, to be satisfied with Whately's position; and the latter soon discovered that Newman's was a spirit beyond his leading. He may have been wrong in saying that Newman was looking "to be the head of a party" himself; and yet there is a side of his character that suggests this view. He had a great love of personal influence. From the first he attracted by his personality rather than by his intelligence—by the authority rather than the rationality of his opinions. He never seems to have understood any other kind of influence. In this kind he was supreme. He did not require to go in search of friends or followers. They gathered spontaneously around him, and there almost necessarily sprang out of this feature of his character a high ambition.—TULLOCH, JOHN, 1885, *Movements of Religious Thought in Britain During the Nineteenth Century*, p. 63.

That great man's extraordinary genius drew all those within his sphere, like a magnet, to attach themselves to him and his doctrines. Nay, before he became a Romanist, what we may call his mesmeric influence acted not only on his Tractarian adherents, but even in some degree on outsiders like myself. Whenever I was at Oxford, I used to go regularly on Sunday afternoons to listen to his sermon at St. Mary's, and I have never heard such preaching since. I do not know whether it is a mere fancy of mine, or whether those who know him better will accept and endorse my belief, that one element of his wonderful power showed itself after this fashion. He always began as if he had determined to set forth his idea of the truth in the plainest and simplest language, language as men say "intelligible to the meanest understanding." But his ardent zeal and fine poetical imagination were not thus to be controlled. As I hung upon his words, it seemed to me as if I could trace behind his will, and pressing, so to speak, against it, a rush of thoughts and feelings which he kept struggling to hold back, but in the end they were generally too strong for him and poured themselves out in a torrent of eloquence all the more impetuous from having been so long repressed. The effect of these outbursts was irresistible, and carried his hearers beyond themselves at once. Even when his efforts of self-restraint were more successful, those very efforts gave a life and colour to his style which riveted the attention of all within the reach of his voice.—DOYLE, SIR FRANCIS HASTINGS, 1887, *Reminiscences and Opinions*, p. 145.

O weary Champion of the Cross, lie still:
  Sleep thou at length the all-embracing sleep:
  Long was thy sowing day, rest now and reap:
Thy fast was long, feast now thy spirit's fill.
Yea, take thy fill of love, because thy will
  Chose love not in the shallows but the deep:
  Thy tides were springtides, set against the neap
Of calmer souls: thy flood rebuked their rill.
—ROSSETTI, CHRISTINA G., 1890, *Cardinal Newman, The Athenæum*, No. 3277, p. 225.

Cardinal Newman had always something to say when he spoke; something most worthy of being said; something which he could say as no one else could. And the light of his whole conversation was his supreme loyalty to truth. . . . In order fully to appreciate Dr. Newman, it was necessary to be with him in his own home, among the devoted fathers and brethren with whom his life was passed. His mornings were usually sacred to his work. But in the afternoon, at the period of which I am speaking, he would take a long walk—he was still a great pedestrian—in which his visitor had the privilege of accompanying him. At six o'clock the community dinner took place; and on the days when his turn came round, "the Father" would pin on the apron of service and wait upon his brethren and his visitor—who, to say the truth, was somewhat uncomfortable in being ministered to—not himself sitting down until they had received their portions. . . . It may be said of him, as Vittoria Colonna said of Michael Angelo, that they who know only his works, know the least part of him.—LILLY, W. S., 1890, *John Henry Newman, In Memoriam, Fortnightly Review*, vol. 54, pp. 423, 425, 437.

If man ever succeeded in anything, Cardinal Newman has succeeded in convincing all those who study his career with an approach to candour and discrimination, that the depth and luminousness of his conviction, that the true key to the enigma of life is God's revelation of Himself in Christ and in His Church, are infinitely deeper in him, and more of the intimate essence of his mind and heart, than his appreciation, keen as it is, of the obstacles which stand in the way of those convictions and appear to bar the access to them. . . . Whether tried then by the test of nobility, intensity, and steadfastness of his work, or by the test of the greatness of the powers which have been consecrated to that work Cardinal Newman has been one of the greatest of our modern great men.—HUTTON, RICHARD HOLT, 1890, *Cardinal Newman, pp.* 5, 15.

Peace to the virgin heart, the crystal brain!
Peace for one hour through all the camps of thought!
Our subtlest mind has rent the veil of pain,
Has found the truth he sought.
Who knows what page those new-born eyes have read?
If this set creed, or that, or none be best?—
Let no strife jar above this sacred head;
Peace for a saint at rest!
—GOSSE, EDMUND, 1890, *Cardinal Newman, The Athenæum, No.* 3277, *p.* 225.

To those who equally honour a great and beautiful character and love their country, nothing surely can have been more striking than the manner in which the whole English nation has been moved during the last fortnight by the death of Cardinal Newman; and this feeling has been absolutely free from any distinctions of creed. . . . It is to Newman even more than to his great fellow-workers that we owe it—to the power and beauty of his life and writings, and even to the manner in which he pointed out our defects. In all these points it is not too much to call him "the founder of the Church of England as we see it." The great institutions which have sprung up, and are still springing up almost of their own accord —the sisterhoods, and now we may hope the brotherhoods, the higher standard of clerical life, the different conception of public worship, the increased freedom of adopting practices of devotion which so many find to be essential to their religious life; the spirit of all this new life we owe primarily to the great man whom the whole nation now mourns.—LAKE, WILLIAM CHARLES, 1890, *Guardian, Aug.* 27; *Memorials, ed. Mrs. Lake, pp.* 301, 302.

No one living knows my brother's life from boyhood to the age of forty as I do. The splendour of his funeral makes certain that his early life will be written; it must be expected that the more *mythical* the narrative the better it will sell. The honour naturally and rightfully paid to him by Catholics makes him a public man of the century. I should have vastly preferred entire oblivion of him and his writings of the first forty years, but that is impossible. In the cause of *Protestants* and *Protestantism* I feel bound to write, however painful to myself, as simply as if my topic were an old Greek or Latin. . . . I could not possibly have written freely of the late Cardinal to grieve him while he lived, but I see a new side of my duty opened to me, now that my words cannot pain him. . . . Now I see that, unless *something* be explained by me, no one will guess at his very eccentric character, and false ideas are likely to gain currency.—NEWMAN, FRANCIS W., 1891, *Contributions Chiefly to the Early History of the Late Cardinal Newman, Introduction, pp.* v, vii.

Newman's strong point was not philanthropy either in word or deed. . . . Newman's genius precluded him from getting on with common people, and made him perhaps feel ill at ease except when he was in an atmosphere of refinement.—ABBOTT, EDWIN A., 1891, *The Early Life of Cardinal Newman, Contemporary Review, vol.* 59, *pp.* 47, 48.

There was such a pathetic tone in his utterance of that which the French describe as "tears in the voice," such a tender appeal of plaintive sweetness, that I remember to this day the first words of the first sermon I heard from his lips—"Sheep are defenceless creatures, wolves are strong and fierce." But I fail to comprehend, regarding the matter in the light of consistency and common-sense, why it was proposed that a statue of Cardinal Newman should occupy the best site in Oxford; why the representation of a deserter should be set up in a barrack-yard of the Church Militant, as a model for the young recruits!—HOLE, S. REYNOLDS, 1893, *Memories, p.* 145.

To the falsification of history, illusion will take the place of reality, fiction of truth. And what would be gained by such an effeminate paltering with facts? To wink in silence is only owl-like wisdom. Not sentimental suppressions, but the simple truth is the only tribute worthy of such a man as Manning. What then is the truth? Not more than three or four years before the illusive and fancy picture of 1890,

Cardinal Manning, not to speak of contemporary letters extending over a long period of years, avowed and put on record his condemnation of Newman in terms so clear and incisive as to leave no room or foothold for an after fiction of friendship. I will only recite one sentence from an autobiographical note dated 1887. "If I was opposed to Newman, it was only because I had either to oppose Newman or to oppose the Holy See. I could not oppose the Pope."
—PURCELL, EDMUND SHERIDAN, 1895, *Life of Cardinal Manning*, vol. II, p. 754.

His [Cardinal Manning] greatest mistake was his treatment of Newman. For the misunderstandings of the two Cardinals he is most to blame, and the severest thing yet to be said of him will be contained in a candid and capable life of Newman. Manning was the leader in the cabinet and the field, and it was his business to have found a place for that beautiful soul lost in the lonely desert of Brompton: instead of shutting him off from every avenue of usefulness and distinction whose gates he was able to close. He has been punished already for his hostility or indifference, or whatever it may be called. His influence fades, while Newman's increases.—SMITH, JOHN TALBOT, 1896, *Cardinal Manning and his Biographer*, The Forum, vol. 22, p. 105.

Early in the evening a singularly graceful figure in cap and gown glided into the room. The slight form and gracious address might have belonged either to a youthful ascetic of the middle ages or a graceful and highbred lady of our own days. He was pale and thin almost to emaciation, swift of pace, but, when not walking, intensely still, with a voice sweet and pathetic both, but so distinct that you could count each vowel and consonant in every word. When touching upon subjects which interested him much, he used gestures rapid and decisive, though not vehement; and while in the expression of thoughts on important subjects there was often a restrained ardour about him; yet if individuals were in question he spoke severely of none, however widely their opinions might differ from his. . . . Nothing more characterised Newman than his unconscious refinement. It would have been impossible for him to tolerate coarse society, or coarse books, or manners seriously deficient in self-respect and respect for others. There was also in him a tenderness marked by a smile of magical sweetness, but a sweetness that had in it nothing of softness. On the contrary, there was a decided severity in his face, that severity which enables a man alike to exact from others, and himself to render, whatever painful service or sacrifice justice may claim.—
DE VERE, AUBREY, 1897, *Recollections*, pp. 256, 278.

Certainly the whole Catholic Church, Anglican as well as Roman, owes a vast debt to the powerful defence that he made of all the great fundamentals of the Catholic faith. No injury done to the English Church by his secession can ever make Anglicans forgetful of all that they, with all true believers, owe to him for doing battle in a latitudinarian age in behalf of the great verities contained in Holy Scripture and the Creeds. To him in no little degree it is due that at the present day there is a more intelligent grasp and a more courageous expression in the Church of England of the mysteries of the faith—the Holy Trinity, the Incarnation, as well as a devout acceptance and reverent use of the Grace of God given in the Sacraments. And therefore his elevation to so high a position in that Church for which he deserted her Communion, was received not only without jealousy, but with no little gratification at the honour done to one who had been the greatest Anglican of his own, if not of any age. Newman was also honoured by his own two colleges at Oxford, Trinity and Oriel, who rejoiced to welcome him back into their societies as an honorary member.
—DONALDSON, AUG. B., 1900, *Five Great Oxford Leaders*, p. 140.

In 1860, he had a slight bend, and seemed to me to look older than he really was. . . . He was, however, very rapid in his movements, still a great pedestrian, and he talked incessantly while walking. I remember what impressed me in his personal appearance was the massive and powerful head of which Froude speaks, and, perhaps, still more the large and luminous eyes, which seemed to pierce through the veil of this world into the illimitable beyond. . . . From the first moment I saw Cardinal Newman, I experienced the inexplicable fascination which all men, high and low, rich and poor, intellectual or otherwise, felt in his presence. It is hard to define the secret of his spell. It consisted partly in the bright, original, startling way in which he touched into life old truths, moral, religious or political. Then there was the extraordinary attraction of voice and manner.—BLENNERHASSETT, SIR ROWLAND, 1901, *Some of My Recollections of Cardinal Newman, Cornhill Magazine*, vol. 84, pp. 616, 620.

APOLOGIA PRO VITÂ SUÂ
1846

Few books have been published of late years which combine more distinct elements of interest than the "Apologia" of Dr. Newman. As an autobiography, in the highest sense of that word, as the portraiture, that is, and record of what the man was, irrespective of those common accidents of humanity which too often load the biographer's pages, it is eminently dramatic. To produce such a portrait was the end which the writer proposed to himself, and which he has achieved with rare fidelity and completeness. . . . The "Apologia" will have a special interest for most of our readers. Almost every page of it will throw some light upon the great controversy which has been maintained for these three hundred years, and which now spreads itself throughout the world, between the Anglican Church and her oldest and greatest antagonist, the Papal See. As to the immediate contest between Professor Kingsley and Dr. Newman, we scarcely deem it necessary to speak. The only abiding significance, we may venture to affirm, of that disagreement will be its having given cause for the production of Dr. Newman's volume. The controversial portion, indeed, of these publications can give no pleasure to the friends of either disputant. Professor Kingsley has added nothing here to his literary reputation. Indeed his pamphlet can only hope to live as the embedded fly in the clear amber of his antagonist's Apology.—WILBERFORCE, SAMUEL, 1864, *Dr. Newman and Apologia Quarterly Review*, vol. 116, pp. 528, 529.

The book is well worth reading, if only as a curious illustration of the utter inadequacy of human intellect and human logic to secure a soul from the strangest wandering, the saddest possible illusion. You cannot read a page of it without admiration for the intellect of the author, and without pity for the poverty even of the richest intellectual gifts where guidance is sought in a faith and in things which transcend the limits of human logic.—McCARTHY, JUSTIN 1872, *Modern Leaders*, p. 169.

It would be impossible to exaggerate the effect of the "Apologia" upon the public mind. It came out in parts, and each new part was looked forward to with eager interest. With the third part the work became purely autobiographical. The writer unveiled his life, his opinions, the influences which had operated upon him, the changes he had undergone, with a candour that carried conviction in every quarter. . . . As a psychological study,—as a remarkable example of searching and faithful introspection the "Apologia" will take its place among the English classics.—JENNINGS, HENRY J., 1882, *Cardinal Newman; the Story of his Life*, pp. 92, 93.

That admirable piece of soul-dissection, so outspoken, with honesty written on every page; that revealing of a soul to which tens of thousands are bound up by ties of gratitude, love, and admiration—the "Apologia" of Cardinal Newman, a book which will henceforth rank with the "Confessions" of St. Augustine.—MULLANY, PATRICK FRANCIS (BROTHER AZARIAS), 1889, *Books and Reading*, p. 47.

As a controversialist Newman's success had perhaps been exaggerated. The success of the "Apologia," for instance, was very little due to its merits as a contribution to the question immediately at issue in the Kingsley dispute; those who were interested in that question knew that there were stronger invectives to be found against the unscrupulousness of Roman methods in Newman's own writings than in the offending words of Kingsley; nor again was its success in any degree theological—probably no single person of average intellect was ever converted by reading it; it was a purely literary success, due in the first place to its engaging frankness, when the public mind was anticipating vulgar subterfuge; and secondly to the lucidity with which it set forth the writer's two positions as a member, first of the English, and afterwards of the Roman communion.—BEECHING, H. C., 1896, *English Prose, ed. Craik*, vol. v, p. 447.

It is the "Apologia" that conquered for Newman the reverence of the younger generation, and left them no choice but to believe in his sincerity and do honour to his motives. It is doubtful if there is anything in literature to compare with it. Here is a man who has practically determined the judgment of an age concerning himself, who has so interpreted himself as he was to himself as to compel his own day and his own people to accept the interpretation. Yet the man was a poet, and the poet's autobiography can never have *Wahrheit* without*Dichtung*, were it only because what has passed through the imagination is transfigured in the passage. The unconscious or the undesigned is ever the truest autobiography; and even more than in any "Apologia" the true Newman may be discovered in the books that come, as it were, unbidden out of his spirit, and seem still to throb as if they had within them the very breath of life.—FAIRBAIRN, A. M., 1897, *Oxford and Jowett, Contemporary Review, vol.* 71, *p.* 836.

Concerning the "Apologia" two things may be said by way of epigraph or conclusion. It fixed the author's place not only in the hearts of his countrymen, but in the national literature. It became the one book by which he was known to strangers who had seen nothing else from his pen, and to a growing number at home, ignorant of theology, not much troubled about dogma, yet willing to admire the living spirit at whose touch even a buried and forgotten antiquity put on the hues of resurrection. No autobiography in the English language has been more read; to the nineteenth century it bears a relation not less characteristic than Boswell's "Johnson" to the eighteenth.—BARRY, WILLIAM, 1904, *Newman (Literary Lives), p.* 133.

GRAMMAR OF ASSENT
1870

His book is composed with elaborate art, which is the more striking the more frequently we peruse it. Every line, every word tells, from the opening sentence to the last. His object, from the beginning to the end, is to combat and overthrow the position of Locke, that reasonable assent is proportioned to evidence, and in its nature, therefore, admits of degrees. . . . The argument is extremely subtle, and often difficult to follow, but the difficulty is in the subject rather than in the treatment. Dr. Newman has watched and analysed the processes of the mind with as much care and minuteness as Ehrenberg the organisation of animalculae. The knotted and tangled skein is disengaged and combed out till every fibre of it can be taken up separately and examined at leisure; while all along, hints are let fall from time to time, expressions, seemingly casual, illustrations, or notices of emotional peculiarities, every one of which has its purpose, and to the careful reader, is a sign-post of the road on which he is travelling.—FROUDE, JAMES ANTHONY, 1870, *Father Newman, or "The Grammar of Assent," Fraser's Magazine, vol.* 81, *pp.* 561, 562.

I find it very instructive, directly and indirectly; as a hint to students of logic generally, as a special key to the character of Dr. Newman's work. . . . He does not mean to go a step beyond assents; he scarcely thinks it possible to go a step beyond them. If he can explain them to us—what assent is, how we are able to assent, what constitutes our obligations to assent —he will deem his work as a teacher accomplished. Whatever wealth of illustration may be at his command, however he may seem to touch upon outlying provinces of thought, this one word really determines his object; he never loses sight of it. The weakness as well as the strength of the book lies, it seems to me, in the persistency with which he pursues this end, and adheres to this name. Assents, he tells us again and again, and I should suppose no one will dispute the assertion, belong strictly and exclusively to *propositions.*—MAURICE, FREDERIC DENISON, 1870, *Dr. Newman's Grammar of Assent, Contemporary Review, vol.* 14, *pp.* 151, 152.

The illustrious author of the "Grammar of Assent" has poured into this, his latest work, the treasures of thought and observation which a whole life-time has gathered together. Here he has summed up, explained, and corrected the lessons of his former writings. Here he has given the last touches to the "Apologia" by supplying the philosophy of its history.—BROWNSON, ORESTES AUGUSTUS, 1871, *Dr. Newman's Grammar of Assent, Catholic World, vol.* 12, *p.* 602.

The work could not have fallen into better hands; and when we say that the learned author has embarked all his genius, culture, and metaphysical acumen in the enterprise, it is superfluous to add that his book is well worth reading. Dr. Newman is master of a simple, clear, untechnical English style; his pages teem with felicitous illustrations drawn from all quarters; and the essay abounds in passages revealing such depths and delicacy of psychological observation, that the reader whose tastes are at all philosophical will be charmed by the book even if he does not accept its teachings. Here our commendation must end.—PATTON, FRANCIS LANDEY, 1871, *Newman's Grammar of Assent, Princeton Review, vol.* 43, *p.* 234.

As before, we shall find, even in what we are compelled to regard as his errors, more instruction than there would be in the true conclusions of many less able and less consistent thinkers. Instead of Newman's term "Assent," I shall invariably use "Belief," which—at least as used in modern psychology—expresses exactly what he intended by "assent."—MELLONE, SYDNEY HERBERT, 1902, *Leaders of Religious Thought in the Nineteenth Century, p.* 78.

SERMONS

For ourselves, we must say, one of Mr. Newman's sermons is to us a marvellous production. It has perfect power, and perfect nature; but the latter it is which makes it so great. A sermon of Mr. Newman's enters into all our feeling, ideas, modes of viewing things. He wonderfully realises a state of mind, enters into a difficulty, a temptation, a disappointment, a grief; he goes into the different turns and incidental, unconscious symptoms of a case, with notions that come into the head and go out again, and are forgotten, till some chance recalls them. . . . He enters into the ordinary common states of mind just in the same way. He is most consoling, most sympathetic. He sets before persons their own feelings with such truth of detail, such natural expressive touches, that they seem not to be ordinary states of mind which everybody has, but very peculiar ones; for he and the reader seem to be the only two persons in the world that have them in common. Here is the point. Persons look into Mr. Newman's sermons and see their own thoughts in them. This is, after all, what as much as anything gives a book hold upon minds. . . . Wonderful pathetic power, that can so intimately, so subtilely and kindly, deal with the soul!—and wonderful soul that can be so dealt with.—MOZLEY, JAMES, 1846, *Christian Remembrancer, Jan.*

Those who never heard him might fancy that his sermons would generally be about apostolical succession, or rights of the Church, or against Dissenters. Nothing of the kind. You might hear him preach for weeks without an allusion to these things. What there was of High Church was implied rather than enforced. The local, the temporary, and the modern were ennobled by the presence of the Catholic truth belonging to all ages that pervaded the whole. His power showed itself chiefly in the new and unlooked-for way in which he touched into life old truths, moral or spiritual, which all Christians acknowledge, but most have ceased to feel when he spoke of "unreal words," of the "individuality of the soul," of the "invisible world," of a "particular Providence," or again of the "ventures of faith," "warfare the condition of victory," "the Cross of Christ the measure of the world," "the Church a Home for the Lonely." As he spoke, how the old truth became new; how it came home with a meaning never felt before! He laid his finger how gently, yet how powerfully, on some inner place in the hearer's heart, and told him things about himself he had never known till then. Subtlest truths, which it would have taken philosophers pages of circumlocution and big words to state, were dropt out by the way in a sentence or two of the most transparent Saxon. What delicacy of style, yet what strength! how simple, yet how suggestive! how homely, yet how refined! how penetrating, yet how tender-hearted! If now and then there was a forlorn undertone which at the time seemed inexplicable, you might be perplexed at the drift of what he said, but you felt all the more drawn to the speaker. After hearing these sermons you might come away still not believing the tenets peculiar to the High Church System; but you would be harder than most men, if you did not feel more than ever ashamed of coarseness, selfishness, worldliness, if you did not feel the things of faith brought closer to the soul.—SHAIRP, JOHN CAMPBELL, 1866, *John Keble.*

People who read the sermons now for the first time, can scarcely appreciate the effect produced by their simplicity and naturalness of diction when they were first delivered or read. Like Arnold in this, if in few other points, Newman spoke on sacred things, usually in the language of common life—plain, even familiar often, but always transparent, always such as to convey the speaker's meaning to the hearer's mind, often such as to enlist imagination and feeling in the service of the speaker. . . .

Regarded simply as compositions, we think that they may disappoint those who read them now for the first time, with tastes and expectations formed by the sermons of more recent preachers. In truth, Newman and Arnold formed the preachers who have in their turn taught the present generation what to expect in a sermon meant to live.—VAUGHAN, E. T., 1869, *J. H. Newman as Preacher, Contemporary Review, vol.* 10, *pp.* 42, 43.

When we read the sermons of Dr. Newman, we admire the subtlety of their insight, the loftiness of their spirituality, the *curiosa felicitas* of a style which, while it often seems to aim at an almost bald simplicity, keeps us spellbound with an unaccountable fascination. Yet so completely have the religious thoughts and even the phraseology, of "Mr. Newman of Oriel," passed into our current homiletic literature, so familiar has even his peculiar pronunciation and method of delivery become, that we can hardly account for the fact that his sermons were once regarded with intense suspicion, and were believed by large sections of the Church to teem with the subtlest insinuation of dangerous heresy.—FARRAR, FREDERIC WILLIAM, 1878, *Thomas Arnold, Macmillan's Magazine, vol.* 37, *p.* 456.

There was not very much change in the inflection of the voice; action there was none. His sermons were read, and his eyes were always bent on his book, and all that, you will say, is against efficiency in preaching. Yes, but you must take the man as a whole, and there was a stamp and a seal upon him; there was a solemn sweetness and music in the tone, there was a completeness in the figure, taken together with the tone and the manner, which made even his delivery, such as I have described it, and though exclusively from written sermons, singularly attractive.—GLADSTONE, WILLIAM EWART, 1887, *Speech at City Temple.*

As tutor at Oriel, Mr. Newman had made what effort he could, sometimes disturbing to the authorities, to raise the standard of conduct and feeling among his pupils. When he became a parish priest, his preaching took a singularly practical and plain-spoken character. The first sermon of the series, a typical sermon, "Holiness necessary for future Blessedness," a sermon which has made many readers grave when they laid it down, was written in 1826, before he came to St. Mary's; and as he began he continued. No sermons, except those which his great opposite, Dr. Arnold, was preaching at Rugby, had appealed to conscience with such directness and force. A passionate and sustained earnestness after a high moral rule, seriously realised in conduct is the dominant character of these sermons. They showed the strong reaction against slackness of fibre in the religious life; against the poverty, softness, restlessness, worldliness, the blunted and impaired sense of truth, which reigned with little check in the recognised fashions of professing Christianity; the want of depth both of thought and feeling; the strange blindness to the real sternness, nay the austerity, of the New Testament. Out of this ground the movement grew. Even more than a theological reform, it was a protest against the loose unreality of ordinary religious morality. In the first stage of the movement, moral earnestness and enthusiasm gave its impulse to theological interest and zeal.—CHURCH, RICHARD WILLIAM, 1891, *The Oxford Movement, p.* 18.

I am one of those who remember well the early days of the "Tracts for the Times;" I possess the Tracts in the original edition; I read them when they came fresh upon the minds of Englishmen; I had taken my degree before the appearance of No. XC. Nay more; I am one of those—not so many of them now—who have heard Newman preach in his own pulpit of St. Mary's, Oxford, and who can bear testimony to the marvellous effect of his preaching and the marvellous manner in which it was produced. Those who never heard him can scarcely believe—so at least I have found—that pulpit eloquence could be supported upon such a foundation; the unvarying note, the absolute immobility of face and limb, the close of a long sentence to be followed by another apparently separated from the preceding one by a sharp fracture; all this does not look much like a true basis for pulpit eloquence—and in a certain sense it was not eloquence; nevertheless in a very real and deep sense it was so; it was like a message from another world, or like an utterance of a primitive saint or martyr permitted to revisit the world of living men.—CARLISLE, H., 1892, *Probability and Faith; Contemporary Review, vol.* 61, *p.* 49.

If we ask by what means this power was

gained at Oxford, the answer must certainly be that it was entirely by his sermons and lectures, expressing as they did his whole character; and these have been so vividly described, and by men of every variety of opinion, that it is difficult, and may seem superfluous, to attempt the task once more. Sir Francis Doyle, Principal Shairp, Professor Mozley, Dean Church and Dean Stanley, Mr. Hutton, Mr. Matthew Arnold, and Mr. Froude have each struck a different note of admiration, and it is indeed difficult to describe their character without exaggeration, and without feeling that no one could entirely appreciate them who did not hear them. There was first the style, always simple, refined and unpretending and without a touch of anything which could be called rhetoric, but always marked by a depth of feeling which evidently sprang from the heart and experience of the speaker and penetrated by a suppressed vein of the poetry which was so strong a feature in Newman's mind, and which appealed at once to the hearts and the highest feelings of his hearers. His language had the perfect grace which comes from uttering deep and affecting truths in the most natural and appropriate words. Then, as he entered into his subject more fully, the preacher seemed to enter into the very minds of his hearers, and, as it were, to reveal to themselves, and to tell them their very innermost thoughts. There was rarely or never anything which could be called a burst of feeling; but both of thought and of suppressed feeling there was every variety, and you were always conscious that you were in the hands of a man who was a perfect master of your heart, and was equally powerful to comfort and to warn you. Is it too much to say of such addresses that they were unlike anything that we had ever heard before, and that we have never heard or read anything similar to them in our after-life?—LAKE, WILLIAM CHARLES, 1897-1901, *Memorials, ed. his Widow*, p. 41.

The finer and more fastidious your mind is, the more you will enjoy Newman's sermons. But the more burdened and broken your heart is, and especially with your secret sinfulness, the less will you find in them that which, above all things in heaven or earth, your heart needs. Had the substance and the spirit of Newman's sermons been but half as good as their style, what a treasure the St. Mary's sermons would have been to all time! As it is, they are a splendid literature in many respects; but one thing they are not, they are not what God intends the Gospel of His Son to be to all sinful and miserable men.—WHYTE, ALEXANDER, 1901, *Newman, an Appreciation in Two Lectures*, p. 93.

POEMS

It is grave and subdued as to tone, somewhat bare of ornament, but everywhere weighty with thought ["Gerontius"]. It is written also with Dr. Newman's usual mastery over the English language, and moves along from the beginning to the end with a solemn harmony of its own. I am here referring to the blank verse; the speeches rather. The lyrical portions (with the exception of two, on which I shall touch by-and-by) are, in my judgment, less successful. The strains as they flow forth from the various ranks of angels are not, if I may use a somewhat pedantic word, differentiated by any intelligible gradations of feeling and of style, and, indeed, do not move me much more than those average hymns which people, who certainly are not angels yet, sing weekly in church. The interlocutory blasphemies of the demons are still worse. I cannot help pronouncing them to be mean and repulsive.—DOYLE, SIR FRANCIS HASTINGS, 1868, *Lectures Delivered Before the University of Oxford*, p. 117.

He has published volumes of verse which I think belong to the very highest order of verse-making that is not genuine poetry. They are full of thought, feeling, pathos, tenderness, beauty of illustration; they are all that verse can be made by one who just fails to be a poet.—McCARTHY, JUSTIN, 1872, *Par Nobile Fratrum—The Two Newmans, Modern Leaders*, p. 170.

"Lead kindly Light" is the most popular hymn in the language. All of us, Catholic, Protestant, or such as can see their way to no positive creed at all, can here meet on common ground and join in common prayer. —FROUDE, JAMES ANTHONY, 1881, *The Oxford Counter-Reformation, Short Studies on Great Subjects, vol.* IV.

His poetry, however, is to be found chiefly in the beautiful thoughts scattered through his prose rather than in the form of verses. These have been the lighter flowers of his literature, and, graceful as they are, are not those by which he is to be judged.—

PAUL, C. KEGAN, 1882, *John Henry, Cardinal Newman, The Century, vol. 24, p. 286.*
Dr. Newman's poetry cannot be passed over without a word—though I am ill-fitted to do justice to it. "Lead kindly Light" has forced its way into every hymn-book and heart. Those who go, and those who do not go to church, the fervent believer and the tired-out sceptic here meet on common ground. The language of the verses in their intense sincerity seems to reduce all human feelings, whether fed on dogmas and holy rites or on man's own sad heart, to a common denominator.
"The night is dark, and I am far from home,
Lead thou me on."
The Believer can often say no more. The Unbeliever will never willingly say less.—BIRRELL, AUGUSTINE, 1888, *Cardinal Newman, Scribner's Magazine, vol. 3, p. 743.*

He will be remembered chiefly by his "Lead kindly Light," which is as far from poetry as I hope most hymns are from the ear to which they were addressed. Else would it be shut to all our petitions.—LOWELL, JAMES RUSSELL, 1890, *To Miss E. G. Norton, Sept. 7; Letters, ed. Norton, vol. II, p. 416.*

Some, and among them the present writer, may dissent from the almost universal admiration of this poem as a congregational hymn, on the ground that it is better fitted for an anxious inquirer in the closet than for an assemblage of Christian believers singing prayers or praises of Him whom they worship as the Father of the Lord Jesus Christ. To some it may even seem that both the words and the spirit of the words reveal a different stage of religion, if not a different religion altogether, from that which is expressed in such a hymn, as "O God our help in ages past." But, whether indiscriminately admired or hypercritically censured, the hymn cannot legitimately suggest that the "kindly light" was, at the time, thought likely by the poet to lead him from the Church of England. Much rather it was the natural and justifiable prayer of one who was entering upon a dangerous, but (as he trusted) heaven-dictated enterprise, in doubt as to the best means for succeeding.... Yet this humble abnegation of foresight—praiseworthy enough perhaps in some penitent and beclouded wanderer groping his way back to the Truth from which he had strayed—would not be praiseworthy, would not be even tolerable, in one who was undertaking to be a leader of souls. We could not praise a teacher who is content not to see "the distant scene," and who finds "one step enough" for him to be in advance of his pupils. But Newman was a poet, and liable to poetic moods. He did not probably, at the time, feel like a guide, and he consequently did not write like a guide. — ABBOTT, EDWIN A., 1891, *The Early Life of Cardinal Newman, Contemporary Review, vol. 59, pp. 53, 54.*

Cardinal Newman towers with only three or four compeers above his generation; and now that the benignity of his great nature has passed from our sight, its majesty is more evident year by year. But Newman is no child of his own age, though he was one of its leaders. He belongs to the Middle Ages, not by his imagination, but by his very personality. If Scott is all chivalry, Newman is all asceticism. Pure mystic speaks in him, the mystic who has not even seen the warrior. His longest poem, the "Dream of Gerontius," is a study of the experience of the Catholic soul after death. No one who has felt the keen touch of that poem upon the hidden spirit could venture to call it archaic. But it is modern only because eternal, as the Confessions of Augustine are modern. Only by accident does the nineteenth rather than the thirteenth century give it birth. Cardinal Newman is in one sense apart even from the mediæval revival: he is simply a true son of the past.—SCUDDER, VIDA D., 1895, *The Life of the Spirit in the Modern English Poets, p. 176.*

"The Dream of Gerontius," as Newman informed me, owed its preservation to an accident. He had written it on a sudden impulse, put it aside, and forgotten it. The editor of a magazine wrote to him asking for a contribution. He looked into all his "pigeon-holes," and found nothing theological; but, in answering his correspondent, he added that he had come upon some verses which, if, as an editor, he cared to have, were at his command. The wise editor did care, and they were published at once. I well remember the delight with which many of them were read aloud by the Bishop of Gibraltar, Dr. Charles Harris, who was then on a visit with us, and the ardour with which we all shared his enjoyment.—DE VERE, AUBREY, 1897, *Recollections, p. 271.*

Newman's great reputation for prose, and the supreme interest attaching to his life, seem to have obscured the fame he might have won, and deserved, as a poet. His poetry is religious without the weakness, or at any rate the limitedness, which mars so much religious verse. He was, in poetry as well as in theology, a greater and more masculine Keble, one with all the real purity of Keble, but with also the indispensable flavour of earth. "I was in a humour, certainly," he says of the Anglican divines, "to bite off their ears;" and one loves him for it. It is worth remembering also that he taught the need of hatred as well as love; and though he explained and limited the teaching, there is meaning in the very form of expression. There was iron in Newman's frame and gall in his blood.— WALKER, HUGH, 1897, *The Age of Tennyson. p.* 148.

No doubt it is somewhat hard for the staunch Protestant to wax enthusiastic over the invocation of a "Kindly Light" which led its author straight into the arms of the Scarlet Woman of the Seven Hills. Against this may be put the fact that when the Parliament of Religions met at Chicago, the representatives of every creed known to man found two things on which they were agreed. They could all join in the Lord's Prayer, and they could all sing, "Lead kindly Light." This hymn, Mrs. Drew tells me, and "Rock of Ages," are two of Mr. Gladstone's "most favourite hymns." —STEAD, W. T., 1897, *Hymns That Have Helped*, p. 107.

"The Dream of Gerontius" described the vision of a dying Christian, and is the most powerful and imaginative of his poems, though, curiously enough, it was not composed until late in life.—MILES, ALFRED H., 1897, *The Poets and the Poetry of the Century, Social, Moral, and Religious Verse,* p. 187.

There is nothing romantic in either temper or style about Newman's poems, all of which are devotional in subject, and one of which—"The Pillar of the Cloud" ("Lead kindly Light")—is a favourite hymn in most Protestant communions. The most ambitious of these is "The Dream of Gerontius," a sort of mystery play which Sir Henry Taylor used to compare with the "Divine Comedy." Indeed none but Dante has more poignantly expressed the purgatorial passion, the desire for pain, which makes the spirits in the flames of purification unwilling to intermit their torments even for a moment. — BEERS, HENRY A., 1901, *A History of English Romanticism in the Nineteenth Century,* p. 362.

This "Dream" is a true and vivid example of what Berkeley intended, when he represented the whole world as shown to the spirit, though not existing outside it, and on that account the more real. It has no local habitation; we do not once think, in reading it, of the Dantean cosmography. It takes place where the soul is, and the Angels, where we love and suffer. But the solid frame of things, as it lately appeared, is no more. Alone the spirit utters its beliefs, while it seems falling into the abyss; alone, amid litanies and absolutions, it passes away, the priest reciting most musically his anthem, "Go forth upon thy journey, Christian soul!"—BARRY, WILLIAM, 1904, *Newman (Literary Lives),* p. 163.

GENERAL

His writings, at least all I have seen of them, leave an unsatisfactory impression on my mind. He appears always to view a subject at some acute angle or another; he never looks at it in a direct or straightforward manner. He never embraces it as a totality. His acuteness loses itself in minuteness, like some meandering rivulet which sinks out of sight in the sand. He throws a peculiar haziness over everything he touches; not exactly that kind of haziness which arises from the employment of quaint and obscure language or phrases; but that which results from a species of intellectual side-glancing at objects instead of steadily looking them full in the face. He is always fishing for pearls in deep water, and always striving to express the most common and familiar thoughts in the formal drapery of philosophical diction. A healthy and rational mode of thinking is out of his beat; partly, I conceive, from constitutional tendencies, and partly from a bad habit of thinking and reasoning. The casual and accidental relations of things are more important to him, as a thinker, than the necessary and essential.—BLAKEY, ROBERT, 1851, *Memoirs, ed. Miller,* p. 203.

Two points are quite certain of Father Newman, and they are the only two which are at present material. He was undeniably a consummate master of the difficulties of the creeds of other men. With a profoundly religious organization which was hard to satisfy, with an imagination which could not help setting before itself simply and exactly what different creeds would come to and mean in life, with an analyzing and most subtle intellect which was sure to detect the weak point in an argument if a weak point there was, with a manner at once grave and fascinating,—he was a nearly perfect religious disputant, whatever may be his deficiencies as a religious teacher.—BAGEHOT, WALTER, 1862, *Mr. Clough's Poems, Works,* ed. Morgan, vol. I, p. 184.

Those who are old enough to remember 1840 will remember that "mystical," not "popish," was the public epithet of dislike for Dr. Newman's mode of treating Christian truth at that period. Its doctrine of "reserve in communicating religious truth" was that which first embroiled nascent Tractarianism with the religious world. Just so in the recent ferment on occasion of "Essays and Reviews." It was not the crudities, blunders, and hasty opinions that volume contains which has stirred all the indignation, but the transcendental treatment of religion from within. Newman's constant effort was to "realize" the doctrines of the Church; it was his favourite word at one time. Jowett is ever idealizing the language of Scripture. To the common understanding both alike are felt to be not only passing beyond its ken, but to be taking truth away with them into some region into which it cannot follow.—PATTISON, MARK, 1863–89, *Learning in the Church of England, Essays,* ed. Nettleship, vol. II, p. 303.

His mind was essentially sceptical and sophistical, endowed with various talents in an eminent degree, but not with the power of taking firm hold on either speculative or historical truth. Yet his craving for truth was strong in proportion to the purity of his life and conscience. He felt that he was entirely unable to satisfy this craving by any mental operations of his own, and that if he was to depend on his own ability to arrive at any settled conclusion he should be for ever floating in a sea of doubt; therefore he was irresistibly impelled to take refuge under the wings of an infallible authority. . . . He bowed to an image which he had first himself set up. There was at once his strength and his weakness. He could deceive himself, and could not help letting himself be deceived. —THIRLWALL, CONNOP, 1867, *To W. Dundas, April 30; Letters Literary and Theological,* ed. Perowne and Stokes, pp. 260, 261.

I cannot help recording my conviction that whenever posterity sits in judgment on the character of Dr. Newman, as it will some day, dutifulness to Bishops will not be reckoned among his *strong* points, or commended as a principle of action in general, from the success with which it was practiced in his case.—FOULKES, EDMUND S., 1872, *Dr. Newman's Essays, Contemporary Review,* vol. 19, p. 383.

To turn from Dr. Newman's Apologia to Mill's autobiography is, in the slang of modern science, to plunge the organism in a totally different environment. With Dr. Newman we are kneedeep in the dust of the ancient fathers, poring over the histories of Eutychians, Monophysites, or Arians, comparing the teaching of Luther and Melanchthon with that of Augustine; and from such dry bones extracting—not the materials of antiquarian discussion or philosophical histories—but living and effective light for our guidance. The terminal limit of our inquiries is fixed by Butler's Analogy. Dr. Newman ends where Mill began.—STEPHEN, LESLIE, 1877, *Dr. Newman's Theory of Belief, Fortnightly Review,* vol. 28, p. 680.

It is not, however, our part here to estimate the need or the value of the work he has done. But it is easy to see how well his rare and peculiar genius fitted him for doing it. If, on the one side, he had the imaginative devotion which clung to a past ideal, he had, on the other side, that penetrating insight into human nature, which made him well understand his own age, and its tendencies. He was intimately acquainted with his own heart, and he so read the hearts of his fellowmen, that he seemed to know their inmost secrets. In his own words he could tell them what they knew about themselves, and what they did not know, till they were startled by the truth of his revelations. His knowledge of human nature, underived from books and philosophy, was intuitive, first-hand, practical. In this region he belonged to the pre-scientific era. He took what he found within him, as the first of all knowledge, as the thing he was most absolutely certain of. The feelings, desires, aspirations, needs, which he felt in his own heart, the intimations of conscience, sense of sin, longing for deliverance, these were his closest knowledge, to accept, not to explain away, or to analyse into nothing. They were his original outfit, they fixed his standard of judgment; they furnished the key by which he was to read the riddle of life, and to interpret the world; they were the "something within him, which was to harmonise and adjust" all that was obscure and discordant without him.—SHAIRP, JOHN CAMPBELL, 1881, *Prose Poets, Aspects of Poetry*, p. 451.

It is hardly an overstrained inference to believe that, with that half-conscious aspiration which arises in the minds of most men, when they contemplate a life in which they recognise the embodiment of their own ideal the John Henry Newman of those days sought to be the Ken of the nineteenth century, striving to lead the Church of England, and, through her, other Christian communities, to the doctrine and the worship of that undivided Church of the East and West, after which Ken yearned even to his dying hour.—PLUMPTRE, EDWARD HAYES, 1882, *The Life and Letters of Thomas Ken*, vol. II.

Of all that he has done, poetry is that which Cardinal Newman has done least well. There are qualities in his mind and circumstances in his career which have been unfavorable to any remarkable development of his genius in this direction. The outward phenomena of nature have ever been subordinated by him to abstract truths, and this has of necessity diverted his observation from the details of physical life, which are in so great a degree the sources of poetic inspiration and the object of poetic description. His life has been intensely interior, and its ascetic character has imparted to his verse a certain severity which is not compensated by finely-chiselled outline of Hellenic form. The influence of women on his thoughts, feelings, and modes of expression in verse is hardly to be traced, and he writes as might a solitary penitent in his cell, or a prophet in his cleft of the rock. The softness and sweetness and melody of versification proper to the poet are with him only occasional, and if we want to read his best poetry we must betake ourselves to his prose. In his sermons and sometimes in his essays the depth and fervor of his religious emotions supply every requisite and overflow every disadvantage, and far from our feeling him severe, rude, or rugged, we are deluged by his ineffable tenderness. Once, indeed,—in his "Lead, Kindly Light,"—he has surpassed himself as a poet, and written what touches every heart and satisfies every ear, and will last as long as the language in which it is composed. It is purely and simply a poetic inspiration —a gem without a flaw.—EARLE, JOHN CHARLES, 1882, *Cardinal Newman as a Man of Letters*, American Catholic Quarterly Review, vol. 7, p. 606.

The published works of Newman fill thirty-five volumes, and abundantly testify to the thoroughness and extent of his knowledge and the versatility of his mind. His "History of the Arians," his "Primitive Church" and his annotations of St. Athanasius, his "Historical Sketches," reveal his intimate acquaintance with the history of the early church. No work of fiction has ever given its readers a clearer view of the outward forms and inward spirit of the Christianity of the third century, especially in Africa, than his "Callista." Its attractiveness for empty hearts and troubled minds, the vigor of its life even in its apparent death, its power to recall the careless and indifferent and to reanimate fainting souls, has never been more happily portrayed. The writer of such a book must have had, in his mind and heart, a picture of the church of that far distant time and clime as vivid and real as that of the church at whose altars he served. . . . His two ablest works,—works which give him a high place among the thinkers on the profoundest subjects that can occupy the human mind, almost as important as the study of the crayfish,—are the "Development of Christian Doctrine," and the "Grammar of Assent." Both works are valuable and interesting, not only because of the power of thought and extent of information and richness of suggestion that are to be found in them, but because they are the operations of a great and earnest spirit upon problems that had for a long time occupied and exercised it as practical matters.—HORNBROOKE, FRANCIS B., 1885, *The Life of Cardinal Newman*, Andover Review, vol. 4, pp. 108, 109.

It is not to be supposed, however, that with all Newman's energy and genius the Tracts were at once successful. For some time they were only "as seed cast on the waters." As we read them now, or try to read them, it seems strange that they should have ever moved any number of minds. If some were found to be "heavy reading" at the time, they are now mainly interesting to the theological antiquarian. But this only shows the more how inflamable the clerical and lay-clerical mind was at the time. — TULLOCH, JOHN, 1885, *Movements of Religious Thought in Britain During the Nineteenth Century*, p. 71.

One of the most winning writers of English that ever existed.—MORLEY, JOHN, 1887, *On the Study of Literature, Studies in Literature*, p. 211.

Dr. Newman's style is pellucid, it is animated, it is varied; at times icy cold, it oftener glows with a fervent heat; it employs as its obedient and well-trained servant a vast vocabulary, and it does so always with the ease of the educated gentleman, who by a sure instinct ever avoids alike the ugly pedantry of the bookworm, the forbidding accents of the lawyer, and the stiff conceit of the man of scientific theory. Dr. Newman's sentences sometimes fall upon the ear like well-considered and final judgments, each word being weighed and counted out with dignity and precision; but at other times the demeanor and language of the Judge are hastily abandoned, and substituted for them we encounter the impetuous torrent—the captivating rhetoric, the brilliant imagery, the frequent examples, the repetition of the same idea in different words, of the eager and accomplished advocate addressing men of like passions with himself. — BIRRELL, AUGUSTINE, 1888, *Cardinal Newman, Scribner's Magazine*, vol. 3, p. 739.

His sermons were read, are still read. They are, or many of them are, admirable discourses; but they are sermons, and sermons they must remain. His "Lead Kindly Light" is an immortal hymn. That and the "Apologia" excepted, it were rash indeed to predict immortality of the rest. I am almost tempted to call him a great journalist, so fragmentary was his writing; so strictly did it answer the appeal, "Give us day by day our daily bread;" so accurately adapted was it to the necessities of the particular occasion on which he wrote. Whether he expressed himself in a column or a volume is accidental, not essential. His books did the work, in a measure and within limits which they were meant to do when written. They affected the thought and to some extent modified the lives of his readers. None the less were they occasional, and none the less are they likely to be ephemeral.

That is why it is so difficult to look upon Newman's place in English literature as a very great one for all time to come.—SMALLEY, GEORGE W., 1890-95, *Studies of Men*, p. 7.

The history of our land will hereafter record the name of John Henry Newman among the greatest of our people, as a confessor for the faith, a great teacher of men, a preacher of justice, of piety, and of compassion.—MANNING, HENRY EDWARD CARDINAL, 1890, *Address on Cardinal Newman*, Aug. 20; *Life of Manning*, ed. Purcell, vol. II, p. 751.

What literary powers were those that thus seem to have been squandered away on temporary objects! Bizarre as his reasoning semed to most of us, how subtly he weaved the weft of it. Dealing for the most part with subjects remote from human interests, he would so order his argument that it would have the attraction of a plot for us. Topics that seemed forbidding both for their theological technicalities and their repulse of reason were presented by him with such skill that they appeared as inevitable as Euclid and as attractive as Plato. All the resources of a master of English style—except, perhaps, one, description—were at his command; pure diction, clear arrangement, irony, dignity, a copious command of words combined with a reserve in the use of them—all these qualities went to make up the charm of Newman's style, the finest flower that the earliest system of a purely classical education has produced.—JACOBS, JOSEPH, 1890, *John Henry Newman, Literary Studies*, p. 122.

In the workings of Cardinal Newman's thought as such, apart from the psychological or literary interest attached to them, not many people of the present day, within at any rate the arena of free discussion, can be said to feel themselves very deeply concerned. The ground, so to speak, on which that thought worked has been undermined on all sides. Many of the questions Newman discussed have assumed totally new aspects; still more, the questions he did not discuss at all have become all-important.—WARD, MARY A., 1891, *Philomythus, The Nineteenth Century*, vol. 29, p. 769.

I protest that *in honesty* any edition of my brother's writing while he was a *nominal* Anglican ought to state in the *title* page, or some equally conspicuous place, that he was *already* a hater of the Reformation, and eager to convert us to Romanism. My brother hated Protestantism, and accepted as a divine mission to supplant it (I do not say by Popery, but) by full Romanism. As warning to incautious parents, I have felt it my duty to exhibit the facts. Scholars like my very able friend Dr. James Martineau may read with profit my brother's works; so perhaps may Mr. Richard Hutton. But parents who would be sorely grieved by their children becoming converts to Romanism will not be wise in exposing the young and inexperienced to the speciousness of his pleadings.—NEWMAN, FRANCIS W., 1891, *Contributions Chiefly to the Early History of the Late Cardinal Newman*, p. 140.

Newman knew well, and taught his followers, that no man can be said to *know* anything of religious importance till he has *done* something in consequence of it. So far as he imbued his party with this very practical truth he helped them to success. Whatever is *done* regularly, in the definite name of religion, drives a nail through the character, and fixes a man in his adherence to what he professes. . . . Newman has left us something to imitate, much more to avoid. Our debt to him is negative rather than positive. Not to despise God's facts, and not to be afraid of God's justice, are the two great lessons to be learned by all Englishmen, and especially by English theologians, from Newman's Anglican career.—ABBOTT, EDWIN ABBOTT, 1892, *Anglican Career of Cardinal Newman*.

We speak of him with regard, respect, affection, almost without reference to schools of thought; we print "Lead, Kindly Light" in all our hymn-books, whether "Ancient and Modern," "Hymnal Companion," Society for the Promoting Christian Knowledge, or what not. When the Cardinal departed this life there was something like a national sorrow, and yet how many Englishmen have practically followed his leading? How many have felt the English Church unsound and unsafe in virtue of these arguments which led him to desert her? What are they who followed him, as compared with the multitude who have recognised all that was beautiful in his character and remarkable in his intellectual powers, and who have sorrowed over him as one who left a grand post of spiritual influence from which it seemed possible that he might have moved the world, in order to adopt a position against which in his best days no one had protested more strongly than himself?—CARLISLE, H., 1892, *Probability and Faith, Contemporary Review*, vol. 61, p. 51.

Yet who can doubt that, when Protestantism is no more, and when the Church stands, as the sole champion of her Master's divinity, face to face with materialism and infidelity, the record of Newman's mind will live, not merely on account of the matchless English with which it is clothed, but because within its pages, according to its author's pregnant motto: *Cor ad cor loquitur?*—WILBERFORCE, WILFRID, 1894, *William George Ward, Dublin Review*, vol. 115, p. 23.

Newman's paragraphs are the result of the most careful analysis on the part of their writer. In them unity, usually philosophical, often complex, is severely observed. The style is highly redintegrating, in spite of the aggregating sentence and bookish vocabulary. But it can never be called impartially redintegrating, as one is sometimes tempted to call De Quincey's. The most careful selection of thought is made, and whatever subsidiary matter may have been generated in the act of composition is sternly repressed in the writing. In this matter we may compare Newman and DeQuincey—both artistic minds. Both men are interested in the various phases of the material they use for any given purpose, though of course Newman less than DeQuincey in the sensuous qualities. But DeQuincey cannot express one phase of his interest at a time; Newman can. We find Newman not indeed depending upon connectives for coherence, but using them freely for increased accuracy.—LEWIS, EDWIN HERBERT, 1894, *The History of the English Paragraph*, p. 151.

As Scott's imagination was fascinated with the picturesque paraphernalia of feudalism—with its jousts, and courts of love, and its coats of mail and buff-jerkins—so Newman's imagination was captivated by the gorgeous ritual and ceremonial, the art and architecture of mediæval Christianity. . . . Newman sought to revive in the Church a mediæval faith in its own divine mission and the intense spiritual consciousness of the Middle Ages; he aimed to restore to religion its mystical character, to exalt the sacramental system as the divinely appointed means for the salvation of souls, and to impose once more on men's imaginations the mighty spell of a hierarchical organisation, the direct representative of God in the world's affairs. . . . Both he and Scott substantially ruined themselves through their mediævalism. Scott's luckless attempt was to place his private and family life upon a feudal basis and to give it mediæval colour and beauty; Newman undertook a much nobler and more heroic but more intrinsically hopeless task —that of re-creating the whole English Church in harmony with the mediæval conceptions.—GATES, LEWIS E., 1895, *ed. Selections from Newman, Introduction*, p. 356.

Newman's prose style may be compared in its distinguishing quality to the atmosphere. It is at once simple and subtle; it has vigour and elasticity; it penetrates into every recess of its subject; and it is transparent, allowing each object it touches to display its own proper color. The comparison holds also in two further points, the apparent effortlessness of its successes, and the fact that, in consequence, its virtue attracts little notice.—BEECHING, H. C., 1896, *English Prose, ed. Craik*, vol. V, p. 443.

The books composed during this long and eventful career, especially in the first half of it, were very numerous, Cardinal Newman's works at the time of his death, and before the addition of Letters, etc., extending to nearly forty volumes. Much of the matter of these is still *cinis dolosissimus*, not to be trodden on save in the most gingerly manner in such a book as this. Yet there are probably few qualified and impartial judges who would refuse Newman, all things considered, the title of the greatest theological writer in English during this century; and there are some who uphold him for one of the very greatest of English prose writers. It is therefore impossible not to give him a place, and no mean place, here. . . . He was perhaps the last of the very great preachers in England—of those who combined a thoroughly classical training, a scholarly form, with the incommunicable and almost inexplicable power to move audiences and readers. And he was one of the first of that class of journalists who in the new age have succeeded the preachers, whether for good or ill, as the prophets of the illiterate.—SAINTSBURY, GEORGE, 1896, *A History of Nineteenth Century Literature*.

He is the greatest subjective writer of our age; his power over it is but the fascination exercised by his revelation of himself. In his more scholastic treatises in his dogmatic works, in his attempts at historical writing—his strained subtleties, his violent prejudices, his wilfulness, and his often startling pettiness, make him one of the authors a dispassionate student finds it hardest to read. But the moment his own experience is distilled into a sermon, or tract, or book, his peculiar and often almost irresistible fascination appears. — FAIRBAIRN, A. M., 1897, *Oxford and Jowett, Contemporary Review*, vol. 71, p. 835.

Plutarch has written "Parallel Lives;" and history, no less than drama, delights in contrast and coincidents. But seldom, perhaps, did it execute in this line a stroke so remarkable as when, in the month of October, 1845, and almost on the same day of the month, it led John Henry Newman to the door of the Catholic Church while Ernest Renan was issuing thence, and bidding his early faith an everlasting farewell. . . . For these two men, although never meeting in the body, nor acquainted with each other's writings, were in fact rivals and antagonists—parallel and opposed; each had fought the battle of belief and unbelief in his own bosom; together they summed up the tendencies of an age. And in variety of gifts, in personal romance, in the influence which went forth from them and subdued more than one generation, who shall say that they were greatly unequal? The most striking resemblance between them is their mastery of style. Newman has long been recognised as one of the crowned and sceptred kings of English prose literature, without a competitor save Ruskin; but as a spiritual teacher, a light in the world of religious development, he is by far the greatest that has risen up during our century. On the other hand, which among illustrious French writers has excelled Renan?— BARRY, WILLIAM, 1897, *Newman and Renan, National Review*, vol. 29, p. 557.

Whose best sermons and controversial essays displayed a delicate and flexible treatment of language, without emphasis, without oddity, which hardly arrests any attention at first—the reader being absorbed in the argument or statement—but which in course of time fascinates, and at last somewhat overbalances the judgment, as a thing miraculous in its limpid grace and suavity. The style which Newman employs is the more admired because of its rarity in English; it would attract less wonder if the writer were a Frenchman. If we banish the curious intimidation which the harmony of Newman exercises, at one time or another, over almost every reader, and examine his methods closely, we see that the faults to which his writing became in measure a victim in later years—the redundancy, the excess of colour, the langour and inelasticity of the periods—were not incompatible with what we admire so much in the "Sermons at St. Mary's Church" and in the pamphlets of the Oxford Movement.—GOSSE, EDMUND, 1897, *A Short History of Modern English Literature*, p. 350.

In spite of having taken a most unpopular step in leaving the national church, Newman always retained the popularity which he had so well earned as a member of that Church. I have myself been one of his true admirers, partly from having known many of his intimate friends at Oxford, partly from having studied his earlier works when I first came to England. I read them more for their style than for their contents. If Newman had left behind him no more than his exquisite University sermons and his sweet hymns he would always have stood high among the glories of England.—MÜLLER, F. MAX, 1898, *Auld Lang Syne*, p. 113.

Newman's work reveals him as one of the great masters of graceful, scholarly, finished prose. It is individual; it has charm, and this is the secret of its power to interest. No writer of our time has reflected his mind and heart in his work as has he. He has light for the intellect, and warmth for the heart.—GEORGE, A. J., 1898, *From Chaucer to Arnold, Types of Literary Art*, p. 655.

He has attached himself to the everlasting world of literature by his gift of imagination and speech. Nothing in English can be compared to his simplicity and self-restraint. An acute critic has placed him for music of language alongside of Cicero; yet this gift is a mere incident, for of more worth is the sincerity of the mind behind the faculty—the truth consistent with and almost one with the expression. The personal element in all he has written is very akin to Dante's characteristic; yet the personalities of each are vastly dissimilar. . . . There are passages of his which act like a sedative on the mind and the heart. We must thank England for giving us this spiritual genius. Amid the strife of many voices his note of solemn unction sounds clear and brings silence, as the music of a bird when all the woods are hushed.—O'KEEFFE, HENRY E., 1900, *Another Aspect of Newman*, Catholic World, vol. 71, pp. 81, 82.

If Arnold's constitutional deficiency was unguardedness and exaggeration, Newman's was impatience and despair. We see his limitations clearly now; of temper, knowledge, mental discipline, even piety. We see haste to be despondent in the hero of his valedictory novel, more nakedly in his letters to his sister, until criticism is disarmed by their agony as the crisis becomes inevitable. That his secular knowledge was limited all his reviews and essays show; ignorant of German as we know him to have been, the historic development of religious reason with its underlying unity of thought lay outside the narrow philosophical basis on which were reared his Anglican conclusions; while Arnold was just the man, *invicem præbens crura sagittis*, to elucidate, correct, counterbalance, these flaws in his temperament and system. And if will governed and narrowed his intellect, so did impatience dominate his piety and self-discipline.—TUCKWELL, W., 1900,*Reminiscences of Oxford*, p. 185.

Apart from their subject matter, Newman's prose writings will assuredly have a permanent place in the front rank of English literature. His poems can scarcely claim so high a rank, though those contained in the "Lyra Apostolica" and his "Occasional Verses" will not readily be forgotten. The fascinating poem, entitled "The Dream of Gerontius," dedicated to his friend, John Joseph Gordon of the Oratory, is perhaps the most remarkable attempt ever made to realize the passage of a soul from this world through death into the unseen. The well-known chant of "The Fifth Choir of Angelicans," "Praise to the Holiest in the height, and in the depth be praise," has found its way into numerous hymnals, and has been sung at the graveside of many an English Christian, including Mr. Gladstone and Dean Church. If the doctrine of purgatory had always been dealt with in the delicate, reverent manner of this wonderful effort to realize the state of the disembodied spirit, Christendom might have been saved not only the horrors of the mediæval conception of purgatorial fires, but all the disastrous reaction and revolt that has followed them.—DONALDSON, AUG. B., 1900, *Five Great Oxford Leaders.*

Newman's "Christian Doctrine" is an investigation into the philosophical justification of all belief in dogmatic Christianity. Christianity as a living creed, exhibiting its life in history, in practical action and in dogmatic expression, proving its objective reality by its vitality, is the subject of the book, which is at once historical and philosophical in the sense in which the two coalesce under the influence of the theory of evolution. There is undoubtedly a plane of theological writing to which the phrase "provincial dogma" is applicable. But Newman's Essay is no more on that plane than are the "Pensées" of Pascal. Both writers accept a dogmatic church. But both have that perception from different points of view of the questions they discuss, that sense of the impossibility of complete intellectual solutions of the deepest problems, and that true estimate of the relation of their own partial solution to the speculations of other thinkers, which mark their work as due to the vision of genius, freely exercised, and wide in range, seeing things as they are, with its own eyes, and not vicariously. Personally I believe that the "Essay on Development" will ultimately be judged to contain materials for a greater work than Newman ever completed anywhere, or outlined elsewhere. And even now I cannot doubt that, by those who really know it, it will be allowed to belong not to "provincial" dogma, but to the literature of the world.—WARD, WILFRID, 1901, *Newman and Sabatier, Fortnightly Review, vol.* 75, *p.* 809.

While Newman was completing this book he was thinking himself into the Roman Catholic Church. It is quite in the modern spirit in its way of approaching the problem; it views the history in the light of the idea of Development.— MELLONE, SYDNEY HERBERT, 1902, *Leaders of Religious Thought in the Nineteenth Century, p.* 62.

Newman was a writer almost by accident. He was essentially a leader of men, an ecclesiastical prince, who used literature as an instrument of his rule. But he was also a mystic and a poet, gifted with literary power of the most winning and magnetic kind. His influence upon pure literature has therefore been great. His mediæval cast of mind, his passionate perception of the beauty of the symbolism embodied in the mediæval church, united with Ruskin's devotion to mediæval art to influence a remarkable group of young painters and poets, known as the "Preraphaelites."—MOODY, WILLIAM VAUGHN, AND LOVETT, ROBERT MORSS, 1902, *A History of English Literature, p.* 342.

Sir Richard Francis Burton
1821–1890.

Born, at Barham House, Herts, 19 March, 1821. Taken abroad soon afterwards. To school at Tours, 1827. To school at Richmond, 1830. Returned to France, 1831. Privately educated in France and Italy, 1831–40. To Trinity Coll., Oxford, Oct. 1840; rusticated, autumn of 1841. To Bombay with commission in H. E. I. C.'s service, Oct. 1842. Joined 18th Bombay Native Infantry at Baroda. Regimental Interpreter, 1843. Journey to Medina and Mecca, 1852. To Somaliland with Speke, 1854–55. In Constantinople, 1856. Left Zanzibar, with Speke, on expedition to Central Africa, June 1857. Returned to England, 1859; Gold Medal of Royal Geographical Soc. Visit to America, 1860. Married Isabel Arundell, 22 Jan., 1861. Consul at Fernando Po, Aug. 1861. Consul at São Paulo, Brazil, 1865; travelled widely in Brazil. Consul at Damascus, Oct. 1869; exploration in Syria. Returned to England, 1871. Visit to Iceland, 1872. Consul at Trieste, 1872–90. Travelled in Land of Midian, 1876, 1877–78; in interior of Gold Coast, 1882. K. C. M. G., 1886. Died, at Trieste, 20 Oct., 1890. *Works:* "Goa and the Blue Mountains," 1851; "Scinde; or, the Unhappy Valley," 1851; "Sindh, and the Races that inhabit the Valley of the Indus," 1851; "Falconry in the Valley of the Indus," 1852; "A Complete System of Bayonet Exercise," 1853; "Personal Narrative of a Pilgrimage" (3 vols.), 1855–56; "First Footsteps in East Africa," 1856; "The Lake Region of Central Africa," 1860; "The City of the Saints," 1861; "Wanderings in West Africa" (under initials: F. R. G. S.), 1863; "Abeokuta," 1863; "The Nile Basin" (from "Morning Advertiser"), 1864; "A Mission to Gelele" (2 vols.),

1864; "Stone Talk" (under pseud. of Frank Baker), 1865; "Wit and Wisdom from West Africa," 1865; "Explorations of the Highlands of Brazil," 1869; "Letters from the Battlefields of Paraguay," 1870; "Zanzibar," 1872; "Unexplored Syria" (with C. F. T. Drake), 1872; "Ultima Thule," 1875; "Two Trips to Gorilla Land," 1876 [1875]; "A New System of Sword Exercise," 1876; "Etruscan Bologna," 1876; "Sind Revisited," 1877; "The Gold Mines of Midian," 1878; "The Land of Midian Revisited," 1879; "A Glance at the 'Passion-Play,'" 1881; "Lord Beaconsfield" [1882?]; "To the Gold Coast for Gold" (with V. L. Cameron), 1883 [1882]; "The Book of the Sword," 1884. *Posthumous:* "The Kasîdah of Hâjî Abdû Al-Yazdi," ed. by Lady Burton, 1894; translations of "Il Pantamerone," 1893; and Catullus' "Carmina," 1894. He *translated:* "Vikram and the Vampire," 1870; Lacerda's "Lands of Cazembe," 1873; Camoens' Works, 1880–84; "Arabian Nights," 1885–86; " Supplemental Nights," 1886–88; Pereira da Silva's "Manuel de Moraes" (with Lady Burton), 1886; and *edited:* Marcy's "Prairie Traveller," 1863; Stade's "Captivity," 1874; Leared's "Morocco and the Moors," 1891 [1890]. *Collected Works:* "Memorial Edn.," ed. by Lady Burton and L. Smithers, 1893, etc. *Life:* by Lady Burton, 2 vols., 1893; by G. M. Stisted, 1896.—SHARP, R. FARQUHARSON, 1897, *A Dictionary of English Authors, p.* 42.

PERSONAL

Burton was a man whose mental capacity was extraordinary, and whose physical powers were far above the average, whilst he also possessed a phenomenal love and power of hard work. It may be asked why a man so exceptionally gifted did not achieve a phenomenal success and die a Peer and Knight of the Garter. The answer is not far to seek; he preferred a position where he was practically independent, and where he could say and do what he liked, to one which, however splendid, would involve certain restraints. He was not a man to endure the wearing of any fetters, not even if they were golden and bejeweled. His independence he valued before all else, and this love of freedom and his unflinching, outspoken honesty prevented his ever becoming a courtier. If he could have stooped ever so little no one can calculate the height (as judged by ordinary standards) to which he must have risen. . . . His scientific, apart from his linguistic and scholarly attainments, were most wonderful, and if he had cared to make them known to the world he would have ranked high as geologist, naturalist, anthropologist, botanist, or antiquarian; in fact, he was admirably equipped in all ways as a scientific explorer, and when you add to the above qualifications his marvellous aptitude for languages and his equally marvellous accuracy, it must be allowed that no traveller of present or past ages outrivals, even if any equals or comes near him. . . . Another point of superiority in Burton to most men was his power of instantly putting a stop to argument and dissension, and this whether the parties were white, black, or of both colors.

Fortunately I have not seen him have cause to do this more than twice or thrice, but on each occasion his influence was magical. As he could control others so he could also control himself, and in my experience of him I have never seen him lose his temper; and the perfect submission with which during the last few years of his life he acquiesced in the regulations of his wife and his doctor, without one word of murmuring or symptom of dissatisfaction, was one of the most touching things I ever witnessed, and also a proof of how completely he had mastered what in his young days had been a fiery temper.—CAMERON, V. LOVETT, 1890, *Burton as I Knew Him, Fortnightly Review, vol.* 54, *pp.* 878, 880, 881.

His pilgrimage in disguise to Mecca, his discovery of Lake Tanganyike, and his translation of the "Thousand and One Nights" (which his wife never read unexpurgated, though it was copied by "a lady amanuensis"), are the three things for which he will chiefly be remembered. In spite of great achievements, his was a life of signal troubles and disappointments. He declared, "My career in India has been in my eyes a failure;" even the famous Mecca trip was but a part of what he had meant to do; the irregular Turkish force which he helped to organise during the Crimean war never saw service, and his various suggestions met with snubs; his expedition with Speke ended in a bitter quarrel between the two, and it was Speke who was chosen to go a second time and have the glory of discovering the sources of the Nile; his name was struck off the Army List without warning when he entered the consular service at perhaps the worst possible post, Fernando Po; when he did at last get a situation to his heart, the consulship at Damascus, after a while he was abruptly cashiered, though his conduct was subsequently approved and he was sent to Trieste where he was left from 1873 till his death in 1890. . . . This is a sad record for a man of such great and varied abilities, of such energy and industry, who knew twenty-nine languages, who understood the East as few Europeans ever have, who was one of the pioneers of modern African exploration, and who wrote, on widely different subjects, works that will always have value. In spite of Lady Burton's protestations, we can see that, to a certain extent, he had himself to blame for his woes; but we will not undertake to say how much.—COOLIDGE, A. C., 1893, *Life of Sir Richard Burton, The Nation, vol.* 57, *p.* 178.

Truly, the story of this good knight and "Isabel his wife" should be writ in other languages than our nineteenth century work-a-day tongue. It should be sung, as a "romaunt" of heroic emprise, of battle with savage foes, of wanderings through the magic lands and mysterious cities of the sun: of glory and mishap, and much persecution; above all, of true love that never failed or wavered, through life or in death. Such a story we might have received as a legend of early mediæval times, and treasured, like the acts of a St. George, or a knightly Quest originated at the "Round Table" of King Arthur. It is difficult to look upon it in the light of modern day, as a tale of marvels enacted concurrently with our own lives. The potent spell of it all lies in the man's ill-rewarded courage and endurance for honour and country's sake; in his lady's love and loyal service at his side, "surpassing woman's power."—GOWING, EMILIA AYLMER, 1894, *Sir Richard Burton, Belgravia, vol.* 84, *p.* 146.

His intellectual gifts, his power of assuming any character he pleased, his facility in acquiring languages, his love of adventure and contempt for danger—all singled him out as a remarkable man. He was very dark, of an almost gypsy aspect. In fact, although he had no known Oriental blood, Lady Burton always thought it strange that he had so many characteristics of the race. He possessed the same power to read the hand at a glance, the same restlessness and inability to stay long in one place, the same philosophic endurance of any evil, and the same horror of a corpse, that distinguish the highest gypsy races. While in the East he could disguise himself so well as to pass for a dervish in the mosques, or as a merchant in the bazars. He undertook a pilgrimage to Mecca, disguised as a pilgrim, and accomplished it in safety, his real identity and nationality never being suspected. It is a proof of the power of the man that he carried the assumed character through to the end—for one mistake or slip would have caused him to pay the forfeit with his life.—CURTIS, GEORGINA P., 1900, *Isabel, Lady Burton, Catholic World, vol.* 72, *p.* 93.

GENERAL

His cast of mind was so original that not only did he never borrow from any one else, but he was disposed to resent another's trespassing upon such subjects as he considered his own. But no man could be more cordial in his admiration of honest work done in bordering fields of learning. He was ever ready to assist, from the stores of his experience, young explorers and young scholars; but here, as in all else, he was intolerant of pretentiousness and sciolism. His virility stamped everything he said or wrote. His style was as characteristic as his hand-writing.—COTTON, J. S., 1890, *Sir Richard Burton, The Academy, vol.* 38, *p.* 365.

A living soul that had strength to quell
Hope the spectre and fear the spell,
Clear-eyed, content with a scorn sublime
And a faith superb, can it fare not well?

. . . .

While England sees not her old praise dim,
While still her stars through the world's night swim,
A fame outshining her Raleigh's fame,
A light that lightens her loud sea's rim,
Shall shine and sound as her sons proclaim
The pride that kindles at Burton's name.
And joy shall exalt their pride to be
The same in birth if in soul the same.

—SWINBURNE, ALGERNON CHARLES, 1891, *Verses on the Death of Richard Burton, New Review, vol.* 4, *p.* 99.

No man of modern times lived a life so full of Romance as Burton. To find his parallel we must turn to the careers of the Elizabethan heroes, notably Sir Walter Raleigh. For Burton was something more than a "gentleman adventurer." He was at once a poet—as the Kasidah, wisely quoted by Lady Burton in full, shows beyond cavil—historian, traveller, profound oriental scholar, and soldier. Even his faults, often virtues in uncongenial surroundings, were those of the Elizabethan age; and his failures were due almost entirely to the fact that he had to live, not under the personage of Gloriana, but in our nineteenth century. . . . That such a man as Burton should have been reduced to his last £15 is a burning scandal to the country whose interests he strove so gallantly to serve. His entire fitness for an Eastern post is demonstrated by the respect the natives of all classes and divisions felt for him, and the fear and love he awakened in his subordinates.—ADDLESHAW, PERCY, 1893, *Life of Sir Richard Burton, The Academy, vol. 44, pp. 333, 334.*

Sir Richard Burton has left behind him an enormous mass of published and unpublished writings, consisting of accounts of countries which he visited, reports to the Royal Geographical Society, treatises on various subjects connected with his expeditions, a translation of Camoëns, and numerous grammars, vocabularies, and other linguistic works. As an Oriental scholar it is possible that his much-discussed edition of the "Arabian Nights" is his most valuable production; and it is therefore probable that the destruction of his manuscript "The Scented Garden," was, at all events, a loss to Eastern scholarship. Generally speaking, his books, although graphic and vivacious, suffer from the want of a more complete digestion, and greater care in compilation, are too impetuous, and have the air of being written *au courant de plume*, without much arrangement or revision. Such volumes, however, as the famous "Pilgrimage to Mecca;" "Scinde; or, the Unhappy Valley;" or the Account of his Mission to the King of Dahomé, would alone be a sufficient monument even of an extraordinary man; but Sir Richard lets them fall by the way as chronicles of his amusements and records of the more picturesque episodes of his career. —NEWTON, MRS. ROBINSON, 1893, *The "Life of Mr. Richard Burton," Westminster Review, vol. 140, p. 482.*

Whether or no Lady Burton was, all in all, justified in burning the "Scented Garden" is at least an open question; but the charge that in so doing she showed "the bigotry of a Torquemada and the vandalism of a John Knox" is overstrained. Miss Stisted's characterization of the act as "theatrical" is unfair.—JOHNSON, E. G., 1897, *Lady Isabel Burton, The Dial, vol. 22, p. 355.*

Burton was attracted to Camoens as the mouthpiece of the romantic period of discovery in the Indian Ocean. The voyages, the misfortunes, the chivalry, the patriotism of the poet were to him those of a brother adventurer. In his spirited sketch of the life and character of Camoens it is not presumptuous to read between the lines allusions to his own career. This sympathy breathes through his translation of the Portuguese epic, which, though not a popular success, won the enthusiastic approval of the few competent critics. . . . Of Burton's translations of "The Arabian Nights" it is difficult to speak freely. While the "Camoens" was only a *succes d'estime*, and "The Book of the Sword" little short of a failure, the private circulation of "The Book of a Thousand Nights and a Night" (1885-6, 10 vols.), brought to the author a profit of about 10,000*l* which enabled him to spend his declining years in comparative luxury. This much at least may be said in justification of some of the baits that he held out to the purchasers. For it would be absurd to ignore the fact that the attraction lay not so much in the translation as in the notes and the terminal essay, where certain subjects of curiosity are discussed with naked freedom. Burton was but following the example of many classical scholars of high repute and indulging a taste which is more widespread than modern prudery will allow. In his case something more may be urged. The whole of his life was a protest against social conventions. Much of it was spent in the East, where the intercourse between men and women is more according to nature, and things are called by plain names. Add to this Burton's insatiable curiosity, which had impelled him to investigate all that concerns humanity in four continents. Of the merits of Burton's translation no two opinions have been expressed. The quaintness of expression that some have found fault with in the "Lusiads" are here not out of place, since they reproduce the topsy-turvy world of the original. If an eastern story-teller could have written in English he would write very much as Burton has done. A translator can expect no higher praise.— COTTON, J. S., 1901, *Dictionary of National Biography, Supplement, vol.* I, *pp.* 354, 355.

Henry Parry Liddon
1829-1890.

Born at North Stoneham, Hampshire, 20th August, 1829, the son of a naval captain, at seventeen went up from King's College School, London, to Christ Church, Oxford, where in 1850 he graduated B. A. Ordained in 1852 as senior student of Christ Church, from 1854 to 1859 he was vice-principal of Cuddesdon Theological College, and in 1864 became a prebendary of Salisbury, in 1870 a canon of St. Paul's, and Ireland professor of Exegesis at Oxford (till 1882). In 1866 he delivered his Bampton Lectures on the "Divinity of our Lord" (1867; 13th ed. 1889). He strongly opposed the Church Discipline Act of 1874, and as warmly supported Mr. Gladstone's crusade against the Bulgarian atrocities in 1876. In 1886 he declined the bishopric of Edinburgh, and in 1887 visited the Holy Land. Canon Liddon was the most able and eloquent exponent of Liberal High Church principles. He died suddenly at Weston-super-Mare, 9th Sept., 1890. An "Analysis of the Epistle to the Romans" was published in 1893; his "Life of Pusey" was edited by Johnston and Wilson.— PATRICK, AND GROOME, eds. 1897, *Chambers's Biographical Dictionary*, p. 590.

PERSONAL

The greatest preacher by far, and perhaps the greatest genius (though he retired a good deal from action), in the English Church is taken from us. You knew him much better than I did, but I have known him well since 1846, and almost from the first anticipated his greatness.—LAKE, WILLIAM CHARLES, 1890, *Letter to Lord Halifax, Sept. 10; Memorials, ed. his Widow*, p. 305.

As a preacher, his influence has been unique in our time—more powerful, as I believe, even than that of the present Bishop of Peterborough or the late Bishop Wilberforce, notwithstanding the close logic of the former and the persuasive rhetoric of the latter; for Liddon combined the two. Profound and ever-increasing stores of learning, careful study and preparation, great power of language, a clear, distinct intonation, and withal that great force which earnest personal conviction brings with it (the ἠθική πίστις of Aristotle) these seem to me to have been some of the elements of his strength. It has been said that his style was formed upon French rather than English models. . . . Of his charm in private life, of the value of his personal friendship, of the brilliancy of his conversation, of his quiet humour and power of sarcasm—ever kept within due bounds—of these things I do not trust myself to speak. Much that I might say seems too private and too sacred for these pages. It is rather of his public life and his work for the Church that I write.—POTT, ALFRED, 1890, *Canon Liddon, New Review*, vol. 3, pp. 306, 307.

I never heard Liddon preach. But I have walked with him many hours and miles. And when Liddon got deeply interested in what he was saying, and stopped, gazed intently on you, and talked in touching tones, accompanied with a graceful little movement of both hands, you had no difficulty in making out the great preacher of great St. Paul's. — BOYD, ANDREW K. H., 1892, *Twenty-Five Years of St. Andrews*, vol. I, p. 142.

The personal factor, by which the claim of St. Paul's to become once more a wide spiritual home for London could make itself heard and felt over the hearts of large multitudes, was to be found in the preaching of Dr. Liddon. That voice reached far and wide. It fixed the attention of the whole city on what was going forward in its midst. It kindled the imagination, so that the big world outside was prepared for great things. It compelled men to treat seriously what was done. No one could suppose that the changes in the services and ritual of St. Paul's were superficial or formal or of small account, so long as that voice rang on, like a trumpet, telling of righteousness and temperance and judgment, preaching ever and always, with personal passion of belief, Jesus Christ and Him crucified.—HOLLAND, HENRY SCOTT, 1894, *Life and Letters of Dean Church, ed. his Daughter*, p. 260.

A twofold memorial will keep his fame before the minds of future generations. First the beautiful monument in the great Cathedral, and next the scholarships at Oxford, founded in his name, for the training of candidates for Holy Orders in the careful and scientific study of theology. But his character and life will never be forgotten so long as English Churchmen gratefully recall the debt they owe to him in the noble band of Oxford theologians and preachers. Single-hearted, perfectly free from all vulgar craving for honour or preferment, courageous in proclaiming truth, the friend of the oppressed, generous in giving almost to lavishness, considerate and tender to lowly men and women, his example as well as his splendid gifts will be for ever linked with the great revival of the Church of England in which he played so noble a part.—DONALDSON, AUG. B., 1900, *Five Great Oxford Leaders, p.* 308.

GENERAL

In all Liddon's discourses we can mark an apologetical aim, but his method is best seen in the volume called "University Sermons," originally published under the title "Some Words for God," and in the "Elements of Religion," a course of lectures delivered during Lent, 1870, in St. James's Church, Piccadilly. These discourses show that he possesses, in a high degree, many of the qualities needed in a modern apologist of Christianity. No apologist in our time, writing from the strict Church standpoint, has done his special work so well. He may be compared without disadvantage with Lacordaire, whom, indeed, he greatly excels in learning and range of thought.— GIBB, JOHN, 1880, *Theologians of the Day, Catholic Presbyterian, vol.* 3, *p.* 3.

His intellect, as such, would never stir. You could anticipate, exactly, the position from which he would start. It never varied. He had won clear hold on the dogmatic expressions by which the Church of the Councils secured the Catholic belief in the Incarnation; and there he stood with unalterable tenacity. Abstract ideas did not appeal to him: for philosophy he had no liking, though, naturally, he could not fail in handling it to show himself a man of cultivated ability. But it did not affect him at all: he never felt drawn to get inside it. He did not work in that region. His mental tone was intensely practical; it was Latin, it was French, in sympathy and type. For Teutonic speculation he had a most amusing repugnance. Its misty magniloquence, its grotesque bulk, its immense clumsiness, its laborious pedantry, which its best friends admit, brought out everything in him that was alert, rapid, compact, practical, effective, humorous. There was nothing against which his entire armoury came into more vivid play—his brilliant readiness, his penetrating irony, his quick sense of proportion, his admirable and scholarly restraint, his delicate grace, his fastidious felicity of utterance. . . . He had the double gift of the preacher. He impressed, he overawed, he mastered, by the sense of unshaken solidity which his mental characteristics assured to him. Men felt the force of a position which was as a rock amid the surging seas. Here was the fixity, the security, the eternal reassurance most needed by those who wondered sadly whether the sands under their feet were shifty or no. And yet, at the service of this unmoving creed was a brain, a heart, alive with infinite motion, abounding in rich variety, fertile, resourceful, quickening, expansive, vital. And, if we add to this a strong will, possessed of unswerving courage, and utterly fearless of the world, we shall see that there was in him all the elements that constitute a great Director of Souls. — HOLLAND, HENRY SCOTT, 1890, *H. P. Liddon, Contemporary Review, vol.* 58, *pp.* 476, 477.

Dion Boucicault
1822–1890

A British dramatist and actor; born in Dublin, Dec. 26, 1822; died in New York, Sept. 18, 1890. His first drama, "London Assurance," was written before he was 19 years of age, and made him famous. He also attained celebrity as an actor and manager in England and the United States; established a school for acting and produced about 300 dramas, many of which were original and many adaptations from the French. He dramatized Washington Irving's "Rip Van Winkle," which Joseph Jefferson enlarged; and produced a series of Irish dramas which were extraordinarily popular, such as: "The Colleen Bawn" (1860); "Arrah-na-Pogue" (1864); and "The Shaughraun" (1875); in which he played the principal parts. "Old Heads on Young Shoulders;" "The Corsican Brothers;" "The Streets of London;" "Flying Scud;" and "After Dark;" were among his later productions.—WARNER, CHARLES DUDLEY, *ed.* 1897, *Library of the World's Best Literature, Biographical Dictionary, vol.* XXIX, *p.* 69.

GENERAL

That despicable mass of inanity. ["London Assurance."]—POE, EDGAR ALLAN, 1846, *The Literati*, *Works*, ed. Stedman and Woodbury, vol. VIII, p. 31.

We have already noticed Mr. Dion Boucicault's share in "Foul Play." This collaboration gratified Charles Reade more thoroughly than any during his lifetime; and although he could chaff Mr. Boucicault as "a sly fox," esteemed both his society and friendship very highly. On one occasion, when a remark was hazarded in disparagement of a drama by this gentleman, he turned contemptuously on the speaker with the query, "Will you find me another man in England who could write such a comedy?" Nor was his belief in Mr. Boucicault ever shaken—indeed, he envied his capacity for commanding both the tears and laughter, the astonishment and delight, of the Gallery.—READE, CHARLES L., AND REV. COMPTON, 1887, *Memoir of Charles Reade*, p. 398.

I remember that when Mr. Dion Boucicault originally produced the "Shaughraun"—it was at Wallack's Theatre in New York ten or twelve years ago—there was an attempt to prove that he had taken his plot from an earlier Irish drama by Mr. Wybert Reeve. At first sight the similarity between the two plays was really striking, and parallel columns were erected with ease. But a closer investigation revealed that all that was common to these two plays was common to fifty other Irish plays, and that all that gave value to the "Shaughraun"—the humor, the humanity, the touches of pathos, the quick sense of character—was absent from the other play. There is a formula for the mixing of an Irish drama, and Mr. Reeve and Mr. Boucicault had each prepared his piece according to this formula, making due admixture of the Maiden-in-Distress, the Patriot-in-danger-of-his-Life, and the cowardly Informer, who have furnished forth many score plays since first the Red-Coats were seen in the Green Isle. Both dramatists had drawn from the common stock of types and incidents, and there was really no reason to believe that Mr. Boucicault was indebted to Mr. Reeve for anything, because Mr. Reeve had little in his play which had not been in twenty plays before, and which Mr. Boucicault could not have put together out of his recollections of these without any knowledge of that.—MATTHEWS, BRANDER, 1888, *Pen and Ink*, p. 42.

Dion Boucicault brought the stage romanticism of Victor Hugo and Dumas down to our day. But the transit was not made in Victor Hugo's vehicle. That which was a conviction with the Master, became an expedient with the imitator. To fix the status of this indefatigable worker, who was always felicitous without being fecund, is not an easy matter. His repertoire affects the student of stage literature now, like a long twilight which gets glory from what has departed. And yet it is in Dumas and Klopstock that we must find the prototypes of this inspired activity, rather than in Lope de Vega. If he was not endowed with that reflex of the Infinite, which creates by an inbreathing, he was at least gifted with the wonderful finite craft which can fashion by an onlaying. This is always the playwright's function, in contradistinction to the dramatist's. But Dion Boucicault had something more than the playwright's craft. He possessed the swift instinct which apprehends the aberrations of the public pulse, and can seize and use for its own purposes those vague emotions which sweep over a community, and are at once irresistible and evanescent. . . . The Dion Boucicault of "London Assurance" is an unknown quantity. The Dion Boucicault of "The Colleen Bawn" is within the measurement of most of us. And here it should be said at once that "The Colleen Bawn" is probably the most romantic, as it was certainly the most successful, Irish play that had been written, up to the time of its production. The success was Dion Boucicault's. The romance belonged to another. . . . He had produced "The Shaughraun." Greater and nobler plays lie like wrecks all along the record. A more phenomenal public triumph cannot be mentioned. . . . It is a matter of approximate verification that Dion Boucicault received as his share of the profits of the "Shaughraun" over eight hundred thousand dollars.—WHEELER, A. C., 1890, *Dion Boucicault*, *The Arena*, vol. 3, pp. 47, 52, 59.

His dramas show little originality, being almost without exception built on some work, play, or romance previously existing.—KNIGHT, JOSEPH, 1901, *Dictionary of National Biography, Supplement*, vol. I, p. 237.

Charles Mackay
1814-1889.

A Scottish poet, journalist, and miscellaneous writer; born at Perth, March 27, 1814; died in London, Dec. 24, 1889. He was editor of the illustrated London News, 1852-59. He lectured in the United States in 1857-58. While special correspondent of the London Times in New York during the Civil War (strongly favoring the Southern cause), he unearthed the Fenian conspiracy (1862). He wrote: "The Salmandrien, or Love and Immortality" (1842); "Voices from the Crowd" (1846); "Voices from the Mountains" (1847); "History of the Mormons" (1851); etc.—WARNER, CHARLES DUDLEY, ed. 1897, Library of the World's Best Literature, Biographical Dictionary, vol. XXIX, p. 359.

PERSONAL

I was charmed with Mackay, the "Poet of the People." He has a fine face, lighted up with noble emotions of the soul.—LE-VERT, OCTAVIA WALTON, 1853. Souvenirs of Travel, vol. I, p. 79.

Throughout his career Charles Mackay was a most energetic and prolific worker,—poems, novels, essays, critical articles, lectures, dissertations on literary antiquities, papers on philology, whether in French or English, coming apparently with equal facility from his pen. His "History of Popular Delusions" was one of his most popular books, and his "Gaelic Etymology of the Languages of Western Europe," and his "Récréations Gauloises et Origines Françaises" were his most important contributions to philological science. A frequent contributor to journalistic literature, his "Voices from the Crowd," which appeared in the "Daily News," are still remembered, while his articles in the "Nineteenth Century" on "Burns and Beranger," and on "Boileau and Pope," show him to have been an able and eloquent critic.—MILES, ALFRED H., 1892, The Poets and the Poetry of the Century, Frederick Tennyson to A. H. Clough, p. 456.

GENERAL

One of the most popular authors of the day. . . . Mr. Mackay is emphatically the lyric poet of progress. He writes with great animation and deep feeling, and no one can fail to see that he has a true heart—a deeply philanthropic spirit; and that he has a firm faith in the ultimate happiness of the race,—in the reign of universal love.—CLEVELAND, CHARLES D., 1853, English Literature of the Nineteenth Century, p. 701.

Like all the great song-writers, Dr. Mackay is a musician, and the composer of all the melodies published with many of his songs. He possesses in a high degree the rare faculty of a true lyric poet, that of working his words and music up into harmony and unison with the feelings they express.—BEETON, S. O., 1870, ed. Great Book of Poetry.

Among the authors of the day, uniting political sympathies and aspirations with lyrical poetry, is Dr. Charles Mackay. Some of his songs are familiar as household words both in this country and in America, and his influence as an apostle or minstrel of social reform and the domestic affections must have been considerable.—CHAMBERS, ROBERT, 1876, Cyclopædia of English Literature, ed. Carruthers.

Like those of many other poets, his longer efforts in verse have lost whatever interest they may have once excited, but his songs and shorter poems still give lyrical expression to popular feeling, sentiment, and philosophy. These are characterized by a clear resonant ring, and animated by a healthy, liberal spirit. "John Littlejohn" is of the happiest class of popular verse, and "Tubal Cain" swings along and drives home its points as with the sweep and force of the blacksmith's hammer.—MILNES, ALFRED H., 1892, The Poets and the Poetry of the Century, Frederick Tennyson to A. H. Clough, p. 457.

George Henry Boker
1823-1890.

Dramatist and Diplomat, born Philadelphia, Penn., 6 Oct., 1823; died there, 2. Jan., 1890. Graduated at Princeton, and, after a period of travel in Europe, made his permanent home in Philadelphia. His first volume of verse, "The Lesson of Life, and Other Poems," was issued in 1847. It was succeeded the following year by "Calaynos," a blank-verse tragedy, which was successfully produced in 1849 at a London theatre.

"Francesca da Rimini" is now the best known of the metrical dramas which, with his miscellaneous poems, were published in two volumes, "Plays and Poems," 1856. Mr. Boker was secretary of the Union League of Philadelphia from 1861 to 1871, and was actively patriotic during the Civil War. "Poems of the War," containing some lyrics widely familiar, appeared in 1864. Later volumes are "Königsmark, and Other Poems," 1869; "The Book of the Dead," 1882; and "Sonnets," 1886. He was U. S. minister to Turkey from 1871 to 1875, and to Russia from 1875 to 1879. Throughout his literary career he was closely associated with Bayard Taylor and R. H. Stoddard. To represent Boker with fairness, extracts should be given from the dramatic work to which he devoted his best powers, and for which the repeated success of "Calaynos" and "Francesca da Rimini" showed that he possessed both literary and practical equipments. The ballads, sonnets, etc., to which this Anthology is restricted, exhibit his lyrical strength and quality.—STEDMAN, EDMUND CLARENCE, 1900, *ed., An American Anthology, p.* 780.

PERSONAL

Young Boker, author of the tragedy of "Calaynos," a most remarkable work, is here on a visit, and spent several hours tonight with me. He is another hero,—a most noble, glorious mortal! He is one of our band, and is, I think, destined to high renown as an author. He is nearly my own age, perhaps a year or two older, and he has lived through the same sensations, fought the same fight, and now stands up with the same defiant spirit.—TAYLOR, BAYARD, 1848, *To Mary Agnew, Oct.* 13; *Life and Letters, ed. Taylor and Scudder, vol.* I, *p.* 136.

An early portrait of Boker bears strong resemblance to Nathaniel Hawthorne in his manly prime. But passing decades, while they have not bent the tall, erect figure, have whitened the thick, military-looking moustache and short curling hair that contrast strikingly with a firm, ruddy complexion. His commanding presence and distinguished appearance are as well known in Philadelphia as his sturdy personality and polished manners are.—LATHROP, GEORGE PARSONS, 1888, *Authors at Home, The Critic, vol.* 12, *p.* 176.

He had one quality which is the distinction of most great writers, of masterminds, like Shakespeare, Byron, Scott, and Browning,—fecundity of conception and rapidity of execution,—and beyond all other American poet's creation was necessary to his intellectual well-being.—STODDARD, RICHARD HENRY, 1890, *George Henry Boker, Lippincott's Magazine, vol.* 45, *p.* 857.

George H. Boker had a great influence on me. We were in a way connected, for my uncle Amos had married his aunt, and my cousin, Benjamin Godfrey, his cousin. He was exactly six feet high, with the form of an Apollo, and a head which was the very counterpart of the bust of Byron. A few years later N. P. Willis described him in the "Home Journal" as the handsomest man in America. He had been from boyhood as precociously a man of the world as I was the opposite. He was *par éminence* the poet of our college, and in a quiet, gentlemanly way its "swell." I passed a great deal of my time in his rooms reading Wordsworth, Shelley, and Byron, the last named being his ideal.—LELAND, CHARLES GODFREY, 1893, *Memoirs, p.* 97.

This rare man, born to fortune and to a fashionable position which he enjoyed, kept up his classics and his literary work to the end. . . . There was something of the grandeur and gloom of Hawthorne about Mr. Boker when he was serious. At a dinner he preferred to be humorous. His temperament was changeful, as is always the case with children of genius. He was a gifted creature, and most generous to poor authors, for whom he drew many a check. . . . I know no man who seemed to me to have led more nobly the dual life of man of the world and man of the library. He had a beautiful head and the manners of Lord Chesterfield.—SHERWOOD, MARY E. W., 1897, *An Epistle to Posterity, pp.* 193, 194.

Excellent as some of his work has been, especially in his sonnets, it is undeniable that Boker's work has not been taken with entire seriousness; the division of his abilities between two such divergent exactions explains in part his lack of a fast reputation. He was versatile beyond question, even attaining to high degree of skill as a mechanic. His personal appearance had something to do with his successes. Early in his life Willis had declared him "the handsomest man in America." He was six feet in height, and Leland calls him "distingué," and, again, "the American Sidney of his time." Modesty was characteristic of him, and he never was first to allude to his writings. In his shyness he has been compared to Hawthorne. . . . As a representative American abroad he was irreproachable, and in attainments and social training he has been favorably compared with Motley. "Respectability" may have proved his bane in literature, though it was the mainspring of his social and political life.—SWIFT, LINDSAY, 1900, *Our Literary Diplomats, The Book Buyer*, vol. 21, p. 48.

GENERAL

Stoddard spent Saturday night with me, and we read the "Song of the Earth" together. He was rapturous in his praises as we went along, swinging on your dactyls, marching through your files of iambics, and sliding over your anapests. He has the soul to comprehend the grandeur of the thing, and not a drop of that damnable spirit of depreciation which curses half our authors.—TAYLOR, BAYARD, 1849, *To George H. Boker, May 29; Life and Letters*, ed. Taylor and Scudder, vol. I, p. 146.

Our only *American* dramatic poet in its highest sense — George H. Boker.— BARRETT, LAWRENCE, 1887, *A Blot in the 'Scutcheon and Other Dramas*, ed. Rolfe and Hersey, p. 13.

Among the dramas which were the fruit of his youth, "Calaynos" and "Francesca da Rimini" achieved a great success, both in England and in this country. The revival of "Francesca da Rimini" at the hand of Lawrence Barrett, and its run of two or three seasons, thirty years after its first production, is one of the most remarkable events in the history of the American stage. Nor should it be forgotten that Daniel Webster valued one of Boker's sonnets so much, that he kept it in memory, to recite; and that Leigh Hunt selected Boker as one of the best exponents of mastery in the perfect sonnet.—LATHROP, GEORGE PARSONS, 1888, *Authors at Home, The Critic*, vol. 12, p. 176.

In the desert of the American drama the work of Boker, then, is doubly welcome. It is not "indigenous" or new or indispensable; it merely offers somewhat of the strength of the word, the flame of color, the intensity of act, of the earlier or later English makers of plays, to whom the bloody pages of mediæval history have been so rich an inspiration. — RICHARDSON, CHARLES F., 1888, *American Literature*, 1607-1885, vol. II, p. 249.

He was the creator of our Poetic Drama, which began with "Calaynos" and ended with "Königsmark." That his tragedies were capable of effective representation was known to those of us who saw Mr. Davenport and Miss Dean in "Francesca da Rimini" years ago, and is known to those of us who have since seen Mr. Barrett and Miss Wainwright in the same play. The conception of his tragedies and comedies, their development, their movement, and their catastrophies, are dramatic. Poetical, they are not overweighted with poetry; emotional and passionate, their language is naturally figurative, and the blank verse rises and falls as the occasion demands. One feels in reading them that the writer had studied the Elizabethan and Jacobean dramatists, and that they harmed as well as helped him. If he could have forgotten them, and remembered only his own genius, his work would have been more original. A born dramatist, he was a genuine balladist, as I could prove by comparing his ballads with those of Macaulay, and a born sonneteer, as I could prove by comparing his sonnets with those of Sidney, Spenser, Daniel, and Shakespeare.—STODDARD, RICHARD HENRY, 1890, *George Henry Boker, Lippincott's Magazine*, vol. 45, p. 866.

While "classical" in form, his works are refreshingly free from the high-stepping twaddle to which at one time our tragic muse seemed hopelessly wedded. It may be said of all his plays that they possess the essentials of true drama,—life, action, and feeling. The best known of these doubtless owes much of its popularity to its fine interpretation on the stage by Lawrence Barrett.—ONDERDONK, JAMES L., 1899-1901, *History of American Verse*, p. 233.

Perhaps our lack of a vigorous dramatic literature is not mainly chargeable to our poets. Certainly, even when merely read carefully, Boker's "Francesca" seems a very remarkably strong play. The versification, and the character drawing, though both lack the dreamy mysterious charm of Stephen Phillips's recent "Francesca," are strong, masculine, and clear. Indeed, Boker's plays are probably the best yet produced among us.—LAWTON, WILLIAM CRANSTON, 1902, *Introduction to the Study of American Literature*, p. 341.

John Boyle O'Reilly
1844–1890.

Born in Dowth Castle Co. Meath, Ireland, 28 June, 1844; died Hull, Mass., 10 Aug., 1890. Son of the master of Nettleville Institute at Dowth Castle. He did some journalistic work in Drogheda, near his birthplace, but was sent to England as an agent of the Fenian society. He was arrested and condemned to death, but his sentence was commuted, and he was sent to Australia. After a year of penal servitude he escaped in a boat, was rescued by an American whaler, and landed at Philadelphia, Penn., 1869. He became editor and joint owner of the Boston "Pilot," and published "Songs of the Southern Seas," 1873; "Songs, Legends, and Ballads," 1878; "Moondyne," novel, 1879; "Statues in the Block," poems, 1881; "In Bohemia," 1886; "The Ethics of Boxing," 1888; "Stories and Sketches," 1888. At the time of his death he was preparing a work on Ireland. In 1896 a statue of Mr. O'Reilly by Daniel French was unveiled in Boston. Below the statue, which is fourteen feet tall, is a group of symbolic figures.—STEDMAN, EDMUND CLARENCE, 1900, ed. *An American Anthology*, p. 812.

PERSONAL

He was throughout all and above all a gentleman. There are a great many definitions of that word, most of them formulated by tailors or by footmen, and some by those who estimate a man's worth by the social standing of his grandfather. He would have stood the tests of all those three critical classes, and if we happen to prefer a higher standard he would not have failed before that. For he was courteous to all men, of whatever estate; he was chivalrous to women and tender to children and all weak and helpless ones; he was magnanimous to his enemies, loyal to his friends, and merciful to all mankind. He believed in humanity and in his age; and his faith was rewarded, for he was appreciated in his life and mourned in his death as no private citizen ever has been mourned. What he did to lift his fellow men to that appreciation will be known in long years to come. If he was not a saint, he worked at least one miracle—he made men grateful.—ROCHE, JAMES JEFFREY, 1890, *John Boyle O'Reilly*, *The Cosmopolitan*, vol. 9, p. 770.

He was a revolutionist always; but he was much more than that. He was a reconstructive, also. I have never known any one who showed such deep and searching and wide interest in the welfare, comfort and progress of the whole human race. He had an almost infinite compassion for the sufferings of mankind, and an unlimited fund of hope for the alleviation of those sufferings. Sometimes, however, he uttered terrible theories looking towards the destruction of human society as it now exists. These theories were only a sort of rendrock, intended merely to blow up the granite walls of inert prejudice, and make an opening for broader paths of progress and enlightenment; but these caused him to be misunderstood. Full of the fighting spirit, athletic, independent, and absolutely uncompromising when he measured existing institutions by the standard of lofty ideas and pure principles, he was yet one of the gentlest among men. I never heard him utter a word of malice or ill will towards any one, even when he was speaking of those who represented the extreme of opposition to his views. . . . He did not obtrude his opinions; but, when moved to talk, he expressed them with a fire, a brilliance, a wealth of wit and humor and good fellowship, which convinced every unprejudiced listener that he was not only sincere, but was also the earnest and cordial friend of every living creature. Furthermore, it was evident that he possessed that quality which we call greatness of mind.—LATHROP, GEORGE PARSONS, 1890, *John Boyle O'Reilly*, *The Critic*, vol. 17, p. 83.

He was the most widely beloved man in Boston, and it will be long before the mention of his name fails to provoke expressions of sorrow and affection. The anecdotes about him are unfailing. He was one of those men who sparkled with witticisms and unexpected sayings, and there is no friend who has not something to tell which is worth hearing.—BATES, ARLO, 1890, *Literary Topics in Boston, The Book Buyer.*

No man dared say twice to him: "We don't mean your kind of Irish or Catholic O'Reilly." All that bore the name was his; bone of his bone and flesh of his flesh; and this man, who cherished no personal enmities, who forgave and succored even the wretch who betrayed him, was merciless in his resentment of an insult to the least of his people, until condign satisfaction had been made. Thus he inspired a wholesome fear in the bully, and won the respect of all honest and fair-minded non-Catholics, for there is nothing your New England Yankee honors above "grit." . . . O'Reilly valued his personal advantages, his early-won literary fame, and immense social popularity and influence chiefly as they promoted the cause of his people.—CONWAY, KATHERINE E., 1891, *John Boyle O'Reilly, Catholic World*, vol. 53, pp. 209, 211.

Boyle O'Reilly easily became one of the most popular men and scholars of Boston. He took an active part in all public affairs, social and political, and soon became as "to the manor born." He was successful as a lecturer from the outset, for he had the genius of the poet, and the wit and warmth of an Irishman—qualities that, with a most attractive presence, made him popular always. But he cared more for his home, his newspaper, and his library than for the platform. Nevertheless, he was able to do a good deal of lecturing, where the distances would permit, without neglecting his other duties.—POND, J. B., 1900, *Eccentricities of Genius*, p. 327.

GENERAL

His verse is masculine, spontaneous, and novel.—ROBERTS, CHARLES G. D., 1888, *ed. Poems of Wild Life*, p. 235, *note*.

Mr. O'Reilly's work is known to all readers. He prefers to be known by it and through it. Otherwise one might be tempted to write indefinitely of his personal character, his unbounded popularity with all classes, his catholic sympathy with the oppressed and suffering of every class, creed and color, his healthy robustness, mental and physical. But all these are patent in his writings, which reflect the man as in a mirror. In the scant leisure of an active journalist's busy life, supplemented by unceasing and earnest labors in the cause of Irish nationality, he has found time to write half a dozen or more books. —ROCHE, JAMES JEFFREY, 1889, *John Boyle O'Reilly, Magazine of Poetry*, vol. 1, p. 47.

In these later poems the ethical tendency of O'Reilly's thought is vigorously developed, the spirit of human brotherhood is prominent, and an impatience with the conventions of society even when embodied in organized charities, is manifest. The interest taken by O'Reilly in athletics which was shown by his exploits with the gloves, the foils, and the paddles, is seen in "The Ethics of Boxing and Manly Sport," published in 1888. Some of the most brilliant of O'Reilly's literary successes were secured upon the platform, where as lecturer, orator, and poet he won a national reputation. His poem at the dedication of the Pilgrim monument at Plymouth in August, 1889, was a wonderful illustration of his sympathetic insight into characters and conditions which as an Irish Catholic he was thought unfitted to appreciate. — YOUNG, ALEXANDER, 1890, *John Boyle O'Reilly, Chautauquan*, p. 343.

Of the four notable poems of his maturity, one was for Ireland, "The Exile of the Gael;" one for America, "The Pilgrim Fathers;" one commemorated Wendell Phillips; and one the negro proto-martyr of American liberty, Crispus Attucks. His only novel, "Moondyne," written but a few years after his escape from Australia, was based, not, as one would naturally expect, on the Irish national struggle, in one phase of which he bore so notable a part, but on phases of English life. Its hero, Joseph Wyville, "Moondyne" to the Australian aborigines, was an Englishman. Its motive was the reform of the English penal system.— CONWAY, KATHERINE E., 1891, *John Boyle O'Reilly, Catholic World*, vol. 53, p. 216.

As an artist in verse he too often fell short; yet the very marked increase of dexterity and delicacy in some of his later pieces demonstrated how well fitted he was by nature to rise to the higher plane of expression. His influence as a writer and as a man was very wide, not only among classes usually little affected by artistic literature, but also among many cultivated, refined, and sensitive minds.—LATHROP, GEORGE PARSONS, 1891, *Open Letters, Century Magazine*, vol. 43, p. 313.

His genius was his fortune. He worked for a small salary until 1873, when he published his first volume of poems, "Songs of the Southern Seas." On reading these delightful poems, it is not probable that anybody asked or cared whether the author was a prince or an exiled stranger.—CONNELL, RICHARD E., 1897, *A Citizen of the Democracy of Literature, Catholic World*, vol. 65, p. 756.